POLICE ADMINISTRATION
STRUCTURES, PROCESSES, AND BEHAVIORS

Tenth Edition

Charles R. Swanson

University of Georgia

Robert W. Taylor

The University of Texas at Dallas

Leonard Territo

University of South Florida

John Liederbach

Bowling Green State University

Please contact https://support.pearson.com/getsupport/s with any queries on this content

Cover Image by Tetra Images/Getty Images

Library of Congress Cataloging-in-Publication Data

Names: Swanson, Charles R., author. | Taylor, Robert W., author. | Territo, Leonard, author. | Liederbach, John, author.
Title: Police administration: structures, processes, and behaviors/Charles R. Swanson, University of Georgia, Robert W. Taylor, The University of Texas at Dallas, Leonard Territo, University of South Florida, John Liederbach, Bowling Green State University.
Description: [Tenth edition]. | Boston: Pearson, 2021. | Includes index. | Summary: "The field of police administration is dynamic and ever changing. Laws are modified, new problems occur, and administrative practices that were once accepted as gospel are challenged, modified, and, in some cases, discarded. Beginning in the turbulent 1960s with the due process revolution, followed by the civil rights movement, the Vietnam War demonstrations, widespread riots in our largest cities, the President's Commission on Law Enforcement and the Administration of Justice, and largescale research on policing, the somewhat static precepts of policing came under increased scrutiny. Like a ball gaining speed as it rolls down a steep hill, change has become more fast paced, urgent, and pervasive"—Provided by publisher.
Identifiers: LCCN 2020042456 (print) | LCCN 2020042457 (ebook) | ISBN 9780135728338 (paperback) | ISBN 9780135728369 (ebook)
Subjects: LCSH: Police administration.
Classification: LCC HV7935 .S95 2021 (print) | LCC HV7935 (ebook) | DDC 363.2068—dc23
LC record available at https://lccn.loc.gov/2020042456
LC ebook record available at https://lccn.loc.gov/2020042457

4 2021

ISBN 10:   0-13-572833-9
ISBN 13: 978-0-13-572833-8

Dedicated to Charles R. "Mike" Swanson (1942–2020)

For our good friend, partner, mentor, scholar, and coauthor for over 50 years. Mike was one of the kindest and most intelligent persons we have ever known, and he will be greatly missed by all of us!

— Bob, Lenny, and John

BRIEF CONTENTS

CONTENTS

Chapter 9   HUMAN RESOURCE MANAGEMENT   290

PART 3   The Management of Police Organizations   340

Chapter 10   ORGANIZATIONAL AND INTERPERSONAL COMMUNICATION   342

Chapter 12   FINANCIAL MANAGEMENT   402

PART 4   The Management of Police Organizations   428

Chapter 13   STRESS AND POLICE PERSONNEL   430

PREFACE

The field of police administration is dynamic and ever changing. Laws are modified, new problems occur, and administrative practices that were once accepted as gospel are challenged, modified, and, in some cases, discarded. Beginning in the turbulent 1960s with the due process revolution, followed by the civil rights movement, the Vietnam War demonstrations, widespread riots in our largest cities, the President's Commission on Law Enforcement and the Administration of Justice, and large-scale research on policing, the somewhat static precepts of policing came under increased scrutiny. Like a ball gaining speed as it rolls down a steep hill, change has become more fast-paced, urgent, and pervasive.

Even while revising this book, we returned to already "finished" chapters to include new and significant changes to policing brought about by the COVID-19 pandemic, the death of George Floyd in Minneapolis, MN, and Breonna Taylor in Louisville, KY, and the resulting social unrest stemming from the Black Lives Matter movement in cities like Seattle, WA, Portland, OR, Chicago, IL, and New York City. Renewed calls to "defund" and even abolish the police highlighted consistent demands to reform the way our communities are secured and safeguarded. These significant additions represent our efforts to keep the book contemporary and up-to-date. Most importantly, they represent our goal to keep the book, strong, yet balanced in addressing some of the most important issues in the history of policing in our country.

Collectively, the four authors of this text have been police officers, detectives, administrators, and educators for over 120 years. We have studied, practiced, researched, taught, and consulted on police administration, and an inevitable by-product of these experiences is the development of certain perspectives. In addition to meticulous research and recent events, our own insights also undergird this book.

NEW TO THIS EDITION

This revision of *Police Administration* includes the following:

- A new and updated format for the book that features a full color design and accompanying digital products;
- Many new, revised, and updated sections, for example, failed police leadership, supplemental budgets, a new discussion on Suicide by Cop (SbC) and new information on evidence-based policing;
- Coverage of timely topics, such as the impact of the COVID-19 pandemic on policing;
- Important developments, such as the closer scrutiny of police officers use of deadly force, new laws

presented to curb police brutality and illegal use of deadly force, highlighted discussions relating to the death of George Floyd, and the impact of social unrest in our cities witnessed through protest and riots by the Black Lives Matter and the Antifa movements;
- New photographs, figures, tables, and box items on current topics and Quick Facts boxes that further illuminate chapter narratives. To illustrate, a highlighted box item features a discussion of the Camden County Police Department in New Jersey, following its dramatic reformation in 2012.

Users of the book will find much that is familiar to them and carefully planned additions to continue moving it forward. The thumbnail sketches of chapters in the following section illustrates, without being exhaustive, what we have done with this revision. In forging this edition, we kept the reader, the profession, and the impact of policing on our larger society foremost in our minds.

CHAPTER 1: THE EVOLUTION OF POLICE ADMINISTRATION

- Added new figures on Sir Robert Peel, the "Buffalo Soldiers," and the "Hole in the Wall" gang
- Fresh and revised content in many areas of the chapter, including new text on August Vollmer, a new box item on John Dillinger, and the attempted assassination of President Ronald Reagan
- New and updated research on terrorism
- A new section addressing the recruitment and staffing of policing in light of current social unrest aimed at controversial police use of deadly use of force
- A new section focusing on the impact of COVID-19 on policing
- Additional new box items, Quick Facts, and photographs

CHAPTER 2: POLICING TODAY

- New and revised material on the impact of the decline in crime over the past decade on police departments nationally with a special focus on new, rising violent crime rates in large cities
- Revised material on the primary elements of community policing with a focus on organizational structure

- New and updated material on evaluation research and community policing, evidence-based policing, hot-spots policing, intelligence-led policing, and predictive policing
- New material entitled "Research on Chicago's CAPS Program"
- A new box item entitled "Advances in Community Policing: Community Advisory and Review Boards"
- Updated material on community policing models in Newport News, Virginia; Chicago, Illinois; and Minneapolis, Minnesota
- New material on the use of social media and policing, with a new box item entitled "The Lip Sync Challenge: Social Media and Police Community Relations"
- New material on police body-worn cameras
- New material on the militarization of the police
- New material on police-community relations crisis and the death of George Floyd
- New box item entitled "Honoring Police Today"

CHAPTER 3: INTELLIGENCE, TERRORISM, AND HOMELAND SECURITY

- New box item entitled "Types of Fusion Centers"
- Updated material highlighting the Nation Fusion Center Association (NFCA) and the National Counterterrorism Center (NCTC)
- New box item on the National Counterterrorism Center (NCTC) and predicting the next terrorist strike
- Updated material on the U.S. Department of Homeland Security and Presidential Directives
- New box item entitled "Crisis in Removing Unlawful Immigrants"
- Updated information relating to the shooting at the Pulse night club in Orlando, Florida and the Walmart Supercenter in El Paso, Texas
- Updated material on the Islamic State in Iraq and Syria (ISIS) and the death of Abu Bakr al-Baghdadi
- New material on identified radical Islamic terrorist groups including al-Qaeda, Hezbollah, the Muslim Brotherhood, al-Shabaab, and the Islamic State (ISIS)
- New and updated material on international terrorist groups and threats including Boko Haram, "El Chapo" Guzman, and the Mexican Cartels
- New and updated research on "Homegrown Terrorist" including material on threats from the left including Antifa and the Black Lives Matter movement
- Updated and new material on right-wing terrorism

CHAPTER 4: POLITICS AND POLICE ADMINISTRATION

- A completely new chapter outline and reordering of material to place upfront and emphasize the role of local political forces on the job of the police administrator
- Updates to materials on controversial police encounters and emerging political issues including the notorious encounters involving Freddie Gray, Michael Brown, Tamir Rice, and Eric Garner
- Revised material concerning the various types of external mechanisms of control and citizen complaints against the police
- Revised material on the office of the county sheriff as a distinct political entity

CHAPTER 5: ORGANIZATIONAL THEORY

- New material on quality-of-life crimes and mutual benefit associations
- New workflow, and organizational chart models for police departments
- New section entitled "Neoclassical, Hawthorne, or Reformatted Bureaucratic Model" of Organizational Theory
- New section on the "bones" and actions of policing
- New material on automated red light and photo radar speeding enforcement
- Additional new box items, Quick Facts, and photographs

CHAPTER 6: ORGANIZATIONAL DESIGN

- New box items on shared leadership, organizational structure and community policing
- Updated material on the factors that influence organizational design
- Updated material on organizational design and the investigative function with pointed discussion on crime and police factors that impact investigation
- Updated material on the organizational structure of state police agencies using the California Highway Patrol as an example
- Revised and updated material on the unique structure of sheriffs' offices in the United States

CHAPTER 7: LEADERSHIP

- New material on the dark side of self-monitoring and leadership
- New material on problems relating to police chief turnover
- New box items, Quick Facts, and photographs

CHAPTER 8: PLANNING AND DECISION MAKING

- New box item on the pitfalls of reactive planning and the walk-back from body-worn cameras within some medium and small police agencies due to cost
- New box item concerning preparation for organizational planning and the need for citizen involvement in the process
- New box item on the Law Enforcement Advancing Data & Science (LEADS) program designed to encourage and aid police officers in conducting their own research
- New box items, Quick Facts, and photographs

CHAPTER 9: HUMAN RESOURCE MANAGEMENT

- Updated all major federal laws and court decisions pertaining to Human Resource Management
- Updated material on gender and other pay disparities
- Updated material on police selection during the COVID-19 pandemic
- New box item on the impact of Seattle's efforts to defund the police department on officers of color leading to the protest resignation of Chief Carmen Best
- Updated material on internal affairs investigations, police use of force, and discipline matrix
- New box item on suits filed that allege "opposing discrimination" by police officer and police unions

CHAPTER 10: ORGANIZATIONAL AND INTERPERSONAL COMMUNICATION

- New chapter introduction
- Reordering and condensing of existing material throughout the chapter

- Revised materials on police encounters with special audiences
- New primary section on electronic mediums of communication including revised and new material on the importance of mobile devices, e-mail, and the use of social media platforms by police such as Facebook, YouTube, Nixle, and Twitter

CHAPTER 11: LABOR RELATIONS

- Labor-management relations in the face of funding cutbacks. These include setting new priorities and making specific recommendations on how best to deal with budget reductions
- New box items, Quick Facts, and photographs

CHAPTER 12: FINANCIAL MANAGEMENT

- Updated and new material on "Economy and Police Budgets" section with a focus on "Impact of COVID-19 and Fiscal Health" section
- New content on Camden, New Jersey: A Case Study in "Defunding" the Police
- New material on 2020 budget cycles and calendars
- New information on police budget modification and adjustments
- New information on line item, program, and performance budgets
- New content on the Black Asphalt Electronic Networking & Notification System
- New box items, Quick Facts, and photographs throughout the chapter

CHAPTER 13: STRESS AND POLICE PERSONNEL

- Updated research on police officer homicide and suicide.
- New box items on shift work and potential health problems, the effect of shift work on officer safety and wellness, and the dangers of "microsleep" or falling asleep without knowing it.
- New and updated material on peer support programs
- Updated material on the Chicago EAP
- New box items, Quick Facts, and photographs throughout the chapter

CHAPTER 14: LEGAL ASPECTS OF POLICE ADMINISTRATION

- Updated all cases relating to legal cases and police administration
- Expansive new box item on defining key terms in U.S. Code 42, Section 1983 litigation cases, police training and liability from an officer's perspective
- Revised and updated material on *Graham v. Connor* (1989) and the new "Stephon Clark Law" passed in California
- New material on "swatting" and police liability
- New and updated material on police sexual violence (PSV)
- New box items on (1) the impact of police body cameras on police liability; (2) the deadly statistics associated with police pursuits and chases; (3) police sexual violence as an emerging law enforcement issue; and (4) police membership in hate groups
- New material on suicide by cop (SbC)
- Updated material relating to case law and use of force by the police
- Updated material on police officers' rights, particularly those focusing on officers who are minority, women and/or gay

CHAPTER 15: ORGANIZATIONAL CHANGE

- Updated introductory material on organizational change and the factors that impact successful change in policing
- Updated material on why change occurs as a reaction to crisis, fluctuating crime rates, technological advances, funding and economic decline, politics, a changing workforce, and a changing and new paradigm shift in policing focusing on new strategies to cope with rising crime rates with less resources
- New box items that focus on (1) organizational change in policing in wake of police-community unrest; (2) the effect of economic downturn on police agencies; (3) the race gap in America's police departments; and (4) confronting the real problem in America's inner cities
- New box item entitled, "Police Recruiting: A Case for Organizational and Cultural Change"
- Revised material on the role of the police culture in organizational change
- Updated material on the impact of COVID-19, information technology, and change on policing in the future

Organization

The overall flow of the book starts with Chapter 1 (The Evolution of Police Administration), which explains how the field of police administration developed and is continuing to develop, and ends with Chapter 15 (Organizational Change), which describes important strategies for going forward. Essentially, these two "bookend" chapters chronicle how we got here and suggest the means to move beyond the here and now.

The chapters in this book are grouped into four parts, generally moving from broader topics to more specific ones:

PART ONE: FOUNDATIONS

The four chapters in Part One are grouped together because they provide a "wide lens" view of the field of police administration. Part One is usefully characterized as providing a "base layer" of information about the field of police administration so the subject specific chapters that follow have a context in which to occur.

Chapter 1, "The Evolution of Police Administration," is a historical overview of how that field developed in the United States, along with general description of where it is now. This description serves to prepare the reader for some of the important topics to be covered in more detail in the chapters that follow. Chapter 2, "Policing Today," covers current policing philosophies, their characteristics, and impact, as well as discussion on some of the most pressing issues confronting policing today. Chapter 3, "Intelligence, Terrorism, and Homeland Security," addresses the terrorism threat and its impact on national laws and policy, as well as its effect on the role of state and local law enforcement agencies. Chapter 4, "Politics and Police Administration," examines the political effect of various institutions, officials, and the public on law enforcement agencies, as well as some major forces impacting on law enforcement agencies, such as the increased scrutiny of police use of force cases that started with Ferguson, Missouri, in 2014 and gained prominence with the series of deadly encounters between the police and unarmed African-American males that followed, highlighted by the death of George Floyd in Minneapolis, Minnesota in 2020.

PART TWO: THE ORGANIZATION AND THE LEADER

Organizations exist to do the things people can't do for themselves in modern society. They must be thoughtfully designed to achieve the purposes for which they have been created. Leaders are responsible for ensuring organizational performance. To do so, they must plan, envision the organization's future, make decisions, select a course of action from alternatives, and direct the human resources (HR) program. HR is of substantial importance to police administration because it is the largest single class of expenditures for police services: at least 80 percent of the police operational budget is encumbered by costs for

it. These connections constitute the basis for grouping five chapters together in Part Two.

Chapter 5, "Organizational Theory," traces the different ways organizations can be structured and the assumptions that different approaches make about people. To illustrate, the classical bureaucratic approach holds that subordinates must be closely watched, resulting in such effects as narrow spans of control, which in term, contribute to "tall" organizational structures that often have seven, eight, or even more horizontal layers. Chapter 6, "Organizational Design," introduces concepts and the decisions that affect how organizations are designed and structured. Chapter 7, "Leadership," is a comprehensive treatment of the subject, including definitions and theories about it, and the difference between authority and power. A major section illustrates why police leaders fail because those lessons are often more illuminating than content about what leaders "should" do. Remember the failed leadership section as "Thou shalt nots" to be rigorously avoided. Chapter 8, "Planning and Decision Making," covers two related skills law enforcement leaders use to help create and sustain improvements. Chapter 9, "Human Resource Management," provides the knowledge necessary to direct the HR program, including the maze of federal laws regulating it, as well as the numerous moving parts HR has including recruitment, testing, selection, training, and promotional testing. Law enforcement leaders need to be well versed in HR because so much is spent on it and so many things can go wrong and create liabilities.

PART THREE: THE MANAGEMENT OF POLICE ORGANIZATIONS

Part Three focuses on a trio of key, organization-wide management processes. Chapter 10, "Organizational and Interpersonal Communication," is included because nothing can be started, guided, receive corrective action, or be terminated without communication. Chapter 11, "Labor Relations," provides information regarding labor relations, including establishing the collective bargaining relationship, bargaining, and contract administration. While some law enforcement executives chafe at the existence of a union in their agency as a restriction on executive actions, others hold that a carefully negotiated contract make administration easier because so many aspects of the management-union membership relationship is regulated in clear terms. Police chiefs and sheriffs know that their agencies run on three important elements: staff, information, and money. When budgets are slashed, the result is fewer officers and deputies to protect the same area and fewer dollars to analyze information. While volunteers can be trained to perform some tasks, severe budget cuts translate into reduced or entirely eliminated functions. Such things explain why knowledge about, and skill in financial management is one of the premier attributes of law enforcement leaders and why Chapter 12, Financial Management, is so important.

PART FOUR: ORGANIZATIONAL ISSUES

This concluding part contains three chapters that are grouped together by being specific issues that touch the entire law enforcement organization. Chapter 13, "Stress and Police Personnel," effects all sworn personnel and often civilian employees as well. Negative stress degrades individual and sometimes unit and agency functioning. Chapter 14, "Legal Aspects of Police Administration," centers on police civil liability, which often arises out of the misuse of force and high-speed pursuits. In recent decades, the old refrain that law enforcement agencies are very traditional and resist change has been dismissed by a newer reality: The pace of change in law enforcement is rapid, if not bordering on chaotic. Police departments across our country face some of the most critical issues and challenges they have ever confronted, and in some cases, future reform may well mean significant functional and structural change dramatically impacting the very role of police in our communities. Such discussion closes the book in Chapter 15, "Organizational Change."

Pedagogical Features

This book is rich with pedagogical or teaching tools that were selected based on research on what tools were helpful. The teaching tools included in this book are as follows:

- **Learning Objectives**
  At the beginning of each chapter, there are behaviorally stated learning objectives which can be used to focus students on what they should learn in the chapter. In this regard, learning objectives provide an important study guide. The objectives are stated in specific terms so that the learning outcome is clearly understood and students will know what they should be able to do when finished with the chapter. The learning objectives also serve as the basis for the chapter summary.
- **Key Terms and Definitions**
  The key terms in each chapter are in bold and at the end of each chapter, there is an alphabetized list of Key Terms. At the end of the book, there is an alphabetized glossary of all Key Terms and their definitions. This feature eliminates the need to search several previous chapters looking for the definition of a term.
- **Photographs, Tables, and Figures**
  The book is replete with these three types of learning tools. Many of the photographs have not appeared in other criminal justice books and some of the tables and figures were prepared by the authors and are unique to this work. The photographs, tables, and figures complement the narrative content.

- **Quick Fact Boxes**

  These boxes are short, informative, and interesting supplements to the content of a chapter, for example, in Chapter 1, "The Evolution of Police Administration," there is a biographical sketch of August Vollmer. If it appeared in the narrative, the flow of the chapter would be disrupted, but the information is illuminating and therefore deserved a place in the chapter. Each chapter contains several Quick Facts boxes.

- **Box Items**

  These boxes contain more extended information, than Quick Facts boxes and provide relevant supplemental information to the chapter. Each chapter has multiple box items.

- **Chapter Summary**

  The chapter summary is based on the learning objectives and reinforces what the student has learned after completing the chapter. Each learning objective is stated and then followed by a statement of what should have been learned by fulfilling that objective.

- **Chapter Review Questions**

  The Chapter Review Questions call attention to other learning opportunities in the chapter that, arguably, could have been included as learning objectives. These are important points of learning that will facilitate additional student growth and can also be the basis of classroom discussions and short essay examination questions.

- **Critical Thinking Exercises**

  Critical interest exercises promote student interest and participation. Each of the 15 chapters has two or more Critical Thinking Exercises that can be assigned to individual students or groups that report back on their conclusions. This could be done in class or as out-of-class experiences. They may also be used to stimulate class discussions and involvement.

Instructor Supplements

Instructor's Manual with Test Bank. Includes content outlines for classroom discussion, teaching suggestions, and answers to selected end-of-chapter questions from the text. This also contains a Word document version of the test bank.

TestGen. This computerized test generation system gives you maximum flexibility in creating and administering tests on paper, electronically, or online. It provides state-of-the-art features for viewing and editing test bank questions, dragging a selected question into a test you are creating, and printing sleek, formatted tests in a variety of layouts. Select test items from test banks included with TestGen for quick test creation, or write your own questions from scratch. TestGen's random generator provides the option to display different text or calculated number values each time questions are used.

PowerPoint Presentations. A PowerPoint lecture package is available for use in class.

To access supplementary materials online, instructors need to request an instructor access code. Go to www.pearsonhighered.com/irc, where you can register for an instructor access code. Within 48 hours after registering, you will receive a confirming e-mail, including an instructor access code. Once you have received your code, go to the site and log on for full instructions on downloading the materials you wish to use.

Alternate Versions

eBooks. This text is also available in multiple eBook formats. These are an exciting new choice for students looking to save money. As an alternative to purchasing the printed textbook, students can purchase an electronic version of the same content. With an eBook, students can search the text, make notes online, print out reading assignments that incorporate lecture notes, and bookmark important passages for later review. For more information, visit your favorite online eBook reseller or visit www.mypearsonstore.com.

ACKNOWLEDGMENTS

Although it is insufficient compensation for their gracious assistance, we wish to recognize here the individuals who helped to make this book a reality.

Bob wishes to give a very special "thank you" to Ms. Jennifer Davis-Lamm, Caruth Police Institute, Dallas Police Department for her outstanding research and energy on this project. Her hard work helped improve the overall quality of this edition. He would also like to thank his wonderful and beautiful wife Mary for all her love and support during the long writing schedule and production of this edition.

Lenny wishes to thank his long-time administrative assistant, Sharon Ostermann, for her work on this edition, as well as providing invaluable assistance in conducting the necessary research to be certain this edition contained the most current and accurate information in policing today.

Her pleasant attitude and considerable intelligence made this revision a much easier task. He would also like to thank his wife Elena, and their children, Lorraine, Kseniya, and Illia, and their grandchildren, Matthew, Branden, Alexander, and Anna for their love and inspiration during the writing of this book.

John would like to thank his wife, Allyson, and son, Ben, for their enduring love and support throughout this project.

Finally, we would like to thank the following reviewers for their comments and suggestions: Jennifer Hammack, Georgia College & State University; Collin Lau, Chaminade University; and John Prendergast, Holy Family University. We would also like to thank our editor, Holly Shufeldt, for her continued guidance, patience, and support during the writing of this book. It has been a pleasure working with her.

ABOUT THE AUTHORS

Charles R. "Mike" Swanson enlisted in the Marine Corps at the age of 17, after which he was a uniformed officer and detective with the Tampa Police Department. As deputy director of Florida, Governor Kirk's Council on Law Enforcement and Criminal Justice, he led a central and seven public safety regional offices to innovations in service delivery and in addition advised the governor on policy issues.

Subsequently, he taught criminal justice courses for a year at East Carolina University and then joined the University of Georgia's Carl Vinson Institute of Government working full-time with Georgia law enforcement agencies in solving practical problems and conducting agency assessments. In more than 200 seminars, he also trained over 10,000 police officers from over 40 states in topics ranging from advanced homicide investigation to organizational theory. Mr. Swanson also designed and led training in China's Shanghai Municipal Institute for senior governmental officials and has been a consultant to agencies in the United States, ranging from Elizabeth, New Jersey, to the Multnomah Department of Public Safety in Portland, Oregon. He has written over 100 consulting reports.

Mr. Swanson has extensive experience in police promotional systems. Notably, as an expert, he led a state patrol agency out of federal district court, designing and administering the new promotional system he developed for some 10 years. The commissioner of the state patrol described it as "Our agency's most important development in human resource management in the last 50 years." None of the approximately 14 agencies for which he designed promotional systems has been successfully sued. Mr. Swanson has extensive experience in job analysis and test validation, developing and administering more than 100 written tests, and exercises for oral, boards and assessment centers. He has also trained assessment center assessors from more than 20 states.

Rising through the ranks to retire as the interim director of the Vinson Institute, Mr. Swanson led its 183 faculty and staff members in a state-wide program of technical assistance, training, and research for state and local units of government in Georgia.

Among his other publications are several other coauthored books: *Terrorism, Intelligence and Homeland Security*, 2nd edition (Upper Saddle River, NJ: Pearson Publishing, 2019), *Criminal Investigation*, 13th edition (New York: McGraw-Hill Education, 2021), *The Police Personnel Selection Process* (1980), *Introduction to Criminal Justice* (1979), and *Court Administration: Issues and Responses* (1980).

Both *Police Administration* and *Criminal Investigation* were previously translated into Mandarin. The Georgia Association of Chiefs of Police twice recognized Mr. Swanson's contributions to the association. He received the first award for 20 years of service to the association and other contributions and later was named their first honorary chief of police. Mr. Swanson is the recipient of the Academy of Criminal Justice Sciences' O. W. Wilson Award for distinguished police research. The University of Georgia twice granted him Distinguished Service awards and a Walter Bernard Hill Award for Distinguished Achievement in Public Service. The governors of Florida, Kentucky, and Georgia have issued proclamations recognizing his contributions to law enforcement in their states.

Mr. Swanson holds a BS and MS in criminology from Florida State University and a PhD in political science with an emphasis in public administration from the University of Georgia.

Sadly, on June 29, 2020, Mike Swanson passed away leaving behind his wonderful wife of 18 years, Paige Mercer Cummings, and two daughters, Traci and Kellie. Mike Swanson loved his family, his church, being a Marine and a former Tampa cop, and the Georgia Bulldogs. We will forever miss his big smile, and never-ending supply of stories, any of which he would be happy to tell or repeat.

Robert W. Taylor is currently a professor in the Criminology Program at The University of Texas at Dallas. Before this position, he was the director of the Executive Masters in Justice Administration and Leadership Program and the former program head for the Public Affairs Program at UT-Dallas. Both are academic programs integrating the traditions of management, governmental affairs, policy analysis, and decision science in the public sector. The program hosted one of the largest graduate degree programs on campus including doctoral (PhD) and master's degrees in Public Affairs and Public Administration.

From January 2008 through 2010, Dr. Taylor was the executive director of the W.W. Caruth Jr. Police Institute at Dallas (CPI). The Institute was established through a $9.5 million grant from the Communities Foundation of Texas. Dr. Taylor was a principle party to the development of the Institute and was appointed the founding director by the University of North Texas System. The primary mission of the Institute is to provide direction and coordination of major training and research projects for the Dallas Police Department. The Institute represents a national "think tank" on policing strategies focused on major urban cities in the United States. From 1996 to 2008, Dr. Taylor was professor and chair of the Department of Criminal Justice at the University of North Texas. He served in this capacity for 13 years, and under his direction, the Department gained national prominence.

For the past 40 years, Dr. Taylor has studied criminal justice administration and specifically police responses to crime and terrorism, focusing on issues in the Middle East. He has traveled extensively throughout the Middle East, meeting several heads of state in that region. He has acted as a consultant to numerous federal, state, and local agencies, and since September 11, 2001, Dr. Taylor has been a consultant to the U.S. Department of Justice working with the Institute for Intergovernmental Research (IIR). He has also worked extensively throughout the Middle East, especially in the countries of Turkey, United Arab Emirates, Bahrain, and Lebanon. He has been an instructor for the U.S. Department of State, Anti-Terrorism Assistance (ATA Program) (2001–2006) and taught internationally in the Executive Seminar on Cyber Terrorism presented to executives of foreign governments. Dr. Taylor has also worked extensively with the U.S. intelligence community. He held appropriate *top secret* national security clearances through the JPASS system (currently archived).

Dr. Taylor has authored or coauthored over 200 articles, books, and manuscripts. Most of his publications focus on police administration and management, police procedures, international and domestic terrorism, drug trafficking, and criminal justice policy. His articles appear in numerous journals including *Defense Analysis* (University of Oxford, England Press), the *ANNALS* (American Academy of Political and Social Sciences), *Police Quarterly, Crime and Delinquency*, and the *Police Chief* (International Association of Chiefs of Police). Dr. Taylor is senior author of four best-selling textbooks, *Terrorism, Intelligence and Homeland Security*, 2nd edition (Upper Saddle River, NJ: Pearson Publishing, 2019); *Cyber Crime and Cyber Terrorism*, 4th edition (Pearson, 2019); *Juvenile Justice: Policies, Practices and Programs*, 5th edition (New York: McGraw-Hill, 2020); and *Police Patrol Allocation and Deployment* (Pearson, 2011). He is also the coauthor of two truly landmark textbooks, *Police Administration: Structures, Processes, and Behaviors*, 10th edition (Pearson Publishing, 2021) and *Criminal Investigation*, 13th edition (McGraw-Hill, 2021). These texts are used in over 700 universities, colleges, and police departments throughout the United States, Europe, the Middle East, Latin America and China, and continue to be developed into new editions.

Dr. Taylor has an extensive background in academic and professional criminal justice, having taught at four major universities and served as a sworn police officer and major crimes detective (lateral rank of sergeant) in Portland, Oregon, for over six years. In 1984, he was appointed as a research fellow at the International Center for the Study of Violence at the University of South Florida, Tampa, Florida, conducting various studies involving international and domestic terrorism, police training and management, public violence and homicide, computerized mapping, and international drug trafficking. He continues to conduct research in these areas and is the recipient of numerous grants and contracts (over $15 million in funded projects). His latest work has concentrated in four areas: (1) police use of force and improved tactical/strategic improvement through advanced training, decision-making, leadership, and management practices particularly addressing areas of officer-involved shootings; (2) international terrorism, especially Middle Eastern terrorist groups, and the spread of radical Islam; (3) evaluation of community policing, evidence-based policing, and other predictive policing strategies in the United States; and (4) police corruption and misconduct, including police sexual violence (PSV), focusing on organizational cover-up and the police subculture.

In 2004, Dr. Taylor was asked by the International Justice Mission in Washington, DC, to assist in the training of the Cambodian National Police on child sex slavery and human trafficking as part of a large project funded through the U.S. Department of State ($1 million). His interest and research in this area has led to a leadership role in designing and developing training efforts in the United States aimed at raising awareness of the human trafficking tragedy for American law enforcement officers, funded in part through the U.S. Department of Justice. Dr. Taylor focuses on the nexus between human trafficking, drug trafficking and the financing of terrorist incidents internationally and domestically.

In 2003, Dr. Taylor was awarded the University of North Texas, Regent's Lecture Award for his work in the Middle East. In March 2008, the Academy of Criminal Justice Sciences presented Dr. Taylor with the prestigious O.W. Wilson Award "in recognition of his outstanding contribution to police education, research and practice."

Dr. Taylor has been a consultant to the U.S. Army and the U.S. Marine Corp, the U.S. Department of Homeland Security, the U.S. Department of Treasury, Federal Law Enforcement Training Center, the U.S. Secret Service, the Bureau of Alcohol, Tobacco, and Firearms, the U.S. Department of Justice, the Federal Bureau of Investigation, the Drug Enforcement Administration, agencies within the U.S. intelligence community, the Police Foundation, the Police Executive Research Forum (PERF), the International Association of Chiefs of Police, and numerous state and local municipalities and private corporations. He has also conducted significant training in the United States protectorates of the U.S. Virgin Islands, Guam and Saipan, and the countries of Canada, England, France, Switzerland, Thailand, Cambodia, Barbados, Northern Cyprus, Bahrain, Venezuela, Russia, Finland, United Arab Emirates, Kenya, Singapore, and Turkey. He is an active member of the Academy of Criminal Justice Sciences (elected National Chair of the ACJS Police Section 2002) and the American Society of Criminology.

Dr. Taylor is a graduate of Michigan State University (Master of Science 1973) and Portland State University (Doctor of Philosophy 1981).

Leonard Territo is a professor emeritus in the Department of Criminology, at the University of South Florida, Tampa, Florida, and was previously distinguished professor of criminal justice at Saint Leo University, Saint Leo, Florida. He also served first as a major and then chief deputy (undersheriff) with the Leon County Sheriff's Office, Tallahassee, Florida. As chief deputy, he was responsible for the daily operation of the office. While serving with the sheriff's office, he was a major homicide investigative advisor on the murders committed by Theodore Robert (Ted) Bundy on the Florida State University campus in Tallahassee. This investigation eventually led to the arrest, conviction, and execution of Ted Bundy. He also served for almost nine years with the Tampa Florida Police Department and had assignments as a patrol officer; motorcycle officer; homicide, rape, and robbery detective; internal affairs detective; and member of the police academy training staff. Dr. Territo is the former chairman of the Department of Police Administration and director of the Florida Institute for Law Enforcement at St. Petersburg Junior College (now St. Petersburg College), St. Petersburg, Florida.

He was selected for inclusion in "Who's Who" in American Law Enforcement, selected as Florida's "Outstanding Criminal Justice Educator" by the Florida Criminal Justice Educators Association, cited for 10 years of "Meritorious Service" by the Florida Police Chiefs Association, given the "Outstanding Teacher Award" by the College of Social and Behavioral Sciences, University of South Florida, Tampa, Florida, and cited for 25 years of teaching and meritorious service to the Tampa Florida Police Academy and awarded the Saint Leo University, Saint Leo, Florida Outstanding Publication Award. He was recently awarded a Lifetime Achievement Award by the Department of Criminology at the University of South Florida.

He has also been qualified as a police policies and procedures expert in both federal and state courts in the following states: Alaska, Arizona, Florida, Georgia, Illinois, Iowa, Kansas, Kentucky, Louisiana, Michigan, New Jersey, Ohio, Oregon, Pennsylvania, Tennessee, Virginia, Washington, Wisconsin as well as the District of Columbia.

Dr. Territo has served as a lecturer throughout the United States and has instructed a wide variety of police subjects to thousands of law enforcement officials. In addition to writing over 50 articles, book chapters, and technical reports, he has authored, coauthored or edited the following books: *Criminal Investigation*, 13th edition (New York: McGraw-Hill Education, 2021), which is by far the bestselling book of its kind in the United States and has recently been translated into Chinese for use by the Chinese police and Chinese criminal justice students;

International Sex Trafficking of Women and Children: Understanding the Global Epidemic (3rd edition) (Looseleaf Law Publications, Inc. 2021); *Stress Management in Law Enforcement* (4th edition) (Carolina Academic Press, 2019); *Criminal Investigation of Sex Trafficking in America* (CRC Press, 2014); *The International Trafficking of Human Organs: A Multidisciplinary Perspective* (CRC Press, 2012); *Crime and Justice in America* (6th edition) (Prentice Hall, 2003); *College Crime Prevention and Personal Safety Awareness* (Charles C Thomas Publishers, 1989); *Hospital and College Security Liability* (Hanrow Press, 1987); *Police Civil Liability* (Hanrow Press, 1984); *Stress and Police Personnel* (Allyn & Bacon, 1980); and *The Police Personnel Selection Process* (Bobbs-Merrill Educational Publishing, 1977).

Dr. Territo has also coauthored a novel with Dr. George Kirkham titled *Ivory Tower Cop* (Carolina Academic Press, 2009), which is a mystery crime novel based on a true story. His books have been used in more than 1,000 colleges and universities in all 50 states and he has had numerous articles published in nationally recognized law enforcement and legal journals. His books have been used and referenced by both academic and police departments in 16 countries including Australia, Barbados, Belarus, Canada, Chile, China, Czech Republic, England, France, Germany, Israel, The Netherlands, Poland, Saudi Arabia, South Korea, and Spain.

John Liederbach earned his PhD in criminal justice from the University of Cincinnati in 2002. He worked as an assistant professor in the Department of Criminal Justice at the University of North Texas from 2001 to 2007. Since 2007, he has worked in the Criminal Justice Program at Bowling Green State University where he was promoted to professor in 2017.

His primary research interest is police behavior, and the focus of his published research is on varieties of police behavior across community types, racial profiling, the processing of citizen complaints, police-media relations, and police crime. He has also published research on white-collar crime, including studies focused on medical malpractice and the mortgage default crisis.

Dr. Liederbach has authored or coauthored 24 peer-reviewed journal articles and over 20 additional scholarly publications. He has published in a variety of journals including *Justice Quarterly*, *Police Quarterly*, and *Criminal Justice Policy Review*. He is coauthor of *Cyber Crime and Cyber Terrorism*, 4th edition (Pearson, 2019) and *Police Patrol Allocation and Deployment* (Pearson, 2011). He teaches graduate courses on law enforcement, research methods, policy analysis, and special topics, as well as undergraduate courses on policing, research methods, and senior seminar.

PART 1   Foundation

These first four chapters cover the history of policing, identify current major policing philosophies, describe how transnational and domestic terrorism have impacted the role of our law enforcement agencies, and discuss the continuing importance of politics. This section also introduces terms and concepts used in subsequent chapters.

Chapter 1, "The Evolution of Police Administration" differs from most other histories of policing because it has a specific, rather than a general, focus. It explains policing's trials and tribulations as the occupation morphed from a colonial night watchman system into complex organizations testing new policing philosophies and challenges. This chapter also chronicles the social, political, economic, and technological forces that continuously shape and reshape American policing.

The underlying thesis of this chapter is that policing is like a sandbar in a river, being shaped and reshaped by the currents of the society in which it is embedded. These include government/governing, special interest groups, courts, wars/military actions, violence/active shooters/mass murders, innovations in technology and policing philosophies, and terrorism.

Chapter 2, "Policing Today," begins with an examination of current police operational philosophies, also referred to as strategies. Included are community policing and the SARA model, harm-focused policing, evidence-based policing, hot spots, intelligence led, and predictive policing. Other sections cover information technologies, such as crime analysis, geographic information systems, using social media, body cameras, and the impact of information technologies. The chapter ends with information on the warrior and guardian styles of policing, unrest with the police, and improving police community relations.

Chapter 3, "Intelligence, Terrorism, and Homeland Security," addresses the significant shifts that have occurred in law enforcement in the wake of the 9/11 attacks on this country, as well as the threats posed by the Mexican drug cartels operating near our border, "home-grown" terrorists, and recent trends in radical Islamic groups, including al-Qaeda and ISIS. This chapter vividly illustrates the dangers of international terrorism, domestic right-wing hate groups, left-wing anarchists, and ecoterrorists.

Chapter 4, "Politics and Police Administration," supports the theme that policing and politics are inevitably intertwined in a democratic society. The chapter provides an overview of the major political actors that shape police administration and officer behavior on the street including local politics, court decisions and actors such as the district attorney, and citizens themselves. The chapter discussions how several recent and highly publicized events worked to exert political influence on police and their organizations.

CHAPTER ONE

THE EVOLUTION OF POLICE ADMINISTRATION

Learning Objectives

1. Define *politics* and give three reasons why it cannot be kept out of police agencies.
2. Identify the most negative and positive things about the patronage/spoils system.
3. Describe the impact of prohibition on policing.
4. Describe how World War II affected law enforcement.
5. Define and explain the unequal badge problem.
6. Explain leakage of intent by mass shooters and how it is accomplished.

INTRODUCTION

STUDYING THE EVOLUTION OF *police administration is crucial because: (1) the past is full of important lessons; (2) ignoring these lessons increases the probability that prior mistakes will be repeated and opportunities forfeited; (3) knowledge of the past breeds esprit de corps, or pride in the heritage of one's chosen profession; (4) it instills an appreciation that each of us stands on the shoulders of the men and women who served before us with dignity, compassion, and valor; (5) there is a more complete comprehension of where and why a profession is when you know where it has been; (6) concepts in this chapter are part of the vocabulary of policing; and (7) it sets the stage for further discussion in some of the chapters that follow.*

THE URBANIZATION OF AMERICAN POLICING

The earliest American colonists were primarily English. They depended on volunteer citizen night watchmen to patrol their villages from dusk to dawn. If there were threats, such as fires, crimes, and pirates, the watchmen raised an alarm. It became the collective responsibility of all residents to respond. Other offices familiar to the colonists, such as sheriff, constable, and coroner, were subsequently added. However, their numbers were very small. In 1625, New Amsterdam, now New York City, created its office of sheriff.[1]

In 1833, Philadelphia became the first city in this country to have a paid, full-time day police force.[2] Gradually, the widespread use of volunteer citizens' night patrols faded away. The paid day and night police departments were entirely separate. In 1844, New York City created the first unified day-night police force. After 1865, police uniforms (Figure 1.1) often incorporated features of those worn by Union soldiers in the Civil War (1861–1865).

To no small degree, the rise of unified, full-time police departments in America was influenced by events in England. During the late 17th and early 18th centuries, England's economy made two key shifts: (1) the industrial revolution (1760–1830)[3] shifted production from manual to machine made goods. Factories in cities replaced homes and small workshops as the dominant places of employment and (2) improved agricultural methods provided enough surplus crops to feed people living in cities, including factories. This further influenced a movement from farming to other occupations.

As the populations of England's cities grew, so did their problems, such as slums, crime, and appalling working conditions. As a result, social unrest escalated. The old ways of dealing with crime and unrest were inadequate. In 1829, Parliament passed the Metropolitan Police Act with the strong support of **Sir Robert Peel** (Figure 1.2), creating the first full-time police department for London. Peel introduced new principles such as candidates should be hired on a probationary basis.

FIGURE 1.1 ▶ The Colorado Springs (Colorado) Police Department circa 1890–1900. The influence of Union uniforms is plainly seen including the style of six belt buckles being worn. Chief Dana is in the middle of the second row. He wears two separated columns of buttons, which Union officers wore to quickly identify them as leaders. In the third row is the lone African-American officer, Horace Shelby.
(The Denver Public Library, Western History Collection, X-14668)

FIGURE 1.2 ▶ Sir Robert Peel. If we consider only policing, Sir Robert Peel (1788–1850) is an important historical figure. However, there is much more to him. Twice elected England's Prime Minister, Peel also championed laws prohibiting employing women and children in mines (1842) and limiting the numbers of hours they could work in factories (1844). In 1950, a horse he was riding fell and killed him, leaving us to wonder what other contributions Peel would have made had his life not been cut short. (IanDagnall Computing/Alamy Stock Photo)

FIGURE 1.3 ▶ A satire of police corruption. "Mulberry Ring" refers to the New York City Police Department, then located at 300 Mulberry Street. (Library of Congress Prints and Photographs Division [LC-USZ62-85436])

He stressed the need for professional conduct by the agency and its officers.[4] The effort to create a force in which the public would have confidence produced some startling numbers. In the first three years of its existence the new police department dismissed 5,000 officers and another 6,000 resigned; many of them were under pressure.[5]

American cities selectively drew on the experience of the London Metropolitan Police. They gradually created centralized, full-time police departments. However, many American politicians during the 1800s had no interest in hiring quality officers. Instead, they chose to use officers to suit their own purposes: graft, control of elections, and harassment of the opposition party.

In New York City during 1892, Presbyterian Minister Charles Parkhurst gave several sermons, which publicly exposed the city's political and police corruption. The sermons reached that city's now-defunct newspaper, *The World,* and a cartoon was drawn and printed (Figure 1.3). Notice the taunting message on the right-side of the cartoon, attributed to corrupt police officers, "To the pulpit, press, courts, & the people, the side doors to the dives are open again." It clearly communicated that the corrupters were more powerful than the reformers.

In the history and image of America, the "wild and wooly" West also looms large (Figure 1.4). Factors contributing to the settlement of the West included the discovery of gold at Sutter's Mill, California (1848), the availability of tracts of land to settlers under the Homestead Act (1862), and the conclusion of the Civil War. Although there were already free African-Americans in the West, that number was increased after 1865, due to (1) assistance from the federal **Freedmen's Bureau** (1865–1872), (2) flight from the South's new sharecropper system that effectively re-enslaved the recently emancipated, (3) the repressive laws enacted to keep "Negroes" segregated and powerless, and (4) the brutality of the **Ku Klux Klan (KKK),**

FIGURE 1.4 ▶ "Big Ned," Con Wagner, and "Ace" Moore were lynched in 1868 by vigilantes in a partially completed cabin near Laramie, Wyoming. Hoisted just off the ground with no fall to break their necks, the men slowly strangled. (Denver Public Library, Western History Collection, Arundel Hull, Z-5808)

FIGURE 1.5 ▶ Prosperous African-American Settlers. This photograph was taken in Nicodemus, Kansas during 1877. This family may have come West with Pap Singleton. (Everett Collection/Shutterstock)

which was formed in 1866 for social purposes, but quickly began using terror, lynching, and other violence to control African-Americans (see Figure 1.5).

The completion of the transcontinental railroad (1869) and the construction of other rail lines provided mass transportation into the West for adventurers and settlers. By the mid-1880s, cattle drives up the Chisholm and other trails from Texas to Abilene, Dodge City, Wichita, and other Kansas "cow towns" were a thing of the past due to the expansion of railroads, settlements, and the use of barbwire to close off open range. Three legendary lawmen policed Abilene, Bat Masterson, Wyatt Earp, and "Wild Bill" Hickok.[6]

West of the Mississippi, episodic war with Native Americans is traditionally dated as lasting from 1823 to 1890. However, the last battle was actually fought in 1918 (see Box 1.1). Eventually, the tribes were forced onto reservations, producing a need for law and order on tribal lands and protection from trespassers. Lacking any appropriated funds to create a reservation law enforcement capability, agents on various reservations scrapped together funds and recruited

Box 1.1: The Battle with Yaquis Indians in Bear Valley, Arizona

The Yaquis mistook the African-American troopers of the 10th Cavalry as Mexican soldiers seeking to intercept them. If caught, the penalty would be death, and so they opened fire. In the skirmish that followed, The Yaquis Indians living in Northern Mexico were in rebellion against their Mexican national government. Yaquis would cross into the United States, take jobs long enough to buy arms and ammunition, return to Mexico, and distributed the weapons to other Yaquis. At other times these goods were taken by raids on isolated ranches. On January 9, 1918, there was a chance meeting in Bear Valley, Arizona, between horse-mounted Yaquis headed south with newly purchased weapons and a patrol from the 10th Cavalry.[7]

At least one Yaquis was killed and nine captured. Those taken prisoner were tried on minor charges, served a 30-day confinement, and were released. Because World War I was still going on, the Bear Valley engagement got little attention in the news media or officially. The 10th Cavalry historically comprised African-Americans with an excellent reputation as fighters. Because of the ferocity with which they fought, Native Americans called them "Buffalo Soldiers."[8] For many years, buffalo soldiers served in all Black units ordinarily commanded by white officers, although there were some African-American officers. (See Figure 1.6.)

FIGURE 1.6 ▶ An unidentified African-American "Buffalo Soldier" of Company A, 25th Infantry Regiment, U.S. Army. African-Americans have fought in every war on the North American continent and also helped explore our West, beginning with the Lewis and Clarke expedition in 1805, and were well-regarded "law men" as well. This photograph was taken between 1884 and 1890. (Goff, O. S./Library of Congress Prints and Photographs Division)

FIGURE 1.7 ▶ Sioux Standing Rock Reservation Police Officer Red Tomahawk (L) wears boots, his pistol partially inside of his coat, and what appears to be a single-shot rifle at his side. Eagle Man (R) wears moccasins, his pistol is on his left hip, in a cross-draw holster. In his right hand is a repeating rifle. (Denver Public Library, Western History Collection, Photograph dated to 1880s, D. Barry, B-836)

Native Americans as police officers. The Congress finally began appropriating money for tribal police agencies in 1879 (see Figure 1.7).[9] Tribal enforcement agencies represent an out-of-the-mainstream example of police administration, as is the U.S. Mint Police (1792).

Western law enforcement agencies were typically small, their jurisdictions limited, and did little record-keeping. Marauding bandits could vanish into vast lands. Communication between agencies was often sparse, slow, and occasionally not operating. Opposing them was an abundance of murderers, rustlers, and stagecoach robbers, a small number of whom were unique.

Given the limitations of Western law enforcement agencies of the period, it is not surprising that the **Pinkerton National Detective Agency**, Wells Fargo detectives, and Union Pacific operatives developed a strong record in catching or killing these robbers. Unrestricted by jurisdiction, these private "lawmen" pursued bandits across jurisdictional lines and were aided by their employers' substantial record systems.

Notorious outlaws "Butch Cassidy" (Robert Parker) and the "Sundance Kid" (Harry Longabaugh) were part of a loose coalition of gangs whose primary hideout was the Hole-in-the-Wall Pass in Wyoming, a place with only one entrance and other natural defense features. Parker was the leader of a loose-knit gang called "the wild bunch" (Figure 1.8).

In 1890, the federal government announced that the frontier was closed and six states were later admitted to the union. Both the territorial governments of Arizona and New Mexico realized that their own aspirations for statehood would be

FIGURE 1.8 ▶ The Wild Bunch. This 1900 photograph of the dressed-up Hole-in-the Wall Gang was taken in Fort Worth, Texas. Also known as the Wild Bunch, they were the most successful train-robbing gang in history. Front row left to right: Harry A. Longabaugh (The Sundance Kid), Ben Kilpatrick (the Tall Texan), Robert Leroy Parker (Butch Cassidy), and standing: Will Carver, Harvey Logan (Kid Curry). Kilpatrick, Carver, and Harvey Logan all died violent deaths, none of them lived to 39 years of age. (Lordprice Collection/Alamy Stock Photo)

Quick Facts: Sitting Bull Killed by Tribal Police

Red Tomahawk, Eagle Man (from above Figure 1.7), and 37 other Native American police officers, along with four volunteers, attempted to arrest Hunkpapa Sioux spiritual leader Sitting Bull in 1890. The basis for the arrest was his rumored involvement with a potential uprising.

His followers opened fire to prevent the arrest. In the ensuing 30-minute battle, eight officers, Sitting Bull, and seven of his followers were killed. Among them was Crow Foot, his 17-year-old son. Sitting Bull had long maintained that contacts with white men could only result in the destruction of the Sioux way of life.

impeded by their image of being populated by thieves, rustlers, and bandits. Drawing on the long experience of the Texas Rangers (1823),[10] they created the Arizona Territorial Rangers (1860) and the New Mexico Territorial Mounted Police (1905) to curb lawlessness.

The significance of the **frontier closing** in 1890 is that it marks the onset of the swift transition from a rural, agrarian society to an urbanized one within only 30 years. The Census of 1920 revealed that 51 percent of Americans lived in an urban incorporated area, *but the definition of that area was a place with a population of 2,500 or more people.*[11]

POLITICS AND ADMINISTRATION IN THE 19TH CENTURY: ILLS OF THE PATRONAGE AND SPOILS SYSTEMS

Politics is the process of acquiring and maintaining control over a government, including its policies, administration, and operations. Politics has no established quality. Its nature comes from how it is used. There are several reasons why there is no way to keep politics out of policing or police departments: (1) police departments must be responsive to democratic control; (2) public policy is expressed in the laws, regulations, operating procedures, decisions, and actions taken or not taken by a governmental agency. Public policy is where politics and administration intersect. It is how governmental agencies are guided and controlled; (3) as a practical matter, politics flourishes in even the smallest agencies. The type of politics we want to keep out of policing is highly partisan party politics. It has had a long and unhealthy relationship with policing.

Historically, a **political machine** or **machine politics** is a tightly controlled political party headed by a boss or a small autocratic group. Their purpose was to repeatedly win elections for personal gain. This usually happened through graft and corruption. These parties had a hierarchical structure running from the boss at the top through the precincts to each neighborhood. There, block captains made sure supporters "voted right," or in-line with the preferences of the prevailing political machine.

The phrase "vote early and often" reflects the spirit of machine politics. It was coined in Chicago. Loyal voters there were rewarded with incentives for their support. These incentives included jobs, promotions, job transfers to more desirable positions, lucrative contracts, and liquor licenses. For new arrivals to America, prized incentives included getting help for their recently arrived immigrant relatives to gain housing, jobs, and citizenship. New York Senator William Marcy (1786–1857) is responsible for a related concept: "To the [election] victor belongs the spoils." This meant the elected had the authority to make patronage appointments and bestow other benefits.

When politicians reward loyal voters, it is called **patronage** or the **spoils system**. The worst use of it is when people are given jobs for their political and personal loyalty instead of their ability. This was a regular occurrence from roughly 1820 to 1883. To curb it, the **Pendleton Act** was passed (1883). It established the U.S. Civil Service Commission to enforce its provisions. The Act required federal employees to pass a competitive examination and be appointed on merit. Momentum for its passage was garnered from the assassination of **President James Garfield** (Figure 1.9) by Charles Guiteau, a mentally disturbed seeker of a patronage job as ambassador to France.[12]

FIGURE 1.9 ▶ An artist's sketch of the assassination of President Garfield at the Baltimore and Ohio train station in Washington, DC. His assassin is being apprehended in the background. (Library of Congress Prints and Photographs Division [LC-USZ62-7622])

Under the 19th-century patronage system, a person seeking employment in a police department usually needed a letter of endorsement from a powerful politician allied with the party in power. The letters were typically written by elected officials, such as members of the city council or county commission, prominent state officials, or power brokers. When a new party came to power, the entire staff of a police agency was often dismissed.[13]

Machine politics and the ugly side of patronage were enhanced by the absence of an effective secret ballot at the polls in many states during much of the 19th century.[14] Each political party distributed ballot tickets for its own candidates. Because these tickets varied in size and color, carrying a ticket into a polling place made voting a public act and subjected voters to harassment and intimidation.[15] Votes were sold for drinks and money, and states began slowly enacting residency requirements to vote.[16]

According to "Boss" Tweed (William M. Tweed, 1823–1878), the mid-1800s ringleader of the most powerful New York City political machine, ballots didn't make a difference, the counters did.[17] As a final insult to the democratic process, state courts, dominated by patronage judges, consistently ruled that ballots could not be released for investigating and prosecuting abuses, such as the widespread use of names of dead people as voters in an election.[18]

There are examples of resistance to corruption during the 19th century. In 1856, San Francisco citizens, outraged by election corruption, graft, and out-of-control crime, formed the Committee of Vigilance to provide "security for life and property." An earlier Vigilance Committee (1851) had only focused on rampant crime. Even with its own constitution and terms on the committee limited to three months, the committee was nonetheless a vigilante group, executing criminals, forcing corrupt elected officials to resign, and ordering people to leave the state immediately. Because the owner of the San Francisco newspaper supported the committee, its early reputation was excellent. However, as historians looked more closely at the committee, its reputation began to suffer. On the other side of the country, the **Lexow Committee** (1894–1895), named after its chairman, was established by the New York Senate to examine police corruption in the New York City Police Department. Its report, which ran some 10,000 pages, was instrumental in that city electing a reform candidate as mayor.

Nationally, some reform candidates were occasionally elected, although machine politics usually defeated them in the next election, and from time to time, the outrage of decent citizens boiled over, leading them to activities such as sacking brothels protected by politicians and engaging in election day violence. However, real progress was not made until the 20th century.

The Reformation Period

As policing entered the 20th century, our cities were staggered under the burdens of machine politics, rampant patronage, government inefficiency, poverty, corruption, crime, slums,

FIGURE 1.10 ▶ At the beginning of the 20th century, children were still being exploited as a labor source. Here, "coal breaker boys" (circa 1890–1910) take a break from their 14-hour days in the mines, where they separated chunks of coal. Note their lunch pails in the foreground. (Library of Congress Prints and Photographs Division [LC-D4-32069])

inadequate health care, riots, and the exploitation of woman and children by industries (see Figure 1.10).[19] State and federal governments were similarly dysfunctional and scandalized. Conditions were so intolerable that they finally became the stimulus for change.

Change came in the form of the **Reformation Period** (1900–1926), which had two immediate needs: (1) arousing the public from its apathy and (2) creating a conceptual cornerstone or model for improvement by separating politics and patronage, in the worst sense, from the administration of governmental agencies.

Arousing the Public from Its Apathy: The Muckrakers

Lincoln Steffens exposed major corruption in Chicago, St. Louis, and other municipalities in his *The Shame of the Cities* (1906). He believed that bribery was not an ordinary felony, but an act of treason that subverted democracy. Sinclair's novel, *The Jungle* (1906), called attention to major abuses in the meat-packing industry, which led to the passage of the Pure Food and Drug Act (1906). Churchill's *Coniston* (1906) addressed political corruption in New Hampshire and Phillips's *The Treason of the*

FIGURE 1.11 ▶ Colonel Roosevelt standing at the middle of his troops on San Juan Hill, Cuba, during the Spanish American War (1898). He previously served as Police Commissioner of New York City (1895–1897), famous there for his "midnight ramble," checking to see that officers were working their assignments. The charge up San Juan Hill propelled Roosevelt into national frame and later into the White House. (Library of Congress Prints and Photographs Division [LC-USZC4-7934])

Senate did likewise with that body. It was President Theodore Roosevelt (1858–1919, Figure 1.11,) who, in a 1906 speech, labeled Steffens, Sinclair, and other writers who exposed social ills, scandals, and corruption as "**muckrakers**." The muckraker tradition among investigative journalists continues today.

The Conceptual Cornerstone

The conceptual cornerstone of the reform movement was provided by Woodrow Wilson (1856–1924) while he was a faculty member at Bryn Mawr College[20] in Pennsylvania.[21] He later served as President of the United States (1913–1921). Wilson called for a dichotomy or separation of politics, in the worst sense of the word, and administration.[22] The idea was very progressive and forward-thinking at the time.[23]

As the work of the muckrakers and the conceptual cornerstone entwined, rapid progress was made. In 1906, the New York Bureau of Municipal Research was formed. Staunton, Virginia, appointed the first city manager in 1908, placing responsibility for day-to-day operations in the hands of a trained professional not beholding to any political party. Two years later, the **city manager movement** was well underway, and appointees were usually experienced engineers or business managers. Further impetus was created in 1914, when the International City Manager Association was founded and the University of Michigan offered a degree in municipal administration.

In 1916, the National Municipal League issued a model city charter calling for a strict separation of politics and administration, which had a trickle-down effect on the police and other departments. City managers worked hard to see that capable people were appointed to leadership positions. In 1922, the Cleveland Foundation completed a major study of crime in that city, which at that time was the fifth largest in the nation.[24] Separate groups worked on different aspects of the criminal justice system. **Raymond Fosdick** (1883–1972) guided the group working on the police department, which was soundly criticized. Fosdick concluded that it was mostly just a larger version of what existed there in 1866—the record system was meager, precincts were too numerous, there was confusion in the lines of authority, and widespread corruption was common. The Cleveland study is noteworthy because it appears to be the model, albeit one that was slowly adopted, of using outside experts to study police agencies.

As the separation of politics and administration gained traction, attention was focused on new ideas. For instance, scientific management sought to find the one best way to do things, the bureaucratic model was carefully articulated, and administrative theory formulated generic principles and methods of administration (see Chapter 5, Organizational Theory). The shift to these new ideas was marked by the publication of White's *Public Administration* (1926) and Willoughby's *Principles of*

Public Administration (1927). However, neither of the two abandoned the politics/administration dichotomy and they both endorsed the city manager's 1924 code of political neutrality.

During the Reformation Period, progress was made toward reducing corruption, fraud, waste, and abuse in government; creating a cadre of qualified personnel to hold public jobs, refining the civil service system; emphasizing proper recruitment, selection, training, and promotion of governmental employees; rescuing the public's business from highly partisan/machine politics; and developing new theories, models, and practices related to organizations. The Reformation Period represents more than mere history; it was the landmark that unleashed a process of improvement that has been continuous in terms of political and police professionalization. Chapter 2, "Policing Today" and Chapter 9, "Human Resource Development" cover some of these developments.

POLICE PROFESSIONALIZATION

Profession and Professional

The word **profession** comes from the Latin *pro* (forth) and *fateri* (to acknowledge or confess), meaning to announce a belief. In its earliest use, the word referred to public statements or declarations of faith.[25] By 1541, *profession* meant a learned occupation, but just 25 years later, its meaning was reduced to how a person habitually earned a living. In 1675, there was another shift, professing to be duly qualified. The serious work on professions is centered on specifying what criteria must be met

to constitute a profession. Table 1.1 illustrates three different views about such criteria.

Being seen as a profession was fundamental to transforming the public view of officers from corrupt thugs and heavy-handed brutes to something noble: professionals. Every opportunity to develop this view was seized upon. For example, when cars first became available, they were largely purchased by people with a degree of affluence, those thought of as being upper class. Knowing that such people were influential in molding opinions, Chiefs quickly assigned their best officers to traffic enforcement duties.

For years thereafter, many Chiefs, almost as a reflex, continued this practice, even after cars became commonplace. It was good public relations, and Chiefs knew that some of the goodwill created for the department would rub off on them. It was an advancement for policing, but the practice fell short of modern policing methods. August Vollmer led the way toward it.

August Vollmer

In this country, the father of modern policing is **August (Gus) Vollmer** (Figure 1.12 and see Box 1.2). Without detracting from the genius of his efforts, note that his successes paralleled the advances of the Reformation Period of 1900–1926.

Vollmer was elected Marshal of Berkeley (CA) in 1905. Four years later Berkeley incorporated and he was appointed that city's first Chief of Police, a position he held until his retirement in 1932. Vollmer interrupted his time in Berkeley, serving as Police Chief in Los Angeles, 1923–1924. He voluntarily returned to Berkeley, frustrated by deeply rooted problems and the antipathy toward him as an "outsider."

Carte summarized the work of this giant: Under Chief Vollmer's leadership, the Berkeley Police Department (BPD) became the model for professional policing. Vollmer championed hiring African-Americans and women as officers. He mobilized officers, moving them first to bicycles and then to patrol cars

TABLE 1.1 THREE VIEWS OF THE CRITERIA MAKING UP A PROFESSION[26]	
Most Commonly Identified Criteria	**Merton's Criteria**
1. An organized body of theoretical knowledge	1. Knowing (systematic knowledge) 2. Doing (trained capacity and technical skill) 3. Helping (knowing and doing)
2. Advanced study is needed to master knowledge	
3. A code of conduct guides action	
4. Prestige	
5. Standards of admission	
6. A professional association	**Becker's Criteria**
7. Altruism is the driving force for wanting to practice the profession	If you can get people to call you one, you are one.

FIGURE 1.12 ▶ Chief August Vollmer, Berkeley Police Department, circa 1925. (Courtesy Berkeley Police Department, Byron White, Public Information Officer)

Box 1.2: Milestones in August Vollmer's Life

Vollmer (1876–1955) was born in New Orleans to German immigrant parents. His formal education ended in the sixth grade. "Gus" served with the Marine Corps in the Philippines during the Spanish-American War (1898), fighting in 25 engagements with enemy forces.

In 1921, he was elected President of the International Association of Police Chiefs. Vollmer retired from the Berkeley Police Department in 1932. He remained active as a consultant and writer for many years. Suffering from failing eyesight, Parkinson's disease, and cancer, this extraordinary man ended his own life at 79 years of age.

---

with radios, introduced a police signal system to dispatch calls, created a network of callboxes, established a modern records system, used crime analysis to establish and staff geographical beats, founded the first scientific crime laboratory in the United States in 1916, and the first lie detection machine used in investigation was built in the BPD in 1921.[27]

Chief Vollmer is the father of modern policing in the United States. This remarkable man rose from humble beginning and a sixth-grade education to become a giant of innovation and a champion of a college degree for officers. Remarkably, he also introduced other important innovations, including using intelligence testing for selecting applicants, creating the first Juvenile Division, and was the driving force to establish the first criminology program at the University of California, Berkeley.

Despite these achievements, Vollmer is better known for his tireless efforts to improve the caliber of police personnel. He established formalized police training in 1908, encouraged officers to attend college classes, introduced intelligence and psychological testing for officers, and, around 1919, began recruiting college students.[28] Although they never constituted a majority, the "college cops" set the tone for the BPD over the coming decades. The most influential of these was **O. W. Wilson**.[29]

Orlando Winfield Wilson (1900–1972) both studied under Vollmer and worked for him as a patrol officer. After graduating from the University of California at Berkeley, he spent the next 14 years serving as Chief of the Fullerton, California, and Wichita, Kansas, Police Departments.

O. W. Wilson advocated many of the things Vollmer did, earning him a reputation as a progressive leader. In 1939, he joined the University of California-Berkeley faculty as professor of police administration. From 1943 to 1947, Wilson served as an Army Colonel in England, Italy, and Germany, often helping to reorganize police agencies.

He returned to Berkeley and became the Dean of the School of Criminology (1950–1960). In his last leadership role in a police department, O. W. Wilson became Superintendent of Chicago's scandal-ridden police department (1960–1967), earning him a reputation as a fair but tough-minded reformer.

Long established as an advocate of professionalism, O. W. Wilson's well-regarded *Police Administration* (1943) was another jewel in his crown and highly influential in policing circles for decades.[30] After Chief Wilson's death, the book was revised by various authorities and their names were added as co-authors with Wilson.

The Pendleton Act of 1883 to the Military Model

The Pendleton Act of 1883 eliminated some ills of the patronage/spoils system. In the three decades following the adoption of the Pendleton Act, state and local governments also adopted similar measures, although the spoils systems lasted well into the 1900s. The federal Hatch Act (1939) placed another wedge between politics and administration by forbidding federal employees from engaging in partisan political activities, which also spurred similar measures, or "Little Hatch Acts," that were enacted by state and local governments.

Although the rise of federal and state civil service systems seems intuitively attractive, some observers were not so enthusiastic. Fosdick, writing in 1920, concluded that the civil service system sometimes made it difficult to terminate officers who committed serious breaches because the evidence did not satisfy civil service requirements.

Civil service and Vollmer's notion of educated, professional officers also conflicted. The former's emphasis was on keeping politics out of policing, whereas Vollmer's concept of merit was competent performance. Perhaps as much as 80 percent of an agency's budget is spent on personnel and related support costs, so personnel issues continue to be prominent for chiefs today (see Chapter 7, Leadership; Chapter 9, Human Resource Management; and Chapter 12, Financial Management).

While some worked at ending the spoils system, other reformers sought to enhance professionalization by using a new model that presumably would lead to more efficient operations. They concluded the country was besieged by crime and that police, as our front line of defense against it, should be more analogous to the military.

The **military model** (Figure 1.13) resulted in more staff positions to do specialized work, an emphasis on both line inspection of officers and staff inspections of functions, written policies and procedures, enhanced training, increased accountability, and the widespread adoption of the bureaucratic form of organization (see Chapter 5, Organizational Theory), which

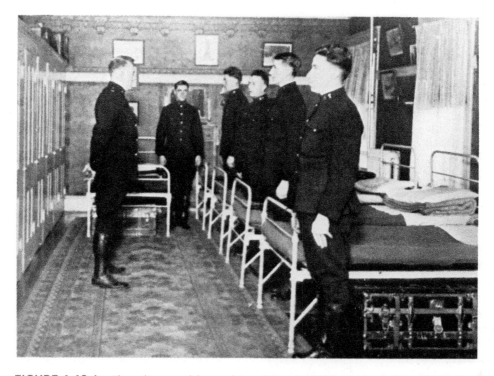

FIGURE 1.13 ▶ The military model at work in policing. A 1906 Pennsylvania State Police barracks inspection. (Courtesy of the Pennsylvania State Police)

remains in use today. The implementation of the military model required expanded authority for chiefs, who were then able to put an end to precincts operating so independently that they sometimes looked like separate agencies.

The military model was so persuasive that some jurisdictions hired military officers to head their law enforcement agencies. For instance, retired Marine Major General Smedley Butler was hired as Director of Public Safety in Philadelphia, serving during 1924–1925. General Butler is among an elite group of 19 men in our nation's history who were awarded two Congressional Medals of Honor for valor.

PROHIBITION TO THE 1930s

The Roaring '20s and Prohibition

The 1920s are often referred to as the "roaring '20s" because of the tremendous changes that occurred in America in that decade. Following World War I, military de-mobilization made available hundreds of thousands of young men to work in the rapidly expanding economy, as our factories shifted from the production of military necessities to consumer goods. Henry Ford made millions by producing affordable cars. The construction of highways quickly paralleled this development, as did the proliferation of motels, gas stations, cafes, and other businesses catering to travelers. Some state highway patrol agencies were created to foster the safe movement of vehicles along these new road systems. Suburbs, formerly limited to areas served by trolley and train lines, could spring up anywhere there were

roads. Some suburbs evolved into towns, resulting in more small police departments, and big-city police agencies added more officers.

Women rebelled at the existing strict social customs that dictated and limited norms of dress and behavior. A new sound, jazz, swept the nation, abetted by the rapid expansion of radio stations, which also created national sports heroes, such as baseball's Babe Ruth and golf's Bobby Jones. Also during the second decade of the 20th century, the first "talkie" movie was made, the rural electrification movement began, and telephone service expanded dramatically. Amid these changes, the "noble experiment" of **prohibition** was a defining force throughout the 1920s.

In the first half of the 19th century, ministers used their pulpits to denounce drinking, claiming that those who imbibed excessively were sinners who had lost their way with God. Thus, the **temperance movement**, which began in the second half of the 19th century, grew out of churches.

There were substantial reasons to oppose alcohol, since drunkenness was made worse by other vices commonly found in saloons, such as prostitution and gambling. Drinking contributed to both significant family and public health problems. In the 1800s, deaths by liver cirrhosis and chronic alcoholism were 25 per 100,000 people,[31] twice what it is now. Given these problems, the existence of a national prohibition law (1919–1933) can in part be viewed as pro-family legislation.[32]

In the second half of the 18th century, temperance crusaders turned from using moral persuasion to legal coercion.[33] Some 17 states adopted prohibition laws, although by 1903, all but three had abandoned them.[34,35]

CARRIE NATION

FIGURE 1.14 ▶ The family Bible recorded her name as Carry Nation (1846–1911), although it is habitually misspelled as "Carrie." She referred to herself as "a bulldog running along at the feet of Jesus, barking at what He doesn't like." (Library of Congress Prints and Photographs Division [LC-B2- 1131-3])

Making alcohol illegal was preceded by the formation and mutual support of various temperance movement organizations, including the Prohibition Party (1869), which promoted candidates for election, and the Woman's Christian Temperance Union (WCTU, 1874). Perhaps the best-known WCTU temperance activist was **Carry Nation** (see Figure 1.14) who went into saloons with a hatchet, ripping kegs open and scolding drinkers. She was arrested more than 30 times for these "hatchetations."

Prohibition was ratified as the 18th Amendment to the Constitution in 1919; the same year Congress passed the **National Prohibition Act**, more commonly known as the **Volstead Act**, as the legal means for enforcing the new amendment. The making, manufacturing, selling, bartering, transporting, importing, exporting, and delivery of alcohol were made illegal, with the exception that 200 gallons of alcohol could be made annually by homeowners for their own consumption.

However well intended, national prohibition resulted in a large, illicit market for alcohol that gangsters fought violently to control. They smuggled "booze" from Canada and across the ocean in "rum runner" boats, set up illegal breweries and stills, and hijacked their rivals' liquor convoys. Illegal bars called **speakeasies** were established, so named because at their entrances customers spoke the password softly before entering and drinking. In New York City alone, there were an estimated 32,000 speakeasies[36]. "**Bootlegger**" was a flexible term meaning people who made, smuggled, or transported liquor.

The prohibition era is a prime example of the law of unintended consequences. It did more to damage the image and reputation of policing than any other single event. To protect their operations, gangsters bribed police, judges, and other public officials to "look the other way" on a massive scale. The police professionalization movement was hampered and law enforcement suffered a self-inflicted black eye that lingered for decades afterward. Still, officers of integrity continued to enforce the law (see Figure 1.15). In Chicago, Eliot Ness, a federal Treasury agent, and 10 agents he handpicked were known as the **untouchables** because they couldn't be "bought." Nonetheless, prohibition created an environment in which organized crime could flourish in the United States,[37] and organized gangsters could widely influence politicians and police officers alike. Perhaps more importantly, many Americans developed a diminished regard for the law and authority during this period, because average citizens were defined as "criminals" and subsequently flaunted the law with regularity. Recognizing widespread disobedience to the Volstead Act and the many ills associated with it, Congress abolished the Volstead Act in 1931. Two years later, the 21st Amendment repealed the 18th Amendment. Still, the damage done to public esteem for government and its officials lingered on for years, and organized crime groups that prospered during the prohibition era continue to plague our society.

The Lawless Years: Late 1920s to 1930s

Overlapping with the later portion of the prohibition period, the lawless or gangster era lasted from the late 1920s and into the mid-1930s, when criminals filled their pockets as a result of spectacular bank robberies and kidnappings, known as the "**snatch racket**." These bandits operated in the same era as prohibition gangsters, but were independent of them, specializing in robbing "soft targets," small banks, and snatching wealthy people from their unprotected homes.

In the crash of October 1929, the stock market lost 80 percent of its value, wiping out billions of dollars of wealth. Millions of people became unemployed, and lost their homes, farms, and businesses. Consumer spending dried up. The severe droughts in the American prairie states during 1930–1936 created a "**dustbowl**" as fertile topsoil got blown away.

More people lost everything and immigrated, seeking a better life elsewhere, many going to California. Collectively, these immigrants were called **Okies** because so many of them, between 400,000 and 500,000, fled Oklahoma; the hardships of these families were memorialized in John Steinbeck's *The Grapes of Wrath*[38] (1939; Figure 1.16).

FIGURE 1.15 ▶ New York City police pour alcohol seized in a 1921 speakeasy raid into the sewer system. (Library of Congress Prints and Photographs Division [LC-USZ62-123257])

FIGURE 1.16 ▶ Her hard life is carved into the face of this 32-year-old mother. With her seven children, she lived in a migrant pea picker camp near Nipomo, California. Note the condition of the clothes, the kerosene lantern, and the canvas tent. Because the early pea crop failed, the camp is destitute. The parents of this family have just sold the tent and will use the money to buy food for their family. (Library of Congress Prints and Photographs Division [LC-USF34-9093-C])

In response to these migrations, some cities established **"bum blockades"** manned by police officers to turn back everyone who lacked sufficient funds to support themselves[39] so they wouldn't be a drain on local resources. In California, the police sold license plates at state line blockades as a partial test of finances. The bum blockades fueled negative opinions of the police among those who were turned away.

During the Great Depression, as a means to ensure that jobs went to local taxpayers and to help the local tax base, city and county governments enacted **residency requirements** mandating that employees live within the jurisdiction of the employing unit of government, and existing employees had to meet the same standard to keep their jobs.[40] Critics of the requirement argue that it placed officers and other city employees in a difficult situation. They had to choose between living in better neighborhoods, which they found difficult to afford, or living in lower income areas where their children may have to attend marginal schools.[41]

However difficult the 1930s were, law enforcement, surprisingly, gained some momentum, moving away from its tarnished image and toward increased legitimacy and authority in society. President Herbert Hoover appointed the **National Commission on Law Observance and Law Enforcement** in 1929, the first comprehensive study of crime and policing in America's history. It was commonly referred to as the **Wickersham Commission**, taking the name of its chairman. The Wickersham Commission issued its report in 1931, consisting of 14 volumes, much of it written by August Vollmer. Among its recommendations was support for civil service protection for the police and enhanced training and education. Major academic police programs sprang up or expanded at the University of California-Berkeley; Michigan State University; and Northwestern University.[42]

The importance of separating police and politics gained additional impetus as law enforcement associations emerged. In 1934, the **International Association of Chiefs of Police (IACP)** was formed.[43] The IACP issued a newsletter, creating a common perception of what was important to the profession. The FBI established its crime laboratory in 1932, which provided free analysis of evidence submitted by state and local police agencies. Two years later, the FBI launched its prestigious **National Police Academy (NA, 1934)** to train police executives, resulting in a core of knowledgeable leaders. As the next decade began in 1940, the **National Sheriffs Association (NSA)** came into being.

The kidnapping and murder of the infant son of "Lucky Lindy" Lindbergh, the first man to complete a trans-Atlantic flight, led to the adoption of the federal Kidnapping Act (1932), which gave the Federal Bureau of Investigation (FBI) jurisdiction over such crimes.

In some circles, bank robbers achieved celebrity status, with colorful names such as "Pretty Boy" Floyd, "Creepy Karpis," and "Handsome Harry" Piermont. These bandits moved rapidly from one state to another, frustrating state and local investigators who lacked wider jurisdiction. Congress passed the federal Bank Robbery Act (1934) and tasked the FBI with its enforcement. Relatively quickly, the FBI apprehended or killed notorious bank robbers resisting arrest, making it a very dangerous occupation. **John Dillinger** (1903–1934), who may have robbed two dozen banks, was killed in a gunfight with FBI agents outside of a Chicago theater, marking the end of the lawless era.[44]

Box 1.3: John Herbert Dillinger, Public Enemy Number 1

As a young boy in Indianapolis, "Johnny" ran with young toughs committing petty crimes. In prison, he was respected and made friends with prisoners, some of whom were later part of one or another of his gangs. A fast worker, Dillinger helped slower prisoners make their quota too, as they were assigned various work tasks in labor fields.

A prolific bank robber as an adult, he was brought down by a Romanian prostitute who morphed into an entrepreneurial madam with a string of brothels. She became an FBI informant hoping it would prevent her deportation because of her profession.

On July 22, 1934, after a tip from the above prostitute, John Dillinger exited Chicago's Biograph Theater as "Public Enemy Number 1." According to the FBI, "he reached for a pistol from his trouser pocket" and was killed by the agents. He was the last of the major "gangster era" figures to be brought down. Interestingly, although she collected a reward for informing on Dillinger, the above prostitute was still deported.

(GL Archive/Alamy Stock Photo)

Sources: FBI History, "Famous Cases & Criminals. See: https://www.fbi.gov/history/famous-cases/john-dillinger Elliott J. Gorn, *Dillinger's Wild Ride: The Year That Made America's Public Enemy Number One* (Oxford University Press, 2009).

The Ku Klux Klan: Formation to the 1930s

Perhaps as soon as the first slave ship reached our shores, the pernicious and voluntary malignancy of racial hatred began infecting some people in all walks of life, including law enforcement. Its toxicity endures to this day, although it is typically less overt, but even after all this time, it is still not eradicated

The KKK (Figure 1.17) was formed in Pulaski, Tennessee in 1866 by bored Confederate Army veterans who wanted to create a mysterious stir at parties.[45] They made up names for themselves such as Grand Cyclops and Imperial Wizard, and wore masks and robes made from sheets by the wife of a founding member. However, quite quickly the agenda shifted from fun to repressing former slaves, referred to as "freedmen," first by intimidation tactics and then by outright violence.

The KKK essentially took over some of the duties that **slave patrols** held until the end of the civil war. Those patrols, usually of three to six persons[46] could enter any plantation and search, without warrant, slave quarters, disperse all slave meetings, hunt down fugitive slaves, and administer impromptu punishments as they saw fit.[47] Many Southerners tolerated or approved of the Klan's activities. Freeing the slaves upset the status quo and created what many perceived to be chaos. The KKK repression of African-Americans maintained white supremacy and "restored order," warded off feared depredations by them, and created some resemblance to the pre-Civil War South.[48]

Through the decades, a fraction of police officers were KKK members. Other officers, while not KKK members, harshly discriminated against Blacks. While acknowledging that, it should not be lost that there have always been more "fair-minded officers."

Southern state and local legislatures adopted **Black Codes** in reaction to losing the Civil War. The codes were intended to keep African-Americans "in their place." During 1880–1960, **Jim Crow laws** added more restrictions. The name Jim Crow was taken from a minstrel show character played by white actors who blackened their faces with burnt cork, presenting a caricature of African-Americans.

Together, the Black Codes and Jim Crow laws made a mockery of equality. It was all but impossible for African-Americans to vote, and they were prohibited from assembling unless a white person was present. Separate facilities, including telephone booths, restrooms, drinking fountains, and cemeteries, were mandated. It was illegal to teach Blacks how to read or write, and mixed marriages were forbidden. Enforcement of these laws caused the police to drop even lower in the estimation of African-Americans. To assert their power and intimidate Blacks, KKK members periodically held parades (see Figure 1.17).

The federal **Forces Act** (1870) was passed in response to the actions of the KKK. Prosecutions under the Act resulted, for the most part, in the disintegration of the Klan, although

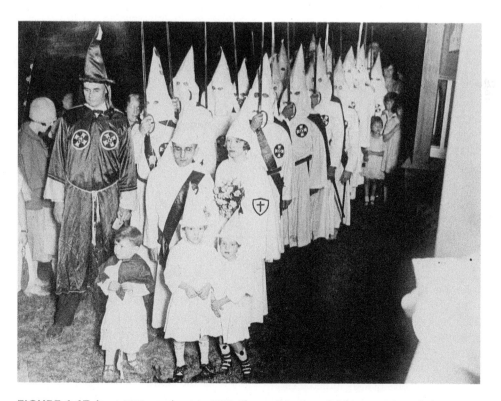

FIGURE 1.17 ▶ A KKK parade, circa 1921. The participation of children was intended to indoctrinate them in hate. (Library of Congress Prints and Photographs Division [LC-F81-43556])

Box 1.4: A Fair-Minded Officer Catches a Break

Around 4:10 a.m. on an October night, a lone white officer stopped a car in a rural area. It was running off both sides of a two-lane road. As he stepped out of his patrol car, six African-American men in various stages of intoxication got out of the stopped vehicle. They slowly inched toward the officer making violent threats. Later, the officer injected some humor into what was a dangerous situation, "Those guys were whipping themselves up. The only threats they didn't make were salting my well and burning my picket fence."

Backup was a long way off and the officer was mentally racing through his options when a car pulled up behind his.

Two more Black men got out. The officer thought, "I need this like Custer needed another Indian." Each of the new arrivals stood on either side of the officer. In a command voice, the larger one immediately issued an order, "You do exactly whatever this man says, he's our officer."

After everything was handled, the larger man motioned toward the officer, "I don't like you worth a damn just because of that blue shirt you wear. But, folks talk and say you're fair and give some breaks. That's why we stopped."

---

arguably state and local legislative bodies had substantially achieved white supremacy through the Black Codes. Since the reconstruction following the Civil War, the KKK has reinvented itself several times (see Chapter 3, Intelligence, Terrorism, and Homeland Security).

THE 1940S AND 1950S: WAR, FEAR OF COMMUNISM, THE PROFESSIONAL MODEL REASSERTED, AND THE KOREAN WAR

This period is dominated by World War II (1941–1945) and the Korean War (1950–1953). The mobilization of able-bodied men for military service created opportunities for women in policing and the defense industry. The police took on new responsibilities as part of the war effort, the civil rights movement was born, there was substantial fear of communism, and the publication of O. W. Wilson's **Police Administration** reaffirmed the professional model of policing.

The 1940s: World War II and Some Progress for Women in Policing

In reaction to the Japanese surprise attack on Pearl Harbor, Hawaii (December 7, 1941), the United States issued a declaration of war against Japan the following day. Three days later, fellow Axis powers, Germany and Italy, declared war against the United States. In 1942, war was declared against three allies of Germany, including Romania, Hungary, and Bulgaria.

The men in public safety agencies had no exemptions from compulsory military service. They volunteered and were drafted in great numbers. Departments quickly turned their attention to the new staffing realities. With the absence of able-bodied men, police departments were left with officers who did not meet military physical standards and/or were too old for military service. For the duration of the war, there would not be better police applicants and recruiting women became a necessity (Figure 1.18).

Although small numbers of women were hired as police officers beginning around 1920, the war cracked the door open just a little wider for the hiring of women. If hired, women were often assigned to supportive roles to sworn male officers[49] or specialty duties such as dealing with juvenile delinquents and the shoplifting detail. This practice was the norm for several decades thereafter. The **Civil Rights Act of 1964** invalidated Jim Crow laws. Title VII of the Act forbade businesses to discriminate in hiring, promoting, and firing based on sex, race, color, religion, and national origin, but state and local units of government were excluded from this requirement until the passage of the **Equal Employment Opportunity Act of 1972**, which amended Title VII. Functionally, this opened the door for women to be used in all types of assignments, including patrol, and also fostered more minority hiring.

Police duties during World War II expanded. One common responsibility was directing the work of air wardens. Concerned about air raids and shelling from submarines, **air raid warden** units were formed around the country, staffed by women, civic and fraternal groups, Boy Scouts, and other volunteers. Among their duties were checking to make sure no lights were showing, which our enemies could see and use to navigate toward their targets. Downtown areas were dark, and windows everywhere were outfitted with dark shades. Nonetheless, a few attacks did occur (see Box 1.6).

Another common responsibility of police during this period was investigating the forgery and use of forged **ration books**. To be able to maintain the millions of service members involved in fighting a war on two fronts (Europe and the Pacific), certain commodities were rationed or limited to civilians, such as gas, butter, and meat, and redirected to the armed forces. Forged ration books allowed some people to get more of the restricted commodities than they were allowed. Unchecked, forged books would create actual shortages of necessary materials for soldiers as well as morale problem on the home front.

FIGURE 1.18 ▶ During World War II (1941–1945) women were joining the civilian workforce in order to replace the millions of men who were serving in the military. This photo depicts women taking an entrance examination in the hopes of joining the New York City Police Department.
(Library of Congress Prints and Photographs Division [LC-USZ62-136823])

Box 1.5: Japanese Attacks on the American Homeland

In 1942, a Japanese sub surfaced off the coast of California. Sixteen shells from a deck-mounted gun were fired at the Ellwood Oil Field near Santa Barbara, causing little damage. That same type of attack occurred again later that year when a Japanese sub followed fishing boats transiting from the Pacific Ocean up the Columbia River in Oregon.

Intending to start a forest fire, a seaplane launched from a Japanese sub dropped incendiary bombs on a heavily wooded section of Oregon. Japan also launched 9,000 balloons into the Pacific jet stream. Fire bombs and/or anti-personnel mines were suspended underneath the balloons. Only 342 are known to have reached the United States. Some of the balloons were carried as far as Arizona, Kansas, and Michigan, but none caused major fires. During 1945, in Oregon, a Sunday school teacher and five of her 11- to 14-year-old students were killed by a balloon bomb, the only mainland American civilian casualties that occurred during World War II.[50]

When the war ended, veterans came home, the domestic market for goods heated up, and jobs were plentiful in an expanding economy. Some war veterans made a smooth transition from the military to police departments because of the preference given to military veterans in hiring and their familiarity with responsibility, wearing a uniform, a hierarchical organizational structure, and formal ranks.

Now past the pain of the depression and the war, prosperity was within the grasp of many Americans. New highways were built, and factories that had produced tanks now churned out cars. Many people who suddenly joined the middle class left the cities for the newly developing suburbs, purchased with the help of veterans' benefits. The Levitt brothers built so many suburban homes that a generic name for any suburb became "Levitt Town."

Although a novelty in the late 1940s, television expanded in the 1950s as quickly as radio stations did following World War I. The New York City Police Department (NYPD) rapidly seized on TV for administration and investigative purposes. An example is live lineups of criminal suspects were broadcast to police precincts near where victims and witnesses lived so that it became convenient for citizens to come and view suspected perpetrators.

The 1950s: Fear of Communism, the Professional Model Reasserted, and the Korean War

For the most part, interest in the police decreased during the 1950s, as new concerns emerged. Among them were fears we were losing our traditional values. Many community leaders, including ministers, argued rock-n-roll was inspired by the devil so he could take the souls of our children.[51]

Two terrorist attacks during the 1950s provided a warning of terrible things yet to come. In 1950, two Puerto Ricans attempted to assassinate President Truman. One police officer and one Puerto Rican were killed. Four years later, from a House of Representatives balcony, four Puerto Rican nationalists shot at Representatives conducting official business. Miraculously, no representative was killed however, five did suffer non-fatal wounds. All four perpetrators were captured, tried, convicted, and served long prison terms before receiving Presidential pardons in the late 1970s. Both attacks were calls for Puerto Rico's independence.

In 1953, Ethel and Julius Rosenberg were executed for divulging nuclear bomb secrets to the Soviet Union. The Soviet Union beat the United States into space in 1957 with the first satellite, Sputnik, causing concerns about communists using the bomb to rule the world from space. In addition, Fidel Castro's rise to power in Cuba (1959) put communism on our doorstep. Between 1950–1954, Senator Joseph McCarthy ran roughshod, searching everywhere for communists, until he was discredited

O. W. Wilson's *Police Administration* (1950) essentially reinforced use of the military model. Its operational philosophy was R2I: Respond to Incident. Crime was thought to be prevented and apprehensions made by random, aggressive patrol in all areas of the city around the clock. *Police Administration* quickly became the "bible" for law enforcement executives, who were guided by it as they sought to find the optimum way to organize and staff the units in their agency and achieve the most efficient operations. Written policies and procedures manuals became more common and comprehensive.

On the street, officers who were combat veterans watched rookie officers closely. The veterans would tolerate rookies who drank too much, ran around on their spouses, or were financial "deadbeats," but if rookies couldn't be counted on when the job got rough, the veterans would run them off.[52] This value may account for some portion of the belief in police circles that women were ill-equipped for patrol work, for example, "If even some men can't do the job, why do you think women could?"

In that era and several following decades, it was widely thought that physically women wouldn't be able to handle the rough hands-on part of policing. The "weaker sex" continues to invalidate stereotypes of them. The 62-day Ranger School is the Army's hardest training and its premier leadership course. Ranger School was opened to women in 2015. By early 2019, 30 had successfully completed the training, earning the right to wear the coveted black and gold Ranger tab.[53]

The Korean War (1950–1953) saw the recall of many World War II veterans, including some law enforcement officers, who had joined or stayed in Reserve and National Guard units. Because the Korean War was confined to one peninsula and was a war fought on a smaller scale, the impact on police staffing was less than that of World War II.

Rosa Parks (1913–2005), an African-American woman riding a public bus in Montgomery, Alabama, refused to give up her seat to a white man and was arrested for her defiance on December 1, 1955 (see Figure 1.19). Reverend **Martin Luther**

FIGURE 1.19 ▶ Mourners file past the casket of Rosa Parks, the mother of the Civil Rights movement, in the Rotunda of the U.S. Capitol, Washington, DC. Honoring a private citizen in that manner is rare. She is the first woman to be so recognized. (Mandel Nfgan/AFP/Getty Images)

King, Jr., a 26-year-old minister in that city, organized a bus boycott by African-Americans that lasted 381 days and reduced bus revenues by 80 percent.[54] The incident helped to give rise to the Civil Rights Movement that emerged more obviously during the subsequent decade and beyond.

During the 1950s and extending into the mid-1960s, a small number of Southern cities still had the problem of the "**unequal badge.**" In those cities, African-American officers were not allowed to arrest a white person because of the fear it might trigger a riot. Minority officers could not drive patrol cars for a similar reason; it was believed that white motorists would not accept a ticket from an African-American officer.[55] This resulted in the practice of White officers dropping their African-American counterparts off at their walking beats in minority business districts at the beginning of a shift and picking them up afterward. Minorities subtly retaliated by getting into the back seat when being picked up, making it appear white officers were their chauffeurs.

In 1959, the California **Peace Officers Standards and Training Commission (POST)** was created by legislation to set minimum standards for the selection and training of police officers. Although some states followed suit during the early 1960s, many POST units were not created until the late 1960s and early 1970s when federal grant funds from the now-defunct federal Law Enforcement Assistance Administration (LEAA) were available. POST units played an important role in police professionalization. They essentially constitute a professional licensing board and can revoke an officer's certificate to hold a job with any public law enforcement agency in the state that issued it.

THE TURBULENT 1960S: RIOTS, PROTESTS, ASSASSINATIONS, AND THE ISOLATION OF POLICE RANK AND FILE

World War II regained international attention with the trial (1961) of Adolph Eichmann in Israel for his role in the Holocaust. Closer to home, the Bay of Pigs, which was an American-sponsored Cuban invasion (1961) intended to topple communist dictator Fidel Castro, failed. Further concerns about the "commies" controlling outer space were sparked when the Soviet Union launched the first man into orbit (1962). The Soviets ignited the Cuban Missile Crisis in October 1962 by placing nuclear weapons in Cuba, and war seemed terrifyingly imminent. Although Russian Premier Khrushchev quickly removed the weapons, the practical effect was that Castro's hand was strengthened. The United States agreed not to invade or sponsor further invasions of Cuba.

Domestically, the 1960s was a staggering decade for our society as smoldering racial, social, and economic tensions erupted. In 1965, these tensions boiled over in Los Angeles' Watts neighborhood. A white California Highway Patrol motorcycle officer

stopped Marquette Frye, an African-American, for drunk driving. Frye's brother was also in the car and the men's mother soon appeared. Los Angeles officers arrived to assist as African-Americans congregated at the scene. Events spiraled out of control, rocks were thrown at the officers, and all three Fryes were arrested. Six days of looting, sniping, and arson followed in Watts. Thirty-four people were killed, most of them minorities, and losses amounted to $200 million before an uneasy peace was restored.

Over the next three years, more than two dozen major cities were struck by similar riots. The 1967 Detroit riot could not be controlled by local officers and elements of the state police and Michigan's National Guard. Ultimately, it took the presence of two brigades, one each from the 82nd and 101st Airborne Divisions to restore order. The following year in Washington, DC, a riot broke out the same day the Reverend Martin Luther King was assassinated in Memphis, Tennessee. It was only quelled with the assistance of nearly 14,000 troops (see Figure 1.20). Rioters came within two blocks of the White House before being forced back.

The causes cited across all riots were fundamentally the same: high rates of minority unemployment; poor housing; white store owners who took money from the minority communities but gave no reciprocity, such as jobs for them; a segregated and unequal society; and police officers viewed as hostile and repressive, a force of occupation to maintain the status quo.

The first mass murder on an American university campus occurred at the University of Texas in 1966. In today's lexicon, there was an active shooter on campus. **Charles Whitman** brought an assortment of firearms, including a scoped rifle, to the 28th floor of a campus building and began shooting. Before he was stopped, Whitman killed 14 people and wounded 32 others. He died a few days later of wounds inflicted by the police. The incident helped transform campus security departments from simply being unarmed watchmen to professional police agencies.

In 1967, the first national study of police since the Wickersham Report (1931) was completed. President Johnson's Commission on Law Enforcement and Administration of Justice issued a summary report, *The Challenge of Crime in a Free Society*. The study was supplemented by task force reports on the police, organized crime, and other topics. The organization of the Commission's report paralleled the Cleveland Foundation's use in 1922 of subordinate working groups to study specific areas. Among the recommendations made was that police officers should have college degrees.

The 1968 report from the **National Advisory Commission on Civil Disorders**, the Kerner Commission, also took the name of its chair, Ohio Governor Otto Kerner. The report simply confirmed what everyone knew were the causes of riots. It also acknowledged the confusing demands being placed on law enforcement: One side saw the police as maintaining order at the expense of justice, whereas the other demanded tougher enforcement.[56]

The Kerner Commission didn't start the national discussion about what the role of police officers should be, but it certainly

FIGURE 1.20 ▶ Army soldier on duty during the 1968 riot in Washington, DC. The smoldering building in the background is an indicator of the wider damage. (Library of -Congress Prints & Photographs Division [LC-U9-18949-12])

added to it, as did recommendations in *The Challenge of Crime in a Free Society*. As previously stated, at the core of the military model was the belief that there was a war on crime led by the police. Their duty was ferreting out crime, conducting investigations, making arrests, and assisting with the prosecution of offenders. Others suggested that the police needed to be something more than that or risk being forever seen as the "bullies" of a culturally divided society. During the 1960s, the police, albeit slowly and under pressure, began a metamorphosis from just being crime fighters. Their role enlarged to being conflict managers, community relations specialists, and a conduit to social welfare agencies.

Meanwhile, other events in the 1960s were also changing the world-view of police officers. There were hippies, psychedelic drugs, massive demonstrations against the Vietnam War, draft evaders and military deserters, civil rights marches and demonstrations, the beginning of the gay rights movement, the burgeoning women's rights movement, the passage of civil rights legislation discussed earlier, and Supreme Court decisions, such as the restrictions placed on police interrogations by *Miranda v. Arizona* (1966). Native Americans sought more control over their lands and **Cesar Chavez** unionized mostly Mexican farm workers in the Southwest to provide them with better working conditions and wages.

The first U.S. deployment of a major combat unit to South Vietnam was 3,500 Marines in 1965. However, the presence of small units of Americans dated back roughly a decade, with some casualties. Chicago police clashed repeatedly with anti-Vietnam demonstrators at the 1968 Democratic National Convention. A portion of both sides used excessive force. Some demonstrators threw apples into which razor blades had been inserted and threw vials containing urine and garbage can lids at the police. In response, police occasionally used tear gas and charged into crowds freely swinging their nightsticks.

Further evidence that our society was unraveling during the 1960s were the assassinations of President Kennedy (1917–1963) in Dallas;[57] Robert Kennedy (1925–1968), the dead President's brother, who was campaigning for the presidency in Los Angeles; and the civil rights leader, Reverend Martin Luther King, Jr. (1929–1968), who was supporting a sanitation workers strike in Memphis. On April 4, 1968, the Reverend Martin Luther King, Jr., stepped outside of his hotel room and was shot to death by James Earl Ray (1928–1998, see Figure 1.21). The day before, in Memphis, the Reverend King gave perhaps his most notable address, "I've Been to the Mountaintop."

A new world was unfolding that the police did not understand and in which they felt isolated and unsupported. In this milieu, police professionalism took on new urgency. Before the 1960s, police departments required applicants to have a tenth-grade to a high school degree, or its counterpart, the General Equivalency Degree (GED). The first major law enforcement agency to require a college degree was the Multnomah County Sheriff's Office (Oregon) in 1965.[58] If any college was required for applicants, it usually amounted to 6 to 12 semester hours. Other departments hired officers with the understanding that they would complete a certain number of hours within a specified time-period after appointment or forfeit their jobs.

Police locker rooms were polarized as a less-educated portion of older officers occasionally taunted younger, college-attending officers. They harassed them with orders to "Talk some psychology" or "Say some sociology to me." The kindest epithets hurled at officers working on a degree were "egghead"

FIGURE 1.21 ▶ The Lorraine Hotel, Memphis, Tennessee. Reverend King, a Nobel Peace Prize winner (1964), occupied room 306. (Library of Congress Prints and Photographs Division [LC-DIG-highsm-04695])

and "educated idiot." On campus, degree-seeking police officers were subject to cries of "police spy" if their occupation was discovered by other students. While a very small number of departments required a college degree as an entry-level credential, the majority remained at a high school education or a General Equivalency Degree (GED).

Nonetheless, in policing, "professional" slowly became synonymous with "education" from roughly 1965–1967 onward. It was thought a police college education would (1) improve community relations, (2) reduce use of force, (3) improve discretionary decision-making, (4) reduce corruption, and (5) redefine the role of policing.[59] From the late 1960s until the mid-1970s, there was a quick proliferation of police administration and criminal justice programs in community colleges and universities. Much of the funding for this expansion came from federal grants.

Some impetus to college education for officers came in programs adopted by progressive communities. Those officers with college degrees got an additional 5 or 10 percent above the normal salary and those without a degree could work on one and get some reimbursement for the tuition cost, based on their final grade. Tuition for an "A" was reimbursed 100 percent, a "B" 50 percent, and a "C" 25 percent. Officers were not normally reimbursed for the cost of their books. Beginning in 1968, the federal Law Enforcement Education Program (LEEP), an arm of LEAA, provided up to $2,400 a year to help defray college education costs for criminal justice majors. Repayment could be accomplished by a 25 percent loan forgiveness formula for each year of service with a public criminal justice agency, up to a maximum of four years/100 percent.

Character and background checks began to scrutinize more factors, and the use of polygraphs and credit checks became more standard. Some psychological screening was done, although it often involved the general practitioner conducting the entry-level physical exam to simply state that no abnormalities were observed. The most important leap in the quality of applicant screening was the result of standards set by emerging POSTs.

The professionalization movement during the 1950s and 1960s shaped the role of the police and created a sense of pride and unity among many officers. However, in the second half of the 1960s, the basis for police unity shifted due to the following: (1) riots and civil rights demonstrations, (2) Supreme Court decisions "handcuffing" the police, (3) a rising crime rate, (4) an increasingly critical press, (5) a perceived lack of public support, and (6) the creation of civilian review boards to investigate allegations of police misconduct. Few things promote group solidarity as much as the perception of being under attack. As these factors accumulated, police unity was fueled by these "attacks." The police turned to the one bastion they could trust, each other.

Officers also saw administrators bringing unwanted change into their world. "Bosses" who seldom left their offices were judged as out-of-touch with the realities of street police work. The police rank and file felt they were isolated and unsupported, creating a "we against them" mentality that propelled them to join unions as states began passing public sector collective bargaining laws in the 1960s. Unions created a new power center in police departments, exciting officers and alarming administrators (see Chapter 11, Labor Relations).

THE 1970S: RESEARCH, EXPERIMENTATION, AND RISING TERRORISM

Wadman and Allison characterized the 1970s "… as a period of malaise in American history . . . the Vietnam War ended without a sense of closure, the **Watergate Scandal** intensified distrust of government . . . the economic downturn reduced budgets, limiting the ability of the police to innovate . . . and traditional police concepts made it difficult for communities to influence."[60] President Richard Nixon's 1974 resignation while facing impeachment grew out of the burglary of the Democratic National Committee headquarters at the Watergate Office Complex in Washington, DC. The burglary was initially tied to the Republican Committee to Reelect the President and then to members of President Nixon's staff.

As a result of the Watergate political scandal, 61 percent of Americans expressed distrust of government—a burden on all public agencies, including the police. Prior events may have also fed this distrust, including the killing of four Kent State University students by members of the Ohio National Guard (1970) who fired on the demonstrators,[61] as well as disillusionment with the Vietnam War. Because police officers also tried to control protests, they were often bitterly resented by demonstrators who labeled them "pigs."[62]

Once again, the country seemed to be coming unglued. Presidential candidate George Wallace was shot and paralyzed while campaigning in Maryland (1972),[63] and there were two assassination attempts on President Gerald Ford's life in an 18-day period (1975). Against this social backdrop, important things were occurring in policing. The previously mentioned *Challenge of Crime in a Free Society* found, "There is no subject connected with crime or criminal justice into which further research is unnecessary."[64] Doig reached the same conclusion, declaring that law enforcement was a *terra incognita*, an unknown land.[65] During the 1970s, with grants from LEAA, there was a torrent of research. An early trilogy of major experiments rocked policing: (1) the **Kansas City Preventive Patrol Study**, (2) the **RAND Criminal Investigation Study**, and (3) the **team policing** experiment.

The Kansas City Preventive Patrol Study examined three types of patrol services to see what difference each made:

1. *Reactive districts* received no regular patrol; officers who responded to calls entered and left the district by the shortest routes.

2. *Proactive districts* were saturated with two to three times the normal amount of patrolling.

3. *Control districts* maintained regular or normal patrolling.

The study found no significant differences in reported crime, arrests, traffic accidents, fear of crime, or security measures among the three types of districts. As local governmental leaders learned of the results, some refused to fund requests for additional police officers. The findings were controversial and dismissed by police leaders and some scholars as methodologically flawed.

The RAND (Corporation) Criminal Investigation Study sought to determine what factors contribute to the success of criminal investigations, and just what it is that detectives do. Focusing on serious crimes, the study concluded that the preliminary investigations conducted by patrol officers provided the information that led to the solution of most crimes. Critics of detectives said it confirmed suspicions of their value, while police leaders labeled it "one, un-replicated study." Like the Kansas City Study, the finding also became an issue in police budgets for a period of time.

Team policing was a bold reform effort to reshape how police resources were used and to reduce the amount of specialization by using patrol officers in a variety of roles, such as plainclothes assignments.[66] Roughly 20 to 30 officers were formed into teams, under the 24-hour direction of a single commander who controlled how they were deployed. By the end of the 1970s, team policing vanished due to the problems of implementation and the opposition of mid-level police managers who correctly saw that it reduced their importance. The experiment increased appreciation of the capabilities of patrol officers and helped set the stage for community policing, which became very popular during the 1980s.

Around 1970, there was a movement toward new organizations. In 1969, the **International Association of Police Women (IAPW)**, with roots that date back to 1926, adopted its current name. A number of state-level women officers associations belong to IAWP. The **National Association of Women Law Enforcement Executives (NAWLEE)** also advocates for women's issues in policing. The formation of the federal **National Criminal Justice Reference Service (NCJRS**, 1972) created an easily accessible body of cutting-edge information for criminal justice students, scholars, and practitioners. **HAPCOA**, the Hispanic American Police Command Officers Association, was formed in 1973 to assist in the recruitment, training, and promotion of qualified Hispanic men and women and to advocate for Hispanic law enforcement issues. The **Police Executive Research Forum (PERF**, 1975) was formed by the largest city, county, and state agencies for the purpose of pursuing research and public policy work of particular interest to its members. The **National Organization of Black Law Enforcement Executives (NOBLE**, 1976) focuses on crime in low-income urban areas. The **Commission on Accreditation of Law Enforcement Agencies (CALEA**, 1979) was established with the support of the IACP, NSA, PERF, and NOBLE as an independent accrediting body for law enforcement agencies. CALEA accreditation can reduce liability insurance costs, be used as a tool in attracting new businesses to a community and stimulates community pride and confidence in a community's police department. Although its formation falls in a later era, the **National Association of Asian American Law Enforcement Commanders (NAAALEC)** was created in 2002 to promote a positive police image in Asian/Pacific communities and to speak on topics of common concerns for its membership.

Although terrorism is an ancient strategy, transnational terrorism began a march toward the present during the 1970s (see Chapter 3, Intelligence, Terrorism, and Homeland Security). On Black Sunday (1970), operatives of the **Popular Front for the Liberation of Palestine (PFLP)** hijacked four planes. The **Black September Organization (BSO)**, a Palestinian group, killed 11 Israeli athletes and team officials at the 1972 Olympic Games in Munich, some of whom died in a botched rescue attempt. Four years later, the PFLP, aided by two Germans from the Revolutionary Cells, hijacked an Air France jet and forced it to fly to the Entebbe Airport in Uganda.[67] The hijackers released all non-Jewish passengers but held their Jewish hostages in the terminal. The hijackers demanded the release of 53 Palestinians held in several countries in exchange. The Israel Defense Force (IDF) conducted a spectacular raid, freeing the hostages.[68] The success of the Entebbe raid may have encouraged President Jimmy Carter to approve a military plan to free 53 American hostages held in Iran for more than a year. The raid failed and played a part in his defeat by Ronald Reagan.[69]

1980S TO THE 9/11 ATTACKS: THE COMMUNITY-ORIENTED POLICING ERA

Innovation in policing strategies occurred at a rapid pace during this 20-year period. Some came from the convergence of several phenomena, including the rise of terrorism from foreign and domestic sources. The 2001 al-Qaeda attacks produced the worst single day loss of life by American police officers. Seventy-two police officers died attempting to save victims trapped within the Word Trade Center complex of buildings. The call for more transparency in policing due to high-profile incidents involving law enforcement decision-making at Ruby Ridge, Idaho and in Waco, Texas, also produced innovations to gain and maintain community trust. Chapter 8, Planning and Decision Making, addresses the impact of police decision making.

New strategies in policing also emerged. These new paradigms include **community-oriented policing (COP)**, **zero tolerance policing (ZTP)**, **COMPSTAT**, **evidence-based policing (EBP)**, and **hot-spot policing (HSP)**. COP is the development of police strategies and programs in partnership with communities in order to deliver custom-tailored police services and solutions to problems, as well as a renewed focus on crime prevention rather than crime detection. ZTP was based on the premise that when small infractions of the law are ignored, it creates a climate conducive to more serious crimes being committed. The extension of this thinking was ZTP, which required non-discretionary enforcement for all crimes. COMPSTAT, which was implemented in the New York City Police Department during 1994, is a management control system designed to develop, analyze, and disseminate information about reported crime and

to track efforts to deal with it.[70] Evidence-based policing (EBP) is based on data analysis of a constellation of sources, including intelligence, agency records, and scientific research. With the results of the analysis, strategies are selected or developed to attack the targeted problem.

Sherman pioneered the notion of hot-spot policing by analyzing crime data. He concluded that a relatively few places/addresses in a city produced roughly half of all crimes. By concentrating on those locations or "hot spots," such as open-air drug markets, specific bars, and other areas, crime could be reduced. Some of these new strategies were later identified as "best practices," publicized, and adopted by many agencies.

Each of these paradigms is further discussed in detail in Chapter 2, Policing Today, along with other emerging approaches such as directed patrol and intelligence-led policing. However, it should be noted that of all of these approaches, COP had the quickest, and to date, the most widespread impact on policing. It produced an important impact on not only police operations, but also on the structure and culture of police organizations. Certainly, policing has dramatically changed since the days of August Vollmer and O. W. Wilson; policing has become much more proactive, focused on preventing not only crime but terrorism as well. Perhaps, no greater challenge confronts American law enforcement today than the imperative to prevent the next terrorist attack in the American homeland or on our citizens and interests abroad.

Terrorism to 9/11

During the 1980s and 1990s, there were terrifying crimes and acts of terrorism in this country. Those mentioned in this section are illustrations from a longer list of events.

Twenty-six-year-old John Hinckley became obsessed with a 19-year-old movie actress, Jodie Foster. In a 1981 "love offering" to Foster, which Hinckley hoped would gain her affection, he shot President Reagan in an assassination attempt and wounded three others (see Figure 1.22). All those wounded recovered, but with varying degrees of permanent injuries. Press Secretary James Brady suffered a head wound resulting in permanent and disabling brain damage. When he died in 2014, the medical examiner ruled it was a homicide, his death caused by the wound he suffered in 1981. Hinckley was found not guilty of all criminal charges because he was legally insane. He was confined for psychiatric care at St. Elizabeth Hospital, Washington, DC, for 35 years and was released in 2016.[71]

In 1986, a mail carrier in the Edmond, Oklahoma Post Office and his supervisor were in conflict. The carrier went to the Post Office with several guns and begun shooting supervisors and other employees. After killing 14 of them and wounding 7 others, the carrier killed himself. This incident led to the use of the term "going postal" to mean someone who was out-of-control mad or filled with rage.

Almost a decade later, anti-government right-wing activist **Timothy McVeigh** used a rental truck loaded with explosives to bomb the federal building in Oklahoma City. The explosion

FIGURE 1.22 ▶ March 30, 1981, President Ronald Reagan waves to a crowd after exiting the Washington Hilton Hotel. Seconds later, John Hinkley, standing with a group of reporters, fired six shots with a .22 caliber pistol. President Reagan was hit in the lung with a ricochet. When wheeled into the operation room, the President looked around and playfully asked for reassurance, "Tell me you are Republicans." (Everett Collection Inc/Alamy Stock Photo)

killed 168, including 19 children, and wounded 500 other people.[72] Following his conviction, McVeigh was executed by lethal injection in 2001. Foreign terrorist groups continued their attacks on U.S. persons and interests abroad. In 1996, a Hezbollah truck bomb in Saudi Arabia killed or wounded 20 Americans when it exploded in a housing area for service members.[73] Two years later, al-Qaeda exploded bombs at the American Embassies in Kenya and Tanzania, which killed 252 people.[74] In 2000, al-Qaeda operatives steered a launch alongside the USS Cole, docked in Yemen, and detonated the launch's explosives, killing 17 sailors and causing extensive damage to the Cole.[75] In 2019, Jamal al-Badawi, a key figure in the Cole bombing, was driving alone in Yemen when he was killed by a drone.

On September 11, 2001 (9/11), al-Qaeda launched four attacks on the United States. It used hijacked domestic passenger flights. Two hijacked planes hit New York City's World Trade Centers and one the Pentagon. United Airline Flight 93 was denied hitting any target. Some of its passengers received calls and knew how their hijacked plane would be used. Heroically, these patriots fought the hijackers, attempting to regain control of the plane or deny the hijackers its use. Flight 93 crashed in rural Pennsylvania, killing all aboard, but no others on the ground. The 9/11 attacks produced 72 deaths of police officers, the single worst day in our history for such losses.[76] Dozens of 9/11-involved officers have also

died since the attacks. Their lives were shortened by the injuries they received.

The call for more transparency in policing was due to high-profile incidents involving law enforcement decision making at **Ruby Ridge, Idaho** and in **Waco, Texas**, also produced innovations to gain and maintain community trust. Chapter 8, "Planning and Decision Making," addresses the impact of police decision making.

The structure and culture of police organizations is often in a state of change for one reason or another. Perhaps, no greater challenge confronts American policing now than the imperative to prevent the terrorist attacks on the American homeland and our people and interests abroad.

THE NEW OPERATING ENVIRONMENT: POST-9/11 TO 2020

The new operating environment spans from post-9/11 to 2020. There are some periods in the history of police administration that are relatively stable, while others have some continuity mixed with notable developments. The post-9/11 to 2020 era had some continuity, but there were also major events that substantially impacted law enforcement in ways that could not have been foreseen. These events demonstrate a point made early in this chapter: policing is like a sandbar in a river, being shaped and reshaped by the currents of the society in which it is embedded. This section examines these subjects: (1) active and mass shootings, (2) terrorism continues, (3) police react to shaken confidence in their use of force, (4) recruiting and staffing difficulties, and (5) the coronavirus-19 (COVID-19) and Law Enforcement.

1. Active and Mass Shootings

Post-9/11, active shooter, and mass shootings have become almost a daily feature within the popular news media. This regularity has the potential to "normalize" terrible events and may desensitized us to them unless the casualty count is high, such as the Mandalay Bay Hotel shooting in Las Vegas during 2017, when a lone gunman killed 48 and wounded 413.

The U.S. Department of Homeland Security (USDHS) defines an active shooter as "an individual engaged in killing or attempting to kill people in a confined and populated area."[77] Note that although the term "active shooter" is used, other types of weapons also fall within the previous definition. For instance, a bullied 16-year-old Pennsylvania high school student used kitchen knives to stab 22 students and a security guard. Following his conviction, the student was sentenced up to 60 years imprisonment.[78] Reduced to its essence, an active shooter is a presently on-going potentially deadly event. In 2019, there were 417 such attacks.[79] In most cases there is no method as to the selection of victims."[80]

There is no legal definition of mass shootings. The closest to it is provided in the federal *Investigative Assistance for Violent Crimes Act of 2012*.[81] It defines a mass killing as when three or more fatalities, excluding the death of the perpetrator, result from an active shooter attack. The Act also gave the FBI authority to provide assistance in mass killing investigations. The strictest definition of a mass shooting, which is widely used, is four or more fatalities, excluding the perpetrator.[82]

It is known that 80 percent of those contemplating killing themselves give some sign of their intentions before acting.[83] The FBI studied the behavior of mass shooters over a 14-year period. The study revealed that 56 percent of mass shooters also gave some notice of their violent intentions prior to attacking.[84] This "leakage of intent" was expressed in social media posts, verbal statements, letters, essays, or by other means.[85]

This is an area ripe for exploration by a collaborative effort of schools, parents, school social workers, employers, law enforcement agencies, and others. Some new enabling legislation may be needed to authorize police to take a mentally disturbed persons into custody and before a Judge immediately.

As a probabilistic statement, some lives will be saved if interest can be aroused and more importantly sustained to address the problem.

2. Terrorism Continues

Roughly six weeks after the 9/11 attacks, the Congress quickly passed major legislation, the USA Patriot Act, specifically aimed at combating terrorism. Other acts for the same purpose followed. The Patriot Act expanded state and local law enforcement's powers and roles in combating terrorism. This expansion and other aspects of terrorism are discussed in Chapter 3, "Intelligence, Security, and Homeland Security."

In 2014, the Islamic State (IS) controlled vast land in Iraq and Syria, some 41,000 square miles or an area roughly the size of Indiana and ruled its population of 8,000,000.[86] It had attracted 40,000 fighters from 120 countries. Its monthly income of $81 million was derived from stolen antiquities, looting captured banks, taxes and fees placed on its population, smuggling, and extortion.[87] IS used a portion of its bankroll to fund "affiliates." By 2019, IS had lost all of the territory it had controlled. Its fighters had gone on to Yemen, Libya, Philippines, Afghanistan, Algeria, Pakistan, Egypt, and elsewhere,[88] including sleeper cells that preserved a cadre of seasoned fighters. Although damaged, IS isn't defeated. It is skilled in using social media and its slick magazine to advance its purposes. It is more likely than not that the world will hear from IS again. Many other terrorist organizations also want to do America harm, including al-Qaeda.

3. Policing Reacts to Shaken Confidence in Officers' Use of Force

Between 2014 and 2020, a series of police use of force cases were perhaps the transcendent event for law enforcement in the last decade. Some of the actions by police were highly criticized, a few produced riots, others resulted in criminal charges being levied against officers, and a few of them were convicted. Several of these cases are examined in Chapter 2, "Policing Today"... A consequence of these highly publicized events is that police use of force has become part of a national conversation on structural racism and the degree to which police practices contribute to perpetuate racial inequalities and discrimination.

Many African-American citizens have vocalized disturbing concerns in the aftermath of highly publicized and controversial police shootings: "Could this happen here, to me, or to someone in my family?" The U.S. Department of Justice has quickly moved to place more emphasis on investigating police use of force cases, particularly those involving deaths of unarmed Black males.

In addition, many local and state law enforcement agencies quickly initiated reviews and made thoughtful changes to their use of force policies. As an example, in 2015, the Los Angeles, California, Police Commission began the process of creating a use of force policy that emphasizes de-escalation and advocated minimum force whenever possible. Two years later, Special Order 5, "Policy on the Use of Force-Revised" was issued with an even-stronger emphasis on de-escalation: "Officers shall attempt to control an incident by using time, distance, communications, and available resources in an effort to deescalate the situation, whenever it is safe and reasonable to do so." [89] Then too, the entire State of California passed new legislation regarding limiting the use of deadly force by police. Named after an unarmed Black man killed by police officers in Sacramento, CA, the Stephon Clark Law moves the "objectively reasonable" standard in *Graham v Connor* (1989) to "necessary only in defense of human life." Hence, the burden to show that use of deadly force was necessary shifts to the individual police officer. This significant change, as well as a more thorough discussion of *Graham v Conner* is discussed in Chapter 14, Legal Aspects of Police Administration.

Newly minted reforms aside, this text was completed as the nation once again convulsed during 2020 in the aftermath of several more highly questionable and deadly police citizen encounters including the death of George Floyd in Minneapolis, Breonna Taylor in Louisville, and Jacob Blake in Kenosha (WI). These most recent cases are covered in more detail in boxed-items within Chapter 2. These most recent encounters have led collectively to large-scale street protests, the legitimization of the Black Lives Matter movement, and what many commentators perceive as a "national reckoning" on the issue of racial justice. In some respects, these most recent protests echo those of earlier eras in American history particularly those of the 1960s and 70s. The American public has been forced to once again re-examine and question the role and legitimacy of police against the backdrop of calls to "de-fund" them and create new societal mechanisms to more effectively deal with problems such as public health, inequality, homelessness, substance abuse, and domestic violence. The current controversy and public outrage has the potential to fundamentally alter the work of police in ways that rival earlier shifts to de-politicize police, professionalize them, and make them more connected and responsive to local communities, especially those of color.

4. **Recruiting and Staffing Difficulties**
    Law enforcement agencies are at the doorstep of a national workforce crisis in hiring and retaining sworn personnel.[90] After the well-publicized and controversial police use of force deaths, public confidence in the police dropped in polls to nearly a 25-year low. In fact, a 2019 survey of 411 law enforcement agencies by the Police Executive Research Forum (PERF) identified a "triple threat" to police recruiting and staffing:
    (A) *Fewer people are applying to become full-time officers.* Of the 411 departments surveyed, 63 percent reported fewer applications. An example is the online applications to the Metropolitan Nashville, Tennessee, Police Department have dropped 60 percent since 2010.[91]

Quick Facts: Ambush Attacks on U.S. Police Officers and Intelligence Warnings for 2020

FBI statistics show 53 police officers were killed in ambushes between 2014 and 2018. There are also incidents of officers being wounded in surprise/ambush incidents. Three such attacks are summarized below.

A man fired a total of 11 shots at a Philadelphia officer who was sitting in his marked patrol car at a lane in an intersection. In 2018, the attacker was sentenced to 48.5 to 97 years confinement. Some of the shots were fired with the gun thrust through the driver's side window. Although wounded three times, the officer courageously exited his vehicle and shot the man, who was taken into custody. In the Flint, Michigan, Airport, a man shouted "allahu akbar" (God is Great) as he suddenly attacked a police Lieutenant from behind, stabbing him several times with a long knife. Immediately taken into custody at the scene, the attacker received a life in prison sentence in 2019. And in 2020, two Los Angeles County Sheriff's Deputies were surprise attacked by a lone Black gunman that slowly walked up to their parked car in Compton, CA and fired several shots from a pistol directly at the officers, severely wounding both. The suspect remains unidentified and at large during the writing of this edition.

In a number of countries, including the United States, first responders received warnings of potential 2020 terrorist ambush attacks on them. These warnings originated in intelligence agencies and were released through various channels. Police, fire, and medical responders are all highly visible targets operating on a continuous basis throughout their communities and therefore were "soft targets." Accompanying the warnings were suggestions to first responders, such as using countermeasures to detect potential ambushes.

Family members of current officers and the military have long been a traditional source of job applicants, but this source of personnel seems to be drying up. A strong economy and job growth provide many options for those seeking employment, creating strong alternatives to police work. The use of military rank and an organizational structure emphasizing control does not align with the orientations of some potential applicants.[92]

(B) *More officers are retiring earlier*; 8.5 percent of officers are eligible now and in five years, 15.5 percent can retire.[93] These retirements can reduce the effectiveness of law enforcement agencies by dangerously lowering the experience level of departments. Increased retirements may be due to such factors as new efforts to establish civilian oversight of police discipline, increased reviews of police use of deadly force by the U.S. Department of Justice, ambush attacks on police officers, and the reenergized push for more police transparency. In *Chapter 4, Politics and Police Administration*, the transparency movement is examined.

(C) *More officers with one to five years of experience are resigning.* The three most common reasons across the 411 law enforcement agencies surveyed were: (1) take a job with another local law enforcement agency, (2) pursue a career outside of law enforcement, and (3) accept a federal law enforcement appointment.[94] This finding means that not only are other police departments competitors for hiring applicants, but also for retaining them. Each resignation is a financial loss for police departments, the replacement cost, which includes recruiting, testing, selection, background and health evaluations, as well as academy, firearms, and field training.

Recruiting is further discussed in *Chapter 9, Human Resource Management,* including what police departments are doing to overcome this workforce crisis.

5. **The Coronavirus-19 (COVID-19) and Law Enforcement**
   While our understanding and the history of the COVID-19 pandemic is still unfolding, it is believed that the virus originated in Wuhan, the capital of China's Hubei province. At first, in late 2019, what would become known as COVID-19 was described as an illness that resembled severe acute respiratory syndrome (SARS). The virus is spread when an infected person coughs or sneezes, producing airborne droplets, or through droplets of saliva or discharge from the nose.

The U.S. health system was not prepared for the overwhelming needs created by the COVID-19 pandemic. The first cases of the virus began to appear in the United States in early 2020 and since then, hundreds of thousands of Americans have died and many millions more have been infected.[95] The rapid acceleration of the virus caused immediate medical shortages worldwide. There weren't enough test kits, hospitals didn't have enough beds, there were not sufficient ventilators for the most serious cases, and in some hospitals, they ran out of personal protective equipment (PPE) and medical personnel were forced to substitute plastic garbage bags for PPE. The world had never witnessed such a dramatic and far-reaching pandemic. For first responders like the police, the daily risk of contracting COVID-19 is extremely high, primarily because their work entails frequent direct contact with individuals and sometimes small groups. Across the country, police and other first responders have contracted COVID-19 or are being quarantined. So much so that the numbers of deaths to police officers far exceeds the number of deaths to officers from all other causes combined. Indeed, some entire police precincts and fire stations have been quarantined. A more thorough discussion of the changes brought about from COVID-19 is discussed in the final chapter of the book, Chapter 15, Organizational Change.

Quick Facts: COVID-19 and Unemployment

With many businesses closed, unemployment claims soared. In the week ending March 28, 2020, 3.28 million people filed new unemployment claims in one week. This eclipsed the previous high of 695,000 for the week ending October 2, 1982. However, as the pandemic grew, so did the number of unemployment claims, averaging over 5.5 million per week. By the end of 2020, about 50 million claims are estimated to be filed, representing nearly 35 percent of our county's workforce population, the highest number of unemployed people in the history of our country.

Chapter Summary

Summary by Learning Objectives

1. **Define *politics* and give three reasons why it cannot be kept out of police agencies.**

   Politics is the process of acquiring and maintaining control over a government, including its policies, administration, and operations. The three reasons politics cannot be kept out of policing are: (1) police departments must be subject to democratic control, (2) public policy is where politics and administration intersect, and (3) politics exists, even in small police departments; what we want to do is keep the worst sort of politics—highly partisan—out of policing because of its long and most often unhealthy relationship with policing.

2. **Identify the most negative and positive things about the patronage/spoils system.**

   The worst abuse of the patronage/spoils system is when unqualified people are rewarded, for example, given a job for their political loyalty instead of their ability. Patronage that is not excessive or create inefficiencies is useful: Elected officials can appoint persons who agree with their policies, making governing easier.

3. **Describe the impact of prohibition on policing.**

   It did more damage to the image and reputation of policing than any other event. To protect their operations, gangsters bribed judges, policemen, and other public officials to "look the other way" on a massive scale.

4. **Describe how World War II affected law enforcement.**

   The men in public safety agencies had no exemptions from compulsory military service and they volunteered and were drafted in great numbers. Departments quickly turned their attention to the new staffing realities: (1) the remaining officers did not meet military physical standards and/or were too old for military service. For the duration of the war, there would not be better police applicants and (2) women could be part of the staffing solution.

5. **Define and Explain the unequal badge problem.**

   During the 1950s through the mid-1960s, a small number of Southern police departments had an informal practice that minority officers were not to arrest majorities for fear a riot would result. A variation of this was in some of those cities minorities couldn't drive a patrol car based on the reasoning that a white motorist would not accept a traffic citation from an African-American officer. A majority officer would drive a minority to his walking beat and pick him up at the end of the shift. Minorities would subtly retaliate by getting in the back seat when being picked up, so it appeared the majority officer was a chauffeur.

6. **Explain leakage of intent by mass shooters and how it is accomplished.**

   It is known that 80 percent of those contemplating killing themselves give some sign of their intentions before acting. The FBI studied the behavior of mass shooters over a 14-year period. The study revealed that 56 percent of mass shooters also gave some notice of their violent intentions prior to attacking. This "leakage of intent" was expressed in social media posts, verbal statements, letters, essays, or by other means.

   This "leakage of intent" was also identified in an FBI study discovered that covered active shooters over a 14 year period: 56 percent expressed their violent intentions prior to attacking. Leakages are made by social media posts, verbal statements, letters, essays, or by other means.

Chapter Review Questions

1. What contributions were made by Sir Robert Peele that can still be applied to modern day policing?

2. What advantages did the Pinkerton National Detective Agency, Wells Fargo Detectives, and Union Pacific Operatives have over Western law enforcement agencies of the period?

3. There are several reasons discussed as to why there is no way to keep politics out of police departments. What are they?

4. What was accomplished with the passage of the Pendleton Act of 1883?

5. What was the function of the Lexow Committee?

6. What were some of the early operational and administrative accomplishments of Chief August Volmer?

7. What was the purpose of the Kansas City Preventive Patrol Study?

8. What were the main goals of Team Policing?

9. What are the major strategies behind Community Oriented Policing (COP), Zero Tolerance Policing (ZTP), Evidence Based Policing (EBP) and Hot Spot Policing (HSP)?

10. Why are law enforcement agencies having difficulty in staffing, recruiting, and retaining sworn personnel?

Critical Thinking Exercises

1. How do you think our unique history as a country has impacted policing today?

2. Assume your family was fleeing from catastrophic conditions in Oklahoma during the time of the bum blockades and were turned back from town after town while seeking medicine for your diabetic younger brother. What would you do?

3. As the Chief of Police of a 100-officer department, you have been closely monitoring the unprovoked ambush-type murders of police officers. Officers in your department are on edge about this development. What actions would you take to increase the likelihood that such incidents do not occur and officers have a better chance of surviving them?

Key Terms

air raid warden
Black Codes
Black September Organization (BSO)
bootlegger
bum blockades
Challenge of Crime in a Free Society
Chavez, Cesar
city manager movement
Civil Rights Act of 1964
Commission on Accreditation of Law Enforcement Agencies (CALEA)
community-oriented policing (COP)
Dillinger, John
dustbowl
Equal Employment Opportunity Act of 1972
evidence-based policing (EBP)
Forces Act
Fosdick, Raymond
Freedmen's Bureau
frontier closing
Garfield, President
Hispanic American Police Command Officers Association (HAPCOA)
hot-spot policing (HSP)
International Association of Chiefs of Police (IACP)
International Association of Police Women (IAPW)

Jim Crow laws
Kansas City Preventive Patrol Study
King, Martin Luther Jr., Reverend
KKK
Lexow Committee
machine politics
military model
muckrakers
National Advisory Commission on Civil Disorders
National Association of Asian American Law Enforcement Commanders (NAAALEC)
National Association of Women Law Enforcement Executives (NAWLEE)
National Commission on Law Observance and Law Enforcement
National Criminal Justice Reference Service (NCJRS)
National Organization of Black Law Enforcement Executives (NOBLE)
National Prohibition Act
National Sheriffs Association (NSA)
Nation, Carry
Okies
patronage
Peel, Sir Robert
Pendleton Act

Police Executive Research Forum (PERF)
Pinkerton National Detective Agency
Police Administration
political machine
politics
Peace Officers Standards and Training Commission (POST)
profession
prohibition
RAND Criminal Investigation Study
ration books
Reformation Period
residency requirements
slave patrols
snatch racket
speakeasies
spoils system
team policing
temperance movement
unequal badge
untouchables
Vollmer, August (Gus)
Volstead Act
Waco
Whitman, Charles
Wickersham Commission
Wilson, O. W.

Endnotes

[1] New Amsterdam was settled by the Dutch. To be precise, the office they created was schout, their cultural equivalent of a sheriff.

[2] Raymond Fosdick, *American Police Systems* (Montclair, NJ: Patterson Smith reprint, 1969), pp. 63–64.

[3] These were three early English industrial revolutions. The first was during 1760–1830. Some sources cite other dates for the first industrial revolution, 1760-1840 and 1750-1850.

[4] Many sources list these principles, including the New Westminster Police Service (British Columbia, Canada), www.NWpolice.org/Peel.html, January 9, 2010. Also see Douglas Hurd, Sir Robert Peel: *A Biography* (London: Weidenfeld & Nicolson, 2007). Susan Lentz maintains that the principles are the invention of 20th-century textbook writers, see "The Invention of Peel's Principles," Journal of Criminal Justice, Vol. 35, No. 1 (January 2007), pp. 69–79.

5 Melville Lee, *A History of Police in England* (Montclair, NJ: Patterson Smith reprint, 1971), p. 240.

6 At one time or another, three legendary lawmen of the West were employed in Abilene: Bat Masterson, Wyatt Earp, and "Wild Bill" Hickok. An excellent recent biography of Hickcok is Tom Clavin, Wild Bill (New York: St. Martin's Press, 2019).

7 Colonel H. B. Wharfield, "A Fight with the Yaquis at Bear Valley, 1918," Arizona 4, No. 3 (Fall 1983), pp. 1–8.

8 Ibid.

9 For an excellent summary of the development of tribal police systems, see David Etheridge, *Indian Law Enforcement History* (Washington, DC: Bureau of Indian Affairs, Division of Law Enforcement Services, February 1, 1975), p. 80.

10 See M. David Desoucy, *Arizona Rangers* (Mount Pleasant, SC: Arcadia Publishing, 2008), Chuck Hornung, *Fullerton's Rangers: A History of the Mexico Territorial Mounted Police* (Jefferson, NC: McFarland & Company, 2005), and Mike Cox, *The Texas Rangers: Wearing the Cinco Peso, 1821–1900* (New York: Forge Books, 2008). "Texas Ranger" was not used in any legislation until 1874, although the term "Ranger" had been widely used by Texas citizens for many years.

11 U.S. Census Bureau, Table 1, Urban and Rural Population 1900 to 1990, https://www.census.gov/population/censusdata/urpop0090.txt, accessed August 16, 2015.

12 The site of the assassination is where the present National Gallery of Art is located, 401 West Constitution Avenue, Washington, DC.

13 Thomas A. Reppetto, *The Blue Parade* (New York: Free Press, 1978), pp. 41–42.

14 Peter H. Argersinger, "New Perspectives on Election Fraud in the Gilded Age," *Political Science Quarterly* 100, No. 4 (Winter 1985–1986), p. 672.

15 Loc. Cit., This is the reason that in all states today, any political signs or activities on behalf of a candidate or party cannot be displayed or conducted with a specified number of feet from a polling station.

16 Loc. cit.

17 Ibid., p. 678.

18 Ibid., 680–681.

19 Alice b. Stone and Donald C. Stone, "Early Development of Education in Public Administration," *American Public Administration: Past, Present, and Future*, edited by Frederick C. Mosher (Tuscaloosa: University of Alabama, Press, 1975), pp. 17–18.

20 Bryn Mawr was the first institution of higher learning education to offer graduate degrees to women. In 1888, that college awarded its first PhD to one.

21 William Penn, the founder of Pennsylvania, was a strong advocate of education. The prevailing religious traditions of early Pennsylvania shaped formal education in the state. Most of the early universities and colleges were developed by the prevailing Quaker tradition exclusively for men. However, Bryn Mawr College was an exception, founded in 1885, again by the Quakers, was one of the nation's first colleges offered to provide more rigorous education exclusively for women.

22 Parenthetically, Woodrow Wilson is the only President (1913–1921) to have an earned Ph.D. He also signed the legislation making Mothers' Day a national holiday.

23 Woodrow Wilson, "The Study of Administration. *Political Science Quarterly*, 2 (1887) pp 197–222.

24 Raymond Fosdick and Others, edited by Roscoe Pound and Felix Frankfurter, *Criminal Justice in Cleveland, Report of the Cleveland Foundation* (Cleveland: The Cleveland Foundation, 1922). The 81 detectives, supposedly the "cream of the department," were substantially short of that. After administering the Army Alpha Test for Mental Ability to all officers, Fosdick discovered 25 percent of all detectives had "inferior intelligence," while the personnel in the traffic and mounted patrol units had higher test scores.

25 E. W. Roddenbury, "Achieving Professionalization," *Journal of Criminal Law, Criminology, and Police Science* 44 (May 1953–1954), p. 109.

26 See Sylvia R. Cruess, Sharon Johnson, and Richard L. Cruess, "Profession," *Teaching and Learning in Medicine*, Vol. 6, No 4, (Winter 2004), pp. 74–76, Robert K. Merton, "Some Thoughts on the Professions in American Society (Address before the Brown University Graduate Convocation, Providence, R.I., June 6, 1960), and Howard Becker, "The Nature of a Profession," in the Sixty-First Yearbook of the National Society for the Study of Education (Chicago: National Society for the Study of Education, 1962).

27 Gene Edward Carte, "August Vollmer and the Origins of Police Professionalism," *Journal of Police Science and Administration*, No. 3, (1973), p. 274. For an excellent read on the life and impact of *August Vollmer on American policing*, see Willard M. Oliver, August Vollmer: The Father of American Policing (Durham, NC: Carolina Academic Press, 2017).

28 Larry T. Hoover ascribes the development of a police academic establishment to O. W. Wilson. See "From Police Administration to Police Science: The Development of a Police Academic Establishment in the United States," *Police Quarterly*, Vol. 8, No. 1, (2005)

29 The Academy of Criminal Justice Sciences Police Section bestows an annual award in O. W. Wilson's name for distinguished police scholarship.

30 After Chief Wilson's death, the book was revised by various authorities, their names added as coauthors with Wilson. The last edition appears to be 1997. William J. Bopp wrote at least four publications on O. W. Wilson, including "O. W. Wilson: Portrait of an American Police Administrator," The Police Journal: Theory, Practice, and Principles, July 1, 1988, Vol. 61, Issue 3, pp, 2019–225.

31 Jack S. Blocker, "Did Prohibition Really Work," *American Journal of Public Health*, Vol. 96, No. 2, (February 2006), p. 235. 36

32 Marcia Yablon, "The Prohibition Hangover," conference paper, Law & Society Annual Meeting, Humboldt University, Berlin, Germany, July 25, 2007.

33 Holland Webb, "Temperance Movements and Prohibition," *International Social Science Review*, Vol. 74, No. 1 and 2, (1999), p. 61.

34 No Author, "Abandoning Prohibition," *The Nation* Vol. 76, No. 1977, (May 21, 1930), pp. 409–410.

[35] Oddly, at the same time, Americans began drinking more; between 1900 and 1913 the annual production of alcohol grew dramatically. Beer jumped from 1.2 billion to 2 billion gallons and liquor grew from 97 to 147 million gallons. Blocker, "Did Prohibition Really Work?" p. 235.

[36] Seth Kugel, "Tell Them Seth Sent You," *New York Times*, April 29, 2007.

[37] Jack Kelly, "Gangster City," *American Heritage*, Vol. 46, No. 2, (April 1995), p. 65.

[38] Toni Alexander, "Welcome to Old Times: Inserting the Okie Past into California's San Joaquin Valley Present," *Journal of Cultural Geography*, Vol. 26, No. 1, (February 2009), p. 74.

[39] Cecilia Rasmussen, "LAPD Blocked Dust Bowl Migrants at State Borders," *The Los Angeles Times*, March 9, 2003.

[40] Kevin M. O'Brien, "Do Municipal Residency Requirements Affect Labour Market Outcomes?" *Urban Studies*, Vol. 34, No. 11, (November 199)7, p. 1159.

[41] Kevin Johnson, "Police, Firefighters Challenge Residency Rules," *USA Today*, October 3, 2006.

[42] Frank J. Remington, "Development of Criminal Justice Education as an Academic Discipline," *Journal of Criminal Justice Education*, Vol. 1, No. 1, (March 1990), pp. 9–20.

[43] IACP's roots are traceable back to the National Chiefs of Police Union (1893), which largely focused on the apprehension of fugitives.

[44] In Chicago, Dillinger dated Romanian immigrant Ana Cumpanas, a brothel operator known as Anna Sage. Subsequently, he was involved with one of her employees. Fearing deportation and perhaps stung by being dropped by Dillinger, Sage betrayed him to the FBI. According to FBI records, on July 22, 1934, Sage wore an orange skirt and a white blouse to a movie with Dillinger at the Biograph Theater to help agents identify him. This contrasts with the numerous media reports stating she wore a red dress, which probably made better reading. Sage's betrayal did her little good. After receiving a $5,000 reward, she was deported to Romania. Annually, gangster buffs hold a ceremony on July 22 at the Biograph, complete with food, drinks, bagpipes, and speakers, to commemorate Dillinger's death. Dary Matera authored the most recent biography of him. See *John Dillinger* (New York: Carroll & Croft, 2005).

[45] Elaine Frantz Parsons, "Midnight Rangers: Costume and Performance in the Reconstruction-Era Ku Klux Klan," Vol. 93, No. 3, *The Journal of American History*, (December 2005), p. 812. Some of the founding KKK members may have earlier been part of a musical group, the "Midnight Rangers;" in that era, "rangers" were roaming groups of armed men of dubious legality. Also see, Patrick O'Donnell, *Ku Klux Klan: America's First Terrorists Exposed* (Idea Men Productions: West Orange, NJ, 2006).

[46] Occasionally, women accompanied these patrols although their role is not clear.

[47] The topic of slave patrols has received little attention. See K.B. Turner, David Giacopassi, and Margaret Vandiver, "Ignoring the Past: Coverage of Slave Patrols in Criminal Justice Texts," *Journal of Criminal Justice Education*, Vol. 17, No. 1, (March 2006).

[48] Danial Kato, "Law and (Dis)Order: Why the KKK was So Successful in 1868?" Conference Paper, Western Political Science Association, 2007, Las Vegas, Annual Meeting, pp. 35.

[49] Jennifer Gossett, "History of Women in Policing" in *The Encyclopedia of Women and Crime*, Wiley Online Library, May 6, 2019.

[50] Bert Webber, *Silent Siege: Japanese Attacks Against North America in World War II* (Fairfield, WA: Ye Galleon Press, 1984).

[51] Many saw the new rock'n'roll sound popularized by such performers as Little Richard, Elvis Presley, and Jerry Lee Lewis as inspired by the devil to seize the souls of our children. The emergence of doo-wop music in the mid-1950s, a smooth harmonized group sound, provided further "evidence" of the evil of rock'n'roll.

[52] There is one exception to a bill deadbeat being accepted. Historically, many employee credit unions wouldn't issue a loan unless the applicant had cosigners. If an officer defaulted on such a loan and his cosigners had to pay it off, his reputation went to absolute zero and he might find that his backups were slow getting to him, a hint that it was time to find another occupation.

[53] The coveted black and gold Ranger Tab is a qualification tab authorized on successful graduation from the U.S. Army Ranger School. It is considered one of the highest achievements in the U.S. Army as, on average only 3,000 soldiers are offered the opportunity to earn the badge.

[54] One of the casualties of that boycott was a city of Montgomery White librarian, Juliette Morgan, who wrote a letter printed in the Montgomery Advertiser praising the restraint of African-Americans in protesting for equal treatment. The KKK is thought to be responsible for burning a cross on her lawn and invectives were hurled at her from all quarters. Although Juliette Morgan was not a healthy person, the intense hostility displayed toward her must have played a role in her suicide 18 months later. See Mary Stanton, *Journey Toward Justice: Juliette Hampton Morgan* (Athens, Georgia: University of Georgia, 2006).

[55] The lead author on this book was a field training officer for the first group of African-Americans Tampa Police Department officer trained for general patrol duties in 1964 and witnessed attempts by White motorists to refuse his trainee's traffic citation. Such events were not unusual. See Elliot M. Rudwick, *The Unequal Badge: Negro Policemen in the South* (Atlanta: Southern Relations Council, 1962) and Jack Kuykendall and David E. Burns, "The Black Police Officer: A Historical Perspective," *Journal of Contemporary Criminal Justice*, Vol. 1, No. 4, (1980).

[56] This quote has been restated for succinctness. See U.S. National Advisory Commission on Civil Disorders, Report of the National Advisory Commission on Civil Disorders (Washington, DC: U.S. Government Printing Office, 1968), p. 157.

[57] Some believe that the assassination of President Kennedy was Castro's retaliation for the Central Intelligence Agency's attempted assassination of him in 1961, coordinated by mobster "Handsome Johnny" Roselli

(1905–1976). Roselli broke into crime with Capone's outfit in Chicago. The men allegedly involved in the assassination were apprehended and executed in Cuba. Several months after testifying before a Senate committee on this affair, Roselli's decomposing and legless body was found in a steel barrel near Dumfounding Bay, Florida. There is, of course, no shortage of theories about JFK's assassination. The topic continues to command attention; see Amy Zegart, "A Plot to Assassinate Castro Was Approved by CIA Director Allen Dulles," *The New York Times*, (January 26, 2007).

58 Garr Nielsen, Multnomah County, Oregon, The Police Chief, Vol. 73, No. 8. (August 2006). Reviewed online. No page numbers.

59 James Q. Wilson, "The Police and Their Problems," *Public Policy*, Vol. 12, (1963), pp. 189–216.

60 Robert C. Wadman and William Thomas Allison, *To Serve and Protect* (Upper Saddle River, NJ: Prentice Hall, 2000), p. 151.

61 On May 4, 2070, the Ohio National Guard opened fire on a crowd gathered to protest the Vietnam War on the campus of Kent State University. The incident is recaptured by the History Channel (History.Com Editors), *Kent State Shooting*, September 8, 2017. See: https://www.history.com/topics/vietnam-war/kent-state-shooting

62 Vietnam veterans attending college often chose to conceal their service because the anti-war movement, which permeated campuses, would lead to them being spit at or reviled as "baby killers," a shameful reward for their service. At the same time, law enforcement personnel attending universities part-time did not reveal their occupation because of student "paranoia about police spies" investigating anti-war activities or drug use.

63 His assailant was released from prison in 2007.

64 Nicholas deB Katzenback, *The Challenge of Crime in a Free Society* (Washington, DC: Government Printing Office, 1967), p. 12.

65 Jameson W. Doig, "Police Problems, Proposals, and Strategies for Change," *Public Administration Review*, 28, (September/October 1968), p. 393.

66 National Research Council of the National Academies, *Fairness and Effectiveness in Policing: The Evidence* (Washington, DC: The National Academies Press, 2001), p. 176.

67 Joe Schwartz, Israel's Defense, First Things: A *Journal of Religion and Public Life*, No. 191, (March 2009), p. 29. His assailant was released from prison in 2007.

68 After the raid, Ugandan Army officers murdered an Israeli passenger who previously had been taken from the terminal to a hospital.

69 It also led to U.S. Navy Seal Team 6 (ST6) being designated as a primary counter-terrorism group (1981). Six years later, ST6 was folded into the U.S. Navy Special Warfare Development Group (NSWDG) with responsibility for maritime environment terrorism.

70 David Weisburd et. al., *CompStat and Organizational Change: A National Assessment* (Washington, DC: National Institute of Justice, 2008), p. 5.

71 Spencer S. Hsu and Ann E. Marimow, "Would-Be Reagan Assassin John Hinckley Jr. To Be Freed After 35 Years, The Washington Post, July 27, 2016, https://www.washingtonpost.com/local/public-safety/ would-be-reagan-assassin-john-w-hinckley-jr-to-be-freed-after-35-years/2016/07/27/04142084-5015-11e6-a422-83ab49ed5e6a_story.html, accessed December 22, 2019.

72 No author, Oklahoma City "Bombing Fast Facts," CNN, April 8, 2019, https://www.cnn.com/2013/09/18/us/ oklahoma-city-bombing-fast-facts/index.html, accessed January 17, 2020.

73 Raphael Perl and Ronald O'Rourke, Terrorist Attack on USS Cole: Background and Issus for Congress (Washington, D.C.: Congressional Research Service, January 30, 2001), p. 1 and Hearing Before the Committee on Armed Services, United States Senate, 107th Congress, First Session, May 3, 2001 (Washington, D.C.: Government Printing Office, 2002), May 3, 2001 (Washington D.C.: Government Printing Office, 2002), May 3, 2001, No page numbers.

74 David B. Muhlhausen and Jena Baker McNeill, Terror Trends: 40 Years' Data on International and Domestic Terrorism, The Heritage Foundation, May 20, 2011, p. 3 and Hearing on Armed Forces, United States Senate, 107th Congress, First Session, no page numbers.

75 Ibid. p. 6.

76 Ibid. p. 7.

77 U.S. Department of Homeland Security, Active Shooter: How to Respond (US Printing Office, October 2008) p. 2. See: https://www.dhs.gov/xlibrary/assets/active_shooter_ booklet.pdf

78 Elizabeth Daley, "Knife-Wielding Student Wounds 22 in Pennsylvania School, Reuters News, April 9, 2014. See: https://www.reuters.com/article/usa-pennsylvania-stabbing/knife-wielding-student-wounds-22-in-pennsylvania-school-idINDEEA3809820140410

79 Jason Silverstein, "There Were More Mass Shooting than Day in 2019," CBS News, January 2, 2020. See: https://www.cbsnews.com/news/ mass-shootings-2019-more-than-days-365/

80 Ibid.

81 U.S. Congress, *Investigative Assistance for Violent Crimes Act of 2012*, updated and enacted as law on January 134, 2013.

82 Ibid.

83 Federal Bureau of Investigation, "Active Shooter Study: Active Shooter Incidents in the United States from 2000-2018. *FBI.gov*. See: https://www.fbi.gov/file-repository/ active-shooter-incidents-2000-2018.pdf/view

84 Ibid.

85 See James Silver, John Horgan, and Paul Gill. "Foreshadowing Targeted Violence: Assessing Leakage of Intent by Public Mass Murderers." *Aggression and Violent Behavior* (December, 2017). https://www.sciencedirect. com/science/article/pii/S1359178917300502

86 See Robert W. Taylor and Charles R. Swanson, Terrorism, Intelligence and Homeland Security, 2nd edition (New York: Pearson, 2019), Chapter 4 and Graaeme Wood, "What ISIS Really Wants," *The Atlantic*, March 2015.

87 Ibid.

88 With most of its resources (including finances and armed fighters) depleted through battles in Iraq and Syria against Western forces, the Islamic State (IS) continues to operate primarily through its affiliates. IS remains a significant threat to the United States and American interests abroad.

See Ben Wedeman, "Baghdadi is Gone, but ISIS Isn't Dead yet...and Could be Poised for a Resurgence." CNN, October 28, 2019.

[89] http://lapd-assets.lapdonline.org/assets/pdf/special-order4-use-of-force-revised.pdf. Revised February 5, 2020.

[90] Police Executive Research Forum, *The Workforce Crisis, and What Police Agencies are Doing About It.*, September 2019. See: https://www.policeforum.org/assets/WorkforceCrisis.pdf

[91] Ibid.

[92] Ibid.

[93] Ibid.

[94] Ibid.

[95] World Health Organization - WHO, *Coronavirus Disease (COVID-19) Dashboard.* See: https://covid19.who.int/?gclid=EAlalQobChMIz9DmwpH26wlVvxitBh31sAzGE AAYAiAAEgLgk_D_BwE. Data and information relating to these precise figures was retrieved on December 31, 2020.

## CHAPTER TWO

POLICING TODAY

Learning Objectives

1. Define community policing.
2. Describe the four-step problem-solving model called SARA.
3. Describe CompStat.
4. Discuss newer police strategies, including evidence-based policing, hot-spots policing, intelligence-led policing, and predictive policing.
5. List and briefly describe some of the more common crime analysis techniques.
6. Describe geographic information systems and explain how such a system would enhance police service.
7. Explain the impact of information technology on policing.
8. Describe how distrust between police and citizens can affect police strategies.

INTRODUCTION

IN THE PAST DECADE, our society has changed measurably. Economic downturns and other social issues have, arguably, widened income disparities; politics have become increasingly divisive; and issues of race and equality are at the forefront of the national consciousness in a way that hasn't been seen since the 1960s. Throughout it all, crime levels have largely been on the decline—police departments across the country have enjoyed the lowest crime rates in decades However, beginning in early 2020, these rates have increased. Many urban areas are seeing huge increases in both violent crime and property offenses, causing law enforcement agencies to reexamine their strategies and reallocate resources. In some cases, departments have shifted from targeted enforcement models back to community policing blends—in other cases, departments have utilized technology in new and different ways.

Furthermore, the landscape of policing itself looks much different than it did just a few years ago: Various social movements have begun to call on law enforcement agencies to increase transparency and respond to perceptions of biased policing; the trend of police militarization, an outgrowth of SWAT-style techniques and armaments, is being challenged; and the use of technology has transformed many police functions.

This is an interesting era for crime-fighting methodologies—making understanding their evolution even more important. Tracing the genesis of these methods from the reactive and ineffective traditional model of policing common previous to the 1980s, one sees how the shift in focus on social problems and attempts to engage the wider community to assist in curbing crime and disorder emerged into what is now commonly called "community policing." Community policing still provides a strong philosophical model among police agencies in the United States today. In the early 1990s, community policing was greatly enhanced through a management accountability process known as CompStat (Computer Statistics), originally started under the leadership of then Commissioner Bill Bratton in New York City. The variety of tactics and strategies being used to address today's unique problems draw greatly from both of these models, as well as utilizing technology and research-bolstered techniques to maximize their effectiveness.

This chapter begins with an examination of current police operational philosophies. Included are community policing and the Scanning, Analysis, Response and Assessment (SARA) model, harm-focused policing, evidence-based policing, hot-spots policing, intelligence-led policing, and predictive policing. Other sections in the chapter cover information technologies, such as crime analysis, geographic information systems, using social media, body cameras, and the impact of information technologies. The chapter ends with information on the warrior and guardian styles of policing, police militarization, unrest with the police, and improving police community relations.

COMMUNITY POLICING

As explained in Chapter 1, the failure of traditional law enforcement methods to curb rising crime rates during the 1970s and 1980s and to reintegrate the police with society gave rise to a new movement, generally referred to as community-oriented policing (COP) or **community policing**. Today, community policing represents the dominant strategy of policing in America. According to a 2017 U.S. Department of Justice budget request, approximately 81 percent of the nation's population is served by law enforcement and police agencies practicing community policing.[1] Although COP is a core operational philosophy, it is also an environment to implement other compatible strategies, tactics, programs, and/or philosophies such as problem-oriented policing, hot-spots policing, pulling levers policing, COMPSTAT, and evidence-based policing, some of which are discussed later in this chapter.[2]

One of the first major critics of the traditional policing model was Herman Goldstein.[3] In his classic work *Policing a Free Society*, Goldstein questioned the effectiveness of traditional police methods in safeguarding the constitutional rights and privileges celebrated in American society (e.g., freedom of speech and expression, due process, and the right to privacy) versus the control of crime and the decay of social order. Goldstein pointed out that these two goals may be incompatible under the traditional police model and called for a closer link between the police and the community.

During the same time period, Wilson and Kelling's "broken windows" thesis emerged as a dominant theme in American policing debate.[4] In the thesis they argued that crime seemed to increase dramatically in neighborhoods where visible signs of social decay and disorder were present (e.g., graffiti on bridge structures, unkept lots with overgrown weeds, visible drug and prostitution activities, and warehouses with broken windows). Wilson and Kelling argued that areas with these types of crimes are signs of decaying neighborhoods and therefore a breeding ground for more serious crimes. The philosophy of **zero-tolerance policing (ZTP)** focuses on targeting police responses to less serious crimes in these areas, addressing the counterintuitive argument that disorder may elicit more fear than actual crime.[5] Where adopted, officers are not given any discretion in dealing with minor crimes of disorder; an arrest has to be made. In more recent times, ZTP has been re-labeled as "disorder policing" in some circles.

Although ZTP has been given credit for reducing crime in some jurisdictions, most notably New York City, the empirical evidence of its effectiveness raises some questions,[6] as does the assumed progression from disorder to serious crimes.[7] Moreover, the strategy may have some unintended consequences: In New York City, the implementation of ZTP was accompanied by an increase in citizen complainants and lawsuits alleging police misconduct and abuse of force.[8] Still, some policymakers continue to adopt ZTP, which can be used as the dominant strategy in an agency or within the framework of other policing strategies such as community-oriented policing. Others maintain that the two strategies are incompatible and that working closely with the community can achieve ZTP results without generating increases in complainants and lawsuits.[9]

Kelling and Coles went on to argue that "broken windows needed fixing" and that the police must be directed to do more than just "crime control."[10] Indeed, they argued that other functions of the police were as important and maybe more important than strictly enforcing the law and maintaining order. In this context, police should focus more on a service orientation, building key partnerships with churches, youth centers, and other neighborhood groups in an effort to forge new alliances with the community. Crime was seen not as the sole purview of the police but rather as an entire community responsibility. Police administrators began to look for new techniques and operational strategies that emphasized more service than arrest. Decentralization of services, characterized by storefront operations and neighborhood centers, began to be commonplace in police organizations. Old programs, such as the horse patrol, bike patrol, and the "walking beat" officer, were reintroduced to American policing as ways to bring the police and the community closer together.

Although Braiden[11] argues that community policing was "nothing new under the sun" because it only echoed the ideas expressed by Sir Robert Peel in the early 1800s, community policing did represent a refreshing approach to earlier problems. Community policing embraced the Peelian principle of police as members of the public giving full-time attention to community welfare and existence. Therefore, policing was linked to a myriad of social issues other than simply crime, including poverty, illiteracy, racism, teenage pregnancy, and the like.[12]

Although precise definitions of community policing are hard to find and also vary, it is generally an operational and management philosophy that can be quickly identified. Community policing is characterized by ongoing attempts to promote greater community involvement in the police function. For the most part, the movement focused on programs that fostered five elements: (1) a commitment to crime prevention, (2) public scrutiny of the police, (3) accountability of police actions to the public, (4) customized police service, and (5) community organization.[13]

Community policing advocates argue that **traditional policing** is a system of response; that is, the police respond to calls for services *after* the activity occurs. Police response is then reactive and incident driven (calls for assistance and people reporting crimes) rather than proactive and preventive. Further, a randomized motor patrol neither lowers crime nor increases the chances of catching suspects. Simply, increasing the number of police, then, has limited impact on the crime rate because improving response time on calls for service has little relevance to preventing the original incident.[14] In addition, the role of the individual police officer is largely limited within the confines of random patrol and response to incidents. In some jurisdictions the calls for service are so high that the amount of time available to random, preventative patrol is negligible.

In present practice, COP is a proactive approach to crime control with three complimentary elements: (1) community partnerships; (2) problem-solving, using the Scanning, Analysis, Response, and Assessment (SARA) model; and (3) organizational transformation (see Figure 2.1). The most common types of restructuring associated with community policing include the following:

- A decentralization of authority, allowing all levels of a department to have an increased level of independence and decision-making.

- A flattened hierarchy, which collapses bureaucratic layers and allows for increased efficiency and better communication.

- A reduced number of specialized units, with resources instead being devoted to the direct delivery of police services to the public.

- An emphasis on teamwork, which promotes problem-solving and the provision of services by groups of employees.

- Increasing non-sworn personnel, which provides cost savings because their salaries are typically less than sworn officers and which also allows sworn officers to be used more effectively.[15]

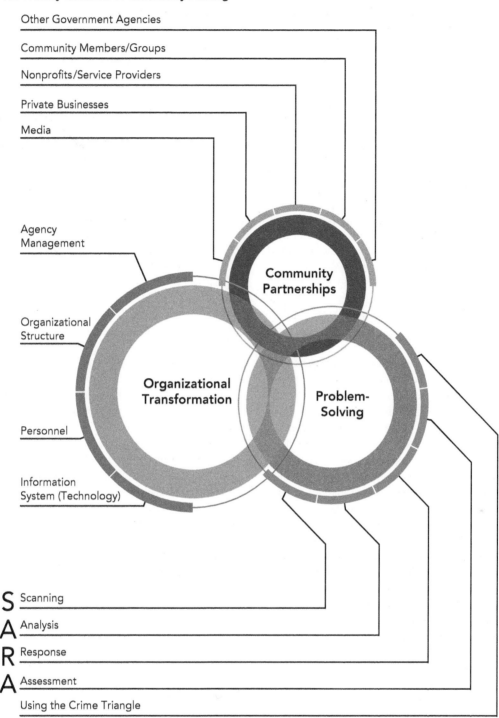

The Primary Elements of Community Policing

Other Government Agencies

Community Members/Groups

Nonprofits/Service Providers

Private Businesses

Media

Agency Management

Organizational Structure

Personnel

Information System (Technology)

Community Partnerships

Organizational Transformation

Problem-Solving

S Scanning

A Analysis

R Response

A Assessment

Using the Crime Triangle

FIGURE 2.1 ▶ Primary Elements of Community Policing. *Source:* Community Oriented Policing Services, "Community Policing Defined," p. 2 (2014). www.cops.usdoj.gov/pdf/vets-to-cops/e030917193-CP-Defined.pdf

EVALUATION RESEARCH ON COMMUNITY POLICING

Since the 1980s, considerable empirical data has been generated regarding the effectiveness of community policing. Few, however, actually show positive effectiveness of the policing paradigm as a successful methodology to reduce crime and disorder. The evidence is at best largely mixed as it relates to positive outcomes. While a portion of the evidence shows some indication that community policing may be related to decreases in crime—as is often the case in social science research—design limitations make it difficult to generalize to other places and time.

Box 2.1: Harm-Focused Policing

When we attempt to quantify the success of a policing program, we often talk about things that *didn't* happen: Certain crimes *didn't* occur at certain rates or we *prevented* these things from happening. This is a very one-dimensional perspective to look at policing—the technique may be adequate to compare crime rates from year to year, but it does not give a full picture of the role of the police within a specific community, nor does it recognize that all crimes are not equal across the spectrum. According to at least one police scholar (Dr. Jerry Ratcliffe), the field of policing is missing an opportunity to better capture the complex nexus between crime and the criminal justice system by not developing a harm-based evaluation system that explores all of these intricacies. Not only does harm-focused policing take a look at crime numbers and the harm that crime itself causes, but it also explores the inherent harms in different types of police activities. Ratcliffe explains that, for example, in hot-spots policing, increased "stop-and-frisk" scenarios might drive down narcotics crime in the area. But as increased patrols tend to unfairly target minorities, the social implications of arresting and sending nonviolent offenders through the criminal justice system might have a ripple effect: It might inflame racial tensions, decrease police legitimacy, and increase social problems like poverty among families whose loved ones were arrested. In that case, a slightly decreased number of drug-related crimes as a result of hot-spots policing may not be offset by the social harms it has simultaneously inflicted on the community.

Ratcliffe believes that his harm-focused model is an ideal complement to both intelligence-led policing and evidence-based policing; the model would provide statistics and information on which to focus intelligence-led practices and would provide much in the way of scientific data for evidence-based policies and strategies. This new and innovative policing model, though complex, provides a rich perspective to view the ways that crime and law enforcement actions impact a community.

Findings are also limited when it comes to perceptions and fear of crime. While it is generally accepted that community policing helps community members feel safer and reduces the levels of fear of crime, in reality, actual crime incidents in several COP communities reveal no significant changes.[16] In some research findings, favorable decreases in disorder offenses as a result of community policing are clear and consistent evidence that COP improves community relations. And, it appears that community policing models benefit individual police officer attitudes toward both their work and the community. It's not as certain, however, whether community policing actually reduces calls for service or whether it significantly changes police officer behavior. Hence, definitive statements on the impact of community policing are difficult because the concept itself looks very different from agency to agency. Some departments emphasize community outreach and programming that directly affect quality of life, while others favor increased patrols and increased reliance on CompStat. There's no standard definition of what a community policing model should look like, and implementation varies across agencies compounding problems relating to evaluation of the community policing model.[17]

COMMUNITY POLICING AND COMPSTAT

Although community policing has *not* had the drastic effects its supporters had hoped, the premise behind the philosophy has in turn led to the quality movement within policing: making the police be more efficient and effective. Today, most ambitious police methodology focuses precisely on that concept—**CompStat**. The word CompStat is derived from "comp," stemming from the word "computer," and "stat," which originates from "statistics." The process was originally developed in New York City by the then Commissioner William Bratton in the mid-1990s,[18] and continues in some form today in most major cities. CompStat is a process that looks at the individual needs of the community and then designs proactive strategies to stop or prevent crime. To accomplish this goal, Bratton required his department (New York in the 1990s and Los Angeles in the 2000s) to analyze crime data weekly and required police administrators to meet regularly to share information between divisions and precincts. A key component of CompStat is to force police commanders to address crime and social problems in their areas of responsibility and to address them immediately. Police commanders are then held accountable for the success or failure of their plans and decisions. Combining the two strategies of in-depth analysis with management accountability is the heart of the process.

Essentially, CompStat is a collection of modern management practices, military-like deployment efforts, and strong enforcement strategies all based on the availability of accurate and timely statistical crime data. Four core principles highlight a police department's model of CompStat:

1. *Accurate and timely intelligence and statistical crime information based on geographical settings and/or areas.* High-tech computer systems and geographical mapping programs are most helpful in providing the aggregate and individual data often required for effective CompStat efforts. However, more rudimentary aspects of visual crime analysis can be accomplished through daily pin mapping and bulletins.

2. *Rapid deployment of resources, particularly combining the immediate presence of uniform patrol working in*

Box 2.2: Traditional vs. Community Policing: Questions and Answers

	Traditional	Community policing
Question: *Who are the police?*	A government agency principally responsible for law enforcement.	Police are the public and the public are the police: The police officers are those who are paid to give full-time attention to the duties of every citizen.
Question: *What is the relationship of the police force to other public service departments?*	Priorities often conflict.	The police are one department among many responsible for improving the quality of life.
Question: *What is the role of the police?*	Focusing on solving crimes.	A broader problem-solving approach.
Question: *How is police efficiency measured?*	By detection and arrest rates.	By the absence of crime and disorder.
Question: *What are the highest priorities?*	Crimes that are high value (e.g., bank robberies) and those involving violence.	Whatever problems disturb the community most.
Question: *What, specifically, do police deal with?*	Incidents.	Citizens' problems and concerns.
Question: *What determines the effectiveness of police?*	Response times.	Public cooperation.
Question: *What view do police take of service calls?*	Deal with them only if there is no real police work to do.	Vital function and great opportunity.
Question: *What is police professionalism?*	Swift effective response to serious crime.	Keeping close to the community.
Question: *What kind of intelligence is most important?*	Crime intelligence (study of particular crimes or series of crimes).	Criminal intelligence (information about the activities of individuals or groups).
Question: *What is the essential nature of police accountability?*	Highly centralized; governed by rules, regulations, and policy directives; accountable to the law.	Emphasis on local accountability to community needs.
Question: *What is the role of headquarters?*	To provide the necessary rules and policy directives.	To preach organizational values.
Question: *What is the role of the press liaison department?*	To keep the "heat" off operational officers so they can get on with the job.	To coordinate an essential channel of communication with the community.
Question: *How do the police regard prosecutions?*	As an important goal.	As one tool among many.

Source: Malcolm K. Sparrow, "Implementing Community Policing," *Perspectives on Policing* (Washington, DC: U.S. Department of Justice, National Institute of Justice, November 1988). See: https://www.ncjrs.gov/pdffiles1/nij/114217.pdf

concert with directed undercover operations. Rapid deployment of other city and governmental resources, such as nuisance and abatement personnel, sanitation workers, and alcoholic beverage and licensing enforcement, is an additional aspect of this principle.

3. *Effective tactics and strategies of enforcement that focus on visible street crimes or "quality-of-life" crimes,* such as loitering, drinking in public, street prostitution, or even jumping subway turnstiles.

4. *Relentless follow-up and assessment,* which include placing accountability and responsibility not only on the individual police officer on the beat but also on individual police managers of traditionally defined areas, such as division heads, precinct captains, or shift commanders.[19]

CompStat focuses on using the most accurate and timely information and data available to the police, opening lines of communication both horizontally and vertically within the organization, activating the community at large, and improving the overall efficiency and effectiveness of the police. CompStat is problem-oriented and preventive and stresses the need to focus on current problems rather than on past incidents. In this manner, CompStat significantly departs from the traditional police model by taking a preventive/proactive approach rather than a reactive, incident-driven approach. CompStat meetings tend to focus on an individual area or a community's problems with an eye toward remedying the situation or variables/people that encourage, cause, or commit crime, thereby preventing continuing problems and crime.

The CompStat process is not limited to large, metropolitan agencies. Indeed, CompStat can be implemented in cities of all sizes with diverse populations and varying crime rates. The process helps police executives clarify their agency's mission and focus its efforts on the most important issues first, identifying problems early and developing effective strategies for remediation and prevention. Most importantly, the CompStat process allows the organization to quickly learn what works and what does not, while providing a flexible methodology to try innovative programs and promising strategies.[20]

CompStat doesn't look the same in every agency, nor should it. When it was first widely implemented, many police chiefs thought that CompStat meetings should be high stakes, discipline-oriented meetings that involved a lot of yelling and finger-pointing, which only served to marginalize the process and make meeting highly unpopular and intimidating to mid-level and even command staff. Today's CompStat meetings are much lighter in tone than in Bratton's version—and many agencies now include outside stakeholders who contribute alongside of commanders, patrol officers, and crime analysts. Depending on the problem, outside stakeholders might include key representatives from a variety of institutions, including public health, the chamber of commerce, public housing, and even private security agencies. For instance, in a city that is economically oriented to tourism, criminals could easily identify rental cars. When the rentals were stopped by traffic or at lights, the criminals would slash the tires and rob the immobile car occupants. They didn't fear prosecution if apprehended because the visitors were unlikely to return to that city in order to testify. By including a group of stakeholders that included the tourism bureau and the car rental industry, multiple strategies were devised that substantially obviated the problem.

CompStat meetings consistently generate clear performance measurements that emphasize metrics related to crime reduction and quality of life, as opposed to police activity indicators like arrests made and tickets issued.[21] Many policing experts point to CompStat as the single most important advance in police administration in the past century. Whether that will continue to be the case in the future lies within CompStat's ability to incorporate technological advances, disseminate tactical information, and balance its focus on crime with other values critical to law enforcement, such as fair and impartial policing, officer behavior, and community relations.

COMMUNITY POLICING MODELS

Community policing has evolved greatly in the years since its implementation, and as mentioned previously, it takes many different forms across agencies. And though some of the benchmark case studies in policing literature tend to focus on programs that were created decades ago, it remains important to see the genesis of community policing in order to understand how the concept is relevant to today's police organizations. Three case studies that still have a major impact on today's community policing philosophies include Newport News, Virginia; Chicago, Illinois; and Minneapolis, Minnesota.

Newport News, Virginia

In 1983, under the direction of a new chief, Darrel Stephens, the Newport News Police Department developed a new approach to policing. Known as **problem-oriented policing (POP)**, this innovative style of community policy focused on the department's traditional response to major, recurring problems. Its goal was to reassess the traditional, incident-driven aspects of police work, and fundamentally change the way the Newport News Police Department viewed its mission. The resulting self-analysis yielded an important four-step, problem-solving methodology (commonly referred to as **SARA**) that has become an integral part of current community policing operations (see Figure 2.2).

> *Scanning*—Instead of relying on broad, law-related concepts, such as robbery, burglary, and auto theft, officers are encouraged to group individual, related incidents that come to their attention as "problems" and define these problems in more precise and useful terms.

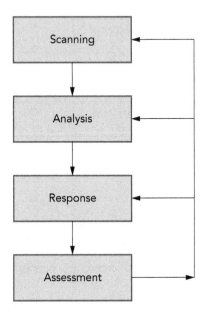

FIGURE 2.2 ▶ SARA, the problem-solving system used in Newport News, Virginia, Police Department. *Source:* William Speiman and John E. Eck. "Problem Oriented Policing," in *Research in Brief* (Washington, DC: National Institute of Justice, October 1988), p. 4.

For example, an incident that typically would be classified simply as a "robbery" might be seen as part of a pattern of prostitution-related robberies committed in center-city hotels. In essence, officers are expected to look for possible problems and accurately define them as part of their daily responsibility.

Analysis—Officers working on a well-defined problem then collect information from a variety of public and private sources, not just traditional police data, such as criminal records and past offense reports. Officers rely on problem analysis guides that direct officers to examine offenders, victims, the social, economic, and physical environment, and previous responses to the problem. The goal is to understand the scope, nature, and causes of the problem and formulate a variety of options for its resolution.

Response—The knowledge gained in the analysis stage is then used to develop and implement solutions. Officers seek the assistance of citizens, businesses, other police units, other public and private organizations, and anyone else who can help develop a program of action. Solutions may go well beyond traditional police responses to include other community agencies and/or municipal organizations.

Assessment—Finally, officers evaluate the impact and the effectiveness of their responses. Were the original problems actually solved or alleviated? What went right and just as importantly, what didn't work and why? Officers then can use the results to revise a response, to collect more data, or even to redefine the problem.[22]

Goldstein[23] further explains this systematic process in his book *Problem-Oriented Policing*, which has become a classic in the field. Goldstein's work attempts to give greater meaning

to each of the four SARA steps. To illustrate, a *problem* is expanded to mean a cluster of similar, related, or recurring incidents rather than a single incident. The assumption is that few incidents are isolated; instead, they are part of a wider set of urban social phenomena. Examples of such community problems are the following:

- Disorderly youth who regularly congregate in the parking lot of a specific convenience store
- Street prostitutes and associated "jack roll" robberies of patrons that continually occur in the same area
- Drunk and drinking drivers around the skid-row area of the city
- Panhandlers, vagrants, and other displaced people living on the sidewalk in a business district
- Juvenile runaways, prostitutes, and drug dealers congregating at the downtown bus depot
- Robberies of commercial establishments at major intersections of a main thoroughfare of a suburban area that is a corridor leading out of a large central city[24]

Note that each of these problems incorporates not only a potential or real crime but also a wider community/social issue. Further, each problem has been identified with a specific location. Goldstein[25] emphasizes that the traditional functions of crime analysis under the problem-solving methodology can be expanded to have a much wider and deeper importance. The pooling of data and subsequent analysis provide the basis for problem identification and response strategies. Therefore, the accuracy and timeliness of such information becomes a necessity for the department. However, the ultimate challenge in problem-oriented policing is not the identification of problems but rather the integration of the community with the police in developing effective ways of dealing with them (see Figure 2.3).

FIGURE 2.3 ▶ Officers focus on problem-solving in traditionally high-crime areas, such as low-income, densely populated urban settings. Providing quality policing and enhancing police and community relationships are important parts of the community policing movement. (Larry Kolvoord/The Image Works)

Chicago, Illinois

In January 1993, Mayor Richard Daley and then Police Superintendent Matt L. Rodriguez announced the first major operational changes to implement community policing in the city of Chicago. The new program, the **Chicago Alternative Policing Strategy (CAPS)**, was designed to move the department from a traditional, reactive, incident-driven agency to a more proactive and community-oriented department. At first, CAPS was hailed as a method to combat crime, drugs, and gang activity in the inner city. However, as the implementation plan unfolded, a much broader mission statement evolved that focused on a combined effort with the community to "identify and solve problems of crime and disorder and to improve the quality of life in all of Chicago's neighborhoods."[26]

As in many large cities implementing community policing, Chicago developed five prototype districts to serve as "laboratories" for testing new police ideas, innovations, and strategies (see Figure 2.4).

These districts could then refine the successful new programs and hence improve the overall CAPS model. Essentially, the new CAPS program echoed the methodology for implementing community policing in several other large metropolitan cities at the time. For instance, in Houston, Texas, and New York City, under the direction of the then Commissioner Lee P. Brown, the transition to community policing occurred only in select neighborhoods or districts and was known as **neighborhood-oriented policing**. Similar programs evolved in Phoenix, Arizona; Miami,

Florida; Philadelphia, Pennsylvania; and Newark, New Jersey. Only a few cities attempted to implement community policing strategies on a department-wide basis (e.g., Portland, Oregon and Baltimore, Maryland). Most cities, and particularly large metropolitan communities, realized that the implementation of community policing demanded dramatic modification in the existing philosophy, structure, operation, and deployment of police.[27] The gradual evolution toward full-scale adoption essentially continued to redefine both the means and ends of community policing.[28]

CAPS had a number of key features aimed at improving and expanding the overall quality of police services in the city of Chicago, as well as reducing crime.[29] These key features included the following:

- *Crime control and prevention*—CAPS emphasized both crime control and crime prevention. Vigorous and impartial enforcement of the law, rapid response to serious crimes and life-threatening emergencies, and proactive problem-solving with the community were the foundations of the city's policing strategy.

- *Neighborhood orientation*—CAPS gave special attention to the residents and problems of specific neighborhoods, which demanded that officers knew their beats (i.e., crime trends, hot-spots, and community organizations and resources that are within the geographical areas in which they are assigned) and developed partnerships with the community to solve problems. Beat officers worked the same beat on the same watch everyday, so they could more intimately know the beat's residents, its chronic crime problems, and the best strategies for solving those problems.

- *Increased geographic responsibility*—CAPS involved organizing police services so that officers are responsible for crime control in a specific area or beat. A district organizational structure using rapid-response cars to handle emergency calls allowed newly created beat teams to engage in community policing activities. The beat teams shared responsibility for specific areas under the leadership of a supervising beat sergeant.

- *Structured response to calls for police service*—CAPS system of differential responses to citizen calls freed beat team officers from the continuous demands of 911 calls. Emergency calls were handled primarily by rapid-response sector cars, whereas nonemergency and routine calls were handled by beat officers or by telephone callback contacts. Sector officers also attended to community matters, and sector and beat teams rotate, so that all officers participated in community policing.

- *Proactive, problem-solving approach*—CAPS focused on the causes of neighborhood problems rather than on discrete/individual incidents of crime or disturbances. Attention was given to the long-term prevention of these problems and to the signs of community disorder and decay that are associated with crime (e.g., "hot-spots" such as drug houses, loitering youth, and graffiti).

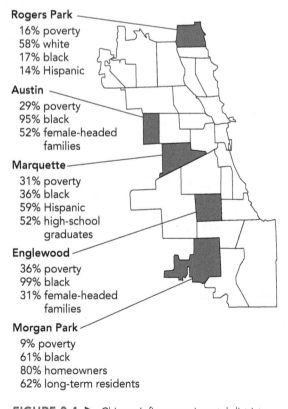

Rogers Park
16% poverty
58% white
17% black
14% Hispanic

Austin
29% poverty
95% black
52% female-headed families

Marquette
31% poverty
36% black
59% Hispanic
52% high-school graduates

Englewood
36% poverty
99% black
31% female-headed families

Morgan Park
9% poverty
61% black
80% homeowners
62% long-term residents

FIGURE 2.4 ▶ Chicago's five experimental districts.
Source: Susan M. Harnett and Wesley G. Skogan, "Community Policing: Chicago's Experience," *NIJ Journal* (April 1999), p. 3.

Quick Facts: Research on Chicago's CAPS Program

Researchers at Northwestern University in Chicago found that CAPS had a significant impact in crime levels and police community relations. The report, published in 2004, found decreased crime; decreased fear of crime; and increased levels of trust between the community and the police.

Source: Chicago Community Police Evaluation Consortium, "Community Policing in Chicago, Year Ten," April 2004, Illinois Criminal Justice Information Authority, https://www.ipr.northwestern.edu/publications/papers/urban-policy-and-community-development/docs/caps/Yr10-CAPSeval.pdf.

- *Combined community and city resources for crime prevention and control*—CAPS assumed that police alone cannot solve the crime problem and that they depend on the community and other city agencies to achieve success. Hence, part of the beat officer's new role was to broker community resources and to draw on other city agencies to identify and respond to local problems. Former Mayor Daley made CAPS a priority of all city agencies. Hence, the mayor's office ensured that municipal agencies were responsive to requests for assistance from beat officers.

- *Emphasis on crime and problem analysis through the CompStat process*—CAPS required more efficient data collection and analysis to identify crime patterns and target areas that demand police attention. Emphasis was placed on crime analysis at the district level, and beat information was recorded and shared among officers and across watches or shifts. To accomplish this task, each district implemented a local area network of advanced computer workstations employing a crime analysis system called ICAM (Information Collection for Automated Mapping). This new technology allowed beat officers and other police personnel to analyze and map crime hot-spots, track other neighborhood problems, and share this information with the community. The CAPS project also instituted a rigorous CompStat process designed to take CAPS to the next level through management accountability.[30]

- *Training*—The Chicago Police Department has made a significant commitment to training police personnel and the community in the CAPS philosophy and program. Intensive training on problem-solving and community partnerships was provided to district patrol officers and their supervisors. Innovative classroom instruction for the community and a program of joint police–community training were also developed.

- *Communication and marketing*—The Chicago Police Department was dedicated to communicating the CAPS philosophy to all members of the department and the community. This was a fundamental strategy of the CAPS program. To ensure such communication, an intensive marketing program was adopted that included a newsletter, roll-call training, a regular cable television program, information exchanges via computer technology (Internet and fax machines), and various brochures and videos. Feedback was collected through personal interviews, focus groups, community surveys, a CAPS hotline, and several suggestion boxes. The information collected through this marketing program assisted in the refinement and development of the CAPS program.

- *Evaluation, strategic planning, and organizational change*—The CAPS program underwent one of the most thorough evaluations of any community policing initiative in the United States. A consortium of four major Chicago-area universities (Northwestern, DePaul, Loyola, and the University of Illinois at Chicago) conducted an evaluation of the process and results in the prototype districts.

CAPS represents one of the largest and most comprehensive community policing initiatives in the country. During its first 10 years of operation, evaluation findings indicated that major crime and neighborhood problems were reduced, drug and gang problems were reduced, and public perception of the quality of police services was improved.[31] Under this orientation, the community is viewed as a valuable resource from which powerful information and ties can be gathered. It aims "to increase the interaction and co-operation between local police and the people and neighborhoods they serve" to combat crime.[32] Hence, the major goals of community policing are not only to reduce crime but also, more significantly, to increase feelings of safety among residents.[33] These two goals appear to be separate but are actually very closely linked in the community policing process. This approach attempts to increase the visibility and accessibility of police to the community. Through this process, police officers are no longer patrol officers enforcing the laws of the state but rather neighborhood officers. These officers infiltrate local neighborhoods, targeting specific areas in need of improvement. By involving themselves within the community, the officers are more available to meet and discuss the specific problems and concerns of each neighborhood and work to develop long-term solutions.[34] These solutions are the root of the proactive approach to policing. By listening to the public, the police will be better informed of the specific problems in each area. As cooperation between police and citizens in solving neighborhood problems increases, residents feel more secure.[35]

The Chicago program was a much lauded and often imitated initiative with support from within the community and accolades from around the country. But despite all the promises, results, and potential, the program became a shell of itself: budget cuts diverted necessary resources from the program; organizational restructuring disrupted continuity and institutional knowledge; and the community was left with a mishmash of disconnected and ineffective programs. The result? A palpable erosion of the trust and goodwill that the Chicago Police Department worked so hard to foster through CAPS. Increased violence and homicide rates and poor police/community relations are forcing the Chicago Police Department to re-examine their community policing initiatives—and to think of programs like CAPS a little differently. In a recent report from its Police Accountability Task Force, the Chicago Police Department was taken to task for treating CAPS as an alternative to policing as opposed to as an integral part of an effective policing strategy.[36] In April 2020, after a several changes in the top leadership spot, David O. Brown, former chief of police in Dallas, Texas and a strong advocate of community policing

Superintendent of Police in Chicago. Facing sky-rocking violent crime rates and significant racial and social unrest, Chicago may see a turn to CAPS once again.

Minneapolis, Minnesota

Comparing the core principles of CompStat with the problem-solving model of Newport News, presented earlier, reveals a significant amount of similarity. Indeed, CompStat may well be the natural evolution of the problem-solving model in today's more sophisticated cities. It is important that Chicago's CAPS program incorporated CompStat as a vehicle to enhance crime fighting and management accountability. While a number of jurisdictions, including Los Angeles, Philadelphia, New Orleans, Albuquerque, Sacramento, Boston, and Dallas, continue to refine the CompStat principles, none has been more successful in implementing the process than the Minneapolis Police Department.

Box 2.3: Advances in Community Policing: Community Advisory and Review Boards

Community policing has evolved and taken many forms since the early 1980s; today, one of the most popular forms involves the use of community advisory boards or panels. Police departments that utilize a community advisory board generally recruit a diverse group volunteer citizens to serve as community representatives; voice community concerns; give input into police policies and procedures; participate in research; support community outreach endeavors; provide feedback on police initiatives; help identify crime trends; and much more.

Departments around the country have used community advisory groups with positive results. Chicago's Community Policing Advisory Panel (CPAP) gave community members a critical role in filling the void left by their CAPS program; they worked with police to construct a framework for a durable community policing program, currently being implemented under Superintendent Eddie Johnson.

In Dallas, Texas, Chief U. *Reneé* Hall assembled a Community Advisory Board that meets in different locations around the city and reviews training initiatives; discusses community concerns; and works together to solve problems. In Hennepin, Minnesota, the Hennepin County Sheriff's Office uses a community advisory board as part of a slate of initiatives to increase transparency and to involve the community in efforts related to police reform. Chief of Staff Julianne Ortman stated, "The key to success is having a partner that provides services to folks in the community we don't otherwise have contact with, then building from there in order to educate them about how to work with law enforcement. We are trying to building understanding and partnership across the country to help us stay ahead of the curve with prevention and awareness."

The International Association of Chiefs of Police recommends that to form lasting and effective community advisory boards, police departments should do the following:

- Plan how to communicate the role of the advisory board with officers, command staff, or elected officials.

- Advertise the formation of the advisory board widely and appropriately for each population of your city, and notify the community when the department starts accepting applications.

- Create an inclusive space designed to accommodate the community's diverse needs, such as accessibility for persons with disabilities, interpretation services, even childcare or meals for children so that parents with various economic backgrounds can participate.

- Host meetings in different locations so members start to understand the diversity of needs in your city.

- Select applicants that represent different sectors of the community; together, the board should represent the interests, skills, and experiences of the whole community.

- Try to acquire between 10 and 20 board members—enough to represent your community, but not enough to stymie discussions.

- Consider involving a third-party facilitator to help develop the board's processes, including establishing a clear mission and ground rules and setting up guidelines for members' interactions with the media.

Additionally, police departments should be aware that such boards cannot just be symbolic. Input and suggestions from community advisory boards *must* make their way into decision-making processes in law enforcement agencies, or departments risk damaging the trust and the partnerships they're attempting to build.

Source: International Association of Chiefs of Police, "Promoting Community Involvement in Law Enforcement: Community Advisory Boards," May 6, 2019, https://www.theiacp.org/news/blog-post/promoting-community-involvement-in-law-enforcement-community-advisory-boards.

In Minneapolis, the CompStat program was referred to as **CODEFOR** (**C**omputer **O**ptimized **DE**ployment—**F**ocus **O**n **R**esults). This strategy was designed specifically to reduce crime and involves every geographical and structural unit within the Minneapolis Police Department. CODEFOR combined the latest technology in computer applications and geographical mapping with field-proven police techniques. Computer-generated maps identify high-intensity crime areas, and police resources are coordinated to such locations in a timely manner. Each week, police managers gather together and ask directed questions regarding the crime rates in each of their areas (see Figure 2.5).

In CODEFOR's heyday, departmental executives and commanders grilled precinct captains on the crimes in their areas. Precinct captains, while not expected to be able to eliminate crime entirely, were expected to articulate a sensible strategy for reversing a trend or eliminating a hot-spot. In many cases, those leaders who repeatedly failed to rise to the occasion—not unlike what might happen to the manager of a struggling department in a corporation—found themselves promptly reassigned. Police managers were held accountable for reducing crime in their areas. A more enlightened understanding of why the process worked was that it got the top police managers involved with crime once again. In addition to the solution of internal problems, attendance at community meetings, scheduling, and a myriad of other administrative tasks, managers were forced to direct their efforts to addressing crime in their geographical districts of responsibility. This emphasis on crime awareness and crime fighting sparked renewed feelings of self-worth among managers as well as an increase in communication between the beat officer and the precinct captain. Obviously, a more team-oriented spirit naturally arises which increases morale and supports the primary goals of CompStat under the CODEFOR program.[37]

The Minneapolis Police Department was one of the first departments not only to generate specific crime statistics each week by geographical area but also to use a much more refined process of tabulating success or failure. Interestingly, the reports were also provided over the Internet on a monthly basis for public consumption and evaluation.[38]

These three case studies presented represent some of the most iconic and groundbreaking community policing initiatives in American policing. Understanding the genesis of this major paradigm shift in law enforcement is crucial to replicating their successes, maintaining public trust and police legitimacy, and avoiding mistakes that have unintentionally harmed police/community relations over the past decade.

POLICING STRATEGIES TODAY

Discussions of policing strategies today employ a number of catchphrases and acronyms—it seems that every major jurisdiction employs a strategy that they credit with decreasing crime rates. As previously discussed, though, community policing programs and other contemporary policing initiatives have also revealed similar levels of inefficiency.

In particular, research has provided little in terms of support for problem-oriented policing as presented through broken windows and zero-tolerance philosophies.[39] Furthermore, despite the widespread popularity of community policing strategies, most studies evaluating this type of policing have not found that it greatly impacts crime or disorder. At best, community policing reduces citizens' fear of crime[40] and produces core challenges to police organizations as they attempt to restructure and adapt to community policing ideologies.[41]

Nevertheless, there are some new approaches and tactics being used with promising results. **Evidence-based policing** is becoming a major player, with more and more departments across the country engaging with police science and research to determine effective strategy.

Geographic-based and focused policing approaches, such as **hot-spots policing** and directed patrols, represent the most strongly supported policing practices in the United States,[42] aided by the use of geographical information systems (GIS), crime analysis, and artificial intelligence. Similarly, **intelligence-led policing (ILP)** and proactive policing models are also gaining attention as police departments look for ways to do more with fewer resources. Although currently under-researched and new, the geographic-based policing approaches have emerged as innovative strategies for reducing crime and increasing citizen satisfaction with police services. Unfortunately, the sheer number of new and innovative paradigms to combat crime appears to be escalating by the year. Students and scholars alike often have problems segregating and differentiating the various types of policing strategy that may be employed in one city, or for that matter, in one sector of a city. Many of the police strategies employed today are similar, particularly those that are geographically based, with only minor additions or tactical differences. Indeed, many of the "strategies" could be much more easily classified as a police tactic aimed at reducing crime in a specific neighborhood over a specific period of time. The myriad of new names and models has given rise to the thought that the real differences between policing strategies may be more "rhetoric than reality."

Evidence-Based Policing

In recent years, researchers have focused on building a knowledge base as it pertains to what is known about the effectiveness of criminal justice strategies. The ultimate goal is to provide practitioners with sound empirical evidence to help them make informed decisions regarding related policies and programs. Evidence-based policing is a reflection of this philosophy. According to Sherman, "evidence-based policing is the use of the best available research on the outcomes of police work to implement guidelines and evaluate agencies, units, and officers."[43] Rather than focusing on "how" to do police work, as in community policing, or utilizing a generalized problem-solving approach to crime, as in problem-oriented policing, evidence-based policing is a paradigm that utilizes the scientific method to identify, implement, evaluate, and modify the methods that are most effective in reducing crime.[44]

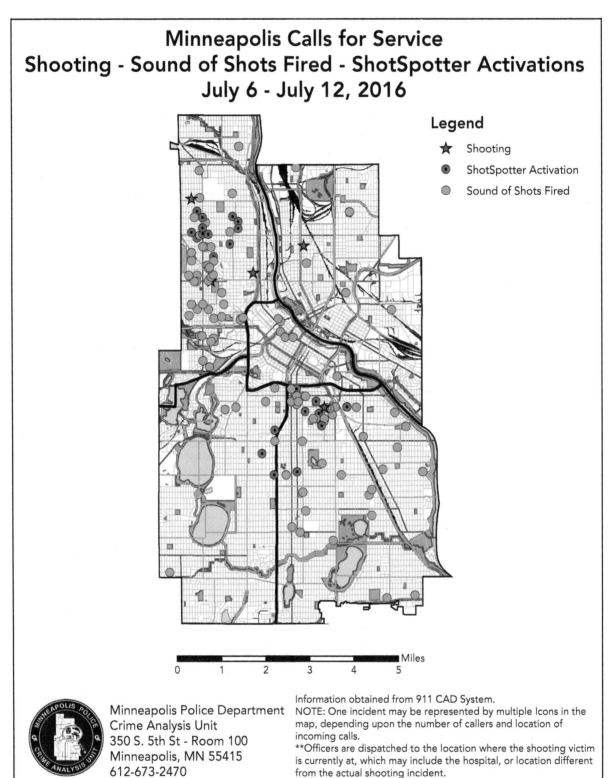

Minneapolis Calls for Service
Shooting - Sound of Shots Fired - ShotSpotter Activations
July 6 - July 12, 2016

Legend

★ Shooting

◉ ShotSpotter Activation

○ Sound of Shots Fired

Minneapolis Police Department
Crime Analysis Unit
350 S. 5th St - Room 100
Minneapolis, MN 55415
612-673-2470

Information obtained from 911 CAD System.
NOTE: One incident may be represented by multiple Icons in the map, depending upon the number of callers and location of incoming calls.
**Officers are dispatched to the location where the shooting victim is currently at, which may include the hospital, or location different from the actual shooting incident.

FIGURE 2.5 ▶ Minneapolis' CODEFOR program continues to merge community policing with CompStat. Police executives are held accountable for their strategic response to calls for service and crime. Minneapolis routinely shares its crime bulletins and analysis maps with the public on a weekly basis via their website and social media. *Source:* http://www.ci.minneapolis.mn.us/police/crime-statistics/codefor/650_MinneapolisShotsFired.pdf, retrieved on July 16, 2016.

Sherman's model focuses on the *"Triple-T Strategy"*: Targeting, Testing, and Tracking. *Targeting* involves assessing relative levels of harm and allocating police resources based on this measure; in other words, focusing on those issues that the police can lawfully address that will have the most impact. *Testing* looks at examining research for evidence of success (or failure) to determine how a strategy is working. And *tracking* is an effort to continually check performance and implementation, through programs that might include CompStat and even review of body-worn camera data.[45]

Essentially, evidence-based policing means that police agencies should assess research related to "what works and what doesn't work"—and adjust their organizational strategies appropriately. This seems intuitive; however, law enforcement agencies have been historically slow and even resistant to discontinue programs that have been clearly shown through effective evaluation research that they do not work (e.g., Drug Abuse Resistance and Education (DARE) programs, gun buyback programs, and the random moving patrol car). And, in the case of programs that *do* work, like hot-spots policing, departments implement bits and pieces of the philosophy while still maintaining more traditional policing methods overall.[46]

Adopting an evidence-based policing model would have many benefits to willing law enforcement agencies. Using scientifically backed principles to decide on tactics and strategies is more ethically sound than simply choosing whatever is new, popular, and preferred. Furthermore, using programs and strategies that are proven to work will reduce crime and increase quality of life, thereby inherently enhancing police legitimacy. Evidence-based policing also reinforces the concept of police transparency—it's much easier to explain motives, goals, objectives, and plans to the public when there is solid evaluation research to support the effort. Research also plays a very important role in police professionalism: Using evidence-based strategies for hiring, training, and developing/implementing policies and procedures may strengthen the personnel base, decrease inappropriate use of force, and advance the notion of fair and impartial policing. As echoed by the National Research Council (in 2004), current policing strategies in the United States are problematic at best, and future efforts must focus on more effective, evidence-based models:

1. Standard models of policing emphasizing random patrols and unfocused enforcement is not effective in reducing crime.
2. Community policing strategies aimed at reducing crime, fear of crime, and disorder have had mixed results.
3. Police strategies focused and tailored on specific types of crime, criminals, and geographic locations are more effective.
4. Problem-oriented policing is effective.
5. Future models of policing should be supported by strong and independent evaluation research.[47]

A law enforcement agency that seeks to operate under the philosophy of evidence-based policing probably, at a bare minimum, looks at the latest research for basic knowledge regarding its organizational directives and strategies and incorporates it into their operation on multiple levels from training to crime analysis. Agencies truly committed to the evidence-based model would further emphasize crime analysis and proactive versus reactive policing policies; would base policies and procedures on proven strategies; and work with at least one major academic partner with whom it shares statistics, policies, and plans for the purposes of ongoing and unbiased evaluation.

Shifting to an evidence-based culture in law enforcement will be a slow change; police agencies are notoriously resistant to major transformative change, particularly ones that force them to reassess the way things have been done for years. Institutionalizing research means that police agencies have to work outside their area of comfort, with expert researchers often from academic and research institutions that do not have a political position in the outcome. The relationship between academics and police agencies has been one fraught with historical conflict and mistrust. Today, however, there are a number of relatively isolated but growing collaborations that highlight partnerships between researchers and police. In New York City, the relationship between NYPD and the John Jay School of Criminal Justice flourishes. The Chicago Police Department continues its evaluation research project of CAPS with Northwestern University and the Providence, Rhode Island Police Department continues to collaborate with Roger Williams University for the improvement of their programs. However, there are a number of important and new collaborations in Texas. Sam Houston State University has historically assisted the Houston Police Department in a variety of evaluation projects over the past 30 years; and the Arlington Police Department has emphasized evidence-based practices for several years and is seen as a national model for practical research and evaluation. Under former chief Theron Bowman and continued leadership by Chief Will Johnson, the agency participated in a complex and rigorous study of compressed work weeks in policing, employing randomized controlled trials to aid in the understanding of how different types of shifts affect officer performance, safety, and health. The six-month study required significant resources from the department, but APD remained committed to seeing the outcomes through and adapting its agency policies accordingly. It also participated in programs that highlighted risk-terrain modeling for robbery reductions, national traffic safety studies, and patrol deployment algorithms.[48] Continued research into unmanned aircraft systems, best practices from social media in law enforcement, and body-worn camera deployment again highlight evidence-based policing projects team with local universities for research and evaluation. However, one of the most noted national collaborations was highlighted in Dallas, Texas, in 2008 with the development of the Caruth Police Institute; a collaboration between the Dallas Police Department and the University of North Texas at Dallas and the University of Texas at Dallas. Under the leadership of then chief David M. Kunkle, a transformative gift of nearly $10 million was presented for the development of the institute among private foundations, local universities, and the Dallas Police Department. The institute is physically located inside the Dallas Police Department and staffed primarily by faculty at the new University of North Texas at Dallas, with an affiliated relationship with the University of Texas at Dallas, which offers a doctoral program in criminology as well as major assistance with research and evaluation projects. The Caruth Police Institute focuses on fulfilling the complex research, career advancement, and leadership development needs of the Dallas Police Department. This placed the Dallas Police Department in the unique position of being a national resource for innovative strategies in policing. The venture signifies a bold new relationship between academia and major police departments characterized by cutting-edge research, education, and professional development services.[49]

Tools for agencies seeking to bolster their evidence-based credentials are not in short supply. Academic institutions are forever seeking crime data and access to law enforcement agencies, as well as internships and research opportunities for students. And the Center for Evidence-Based Crime Policy offers a number of resources, including the Evidence-Based Policing Matrix developed by Dr. Cynthia Lum and colleagues (see Figure 2.6). This visual guide classifies police interventions based on the nature and type of target (individuals, groups, neighborhoods, etc.), whether it's proactive or reactive, and the level of focus within each strategy (i.e., general prevention versus focused tactics); included studies must be at least moderately scientifically rigorous. The result of this ongoing collation of data is that practitioners can see at a glance where successful programs cluster—and generally, the data indicates that successful interventions cluster in micro-places or neighborhoods, and are highly focused on specific issues.[50]

Hot-Spots Policing

Much like evidence-based policing, hot-spots policing reflects the direct application of empirical data (through various crime analysis and information technologies) that show that crime is *not* randomly dispersed but rather is concentrated in specific areas.[51] In their seminal work, Sherman and colleagues found that only a few locations were responsible for a majority of police calls for service and reported crime—particularly predatory crimes such as muggings, vehicle thefts, burglary, robbery, and rape.[52] In addition, they found that all robberies occurred at 2.2 percent of places, all rapes occurred at 1.2 percent of places, and all auto thefts occurred at 2.7 percent of places.[53] These areas or "places" with a higher than average number of crimes are "hot-spots" and represent areas that reflect not only higher than normal crime rates but also are often inhabited by lower-income and high-density populations.[54] Similar to these findings, drug distribution also appears to cluster. In Jersey City, New Jersey drug "hot-spots" were responsible for a disproportionate number of arrests and calls for service to the police. Furthermore, these areas also experienced a greater amount of issues related to crime and disorder compared to other areas; that is, serious crime, disorder, and street-level drug problems cluster in certain areas within the city. Deploying more police resources to these areas reduces the clustering effect.[55]

Although the concept of crime hot-spots has been documented for many years, hot-spots policing is a relatively innovative approach to crime. This type of policing forces the police to

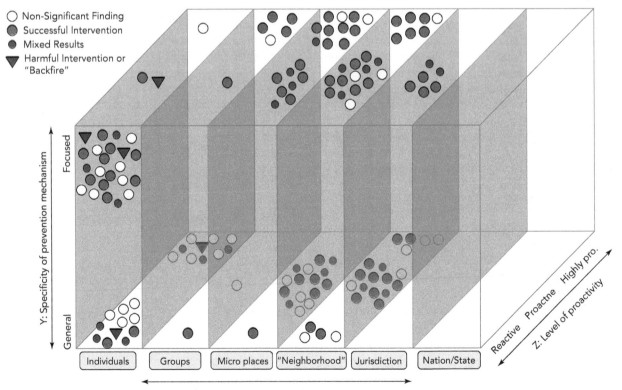

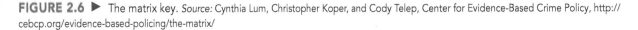

FIGURE 2.6 ▶ The matrix key. *Source:* Cynthia Lum, Christopher Koper, and Cody Telep, Center for Evidence-Based Crime Policy, http://cebcp.org/evidence-based-policing/the-matrix/

identify specific areas with unusual concentrations of crime and then direct their resources at those places. This is certainly not a novel idea, and the traditional patrol sergeants of the 1960s could have argued that a map, a few colored pins, and a series of crime reports could have told us "where to send officers" on routine patrol. However, this is still an important police strategy, particularly in reducing more predatory crimes, recently reinforced by a study in Charlotte, North Carolina. The deployment of street crime units in hot-spot robbery areas not only significantly reduced crime but also reduced the level of fear expressed by citizens.[56] However, the strongest support for "hot-spots" policing comes from the National Academy of Sciences:

> Studies that focused police resources on crime hot-spots provide the strongest collective evidence of police effectiveness that is now available. On the basis of a series of randomized experimental studies, we conclude that the practice described as hot-spots policing is effective in reducing crime and disorder and can achieve these reductions without significant displacement of crime control benefits. Indeed, the research evidence suggests that the diffusion of crime control benefits to areas surrounding treated hot-spots is stronger than any displacement outcome.[57]

Despite the evidence in support of hot-spots policing, it is uncertain as to what specific tactics have the most influence in problem areas, given the wide array of intervention tactics that are used within the model.[58] For example, hot-spots policing tactics include directed patrols, saturation patrol, aggressive traffic enforcement, zero-tolerance, and disorder enforcement, as well as specific drug "buy and bust" programs, even focused problem-oriented policing techniques. In addition, some scholars argue that hot-spots do not actually exist in the real world; that is, hot-spots are an "amalgam" of different types of locations that simply cluster on a map; they are a product of data construction.[59] These data points could be addresses, buildings, apartment complexes, block faces, census tracks, or individual police sectors; however, they are a temporary product of the data world, a logical fallacy that is impossible to operationally identify using agreed-upon, replicable, and scientific criteria.[60]

Today, many police departments are utilizing a hot-spots strategy banking on those studies that show that it reduces and prevents crime; however, they are also utilizing a plethora of patrol and arrest techniques that most likely have varying effects on crime in specific places. Future research in this area should focus on parceling-out the various techniques and tactics used in each type of hot-spot and measuring the impact of each. Hypothetically, we may well find that it is not one approach but rather the cumulative impact of visible police patrol and the employment of various arrest tactics that most likely impacts crime the most in a specific area.

Directed and Saturation Patrols

Directed and saturation patrols are tactics commonly used in policing. Although these strategies are considered low on the scale of diverse approaches, they are often used in conjunction with hot-spots policing. While directed patrol usually involves the "directing" of patrol officers to specific locations during their patrol shift, saturation patrol concentrates *additional* officers on specific locations at specific times. The idea is to maximize visible patrol efforts in a specific area. Both types of patrol involve the assignment of officers to problematic areas for proactive enforcement at high-risk times.[61] In theory, increased police presence through directed and saturation patrols in these areas and times is expected to arrest offenders responsible for a great majority of these crimes and generate reductions in crime. It is, however, unknown as to whether crime is actually reduced or simply moved to another location (displaced); when police visibility is increased, offenders often move to other areas of the city.

There is also conflicting evidence that calls into question the effectiveness of directed and saturation patrols as an effective crime control strategy versus more aggressive arrest tactics. Fritsch, Caeti, and Taylor evaluated police strategies aimed at reducing gang violence in Dallas, Texas.[62] Their initiative targeted five areas that housed seven of the most violent gangs in the city. Officers spent a majority of their time utilizing three suppression tactics, including aggressive curfew enforcement, aggressive truancy enforcement, and saturation patrol, making patrols highly visible in the targeted areas. Although aggressive curfew and truancy enforcement were related to significant reductions in gang violence, saturation patrols did not produce the same effects. Once again, more aggressive arrest techniques in specific areas during specific times aimed at specific predatory crimes may be the most effective tactic in reducing crime.

Intelligence-Led Policing

Unlike directed and saturation patrols, intelligence-led policing (ILP) is not a tactic, nor is it a crime-reduction strategy, but rather a business model for policing. It is "an information-organizing process that allows police agencies to better understand their crime problems and take a measure of the resources available to be able to decide on an enforcement tactic or prevention strategy best designed to control crime."[63] More specifically, intelligence-led policing utilizes criminal intelligence analysis as a means to accomplish crime prevention and reduction through best practices and partnerships with other entities.

There are a number of reasons as to why intelligence-led policing has become popular in recent years. First, widespread recognition of the ineffectiveness of the standard policing model and the difficulty in implementing problem-oriented policing has caused police departments to look for alternatives. Second, departments are increasingly faced with financial constraints though demands remain high and the opportunities to employ additional resources and personnel are limited. Third, more sophisticated technologies in information retrieval and analysis of police information have generated interest in systematic approaches to crime.[64]

Although intelligence-led policing emerged in the United States after the September 11, 2001, terrorist attacks, the movement toward this approach actually began prior to the 1990s and originated in the United Kingdom.[65] At that time, it was recommended by the Audit Commission that police services should *focus on the offender* rather than reported crime. The

British government subsequently passed legislation requiring police departments to adopt the National Intelligence Model, which promoted intelligence-led policing.

It is important to note that intelligence is more than simply data; it also involves information. While data are "identifiable, objective facts about events," information is the addition of context and analysis that puts data into comprehensible forms.[66] Data and information do not become intelligence until they are interpreted, evaluated, and used as a means to inform crime prevention and reduction strategies. In ILP, these objectives are believed to be obtainable primarily through the proactive and objective identification and targeting of the criminal subpopulation.[67]

An example of intelligence-led policing in practice is Operation Nine Connect. Ratcliffe and Guidetti report that the New Jersey State Police implemented a gang crackdown targeting Nine Trey—a subset of the much larger and well-known "Bloods" gang.[68] Together, officers involved in the crackdown conducted over 8,000 hours of electronic surveillance and more than 2,300 hours of physical surveillance, as well as spent over 1,200 hours transcribing wiretaps and approximately 300 hours developing and maintaining confidential sources. The result was the initial arrest of 60 gang members and the subsequent arrest of at least 30 others.

Despite the popularity and the successes of intelligence-led policing, there are a number of limitations associated with this type of approach, including data entry problems and lack of training in advanced analytic techniques within the police. In addition, Ratcliffe notes the organizational problems of intelligence-led policing, such as the lack of continuity in structure across intelligence units and the confusion over the principles of intelligence-led crime reduction.[69] In addition, as discussed later in Chapter 3, some argue that ILP could be in conflict with civil and constitutional safeguards that ensure individuals are "innocent until proven guilty." Focusing on specific individuals as offenders tests this important principle of our democracy.

Predictive Policing

Similar to intelligence-led policing, **predictive policing** is a proactive approach to crime and disorder that uses information and analytical tools to achieve the goal of crime prevention while requiring fewer resources.[70] Not only does predictive policing improve upon intelligence-led policing, it also reflects the principles of problem-oriented, community, and evidence-based policing.[71] According to Beck and McCue, "With new technology, new business processes, and new algorithms, predictive policing is based on directed, information-based patrol; rapid response supported by fact-based prepositioning of assets; and proactive, intelligence-based tactics, strategy, and policy."[72] Consequently, one of the key components of predictive policing is the use of advanced analytics that evaluate and examine data and information through advanced statistics and artificial intelligence. In other words, predictive policing utilizes numerous technologies and techniques such as data mining, crime mapping, and geospatial prediction to plan for and respond to future crime.

Advanced analytics have been used in a variety of capacities from preventing violent crimes to improving deployment, response planning, and policy decision-making. For example,

police in Richmond, Virginia, used advanced analytics and predictive policing to reduce random gunfire on New Year's Eve. Based on information collected from previous years, police were able to predict the time, location, and type of incident most likely to occur on that particular night. In preparation, officers were placed at those locations to prevent and quickly respond to such crimes. The end result was a 47 percent reduction in random gunfire and a significant increase in the number of seized weapons.[73]

Although predictive policing is a new and promising approach, it too has generated a number of questions and concerns. A major criticism is the novelty of predictive policing given its semblance to other policing models, particularly ILP. Moreover, the central tenets of predictive policing closely resemble what crime analysts have been doing for years. Still, others argue that the outcomes of the model are vague and unclear.[74]

INFORMATION TECHNOLOGIES IN POLICING

The evolution of policing strategies has included the development and use of sophisticated information technologies. Today, information technologies assume a new and more vital role. For instance, police operations are incredibly data and information intensive. Rather than utilizing computers for data storage, police departments are now using them as information and knowledge-based systems.[75] This is especially important as police agencies rely more heavily on intelligence as well as the identification and targeting of crime hot-spots and repeat offenders. Crime analysis, geographic information systems (GIS), and artificial intelligence represent the most widely used information technologies in policing today.

Crime Analysis

As the dynamics of policing move toward an information-driven and evidence-based agenda, the need for accurate analyses is becoming increasingly important. Consequently, crime analysis has emerged as a means to satisfy this requirement. **Crime analysis** is the process of identifying patterns and relationships between crime data and other relevant data sources to prioritize and target police activity.[76] The uneven distribution of crime in terms of space and place, type of offenders, and victimization theoretically allows analysts to draw inferences from patterns of crime, which can be used as a foundation for allocating police resources. In other words, crime analysis generates associations and relationships between variables (such as space, time, offenders, and victims) that are related to crime. The purpose of crime analysis is to organize massive quantities of raw information from databases used in automated records systems and to forecast specific, future events from the statistical manipulation of these data. In theory, crime analysis provides a thorough and systematic analysis of data on which to make rational decisions regarding past, present, and future actions.[77] Crime analysis is critical when deploying resources based on new policing strategies such as "hot-spots" policing, directed and saturation patrols, and predictive policing (see Figure 2.7).

Quick Facts: Crime Rates Dramatically Rise in 2020

According to a 2020 Police Executive Research Forum (PERF) analysis, violent crimes appears to have dramatically increased across the United States. Indeed, 84% of major American cities reported an increase in homicides in 2020, and 77% of the cities reported an increase in aggravated assaults. Homicides were particularly pronounced in major cities, with increases greater than 50% in Milwaukie, Wisconsin; Minneapolis, Minnesota; Louisville, Kentucky; Portland, Oregon; Fort Worth, Texas; Memphis, Tennessee; Prince George's County, Maryland; Boston, Massachusetts; and Chicago, Illinois. Sadly, the same trend followed for medium-size cities as well, with number of homicides jumping in cities like Topeka, Kansas; Baton Rouge, Louisiana; Colorado Springs, Colorado; and Madison, Wisconsin; Cedar Rapids, Iowa; Redlands, California; and Yakima, Washington. Not surprisingly, aggravated assault soared nearly 10% across the nation as well. The good news from the PERF analysis revealed that armed robberies and rape appeared to decline in 2020 over 2019 rates by 11% and 15%, respectively.

While there has been talk of increasing crime rates in the United States as a result of changing police behavior (a decrease in proactive police techniques and arrests due to increased public scrutiny, calls to defund the police, and reduced numbers of police on the street), the causal link between increased violent crime and decreased police activity have <u>not</u> been established by research. Certainly, the answer for the causal link may well lie in several simultaneous challenges that confronted police departments in 2020, such as the COVID-19 pandemic, the resulting economic fallout from the pandemic, and the widespread and sometimes violent protests against racial injustice stemming from controversial police shootings which in turn led to decreased police funding, an exodus of police officers from the profession, and calls for radical police reform in some cities.

Sources: "PERF Analysis Reveals a Spike in Some Violent Crimes This Year," November 18, 2020. See: https://www.policeforum.org/criticalissuesnov18

Nathan James, "Recent Violent Crime Trends in the United States," Congressional Research Service, June 20, 2018, https://fas.org/sgp/crs/msic/R45236.pdf.

Crime analysis is not limited solely to reported crime information. Attention has also been given to the statistical analysis of intelligence information. Kinney[78] reports that criminal intelligence analysis supports investigators, decision-makers, and policymakers in their attempts to prevent and control crime. The following are some of the more common crime analysis techniques:

- *Tactical crime analysis or crime-specific analysis*—a tabular or graphic display of reported crimes with a given pattern of time and/or location. It is often used to detect patterns of crime (e.g., robberies, burglaries, and auto thefts) that cluster in specific locations during various time periods. The focus of tactical crime analysis is on recent criminal incidents through the examination of characteristics such as how, when, and where the activity has occurred in order to identify potential suspects and improve case clearance Statistics.[79]

- *Strategic crime analysis*—the study of crime and/or social problems in a specific area in an effort to determine long-term patterns of activity as well as to evaluate police responses and organizational procedures.[80] Strategic crime analysis is often used to determine the effectiveness of police over a given period of time, or in the evaluation of specific policing strategies as discussed earlier.

- *Link analysis*—a graphic portrayal of associations and relationships among people, organizations, events,

FIGURE 2.7 ▶ A series of "hot-spots" indicating vehicle crimes mapped by census track to varying hot-spot thresholds. Note that "hot-spots" become much more apparent as the data used to create the maps are refined. *Source:* John E. Eck, Spencer Chaney, James G. Cameron, Michael Leitner, and Ronald E. Wilson, *NIJ Special Report: Mapping Crime: Understanding Hot-Spots* (Washington, DC: National Institute of Justice, August 2005). See: http://www.ncjrs.gov/pdffiles1/nij/209393.pdf

activities, and locations from a given point in time. This technique is a powerful analytic tool used to reveal the hidden connections among criminals and the structure of clandestine, organized criminal entities often found in street gangs, La Cosa Nostra families, white-collar crime syndicates, large drug trafficking cartels, and terrorist organizations. Link analysis is invaluable in complex investigations, particularly those that have a "conspiracy" aspect, as is often found in racketeering and continuing criminal enterprise cases. Link analysis is also a powerful tool used extensively in ILP.

- *Digital evidence analysis*—reports from smartphones can yield location data, messaging, call histories, search engine history and much more in all types of investigations.

- *Visual investigative analysis (VIA)*—charting that depicts key events of criminal activity in chronological order. VIA is used to show the degree of involvement of subjects. This method is especially convincing in conspiracy cases and can also be used as a planning tool to focus the resources of an investigative effort.[81] At a conference focusing on school shootings, a graphical VIA was presented on the Virginia Tech University shooting incident.[82] Interestingly, the VIA effort displayed a horizontal graph, over 60 feet long, with over 1,200 entries.

- *Case analysis and management system (CAMS)*—computerized case management in which large amounts of data are compiled and indexed for each retrieval of specific items. This system is used to clarify relationships and calculate the probability of associations.[83]

- *Intelligence analysis*—the identification of networks of offenders and criminal activity, often associated with organized crime, gangs, drug traffickers, prostitution rings, and terrorist organizations. Recent interest in intelligence analysis has given rise to the development of large, centralized intelligence processing hubs, referred to as fusion centers (discussed later in Chapter 3, Intelligence, Terrorism, and Homeland Security). Intelligence analysis

also becomes the basis for intelligence-led policing (see Figure 2.8).

Crime analysis is a flexible and dynamic process designed primarily to identify trends and patterns associated with crime and social problems. It is designed to be a perpetual and continuous process and to assist law enforcement executives in making more informed decisions in their response to crime. The technology of crime analysis takes advantage of research and statistical methodologies, often in an automated process. It does not necessarily have to be relegated to advanced statistical techniques, but it can be accomplished quite well with a basic understanding of Microsoft Office programs, such as Word and Excel. Indeed, Mark Stallo's inviting work focuses on developing a relatively sophisticated crime analysis model based solely on the application of Microsoft Office products to reported police data.[84]

Geographic Information Systems (GIS)

The use of **geographic information systems (GIS)** in law enforcement to map criminal events coincided with the results of several environmental criminology studies that illustrated crime patterns. Prior to computerized mapping systems, police commonly used pin maps as a means of tracking crime. Unfortunately, this practice has many limitations due to the difficulties in determining clusters and general trends using point data.[85] However, with the advent of sophisticated computerized mapping, researchers have found a widespread adoption of GIS tools across police departments, particularly larger agencies[86].

There are two types of crime mapping: statistical spatial analysis and spatial modeling. While statistical spatial analysis focuses on the spatial relationship between crime points in a particular area, spatial modeling is concerned with the technology and application of data.[87] As previously mentioned, GIS has made these two components of crime mapping easy to use in the realm of policing. Given its functionality, it has become an influential mechanism in hot-spots policing as well as Crime Prevention Through Environmental Design (CPTED), situational policing, directed patrols, and crime analysis.

FIGURE 2.8 ▶ Intelligence analysis tools are becoming the basis for intelligence-led policing. (Denver Police Department, 2019)

Of course, GIS has a myriad of other uses in policing. Police agencies can use GIS in dispatching police units by providing directions to locations; address histories; and locations of nearby fire and waste hazards, fire hydrants, alarm boxes, high-power lines, water lines, and the like. Police managers can not only use GIS to provide graphic analysis of specific crime patterns and to evaluate new policing strategies but also to track individual officer performance by area.[88] Not surprisingly, GIS has emerged as a powerful tool that helps police executives make better-informed decisions. Due to its wide range of uses, it is likely that crime mapping and geographic information systems will remain key tools in police operations and in the evaluation of police strategies.

The Internet

Clearly, one of the most important technological advantages of the information age is the Internet. The Internet is a worldwide network of computer systems and other computer networks that offers the opportunity for sending information to and receiving information from a vast audience from around the world. The unique benefits of the Internet are speed and efficiency combined with global reach. There are essentially no barriers to sending information and receiving information from as close as next door to around the world. Of particular importance to police agencies is the ease and speed with which information can be kept current.

Local police agencies have capitalized on the use of the Internet, with most major departments establishing their own home pages (see Figure 2.9). In addition, most departments have encouraged their communities to keep abreast of police activities through the Internet. A list of emergency services and phone numbers, names and descriptions of the most "wanted" fugitives in the community, periodic updates on a specific (usually high-profile) case, employment announcements and opportunities within the department, residential and commercial crime alerts, and even online crime reporting are now available through various departments on the Internet.

As worldwide communication and global reach via the Internet expand, policing will likely experience dramatic changes. For instance, the United Nations recently linked various criminal justice research institutes from different countries, allowing for the first time a free exchange of information among countries on issues impacting the world community (e.g., international terrorism, environmental crime, gangs, and computer fraud). New and combined training sessions, various telecommunication partnerships, and interactive information exchanges (podcasts and webinars) are now commonplace on the Internet. The greater access to information provided by the Internet has made a major difference in the future, not only for police agencies and researchers but also for individual communities addressing wider criminal justice issues. Certainly, the Internet has been one of the strongest catalysts for social, economic, and political change in the world.

Social Media and Policing

One of the most surprising technological advances in law enforcement from the past decade can be found in the realm of **social media**, taking police agencies into a whole new world of "likes," "shares," and "re-Tweets." Facebook and Twitter, particularly, have been a boon to police departments across the country, allowing for instantaneous outreach to the community. In one of the best examples of the possibilities that lie within this integrated technology, the Boston Police Department utilized Twitter and Facebook in the immediate aftermath of the Boston Marathon Bombings in 2013. These social media platforms were crucial to distributing public information, coordinating media briefings, giving traffic information related to street closures, coordinating volunteers, and soliciting videos and pictures from the event that, in some cases, contained evidence of the crime.[89]

Boston is not alone in their successful use of social media; it has now become standard for police agencies to use Facebook and Twitter, NextDoor, Instagram, and other social networks to connect with citizens, personnel, other police agencies, and

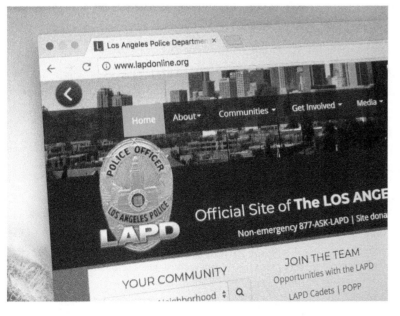

FIGURE 2.9 ▶ Los Angeles Police Department home page that encourages their communities to interact with them via online links. (Jarretera/Shutterstock)

the media. The following examples highlight the use of social media as employed by law enforcement organizations:

- *Communication in emergency situations*—informing the public of a situation; releasing new information as it is available; describing areas to avoid; communicating risks and giving suggestions to avoid those risks; missing persons; and Amber alerts.

- *Agency transparency*—informing the public of use of force complaints brought against the department; releasing officer disciplinary information; explaining the actions of the police agency in a crisis situation; providing insight into day-to-day policing; and announcing new initiatives and strategies.

- *Community outreach*—publicizing community policing events; announcing community events; publicizing policing successes; and humanizing policing through anecdotes, humor, and the like.

- *Networking with other police agencies*—sharing best practices; making investigative contacts.

- *Investigation*—suspect identification; request submission of crime tips or photographic/video evidence; examination of social media sites for criminal activity; and use of social media in undercover operations and stings.

- *Recruitment and personnel selection*—the requirements for appointment and related information are listed, including education, the pay scale, how prior service in another law enforcement effects where applicants are placed on the pay scale, whether candidates are expected to pay for their own academy training before being eligible for hiring, and annual leave and holidays. Further, an applicant's use of social media may be reviewed to determine conflicting interests or behaviors to the police mission. For instance, an applicant's membership in a right-wing, hate group may disqualify the candidate from police service.

- *Public relations*—social media allows law enforcement agencies to craft news releases long before the media gets information.

For proponents of evidence-based policing, determining the value of social media policing is difficult. How does an agency measure the value and contribution of social media to the police mission? Is it the number of followers an agency has? The number of missing persons found as a result of shared Facebook posts? The number of suspects arrested through YouTube posts? Does it increase police legitimacy, and if so, where is the evidence to suggest such a claim? Few scientifically validated studies have been undertaken to pinpoint the value of police use of social media, but nonetheless, agencies continue to implement social media strategies at a breaking speed.

Social media demands significant resources from law enforcement agencies. For instance, officer accounts need to be monitored to prevent abusive, inflammatory, and/or discriminatory posts. Agencies must constantly reinforce that emergencies should not be reported via social media. Grammatical errors can become news headlines and the threat from hacking is always a real possibility. These types of events can open police departments to potentially devastating public relations nightmares and potential liability, especially when police departments rush to update an incident on social media before all the facts are known, implicating innocent people in criminal activity. Training for officers and police executives entrusted with official social media communications should be rigorous, and departments should have specific policies and procedures that govern their use of social media. Finally, police tout social media as a way to increase transparency and legitimacy, but it is increasingly being used to allow agencies to "manage the message"—or release a story in order to pre-empt the media and control the message. In some cases, monopolizing the message may backfire on perceptions of legitimacy and openness.

Obviously, social media in law enforcement is a phenomenon that has permeated the operations of police agencies at every level. As a means to generate goodwill between the police and the public, its value is indispensable—it allows agencies to connect with the people they serve in a creative and instantaneous manner. In the future, social media will continue to shape the way that communities and the police interact.

Quick Facts: Social Media Adoption in Law Enforcement

Today, social media has become a critical part of law enforcement, reflecting the need for transparency as well as serving a variety of functions within the department:

- The most common use of social media is for notifying the public of public safety concerns, at 91 percent; at a close second is community outreach and engagement at 89 percent.

- About 29 percent of agencies using social media report that they always communicate in an informal tone in their posts.

- About 80 percent of agencies surveyed have a written social media policy.

- For most agencies (55 percent), content is approved by a central group before it is posted.

Source: Kaitlyn Perez, "Social Media has Become a Critical Part of Law Enforcement," National Police Foundation. See: https://www.policefoundation.org/social-media-has-become-a-critical-part-of-law-enforcement/?gclid=EAlaIQobChMIkKO Mso-Z7QIVYR6tBh3-WwAyEAAYASAAEgKqUvD_BwE and KiDuek Kim et al., "2016 Law Enforcement Use of Social Media Survey," International Association of Chiefs of Police and the Urban Institute, February 2017, http://www.urban.org/sites/default/files/publication/88661/2016-law-enforcement-use-of-social-media-survey.pdf.

Box 2.4: The Lip Sync Challenge: Social Media and Police Community Relations

During the summer of 2018, the #LipSyncChallenge embroiled law enforcement agencies (and the occasional fire department) throughout the country. Posted on Twitter, Facebook, and YouTube, the viral challenge involved police officers vamping their way through current pop hits, oldies, epic rap mash-ups and more—officers danced to "Uptown Funk" in Norfolk, Connecticut, and were cheered by crowds during a performance of Macklemore's "Downtown." As one department posted their masterpiece, they challenged another to do the same—and for several weeks, social media feeds were full of lip synch videos of varying quality and talent.

And while they were a fun distraction, departments were also hoping that the videos were functioning as a public relations tool. It's hard to watch Seattle's entry (the aforementioned "Downtown") without cracking a smile and generating some good feelings. Police departments who participated hoped that it would shed officers in a different, more humanizing light: that these officers weren't like those involved in police brutality cases; that these officers were more like the people watching. It's easy to be relatable when you're groovin' to a Flo Rida tune, but some community advocates warn that years of distrust can't simply be mended with a YouTube video.

Body-Worn Cameras

Another technological transformation in policing organization is that related to body-worn camera technology (see Figure in Box 2.4). The small cameras, which can be mounted on eyeglasses, headgear, or on the chest, have become the norm in American policing—largely seen as a panacea to public distrust of police due to use of force and/or perceived abuses of power. By 2016, almost half of police agencies in the United States used the devices[90]—a quick increase, as in 2013, only about a third did so.[91] And while public discourse around the cameras has largely focused on their use as a means of transparency related to use of force complaints (or even as a preventative measure against unnecessary use of force), most police departments brought the cameras online as a means to improve officer safety. In fact, 80 percent of agencies surveyed in 2016 (a year following repeated public outcry due to police shootings of unarmed black men) affirmed that reason, with agency liability and officer accountability coming in fourth and fifth on the list of reasons. Reducing use of force came in toward the bottom of the list—only 34 percent of agencies reported that as a motivation for their implementation.[92]

Regardless, body-worn cameras do offer some potential benefits for law enforcement agencies, including the following:

- Increased transparency: in theory, confidence in law enforcement may be bolstered if evidence exists to settle questions about police encounters, particularly in instances where deadly and even nonlethal force is used.

- Civility: citizens may change their behavior toward officers if they know that encounters are being recorded. This may provide a de-escalating effect on the situation.

- Quicker resolutions: provides hard evidence in cases of complaints and lawsuits.

- Training opportunities: the opportunities for video case studies to inform policing techniques, tactics, safety procedures, and general policies are vast.[93]

Research has not fully borne out whether body-worn cameras are the panacea they have been built up as: though some

Body-worn cameras offer increased transparency of police activity and may provide a de-escalating effect on the situation.

positive outcomes have been found related to police/community relations and use of force, methodology and sample sizes have called findings into question. There is, largely, no clear indication that body-worn cameras make policing more transparent; make officers safer; or make use-of-force encounters less likely. There are some indications that police agencies are pushing back on their use, however: the rising costs of the cameras and their software plus the amount of resources it takes to review and store thousands of hours of footage have been daunting for many agencies.[94]

The Impact of Information Technologies

Clearly, information technologies in policing have assumed a new and more vital role. They have taken on a new dimension, one that is central to the support of new policing strategies. The new task for information technologies is *analysis*, in addition to the storage and maintenance of information as in the past. The analytic support for various police strategies, however, must permeate the entire organizational structure and not be just a function of the crime analysis division. Information technology functionality must be much more flexible—ranging from support for quick, officer-level field inquiries to longitudinal mapping of a specific neighborhood to specific managerial performance measurements. Information technologies can no longer be separated from the integral parts of police management and decision-making. They can no longer be relegated solely to the storage, maintenance, and retrieval of vast amounts of police data. Most new policing strategies (e.g., community policing, evidence-based policing, and predictive policing) are information-based and information-intensive and require the ability to identify problems, suggest specific police responses, and evaluate their effectiveness. This function cannot follow the same information-processing path as before.

Today's police officers must be equipped with information and training. The job still requires the ability to relate to various people under stressful conditions in often hostile environments. New policing strategies involve new tactics that call for individual judgment and skill in relating to problems that are both criminal and noncriminal. The police officer of the future must be able to relate to diverse groups of people in ways that stretch the imagination. To meet this challenge, police executives must ensure that three conditions exist. First, information technology development and design must support the emerging strategies in policing, particularly meeting the analytic demands embraced within such strategies. Second, police officers and executives must manage technology rather than allow themselves to be managed by it. Finally, individual police officers must understand their role in the community as aided by, but not controlled by, information technologies.

A CHANGING PARADIGM: FROM WARRIOR TO GUARDIAN

Policing is in a state of flux. A spate of high-profile use-of-force incidents between 2014 and 2020 resulted in the deaths of several unarmed African Americans. These events have fueled criticisms of, and anger toward, law enforcement agencies across the country. The result was a series of protests, increased anti-policing sentiment, calls for police reforms, and is correlated with a series of ambushes and murders of police officers. It is essential to recognize that the best policing strategy means nothing if the community does not have confidence in the police. Indeed, the events of 2014–2020 provided further evidence that at least part of our communities—particularly parts of the minority community—has lost faith in police organizations.[95]

There is an increasing number of people who believe that the militarization of U.S. policing is inconsistent with the community policing philosophy and a threat to it. In 1829, Robert Peel developed plans for the London Metropolitan concepts from the British military. However, he wanted there to be a distinction between the police and the military. Peel viewed the police as having a protective role toward the public versus the British military fighting an armed enemy in a distant land.[96] To make that distinction abundantly clear, Peel's officers wore blue uniforms, a marked contrast to the bright red British army coats

and he did not allow them to carry guns.[97] While a military's mission is predicated on the use of force, Peel's principles of policing emphasize crime prevention, the need for public approval, the willing cooperation of the public, and the minimal use of physical force by the police in the performance of their duties. These philosophical statements are echoed in the tenets of today's community and evidence-based policing models.

Peel's efforts to separate the role of the police from the military essentially distinguishes between the guardian and warrior roles. Although there was some earlier use of police uniforms in America, the adoption of blue uniforms was to some degree a by-product of the availability of surplus union army uniforms after the Civil War and thus essentially not a major movement until after 1865. Traditional law enforcement uniforms serve as a symbol of police authority and provide the public with a quick way to locate an officer if one is nearby, e.g., to help find a wandering child at a school fair. Presently, the wearing of black military-style Battle Dress uniforms (BDUs) by some officers is troubling to militarization critics because: (1) those uniforms blur the line between police and the military, which have distinctly different roles; (2) the BDUs worn by officers are often black, a color often associated with the "bad guys," such as ninja assassins, and (3) the BDUs may re-enforce the police warrior culture.

A 1988 study covering 16 years of National Football League penalties revealed teams wearing black drew more penalties than their opponents, suggesting black uniforms made players more aggressive.[98] Studies of dark uniforms and aggression were conducted in the National Hockey League in 2011, which found a relationship between uniform color and aggression, and 2012, which reached the opposite conclusion.[99] A 2013 study found no significant differences in aggressive measures between departments whose officers wore dark versus departments whose personnel wore light-colored uniforms, and a 2008 study concluded black police uniforms elicited more favorable public impressions than light-colored uniforms.[100] Still, there is a view that black BDU-wearing officers appear more formidable, are more aggressive, and less approachable, undercutting public support for policing. An unanswered question is whether a yet-to-be-done study in the post-Ferguson environment would provide a clear answer about any relationship between police behavior and uniform color, as well as public perceptions of the topic.

The Historical Drift Toward Militarization

The historical drift toward militarization is rooted in the social unrest, soaring crime, massive demonstrations, social changes, and political rhetoric that swept America in the 1960s and 1970s. Initially, SWAT teams were created primarily as a mechanism to deal with riots. Over time, there was mission creep as SWATs effectively took on high risk responsibilities (e.g., drug raids and barricaded subjects). These responsibilities required adoption of new tactics and equipment with greater capabilities, some of which were adapted from military models and provided from surplus military inventories. This was an ongoing process that moved SWATs to become increasingly militarized (e.g., using explosives to breach reinforced doors on drug raids and flash-bangs/stun grenades when serving some warrants). Militarization critics, including some Chiefs of Police and Sheriffs, are concerned that militarization re-enforces the warrior role of law enforcement at the expense of serving and protecting the public, unlike the military's role of engaging and destroying the enemy.

In 1997, bank robbers in North Hollywood, California, armed with fully automatic weapons and body armor confronted police officers equipped only with pistols and shotguns. This incident placed individual officers at a significant disadvantage and the movement toward arming patrol officers with military AR-15s as "patrol rifles" became a major movement in policing, which continues to the present. The highly publicized robbery was caught on video tape and marks an important milestone on the road to the militarization of police over the past decade.[101]

The President's Commission on Law Enforcement and Administration of Justice (1967) issued an overall report as well as ones on the components of the criminal justice system. It had the effect of focusing attention on crime and into our national conversations, policies, and laws. In 1965, President Johnson declared a war on crime, and seven years later, President Nixon confirmed that "war" was an appropriate term to use with respect to fighting crime.[102]

In 1982, President Reagan maintained illicit drugs a threat to national security.[103] William Bennett became the first Director of the White House National Drug Control Policy in 1989 and was known as the "drug czar."[104] He is on record as favoring "limiting Constitutional liberties if there was a compelling reason to do so" in the war on drugs.[105] Years later, he observed "it's a funny war when your enemy is entitled to due process and a fair trial."[106]

Until the 1980s, the use of SWAT teams was unexceptional in terms of number of deployments or "callouts." However, during that decade callouts began an explosive expansion. Arguably, this expansion also had the effect of reinforcing the criticism that police officers were too quick to become confrontational, what today is called the warrior mindset. BDUs were first adopted in policing by SWAT teams because they were practical. They also visually communicated the police officers wearing them were highly trained and not to be taken lightly. SWAT members have historically responded to incidents that were beyond the capability of patrol officers and which they were not trained to handle. These incidents often resulted in highly skilled use of force that both took and saved lives. While the mission of SWAT teams vary by agency, among the missions for which they train are building searches, hostage incident/rescue, barricaded suspects, serving high risk warrants, assaults on bus/train/aircraft, and rescue of persons downed. Although SWAT is the most common designation, such units carry different "labels" in law enforcement agencies, such as Emergency Response Team or Special Response Team. The International Association of Chiefs of Police (IACP) studied SWAT operations nationally for 2009–2013. Among its findings: (1) the U.S. military was a source of training for only 7.1 percent of respondents; (2) armored vehicles were deployed with SWAT teams an average of 10 times annually; (3) the most common complaint about SWAT teams was property damage (38 percent) and the least common was unlawful tactics (2 percent) with excessive force constituting 14 percent of all complaints.[107] The results of the IACP study suggest that concerns about police militarization are less about SWAT teams specifically and more about policing generally.

In addition to highly publicized wars on crime and drugs, some police rhetoric over past decades also reinforced the warrior model. Daryl Gates was the Los Angeles Police Chief from 1978 until 1992. Two years before leaving that post he suggested drug offenders should be shot for treason.[108] William Bennett echoed Gates by asserting he had no moral objection to convicted drug dealers being beheaded, although it would be legally difficult.[109] He also advocated evicting people from public housing on mere suspicion of using drugs.[110] The war on crime perspective threads through the administrations of Presidents George H. Bush, Bill Clinton, and George W. Bush. The last of these famously said if you quit drugs, you join the fight on terrorism.[111] His administration also ran ads that claimed drug use supported terroristic acts. While this is true to a degree, a connection to specific terrorist groups was never made. Still, the rhetoric fanned the some flames against crime, drugs, and terrorism simultaneously.

An unscientific peek into the police culture suggests a warrior, "hard-liner" orientation by some officers. The messages on their occasionally worn T-shirts provide a basis for that observation. A former chief of police reports that at a SWAT team conference he saw a shirt with the message "We don't do drive-by shootings" on one side and on the other there was a demolished house and under it "We stop."[112] The message is eerily similar to a quote from the Vietnam War: "To save this village we had to destroy it." T-shirts worn by officers or sold as fund raisers elsewhere reflect an insensitivity to those they serve: "Baby Daddy Removal Team," "You huff and you puff and we'll blow your house down," and "We get up early just to beat the crowds." More distantly, just before the 1996 Democratic National Convention in Chicago, an enterprising local printer made shirts that quickly became popular with police: "We kicked your father's ass in 1968 … wait 'til you see what we do to you." The police shirt that reads "We trust in God, but all others get searched" arguably gets a pass as merely clever.

Perhaps nothing reinforces the perceived need for the "warrior" mentality more than the murders of officers. On September 11, 2001, the loss of 343 firefighters, 8 paramedics, and 60 police officers was a horrific example of just how dangerous public safety and emergency service jobs can be. Collectively, they rushed into incredible danger and an unknown number surely stayed to lead people out at the cost of their own lives. Hero is sometimes an overused word. However, there are no words sufficient to honor those 411 people.

A total of 1,582 police officers have died in the line of duty in the past decade, that is, an average of one death every 55 hours or 158 officers died in the line of duty per year from 2009 to 2019.[113] There were 134 law enforcement officers killed in the line of duty in 2019.[114] Police academies may also contribute to the warrior mindset. Fifteen percent of all law enforcement academies are primarily stress based and another 38 percent more stress than non-stress. Together, 53 percent of all academies are primarily stress oriented and the stress is not classroom instruction about dealing with it, so much as it is learning to "bear up" under it.[115] Stress training in police academies may well generate an "us versus them" mindset in rookie officers, which has the potential of creating barriers between the police and the community. Even when community policing is part of an academy curriculum, the stress training may create latent psychological obstacles to the kind of police–citizen relationships necessary to fully operationalize a community policing philosophy.[116]

Current Unrest with the Police

A federal program also has contributed to growing concerns about police militarization The National Defense Authorization Act (1997) allows the Secretary of Defense to provide weapons, vehicles, and other materials to federal and state law enforcement agencies for counter-drug and counter-terrorism activities. These are drawn from surplus stock Department of Defense. Perhaps a majority of this equipment is much needed and used well. As an example, police acquisition of large tents provides shelter and rest areas for volunteers searching for lost children, hunters, hikers, and others in wilderness areas (Figure 2.10). Armored vehicles are legitimately needed by the police to rescue hostages, the public and officers under fire, those who are wounded and lying in the open and may be fired upon at again, and the presence of such vehicles at a barricaded subject situation sometimes causes the peaceful surrender of the subject. In 2016, a lone terrorist murdered 49 people at an Orlando, Florida, nightclub and some of the wounded were in critical condition and the toll could have increased. Using an armored vehicle, the police were able to rescue some 30 people trapped in various rooms in the nightclub. Critics of the police don't have a blind eye to a genuine police need for such equipment. However, when the police use the equipment inappropriately or in a way that seems to menace the exercise of constitutional rights criticisms are rightfully expressed.

Militarization critics recognize that the police need to monitor demonstrations by citizens exercising their First Amendment rights because those events have the potential to spiral out of control quickly and create losses of life and property. Their concern is that an early and unnecessary show of armored vehicles and other military capabilities could be viewed as an intolerance of dissent by government, which could produce an unintended result, rioting. In Ferguson, Missouri, the police response to the 2014 largescale demonstrations following the shooting death of Michael Brown by a police officer has been subject to much criticism. Some of that criticism is due to the presence of 50 police agencies, many small, who had not trained together. Nonetheless, it has set off a national discussion of how the police responded.

A central criticism of the response by police in Ferguson is that it was heavily militarized. That appearance stirred the emotions of citizens, creating fear and anger, and interfering with press documentation of events. Armored vehicles drove on the streets and the community called the "tanks" "an act of aggression." One person said "It looked like the police were invading."[117] The "overwatch" tactic borrowed from the military provided sniper cover for the protection of officers. It too was heavy-handed. Sometimes, the sniper rode on top of an armored vehicle, scanning the crowd through his rifle scope to monitor the crowd. Overwatch is not considered a crowd control tactic. Some officers wore camouflage BDUs that further set a militarized response.

In *Militarizing the Criminal Justice System*, Kraska observes that as the police and the public view each other over militarization, the police could begin to lose legitimacy in the eye of the public.[118] If "we versus them" continues unabated in law enforcement, the public may increasingly view the police as an army of occupation. If the police lose the public, the Republic may well be endangered. Militarization represents traditional policing in all of its negative manifestations—aggressive, reactive,

FIGURE 2.10 ▶ The Ferguson, Missouri, Police Department responds to rioting after one of its on-duty officers fatally wounded an unarmed African American teenager who reportedly was trying to take the officer's gun. The clouds appear to be from the deployment of tear gas. Demonstrators later won an injunction to prevent the police from using it. The events in Ferguson became a focal point for critics concerned with police militarization. (Larry W. Smith/epa european pressphoto agency b.v./Alamy Stock Photo)

Quick Facts: How Much Military Equipment Has Been Transferred to State and Local Law Enforcement Agencies?

Between Fiscal Years 2009 and 2014, the federal government provided nearly $18 billion dollars in funds and resources to support state and local law enforcement agencies. These resources are transferred by various federal programs operated by the Departments of Homeland Security, Justice, Defense and Treasury, as well as the Office of National Drug Control Policy.

Some of the equipment is routine, such as office furniture and computers, personal protective equipment, basic firearms, tents, generators, tarps, tool kits, first aid kits, blankets, safety glasses, storage lockers, shelving, and forklifts. The White House asserts that in the 12-month period ending August 2014, such items made up 96 percent or 1.8 million items transferred, which are non-controlled, meaning that they are not returned to the federal government at the end of their useful life.

Some 460,000 pieces of returnable controlled items have been transferred to state and local police agencies, including 92,442 small arms, 44,275 night vision devices, 5,235 high mobility, multi-purpose vehicles, 617 mine resistant, ambush-protected vehicles, and 616 aircraft.

Source: Executive Office of the President, Review: Federal Support for Local Law Enforcement Equipment Acquisition, December 2014, pp. 1, 7, and 8.

and based on force. There is very little that represents the tenets of proactive de-escalation, conflict resolution, the prevention of harm, and the protection of civil and human rights so passionately expressed in modern tenets of policing.

A 2019 Pew Research Center poll found Americans trust in the federal government is very low. Only 17 percent believed they could trust it to do the right thing "most of the time" (14 percent) or "always" (3 percent). This is a long fall from a 1958 poll of 75 percent trusting the federal government.[119] In contrast, despite police officers being involved in relatively recent nationally controversial use of force cases, including some which resulted in officers being criminally charged, a different 2019 Pew Research Center poll revealed strong support for police officers, local government officials, and military leaders. Of those surveyed, 79 percent believed police officers cared about them "most" or "all of the time." Overall, 84 percent of all respondents thought the police did a good job of protecting people from crime, all, most, or some of the time. Less glowing were the results from asking "how often officers treat racial and ethnic groups equally." Sixty-two percent believed the police did so at least some of the time. Racial minorities were viewed as being treated equally 37 percent only a little or none of the time.[120]

Trust is a perishable commodity. It is to be prized and must be protected. There is a case to make for the use of some military equipment, such as using armored vehicles to rescue citizens and wounded officers, as well as freeing hostages. Part of the public's negative reaction to militarization is driven by police policies that permit or require the roll-out of armored equipment to an excessive degree and officers wearing military clothing. It produces a fear that police are indeed, morphing into an occupying force, which is inherently at odds with the Peelian dictum that the police are the public and the public are the police.

IMPROVING POLICE–COMMUNITY RELATIONS

In 2014, President Barak Obama called together a task force to address community–police relations and offer guidelines for reforms in the wake of the unrest in Ferguson, New York, and Baltimore. Their recommendations, organized as "pillars," are linked closely to policing strategies discussed in this chapter, and provide opportunities for departments to strengthen and shift their current crime reduction and prevention initiatives:[121]

1. ***Building Trust and Legitimacy:*** This is the foundation on which all police/community interactions rely. Evidence shows that when people perceive authorities to be acting in procedurally just ways, they are more likely to obey the law. Procedurally just behavior is described as being based on four principles: treating people with dignity and respect; giving individuals a "voice" during encounters; being neutral and transparent in decision-making; and conveying trustworthy motives. Specific recommendations include embracing a guardian versus a warrior mindset acknowledging past injustices; and increasing transparent and proactive communication with the public.

2. ***Policy and Oversight:*** Simply stated, policies in police agencies must reflect community values. Clear and concise policies must be developed that regulate the use of force, police control of mass demonstrations (particularly in regards to equipment used, such as armored personnel carriers or other "military grade" weaponry), consent to search, racial profiling, internal investigations of improper use of force, in-custody deaths, and officer-involved shootings.

Box 2.5: "I Can't Breathe": Community–Police Relations in Crisis and the Case of George Floyd

George Floyd, a 46 year-old black man, encountered officers from the Minneapolis Police Department (MPD) on May 25, 2020. Police initially responded to a call alleging that Floyd and two other men used counterfeit money at a convenience store. Two officers arrived on scene and confronted Floyd inside his parked vehicle. Floyd exited his vehicle and was placed in handcuffs. Police sat Floyd on the sidewalk against the exterior wall of a commercial building before they walked him across the street to another police vehicle. Almost immediately, Floyd began to say to the officers that he was claustrophobic and could not breathe. Additional MPD officers arrived on-scene including 19-year police veteran, Officer Derek Chauvin.

Officer Chauvin forcibly removed Floyd from the police vehicle and placed him face-down on the pavement. Floyd laid face to the ground and handcuffed while Chauvin pinned his knee against Floyd's neck, as two other MPD officers assisted in keeping a growing crowd from interfering. Additionally, a fourth officer communicated with by-standers and prevented them from interfering.

Officer Chauvin kept his knee firmly pinned on Floyd's neck for several minutes as Floyd pleaded, "Please, please, please; I can't breathe. Please man." Several bystanders attempted to intervene and communicated to the officers that Floyd was now unconscious and unresponsive. Still, Officer Chauvin kept his knee pinned against Floyd's neck for almost nine minutes before an ambulance arrived on scene. Floyd was pronounced dead at the hospital about one hour later.

While all the facts in their case continue to evolve, what is clear is that a citizen video of the Floyd encounter is heartbreaking, extremely difficult to watch, and has stoked nationwide protests similar to those that occurred in the wake of the Freddie Gray and Michael Brown cases just five years earlier and also described within this chapter. After several days of national protests primarily organized by the Black Lives Matter (BLM) movement, Officer Chauvin was criminally charged with second-degree murder and three other officers were charged with aiding and abetting to second degree murder and manslaughter.

The death of George Floyd obviously serves as another flashpoint in the continued nationwide conversation about race, brutality and the use of force in policing. Indeed, many commentators described Floyd's death as the major inflection point that may spur long-sought structural reforms designed to mitigate police brutality, improve police selection and training, and create stronger systems of accountability and discipline. This encounter also diverges from many previous notorious events in that police administrators and officers across the nation quickly condemned the actions of the Minneapolis PD officers. Indeed, police officers and executives in some jurisdictions joined in peaceful protests that emerged quickly after Floyd's death. The Floyd case, along with other police shooting deaths (Breonna Taylor in Louisville, Kentucky on March 13, 2020 and Stephon Clark in Sacramento, California on March 18, 2018) have captured the nation's attention and will be observed closely as Floyd's death continues to be mourned and the case against the involved officers

© Michael Siluk/Alamy Stock Photo

unfolds within the courts of both public opinion and the law. Most certainly, outraged activists within the Black Lives Matter movement will continue to work for police reform and insist that the names of those African Americans killed during encounters with the police (or by those who take police power on themselves) are not forgotten.

Sources: "The Death of George Floyd: What Video Shows About His Final Minutes." Available at youtube.com/watch?v=FMGUAHBFmjk. Accessed June 9, 2020

Los Angeles Times Editorial Board, "A Very Abbreviated History of Police Officers Killing Black People," *Los Angeles Times*, June 4, 2020. Available at https://www.latimes.com/opinion/story/2020-06-04/police-killings-black-victims. Accessed September 4, 2020.

Varn, T. (2020). "Death of George Floyd Draws Quick Condemnation from Tampa Bay's Top Cops." *Tampa Bay Times*, May 28 (p. 1).

Waldrop, T. (2020). "The Charges Against 4 Officers Involved in George Floyd's Death, Explained." Available at cnn.com/2020/06/04/us/George-floyd-officers-charges-explained/index.html. Accessed June 9, 2020.

Box 2.6: Youth Outreach Programs

The recommendations from the President's Task Force on 21st Century Policing made it clear that engaging with youth should be a priority both to increase police legitimacy, tackle systemic quality of life issues, and to reinvigorate community/police dialogue. Most department run a variety of programs aimed at disadvantaged youth of all ages, particularly those from areas identified as policing hot-spots throughout the city.

Though evaluations of these programmatic effects on crime will be longitudinal—and therefore data is not readily available—participation is robust, and activities are highly rated by participants and observers alike. A police department should take a holistic approach to youth engagement, exposing kids to career options, educational activities, athletics, special needs programs, and the arts in the following programs:

Junior Police Academy—includes Basic Academy, aimed at 4th–7th grades and Advanced Academy, 8th–10th grades. Participants discuss life skills, learn about positive behavioral choices, and have hands-on interactions with police officers from a variety of units within DPD.

Explorer Program—aimed at ages 14–21, this program is held in conjunction with the Boy Scouts of America and emphasizes leadership, service activities, and interest in law enforcement careers.

Junior Explorer Program—aimed at ages 10–13, emphasizes good citizenship, community service, personal responsibility, and leadership skills.

Special Olympics—sponsorship of Special Olympic programs as well as other special needs events provides an opportunity to address problems confronting this very important, yet often overlooked, youth population group.

Blue in the School—character education for 4th graders taught by police officers, and emphasizing communication skills and healthy, positive lifestyle choices.

Police Athletic/Activities League (PAL)—includes Midnight Basketball, Soccer Camp, Boxing Club, Community Biking Program, Fitness Adventure, Tennis Camps, Free Play, PAL Gardening, Robotics, Guitar Lessons, PAL Singers (youth choir), "Movin' in the Right Direction" musical, Male Mentoring, Girl Empowerment/DIVA Mentoring, Chess Club, Stuff the Squad Car (school supply & Christmas toy collection drives), Anti-Bullying Presentations, Career Day Presentations, Summer Internship Programs, and a leadership program held on a local university campus, which includes leadership development courses, interview skills, college planning, and discussions on how to impact police–community relations.

Police departments focus on youth outreach programs, like Special Olympics, in an effort to improve police–community relations trained participants for a 12-mile bike ride. (Steve Skjold/Alamy Stock Photo)

3. ***Technology and Social Media:*** The implementation, use, and evaluation of technology and social media are acknowledged as a valuable tool for policing, emphasizing that these areas contain valuable opportunities to engage the public and increase police transparency. Technology, such as visual and audio recording devices, biometric devices, and less than lethal technology, should be implemented with community input and should be held to national standards that maintain civil and human rights protections.

4. ***Community Policing and Crime Reduction:*** The taskforce heralded the potential of community policing to build trust and collaboration, while also reinforcing that communities will only support policing models that reflect their own values. The task force also placed significant emphasis on programming that enhances positive youth/police interactions.

5. ***Training and Education:*** Improving training in police agencies to address a wide range of challenges, particularly those involving minority communities, must include wider community input.

6. ***Officer Wellness and Safety:*** Recognizing and promoting the importance of officer safety at all levels of a police organization increases officer awareness. Task force recommendations focused on increased funding and national support for initiatives supporting the safety of officers, as well as institutional support for their physical and emotional needs throughout their careers.

Ultimately, there is no means by which police agencies can be forced to adopt these recommendations, unless they are under a consent decree in which the Department of Justice is monitoring their operations. That has been the case in a number of jurisdictions, including Ferguson, MO, Detroit, MI, Los Angeles, CA, Portland, OR, and Cleveland, OH, in which the federal government threatens to sue the agency under civil rights clauses of the constitution unless significant reforms are enacted. Short of that, however, agencies are left to implement these types of future changes on their own, considering community political pressures and the myriad of evidence-based strategies available today.

What's clear is that change will have to fundamentally occur within not only police organizations but within the police culture as well. Change, too, must occur within our communities. Citizens who do not accept the legitimacy of police are more likely to escalate simple traffic stops to angry confrontations—and unfortunately, as witnessed in the past, police officers with their own biases and entrenched notions of police identity are frequently engaging such incidents with increased violence rather than attempting to de-escalate such instances. American policing must re-invent itself, emphasizing crime prevention (as opposed to arrests), and incorporating citizen response and input. In a similar manner, communities (particularly minority communities) must realize that policing is an inherently dangerous profession and that individual officers serve everyday at the peril of their own lives. New threats from foreign terrorists, mad bombers, and spree killers simply escalate this situation.

This chapter documents the significant movement of major paradigm shifts in the evolution of policing, from traditional patrol and Broken Windows models to community policing, CompStat, and various hybrid blends of evidence-based police practices. The remarkable strides made as part of those seismic shifts give hope that policing organizations and communities within our country can rise to meet the current challenges facing our society.

Box 2.7: Honoring Police Today

On July 7, 2016, American policing was forever changed by an incident that took place in Dallas, Texas. Known in law enforcement circles simply as 7/7, it was the night that five police officers were ambushed and killed by Micah Johnson for reasons that are still not entirely clear, though largely attributable to his hatred of white law enforcement officers. During a peaceful *Black Lives Matter* protest, Johnson began shooting officers with a high-powered rifle from a nearby building window. Armed with at least two high-powered rifles and several handguns, Johnson took the lives of dedicated members of the Dallas Police Department and the Dallas Area Rapid Transit Police Department. Those lost included:

- Lorne Ahrens, a senior corporal with the Dallas Police Department
- Michael Krol, a police officer with the Dallas Police Department
- Michael Smith, a sergeant with the Dallas Police Department
- Brent Thompson, a police officer with DART Police Department
- Patrick Zamarripa, a police officer with the Dallas Police Department

This shooting represents the deadliest incident for American law enforcement since the September 11, 2001, attack on the World Trade Center by Middle East terrorists. A discussion of policing today is not complete without acknowledging the terrible sacrifice made by these officers, all of whom were truly embodying the concept of police officers as guardians while they protected the free speech of those protesting—and then switched roles in seconds to become warriors, shielding citizens, covering their fellow officers, and eventually succumbing to a violent death.

Image: Fort Worth Star Telegram.

Chapter Summary

Summary by Learning Objectives

1. Define community policing.

A policing philosophy that focuses on general neighborhood problems as a source of crime; community policing is preventive, proactive, and information-based.

2. Describe the four-step problem-solving model called SARA.

The problem-solving model called SARA comprises four specific steps: (1) *Scanning*—Instead of relying on broad, law-related concepts, such as robbery, burglary, and auto theft, officers are encouraged to group individual, related incidents that come to their attention as "problems" and define these problems in more precise and useful terms. For example, an incident that typically would be classified simply as a "robbery" might be seen as part of a pattern of prostitution-related robberies committed by transvestites in center-city hotels. In essence, officers are expected to look for possible problems and accurately define them as part of their daily routine. (2) *Analysis*—Officers working on a well-defined problem then collect information from a variety of public and private sources, not just traditional police data, such as criminal records and past offense reports. Officers rely on problem analysis guides that direct officers to examine offenders, victims, the social and physical environment, and previous responses to the problem. The goal is to understand the scope, nature, and causes of the problem and formulate a variety of options for its resolution. (3) *Response*—The knowledge gained in the analysis stage is then used to develop and implement solutions. Officers seek the assistance of citizens, businesses, other police units, other public and private organizations, and anyone else who can help develop a program of action. Solutions may go well beyond traditional police responses to include other community agencies and/or municipal organizations. (4) *Assessment*—Finally, officers evaluate the impact and the effectiveness of their responses. Were the original problems actually solved or alleviated? They may use the results to revise a response, to collect more data, or even to redefine the problem.

3. Describe CompStat.

Essentially, CompStat is a collection of modern management practices, military-like deployment efforts, and strong enforcement strategies all based on the availability of accurate and timely statistical crime data. Four core principles highlight a police department's model of CompStat:

- *Accurate and timely intelligence and statistical crime information based on geographical settings and/or areas.* High-tech computer systems and geographical mapping programs are most helpful in providing the aggregate and individual data often required for effective CompStat efforts. However, more rudimentary aspects of visual crime analysis can be accomplished through daily pin mapping and bulletins.

- *Rapid deployment of resources, particularly combining the immediate presence of uniform patrol working in concert with directed undercover operations.* Rapid deployment of other city and governmental resources, such as nuisance and abatement personnel, sanitation workers, and alcoholic beverage and licensing enforcement, is an additional aspect of this principle.

- *Effective tactics and strategies of enforcement that focus on visible street crimes or "quality-of-life" crimes,* such as loitering, drinking in public, street prostitution, or even jumping subway turnstiles.

- *Relentless follow-up and assessment,* which include placing accountability and responsibility not only on the individual police officer on the beat but also on individual police managers of traditionally defined areas, such as division heads or precinct captains.

CompStat focuses on using the most accurate and timely information and data available to the police, opening lines of communication both horizontally and vertically within the organization, activating the community at large, and improving the overall efficiency and effectiveness of the police. CompStat is problem-oriented and preventive and stresses the need to focus on problems rather than on past incidents.

4. Discuss newer police strategies, including evidence-based policing, hot-spots policing, intelligence-led policing, and predictive policing.

Evidence-based policing is a style of policing using the best available research to guide, manage, and evaluate police operations within a community; hot-spots policing is a geographically based approach to crime-fighting focused on in-depth analysis of "places" and times, and deploying police officers to those locations that account for the majority of calls for service and crime in a community. *Intelligence-led policing* (ILP): arose from the 9/11 terrorist attacks, and is focused on offenders, not crime incidents, using intelligence analysis to prevent crime. *Predictive policing* is a proactive policing style that uses information and analytical tools to prevent crime while using the fewest police resources possible.

5. **List and briefly describe some of the more common crime analysis techniques.**

Some of the more common crime analysis techniques are as follows:

- *Tactical crime analysis or crime-specific analysis*—a tabular or graphic display of reported crimes with a given pattern of time and/or location, often used to detect patterns of crime (e.g., robberies, burglaries, and auto thefts) that cluster in specific locations during various time periods.

- *Strategic crime analysis*—the study of crime and/or social problems in a specific area in an effort to determine long-term patterns of activity as well as to evaluate police responses and organizational procedures. Strategic crime analysis is often used to determine the effectiveness of police over a given period of time or in the evaluation of specific policing strategies.

- *Link analysis*—a graphic portrayal of associations and relationships among people, organizations, events, activities, and locations from a given point in time.

- *Digital evidence analysis*—reports from smartphones can yield location data, messaging, call histories, search engine history and much more in all types of investigations.

- *Visual investigative analysis (VIA)*—charting that depicts key events of criminal activity in chronological order. VIA is used to show the degree of involvement of subjects.

- *Case analysis and management system (CAMS)*—computerized case management in which large amounts of data are compiled and indexed for each retrieval of specific items. This system is used to clarify relationships and calculate the probability of associations.

- *Intelligence analysis*—the identification of networks of offenders and criminal activity, often associated with organized crime, gangs, drug traffickers, prostitution rings, and terrorist organizations.

6. **Describe geographic information systems and explain how such a system would enhance police service.**

GIS has become an influential mechanism in hotspots policing as well as Crime Prevention Through Environmental Design (CPTED), situational policing, directed patrols, and crime analysis. GIS has a myriad of other uses in policing. Police agencies can use GIS in dispatching police units by providing directions to locations; address histories; and locations of nearby fire and waste hazards, fire hydrants, alarm boxes, high-power lines, water lines, and the like. Police managers can not only use GIS to provide graphic analysis of specific crime patterns and to evaluate new policing strategies but also to track individual officer performance by area.

There are two types of GIS crime mapping: statistical spatial analysis and spatial modeling. While statistical spatial analysis focuses on the spatial relationship between crime points in a particular area, spatial modeling is concerned with the technology and application of data.

7. **Explain the impact of information technology on policing.**

The impact of information technologies on policing cannot be overstated; they take a central support role for policing strategies, allow for community interaction, and provide better analysis and problem-solving capabilities.

8. **Describe how distrust between police and citizens can affect police strategies.**

Police/community co-operation is the cornerstone of many new police strategies; without police legitimacy and community trust, many of these strategies simply will not work.

Chapter Review Questions

1. Define *community policing*.
2. Describe the four-step problem-solving model commonly referred to as SARA.
3. Identify the problems commonly associated with traditional policing.
4. What is the CAPS program? Discuss some of the key features aimed at improving and expanding the overall quality of police services in the City of Chicago, as well as reducing crime.
5. Define *CompStat* and identify the core principles of CompStat as presented in the New York Police Department model.
6. Define some of today's new police strategies, such as hot-spots policing, intelligence-led policing (ILP), and harm-focused policing.
7. What is evidence-based policing? Describe the *Triple T Strategy* proposed by Larry Sherman as a part of the evidence-based policing philosophy.

8. List and briefly describe some of the more common crime analysis techniques.

9. Describe a geographic information system and explain how such a system enhances police service.

10. What are the benefits and issues that surround the use of social media by police agencies?

11. What factors have contributed to the militarization of the police over the past two decades?

12. How can we improve police–community relations in the United States?

Critical Thinking Exercises

1. Visit your town or city's law enforcement website. Can you tell by the information published what type of policing strategies they employ? Do you think this is an appropriate strategy for your city? Why or why not?

2. Why is police legitimacy so closely tied to community policing? Can you have a good community policing program without police legitimacy? Why or why not?

3. Find a law enforcement agency's Twitter or Facebook page. What examples of policing strategies can you see throughout their posts?

Key Terms

Chicago Alternative Policing Strategy (CAPS)
CODEFOR
community policing
CompStat
crime analysis

directed and saturation patrols
evidence-based policing
geographic information systems (GIS)
hot-spots policing
intelligence-led policing (ILP)
neighborhood-oriented policing

predictive policing
problem-oriented policing (POP)
SARA
social media
traditional policing
zero-tolerance policing (ZTP)

Endnotes

[1] U.S. Department of Justice, Office of Community Oriented Policing (COPS Office), Community Policing (COPS), 2017. See: https://www.justice.gov/jmd/file/822291/download.

[2] See David Weisburd and Anthony Braga (eds.), Police Innovation: Contrasting Perspectives, 2nd Edition (Cambridge, UK: Cambridge University Press, 2019.

[3] See Herman Goldstein, *Policing in a Free Society* (Cambridge, MA: Ballinger, 1977).

[4] See James Q. Wilson and George L. Kelling, "The Police and Neighborhood Safety: Broken Windows," *Atlantic Monthly*, No. 249 (1982), pp. 29–38.

[5] See Y. Xu, M. L. Fiedler, and K. H. Flaming, "Discovering the Impact of Community Policing," *Journal of Research in Crime and Delinquency* 42, No. 2 (2005), pp. 147–186.

[6] Hyunseok Jang, Larry T. Hoover, and Brian A. Lawton, "Effectiveness of Broken Windows Enforcement on Clearance Rates," *Journal of Criminal Justice* 36, Issue 6 (November/December 2008), p. 529. See also, National Research Council of the National Academies, *Fairness and Effectiveness in Policing: The Evidence* (Washington, DC: The National Academies Press, 2001), pp. 228–230.

[7] B. E. Harcourt and J. Ludwig, "Broken Windows: New Evidence from New York City and a Five City Social Experiment," *University of Chicago Law Review* 73, Issue 1 (Winter 2006), pp. 271–320. The questioning of this link also appears in the news media; illustratively, see Daniel Brook, "The Cracks in Broken Windows," *The Boston Globe*, on-line, February 19, 2006.

[8] Judith A. Greene, "Zero Tolerance: A Case Study of Police Policies and Practices in New York City," *Crime and Delinquency* 45, No. 2 (1999), pp. 171–210.

[9] Ibid., p. 171.

[10] George L. Kelling and Catherine M. Coles, *Fixing Broken Windows: Restoring Order and Reducing Crime in Our Communities* (New York: Touchstone Publishing, 1996).

[11] Chris Braiden, "Community Policing: Nothing New Under the Sun" (Edmonton, Alberta: Edmonton Police Department, 1987).

[12] Ibid. See Peel's Principle 7, as expressed on p. 2.

[13] Jerome H. Skolnick and David H. Bayley, *Community Policing: Issues and Practices Around the World* (Washington, DC: U.S. Department of Justice, 1988), pp. 67–70.

[14] A number of researchers have documented the failures of traditional policing methods. Most notably, see A. J. Reiss, *The Police and the Public* (New Haven, CT: Yale University Press, 1971); G. L. Kelling, T. Pate, D. Dickman,

and C. Brown, *Kansas City Preventive Patrol Experiment* (Washington, DC: Police Foundation, 1975); M. T. Farmer, ed., *Differential Police Response Strategies* (Washington, DC: Police Executive Research Forum, 1981); L. W. Sherman, P. R. Gartin, and M. E. Buerger, "Hot-Spot of Predatory Crime: Routine Activities and the Criminology of Place," *Criminology* 27 (1989), pp. 27–55; and W. H. Bieck, W. Spelman, and T. J. Sweeney, "The Patrol Function," in *Local Government Police Management,* ed. William A. Geller (Washington, DC: International City Management Association), pp. 59–95.

[15]Gary W. Cordner. "Community Policing," in *Critical Issues in Policing, Seventh Edition,* eds. Geoffrey Alpert and Roger Dunham (Long Grove, IL: Waveland Press, 2015), pp. 481–498.

[16]Journal of Experimental Criminology, "Community-Oriented Policing to Reduce Crime, Disorder and Fear and Increase Satisfaction and Legitimacy Among Citizens: A Systematic Review." -See more at: http://journalist-sresource.org/studies/government/criminal-justice/the-impact-of-community-policing-meta-analysis-of-its-effects-in-u-s-cities#sthash.ksuElqOq.dpuf

[17]Early discussions relating to the problems associated with evaluating community policing were highlighted in the following article: Robert W. Taylor, Eric J. Fritsch, and Tory Caeti, "Core Challenges Facing Community Policing: The Emperor Still Has No Clothes." *ACJS Today* 17, No. 1 (May/June 1998).

[18]For a discussion of CompStat as a new police strategy to reduce crime, see William Bratton and Peter Knobler, *Turnaround: How America's Top Cop Reversed the Crime Epidemic* (New York: Random House, 1998); William Bratton and William Edwards, "What We Have Learned about Policing," *City Journal* (spring 1999): William F. Walsh, "CompStat: An Analysis of an Emerging Police Managerial Paradigm," *Policing: An International Journal of Police Strategies and Management* 24, No. 3 (2001), pp. 347–362; William F. Walsh and Gennaro F. Vito, "The Meaning of CompStat," *Journal of Contemporary Criminal Justice* 20, No. 1 (2004), pp. 51–69; John E. Conklin, *Why Crime Rates Fell* (Boston, MA: Pearson Education, 2003).

[19]Much of this section has been adapted from Raymond Dussault, "Maps and Management: Compstat Evolves," *Government Technology* (April 2000), pp. 1–2.

[20]William F. Walsh and Gennero F. Vito, "The Meaning of CompStat," *Journal of Contemporary Criminal Justice* 20, No. 1 (2004), pp. 51–69.

[21]Police Executive Research Forum, "COMPSTAT: Its Origins, Evolution, and Future in Law Enforcement Agencies" (2013), http://www.policeforum.org/assets/docs/Free_Online_Documents/Compstat/compstat%20-%20its%20origins%20evolution%20and%20future%20in%20law%20enforcement%20agencies%202013.pdf (accessed June 23, 2015).

[22]The SARA methodology was adapted from William Spelman and John E. Eck, *Newport News Tests Problem-Oriented Policing* (Washington, DC: National Institute of Justice, SNI 201, January/February 1987), pp. 2–3, and Spelman and Eck, "Police and Delivery," p. 61.

[23]Herman Goldstein, *Problem-Oriented Policing* (New York: McGraw-Hill, 1990).

[24]This list was adapted, in part, from Goldstein, *Problem-Oriented Policing,* pp. 66–67.

[25]Ibid., pp. 36–37.

[26]City of Chicago, Department of Police, "Fact Sheet—the Chicago Alternative Policing Strategy (CAPS)" (July 1995).

[27]Arthur J. Lurigio and Wesley G. Skogan, "Winning the Hearts and Minds of Police Officers: An Assessment of Staff Perceptions of Community Policing in Chicago," *Crime and Delinquency* 40, No. 3 (July 1994), p. 319.

[28]Mark Moore, "Problem-Solving and Community Policing," in *Modern Policing,* eds. M. Tonry and N. Morris (Chicago: University of Chicago Press, 1992), pp. 99–158.

[29]The key features of the CAPS program presented in this text are adapted from Lurigio and Skogan, "Winning the Hearts and Minds of Police Officers," p. 318, and Chicago Police Department, "Fact Sheet," pp. 1–2.

[30]Ibid.

[31]Ibid.

[32]Stephen Mastrofski, Roger Parks, and Robert E. Worden, "Community Policing in Action: Lessons from an Observational Study," *Research Preview* (Washington, DC: National Institute of Justice, June 1998).

[33]Ibid.

[34]Quint C. Thurman and Jihong Zhao, "Community Policing: Where Are We Now?" *Crime and Delinquency* 43, No. 3 (July 1997), pp. 554–564.

[35]Mastrofski et al., "Community Policing in Action," p. 7.

[36]Nissa Rhee, "The Rise and Fall of Community Policing in Chicago," *The Chicago Reader*, September 22, 2016, https://www.chicagoreader.com/chicago/caps-cpd-community-policing-analysis/Content?oid=23635982.

[37]Interview with Chief Robert K. Olsen, October 7, 2002.

[38]Refer to www.ci.minneapolis.mn.us/citywork/police/index.html

[39]D. Weisburd and J. E. Eck, "What Can Police Do to Reduce Crime, Disorder, and Fear?" *The Annals of the American Academy of Political and Social Science* 593 (2004), pp. 42–65.

[40]Ibid.; Lawrence W. Sherman, "Policing Communities: What Works?" *Crime and Justice* 8 (1986), pp. 343–386.

[41]See Robert W. Taylor, Eric J. Fritsch, and Tory J. Caeti, "Core Challenges Facing Community Policing: The Emperor *Still* Has No Clothes," *ACJS Today*, No. 1 (May-June, 1998), Volume XVII: 1, pp. 1–5.

[42]See Larry W. Sherman, "Policing for Crime Prevention," in *Preventing Crime: What Works, What Doesn't, What's Promising—A Report to the Attorney General of the United States* eds. L.W. Sherman, D. Gottfredson, D.L. MacKenzie, J.E. Eck, P. Reuter, & S. Bushway (Washington, DC: United States Department of Justice, Office of Justice Programs, 1997).

[43]Larry W. Sherman, "Evidence-Based Policing," *Ideas in American Policing* (Washington, DC: U.S. Department of Justice, Police Foundation, July 1998), pp. 3–4.

[44]Ibid.

[45]Lawrence W. Sherman. "The Rise of Evidence-Based Policing: Targeting, Testing, and Tracking." The Rise of Evidence-Based Policing, Crime and Justice, Volume 42: *Crime and Justice in America: 1975–2015.*

[46]Cynthia Lum and Christopher S. Koper. "Evidence-Based Policing." *Critical Issues in Policing, Seventh Edition,*

eds. Geoffrey Alpert and Roger Dunham (Long Grove, IL: Waveland Press, 2015), pp. 260–273.

[47]Ibid.

[48]"Evidence Based Policing Hall of Fame: Dr. Theron Bowman." Center for Evidence Based Crime Policy. Retrieved from http://cebcp.org/hall-of-fame/on July 18, 2015.

[49]See the Caruth Police Institute website at: http://www. untdallas.edu/cpi

[50]"The Matrix." Center for Evidence-Based Crime Policy. Retrieved from http://cebcp.org/evidence-based-policing/the-matrix/on July 15, 2015.

[51]David Weisburd, "Hot-Spots Policing Experiments and Criminal Justice Research: Lessons from the Field," *Annals of the American Academy of Political and Social Science* 599 (2005), pp. 220–245.

[52]Lawrence W. Sherman, P. R. Gartin, and M. Buerger, "Hot-Spots of Predatory Crime: Routine Activities and the Criminology of Place," *Criminology* 27 (1986), pp. 27–55.

[53]Ibid.

[54]John E. Eck, S. Chainey, and J. Cameron, *Mapping Crime: Understanding Hot-Spots* (Washington, DC: National Institute of Justice, 2005).

[55]David Weisburd and Lorraine G. Mazerolle, "Crime and Disorder in Drug Hot-Spots: Implications for Theory and Practice in Policing," *Police Quarterly* 3 (2000), pp. 331–349.

[56]S. L. Rutherford, K. R. Blevins and V. B. Lord, "An Evaluation of the Effects of a Street Crime Unit on Citizens' Fear of Crime," *Professional Issues in Criminal Justice* 3 (2008), pp. 21–36.

[57]Wesley Skogan and Kathleen Frydl (eds), *Fairness and Effectiveness in Policing: The Evidence* (Washington, DC: National Academy of Sciences, Committee to Review Research on Police Policy and Practice, 2004), p. 250. See also, Anthony A. Braga, *U.S. COPS Office Crime Prevention Research Review: Police Enforcement Strategies to Prevent Crime in Hot-Spot Areas* (Washington, DC: U.S. Department of Justice, 2008).

[58]Anthony A. Braga, "The Effects of Hot-Spots Policing on Crime," *Annals of the American Academy of Political and Social Sciences* 578 (2001), pp. 104–125.

[59]Ralph B. Taylor, "Hot-Spots Do Not Exist and Four Other Fundamental Concerns About Hot-Spots Policing," in Natasha A. Frost, J. D. Freilich, and T. R. Clear, *Contemporary Issues in Criminal Justice Policy* (Belmont, CA: Wadsworth Cengage Learning, 2010).

[60]Ibid., p. 272.

[61]C. S. Koper and E. Mayo-Wilson, "Police Crackdowns on Illegal Gun Carrying: A Systematic Review of Their Impact on Gun Crime," *Journal of Experimental Criminology* 2 (2006), pp. 227–261.

[62]Eric J. Fritsch, Tory J. Caeti, and Robert W. Taylor, "Gang Suppression through Saturation Patrol, Aggressive Curfew, and Truancy Enforcement: A Quasi-experimental Test of the Dallas Anti-gang Initiative," *Crime & Delinquency* 45 (2000), pp. 122–139.

[63]Jerry H. Ratcliffe and Robert Guidetti, "State Police Investigative Structure and the Adoption of Intelligence-led Policing. *Policing: An International Journal of Police Strategies and Management* 31 (2008), p. 111.

[64]Ibid.

[65]Jerry H. Ratcliffe, *Intelligence-Led Policing* (Portland, OR: Willan Publishing, 2008).

[66]C. Clarke, "Proactive Policing: Standing on the Shoulders of Community-Based Policing," *Police Practice and Research*, 7 (2006), pp. 3–17.

[67]Jerry H. Ratcliffe and Robert Guidetti, "State Police Investigative Structure and the Adoption of Intelligence-led Policing."

[68]Ibid.

[69]Jerry H. Ratcliffe, "The effectiveness of police intelligence management: A New Zealand case study." *Police Practice and Research* (In Press).

[70]Craig D. Uchida, *A National Discussion on Predictive Policing: Defining our Terms and Mapping Successful Implementation Strategies* (Washington, DC: National Institute of Justice, 2010).

[71]Beth Pearsall, "Predictive Policing: The Future of Law Enforcement?" *NIJ Journal* 266 (2010), pp. 16–19.

[72]Charlie Beck and Colleen McCue, "Predictive Policing: What Can We Learn from Wal-Mart and Amazon about Fighting Crime in a Recession?" *The Police Chief* 76 (November 2009). Retrieved from http://policechiefmagazine.org/magazine/on July 20, 2010.

[73]Beth Pearsall, "Predictive Policing: The Future of Law Enforcement?"

[74]Craig D. Uchida, *A National Discussion on Predictive Policing: Defining our Terms and Mapping Successful Implementation Strategies.*

[75]J. W. Brahan, K. P. Lam, H. Chan, and W. Leung, "AICAMS: Artificial Intelligence Crime Analysis and Management Systems," *Knowledge-Based Systems* 11 (2009), pp. 355–361.

[76]N. Cope, "Intelligence Led Policing or Policing Led Intelligence?" *British Journal of Criminology* 44 (2004), pp. 188–203.

[77]Several scholars have provided definitions of crime analysis. See J. B. Howlett, "Analytical Investigative Techniques," *Police Chief* 47 (December 1980), p. 42; Rachel Boba, *Crime Analysis and Crime Mapping* (Thousand Oaks, CA: Sage, 2005), p. 5; S. Gottlieb, S. Arenberg, and R. Singh, *Crime Analysis: From First Report to Final Arrest* (Monclair, CA: alpha, 1994); Mark A. Stallo, *Using Microsoft Office to Improve Law Enforcement Operations: Crime Analysis, Community Policing, and Investigations* (Dallas, TX: Act, Now, 2010).

[78]J. A. Kinney, "Criminal Intelligence Analysis: A Powerful Weapon," *International Cargo Crime Prevention* (April 1984), p. 4.

[79]Boba, *Crime Analysis and Crime Mapping*, p. 14.

[80]Ibid., pp. 15–16.

[81]Ibid.

[82]Incident occurring on Virginia Tech University, April 16, 2007 resulting in over 30 deaths from gunman, Seung-Hui Cho.

[83]Ross, "Criminal Intelligence Analysis," p. 49.

[84]Mark A. Stallo, *Using Microsoft Office to Improve Law Enforcement Operations.* See http://www.actnowinc.org/books.html (July 20, 2010).

[85]Jerry H. Ratcliffe, "Crime Mapping and the Training Needs of Law Enforcement," *European Journal on Criminal Policy and Research* 10 (2004), pp. 65–83.

[86]David Weisburd and C. Lum, "The Diffusion of Computerized Crime Mapping in Policing: Linking Research and Practice," *Police Practice and Research* 6 (2005), pp. 419–434.

[87]J. R. Battin, "Is Hot-Spot Policing Effective Empirically?" *Professional Issues in Criminal Justice* 4 (2009), pp. 35–50.

[88]For more information relating to the applications of GIS technology to policing, see Nancy G. La Vigne and Julie Wartell, *Mapping Across Boundaries: Regional Crime Analysis* (Washington, DC: Police Executive Research Forum, 2001).

[89]https://www.ncjrs.gov/pdffiles1/nij/244760.pdf

[90]Hyland, Shelley. "Body Worn Cameras in Law Enforcement Agencies, 2016." U.S. Department of Justice Bulletin, November 2018. Retrieved from https://www.bjs.gov/content/pub/pdf/bwclea16.pdf.

[91]Chapman, Brent. "Body Worn Cameras: What the Evidence Tells Us." *National Institute of Justice Journal*, No. 280 (December 2018). Retrieved from https://www.nij.gov/journals/280/Pages/body-worn-cameras-what-evidence-tells-us.aspx.

[92]Hyland, Shelley. "Body Worn Cameras in Law Enforcement Agencies, 2016." U.S. Department of Justice Bulletin, November 2018. Retrieved from https://www.bjs.gov/content/pub/pdf/bwclea16.pdf.

[93]Chapman, Brent. "Body Worn Cameras: What the Evidence Tells Us." *National Institute of Justice Journal*, No. 280 (December 2018). Retrieved from https://www.nij.gov/journals/280/Pages/body-worn-cameras-what-evidence-tells-us.aspx.

[94]Kindy, Kimberly. "Some U.S. police departments dump body worn camera programs amid high costs." *Washington Post*, January 21, 2019. Retrieved from https://www.washingtonpost.com/national/some-us-police-departments-dump-body-camera-programs-amid-high-costs/2019/01/21/991f0e66-03ad-11e9-b6a9-0aa5c2fcc9e4_story.html?utm_term=.46a72c34cf90.

[95]Justin McCarthy. "Nonwhites Less Likely to Feel Police Protect and Serve Them." *Gallup: Politics*, November 17, 2014.

[96]The concept of the "warrior" versus "guardian" role and mindset has been developed over the last decade. For further information regarding these concepts, please see the works of Radley Balko, "Overkill: The Rise of Paramilitary Raids in America" Unpublished white paper (July 17, 2006); "Rise of the Warrior Cop: Is It Time to Reconsider the militarization of American Policing?" *The Saturday Essay* (August 7, 2013); and *Rise of the Warrior Cop: The Militarization of America's Police Forces* (Jackson, TN: Public Affairs, 2013).

[97]"Will the Growing Militarization of Our Police Doom -Community Policing?" *The e-Newsletter of the COPS Office* 6, No. 12 (December 2013), pp. 1–2; http://cops.usdoj.gov/html/dispatch/12/20/13.

[98]See Mark G. Frank and Thomas Gilovich, "The Dark Side of Self- and Social Perception: Black Uniforms and Aggression in Professional Sports," *Journal of Personality and Social Psychology* 54, No. 1 (1988), pp. 74–85.

[99]See George D. Webster, Geoffrey R. Erland, and Joshua Correll, "Can Uniform Color Color Aggression? Quasi–Experimental Evidence from Professional Ice Hockey,"

Social Psychology and Personality Science 2, No. 3 (May 2011), pp. 306–310; and David F. Caldwell and Jerry M. Burger, "On Thin Ice: Does Uniform Color Really Affect Aggression in Professional Hockey?" *Social Psychology and Personality Science* 3, May 1 (2011), pp. 306–310

[100]Richard R. Johnson, "An Examination of Police Uniform Color and Police-Citizen Aggression," *Criminal Justice and Behavior* 40, No. 2 (2013), pp. 228–244; and Ernest Nickles, "Good Guys Wear Black: Uniform Color and -Citizen Impressions of the Police," *Policing: An International Journal of Police Strategies and Management* 31, No. 1 (March 2008), pp. 77–92.

[101]See Radley Balko, Rise of the Warrior Cop: The Militarization of America's Police Forces (Jackson, TN: Public Affairs, 2013) and Radley Balko, Our Militarized Police Departments: Hearing Before the Subcommittee on Crime, House of Representatives, 110th Cong. (2007) (Testimony of Radley Balko). http://reason.com/archives/2007/07/02/our-militarized-police.

[102]Michael S. Sherry, In the Shadow of War (New Haven, CT: Yale University Press, 1997), p. 309.

[103]President Reagan, June 24, 1982, "Remarks on Signing Executive Order 12368, Concerning Federal Drug Abuse Policy Functions," The American Presidency Project, http://www.presidency.ucsb.edu/ws/index.php?pid=42671%23axzz1P5p1SNqO.

[104]Steve Daley, "Bennett Overwhelmingly Confirmed as Drug Czar," *Chicago Tribune*, March 10, 1989, http://articles.chicagotribune.com/keyword/william-bennett/featured/3.

[105]Douglas Jehl, "Bennett Would Limit Rights in War on Drugs: Says 'Compelling Reasons' Would be Needed; Military Might Be Given a Wider Role in Arrests," *Los Angeles Times*, March 3, 1989, http://articles.latimes.com/1989-03-03/news/mn-238_1_compelling-reason.

[106]Norm Sampler, "Losing the Hearts and Minds in the Drug War." *The Huffington Post*, November 14, 2011, http://www.huffingtonpost.com/norm-stamper/war-on-drugs_b_1088931.html.

[107]International Association of Chiefs of Police and the National Tactical Officers Association, National Special Weapons and Tactics (SWAT) Study: A National Assessment of Critical Trends and Issues from 2009 to 2014 (Alexandria, VA: International Association of Chiefs of Police, 2016), pp. 11 and 18.

[108]Ronald J. Ostrow, "Casual Drug Users Should be Shot, Gates Says," *Los Angeles Times*, September 6, 1990, http://articles.latimes.com/1990-09-06/news/mn-983_1_casual-drug-users.

[109]No author, "Drug Czar Says Beheading Dealers 'Morally Plausible," *Chicago Tribune*, June 16,1989, http://archives.chicagotribune.com/1989/06/16/page/25/article/drug-czar-says-beheading-dealers-morally-plausible.

[110]Howard Kohn, "Cowboy in the Capital: Drug Czar Bill -Bennett," *Rolling Stone*, November 2, 1989, http://www.rollingstone.com/culture/features/cowboy-in-the-capital-drug-czar-bill-bennett-19891102.

[111]Duncan Campbell, "Bush Tars Drug Takers with Aiding Terrorists," *The Guardian*, August 7, 2002, https://www.theguardian.com/world/2002/aug/08/usa.duncancampbell.

[112]Radley Balko, "What Cop T-Shirts Tell Us About Police Culture," *Huffington Post*, June 22, 2013, http://www.huffingtonpost.com/2013/06/21/what-cop-tshirts-tell-us-_n_3479017.html.The information about T-shirts is drawn with restatement from this source and some additions.

[113]*National Law Enforcement Officers Memorial Fund*. See: http://www.nleomf.org/facts/officer-fatalities-data/year.html?referrer=https://www.google.com.

[114]Ibid.

[115]Cynthia Lum and Daniel S. Nagin, "Reinventing American Policing," The Crime Report, June 24, 2015, http://thecrimereport.org/2015/06/24/2015-06-reinventing-american-policing-a-seven-point-blueprin, accessed July 5, 2016.

[116]No author, Recruit Training: "Are We Preparing Officers for a Community Policing Department?" Community Policing Dispatch (The e-newsletter of the Cops Office), Vol. 6, Issue, 6, June 2013, p. 2, http://cops.usdoj.gov/html/dispatch/06-2013/preparing_officers_for_a_community_oriented_department.asp, accessed July 5, 2016.

[117]U.S. Department of Justice, Office of Community Oriented Policing Services, After-Action Assessment of the Police Response to the August 2014 Demonstrations in Ferguson, Missouri (Washington, DC: Office of Community Oriented Police Service, 2015).

[118]Peter B. Kraska, Militarizing the American Criminal Justice System: The Changing Roles of the Armed Forces *and* the Police (Boston, MA: Northeastern University Press, 2001).

[119]Pew Research Center, "Public Trust in Government: 1958-2019" April 11, 2019. See: https://www.people-press.org/2019/04/11/public-trust-in-government-1958-2019/.

[120]Pew Research Center, Where Public Confidence Stands About Eight Groups That Have Positions of Power and Responsibility, September 19, 2019. See: https://www.people-press.org/2019/09/19/where-public-confidence-stands-about-eight-groups-that-have-positions-of-power-and-responsibility.

[121]No author, Final Report of the President's Task Force on 21st Century Policing, May 2015, http://www.cops.usdoj.gov/pdf/taskforce/taskforce_finalreport.pdf, accessed July 5, 2016.

## CHAPTER THREE

INTELLIGENCE, TERRORISM, AND HOMELAND SECURITY

Learning Objectives

1. Define *intelligence*.
2. Describe the Intelligence Cycle as presented in the *National Criminal Intelligence Sharing Plan (NCISP)*.
3. Define a *fusion center* and briefly list its four primary goals.
4. Describe some of the major criticisms aimed at fusion centers and other law enforcement responses to terrorism.
5. List the four primary areas of responsibility within the Department of Homeland Security (DHS).
6. Define *terrorism*.
7. Briefly describe the concept of "jihad" and name some of the more radical Islamic groups active throughout the world.
8. Describe the concept of a "homegrown terrorist."
9. Discuss why Outlaw Motorcycle Gangs (OMGs) are considered an international threat to the United States. Identify the "Big Four" OMGs that are active in the United States.
10. Define a *hate crime*.
11. Define and identify groups that are commonly called *ecoterrorists*.

INTRODUCTION

ON SEPTEMBER 11, 2001, *our world changed forever. For the first time in the past 60 years, America came under attack by an outside and foreign enemy (see Figure 3.1). Our security weaknesses were exploited, our vulnerability was exposed, and our fear became real. For law enforcement and police officers throughout the United States, the attacks on the World Trade Center and the Pentagon posed yet another new challenge to the already difficult task of reducing crime and maintaining order in our communities (revisit Chapters 1 and 2 to refresh your understanding of the changing role of police in America).*

The 9/11 attacks and the ongoing war on terror have demonstrated that terrorism respects no jurisdictional boundaries, whether these attacks take the form of aircraft hijackings, the use of biological agents, or more sophisticated attempts to infiltrate crucial infrastructures. This realization has forced local police administrators to focus considerable attention on the need to improve law enforcement intelligence operations. The notion that state and local law enforcement agencies must enhance their intelligence gathering and analysis capabilities represents a fundamental shift in the strategic dimension of local policing that involves making these agencies "intelligence-led" organizations reminiscent of the military model used for gathering, assessing, and distributing critical information.[1]

While much of the effort to reform intelligence operations after 9/11 focused on the need to restructure and better coordinate the intelligence infrastructure and model at the federal level, there has also been a significant effort to define the role state and local law enforcement agencies play in homeland security.

FIGURE 3.1 ▶ Piloted by a terrorist, the second plane is moments from deliberately crashing into New York City's Twin Towers. The 9/11 events changed our world forever ... as one of the defining moments of the 21st century: A total of 2,752 men, women, and children lost their lives in this horrific terrorist attack. According to former Attorney General John Ashcroft, there is no priority higher than the prevention of terrorism. It is a priority that make demands on our police and law enforcement officers. (SETH MCALLISTER/AFP/Getty Images)

INTELLIGENCE AND TERRORISM

Historically, the missing dimension in quality intelligence has been analysis.[2] The transformation of raw data, whether acquired through human, technical, or open sources, must be collated, scrutinized, and processed accurately and quickly. The ultimate goal of this analytical process is a finished product more intelligible, accurate, and usable than the data and information drawn on to prepare it. Herein is the definition of **intelligence**—data and information that have been evaluated, analyzed, and produced with careful conclusions and recommendations. Intelligence, then, is a *product* created from systematic and thoughtful examination, placed in context, and provided to law enforcement executives, with facts and alternatives that can inform critical decisions.[3]

There are three major perspectives on the purpose of intelligence and analysis. Each voices a different focus on the ability of intelligence officers and agents to provide sound information on which responsible decision making can be based:

1. The first perspective is associated with the writings of Sherman Kent; it holds that the role of intelligence is to limit surprise from national security policymaking.[4] In other words, the analysis of data (or the making of intelligence) should render facts and figures, identify trends and patterns, and provide statistical support on *past* events. There are no follow-up investigations, postaudits, or continued evaluations concerning the policy implemented in response to the data provided. In essence, this type of analysis provides the facts and leaves the decisions to decision makers.

2. In the second perspective, analysts not only should be responsible for providing historical data but also should force policymakers and decision makers to confront alternative views of specific events, potential threats, and/or foreign situations. The emphasis is on connecting the political ends with the course of events. Analysts cannot limit themselves simply to giving situational reports and briefings; they must inherently focus on the dynamics of the political arena in order to give meaning to data. This can be particularly true regarding threats (such as terrorism) from foreign sources, in which state and local police executives may be relatively naïve to the geo-global dimensions of a specific region outside the United States. Most important, analysts need to place intelligence into the relevance and perspective of state and local governments. For instance, increased violence in the West Bank may be of little consequence to rural areas in the United States but much more meaningful to areas outside Detroit, Michigan, where nearly 300,000 Palestinians reside.

3. The final and sharply contrasting perspective concerning the purpose of analysis is somewhat latent. Its emphasis is not on providing past data on which to base decisions or policy; rather, the focus is squarely on the *prediction* of future events. This shift in emphasis can be viewed as an outgrowth of the second perspective as more technological advances have come to pass. With the advent of advanced analytical software and artificial intelligence systems, more robust records management systems, and relatively easy access to huge data banks (see Chapter 2, Policing Today), it should now be possible to provide accurate and reliable predictions concerning specific events.[5] The ultimate goal is twofold: (1) provide accurate information concerning the future in order to avoid decision and policy pitfalls and bureaucratic blunderings and (2) chart out courses of action directly aimed at achieving specific objectives. This, of course, requires a new way of thinking about policing—one that emphasizes prediction and prevention rather than detection and apprehension.

The Intelligence Process and Cycle

The *National Criminal Intelligence Sharing Plan (NCISP),* originally released in 2003 and slightly revised in 2005 and 2012, contained 28 specific recommendations for major changes in local policing.[6] However, the key concept from the document emphasized the strategic integration of intelligence into the overall mission of the police organization—intelligence-led policing (refer to Chapter 2). Rather than react and respond to past calls for service, the NCISP placed much more emphasis on predictive analysis derived from the discovery of hard facts, information, patterns, intelligence, and good crime analysis. By concentrating on key criminal activities, problems, and individuals targeted through analysis, significant attention could be directed to alleviate the crime problem. In order to protect the civil liberties of all individuals, the intelligence process was developed with key evaluation points aimed at verifying source reliability and validity at the beginning of the collection cycle. The goal was to develop a universal process that would integrate both law enforcement and national security intelligence agendas, while providing mechanisms for securing individual freedoms and allowing law enforcement agencies to be proactive in preventing and deterring crime and terrorism. The end result was the "Intelligence Cycle," presented by the FBI in an effort to bring varied pieces of information together in an effort to draw logical conclusions from a thorough and systematic process (see Figure 3.2). As important, the Intelligence Cycle also provides a means of communicating and sharing intelligence among individuals and agencies through the dissemination process.

Fusion Centers

The transformation of local police agencies into intelligence-led organizations involves four key objectives: (1) the creation of a task and coordination process, (2) the development of core intelligence products to lead the operation, (3) the establishment

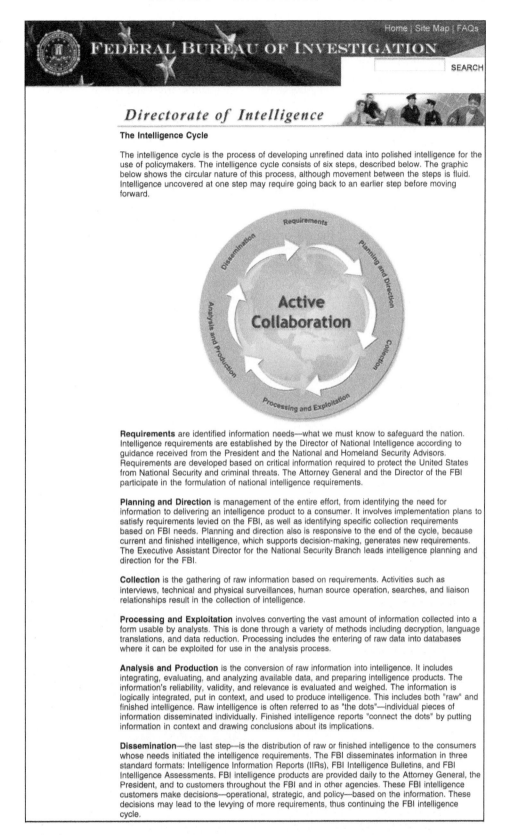

FEDERAL BUREAU OF INVESTIGATION

SEARCH

Directorate of Intelligence

The Intelligence Cycle

The intelligence cycle is the process of developing unrefined data into polished intelligence for the use of policymakers. The intelligence cycle consists of six steps, described below. The graphic below shows the circular nature of this process, although movement between the steps is fluid. Intelligence uncovered at one step may require going back to an earlier step before moving forward.

Active Collaboration

Requirements
Planning and Direction
Collection
Processing and Exploitation
Analysis and Production
Dissemination

Requirements are identified information needs—what we must know to safeguard the nation. Intelligence requirements are established by the Director of National Intelligence according to guidance received from the President and the National and Homeland Security Advisors. Requirements are developed based on critical information required to protect the United States from National Security and criminal threats. The Attorney General and the Director of the FBI participate in the formulation of national intelligence requirements.

Planning and Direction is management of the entire effort, from identifying the need for information to delivering an intelligence product to a consumer. It involves implementation plans to satisfy requirements levied on the FBI, as well as identifying specific collection requirements based on FBI needs. Planning and direction also is responsive to the end of the cycle, because current and finished intelligence, which supports decision-making, generates new requirements. The Executive Assistant Director for the National Security Branch leads intelligence planning and direction for the FBI.

Collection is the gathering of raw information based on requirements. Activities such as interviews, technical and physical surveillances, human source operation, searches, and liaison relationships result in the collection of intelligence.

Processing and Exploitation involves converting the vast amount of information collected into a form usable by analysts. This is done through a variety of methods including decryption, language translations, and data reduction. Processing includes the entering of raw data into databases where it can be exploited for use in the analysis process.

Analysis and Production is the conversion of raw information into intelligence. It includes integrating, evaluating, and analyzing available data, and preparing intelligence products. The information's reliability, validity, and relevance is evaluated and weighed. The information is logically integrated, put in context, and used to produce intelligence. This includes both "raw" and finished intelligence. Raw intelligence is often referred to as "the dots"—individual pieces of information disseminated individually. Finished intelligence reports "connect the dots" by putting information in context and drawing conclusions about its implications.

Dissemination—the last step—is the distribution of raw or finished intelligence to the consumers whose needs initiated the intelligence requirements. The FBI disseminates information in three standard formats: Intelligence Information Reports (IIRs), FBI Intelligence Bulletins, and FBI Intelligence Assessments. FBI intelligence products are provided daily to the Attorney General, the President, and to customers throughout the FBI and in other agencies. These FBI intelligence customers make decisions—operational, strategic, and policy—based on the information. These decisions may lead to the levying of more requirements, thus continuing the FBI intelligence cycle.

FIGURE 3.2 ▶ The intelligence cycle. (Courtesy of Federal Bureau of Investigation)

of standardized training practices, and (4) the development of protocols to facilitate intelligence capabilities. This approach is intended to improve the capability of local law enforcement in regard to responding to terror threats and traditional anticrime efforts. Intelligence-led policing blends community partnerships with crime fighting and police accountability in an effort to maximize police efficiency and effectiveness in terrorism prevention and crime reduction. There is evidence to suggest that this initiative has started to alter the face of traditional policing in the United States. A national survey found that a majority of responding local and state police agencies have conducted terrorism threat assessments since 9/11, and about one-third of these agencies have collaborated with the FBI's joint terrorism task force to assist in local crime investigations.[7] The movement to integrate information and develop an overarching process of managing the flow of information and intelligence across all levels and sectors of government and private security has been the impetus to create **fusion centers** (see Figure 3.3) inside local and state police agencies. Fusion centers act as effective and efficient mechanisms for exchanging information and intelligence, maximizing police resources, streamlining public safety operations, and improving the ability to fight crime and terrorism by merging data from a variety of sources.[8] Fusion centers serve as clearinghouses for all potentially relevant homeland security information that can be used to assess local terror threats and aid in the apprehension of more traditional criminal suspects.

Originally launched in New York City under the direction of then police commissioner Raymond Kelly in 2002, the concept of a fusion center blended the power of information technology with terrorism prevention and crime fighting. With a price tag exceeding $11 million, the Real Time Crime Center (RTCC) in New York City combs through tens of millions of criminal complaints, arrest and parole records, and 911 call records dating back a decade in an effort to provide NYPD officers with the information tools necessary to stop a terrorist event or investigate a crime.[9] Fusion centers distribute relevant, actionable, and timely information and intelligence, incorporating a simultaneously vertical (i.e., federal, state, and local) and horizontal (i.e., within the agency, with other local agencies, and across disciplines such as fire, EMS, public works, and private partners) approach within a given jurisdiction. Fusion centers are composed of talented and trained individuals using sophisticated application software in crime analysis and mapping to manage and manipulate information and intelligence into a usable product. The resulting analysis acts as a basis for the deployment of police resources and directed operations in a real-time format—that is, almost immediately. The fusion center not only acts as a centralized host for intelligence information and analysis but also serves as a conduit for disseminating critical information to other regional, state, and national authorities. This is a particularly important point that fulfills the NCISP in protecting the homeland. Both large and small, as well as local, state, tribal, and federal law enforcement agencies are encouraged to work toward the systematic sharing of intelligence information relating to criminal and terrorist threats. See Figure 3.4.

FIGURE 3.3 ▶ Fusion centers are high-tech, information-intensive operational centers that analyze and disseminate intelligence relating to terrorism and crime to police officers on the street. (Raad Adayleh/AP Images)

FIGURE 3.4 ▶ Ten simple steps that assist individual police agencies become part of the National Criminal Intelligence Sharing Plan. *Source:* https://it.ojp.gov/gist/100/10-Simple-Steps-to-Help-Your-Agency-Become-a-Part-of-the-National-Criminal-Intelligence-Sharing-Plan, Criminal Intelligence Coordinating Council, updated 2019.

1. **Recognize your responsibilities and lead by example**

   Recognize the value of sharing intelligence information within your own agency, and encourage the practice of sharing information with other law enforcement and public safety agencies. Use the guidelines and action steps outlined in the National Criminal Intelligence Sharing Plan ("Plan") to implement or enhance your organization's intelligence function.

2. **Establish a mission statement and a policy to address developing and sharing information and intelligence data within your agency**

   The Plan provides model policies and guidelines for implementing or reviewing an agency's intelligence function. Examples include Criminal Intelligence Systems Operating Policies federal regulation 28 CFR Part 23, the International Association of Chiefs of Police's Criminal Intelligence Model Policy, and the Law Enforcement Intelligence Unit's (LEIU) Criminal Intelligence File Guidelines.

3. **Connect to your state criminal justice network and regional intelligence databases, and participate in information sharing initiatives**

   Many states provide access to other government databases, including motor vehicles, corrections, and others. Regional intelligence databases and sharing initiatives promote communication and collaboration by providing access to other agencies' and organizations' investigative and intelligence data.

4. **Ensure privacy issues are protected in policy and practice**

   The protection of individuals' privacy and constitutional rights is an obligation of government officials and is crucial to the long-term success of criminal intelligence sharing. The Plan provides guidelines that support policies that will protect privacy and constitutional rights while not hindering the intelligence process. Implementing and supporting privacy policies and practices within your agency will also reduce your organization's liability concerns.

5. **Access law enforcement websites, subscribe to law enforcement listservs, and use the Internet as an information resource**

   Many websites on the Internet and others on closed networks provide valuable intelligence assessments and news. Listservs provide instant and widespread communication for investigators.

   Listservs allow both the receipt and distribution of intelligence information. The Internet provides a wealth of opensource information, including government information and access to private agencies that share with law enforcement.

6. **Provide your agency members with appropriate training on the criminal intelligence process**

   Some training models or modules are already found in Internet-based and interactive CDs, such as the International Association of Law Enforcement Intelligence Analysts (IALEIA), National White Collar Crime Center, and LEIU "Turn Key Intelligence." A listing of available intelligence training sources and specifically scheduled classes is found on the IALEIA website: www.ialeia.org. This listing allows individuals to directly contact training source agencies and organizations for more information on classes and schedules.

7. **Become a member of your in-region Regional Information Sharing Systems® (RISS) center**

   RISS operates the only secure web-based nationwide network for communication and exchange of criminal intelligence information by local, state, federal, and tribal participating law enforcement member agencies. RISS partners with other law enforcement systems to electronically connect them to RISSNETTM, including High Intensity Drug Trafficking Areas (HIDTA) Investigative Support centers and other federal and state agency systems.

8. **Become a member of the Federal Bureau of Investigation's (FBI) Law Enforcement Online (LEO) system**

   The FBI's LEO system is a sensitive but unclassified, real-time information sharing communications system for all levels of the law enforcement community and is available at no cost to its users. LEO provides secure e-mail capability, a national alert mechanism, and access to over 125 special-interest groups for sharing information by providing access to other networks, systems, databases, and other services.

9. **Partner with public and private infrastructure sectors**

   Regular communication with the entities that control America's critical infrastructures, such as energy, agriculture, transportation, and shipping, is critically important to ensuring the safety and security of the citizens in your community.

10. **Participate in local, state, and national intelligence organizations**

    In most areas of the country, there are locally based intelligence organizations that welcome participation from all agencies and are often affiliated with state and national organizations.

Box 3.1: Types of Fusion Centers

There are two types of fusion centers:

- **Primary Fusion Centers:** A primary fusion center typically provides information sharing and analysis for an entire state. These centers are the highest priority for the allocation of available federal resources, including the deployment of personnel and connectivity with federal data systems.

- **Recognized Fusion Centers:** A recognized fusion center typically provides information sharing and analysis for a

major urban area. As the Federal Government respects the authority of state governments to designate fusion centers, any designated fusion center not designated as a primary fusion center is referred to as a recognized fusion center.

Source: Courtesy Department of Homeland Security, Fusion Center Locations and Contact Information (DHS: Washington, D.C. December 27, 2019), https://www.dhs.gov/fusion-center-locations-and-contact-information, accessed January 20, 2019.

Almost every state and several large metropolitan cities have undertaken the development of fusion centers with significant funding assistance from the Department of Homeland Security. For instance, the Chicago Police Department Deployment Operations Center (DOC) was one of the first centers to combine real-time intelligence analysis with the deployment process. In Los Angeles, both the city and the county have well-developed fusion centers, and in Dallas, Texas, the Metropolitan Operations and Analytical Intelligence Center (MOSAIC) provides real-time tactical information to officers on the street 24/7.

The goals of a fusion center are fourfold:

1. Fusion centers support the broad range of activities undertaken by a police department relating to the detection, examination, and investigation of a potential terrorist and/or criminal activity. Ideally, the center serves as a hub of antiterrorist and anticrime operations in a specific region, focusing on the recognition of patterns, indications and warnings, source development, interdiction, and the coordination of critical criminal justice resources. These are critical activities for any police agency attempting to be proactive and intelligence-led to be successful in deterring, detecting, disrupting, investigating, and apprehending suspects involved in terrorist and criminal activity directly related to homeland security. As important, in 2018, both Fusion Center Directors from across the country and the federal government identified the protection of privacy, civil rights, and civil liberties (P/CRCL) as a key priority for all fusion centers.[10] Figure 3.5 represents one of several information technology solutions that are commonly used in fusion centers to help identify patterns and indicators associated with terrorism and/or crime.

2. Fusion centers support operations that protect **critical infrastructure and key resources (CI/KRs)** in a given region, support major incident operations, support specialized units charged with interdiction and investigative operations, and assist in emergency operations and planning. The aim of a fusion center is to reduce the vulnerability of the high-value and high-risk targets identified within a jurisdiction. For example,

in any major city, there are several important CI/KRs—bank buildings, corporate headquarters, bridges and overpasses, water supply tanks and systems, electronic switching hubs, rail and subway stations, and a myriad of other important infrastructure entities. Fusion centers maintain huge databases that are immediately retrievable for use in thwarting an attack or dealing with an emergency. For instance, the Los Angeles Police Department has implemented the "Archangel Project," aimed at developing a large database for all CI/KRs in the region. Its primary purpose is to maintain as much accessible and critical data as possible on any one given piece of critical infrastructure, so that during an emergency or a potentially threatening event, police resources can be directed appropriately. Hence, building schematics and event histories, alternative road and highway routes, and maps of water supply mains, electrical grids, switching stations, and the like are maintained and accessible within the fusion center. Fusion centers are **all-hazard** in scope—that is, they are developed to support operations during an emergency that is either human-made, such as a terrorist event, or natural, such as a hurricane, flood, or tornado.

3. Fusion centers often maintain public "tip lines," which give them the capability to promote more public involvement in and awareness of terrorist threats. The goal is to identify and recognize warning signs and potential threats in a timely manner in order to preempt potential terrorist attacks and reduce the vulnerability of the CI/KRs in a given region. Fusion centers accomplish this task on a daily basis, focusing on the analysis of crimes that are often linked to terrorist cells and activity for funding, such as narcotics trafficking, credit card abuse, armament and gun theft, prostitution, and human trafficking, by distributing information relating to these linkages to all agencies within a given region. The timeliness of gathering, analyzing, and disseminating information is vital to successfully preventing acts of violence and threats to homeland security.

FIGURE 3.5 ▶ IBM i2 ANB (**A**nalyst **N**ote **B**ook) is a stand-alone, desktop tool for intelligence and data analysis, representing state-of-the-art data analytics in crime and intelligence analysis. *IBM iBase IntelliShare Software* enables multiple web-based users to analyze data in a central repository. Further, individual dashboards can be created to reveal a number of widgets and windows that provide single and unified views of intelligence data. Such intelligence tools can be used in a wide range of investigations, including the following:

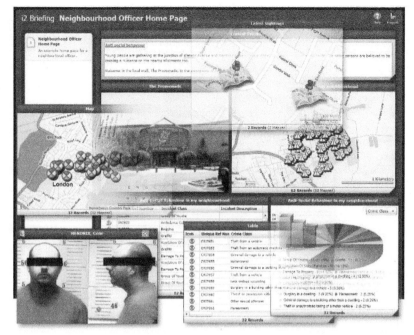

- Counterterrorism
- Drug Trafficking
- Money Laundering
- Securities Fraud
- Insurance Fraud
- Forensic Accounting
- Major Incident Management
- Immigration Violations and Human Trafficking
- Identity Theft
- Threat Assessment and Emergency Management

Application Programs

Since 1990, i2 Corporation has been a worldwide leader of visual investigative analysis software for law enforcement, intelligence, military, and Fortune 500 organizations. The application software performs an array of sophisticated analytical techniques, including social network analysis, commodity flow, telephone record analysis, link analysis, and the like, often used in real-time fusion centers to convey analytical findings in intuitive charts that organize support data. i2 is part of IBM and has developed a number of new analytic tools for intelligence analysis and sharing, such as the IntelliShare dashboard described here. © Copyright IBM Corporation 1994, 2020.

4. Fusion centers assist police executives in making better-informed decisions, especially during emergencies or critical incidents. Fusion centers are ongoing deployment operations centers with the real-time ability to monitor critical resources. This includes real-time status monitoring of major events, communicating with area medical facilities and trauma units, coordinating the allocation and deployment of multi-agency personnel resources (including military reserve units), monitoring changing weather conditions, and directing all support services through a centralized operations center.

Fusion centers embody the core of collaboration between agencies in law enforcement, as well as members of private security and the general public. The National Governors Associated Center for Best Practices revealed that states ranked the development of intelligence fusion centers as one of their highest priorities in reducing crime and preventing terrorism in the homeland.[11]

The National Fusion Center Association (NFCA) and the National Counterterrorism Center (NCTC)

As of 2019, there were 79 state and major urban fusion centers within the United States.[12] Almost every state has a statewide fusion center, as well as most major urban areas. The National Fusion Center Association (NFCA) is a formal group that represents the interest of state and local urban area fusion centers nationally. In addition, the NFCA promotes the development and sustainment of fusion centers to enhance public safety, the ethical and lawful collection of intelligence gathering, analysis, and dissemination.[13] The goal of the NFCA is to prevent the next terrorist attack on the homeland. To this end, the **Homeland Security Data Network (HSDN)** allows the federal government to move information and intelligence to the states at the "secret" level, thereby allowing the quick exchange of critical data and information pertaining to an immediate terrorist threat within any jurisdiction of the United States. Through HSDN, fusion center staff can access the **National Counterterrorism Center (NCTC)** via a secure and classified portal to the most current terrorism-related information. The NCTC acts as the nations "hub" for intelligence activity both domestically and internationally, coordinating intelligence information derived by individual members of the intelligence community. It also serves as the single point for the strategic and operational planning of counterterrorism activity. See Figure 3.6. This is often accomplished through interagency meetings and secure teleconferences about terrorist groups, capabilities, plans and intentions, and emerging threats to U.S. interests. The NCTC is located in Washington, DC, and is part of the Office of the Director of National Intelligence. One of the most important duties of the center is to maintain

Box 3.2: National Counterterrorism Center (NCTC): Predicting the Next Terrorist Strike Using Mobilization Indicators

One of the primary duties of the National Counterterrorism Center (NCTC) is to provide ongoing intelligence and warning relating to a potential terrorist strikes on the homeland. In 2019, in collaboration with the FBI and the Department of Homeland Security, the NCTC developed a handbook that outlined mobilization indicators and risk factors that increase the likelihood of a terrorist attack by an individual homegrown violent extremist or group. The booklet provides a list of nearly fifty observable indicators compiled by subject matter experts that assess the potential for a terrorist strike. The first six of these indicators are most important and highly diagnostic:

- An individual or group that prepares and disseminates a martyrdom video/statement, last will or final statement.
- An individual or group that seeks religious or political justification for a planned violent act.
- An individual or group that attempt to mobilize others to violence, especially family members and/or peers.
- An individual or group that seeks help from family, peers, or authority figures to enable travel to join a terrorist group overseas.
- An individual or group that prepares to travel to fight with or support a known terrorist group.
- An individual or group that communicates their intent to engage in violent extremist activity; a threat with justification for action, such as a social media post, tweet, hashtag or website manifesto.

The NCTC stresses the importance of considering these indicators in the totality of the circumstances; some factors my increase the risk of terrorist violence much more than others, dependent upon the individual or group's social awareness and acceptance, access and familiarity with weapons and/or explosives, and past history of violence.

Source: National Counterterrorism Center (NCTC), *Mobilization Indicators*, 2019. See https://www.dni.gov/files/NCTC/documents/news_documents/NCTC-FBI-DHS-HVE-Mobilization-Indicators-Booklet-2019.pdf and https://www.dni.gov/index.php/nctc-home.

---

the national repository of known and suspected terrorists and provide assessments to potential threats by these individuals.[14]

Clearly, the 9/11 attacks and the impact of terrorism on our country have transformed the role of the police in our communities. We have witnessed an unprecedented movement on the part of the federal government to employ local, tribal, and state police agencies into the counterterrorism mission. Police executives need to recognize that this trend will not wane in the future, but that the public as well as federal officials will increasingly expect local police to take a broader and more important role in safeguarding their communities against terrorists.[15]

Policing Terrorism

According to policing scholar George Kelling and former NYPD Commissioner Bill Bratton, cities must create a hostile environment for terrorists by instilling effective intelligence gathering and analysis into the everyday workings of local police departments.[16] Additionally, Mathieu Deflem's work on the policing of terrorism emphasized the prevention and response to terrorism as an issue of crime control for every police department and suggests the development of professional standards for investigating terrorist incidents as a crime methodology, rather than singularly a counterterrorism effort.[17] This theme is certainly reinforced by federal authorities as presented in the late 2008 report presented by the U.S. Department of Justice, Office of Community Oriented Policing Services, acting as a police chief's guide to policing terrorism.[18] Central to this document and the mission of policing

in preventing terrorism and reducing crime must be the systematic collection, analysis, and sharing of intelligence information between agencies. Several important steps for any local police department to consider in developing its intelligence collection methodology and enhancing its role to prevent terrorism are echoed earlier in Figure 3.4 and include the following:

- Create an intelligence unit that focuses on counterterrorism and/or appoint a terrorist liaison officer.
- Send officers for training in intelligence gathering, analysis, and sharing. Know the legal and privacy issues surrounding police use of intelligence information.
- Join the local Joint Terrorism Task Force (JTTF) sponsored by the FBI field office in the local jurisdiction. Depending on the size of the department, this may not always be feasible or cost-effective since the FBI provides pay for only overtime and equipment; officer salaries are continued by the home department. Therefore, smaller agencies may wish to only designate an officer to coordinate information between the department and the nearest task force.
- Develop an information-sharing environment between agencies of law enforcement within and across jurisdictions. Implement fusion centers when appropriate to analyze and funnel terrorist information to appropriate authorities.
- Participate in the National SAR Initiative (NSI), which is focused on developing and using the Suspicious Activity Reporting System (SARS). In accordance with

FIGURE 3.6 ▶ The National Counterterrorism Center (NCTC) serves as the primary organization in the U.S. government for integrating and analyzing intelligence relating to terrorism. https://www.fbi.gov/about/partnerships

the National Criminal Intelligence Sharing Plan and the National Strategy for Information Sharing (NSIS), developed within the U.S. Department of Justice, this system promotes an Information Sharing Environment (ISE) important to establishing the timely sharing of SAR information with law enforcement agencies, fusion centers, and the JTTF[19] (see Figure 3.7).

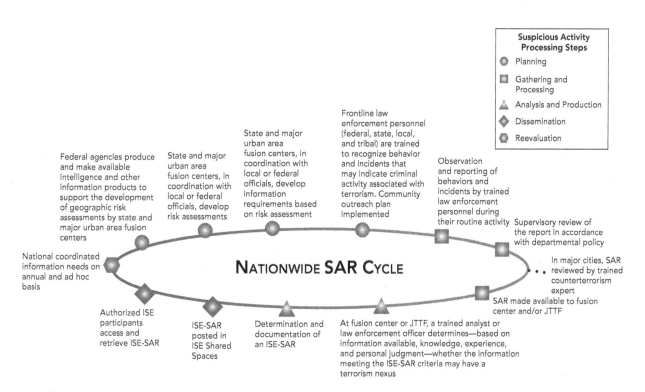

FIGURE 3.7 ▶ The SAR cycle chart. This diagram focuses on activities of local, state, and tribal agencies. By following these steps, agencies can be assured that their SAR activities are in alignment with and can support crucial information sharing. This diagram will also help identify gaps in an agency's current process that may need to be addressed and/or corrected. (Suspicious Activity Reporting: Process Implementation Checklist, p. 4. See http://it.ojp.gov/docdownloader.aspx?ddid=1147)

- Promote intelligence-led policing and implement community policing efforts with immigrant communities, especially immigrant Muslim communities.

Criticisms Aimed at Fusion Centers and Other Law Enforcement Responses to Terrorism

As with any new direction, there have certainly been setbacks and problems that have plagued not only the development and transition of the Department of Homeland Security but also befuddled the government's response to terrorism. For instance, there continue to be problems relating to the sharing of information between local law enforcement and the FBI. A 2010 assessment of state and local fusion centers conducted by the U.S. Department of Homeland Security revealed widespread deficiencies in the centers' basic counterterrorism information-sharing capabilities.[20] Especially noted in the study was the need to improve the coordination of federal communication and collaboration within and between fusion centers. One local fusion center director noted that information flow appears to be one way—from the local agency to the FBI.[21]

Fusion centers have also not been without their detractors. Monahan and Palmer note, after an exhausting and comprehensive analysis from 2002 to 2008, that three primary concerns continue to plague these information and intelligence hubs.[22] First, fusion centers are expensive and almost any cost-benefit analysis will reveal significant money spent for very little, tangible evidence of success. The effectiveness of fusion centers, particularly given their financial outlay, is seriously questioned. Few terrorist incidents have actually been prevented due to the work of fusion centers. Second, many fusion centers appear to suffer from "mission creep"; that is, because there are few cases focused on terrorism, many centers have expanded their role to include crime fighting and reduction. According to Monahan and Palmer, the expansion of fusion centers into this mission is well beyond the initial intention of funding "all-hazard" centers for the coordination of intelligence and information to prevent terrorism. And finally, fusion centers come desperately close to violating the civil liberties of people, especially relating to racial and ethnic profiling and breaches of privacy. The American Civil Liberties Union (ACLU) has also highlighted possible privacy and individual infringements stemming from fusion centers.[23]

Fusion centers have access to an enormous amount of personal information regarding individuals. Data banks involving criminal and arrest records, financial records, civil litigation, credit reports, water bills, and even Internet sites such as Facebook and MySpace are now available to police personnel. Quoting a spotty historical past by police relating to intelligence gathering and analysis, the ACLU suggests a number of major changes:

1. **Eliminate ambiguous lines of authority**—In many cases, there appears to be a blurred line between the federal government and individual states or local agencies housing fusion centers. There simply is not a clear portrait of who is actually in charge of fusion centers. Although individual fusion centers were developed by state and local governments, the federal government provided much of the original funding and dispatches its own intelligence analysts and agents to work alongside state/local officials. Most state/local agencies cannot access classified information, and, hence, must rely on the DHS employee or the FBI to provide this intelligence.

2. **Eliminate private sector involvement in the fusion process**—Private sector participation in fusion centers is designed to encourage a number of public safety, transportation, social service, and private sector entities to join together in the fusion process. Because one of the goals of fusion centers is to protect the nation's critical infrastructure—85 percent of which is owned by private interests—fusion centers are strongly encouraged to seek information from "nontraditional sources" (e.g., private corporations, hospitals, and transportation companies). Allowing private sector corporations access to classified materials and other sensitive law enforcement information may violate individual Constitutional and personal rights. Police and law enforcement entities undergo rigorous training, are sworn to objectively serve their community, and are paid through public salaries, whereas private companies and their employees are motivated to maximize profits. In short, the availability for personal information to be shared between public and private officials, for the sake of forging public and private partnerships, may be a violation of individual rights to privacy guaranteed by our Constitution.

3. **Eliminate military participation in the fusion process**—The Posse Comitatus Act of 1878 clearly prohibits the U.S. military from acting in a law enforcement capacity on American soil, except under express authority from Congress. Hence, fusion centers should be prohibited from using active-duty military personnel. However, many fusion centers incorporate the National Guard and the Coast Guard and are a bridge between military and civilian intelligence centers. At least one center in North Dakota is actually located within National Guard facilities. The ACLU argues that military personnel operating in a law enforcement capacity (fusion centers) would erode not only the Posse Comitatus Act but also reduce the Constitutional barriers between the military and American citizenry.

4. **Eliminate illegal data mining in the fusion process**—Data fusion can lead to illegal data mining, that is, accessing private sector databases that are not controlled or authenticated. This action clearly jeopardizes an individual's Constitutional right to privacy, as well as subjects the individual to unwarranted scrutiny by the police *without* probable cause. Intelligence gathering and fusion center processes include anticipating, identifying, monitoring, and preventing future criminal and terrorist activities without probable cause. How police agencies focus on one group versus another, and who becomes the target of an investigation, are key questions concerning this issue.

5. **Eliminate excessive secrecy**—A fusion center's ability to gather vast amounts of personal information on individuals, with very little oversight, not only undercuts the function and purpose of the intelligence process but also increases the danger that incompetence and malfeasance will flourish. Fusion centers must be held accountable and transparent to public scrutiny.

Clearly, the power struggle between federal and state/local agencies continues today. Despite the lessons learned from 9/11, there are still major issues in this area. Further, while over a half a billion dollars have been spent to improve the nation's ability to thwart terrorist attacks, the Congressional Research Service (CRS) Reports for Congress indicates that fusion centers are ineffective and continue to suffer from lack of interoperability and a host of political power issues between government levels.[24] The CRS reports that while fusion centers were primarily designed to "fuse" federal, state, and local intelligence regarding potential terrorist attacks, they have gravitated more toward collecting and analyzing information on criminals and offenders in local regions—precisely the concern of the ACLU. The CRS document supports the ACLU stance that fusion centers pose significant risks of civil liberty and privacy incursion. Most revealing of the criticism against fusion centers was a 2012 report by the U.S.

Senate Permanent Subcommittee on Investigations.[25] The subcommittee found that the quality of intelligence information forwarded by many fusion centers was "oftentimes shoddy, rarely timely, sometimes endangering citizens' civil liberties and Privacy Act protections" and often taken from previously published public sources.[26] Most damaging was the finding that many times, the "intelligence" was not even related to terrorism and that DHS was unable to provide an accurate amount as to how much it had granted to states and cities in support of fusion center efforts. Instead, it provided a range from $289 million to $1.4 billion, without any details regarding a cost-benefit analysis or study on efficiency and effectiveness.[27] Fusion centers can serve a significant purpose in detecting and investigating terrorists, but their current practices are in need of constant monitoring and supervision. And, the public is certainly entitled to an accounting of federal dollars spent on the development of fusion centers with an honest evaluation of the effectiveness of such entities.

The USA Freedom Act was designed to end bulk surveillance on metadata derived from telephone records and other sources relating to American companies and individuals. Specifically, the act prohibits the government from collecting such data generated by communications providers. The government can only access such data with approval by the FISA court.

Box 3.3: USA Freedom Act: High-Tech Companies vs. the U.S. Government

After 9/11, Congress quickly passed the USA PATRIOT Act that provided new tools to assist law enforcement in securing the country against terrorist attacks. The PATRIOT Act expanded the traditional methodologies of surveillance used by law enforcement and intelligence agencies with significantly reduced checks and balances relating to record searches, wiretaps, search warrants, pen trap and trace orders, and court orders. However, in 2015, a major shift signaling a significant change in American attitudes toward safeguarding civil liberty versus the nation was marked by the expiration of parts of the PATRIOT Act, and the development of new laws curtailing international and domestic intelligence agencies like the Central Intelligence Agency (CIA), the National Security Agency (NSA), and the Federal Bureau of Investigation (FBI). Sparked by a former NSA contractor in 2014, Edward Snowden revealed the presence of a powerful national intelligence apparatus involving the collection of phone and computer records (metadata) from almost every large communications provider in the country. Worse yet, federal bureaucrats denied the existence of the apparatus in Congressional Hearings in 2014–2015.

A new bill, known as the USA Freedom Act, was signed by then-President Obama on June 2, 2015, that strengthened civil liberty safeguards and allowed three key provisions of the PATRIOT Act to expire: (1) The NSA (or any other agency) could no longer collect newly created logs of Americans' phone calls in bulk; (2) The FBI could no longer be able to invoke the PATRIOT Act to obtain new investigations or new wiretaps on potential suspects without affiliation or linkage to a known terrorist group; and (3) the

FBI could no longer be required to obtain a court order to obtain business records relevant to a terrorist organization. The new law represented some of the most significant surveillance reforms in decades in the United States and came on the heels of information technology companies like Apple and Microsoft that provided new personal security tools for customers that could prevent "snooping" from both the government and the Internet Service Provider itself. The Patriot Act had a sunset provision, which would have allowed all of its remaining provisions to "die" on December 15, 2019 without any official action. However, in November 2019, the House and Senate passed a short-term funding resolution to keep the federal government operating. Buried in this resolution was a provision that extended some portions of the Patriot Act into 2020. It is likely to receive further legislative attention during 2020.[28] The conflict between big high-tech companies and the government continued into early 2016, as a U.S. magistrate ordered Apple to produce software that would give FBI agents the ability to access data stored within the new iPhone. Specifically, agents wished to access the data on Syed Rizwan Farook's iPhone, a U.S. citizen accused of killing 14 people at a holiday party in San Bernardino, California on December 2, 2015. Agents were interested in viewing potential e-mails from members of terrorist organizations (e.g., ISIS, al-Qaeda) in the Middle East with Farook, as well as Farook's conversations on an online dating site in which Farook met his wife, Tashfeen Malik, an accomplice in the San Bernardino massacre. Farook and Malik were both killed in a shoot-out with police after the attack.

HOMELAND SECURITY

In November 2002, President George W. Bush ushered in the largest federal bureaucratic reorganization in 55 years to create the cabinet-level Department of Homeland Security (DHS). Headed by the former governor of Pennsylvania, Tom Ridge, the new department focused the antiterrorism effort in the United States, absorbing many of the enforcement agencies within the Departments of Treasury and Transportation (Transportation Security Administration; U.S. Coast Guard; U.S. Customs; Bureau of Alcohol, Tobacco, and Firearms; U.S. Secret Service; and Federal Emergency Management Administration [FEMA]). In addition, the department created a division to analyze intelligence gathered by the FBI, CIA, and other police and military agencies. There are four primary areas of responsibility within the Department of Homeland Security:

- Border security and transportation
- Emergency preparedness and response
- Chemical, biological, radiological, and nuclear countermeasures
- Intelligence analysis and infrastructure protection

The building of the department has been slow, with a variety of changes and setbacks coming from changes in leadership, violations of ethical behavior, and severe criticism stemming from poor agency responses to several national emergencies. For instance, FEMA's lackluster response to the city of New Orleans during Hurricane Katrina in 2005 was eclipsed in 2010 with, again, a very slow and poor response to the largest oil leak in U.S. history crippling the Gulf Coast of Louisiana (British Petroleum's Deep Horizon oil rig explosion and resulting oil spill). In 2012 and again in 2015, the U.S. Secret Service was rocked by scandals involving agents that were drinking heavily and engaging with prostitutes and strippers overseas prior to official duty in safeguarding the President.[29] The head of the Transportation Security Agency (TSA) was reassigned after it failed 95 percent of its security tests at several dozen busy airports, including failing to detect guns and other contraband.[30]

Homeland Security and Recent Presidential Directives

On January 20, 2009, Senator Barack Obama from the state of Illinois was sworn in as the 44th President of the United States. One of his first duties was to appoint then-Governor of Arizona, Janet Napolitano, as the third Secretary of the Department of Homeland Security. Napolitano had received praise in her role as governor in the areas of terrorism and immigration reform.[31] As then-Secretary of the Department of Homeland Security, Napolitano played an integral role in bolstering border security by increasing forces along the border, and, in addition, increasing resources and technology to aid in the fight against terrorism.

With the election of Donald J. Trump to the White House in 2016, immigration reform and securing the southern border of the United States have become a centerpiece of his presidency. Eliminating loopholes in the immigration system and moving the country to a merit-based entry process for those that would like to live in the United States have become controversial issues across the country. President Trump was committed to improving the security of the country by constructing a border wall and removing unlawful immigrants already residing in the United States. With the election of President Joe Biden in November 2020, border security may diminish in importance as the country continues to address COVID-19 responses, racial tensions, and growing economic issues confronting the country.[32]

The Department of Homeland Security is the third-largest department and has the ninth-largest budget in the federal government, boasting over 240,000 employees and a total budget authority that exceeds $90 billion (FY 2020), with an additional $17 billion earmarked for grants aimed at funding antiterror and border security initiatives at the state and local levels (see Figure 3.8). Much of this money will be provided to local and state law enforcement agencies for the development of programs that address one of the four primary responsibilities of DHS.

Beyond the ultimate mission of ensuring the nation's safety and preventing terrorism, DHS is responsible for immigration policy, airport security, and the protection of the president.

Box 3.4: Crisis in Removing Unlawful Immigrants

Triggered by a change in national policy, the U.S. Customs and Border Protection (CBP) began separating parents and children who sought asylum in the United States in 2018. Many of families were fleeing from violent and oppressive countries. At least 2,648 children including infants and toddlers were taken from their parents. Some children were held for more than a year. Mental health concluded greater damage was done to the separated children than previously thought. Although under court order to reunite all families, at least 30 children are still detained because the location of their already deported parents is unknown. The conditions are appalling as well. At a Customs and Border Protection (CBP) facility in McAllen, the children sleep on mats on the floor. For warmth, they slip under silver colored Mylar blankets (so-called space blankets) designed years ago by the National Aeronautics and Space Administration (NASA). (Photograph courtesy of U.S. Customs and Border Protection).

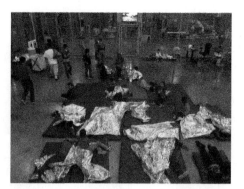

Source: Staff Report prepared for Chairman Elijah E. Cummings, Committee on Oversight and Reform U.S. House of Representatives, July 29, 2019, pp. 1–2. (Courtesy CBP/Handout/Reuters)

POLITICAL VIOLENCE AND TERRORISM

The events of 9/11 and continuing incidents of mass violence in America have had a profound impact on federal, state, and local law enforcement agencies, as police administrators are confronted with the most pressing and significant external issue of their careers: how to investigate, interdict, and prevent terrorism. Police departments around the country have had to address new threats of violence that are sometimes the result of federal actions or international foreign policy actions in which they have no authority. For instance, since 9/11, virtually every large metropolitan police department has been placed on the highest alert. Operational demands required police agencies to perform new activities, including increasing infrastructure security around critical buildings and airports, building antiterrorism barriers, beefing up intelligence gathering and analysis functions, monitoring activity in Middle Eastern communities, and participating in joint terrorism task forces. Even though an extensive federal structure has been developed to counter the terrorist threat, the first level of prevention (and response) remains with uniformed police officers on the street.

Defining Terrorism

In the popular mind, terrorism is viewed as the illegitimate and violent actions of specific groups that violate the authority of rightfully established governments. **Terrorism** encompasses the threat of and/or use of violence to achieve a specific set of political objectives or goals.[33] Historically, defining terrorism has been a very difficult venture, shaped and altered by a number of factors, including our own national interests, government interpretations, the news media, hidden political agendas, and emotional human rights rhetoric.[34] Such phrases as "guerrilla warfare," "revolutionary movement," "communist-supported terrorism," and "radical Islamic fundamentalist" only heighten ideological sentiment and play to emotion rather than intellect. Hence, we find the cliché that one person's terrorist is another

person's freedom fighter to be truly an observation based on perspective and perception.[35] This is certainly the case in the United States, as some actions, such as the first attack on the World Trade Center (1993), the bombing of the Alfred P. Murrah Federal Building in Oklahoma City (1995), the downing of TWA flight 800 (1996), the attacks on 9/11 (2001), the killing of 13 soldiers at Fort Hood, Texas (2009), the Boston Marathon Bombing (2013), the attack on the Dallas Police Department using homemade bombs, automatic weapons, and an armored truck (2015), the killing of 14 people in San Bernadino, California (2015), the mass shooting of patrons at the Pulse night club in Orlando, Florida (2016), and the slaughter of 22 people including several children at a Walmart Supercenter in El Paso, Texas (2019) are "terrorist," whereas the sporadic bombings at abortion centers or mosques across the country are not.

Large, high-profile terrorist events greatly impact how members of society interact. Random acts of terrorism upset the framework of society, leaving only futile questions without rational answers. Essentially, terrorism tests the basic social structure of dependence and trust. If random bombings and acts of violence occur on a frequent basis at the most secure institutions of a society (e.g., federal buildings, police departments, churches, synagogues, and hospitals), then people tend to lose faith in the existing social and government structure. Safety and security are severely compromised and questioned. Terrorism destroys the solidarity, cooperation, and interdependence on which social functioning is based and substitutes insecurity and distrust.

Terrorism, then, plays to emotion, not intellect.[36] It strikes at the very heart of who we are as Americans. For the first time in modern history (9/11), the United States was rocked by an attack on its own land. People were afraid as their daily lives were impacted and changed forever. The privileges and lifestyle that we so enjoyed in this country appeared to be jeopardized. The ability to travel freely was restricted. Few of us can recall where we were on September 2, 2001, but almost all of us can give vivid details of where we were and what we were doing in the morning hours of September 11, 2001. Even if we were in junior high or grade school, this event was so powerful and impactful on the United States as to be called a modern day "Pearl

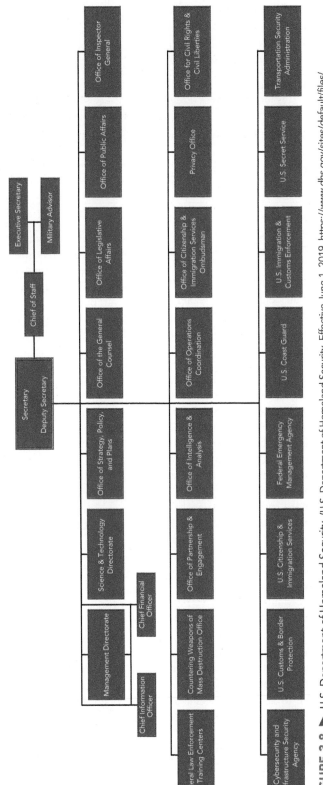

U.S. Department of Homeland Security

FIGURE 3.8 ▲ U.S. Department of Homeland Security. (U.S. Department of Homeland Security. Effective June 1, 2019. https://www.dhs.gov/sites/default/files/publications/18_1204_DHS_Organizational_Chart.pdf)

Harbor," comparing it to the surprise attack by the Japanese in 1941 that heralded U.S. entry into World War II.

The overwhelming question plaguing so many of us was, why? We are a great nation that has helped almost every other nation in need. We give billions of dollars away each year in foreign aid. And we consistently stand for the human rights of all people, emphasizing the dignity of the human spirit and integrity of all people to live free, so why were we the victims of such rage on September 11, 2001, and continuing today, from a group of people that few of us even knew?

Interestingly, the answer may be found in the question. Historically, we have known little about the Middle East. This view is confirmed by the late Osama bin Laden and the al-Qaeda group announcements to the world that one of the primary reasons for the attack was our lack of knowledge about the true political and economic conditions of the Middle East. Indeed, bin Laden made it very clear that they believed our goals in the Middle East were much more motivated by our own self-interest and quest for oil than in safeguarding the human rights of the people in that land. These may be particularly stinging remarks, considering the wars in Iraq and Afghanistan. He maintained that the stationing of American troops in the Middle East—in particular, near the holy city of Mecca (in Saudi Arabia)—was an egregious affront to his religion. He maintained that the people of the Middle East suffer under puppet governments supported by the United States and that these governments practice state terrorism against their own people. Today, we hear similar reasons given for attacks against the United States; only the focus is much more anti-American regarding our involvement in Iraq, Afghanistan, Syria, and other parts of the Middle East.

Here, we see quite profoundly the perspective that terrorism can be different things to different people. Theoretically, scholars have been debating the definition of terrorism for the past 50 years.[37] The goal here is to provide a conceptual framework on which to classify and understand terrorism, particularly in the Middle East. The work of Edward Mickolus provides such a framework.[38]

Terrorism is situationally defined—that is, a number of factors play on the difficulty of defining terrorism, including competing political agendas, national interests, economic security, the news media, fundamental cultural and religious beliefs, and the use of misinformation. By exploiting any one of these, it is possible to distort the facts. Even more disturbing and most compromising is the moral judgment passed on those who are labeled terrorists, for we in America assume that terrorism is "what the bad guys do." Hence, what better way is there to distort the sovereign interest of people than to associate them with illegitimate action or sources? In the Middle East, all of these factors are at play, making for a very complicated and difficult analysis. Those perpetrating terrorism against the United States do not view themselves as criminals. Indeed, many are at war and may well be agents provocateur and within the employ of a foreign government. This is an audience that American law enforcement has had little experience with, and these groups pose special challenges to the everyday police officer now charged with thwarting attacks against our homeland and with securing our infrastructure. Conceptualizing terrorism from a different perspective provides us with an opportunity to learn about our adversaries and hopefully exploit their

weaknesses. Mickolus conceptualizes terrorism in four distinct typologies, based on actors:

- **International terrorism**—Actions conducted in the international arena by individuals that are members of a nation state. This usually includes members of intelligence and secret services employed by governments, such as the Cuban DGI, the old Soviet KGB (now called the Federal Counterintelligence Service - FSK), the Syrian Secret Police, the British M-9, the Israeli Mossad, and even the CIA.

- **Transnational terrorism**—Actions conducted in the international arena by individuals that have no nation-state. The predominate groups for the past 60 years are associated with the Palestinian cause (e.g., Popular Front for the Liberation of Palestine [PFLP], al-Fatah, Black June, Black September Organization, and Abu Nidal). However, other groups have also been active in the Middle East, such as the Kurdish Workers Party (PKK), the Armenians, and various groups from the breakaway lands of the former Soviet Union. The radical Islamic groups, such as al-Qaeda, HAMAS, and Hezbollah, are also classified in this typology. The new **Islamic State (ISIS)** is also a very good example of a transnational terrorist group.

- **Domestic terrorism**—Actions conducted by groups within a nation, usually against the government or specific groups within the nation-state. This may be one of the most difficult aspects of attempting to define the concept of terrorism. When do the rights of a government to control splinter elements within its own country end and the rights of the people to rebel become legitimate? This is a difficult question and one most often "flavored" by the myriad of factors already discussed. In any event, within the United States, groups associated with an extremist perspective (whether from the far left, the far right, or single issue) often fall within this typology. Examples of such groups include the Weather Underground, the Earth Liberation Front, the Animal Liberation Front, the Ku Klux Klan, the Neo-Nazis, the National Alliance, many of the radical militias (e.g., the Republic of Texas Militia and the Hutaree Militia of Eastern Michigan), and a myriad of anarchist groups (like Antifa and the Black Blocs) sprouting up across the country. Most recently in 2016, armed aggressors affiliated with the militia movement calling themselves "Citizens for Constitutional Freedom" occupied the Malheur National Wildlife Refuge in rural Harney County, Oregon. While the occupation ended with the death of one of the leaders of the group during a police confrontation, the incident sparked national debate over the word "terrorist," as the Harney County Sheriff's Office characterized the group as "criminals engaged in trespassing" while the Oregon Governor, Kate Brown, referred to them as "terrorist."[39] The incident was compared to the Ruby Ridge shooting in northern Idaho (1992), the Mount Carmel siege with David Koresh in Waco, Texas (1993), and the Montana Freemen-Christian Patriot standoff in Jordon, Montana (1996) wherein suspects were consistently labeled "terrorist" by the FBI. More recently, the protests and riots stemming from the death of George Floyd during 2020 organized by the Black Live Matter movement and Antifa further complicate definitional issues relating to terrorism. See Box 3.5.

• *State terrorism*—Actions conducted by governments against their own population. Unfortunately, history is replete with suppressive governments that victimize their own populations. Certainly, the regimes of Adolph Hitler, Joseph Stalin, and Pol Pot represent these types of regimes, often characterized by ethnic and political cleansing. More recently, we have seen these types of activities in smaller countries throughout the Far East and Latin America. In the Middle East, Saddam Hussein in Iraq and Haffez al-Assad and now his son, Bashar al-Assad in Syria, represent these types of entities. Interestingly, many (including the leadership of ISIS and the deceased Osama bin Laden) in the Middle East refer to the governments of Israel, Jordan, Kuwait, Egypt, and Saudi Arabia as suppressive regimes controlled by rich elites that suppress the legitimate rights of their people through the use of kidnapping, death squads, and brutal police tactics. By proxy, the same people also argue that the United States is guilty of state terrorism because it financially and militarily supports these governments. They are quick to point to the military use of power against the Palestinian people in the West Bank and Gaza by the Israelis, the use of armed soldiers in Jordan and Egypt to quell mass demonstrations, and the huge differential between classes in Saudi Arabia. Again, and to re-emphasize, the Middle East is a hodge-podge of cultural, religious, and ethnic groups, all struggling for power and recognition. Precisely defining the terrorist and placing moral judgment is a very difficult task, at best.[40]

From a law enforcement perspective, it is important to understand this conceptualization of terrorism. It provides a framework on which to understand the motivations behind people's actions, particularly in the Middle East and for those expressing a radical Islamic philosophy. Further, it provides a basis on which to develop a conversation or an interview with members of Middle Eastern communities living within the United States, some of whom may be sympathetic to the causes of specific Middle Eastern or radical Islamic groups.

Box 3.5: Are They "Terrorist" Organizations?—Examining the Black Lives Matter and Antifa Movements

The **Black Lives Matter** (BLM) Foundation, Inc. began in 2012 in response to the shooting of 17-year-old Trayvon Martin in Sanford, Florida by George Zimmerman, a 28-year-old neighborhood watch coordinator. Zimmerman is a mixed-race Hispanic. The two had a physical altercation stemming from contact initiated by Zimmerman who was on patrol, armed with a licensed firearm as he had done over the past several years. He was suspicious of Martin because of past reported break-ins and stalkers in Zimmerman's Twin Lakes community. During the encounter a fight ensued in which Zimmerman was injured, suffering a fractured nose and several head lacerations. During the fight, Zimmerman fired his weapon (a Kel Tec 9 mm pistol) in contact with Martin's chest, killing him almost instantly. Zimmerman was charged with second degree murder. In a highly publicized trial, amid allegations of racism, and inappropriate and intentional distortion of the incident by two major news groups (ABC and NBC), Zimmerman claimed that he was acting in self-defense and that under Florida's "Stand Your Ground" statute, he had an affirmative duty to protect himself by shooting Martin during the encounter. On July 13, 2013, Zimmerman was found *not guilty*, and the BLM movement was borne from this verdict.

While it is somewhat confusing, it is important to understand that the BLM Foundation, Inc., is a formal organization and group, while the activities of protest supporting significant improvement in lives of Black people in America, less police use of force and brutality against people of color, and awareness of white privilege is a much broader, social movement claiming the general phrase, "Black Lives Matter."

According to their website, BLM Foundation, Inc. is a global organization in the United States, the United Kingdom, and Canada, whose mission is to "eradicate white supremacy and build local power to intervene in violence inflicted on black communities by the state and vigilantes." It is <u>not</u> a designated terrorist group by either the U.S. Department of State or the Department of Justice. However, as far back as 2016, a formal petition by the "We the People" lobby groups was presented to President Barack Obama's administration requesting the designation of 'BLM' as a terrorist organization because it "uses violence and intimidation in pursuit of political aims." The petition had over 141,000 signatures. However, and most important to understand, there simply is no process for designating domestic terrorist organizations in the United States, and both scholars and practitioners have argued about the definition of terrorism for decades. Further, labelling any domestic organization "terrorist" seriously infringes upon Constitutional First Amendment free speech protection. Hence, domestic groups on the left and right such as the Ku Klux Klan, Proud Boys, Skinheads, the Neo-Nazi Party, the Animal Liberation Front (ALF), and the Earth Liberation Front (ELF) have <u>no formal designation</u> as a terrorist group. However, several members of these groups have been investigated for engaging in acts of domestic terrorism including rioting, vandalism, bombing, murder, and conspiracy, and are the central subject of various Joint Terrorism Task Force (JTTF) investigations. For example, Timothy McVeigh was widely considered a domestic terrorist by law enforcement agencies, however, was not formally designated as such, even though he was closely associated with the white Patriot movement of the day. He was convicted of murder, conspiracy, and using

a weapon of mass destruction stemming from the 1995 bombing of the Alfred P. Murrah Federal Building in Oklahoma City. (Aaron of L.A. Photography/Shutterstock)

The Impact of George Floyd's Death

In 2020, the death of another unarmed black man, George Floyd at the hands of Officer Derek Chauvin in Minneapolis, MN gave new impetus to the BLM movement, spawning a much larger outcry involving significant protest against police brutality. The BLM Foundation, Inc. was instrumental in organizing several large protests in major cities across the United States. Many of these protests were peaceful, yet several resulted in widespread rioting, burning, and destruction of property as well as direct confrontation with police. For instance, in Seattle, Washington (a city with a history of left-wing mass protests including the 1999 Seattle World Trade Organization Protests and 2011/12 Occupy Seattle protests) became the national center between BLM protesters and the police. After days of unrest, protesters began to converge on a community neighborhood known as Capitol Hill. A several block area and adjoining park was self-declared by protesters as the <u>C</u>apitol <u>H</u>ill <u>A</u>utonomous <u>Z</u>one (CHAZ) or the (<u>C</u>apitol <u>H</u>ill <u>O</u>rganized <u>P</u>rotest (CHOP). The zone was allowed to exist for nearly a month under local administrators even though open violence between the police and the occupying protestors continued to escalate. Mayor Jenny Durkan enacted a 30-day ban on the use of tear gas by police. And finally, on July 1, the occupiers were cleared by police, however not before widespread rioting, violence, vandalism and destruction marked the area. A block-long mural of Black Lives Matter set the background for police encounters involving tear gas, flash bangs, and pepper spray.

The BLM Movement in General

The wide-spread BLM movement started as a relatively peaceful political protest by white and black communities throughout the United States. The movement was highlighted by large numbers of people from every cultural, economic, and racial strata of America participating in demonstrations and walks across the United States. America has embraced the overall goals and objectives of the movement as represented by mainstream corporate, entertainment and sports initiatives aimed at publicizing BLM goals and objectives. In honor of Martin Luther King's "I have a dream" historic march in 1963, a second protest in Washington, DC was organized with over 200,000 people in attendance on August 28, 2020. However, as time from specific incidents marched on, the movement began to wane, leaving only hard-core protestors that seemed to become more violent and riotous in their efforts. Examples of widespread violence and property destruction were fueled by additional police-involved shootings of black suspects in Kenosha, Wisconsin, St. Paul, Minnesota, Baton Rouge, Louisiana and New York City. Each city suffering considerable damage to buildings and neighborhoods. However, no better example of how the movement had degraded into a much more violent confrontation between police and "protestors" than in Portland, Oregon, where over 100 days of consecutive protesting/rioting continued, resulting in burned-out buildings, significant property damage, vandalism, loss of life, injury to police officers, and opposing political banter at the national level. The consecutive nights of rioting appeared to be fomented more by radical white and black members of socialist groups than BLM protestors. At the helm of much of this violence was a shadowy, radical and violent conglomeration of people known as "Antifa."

Antifa Emerges

Unlike the BLM Foundation, Inc., Antifa <u>is</u> loosely considered a "terrorist organization" by Federal law enforcement (like the FBI), and state and local police agencies, even though there is no official designation. Again, neither the government (nor the FBI) has a mechanism to formally designate any organization as a "domestic terrorist organization" since it may infringe upon Constitutional First Amendment free speech protection.

Antifa, stands for "antifascist" and traces its roots back to the 1980's as a number of loosely defined groups began

to emerge as an opposition to white hate groups. The earliest formal Antifa group was founded in Portland, Oregon as "The Rose City Antifa" in 2007, explaining in part, "why" Portland became such a center for continued violence and rioting. The first national recognition of the group emerged during 2016-2017 era, during a number of protests and confrontations between white supremacists and their opponents, exemplified in Charlottesville, Virginia on August 12, 2017.

Since 2017, Antifa has emerged as a relatively decentralized movement, adopting the principles of anarchism, socialism, and communism. Members often express *violent means to accomplish their goals* focused around ending racism against the black community, supporting the rights of indigenous peoples, environmentalism, and gay rights. Unlike the BLM Foundation, Inc., Antifa does <u>not</u> have a strong, centralized organizational structure or statement of ideology; there are few Antifa principles that exist across all members of the movement.

Definitional and Labeling Issues Continue

So, how do we formally define terrorism and how do we label one group "terrorist" and not another. The fact of the matter is that there is *no uniform way to define such groups within the United States (domestically) as terrorist*. Our Constitution ensures public dissent and our government protects every citizen's right to protest lawfully. Any attempt to define one group over another

as "terrorist," threatens that Constitutional right and undermines the very core of our democratic processes. Remember, that terrorist appeals to emotion, and not intellect and that one man's freedom fighter may well be defined as another man's terrorist...comments that clearly reflect the fluid and changing dynamic of the label, "terrorist!" (Julio Cortez/AP Images)

Sources: Black Lives Matter homepage. See: https://blacklivesmatter.com/

Congressional Research Service, "Are Antifa Members Domestic Terrorist? Background on Antifa and Federal Classification of Their Actions," *In Focus,* June 9, 2020. See https://fas.org/sgp/crs/terror/IF10839.pdf

Daniella Silvan and Matteo Moshella, "Seattle Protesters Set Up "Autonomous Zone" after Police Evacuation" *ABC News,* June 11, 2020. See: https://www.nbcnews.com/news/us-news/seattle-protesters-set-autonomous-zone-after-police-evacuate-precinct-n1230151

Gary LaFree, "Is Antifa a Terrorist Group?" *Society* 55 (May, 2018). See https://link.springer.com/article/10.1007/s12115-018-0246-x
Kirk Johnson, "Another Fatal Shooting in Seattle's CHOP Protest Zone," *The New York Times,* June 29, 2020.

We the People, "Formally Recognize Black Live Matter as a Terrorist Organization" January 22, 2017. See https://petitions.whitehouse.gov/petition/formally-recognize-black-lives-matter-terrorist-organization

RADICAL ISLAMIC TERRORISM

The list of potential international terrorist threats against the United States is almost unlimited, considering the numerous political conflicts continuing in the international arena. Many of these threats are fueled by political, religious, and/or ideologically motivated causes. Certainly, terrorism from various Middle Eastern groups has posed significant problems to American law enforcement. Historically, the root of conflict in the Middle East was the establishment of Israel in 1948 and the subsequent U.S. support provided to that country. While peace between the two major groups (Israelis and Palestinians) was formally established in 1995, both sides still have major radical movements opposing the process that often act out in the international arena, including the United States. In 2019, continued violence between Israel and the Palestinian Islamic Resistance Movement (HAMAS) appeared to break-out every few months. While these violent episodes can be quite lethal, most are isolated and short-lived and form a relatively consistent pattern: Political and military tension between the two parties yield to international mediators and a new cease-fire deal that brings tangible economic aid for Palestinians from regional Arab countries, such as Qatar, Bahrain, or Saudi Arabia.[41]

The most significant activities against the United States in the past 25 years have been led by fundamental Islamic groups acting from clandestine areas in Afghanistan, Iraq, Lebanon, Yemen, and Iran. The first major incident witnessed in the United States connected to fundamental Islam was the bombing of the World Trade Center on February 26, 1993, which killed six people. FBI experts contend that, if the bomb had been just slightly larger and more skillfully placed, the entire building may have collapsed, causing untold devastation and death. Unfortunately, this was just a preview of the horrible events to come just eight years later. Linkages to Islamic fundamentalist groups in Egypt were developed, resulting in several indictments of Arab nationals living in the United States. One of those convicted was the blind cleric Sheik Abdul Omar Rahman, a spiritual leader and scholar who helped spawn a number of other groups.

Al-Qaeda (AQ)

The most infamous of these groups is the **al-Qaeda** (AQ) organization formally led by Osama bin Laden and now, Ayman al-Zawahiri. It is actually a network of many different fundamental Islamic groups in diverse countries. Their ideology is based primarily on the writings of Muhammad Ibn al-Wahhab (1703–1792), Hassan al-Banna (1906–1949), and Sayyid Muhammad Qubt (1906–1966), three early Islamic scholars calling for a violent purification movement throughout the Middle East and the greater Islamic world. This religious movement is commonly called "Wahhabism" and later "Salafism" and can be traced back to the late 1700s in what is now Saudi Arabia and Egypt. According to these radical philosophers, the Middle East must be purged of Western influence. To this end, leaders call for a "holy war," or **jihad**, calling on everyday Muslims to join in their fight against the West. Bin Laden and other members of the al-Qaeda network perverted parts of the Qur'an to justify their philosophy and do not represent mainstream Islam. It is important to understand that Islam is the world's second-largest religion, with over 1 billion peaceful followers, living primarily in Africa, Asia, and Europe. The actions of radical Islamic fundamentalists represent only a small but growing percentage of all of Islam. Unfortunately, the movement has flourished in Egypt and Saudi Arabia for the past 100 years, countries where American influence is easily observed. Members of the al-Qaeda organization are politically motivated to overthrow the "heretic governments" that they see as puppets of Western influence and replace them with Islamic governments based on the rule of the Shariah (the first book of the Qur'an, strictly regulating all aspects of life).

Osama bin Laden (1957–2011), the son of a wealthy building contractor in Saudi Arabia, rose to power within the fundamental Islamic movement as a student of Ayman al-Zawahiri. However, it was not until the 1979–1989 Soviet-Afghan War that bin Laden actually took a recognized leadership role in the organization. Triumphant over the Soviets and enlisting the aid of American interests in Afghanistan, bin Laden amassed a number of hardened mujahideen (holy warriors) fighters. He became obsessed with Western influence in the Middle East and declared a holy war on the United States in 1996.[43] Fueled by Middle Eastern oil wealth and an increasing radicalization of Islam, bin Laden set out to destroy those entities that he believes have adulterated his homeland. The activities of al-Qaeda have been significant and numerous, culminating on September 11, 2001, with the attacks on the World Trade Center and the Pentagon.

Since Operation Enduring Freedom, which first sent troops to Afghanistan in 2001, and the recent wars in Iraq and Afghanistan (2003–2015), most scholars and government officials have believed that the stability and operational capability of al-Qaeda have been diminished in the international arena. Certainly, the leadership has been dismantled and most have either been killed or are on the run. According to the U.S. Department of State, much of the 2014 spike in global terror attacks could be attributed to civil conflict in Iraq, Syria, Pakistan, and Afghanistan—areas where AQ played a prominent role.[44] However, today, much of the operational capability of al-Qaeda as a single group has been destroyed, especially with the advent of a much larger and much more violent radical Islamic movement in the Middle East.

The Islamic State (ISIS)

Many of the radical Sunni fighters loyal to al-Qaeda suffered dramatic losses to U.S. forces during the Iraq War. Coupled with the loss of political power and the establishment of a majority Shiite-led government in Iraq, many fled to neighboring countries, and in particular Syria, where violent revolution already in progress was pitting Sunnis against a Shiite-backed al-Assad government. The early name of this group became widely known as ISIS (or the Islamic State in Iraq and Syria). Syrian rebel groups quickly welcomed these hardened fighters; however, they soon realized that the Iraqi group had a much larger goal than toppling the al-Assad regime—their

---

Quick Facts: Terrorism in the United States

Although terrorism is something of an ever present specter in the American consciousness, the United States is actually a relatively safe haven from terrorist attacks compared to its global counterparts. The United States ranks 41st in the world when considered on a scale that measure property damage, loss of life, injury, and other socioeconomic indicators. The top five terror targets are (in order): Iraq, Pakistan, Afghanistan, India, and Yemen. The United States also ranks as a safer place than Great Britain, which is 28th on the list. More recent attacks (2015–2020) in Paris, Brussels, Vienna, and other parts of Europe continue to highlight the relative safety of the United States.[42]

goal was to establish a new "Islamic State," or "Islamic Caliphate" that transcended traditional country borders in the Middle East and established radical Islamic tenets as the center piece of a worldwide organization. ISIS had established a shocking history characterized by a rapid and successful invasion of Iraq, marked by horrifying brutality, slavery and a practice of genocide against some religious groups such as the Yazidis, mass executions and beheadings, and the devastation of historical religious sites and antiquities.

ISIS has been successful in carving out a portion of land in the heart of the Middle East (from Syria across Iraq to Iran) in which to build a new country and recruit other like-minded Sunnis worldwide. The rise of the ISIS was quick and historical, occurring along the banks of the Tigris and Euphrates Rivers, a region commonly known as the cradle of civilization.

In July 2014, the leader of the ISIS, Abu Bakr al-Baghdadi, declared himself "caliph" over the area he controlled and announced the establishment of the new "**caliphate**." He then changed the name of the group to the Islamic State, and within a month (August 2014), he led attacks on Kurdish territories in northern Iraq, prompting an immediate response by the United States—retaliatory air strikes and bombing of IS-held areas. He called upon all Muslims around the world to pledge support and allegiance to him and his country. These were powerful words in the Muslim world, and ones that positioned al-Baghdadi and the Islamic State as a unique challenge to Western nations and a direct threat to the stability of the entire Middle East. This is particularly true as other radical Islamic groups align with the Islamic State. Boko Harem (Nigeria—discussed later in this chapter), Abu Sayyaf (The Philippines), Ansar al-Tawhid (Pakistan/Afghanistan), al-Qaeda on the Arabian Peninsula (AQAP) (Yemen), Answar

al-Sahria (Libya), and other have already recognized and become affiliates to al-Baghdadi's proclamation. The Islamic State is not just another radical Islamic group; rather it is a significant movement across the world (some scholars estimate the movement includes over 8 million people) that sees itself as the provocateurs of the coming apocalypse, paving the way for the final Islamic rule in the Middle East and the rest of the world.[45]

While the grand ideas of a new Islamic caliphate are now gone as a result of serious military and political defeats in Syria and Iraq, ISIS appears to be planning future "Islamic revolutions" from a more international perspective. Even though al-Baghdadi is now gone and the group is significant hurt militarily, ISIS is far from finished. It now appears to have shifted much of his activity away from Syria and the Middle East and focused on individual activities in countries across Africa, Asia, and Europe. As such the new plan for ISIS calls for renewed violence in countries across the globe. For instance, security experts refer to new unrest in countries like Algeria, Afghanistan, Sudan, Mali, Somalia, Thailand, and the Philippines as potential new sites for ISIS global operations. Supporting such propaganda is the ISIS-claimed suicide bombing attacks on Easter Sunday, April 21, 2019 in Sri Lanka. A coordinated attack involving over 40 suspects on churches and luxury hotels in Colombo, Sri Lanka resulted in a death toll of 359 people, possibly marking the beginning of a new global surge of terror sponsored by ISIS.[46] Following the pattern of other radical Islamic groups, ISIS is not going to disappear; it's estimated that 18,000 fighters in Syria may simply morph into another existing group or become a new movement based on old principles.

Thus, although ISIS has been seriously weakened, it continues to flourish as a movement. See Figure 3.9. American

FIGURE 3.9 ▶ On October 27, 2019, the leader of ISIS, Abu Bakr al-Baghdadi killed himself by exploding a suicide vest during a raid in northwestern Syria. The raid was conducted by soldiers in the U.S. Army 75th Ranger Regiment and the U.S. Delta Force. Al-Baghdadi had been the so-called caliph of ISIS sense 2014. His death marks a significant blow to the future of ISIS. (United States Department of Defense)

soldiers are the continual targets of ISIS, as well as reported bombings of government buildings, security positions, and non-Islamic schools throughout the Middle East. ISIS bombers and soldiers continue to strike at locations both in the Middle East (Saudi Arabia, Yemen, Tunisia, Brussels, and Turkey) as well as in Europe (Madrid, London, Brussels, Vienna, and Paris) (see Figure 3.10) and the United States (Garland, Texas, and San Bernadino, California 2015, Orlando, Florida 2016, and Pittsburg, Pennsylvania 2018). From website announcements and flyers to the recruitment of new fighters, ISIS continues to grow in sustained acts of violence against Western interests. Most alarming are the number of attacks being planned or those implemented over the past several years from U.S.-born, radical Islamic terrorists. A White House report in late 2018 warns that ISIS "remains the foremost radical Islamic group and the primary transnational terrorist threat to United States."[48] ISIS as well as al-Qaeda continue to be very adaptive movements, and future attacks inside the United States may well be inspired by these groups, particularly if they can retain their prominence in the Middle East and use social and mainstream media to plan, encourage, and promote their violent message.[49]

"Homegrown" Islamic Terrorists

A trend observed in the radical Islamic terrorist movement is the development of **"homegrown" terrorists**. The term refers to extremists who are legal U.S. residents or even citizens, and who are linked to or inspired by a specific, often intolerant ideology. This ideology may be motivated by political or religious sources and may be centered in domestic or foreign movements. Indeed, some of them have made connections with well-known, international terror groups, such as ISIS and al-Qaeda.[50] These individuals may receive ideological encouragement, but not financial or material support, making them ancillary to the primary group and very difficult to detect by intelligence and law enforcement services.

For instance, Major Nidal Hasan, perpetrator of the 2009 Fort Hood shootings that killed 13 people and wounded more than 30 others, is a prime example of this type of terrorist—a man who was radicalized due to a belief that American wars in Iraq and Afghanistan were wars against the Muslim faith. Hasan had expressed his opposition to these wars, despite his position as a psychiatrist in the U.S. Army and carried out his attack about a month before he was to be deployed to Afghanistan. Hasan

---

Box 3.6: Radical Islamic Groups Active Throughout the World[47]

Radical Islamic ideologies represent a significant threat to Israel, Europe, and the United States. The philosophy represents the most virulent of radical Islamic fundamentalism and has been the base foundation for several active terrorist groups throughout the world. These groups remain active and continue to pose a significant threat of attack in the United States and against American interest abroad.

Abu Sayyaf Group (ASG). ASG is a violent Islamic separatist group operating in the southern Philippine island of Mindanao. Split from the Moro National Liberation Front, the group has been active in narcotics, arms, and human trafficking as well as kidnapping as a means to fund their operations in Southeast Asia. In 2019, President Rodrigo Duterte declared an "all out war" against the ASG, which has led to significant military operations against the ASG as well as other radical Islamic groups operating in the Philippines.

Al-Qaeda. Established in 1988 by Usama bin Laden in Afghanistan as a resistance movement against the invasion by the Soviet Union, al-Qaeda remains a viable terrorist group aimed at destroying Western influence (particularly the United States) and establishing a worldwide Islamic state. The group has been significantly reduced in number and resources due to military involvement in Iraq and Afghanistan. Al-Qaeda is currently headed by its long-time spiritual leader, Ayman al-Zawahiri, and remnants are still committed to their Jihadist cause. In 2017, al-Qaeda was suspected to have gained alliance with ISIS, as Iraqi forces

closed in on Mosul, ISIS' last key stronghold in the region. Today, al-Qaeda operates globally through its multiple, regionally based factions such as al-Qaeda in the Arabian Peninsula (AQAP), al-Qaeda in Iraq (AQI), al-Qaeda in Islamic Maghreb (AQIM), and al-Qaeda in the Indian Subcontinent (AQIS).

Al-Qaeda in the Arabian Peninsula (AQAP). AQAP is a militant group following the ideological philosophies of the larger al-Qaeda. AQAP is based primarily in Yemen and has been linked with other radical Islamic groups in that country, such as the Yemeni Islamic Jihad and the Aden-abyan Islamic Army. It has been strongly opposed to the House of Saud in Saudi Arabia and has been involved in several terrorist attacks in Saudi Arabia and Yemen. Interestingly, AQAP claimed responsibility for the Christmas Day attempted bombing of Northwest Airlines Flight 253 on December 25, 2009 by Umar Farouk Abdulmutallab. In that incident, Abdulmutallab attempt to set off plastic explosives sewed into his underwear. The explosives failed to detonate and Abdulmutallab was arrested. The group also took credit for the December 2019 attack on Naval Air Station Pensacola (Florida) by Mohammed al-Shamrani, resulting in the shooting death of three people.

Al-Qaeda in Iraq (AQI). AQI is also known as the Islamic State of Iraq and more recently as the Islamic State of Iraq and the Levant (ISIL) was established in 2004 by Abu Musab al-Zarqawi, a long and strong-time supporter of Usama bin Laden. AQI was a primary force against the U.S. military in Iraq, even after al-Zarqawi and other leaders were killed; remnants in Iraq continue to perform acts of terrorism against the established government of Iraq and threaten U.S. interests in the area. Much of the membership of AQI is now associated with the **Islamic State**.

Al-Qaeda in the Indian Subcontinent (AQIS): Also known as Ansar al-Islam, AQIS was founded in 2014 and carried on significant terrorist attacks in Pakistan, Afghanistan, India, Myanmar, and Bangladesh. The group is composed primarily of former Taliban fighters loyal to Ayman al-Zawahiri and seeks to establish "jihad and Shariah law across the Indian subcontinent."

Al-Qaeda in Islamic Maghreb (AQIM). The Maghreb is a geographical region of northwest Africa, comprising the Atlas Mountains and the modern day countries of Mauritania, Morocco, Algeria, Tunisia, Western Sahara, and Libya. AQIM has declared itself as an affiliate of the original al-Qaeda and carries out operations in an attempt to overthrow the Algerian government and institute an Islamic state throughout the Maghreb.

HAMAS. The Palestinian Islamic Resistance Movement or Harakat al-Muqawamah al Islamiyyah (Arabic) is the largest and most politically powerful group expressing radical Islamic ideologies to justify the liberation of Palestine and the destruction of Israel. The group was originally led by the now-deceased Sheik Ahmed Hassan Yassin and conducted a campaign of suicide bombing throughout the Gaza Strip and the West Bank in Israel during the late 1990s to mid-2000s. Significant linkages between HAMAS and groups within the United States have been confirmed over the past decade. HAMAS remains a very active military unit within the Gaza and routinely engages Israel in violent attacks of terrorism.

Hezbollah. Arabic for "Party of God," Hezbollah is primarily focused in Lebanon and Syria. The group represents the radical Shiite fundamentalist perspective as opposed to the other radical Sunni Islamic perspective. The group is led by Hassan Nasrallah and was linked directly to the bombing of the barracks in Beirut in 1983, killing 241 U.S. Marines. The group is philosophically, politically, and economically backed by Iran. While much controversy has resulted from the groups political success in Lebanon as a "legitimate" resistance movement, most Western nations in Europe (including Great Britain, France, and Germany) and the Middle East (Bahrain, Israel, United Arab Emirates), as well as Australia and the United States have declared Hezbollah a terror group.

Harakat ul-Mujahidin (HUM). Formerly part of the larger radical Islamic movement in Pakistan and Afghanistan called Harakat al-Ansar, HUM operates primarily in Kashmir and can link direct associations with bin Laden and original al-Qaeda fighters in Afghanistan and Pakistan. The group maintains close ties to Jaish e-Mohammad (JEM) or the "Army of Muhammad" in Afghanistan. These groups have maintained significant training camps in Pakistan and represent the primary groups that fought against U.S. forces in Afghanistan. Since the war in Afghanistan has subsided, many of the warriors for HUM have joined the ranks of al-Qaeda in the Indian Subcontinent (AQIS). The group is still very active in the Kashmir region of Pakistan

Islamic State in Iraq and Syria (ISIS), Islamic State (IS). Much of the original membership came from al-Qaeda in Iraq (AQI); however, the group represented a major radical Islamic movement across Iraq and Syria. Led by Abu Bakr al-Baghdadi, the movement claimed to be the new "caliphate" and continues to pose the most significant threat facing Western interests in the Middle East and globally. With most of its resources (including finances and armed fighters) depleted through battles in Iraq and Syria against Western forces, the group continues to operate primarily through its affiliates. ISIS remains a significant threat to the United States and American interests abroad.

Jemaah Islamiya (JI). JI is an Indonesia-based terrorist group active throughout Southeast Asia. JI is headed by Abu Baker Bashir, an Indonesian of Yemini descent, and a highly charismatic cleric and leader. The group has active cells in Thailand, Singapore, Malaysia, and Indonesia and has been linked to the Moro Islamic Liberation Front in the Philippines. The group has been responsible for several high-profile terrorist incidents in Southeast Asia including the 2002 bombing of a nightclub in Bali killing 202 people and the 2003 car bombing of the JW Marriott Hotel in Jakarta, Indonesia that killed 12 people. JI remains an active group throughout Southeast Asia.

Lashkar-i-Tayyiba (LT). The Lashkar-i-Tayyiba or "Army of the Righteous" is one of the largest and best trained fighting groups in the Pakistan-Afghan region. It is headed by Hafiz Mohamed Saeed and has conducted a number of terrorist attacks against India (Mumbai). The group is focused on fighting India control over the Jammu and Kashmir regions of Pakistan, and as such as been linked with AQIS terrorist operations.

Muslim Brotherhood (MB). An Islamic fundamental group stemming from the writings of Hassan al-Banna and Sayyid Qutb in 20th-century Egypt. The group has been very successful in recent Middle East politics, winning the majority of parliamentary seats in the government of Egypt and moving vigorously in other North African countries (2011–2014). Considered by the FBI as the "father of all militant Islamic groups," the Muslim Brotherhood has established cells in the American Islamic community within the United States. The group continues to be very active politically throughout the Middle East and, interestingly, has officially rejected violence and terrorism associated with the al-Qaeda and ISIS movements.

Quick Facts: Al-Shabaab Terrorists Attack Kenya Airfield, Host to American Special Operations Personnel

On January 5, 2020, al-Shabaab (The Youth) terrorists left their sanctuary in Somalia and executed a surprise attack on a Kenya airbase close to their border. For several years, the airbase has hosted a contingent of American special operations personnel, including Marine Raiders, Navy Seals, and Army Green Berets. Three Americans were killed, aircraft destroyed, and a fuel dump set on fire before al-Shabaab slipped back into Somalia.

At its core, al-Shabaab is a fundamentalist Islamic jihadist group that believes in strict obedience to Sharia law and opposition to Western influences. It is in Somalia to carve out

Source: No author, "Chaos as Militants Overran Airfield, killing Three Americans in Kenya," *The New York Times*, January 23, 2020.

FIGURE 3.10 ▶ Chilling photo of two gunmen just prior to entering the Paris, France offices of satirical magazine Charlie Hebdo and killing 12 people in 2015. The gunmen were later linked to members of the Islamic State (ISIS). (ABACA/Newscom) In late 2020, two people were stabbed near the former offices of Charlie Hebdo, as well as a third person was beheaded in Paris. Coupled with shooting incidents on innocent victims in London and Vienna, these attacks point to a potential resurgence in violence by Islamic militants across Europe.

had been in contact with radical Muslim cleric and suspected al-Qaeda propaganda officer Anwar al-Awlaki via a series of e-mails before his attack.[51]

In other cases, terrorist groups target first-generation foreign nationals living in the United States to join their ranks. The perpetrators of the Boston Marathon bombings in 2013 are good examples of this activity and are considered homegrown terrorists. Tamerlan Tsarnaev, who apparently masterminded the attack with the help of his younger brother Dzhokhar, was another young Muslim who had been radicalized by his anger over perceived injustices against the Muslim faith by the United States. Though no direct connections between the two Chechens and any specific terrorist group have been identified in the year after the bombing, the two did view al-Qaeda training videos on the Internet and espoused doctrine that was common among al-Qaeda sympathizers.[52] See Figure 3.11.

Similarly, first-generation "homegrown" terrorists were actually known by intelligence and law enforcement services; however, no previous illegal actions had been taken by the suspect. Such was the case in 2015 when Elton Simpson and Nadir Soofi (a first-generation Pakistani) entered the Curtis Culwell Center in Garland, Texas, armed with assault rifles threatening participants in a controversial event designed to show cartoons of the Muslim Prophet Muhammad. Simpson had been convicted of a terror-related charge in 2011 after discussing plans to travel to Somalia to engage in "violent jihad" or a "holy war" and Soofi had expressed similar convictions but not threatened actual violence.[53] Both suspects had been a concern for their radical Islamic beliefs and both had been living together in a Phoenix, Arizona, apartment prior to the shooting incident. Both Simpson and Soofi linked themselves to ISIS, which was indeed confirmed by ISIS supporters via various website outlets.[54]

FIGURE 3.11 ▶ The Boston Marathon Bombing in 2013 shocked the American public as two first-generation foreign nationals and brothers from Chechnia, Tamerlan and Dzhokhar Tsarnaev, carried out the crude attack killing 3 and injuring another 264 people. Tamerlan Tsarnaev was killed by police at the time of his arrest and Dzhokhar was convicted of 30 charges relating to terrorism and sentenced to death in 2015. He is currently awaiting execution in a Federal maximum-security prison in Colorado. *Source:* (a) FEMA, (b) FBI.

In the United States, such homegrown terrorists have largely flown beneath the radar—many have no criminal records (unlike Simpson), and while their European counterparts tend to be more socially marginalized, it's more likely that American-grown extremists come from a broad variety of educational and socioeconomic statuses. Consider that Major Nidal Hasan had completed medical school; Tamerlan Tsarnaev had gone to college for a time to pursue engineering; and his brother, Dzokhar, was enrolled in American university at the time of the attacks. Even Nadir Soofi had been a premed student at the University of Utah and was described by neighbors and friends as being outgoing, loved cars, was intelligent, and "had a normal American upbringing."[55]

In December 2015, a 28-year-old U.S. citizen, Syed Rizwan Farook and his wife, Tashfeen Malik (age 29), a legal immigrant to the United States, walked into a morning holiday party for disabled persons at the Inland Regional Center in San Bernardino, California, and opened fire with semiautomatic weapons and pistols. The attack left 14 individuals dead and another 17 wounded. Farook and Malik were later killed in a shoot-out with police later that evening. Interestingly, Farook was recently married, a graduate student at California State University-Fullerton, and worked for the county as an environmental health specialist. Neighbors and friends referred to Farook as a "normal guy;" however, both Farook and Malik had expressed allegiance to ISIS leader Abu Bakir Bashir in recent Facebook posts.[79]

One of the more recent attacks within the homeland occurred in Orlando, Florida in June 2016. Omar Mateen, a first-generation Afghani Muslim who had pledged allegiance to ISIS burst into Pulse, a gay night club, and killed 49 people and injured another 53. See Figure 3.12. Mateen was only 29 years old, a former security guard, and married to Noor Salman whom the federal government charged with aiding and abetting her husband before the attack. Salman was fully aware of the premeditated attack and dropped-off Mateen at the Pulse nightclub. While Mateen was eventually killed by police at the club after a three-hour stand-off, Salman stood trial for her involvement. Early thoughts on the motivation for the attack focused on anti-LGBTQ (Lesbian, Gay, Bi-Sexual, Transgender and Queer) hate crime. However, during the trial, Salman presented evidence that showed her husband's true motive was apparently revenge

Box 3.7: Recent Homegrown Terrorist Incidents

Recent instances that made national news involving U.S. citizens and residents that convert to radical Islamic extremism, plot and commit terrorist acts, or fight for the jihadist movement both inside the United States and in foreign counties:

July 2009—A North Carolina man, Daniel Boyd, along with six other individuals were arrested for operating a terrorist training camp in North Carolina.[56] Daniel Boyd, a U.S. citizen, his two sons, and four others had allegedly been training in their rural lakeside home for "violent jihad." Boyd and his brother had lengthy ties to radical Islamic groups, having been arrested in 1991 in Pakistan on bank robbery charges and were found with identification indicating they were members of the Islamic terrorist group Hezbollah.[57] Further, Boyd had traveled to the Middle East nearly 20 years prior to train at terrorist camps in Pakistan and Afghanistan and fought the Soviets (in the Soviet–Afghan War) for three years before returning to the United States.[58] Members of his group also traveled to Israel in 2007 with the intent of joining the Palestinian Islamic jihad movement in that country but later returned without incident. The seven men were charged and convicted with providing material support to terrorists.

September 2009—A 19-year old Jordanian citizen, Hosam Maher Husein (Sam) Smadi, was arrested by the Federal Bureau of Investigation in downtown Dallas, Texas, for attempting to detonate an inert/inactive device. The Jordanian had been living and working in Italy, Texas, illegally on an expired tourist visa.[59] He had been under constant surveillance by the FBI and had placed what he believed to be an active car bomb under the Fountain Building in downtown Dallas, a 60-story, glass skyscraper.[60] The decoy device and all materials had been supplied to him by the FBI, who kept him under constant surveillance after discovering him as a potential terrorist in an online chat room with a group of extremists. Smadi was subsequently charged with attempting to use a weapon of mass destruction and pleaded guilty to this charge in June 2010.[61]

September 2009—Najibullah Zazi, an Afghan citizen and U.S. legal resident living in Colorado, was arrested on charges of conspiring to use weapons of mass destruction with others against the United States.[62] It was later reported that Zazi had traveled to Pakistan to receive weapons and explosives and for training in their use and tactics. Zazi pleaded guilty to terrorism charges including conspiracy to use weapons of mass destruction, conspiracy to commit murder overseas, and providing material support for a terrorist organization.[63] He admitted to planning to use explosives when he arrived in New York in September 2009 to make a political statement about civilian killings in Afghanistan.[64] Law enforcement authorities were alerted to Zazi while monitoring various online chat rooms. Zazi actually planned his attack on the web and communicated it with others online.

October 2009—David Coleman Headley, a U.S. citizen of Pakistani descent, was arrested for plotting the attacks in Mumbai, India, that killed 170 people, including 6 Americans. Headley, whose original name is Daood Gilani, had his name changed in order to make his overseas traveling easier.[65] Headley actively scouted targets in Mumbai before the attacks and has admitted to planning and scouting targets against a Danish newspaper that printed images of Muhammad in 2005, an attack that was never carried out.[66] The Chicago native pled guilty to conspiring to bomb public places in India, murder people in India and Denmark, and to providing material support to terrorist groups.[67]

November 2009—Five young men from Virginia (all born in the United States) were arrested in Pakistan for attempting to join Jihadist terrorist groups, specifically al-Qaeda.[68] They had been reported missing by their parents in Virginia on the advice of the local Muslim community after the men had traveled to the Middle East without informing their parents.[69] The "Virginia 5" were reported to have been arrested in a safe house of an anti-India terrorist group in possession of Jihadist literature. They were also reported to be building schematics and maps of local areas. Officials believe that they were in the planning stages of a major attack in Pakistan.

November 2009—Major Nidal Malik Hassan, a psychiatrist for the U.S. Army, killed 13 people and wounded

Major Nidal Malik Hassan (Handout/MCT/Newscom)

30 others at Ft. Hood, Texas, in a Soldier Processing Center. Major Hassan was reportedly unhappy about the continuing wars in the Middle East and feared an approaching deployment to Afghanistan to assist in the war against his fellow Muslims.[70] Major Hassan had showed signs through his career of resistance to the war effort in the Middle East, as well as many disagreements about U.S. foreign policy. Hassan had even been in contact with the radical Muslim cleric Anwar al-Awlaki.[71] Army officials cited numerous failures in supervision and information sharing to recognize these signs and connect the dots that should have produced increased vigilance on Hassan's mental state and potential terrorist activities.[72]

March 2010—Colleen LaRose, more commonly known as "Jihad Jane," was a U.S. citizen born in 1963 and living in Philadelphia. She was apprehended for conspiracy to provide material support to terrorists, conspiracy to kill in a foreign country, attempted identity theft, and making false statements to a government official.[73] Ms. LaRose had been exchanging e-mails for years in an attempt to recruit fighters for "violent jihad" in South Asia and Europe. Her U.S. citizenship and Caucasian appearance made her appealing to Islamic extremists who used her within the United States.[74] She had also made posts on various online message boards and blogs expressing sympathy with various terrorist groups and movements, and a desire to help in any way possible, including fighting and killing, to help ease the suffering of the Muslim people during their jihad or "holy war." LaRose even traveled to South Asia to marry a known and active jihadist in that area. She supplied her American boyfriend's passport to her new "husband" in an attempt to avoid travel restrictions in the United States and Europe.[75] She planned to use her European looks to blend into the Swedish population and to kill a Swedish artist who depicted the face of Muhammed on a dog in 2007.[76]

April 2013—Two bombs exploded during the Boston Marathon, killing three people and wounding another 250 spectators and runners. The bombs were crudely constructed using ordinary pressure cookers as an improvised explosive device (IED) stuffed with explosive material (black powder) and scrape metal (e.g., BBs, nuts, and bolts). A blasting cap was then placed through the cooker cover and attached to a simple timing device or cell phone. Within two hours after the bombing, a police officer for Massachusetts Institute of Technology (MIT) was killed while confronting two potential suspects, and an ensuing gun battle with police in Watertown, Massachusetts, ensued. One suspect, 27-year-old Tamerlan Tsarnaev was shot and killed during the incident. The other suspect (Tamerlan's brother), 20-year-old Dzhokhar Tsarnaev was arrested hiding in a boat parked in the backyard of a Watertown resident later that same night. During the initial investigation, Dzhokhar alleged that Tamerlan was the mastermind of the entire bombing and that they had learned how to build the bombs from online instructions hosted by an al-Qaeda affiliate in Yemen. Both Tsarnaev brothers were born in remote areas of the former Soviet Union, near Chechnya, and grew up in Kyrgyzstan. Both were Muslims who became increasingly radicalized by watching jihadist speakers on the Internet. Dzhokhar Tsarnaev was convicted of 30 charges relating to homegrown terrorism, including use of weapon of mass destruction and the malicious destruction of property resulting in death. He was found guilty of all 30 charges on April 8, 2015, and sentenced to death.

October 2014—Zale Thompson attacked four NYPD police officers posing for a photograph. He critically injured two officers as he swung a hatchet at them. Thompson, an African-American male, had previously converted to Islam and adopted radical jihadi beliefs having posted numerous threats against police officers online. He was killed during the melee.

June 2015—Two gunmen, Elton Simpson and Nadir Soofi, opened fire outside the Curtis Culwell Center in Garland, Texas. The attackers were motivated by the Charlie Hebdo Shooting in Paris, France, and the Copenhagen Shooting in Denmark earlier in the year. All three attacks involved heavily armed suspect (assault rifles and pistols) sparked by the insensitivity of developing cartoon depictions of the Islamic Prophet Muhammad. Two days after the incident, members of the Islamic State claimed responsibility for the attack through a Twitter post.[77]

July 2015—A lone gunman, Mohammad Youssuf Abdulazeez (24 years old), armed with an assault rifle with a 30-round magazine, opened fire outside a military recruiting office in Chattanooga, Tennessee, killing five soldiers and severely wounding three others. Abdulazeez, born in Kuwait, was a naturalized citizen of the United States for the past 17 years. He had traveled back to the Middle East in the past two years; however, he was not a member of any known terrorist organization, nor mentioned on any governmental terrorist watch list. According to numerous friends in the Chattanooga community, Abdulazeez was "very intelligent" and a "good kid." He was killed by police responding to the shooting incident.[78]

December 2015—A 28-year-old U.S. citizen, Syed-Rizwan Farook and his wife, Tashfeen Malik (age 29), a legal immigrant to the United States, walked into a morning holiday party for disabled persons at the Inland Regional Center in San Bernardino, California and opened fire with semiautomatic weapons and pistols. The attack left 14 individuals dead and another 17 wounded. Farook and Malik were later killed in a shoot-out with police later that evening. Interestingly, Farook was recently married, a graduate student at California State University-Fullerton, and worked for the county as an environmental health specialist. Neighbors and friends refereed to Farook as a "normal guy"; however, both Farook and Malik had expressed allegiance to ISIS leader Abu Bakir Bashir in recent Facebook posts.

June 2016—Pulse nightclub shooting by Omar Mateen in Orlando, Florida. See Figure 3.12. A first-generation Afghani Muslim who had pledge allegiance to the Islamic State opened fire in a crowded, predominately gay night club in Orlando, Florida leaving 49 people dead and another 53 wounded. It was the deadliest shooting by a single shooter in U.S. history until the Las Vegas Route 91 Harvest Music Festival shooting by Stephen Paddock that left 58 people dead and over 850 injured/wounded in late 2017. The Las Vegas shooting had no apparent linkage to terrorism, and Paddock's motivations remain unknown.

January 2017—Ambush shooting death of Denver transit officer Scott Von Lanken by Joshua Cummings, a 37-year-old Muslim convert and former Army sergeant. The U.S. Department of Homeland Security had been warned by Denver-area mosque that Cummings had become highly radicalized in Islamic beliefs and was dangerous. According to reports, Von Lanken was in uniform and giving directions to individuals at the Denver Union Station when Cummings approached him from the rear, pulled a 9 mm Lugar from his belt, and shot Von Lanken in the head at point-blank range.

October 2017—Eight people are killed and another dozen injured when 29-year-old Sayfullo Habibullaevic Saipov drives a rented pick-up truck won a bicycle path crowded with people near the World Trade Center in New York. Saipov, an Uzbeki immigrant to the United States, left a note stating that the attack was made in the name of ISIS.

October–November 2018—A total of 16 packages containing pipe bombs were sent to national politicians and government leaders including former President Barack Obama, Vice-President Joe Biden, and President Donald Trump. Cesar Altieri Sayoc, Jr., was the son of Filipino immigrant born in Brooklyn, NY had a long criminal history and was deeply troubled by anxiety and paranoia. He was convinced that the current political structure of the United States was dangerous, unpatriotic and evil. He was arrested in Florida and plead guilty to 65 felony counts, including using weapons of mass destruction in an attempted domestic terrorist attack.

August 3, 2019—A lone gunman targeting Hispanic and Latino Americans shot and killed 23 people and injured another 23 at a Walmart Shopping Center in El Paso, Texas. Patrick Crusius, a 21-year-old from Allen, Texas was arrested shortly after the shooting. He had previously published a manifesto on the internet boasting a white nationalist sentiment with anti-immigration themes.

December 6, 2019 — Mohammed al-Shamrani shot and killed three people at the Naval Air Station in Pensacola,

FL. Al-Shamrani was directly linked (via telephone records) to the group that immediately took credit for the attack, Al-Qaeda on the Arabian Peninsula (AQAP).

FBI Press Release, "Shooting at Naval Air Station Pensacola Called "Act of Terrorism." January 13, 2020. See: https://www.fbi.gov/news/stories/naval-air-station-pensacola-shooting-called-act-of-terrorism-011320

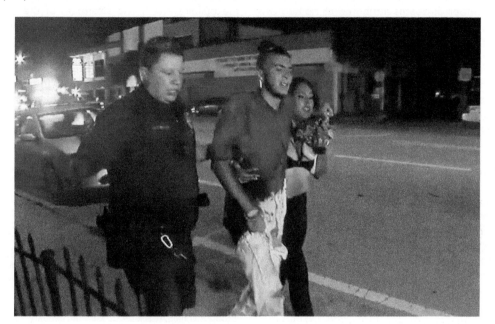

FIGURE 3.12 ▶ An injured man is escorted out of the Pulse nightclub after the rampage shooting by Omar Mateen on June 12, 2016. The motivation for the shooting was first attributed as an LBGTQ hate crime as the Pulse is a predominately gay nightclub; however, later evidence proved that the crime was in allegiance to ISIS. (Steven Fernandez/AP Images)

for U.S. bombing campaigns on ISIS targets in the Middle East. Omar Mateen had openly pledged allegiance to Abu Bakr al-Baghdadi social media sites. His last post on Facebook stated, "In the next few days you will see attacks from the Islamic State in the USA."[80] Interestingly, Noor Salman was acquitted of all charges as she introduced evidence showing that she had been a victim of her husband as well, suffering frequent beatings and sexual assault.[81] The attack at the Pulse nightclub remains one of the most deadly mass shootings in American history.

The future of homegrown terrorism is one that will see shifts in the composition of participants, as well as in the networking that they engage in with ISIS, al-Qaeda, and other affiliated movements. As the United States continues to see successes in dismantling the major arteries of these terrorist organizations, homegrown terrorists will seek new ways to interact with them. In the past, some had physically attended training camps or, as in the cases of Hasan and Simpson, communicated directly with terror operatives. As surveillance has intensified and travel has become more scrutinized, those who seek out these radically inclined connections will retreat further into the Internet, particularly the "**deep web**," utilizing gaming sites that appear

innocuous on the outside but allow encrypted conversations using their platforms, social media sites, and chat rooms to communicate.[82] The deep web is a vast part of the World Wide Web, not accessible through regular Internet browsing or search engines. Most of the information in the deep web is hidden, accessible from dynamic websites requiring the use of an application called *Tor*. The **Tor network** is synonymous for the deep web. This secretive online world remains mostly untraceable and difficult to access for the regular Internet user and even law enforcement and intelligence operatives. This subsequently allows a large illegal domain to thrive and a hidden venue for secret communications between terrorists, particularly astute worldwide terrorists sharing a common radical Islamic philosophy.[83]

Crude Devices and Nonsophisticated Weapons Aimed at Mass Casualty

Another important trend among homegrown terrorists is the use of crude devices or easily obtained weapons (such as assault rifles and other firearms) to carry out their attacks. The

Quick Facts: The Changing Nature of Homegrown Terrorism

In the last three years (2017, 2018, and 2019), the number of homegrown terrorist incidents in the United States has actually reduced as attacks stemming from far-right and hate extremists have dramatically escalated. According to New America, a research institution that tracks political violence, the number of deaths attributed to homegrown jihadist terrorist in the United States since 9/11 is 104 people. During the same timeframe, the number of deaths perpetrated by far-right and hate extremists in the United States is 86, with a dramatic rise over the last three years. Unfortunately, the FBI lumps both types of incidents together in a broad category call "domestic terrorism," complicating the ability to conduct more accurate and specific research on the different motivations to terrorist attacks in our country.

In October 2020, the U.S. Department of Homeland Security reported that "racially and ethnically motivated violent extremists--specifically white supremacist extremists (WSEs) -- will remain the most persistent and lethal threat in the Homeland. The report also stated that left-wing anarchist, anti-government, and anti-authority ideologies are on the rise, reinforcing the concept that the nature of 'homegrown' terrorism has changed from jihadist threats of the past to more racially and ethnically motivated violent extremists domestically, including white supremacists.

The warning from this report was quite prophetic. On January 6, 2021, a large crowd of supporters for President Donald Trump stormed the U.S. Capital in Washington, D.C. Five people died from the event, and dozens more were injured as the mob breached the Senate and House of Representatives meeting chambers. The rioters vandalized and looted many offices within the Capital as well as the building itself. The aftermath of the event has led to impeachment hearings on Trump, as well as a renewed emphasis on domestic, right-wing terrorism. The FBI opened more that 400 cases against individuals identified at the event. Dozens of people were arrested. Members of the anti-government paramilitary group "Oath Keepers" and right-wing hate group "Proud Boys" were indicted on conspiracy charges for allegedly planning specific aspects of the attack on the U.S. Capital.

Sources: Peter Bergen, "Homegrown Terrorism: A Plague We Cannot Ignore." *CNN*, October 28, 2018. See https://www.cnn.com/2018/10/28/opinions/homegrown-terrorism-a-plague-we-cannot-ignore-bergen/index.html; New America, *Terrorism in America After 9/11.* See https://www.newamerica.org/in-depth/terrorism-in-america/what-threat-united-states-today/; and U.S. Department of Homeland Security, Homeland Threat Assessment (Washington, DC: U.S. Department of Homeland Security, October 2020), 18. See: https://www.dhs.gov/sites/default/files/publications/2020_10_06_homeland-threat-assessment.pdf. CNN, David Shortell, Katelyn Polantz, and Zachary Cohen, "Members of Extremist Oath Keepers Group Planned Attack on US Capital, January 19, 2021.

bombs used in the Boston Marathon attacks were basically pressure cookers, found in any large retailer, filled with nails and ball bearings. They were reportedly made using instructions found online. Major Nidal Hasan used legally obtained firearms. Simpson and Soofi were armed with pistols and assault rifles commonly found at local gun stores, and Omar Mateen used an AR-15 assault rifle during the Orlando Pulse night club attack, which has become "the signature weapon" of terrorists and mass killers in the United States.[84] Other terror attacks in the past few years have utilized vehicles as weapons, as well as a litany of homemade explosives. Purchasing materials to make more complex weaponry is made more difficult by policy changes restricting certain hazardous or biologic materials—or, if not restricting them outright, triggering a level of scrutiny that would-be terrorists might avoid.[85]

It's for these reasons that then-Attorney General Eric Holder stated that these were the types of potential attacks that keep him up at night; he singled out the homegrown, lone wolf terrorist, stating that he was "very concerned about individuals who get radicalized in a variety of ways … sometimes self-radicalized."[86] **Lone wolves** include homegrown terrorists, but the term also encompasses those who identify with ideologies other than radical Islam; lone wolves can be right-wing extremists, anti-abortion radicals, and leftist environmentalists. They typically operate the same way that homegrown terrorists do—by networking online, seeking out their own information, and utilizing easily made or easily obtained weaponry for their attacks, though they may have more of a tendency than their radical Muslim counterparts to broadcast their intentions in some way.[87] They generally act on their own accord, in the name of some deeply held ideological belief system. While incidents of lone wolf terrorism are still statistically rare, they can have a devastating impact on local communities and inflame public fears.[88]

OTHER INTERNATIONAL THREATS

Certainly, the Middle East is not the only area ripe with terrorist activity aimed at the United States. Indeed, the huge growth of Islam in Southeast Asia (e.g., Thailand, Indonesia, Malaysia, and the Philippines) continues to also spawn radical movements aimed at destroying Western interests in the area. Jemaah Islamiya (JI) continues to be an active radical

Islamic group in Southeast Asia under the leadership of Abu Bakar Bashir (released from his Indonesian prison for participation in bombings in Jakarta [2003] and Bali [2002]). In July 2014, Abu Bakar Bashir pledged allegiance to ISIS, as did several other leaders of radical Islamic groups throughout Southeast Asia. Abu Sayyaf, another Islamic group based in the Philippines followed suit and released a video swearing allegiance to ISIS as well.[89] And terrorism on the left appears to be escalating throughout Western Europe, fueled in part by the current downturn in the global economy, causing high unemployment and a reduction of government benefits to various populations. Incidents in Germany, Italy, and France have indicated a "reawakening" of the Red Brigades, the Greens, and other cell groups expressing a left-wing, Marxist orientation.[90] On the other end of the political spectrum, alternative, far-right nationalist groups also appear to be escalating across Europe. Elections in 2018 and 2019 have revealed a dramatic increase in far-right political success in France, Spain, Italy, Germany, Austria, and the Scandinavian countries of Sweden, Finland, and Denmark.[91] The political success of the far-right often brings a new generation of radical groups that focus attention on anti-immigration and hate,

Then, too, a phenomenon called **"narco-terrorism"** continues to plague American police agencies as well as the international community. The most illustrative cases are seen in South America and Mexico surrounding the highly lucrative cocaine business. Drug lords in the Medellin and Cali cartels continue to be allied with the M-19 group in Colombia and Sendero Luminoso (Shining Path) in Peru for protection in cultivating and trafficking cocaine to the United States. Similar arrangements between drug dealers and anti-Western political groups (or states) have been observed in Cuba, Nicaragua, Panama, Bulgaria, and Burma.[92] One of the most successful of these collaborations is the development of the notorious street gang Mara Salvatrucha (MS-13). Originally composed of former soldiers and fighters from civil wars in El Salvador and Honduras during the 1970s and 1980s, MS-13 has become a violent and sophisticated gang associated with drug and human trafficking from Latin America. More problematic to local police agencies is the connection between ethnic drug dealers (Haitians, Jamaicans, and Cubans) and foreign governments, which results in significant financing and armament supplying in support of drug trafficking to the United States.[93]

Boko Haram

Although having existed for over a decade (since 2002), the Nigerian group Boko Haram gained international notoriety when the group kidnapped 276 schoolgirls in Chibok, Nigeria, in April 2014. The incident brought international condemnation as well as a cooperative venture by Western countries (primarily the United States, Great Britain, and France) aimed at reducing the impact of Boko Haram in northeastern Nigeria. Aside from this infamous kidnapping,

FIGURE 3.13 ▶ A member of Boko Haram states demands for the exchange of new girls kidnapped in Nigeria in 2015. The group has expressed its allegiance to the greater caliphate called the Islamic State and has become a significant threat in Africa. (AP Images)

the group has also been responsible for a number of other kidnappings for ransom, the wholesale slaughter of hostages taken from Borno, Nigeria, in June 2015, and several bombings using **improvised explosive devices (IEDs)**. Boko Haram means "Western education is forbidden." Its primary goal at inception was the destruction and overthrow of the current Nigerian Government. However, under the leadership of Abubakar Shekau, the group now represents the radical Islamic movement in Nigeria. It has become increasingly more violent and radicalized in the past few years, aligning itself operationally and philosophically with the greater Islamic State in the Middle East, now rebranded as the Islamic State in West Africa.[94] An estimated 15,000 innocent civilians have been killed by Boko Haram in the past seven years, with the vast majority occurring in 2014 and 2015.[95] As important, Boko Harem has dramatically increased the kidnapping and enslavery of women and children over the last two years (see Figure 3.13). As an example, in just one raid, the Nigerian Army reported rescuing more than 1,000 captives, many of whom were forced into sexual servitude as well as becoming Boko Haram fighters; some were also being trained as future suicide bombers.[96] Members of Boko Haram have declared areas in Nigeria, Northern Cameroon, Niger, Chad, and Mali that they control to be part of the Islamic State "Caliphate" in greater Africa.

The Mexican Cartels

Violence along the U.S.–Mexican border has dramatically decreased in the past five years, so much so, that many refer to places like Ciudad Jaurez and Nogales as "back to normal."[97] For instance, in Ciudad Juarez, once considered the most dangerous city in the world (across the Rio Grande River from El Paso, Texas), 1,247 people were killed in 2018.[98] While this number of homicides is huge from an American city perspective, it is less than half of the homicide rate in 2010 when

Box 3.8: The Legend of Joaquin Guzman Loera—"El Chapo"

One of the most notorious Mexican cartel leaders in the world today is Joaquin Guzman Loera, more commonly known as *"El Chapo."* Guzman was born in Culiacan, the capital of the state of Sinaloa, Mexico, into a poor, working class family. He quickly rose through the ranks of the Mexican drug cartels to become of the world's largest and most successful drug traffickers in history.[99] According to some DEA reports, El Chapo was responsible for the death and destruction of millions of people across the globe though drug addiction, violence, and corruption.[100] However to many Mexicans, he is a modern-day folk hero—a person who successfully rose from poverty to fight the deeply unpopular Mexican government, and a person who, mythically, cannot be imprisoned having escaped his captors countless times in Mexico. Many people, especially those from poor agrarian backgrounds inside Mexico, look to their government as a highly corrupt and aloof elite class. Like his American counterparts, El Chapo represents the hero outlaw, such as the Al Capone, the Lucky Luciano, the Don Corleone, or the Tony Soprano of Mexico—the persons who rose from nothing to outsmart the rich and powerful government to run an effective international drug trafficking and crime syndicate.[101]

El Chapo represents the new state of order in some developing countries, a person not afraid to use his massive wealth and influence (albeit from criminal enterprise) to help the lower classes achieve some status in an otherwise ruthless and corrupt governmental condition. Consequently, he is viewed as the "Robin Hood" of the modern era.[102] The concept is not new to the South American drug world, as Pablo Escobar and Carlos Lehder held similar positions of respect in Colombia during the 1980–early 1990s "cocaine cowboy" era. El Chapo maintains his mythical position as he once again escaped from Mexico's most secure prison via an elaborate tunnel on July 11, 2015; however, he was recaptured in early 2016 by Mexican Navy Special Commandos in western Mexico. He was extradited to the United States in January 2017 and was subsequently convicted of leading the murderous Sinaloa Cartel in a federal court in New York City in 2019. He is currently serving a life plus 30-year sentence in the federal supermax prison—Administrative Maximum U.S. Penitentiary—in Florence, Colorado.

Source: Polaris/Newscom; PGR/NOTIMEX/Newscom; PGR GDA Photo Service/Newscom.

3,057 people were murdered in Ciudad Juarez; that was an average of over eight people killed every day! Most of these murders could be attributed to narco-terrorism and violence between cartels vying for control of the primary transportation routes for billions of dollars worth of illegal drugs entering the United States from Mexico annually. The primary groups operating on the border were the Tijuana Cartel; the Vicente Carrillo Fuentes Organization, also known as the Juarez Cartel; the Gulf Cartel; and the Sinaloa Cartel, composed of several smaller groups including the Guzman-Loera Cartel and the Pacific Cartel.

These primary narco-trafficking cartels had direct linkages to Hispanic street gangs operating within the United States (such as the Mexican Mafia, La Familia, and the MS-13 gang), used for street trafficking and enforcement.

The Sinaloa and Juarez cartels are frequently involved with gangs that are involved in a variety of Mexican transnational crimes; meaning they use street gangs such as the Barrio Azteca, Surenos, Nortenos, and Tango Blast to conduct primary drug, weapons, and human trafficking across the Mexican Border.[103] Los Zetas is a rival group that is also very active on the border. Members of Los Zetas have acted as highly select assassins after deserting from the Mexican Army after receiving extensive training. While originally hired as "enforcers" for the Gulf Cartel, Los Zetas were also violent leaders in the narco-trafficking business along the U.S.–Mexico border.[104] This gang's brand of narco-terrorism was particularly vicious, often marked by mass murders and mutilated bodies set for display in an effort to frighten rival groups. As a result, Mexico recorded its highest number of homicides ever, reporting 29,168 murders in 2017. The number was the highest since the government began keeping records and revealed a homicide rate of 20.5 murders per 100,000 residents. Amazingly, this homicide rate is still significantly below other Latin countries, such as Brazil, Colombia, Venezuela, or El Salvador.[105].

Clearly, the violence in Mexico and particularly along the border will remain a top priority for intelligence agencies and American law enforcement. The violence does not appear to be spilling over into major U.S. cities. During 2017, El Paso was once again designated the "safest city in America," and significant drops in murder rates were reported nationwide with significant decreases in major cities like Chicago, Baltimore, St. Louis, Phoenix, and Dallas during this same period of time.

Outlaw Motorcycle Gangs (OMGs)

The history of outlaw motorcycle gangs in the United States and the rest of the world is a history of violent confrontations between rival gangs themselves and the police. According to the FBI's *2015 National Gang Report (NGR)*, there may be as many as 50,000 members in the United States alone, with affiliations to approximately 3,000 active outlaw motorcycle clubs.[106] In addition, larger OMGs have established new chapters and have attracted many new members. This increase has spawned new violence for geographic dominance in all types of criminal activity, including drug, weapon, human and sex trafficking, as well as smuggling of goods such as cigarettes and cell phones, theft and fencing of motorcycle parts, robbery and fraud.[107] Although, outlaw motorcycle gangs represent only a small percentage against traditional street gangs, they still pose a significant threat.

Calling themselves "1 percenters," representing 1 percent of all the people that are members of the American Motorcycle Association, outlaw motorcycle clubs gained in popularity after World War II as young combat soldiers, often disenfranchised by the war and unemployed, sought the thrill-seeking, crime-ridden subculture focused around riding a motorcycle. The 1947 Fourth of July week-end that occurred in the small town of Hollister, California, has become part of OMC folklore as well as the subject of many Hollywood movies. The incident was not nearly as infamous as Hollywood made it out to be; however, the reported havoc caused by some 4,000 outlaw motorcycle members descending on a small rural city did nothing more that recruit new members to the lifestyle. The ranks of OMGs have filled through the years with returning veterans from the Korean, Vietnam, and Iraq/Afghanistan Wars.

Today, there are four primary outlaw motorcycle clubs in the United States, with all having chapters in foreign countries: The Hell's Angels (the largest group focused in California with 425 chapters in 50 different countries), the Pagans (located primarily on the east coast of the United States and throughout Canada), the Outlaws (focused in Chicago with 275 chapters in 23 countries), and the Bandidos (focused in Texas with 210 chapters in 22 countries). Each club has their own insignia often proudly displayed on members' leather vests and jackets, commonly called the club's "**colors**." Most people in the United States would not immediately think of outlaw motorcycle gangs as "an international threat." However, during the past 25 years, almost all of the major outlaw motorcycle gangs have been classified by authorities as international criminal enterprises. Indeed, there have been several gang battles overseas. For instance in 1984, a shoot-out between the Bandidos and a rival gang called the Comancheros killed seven people and wounded another 28 in Milperra, Australia, and between 1994 through 1997, in what is commonly called, "The Great Nordic Biker War," long-time enemies belonging to the Hell's Angels and the Bandidos shook the Scandinavian countries of Denmark, Finland, Sweden, and Norway. At least 12 people died and over 100 were injured in the four-year war. On the domestic side, in 2015, in Waco, Texas, over 170 rival OMG members were arrested and charged in a shoot-out at a popular *Twin Peaks* restaurant. Nine bikers were killed and another 18 were wounded in the gun battle that at one time had over 30 gang members shooting at one another. Over 100 weapons, including various pistols and assault rifles were confiscated by police at the scene, as well as nearly 500 spent shell casings.[108] The incident marked one of the bloodiest confrontations in OMG history. See Figure 3.14.

Outlaw motorcycle gangs are engaged in variety of organized crime activities, including international drug, gun, stolen property, and human trafficking. They also have a long history associated with hate. Many of their symbols mimic Nazi-era insignias such as lightning bolt tattoos, *Waffen SS* initials, the number "88" signifying the 8th letter of the alphabet—"H" or "HH" for Heil Hitler. The role of women in OMG is also quite dubious. Many are referred to as "sheep" and are "owned by the club." It is not unusual to see a women tattooed with "Property of…" somewhere on her body as she dances in a biker-owned strip bar. While the above four OMGs dominate, there are also a number of smaller clubs such as the Vagos, Sons of Silence, Mongols, and the Red Devils. OMGs are often associated with right-wing extremist groups around the world, such as the Aryan Nation, Aryan Brotherhood, the Order, and various Neo-Nazi factions. For this reason, there were no known African-American or Mexican-American outlaw motorcycle gang members in any of the "Big Four" clubs. However, in just the last five years, the National Gang Intelligence Center has identified several large, black motorcycle gangs such as the Chosen Few, Hell's Lovers, Outcasts, Sin City Disciples, and Wheels of Soul. These groups have a black male only membership and have been involved localized assaults and homicides.[109]

FIGURE 3.14 ▶ Members of an outlaw motorcycle gang were arrested after a devastating shooting in Waco, Texas, in May 2015. Nine people were killed and another 18 were wounded outside a local restaurant as members from rival gangs (The Bandidos and the Cossacks) engaged in a bloody shoot-out between themselves and then police as they arrived on the scene. (Rod Aydelotte/Waco Tribune-Herald via AP Images)

RIGHT-WING EXTREMISM

The resurgence of right-wing, white supremacist groups across the country, was highlighted in the bombing of the Alfred P. Murrah Federal Building in Oklahoma City on April 19, 1995. The blast killed 169 people, including 19 children, and injured more than 500 others. Convicted and sentenced to death, Timothy James McVeigh held "extreme right-wing views and hated the federal government."[110] According to the FBI, the former army sergeant often wore military fatigues, sold weapons at gun shows, and attended militia meetings.[111] Although the incident will shortly mark it 25-year anniversary, the bombing of the Murrah Building remains a cold reminder of the potential of hate in America.

The bombing focused attention on a number of right-wing groups and state militias that have traditionally expressed strong antigovernment and white supremacist propaganda. These groups have also supported violence against minorities (African-Americans, Asians, and Jews), homosexuals, and members of the U.S. government (Bureau of Alcohol, Tobacco, Firearms, and Explosives). While the number of members of each of these groups is relatively small, they pose a significant threat because of their ability to communicate and coordinate activities. The groups have multiple names and members, publish regular newsletters, maintain websites, and operate automated bulletin board systems. In some cases, documented collusion between these groups and local law enforcement officials has posed a significant threat. Many people are attracted to these groups because they identify themselves with fundamentalist Christianity. Much of their rhetoric focuses on patriotism as interpreted by their leaders, usually using a perversion of the Constitution or the Bible. These groups consist of well-armed ideologues who possess the potential for increased terrorism, at least in geographical pockets throughout the United States.[112]

Hate Crimes

Right-wing extremist groups represent a movement that promotes whites, especially northern Europeans and their descendants, as intellectually and morally superior to other races.[123] On October 28, 2009, then-President Barack Obama signed the Matthew Shepard and James Byrd, Jr., Hate Crimes Prevention Act into law. This act expanded the 1969 federal hate crime statute based primarily on race and religion to include crimes based on a victim's sexual orientation, gender identity or disability. It is not coincidental that as right-wing, extremist groups have grown in strength, so have the number of reported hate crimes. **Hate crimes**, then, are harms inflicted on a victim by an offender whose motivation derives primarily from hatred directed at a perceived characteristic of the victim (e.g., the person's race, religion, ethnicity, gender, and/or sexual orientation). These crimes are particularly

Quick Facts: The Threat from Right-Wing Terrorism

Since the 9/11 attacks, nearly twice as many people have been killed by white supremacists and antigovernment fanatics than by radical Islamic terrorists in the United States. Clearly, public perception does not match the facts: The terrorist threat inside the county is much greater from right-wing hate groups than radical Muslim extremists.[113]

In a 2019 article, noted terrorism expert Bruce Hoffman warned that far-right, antigovernment extremism is growing and evolving rapidly in the United States and abroad.[114] The 2019 attack on two different mosques by white supremacist Brenton Harrison Tarrant in Christchurch, New Zealand supports Hoffman's statement. Unique to this attack, Tarrant actually live-streamed his shooting rampage on the *Al-Noor Mosque* on Facebook Live. Over 17 minutes of the attack shows Tarrant indiscriminately shooting attendees at the Friday prayer. In all, Tarrant killed 51 people and wounded another 50 in the worst terrorist attack in the history of New Zealand. Domestically, on an October Saturday morning in 2018, 46-year-old Robert Bowers burst into the *Tree of Life Synagogue* in Pittsburgh, Pennsylvania and opened fire on innocent people attending worship services. Witnesses state that Bowers yelled anti-Semitic epithets, including "All Jews must die," as he opened fire on the innocents, leaving 11 dead and another 6 seriously wounded, including 4 police officer responding to the scene. The incident remains the deadliest attack on the Jewish community in America. Clearly, hate and right-wing terrorism is escalating not only in the number of incidents and groups but also the number of fatalities from such attacks. The Southern Poverty Law Center reports a 30 percent increase in the number of U.S. hate groups over the past four years and 7 percent increase in hate groups in 2018 alone.[115] A total of 1,020 organizations were identified in 2018, a high for the past 20 years. Much of this increase was blamed on President Trump's administration and continued political endeavors that emphasizes a white nationalist fervor during a time of demographic change in America, as well as on right-wing media outlets and the expansive use of social media for allowing diverse groups to communicate with each other, finding common

Patrick Crusisus is currently awaiting trial on capital murder charges in Texas stemming from the 2019 mass shooting in El Paso, Texas. (El Paso Police Department/Handout/Getty Images)

ground for recruiting new members, and identifying common issues on which to spread hate and divisiveness.[116]

Sadly, Hoffman's predictions appeared to have traction domestically as 22 people at a Walmart Supercenter in El Paso, Texas were gunned down on an early Sunday morning, August 3, 2019. Another 23 were injured in one of the worst attacks of domestic terrorism in the United States. The gunman, Patrick Crusius, 21 years of age, stated that he targeted Mexican people as he drove from his home near Dallas, to the largest concentration of Hispanic citizens in a Texas city—El Paso, located directly on the on the border with Mexico. Law enforcement officials found numerous online messages that expressed racist and anti-immigration hate toward Latinos and Mexicans; eight of the victims of the attack were Mexican Nationals. Crusius is also the assumed author of a four-page manifesto posted online on *8chan,* an online chat and message board linked to white supremacism, neo-Nazism, the alt-right, racism, and multiple mass shootings.[117] The writing, entitled *The Inconvenient Truth,* was posted just 20 minutes before the El Paso shooting and was filled with white supremacist language and hatred against "race mixing," immigration, and the "Latino explosion." Crusius has showed no remorse for his actions.[118]

Box 3.9: Major Right-Wing Militant Groups in the United States

Aryan Nation—This is a white supremacist organization with strong separatist ideology, founded by Richard Butler of Hayden Lake, Idaho, a major figure in the Christian Identity Church, a pseudo-religious justification for white supremacy. The Nation recruits members from white prison gangs. Their goal is to develop an all-white homeland, to be called the "Northwest Mountain Republic," in Washington, Oregon, Idaho, Montana, and Wyoming. In September 2000, a jury awarded $6.3 million to a mother and son who were assaulted by Aryan

Nations guards outside their Idaho compound.[119] The Aryan Nations were forced to sell the land on which the compound was built. With the death of Richard Butler in 2004, the group and its philosophical position continue; however, its numbers have dwindled and the group's future is filled with uncertainty.

The Base— A militant, white nationalist, neo-Nazi network that emerged in 2018 believing in the use of violence, guerrilla warfare, and small terrorist attacks to rapidly overthrow existing social and governmental order (the downfall of the state), necessary to establish a new world order based on white supremacist principles. In January 2020, six members were arrested for plotting to kill federal agents in Georgia and Maryland.

Covenant, Sword, and Arm of the Lord—This paramilitary group operated primarily in Texas, Arkansas, and Missouri. Eight members were arrested with illegal weapons, explosives, land mines, and an antitank rocket launcher. They were extreme Christian fundamentalists with survivalist mentalities.

Ku Klux Klan (KKK)—This is primarily a southern states organization, with the largest memberships in Alabama, Georgia, Kentucky, South and North Carolina, and Mississippi. Several of the chapters have forgone the traditional cross burning and hooded robes in favor of automatic weapons, paramilitary training camps, and camouflage uniforms. In 2008, a jury awarded $1.5 million in compensatory damages and $1 million in punitive damages to plaintiff Jordan Gruever, represented by the Southern Poverty Law Center against the KKK.[120] The jury found that five KKK members had brutally beaten Gruver, then a 16-year-old of American Indian descent, at a Kentucky county fair. The case, similar to the one against the Aryan Nations in 2000, had a significant impact on the Klan, as its numbers and donations fell dramatically. Current estimates of KKK membership hover around 5,000; however, increases in splinter groups appear to be growing. The group still maintains the white supremacist and anti-Semitic beliefs prominently characterizing the KKK historically.

Minutemen—This paramilitary organization was strongest during the 1960s. Small enclaves still exist that express strong anticommunist rhetoric and violence against liberals. Their insignia of the crosshairs of a rifle scope usually earmarks this group from other right-wing extremists.

National Alliance—This is a Neo-Nazi group founded by William L. Pierce, who started a new white enclave in rural West Virginia. Pierce was the author of *The Turner Diaries*, the saga of a family that survives the impending race war against African-Americans and retreats to the mountains for safety. Pierce's death in 2002 heralded the rise of Erich Gliebe as national chairman. His primary goal had been to foster international membership expressing the white supremacy doctrines of the past, particularly those stemming from Nazi Germany. However, following several public incidents involving strippers, Gliebe stepped down. Will White Williams II took over the top leadership position of the group in late 2018.

Posse Comitatus—This is a loose-knit group attracting rural farmers. Strong antigovernment sentiment claims that the Federal Reserve System and income tax are unconstitutional. Posse leaders have fused tax-protest doctrine with virulent anti-Semitism. Leader Gordon Kahl murdered two U.S. marshals in North Dakota and was subsequently killed in a shoot-out in 1983.

Proud Boys—Established in 2016, this far-right political group self-described as a "western chauvinists" sprang to national attention in 2017 as members organized the "Unite the Right" rally in Charlottesville, VA. The group was often mentioned during the Trump-Biden campaigns of 2020 because of their racists and "alt-right" statements, and alleged associations to law enforcement. "Proud Boys," along with an associated paramilitary group, "Oath Keepers" were indicted in the January 6, 2021 riot breaching the U.S. Capital stemming from their activities in planning the attack.

Skinheads—This is a violence-prone, Neo-Nazi youth gang whose members are noted for their shaved heads. They express a strong white supremacist, racist, and anti-Semitic ideology and have close linkages to the Ku Klux Klan.

The Order—This is the most violent of the Neo-Nazi groups, with several ties to the Aryan Nations. It is responsible for the murder of a Jewish radio personality in Denver in 1984; at least two armored car robberies totaling $4 million in Seattle, Washington, and Ukiah, California; and a large bombing attempt in Coeur d'Alene, Idaho. The Order has been very quiet during the past decade.

White Aryan Resistance (WAR)—This is the main white supremacist group in California, headed by Tom Metzger, former Grand Dragon of the California Ku Klux Klan. It currently produces *Race and Reason,* a white supremacist program shown on public access cable television.

White Revolution—This group was founded in September 2002 by Billy Roper after he was expelled from the National Alliance during a power struggle with Erich Gliebe. The Arkansas-based White Revolution is a racist organization that promotes cooperation between white supremacist groups in the United States and in Europe.

State militias—Active paramilitary organizations exist in almost every state (e.g., the Michigan Militia, the Republic of Texas Militia, and the Arizona Vipers), expressing a strong white, Protestant, local constitutionalist perspective of government. They conduct a variety of paramilitary camps and are preparing for an "impending race war." Many groups have legitimate firearms licenses allowing automatic weapons and explosives. One group in Arizona is known to have purchased a World War II-era tank. Strong linkages to local police agencies have been documented. Members are strong gun owner advocates with a superpatriotism and antifederal government sentiment. Since 2009, their financial strength and membership rolls have grown apparently due to deep-seeded conflict over immigration reform and the desire to secure the Mexican-American border. The Southern Poverty Law Center estimates that there are close to 800 militia groups active in the United States. None are more potentially violent than the *Hutaree or Christian Warrior Militia* based in eastern Michigan's Lenawee County. Established in 2008, the group was heavily para-military, participating in extensive training for a future war "preparing for the end time battles" with forces of the anti-Christ.[121]

Nine members of the group (located in Michigan, Ohio, and Indiana) were indicted by a grand jury in Detroit for conspiring to murder police officers and civilians using explosives and firearms.[122] Their intent was apparently to "replace" all factions of the government, starting with police officers.

In October 2020, members with direct ties to these State militias were arrested for plotting to kidnap and execute Michigan Governor Gretchen Whitmer. There were also plans to kidnap Viriginia Governor Ralph Northam as well, in part because of his lockdown orders to slow the spread of Covid-19. Members of "The Wolverine Watchmen Militia" were indicted in this plot to kidnap and kill the state governors.

Southern Poverty Law Center, "The Base." See: https://www.splcenter.org/fighting-hate/extremist-files/group/base

Souther Poverty Law Center, "Proud Boys". See: https://www.splcenter.org/fighting-hate/extremist-files/group/proud-boys and Will Carless, "Proud Boys Echoed, Retracted by DC Cops," *USA Today* November 13, 2020.

Kayla Ruble and Devlin Barrett, "FBI: Whitmer Plotters Also Discussed Kidnapping Virginia Governor Ralph Northam," Washington Post, October 12, 2020. See: https://www.washingtonpost.com/national-security/ralphnortham-gretchen-witmer-kidnapping-plot/2020/10/13/26b4e31a-0d5f11eb-b1e8-16b59b92b36d_story.html. and Darcie Moran and Joe Guillen, "AG: Michigan Plot Ringleader Wanted to Televise Killings," *USA Today*, November 13, 2020.

Box 3.10: Charleston, South Carolina Church Massacre

Around 8:00 pm on Wednesday, June 17, 2015, a young white man, Dylann Storm Roof entered the Emanuel AME Church in Charleston, South Carolina, and began shooting African-Americans in a Bible study group, resulting in nine deaths. He then fled the scene in a black four-door sedan.[124] Roof was armed with a handgun that the FBI reports should not have been able to purchase.[125]

Roof was quickly arrested and subsequently confessed to the grotesque massacre of church members. Roof's motive was to start a race war and in that context he saw himself as a heroic figure, doing what others did not dare to do. His website was filled with complimentary comments about Nazis and rants about African-Americans, Jews, Hispanics, and East Asians. A survey taken 10 days after the massacre revealed that 87 percent of Americans saw the murders as a hate-based crime.[126] Roof's murderous rampage did not give rise to hatred, but public forgiveness by the church members, including relatives of slain members, a demonstration of unshakeable Christian belief. However in January 2017, the unrepentant and avowed white supremacist Roof was sentenced to death after a jury found him guilty of 33 counts of murder stemming from the 2015 attack at the Emanuel AME Church in Charleston.

Roof's actions are characteristic of the lone wolf attack, which seemingly comes out of nowhere, with no warning. Even his website did not provide an indication that an actual attack would be carried out. Lone wolves do not have to

coordinate with anyone; there is no group decision-making or supporters who might mediate the wolf's deadly intent.[127]

As an indication of the harm that can be wrought by a lone wolf, the first midair plane bombing, airplane hijacking, anthrax attack, and product contamination were all executed by lone persons.[128]

Source: Splash News/Newscom.

heinous because of their unique impact on victims as well as on the community. Victims often suffer from the suspect's underlying criminal behavior, such as the physical injury caused by violence or the property damage associated with vandalism. In addition, they are victims by the thought that such acts were *not* random, that at least some people in our society detest them because of who they are: African-American, Jewish, Islamic, lesbian-gay-bisexual-transgender-queer (LGBTQ), and so on. Hate crimes are often brutal and injurious, and victims are not only physically hurt but also emotionally traumatized and terrified. Others in the community who share the victim's characteristic may also feel vulnerable, and this may escalate the conflict as they attempt to retaliate for the original offense.

In the past, police officers have not been adequately trained to handle such incidents, treating them as routine assaults or vandalism. However, enacted federal legislation has resulted in the development of the National Institutes Against Hate Crimes and Terrorism, located at the Simon Wiesenthal Center in Los Angeles, California. The institute provides training for teams of criminal justice professionals from the same jurisdiction to combat hate crimes. Its goal is to provide new strategic approaches to combating hate crimes based on an understanding of the unique elements that differentiate such crimes from other acts. The center has been highly successful in training over 500 participants and providing an ongoing support center for follow-up communication, program evaluation, and professional development via website updates and videoconferences.[129]Legal definitions of hate crimes vary. The federal definition addresses civil rights violations under 18 U.S.C. Section 245. A hate crime is a criminal offense committed against persons, property, or society that is motivated, in whole or in part, by an offender's bias against an individual's or a group's perceived race, religion, ethnic/national origin, gender, age, disability, or sexual orientation.[130] Most states have a hate crime statute that provides enhanced penalties for crimes in which victims are selected because of the perpetrator's bias against the victims' perceived race, religion, or ethnicity. Some states also classify as hate crimes those in which a victim is selected on the basis of a perception of his or her sexual orientation, gender, or disability. In some states, the passage of hate crime statutes has been controversial as politicians have debated the constitutionality of enhanced penalties based on a suspect's association with an extremist group or the inclusion of homosexuality as a protected class.

Digital Hate

Many white supremacist groups have used the Internet to recruit potential members and spread their message of hate. See Figure 3.15. Over 1,500 websites can be identified and attributed to extremist organizations that incite racial hatred and religious intolerance as well as terrorism and bomb making. More disturbing is the directed effort by many of these groups to attract young people into their ranks. Based in part on links to other social youth movements involving music and dress (e.g., Skinheads, Black cults, and heavy-metal music), aggressive recruitment on college campuses and the development of web pages designed to attract young people are now quite common. In addition, white-power rock concerts are often sponsored by extremist groups, such as the National Alliance and the World Church of the Creator. These concerts provide face-to-face opportunities for meeting and recruitment.

White supremacist groups have also created sophisticated computer games aimed at attracting teenagers. *Ethnic Cleansing*, the most high-tech game of its kind, encourages players to kill Blacks, Jews, and Hispanics as they run through urban ghettos and subway environments. In the game, players can dress in Ku Klux Klan robes and carry a noose. Every time a Black enemy is shot, he emits a monkeylike squeal, while

FIGURE 3.15 ▶ Selected hate sites on the Internet.
Sources: The New Lexicon of Hate: The Changing Tactics, Language and Symbols of America's Extremists (Los Angeles: Simon Wiesenthal Center, 1999), www.wiesenthal.com. See also Robert W. Taylor, Eric J. Fritsch, and John Liederbach, *Digital Crime and Digital Terrorism*, 3rd edition (Upper Saddle River, NJ Pearson, 2015).

Jewish characters shout, "Oy vey!" when they are killed.[131] Quite predictably, the game has spurred significant controversy between game developers and censor advocates. However, very little can be done to ban the game, since many other video games are designed to allow enthusiasts to create new levels and characters, while free software tools enable programmers to build new platforms easily.

These types of games and directed recruitment efforts have been effective tools in swelling the ranks of some extremist organizations.[132] According to one Skinhead source, young people represent the future—"they are the frontline warriors in the battle for white supremacy."[133]

ECOTERRORISTS AND ANIMAL RIGHTS GROUPS

Many of the single-issue terrorist groups, such as the **Earth Liberation Front (ELF)** and the **Animal Liberation Front (ALF)**, arose from relatively peaceful movements and call for a renewal of the planet's geophysical and biological environment. These groups are commonly called "ecoterrorists" since their primary motivation focuses on improving the ecology of the world. The notable difference between the terrorist group and the more passive movements (e.g., Earth First and People for the Ethical Treatment of Animals [PETA]) is in the advocacy of violence and destruction to accomplish their ends. Single-issue groups, such as ELF and ALF, pose one of the most significant new threats in domestic terrorism. Both organizations work in small groups with no central hierarchy. They have no formal membership lists, and they work independently in a cell-structured manner similar to other violent groups. The ELF and ALF declared solidarity in 1993 and members of either group usually carry out acts on behalf of both groups. To date, most of their activities have been aimed at the destruction of property and vandalism.

Both groups began in England and migrated to the United States during the 1980s. Like so many other groups, ELF was inspired by the fictional writings of one author, Edward Abbey, whose 1975 novel, *The Monkey Wrench Gang,* told the story of a group of ecologists who were fed up with industrial development in the West. In the novel, environmental activists travel through the western U.S. spiking trees, burning billboards, sabotaging bulldozers, and damaging the property of people they deem to be destroying the environment. This type of low-level activity has become so popular that, among activists, the term "monkey wrenching" has become a key touchstone for ecoterrorism.[134] The FBI designated ELF a terrorist organization in January 2001. This action was based primarily on the arson attack of a ski resort under construction near Vail, Colorado, in 2001. ELF burned three buildings and caused the destruction of four ski lifts. The group quickly claimed responsibility for the attack, which caused an estimated $12 million in damages. Ironically, the fire almost swept through the adjoining forest and would have destroyed the very habitat ELF was attempting to "save" for the preservation of wildlife. Of course, this was not the only attack from ELF, but it does represent one of the most financially destructive incidents directly attributed to the group. More recently, ELF has had a resurgence in England, firebombing several cars in London (2014) in response to the death of Remi Fraisse, an environmental activist, and a major arson attack of a U.S. Forest Service Research Station in Pennsylvania causing over $700,000 in damages and destroying 70 years of research in 2012.[135]

ALF grew substantially during the 1990s and took on a much more destructive perspective. Instead of just tossing blood or spray-painting individuals wearing furs, the group began a campaign to "free" animals from cages and destroy animal-linked farms, business, and laboratories. Breeding companies were attacked when the animals were released from their cages and the surrounding areas destroyed by fire and/or vandalism. Several of the targets were major research universities in Michigan and California, which not only suffered significant physical damage to buildings but also lost years of research findings and records.[136] However, in January 2006, after a nine-year investigation, the FBI indicted 11 people in connection with a five-year wave of arson and sabotage claimed by the Earth Liberation Front and the Animal Liberation Front. Detailing nearly 20 attacks from 1996 to 2001, causing no deaths but nearly $25 million in damage to lumber companies, a Vail ski resort, meat plants, and electric towers throughout the Pacific Northwest, the "vast ecoterrorism conspiracy" was dealt a very severe blow, one that placed a significant dent in the movement.[137] In the last few years, ALF activities have been limited to a few isolated events involving, again, the firebombing of a UCLA researcher's house in 2006 for research with animals and the arson of four houses in the Seattle region, causing nearly $7 million in damages because the houses were not deemed to be "built green" (2009),[138] and a 2011 arson of the Rocky Mountain Fir and Fireworks Corporation in Boise, Idaho causing over $100,000 in damages.[139]

While both groups, ELF and ALF, maintain websites on the Internet, their radical activity has seriously declined over the last 10 years. Today, much of their activity is relegated to disseminating literature and political activism supporting their cause in various countries throughout the world.

Chapter Summary

Summary by Learning Objectives

1. **Define *intelligence*.**

   Intelligence is data and information that have been evaluated, analyzed, and produced with careful conclusions and recommendations. Intelligence, then, is a *product* created from systematic and thoughtful examination, placed in context, and provided to law enforcement executives, with facts and alternatives that can inform critical decisions.

2. **Describe the Intelligence Cycle as presented in the *National Criminal Intelligence Sharing Plan* (NCISP).**

   The *National Criminal Intelligence Sharing Plan* (NCISP) contains 28 specific recommendations for major changes in local policing. The key concept from the document emphasized the strategic integration of intelligence into the overall mission of the police organization—intelligence-led policing. Rather than react and respond to past calls for

service, the NCISP places much more emphasis on predictive analysis derived from the discovery of hard facts, information, patterns, intelligence, and good crime analysis. By concentrating on key criminal activities, problems, and individuals targeted through analysis, significant attention can be directed to alleviate the crime problem. In order to protect the civil liberties of all individuals, the intelligence process was developed with key evaluation points aimed at verifying source reliability and validity at the beginning of the collection cycle. The goal was to develop a universal process that would integrate both law enforcement and national security intelligence agendas, while providing mechanisms for securing individual freedoms and allowing law enforcement agencies to be proactive in preventing and deterring crime and terrorism. The end result was the "Intelligence Cycle," presented by the FBI as a means of developing data into refined and polished intelligence and communicating or sharing that intelligence among individuals and agencies through the dissemination process.

3. **Define a *fusion center* and briefly list its four primary goals.**

Fusion centers act as a hub for exchanging information and intelligence, maximizing police resources, streamlining public safety operations, and improving the ability to fight crime and terrorism by merging data from a variety of sources. Fusion centers serve as clearinghouses for all potentially relevant homeland security information that can be used to assess local terror threats and aid in the apprehension of more traditional criminal suspects. The four primary goals of a fusion center are as follows: (1) fusion centers support the broad range of activities undertaken by a police department relating to the detection, examination, and investigation of a potential terrorist and/or criminal activity; (2) fusion centers support operations that protect critical infrastructure and key resources (CI/KRs) in a given region, support major incident operations, support specialized units charged with interdiction and investigative operations, and assist in emergency operations and planning. The aim of a fusion center is to reduce the vulnerability of the high-value and high-risk targets identified within a jurisdiction; (3) fusion centers often maintain public "tip lines," which give them the capability to promote more public involvement in and awareness of terrorist threats. The goal is to identify and recognize warning signs and potential threats in a timely manner in order to preempt potential terrorist attacks and reduce the vulnerability of the CI/KRs in a given region; and (4) fusion centers assist police executives in making better-informed decisions, especially during emergencies or critical incidents.

4. **Describe some of the major criticisms aimed at fusion centers and other law enforcement responses to terrorism.**

The major criticisms aimed at fusion centers and other law enforcement responses to terrorism include the following: (1) problems relating to the sharing of information between local law enforcement and the FBI. The sharing of information appears to be one way, from local police agencies to the FBI; (2) fusion centers are expensive and almost any cost-benefit analysis (including a 2012 U.S. Senate Permanent Subcommittee investigation) revealed significant money spent for very little, tangible evidence of success. The effectiveness of fusion centers, particularly given their financial outlay, has seriously been questioned; (3) many fusion centers appear to suffer from "mission creep"; that is, because there are few cases focused on terrorism, many centers have expanded their role to include crime fighting and reduction; and (4) many

fusion centers come desperately close to violating the civil liberties of people, especially relating to racial and ethnic profiling and breaches of privacy.

5. **List the four primary areas of responsibility within the Department of Homeland Security (DHS).**

There are four primary areas of responsibility within the Department of Homeland Security (DHS): (1) border security and transportation; (2) emergency preparedness and response; (3) chemical, biological, radiological, and nuclear countermeasures; and (4) intelligence analysis and infrastructure protection.

6. **Define *terrorism*.**

In the popular mind, terrorism is viewed as the illegitimate and violent actions of specific groups that violate the authority of rightfully established governments. Terrorism encompasses the threat of and/or use of violence to achieve a specific set of political objectives or goals. Historically, defining terrorism has been a very difficult venture, shaped and altered by a number of factors, including our own national interests, government interpretations, the news media, hidden political agendas, and emotional human rights rhetoric. Terrorism is situationally defined—that is, a number of factors play on the difficulty of defining terrorism, including competing political agendas, national interests, economic security, the news media, fundamental cultural and religious beliefs, and the use of misinformation. For this reason, scholars have conceptualized terrorism in four distinct typologies, based on the actors: (1) *international terrorism*—actions conducted in the international arena by individuals that are members of a nation state; (2) *transnational terrorism*—actions conducted in the international arena by individuals that have no nation-state; (3) *domestic terrorism*—actions conducted by groups within a nation, usually against the government or specific groups within the nation-state; and (4) *state terrorism*—actions conducted by governments against their own population.

7. **Briefly describe the concept of "jihad" and name some of the more radical Islamic groups active throughout the world.**

The concept of "jihad" or "holy war" is rooted in an early religious movement commonly called "Wahhabism" and later "Salafism" and can be traced back to the late 1700s in what is now Saudi Arabia and Egypt. The ideology is based primarily on the writing of radical Islamic philosophers, Muhammad Ibn al-Wahhab, Hassan al-Banna, and Sayiid Muhammad Qubt and calls for the purging of Western influence throughout the entire Middle East. The concept is justified throughout passages in the Qur'an that are perverted and misinterpreted to justify a "holy war" against the West. It is important to note that radical Islamic fundamentalists represent only a small but growing percentage of all Islam. Some of the groups that espoused "jihad" throughout the world are al-Qaeda, the Islamic State, Abu Sayyaf Group, HAMAS, Jemaah Islamiya, Lashkar-i-Tayyiba, and the Muslim Brotherhood.

8. **Describe the concept of a "homegrown terrorist."**

   The term "**homegrown terrorist**" refers to extremists who are legal U.S. residents or even citizens, and who are linked to or inspired by a specific, often intolerant ideology. This ideology may be motivated by political or religious sources and may be centered in domestic or foreign movements. Indeed, some of them have made connections with well-known, international terror groups, such as ISIS and al-Qaeda. These individuals may receive ideological encouragement, but not financial or material support, making them ancillary to the primary group and very difficult to detect by intelligence and law enforcement services.

9. **Discuss why Outlaw Motorcycle Gangs (OMGs) are considered an international threat to the United States. Identify the "Big Four" OMGs that are active in the United States.**

   Most people in the United States would not immediately think of outlaw motorcycle gangs as "an international threat." However, during the last 25 years, almost all of the major outlaw motorcycle gangs have been classified by authorities as international criminal enterprises primarily because of recent and wide-spread gun battles between OMG's and shoot-outs with the police. As an example, in 2015, in Waco, Texas, over 170 rival OMG members were arrested and charged in a shoot-out at a popular *Twin Peaks* restaurant. Nine bikers were killed and another 18 were wounded in the gun battle that at one time had over 30 gang members shooting at one another. There are four primary outlaw motorcycle gangs in the United States, with all having chapters in foreign countries: The Hell's Angels (the largest group focused in California with 425 chapters in 50 different countries), the Pagans (located primarily on the east coast of the United States and throughout Canada), the Outlaws (focused in Chicago with 275 chapters in 23 countries), and the Bandidos (focused in Texas with 210 chapters in 22 countries). Clearly, OMGs pose an international as well as a domestic threat.

10. **Define a *hate crime*.**

    A hate crime is a criminal offense committed against persons, property, or society that is motivated, in whole or in part, by an offender's bias against an individual's or a group's perceived race, religion, ethnic/national origin, gender, age, disability, or sexual orientation. Most states have a hate crime statute that provides enhanced penalties for crimes in which victims are selected because of the perpetrator's bias against the victims' perceived race, religion, or ethnicity. Some states also classify hate crimes as those in which a victim is selected on the basis of a perception of his or her sexual orientation, gender, or disability. In some states, the passage of hate crime statutes has been controversial as politicians have debated the constitutionality of enhanced penalties based on a suspect's association with an extremist group or the inclusion of homosexuality as a protected class. There is also a federal statute that addresses civil rights violations under 18 U.S.C. Section 245.

11. **Define and identify groups that are commonly called *ecoterrorists*.**

    Groups commonly called "ecoterrorists" are primarily motivated on improving the ecology of the world. Many of these single-issue terrorist groups arose from relatively peaceful movements and the call for a renewal of the planet's geophysical and biological environment. The two most notable "ecoterrorist" groups are the Earth Liberation Front (ELF) and the Animal Liberation Front (ALF). Despite recent and significant law enforcement and prosecution successes against these groups, both are still active today, with most of their activities aimed at the destruction of property and vandalism.

Chapter Review Questions

1. Define *intelligence*, and identify the two ultimate goals of intelligence.
2. List and briefly explain the six steps of the Intelligence Cycle as presented in the *National Criminal Intelligence Sharing Plan (NCISP)*.
3. What is a fusion center and briefly list their four primary goals?
4. What are the 10 simple steps that assist individual police agencies become part of the National Criminal Intelligence Sharing Plan?
5. What are critical infrastructure and key resources (CI/KRs)? Give some examples.
6. What is the National Counterterrorism Center (NCTC)?

7. What are the four primary areas of responsibility within the Department of Homeland Security?

8. Briefly discuss some of the issues and criticisms relating to police and intelligence generally, and with fusion centers specifically.

9. Define *terrorism*.

10. Briefly describe the concept of "jihad" and name some of the more radical Islamic terrorist groups active throughout the world.

11. What is ISIS and who is Abu Bakr al-Baghdadi?

12. What is a "homegrown" terrorist? Give some examples and recent incidents involving homegrown terrorists.

13. What is Boko Haram?

14. Who is "el Chapo" and what is his importance to the Mexican Cartels?

15. Why are Outlaw Motorcycle Gangs (OMGs) considered an international threat to the United States. Identify the "Big Four" OMGs that are active in the United States.

16. What is a *hate crime?* In your answer be sure to identify some of the major right-wing groups active in the United States.

17. What is an *ecoterrorist?* Identify some of the major groups called ecoterrorists.

Critical Thinking Exercises

1. **Historical Problems in the Levant.** Research the Middle Eastern area known as the Levant—an area of land between Egypt, Anatolia, Mesopotamia, and the Arabian Desert. The Levant is an ancient land of great historical civilizations—from the center of the Ur civilization (2100 BC) to the kingdom of Babylonia (1700 BC), to the ancient Greek and Roman Empires (300 BC to 400 AD), to the great Ottoman Empire of the 20th century. The Levant has been the crossroad for communication, trade, and commerce between the Middle East and the rest of world (Europe). The Levant is a geographical area composed of the modern-day countries of Israel, the Palestinian territories of the Gaza and West Bank, Syria, Jordan, and Lebanon. It is a fertile area located on the southeastern shores of the Mediterranean Sea. Great spiritual meaning has also been given to the area of the Levant as it represents the lands of Abraham, Moses, Jesus, and Muhammad. It is also an area that has witnessed significant historical conflict. Study the countries of the Levant and focus on the conflict in Syria and Iraq. Try to identify which groups discussed in this chapter are actively fighting or supporting a specific side in these countries. Now research the history of the al-Assad family in Syria. Who is Bashar al-Assad and do you think he will abdicate his monarchy in the near future? Why or why not?

2. **Mass Shooters and Lone Wolves.** Scour the Internet for mass shooters and lone wolf attacks in the United States. Are there any common denominators between the shooters and their horrific events of the past decade? Review the CNN story and videos entitled, "Deadliest Mass Shootings in Modern U.S. History Fast Facts" updated in 2019, at https://www.cnn.com/2013/09/16/ us/20-deadliest-mass-shootings-in-u-s-history-fast-facts/index.html. Note that the article makes a difference between mass murders (single incident) and spree killing (multiple incidents). Discuss the problem of mass shootings and spree killings in class. What do you think can be done to prevent such horrific incidents in the future?

3. **Research Intelligence on Terrorist Organizations and Groups Globally.** Visit and preview the Terrorism Research and Analysis Consortium (TRAC), created by the Beacham Group, LLC on the Internet at: www.terrorismresearch.org. Watch the preview and explore the site. TRAC is one of the most comprehensive terrorism research sites on the Internet and provides an efficient series of filters in which to study various types of terrorist targets, tactics, and groups. Play with the filters, watch some of the posted videos, read some of the articles on ideology, and read the intelligence reports about the latest information on active groups in any area of your choosing. Consider subscribing, or having your university or college subscribe to the site. TRAC was specifically designed to fulfill the research and intelligence needs of faculty, scholars, students, government, and defense professionals studying terrorism.

4. **The National Counter Terrorism Center (NCTC).** The Office of the Director of National Intelligence houses the National Counter Terrorism Center (NCTC). The two core missions of the NCTC are to serve the primary organization in the United States for the analysis and integration of terrorism intelligence, and the second mission is to conduct strategic operational planning for counter terrorism activities. Visit the NCTC website at: www.nctc.gov. Name the key partners associated with the NCTC and view the Counter Terrorism Calendar. Now explore career possibilities

within the intelligence field. What types of career opportunities exist within the Intelligence Community at the federal level? As important, what knowledge, skills, and abilities are required to fulfill these types of positions and are you qualified? Develop an action plan for yourself to accomplish education and training goals that would qualify you for an intelligence analyst position within the NCTC.

Key Terms

al-Qaeda
all-hazard
caliphate
colors
critical infrastructure and key resources (CI/KRs)
deep web
Earth Liberation Front (ELF)

Animal Liberation Front (ALF)
fusion centers
hate crimes
homegrown terrorism
Homeland Security Data Network (HSDN)
improvised explosive devices (IEDs)
intelligence

Islamic State (ISIS)
jihad
lone wolf (wolves)
narco-terrorism
National Counterterrorism Center (NCTC)
terrorism
Tor network

Endnotes

[1] Marilyn Peterson, *Intelligence-Led Policing: The New Intelligence Architecture* (Washington, DC: U.S. Department of Justice, BJA, September 2005) NCJ 210681; and K. Riley, G. Terverton, J. Wilson, and L. Davis, *State and Local Intelligence in the War on Terror* (Washington, DC: The RAND Corporation, 2005).

[2] For a more thorough discussion of the role of intelligence in combating terrorism, see Robert W. Taylor, "Terrorism and Intelligence," *Defense Analysis* 3, No. 2 (1987), pp. 165–175.

[3] Peterson, *Intelligence-Led Policing: The New Intelligence Architecture*, p. 3.

[4] For a more thorough discussion of the first two schools of thought, refer to R. Godson, ed., *Intelligence Requirements for the 1980s: Analysis and Estimates* (Washington, DC: National Strategy Information Center, 1983).

[5] Early models of predictive intelligence are discussed in R. Hever, *Quantitative Approaches to Political Intelligence* (Boulder, CO: Westview Press, 1978).

[6] *National Criminal Intelligence Sharing Plan* (Washington, DC: U.S. Department of Justice, 2003, and revised in July 2005).

[7] K. Riley, G. Treverton, and L. Davis, *State and Local Intelligence in the War on Terror.*

[8] *Fusion Center Guidelines: Developing and Sharing Information and Intelligence in a New Era* (Washington, DC: U.S. Department of Justice, 2006).

[9] Joseph D' Amico, "Stopping Crime in Real Time," *Police Chief* (September 2006), pp. 20–24.

[10] Department of Homeland Security, *State & Major Urban Area Fusion Centers: Fact Sheet,* December 17, 2018. See https://www.dhs.gov/national-network-fusion-centers-fact-sheet

[11] *Fusion Center Guidelines: Developing and Sharing Information and Intelligence in a New Era.*

[12] U.S. Department of Homeland Security, "Fusion Center Locations and Contact Information." See http://www.dhs.gov/fusion-center-locations-amd-contact-information.

[13] See https://nfcausa.org/.

[14] For a complete description of the National Counterterrorism Center, visit: www.nctc.gov.

[15] Samuel Walker and Charles M. Katz, *The Police in America,* 5th ed. (Boston: McGraw-Hill, 2005).

[16] George L. Kelling and William K. Bratton, "Policing Terrorism," *Civi Bulletin* 43, New York: Manhattan Institute for Policy Research (September 2006), p. 2.

[17] Mathieu Deflem, *The Policing of Terrorism: Organizational and Global Perspectives* (New York: Routledge Publishing, 2012).

[18] See Graeme R. Newman and Ronald V. Clarke, *Policing Terrorism: An Executive's Guide* (Washington, DC: U.S. Department of Justice, October, 2008).

[19] See Nationwide SAR Initiative (NSI), http://nsi.ncirc.gov/default.aspx (June 2010).

[20] U.S. Department of Homeland Security, *2010 Baseline Capabilities Assessment of Fusion Centers.* See http://www.dhs.gov/2010-baseline-capabilities-assessment-fusion-centers-and-critical-operational-capabilities-gap.

[21] Information received during conversations with various fusion directors at the Fourth National Fusion Center Conference, New Orleans, LA (February 23–25, 2010).

[22] For a thorough critique focusing on fusion centers, see Torin Monahan and Neal A. Palmer, "The Emerging Politics of DHS Fusion Centers," *Security Dialogue* 40, No. 6 (December, 2009), pp. 617–636.

[23] Michael German and Jay Stanley, "What's Wrong with Fusion Centers? Retrieved June 8, 2008 from http://www.aclu.org/pdfs/privacy/fusioncenters_20071212.pdf.

[24] John Rollins, *Fusion Centers: Issues and Options for Congress* (Washington, DC: Congressional Research Services, January 2008).

[25] U.S. Senate Permanent Subcommittee on Investigations, *Federal Support for and Involvement in State and Local Fusion Centers.* See http://www.hsgac.senate.gov/search/?q=federal+support+for+and+involvement+in+state+and+local+fusion+centers.

[26] Ibid., p. 1.

[27] Ibid., p. 5.

[28] Adam Mazmanian, "Trump Signs Continuing Resolution, Averting a Midnight Shutdown," FCW, November 21, 2019.

See https://fcw.com/articles/2019/11/21/senate-passes-cr-shutdown.aspx.

[29]See "Norah O'Donnell and Jillian Hughes, "New Code of Conduct Issued for Secret Service Agents," *CBS News*, April 27, 2017 and Alicia Caldwell, "REPORT: Secret Service Agents 'Likely' Impaired by Alcohol," *The Huffington Post*, May 14, 2015. See http://www.huffingtonpost.com/2015/05/14/secret-service-agents-wer_n_7281024.html.

[30]See https://www.nbcnews.com/news/us-news/investigation-breaches-us-airports-allowed-weapons-through-n367851.

[31]See http://change.gov/newsroom/entry/key_members_of_obama_biden_national_security_team_announced/(May 31, 2010).

[32]The White House, "Immigration," June 1, 2019. See https://www.whitehouse.gov/issues/immigration/

[33]Richard Schultz, "Conceptualizing Political Terrorism: A Typology," *Journal of International Affairs* 4, No. 8 (spring/summer 1978), p. 8.

[34]Robert W. Taylor and Harry E. Vanden, "Defining Terrorism in El Salvador: La Matanza," *Annals of the American Academy of Political and Social Science* (September 1982): pp. 106–117.

[35]Ibid., p. 109.

[36]Ibid.

[37]For a discussion on the various definitions of terrorism, see Richard Schultz, "Conceptualizing Political Terrorism: A Typology," *Journal of International Affairs* 4, No. 8 (spring 1978); Martha Crenshaw Hutchinson, *Revolutionary Terrorism* (Stanford, CA.: Hoover Institute Press, 1978); Brian Jenkins, *The Study of Terrorism: Definitional Problems* (Santa Monica, CA: The RAND Corporation, 1980); James M. Poland, *Understanding Terrorism: Groups, Strategies, and Responses* (Upper Saddle River, NJ: Prentice Hall, 1988); Paul Wilkinson, *Political Terrorism* (New York: Wiley Press, 1974); Bruce Hoffman, *Inside Terrorism* (New York: Columbia University Press, 1998); and Jonathan R. White, *Terrorism: An Introduction* (Belmont, CA: West/Wadsworth, 2003).

[38]The conceptualization of terrorism is presented in a number of works. See Edward Mickolus, "Statistical Approaches to the Study of Terrorism," in *Terrorism: Interdisciplinary Perspectives*, Yonah Alexander and Maxwell Finger, eds. (New York: McGraw-Hill, 1977), pp. 209–269. For additional reading on this subject, see David Milbank, *International and Transnational Terrorism: Diagnosis and Prognosis* (Washington, DC: CIA, 1976), and Richard Schultz, Jr., and Stephen Sloan, *Responding to the Terrorist Threat: Security and Crisis Management* (New York: Pergamon Press, 1980).

[39]See CBS News, "Armed militia takeover in Oregon Sparks Debate on Meaning of Terrorist" (New York: CBS, January 3, 2016) and Rob Manning, "Oregon Governor Brown on Burns: "Spectacle Must End." (Portland, OR: Oregon Public Broadcasting, January 20, 2016).

[40]Ibid.

[41]Neri Zilber, "The Next Round in Gaza Will Be Deadlier," Foreign Policy, May 8, 2019. See https://foreignpolicy.com/2019/05/08/the-next-round-in-gaza-will-be-deadlier/

[42]See Robert W. Taylor and Charles R. Swanson, *Terrorism, Intelligence and Homeland Security* (Upper Saddle River, NJ: Pearson, 2016), Jennifer Harper, "As a Target for Terrorists, U.S. Ranks 41st in the World," *The Washington Post*, December 4, 2012, and David Inserra, "Here's How Safe We Are 17 Years After 9/11" *The Herigate Foundation: Commentary on Homeland Security*, September 11, 2018. See https://www.heritage.org/homeland-security/commentary/heres-how-safe-we-are-17-years-after-911

[43]For detailed information on the life of Osama bin Laden, see Yossef Bodansky, *Bin Laden: The Man Who Declared War on America* (Rocklin, CA: Prima, 1999).

[44]U.S. Department of State, *Country Report on Terrorism, 2014*, released June 19, 2015.

[45]Graeme Wood, "What ISIS Really Wants," *The Atlantic*, March 2015. See https://www.theatlantic.com/features/archive/2015/02/what-isis-really-wants/384980/?fb_ref=Default.

[46]Jeffrey Gettleman, Dharisha Bastians, and Mujib Mashal, "ISIS Claims Sri Lanka Attacks, and President Vows Shakeup," *The New York Times*, April 23, 2019. See https://www.nytimes.com/2019/04/23/world/asia/isis-sri-lanka-blasts.html?action=click&module=RelatedLinks&pgtype=Article. See also Ben Wedeman, "Baghdadi Is Gone, but ISIS Isn't Dead Yet...and Could Be Poised for a Resurgence," *CNN*, October 28, 2019.

[47]Robert W. Taylor and Charles R. Swanson, *Terrorism, Intelligence and Homeland Security* (Upper Saddle River, NJ: Pearson, 2016) and the National Counter Terrorism Center (NCTC) website. See http://www.nctc.gov/site/index.html.

[48]The White House, *National Strategy for Counterterrorism*, October 2018, pp. 8–9. See https://www.whitehouse.gov/wp-content/uploads/2018/10/NSCT.pdf

[49]Ibid.

[50]Ally Pregulman and Emily Burke, "Homegrown Terrorism," *AQAM Futures Project Case Studies Series*, April 2012, http://csis.org/files/publication/120425_Pregulman_AQAMCaseStudy7_web.pdf.

[51]Rick "Ozzie" Nelson and Ben Bodurian, "A Growing Terrorist Threat? Assessing 'Home-grown Extremism' in the United States." *Center for International and Strategic Studies*, March 8, 2010, retrieved from www.csis.org/files/publication/100304_nelson_growingterroristthreat_web.pdf on July 15, 2015.

[52]Katherine Q. Seelye, "Bombing Suspect Cites Islamic Extremist Beliefs as Motive," *The New York Times*, April 23, 2013, www.nytimes.com/2013/04/24/us/boston-marathon-bombing-developments.html?hp&pagewanted=all&_r=1&.

[53]Holly Yan, "Texas Attack: What We Know About Elton Simpson and Nadir Soofi," *CNN Video AP*, May 5, 2015.

[54]Catherin Schoichet and Michael Pearson, "Garland, Texas: Shooting Suspect Linked Himself to ISIS in Tweets," CNN Video AP (May 4, 2015).

[55]Matt Pearce and Nigel Duara, "Texas Gunman's Mother: 'He Had a Normal American Upbringing,'" *Los Angeles Times*, May 5, 2005. See http://www.latimes.com/nation/la-na-texas-gunman-20150505-story.html#page=1.

[56]Alejandro J. Beutel, "Data on Post-9/11 Terrorism in the United States," *Muslim Public Affairs Council: Policy Memo Backgrounder* (April 1, 2010), pp. 1–16.

[57]See M. J. Stephey, "Daniel Boyd: A Homegrown Terrorist?" *Time Online*, July 30, 2009, retrieved online from www.time.com/time/nationa/article/0,8599,1913602,00.html on April 23, 2010.

[58]See M. Baker, "Daniel Boyd, Six Others in North Carolina, Charged with Terror Conspiracy," *The Huffington Post*, July 27, 2009, retrieved online from www.huffingtonpost.com/2009/07/27/daniel-boyd-six-others-in_n_245792.html on April 23, 2010.

[59]See A. Gary, "Hosam Maher Husein Smadi Arrested for Dallas Bomb Plot," *The Huffington Post*, September 24, 2009, retrieved online from www.huffingtonpost.com/2009/09/24/hosam-maher-husein-smadi-_n_299340.html on April 25, 2010.

[60]See J. Trahan, T. J. Gillman, and S. Goldstein, "Dallas Bomb Plot Suspect Told Landlord He Was Moving Out," *The Dallas Morning News*, September 26, 2009, retrieved from www.dallasnews.com/sharedcontent/dws/dn/latestnews/stories/092409dnmetbombarrest.1b177db8b.html on April 25, 2010.

[61]Ibid.

[62]Rick "Ozzie" Nelson and Ben Bodurian, "A Growing Terrorist Threat? Assessing 'Home-grown Extremism' in the United States." *Center for International and Strategic Studies*, March 8, 2010, retrieved from www.csis.org/files/publication/100304_nelson_growingterroristthreat_web.pdf on April 22, 2010.

[63]"Najibullah Zazi," *The New York Times*, updated February 22, 2010, retrieved online from http://topics.nytimes.com/topics/reference/timestopics/people/z/najibulla_zazi/index.html on April 18, 2010.

[64]Michael Leiter, Director of National Counterterrorism Center, "*Hearing Before the Senate Homeland Security and Governmental Affairs Committee: Eight Years After 9/11: Confronting the Terrorist Threat to the Homeland*," September 30, 2009. Transcript online at www.nctc.gov/press_room/speeches/hbshsgac_8years_9-3—29.pdf, retrieved April 22, 2010.

[65]See G. Miller, "Al Qaeda's New Tactic Is to Seize Shortcuts," *Chicago Tribune*, March 19, 2010, retrieved online from www.chicagotribune.com/news/nationworld/la-fg-qaeda19-2010mar19,0,3312538.story on April 18, 2010.

[66]See P. Belien, "Jihad Against Danish Newspaper," *The Brussels Journal*, October 22, 2005, retrieved online from http://www.brusselsjournal.com/node/382 on April 16, 2010.

[67]Rick "Ozzie" Nelson and Ben Bodurian, "A Growing Terrorist Threat? Assessing 'Home-grown Extremism' in the United States."

[68]Spencer Ackerman, Pakistani Court Indicts "Virginia Five," *The Washington Independent*, March 17, 2010, retrieved online from http://washingtonindependent.com/79466/pakistani-court-indicts-virginia-five on April 10, 2011.

[69]See S. Ackerman, "A Mixed Picture on Domestic Radicalization?" *The Washington Independent*, December 10, 2009, retrieved online from http://washingtonindependent.com/70388/a-mixed-picture-on-domestic-radicalization on April 24, 2010.

[70]See G. Whittell, "Profile: Major Nidal Malik Hassan was trained to treat post-traumatic stress," *The Times*, November 6, 2009, retrieved online from www.thetimes.co.uk/tto/news/world/americas/article2001549.ece on April 20, 2010.

[71]Rick Nelson and Ben Bodurian, "A Growing Terrorist Threat? Assessing 'Home-grown Extremism' in the United States."

[72]See "Major Hassan's Smooth Ascension," *The New York Times*, January 15, 2010, retrieved online at www.nytimes.com/2010/01/16/opinion/16sat2.html on April 23, 2010. Appeared in print (January 16, 2010), p. A-20.

[73]Department of Justice, "Pennsylvania Woman Indicted in Plot to Recruit Violent Jihadist Fighters and to Commit Murder Overseas," Federal Bureau of Investigation Philadelphia Office Press Release, March 9, 2010, retrieved online at http://philadelphia.fbi.gov/dojpressrel/pressrel10/ph030910a.htm on April 24, 2010.

[74]See H. Khan, E. Friedman, and J. Ryan, "'Jihad Jane's' Arrest Raises Fears About Homegrown Terrorists," *ABC News*, March 10, 2010, retrieved online at http://abcnews.go.com/GMA/politics/jihad-jane-arrest-colleen-larose-raises-fears-homegrown/story?id=10056187 on April 22, 2010.

[75]Department of Justice, "Pennsylvania Woman Indicted in Plot to Recruit Violent Jihadist Fighters and to Commit Murder Overseas."

[76]See "Profile: 'Jihad Jane' from Main Street," *BBC News*, last updated March 11, 2010, retrieved online at http://news.bbc.co.uk/2/hi/americas/8561888.stm on April 26, 2010.

[77]See http://dfw.cbslocal.com/2015/05/03/breaking-shooting-in-garland.

[78]Catherine E. Shoichet and Gary Tuchman, "Chattanooga Shooting: 4 Marines Killed, a Dead Suspect and Questions of Motive," *CNN News* (July 17, 2015). See http://www.cnn.com/2015/07/16/us/tennessee-naval-reserve-shooting/.

[79]Saeed Ahmed, "Who Were Syed Rizwan Farook and Tashfeen Malik?" *CNN Reports* (December 4, 2015). See http://www.cnn.com/2015/12/03/us/syed-farook-tashfeen-malik-mass-shooting-profile/.

[80]Jane Coaston, "New Evidence Shows the Pulse Nightclub Shooting Wasn't About Anti-LGBTQ Hate." Vox, April 5, 2018. See https://www.vox.com/policy-and-politics/2018/4/5/17202026/pulse-shooting-lgbtq-trump-terror-hate

[81]Huma Yasin, "Noor Salman Should Never Have Been Prosecuted in the First Place," *The Washington Post*, March 30, 2018. See https://www.washingtonpost.com/news/posteverything/wp/2018/03/30/noor-salman-should-never-have-been-prosecuted-in-the-first-place/?noredirect=on&utm_term=.b5bd537632ab

[82]Frank Gardner, "How Do Terrorists Communicate?" *British Broadcasting Company*, November 2, 2013, www.bbc.com/news/world-24784756.

[83]Robert W. Taylor, Eric J. Fritsch, and John Liederbach, *Digital Crime and Digital Terrorism* (Upper Saddle River, NJ: Pearson, 2014).

[84]James Rothwell, "Orlando Gunman used AR-15 Assault Rifle to Kill His Victims—The Weapon of Choice for Mass Shooters," *The Telegraph*, June 12, 2016. See https://www.telegraph.co.uk/news/2016/06/12/orlando-shooting-gunman-omar-mateen-used-ar-15-assault-rifle-to/

[85] Pregulman and Burke, "Homegrown Terrorism."

[86] Evan Perez and LeeAnn Caldwell, "Holder Fears 'Lone Wolf' Terrorist Attack, Doesn't Want TSA Armed," *CNN*, November 5, 2014. See www.cnn.com/2013/11/05/politics/holder-terror-snowden-interview/.

[87] Sarah Teich, "Trends and Developments in Lone Wolf Terrorism in the Western World: An Analysis of Terrorist Attacks and Attempted Attacks by Islamic Extremists," *International Institute for Counterterrorism*, October 2013. See www.ict.org.il/LinkClick.aspx?fileticket=qAv1zIPJlGE%3D&tabid=66.

[88] Jeffrey C. Connor and Carol Rollie Flynn, "What to Do About Lone Wolf Terrorism? Examining Current Trends and Prevention Strategies," Foreign Policy Research Institute, E-Notes, November 26, 2018. See https://www.fpri.org/article/2018/11/what-to-do-about-lone-wolf-terrorism-examining-current-trends-and-prevention-strategies/

[89] The ISIS Study Group, "People Are Waking-Up to the Southeast Asia ISIS Threat—But Things Are Still Being Missed," (November 30, 2014). See http://isisstudygroup.com/?p=3314.

[90] See Robert Kupperman and Jeff Kamen, "A New Outbreak of Terror Is Likely," *New York Times* (April 19, 1988), p. 6, and Alan Riding, "Rifts Threaten Plan to Remove Borders," *CJ International* 6, No. 5 (September/October 1990), p. 3.

[91] BBC News, "Europe and Nationalism: A Country-by-Country Guide," April 29, 2019. See https://www.bbc.com/news/world-europe-36130006

[92] David W. Balsiger, "Narco-Terrorism 'Shooting Up' America," in *Annual Edition: Violence and Terrorism 1990/91* (Guilford, CT: Dushkin, 1990), pp. 164–166.

[93] Ibid.

[94] *Al Arabiya*, "Boko Haram Voices Support for ISIS' al-Baghdadi" (July 13, 2014).

[95] Jack Moore, "Nigerian Military Enters Final Stages of Boko Haram Offensive," *Newsweek* (April 23, 2015).

[96] CNN, "Boko Haram Fast Facts," April 24, 2019. See https://www.cnn.com/2014/06/09/world/boko-haram-fast-facts/index.html

[97] Nick Valencia, "After Years of Violence and Death, 'Life Is Back' in Juarez," *CNN* (April 21, 2015).

[98] Jesus A. Rodriguez, "El Diario: 1,247 Homicides Reported in Juarez in 2018," *KVIA News*, January 3, 2019. See https://www.kvia.com/news/border/el-diario-1-247-homicides-reported-in-juarez-in-2018/962777824

[99] Pamela Engel, "The Astonishing Rise of the World's Most Notorious Drug Lord," *Business Insider* (July 18, 2015).

[100] William Neuman and Azam Ahmed, "Public Enemy? Escaped 'El Chapo' Is Folk Hero No. 1," *New York Times* (July 18, 2015).

[101] Ibid.

[102] Catherine E. Shoichet, Don Melvin and Mariano Castillo, "The Legend of 'El Chapo': Cartel Chief Cultivated Robin Hood Image," *CNN* (July 14, 2015). See http://edition.cnn.com/2014/02/22/world/americas/mexico-el-chapo-profile/.

[103] National Gang Intelligence Center, 2015 National Gang Report (Washington, DC: FBI, 2016). See https://www.fbi.gov/file-repository/stats-services-publications-national-gang-report-2015.pdf/view

[104] See George Grayson, "Los Zetas: the Ruthless Army Spawned by a Mexican Drug Cartel." U.S. Foreign Policy Research Institute. http://www.fpri.org/enotes/200805.grayson.loszetas.html, and Michael Ware, "Los Zetas called Mexico's most dangerous drug cartel," *CNN News* (August 6, 2009) http://www.cnn.com/2009/WORLD/americas/08/06/mexico.drug.cartels/index.html.

[105] Eli Meixler, "With over 29,000 Homicides, 2017 was Mexico's Most Violent Year on Record," *Time*, January 22, 2018. See http://time.com/5111972/mexico-murder-rate-record-2017/

[106] Federal Bureau of Investigation, *National Gang Intelligence Report, 2013*. See https://www.fbi.gov/stats-services/publications/national-gang-report-2013/view. See also the 2015 National Gang Report, https://www.fbi.gov/file-repository/stats-services-publications-national-gang-report-2015.pdf/view

[107] Ibid.

[108] Ibid.

[109] Ibid.

[110] "Families Scoff at Suspect's New Images," *Sunday Oklahoman* (July 2, 1995), p. 24.

[111] Ibid.

[112] Louis A. Radelet and David Carter, *Police and the Community*, 5th ed. (New York: Macmillan, 1994), p. 248.

[113] Scott Shane, "Homegrown Extremists Tied to Deadlier Toll than Jihadists in U.S. Since 9/11," *The New York Times*, June 24, 2015. See http://www.nytimes.com/2015/06/25/us/tally-of-attacks-in-us-challenges-perceptions-of-top-terror-threat.html.

[114] Bruce Hoffman, "How Serious Is White Nationalist Terrorism," *Council on Foreign Relations*, March 29, 2019. See https://www.cfr.org/article/how-serious-white-nationalist-terrorism

[115] Southern Poverty Law Center, Intelligence Report, Rage Against Change, Spring 2019, Issue 166.

[116] Ibid.

[117] Julia Carrie Wong, "8chan: The Far-Right Website Linked to the Rise of Hate Crimes," *The Guardian*, August 4, 2019. See https://www.theguardian.com/technology/2019/aug/04/mass-shootings-el-paso-texas-dayton-ohio-8chan-far-right-website

[118] Brian Todd, Christina Maxouris, and Amir Vera, "The El Paso Shooting Suspect Showed No Remorse or Regret, Police Say," *CNN*, August 6, 2019. See https://www.cnn.com/2019/08/05/us/el-paso-suspect-patrick-crusius/index.html.

[119] *Keenan v. Aryan Nations*, CV 99-441 (September 8, 2000).

[120] See *Gruver v. Imperial Klans of America*, Civil Action Number 07-CI-00082 (November 14, 2008).

[121] See http://hutaree.com/.

[122] See *United States v. Hutaree Members*, copy of federal indictment. See http://commons.wikimedia.org/wiki/File:Federal-hutaree-indictment-mar-2010.pdf) (June 10, 2010).

[123] *The New Lexicon of Hate: The Changing Tactics, Language and Symbols of America's Extremists* (Los Angeles: Simon Wiesenthal Center, 1999).

[124] Federal Bureau of Investigation, "Seeking Suspect in Church Shootings in Charleston", South Carolina," June 18, 2015, p. 1, https://www.fbi.gov/news/news_blog/seeking-suspect-in-church-shootings-in-charleston-south-carolina (accessed October 20, 2015).

[125]Statement by FBI Director James Comey Regarding Dylann Roof Gun Purchase, July 10, 2015, https://www.fbi.gov/news/pressrel/press-releases/statement-by-fbi-director-james-comey-regarding-dylann-roof-gun-purchase (accessed October 20, 2015).

[126]Janell Ross, "Why Blacks See Dylann Roof as a Terrorist and Whites Don't," *The Washington Post*, July 3, 2015, p. 1, https://www.washingtonpost.com/news/the-fix/wp/2015/07/03/why-blacks-see-dylann-roof-as-a-terrorist-and-whites-don't (accessed October 20, 2015).

[127]Robert Taylor and Charles Swanson, *Terrorism, Intelligence, and Homeland Security* (Boston, Pearson, 2015, p. 112.)

[128]See Jeffrey D. Simon, *Lone Wolf Terrorism: Understanding the Growing Threat* (Amherst, NY: Prometheus Books, 2013) and Mark Thompson, "The Danger of the Lone-Wolf Terrorist," (February 27, 2013), www.nation.time.com/2013/02/27/the-danger-of-the-lone-wolf-terrorist (accessed October 20, 2015).

[129]For more information, see the National Institutes Against Hate Crimes and Terrorism. Visit their website at: http://www.museumoftolerance.com/site/c.tmL6KfNVLtH/b.5052739/.

[130]*Responding to Hate Crimes: A Police Officer's Guide to Investigation and Prevention* (Washington, DC: U.S. Department of Justice and International Association of Chiefs of Police, 1999).

[131]Victor Godinez, "Hate Group Wooing Teens by Making a Game Out of Racism," *Dallas Morning News* (March 14, 2002), p. A2.

[132]Robert W. Taylor and Eric. J. Fritsch, *Juvenile Justice: Policies, Programs, and Practices*, 4th ed. (New York: McGraw-Hill, 2015). See also Robert W. Taylor, Eric J. Fritsch, and John Liederbach, *Digital Crime and Digital Terrorism*, 3rd ed. (Upper Saddle River, NJ: Pearson Prentice Hall, 2015).

[133]An interview with leader of the Texas Militia in Dallas (December, 2014), reflecting much of the sentiments expressed by Tom Metzger, a leader of the White Aryan Resistance (WAR).

[134]Jonathan R. White, *Terrorism and Homeland Security*, 6th ed. (Belmont, CA: Wadsworth Cengage Learning, 2009), p. 233.

[135]University of Maryland, *Global Terrorism Data Base*, Incident Summary Number 201411250074 and 2012201208110011. See www.Start.umd.edu/gtd/Search.

[136]Cindy C. Combs, *Terrorism in the Twenty-First Century*, 3rd ed. (Upper Saddle River, NJ: Prentice Hall, 2003), pp. 164–166.

[137]See Blaine Harden, "11 Indicted in 'Eco-Terrorism' Case," *Washington Post* (January 21, 2006), p. A-3.

[138]See "Terror at UCLA," *Critical Mass* (August 22, 2006) and "Luxury Homes Burn in Apparent Eco-Attack," *Associated Press* (March 3, 2008).

[139]University of Maryland, *Global Terrorism Data Base*, Incident Summary Number 201109260012. See www.Start.umd.edu/gtd/Search.

## CHAPTER FOUR

POLITICS AND POLICE ADMINISTRATION

Learning Objectives

1. Identify three distinct styles of law enforcement discussed by James Q. Wilson and discuss how those different styles are believed to correspond to different types of local political cultures.

2. Explain the legally defined roles of city councils.

3. Explain how the policies and procedures of state prosecutors have an observable influence on police practices and procedures.

4. Discuss the ways in which the judiciary impacts local police practices.

5. Explain the significance of U.S. Supreme Court decisions in each of the following cases: *Mapp v. Ohio*, *Gideon v. Wainwright*, *Escobedo v. Illinois*, and *Miranda v. Arizona*.

6. Understand the differences between the various forms of citizen oversight of police.

7. Discuss the ways in which the office of the county sheriff differs from that of local municipal police agencies in terms of political considerations.

8. Define racial profiling and how the recent cases of Freddie Gray and Michael Brown have underscored the importance of this issue to local police administrators.

9. Discuss the advantages of body-worn cameras cited by police administrators.

10. Discuss the major concerns of police administrators as they relate to the ongoing integration of local and federal enforcement of illegal immigration.

INTRODUCTION

POLICE ADMINISTRATION WITHIN A DEMOCRACY IS POLITICAL. *The study of connections between politics and police administration is important because (1) it is essential that the police are subject to democratic control. (2) The political culture of cities and counties shapes who is chosen to lead law enforcement agencies and the core style of policing. (3) Police leaders must be able to distinguish between politicians and citizens who genuinely want to contribute to policing versus those whose real aim is to raise their visibility in the community or win voters. (4) Law enforcement is under siege from groups demonstrating against police use of what is perceived as excessive and racially directed force. The demonstrations and voices raised are not only opinion molding, but have political impact as well. Law enforcement must develop counter narratives delivered by different means to relevant audiences. (5) Policing must work continuously to be transparent, which contributes to the counter narrative. (6) As one strategy to countering negative messaging, the police must connect with political leaders and opinion shapers who will advocate for the police when appropriate.*

THE POLICE CHIEF AS POLITICAL ACTOR

The police administrator is in many ways a political actor who must perform a delicate balancing act involving the management of competing political forces. The term **politics** has different meanings depending on context and the type of influence put on the police administrator. Quite often, the term politics is used to describe negative influences on the work of police administrators. These include external partisan forces designed to sway the administrator and the management of police organizations in favor of one political party or even personal agenda over another. In this case, the police administrator may refer to the influence of some outside force on his or her decisions as "political"—something external to the goals of the organization that is negative. One example of this is the imposition of personal politics (see Box 4.1).

Personal politics sometimes explains why certain officers are promoted and others remain at their current rank. Typically, the Chief shares the identities of those who are promotable with his immediate staff. A few staff members will have more influence than others with the Chief. Occasionally, this is due to their own strong performances. Alternatively, their influence may have begun from the time they were rookies in the Police Academy, because they now socialize together, or some other reason. The exercise of personal politics is inherent in human nature and so virtually impossible to eliminate. However, desirable assignments and promotions based on favoritism can damage morale and the reputations of recipients.

The term politics can also be used in the positive sense to refer more generally to the means of governance of a particular jurisdiction. Aristotle's original understanding of the term was "science of the polis," seeking the good of both citizen and the city-state.[1] This type of politics involves democratic control of the police and is fundamental to our way of governing.

Box 4.1: Personal Politics

A four-year old girl drowned in the city-owned retaining pond immediately adjacent to her home. The mother saw her wandering toward the pond and ran to her, but fell and injured herself. The daughter drowned before the injured mother could reach her.

The parents sued the city, which settled out of court. By the agreement of the parties involved, the settlement was sealed. The father was an unranked, six-year veteran of the police department. Suddenly, he was promoted to Sergeant without competing for the position. The "locker room wisdom" was that the settlement must have included a promotion for him. A limited number of officers saw the dad as taking inappropriate advantage of his daughter's death.

Two years later, he was promoted to Lieutenant under the same circumstances as his prior promotion. Criticism of how he got the promotions became loose talk in the locker room.

Although nothing was ever said directly to the dad, there was coolness toward him by some officers who did not regard him as a "real Lieutenant." Years later, the dad took early retirement, still a Lieutenant.

What is your takeaway from this situation? Would it be different if the promotions were offered by the cash-strapped city to eliminate some of the large settlement to be paid within 30 days? If the dad had taken the promotional tests for Captain and was always promotable, was it fair to skip over him?

FIGURE 4.1 ▶ Mayoral candidate Jane Castor, a retired 31-year veteran of the Tampa Police Department, addresses members of the Tampa Police Benevolent Association (PBA). From the time she was a senior commander, through her nearly six years as the Chief, major crime was slashed by 70 percent. (ZUMA Press Inc / Alamy Stock Photo)

It is similar to our military being under the ultimate control of a civilian, the President. It is commonly asserted that there is no place in policing for politics. But, any local police chief needs the positive support of political structures and individuals to be an effective leader. For example, city councils and county legislators must approve budgets effecting the pay of municipal police officers, county police, and/or sheriff's personnel. In Tampa during 2019, the Tampa Police Benevolent Association (PBA) was active in supporting former Tampa Police Department (TPD) Chief Jane Castor for Mayor (see Figure 4.1).

Police Chiefs also sometimes take positions on political issues. In 2019, Houston Police Chief Art Acevedo testified before Congress on gun control. Before the House Judiciary Committee, he labeled gun violence an epidemic and advised the Representatives to quit praying and to get on with passing more restrictive gun laws.[2] Likewise, the Chief of one small town police agency in the state of Washington recently announced that his agency would *not* enforce new state restrictions on gun ownership. The town's city council is considering an ordinance that would make it a "sanctuary city" for the Constitutional right to bear arms.[3] Some Washington sheriffs have announced they will also not enforce the new restrictions. This pattern of civil disobedience is found in other states as well.

It is commonly understood and expected that police administrators make decisions that are at least in part political in nature. A basic characterization of their job is representing the department to the community and its leaders, commonly known as "politicking." Many actions taken by Chiefs are largely unnoticed, while others attract some or more attention inside the department. Occasionally, Chiefs will lose control of an administrative decision when it gets entangled with politics outside of their departments (see Box 4.2).

Readers should recognize based on the previous discussion that the political forces described in this chapter can be perceived by the police administrator as positive or negative (or both) depending on the situation. In the bigger picture, the police administrator must be able to identify and deal with a variety of political concerns that exert both positive and negative pressures on any police organization. Again, the work of police administrators within a democracy is inherently political.

The rest of the chapter is organized in three primary sections. The first section presents six different but related political forces on police administration. The second section describes the unique case of the County Sheriff as a distinct political entity within American law enforcement. The third primary

Box 4.2: How the Administrative Decision Became a Political Decision

The Chief of Police, after input from Command Staff, was expected to announce an impending decision about proposed changes to the department shift schedule. The traditional shift plan included five days with three 8-hour shifts, followed by two days off. Members of the Patrol Officers Association (POA) wanted to abandon this traditional shift schedule in favor of a proposed 10-4 shift plan, or four 10-hour days followed by three days off. The POA voted 118-9 to drop the traditional plan in favor of the proposed 10-4 plan and notified the Chief.

A follow-up meeting between staff members and the Chief resulted in some "tight faces" among members of the staff who were seemingly worried that the Chief would not adopt the favored 10-4 shift plan. The Association met again to discuss this development.

Although the state in which the department was located did not allow collective bargaining for public employees, the association had great unity and was in good financial shape. "Joe," their Executive Director, previously led a police union in a neighboring state. He was confident the community could be a potent ally if a 10-4 campaign was conducted in the right way.

At the direction of the Association's Board of Directors, Joe met with the news media, business leaders, civic clubs, and community groups. Joe coached Little League baseball for the past several years. Informally, he talked with the many parents he knew about the upcoming shift plan decision. Joe was careful to praise the Chief's leadership and what he meant to the department.

Inevitably, people would ask, "What do you think the best shift plan is?" Joe replied "That's above my pay grade, but the folks I represent are hoping for the 10-4." Then he would set the political hook, "The 10-4 is family friendly. The three consecutive days off would give officers bigger chunks of time to be with their spouses and kids, visit relatives a little further away, take mini-vacations, and return to their jobs well-rested."

The newspaper wrote an editorial endorsing the 10-4 plan. Letters to the editor supporting the "family friendly" 10-4 shift plan quickly appeared. The members of several civic clubs began talking to City Council and "movers and shakers' in the community about their support for the 10-4 plan. One well-heeled supporter put up a billboard supporting the 10-4 plan.

Seemingly, the Mayor invited the Chief to meet with him just to learn where he was on this shift business. The Chief told the Mayor he had some serious doubts about adopting the 10-4 plan, "It will cause a big increase in overtime and the department might not be as effective." The Mayor asked, "If that's so, why are so many departments using it?" The Chief croaked a hopeful reply, "Maybe they have deeper pockets than we do." The Mayor suggested if the Chief implemented the 10-4 before he retired in 11 months, it would be a great memorial to his leadership. Moreover, the Chief could simply direct the Command Staff to run with it so it would not eat up his time.

Out-flanked by the Patrol Officers Association, the news media, some council members, a community uprising, and quite possibly members of his own Command Staff, the Chief realized the decision was already made before he entered the Mayor's office. He began posturing as if he had really warmed to the 10-4 shift plan.

section is an overview of emerging issues of concern for police administrators that have increasingly involved the imposition of politics on the police organization. These include racial profiling and discrimination, police-worn body cameras, and immigration enforcement.

POLITICAL FORCES AND POLICE ADMINISTRATION

Some issues police executives deal with are inherently political. Others, as we saw earlier in this chapter, become caught up in politics. Portions of those issues have "devil's choices," meaning there are no good options for handling them. A Chief will have to choose the best solution from marginal or worse options. This situation may also be due to issues that involve multiple competing interests in the community seeking to have their "solution" adopted. No matter what the Chief does, some factions will be disappointed or even adversarial. Law enforcement executives must be aware of the political forces at work in their communities, but avoid being

captured by them and risk the credibility and legitimacy of the agency. This section of the chapter presents an overview of the most influential political forces on police administration including (1) local politics, (2) state government, (3) courts, (4) citizens, (5) non-government institutions, and (6) the media.

Local Politics

From the outset, most Americans had a firm belief that the police should be controlled by local officials. For them, a national police agency such as the Italian *Carabinieri* was inconceivable, and a state police, such as the German *Polizei,* was undesirable.[4] Thus, the structure and organization of policing in America is very unique among nations. There are an estimated 17,965 autonomous police agencies in the United States.[5] This system of policing can best be described as decentralized, where police powers are distributed locally throughout the nation and administered as part of local systems of government. The decentralized organization of American policing ensures that local politics is likely to be the most significant political influence on police administrators.

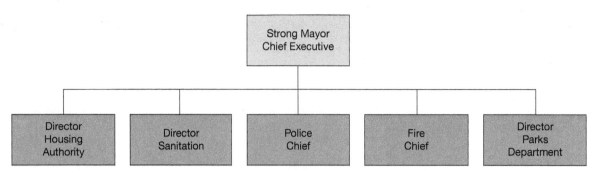

FIGURE 4.2 ▶ The strong mayor form of government. The mayor serves as the chief executive and appoints all department heads. The department heads serve at the pleasure of the mayor.

The special dimension of police politics varies from local community to local community. But, law enforcement activities are governed for the most part by the dominant values of the local political culture. James Q. Wilson, in his now classic study of the police in eight communities, identified three distinct styles of law enforcement, all of which reflected the political culture of the communities they served: (1) the "watchman" style of law enforcement emphasizes the maintenance of order and is found most often within economically declining cities with traditional political machines; (2) the "legalistic" style of law enforcement is found in cities with mixed populations and reform-oriented, professional governments; and (3) in homogeneous suburban communities, the "service" style of law enforcement is often oriented toward the needs of citizens.[6] In Wilson's studies, these variations in the **local community political culture** influenced the enforcement action taken by the police in situations involving vice, juvenile offenses, order maintenance, and traffic enforcement.

To some extent, the type of local government that a community has impacts the way police chiefs are selected, the freedom they enjoy in the performance of their status, and their **tenure** or length of term as chief. For example, with a **strong mayor** form of government, the mayor is elected to office and serves as the chief executive of the city. The city council constitutes the chief legislative and policymaking body. The mayor nominates a candidate to serve as police chief, and sometimes majority approval is needed from the city council. Once approved, the candidate assumes the position of police chief and serves at the discretion of the mayor (see Figure 4.2).

Ideally, the person the mayor selects as police chief should possess the full range of skills necessary to operate the police department. However, the kind of person selected to serve as police chief is to a large extent determined by the mayor's professional qualifications, philosophy about the role of law enforcement, and political commitments. If the mayor is endowed with sound business or public administration skills and has a "good government" philosophy, then the chief of police will very likely be selected on the basis of professional abilities rather than on outside political factors. Unfortunately, on too many occasions in the past, this appointment has been a method of repaying political favors.

In the strong mayor form of local government, the tenure of the chief of police is often linked directly to the mayor. The nature of the relationship is such that the chief is quite dependent on the mayor for support and guidance on budgetary matters, enforcement practices, and many other areas important to the overall success of the police department. If there is mutual respect between the police chief and the mayor, a strong professional and political bond will be formed. If the reverse holds true, however, significant antagonisms are almost certain to emerge.

Another form of local government found in the United States besides the strong mayor is the **city manager** form (see Figure 4.3). The proponents of the city manager form claim that it provides the most conducive atmosphere in which professional law enforcement can operate and minimize external interference.

There are many perceived advantages of the city manager form of government. First, the city manager is accountable to the elected members of the city council as a body rather than to any individual council member. Second, individual council members are prevented (by law or council rules) from giving administrative, operational, or policy direction to the city manager. Third, the council may not give specific administrative direction to the city manager, who generally has exclusive executive authority over city employees. Four, the city manager has full authority to hire, promote, and discipline city personnel. Five, the city manager has broad authority within state municipal financial statutes to manage the budget and to depart from line item appropriations to meet unanticipated needs. Six, the council hires the city manager and may dismiss the city manager at its discretion without stating its cause. The city manager model is significant because it has clearly been successful as a model within American politics, mostly because it separates the political policymaking body (city council) from the independent chief executive (mayor).[7]

The city manager is more often than not a professional administrator who is recruited for certain skills and training and is appointed by the city council. A person with this background tends to make honest efforts to select a competent individual to

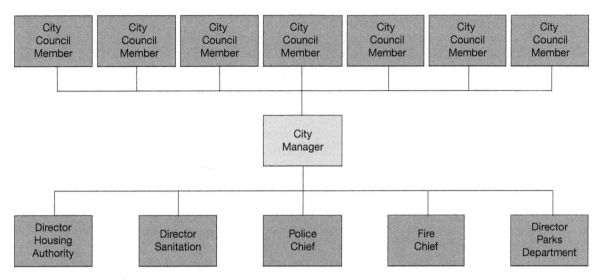

FIGURE 4.3 ▶ The city manager form of government. The city manager is appointed by the council (typically the majority), and the manager serves at the pleasure of the city council. The city manager in turn appoints all department heads, and they serve at the pleasure of the manager.

serve as police chief, because the manager's professional reputation is tied to the effective management of the city.[8] This does not mean that the city manager form of government removes the chief from local politics, but it does create more distance and insulation than the one-to-one political relationship commonly found in the strong mayor form of government.

Another mechanism by which local politics influences the police administrator is through local **city council**. The legally defined roles of a city council is fairly consistent throughout the United States. City council acts as the chief legislative and policymaking body. The council carries out its legislative function through its ordinance power, subject to constitutional and statutory provisions, including the city charter. When within the council's authority, its enactments have the force of law and are binding on both administration and electorate. In addition to legislative and policymaking functions, the council exercises control over budgets.[9] Thus, the immediate impact of a council's actions on the operation of a law enforcement agency is considerable.

The record of negative involvement by council members and other elected officials in police operations is well-established. One observer of this problem has noted:

Local political leaders frequently promote more abuses of police power than they deter. In seeking favored treatment for a violator of the law or in exerting pressure for police assistance in the sale of tickets to a fund-raising dinner, the politician only encourages the type of behavior he/she is supposed to prevent. Although such political interference into police work is not as extensive as it once was, it still exists.[10]

The various forces of local politics also decidedly influence job tenure, or the length of time that police chiefs maintain their position. Research shows that the period of time that police chiefs maintain their position is usually quite brief. A study conducted in California showed that the average tenure of a police chief in that state was less than three years.[11] Even though the tenure of police chiefs across the nation has somewhat improved since this study was conducted, the national average is still only about five years,[12] with most chiefs still having no contract or agreement to serve.

The shaky nature of the position (and no doubt the difficulties inherent in constantly replacing chiefs of police) has demonstrated the need for some type of protection for police chiefs against the arbitrary and unjustified removal from office by an elected or political officeholder.[13] In some states, such as Illinois, statutory protections have been implemented to protect police chiefs against such actions. Special boards or commissions have been created for the sole purpose of establishing recruitment, selection, and retention policies for chiefs of police. In Illinois, the law prohibits the removal or discharge of a member of the fire or police department (including the chief) without cause; the individual must also be given written charges and an opportunity to be heard in his or her defense. While this is a state mandate, these protections are available only when there is no local ordinance that provides a different procedure. If such an ordinance exists, the statute requires the municipal appointing authority to file the reasons for the chief's removal but does not require a showing of cause or a hearing. New Hampshire affords significant protection to police chiefs. It requires written notice of the basis for the proposed termination, a hearing on the charges, and a finding of cause before the dismissal can be implemented. Minnesota, on the other hand, provides no mandatory protections for police chiefs. The state does require they be included in any civil service system adopted by a municipality. A few other states have attempted to provide police chiefs with at least some job security whenever they have been promoted from within the ranks of the police department. Both Illinois and Ohio allow chiefs who resign or who are removed from their positions to return to the ranks they held within their departments before being appointed chiefs. Most states, however, offer very little protection. Chiefs across the country are sometimes forced to look for job protections in local civil service codes, local municipal ordinances, and any existing individual employment contracts.[14]

For the most part, the ability to endure the realities of the position of chief of police requires a unique blend of talent, skill, and knowledge that is often not "guaranteed" in statute or law. The reality is that few protections exist for persons occupying the highest position of a police agency except for those developed in the person themselves. Personal characteristics and qualities of excellent management and leadership are generally the reasons a chief remains in office.

The lack of job security and statutory protections seems to have real consequences—some of them quite negative—on how police chiefs administer their position and perform on the job. For example, police chiefs who lack protection from arbitrary and unjustified termination cannot independently fulfill their responsibilities. They will also likely be less willing to implement innovative programs that are controversial. This is so because a failure could jeopardize their position.

Researchers of the Police Executive Development Project at Pennsylvania State University found that top police executives showed greater devotion to their own job security than for the citizens they served. Their findings also indicated that top police executives showed greater submission to authority than did the general public. This type of attitude is formed as a result of working in a rigid organizational structure that demands and rewards obedience to authority.[15] The results of the project indicated that the average police executive failed to possess initiative, self-reliance, and confidence because of a lifelong habit of submission and social conformity. Without some form of contract protection, it is difficult to expect any police chief to jeopardize his or her job by implementing a vision or a program that has any chance of failure.

In the end, it may be most accurate to define the influence of local politics as a double-edged sword. Local politics is the most direct means by which the citizens of a democracy can influence the management of the police organization. Local politics may also constitute the most direct threat to the goal of nonpartisan, innovative, and effective police management.

State Government

State government may influence the administration of local police in several ways, including preemployment and training standards, the establishment and promotion of state-wide law enforcement priorities or reforms, and overall planning. The first state to impose minimum standards of training for police officers was California (1959). This move was soon followed by the states of New York, Oklahoma, and Oregon. In 1970, the law enforcement assistance administration (LEAA) made available discretionary grants to those states that wanted to implement minimum standards programs. Today all 50 states have mandated training for law enforcement officers.

Requirements related to the minimum standards for employment for police officers are administered through state organizations, often termed police officers standards and training commissions (POSTs). POSTs generally operate under four broad mandates. First, to establish minimum standards for employment in a state, county, or local law enforcement agency. Second, to articulate academy and annual training requirements for police officers. Third, to conduct and encourage research designed to improve all aspects of law enforcement.[16] Fourth, to suspend or revoke the certification of police officers for certain disciplinary or criminal violations.

A separate but related way in which states may influence the work of the local police chief is the establishment and promotion of state-wide law enforcement priorities or reforms. One example of this type of influence is the recent and strikingly rapid spread of the proprietary Blue Courage training program across several states including Ohio. Blue Courage was developed by former and active law enforcement professionals to "change the police culture from warriors to guardians" and "recommit American police culture to democratic ideals."[17] The program in Ohio has been directed largely by the Office of the Ohio Attorney General and is part of a state-mandated training expansion on the topics of implicit bias and procedural justice. The Ohio Attorney General's advisory group on law enforcement training recommended an increase in continuing police training. The Ohio state legislature subsequently mandated additional training hours, some of which could be fulfilled by the Blue Courage training program.[18] This process is an example of state-level political actors promoting an agenda for reform that ultimately filters to the administration of local police agencies.

Most recently, state legislatures have expressed a strong interest in fostering community safety and improving officer efficiency.[19] Between 2014 and 2017, laws were enacted by 14 states that allow police officers to issue citations for many minor crimes and decriminalized other laws.[20] These and other state actions frees officer's time to remain in-service and respond to calls or engage in eliminating open air drug markets, resuming directed patrol or participating in other programs. Also, some 30 states have adopted Blue Alert systems that rapidly disseminate information to other law enforcement agencies about an attack on one or more law enforcement officers.[21] Taking notice of the murders and aggravated assaults of law enforcement officers, some states have passed laws addressing these criminal acts. Among the states that have passed laws with enhanced sanctions for crimes against police officers are Arkansas, Arizona, California, Georgia, Kentucky, Mississippi, North Dakota, Tennessee, Utah, and Colorado.[22]

Courts

Courts play an obvious role in the formation and dissemination of criminal justice policy including the administration and day-to-day operations of local police agencies. We can describe these influences in at least three ways. First, there is the role of the state's attorney or prosecutor. Second, there are the decisions of state-level trial judges. Third, there are the decisions of the Supreme Court of the United States (SCOTUS).

The state's attorney or **prosecutor** works hand-in-hand with local police to investigate alleged crimes and file criminal charges or present evidence to a grand jury. The prosecutor provides supervision of criminal cases investigated by police and enacts specific procedures for the review of all arrests before their presentation in court. The initial contact of police officers with prosecutors occurs when the former brings a complaint to be charged. This encounter may be critical because it is an important point for making decisions about the disposition of the case and whether the complaint will be dismissed or reduced to a lesser offense. This discretionary power given to the prosecuting attorney has tremendous influence on the ways that certain laws are enforced or ignored. Police chiefs who perceive that the prosecutor consistently reduces or fails to aggressively enforce certain types of violations may divert their enforcement efforts and resources elsewhere. Then again, some chiefs may decide to "go public" and try to mobilize community support for enforcing the ignored violations. However, few police chiefs take this course of action because it could result in a serious deterioration in the working relationship with the local prosecutor. This is a situation most Chiefs would prefer to avoid.

For their part, local prosecutors have traditionally been reluctant to file criminal charges against rogue police officers in cases of misconduct or corruption because of the need to maintain close and productive working relations with local police.[23] When cases of alleged police misconduct become public knowledge or lead to indictments, a prosecutor's relationship with the police can be severely strained and may require sustained effort to repair. The resulting tension may become high if officers believe that the prosecutor is "sticking it to" the police department by "dragging the thing out," or by not allowing affected officers to plea bargain to lesser charges, or if the prosecutor is suspected of furthering his or her career at the officers' expense. The influence of the prosecutor on local police is for better or worse built in to the system. Police cannot independently turn arrests into criminal convictions, and the prosecutor needs evidence and testimony provided most often through local police to accomplish their work.

Another way in which courts influence the work of the police administrator is through the decisions of trial court judges. Once the police have made an arrest and brought the arrestee before a judge, from pretrial release onward the case is within the domain of the **judiciary**. In its assessment of the relationships of the judiciary and the police, one government report noted that trial judges have acted as chief administrative officers of the criminal justice system, using their power to dismiss cases as a method of controlling the use of the criminal process. However, except in those rulings involving the admissibility of evidence, this has been done largely on an informal basis and has tended to be inconsistent, often reflecting the personal values of the individual trial judge.[24]

In contrast, the function of trial judges in excluding evidence that they determine has been obtained illegally places them very clearly in the role of controlling police practices. Trial judges have not viewed this role as making them responsible for developing appropriate police practices. However, many trial judges indicate that they have no more responsibility

for explaining decisions to police than they have to private litigants.[25] Occasionally, judges grant motions to suppress evidence to dismiss cases they feel should not be prosecuted because the violation is too minor or for some other reason. The use of a motion to suppress evidence in this manner confuses the standards that are supposed to guide the police and has a disturbing, if not demoralizing, effect on them.[26] If judges consistently interject their personal biases into the judicial process and make it very clear to the police they will dismiss certain categories of violations, the police may discontinue enforcing that law.

For example, one of the co-authors of this book had previously been a motorcycle officer whose primary functions were traffic enforcement and accident investigation. It became apparent during the course of investigating traffic accidents that one of the major causes of rear-end collisions was drivers who were following too close. However, it was the practice of his agency not to issue traffic citations for following too close unless an accident had occurred. In an effort to be proactive, he decided to start issuing traffic citations to motorists who were clearly following too close but to do so before accidents occurred. At the end of his shift, like he routinely did, he submitted his traffic citations to his supervisor, who wanted to know where the accident reports were. He explained that there were no traffic accidents and that this was his effort to be proactive and prevent rear-end collisions. The sergeant just smiled and accepted the tickets without saying a word. When the court date came to appear before the judge, along with the unhappy citizens who had received the traffic citations, he started to testify about the following too close violations he had witnessed and the rationale for issuing the tickets. When the judge realized that the traffic citations were issued without any accidents having occurred, he summarily dismissed all of the cases. The judge never told him to stop writing traffic citations for this particular traffic violation, but suffice it to say, no more traffic citations were written for following too close unless there were rear-end collisions.

A third way in which courts influence the work of the police administrator is through the decisions of the Supreme Court of the United States (SCOTUS). The influence of these decisions may best be described as part of a larger process commonly referred to as the federalization of crime policy. Up to the 1960s, it was said that criminal justice was almost completely the responsibility of state and local governments. Federal criminal statutes were limited in their coverage, federal assistance to local law enforcement was generally in the areas of training and the processing of evidence, and the SCOTUS concerned itself with only the most notorious violations of Constitutional rights by state and local authorities.[27] A number of trends emerged during the 1960s and 1970s that led to an increase in the influence of federal law enforcement and judicial powers, including the promotion of national-level efforts to cripple networks of organized crime, mitigate problems associated with the use and sale of illegal drugs, and efforts to address public concerns about skyrocketing rates of violent crime.[28]

FIGURE 4.4 ▶ The U.S. Supreme Court led by Chief Justice Earl Warren was responsible for some of the most important decisions affecting law enforcement in the 1960s. (Library of -Congress Prints and Photographs Division [LC-USZ62-41653])

The trends toward federalization were in no small measure pushed by a series of Supreme Court opinions during the 1960s made under the leadership of Chief Justice Earl Warren. This series of decisions dramatically strengthened the rights of accused persons in criminal cases and is commonly referred to as the "due process revolution" (see Figure 4.4). Fundamentally, the Supreme Court's role in the due process revolution was a response to a vacuum in which the police themselves had failed to provide the necessary leadership. The era of strong social activism by various special-interest groups was not yet at hand, and neither the state courts nor the legislatures had displayed any broad interest in reforming the criminal law. What institution was better positioned to undertake this responsibility? The Court may even have felt obligated by the inaction of others to do so. Therefore, it became the Warren Court's job to provide the reforms so genuinely needed but so unpopularly received by some in the law enforcement community.

Several key decisions were made by a split vote of the Court. These decisions often drew heavy criticism from law enforcement officers and others as "handcuffing" police in their struggle with lawlessness. These decisions included:

- *Mapp v. Ohio* (1961), which banned the use of illegally seized evidence in criminal cases in the states by applying the Fourth Amendment guarantee against unreasonable searches and seizures

- *Gideon v. Wainwright* (1963), which affirmed that equal protection under the Fourteenth Amendment requires that legal counsel be appointed for all indigent defendants in all criminal cases

- *Escobedo v. Illinois* (1964), which affirmed that a suspect is entitled to confer with an attorney as soon as the focus of a police investigation of the suspect shifts from investigatory to accusatory

- *Miranda v. Arizona* (1966), which required police officers, before questioning suspects, to inform them of their constitutional right to remain silent, their right to an attorney, and their right to have an attorney appointed if they cannot afford to hire one. Although the suspect may knowingly waive these rights, the police cannot question anyone who, at any point, asks for a lawyer or indicates

"in any manner" that he or she does not wish to be questioned.[29]

The impact of these decisions on police work was staggering. In an effort to curb questionable and improper tactics, the Supreme Court barred the use of illegally obtained evidence in a criminal prosecution to prove guilt. This action, known as the exclusionary rule, rested primarily on the judgment that deterring police conduct that violates Constitutional rights outweighs the importance of securing a criminal conviction. A need for new procedures in such areas as interrogations, lineups, and seizures of physical evidence was created.

Although the decisions of the due process revolution initially were criticized by many police officers, over the years that view has changed as new generations of law enforcement officers joined the profession. These "newer" officers tended to view the decisions of the SCOTUS as simply the correct way to do things. Also, officers from the due process revolution have retired or left the profession because they could not abide or adapt to the new procedures mandated by the Supreme Court. Finally, there was a growing willingness among law enforcement leaders to acknowledge not only that some of their tactics needed changing but also that *Miranda* and other decisions had accomplished it. There is a sense in which the due process revolution furthered police professionalization. The SCOTUS has become more conservative since the 1970s, so much so that scholars have defined an erosion of many of the landmark cases decided during the Warren era.[30] Still, the trends toward federalization and the landmark decisions of the SCOTUS continue to exert significant influences on street-level police officers and the administration of local police agencies no matter the balance between "conservative" and "liberal" judges on the SCOTUS.

Citizens

The essence of police work is "people work," and so the job of the police administrator is obviously influenced by those who are policed—citizens. The citizen influences policing and its administration directly through face-to-face encounters. Citizens also obviously influence policing and its administration more indirectly through their collective membership in communities. These aggregate or group-level influences were outlined earlier within the section on how the local politics of communities influences styles of policing on the street.

Another way that citizens may exercise **citizen oversight** of the administration of police agencies is through the operation of organizations designed to identify and address citizen complaints against the police and more generally review the operation of police agencies. Traditionally, complaint investigations and review has been handled exclusively by sworn police, specifically administrators, first-line supervisors, and officers working in Internal Affairs Units (IAUs). By the late 1960s however, questions concerning the integrity and fairness of internal investigations led to a movement to reform the process and include some sort of citizen oversight. Citizen oversight is defined as a process by which people who are not sworn officers

---

Quick Facts: St. Louis Police Threaten to Quit or Slowdown if Civilian Oversight Passes

A bill to create a seven-member civilian oversight board for the St. Louis, Missouri Police Department, is looking like a sure bet to pass. The majority of the Board of Aldermen and even Mayor Francis are attaching their names to it.

Jeff Roorda, a spokesperson for the St. Louis Police Officers' Association, announced that St. Louis police officers will quit the department or do only the bare minimum on patrol if the city creates the proposed civilian oversight board.[32]

---

are involved in some way in the review of citizen complaints against police officers. Citizen oversight rests on the assumption that because of the police subculture, police officers cannot objectively investigate complaints against fellow officers.[31] As a result, various forms of citizen oversight of police have become institutionalized within large urban jurisdictions since the 1970s.

The movement toward civilian oversight of the police has progressed unevenly and has resulted in a patchwork of structures for the review of complaints. These structures have been described as a continuum ranging from those that are still primarily controlled by the police organization (or internal complaint review systems incorporating some citizen involvement) and those that are largely controlled by some sort of civilian oversight body (or external complaint review systems).[33] The external complaint systems with civilian oversight can take one of three primary forms:

- *First Tier* external review has a civilian oversight agency (e.g., ombudsman) that receives, investigates, adjudicates, and recommends appropriate discipline to police administrators.
- *Second Tier* external review has a civilian oversight agency that carries out the same function as those in the first tier, except the complaint investigations are conducted internally by the police agency.
- *Third Tier* external review has a civilian oversight agency with authority that is identical to those found in Tiers 1 and 2; however, the city's chief administrator (mayor or city manager) acts as an arbiter of disciplinary disputes between the police department and the civilian oversight agency.[34]

Any system of external review has both advantages and disadvantages. There is no one perfect system. The effective control of police officer misconduct remains a high priority for police administrators as popular media accounts illustrate continued tension between police and the public, particularly within many urban jurisdictions. The situation ensures ongoing debate as to how involved citizens and civilian oversight bodies should be in the review of police organizations and complaints against police. It is important to note that many police and sheriffs' departments are not pleased with trends involving citizen oversight of their agencies and have expressed some concerns (see Table 4.1).

Non-governmental Institutions

A variety of non-government institutions may also exert influence on the work of the police administrator. These include public interest organizations, local Chambers of Commerce, and religious-affiliated organizations such as churches.

Several years ago, the local chapter of the American Civil Liberties Union (ACLU) in Oakland, California had volunteers systematically call different units of the Oakland Police Department and ask how to file a citizen complaint. The callers found that few Oakland officers handling their calls gave out correct information. Many were apparently uninformed about the department's complaint process. Some others may have deliberately not given out the right information. The ACLU report blasting the Oakland Police Department for this failure was only one in a long series of investigations on police misconduct by that organization.

The ACLU is a private, nonprofit **public interest organization**. Private groups play an important role in police accountability. For the most part, they have been involved in attacking police misconduct. The National Association for the Advancement of Colored People (NAACP) has a long record of fighting police use of excessive force against African-Americans. The ACLU was responsible for some of the most important Supreme Court cases involving the police. For example, ACLU briefs were the basis for the Court's decisions in the landmark *Mapp* and *Miranda* cases discussed earlier in this chapter. The ACLU has been the leading advocate of citizen review of the police in New York City, Los Angeles, and many other cities. At the same time, the ACLU has defended the rights of police officers in cases involving, for example, grooming standards and department investigations of alleged police misconduct. The ACLU even published a handbook on *The Rights of Police Officers*.[35]

Local chambers of commerce and service clubs typically are supportive of efforts that lead to efficient government. Although such groups are characterized as being apolitical, they do exercise considerable influence. Their support for improving the quality of law enforcement is frequently heard in the chambers of city hall and is demonstrated through various community projects intended to assist local law enforcement. Perceptive police chiefs realize the benefit to be gained from the support

TABLE 4.1	CONCERNS MANY POLICE AND SHERIFF'S DEPARTMENTS—AND UNION LEADERS—EXPRESS ABOUT CITIZEN OVERSIGHT—AND POSSIBLE RESPONSES

Assertion: Citizens Should Not Interfere in Police Work	
Concerns	**Responses**
• The chief must be held accountable for discipline to prevent misconduct.	• Most oversight bodies are only advisory.
• Internal affairs already does a good job.	• Even when the department already imposes appropriate discipline without citizen review, an oversight procedure can reassure skeptical citizens that the agency is doing its job in this respect.
	• The next chief or sheriff may not be as conscientious about ensuring that the department investigates complaints fairly and thoroughly.

Assertion: Citizens Do Not Understand Police Work	
Concerns	**Responses**
• Oversight staff lack experience in police work.	• Board members typically have pertinent materials available for review, and ranking officers are usually present during hearings to explain department procedures.
	• Oversight administrators need to describe the extensive training they and their staff receive.
	• Citizen review is just that—*citizens* reviewing police behavior as private citizens.
• Only physicians review doctors, and only attorneys review lawyers.	• Doctors and lawyers have been criticized for doing a poor job of monitoring *their* colleagues' behavior.

Assertion: The Process Is Unfair	
Concerns	**Responses**
• Oversight staff may have an "agenda"—they are biased against the police.	• Oversight staff need to inform the department when they decide in officers' favor.
	• Oversight staff and police need to meet to iron out misconceptions and conflict.
• Not sustained findings remain in officers' files.	• Indecisive findings are unfair to both parties and should therefore be reduced in favor of unfounded, exonerated, or sustained findings.
• Adding allegations unrelated to the citizens' complaint is unfair.	• Internal affairs units themselves add allegations in some departments.
• Some citizens use the system to prepare for civil suits.	• Board findings can sometimes help officers and departments defend against civil suits.

Source: Citizen Review of Police: Approaches and Implementation, NIJ Issues and Practices, U.S. Department of Justice, Washington, DC, March 2001, p. 110.

of such groups, encourage personnel to become active members in these clubs, and frequently join one or two themselves. Support from these groups is not surprising when one considers that many are composed of men and women who are well educated and deeply involved in many aspects of community leadership. Such groups often have mobilized behind a police chief to get much-needed budget increases for salaries, additional personnel, and equipment.

Religious leaders and church congregations represent one of the most potentially powerful political pressure groups in the community. Their influence can, and frequently does, extend into the voting booth. This fact assures a high degree of responsiveness from local elected officials. Church leaders and their congregations almost always find an open door and a receptive ear at the office of their local police chief when they present their concerns. The problems that are frequently of greatest

concern to such groups are vice-related, such as prostitution, massage parlors, X-rated theaters, and adult bookstores. It is true that individual communities impose different standards and have varying levels of tolerance, but if the church leaders of a community mobilize and call on their police chief to eradicate or reduce what they perceive to be a serious problem, there is a high probability that they will receive some positive response. And, if the police chief suggests that the police department cannot cope realistically with the problem because of limited personnel and resources, these groups will likely begin applying pressure on the city officials to give the police chief the needed resources. Thus, the religious leaders of the community can be powerful allies of the police chief in certain types of enforcement efforts. On the other hand, this pressure group may force the chief to redirect resources away from areas that may have a higher priority.

Media

It is the responsibility of the police department, and especially its top leadership, to establish and maintain a friendly association with all media representatives.[36] Both the electronic and print news media can be powerful friends or devastating opponents of a local police department. This is determined by the attitudes, policies, and working relationships among editors, news directors, and the police chief. When friction does occur between the police and the news media, as it invariably does in every community, it frequently flows from the events surrounding a major crime or an unusual occurrence.

Often in the case of major crimes or incidents, police departments do not want to release information that will jeopardize the safety of the public or its officers, impair the right of a suspect to a fair and impartial trial, or slow the progress of an investigation. On the other hand, the news media have a different orientation and duty: to inform the public. Although their goals are often compatible, the police and the news media can sometimes fundamentally disagree. The following case illustrates this point.

One of the authors was involved in the investigation of the murders committed by Theodore Robert (Ted) Bundy in Tallahassee, Florida, and learned firsthand how differences in philosophy can play out to the detriment of a criminal investigation and cause conflict between the media and law enforcement. The facts are as follows:

At approximately 2 a.m. on a Sunday morning, Bundy entered an unlocked door to the Chi Omega sorority house, located near the campus of Florida State University. Prior to entering, he had armed himself with a nearby tree limb. He went to the second floor where he encountered a lone woman asleep in her bed. He clubbed her with the tree limb, rendering her immediately unconscious. He strangled her with the pantyhose he had brought to the scene with him. He left her room, went to a second room, and proceeded to batter a second sleeping woman with the tree limb. Like the previous victim, he rendered her unconscious and strangled her. He also bit off the nipple of her right breast, bit her twice on the left buttocks, and sodomized her with a hairspray bottle. He left her room, went down the hall and entered a third room where he encountered two more sleeping women, and proceeded to batter each of them. Still armed with the tree limb, he started walking down the flight of stairs leading to the front door of the sorority house. He briefly encountered a member of the sorority returning from an evening out. She knew nothing of the crimes, and Bundy was able to discreetly leave the premises. She turned out to be the only eyewitness to these crimes.

The investigation involved three different law enforcement agencies: the local sheriff's office, the municipal police department, and the campus police. At the end of the first day, it was agreed that all 35 criminal investigators who had worked independently of each other on the case would meet to discuss facts they had gathered. It was made clear to all those present

that highly specific information such as the name of the only eyewitness and the ways in which the victims were killed and assaulted should not be released to the media because this information would jeopardize the safety of the eyewitness, who said she would be able to identify the man if she ever saw him again. It could also result in the possible destruction of physical evidence by the suspect or perhaps encourage him to flee the area.

In spite of this admonition, the following day the local newspaper printed every detail of the crime, including the name of the young woman who had observed the suspect leaving the Chi Omega sorority house. Once she read the headlines, which identified her by name and location, she packed her bags and went home. Her reaction was perfectly understandable considering her personal safety concerns. The sheriff who was heading this investigation was very upset by the release of this information, which very likely had been provided to the newspaper by one or more of the investigators at the meeting the day before. He went to the local newspaper to talk to the editor to find out why it was necessary to divulge all of this highly specific information, which endangered the victim's life, and also raised the possibility the suspect might now destroy important physical evidence. The editor's comment was that the public had the right to know all of the facts available on the case and he would continue to publish any information provided from any source as long as it was reliable. The story encapsulates perfectly the tension arising from the fundamentally different goals of police and media at high-profile crime scenes. There is also little question, from a purely business perspective, that the more sensational and salacious the information printed about the crime, the more papers that would be sold. An old axiom in the media is "If it bleeds it leads" and this is true for both the print and electronic media. Bundy was eventually arrested, convicted, sentenced to death, and subsequently executed in the electric chair. Prior to his death, he confessed to murdering 35 young women in three states.

Studies show that conflicts between police and the media can be mitigated by police administrators who communicate to the media clear "rules of engagement" on where the media will be allowed to congregate, as well as when and how the media will be provided information.[37] The work of the police administrator can be helped by the use of a **public information officer** (PIO). The primary mission of the PIO is to act as a bridge between police and media. In many smaller or medium-sized police agencies, the police chief or highest-ranking officer may be the most appropriate choice to perform these duties. There is a growing list of resources available to police administrators to aid communication and cooperation at critical incident scenes. These include *Jane's Crisis Communications Handbook*, a resource that provides comprehensive and practical procedures to assist both public and private sector executives in the management of media relations.[38]

THE COUNTY SHERIFF AS A DISTINCT POLITICAL ENTITY

The bulk of this chapter describes various political forces on the police administrator of the typical local municipal police agency. The content is equivalent to how scholars have approached these topics and focused almost exclusively on the work of the chief of police in charge of a local municipal police agency. This focus sometimes ignores the office of the county **sheriff** within the realm of American criminal justice. The gap in knowledge and coverage on the work of the county sheriff is a problem because the office is a mainstay of the American law enforcement industry. Of the 50 states, 48 have sheriffs' offices; county level policing employs about 360,000 personnel including over 173,000 full-time sworn officers (see Figure 4.5).[39]

There are some political and organizational differences between local municipal police agencies and the office of the county sheriff that are important to the study of police administration. These differences involve the office's inherently political nature, its broad scope of legal authority, and the comparatively large geographical jurisdiction patrolled by sheriff's deputies. The most important of these differences for our purposes is the fact that the county sheriff gets authority directly through public election rather than administrative appointment. The sheriff became a popularly elected office immediately following the American Revolution and remains overwhelmingly so today.[40]

As elected officials, sheriffs are important political figures. In many rural areas, the sheriff is the most powerful political force in the county. As a result, sheriffs are far more independent than appointed law enforcement executives because, as discussed earlier, police chiefs in most cases can be removed by the mayors or city managers who appoint them. However, sheriffs are also subject to powerful political forces within their communities. Indeed, because the office is usually an elected position, there is a lot of media scrutiny. Individuals seeking the position of sheriff must run for public office the same as any other public official. The office of sheriff is the only local law enforcement position recognized and decreed by many state constitutions, a holdover from the days when local sheriffs were the only law of the land.

The extent to which politics, in the negative sense, influences the election of the sheriff and the subsequent operations of the office varies radically from community to community and even within particular election cycles. For example, in states in which sheriffs—because they are constitutional officers—are not bound by normal purchasing restrictions, some potential for abuse exists. If a candidate running for the office of sheriff has accepted a large donation from a certain business, there would likely be an expectation of reciprocity in return for such "support." This could result in purchases of cars from "loyal" car dealers, food for jail inmates from certain distributors, uniforms from a specific uniform company, and so forth. However, a sheriff who becomes too partisan in his or her purchasing risks disappointing other vendors. As such, momentum for the support of a different candidate in the next election usually occurs. The "real politics" of such a situation is that, while more purchases will be made from key supporting organizations, the incumbent must "spread around" enough purchasing to appease other vendors.

Then, too, there is the potential within any political environment for dirty campaigns, and sheriff's races are no exception. For example, several years ago, an incumbent sheriff who realized he might not be reelected because of strong opposition from a highly qualified opponent contacted one of his vice squad officers to see if he could create a situation that would be embarrassing to his opponent. The vice squad officer contacted a young and exceptionally attractive prostitute, who also served as his informant. He asked her to approach the man running against the incumbent sheriff at his place of business and try to entice him into joining her in a nearby hotel to have sex. The pre-selected hotel room had been set up with audiovisual equipment, so that the entire event could be recorded. Once the planned act was consummated and recorded, the videotape would be sent to the candidate's wife, along with copies to his minister and other key people in his life. It was felt that such a tape would be sufficiently disruptive to the candidate's personal life to make him ineffective as a campaigner. The prostitute, as instructed, did go to the business of the candidate and attempted to entice him to join her. The candidate, who was a politically connected individual, saw through this transparent farce and told the woman to leave his business. However, as soon as she left, he very discreetly followed her for a couple of blocks and saw her getting into an unmarked sheriff's department vehicle, which was being driven by the vice squad officer, whom he recognized. When the election was held, the incumbent sheriff lost. Since this was only one of many "dirty tricks" attempted by a number of employees of the sheriff's department, the newly elected sheriff immediately "cleaned house" and fired everyone who he could prove (or suspected) was involved in the efforts to embarrass him.

Inside the sheriff's department, politics can also be a decisive factor in the operational effectiveness of the organization. It is no accident that increased enforcement activity by the local sheriff's department usually precedes an election. The activity usually focuses on highly visible suspects or signs of disorder. Characteristic events include the roundup of local prostitutes, the crackdown on street corner vagrants, and the closing of "X-rated" video stores, all of which just happen to ensure considerable positive media attention. The interpretation is obviously that the incumbent sheriff is "tough" on crime. Sheriffs serving in smaller counties may even instruct their deputies to decrease the number of traffic citations that are given, except for the most serious violations such as DUI and reckless driving, and to start issuing more traffic warnings rather than citations, especially to those motorists who live in the county. This, of course, is based upon the assumption that unhappy citizens could translate this dissatisfaction in a vote against the incumbent sheriff.

One of the most important political processes that impact the police organization is the absence of local or state civil service boards. In many states, employees of the county sheriff's department serve at the pleasure of the current sheriff. Therefore, if the incumbent sheriff either decides not to run for office or

Quick Facts: Variety in Term Lengths for Sheriffs

In 43 states, sheriffs are elected to four-year terms. In two states, Arkansas and New Hampshire, their terms are two years in length. In New Jersey, a sheriff's term is three years in length and in Massachusetts, it is six years in length. Alaska has no county government. Thus, they do not have any Sheriff's Offices. In Connecticut, sheriffs have been replaced with a State Marshall system, and in Hawaii, there are no sheriffs, but deputy sheriffs serve in the Sheriff's Division of the Hawaii Department of Public Safety.[41]

FIGURE 4.5 ▶ Recent graduates of the Los Angeles County Sheriff's Department police academy. This organization is one of the largest of its kind in the United States with nearly 18,000 sworn and professional staff. (Courtesy of Los Angeles County Sheriff's Department)

is defeated in the next election, the newly elected sheriff may decide to fire a high percentage of the employees currently working at the sheriff's department. However, if wholesale dismissals do occur, this will result in a lack of continuity in the skill level of employees and affect the quality of service being delivered to the public. It also creates enormous job insecurity and provides a mechanism whereby unqualified persons may be elected to one of the highest positions of law enforcement in the community. Thus, the very nature of the electoral process and the enormous power inherent in the office can foster an environment in which politics prevails.

EMERGING POLITICAL ISSUES

This last section of the chapter provides an overview of emerging political issues for police administrators including: (1) racial/ethnic profiling and discrimination, (2) police-worn body cameras, and (3) local immigration enforcement. The discussion should make clear that these and other topics have increasingly involved the influence of politics on the administration of any law enforcement organization.

Racial/Ethnic Profiling and Discrimination

Nothing has fueled the political fire between police and minorities more than the use of race and ethnicity as criteria in police decision-making, a phenomenon often referred to as "racial and ethnic profiling."[42] Weitzer and Tuch define **racial profiling** as "the use of race as a key factor in police decisions to stop and interrogate citizens."[43] The term has several meanings, most of which are associated with law enforcement officers making the decision to stop an individual because of race or ethnicity. Officers often use the "pretext" or "suspicious vehicle stop" argument to justify their actions as legal (e.g., using a legal pretext, such as an illegal lane change or broken license plate light, to stop the vehicle and then gain a basis to search for illegal drugs).[44] However, if a specific crime occurs (e.g., a rape, robbery, or a murder) and the suspect description by a witness

FIGURE 4.6 ▶ Racial profiling in traffic stops has become an increasingly controversial issue in police procedure. (Michael Matthews - Police Images/Alamy Stock Photo)

includes race, gender, or ethnicity, it is lawful for the police to stop a citizen on the basis of how closely the individual resembles the characteristics or description within the "profile" (see Figure 4.6).

Media accounts of illegal treatment of minority citizens during the 1990s led many state governments to enact legislation that banned racial profiling and held police organizations accountable for targeting minority citizens. In addition to the legislation, in 1999, Attorney General Janet Reno convened the Strengthening Police-Community Relations Conference held in Washington, DC, for the purpose of assisting police organizations in collecting data on this issue. By 2000, more than 4,000 law enforcement agencies across the United States were involved in data collection efforts. As early as 1999, several states—including North Carolina—adopted legislation that required data collection on every police-initiated stop. In North Carolina, Senate Bill 76 required all state law enforcement agencies to track the race and ethnic backgrounds of motorists stopped to monitor officers who might be targeting minority drivers. Prior to Senate Bill 76, officers recorded the race/ethnicity of motorists who were formally cited for a violation (e.g., citations and written warnings). By 2015, the majority of states had passed similar legislation.[45]

Our coverage of racial/ethnic profiling and discrimination within this chapter could involve a systematic review of the multitudes of research studies over the last two or three decades that have examined the issues primarily in terms of whether, and if so to what extent, police officers engage in racial/ethnic profiling and discrimination. Such a review is beyond the scope of this chapter and would involve discussions focused primarily on issues of data collection, research methods, and/or the analysis of data rather than the management of political forces important to the day-to-day work of the police administrator. Instead, we cover these important

issues through the lens of two recent and widely recognized police-citizen encounters: (1) the 2015 arrest of Freddie Gray in Baltimore MD and (2) the 2014 shooting of Michael Brown in Ferguson, MO. These cases were chosen because they have become landmarks. They are widely recognized and have produced volumes of information through both official sources and the news media. Nationally prominent high-profile cases such as these do not come along everyday within every jurisdiction. But allegations involving racial/ethnic profiling and police discrimination commonly occur. These cases provide an important context for police administrators who must confront politically charged issues and limit the potential for significant community backlash. We also cover the latter case and the shooting of Michael Brown as a transition to a discussion of another trend important to police administrators, the trend toward police-worn body cameras.

The Case of Freddie Gray

In 2015, a 25-year-old African-American male named **Freddie Gray** was arrested by Baltimore police officers after he ran from them. He eventually died as a result of a fatal spinal cord injury he suffered while in police custody. Large-scale rioting broke out shortly after his funeral. The following are the facts of the case as set forth by the District Court of Maryland, Baltimore City.[46]

On the morning of April 12 near the corner of North Avenue and Mount Street Baltimore Police Department (BPD) Officers Brian Rice, Garrett Miller and Edward Nero made eye contact with local resident Freddie Gray. Gray immediately ran from police. Rice dispatched that he was involved in a foot pursuit, at which time bike patrol Officers Miller and Nero also pursued Gray. Gray eventually surrendered to the pursuing officers in the vicinity of the 1700 block of Presbury Street.

Officers Miller and Nero handcuffed Gray's arms behind his back and moved him to a location a few feet away from where he had initially surrendered. Gray was placed in a prone position. Gray indicated that he could not breathe and requested an inhaler to no avail. Officers Miller and Nero placed Gray in a seated position and found a knife clipped to the inside of his pants pocket. The blade of the knife was folded into the handle. The knife was not a switchblade knife and is lawful under Maryland law. The officers removed the knife and placed it on the sidewalk. Gray was placed back down on his stomach and began to flail his legs and scream as Miller placed him in a restraining technique known as a "leg lace" while Nero physically held him down against his will. The BPD wagon arrived in order to transport Gray.

Lt. Rice, Officer Miller, and Officer Nero failed to establish probable cause for Gray's arrest as he had committed no crime. Thus, his arrest had been illegal. The police transport wagon driven by BPD Officer Goodson arrived, and police loaded Gray into it without properly securing him via seatbelt. The failure to properly secure Gray in the wagon was a violation of BPD General Orders. Rice eventually directed the BPD wagon to stop at Baker Street, where police removed Gray from the wagon, placed flex cuffs on his wrists, placed leg shackles on his ankles, and completed required paperwork. Miller, Nero, and Rice loaded Gray back into the wagon, placing him on his stomach, head first onto the floor of the vehicle. Police once again failed to properly secure Gray into the wagon in violation of BPD policies. Rice directed Goodson to transport Gray to the Central Booking and Intake Facility. Following transport from Baker Street, Gray suffered a severe and critical neck injury as a result of being handcuffed, shackled, and left unrestrained inside the BPD wagon. Goodson proceeded to the vicinity of Mosher Street and Fremont Avenue, where he parked the wagon and walked to the back of it in order to observe Gray. At no point did he seek, nor did he render, any medical assistance to Gray. Goodson returned to the driver's seat and proceeded toward the Central Booking and Intake Facility, with Gray still not properly secured.

Several blocks later, Goodson called into dispatch that he needed to check on the status of this prisoner and requested additional units at Dolphin Street and Druid Hill Avenue. Officer William Porter arrived on the scene near Dolphin Street and Druid Hill Avenue. Both Goodson and Porter proceeded to the back of the wagon to check on Gray. Gray requested "help" and indicated that he could not breathe. Porter asked Gray if he needed a medic. Gray indicated at least twice that he needed a medic. Porter then physically assisted Gray from the floor of the van to the adjacent bench seat. However, despite Gray's appeal for a medic, both officers once again failed to properly secure Gray. They also once again failed to render or request medical assistance.

Porter subsequently left the scene to assist in the arrest of another prisoner at North Avenue. Despite Gray's obvious and recognized need for medical assistance, Goodson, in a grossly negligent manner, chose to also respond to the call on North Avenue. Gray was still unsecured in the back of the wagon,

and police once again failed to render or summon medical assistance.

Goodson arrived on scene at North Avenue, where he was eventually met by Nero, Miller, Porter, Rice, and BPD Sgt. White. Goodson walked to the back of the wagon and again opened the doors to observe Gray. Police observed Gray unresponsive on the floor of the wagon. White spoke to the back of Gray's head. Gray did not respond, and his condition had obviously deteriorated. White made no subsequent attempt to look, assess, or determine Gray's condition. No police officer on scene rendered medical assistance. No police officer on scene summoned medical assistance. Goodson proceeded to the Western district BPD station after police had loaded the additional prisoner from the North Avenue call. He once again—for a fifth time—failed to properly secure Gray in the wagon. Upon arrival at the station, police unloaded and escorted the prisoner from the North Avenue call before they attended to Gray. Gray had stopped breathing by the time police tried to remove Gray from the wagon. A medic was finally called to the scene who quickly determined that Gray was in cardiac arrest and was critically and severely injured.

Gray was rushed to the University of Maryland Shock Treatment Unit, where he underwent emergency surgery. He died seven days later. His death was determined by the Maryland State Medical Examiner to be a homicide believed to be the result of injuries sustained while he was left unrestrained in the police wagon.

On April 27, 2015, funeral services were held for Freddie Gray. That same afternoon rioting started in the same part of Baltimore where he had been arrested. The riots resulted in extensive burning and looting of hundreds of businesses in the area as well as dozens of police officers being injured primarily by bricks, stones, and other objects being thrown at them. Over the next couple of days, an additional 5,000 police officers were brought to Baltimore from other Maryland cities and counties, as well as officers from New Jersey and Pennsylvania. Also called in for assistance was the Maryland National Guard. A curfew was imposed from 10:00 p.m. to 5:00 a.m. for five days, and eventually the rioting was brought under control (see Figure 4.8).

Upon receiving the medical examiner's report ruling that Freddie Gray had died as a result of a homicide, the decision was made by Baltimore State's Attorney Marilyn Mosby to charge the six officers criminally (see Figure 4.7). Prosecutors concluded that Gray should never have been arrested. They also determined that police had lacked probable cause to initially pursue Gray and that Gray had been legally in possession of the knife. Prosecutors alleged that Gray sustained fatal spinal cord injuries during his transport. Six BPD officers at various times had failed to render and/or summon necessary medical aid.[47] The officer driving the van was charged with second-degree murder for his indifference to the risk that Gray might be killed. The other involved officers were charged with crimes ranging from manslaughter to false imprisonment. The prosecutor pursued separate criminal trials of the accused officers. The case against one of the accused officers ended in a mistrial. Three of the other accused officers were found not guilty at trial. Remaining criminal charges against the officers were dropped in July 2016. In September 2017, the U.S. Department of Justice declined to bring federal charges against the officers involved in the case.[48]

The impact of the Freddie Gray case goes well beyond the legal outcomes, however. Whether one views the Gray case as an example of criminal police misconduct, the opposing reactions of police, the legal community, and local citizens and community activists clearly highlight how the issues of race and discrimination can impact police-community relations and the work of police administrators. As a result of the death of Freddie Gray, a considerable political divide has emerged among local prosecutors, members of the minority community, and the police union representing these officers (see Figure 4.8). For example, the Baltimore Chapter of the Fraternal Order of Police called the speed at which the prosecutor moved on the case politically motivated. "The actions taken today by the State's Attorney are an egregious rush to justice," said Michael E. Davey, the Union's lawyer. "We believe that these officers will be vindicated as they have done nothing wrong."[49] There is also a strong feeling among some pro-police advocates that the prosecutor's decision was a political one as well as an effort to appease those who were rioting and looting in the hopes that they would discontinue their actions. On the other hand, there are those in the community who believe that the criminal charges placed against these six officers were justified and would like to see these officers punished and imprisoned. The case will stand for some time as an example of the political divide that only seems to widen as a result of notorious encounters between police and minority citizens.

The Case of Michael Brown

Michael Brown was an 18-year-old African-American resident of Ferguson, MO located outside of St. Louis. Brown and one of his friends entered a local market and according to witnesses pushed the clerk after he had shoplifted a box of cigarillos. A person inside the store called police. Police dispatchers described the suspect and relayed information that he was walking along a nearby avenue. Ferguson Police Department (FPD) Officer Darren Wilson observed Brown and his friend walking in the road. He rolled down his window and told them to exit the roadway. There was a verbal altercation between Brown and Wilson. At this point, there was considerable discrepancies between witnesses and the story of how the shooting unfolded according to Wilson. Wilson contended that Brown had attacked him and grabbed his neck. Brown and his friend attempted to flee on foot. Wilson gave chase on foot, and

FIGURE 4.7 ▶ Baltimore, Maryland, State's Attorney, Marilyn Mosby, announcing the criminal charges being placed against the six Baltimore, Maryland, police officers on the death of Freddie Gray. (Alex Brandon/AP/Corbis)

FIGURE 4.8 ▶ Rioting breaks out in Baltimore, Maryland, after the funeral of Freddie Gray. (Andrew Burton/Getty Images)

he stated that Brown stopped and charged him. Wilson fired several shots as Brown charged him. Brown's friend contradicted Wilson's version of the event. He stated that Brown had turned around and surrendered with his hands up, and then Wilson shot him several times. Brown was hit six times in the front of his body.

The shooting of Brown resulted in weeks of large-scale protest in Ferguson. Protesters coined the now familiar phrase "Hands Up Don't Shoot!" that became the theme of civil unrest. A grand jury was convened to investigate the shooting. Because there was no video recording from either a dash camera or a BWC, the grand jury had to rely upon physical, ballistics, forensic, and crime scene evidence, medical reports, autopsy reports as well as hearing the testimony of dozens of witnesses. In the end, the grand jury concluded that Officer Wilson was justified in using deadly force in defense of his life. The U.S. Department of Justice, Civil Rights Division, which conducted its own investigation, came to the same conclusion.[50] However, in spite of the overwhelming evidence to support these findings, there were many in the media and the community who disputed the grand jury findings. This is precisely the kind of case where a video recording of the events would have been very useful to reconcile some of the conflicting accounts by eyewitnesses.[51] Following the grand jury's decision to exonerate Officer Wilson, a riot erupted in Ferguson, Missouri, followed by major demonstrations in numerous cities throughout the United States (see Figure 4.9).

The investigation of the shooting conducted by the U.S. Department of Justice (DOJ) was expanded to examine the operations and practices of the Ferguson Police Department after serious allegations were raised by members of the African-American community that racial profiling was being employed by this agency. The DOJ investigators determined that there were several problem areas associated with the potential profiling of African-American residents of the city of Ferguson including discriminatory police and municipal court practices, the use of enforcement for purposes of generating municipal revenue, and wide-scale distrust between police and local citizens.[52]

The DOJ report indicated that Ferguson's law enforcement practices were shaped by the City's focus on revenue rather than public safety needs, and that this emphasis on revenue had compromised the institutional character of Ferguson's police department. These factors contributed to a pattern of unconstitutional policing. This also shaped its municipal court and has led to procedures that have raised due process concerns and inflicted unnecessary harm on members of the Ferguson community. Further, Ferguson's police and municipal court practices both reflected and exacerbated existing racial bias, including racial stereotypes. Ferguson's own data established clear racial disparities that adversely impact African-Americans. The evidence showed that discriminatory intent is part of the reason for these disparities. Over time, Ferguson's police and municipal court practices had sown deep mistrust between parts of the community and the police department, undermining law enforcement legitimacy among African-Americans in particular.[53]

The City's emphasis on revenue generation had a profound effect on FPD's approach to law enforcement. Patrol assignments and schedules were geared toward aggressive enforcement of Ferguson's municipal code, with insufficient thought being given to whether enforcement strategies promoted public safety or unnecessarily undermined community trust and cooperation. This culture within the FPD influenced officer activities in all areas of policing beyond just ticketing. Officers

FIGURE 4.9 ▶ Police guard the Ferguson, Missouri Police Department and Municipal Court building as rioting erupts following the grand jury announcement exonerating Officer Darren Wilson in the shooting of Michael Brown. (Scott Olson/ Getty Images)

expected and demanded compliance even when they lacked legal authority. They tended to interpret the exercise of free-speech rights as unlawful disobedience, innocent movements as physical threats, and indications of mental or physical illness as belligerence.

Ferguson had allowed its focus on revenue generation to fundamentally compromise the role of Ferguson's municipal court. The municipal court did not act as a neutral arbiter of the law or a check on unlawful police conduct. Instead, the court primarily used its judicial authority as the means to compel the payment of fines and fees that advanced the City's financial interests. This has led to court practices that violate the Fourteenth Amendment's due process and equal protection requirements. The court's practices also imposed unnecessary harm, overwhelmingly on African-American individuals, and run counter to public safety.

Most strikingly, the court issued municipal arrest warrants not on the basis of public safety needs, but rather as a routine response to missed court appearances and required fine payments. In 2013 alone, the court issued over 9,000 warrants on cases stemming in large part from minor violations such as parking infractions, traffic tickets, or housing code violations. Jail time would be considered far too harsh a penalty for the great majority of these code violations, yet Ferguson's municipal court routinely issued warrants for people to be arrested and incarcerated for failing to timely pay related fines and fees. Under state law, a failure to appear in municipal court on a traffic charge involving a moving violation also results in a license suspension. Ferguson has made this penalty even more onerous by only allowing the suspension to be lifted after payment of an owed fine is made in full. Until recently, Ferguson also added charges, fines, and fees for each missed appearance and payment. Many pending cases still include such charges that were imposed before the court recently eliminated them, making it as difficult as before for people to resolve these cases.

Ferguson's law enforcement practices overwhelmingly impacted African-Americans. Data collected by the FPD from 2012 to 2014 showed that African-Americans accounted for 85 percent of vehicle stops, 90 percent of citations, and 93 percent of arrests made by FPD officers, despite comprising only 67 percent of Ferguson's population. African-Americans were more than twice as likely as white drivers to be searched during vehicle stops even after controlling for nonrace-based variables such as the reason for the vehicle stop. These disparities were also present in FPD's use of force. Nearly 90 percent of documented force used by FPD officers was used against African-Americans. In every canine bite incident for which racial information is available, the person bitten was African-American.

The DOJ investigation indicated that this disproportionate burden on African-Americans could not be explained by any difference in the rate at which people of different races violated the law. Rather, the investigation revealed that these disparities occur, at least in part, because of unlawful bias against and stereotypes about African-Americans. It found substantial evidence of racial bias among police and court staff in Ferguson. For example, the DOJ investigators discovered e-mails circulated by police supervisors and court staff that stereotype racial minorities as criminals, including one e-mail that joked about an abortion by an African-American woman being a means of crime control.

Since the shooting death of Michael Brown, the lack of trust between the FPD and a significant portion of Ferguson's residents, especially African-Americans, has become undeniable. The causes of this distrust and division, however, have been the subject of debate. Police and other city officials, as well as some Ferguson residents, have insisted that the public outcry is attributable to "outside agitators" who do not reflect the opinions of "real Ferguson residents." That view is at odds with the facts gathered during the investigation. The investigation has shown that distrust of the FPD is longstanding and largely attributable to Ferguson's approach to law enforcement. This approach results in patterns of unnecessarily aggressive and at times unlawful policing, reinforces the harm of discriminatory stereotypes, discourages a culture of accountability, and neglects community engagement. The FPD had moved away from the modest community policing efforts it previously had implemented, reducing opportunities for positive police-community interactions, and losing the little familiarity it had with some African-American neighborhoods. The confluence of policing to raise revenue and racial bias thus had resulted in practices that not only violate the Constitution and cause direct harm to the individuals whose rights are violated but also undermined community trust, especially among many African-Americans. As a consequence of these practices, law enforcement has been defined as illegitimate, and the partnerships necessary for public safety were, in some areas, entirely absent.

Box 4.3: The Movement to Define Police "Violence" as a Public Health Issue

The American Public Health Association (APHA) is a 25,000-member organization of public health professionals. Members include physicians and other medical professionals, social workers, and employees of public health agencies nationwide.

The APHA recently adopted a policy statement addressing law enforcement "violence" as a public health issue. The policy defines law enforcement violence as physical, psychological, and sexual violence perpetrated by police that results in deaths, injuries, trauma, and stress. The policy references data that focuses on the disproportionate use of force (or "violence") by police officers within encounters involving marginalized populations. This movement emphasizes the relationship between demographics and factors within the structure of communities that increase the incidence of police violence against citizens.

This movement is consistent with decades of criminological research that locates the primary causes of crime within communities rather than individuals. The basic idea is that marginalized populations are disproportionately impacted by police violence due to a range of factors including the war on drugs, police militarization, and the tendency of police agencies to allocate more officers within high-crime/low-income neighborhoods.

The movement to define police violence as a public health issue does, however, seem to overlook some of the more direct influences on police "violence." Criminal justice scholarship has consistently identified "situational risk" as the most significant factor in determining when and why police use force within any particular police-citizen encounter. Situational risk refers to factors such as whether citizens possess weapons, or the degree to which citizens resist police actions though demeanor, non-cooperation, or acts of physical violence against police.

The disproportionate use of force by police within encounters involving persons of marginalized populations is an obvious issue of concern. The APHA and other groups driving the movement emphasize demographic and community-level factors as causes. But criminal justice scholarship focuses on the more immediate factors that influence police to enforce the law and/or defend themselves and others from situational risks including citizens who resist police attempts to control situations, citizens who are armed, and citizens who respond to police tactics to control them with acts of violence against police.

Public health initiatives designed to address the disproportionate incidents of police violence against marginalized populations need to emphasize demographic and structural causes. But the more immediate factors within individual police-citizen encounters that elevate the risks of violence cannot be ignored. Police most commonly perpetrate "violence" in response to situational threats that endanger the safety of themselves and others. More data is necessary to explore *why* police encounters involving marginalized populations tend to escalate in violence and result in injuries, trauma, and stress to citizens.

Source: The American Public Health Association (APHA). Available at https://www.apha.org/policies-and-advocacy/public-health-policy-statements/policy-database/2019/01/29/law-enforcement-violence.

Police-Worn Body Cameras

There was previously a slow but steady trend toward police departments utilizing body-worn cameras (BWCs) for their police officers. However, this trend dramatically increased in the aftermath of the Michael Brown shooting and related political fall-out that stemmed from the protests and the report of the DOJ. This case may be defined as an important catalyst in the increased trend toward the use of police-worn body cameras. This is the second of our three emerging political issues of concern for police administrators

The question that is consistently raised in police-citizen interactions is what can be done to prevent officers from using excessive force in the first place, and equally important, what can be done to determine what actually happened in any specific interaction between a police officer and citizen when there is an allegation of excessive force or other misconduct. One of the technological innovations that can assist both law enforcement agencies as well as citizens in coming to a conclusion as to what did transpire is through the use of police body-worn cameras (BWCs) (see Figure 4.10). Police administrators who are in favor of the use of these devices argue that they can provide valuable evidence in court and provide a clear and objective image of exactly what transpired between their officers and individuals who may be taken into custody. There is also the implied suggestion that such devices will deter officers who might be inclined to engage in misconduct from doing so, as well as discourage citizens inclined to make false allegations when they know the entire interaction is being recorded.

Even the ACLU, which generally is wary of surveillance, recently expressed support for the use of such cameras. However, they do acknowledge that privacy concerns of the police and public and its import comes with conditions. "I absolutely know this tool will transform policing," Scott Greenwood, a police accountability attorney and general counsel for the ACLU, said in an interview. "It's an unalloyed good, provided that there are policies in place that mandate the use of devices rather than leaving it up to the discretion of the officers."[54]

Because increasing numbers of police departments are presently using the cameras, both objective and anecdotal information seems to be accumulating pointing to the benefits of cameras. For example, the Institute of Criminology at the University of Cambridge recently conducted a body camera study with the Rialto Police Department, California, and the results were that complaints against officers dropped by 88 percent and officers wearing cameras used force almost 60 percent less.[55,56]

On the other hand, the use of BWCs also raises some significant privacy concerns. Police officers routinely patrol their communities, responding to calls for assistance as well as initiating citizen contacts. This work often takes police inside people's homes and businesses, as well into alleys, fields, cars, and a wide variety of other locations. Additionally, what officers actually see and hear on some of these calls can be very graphic and personal. With these thoughts in mind, agencies implementing the use of BWCs should consult closely with their legal advisor to ensure the operational protocol properly addresses privacy concerns.[57]

A second aspect of the privacy issue is state laws governing audio or video recording of parties involved in the communication. States can be described as a one-party consent state or a two-party consent state. In one party state, only one party to the communication has to consent for the recording to be legal.[58] In a two-party consent state, all parties to the communication must consent for the recording to be legal. In those states, it stands to reason that the police would have to obtain consent from the citizen before recording the encounter. It is imperative that the privacy issue be thoroughly reviewed with legal counsel and legal advice strictly followed. The reasonable expectation of privacy doctrine will certainly be at the forefront of this issue, but it is not always crystal clear for operational purposes.[59]

Another issue of concern for police administrators who have implemented or are considering the implementation of BWCs involves software and the capability to redact or block certain segments of video depicting police-citizen encounters. Any camera system selected must have easy-to-use redaction software for both the video and the audio or be compatible for redaction with other software. It is very likely that many recordings will be released to the public, for example, via each state's open record law. At the same time, there may be certain sections of the released video or audio that the law requires to be redacted or blocked out. Absent user-friendly software for redaction purposes, the agency could experience significant complications. Demonstration visits from the vendors should include a thorough demonstration of the software's redaction capability.[60]

Digital recordings also can consume a lot of hard drive space. An in-house analysis by one agency with 200 sworn officers indicated that 33 terabytes of storage would be needed each year, based on a conservative estimate of one hour of recording per officer work shift.[61] The amount of space needed will be contingent on three primary variables: (1) the number of officers using the BWCs, (2) the policy requirement for recording, and (3) the retention requirements for the recordings. Smaller agencies will likely need less storage capacity than medium and large agencies. Continuous recording will result in a massive amount of stored data, but recording only during citizen contacts will significantly reduce the storage space required. How long the recordings must be saved will probably be determined by state laws governing the retention of official records.

The in-house storage of video data requires significant expenditure of resources, including servers, redundancy, proper physical space, and IT personnel. Using cloud storage can reduce the cost by as much as 30–50 percent and give the agency access to cutting-edge technology and the best security available.[62] Considerable preplanning for storage is critical for proper maintenance of the data.[63]

Agencies contemplating the use of BWCs should calculate the total costs of the implementation, including start-up costs and maintenance costs. Start-up expenses, at a minimum, include the cameras, any accessories, policy development, data storage, training, and related infrastructure or technical costs, such as space requirements for equipment and technical training of appropriate employee(s) to oversee the system. Maintenance costs, at a minimum, will include manpower associated with managing and maintaining the equipment. Additionally, camera replacement due to breakage (physical altercations with suspects) and technical malfunctions will need to be considered. The ongoing cost associated with storage of the data must be calculated, and the potential increase in open records requests and the resultant workload increase must be considered. The personnel cost could increase substantially after factoring in redaction requirements.[64]

FIGURE 4.10 ▶ Near the right ear note that the camera is attached to the frame of the sunglasses. The camera can easily be moved from one type of glasses to another. The model also wears a body camera on his chest. It could easily be attached to an epaulette on a shirt or coat. (Courtesy WOLFCOM®, a Los Angeles-based company that is a leader in body-camera applications)

Politics and Other Deadly Encounters Between Police and African-Americans

The cases of Freddie Gray and Michael Brown have clearly become landmarks. These landmark cases however occurred within the context of a steady stream of controversial police shootings of African-Americans during the same general period of time. These cases often become the subject of public and media attention precisely because they had been recorded by citizens using the cameras attached to their mobile devices. We provide brief overviews of three of these recent cases as an adjunct to our discussion of the emerging issues of racial profiling, discrimination, and the trend toward body-worn cameras. Although the facts of each of these situations have been quite different, the political fallout has been similar in that it has negatively impacted police-community relations.

1. On July 17, 2014, Eric Garner a 350-pound African-American man was on a street corner in New York City selling "loosies," which is the term used for selling one cigarette at a time. While he was engaging in this act, the price of a pack of cigarettes in New York City was approximately $13.00 because of substantial city taxes. A single "loosie" costs 75 cents, but two could be purchased for a dollar. On the face of it, selling loosies would appear to be a minor crime, except for the fact that it deprives shop owners of the income from selling them and more importantly, the city loses substantial tax revenue from the practice. Arguably, it was the motivation to fully collect all legal tax dollars that contributed to Garner's death.

   A police officer observing Garner engaged in selling these loosies approached him, determined he was violating the law, and advised him he was under arrest. When the officers tried to physically take him into custody, he resisted. This officer, along with several other officers at the scene, took him to the ground and placed him in handcuffs. One of the officers who wrestled Garner to the ground while holding him around the neck claimed he was using an approved "take down" maneuver taught in the police academy. Others in the community claimed it was an illegal chokehold. While being held down on the pavement, Garner complained several times that he could not breathe. He subsequently died.

   All the officers, except the one holding Garner around the neck, were given immunity for their testimony. However, the grand jury declined to indict the officer who was holding him around the neck on the pavement. This was also the same officer who had made the initial contact with Garner and told him he was under arrest. As a result of the grand jury absolving this officer, several large demonstrations and marches were held in NYC and around the country to demand justice for Eric Garner.[65]

2. At approximately 3:22 p.m. on November 22, 2014, Cleveland (Ohio) Police Officers responded to a 911 call that someone had been taking a gun out of his waistband and pointing it at people in a local park. The dispatcher did not pass on critical information that had been given by the person telephoning in the information that the "guy" was likely a juvenile and the gun was "probably fake." Responding police officers immediately sped toward the juvenile, who was now standing by himself near a gazebo. As the officers came to a stop and exited the car, the African-American juvenile later identified as 12-year-old Tamir Rice reached for, or pulled out a gun, which would later be determined to be an air-soft pellet gun. The orange tip on the gun that would have alerted the officer it was not an actual weapon was missing. The police officers reported that they told Tamir to "Show your hands" three times before a shot was fired. Witnesses who were at the scene say they did not hear the officers issue a warning.[66] Seconds after the encounter, one officer shot and fatally wounded Rice, who died the next day.

   The Cuyahoga County Sheriff's Office investigated and produced a report of several hundred pages. A Cleveland Police Union Official said the officers' actions were justified. The Prosecutor presented all the evidence gathered from the shooting to a grand jury to consider whether rookie Officer Timothy Loehmann, who shot Tamir, should face criminal prosecution along with his training partner, Officer Frank Garmback.[67] The grand jury concluded that the shooting was justified and as a result, the prosecutor decided not to file charges against either officer. However, recently the City of Cleveland settled the case with the Rice family for $6 million.

3. On April 4, 2015, A Caucasian North Charleston, South Carolina, police officer Michael Slager made a traffic stop of a vehicle with a broken tail light. The driver, African-American Walter Scott, ran from the officer after a brief conversation. The two men ran into a park-like setting, and Scott continued to run when he was reportedly ordered to stop by the officer. A civilian passing by used a cellphone to videotape the two men struggling and then Scott running away. The officer fired eight times at the fleeing Scott, causing his death. The autopsy report revealed that Scott had sustained multiple gunshot wounds to his back. The video also depicts the officer moving one or more items at the scene closer to the body. The officer claimed that during his initial encounter with Scott he had to use a Taser and that Scott had initially tried to take his gun. The video evidence made clear that Slager had altered the crime scene after he shot Scott to make it look as if Scott had taken his Taser. Slager was fired and charged with murder. The murder trial ended in a hung jury. Slager was later indicted and plead guilty to federal civil rights charges stemming from the shooting. Slager was sentenced to 20 years in prison in December 2017 for the underlying charge of second-degree murder. Large demonstrations protesting the shooting of Scott were held across the nation, including in New York City where people marched to Times Square.[68]

Illegal Immigration

The third emerging political issue of concern for police administrators is illegal immigration. In recent years, local police have become increasingly involved in the identification and arrest of undocumented immigrants. The term "**undocumented immigrant**" generally includes several categories of individuals who are subject to removal from the United States for a variety of reasons defined by the federal Immigration and Nationality Act. In general, an individual may be considered "removable" because he or she does not qualify for admission in to the United States, has entered the country illegally by crossing the border without formal inspection, or has violated the terms of a legal admission, for example, by entering the country on a student visa and then dropping out of school.[69]

Enforcement action taken against this category of immigrants is normally the job of federal agents of the Immigration and Customs Enforcement (ICE). However, a federal program to train local police officers in such duties has existed since 1996. Florida, the first state to join the federal program in the wake of the September 11, 2001 terrorist attacks, tailored its version to help block possible terrorist infiltrators. Interest in the program has taken off recently as the national debate over illegal immigration has heated up. Federal funds have been available to create a program to train local and state police officers in immigration duties (see Figure 4.11). Federal funding for this program increased from $5 million in 2006 to $68 million in each of the fiscal years 2011, 2012, and 2013.[70]

The integration of local and federal enforcement efforts holds some degree of allure. Alabama for example decided to join the program because local officials believed ICE's small staff in the state was unable to cope with the swelling numbers of undocumented immigrants. The Governor pledged to double the number of state troopers trained to deal with undocumented immigrants, saying: "Alabama welcomes those who enter the country legally, but we won't stand idly by when we catch illegal immigrants in our state."

The integration of local police enforcement of immigration laws and the degree to which this issue has been politicized has increased since the election of President Donald J. Trump in 2016. The enforcement of laws against illegal immigration was a cornerstone of his campaign that culminated in his pledge to build a wall across the southern U.S. border with Mexico.[71] Scholarship has increasingly underscored some of the potential problems associated with the integration of local and federal enforcement of immigration laws. For example, site visits to document the implementation of federal programs to increasingly involve local police in immigration enforcement in Arkansas confirmed that local officers were checking

Quick Facts: The Number of Undocumented Immigrants in the United States by Ethnicity

The most recent estimate of the illegal alien population residing in the United States is 12 million persons. On average, the population of illegal aliens in the United States grew by 70,000 per year from 2010 to 2015. Nearly 80 percent of the illegal alien population resided in the United States for more than 10 years. Nearly 25 percent of the illegal alien population resides in California. Roughly 55 percent of the illegal alien population is from Mexico.[73]

FIGURE 4.11 ▶ An undocumented immigrant being taken into custody by Immigration and Customs Enforcement (ICE) special agents. (Photo courtesy ICE)

immigration status in a variety of operations including routine traffic stops, worksite investigations, drug raids, and within county jails. National surveys of law enforcement executives indicate that the integration of local law enforcement of immigration laws often conflicts and even challenges the commitment of local police agencies to community policing practices.[72] The issue for police administrators may come down to articulating and enforcing a balance between the interests of immigration enforcement, civil rights, and the goal of developing and maintaining local community partnerships to reduce crime. This balance is increasingly difficult to maintain in the case that citizens become fearful and increasingly distant from local police due to programs and policies designed to more strictly enforce federal immigration laws within local jurisdictions. Police administrators are likely to be on the frontline of this debate for the foreseeable future.

The ICE partnership empowers local officers to temporarily detain someone who has violated federal immigration law—something they are typically not allowed to do. That is a valuable tool in states where there are few ICE agents.

Chapter Summary

Summary by Learning Objectives

1. **Identify three distinct styles of law enforcement discussed by James Q. Wilson and how those different styles are believed to correspond to different types of local political cultures.**

   (1) The "watchman" style of law enforcement emphasizes maintenance of order and is found in economically declining cities with traditional political machines; (2) the "legalistic" style of law enforcement is found in cities with heterogeneous populations and reform-oriented, professional governments (law enforcement of both a reactive and proactive nature characterizes this style); and (3) in the homogeneous suburban communities, the "service" style of law

enforcement is oriented toward the needs of the citizens.

2. **Explain the legally defined roles of city councils.**

   The city council acts as the chief legislative and policymaking body. Through its ordinance power, subject to constitutional and statutory provisions, including the city charter, the council carries out its legislative function.

3. **Explain how the policies and procedures of state's prosecutors have an observable influence on police practices and procedures.**

   Police chiefs who perceive that the prosecutor consistently reduces or fails to vigorously enforce certain types of violations may very likely divert their enforcement efforts and resources elsewhere.

4. **Discuss the ways in which the judiciary impacts local police practices.**

   If judges consistently interject their personal biases into the judicial process and make it very clear to the police that they will dismiss certain categories of violations, the police may discontinue enforcing that law.

5. **Explain the significance of U.S. Supreme Court decisions in each of the following cases: *Mapp v. Ohio*, *Gideon v. Wainwright*, *Escobedo v. Illinois*, and *Miranda v. Arizona*.**

   Mapp v. Ohio (1961) banned the use of illegally seized evidence in criminal cases in the states by applying the Fourth Amendment guarantee against unreasonable searches and seizures. *Escobedo v. Illinois* (1964) affirmed that a suspect is entitled to confer with an attorney as soon as the focus of the police investigation of the suspect shifts from investigatory to accusatory. *Gideon v. Wainwright* (1963) affirmed that equal protection under the Fourteenth Amendment requires that legal counsel be appointed for all indigent defendants in all criminal cases. *Miranda v. Arizona* (1966) required police officers, before questioning suspects, to inform them of their constitutional right to remain silent, their right to an attorney, and their right to have an attorney appointed if they cannot afford to hire one.

6. **Understand the differences between the various forms of citizen oversight of police.**

   There are three tiers of civilian oversight. *First Tier* external review has a civilian oversight agency (e.g., ombudsman) that receives, investigates, adjudicates, and recommends appropriate discipline to police administrators. *Second Tier* external review has a civilian oversight agency that carries out the same function as those in the first tier, except the complaint investigations are conducted internally by the police agency. *Third Tier* external review has a civilian oversight agency with authority that is identical to those found in Tiers 1 and 2; however, the city's chief administrator (mayor or city manager) acts as an arbiter of disciplinary disputes between the police department and the civilian oversight agency.[74]

7. **Discuss the ways in which the office of the county sheriff differs from that of local municipal police agencies in terms of political considerations.**

   The primary difference between the office of the county sheriff and the local police administrator is that the sheriff is directly elected whereas the local police chief is typically appointed. This situation makes the sheriff more directly susceptible to the influences of local politics and more similar to other local political actors than is the case with the typical local chief of police.

8. **Define racial profiling and how the recent cases of Freddie Gray and Michael Brown have underscored the importance of this issue to local police administrators.**

   The term has several meanings, most of which are associated with law enforcement officers making the decision to stop an individual because of race or ethnicity. Officers often use the "pretext" or "suspicious vehicle stop" argument to justify their actions as legal (e.g., using a legal pretext, such as an illegal lane change or broken license plate light, to stop the vehicle and then gain a basis to search for illegal drugs). The recent landmark cases of Freddie Gray and Michael Brown have intensified political pressure on local police administrators nationwide. Racial profiling and discrimination have become national issue through public protests and media attention. These and other high-profile encounters between police and African-American citizens have clearly increased public scrutiny of police overall.

9. **Discuss the advantages of body-worn cameras cited by police administrators.**

   Body-worn cameras can provide valuable evidence in court and provide a clear and objective image of exactly what actions transpired between their officers and individuals who may be taken into custody. There is also the implied suggestion that such devices will deter those officers who might be inclined to engage in misconduct from doing so, as well as discouraging citizens inclined to make false allegations when they know the entire interaction is being recorded.

10. **Discuss the major concerns of police administrators as they relate to the ongoing integration of local and federal enforcement of illegal immigration.**

A key concern is that state and local enforcement involvement in immigration can have a chilling effect on the relationship with the immigrant community in their jurisdiction and could lead immigrants to become reluctant to report crimes or cooperate with officers in investigating incident. In addition, many police chiefs and sheriffs have also expressed concerns about the additional numbers of personnel it would take for these federal immigration laws to be enforced in their local communities.

Chapter Review Questions

1. What are the major differences between the strong mayor form of government and the city manager form of government as they relate to the appointment of the police chief?

2. Why can police chiefs not objectively and independently fulfill their responsibilities if they lack job protection?

3. Describe the differences in the status between an elected county sheriff and an appointed police chief.

4. What role do public interest organizations play in police accountability?

5. What was the catalyst for the accelerated change in the decision by law enforcement administrators to purchase body-BWCs for many of their officers working on the street?

6. What conclusions did the U.S. Department of Justice reach in its investigation of the patterns and practices of the Ferguson, Missouri Police Department?

Critical Thinking Exercises

1. The Use of Deadly Force: Within the past three years, there has been a dramatic increase in the number of deadly force encounters between white police officers and young African-American males in your community.

   a. You know from personal experience that the police academy street survival unit of instruction has been radically modified in recent years and has increasingly focused on the street violence being directed toward police officers. You strongly suspect that some of this has resulted in police officers becoming "hypervigilant" to potential dangers to their personal safety on the street and this could possibly be leading them to overreact to situations they encounter, especially with those involving young African-American males.

   b. Serious allegations have been raised that your officers are profiling young African-American males and stopping them on the streets without reasonable suspicion or probable cause that they have been involved in any type of criminal activity.

   c. There are serious allegations being raised by members of the minority community that the police department is incapable of investigating itself, especially as it relates police officers' use of deadly force and have recommended the creation of a citizen oversight committee to evaluate police officer shootings.

   How would you go about addressing each of these problems?

2. Undocumented Immigrants: Recently, there has been a dramatic increase in the number of undocumented immigrants moving into your community. Some powerful local politicians and local citizens of the city have been very critical of the police department's decision not to aggressively enforce immigration laws as it relates to undocumented immigrants unless they are actively involved in the commission of crimes not related to immigration issues.

   a. The objective evidence available indicates that the vast majority of undocumented immigrants are law abiding and supporting themselves by engaging in farm work, construction labor, and domestic work. However, the few who have committed serious crimes have gotten a disproportionate amount of attention from both local and national media

b. You also know that undocumented immigrants are disproportionately targeted by criminals within their groups for financial exploitation, but they are reluctant to report this to the police because they believe it might reveal their illegal status and result in their deportation.

Since you have made a conscious effort not to become involved in enforcing immigration laws, you must provide local politicians and local citizens expressing concern with the rationale for your decision to not enforce these laws.

Key Terms

citizen oversight	Michael Brown	sheriffs
city council	politics	strong mayor
city manager	prosecutor	tenure
Freddie Gray	public information officer	undocumented immigrant
judiciary	public interest organizations	
local community political culture	racial profiling	

Endnotes

1W. H. Hudnut III, "The Police and the Polis: A mayor's Perspective, "in Police Leadership in America: Crisis and Opportunity, ed. William A. Geller (Westport, CT: Praeger, 1985), p. 20.

2ABC Eyewitness News, "Houston Police Chief Testifies About Control to Congress," February 17, 2019; https://abc13.com/politics/hpd-chief-acevedo-testifies-about-gun-control-to-congress/5125228/ (accessed March 22, 2019).

3Erik Lacitis, "Wash. Police Chief Says He Won't Enforce New Gun Laws," The Seattle Times, November 19, 2018; https://www.policeone.com/chiefs-sheriffs/articles/482125006-Wash-police-chief-says-he-wont-enforce-new-gun-law/ (accessed March 22, 2019).

4Robert M. Fogelson, Big-City Police (Cambridge, MA: Harvard University Press, 1975), pp. 14–15.

5President's Task Force on 21st Century Policing, Final Report of the President's Task Force on 21st Century Policing (Washington DC: Police Executive Research Forum, 2015).

6James Q. Wilson, Varieties of Police Behavior (New York: Atheneum, 1973).

7A. H. Andrews, Jr., "Structuring the Political Independence of the Police Chief," in Police Leadership in America: Crisis and Opportunity, ed. William Geller (New York: Praeger, 1985), pp. 9, 10.

8V. A. Leonard and H. W. Moore, Police Organization and Management (Mineola, NY: Foundation Press, 1971), p. 21.

9G. E. Berkeley et al., Introduction to Criminal Justice (Boston: Holbrook Press, 1976), p. 216.

10Leonard and Moore, Police Organization and Management, p. 15.

11J. J. Norton and G. G. Cowart, "Assaulting the Politics/Administration Dichotomy," Police Chief 45, No. 11 (1978), p. 26.

12Interview with staff assistants at the International Association of Chiefs of Police, Washington, DC (December 8, 1995).

13One of the most comprehensive collections of articles and essays focusing on the role of the chief of police is found in Geller, Police Leadership in America.

14Janet Ferris et al., "Present and Potential Legal Job Protections Available to Heads of Agencies," Florida Police Chief 14, No. 5 (1994), pp. 43–45.

15Ibid.

16Information provided by the National Association of State Directors of Law Enforcement Training.

17J. B. Helgott, et al. Evaluation of the Washington State Criminal Justice Training Commission's Warriors to Guardians Cultural Shift and Crisis Intervention (CIT) Training (Seattle University, Department of Criminal Justice, 2015).

18"DeWine announces CPT training requirements," retrieved from https://www.fairborndailyherald.com/category/news/special-report.

19No author, "State Trends in Law Enforcement Legislation," National Conference of State Legislation, no page numbers, September 24, 2018; http://www.ncsl.org/research/civil-and-criminal-justice/state-trends-in-law-enforcement-legislation-2014-2017.aspx (accessed March 24, 2019).

20Ibid

21Ibid.

22Ibid.

23Collins, A., In Brown, C., & Human Rights Watch (Organization) (1998). Shielded from justice: Police brutality and accountability in the United States. New York: Human Rights Watch.

24Ibid., p. 31.

25Ibid.

26Ibid.

27N. G. Holten and M. E. Jones, The Systems of Criminal Justice (Boston: Little, Brown, 1978), p. 416.

28N.E. Marion, A Primer in the Politics of Criminal Justice (Boulder, CO: Lynne-Rienner Publishers, 2010).

29T. R. Dye, Politics in States and Communities (Englewood Cliffs, NJ: Prentice Hall, 1973), p. 214.

30For a more detailed discussion on this topic see C. R. Swanson, N. C. Chamelin, L. Territo, and R. W. Taylor, Criminal Investigation, 11th edition (New York, NY: The McGraw-Hill Companies, Inc., 2012), pp. 143–144.

31Samuel Walker and Charles M. Katz, The Police in America, 7th ed. (New York: McGraw-Hill Companies, 2008), pp. 486–490.

[32]Cassandra Fairbanks, "St. Louis Police Threaten to Quit or Slowdown if Civilian Oversight Passes," *The Free Thought* Project.com, January 31, 2015; http://thefreethoughtproject.com (accessed June 28, 2015).

[33]W. E. Petterson, "Police Accountability and Civilian Oversight of Policing: An American Perspective" in A. Goldsmith (Ed.), *Complaints Against the Police: The Trend to External Review* (New York: Oxford University Press), pp. 259–291.

[34]Ibid.

[35]National Association for Civilian Oversight of Law Enforcement.

[36]E. M. Davis, "Press Relations Guide for Peace Officers," *Police Chief* 39, No. 3 (1972), p. 67.

[37]T. J. Caeti, J. Liederbach, and S. Bellew, "Police-Media Relations at Critical Incidents: Interviews from Oklahoma City," *International Journal of Police Science and Management* 9, No. 2, pp. 86–97.

[38]L. Fernandez and M. Merzer, *Jane's Crisis Communications Handbook* (Alexandria, VA: Jane's Information Group, 2003).

[39]*Law Enforcement Management and Administrative Statistics* (LEMAS) (Washington, DC: US Department of Justice, Bureau of Justice Statistics, 2020. See: https://www.bjs.gov/index.cfm?ty=pbdetail&iid=6707).

[40]D. N. Falcone and L. E. Wells, "The County Sheriff as a Distinctive Policing Modality," *American Journal of Police* 14, pp. 123–149.

[41]One Voice for the Office of Sheriff, National Sheriffs' Association, http://www.sheriffs.org/content/faq (accessed June 22, 2015).

[42]Special thanks to Brooke Nodeland for her assistance in developing this section on racial and ethnic profiling. See also Robin Engle, Jennifer Calnon, and Thomas Bernard, "Racial Profiling: Shortcomings and Future Directions in Research," *Justice Quarterly* 19, No. 2 (June 2002), pp. 249–273.

[43]Ronald Weitzer and Steven Tuch, "Perceptions of Racial Profiling: Race, Class, and Personal Experience," *Criminology* 40, No. 2 (2002).

[44]See *Whren v. United States,* 517 U.S. 06 (1996).

[45]Warren and Tomaskovi-Devey, "Racial Profiling and Searches," p. 349.

[46]Application for Statement of Charges, District Court of Maryland for Baltimore City, 5800 Wabash Ave, Baltimore, MD 21215, DC Case No. 0B02294453.

[47]Scott Calvert, "What Baltimore Prosecutors Say Happened to Freddie Gray on Van Ride," *The Wall Street Journal*, May 1, 2015; available at: http://www.wsj.com/articles/what-baltimore-prosecutors-say-happened-to-freddie-gray-on-van-ride-1430515289.

[48]Rector, K., "DOJ Won't Charge Baltimore Police Officers," *The Baltimore Sun*, September 13, 2017.

[49]Alan Blinder and Richard Perez-Pena, "6 Baltimore Police Officers Charged in Freddie Gray Death," *New York Times*, May 1, 2015.

[50]Department of Justice Report Regarding the Criminal Investigation into the Shooting Death of Michael Brown by Ferguson, Missouri Police Officer Darren Wilson, March 4, 2015; retrieved from: http://apps.washingtonpost.com/g/documents/national/department-of-justice-report-on-the-michael-brown-shooting/1436/.

[51]For a more detailed discussion of the facts of this case, see the *State of Missouri v. Darren Wilson, Grand Jury*, Vol. 5 (September 15, 2014).

[52]U.S. Department of Justice, Civil Rights Division, Investigation of the Ferguson Police Department, March 4, 2015, 1-6; retrieved from: http://www.justice.gov/sites/default/files/opa/press-releases/attachments/2015/03/04/ferguson_police_department_report.pdf.

[53]Ibid., p. 2.

[54]Rachel Weiner, "Police Body Cameras Spur Privacy Debate," *Washington Post*, November 10, 2013; retrieved from: http://www.washingtonpost.com/local/crime/police-body-cameras-spur-privacy-debate/2013/11/10/7e9ee504-2549-11e3-b75d-5b7f66349852_story.html (accessed February 17, 2014).

[55]Stephanie Hayes, "USF to Study Police Officers Wearing Body Cameras," *Tampa Bay Times*, January 11, 2014; retrieved from: http://www.tampabay.com/news/education/college/usf-to-study-police-officers-wearing-body-cameras/2160669 (accessed February 17, 2014).

[56]For a more detailed discussion of the Rialto Police Department's use of body-worn cameras see William Farrar, "Operation Candid Camera: The Rialto Police Department's Body-Worn Camera Experiment," *The Police Chief* (January 2014), pp. 20–25.

[57]Larry E. Capps, "Police Body-Worn Cameras: An Overview," *Police Chief Magazine* (February, 2015), pp. 53–54.

[58]Eugene P. Ramirez, *A Report on Body Worn Cameras* (Los Angeles, CA: Manning & Kass, Ellrod, Ramirez, Trester LLP), 14; http://www.parsac.org/parsac-www/pdf/Bulletins/14-005_Report_BODY_WORN_CAMERAS.pdf (accessed September 8, 2014).

[59]Capps, "Police Body-Worn Cameras," p. 53.

[60]Ibid.

[61]Vern Sallee, "Outsourcing the Evidence Room: Moving Digital Evidence to the Cloud," *The Police Chief* 81, No. 4 (April 2014), p. 44; http://www.policechiefmagazine.org/magazine/index.cfm?Fuseaction=display&article_id=3319&issue_id=42014 (accessed September 8, 2014).

[62]Ibid.

[63]Ibid.

[64]Ibid., p. 54.

[65]J. David Goodman and Al Baker, "Wave of Protests After Grand Jury Doesn't Indict Officer in Eric Garner Chokehold Case," *New York Times*, December 3, 2014; http://www.nytimes.com/2014/12/04/nyregion/grand-jury-said-to-bring-no-charges-in-staten-island-chokehold-death-of-eric-garner.html?_r=0 (accessed June 27, 2015).

[66]Ida Lieszkovsky, "Tamir Rice Investigation Released: The Big Story," *Cleveland.com* (June 13, 2015); http://www.cleveland.com/metro/index.ssf/2015/06/tamir_rice_investigation_relea.html (accessed June 23, 2015).

[67]Ibid.

[68]Denis Slattery, Edgar Sandoval, Laura Bult, and Tina Moore, "More than 400 Anti-Police Brutality Demonstrators March on Union Square to Protest Walter Scott Shooting," *New York Daily News*, Tuesday April 14, 2015; http://www.

nydailynews.com/new-york/nyc-crime/400-anti-police-brutality-protestors-march-union-square-article-1.2185101 (accessed June 23, 2015).

[69]Critical Issues in Policing Series: *Police Chiefs and Sheriffs Speak Out on Local Immigration Enforcement* (Washington, DC: Police Executive Research Forum, 2008), p. 3.

[70]American Immigration Council, "The 287(g) Program: An Overview" (2019); http://www.americanimmigrationcouncil.org (accessed February 27, 2018).

[71]Liptak, K., D. Merica, and T. Kopan, "Trump Stands by Pledge of Building Wall, Blames Democrats for Stalled Immigration Debate," February 23, 2018; http://www.cnn.com/2018/02/23/politics/trump-immigration-cpac-speech-wasll/index.html (accessed February 27, 2019).

[72]Khashu, A., "The Role of Local Police: Striking a Balance Between Immigration Enforcement and Civil Liberties" 2009; available at https://www.policefoundation.org/wp-content/uploads/2015/07/Khashu-2009-The-Role-of-Local-Police.pdf

[73]B. Baker, "Population Estimates: Illegal Alien Population Residing in the United States (January 2015). Office of Immigration Statistics, US Department of Homeland Security.

[74]Ibid.

PART 2 The Organization and the Leader

The five chapters in this section deal with broad aspects of law enforcement agencies, including how to organize them from theoretical and practical perspectives, different approaches to leading departments and what research tells us about these approaches, planning and decision-making models, and the legal and "hands-on" aspects of human resource management in a law enforcement agency.

Chapter 5, "Organizational Theory," is a longer chapter on a difficult and underappreciated subject. All organization structures reflect assumptions, one way or another, about the people that work in them and reveal the leader's preferences for one approach over another. This chapter provides the basis on which leaders can thoughtfully examine what they implicitly or explicitly believe in with respect to how work is organized, and authority is distributed. While continuing to use Weber's hierarchical organizational approach, policing, like most other organizations in the world, is employing practices that are distinctly non-Weberian, such as vertical staff meetings.

Chapter 6, "Organizational Design," examines the practical choices faced by law enforcement administrators when they are modifying their organizations, for example, to achieve their missions. Such choices include determining to what degree they will be "flat" or "tall," what types of units will be grouped together or separated, and the extent of specialization that will exist. Local law enforcement agencies share many of the same characteristics in their organizational structures, such as placing line and staff functions in different groupings. Beyond these basic commonalities, subtle variations are seen. Some law enforcement executives may want the Intelligence and Professional Standards units reporting directly to their office so they "can keep their finger on the department's pulse," while others may want to place more distance between their office and these functions so "they can keep their eye on the big picture." Thus, some aspects of organizational structures reflect the idiosyncratic personal preferences of the law enforcement executive and may not be inherently "right" or "wrong."

Chapter 7, "Leadership," is a critical examination of that subject in law enforcement agencies. It examines what leadership is and does, probes the leader-manager dichotomy, scrutinizes why some police leaders are effective and others fail, and provides comprehensive coverage of leadership theories and the research findings on them. The theories discussed span the distance from "Great Man" explanations to the more recent work on transactional, transformational, ethical, charismatic, servant, spiritual, and authentic leaders.

Chapter 8, "Planning and Decision Making," joins these two topics because planning is decision making for the future and these two subjects have some similarities. It covers the importance of these topics, including a discussion of the five categories of types of plans: Administrative or Management Plans, Procedural Plans, Operational Plans, Tactical Plans and Strategic Plans. Various decision-making models are also presented, to include the Rational Comprehensive or Sequencing Model, the Bounded Rationality Model, the Muddling

Through or Disjointed Incremental Model, the Political and Organizational Model, the Gut Level Model, the Recognition Primed Decision-Making Model and the Thin-Slicing Theory Model. Also including are illuminating case studies of police decision making during crisis events using the police shooting involving the Weaver family at Ruby Ridge, Idaho in 1992 and the stand-off with David Koresh and the Branch Davidians near Waco, Texas in 1993.

Mastery of Chapter 9, "Human Resource Management," is a necessity. The larger a law enforcement agency is, the more likely it has taken on some of the functions performed by the unit of government's central personnel office. An important aspect of human resource (HR) management is understanding the applicable laws and regulations. Many local, state, and federal laws create legal rights for officers and other employees and violations of these can create unnecessary conflict and cause lingering labor relations problems. This chapter examines the applicable federal laws prohibiting discrimination and provides summaries of relevant legal decisions. It is generally thought that the preponderance of personnel problems is created through a faulty selection process; Chapter 9 examines this process in detail. Successive waves of generations hired into policing reveal important differences in their expectations, and law enforcement agencies must successfully craft messages to attract and retain them. Other areas covered by this wide-ranging chapter include military call-ups of reservist officers, discipline, performance appraisal, and retirement counseling. Promotional systems and testing also receive significant treatment.

CHAPTER FIVE

ORGANIZATIONAL THEORY

Learning Objectives

1. State why formal organizations, such as police departments, exist.
2. Identify the three stems of traditional organizational theory.
3. In a police context, define street-level bureaucrats and the two modes out of which they operate.
4. Explain how a reaction to a line of thinking gave rise to the human relations school.
5. Identify three statements in Theory Y consistent with practices in today's well-run police departments.
6. Identify the major components of an open system view of a police department.

INTRODUCTION

ORGANIZATIONAL THEORY, WHICH DRAWS

on many disciplines, is a tough subject. It is reasonable to ask why it is important to take time to become familiar with it. Knowledge of organizational theory is important because it (1) makes organizations more understandable; (2) reveals how authority is distributed across the organization; (3) explains why some police departments are less or more open to change and innovation; (4) makes assumptions, one way or another, about followers; (5) incorporates notions about the environments that the police department faces (e.g., political and legal) and how these can impinge on the department; and (6) provides an essential tool for leaders to decide where and how work will be done and the structure and relationship of the work units needed to do it.

FORMAL ORGANIZATIONS

Formal organizations are not a recent innovation.[1] Alexander the Great and Julius Caesar used them to conquer, the pharaohs employed them to build pyramids, the emperors of China constructed great irrigation systems with them, and the first popes created an organization to deliver religion on a worldwide basis.[2] The extent to which contemporary America is an organizational society is such that:

We are born in organizations, educated by organizations, and spend most of our lives working for organizations. We spend much of our time…playing and praying in organizations. Most of us will die in an organization and when the time comes for burial, the state must grant its permission.[3]

The basic rationale for the existence of organizations is that they do those things that people are unwilling or unable to do alone. Parsons notes that organizations are distinguished from other human groupings or social units in that, to a much greater degree, they are constructed and reconstructed to achieve specific goals; corporations, armies, hospitals, and police departments are included within this meaning, whereas families and friendship groups are not.[4] Schein defines an organization as the rational coordination of the activities of a number of people for the achievement of some common explicit purpose or goal, through division of labor and function and a hierarchy of authority and responsibility.[5]

Burns and Stalker break organizations into a dichotomy: **mechanistic** and **organic**:[6]

1. Mechanistic organizations are described as running like a machine. They are machine-like in that the shared purpose of organizational values, structures, policies, procedures, processes, training, jobs, and reward systems is for the organization to consistently perform all tasks.

   Collectively, these features are a control system, theoretically ensuring error-free results. Mechanistic organizations incorporate many of the features of the bureaucratic structure, for example, a hierarchy, chain of command, and specialization. Much of the communication is top-down, for example, directives about new policies and procedures. Examples of mechanistic organizations include municipal water departments and vehicle assembly lines.

   Mechanistic organizations are also "closed systems," that is, their boundaries are characterized as impermeable to outside influences. No mechanistic organization actually has completely impermeable boundaries. Illustrations of outside influences piercing their boundaries include regulatory agencies, insurance companies, occupational and health inspectors, the Internal Revenue Service, court orders, the news media, public opinion, criminal investigations, Presidential Executive Orders, and prosecutors.

Quick Facts: San Francisco: No More Prosecutions for Minor Quality-of-Life Crimes

Reduced to a single sentence, Broken Windows policing postulates that visible signs of minor crimes, such as graffiti, lead to further crimes, including those that are more serious. In 2019, San Francisco's new elected District Attorney announced his office would no longer prosecute minor, quality-of-life crimes, for example, public drinking, graffiti, panhandling, bike riding on a sidewalk, and jumping over subway turnstiles to avoid paying the fare. Earlier in 2019, San Francisco also became the first American city to prohibit the use of facial recognition software by law enforcement and government in an ordinance titled "Stop Secret Surveillance."

Mechanistic organizations perform well when faced with a stable environment, which creates no need to change, and employees repetitively perform the tasks respectively assigned to them. Tightly controlling their employees, mechanistic organizations are low on creativity and innovation. Consequently, they are slow to adapt to new conditions. Commonly, mechanistic, closed system, and bureaucracies are used synonymously.

2. Organic organizations understand they have permeable boundaries and are codependent with the larger, unstable environment in which they are located. As compared to mechanistic organizations, they have a flatter organizational structure that features decentralization of authority and empowerment of employees, horizontal and face-to-face communications are more frequent, employees are encouraged to use "out-of-the-box" thinking, for example, in problem analysis and decision making. These features allow organic organizations to be more adaptable and "nimble on their feet" in their unstable environment. Organic and open systems are used synonymously. Mechanistic and organic organizations can be thought of as opposite ends of a continuum

Blau and Scott identified four types of formal organizations by asking the question of *cui bono,* or who benefits: (1) **mutual benefit associations**, such as police labor unions, where the primary beneficiary is the membership; (2) **business concerns**, for example, Lynn Peavey, which sells crime scene equipment and supplies, where the owner is the prime beneficiary; (3) **service organizations**, examples of which are homeless shelters and community mental health centers, where a specific client group is the prime beneficiary; and (4) **commonweal organizations**, including the U.S. Department of Defense and law enforcement agencies, where the beneficiary is the public at large.[7]

Each of these four types of formal organizations has its own unique issues.[8] Mutual benefit associations, such as police unions, face the crucial problem of maintaining the internal democratic processes—providing for participation and control by their membership (see Box 5.1). For businesses, the central issue is maximizing profits in a competitive environment. Service organizations are faced with the conflict between restrictions imposed by administrative regulations versus providing the services judged by the professional to be most appropriate. In the case of a community mental health center, an illustration is that, following a reduction in funding, a policy is issued that mandates treating all clients in group sessions, when the psychiatric social worker believes the only effective treatment for a particular client is to be seen individually.

The key issue for law enforcement agencies and other types of commonweal organizations is finding a way to accommodate pressures from two sources: (1) external democratic control and (2) internal control. The public expects to have external democratic control of its police department through its elected and appointed officials.

This external democratic control feature also has the expectation that the internal workings of the police department will be effective and efficient, but not also democratic. This is because democratic control by the members of a police department would inevitably lead to the department being in conflict at various times with the will of the community (e.g., one favoring a tough approach to crime control versus the other being in favor of a more moderate approach). Internally, large numbers of officers at the lower levels of the police department do not want to be treated like "cogs in a machine." They desire some voice in how the department operates. Participatory management is one means by which officers at the lower level can have their views known, but not have internal democratic control.

Thus, the challenge for police leaders is how to maintain an organization that meets society's needs and the needs of the officers and civilian staff who work in it. This requires an understanding of such things as the different ways of organizing and the contrasting assumptions that various organizational forms make about the nature of people. Such knowledge is found within organizational theory.

Box 5.1: The Kirkwood, Missouri, Police Union as a Mutual Benefit Association

The 46 Officers and 7 Sergeants of the Kirkwood Police Department (KPD) organized as a union. Previously, there had not been a police union in the KPD. In its first contract negotiation with the city, the union's parent organization, The Fraternal Order of Police Lodge 15, provided legal representation.[9] Salaries were not an issue in this first contract because the previous year Kirkwood had given officers a generous raise. Likewise, a 12-hour shift popular with officers was adopted before negotiations began. The union was successful for raising physical fitness training from one hour a week to six hours every two weeks and getting the city to agree to a fair method of calculating compensatory ("comp") time, with a maximum accumulation of 120 hours. Officers personally must buy new shoes each year at $150–$200 a pair. The city refused to accept the responsibility for buying them, although it does provide all other items of clothing. After negotiating their first contract with the city, morale of union members was high. They received some benefits important to them and feel the first contract is something on which to build.

TRADITIONAL ORGANIZATIONAL THEORY

Traditional theory is associated with organizations described as classical, bureaucratic, mechanistic, and closed systems, which assume little influence from outside of the organization. Its underlying assumption is that there is one best way to structure and operate an organization. This body of knowledge evolved over centuries and crystallized between 1900 and the 1950s. The three stems of traditional organizational theory are: (1) scientific management, (2) the bureaucratic model, and (3) administrative or management theory.

The First Stem: Taylor and Scientific Management

The father of scientific management is Frederick W. Taylor (1856–1915), and the thrust of his thinking was to find the "one best way" to do work (see Figure 5.1). In addition to its status as a theory of work organization, Taylor's scientific management is also a theory of motivation in its belief that employees will be guided in their actions by what is in their economic self-interest.

Natural soldiering came from the natural inclination of employees not to push themselves; **systematic soldiering** came from workers not wanting to produce so much as to see their quotas raised or other workers thrown out of their jobs.[12] To correct these deficiencies, Taylor called for a "complete mental revolution"[13] on the part of both workers and managers, although it is certain that he faulted management more for its failure to design jobs properly and to give workers the proper

FIGURE 5.1 ▶ Frederick W. Taylor's meticulously combed hair and well-groomed appearance hint at his obsession with details. (Library of Congress Prints and Photographs Division [LC-USZ62-79079])

Quick Facts: Taylor's "One Best Way" Permeated His Life

A Pennsylvanian born of Quaker-Puritan parents, Taylor was so discontented with the "evils" of waste and slothfulness that he applied careful analysis to finding the best way of playing croquet and of taking a cross-country walk with the least fatigue that was to be the hallmark of his later work in factories.[10]

From 1878 to 1890, Taylor worked at the Midvale Steel Company in Philadelphia, rising from the ranks of the laborers to chief engineer in just six years.[11] Taylor's experience at Midvale gave him insight into the twin problems of productivity and worker motivation. He saw workers as deliberately restricting productivity by "natural soldiering" and "systematic soldiering."

---

economic incentives to overcome soldiering than he did workers for not producing.[14]

Taylor's scientific management is only loosely a theory of organization because its focus was largely on work at the bottom part of the organization rather than being a general model. Scientific management's method was to find the most physically and time-efficient way to sequence tasks and then to use rigorous and extensive controls to enforce the standards. Although some critics of scientific management rallied against it as an "exploitation of labor," they didn't consider that Taylor's central objective was to produce the maximum prosperity for both the employee and for each employee. [15]

For Taylor, authority was based not on position in a hierarchy but rather on knowledge; **functional supervision** meant that people were responsible for directing certain tasks, despite the fact that this meant the authority of the supervisor might cut across organizational lines.[16] The **exception principle** meant that routine matters should be handled by lower-level managers or by supervisors and that higher-level managers should only receive reports of deviations above or below standard performances.[17] The integration of cost accounting into the planning process became part of some budgeting practices discussed in Chapter 12, Financial Management.

Despite the success of scientific management in raising productivity and cutting costs, "Taylorism" was attacked from several directions. Union leaders saw it as a threat to their movement because it seemed to reduce, if not eliminate, the importance of unions. The management of Bethlehem Steel ultimately abandoned task management, as Taylor liked to refer to his system because managers were uncomfortable with such an accurate appraisal of their performance[18] and some liberals saw it as an exploitation of workers.

Upton Sinclair, one of the muckrakers (see Chapter 1, The Evolution of Police Administration), charged that Taylor had given workers a 61 percent increase in wages while getting a 362 percent increase in productivity.[19] Taylor replied to this charge by saying that employees worked no harder, only more efficiently. In hearings before the U.S. House of Representatives in 1912, Taylor's methods were attacked thoroughly, and he died three years later a discouraged man. Nonetheless, Henry Ford recast scientific management and used it to increase production and lower costs for the mass-produced model T Ford (1909–1927).

Box 5.2: Traffic Ticket Quotas or Performance Standards: The New Scientific Management?

Ticket quotas is an episodically recurring issue in law enforcement. Historically, pressure to "improve ticket productivity," comes from city hall and may be covered in a low-key way at rollcalls, but not attributed to city hall or reduced to writing. At rollcall, the "pitch" may be an appeal to be "extra vigilant" about violations to ensure the safety of pedestrians and the motoring public. As a matter of reality, the fines levied are sometimes an important part of small-town budgets.

In Georgia, there is a presumption that if a law enforcement agency writes speeding tickets for which the fines are more than 35 percent of the agency's annual operating budget, the detection devices are being used for something other than public safety. If it is determined that traffic enforcement is being used as a funding mechanism by local units of government, the Georgia State Patrol may assume those duties until the issue is resolved. Each year, Georgia law enforcement agencies must report on how much in traffic fines were collected by their courts. Nonetheless, in Georgia and across the county, some communities have the appearance of being revenue oriented, sometimes called policing for profit. A number of states have laws similar to Georgia's.

Box 5.3: Community Policing or Policing for Profit?

Beverly Hills (Missouri) provides an opportunity to examine the question of whether the police department is focused on community policing or policing for profit. The Beverly Hills Police Department (BHPD) serves a population of 547 in an area of 0.9 miles. BH also uses traffic enforcement cameras. In a single year, BHPD officers wrote 3,250 traffic citations.[20]

The Police Chief maintains having 14 officers is crucial to Beverly Hills' community policing program. The BHPD also provides police services to neighboring Velda Village Hills (VVH). VVH has a population of 1,055 and an area of 0.12 miles. Combined, the two cities have a population of 1,629 and an area to police of 1.03 miles. The average number of officers in towns under 10,000 in that region is 1.9 per thousand of population. In two years, the BHPD arrested an average of 1,087 people annually for minor crimes, which is 100 times greater than the national average.[21]

Quotas are resisted by officers, their local peace officers' associations, or unions. They maintain that no one really knows how many good cases they will see on a daily or monthly basis. They argue that the number and types of offenses vary within their city by geographical area, time of day, and the demographic characteristics of drivers. For example, older people commit fewer driving violations than do younger operators. Moreover, officers are also quick to point out that quotas force them to make marginal cases to get good evaluations, thereby decreasing public goodwill and support.

In a few cities, writing a certain number of traffic citations was briefly a performance measure stated in the budget request. In Michigan and Illinois, it is a violation of state law to have ticket quotas for law enforcement officers. Whether called quotas or performance standards, the fact remains that both terms refer to a mandated system of production. In some jurisdictions, officers have been disciplined for not hitting the "numbers" required.

Scientific management did not disappear with Taylor. There remained a core of people devoted to its practice, including Henry L. Gantt (1861–1919). Gantt gained a measure of immortality by developing a basic planning chart, illustrated in Box 5.4. It remains in wide use today and still bears his name. It was developed in 1917, while Gantt worked at the Frankford Arsenal. That Gantt chart contained the then-revolutionary idea that the key factor in planning production was not quantity but time.[22] Some international interest in scientific management also remained after Taylor's death. In 1918, France's Ministry of War called for its use. Its adoption was also urged in Russia by Lenin in a *Pravda* article.[23] It is ironic that a communist society should call for the use of a management system based on the principle that economic self-interest guides the behavior of workers.

Although scientific management has long since ceased to be a dominant force, it does not mean that it's now just history. In addition to Gantt charts, many of the techniques associated with scientific management remain in use. Time and motion studies have been used to analyze how detectives use their time, identifying wasteful activities such as waiting for a vehicle to become available at the motor pool. Workflow analysis, shown in Figure 5.2, remains used in many different types of organizations. Other modern successors to scientific management were developed during World War II to support the war effort, and the refinement and more general application of these techniques is a post-1945 movement. The new techniques have alternatively been referred to as management science and operations research (OR), and their central orientation has been the application of quantitative and technical analysis to decision making.[24] Thus, the most enduring contribution of Taylor is as a promoter of both rationalization in organizations and management control systems.[25]

In 1997, Taylor's *The Principles of Scientific Management* (1911) was rereleased due to continuing interest in his methods and Kanigel wrote a balanced criticism of Taylor's work,[26] as did Caldari in 2007.[27] Read together, they serve to essentially rehabilitate both Taylor's work and his reputation.

Box 5.4: A Portion of a Gantt Chart for the "Anywhere Police Department's" Sergeants Written Promotional Test

The left side of the chart shows two major headings, on lines 1 (Data Collection/Analysis/Document Findings) and 2 (Meetings, Discussions, Write Findings). "COL" is an abbreviation of collect. As the start/finish dates are entered for each task, the software automatically calculates the number of workdays required to complete a task, which does not include weekends. The right side of the chart shows a timeline for each task to be completed. It is built automatically from entries on the left side. This example was prepared using Quick Plan, which has other capabilities, including allocating resources to tasks. (Courtesy of Quick Plan)

WBS	TASK	START	FINISH	DAYS	DURATION
		Feb 5, 2020	Mar 12, 2020	27	37
1	▼ Data Collection/Analysis/Documemnt Findings	Feb 5, 2020	Feb 24, 20...	14	20
1.1	⬚ COL Test Quests. Challenged, Last 3 Tests	Feb 5, 2020	Feb 7, 2020		
1.2	COL Reading Level of Sources Last 3 Tests	Feb 5, 2020	Feb 7, 2020	3	3
1.3	COL Reading Grade, Last 3 Tests	Feb 5, 2020	Feb 7, 2020	3	3
1.4	COL Validity & Reliability Data, Last 3 Tests	Feb 5, 2020	Feb 7, 2020	3	3
1.5	COL Evals., Last 3 APD Sgts Test Admin.	Feb 10, 20...	Feb 12, 20...	3	3
1.6	COL Complaints Last 3 Test Administrations	Feb 10, 20...	Feb 12, 20...	3	3
1.7	COL Complaints Source Lists Last 3 Tests	Feb 11, 2020	Feb 13, 20...	3	3
1.8	COL Complaints Testing Time Limit	Feb 12, 20...	Feb 14, 20...	3	3
1.9	COL Complaints About Last 3 Testing Sites	Feb 12, 20...	Feb 14, 20...	3	3
1.10	Analysis, Write Findings, Share With Team	Feb 17, 2020	Feb 24, 20...	6	8
2	▼ Meetings, Discussions, Write Findings	Feb 24, 20...	Mar 12, 20...	14	18
2.1	Input from APD Police Association	Feb 24, 20...	Feb 25, 20...	2	2
2.2	Discussions With HR and APD Legal Officer	Feb 26, 20...	Feb 27, 20...	2	2
2.3	Discussion, Document, Share with Team	Mar 6, 2020	Mar 12, 20...	5	7

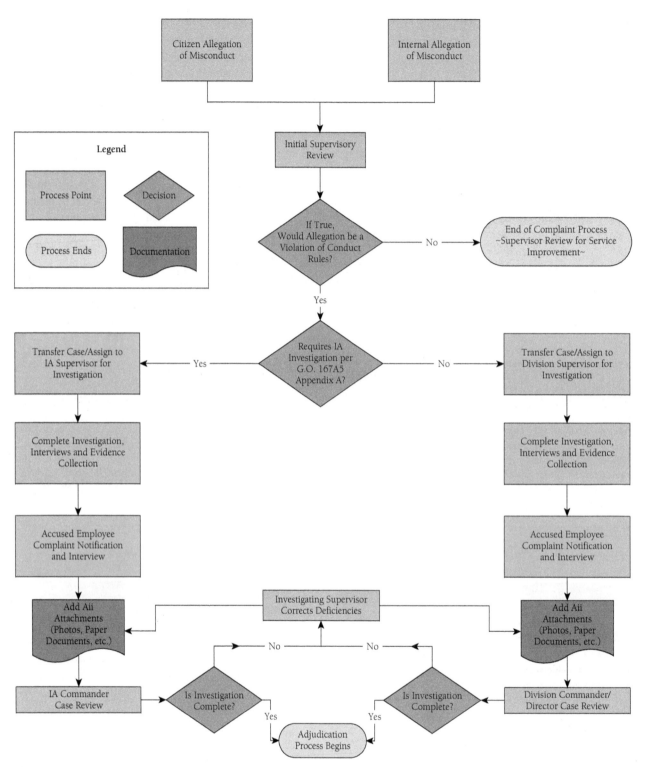

FIGURE 5.2 ▶ Workflow analysis flow for investigating credible allegations of employee misconduct. (Courtesy Greenville, South Carolina, Police Department, General Order 167A5, Workflow for Investigating Credible Allegations of Employee Misconduct, July 1, 2015. This policy is reviewed annually in July)

The Second Stem: Weber and the Classic Bureaucratic Model

In popular use, *bureaucracy* has come to mean slow-performing organizations using unnecessarily complicated procedures with answers that don't seem to quite meet our needs.[28] This meaning is far from the image of the ideal or pure bureaucracy developed by **Max Weber** (1864–1920, see Figure 5.3). For Weber, the choice was "only between bureaucracy and dilettantism in the field of administration."[29] In this

FIGURE 5.3 ▶ Max Weber. He suffered from insomnia, nervousness, and depression. Nonetheless, his interests crossed multiple disciplines and he founded sociology. Weber was also at the forefront of studying organizations. (Library of Congress Prints and Photographs Division [LC-USZ62-74580])

regard, Weber claimed that the pure bureaucratic model was superior to all other methods of organizing with respect to efficiency, control, and stability.[30]

Weber did not invent the bureaucratic model; it had existed for centuries. He only described it and didn't like all that he saw.[31] Thus, whereas Weber spawned the formal study of organizations, it scarcely seems fair to lay at his feet any real or fancied inadequacies of the model or its operation. Moreover, although it would be difficult to overstate Weber's contributions, it must be borne in mind that, although some people read him in the original German,[32] his work was not translated into English and therefore not generally available until 1947, long after the bureaucratic model was well entrenched.

Two dimensions of Weber's work are often overlooked. First, he feared that the bureaucratic model's efficiency constituted a threat to individual freedom by its impersonal nature and oppressive routine.[33] Second, Weber deplored the career professional of moderate ambitions who craved security; Weber saw this type of person as lacking spontaneity and inventiveness, the modern-day "petty bureaucrat."[34]

The bureaucratic model rests on **rational-legal authority**. In a police context, rational legal authority is the legal basis for the existence of the department. Authority is granted to positions within the organization, such as sergeants, lieutenants, and captains. The occupants or office holders of those positions use that authority to fulfill their responsibilities and to accomplish the goals of the department.[35]

With added commentary to illustrate the application of the **bureaucratic model** to policing, Weber's model includes the following characteristics:

1. The organization of offices follows the principle of hierarchy: Each lower office/unit is under the control and supervision of a higher one. It also creates the chain of command, creating an unbroken line of authority and responsibility from the top to the bottom of an organization. In police departments, the principle of hierarchy is reinforced by the rank hierarchy, running from the Chief, to the Assistant/Deputy Chiefs, Majors, Captains, Lieutenants, Sergeants, and Corporals.[36] This arrangement of successively higher offices also creates horizontal "layers" in a police department. The greater the number of layers, the more vertical or "taller" it is. As organizations get taller, they become more complex because of those layers. Hierarchy also establishes various "channels," such as the chain of command and communication.

2. There is a right of appeal and statement of grievances from the lower to the higher offices. These rights are typically provided for by ordinances enacted by City Councils for all employees and administered by the respective departments, including the police. Police unions have gained additional rights for sworn personnel and may represent officers in Internal Affairs/Professional Standards investigations. If an officer is formally charged, the union may also represent an officer. "May" is a key word. Police unions evaluate cases and decide whether to provide representation.

3. A division of labor allows for special areas of "competency," which is understood to mean specialization. Small police departments with roughly 10 or fewer sworn officers have little or no specialization. All officers are needed to provide basic police services. As the number of sworn officers increases, at some point so does the need and amount of specialization, for example, detectives. Specialization is usually directed at addressing specific local needs and results in the creation of units tasked with different missions, responsibilities, and personnel with the relevant skills.

    As the division of labor/specialization increases, the width and horizontal complexity of departments increases. Illustrations of specialized units include Narcotics, Media Relations, Crime Analysis, Harbor Patrol, Scuba and Tactical Teams, Special Victims Unit, and the Bomb Squad. At some point, as the numbers of specialized units in police departments continue to increase, there is a secondary impact. Those departments must grow vertically (taller) to coordinate the different specialized units.

4. Official policies and procedures establish a system of rational rules. Illustratively, the Cobb County (Georgia) Police Department's statement on "Military Deployment and Reintegration" is an example of such a policy. Likewise, the Omaha (Nebraska) Police Department has a procedure for investigating reports of child abuse, sexual abuse, and neglect, as well as serious or suspicious injuries to children. Procedures vary depending on the child's age and location. A common format is for a police policy to be stated, immediately followed on the same page by the procedures to be followed when implementing it.

5. Administrative actions, decisions, and rules are recorded in writing, creating an institutional memory. All organizations, including secretive intelligence agencies, value and depend on written records.

6. The authority associated with a position is the "property" of the job and not the occupant of the position. Captains assigned to the Patrol Division as Shift Commanders operate under the authority granted to that position. That authority is used by Shift Commanders, but it does not belong to them. It is the "property" of the position. When reassigned to a different position, shift commanders can't take that authority with them.

7. Employees are appointed based on qualifications, and specialized training is necessary. The entry-level job is a sworn officer and the first assignment is usually to the Patrol or Traffic Divisions. Chapter 9, "Human Resource Management," has content on the hiring and promotional processes.

8. Organizational members do not own it.[37] However, the most visible representatives of state, county, and municipal/town/village governments are their uniformed law enforcement officers, driving in marked cars and frequently seen as they patrol, respond to calls, direct traffic, work accidents, and come upon things they must handle.

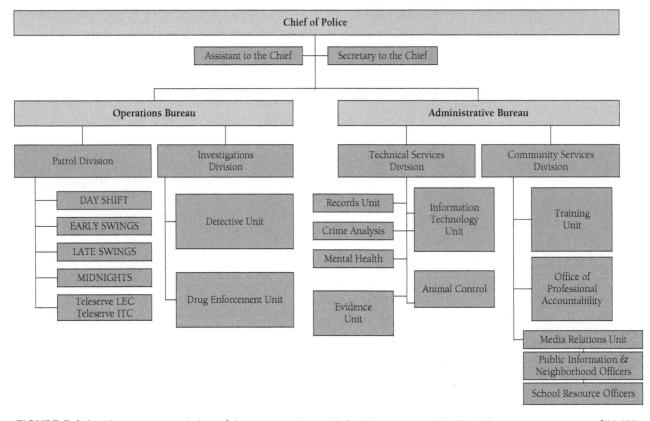

FIGURE 5.4 ▶ The organizational chart of the Lawrence (Kansas) Police Department (LPD). The LPD serves a community of 80,890 with a Chief, 3 Captains, 10 Lieutenants, 17 Sergeants, 111 Patrol Officers, and 22 full-time civilians. (Courtesy of Chief Roy Vasque, Lawrence Police Department)

Not all of the characteristics of Weber's bureaucratic model can be revealed by a single organizational chart. However, Figure 5.4, the Lawrence, Kansas, Police Department's (LPD) organizational chart, does depict two important features: (1) the principle of hierarchy and (2) a division of labor that results in specialization. In 2018, this community policing department achieved 20-year lows in robbery, burglary, and motor vehicle theft. When comparing the LPD's measures of crime and case clearances to those of four similar sized police departments, the LPD has compiled an enviable record.

The Neoclassical, Hawthorne, or Reformatted Bureaucratic Model

In the 1920s, traditional theories, most notably those of Taylor and Weber, dominated organizations. Key limitations of the traditional theory are: (1) its emphasis on control, (2) Weber's fixation with the "bones," meaning structure of organizations, and (3) its neglect of "how to" effectively lead and motivate workers. In balance, Weber's organizational structure remains the most widely used structure today.

Elton Mayo and Fritz Rothelisberger led a series of studies (1928–1932) at Western Electrics' Hawthorne Plant in Chicago. Initially, the studies focused on reducing worker fatigue. The Hawthorne Plant's management style was based on Taylor's scientific management, such as workers were expected to (1) do their job and (2) meet or exceed their production quotas. To achieve productivity gains, Hawthorne plant workers were offered a financial incentive to exceed their quotas. However, it was largely ineffective.

The Hawthorne studies and the rise of the human relations school are covered later in this chapter. Those studies illustrated how little managers knew about workers. One illustration makes that point. Today, it is ordinary that managers know the people they lead, about their lives, families, and aspirations through casual conversations with them. One of the then-stunning findings of the Hawthorne studies was that worker productivity increased when they got some attention from managers. More immediately germane to the present discussion are two related major impacts.

First, the Hawthorne studies significantly hastened what would otherwise have occurred later: the introduction of humanistic values into thinking, writing, researching, and theorizing about all types of organizations. Second, neither the Hawthorne studies nor the subsequent human relations school disavowed the hierarchical structure. However, they successfully draped new thoughts and practices over it. This happened over a period of years, roughly the 1930s to roughly 1960, to such an extent that new organizational terms were coined to describe the change, including neoclassical organization theory, Hawthorne theory, and the reformatted bureaucracy.[38]

We continue to move away from the three stems of traditional organizational theory. Like portions of interstates and mega roads around metropolitan cities, which are always in the process of becoming something else, so it is with developing new processes to append to the hierarchical structure we so widely use. The choice of an organizational structure and the way an organization is led are separate decisions. Acknowledging this separation helps us understand the continued pervasiveness of the hierarchical structure.

The "Bones" and Actions of Policing's (New) Neoclassical Model

Like most of the rest of the world's organizations, overwhelmingly the "bones" of policing haven't shifted away from the hierarchical structure. What's changed is policing itself. Examples include:

1. *New responsibilities and conditions are impacting policing.* The extent of the coronavirus (2019-nCoV) in the United States is yet to unfold at this writing. Some professions, such as emergency medical technicians, nurses, physicians, hospital staff, jail and corrections officers, and many others, including the law enforcement community face the possibility of repeated exposures. Speculatively, officers will be asked to help maintain containment and quarantine areas, refuse entry into the city limits to those who appear to be symptomatic, and provide expedited escorts for trucks bringing needed test kits and medical supplies into the community.

   The continuing influx of undocumented immigrants unexpectedly resulted in the rise of sanctuary units of governments. The policies under which they operate has disrupted the Immigration and Customs Enforcement (ICE) and Customs and Border Patrol (CBP) relationships with state and local sanctuary governments, resulted in thousands of criminals being released, endangered public safety, and produced other ills. The issuance of a Presidential Executive Order in 2019, Enhancing Public Safety in the Interior of the United States, is intended to get communities re-involved with supporting ICE and CBP. The "carrot and stick" in the executive order is that communities that don't cooperate will no longer be able to get any federal funding, except for law enforcement.

   More distant to the coronavirus and the rise of sanctuary governments is the impact of the federal government tasking state and local law enforcement agencies with intelligence and other responsibilities in combatting terrorism, as well as the rise of fusion centers discussed in Chapter 3, "Intelligence, Terrorism, and Homeland Security."

2. *Technology* is the driver of modern policing. Law enforcement agencies are making large investments in new technologies that (a) are relevant to policing's mandated responsibilities, (b) respond to the needs of the community, (c) enhance productivity, and (d) are cost-effective. Examples include facial recognition software, drones, familial DNA, armed robots, thermal imaging social media, Automatic License Plate Recognition (ALPR), body worn cameras that automatically activate whenever an officer's gun is drawn, ShotSpotter gunshot detection systems, TruNarc, a handheld, laser-operated drug analysis device that very quickly can definitively identify more than 498 illicit and abused drugs, and automated traffic enforcement devices.

3. *Increasing police transparency* in this section addresses specific concerns. Transparency is clearly a tool that can enhance both community trust and confidence in

---

Quick Facts: Automated Red Light and Photo Radar Speeding Enforcement Devices

Annually, 750 deaths and 260,000 injuries are produced by crashes precipitated by vehicles running red lights. Another 9,378 fatalities resulted from accidents in which at least one vehicle involved was speeding.

Combined and averaged, those two traffic violations result in nearly 28 deaths every day of the year. Over 400 communities use red light cameras and 130 communities use photo radar to enforce speed limits. Some states prohibit the use of the latter. Instead of being seen as promoting public safety, these devices are often viewed as just a revenue source and therefore are not popular. To eliminate opposition to them, some states enact statutes that citations from automated devices don't count toward driver license revocation points. Ironically, this supports the revenue source objection.[39]

---

local law enforcement agencies. Few would disagree with that general proposition, but, as is the case with many things, it's the details that split people into different factions. The details of transparency are revealed in two key questions: "What is the definition of transparency?" and "How much information can be released at what time after a major incident without creating other problems or violence?" Accountability and transparency are entwined concepts, commonly focusing on the release of specific police records, including body worn and dash camera recordings of controversial events, such as a fatal shooting by police. State and local legislation to enhance police transparency often fall under enactments with "Police Accountability" or "Release of Police Records" in their titles. In 2019, California implemented the most wide-sweeping police "transparency" law. It authorized the wide release of police records for acts of force, sexual assault, and acts of dishonesty. Some laws authorize the release of the names of officers involved, although certain other information may be redacted, such as the names of family members and the officers' home addresses and telephone numbers. Laws may also require that such releases shall be made public within 96 hours of the incident involved, a period in which emotions are commonly running high.

Five major unintended harms from the rapid release of information are likely to occur:

a. Some officers involved in an incident, followed by quick information release, may subsequently become the target of a criminal investigation that was unforeseeable at the time of the release. If indicted, officers right to a fair trial is jeopardized;

b. For an unknown period of time, many officers will be reluctant to get involved in some situations they see while patrolling because those situations might explode into a major event with daily national news media attention. Recent history confirms this possibility. A rapid succession of controversial, unarmed African American deaths in police custody or shootings by officers began in Ferguson, Missouri in 2014 with the death of Michael Brown Jr., provoking a national outcry and demonstrations across the country, including uninvolved cities. A Pew Research Center study revealed 72 percent of officers polled believed sworn personnel in their departments are "less willing to stop and question people who seem suspicious."[40] This behavior became known as the "Ferguson effect";

c. Acts of violence will be directed at the officers involved in an incident and/or or other officers. Other reactions to a released recording include harassment of children at school, vandalism to cars and homes, and/or shots fired into them;

d. The stress levels of both involved and uninvolved officers will increase; and

e. There will be some police retirements and recruiting and retention will be more difficult.

The severity of the harms caused will be dependent on six factors: (1) how severe and controversial an incident is, (2) the amount and tone of news media attention on the incident, (3) the degree to which local leadership or persons external to the community calm or incite emotions, (4) how the community responds, (5) any discipline that is administered is perceived as just, and (6) the degree to which the 96-hour release has a calming effect or is widely seen as evidence of police misconduct and potentially incites the community.

Parenthetically, community engagement programs, even as modest as "Coffee with a COP" can also be additive to building public trust and confidence.

4. *Aligning police departments' operational models with how officers are tasked and empowered.* As an illustration, the adoption of an operational model, such as community policing, triggers the

need for massive changes. Examples include new vision and value statements, decentralization of authority, a participatory style of managing, rewriting policies and procedures, redesigning jobs, revision of many training modules, training officers in community engagement and service delivery, as well as the new emphasis on initiative and their broad empowerment to use discretion and decision making in solving community problems collaboratively. First-line supervisor responsibility shifts from an emphasis on control to supporting officers, for example, finding resources they need, and middle managers must also be trained so they do not feel irrelevant to the changes permeating every corner of the police department. Administrative practices also facilitate the implementation of community policing, for example, **vertical staff meetings** and **vertical problem-solving** committees, and SARA.[41] A Police Chief's conventional staff meeting is horizontal, involving the layer of the department's most senior ranking officers who are ordinarily direct reports to the Chief and generally called the command staff. In contrast, if a Chief of Police is considering a policy change that will impact the Patrol Division, the chief will hold a vertical staff meeting, which in this illustration will include the Major commanding the Patrol Division and also one or more Captains, Lieutenants, Sergeants Corporals, and Officers to get input from those who would be most affected by the proposed policy. A vertical problem-solving committee operates in the same manner, but the focus is getting input about defining and resolving a specific problem from the people who have the relevant knowledge, experience, and insight to be help.

5. *Many law enforcement agencies have moved rapidly into* **e-government**,[42] facilitating the use of government services online. A large number of police websites allow citizens to obtain crime maps of their neighborhoods, search police reports, request copies of traffic accident and incident reports, locate the residence of sexual offenders, file a complaint against or extend recognition to officers, file minor crime reports and print them out, and request special checks on their homes while away.

The preceding paragraphs illustrate the continuing movement away from adherence to traditional organizational theory/closed system views and practices to a neoclassical/neo-Weberian views to the (new) neoclassical model. Traditional practices and views are no longer simply accepted or tolerated. Instead, their usefulness is questioned, challenged, altered, discarded, or new measures put in place as needed.

The Police as Street-Level Bureaucrats

In a policing context, **street-level bureaucrats** refers to field officers who are the face of government when directly engaged with victims, witnesses, suspects, visitors to the community, and others. Theoretically in these encounters, officers are uniformly implementing public policy as expressed in laws, their departments' written policies and procedures, district attorney guidance, court decisions, and other sources. However, as a practical matter, officers use their discretion to implement public policy.[43] As street-level bureaucrats, officers work out of two contrasting modes: (1) "state agents," who believe in following the law and policies and (2) "citizen agents," who will bend or ignore them.[44] Although some officers may operate largely out of one mode or the other, most use both.[45]

Police leaders expect that through training and supervision, officers will be state agents and handle similar calls in the same manner, which often happens, but not always. Academy graduates are commonly first assigned to field duties, typically in the Patrol Division. In less than a year, recent academy graduates who solely, or predominately, started off as a state agent are changed by the realities of the policing experience and the views expressed by veteran officers, which contradict some of the values espoused in the academy.[46] In short, newly minted officers go from "Nobody who violates the law deserves a break." to "You have to approach things realistically…Few situations are exactly the same." Sometimes standard procedures don't really apply to the fact situation staring you in the face on the street. A rhetorical question: How many informants would police departments have if they solely relied on "Nobody who breaks the law deserves a break?"

Several important observations flow from the balancing act officers do with the state and citizen agent modes: (1) however official-sounding the law and public policy are, their implementation is to some extent idiosyncratic; (2) the latent power of personal experience on the street is somewhat of an antidote to the expectations of doctrine; and (3) unaccounted for by state agent advocates is the personal circumstances of street officers. For example, some officers who don't have any court cases scheduled, but are compelled by circumstances to make an arrest, will say, "Well, if I have to go to court anyway, nobody catches a break."

The Third Stem: Administrative Theory

Administrative theory, also referred to as management theory and the principles approach, sought to identify generic or universal methods of administration. Its benchmark is the 1937 publication of **Luther Gulick** (1892–1993) and Lyndall Urwick's (1891–1983) edited *Papers on the Science of Administration*. In content, administrative theory is more compatible with the bureaucratic model than with scientific management, because it concentrates on broader principles (see Table 5.1). Administrative theory is distinguished from the bureaucratic model by its "how-to" emphasis. At some risk of oversimplification, administrative theory both operationalizes and reinforces features of the bureaucratic model. Consequently, because of the continuing pervasiveness of the bureaucratic model, the principles either explicitly or implicitly continue to play some role in organizations, including police departments. Other key contributors to this school are Henri Fayol (1841–1925), James Mooney (1884–1957), and Alan Reiley (1869–1947).

Henri Fayol graduated as an engineer at the age of 19 from France's National School of Mines at St. Etienne and began a 40-year career with the Commentary-Fourchambault Company.[47] His contributions are based on writings that were an outgrowth of his experiences as a manager. Fayol's fame rests chiefly on his *General and Industrial Management* (1916). The first English edition of this appeared in Great Britain in 1923, and although his "Administrative Theory of the State" appeared in *Papers on the Science of Administration* (1937), his main work, *General and Industrial Management,* was not widely available in this country until 1949. Fayol's principles included the following: (1) a division of work or specialization; (2) authority, the right to give orders and expect compliance; whoever issues an order or delegates a task is still personally responsible for its execution; (3) discipline, obedience to laws, policies, procedures, and orders to further the accomplishment of the department's mission; (4) unity of command, on any assignment a subordinate shall only be directed by a single supervisor; (5) unity of direction—leaders must establish a direction for the department; unity of command is meaningless without unity of direction; (6) subordination of personal interest to the interest of the department; (7) compensation must be fair and uniform to people with the same jobs, qualifications, and experience; (8) centralization, which allows the active steering of the department in the direction intended; (9) the scalar chain—authority and responsibility must flow in a clear and unbroken line from the top to the bottom of the department through the various ranks, often referred to as the chain of command; (10) order is another manifestation of discipline; the building, equipment, records, and related matters must be properly maintained and accounted for; (11) equity, that quality of leadership and processes that combine kindness and justice; (12) stability of personnel, which allows employees to become familiar with their jobs; (13) initiative at all levels of the organization is a source of productivity; and (14) esprit de corps, harmony, and union of personnel—these constitute a great strength, and efforts should be made to establish them.[48]

Quick Facts: Luther Gulick

Born in Osaka, Japan, to missionary parents, Gulick later taught at Columbia University where he founded the Institute for Public Administration. He was an important adviser to President Franklin Delano Roosevelt (1882–1945) during World War II. During his remarkable career, he would periodically leave the university to take a practitioner's job, distinguishing himself as a first-rate scholar/practitioner.

TABLE 5.1 GULICK'S POSDCORB

Activity	Description
Planning	Identifying the things that need to be done and the methods for doing them to accomplish the goals of the agency.
Organizing	The establishment of a formal structure of authority through which work subdivisions are arranged, defined, and coordinated.
Staffing	Recruiting, screening, hiring, training, and evaluating officers.
Directing	The continuous effort of making decisions, communicating them, and seeing that they are properly implemented.
COordinating	The all-important duty of interrelating the various parts of the work.
Reporting	Keeping those to whom the leader is responsible informed as to what is going on and ensuring subordinates also stay informed.
Budgeting	The process of developing a plan stated in financial terms.

Fayol recognized that his scalar principle could produce disastrous consequences if it were strictly followed because it would hamper swift action.[49] He therefore developed Fayol's "gangplank," or horizontal bridge, as a means of addressing this problem. First-line supervisors and middle managers in different units who interact regularly "cut across" the organization on the gangplank, eliminating the time-consuming process of going up one hierarchy and down another. Inside of and between law enforcement agencies e-mail and texting have become modern gangplanks (also see Chapter 10, Organizational and Interpersonal Communication). In 2002, Wren, Bedian, and Breeze concluded that the richness of Fayol's contributions can best be understood by reading the "small, stepping-stone" publications that led to his theory.[50]

Mooney and Riley's *Onward Industry* (1931) was generally consistent with the work of Fayol, as were the subsequent revisions of this publication, which appeared in 1939 and 1947 under the title *The Principles of Organization*.[51] In "Notes on the Theory of Organization," which was included in *Papers on the Science of Administration,* Gulick coined the most familiar and enduring acronym of administration, **POSDCORB** (see Table 5.1).[52] Gulick acknowledged that his POSDCORB was adapted from Fayol's principles. Likewise, Urwick drew on the work of another Frenchman, A. V. Graicunas, for his view on the span of control. Urwick asserted that no one should directly supervise five or at the most six subordinates whose work was unrelated.

Subsequent research on the maximum number of persons someone can supervise showed that the figure of six is arbitrary and the actual number depends on such factors as the qualification and experience of those supervised and their supervisor, the nature of the work, and its level of difficulty.

Critique of Traditional Theory

Scientific management is decried because of its "man as machine" orientation. On balance, although Taylor's emphasis was on tasks, he was not totally indifferent to the human element, arguing that no system of management can be woodenly applied and all opinions of workers should be considered.[53] The traditional bureaucratic model has no shortage of criticisms.

However, when those criticisms are applied to the (new) neo-classical models they are clearly outdated. We have traveled well beyond traditional organizational theory. Nonetheless, those criticisms are covered here to provide an understanding of how the bureaucratic model has evolved.

Organizational humanism called for a softening or elimination of many features of the pure bureaucratic model. Herbert Simon (1916–2001) took issue with administrative theory. In 1945, he noted that if you narrow the span of control to five or six employees, you make the organization "taller," creating more layers and greater vertical complexity, and that decreases efficiency because a matter going up the chain of command is more time-consuming as each layer considers how to handle it.[54]

In 1957, Robert Merton (1910–2003) noted that rigid enforcement of rules can become dysfunctional. Originally intended to promote efficiency and equity in dealing with clients, the intention of the rules can become lost and sometimes what is left is a slavish devotion to enforcing them. Merton saw this as creating a "bureaucratic virtuoso," who never forgets a single rule, but may not know what value or purpose it serves.

Perhaps foremost among the humanists was Warren Bennis, who leveled the following specific criticisms of it (1966): (1) bureaucracy does not adequately allow for the personal growth and development of mature personalities; (2) it develops conformity and "group think"; (3) it does not take into account the "informal organization" and emerging and unanticipated problems; (4) its systems of control and authority are hopelessly outdated; (5) it has no adequate judicial process; (6) it does not possess adequate means for resolving differences and conflicts between ranks and, most particularly, between functional groups; (7) communication and innovative ideas are thwarted or distorted due to a tall hierarchy; (8) the full human resources are not utilized due to mistrust, fear of reprisals, and so on; (9) it cannot assimilate the influx of new technology entering the organization; and (10) it modifies the personality structure such that each person becomes and reflects the full, gray, conditioned "organization person."[55] These criticisms started important conversations, but lacked the potency to move things beyond that.

Quick Facts: Warren Bennis, Infantry Leader

In 1944, Warren Bennis arrived in Europe as a 19-year-old Lieutenant, commanding a platoon, as the Battle of the Bulge was ending. For subsequent action, Bennis received a Purple Heart for a combat wound and a Bronze Star for Valor. His difficult early years did not diminish a fervor for organizational humanism or perhaps those years helped to produce it.

Less critical than both Bennis and Simon, Hage describes bureaucracy in the mixed terms shown in Table 5.2.[56] In *Complex Organizations* (1972), Perrow argues that the preoccupation with reforming, humanizing, and decentralizing bureaucracies diverts attention from acknowledging how superior they are to other forms of organization. Goodsell, in *The Case for Bureaucracy* (1985), concludes that denunciations of bureaucracy may be fashionable, but not necessarily solid.[57] He asks the question: "How can we believe that all public bureaucracies, all of the time, are inefficient, dysfunctional, rigid, obstructionist,

TABLE 5.2 HAGE'S SUMMARY OF THE MIXED *CHARACTERISTICS OF THE BUREAUCRATIC MODEL*	
High	**Low**
Centralization	Adaptability
Formality	Job Satisfaction
Stratification	Complexity
Production	
Efficiency	

secretive, oligarchic, conservative, undemocratic, imperialist, oppressive, alienating, and discriminatory?"[58] Gouldner is more blunt, declaring the unending criticisms as being qualitative arguments devoid of any "empirical trimmings."[59]

HUMAN RELATIONS SCHOOL

Earlier in this chapter, brief mention of the **human relations school** was made and it is covered now in greater detail. Its significance is that it pivoted research and practice away from traditional organizational theory and toward new ways of leading organizations and motivating employees.

This school was a reaction to the mechanistic orientation of traditional organizational theory, which gave little or no attention to the needs of workers and helped set the stage for organizational humanism. As previously noted, this school rests on the research of Elton Mayo (1880–1949) and Fritz Roethlisberger (1898–1974). Originally started to study worker fatigue, the research (1927–1932) was expanded several times and was carried out near Chicago at the Western Electric Company's Hawthorne Plant.[60] The major contribution of the Hawthorne studies is the view that organizations are social systems. Two key studies were conducted: (1) the telephone relay assembly study and (2) the telephone switchboard wiring study.[61]

In the first study, five women assembling telephone relays were put into a room and subjected to varying physical work conditions.[62] Even when the conditions changed unfavorably, production increased. Mayo and his associates were puzzled by these results. Ultimately, they decided that (1) when the experimenters took over many of the supervisory functions, the work environment became less strict and less formal; (2) the women behaved differently from what was expected because they were receiving attention, creating the **Hawthorne effect**; and (3) by placing the women together in the relay assembling test room, the researchers had provided the opportunity for them to become a closely knit group.[63] On the basis of these observations, the researchers concluded that an important influence on productivity is the interpersonal relations and spirit of cooperation that had developed among the women and between the women and their supervisors. The influence of these "human relations" was believed to be every bit as important as physical work conditions and financial incentives.[64]

In the telephone switchboard wiring study, 14 men were put on a reasonable piece rate; that is, without physically straining themselves, they could earn more if they produced more. The assumption was that the workers would behave as rational economic actors and produce more, because it was in their own best interest. To insulate these men from the "systematic soldiering" they knew to exist among the plant's employees, the researchers also placed these workers in a special room. The workers' output did not increase, which contradicted scientific management's view that given the opportunity to earn more, workers will be more productive. The values of the informal group appeared to be more powerful than the allure of financial betterment: (1) don't be a "rate buster" and produce too much; (2) if you turn out too little work, you are a "chiseler"; (3) don't be a "squealer" to supervisors; and (4) don't be officious; if you are an inspector, don't act like one.[65]

As a result of the Hawthorne studies, it was concluded that (1) the level of production is set by social norms, not by physiological capacities; (2) often workers react not as individuals but as members of a group; (3) the rewards and sanctions of the group significantly affect the behavior of workers and limit the impact of economic incentive plans; and (4) leadership has an important role in setting and enforcing group norms, and there is a difference between formal and informal leadership.[66]

When workers react as members of an informal group, they become susceptible to the values of that group. Thus, the informal group can be a powerful force in organizations. Illustratively, several police unions started as an unorganized, small informal group of dissatisfied officers. Although many factors contribute to the enduring problem of police corruption, such as disillusionment and temptation, an informal group that supports taking payoffs makes it more difficult to identify and prosecute "bad cops." In 1972, the **Knapp Commission** investigated corruption in the New York (City) Police Department (NYPD, see Box 5.5). The Commission distinguished between "meat-eaters" (those who overtly pursued opportunities to profit personally from their police power) and "grass-eaters" (those who simply accepted the payoffs that the happenstances of police work brought their way).[67] The behavior of the grass-eaters can be interpreted within the framework of the power that informal groups have. In its investigation of corruption in the NYPD, the Knapp Commission learned that the motive for grass-eaters taking petty graft was to appear as "one of the boys" and therefore trusted by the meat-eaters.

The foregoing discussion should not be interpreted to mean that informal groups always, or even frequently, engage in troublesome or unethical behavior but rather is an illustration of the potency that such groups have. Astute law enforcement administrators are always alert for opportunities to tap the energy of informal groups to support departmental goals and programs.

Critique of the Human Relations School

Mayo's human relations school has been challenged on several grounds:

1. The research methods were not rigorous and such lapses may have tainted the findings.[68]

2. The human relations school claims conflicts between management and workers can be resolved by "harmony" between them. This overestimates harmony potency. Moreover, it ignores the possibility that properly handled disagreements and conflicts can be a source of creativity and innovation.

3. The single-mindedness with which advocates insisted on the importance of human relations was evangelistic.

4. Entirely too much emphasis was placed on the informal side of organizations and neglected the organization as a whole.[69]

Box 5.5: Francesco "Frank" Serpico

Born in 1936, Frank Serpico joined the NYPD in 1959. A "straight-arrow" officer, he gradually learned of significant corruption within the department. Illustratively, while some officers would accept occasional, petty bribes not to issue summons, the most serious corruption involved officers who were "on the pad," getting regular payments to protect prostitution, gambling, the numbers racket, and narcotics sales.

In 1970, Serpico reported it, but it appeared nothing was being done. He subsequently did a newspaper interview, which appears to have been a contributing factor to Mayor Lindsay appointing the Knapp Commission.

A year later, Serpico was on a narcotics raid, had his head slammed in the door, and was shot in the face. His two backups reportedly left the scene without calling for an ambulance, perhaps because he was already detested on the department for breaking the "blue curtain of silence." Serpico was belatedly promoted to detective and awarded the NYPD's Medal of Honor. Retired in 1972, he went to Europe for a decade and traveled widely before returning to the United States, living a semi-reclusive life in a cabin he built. Serpico still occasionally speaks out on police issues, like excessive use of force.

In 1992, the Mollen Commission began considering corruption in the NYPD and produced its report in 1994. It did not find the systemic selling and buying of protection corruption of the Knapp Commission but did uncover pockets of "crew-based" corruption. However, substantial use of undetected excessive force was identified, which the Mollen report characterized as being justified by officers as morally correct when a "guilty" person who would otherwise go unpunished was the recipient.

Human relations is also criticized as having a pro-management bias from several perspectives. First, it saw unions as promoting conflict between management and labor, a condition antithetical to the values of human relations. Second, by focusing on workers, the Hawthorne studies provided management with more sophisticated means of manipulating employees. Finally, the goal of human relations is indistinguishable from that of scientific management in that both aim for a more efficient organization:

> Scientific management assumed that the most efficient organization would also be the most satisfying one, since it would maximize both productivity and workers' pay...the Human Relations approach was that the most personally satisfying organization would be the most efficient.[70]

In 2010, job satisfaction in the United States was 46 percent, a 20-year low. This low was erased by 2018, when job satisfaction climbed to 54 percent, a two-decade high point.[71] Although the Hawthorne studies never showed a clear-cut relationship between satisfaction and job performance,[72] the assertion of the human relations school that satisfied people are more productive has become a widely held and cherished belief. It is a logically appealing and commonsense position whose endless repetition has accorded it the status of "fact." There is, however, no consistent research evidence to support that job satisfactions causes or is correlated with productivity.

A review of 70 years of research concluded that uncertainty remains as to whether happier workers are more productive.[73] The study essentially confirms the most scornful dismissal of the human relations school as "contented cows give more milk" theory. Researchers found that in nonenforcement situations with the public, officers had greater job satisfaction when they perceived higher levels of public support.[74] In a smaller study, the best predictors of job satisfaction among police officers were job autonomy and regular feedback.[75] Job satisfaction can be decreased or increased by the speed at which a person is able to make progress toward important goals.[76] There is also some evidence that employer-provided support services, such as child care and exercise opportunities, are a shield to job dissatisfaction and may decrease employee turnover.[77]

ORGANIZATIONAL HUMANISM

Organizational humanism (OH) shares the human relations school's distaste for traditional organizational theory. OH differs from traditional organizational theory and the human relations school in three fundamental ways: (1) the work intrinsically, in and of itself, should be satisfying and help to motivate workers; (2) organizations must pay attention to the on- and off-the-job needs of workers; and (3) work shouldn't be just something that people endure to make a living.[78] Covered in this section are Maslow's needs hierarchy; Argyris's immaturity/maturity changes; McGregor's Theory X-Theory Y; and Herzberg's motivation-hygiene theory. Likert's management systems, a four-step continuum from authoritarian to participative work environments, could also fit here, although it is covered in Chapter 7, Leadership. These organizational humanists must be read in the context of their times; their views were written from 1943 (Maslow, the needs hierarchy) until 1966 (Herzberg, motivation-hygiene theory). Presently, some of their views are archaic; in fairness, they could not foresee the rise of the (new) neoclassical views and processes. Still, organizational humanism is an important milestone moving thinking beyond traditional organizational theory and the human relations school and helped to set the stage for new styles of leadership and organizational processes (see Chapter 7, Leadership).

Maslow: The Needs Hierarchy

Abraham Maslow (1908–1970) was a psychologist who developed the **needs hierarchy** to explain individual motivation. The model appeared first in a 1943 article[79] and later received extended coverage in Maslow's *Motivation and Personality* (1954). It is summarized in Figure 5.5.[80]

The needs hierarchy is arranged, like the rungs on a ladder, from the lower-order to the higher-order needs. A person does not move from one level to the next-higher one until most of the prior level's needs are met. Once those needs are met, they cease to motivate a person, and the needs at the next level of the hierarchy predominate. For example, one does not attempt to self-actualize until one has feelings of self-confidence, worth, strength, capability, adequacy, and mastery;[81] these feelings are generated only with the meeting of the self-esteem needs. It is important to understanding the needs hierarchy that the character of something does not necessarily determine what need is met but rather to what use it is put; money can be used to buy food and satisfy a basic need, or it can be put in a savings account to satisfy safety needs. Also, any progress up the hierarchy can be reversed; a police officer who is fired or is given a lengthy suspension may be thrust into a financial situation in which the physiological needs will predominate.

Police agencies that are managed professionally attempt to make appropriate use of theoretical constructs. For example, the fourth level of Maslow's needs hierarchy is self-esteem, which includes the need for recognition as evidenced by compliments and commendations. The Ohio State Highway Patrol uses this need to combat vehicle theft by creating the Blue Max

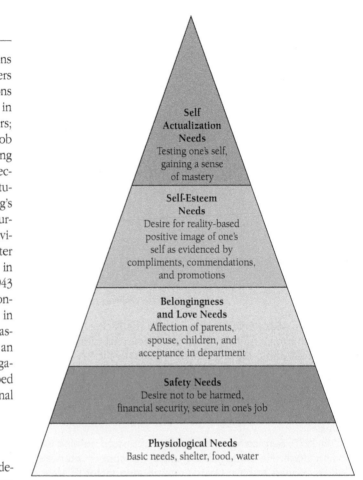

FIGURE 5.5 ▶ Maslow's needs hierarchy.

Award. Each time a state trooper arrests a suspect in a stolen car, he or she receives a lightning bolt decal to place on the side of his or her patrol car. For five such arrests, a trooper receives a license plate that reads "ACE" with a single lightning bolt next to it. Each additional five arrests results in an additional lightning bolt on the license plate. The trooper with the most stolen car arrests at the end of the year receives a citation of merit, a uniform ribbon, and exclusive use of a new patrol car for a year. In 2018, Trooper Matthew D. Boyer received the Blue Max Award for recovering 24 vehicles worth $182,500 and apprehending 24 suspects.[82]

Argyris: Immaturity-Maturity Theory

Chris Argyris (1923–2013) is a leading proponent of more open and participative organizations. In *Personality and Organization: The Conflict Between System and the Individual* (1957), he states a theory of **immaturity versus maturity**. Argyris believes that as one moves from infancy toward adulthood in years of age, the healthy individual also advances from immaturity to maturity. Simultaneously, Argyris views formal organizations as having certain properties that are barriers to the development of maturity: (1) specialization reduces worker initiative because employees repeatedly perform unchallenging tasks and (2) the chain of command and narrow span of control make workers submissive, passive, and dependent.[83]

Argyris believed that when the needs of a healthy, mature worker collided with the properties of the formal organization, dysfunctional things could happen, including the worker becoming frustrated, choosing to produce less, developing psychosomatic illnesses, and choosing to seek employment elsewhere.[84] He doubted that it was possible to have a relationship between the individual and the organization that allowed the simultaneous maximizing of the values of both.[85] Argyris modified his theory in 1966 with a mix model, asserting that organizations could reduce some of their unintended, nonproductive employee practices to free up more productive uses of their energy.[86] He also noted that having some unchallenging work was an asset because it allowed recovery time for workers and routine tasks could get done.[87]

McGregor: Theory X-Theory Y

Douglas McGregor (1904–1964) believed many managerial acts rested on conscious or subconscious assumptions and beliefs about how workers behave.[88] In *The Human Side of Enterprise* (1960), McGregor stated two different sets of assumptions that managers make about people.[89] His **Theory X-Theory Y** reflects two polar opposite characterizations of these assumptions and beliefs (see Table 5.3).[90]

Historically, American police departments were dominated by Theory X assumptions. Even police departments with progressive national images can be experienced as tightly controlling environments by the people who work in them:

A trainer was leading a session for about 35 West Coast Captains and Lieutenants. They were all members of a police department, which had a substantial national reputation for being progressive. She said "We often react to organizations as though they were living, breathing things. The group agreed with this and noted the use of such phrases as "the department promoted me this year" and "the department hired me in 2006." They also understood that in fact someone, not the police department, had made those decisions. The managers were then divided into five groups and asked to make a list of what they thought the police department would say about them if it could talk. When the groups reported back, they identified a total of 42 statements, some of which were duplicates of each other. Those attending this week-long seminar were all college graduates. Many of them held graduate degrees and several had graduated from law school. All groups indicated the police department would make some positive statements, but would also say "They are idiots," "They don't have any sense," "Watch them or they'll screw up royally." The trainer was startled by the number of Theory X statements. She had expected that

TABLE 5.3 MCGREGOR'S THEORY X-THEORY Y ASSUMPTIONS ABOUT WORKERS	
Theory X	**Theory Y**
1. The average human has an inherent dislike of work and will avoid it if possible. 2. Most people must be coerced, controlled, directed, and threatened with punishment to get them to put forth adequate effort toward the achievement of organizational objectives. 3. The average human prefers to be directed, wishes to avoid responsibility, has relatively little ambition, and wants security above all.	1. The expenditure of physical and mental effort in work is as natural as play or rest. 2. External control and the threat of punishment are not the only means for bringing about effort toward organizational objectives. People will exercise self-direction and self-control in the service of objectives to which they are committed. 3. Commitment to objectives is a function of the rewards associated with their achievement. 4. The average human learns, under proper conditions, not only to accept but also to seek responsibility. 5. The capacity to exercise a relatively high degree of imagination, ingenuity, and creativity in the solution of organizational problems is widely, not narrowly, distributed in organizations. 6. Organizations only partially utilize the abilities of their employees; unleashing that energy leads to greater organizational achievements and more fulfilled employees.

with the rich human resource in the seminar to find many more Theory Y comments.

Theory X assumptions are readily recognized as being those that underpin traditional organizational theory. For example, we can relate a narrow span of control to Theory X's first two propositions. In contrast, Theory Y is formed by a set of views that are supportive of Argyris's mix model; they postulate that the interests of the individual and the organization need not be conflictual but can be integrated for mutual benefit. The principal task of management in a Theory X police department is control. In a Theory Y department, it is supporting subordinates by giving them the resources to do their jobs and creating an environment where they can be self-controlling, mature, contributing, and self-actualizing—within the context of the agency's mission and goals.

Herzberg: Motivation-Hygiene Theory

Motivation-hygiene theory was developed from research conducted by **Frederick Herzberg** (1923–2000), Bernard Mausner, and Barbara Snyderman on job attitudes at 11 work sites in the Pittsburgh area and reported in *The Motivation to Work* (1959). The major statement of the theory, which evolved out of this earlier research, is found in Herzberg's *Work and the Nature of Man* (1966).

Herzberg saw two sets of variables operating in the work setting: (1) hygiene factors, which he later came to call maintenance factors, and (2) motivators. Table 5.4 identifies Herzberg's hygiene factors and motivators. The hygiene factors relate to the work environment; the motivators relate to the work itself. Herzberg borrowed the term hygiene from the health care field and used it to refer to factors that, if not treated properly, could lead to a deterioration in performance, creating an "unhealthy" organization. Hygiene factors that are not treated properly are a source of dissatisfaction. However, even if all of them are provided, a police department does not have motivated officers, just ones who are not dissatisfied. Hygiene factors and motivators operate independently of each other; the police manager can motivate subordinates if they are somewhat dissatisfied with their salaries. However, the greater the level of dissatisfaction, the more difficult it becomes to employ the motivators successfully.

Note that law enforcement leaders have more control over motivators than they do over basic hygiene factors. When leaders exercise control over hygiene factors, they can do a considerable amount of good in reducing dissatisfaction and facilitating the use of the motivators, or they can cause considerable unhappiness:

The commander of the uniformed division of a 100-officer department simply announced that officers were going to be placed on permanent shifts. There was no prior mention this was being considered. The newly appointed Chief, an outsider, approved the plan because in his last department he had championed permanent shifts, which was a popular change.

Surprised and angered by this move, the officers and their wives mobilized to oppose the plan, and after a mass meeting with the commander, the plan was abandoned. The legacy of this incident was a period of barely subdued hostility, distrust, and low morale. The new Chief was viewed as weak and patrol officers saw it as another example of the Patrol Commander's impulsiveness.

The nature of police work is challenging, and some motivational effect is thus naturally occurring. Police managers can build on this by varying assignments appropriately. Measures that employ various other motivators include an active awards system, the creation of a master patrol officer designation, an annual police awards banquet, an active staff development program, and a career system with various specialization tracks.

Maslow's needs hierarchy and Herzberg's motivation-hygiene theory can be interrelated; the physiological, safety, and love and belongingness needs of Maslow correspond to Herzberg's hygiene factors; the top two levels of the needs hierarchy—esteem and self-actualization—correlate with Herzberg's motivators.

Critique of Organizational Humanism

In one way or another, organizational humanism (OH) theories depend to some degree on open and honest communication between organizational members who respect and trust each other. An attractive theme, it gives insufficient weight to the

TABLE 5.4 HERZBERG'S MOTIVATION-HYGIENE THEORY	
Hygiene/Maintenance Factors	**Motivators**
Supervisory practices	Achievement
Policies and administration	Recognition for accomplishments
Working conditions	Challenging work
Interpersonal relationships with subordinates, peers, and superiors	Increased responsibility
Status	Advancement possibilities
Effect of the job on personal life	Opportunity for personal growth and development
Job security	
Money	

Source: "Herzberg's motivation-hygiene theory" from *Work and the Nature of Man* by Frederick Herzberg (Cleveland: World Publishing, 1966), pp. 95–96.

consequences that can occur when authenticity meets power. Illustratively, moviemaker Samuel Goldwyn told his staff, "I want you all to tell me what's wrong with our operation even if it means losing your job."[91]

An underlying assumption of OH is that people want more rewards than just money from doing their work. Ignored is the reality that some proportion of workers have a utilitarian involvement with the job. It simply provides the money necessary to live; they save their energies and obtain their rewards from their families, operating their own online businesses, or other nonjob-related sources, such as hobbies.

Despite the lack of research and the fact that the few existing studies do not support Maslow, there remains an almost metaphysical attraction to the needs hierarchy,[92] a condition made even more perplexing by noting that Maslow's work on motivation came from a small clinical study of neurotic people.[93] In turn, Maslow points at Theory X-Theory Y and notes that a good deal of what McGregor bases his conclusions on comes from Maslow's own research "…and above all people I know just how shaky that foundation is…I am concerned that enthusiastic people will swallow it whole."[94]

In contrast to the lack of research on the needs hierarchy, there has been considerable research on Herzberg's motivation-hygiene theory; after reviewing this evidence, Gibson and Teasley concluded the range of findings run from general support to a vigorous condemnation of Herzberg's methodology.[95] The research support for Argyris's immaturity-maturity theory is generally weak. Heavily influenced by Maslow, Argyris's own research only used semi-structured interviews and the theory assumes that each worker's needs are the same as any other worker.[96] A major test of the theory, which included 800 respondents, did not find sufficient evidence to support it.[97]

BEHAVIORAL SYSTEMS THEORY

The successor to organizational humanism was **behavioral systems theory** (BST), founded by **Kurt Lewin** (1890–1947), a psychologist who fled from Germany in the early 1930s.[98] The theorists in this school saw organizations as being composed of the behavior of individuals and groups and were interested in making organizations more democratic and participative. The work of some organizational humanists is sometimes included in BST.

Lewin was interested in group dynamics—how groups form and how their members relate to each other—and he also developed a decision-making tool, **force-field analysis** (see Table 5.5). In force-field analysis, driving forces push for a new condition and restraining forces resist the change. If there are exactly opposing driving and restraining forces, the arrows of these opposing forces meet at the vertical zero, or balance, line. In some instances, there might not be an exactly opposite force, in which case an arrow is simply drawn, as in Table 5.5, to the balance line. After all entries are made and the situation is summarized, the relative power of the driving and restraining forces must be subjectively evaluated. In this regard, the balance line

should be regarded as a spring that will be moved in one direction, suggesting the action that needs to be taken or the decision that needs to be made.

In *The Human Group* (1950), George Homans (1910–1989) advanced the idea that groups have both an internal and an external system.[99] The internal system comprises factors that arise within the group itself, such as the feelings that members of a group develop about each other during the life of the group. In contrast, the external system consists of variables in the larger environment in which the group exists. Members of the same patrol shift may form one or more groups and these groups exist within the context of the law enforcement agency employing them. To illustrate, a chief suspends an officer for three days following a high-speed pursuit in which the officer had an at-fault accident. The officers who work on the same shift as the suspended officer viewed the discipline as unjust and agreed among themselves not to write any traffic citations during the three-day suspension.

Much of Warren Bennis's (1925–2014) effort was in **organizational development (OD)**, a change management process. OD is used to "recalibrate" the work attitudes and values of employees with respect to the changes the organization wishes to make and often involves surveying and training employees. It is intended to take the chaos and uncertainty out of organizational changes. When police departments implement community or intelligence-led policing or servant leadership (see Chapter 7, Leadership), they are engaged in organizational development change (see Chapter 15, Organizational Change).

Critique of Behavioral Systems Theory

Although behavioral systems theory (BST) was relatively short-lived, its theorists helped sustain the movement away from mechanistic views of organizations and toward the people in them. Homans's work on internal and external systems served to set the stage for open systems theory.

ORGANIZATIONS AS OPEN SYSTEMS

Ludwig von Bertalanffy (1901–1972), a biologist, articulated general systems theory (GST) in 1940. However, the application of GST principles to organizational theory did not begin to gain prominence until the 1960s when it was recast as open systems theory (OST) by Katz and Khan in their *The Social Psychology of Organization* (1966).

A system is a grouping of separate but interrelated components working together toward the achievement of a common objective (see Figure 5.6). Organizations can be characterized as closed or open systems. There are no entirely closed or entirely open organizations. These are terms used only to describe the extent to which an organization approximates one or the other. Closed systems operate under assumptions that they are rational, effective, efficient, substantially self-sufficient, can reasonably predict what is going to happen,

TABLE 5.5 FORCE-FIELD ANALYSIS OF CONFLICT INVOLVING A POLICE PROMOTIONAL SYSTEM

Driving Forces	Restraining Forces
Minority officers discontent with lack of minority promotions	Majority and some minority officers support present promotional system
Several discrimination complaints filed by minority officers	Elected and appointed officials willing to initiate change, but wanted the fullest and fairest competition to ensure public confidence in those selected for leadership positions
Minority employees association formed and their attorney had presented plan that would grant preferential treatment to minorities temporarily	Majority officers association took no official policy stand but association's President appeared before Council to oppose changing the current promotional process
Elected and appointed community officials want to respond to legitimate employee and community concerns	Ill-considered change could splinter the department badly along racial lines
Possibility of litigation and court intervention	Fifty majority employees allegedly prepared to get $5,000 second mortgages on their homes to raise $250,000 for filing a cross suit
	Officers with seniority and/or higher education opposed to reducing the importance of these factors in any new police promotional ordinance
Litigation could result in adverse publicity, damaging the city's progressive reputation and economic development	

and "know what's best." This line of thinking is accompanied by, or breeds, an insensitivity to influences from the larger environment, which reinforces the isolation of a closed system organization.

Open systems theory views hierarchical organizations, such as law enforcement agencies, as being comprised of multiple subsystems interfacing with the larger environment. It both accommodates the hierarchical feature of traditional organizational theory and describes the organization's functioning in an open systems context. By doing so, the effect of factors in an organization's environment should be able to account for explanations of its performance.

Both traditional organizational theory and the early police professionalism movement (see Chapter 1, The Evolution of Police Administration) reinforced a closed system view, which regards whatever is "outside of it" as being inconsequential. In contrast, open systems:

1. Recognize that everything beyond their boundary/structure is part of their environment;[100]

2. Know they have regular ongoing relationships in the larger environment in which they are embedded; this is the quality of being interdependent; numerous factors impinge on law enforcement agencies (see Table 5.6);

3. Have walls or boundaries that are permeable, allowing things, for example, information in and out. Too many inputs will overwhelm an open system and threaten its **homeostasis** or balance; from the Greek, homeostasis literally means "standing still";

4. Use **coding** to prevent being overwhelmed, which functions like a priority system; important inputs get through quickly: calls from a city manager will usually be received by the chief, but citizens asking to talk to

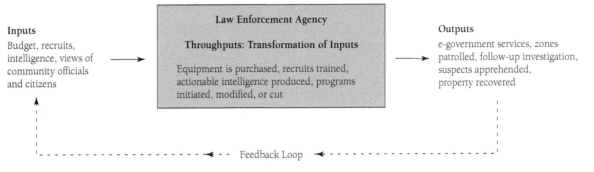

FIGURE 5.6 ▶ A basic open system view of a law enforcement agency with illustrated processes.

Illustrative Environmental Factors	Potential Impacts
Police Unions	Oppose increased cost of health and pension benefits to their members; furloughs and layoffs; wage concessions; freezing cost of living increases for their retirees; early release of violent offenders; parole of "Cop Killers"; increases in hiring standards and some disciplinary actions; support specific political candidates; usually gun control; some tax increases; and legislation requiring the death penalty for those killing officers in the performance of their duties.
Partners	Multiagency single purpose and standing task forces may create friction about budgetary support, credit for successes, and blame for failures; mutual aide compacts allow agencies to share the use of special resources, aircraft, SWAT teams, and bomb disposal units.
Events	Agency resources may be overrun by natural disasters, protests and riots, catastrophic industrial accidents, terrorist attacks, and searching for children lost in wilderness areas. Events may also be positive, e.g., gifts and grants.
Legal Framework	New court rulings, federal, and state laws may require new expenses and procedures and/or provide agencies with new authority. Some federal laws, e.g., Americans with Disability Act (ADA) and Occupational Health and Safety Act (OSHA) provide protection to officers (see Chapter 9, Human Resources).
Governing Body	May slash budgets, impacting agency operations and keeping high-mileage cars in the fleet; declare city a sanctuary for undocumented immigrants putting the agency between official policy and public demands for strict enforcement; and approve take-home cars.
Special Interest Groups/Stakeholders	May call for special unit to deal with the gay, lesbian, bisexual, and transgendered communities; Washington, DC, has a GLBT Police Unit for this purpose; advocate for more officers walking beats in business areas; and demand strict enforcement of loitering, panhandling and noise ordinances.
Technology	Can be used to make agency more transparent, as a recruiting tool, and to provide e-government services.
Other Departments	May see offers to engage in collaborative projects as an attempt by police to "build empire" or use their resources; equipment and supplies selected by purchasing may be seen by rank and file as substandard/inadequate.

TABLE 5.6 ILLUSTRATIVE ENVIRONMENTAL FACTORS POTENTIALLY IMPACTING LAW ENFORCEMENT AGENCIES

the chief often find themselves redirected and speaking to someone else;

5. Have the tendency to become more complex and specialized; as specialization proceeds, its fragmenting effect on the department is countered by the unifying elements of its **internal subsystems** (see Table 5.7);

6. Face the prospect of moving toward decline, disorganization, and death—the **entropic process**.

Only 13 of the businesses existing at the time of the American Revolution remain as autonomous entities, and during a 20-year period, 46 percent of the companies on the Fortune 500 list of America's largest and most powerful businesses disappeared from that list.[101] Law enforcement agencies have no exemption from the entropic process. During financial downturns, thousands of agencies have experienced hiring freezes,

TABLE 5.7 THE INTERNAL SUBSYSTEMS OF A LAW ENFORCEMENT AGENCY

Subsystems	Illustrative Functions
Managerial	Sets direction for agency, controls, directs, coordinates, evaluates, takes corrective action, empowers employees, sets budget priorities and presents and defends operating budget
Supportive	Acquires resources from larger environment and distributes them; budget and grant preparation, recruits, obtains surplus government property, promotes positive image of agency
Production	Components that transform inputs into outputs, patrol, investigation, crime prevention, DUI checkpoints, e-government services
Maintenance	Building, grounds, equipment, special emphasis on employees, fair compensation and benefits, favorable work environment
Adaptive	Scans environment, identifies problems, opportunities, and challenges; develops response strategies and tactics

Source: These subsystems were identified in Danial Katz and Robert L. Kahn, *The Social Psychology of Organizations.* New York: Wiley, 2nd edition, 1978.

furloughs, layoffs, and many were simply shut down (see Chapter 12, Financial Management). To fight entropy, departments continuously import more inputs than they can use (e.g., gasoline), and store it to allow operations to continue if supplies are interrupted. "Buffering" describes this processing of storing some inputs and it allows the department to develop negative entropy, or the capacity to resist decline.

7. Must evolve to avoid decline, the quality of adaptability;

8. Become double-loop learning organizations in order to be adaptive: (1) **single-loop learning** allows organizations to make corrections and carry out their present efforts toward achieving objectives and (2) **double-loop learning**, articulated by Chris Argyris, **goes** deeper, enabling organizations to judge whether they are pursuing the right objectives, programs, and policies.[102] Law enforcement practices associated with double-loop learning include after action reports, staff inspections, and program evaluations;

9. Follow the principle of **equafinality**, which means there are multiple ways to achieve goals; and

10. Can never be more varied than the larger environment.[103] **Isomorphism**, from the Greek meaning equal shape, dictates that the resource-dependent agencies tend to mirror the complexity and demands of their environment and develop policies, programs, and units that are signaled to be important by the environment.

Critique of Open Systems Theory

Some critics question whether GST, which originated in biology and was applied to organizations as OST, can unequivocally be used to explain contrived man-made organizations.[104]

The essence of this criticism is that using explanations of living systems to describe the behavior of artificially created, non-organic organizations pose the danger of a misapplication of knowledge and the creation of false, but persuasive, analogies. These critics argue that the extension of GST into organizations as open systems may fail to account for or understate crucial aspects of organizations. Finally, these critics maintain that organizations may be systems, but they are not natural systems that are subject to immutable laws[105] and do not invariably follow the birth, growth, maturity, and death cycle of biological systems.

In more positive terms, open systems theory provides a framework and language for understanding how law enforcement is loosely connected to and interacts with elected and appointed governmental leaders, prosecutors, the judiciary, federal departments, grant awarding agencies, clients, consultants, and other entities, as well as how they handle inputs such as information.

OTHER PARADIGMS OF ADMINISTRATION

A paradigm is a coherent, internally consistent, and integrated approach to making sense of whatever is being studied. It is like a model. If you are defining a problem in a conventional, habitual, or customary way, you are "thinking inside the box," a condition created by "paradigm paralysis." If trying to solve the problem by thinking "outside of the box," you will have some quirky, unconventional thoughts that may lead you to important innovations or paradigm shifts. This section covers some theories that are not mainstream but are interesting ways of looking at organizations.

Environmental Theories

This group of theories relates organizations to the broader environments in which they are embedded: (1) environmental contingency theory, (2) resource dependency theory, (3) population ecology, (4) old institutional theory, and (5) neo-institutional theory.

ENVIRONMENTAL CONTINGENCY THEORY

Burns and Stalker (1961, 1968) maintain that there is no one best way to structure an organization.[106] Instead, leaders must "read the environment" and decide what type of structure is the best "fit" with the environment being faced. For example, if the environment is stable and the tasks to be performed are routine, a mechanistic form of organization might be the best choice. Very successful organizations can find the best "fit."

Organizations may still survive, with varying degrees of success, with "adequate" or "good" fits, but they are unlikely to excel and may even have to abandon a fit they have chosen. Around 1980, a few police departments tried to "flatten" the seven or eight layers of their hierarchy, which made their structure grow horizontally and shrink in height. These experiments were quickly abandoned because others in the environment (e.g., local, state, and federal agencies) didn't know what unit or who they should contact about any matter. "Fit" is also being used to determine whether a person can be a productive part of an organization or a work team; although ability is a key factor, emotional stability is proving to be even more important.[107]

RESOURCE DEPENDENCY THEORY

The fullest expression of resource dependency theory (RDT) was produced by Pfeffer and Salancik (1978).[108] The basic thrust of RDT is that all agencies must get the resources they need to operate from the larger environment, creating resource dependency. The control of resource distribution by the larger environment is a source of power over agencies and makes them dependent. Failure to capture resources makes an agency more vulnerable and moves it toward entropy. RDT helps agency leaders identify the standing of other agencies competing for resources and who has power in the environment. RDT views organizational success as organizations maximizing their power. Organizations can do so by forming cooperative ventures with other organizations and by making resource providers view their contributions as crucial.

POPULATION ECOLOGY

RDT and population ecology (PE) share the same views on organization resource dependence and the power of the larger environment. However, they use different levels of analysis; RDT focuses on agencies and PE focuses on the larger environment.[109] PE, which fundamentally had a mid- to late-1970s start, seeks to discover why organizations competing in the same resource pool or ecological niche are more, and others less, successful. Hannan and Freeman's *The Population Ecology of Organizations* was a major development in this line of thinking.

OLD INSTITUTIONAL THEORY

"Old" institutional theory (OIT) is associated with traditional organizational theory. In explaining organizations, they tend to rely on historical justifications for structures and processes, OIT was the legal foundation for the existence of public organizations, holding that the structure of an organization dictated the behavior of its members. Therefore, OIT was relatively uninterested on how organizations impacted individuals.[110] The old institutional writings were descriptive and value laden, substantially lacking an empirical base. Nonetheless, along with traditional organizational theory, the old institutionalism was part of the progressive era/good government movement that lasted from roughly 1890 into the 1920s (see Chapter 1, The Evolution of Police Administration).

NEO-INSTITUTIONAL THEORY

Neo-institutionalism was named by March and Olsen (1984)[111] and its beginning dates from the late 1970s until the mid-1980s. There are a half-dozen or more varieties of neo-institutionalism; the political institutional framework (PIF) is briefly described here.[112] PIF's view is that organizations are not simply acted upon by the larger/external political system (e.g., inevitably pressured into the mandatory adoption of strategies, programs, and policies). Instead, organizations are often themselves potent political forces that can resist pressures and shape part of their external political landscape.[113] PIF recognized that politics is "done" both to, and by, organizations.

Networked and Virtual Organizations

Networked and virtual organizations are goal directed and share many characteristics. Advanced information technology is the glue that allows them to function; geographic proximity may not be an issue; dispersion may provide some advantages; and horizontal communication accounts for most message traffic. As a generalization, **networked organizations** (NOs) have relationships that are planned and stable, whereas **virtual organizations** (VOs) have relationships that often arise spontaneously out of special needs and may be temporary.[114]

NOs date from the early 1980s when tall, hierarchical organizations faced a tough economy. They realized that there were some things other organizations or individuals could do cheaper, faster, and better. The result was a period of corporate downsizing as individual jobs and functions were subcontracted out. The separate members of a networked organization are termed nodes and are simultaneously autonomous and collaborative, pooling their resources, and geographically dispersed to one degree or another. The relationships of the nodes are spelled out in contracts. To illustrate, Firm A designs a car; Firm B does the engineering; Firm C builds it with parts provided by supplier nodes; and Firm D markets the vehicle. NOs flatten the organizational

FIGURE 5.7 ▶ The sniper who terrorized the Washington, DC, area for three weeks in 2002 shot from inside of his car's closed trunk using a Bushmaster .223 rifle with a scope for accuracy and a tripod for stability. Note the cut-out in the body of his car so he could take position and shoot without anyone seeing him. (CHRIS GARDNER/ POOL AP/AP Images)

hierarchy and broaden the organizational structure horizontally. This requires continuing horizontal communication, which results in personal relationships developing between people in different nodes. These relationships are added value; people go out of the way to help those they know. NOs may use some overarching or meta-management to coordinate functions (e.g., a board of directors). Although NOs can be used for a single project, they tend to be ongoing enterprises with some node members being replaced from time to time to achieve greater efficiency or for other reasons.

Although NOs and VOs are sometimes used synonymously, others describe VOs as being created more spontaneously, often are not regulated by formal agreements, more informal, and driven by the need to accomplish a single task, for example, neighborhood watch groups. Node members, who can withdraw at any point, participate voluntarily and leadership may not be formally designated; the nodes can be self-directed because of their mutuality of needs.

In 2002, a sniper went on a rampage in the Washington, DC, area; victims were shot with a high-power rifle from a distance, leaving no witnesses and few investigative leads for law enforcement agencies (see Figure 5.7).[115] By the time an arrest was made, there were 14 shootings, 10 deaths, and thousands of local, state, and federal law enforcement officers involved.[116] A total of five different task forces from different involved jurisdictions were in operation and one had three coequal leaders.[117] The task forces were built "on the fly" and nobody had a chance to step back and critically assess what was being done.[118] Task force leaders said that they didn't need more control over the other task forces; they needed more coordination.[119] There was no central hub to coordinate investigative priorities, use of resources, and information sharing.

The sniper case reflects the following elements, many of which reflect virtual organizational theory: (1) there was a spontaneous need; (2) although some agency and personal relationships pre-existed, other relationships were unplanned; (3) the law enforcement agencies were geographically dispersed; (4) in the absence of a central command and control hub, greater horizontal communication was needed; (5) cooperating agencies could withdraw investigators at any point; (6) the enterprise was driven by a single purpose: apprehension; and (8) it is not clear to what extent any of the task forces operated under memorandums of understanding and those that did exist lacked written clarity and had obscure lines of authority and information handling procedures.

Task forces can be established for a single purpose, such as the apprehension of a serial offender, or they can operate continuously, as in the case of the FBI's multijurisdictional Joint Terrorism Task Forces (JTTF) that were developed in the wake of 9/11. Mechanism of these types allows for a reasonable time horizon to plan, organize, and implement them under well-considered written guidance.

One of the situations requiring multiple jurisdiction involvement is serial murder investigations because such crimes may be committed across several counties and states. To illustrate, Ted Bundy killed a number of young women during the 1970s. His method of operation was to kidnap a victim in one county and leave the body in another one to complicate investigations by involving several agencies, which he did in multiple states before being apprehended, convicted, and executed in Florida (1989).

Law enforcement agencies should give some consideration to evaluating the features of networked and virtual organizations, modifying them for off-the-shelf immediate use to meet spontaneous demands.

Sense Making

Sense making in organizations is how we process our experiences and what we do with them. In addition to his other publications, Weick's *Sense Making in Organizations* and *Making Sense of the Organization* marked him as an influential theorist on this topic.

When something happens in the world of officers, the event may be well beyond their experience or anything that could be imagined. Assume an armed robbery occurs at a neighborhood "Mom and Pop" grocery with the suspect wearing a bizarre costume, a superhero mask, an orange wig, waving a flintlock pistol, and Halloween type fangs through which the victim is threatened with death if money is quickly handed over.

Officers try to figure out, "Just what the hell happened?" This is the beginning of sense making. Known information is scrutinized, interpreted, analyzed, and past unusual robberies recalled that might suggest a hint of a connection. Possible explanations are considered, for example, Did a drunk wander away from a party? Was it some nut passing through town? Is there a pirates' convention I haven't heard about? Maybe a recent mental hospital released someone with a pirate fetish? Where did the costume come from? Was the gun real? Could the whole outfit have just been rented or bought someplace? Because the grocery didn't have a surveillance camera, who's going to believe this story?

Internally, officers must create some scenario for their own use about the event. Internally, the officers don't have to believe the scenario and beliefs they create are true. To deal with their own uncertainty, they just have to be plausible. Sense making occurs within an officer or several of them together. These meanings become shared in the locker room or over a beer. A few experiences become organizational lore: "Before you shout me down, I was the first officer on the scene when…" This process of sense making is not episodic, but continuous, as experiences pile up. Like digital information, our interpreted experiences can be stored and retrieved. Over time, objective information may be mixed with our cognitive maps

Accumulated sense making produces **cognitive maps** or "mental understandings." The term may have been coined by Tolman (1948).[120] These maps help us to understand our "landscape" and navigate our "world" so we can do such things as (1) understand the actions of commanding officers, (2) predict what others may do in different situations, (3) know who to take things to for swift handling, (4) decide who shares our values, (5) identify potential mentors, (6) who would make a solid partner, and (7) select career paths in the department that match our interest and abilities.

Chaos Theory

Kiel's *Managing Chaos and Complexity in Government* (1994) was an early effort to apply **chaos theory** to the public sector.[121] In organizational theory, chaos is a state of nonequilibrium. It is precipitated by a crisis event(s) during which the everyday predictability and the usual order of things are disrupted, replaced at some level by a mix of factors, such as (1) widespread uncertainty and fear; (2) the delivery of normal services is not possible; (3) an initial lack of basic information about the event; (4) informational overload caused by inputs

FIGURE 5.8 ▶ Hurricane Katrina devastated New Orleans on an unimaginable scale in 2005. Many residents were rescued from their rooftops by boats and others waded to safety through the floodwaters. (FEMA/Win Henderson)

from political figures, inquiries from federal agencies or the news media, offers of assistance, and urgent citizen appeals; (5) the realization that plans are inadequate or nonexistent for the event; (6) recognition that available resources and modes of operation are insufficient or ineffective; and (7) the need to solve unfamiliar problems whose magnitude, complexity, and durability exceed anything we could imagine, a condition referred to as **cosmology**.[122] Under these circumstances, maladaptive decisions may increase the level of chaos, producing unintended consequences. **Bifurcation** is the flash-point when chaos overwhelms normal conditions in an agency[123] and compels the use of innovative efforts and alliances to restore stability in the community. The 9/11 attacks and Hurricane Katrina possessed the qualities of cosmology and bifurcation (see Figure 5.8).

Contrary to popular view, chaos theory does more than describe under what conditions events spin out of control, and total collapse seems both possible and imminent.[124] Its ultimate value is in how order is restored against seemingly insurmountable adversity. The way off the slippery slope of a chaos event is through self-organization. Police and other agencies don't have to do everything; individuals, neighbors, ad hoc groups, and volunteers from other communities pitch in with helpful acts; they rescue people and pets from debris, open their homes to others, deliver food and water, set up temporary shelters and rudimentary first aid clinics, stand guard, reunite family members, and allow others to use their cell phones. These steps produce the **butterfly effect**, which ripples across the community, energizing people to help themselves and others.

At the organization level, self-organization, or perhaps more precisely, self-reorganization occurs on a continuous basis during a chaos event. Organizations use sense making and, from their understanding of their experiences, use the quality of adaptability, developing new priorities, standards, services, procedures, and alliances. In the wake of a chaos event, organizations evolve into something more complex, with new goals, partnerships, structures, equipment, and communication channels to accommodate what they have learned.

Critique of Other Paradigms of Administration

Environmental contingency theory assumes organizations that are a "misfit" with their operating environment will "shift gears" and move to a "good fit" but fails to provide details on how this occurs and at what velocity. One way to look at a misfit is when the number of risk factors in a community "overpower" the ability of law enforcement agency to provide the desired level of public safety. A study of 133 local law enforcement risk factors (e.g., unemployment, the percent of housing that is renter-occupied, and percent of resident population ages 15–24,

and 25 or more) had a significant impact on resource allocation and performance.[125]

Unsurprisingly, agencies, with higher per capita earning had lower levels of "risk factors," were less crime prone, and better resourced.[126] Such agencies were less cost-efficient than lower resourced agencies because they had lower demands for service and thus fewer outputs.

Donaldson, an advocate of environmental contingency theory, is highly critical of resource dependency theory, population ecology, and neo-institutionalism. He dismisses them as part of the proliferation of theories by academics seeking momentary fame and diverting attention from studying more "worthy" theories (i.e., contingency theory).[127] Some theorists find Donaldson's criticisms too severe and unrelenting.

There are numerous praises of networked and virtual organizations, but they may be overstated with respect to how well NOs and VOs function and their efficiency. The literature is sparse about their failure rates and dysfunctionalities (e.g., the consequences of lingering personality conflicts between node members who have continuing contacts).

Chaos theory teaches us that crisis events that produce cosmology and bifurcation are not situations to be endured and resolved as much as they are the important aspects of organizational life whereby a law enforcement agency can adapt to its environment, maintain, and renew itself, and ultimately adapt through self-organization and emerge stronger.

Chapter Summary

Summary by Learning Objectives

1. **State why formal organizations, such as police departments, exist.**

   The basic rationale for the existence of formal organizations is to do those things that people are unable or unwilling to do alone.

2. **Identify the three stems of traditional organizational theory.**

   The three stems are scientific management, the bureaucratic model, and administrative or management theory.

3. **In a police context, define street-level bureaucrats and the two modes out of which they operate.**

   Police officers working in the field are the face of government. They meet with members of the public and decide how to implement public policy as expressed in laws, departmental policies and procedures, court decisions, and other sources. In doing so, officers operate out of two modes of street-level bureaucrats: (1) "state agents," who believe in following the law and policies and (2) "citizen agents," who will bend or ignore them.

   While some officers may consistently operate in one or the other mode, most officers operate in both modes.

4. **Explain how a reaction to a line of thinking gave rise to the human relations school.**

   This school was a reaction to the mechanistic orientation of traditional organizational theory, which gave little or no attention to the needs of workers.

5. **Identify three statements in Theory Y consistent with practices in today's well-run police departments.**

   Any three of the following statements summarizes this learning objective: (a) the expenditure of physical and mental energy is as natural as play or rest; (b) external control and the threat of punishment are not the only means for bringing about effort toward organizational objectives. People will exercise self-direction and self-control in the service of objectives to which they are committed; (c) commitment to objectives is a function of the rewards associated with their achievement; (d) the average human learns, under proper conditions, not only to accept, but also seek responsibility; (e) the capacity to exercise a relatively high degree of imagination, ingenuity, and creativity in the solution of organizational problems is widely, not narrowly, distributed in organizations; and (f) organizations only partially utilize the abilities of their employees; unleashing that energy leads to greater organizational achievement and more fulfilled employees.

6. **Identify the major components of an open system view of a police department.**

   Inputs (budget, recruits, intelligence, and the views of community citizens and officials) are taken into a police department. In the department, they become *throughputs* (processed in the department)

and *transformed* into equipment being purchased, recruits being hired and new programs started. Those transformations become *outputs*, such as patrol officers responding to calls from citizens, reports written, follow-up investigations conducted, clearance rates, and other results. A *feedback loop* sends the record of results on a monthly schedule, and later as an annual report, to the Mayor, City Manager, and other offices, where it is evaluated and considered when the city is developing its next budget. The next budget becomes a primary input to begin the next cycle.

Chapter Review Questions

1. How are mechanistic and organic organizations different?

2. In a police context, what is rational-legal authority?

3. Gulick's acronym POSDCORB stands for what administrative functions?

4. What key question did Goodsell ask about the numerous denunciations of the classic bureaucratic model?

5. What effect did the Hawthorne studies have on traditional organizational theory?

6. What is the rationale for Maslow's Need Hierarchy as it relates to individual motivation?

7. McGregor has concluded that there are two different assumptions that managers make about workers. What are they?

8. Herzberg's "Motivation Hygiene" theory discusses two sets of variables operating in the work setting. What are they?

9. What is a paradigm?

10. What is Chaos Theory?

Critical Thinking Exercises

1. Assume you are the Chief of Police in a department with 218 sworn and 41 civilians. Give an example of how the exception principle works for you and how you benefit from it.

2. Is the power of an officer's accumulated street experience somewhat of an antidote to a police department's doctrine, for example, its operating philosophy, rules, and regulations? If yes, what, if anything, can and should be done about it? If

no, state your reasons for believing it is not an antidote.

3. Explain what the terms "cosmology, bifurcation, and the butterfly effect" mean to law enforcement agencies in a coastal area three days after the area was devastated by a Category 5 Hurricane with sustained winds in excess of 156 miles per hour.

Key Terms

administrative theory
Argyris, Chris
behavioral systems theory
bifurcation
bureaucratic model
business concerns
butterfly effect
chaos theory
coding

cognitive maps
commonweal organizations
cosmology
double-loop learning
e-government
entropic process
equafinality
exception principle
force-field analysis

functional supervision
Gulick, Luther
Hawthorne effect
Herzberg, Frederick
homeostasis
human relations school
immaturity versus maturity
internal subsystems
isomorphism

Knapp Commission
Lewin, Kurt
Maslow, Abraham
McGregor, Douglas
mechanistic organization
motivation-hygiene theory
mutual benefit association
natural soldiering
needs hierarchy
networked organizations

open systems theory
organizational development (OD)
organizational humanism
organic organization
POSDCORB
rational-legal authority
scientific management
sense making
service organizations
single-loop learning

street-level bureaucrats
systematic soldiering
Taylor, Fredrick W.
Theory X-Theory Y
traditional organizational theory
vertical problem-solving
vertical staff meeting
virtual organizations
Weber, Max

Endnotes

[1] Amitai Etzioni, *Modern Organizations* (Englewood Cliffs, NJ: Prentice Hall, 1964), p. 1.

[2] Ibid., with some additions.

[3] Ibid.

[4] Talcott Parsons, *Structure and Process in Modern Societies* (Glencoe, IL: Free Press, 1960), p.17.

[5] Edgar H. Schein, *Organizational Psychology* (Englewood Cliffs, NJ: Prentice Hall, 1965), p. 9.

[6] See T. Burns and G. Stalker, *The Management of Innovation* (London: Tavistock, 1961), chapter 6, Mechanistic and Organic Systems of Management, pp. 96–125.

[7] Peter W. Blau and W. Richard Scott, *Formal Organizations* (Scranton, PA: Chandler, 1962), p. 43, with some changes.

[8] The treatment of the central issues of the four types of formal organizations is taken from Blau and Scott, *Formal Organizations*, pp. 43, 55, with some changes.

[9] Dennis Hannon, "Kirkwood Police Officers Now Empowered by Union," *Webster-Kirkwood Times*, June 15, 2018, no page number, https://www.timesnewspapers.com/webster-kirkwoodtimes/news/kirkwood-police-officers-now-empowered-by-union/article_cd7b150a-0c87-57b5-9445-b1ff18f08401.html, accessed June 3, 2019.

[10] Daniel A. Wren, *The Evolution of Management Thought* (New York: Ronald Press, 1972), p. 112.

[11] Ibid., p. 114.

[12] Ibid., pp. 114–115.

[13] See the testimony of F. W. Taylor Before the Special Committee of the House of Representatives Hearings to Investigate Taylor and Other Systems of Shop Management, January 25, 1912, p. 1387.

[14] Wren, *Evolution of Management Thought*, p. 115.

[15] Frederick Winslow Taylor, *Principles of Scientific Management*, monograph, 1911.

[16] See Frederick W. Taylor, *Shop Management* (New York: Harper & Brothers, 1911), for a discussion of this concept.

[17] Ibid., p. 126.

[18] Lisa Riordan Seville, "Why Does a City with 600 Residents Need 14 Cops?" *NBC News* (September 7, 2014), pp. 1–2, http://www.nbcnews.com/storyline/michael-brown-shooting/why-does-city-600-residents-need-14-cops-n197676 (accessed August 22, 2015).

[19] Wren, *Evolution of Management Thought*, p. 132. Not only did Bethlehem Steel abandon the system, but it also fired Taylor.

[20] Ibid., p. 131.

[21] Ibid.

[22] L. P. Alford, *Henry Lawrence Gantt* (Easton-Hive Management Series: No. 6, 1972; facsimile reprint of a 1934 edition by Harper and Brothers), pp. 207, 209.

[23] Sudhir Kakar, *Frederick Taylor: A Study in Personality and Innovation* (Cambridge, MA: MIT Press, 1973), p. 2.

[24] Fremont E. Kast and James E. Rosenzweig, *Contingency Views of Organization and Management* (Chicago: Science Research Associates, 1973), p. 7.

[25] Mary Jo Hatch with Ann L. Cunliffe, *Organization Theory* (New York: Oxford University Press, 2nd edition, 2006), p. 33.

[26] Robert Kanigel, *The One Best Way: Frederick Winslow Taylor and the Enigma of Efficiency* (New York: Viking Press, 1997).

[27] Katia Caldari, "Alfred Marshall's Critical Analysis of Scientific Management," *European Journal of the History of Economic Thought* 14, No. 1 (March 2007), pp. 55–78.

[28] Michael Crozier, *The Bureaucratic Phenomenon* (Chicago: University of Chicago Press, 1964), p. 3.

[29] Max Weber, *The Theory of Social and Economic Organization*, trans. A. M. Henderson and Talcott Parsons (New York: Free Press, 1947), p. 337.

[30] Ibid.

[31] Christopher Hood, "The 'New Public Management' in the 1980s: Variations on a Theme," *Accounting, Organization, and Society* 20, No. 2/3 (1995), p. 94.

[32] Wren, *Evolution of Management Thought*, p. 230.

[33] On this point, see Nicos P. Mouzelis, *Organization and Bureaucracy* (Chicago: Aldine, 1967), pp. 20–21 and footnote 29 of that work.

[34] H. H. Gerth and C. Wright Mills, *From Max Weber: Essays in Sociology* (New York: Oxford University Press, 1946), p. 50.

[35] Ibid., p. 328.

[36] In some departments, "Detective" is an assignment, but not a permanent rank. Likewise, Corporal may be a promotion or a Master Police Officer, (MPO), earned by completing three to five years of satisfactory service, satisfactorily completing a mandatory list of training courses, and passing a competency test(s). Illustratively, one of the authors was the primary consultant to the consolidation of a large metropolitan police department and a county police agency. In one, Corporal was a promotion to the first supervisory rank and in the other, the MPO was recognized as a highly skilled officer, but not a supervisor. Corporals may also be awarded the rank for being a Field Training Officer (FTO). That rank is worn

daily, but Corporals only received extra pay while functioning as an FTO.

[37] Ibid., pp. 330–332, with limited restatement for clarity.

[38] These two thoughts were influenced by William G. Scott, "Organization Theory: An Overview and Appraisal," *Academy of Management Journal* 4, No. 1 (April 1961), p. 166. Scott has published two "updates" of the original article, most recently in 2017.

[39] No author, "Automated Enforcement View," National Conference of State Legislatures, July 10, 2018, p. 1 with restatement.

[40] Rich Morin, et al., Behind the Badge, Pew Research Center, January 11, 2017, p. 64; https://assets. pewresearch.org/wp-content/uploads/sites/3/2017/01/06171402/Police-Report_FINAL_web.pdf (accessed December 17, 2019).

[41] SARA, community policing's problem-solving model, was covered in Chapter 2, "Policing Today" and needs no further discussion here.

[42] On this point, see Paul Henman, *Governing Electronically: E-Government and the Reconfiguration of Public Administration, Policy, and Power* (New York: Palgrave Macmillan, 2010).

[43] Zachary W. Oberfield, "Shaping the State: The Development of Street-Level Bureaucrats," Midwestern Political Science Association Annual Meeting, Washington, DC, 2008, p. 1.

[44] Ibid., pp. 3–4.

[45] Ibid., p. 6.

[46] Ibid., pp. 6, 16.

[47] Henri Fayol, *General and Industrial Management*, trans. Constance Storrs (London: Sir Isaac Pitman, 1949), p. vi.

[48] Ibid., pp. 19–41.

[49] Ibid., p. 34.

[50] Danial A. Wren, Arthur G. Bedian, and John D. Breeze, "The Foundations of Henri Fayol's Administrative Theory," *Management Decision* 40, No. 9 (2002), p. 917.

[51] The 1939 edition was coauthored, but the 1947 edition appeared under Mooney's name.

[52] Luther Gulick, "Notes on the Theory of Organization," in *Papers on the Science of Administration*, eds. Luther Gulick and L. Urwick (New York: August M. Kelley, a 1969 reprint of the 1937 edition), p. 13.

[53] Taylor, *Shop Management*, p. 184.

[54] Herbert A. Simon, *Administrative Behavior* (New York: Free Press, 1945), p. 20. For additional criticism of the principles approach, see Dwight Waldo, *The Administrative State* (New York: Ronald Press, 1948).

[55] Warren Bennis, "Organizational Developments and the Fate of Bureaucracy," *Industrial Management Review* 7, No. 2 (spring 1966), pp. 41–55.

[56] J. Hage, "An Axiomatic Theory of Organizations," *Administrative Science Quarterly* 10 (1965–1966), p. 305, table 4.

[57] Charles Perrow, *Complex Organizations* (Glenview, IL: Scott, Foresman, 1972), pp. 6–7.

[58] Ibid., pp. 11–12.

[59] Alvin W. Gouldner, "Metaphysical Pathos and the Theory of Bureaucracy," *American Political Science Review* 49 (June 1955), p. 501, as quoted by Goodsell, *The Case for Bureaucracy*, p. 12.

[60] As early as 1924, researchers from the National Academy of Sciences had experiments underway; for present purposes, the work at the Hawthorne plant is described following the arrival of Mayo.

[61] The designation of this study as the bank wiring study is also found in the literature; banks were telephone switchboards.

[62] There were actually two relay assembly test room studies, one following the other. The second involved a change in the wage incentive and confirmed the importance of the social group.

[63] F. J. Roethlisberger and William J. Dickson, *Management and the Worker* (Cambridge, MA: Harvard University Press, 1st edition, 1939), pp. 58–59, 180–183.

[64] Bertram M. Gross, *The Managing of Organizations* 1 (New York: Free Press, 1964), p. 163.

[65] Roethlisberger and Dickson, *Management and the Worker*, p. 522.

[66] Etzioni, *Modern Organizations*, pp. 34–37.

[67] Whitman Knapp, Chairman, "Commission to Investigate Allegations of Police Corruption and the City's Anti-Corruption Procedures," *Commission Report* (New York, 1972), pp. 4, 65; see also Herman Goldstein, *Police Corruption* (Washington, DC: Police Foundation, 1975).

[68] Also see H. W. Parsons, "What Caused the Hawthorne Effect?" *Administration and Society* 10 (November 1978), pp. 259–283, and Henry Lansberger, *Hawthorne Revisited* (Ithaca, NY: Cornell University Press, 1958).

[69] These points are drawn, with change, from William H. Knowles, "Human Relations in Industry: Research and Concepts," *California Management Review* 2, No. 2 (fall 1958), pp. 87–105.

[70] Etzioni, *Modern Organizations*, p. 39.

[71] Paul Vigna, "Job Satisfaction Among American Workers Continues to Rise, But There Are More Reasons than Salary: Poll," Patriot-News (Harrisburg, PA), September 2, 2019.

[72] Edward E. Lawler, *Motivation in Work Organizations* (Monterey, CA: Brooks/Cole, 1973), p. 62.

[73] John M. Zelenski, Steven A. Murphy, and David A. Jenkins, "The Happy-Productive Worker Thesis Revisited," *Journal of Happiness Studies* 9 (2008), p. 521.

[74] Youngyol Yim and Bryan D. Schafer, "Police and Their Perceived Image: How Community Influences Officers' Job Satisfaction," *Police Practice and Research* 10, No. 1 (February 2009), pp. 17–29.

[75] Holly A. Miller, Scott Mire, and Bitna Kim, "Predictors of Job Satisfaction Among Police Officers; Does Personality Matter?" *Journal of Criminal Justice* 37, No. 5, September 2009, pp. 419–426.

[76] Daisy Chu-Hsiiang Chang, Russell E. Johnson, and Robert G. Lord, "Moving Beyond Discrepancies: The Importance of Velocity as a Predictor of Satisfaction and Motivation," *Human Performance* 23, No. 1 (January/March 2010), pp. 58–80.

[77] Kathryn Wilkins and Magot Shields, "Employer-Provided Support Services and Job Dissatisfaction in Canadian Registered Nurses," *Nursing Research* 58, No. 4 (July/August 2009), pp. 255–263.

[78] Michael E. Milakovich and George J. Gordon, *Public Administration in America* (Belmont, CA: Wadsworth/Thomson, 2004), p. 165.

[79] A. H. Maslow, "A Theory of Human Motivation," *Psychological Review* 50 (July 1943), pp. 370–396.

[80] These five elements are identified in A. H. Maslow, *Motivation and Personality* (New York: Harper and Brothers, 1954), pp. 80–92. Maslow later added a sixth category, "metamotivation," but it never received substantial interest. See "A Theory of Metamotivation," *Humanitas* 4 (1969), pp. 301–343.

[81] Ibid., p. 91.

[82] No author, "Blue Max Award," *Flying Wheel* 57, No. 1 (spring 2019), p. 1; www.statepatrol.ohio/doc/57-1.pdf (accessed January 23, 2019).

[83] Chris Argyris, *Personality and Organization: The Conflict Between System and the Individual* (New York: Harper and Brothers, 1957), pp. 58–66.

[84] Ibid., pp. 76–122.

[85] Chris Argyris, *Integrating the Individual and the Organization* (New York: John Wiley & Sons, 1964), p. 3.

[86] For extended treatment of this subject, see ibid., pp. 146–191.

[87] Ibid., p. 147.

[88] Douglas McGregor, *The Human Side of Enterprise* (New York: McGraw-Hill, 1960), p. 6. See also Louis A. Allen, "M for Management: Theory Y Updated," *Personnel Journal* 52, No. 12 (1973), pp. 1061–1067.

[89] Ibid., p. 7.

[90] Ibid., pp. 33–57.

[91] Warren G. Bennis, *Changing Organizations* (New York, New York: McGraw-Hill Education, 1966), p. 77.

[92] Walter Nord, "Beyond the Teaching Machine: The Neglected Area of Operant Conditioning in the Theory and Practice of Management," *Organizational Behavior and Human Performance* 4 (November 1969), pp. 375—401; see also Lyman Porter, "Job Attitudes in Management," *Journal of Applied Psychology* 46 (December 1962), pp. 375–384; and Douglas Hall and Khalil Nougaim, "An Examination of Maslow's Need Hierarchy in an Organizational Setting," *Organizational Behavior and Human Performance* 3 (February 1968), pp. 12–35.

[93] Maslow, *Motivation and Personality*, pp. 79–80. Also see, David L. Rennie, "Two Thoughts on Abraham Maslow," *Journal of Humanistic Psychology* 48, No. 4 (October 2008), pp. 445–448.

[94] Abraham Maslow, *Eupsychian Management: A Journal* (Homewood, IL: Dorsey Press, 1965), pp. 55–56.

[95] Frank K. Gibson and Clyde E. Teasley, "The Humanistic Model of Motivation: A Review of Research Support," *Public Administration Review* 33, No. 1 (Jan–Feb, 1973), p. 92.

[96] Ansfried B. Weinert, "Testing Argyris' Theory of Organizational Behavior," *Scandinavian Journal of Management Studies* 3, No. 1 (1986), pp. 26–27.

[97] Ibid., p. 41.

[98] Wren, *Evolution of Management Thought*, p. 324. Lewin lived in this country for the 15 years preceding his death in 1947.

[99] George C. Homans, *The Human Group* (New York: Harcourt Brace, 1950), pp. 81–130.

[100] Clint Fuhs, "Toward an Integral Approach to Organization Theory," unpublished paper, p. 6, by permission. Also see ClintFuhs.com.

[101] Michael T. Hannan and John Freeman, "The Population Ecology of Organizations," *American Sociological Review* 82, No. 5 (March 1977), p. 960. Some of the disappearances were from mergers and name changes.

[102] Chris Argyris, "Double Loop Learning in Organizations," *Harvard Business Review* (September/October 1977), p. 116. Also see Crank and Giacomazzi, "A Sheriff's Office as a Learning Organization."

[103] Daniel Katz and Robert Kahn, *The Social Psychology of Organization*, 2nd ed. (New York: John Wiley & Sons, 1978), pp. 23–30, with some change.

[104] The thoughts in this paragraph are taken with restatement from Francis Amagoh, "Perspectives on Organizational Change: Systems and Complexity Theories," *The Public Sector Innovation Journal* 13, No. 3 (2008), pp. 1–7, an online peer-reviewed journal.

[105] Timothy L. Snellnow, Matthew W. Seeger, and Robert R. Ulmer, "Chaos Theory, Informational Needs, and Natural Disasters," *Journal of Applied Communication Research* 30, No. 4 (November 2002), p. 276.

[106] T. Burns and G. M. Stalker, *The Management of Innovation* (London: Tavistock, 1968).

[107] John R. Hollenback, et al., "Structural Contingency Theory and Individual Differences," *Journal of Applied Psychology* 87, No. 3 (2002), p. 599.

[108] J. Pfeffer and G. Salancik, *The External Control of Organizations* (New York: Harper & Row, 1978).

[109] Hatch with Cunliffe, *Organization Theory*, p. 83.

[110] Guy Peters, *Institutional Theory in Political Science: The New Institutionalism*, 2nd ed. (New York: Continuum, 2nd edition, 2005), pp. 6–10.

[111] James G. March and Johan P. Olsen, "The New Institutionalism: Organizational Factors in Political Life," *American Political Science Review* 78, No. 3 (September 1984), p. 734.

[112] James F. Wolf, "Public Administration's Multiple Institutionalized Framework," *Public Organization Review: A Global Journal*, No. 5 (2005), p. 183.

[113] On this point see Seth Abrutyn, "Toward a General Theory of Institutional Authority," *Sociological Theory* 27, No. 4 (December 2009), pp. 449–465.

[114] Hans Jagers, Wendy Jansen, and Wichard Steebakkers, "Characteristics of Virtual Organizations," in Pascal Sieber and Joachim Griese, Editors, *Organizational Virtualness* (Bern, Switzerland: Institute of Informational Systems, 1998), p. 65.

[115] Gerard R. Murphy and Chuck Wexler, with Heather J. Davies and Martha Plotkin, "Managing a Multijurisdictional Case," Identifying the Lessons Learned from the Sniper Investigation (Washington, DC: Police Executive Research Forum, 2006), p. V.

[116] Ibid., p. 113.

[117] Ibid., pp. 20–21.

[118] Ibid., p. 23.

[119] Ibid., p. 22.

[120] E. C. Tolman, "Cognitive Maps in Rats and Men," *Psychological Review* 55, No. 4 (1948), pp. 189–208.

[121] L. Douglas Kiel, *Managing Chaos and Complexity in Government* (San Francisco: Jossey-Bass, 1994).

[122] Snellnow, Seeger, and Ulmer, "Chaos Theory, Informational Needs, and Natural Disasters," p. 271.

[123] Ibid.

[124] E. Sam Overman, "The New Sciences of Administration: Chaos and Quantum Theory," *Public Administration Review* 56, No. 5 (Sep.–Oct., 1996), p. 487.

[125] Jeffrey W. Goltz, "Determinants of Performance of Police Organizations in the State of Florida: An Evidence Based Confirmatory Approach," *International Journal of Public Policy* 3, No. 5/6 (2008), table 2, pp. 423 and 428.

[126] Ibid.

[127] Lex Donaldson, *American Anti-Management Theories of Organization: A Critique of Paradigm Proliferation* (New York: Cambridge University Press, 1995).

## CHAPTER SIX

ORGANIZATIONAL DESIGN

Learning Objectives

1. Explain the principle of hierarchy as it relates to organizational design.
2. Describe the concept of span of management.
3. Distinguish between vertical and horizontal differentiation.
4. Discuss the differences between tall organizational structures and flat organizational structures.
5. List and describe four basic types of police organizational design.
6. Discuss the major crime factors that impact investigative function; list the various models of investigative style.
7. Identify the basic causes for tension between line and staff and suggest strategies to be used as solutions.
8. Describe the characteristics of an informal organization.

INTRODUCTION

IN CHAPTER 5, ORGANIZATIONAL THEORY,
*we discussed the major theoretical concepts
associated with organizations and the ways in
which they function. In this chapter, we will see how
these theories are applied in police organizations.
The topics we will be specifically discussing are
(1) the ways in which police administrators can
modify or design their organizations in order to
fulfill their missions; (2) the principle of hierarchy,
which requires each lower level within the
organization to be supervised by a higher level;
(3) the differences between the span of control
and span of management; (4) some of the more
common ways in which activities and personnel are
grouped within a police department; (5) the impact
of community policing and intelligence-led policing
(ILP) philosophies on organizational structure; (6)
the placement of the investigative function within
the organizational design; (7) the organizational
differences between municipal departments
and sheriff's departments; (8) understanding the
importance of line and staff relationships; why there
are sometimes problems and how they can be
resolved; and (9) the importance of understanding
the informal organization and its potential impact
on the formal organization.*

ORGANIZING: AN OVERVIEW

Police administrators modify or design the structure of their organization in order to fulfill the mission that has been assigned to the police. An organizational chart reflects the formal structure of task and authority relationships determined to be most suited to accomplishing the police mission. However, within the need to accomplish the mission, there can also be accommodations of a law enforcement executive's preferences for the arrangements of units in a particular way.

This reality explains both the similarities across law enforcement organizations of a similar type and their diversity. Stated more simply, while there are some underlying concepts, there is also "more than one way to skin a cat."

The process of determining this formal structure of task and authority relationships is termed **organizing**. The major concerns in organizing are (1) identifying what jobs need to

be done, such as conducting the initial investigation, performing the latent or follow-up investigation, or providing for the custody of physical evidence seized at the scene of a crime; (2) determining how to group the jobs, such as those responsible for patrol, investigation, and the operation of the property room; (3) forming grades of authority, such as officer, detective, corporal, sergeant, lieutenant, and captain; and (4) equalizing responsibility and authority, illustrated by the example that if a sergeant has the responsibility to supervise a team of detectives, that sergeant must have sufficient authority to discharge that responsibility properly or he or she cannot be held accountable for results[1] (see Figure 6.1).

SPECIALIZATION IN POLICE AGENCIES

Central to this process of organizing is determining the nature and extent of specialization. Some 2,300 years ago, Plato observed that "each thing becomes … easier when one man, exempt from other tasks, does one thing."[2] **Specialization**, or the division of labor, is also one of the basic features of traditional organizational theory.[3] As discussed more fully later in this chapter, specialization produces different groups of functional responsibilities, and the jobs allocated to meet those different responsibilities are staffed with people who are believed to be especially qualified to perform those jobs, for example, by experience and training. Thus, specialization is crucial to effectiveness and efficiency in large organizations. However, specialization makes the organizational environment more complex by complicating communication, by increasing the number of units from which cooperation must be obtained, and by creating conflict among differing interests and loyalties. Also, specialization creates greater need for coordination and, therefore, additional hierarchy and can lead to the creation of narrow jobs that stifle the willingness or capacity of personnel to work energetically in support of broader goals. Police departments are not insensitive to the problems of specialization and attempt through various actions to keep the interest and motivation of employees at a high level. Personnel can be rotated to different jobs, they can be given additional responsibilities that challenge them, they can be involved in organizational problem solving, and police departments can experiment with different forms of organizational structures. Although specialization is an essential feature of large-scale organizations, maintaining its positive impact requires thoughtful action.

One of the first police executives to explore systematically the relationship between specialization and the organizational structure was O. W. Wilson.[4] He noted that most small departments do not need to be concerned with widely developed specialization because their patrol officer is a jack-of-all-trades. Moreover, specialized assistance can be obtained from a neighboring large department or a state investigative agency. Conversely, in large departments, the volume of particular tasks, for example, homicide or cybercrime investigation, virtually

FIGURE 6.1 ▶ Grades of authority are designated by rank, starting with the police officer and following the chain of command up to Chief of Police. (Marmaduke St. John/Alamy Stock Photo)

require specialized units.[5] Specialization presents a number of advantages for large departments:

Placement of responsibility—The responsibility for the performance of a given task can be placed on specific units or individuals. For instance, a traffic division is responsible for the investigation of all traffic accidents, and a patrol division is responsible for all requests for general police assistance.

Development of expertise—A narrow field of interest, attention, or skill can be the subject of a specialized unit. For instance, many police agencies have highly skilled special weapons and tactics (SWAT) teams that train regularly to respond to critical incidents, such as terrorist activities, hostage situations, or serving high-risk search/arrest warrants (see Figure 6.2). Advanced training in this area yields increased officer safety and produces a high degree of expertise. Specialization is also helpful during the investigation of narrowly defined, technical crimes, such as computer fraud, arson, and bombings.

Promotion of group esprit de corps—Any group of specially trained individuals sharing similar job tasks and, to some degree, depend on each other for success tends to form a highly cohesive unit with high morale.

Increased efficiency and effectiveness—Specialized units show a higher degree of proficiency in job task responsibility. For instance, a white-collar fraud unit will ordinarily be more successful in investigating complex computer fraud than a general detective division.[6]

Specialization appears to be a sure path to operational effectiveness. It allows each employee to acquire expertise in one area, so as to maximize his or her contribution to the overall department.

However, as noted earlier, specialization has also been associated with increased friction and conflict within police departments. As units such as traffic, detective, and SWAT teams develop, an increase in job factionalism and competition also develops. The result may be a decrease in a department's overall job performance as individuals within each group show loyalty primarily or only to their unit. This traditional problem can be observed in the relationship between patrol officers and detectives. Patrol officers are sometimes reluctant to give information to detectives because they feel detectives will take credit for their work. Specialization also increases the number of administrative and command relationships, complicating the overall organizational structure. Additionally, each unit requires a competent leader. In some instances, this competent leader must also be a qualified specialist. A thorny problem here is when the specialist does not qualify for the rank usually needed to head a major unit. An example of such a problem is observed in the staffing of an air patrol unit in which the commanding officer may be a lieutenant or a sergeant because that individual is the highest-ranking officer with a pilot's license. In this case, the level of expertise (high) does not coincide with the level of rank (lower), which may cause difficulties when the individual tries to deal with other commanding officers of units who hold the rank of captain or major.

Finally, specialization may hamper the development of a well-rounded police program. As specialization increases, the resources available for general uniformed patrol invariably decrease, often causing a lopsided structure wherein the need for general police services becomes second to the staffing of specialized programs and units.[7] When this happens, the great danger is that so many positions are siphoned off from patrol, which is the primary line unit, that its ability to provide services is crippled, and response times on calls and public dissatisfaction with the police increase.

FIGURE 6.2 ▶ Specialization occurs when unique tasks require extensive and detailed training, such as helicopter units, search and rescue units, and SWAT operations. (Enigma/Alamy Stock Photo)

THE PRINCIPLE OF HIERARCHY

This discussion of the principle of hierarchy builds on its coverage in Chapter 5, Organizational Theory. The **principle of hierarchy** requirement that each lower level of organization be supervised by a higher level results not only in the use of multiple spans of control but also in different grades of authority that increase at each successively higher level of the organization. This authority flows downward in the organization as a formal grant of power from the chief of police to those selected for leadership positions. These different grades of authority produce the chain of command.[8] Although there are many similarities from one department to another, the American police service does not have a uniform terminology for grades of authority and job titles.[9] In recent years, some police departments have moved away from using traditional military-style ranks and have adopted, instead, alternative titles as summarized in Table 6.1. However, in many departments, there remains a distinction between rank and title.[10] In these, *rank* denotes one's place in terms of grade of authority or the rank hierarchy, whereas *title* indicates an assignment. Where this distinction is made, a person holding the title of division commander or director, for example, may be a captain, major, or colonel in terms of the rank hierarchy. Although some smaller departments have flattened or made the organizational structure less tall be eliminating one or two ranks, the complexity of large police agencies seemingly requires a taller hierarchy to coordinate its many parts. For instance, several departments have

eliminated the rank of "captain" and placed more responsibility on deputy chiefs and lieutenants. This is particularly true in departments that have adopted a more "community-based" approach to policing.[11] Then too, over the last two decades, several large police departments have merged with the surrounding county to become **city-county consolidated governments**. Policing in these types of governmental structures reflects various ranks and structures. For instance, the county sheriff's rank and title names continue in the Las Vegas, Nevada Metropolitan Police Department, whereas the chief executive of the police in the Louisville, Kentucky Metropolitan Police Department is referred to as the Chief and Director of Police Services. In Kansas City, Missouri, the consolidated police department maintained the more traditional rank and titles of a city department with the Chief of Police at the helm of that agency[12] (refer to Table 6.1).

SPAN OF CONTROL VERSUS SPAN OF MANAGEMENT

The term **span of management** instead of "span of control" is used to describe the number of personnel a supervisor can personally manage effectively. The term "span of management" is broader than "span of control" and encompasses factors relating to an individual's capacity to oversee the activities of others directly, such as the police manager's ability, experience, and level of energy.

| **TABLE 6.1** TRADITIONAL POLICE RANKS VERSUS ALTERNATIVE TITLES ||
Traditional Ranks	**Alternative Titles (Including County Agencies)**
Chief of police	Commissioner/Director/Superintendent/Sheriff
Deputy chief	Assistant director/Undersheriff/Chief Deputy Sheriff
Colonel	Division director/Inspector/Commander
Major	Inspector/Commander
Captain	Commander
Lieutenant	Manager
Sergeant	Supervisor
Detective	Investigator/Inspector
Corporal	Senior officer/Master patrol officer
Officer	Public safety officer/Agent/Deputy Sheriff

"Span of management" more suitably describes the process of the number of personnel a supervisor can manage than does the term "span of control." Control is only one aspect of the management process. The term "span of management" encompasses more of the factors relating to the problem of an individual's capacity to oversee the activities of others.

How wide a span of management is depends on many factors. Some state that the ideal number of subordinates reporting to a supervisor is 8 to 12, but the number varies widely depending upon a number of factors[13] (see Table 6.2).

Although many law enforcement agencies prefer lower spans of management, with multiple layers of hierarchy, as indicated earlier, there is some movement toward flatter organizational structures with wider spans of management. Organizational humanists argue that this type of structure can produce better communication within the organization, increase the sense of fiscal and personal responsibility, provide greater organizational flexibility, and increase delegation by supervisors. Humanists also hold that employees also favor flatter structures with higher spans of management because they receive less detailed and micromanaged supervision. Arguably, when this occurs (1) personnel have more authority and responsibility, (2) feel trusted by their supervisors, and (3) employees have a good environment in which to grow, and therefore become more fulfilled and satisfied with their work.[14]

ORGANIZATIONAL STRUCTURE AND DESIGN

Tansik and Elliot suggest that, when we consider the formal **structure** (or pattern of relationships) of an organization, we typically focus on two areas:

1. The formal relationship and duties of personnel in the organization, which include the organizational chart and job descriptions.

2. The set of formal rules, policies, procedures, and controls that guide the behavior of organizational members within the framework of the formal relationships and duties.[15]

Organizational design focuses on two spatial levels of differentiation—vertical and horizontal—depicted in Figure 6.3. **Vertical differentiation** is based on levels of authority, or positions holding formal power within the organization; Table 6.3 reflects one range of vertical differentiation found in police agencies. Persons with vertical authority have the power to assign work and exercise control to ensure job performance.[16] In Figure 6.3, the deputy chief has a span of management of three, all of whom are captains and to whom he or she can give assignments and expect performance.

Quick Facts: Organizational Structure Impacts Police Misconduct and Excellence in Police Service

A study of nearly 500 police departments nationwide revealed that the existence of a full-time professional standards/internal affairs unit, and relevant in-service training tends to reduce both the number of complaints against officers and the number of sustained complaints against them. An organizational structure that provides closer supervision of officers may also produce similar results. A 2016 study reconfirmed these findings and added that police agencies should "consider seeking accreditation by the Accreditation for Law Enforcement Agencies ... as a method of demonstrating their commitment to excellence in law enforcement."[17]

TABLE 6.2 FACTORS IMPACTING THE SPAN OF MANAGEMENT
Factors Enabling an Increased Span of Management
Factor 1: The simplicity of the work The simpler the task, the less need there is for supervision. The more diversified, complex tasks require more supervision. Traditionally, the patrol function has a larger span of control since the work is similar on each beat, and one supervisor can oversee the work conducted on several beats.
Factor 2: Efficient use of information technology Readily available information technologies can obtain needed information to do the job as well as receive direction from supervisor increases the span of control. In-car computers, cameras, and individual communication systems enable officers to be in constant touch with supervisors.
Factor 3: The quality, skills, and capabilities of subordinates Recruiting quality employees having the necessary education, training, and experience to be able to learn and do the assigned work requires providing less supervision by the department. In contrast, hiring the less educated and unskilled subordinates will require extensive coaching by the supervisors to teach these employees the job.
Factor 4: The skills and capabilities of the supervisor Departments that invest in developing supervisors and managers find that the more knowledgeable and skillful the supervisor—along with the ability to clearly communicate the work—the more people he or she can supervise.
Factor 5: The quality of the department's training program Subordinates fully knowledgeable of the laws, procedures, and administrative processes require less supervision.
Factor 6: The harmony of the workforce When the subordinates are of like minds and working toward the same objectives in harmony, fewer incidents require supervision intervention.
Factors Narrowing the Span of Management
Factor 1: Change taking place in the work environment When the work is forever changing, and new procedures and processes are introduced into the work, the greater the need for narrow supervision.
Factor 2: Dispersed workforce, either by time or geographically The greater the geographic distances and the difference in time that the force works, the smaller the supervision ratio. This is often observed in the investigative division, which frequently requires more supervisors in relation to the number of investigators.
Factor 3: New and inexperienced workforce Law enforcement in the next few years is experiencing significant retirement numbers in the supervisory and management ranks. This requires promoting younger persons with lesser experience directing the work of others.
Factor 4: Administrative requirements The greater the administrative burden on each level of management, the greater the need for a narrow span of control. Jobs free of bureaucratic requirements can focus on the work.
Factor 5: The extent of coordination When employees' work must be coordinated and the subordinates depend upon each other to accomplish the work, the narrower the supervision requirements. This relationship exists in many of the tactical and technical positions in a police department.
Factor 6: Employees' expectations The higher the employees' expectations for feedback, career and development coaching, and management interaction, the narrower the requirement for supervision. Many observe that the new workforce entering policing today looks for immediate feedback from management on their progress.

Source: Adapted from Troy Lane, "Span of Control for Law Enforcement Agencies," *The Police Chief* 73, No. 10 (October 2006). Retrieved and adapted on January 8, 2020; http://policechiefmagazine.org/magazine/index.cfm?fuseaction=display&article_id=1022&issue_id=102006.

Horizontal differentiation, on the other hand, is usually based on activity. However, in some cases, horizontal differentiation is based on specific projects or even geographical distribution. For instance, many state police departments are responsible for large geographical areas. Their organizational structure often reflects horizontal differentiation based on location rather than function. Some of the more common ways in which activities of personnel are grouped within a police organization (on a horizontal dimension) are as follows:

Grouping by clientele—The simplest method of grouping within a police department is by clientele. Personnel are assigned by the type of client served, such as juvenile division, senior citizen crime detail, mayor's security unit, gang squad, and human trafficking unit. Each group focuses on the needs of a special clientele, which can be either temporary or permanent. In this manner, officers become familiar with the specific enforcement problems and patterns associated with different client populations.

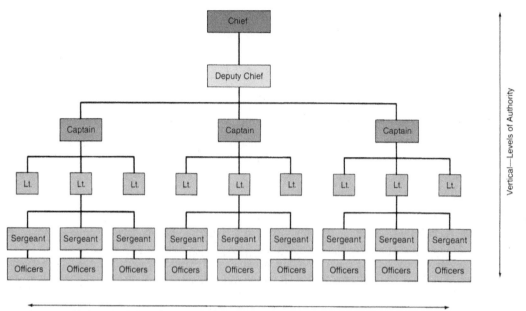

FIGURE 6.3 ▶ Organizational chart showing vertical and horizontal levels of differentiation. In some departments, especially large ones, a number of other ranks may be present within the chart.

Grouping by style of service—A police department usually has a patrol bureau and a detective bureau. The grouping of uniformed patrol officers on the one hand and of plainclothes investigators on the other illustrates how the former are grouped by the nature of their services (conspicuous, preventive patrol, and preliminary investigations) and how the latter are grouped also by this same principle (follow-up investigations). This form of grouping also takes advantage of specialization of knowledge and skill and permits the pinpointing of responsibility for results.

Grouping by geography—Where activities are widespread over any given area, it may be beneficial or even necessary to provide local command. Instances of this type of operation are large-city precincts or district-type operations and state police/patrol posts that are located throughout a state. An example of this appears in Figures 6.4. Even in the

headquarters building, activities that are related usually share the same floor. Instances of this arrangement are records, communications, and crime analysis in close proximity to each other. This permits supervisors to become familiar with operating problems of related units and to coordinate the various efforts by more direct and immediate control.

Grouping by time—This grouping occurs when the need to perform a certain function or service is greater than one normal work period for a single shift, for example, the difference between one 8-hour shift of services versus grouping several shifts together to provide 24-hour patrol services. Grouping by time tends to create problems of coordination and unity of direction because top administrators work normal day hours, whereas many of their officers perform their functions on the evening and midnight shifts. The need to delegate sufficient authority becomes

TABLE 6.3 LINE, AUXILIARY/SUPPORT, AND ADMINISTRATIVE STAFF FUNCTIONS

| Line | Staff | |
	Auxiliary/Support	Administrative
• Uniformed patrol	Crime laboratory	Personnel
• Investigations	Detention and jail	Training
• Vice and narcotics	Records	Planning and research
• Traffic enforcement	Identification	Fiscal/budgeting
• Juvenile service	Communications	Legal services
	Property maintenance, transportation, and vehicle maintenance	Media relations

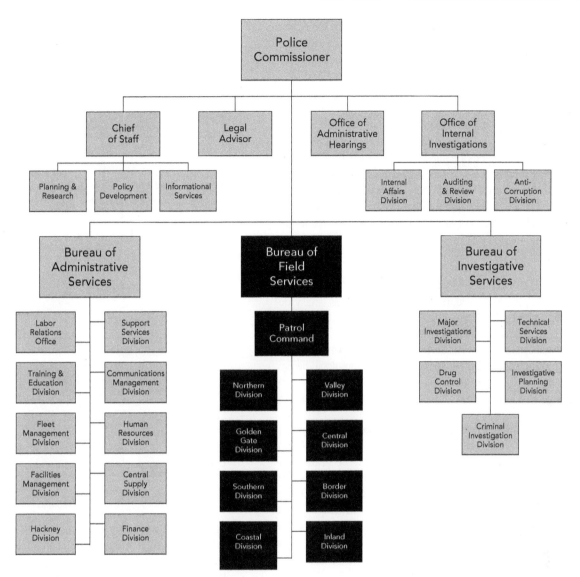

FIGURE 6.4A ▶ Organizational chart for the California Highway Patrol (Field) with modification, showing five levels of control. (Courtesy of the California Highway Patrol, Sacramento, CA)

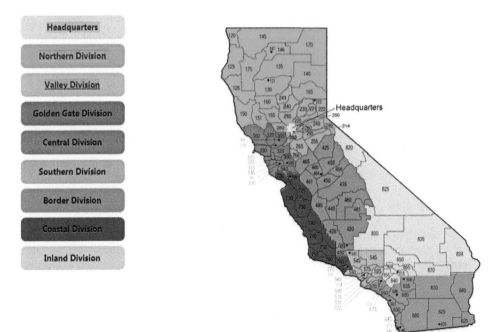

FIGURE 6.4B ▶ Geographical organization of area offices for the California Highway Patrol. (Courtesy of the California Highway Patrol, Sacramento, CA)

critical under these circumstances. For example, police policy manuals often or usually require the approval of a Lieutenant or Captain before a Sergeant can suspend an officer. In some exigencies, such as an officer getting drunk on duty and becoming a danger to himself and others, a policy manual may authorize a Sergeant to immediately suspend the officer and then notify their appropriate senior official.

Grouping by process—This involves the placing of all personnel who use a given type of equipment in one function. Examples include a word processing center, crime laboratory personnel placed in a section to handle certain types of scientific equipment, and automotive maintenance units. This type of grouping lends itself to expertise involving a single process and makes the most efficient use of costly equipment.[18]

Top-Down vs. Bottom-Up Approaches

The level of complexity within a police organization is largely determined by the amount of horizontal and vertical differentiation that exists.[19] Size is often, but not necessarily, related to complexity. Some organizations, even relatively small police departments, can be highly differentiated and quite complex in organizational design.

According to Hodge and Anthony,[20] the differentiation process can occur in two basic ways in police agencies: (1) bottom-up or (2) top-down.

The bottom-up, or synthesis, approach focuses on combining tasks into larger and larger sets of tasks (see Figure 6.5A). To illustrate, an officer's task set may primarily be in the relatively small geographical zone he or she patrols. The task set of Sergeants is to supervise squads of patrol officers. Patrol Lieutenants may supervise a number of Patrol Sergeants, while a Captain often commands an entire shift city-wide. In turn, the Major in charge of the Patrol Division leads all three Captains and is responsible for all patrol services, 24 hours a day.

The top-down, or analysis, approach looks at the overall work of the organization at the top and splits this into increasingly more specialized tasks as one moves from the top to the bottom of the organization (see Figure 6.5B). The top-down approach considers the overall police mission—to protect and to serve the public.

At the top level of a police agency, this can be defined into various administrative tasks, such as representing the department to the larger environment (e.g., elected and

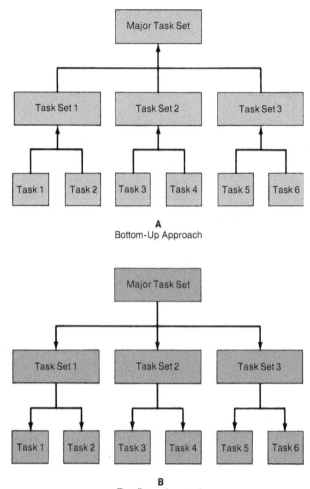

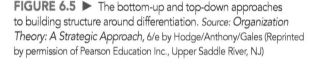

FIGURE 6.5 ▶ The bottom-up and top-down approaches to building structure around differentiation. *Source: Organization Theory: A Strategic Approach,* 6/e by Hodge/Anthony/Gales (Reprinted by permission of Pearson Education Inc., Upper Saddle River, NJ)

appointed officials and the public), envisioning goals, setting priorities, and presenting the department's budget request. Middle management/leaders perform activities such as setting goals with subordinates, conducting studies that improve the police department, writing policies for the approval of the command staff, preparing unit reports, implementing improvements

---

Quick Facts: Bottom-Up Approaches Improve Performance and Officer Morale

The organization of police departments along hierarchical, classical management lines makes it difficult to solve common internal problems in policing, such as performance improvement, complaints against officers, and low morale. The main reason for this fact is that top-down reform invites resistance from rank-and-file officers who feel that their ideas are disregarded and not valuable to leadership. By contrast, individual approaches to officers from supervisors that reflected a more bottom-up perspective was much more successful to organizational effectiveness and efficiency. Bottom-up approaches tend to harness the experience of individual officers, produce an often-needed team-oriented environment with officer squads, reduce opposition to innovation in police strategies and operations, generally increase overall officer morale, and most surprisingly, reduce the number of incidence of use of excessive force in metropolitan police departments.[21]

within their domain, and writing performance appraisals. At the very bottom of a large police department, tasks sets are illustrated by crime scene processing, evidence intake and storage, examining tool marks in the crime lab, follow-up investigation on burglaries, surveillance of open air drug markets, analysis of crime patterns, patrol, investigate traffic and pedestrian accidents, and serve as field training officers.

Both approaches are commonly found in police organizations. The top-down analysis is often used in growing organizations because it is easy to visualize the set of tasks to be accomplished and then to break these sets down into specific tasks and subtasks. The bottom-up approach is often used during periods of retrenchment when organizational growth has declined because combining tasks such as those found in patrol and traffic bureaus can consolidate jobs or even units.

The policing style or philosophy can also impact top-down or bottom-up approaches. This is exemplified in philosophical changes from community and problem-oriented policing to ILP over the past decade. Whereas community and problem-oriented policing is a bottom-up philosophy that places street officers at the forefront of problem identification and subsequent solution, CompStat and ILP are much more hierarchical and emphasize the top-down approach. Increasing accountability at supervisory and command levels is an important element of CompStat, often characterized by strong role definitions, tighter lines of control, and smaller spans of management. And in ILP, criminal intelligence flows up the organizational pyramid to executives who set priorities and develop strategies aimed at prevention and enforcement and then communicate these priorities back down the organizational chain for operational tasking.[22]

Some organizations have narrow spans of management with tall structures and many levels, whereas others reduce the number of levels by widening the span of management at each level. Many narrower spans of control make a police department "taller." The California Highway Patrol (CHP) appears to have five levels, as shown in Figure 6.4A. These levels are commissioner, deputy commissioner, assistant commissioner, field division chief, and area office commander. From a more functional perspective, each area office also has a chain of command consisting of four layers—captain, lieutenant, sergeant, and officer. Thus, when the rank layers in the area offices are considered, the CHP is a tall organization with a number of different levels of authority. Seven to nine levels of rank are fairly typical of large police organizations. Figure 6.4B displays each CHP area office by geographical grouping, as described earlier in this chapter.

The complexity of a police department is increased by the proliferation of levels because they can negatively affect communication up and down the chain of command. For example, during urban riots, police departments found that an initially small incident grew rapidly beyond the ability of a small group of officers to control it. The process of getting approval from senior police officials to send additional officers took so long that, by the time the officers arrived at the scene, the once-small incident had grown into an uncontrollable riot. Thus,

most departments shifted the authority to deploy large numbers of police officers downward, in some cases all the way to the individual police officer at the scene. This example illustrates several important principles:

1. Narrow spans of control make police departments taller.
2. Taller organizations are complex and may react slowly during crisis situations, as effective communication is hampered by the number of different levels present within the chain of command.
3. Successful tall departments must develop policies and procedures that overcome problems created by increased complexity.

Many police agencies, such as the Phoenix, Arizona Police Department, have redesigned their organizations to reflect larger spans of control or management and, hence, flatter organizational structures. Figure 6.6 shows only three major organizational levels—chief, division, and bureau. Although this structure is flatter than that of the CHP, traditional grades of authority, such as commander, lieutenant, sergeant, and officer ranks, continue to exist in the Phoenix Police Department. With higher educational standards for entry-level police officers and efforts toward professionalism, police organizational structures may reflect additional changes of this nature. Ultimately, however, the capacity to flatten out police organizational structures depends to no small degree on reducing the number of traditional ranks, a movement sure to be met with resistance from the rank and file and unions because it means less opportunity for upward mobility.

McFarland[23] argues that flat structures associated with wider spans of control offer numerous advantages over the more traditional tall structures. First, they shorten lines of communication between the bottom and top levels. Communication in both directions is more likely to be faster and more timely. Second, the route of communication is more simple, direct, and clear than it is in tall organizations. Third, distortion in communication is minimized by a reduced number of people being involved. Fourth, and probably most important, flat structures are generally associated with employees with higher morale and job satisfaction as compared to employees in tall, structured organizations.

Flat structures do, however, place demanding pressures on supervisors, require high-caliber managers, and work best in organizations in which employees are held strictly accountable for measurable and objective results. Considering the role of the police and the continuing problems associated with evaluating police services, such a structure may cause inordinate stress on personnel. Top executives can attempt to direct the development of police agencies in such a way as to maintain structural balance. Some amount of hierarchy is needed for coordination, but the extremely tall police organization should be carefully scrutinized. In balance, no major city has successfully flattened out both the numbers of organizational layers or units and the traditional rank structure to any significant and continuing degree. Thus, any substantial flattening of a police organization is likely to be an experiment in organizational design rather than an institutionalized reform.

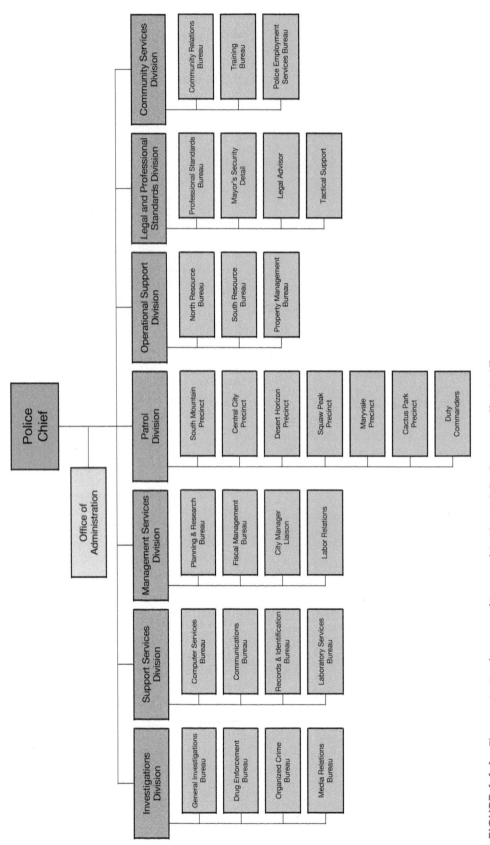

FIGURE 6.6 ▶ Flat organizational structure. (Courtesy of the Phoenix Police Department, Phoenix, AZ)

BASIC TYPES OF POLICE ORGANIZATIONAL DESIGN

Four basic structural types of design can be found within police organizations. They are line, line and staff, functional, and matrix. These types exist separately or in combination.

Line Structure

The **line structure** is the oldest, simplest, and clearest form of organizational design. As illustrated in Figure 6.7, authority flows from the top to the bottom of the organization in a clear and unbroken line, creating a set of superior- subordinate relations in a hierarchy commonly called the *chain of command*. A primary emphasis is placed on accountability by close adherence to the chain of command.

The term "line" originated with the military and was used to refer to units that were to be used to engage the enemy in combat. "Line" also refers to those elements of a police organization that perform the work the agency was created to handle. Stated somewhat differently, line units contribute directly to the accomplishment of the police mission. Thus, the primary line elements of a police department are uniformed patrol, criminal investigation, and traffic. Within police agencies, the line function can also be referred to as "operations," "field services," or a similar designation.

The pure line police organization does not have any supporting elements that are internal or part of it, such as personnel, media relations, training, or fiscal management. Instead, the line police organization uses its total resources to provide services directly to the public. Typically found only in small towns and small counties, the line is the most common type of police organization because of the sheer frequency of small jurisdictions. However, most police officers work in larger departments that retain the basic line elements but to which are added

various types of support units. These larger police departments are often referred to as the *line and staff* form of organization.

Line and Staff Structure

As more demands for services are placed on police departments, there is a need to add internal support functions, so that the line functions can continue to provide direct services to the public. The addition of support functions to the line elements produces a distinct organizational form: the **line and staff structure**. The addition of a staff component to the line structure offers a number of advantages because such units are helpful in the following:

1. Providing expert advice to line units in special knowledge areas as demonstrated by the opinions of legal advisors;
2. Relieving line managers from performing tasks they least prefer to do or are least qualified to do, such as financial management and providing legal guidance;
3. Achieving departmentwide conformity in activities that affect the entire organization, such as disciplinary procedures; and
4. Reducing or eliminating special problems, such as corruption, because of the greater expertise they bring to bear on the issue and the greater amount of time they have to devote to the problem.[24]

Staff functions are sometimes further broken down into two types: auxiliary or support and administrative staff. Under this arrangement, auxiliary/support units, such as communications and crime laboratory services, are charged with the responsibility of giving immediate assistance to the operations of line elements. In contrast, administrative staff units, such as personnel and training, provide services that are of less immediate assistance and are supportive of the entire police department. Table 6.3 identifies typical line, auxiliary/support, and administrative staff functions.

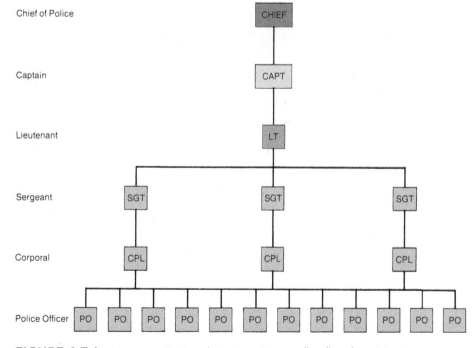

FIGURE 6.7 ▶ Line organizational structure in a small police department.

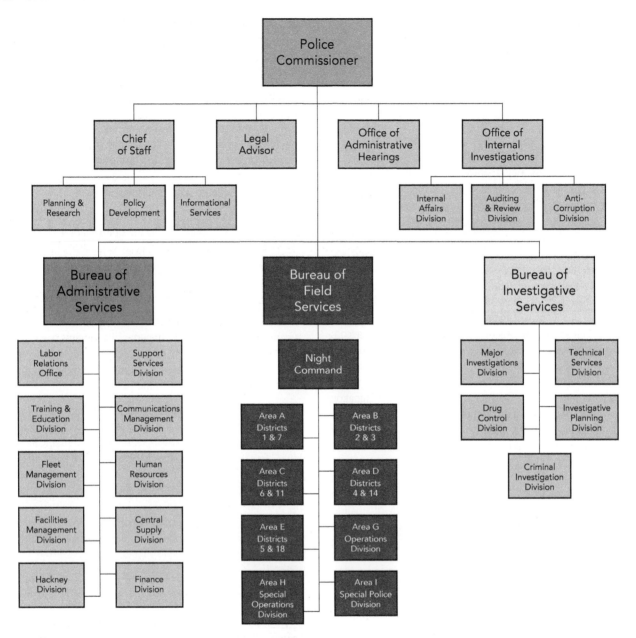

FIGURE 6.8 ▶ Line and staff structure in a police department. Note that line functions are grouped in the middle of the structure highlighted as "Bureau of Field Services." (Courtesy of the Boston, Massachusetts, Police Department)

Depending on factors such as the history of the police department and the chief's preferences, there is some variation as to how these functions are categorized. Less frequently, legislative enactments may establish the organizational structure, which is another source of variation in how functions are categorized.

Figure 6.8 shows a line and staff structure. In it, the Bureau of Field Services (composed of the patrol districts) is the "heart" or primary line function of the organization and is highlighted to show that purpose. The investigative services bureau is also a line function but smaller than the Bureau of Field Services. The Bureau of Administrative Services and upper-echelon offices represent staff functions within the organization. Note in Figure 6.8 that two types of staff members report directly to the chief of police: the generalist, illustrated by the chief of staff, and the specialist, illustrated by the legal advisor and internal investigations office.

Functional Structure

The **functional structure** is one means by which the line authority structure of an organization can be modified. Hodge and Johnson[25] state that functional structure "is a line and staff structure that has been modified by the delegation of management authority to personnel outside their normal spans of control." Figure 6.9 shows a police department in which the intelligence unit is responsible to three captains whose main responsibility is for other organizational units.

Some of the problems in police organizations can be reduced by using functional design. By requiring specific units to be responsible to a variety of other unit commanders, critical information is assured of reaching other line officers. Sharing is promoted, while competing loyalties are diminished. Good examples of functional design can be observed in police departments moving toward geographical responsibility for supervisors on a 24-hour basis. A commander or shift (watch) supervisor (often a lieutenant or Captain) assigned to the day watch may be responsible for solving violent street crimes (e.g., robberies) that occur in a specific area on all three shifts. However, officers on the evening and night shifts get their overall supervision from the Lieutenant or Captain assigned to their shifts, creating the potential for conflict between the orders from the day shift Captain on what strategies to use in combating violent crimes versus the orders that officers on the evening and night shifts get on the same subject from their own shift leaders. This creates more than a conflict between shift leaders because it causes confusion and some stress with officers as to whose orders they should follow.

Dallas and Fort Worth, Texas, as well as San Diego, California, are just a few departments that have noted these types of problems stemming from the implementation of geographical responsibility for managers, resulting in a functional design. In some areas, this type of formalized geographically based, or "geo" policing is referred to as **sector policing**. While the name might be different, the approach is still focused on providing a proactive and geographically based structure for police strategies, personnel deployment, and accountability.[26]

Box 6.1: Factors Influencing Law Enforcement Organizational Design[27]

While there are many similarities across the nation in the organizational structure of law enforcement agencies of roughly the same type and size, there is also an abundance of variation. The factors listed below illustrate how some different factors influence the way police agencies are designed/organized.

1. The mission of the agency, for example, a municipal police department versus a sheriff's office, port authority, airport, or mass transit law enforcement agency.

2. The agency's past experience with different organizational designs. Past changes that have succeeded or not achieved what was expected become part of the agency's legacy. "We already tried that and it didn't turn out so good."

3. The preferences of the Chief of Police, for example, some chiefs want the intelligence unit to report to their office so they can "be on top of things."

   Others want the number of units directly reporting to them kept them at an absolute minimum to allow them to focus on "the big picture."

4. The legal, political, social, and physical environment in which the agency operates.

   Some organizational structures are created by local ordinances, largely as a means of giving elected officials control over changes.

   A very active ministers' alliance in a town may create pressure for the police to closely monitor strip clubs, sex toy shops, and similar businesses, resulting in the creation of a Vice Control unit. A rural sheriff's office in Montana where there are many opportunities for year-round recreation in the backcountry must have a well-developed search and rescue capability. The impact of the physical environment is also illustrated by whether a city is primarily horizontal or vertical. Additionally, rivers, bridges, railroad tracks, and other environment characteristics dictate the boundaries of patrol zones.

5. The size of the population served and its demographics, for example, policing a retirement community is different than a city with a strong young demographic from which many crimes spring, such as those committed by gangs. The distribution or redistribution of a portion of the population within an agency's geographic area of responsibility coupled with the physical environment may require the establishment of substations/precincts, relocating them, or eliminating some. Actions that illustrate these possibilities include rehabilitation of old buildings in a business district for sale as apartments, rezoning of property from one type of use to another, annexations by a municipality of a portion of the county, and major hazardous waste contaminations all represent actions that could affect the delivery of police services. Hinkley, California, Gilman, Colorado, Picher, Oklahoma, and Niagara Falls, New York discovered significant hazardous waste contamination that closed neighborhoods or large portions of the city.

6. The number, types, and distribution of crimes, as well as the characteristics of the victims all impact the design of police departments. Many years ago, a special unit to investigate crime against juveniles was a novelty. Now, the principle that special populations may best be served by specialized units is well established.

   The evolution of this concept has produced Domestic Violence Units and a few departments have formed units to investigate crimes against lesbian, gay, bisexual, and transgender (LGBT) persons and their allied communities. As specialization increases, it often produces the need for the law enforcement agency to grow vertically creating the need for one or more new layers/levels in the organizational structure.

7. The degree to which the police introduce and rely on technology, such as automated license plate readers, photo traffic enforcement, license plate scanners, thermal imaging—useful in searching for lost persons and marijuana investigations, gunshot detection systems, and handheld spectroscopy devices that can identify powdery substances with great accuracy.

   A technology that is on the near horizon for actual use is RF Safe-Stop, which can electronically "confuse" the operating system of a fleeing car and cause it to stop. In tests, it has been effective at 50 meters/164 feet.

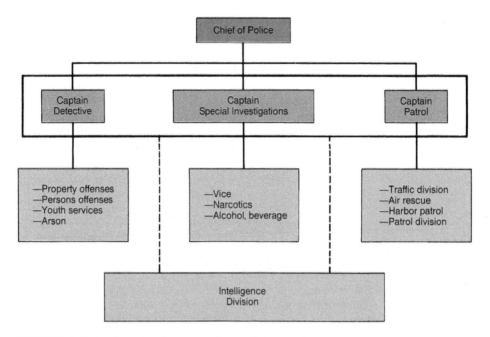

FIGURE 6.9 ▶ Functional structure in a police organization.

In conclusion, the major disadvantage of the functional design is that it increases organizational complexity. In Figure 6.9, members of the intelligence division receive instructions from several superiors. This can result in conflicting directions, and thus extensive functionalized structures are seldom found in police agencies. Law enforcement executives should explore the use of the functional design but be ever cautious of the confusion that can result if the process is not properly monitored and controlled.

Matrix Structure

One interesting form of organizational design is variously referred to as the **matrix (or grid) structure**. In some cases, the style has been inclusively part of "project" or "product" management. The essence of matrix structure is in the assignment of members from different functional areas (e.g., patrol, detective, and support services) to specific projects (e.g., task forces and crime-specific programs). The most typical situation in which the matrix approach is used is when a community has had a series of sensationalized crimes and the local police department announces it has formed a task force to apprehend the violator. One notable example of this occurred in East Los Angeles in 2014, where a task force comprising over 800 federal, state, and local law enforcement officers arrested 25 members and indicted another 38 individuals of a multigenerational street gang name "Big Hazard" on charges of federal racketeering and maintaining a criminal enterprise. The violent street gang was linked to multiple murders, extortions, robberies, drug trafficking, prostitution, and many other crimes in the Boyle Heights area of Los Angeles over the last 70 years.[28] The advantage of this type of organizational design is in the formation of specific groups of individuals, combining varied talents and levels of expertise in order to fulfill a designated mission or goal. Quite

often, the matrix structure is used for relatively short periods of time when specific programs are conducted. After the assignment is completed, individuals return to their respective units.

Figure 6.10 displays the matrix design applied to a police organization. This chart reflects the basic line and staff elements found in most police agencies. However, four specific projects have been initiated that require the use of personnel from five different units, which further requires each project to organize along the lines suggested by Figure 6.11.

Because the matrix structure greatly increases organizational complexity, it has been successful only in the short-term delivery of police services.

ORGANIZATIONAL STRUCTURE TODAY

The impact of community policing during the late 1990s had a dramatic impact on organizational structure. It was most apparent in agencies that adopted **decentralization** strategies. The purpose behind such strategies was that police departments could more effectively serve their communities through an organizational design focused on individual areas and neighborhoods rather than the entire city. Further, decentralization in organizational structure was seen as being much more flexible and having a fluid design in which to provide essential public and human services.[29]

Electing to compartmentalize the activities of the community policing concept, some departments opted to provide such services solely through one unit or bureau. For instance, the Anaheim Police Department in Anaheim, California, had a single bureau devoted to community policing. Through this one unit, the Community Policing Team developed strategies that employed a total community effort involving the police department, city and county government,

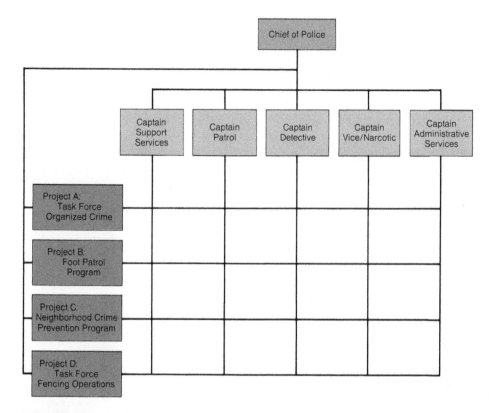

FIGURE 6.10 ▶ Matrix structure in a police organization.

schools, churches, and businesses. These alliances formed neighborhood partnerships. The mission of the Community Policing Team was to develop, promote, and implement community-based partnerships aimed at addressing various criminal and social problems confronting the city of Anaheim.[30] The important note here is that the entire community policing effort was relatively confined to the one unit—the Community Policing Team.

In contrast, other departments (e.g., those in Portland, Oregon; Madison, Wisconsin; Charlotte-Mecklenburg, North Carolina; and Minneapolis, Minnesota) opted to implement the community policing concept holistically; that is, community policing was reflected in all aspects of the organization, and,

therefore the organizational structure did not reflect a single unit devoted to community policing. Instead, the community policing philosophy was simply pervasive throughout the organization. In these cases, the organizational chart was reflective of the philosophical changes imbued in community policing.

Traditional Design vs. Structural Change

Although a number of community policing methods have been adopted across the country, several structural problems have been identified.[31] To illustrate, community policing depends on granting officers' greater authority and

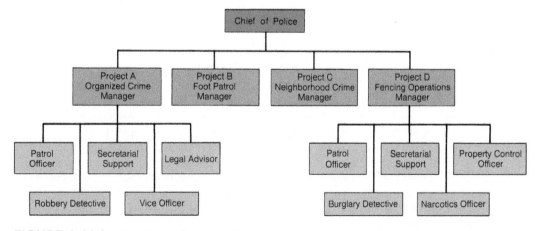

FIGURE 6.11 ▶ The detailed organization of projects.

latitude in decision making, particularly with respect to developing police strategies to impact on problems of concern to people in the area in which officers patrol. This practice conflicts with traditional bureaucratic theory's desire to have close supervision of officers through narrow spans of control/management, which in turn produces taller, multi-layered, organizational structures. In contrast, community policing requires a shorter and flatter organizational design. Services are decentralized and community-based. Necessarily, such a design will be less formalized, less specialized, and with less emphasis on bureaucratic rules. Cordner[32] suggests that police agencies shift from substantial reliance on traditional written rules and regulations to a straightforward situation-oriented approach. Some portion of

Box 6.2: Organizational Structure Impacted by Policing Philosophy

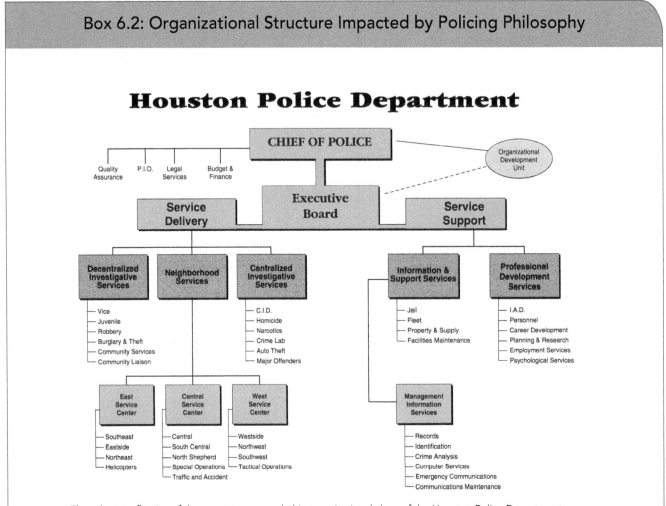

Though not reflective of the current command, this organizational chart of the Houston Police Department reflected emphasized service delivery and support through a community-represented "executive board." Source: Courtesy of the Houston, Texas, Police Department.

Under the leadership of then-Chief Lee P. Brown (1990), the Houston Police Department acted as a model for community policing departments. Reflective of these philosophical changes, the organizational chart of the department provided a new and dynamic look. Note that the focus of the department was on service delivery and support rather than the traditional modes of assignment, such as patrol and investigations. The police department was viewed more as a community organization than as a control agency. As such, the organization was operated similarly to a service corporation that is fully responsible to an executive board comprising police and community leaders. In this manner, community policing made individual police officers accountable directly to the people of Houston. The chief of police acts more as a chairman of the board or a chief executive officer for a major corporation than as a traditional police manager. Innovation in organizational structure has somewhat waned in the last several years, as many departments have continued to use, or returned to some degree to a more traditional, bureaucratic structure to cope with problems such as deep personnel cuts, local responsibilities for combating terrorism, and other factors.

traditional rules and regulations, with their strong control orientation, actually get in the way of community policing.

Community policing advocates empowering the individual officer with greater authority, responsibility, and discretion and responsibility than does traditional policing. As a consequence, direction from the organization must emphasize shared values, participatory decision making, and a collegial atmosphere. For written rules and regulations to be fully useful in a community policing context, some number of them must be rewritten to further that policing philosophy as opposed to retaining ones that interfere with how officers do their jobs.

Stated somewhat differently, the organization of community policing is open and sensitive to the environment, with a built-in need to frequently interact with members of the wider community and to be responsive to its needs or "results-oriented" and therefore accountable to it rather than being hampered by insufficient authority and rules and regulations that are a barrier to performance. The differences in organizational structure between traditional policing and community policing are further outlined in Table 6.4.

Some argue that community policing calls for too radical a change in organizational design—that such changes may be impossible under existing union and civil service constraints. Further, organizations tend to follow Michael's "iron law of oligarchy," which indicates that modern, large-scale organizations tend toward specialization and centralization.[33] However, these organizational traits appear to be in conflict with other community policing or intelligence-led structures. Large police departments require a certain amount of specialization to handle diverse tasks efficiently, such as examining various types of physical evidence or handling unique situations, and the amount

of hierarchy required to coordinate the various specialized parts produces a tendency toward centralization. As stated in Chapter 5, "Organizational Theory," the prospects for police agencies totally abandoning the bureaucratic structure are not strong. What is now being done is preserving the best features of bureaucracy, such as having an organization that is responsive to lawful orders, and supplementing or "dropping over" its processes, policies, procedures, rules, and regulations that blunt the worse features and support initiatives, such as community policing.

Intelligence-Led Policing (ILP) and Organizational Structure

The CompStat movement during the early 2000s was credited with significantly reducing crime in major cities across the United States, but it had very little impact on the organizational structure or design of police agencies. However, the movement toward ILP has placed much more emphasis on the "functional structure" of organizations as previously described (see Figure 6.9). Requiring police agencies to be much more proactive and preventative based, the focus is on integrating the intelligence function throughout the organization. ILP requires accurate and timely information, the source of which is often through the development of partnerships and problem-solving methodologies employed with other departments and agencies. ILP also requires energetic and competent analysts to communicate their findings to decision makers, and much more importantly, that decision makers then communicate their strategies to lower levels of the organization, again, much more "top-down" in style.[34] In contrast to community policing,

Box 6.3: Shared Leadership, Organizational Structure and Community Policing

There are academics, critics, and police executives throughout the United States that believe that hierarchal police organization designs restrict innovation, dampens communication, and undermines law enforcement organizations trying to fully implement community policing into their policing strategies. Structure *has to* support the organization's strategy.

For example, in community policing initiatives, an officer may be presented with a situation that requires an innovative solution. In a traditional police organization, she would have to ask her sergeant—who may have to ask his lieutenant, who may then seek approval from command staff. That process can, in some larger departments, take weeks. By then, opportunities to solve the problem or build trust may have passed. However, a more flexible approach that's more congruent with community policing, known as "shared leadership", could offer a quicker route to community satisfaction.

In this organizational design, a leadership team comprised individuals from all divisions, ranks, and departmental functions has authority to solicit input from both the community and the rank and file; to effect change; and to make

binding decisions. Departmental leaders have to commit to accepting the decisions of others and to genuinely accept the concept of participative empowerment among all ranks.

The Broken Arrow Police Department in Broken Arrow, Oklahoma, integrated a shared leadership model because leadership realized that in order to truly embrace community policing and intelligence-led philosophies, they'd have to interpret data in a timely matter and make adaptive responses at all levels. They assessed their model and found that they made positive gains in police/community relations, employee morale, trust of leadership, pride in the agency among officers, and increased productivity. The program also led to the unforeseen development of increased interest in leadership among those on the team. In short, though police organizational structures are tried and true, innovation may best suit the strategies being adopted by today's police agencies.

Source: Wuestewald, Todd and Steinhelder, B. "Shared leadership: can empowerment work in police organizations?" *Police Chief Magazine;* retrieved from https://www.policechiefmagazine.org/shared-leadership-can-empowerment-work-in-police-organizations/.

TABLE 6.4 DIFFERENCES BETWEEN TRADITIONAL AND COMMUNITY POLICING	
Traditional Policing	**Community Policing**
1. *Bureaucratic and control based:* characterized by detailed standard operating procedures and rigid written policies; high formalization of the organizational pyramid	1. *Nonbureaucratic:* based on the corporate model; more flexible and adaptive than traditional paramilitary structure; focus on building teams within a more collegial environment
2. *Centralized and hierarchical organizational structure:* highly centralized with authority flowing from top to bottom, particularly in operations; characterized by tall organizations with multiple ranks and levels; communication is slow and almost always downward	2. *Decentralization, shorter and flatter organizational structure:* authority and function is derived from community-based demands; characterized by decentralized services with multiple neighborhood storefronts and more service-oriented environments; communication is open and free-flowing between ranks both vertical and horizontal in the organization
3. *Autocratic management style:* leadership is based on rank with rights associated with the office; emphasis on control-based methodologies in managing people within the organization; loss of individual leadership capabilities within the organization	3. *Democratic and participatory management style:* leadership is encouraged at all ranks with focus on challenging the status quo, enabling and inspiring others; ennobling shared visions and possibilities, modeling ethical and collaborative behavior, rewarding others, and reflecting on self and individual service
4. *High specialization and task orientation:* police functions performed by smaller units of highly trained and specialized personnel, often characterized by high esprit-de-corps and unique unit identification; personnel loyalty is often observed to the unit versus the larger department (e.g., SWAT-tactical teams, homicide units, motor patrol, gang units)	4. *Generalization:* police officers act as generalists with specialized training in multiple areas; patrol often becomes the primary and emphasized police function with all other units and divisions supporting the patrol function; officers embrace patrol as the primary mechanism for neighborhood and community engagement
5. *Emphasis on random patrol:* the organization employs traditional policing methodologies focused on random-moving patrol vehicles; little use of technology in the patrol function and crime analysis is limited to plotting crime and activities after the fact	5. *Directed patrol based on crime and intelligence analysis:* the patrol function is directed for high impact, preventative-based activities as defined by detailed and real-time crime and intelligence analysis; wide use of technology and highly trained analysts often observed in crime analysis and fusion centers
6. *Large goal oriented:* preoccupation with crime rates and numbers; arrest orientation with focus on paramilitary structure and function of police to combat crime; individual tasks are quantity oriented	6. *Embraces multiple objectives, problem-solving and individual successes:* celebration of innovative strategies that have a positive impact on the community; goals and objectives are community/client driven; individual tasks are quality oriented
7. *Crime-fighting officer perspective within reactive organization, emphasis on mediocrity:* focus is primarily on crime detection, investigation, and arrest *after* the fact; orientation for the organization is based on the traditional "crime-fighting and order maintenance" model; organizations focus on arrest, cases cleared, and similar measures of success in traditional policing	7. *Preventive-based approach to crime within a proactive organization, emphasis on quality:* focus is on the prevention of crime *before* the activity occurs, with emphasis on broader social issues as well as neighborhood problems; crime prevention through environmental design; success is measured in numbers of interactions with the community and the building of new relations and partnerships
8. *Closed organization orientation:* distinct from environment, resistant to environmental influence and change, internally defined agenda, justification of means over ends; stifling of innovation and creativity; loss of individual worth for group think	8. *Open organization model:* organization attempts to effectively interact with the community, open to change, sensitive to environment; focused on long-term and results-oriented goals; emphasis placed on individual and organizational creativity
9. *"Fear of crime" justifies existence and tactics:* police are responsible for fighting the "war" on crime; symbols focused on the power of the police and control of the community	9. *Uses evidence-based approaches to justify police functions:* embraces on-going research to developed cost effective "best practices" in police strategies and tactics; emphasis on knowing contemporary research in policing
10. *High individual and managerial accountability:* organizational demand on accountability focused on numbers; reaction to increased crime rates result in increased traditional solutions such as more patrol, visible arrests, higher profile policing in specific neighborhoods; CompStat becomes a means to an end	10. *Accountability and police focus is a reflection of community demand:* police functions and foci are developed with the community at the neighborhood level; the community is actively engaged in measuring police performance through shared meetings; emphasis is on community engagement and partnerships

Sources: Adapted by Robert W. Taylor (July 2020) from R. W. Taylor, E. J. Fritsch, and T. J. Caeti, "Core Challenges Facing Community Policing," *ACJS Today* XVII, No. 1 (May/June 1998) and C. Murphy, Contemporary Models of Urban Policing: Shaping the Future (Ontario: Ministry of the Solicitor General, 1991), p. 2.

Ratliff asserts that decentralized structures (often stemming from community policing philosophies) reflect a purpose rather than a geographic focus. This tends to produce stovepipes within the organization, separating police specialties from one another, and decreasing communication and information flow between units, a condition critically important for the success of ILP.[35]

The need to employ intelligence activity at almost every level of the organization requires a structure and design that highlights not only effective communication but also the sharing of information and other resources. The primary methodology, from a structural perspective, to accomplish this task is to organize specialized units (such as organized crime units, gang units, terrorism task forces, narcotics and vice squads, and the like) along geographical hierarchies within the intelligence division—the theme being to highlight intelligence operations within a police department as the central element to planned activities rather than haphazard reactions to crime and potential terrorist strikes. Communication throughout the organization rests primarily on the dissemination of information via technology and planned efforts directed from the highest decision makers in the department. This type of structure necessarily requires the development of a strong fusion center that not only acts as the central hub for intelligence analysis but also serves as the primary "brain" for dissemination and feedback.

Quite frankly, few police agencies in the United States have attempted to structure around the ILP model (or the evidence-based model) of policing. Moreover, many agencies have reverted to more centralized and traditional organizational structures with levels of command and spans of management often observed prior to the community policing movement. This may well be a movement away from community-based approaches as well as a natural result of the CompStat movement and the new demands on policing posed by the threat of terrorism. While the structures may be somewhat flatter, communication within and between organizations continues to be problematic, and the strategies aimed at relatively quick solutions to very complex problems. Even Ratcliffe admits that the criterion for success of ILP is on the immediate detection, reduction, and disruption of criminal and potential terrorist activities, and not on the long-term improvement of social conditions that often encourage crime and disorder. As a result of such difficulties, the continued implementation of ILP should provide a dynamic arena for police organizational structure in the future.

ORGANIZATIONAL DESIGN AND THE INVESTIGATIVE FUNCTION

Police agencies across the country have been reeling from budget cuts in an effort to be more streamlined, more efficient, and more cost-effective.[36] Many of these cuts have been targeted at staff and support functions, particularly in investigative units in an effort to increase the number of uniform officers on the street and available for calls for service. Some departments, like Oakland, California have conducted massive overhauls of their organizational structure to include the disbanding of the entire Criminal Investigations

Division and traditional subunits such as homicide, assault, robbery, burglary, sex crimes, vice, narcotics.[37] Other agencies, particularly during the community policing era (NYPD, Dallas Police Department, LAPD) moved to a more decentralized investigative structure, moving traditional detectives to neighborhood precincts and divisions. Interestingly, many agencies are now realizing that decentralization, especially popular during the community policing era, was inefficient and ineffective. Recent research reveals that traditional persons-crimes such as homicide, robbery, and sex crime that are centralized promoted an increased clearance rate by arrest and decreased reported violent crime in most major cities.[38] This new research has caused many departments to "rethink" the concept of decentralization of police services.

There are only a few studies that have focused on organizational design and the criminal investigative function.[39] Plainclothes investigators, or detectives, in most city police department, primarily perform the following tasks:

1. Determine that a crime has been committed;
2. Identify the individual who committed it;
3. Locate and apprehend the individual;
4. Collect evidence of guilt (or innocence) for courtroom use; and
5. Recover wrongfully held persons and property.

The amount of effort that any individual investigator expends on each of the five tasks is a function of the complexity of the investigation and the specific assignment of the investigator. For example, in a burglary investigation, establishing that a crime has actually been committed consumes far less investigative effort than identifying the offender. On the other hand, an investigator visiting a pawnshop may recover a large amount of stolen property without ever determining the identity of the victim or offender. Then too, determining if a person met with an accident, committed suicide, or was murdered is often a very time-consuming and arduous task.

This combination of diversity of assignment and complexity of investigation prevents several problems for determining the organizational role, staffing and structure of investigators within a police department. Unlike the patrol function where calls for service are largely evenly distributed and where essentially the same type of service is provided to the public regardless of geographic deployment, investigative functions are diverse relative to assignment and responsibility.

While significant research has been conducted on the line function of uniform patrol (see Chapter 2), very little work has correspondingly studied the role and assignments of plainclothes personnel in a police department. Most research on the investigative function has examined either the nature of the investigative function in the abstract or the identification of "solvability factors" to assist in the efficient use of investigative personnel. Three of the better known, albeit now relatively old, studies on the nature of the investigative function relevant to organizational design were conducted by (1) President's Commission on Crime and Administration of Justice in 1967[40]; (2) RAND Corporation in 1976[41]; and (3) National Institute of Justice in 2001.[42]

The President's Commission examined the investigative practices of the Los Angeles Police Department. The report *The Challenge of Crime in a Free Society: Science and Technology* identified several factors that must be considered when creating or changing an organizational structure. The study found that the patrol force made a large portion (90 percent) of the arrests. About 25 percent of these were based on detective follow-ups (warrants). Thus, detectives were directly or indirectly responsible for about 35 percent of all arrests. About one-third of all arrests were made within 30 minutes of the commission of the offense while nearly one-half of all arrests were made within 2 hours of the commission of the offense; presumably, uniformed patrol officers were primarily responsible for these arrests. The research also found two-thirds (66 percent) of all arrests being made within one week of the commission of the offense; 94 percent of all arrests occurred within one month of the commission of the offense. Investigative efforts expended over the next 11 months raised that percentage by only 4.5. Thus, 98.5 percent of all offenders who would be arrested had been arrested within one year of the crime coming to the attention of the police. Within this group, about half were arrested by patrol officers without extensive follow-up investigation. The study further reports that 2.8 cases were cleared for each arrest made, indicating that single perpetrators are responsible for multiple offenses. As to the work of the detectives, two-thirds of the cases they cleared involved suspects whose identity was initially determined by responding patrol officers. The LAPD study leads to several conclusions. First, in half of the arrests, the plainclothes investigator's role was largely case preparation not related to the identification of the suspect. Further, the study reveals that investigative effort beyond one month after the commission of the offense, on average, produces only an incremental difference in arrest rates. Finally, reactive investigation of criminal incidents is most successful when the identity of the offender is already known.

The RAND study examined the investigative practices of 153 cities. Once again, the question of investigative division staffing and placement was not directly addressed. However, the study concluded that differences in staffing levels appeared to have no appreciable effect on crime, arrest, or clearance rates. "In other words, if the total number of officers in a department is kept fixed, switching some of them into or out of investigative units is not likely to have a substantial effect on arrest or clearance rates."[43] As to investigative activity, the RAND study found that, on average, investigators spent 45 percent of their time on noncase work, such as travel and administrative matters. More importantly, of the 55 percent of the time actually spent investigating, 40 percent of the time (22 percent overall) was expended on investigating matters that are never solved. Only 12 percent of the time (7 percent overall) was expended on investigating matters that were solved. Another 48 percent of the time (26 percent overall) was spent on cleared cases after arrest.

Twenty-five years after the RAND study, the National Institute of Justice sponsored a study to examine police practice, policies, goals, and perspectives of the criminal investigation process. The grant was given to Michigan State University.

The study marked the first nationally representative research endeavor of police criminal investigation practice in the United States. Generally, the study revealed that the criminal investigation process has remained relatively unchanged over the past 30 years, despite significant paradigm shift in policing. For instance, during this same period of time, policing strategies and philosophies significantly changed with the advent of new technology, team policing, community policing, CompStat, ILP, and evidence-based policing. Further, the study somewhat echoed the finding of previous research in that the role of the individual police officer in solving a crime was highlighted versus the role and function of plainclothes detectives. These findings were supported in 2011, by a study that attempted to reason "why" the function of detectives remained relatively unchanged:

- Detectives spend an inordinate portion of time on clerical and administrative duties; and this remains a significant portion of their job task;
- Activities that have been associated with the major paradigm shifts in policing such as in community policing (attending neighborhood meetings, school policing, crime analysis, etc.) are largely performed by officers and civilian support staff but not investigators or detectives; and
- Detective work varies across investigative units that are functionally differentiated.[44]

One other bit of research on the investigative function bears mention. The Bureau of Justice Statistics' Law Enforcement Management and Administrative Statistics (LEMAS) reports that nationwide, on average, 16 percent of the sworn personnel in police departments are assigned to investigative functions. The LEMAS study[45] does not further disaggregate the data. Thus, national averages for the number of homicide detectives versus the number of undercover narcotics investigators in agencies of varying size are not available. Correspondingly, the previously mentioned RAND study found that over all respondents, 17.3 percent of their sworn force was assigned to investigative units. Over one-half of the participating departments reported 14-20 percent of personnel assigned as investigators. Within this group of investigative personnel, 78 percent worked "reported crime" while 22 percent worked in vice, narcotics, internal affairs, and other proactive investigative units.[46]

Detailed research to compare one department to another in terms of investigator staffing and placement of the investigative function within the organization has simply not been undertaken at the national level. This type of comparison would probably not be valuable since the definition of investigator is speculative and widely varies with the internal policies defined by each department. In addition, the concept of investigator as an officer or detective also varies greatly. In most departments, investigative functionality is relegated primarily to detectives; however, in some agencies, investigative work is a functional assignment of officers. The problem becomes even more acute when attempting to compare unionized departments with contractual documents that treat investigative functions and assignment with a promotional rank (e.g., New York Police Department, Portland, OR, Phoenix, AZ, San Diego, CA, Seattle, WA), or with those agencies that are not unionized under collective bargaining, as is the case with most police departments.

In the past 10 years, the ratio of investigators to total sworn personnel has slightly increased to a national average of 20 percent, largely a reflection of federal grant money available to combat drug trafficking and terrorism.[47]

Crime Factors Impacting Investigation

James Q. Wilson in his highly acclaimed book *Varieties of Police Behavior* noted that uniformed patrol officers could deliver police services in one of several possible styles: law enforcement, order maintenance (watchman), or service.[48] Similarly, it may be hypothesized that investigative units in a police department carry out their respective responsibilities utilizing a variety of analogous responses. How police investigators respond to the incidence of crime is a function of several factors. Depending on the nature of the incident, any particular factor may receive greater or lesser emphasis in the decision to investigate and, more importantly, the level of investigative energy devoted to the matter. The factors to be considered are as follows:

- **The manner in which the crime comes to the attention of the police**—Is the crime reported by the citizen-victim, such as a sexual assault or robbery? Is the response a result of a generic complaint of illegal activity, for example, public drug market, solicitation of prostitution? Is the crime detected by proactive efforts of the police, such as undercover drug sales or stolen property stings? Is the crime detected by police administrative inspections, for example, review of pawnshop tickets or automobile salvage yards?

- **The severity of the crime**—While, in theory, all victims deserve a complete investigation of their criminal complaints, scarce resources necessitate that priorities be established. Many departments employ differential response policies to address priority handling and time allocation to more serious or aggravated crimes, while others are simply addressed by telephone. Consequently, felony offenses tend to take precedence over misdemeanors, crimes involving personal injury may take precedence over property offenses, and offenses involving large monetary amounts of loss receive greater attention than events resulting in little monetary loss.

- **The historical experience in solving similar crimes**—Clearance rates of Part I offenses nationwide give insight to this factor. While the clearance rate for murder is relatively high (64.1 percent in 2013), the solution rate for automobile theft is less than 1 in 10.[49] Thus, certain types of offenses are by their very nature difficult to clear by arrest. Even within certain crime classifications, such as burglary, investigators soon develop an ability to discern between cases for which expending investigative effort might prove worthwhile and futile. Consider a residential burglary with no witnesses, no latent fingerprints, and the owner cannot provide a detailed description of the property taken. Such a case borders on unsolvable regardless of the amount of investigative effort that might be expended. An experienced investigator will simply process the paperwork on this case and conduct little to no investigation. Clearly, this is part of the reason that burglary is one of the least solved crimes in America with less than 10 percent of the cases ever being cleared.[50]

- **Legal considerations**—As a matter of law, unattended deaths require reporting and a response by designated public officials, generally the police and/or medical examiner. An investigation—sometimes simple, sometimes complex—is initiated to determine if the death was a suicide, an accident, the result of natural causes, or a criminal homicide. Similarly, child abuse reports necessitate a police response. Further, the local prosecutor may choose not to prosecute certain cases or not to take the case unless certain witnesses or evidence is available. These law-related issues affect the police investigative effort, and their position within the organizational design of the department.

- **Department policies**—The chief of a police agency may adopt procedural rules that affect the investigative process. For example, commonly, by policy, unsolved murder cases are never placed in a closed status. Also, a policy of mandatory arrest at domestic disturbances generates cases for investigative follow-up. Perhaps most importantly, the degree to which the responding uniformed officer follows up initial leads affects the amount of work the investigative officer will perform on an individual case. Departmental policy is even more apparent in proactive investigative functions such as intelligence, gang, vice, narcotics, and terrorist investigations where cases are not the result of calls for service, but rather officer initiation or intelligence reports presented fusion centers. How many officers are assigned to these units are often the result of federal task force grants and a rather obscure number derived from history and perceived problems associated with these specific areas of enforcement. For instance, if the number of gang-related or narcotics-related aggravated assaults, robberies, and murders increase in a specific area or over a specific time period, investigative allocation relating to these areas often increases. The same can be true when federal grants are available to combat these same types of crime, or issues. This is certainly the case with the New York Police Department after 9/11, when significant manpower and hence, an entirely new division focused on terrorism was added to the organizational chart.

These factors, when considered together, produce several possible models of investigative style. Each style necessitates a different staffing strategy, that is, a different way of computing workload, and more importantly, a new way of placing the unit(s) within the organizational framework of the police department.

- **Style I—Reinforcing Patrol.** Incident driven; staffing determined by number of incidents independent of complexity. A citizen complains, patrol initially responds, but an investigator is subsequently assigned to the matter. Domestic assaults are an illustration. Time spent on each incident is approximately the same. Cases are quickly resolved and closed. Since the time spent on each incident is roughly the same, the number of incidents, not time spent, is the most important factor in determining staffing levels. Where relevant, response time to the scene is examined for some categories of incidents. In some cases response time may not be relevant, for example, patrol makes a domestic assault arrest and refers the case to CID. While response time levels would not be expected to fall within the same range as initial patrol response time, since these units supplement patrol, response times should be reasonably prompt. The slower the response time of the CID unit, the longer the patrol officer is tied to the scene.
- **Style II—Standard Reactive.** Incident and complexity driven. Requires response and follow-up a little or a lot depending on the particular case. Case may or may not ever be solved. Cases may be closed or placed in inactive status when all logical investigative leads have been exhausted. Robbery and burglary are illustrations.
- **Style III—Major Cases.** All incidents are thoroughly investigated and cases are not closed although reasonable investigative leads may diminish over time. Homicides and unknown assailant sexual assaults are illustrations. Staffing of these units is determined similarly to Standard Reactive units. However, allowance may need to be made for two forms of cases in the primary caseload—active and inactive matters. The latter would be those cases where leads no longer exist but are kept open because of policy. Likewise, because of the severity of the types of cases handled and the likelihood that solved cases may result in a trial, the secondary caseload may demand more attention than with other investigative styles. Actual caseload numbers in this unit will likely be low. Units that investigate homicide and rape are traditionally Style III Units.
- **Style IV—Regulatory Inspection.** Primarily inspection/ regulatory work that uncovers the existence of a crime. Actual follow-up investigation may be assigned to others. Pawn shop and auto salvage yard inspections fall into this category. Caseload is determined on the number of locations needed to be inspected. This is one area where average time spent at each site may provide insight into the number of personnel needed. As the number of bars and adult entertainment centers, pawnshops, salvage yards, and the like change, it would be expected that the number of persons assigned to these units would need to be altered. Interestingly, many departments are shifting the inspections and investigations of these businesses to civilian personnel. These are excellent civilianization steps for cost savings within a department.

- **Style V—Passive Notation.** Primarily report-taking/ support functions with only selective investigative effort. Routine stolen property reports and bad check cases are illustrations. Since little follow-up exists to these reports, the number of complaints determine workload. Investigators are expected to carry a large secondary caseload and a relatively small primary caseload. Many of the traditional investigative roles in this style, such as those observed and associated with Sex Offender Registration and Tracking, are also commonly staffed by civilians.
- **Style VI—Discovery Enforcement.** Largely proactive investigations where covert police officers detect the occurrence of crime and identify suspects, usually at about the same time. Individual officer effort largely determines the size of the caseload. The number of investigators assigned to these units is primarily a policy decision. Since investigations are largely proactive in nature, additional officers or investigators will likely be able to make cases at a rate similar to existing staff. In theory, staffing could exceed its marginal utility—an additional officer or detective adds only incrementally to the number of crimes detected. This is particularly true in geographical areas of high vice and drug activity.

Three key elements exist in the above models. First, is the recognition that investigative units vary in the manner in which they operate; thus, organizational models likewise need to differ. Unlike patrol, which is the primary line function of all police departments, there is no universal mathematical model that can be constructed to determine appropriate staffing levels, or exactly "where" the investigative unit should be placed. Second, historical data should be used to determine baseline staffing, and organizational placement of the investigative function. And third, for all but the specialized investigations units within a criminal investigative, representing Style VI-Discovery Enforcement Units (e.g., terrorist investigations, intelligence, gang officers, narcotics, and vice enforcement), caseload should be calculated as the number of new cases per month. In this manner, conflicts between patrol officer investigations versus specialized investigations are minimized.

SOME UNIQUE ORGANIZATIONAL FEATURES OF SHERIFF'S OFFICES

A detailed discussion of "politics and the county sheriff" was addressed in Chapter 4, Politics and Police Administration. However, in addition to some of the unique political features discussed therein, there are also some organizational differences that typically exist between municipal police departments and sheriff's offices. For example, most police departments do not have a single commanding officer positioned between the police chief and all of the operating and administrative bureaus. However, this is not true of sheriff's offices. Most sheriff's offices have a chief deputy/ undersheriff and, with the blessing of the sheriff, this person typically assumes considerable operational command over the entire organization (see Figure 6.12). The position exists because,

Quick Facts: Sheriffs in the United States

There are currently 3,012 sheriff's departments in the United States. A sheriff is generally (but not always) elected to office and represents the highest law enforcement officer of a county. In contrast, a chief of police is usually appointed and serves as the head of a municipal or city department. Interestingly, three states do not have sheriffs. They include:

1. Alaska. There are no county governments in the state.
2. Connecticut. Sheriff's departments have been replaced by a state marshal system.
3. Hawaii. While there are no elected sheriffs in Hawaii, there are "deputy sheriffs" that serve as part of the Sheriff's Division of the Hawaii Department of Public Safety, a unique merging of traditional county functionality with state police.[51]

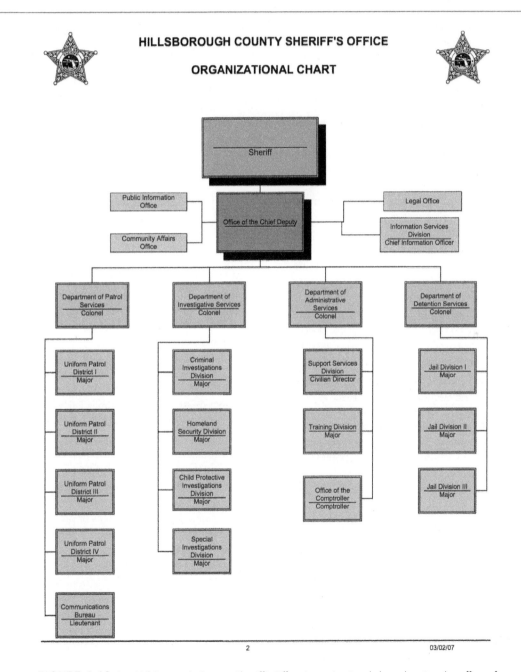

FIGURE 6.12 ▶ Hillsborough County Sheriff's Office (organizational chart showing the office of the chief deputy in charge of the entire organization, but subordinated to the Sheriff). (Courtesy of the Hillsborough County Sheriff's Office, Tampa, FL)

FIGURE 6.13 ▶ Sheriff's departments are often responsible for the county jail, as well as more traditional law enforcement duties. (Image Source/Getty Images)

although the elected sheriff is the chief law enforcement officer of the agency, the sheriff must devote a considerable amount of time addressing the political needs of the sheriff's office within the community to assure that a positive image is created and maintained and public support is maximized. In addition, if the sheriff should decide to run for re-election, he or she must devote considerable time and effort to this endeavor.

In many respects, the role of the chief deputy/undersheriff is very similar to that of the police chief in a municipal police department, in that the person occupying this position assumes direct operational command over the entire organization. However, it is also important to note that, because sheriff's offices typically are responsible for supervising the operation of county jails, the chief deputy/undersheriff should also ideally have a good background in jail administration (see Figure 6.13). This is so because jails consume a substantial portion of the agency's resources for both personnel and operating expenses. Although the position of sheriff, like that of police chief, has traditionally been held by men, this has changed and now women are increasingly being elected as sheriff.

LINE AND STAFF RELATIONSHIPS IN POLICE AGENCIES

The rapid growth in size of many police agencies has been accompanied by a corresponding rapid growth in specialization and a need for the expansion of staff services to provide support for operating units. This expansion and division of responsibility, which occurs in all police departments except those that are a pure line form of organization, is sometimes fraught with difficulty and dissension. If left uncorrected, these conditions will have a serious negative effect on both the quality and the quantity of service a police agency is able to deliver to its citizens. The following represent some of the major causes of conflict between line and staff.

The Line Point of View

One of the basic causes of organizational difficulties, as line operations view them, is that staff personnel attempt to assume authority over line elements instead of supporting and advising them.[52] Line commanders feel that the chief looks to them for accountability of the operation; therefore, staff personnel should not try to control their operation because they are not ultimately responsible for handling line problems. Another commonly heard complaint is that staff personnel sometimes fail to give sound advice because their ideas are not fully thought out, not tested, or "too academic." This attitude is easy for line commanders to develop because of the belief that staff personnel are not responsible for the ultimate results of their product and therefore propose new ideas too quickly.

Communications problems sometimes emerge between the staff specialist and line commanders. Staff personnel on occasion fail to explain new plans or procedures and do not give line commanders sufficient time to propose changes. For example, a major staff project with an ambitious time line for completion was initiated in a patrol division after only a very brief period of time had passed from its announcement until the starting date. Some attempts were made to prepare the personnel for the project by the use of memos, but this task was largely left to line supervisors to do, and they did not have enough information to fully explain the new program. This resulted in confusion. Individual officers were unsure of what they were to do, so they did little. It took several weeks to recognize the problem and several more weeks to explain, train, and guide the personnel to operate under the new plan. After a three-month delay, the plan began to show results. However, the crime picture for this period was the worst in four years. The chief placed the blame at his precinct commanders' doors. They, in turn, blamed staff for poor preparation and lack of coordination.

Line commanders frequently claim that staff personnel take credit for successful operations and point the finger of blame at the line commander when programs fail, reflecting the adage that failure is an orphan and success has many fathers. In one department, a new report-writing program was installed under staff auspices. This program was designed to improve the statistical data that the staff group would use in preparing the various departmental reports and to help the patrol commander to evaluate patrol personnel. During the first year of the program, several flaws showed up that prompted staff to write a report that stated the patrol supervisors were not checking the reports carefully, and as a result erroneous information was appearing that made evaluation impossible. A retraining program was instituted, and the defects were ironed out. The personnel assigned to do the training then wrote a report taking full credit for the improvement. The commander of the patrol division took a rather dim view of this self-congratulatory report because he, along with some of his subordinates, worked very closely with the training section in formulating the retraining program.

Operational commanders sometimes express the concern that staff personnel do not see the "big picture" because they have only limited objectives that reflect their own nonoperational specialties. For example, the personnel unit of one police department developed a test for the rank of lieutenant. Most of the sergeants who took the examination did poorly. Many became frustrated and angry because they had built up fine work records and believed that the examination procedure failed to measure their potential ability for the rank of lieutenant accurately. The members of the personnel unit who developed the examination procedure were not sympathetic and suggested that the department just did not have the caliber of personnel who could pass a valid examination. The line commanders claimed that the personnel unit did not know enough about the department's needs, and if they would put more effort into helping instead of "figuring out reasons why we're no good, then we'd be better off."

The Staff Point of View

Staff personnel contend that line commanders do not know how to use staff. Instead of using their analytic skills, staff personnel feel that line commanders simply want to use them as researchers and writers. As an example, in one medium-sized department, the robbery caseload for detectives was increasing at an alarming rate. When staff were approached to work on the problem, the chief of detectives told them how he saw the problem, asked them to prepare an order for his signature setting out the changes as he saw them, and refused any staff personnel the opportunity to contact the operating field units to determine what the problems were as they saw them.

Many staff personnel also feel that line officers are shortsighted and resist new ideas. As an example, a department had expanded, and numerous personnel were promoted, but some of the personnel promoted to administrative and executive positions could not function effectively because they had not been properly trained to assume their new roles and responsibilities. The results were inefficiency and personal conflict. The planning and research officer had much earlier wanted to install a training program for career development for the ranks of lieutenant and above, so that there would be a trained group to choose from when needed. The planning and research officer blamed the line commanders for being shortsighted and not cooperating earlier to develop career development programs.

Solutions

The problems of line and staff relationships can be corrected. What is needed is a thorough indoctrination and training program and clear definitions as to the tasks of each.

The line is principally responsible for successful operations of the department, and therefore, line employees must be responsible for operational decisions affecting them. Staff, on the other hand, exists to assist the line in reaching objectives by providing advice and information when requested to do so. This does not, however, prohibit staff from volunteering advice they believe is needed.

The use of staff assistance is usually at the option of line commanders, but they must recognize that the chief can decide to use staff services to review any operation and that this decision is binding. As an example, the chief may order a planning and research officer to determine if patrol officers are being properly used. The patrol commander is responsible for making effective use of advice received under such circumstances. If the patrol commander disagrees with staff findings, then an opportunity for reply and review by a higher authority should be available.

Staff exist to help line elements accomplish the objectives of the department. To do this effectively, staff must know what the line elements are doing. Illustratively, the personnel officer who does not know what tasks police officers must perform cannot effectively prepare selection standards for the hiring of personnel. Both staff and line must exert effort to ensure that staff stay in contact with what is going on in line units.

Line personnel are concerned primarily with day-to-day operating objectives within the framework of departmental goals. Staff can perform a valuable task for them by thinking ahead toward future problems and operations before they arise. The possibility of a plane crash in a community that has an airport is a subject that staff, in cooperation with line commanders, can anticipate. Thus, staff can accomplish time-consuming planning and the development of orders and procedures well before they are needed.

Line commanders should know what the various staff functions are and what they can contribute to the improvement of the line units. In some departments, this can be done at meetings by allowing the staff heads to explain what they can do for the line commanders. At the same time, line commanders can make known their expectations about staff support. Such discussions lead to closer coordination and improved personal relationships that are essential for effectiveness. Staff's ideas will be more readily accepted if they demonstrate an understanding of line operations.

Staff activity deals primarily with change. However, people tend to resist change and ideas that threaten the status quo.

Change by itself indicates the possibility that the old way is no longer acceptable. Staff should anticipate and dispel resistance to change by doing the following:

1. Determining to what extent the change proposed will affect the personal relationships of the people involved. Is the change a major one that will affect the social patterns established in the formal and informal organizations discussed later in this chapter? Can the change be broken down into a series of small moves that will have less negative impact than a single, large change? The single big change versus a succession of smaller steps toward completing the change should be carefully considered: A boy had a dog with a long tail, but wanted him to have a short one. The boy didn't want to hurt the dog by chopping the tail all off at once, so he cut it off in sections. Massive change all at once can be detrimental to morale and operations. However, we should not underestimate the importance of fully preparing the police department for change—whether it's large or small—by giving officers a chance for input throughout the process.

2. It is at least arrogant, if not reckless, to impose change without meaningful involvement of those who will be most affected by it. "Meaningful involvement" means the genuine opportunity to shape decisions effecting the change being contemplated. While some changes may be mandated by law, changes in FBI Uniform Crime Reporting guidelines, Supreme Court decisions, or other entities, even under such mandates, the details about the change should involve those most affected. Excluding them communicates the belief that they could not possibly have important insights and recommendations to contribute. Also, it implicitly suggests that only staff members and senior commanders are capable of having cogent thoughts. Although it may not be possible for everyone to participate, the use of representative groups of employees is often effective in helping to facilitate change.

3. Communicating throughout the entire planning stage. The personnel who will be affected by the change will accept it better if (a) they believe it will benefit them personally—that it will make their work easier, faster, or safer (the change should be tied in as closely as possible with the individual's personal goals and interests—job, family, future); (b) the personnel have an opportunity to offer suggestions, ideas, and comments concerning the change as it affects them—provided these suggestions are sincerely wanted and are given serious consideration; and (c) they are kept informed of the results of the change (see Chapter 15, Organizational Change).

To achieve organizational objectives, a line commander should know how to use staff assistance. The specialized skills of staff people can be used to help achieve these goals more efficiently and economically. By involving staff in the problems of the line, staff personnel can become more effective by learning the line commanders' way of thinking. Line commanders must be able to identify their problems precisely before seeking assistance. They must not vaguely define a problem and then expect the staff unit to do all the work. It is also important for staff to keep other staff informed of decisions that will affect them. Keeping others involved and informed before taking action also applies to chiefs..

One thing that people working staff functions typically have is necessary time and research skills to delve into operational problems. As an example, when many police departments were transitioning from revolvers to semiautomatics, a common staff function was to make and support a recommendation to the Chief about which semiautomatic to select. Factors normally considered included the caliber, acquisition cost, reliability, experiences of test shooters from the department, any gender shooting disparities, and the amount and cost of transition training to the firearm selected.

The steps taken by a staff when asked to recommend other equipment would parallel those used to develop a recommendation for the semiautomatic. Researching such potential changes is more complex than immediately meets the eye. Gathering the information includes such activities as (1) gathering any research findings, (2) requesting the applicable policies

---

Box 6.4: Front-End Engagement of the State Patrol Troopers

A State Patrol hired a consultant to develop a new promotional system. After making the necessary appointments and sharing all of the available information, the consultant went around the state meeting with a group of officers from each of the Patrol's 50 posts. Some important ideas were contributed, such as closing off making promotions for favored troopers by making exceptions to the competitive examination promotional roster.

The consultant told the groups two things that proved to be important: (1) occasionally he would react to a trooper's suggestion by saying something like, "I won't recommend that because it would be in conflict with Equal Opportunity Commission guidelines" and (2) "Whatever I tell you today, I believe it to be factually correct. If that changes or turns out not to be the case, I'll send message of correction to all Posts." In the end, a system was developed and implemented in 1998 without opposition from troopers or their association and is still in place. The consultant believes this was due to the high involvement of the rank and file in the actual development of the promotional policy as opposed to giving the troopers a policy and asking them for their input.

Box 6.5: A Lack of Coordination of a Command Staff

A police department received budget authority to hire and train 160 new officers. This represented about four normal-sized recruit classes. The Chief issued a memo calling for two "supersized" recruit classes and set their dates. Although the Majors commanding the personnel and training divisions had previously discussed the new hirings in general with the Chief several times, they were surprised that he had acted without hearing their specific recommendations. When the Chief refused to alter the academy dates, the personnel and training division commanders tried hard to make them work. However, there were too many people marginally qualified and a few who had a more thorough background check would have excluded.

The result was a higher than usual attrition for students in the academy and during the six-month probationary period that followed their graduation: (1) in the third week of the academy, a recruit was fired for pulling a few books off of the shelf at a public library and fondling himself as he watched young girls and (2) a probationary officer was dismissed because he forged a doctor's note to cover his use of a sick day to go play blackjack at a casino. Other problems were also encountered during the first academy, the most serious of which was that some of the best outside instructors had other commitments or family plans and could not participate. While similar problems were also encountered in the second academy, the overall attrition was marginally less.

---

from departments already using the equipment, (3) tabulating surveys of other agencies' practices, (4) making telephone calls to obtain information, (4) sending e-mails to agencies asking them to complete the survey, and other detailed work.

THE INFORMAL ORGANIZATION

The **informal organization** does not appear on organizational charts, but it does exist in every organization because people are not simply objects in boxes connected by lines. Officers have needs, attitudes, and emotions, and informal organizations are built on the friendships that spring up around them. Informal organization members have views and goals that may or may not coincide or support those of the police department. The informal organization has its own communications and behavior patterns, as well as a system of rewards and punishments to assure conformity.[53]

An important attribute for police leaders is to recognize the existence of the informal organization and to inculcate its support of the department as opportunities permit. Sometimes, the informal organization is regarded as a threat to the established authority

of the department or to one or more leaders, such as the chief or sheriff. If a leader actively opposes the informal organization, it strengthens the bond among its members and obviates the opportunity to court its support for departmental activities, for example, new programs. Continuing active opposition to the informal organization sometimes, perhaps often, has an unpleasant ending.

Police leaders must communicate clearly to all employees what the department's goals are and how each of them contributes to achieving them. When this is done properly, several things are accomplished: (1) employees understand their role in the department, (2) they feel valued, and (3) contributing to the department's achievement of goals becomes attractive, and perhaps reduces the likelihood of the informal organization becoming oppositional.

The informal organization has several important characteristics:

Naturalness—The informal organization is natural and spontaneous; it does not ordinarily take on the characteristics of a social group because a commanding officer ordered it to develop.

Instead, the informal group evolves and develops in response to conditions and needs of people in the organization.

Quick Facts: Transition Training Is Crucial

A roughly 100-officer police department near Atlanta had finished the transition training to Glocks. An officer from that department had an off-duty job providing security in uniform at a popular local restaurant. Several days after finishing the transition training, he reported to his extra job through the restaurant's rear door, which led to the large cooking area. At the same time, two robbers came into it from the main restaurant area, seeking to flee out the back. They both fired shots at the officer and ducked behind a steel encased table. The officer also found cover and the three men exchanged multiple shots. Confused about how many shots he had fired, the officer followed his transition training, released the magazine from his pistol, and seated a new one, just in time to hear one of the robbers yell, "He's fired six shots. No more rounds. Let's rush him." The flaw in their thinking was the officer had a revolver and to the officer's credit, he had followed his transition training. Both robbers leaped from behind the steel encased table and charged the officer, who wounded both of them in an exchange of gunfire. However, the officer was not injured.

Interactions (or group dynamics)—Group members interact with each other because they want to; they have a natural, spontaneous desire to do so.

Empathy—Members of a social group have a high degree of attraction and empathy for each other, which comes out of shared attitudes and values. They like to be with each other and know they are safe expressing their true feelings about things at work. While some members of a social group are attracted to each other more than others, the general level of mutual attraction is high.

Social distance—Members of a social group do not feel too much social distance. That is, they do not feel that there are status or other types of barriers (e.g., ethnic, gender, and racial) between themselves and other members. Social distance is the reason that uninhibited interaction often fails to take place in management meetings attended by personnel from several rank levels.

Democratic orientation—The social group has a strongly democratic orientation. The very essence of social group action is the attraction that members have for each other, supplemented by uninhibited communication and

self-expression. Naturalness and freedom characterize effective social groups.

Leadership—Leaders tend to emerge naturally from the group. This does not mean, however, that social groups cannot exist where leaders have been designated from the outside. Much depends on the characteristics and behavior of the leader. When an aggregation of people begins to become a social group, some people initiate interaction more than others and they are usually attractive to a large number of people. These are the natural leaders, but they may not necessarily also be designated as hierarchical leaders.

Group pressures—One aspect of the social group is the pressure exerted to get the members to conform to group standards in thought and action. The phenomenon can be used either to thwart the goals of management or to facilitate their achievement.

Cohesiveness and unity—In order to endure, a social group must have a certain amount of cohesiveness. Members must have sufficient desire to belong, to keep the group together and in continued existence. In short, there must be enough attractiveness in group goals and associations to ensure their observance as a means of maintaining the group.[54]

Box 6.6: The Sheriff and the "Disloyal" Deputies

"Joe" was a first term Sheriff in a Southern state, an area where Sheriffs have historically been very politically powerful. He made erratic decisions, some of which played havoc with the deputies' assignments and their family life. Eleven months before the next election, Joe began hearing that some unidentified deputies were opposed to his re-election and aligning themselves with the challenger in the next election. He told his command staff those deputies were "disloyal piss-ants" and he would deal with them. Subsequently, Joe went on a "witch hunt" trying to find out who these deputies were. Deputies suspected of "disloyalty" were covertly followed on- and off-duty to see where they went and with whom they might be meeting. On mere suspicion, some deputies were reassigned to less desirable duties and subject to strict discipline for even minor infractions. A handful of deputies were left for other employment because of

the sheriff's antics and two "disloyals" were fired for thin reasons. These actions galvanized the remaining deputies, even those whom theretofore been neutral, and support for the challenger increased substantially.

The challenger defeated Joe and went right to work. Among the newly elected, sheriff's initial priorities was offering to rehire deputies that had left for other employment. Several of them took the offer, one because he needed a few more years as a deputy to be vested in the pension system. The new sheriff also worked with the Peace Officers Standards and Training Council to clear the records of the two fired "disloyals." One subsequently came back into law enforcement with a municipality and the other continued to work in his family-owned business. The former sheriff started a private security firm that failed in its third year.

Chapter Summary

Summary by Learning Objectives

1. **Explain the principle of hierarchy as it relates to organizational design.**

   The principle of hierarchy states that each lower level of an organization be supervised by a higher level. This principle results not only in the use of multiple spans of control but also in different grades of authority that increase at each successively higher level of

   the organization. According to the principle of hierarchy, this authority flows downward in the organization as a formal grant of power from the chief of police to those selected for leadership positions. These different grades of authority produce the chain of command. Although there are many similarities from one department to another, the American police service does not have a uniform terminology for grades of authority and job titles. In recent years, some police departments have moved away from using traditional military-style ranks (such as commander, captain, lieutenant, and sergeant) and have adopted, instead, alternative titles (such as director, manager, and supervisor) reflecting changes in both organizational structure and policing philosophy.

2. **Describe the concept of span of management.**

The term span of management instead of "span of control" is used to describe the number of personnel a supervisor can personally manage effectively. The term "span of management" is broader than "span of control" and encompasses factors relating to an individual's capacity to oversee the activities of others directly, such as the police manager's ability, experience, and level of energy. The term "span of management" encompasses more of the factors relating to the problem of an individual's capacity to oversee the activities of others. How wide a span of management is depends on many factors. Some scholars argue that the ideal number of subordinates reporting to a supervisor is 8 to 12 but that number varies widely in practice.

3. **Distinguish between vertical and horizontal differentiation.**

Vertical differentiation is based on levels of authority, or positions holding formal power within the organization. Persons with vertical authority have the power to assign work and to exercise control to ensure job performance. Horizontal differentiation, on the other hand, is usually based on activity. However, in some cases, horizontal differentiation is based on specific projects or even geographical distribution. For instance, many state police departments are responsible for large geographical areas. Their organizational structure often reflects horizontal differentiation based on location rather than function.

4. **Discuss the differences between tall organizational structures and flat organizational structures.**

The complexity of a police department is increased by the proliferation of levels because they can negatively affect communication up and down the chain of command. Tall organizational structures have many levels with narrow spans of control. Taller organizations are complex and may react slowly during crisis situations, as effective communication is hampered by the number of different levels present within the chain of command. Successful tall departments must develop policies and procedures that overcome problems created by increased complexity. Larger spans of management or control yield flatter organizational structures. However, the capacity to flatten out police organizational structures depends to no small degree on reducing the number of traditional ranks, a movement often met with resistance because it means less opportunity for upward mobility. Thus, flatter

structures are associated with wider spans of control that offer numerous advantages over the more traditional tall structures. First, they shorten lines of communication between the bottom and top levels. Communication in both directions is more likely to be faster and more timely. Second, the route of communication is more simple, direct, and clear than it is in tall organizations. Third, distortion in communication is minimized by a reduced number of people being involved. Fourth, and probably most important, flat structures are generally associated with employees with higher morale and job satisfaction as compared to employees in tall-structured organizations.

5. **List and describe four basic types of police organizational design.**

There are four basic structural types of design that can be found within police organizations. They are as follows:

Line Structure: This is the oldest, simplest, and clearest form of organizational design. Authority flows from the top to the bottom of the organization in a clear and unbroken line, creating a set of superior-subordinate relations in a hierarchy commonly called the *chain of command*. A primary emphasis is placed on accountability by close adherence to the chain of command.

Line and Staff Structure: As more demands for services are placed on police departments, there is a need to add internal support functions, so that the line functions can continue to provide direct services to the public. The addition of support functions to the line elements produces a distinct organizational form: the line and staff structure. The addition of a staff component to the line structure offers a number of advantages such as (1) providing expert advice to line units in special knowledge areas as demonstrated by the opinions of legal advisors; (2) relieving line managers from performing tasks they least prefer to do or are least qualified to do, such as training and scientific analysis of physical evidence; (3) achieving departmentwide conformity in activities that affect the entire organization, such as disciplinary procedures; and (4) reducing or eliminating special problems, such as corruption, because of the greater expertise they bring to bear on the issue and the greater amount of time they have to devote to the problem.

Functional Structure: The functional structure is one means by which the line authority structure of an organization can be modified. The functional structure is a line and staff structure that has been modified by the delegation of management authority to personnel outside their normal spans of control. By requiring specific units to be responsible to a variety of other unit commanders, critical information is assured of reaching other line officers. Sharing is promoted, while competing loyalties are diminished. Good examples of functional design can be observed in police departments moving toward geographical responsibility for supervisors on a 24-hour basis. A commander or shift (watch) supervisor (normally a lieutenant) assigned to the day watch may be responsible for solving violent street crimes (e.g., robberies) that occur in a specific area on all three shifts; however, officers on at least two of the shifts (evenings and nights) are not directly assigned to that supervisor.

Matrix Structure: One interesting form of organizational design is variously referred to as matrix (or grid) structure. In some cases, the style has been inclusively part of "project" or "product" management. The essence of matrix structure is in the assignment of members of functional areas (e.g., patrol, detective, and support services) to specific projects (e.g., task forces and crime-specific programs).

6. **Discuss the major crime factors that impact investigative function; list the various models of investigative style.**

Investigative units in a police department carry out their respective responsibilities utilizing a variety of responses. How police investigators respond to the incidence of crime is a function of several factors. Depending on the nature of the incident, any particular factor may receive greater or lesser emphasis in the decision to investigate and, more importantly, the level of investigative energy devoted to the matter. The factors to be considered are as follows: (1) the manner in which the crime comes to the attention of the police; (2) the severity of the crime; (3) the historical experience in solving similar crimes; (4) legal considerations; and (5) department policies. These factors, when considered together, produce several possible models of investigative style:

Style I—Reinforcing Patrol. Incident driven; staffing determined by number of incidents independent of complexity. A citizen complains, patrol initially responds, but an investigator is subsequently assigned to the matter. Domestic assaults are an illustration.

Style II—Standard Reactive. Incident and complexity driven. Requires response and follow-up a little or a lot depending on the particular case. Case may or may not ever be solved. Cases may be closed or placed in inactive status when all logical investigative leads have been exhausted. Robbery and burglary are illustrations.

Style III—Major Cases. All incidents are thoroughly investigated and cases are not closed although reasonable investigative leads may diminish over time. Homicides and unknown assailant sexual assaults are illustrations.

Style IV—Regulatory Inspection. Primarily inspection/regulatory work that uncovers the existence of a crime. Actual follow-up investigation may be assigned to others. Pawn shop and auto salvage yard inspections fall into this category.

Style V—Passive Notation. Primarily report-taking/support functions with only selective investigative effort. Routine stolen property reports and bad check cases are illustrations.

Style VI—Discovery Enforcement. Largely proactive investigations where covert police officers detect the occurrence of crime and identify suspects, usually at about the same time. Individual officer effort largely determines the size of the caseload. Terrorism, narcotics, and vice operations are examples of discovery enforcement.

7. **Identify the basic causes for tension between line and staff and suggest strategies to be used as solutions.**

The rapid growth in size of many police agencies has been accompanied by a corresponding rapid growth in specialization and a need for the expansion of staff services to provide support for operating units. This expansion and division of responsibility, which occurs in all police departments except those that are a pure line form of organization, is sometimes fraught with difficulty and dissension. If left uncorrected, these conditions will have a serious negative effect on both the quality and the quantity of service a police agency is able to deliver to its citizens. One of the basic causes of organizational difficulties, as line operations view them, is that staff personnel attempt to assume authority over line elements instead of supporting and advising them. Another commonly heard complaint is that staff personnel sometimes fail to give sound advice because their ideas are not fully thought out, not tested, or "too academic." Communications problems sometimes emerge as well between the staff specialist and line commanders. Staff personnel on occasion fail to explain new plans or procedures and do not give line commanders sufficient time to propose changes. Line commanders frequently claim that staff personnel take credit for successful operations and point the finger of blame at the line commander when programs fail. Further, operational commanders sometimes express the concern that staff personnel do not see the "big picture" because they have only limited objectives that reflect their own nonoperational specialties. On the other hand, staff personnel contend that line commanders do not know how to use staff. Instead of using their analytic skills, staff personnel feel that line commanders simply want to use them as researchers and writers. Many staff personnel also feel that line officers are shortsighted and resist new ideas. The problems of line and staff relationships can be corrected. What is needed is a thorough indoctrination and training program and clear definitions as to the tasks of each. The line is principally responsible for successful operations of the department, and therefore line employees must be responsible for operational decisions affecting them. Staff, on the other hand, exist to assist the line in reaching objectives by providing advice and information when requested to do so. This does not, however, prohibit staff from volunteering advice they believe is needed. Staff exist to help line elements accomplish the objectives of the department. To do this effectively, staff must know what the line elements are doing. Both staff and line must exert effort to ensure that staff stay in contact with what is going on in line units. Line personnel are concerned primarily with day-to-day operating objectives within the framework of departmental goals. Staff can perform a valuable task for them by thinking ahead toward future problems and operations before they arise.

8. **Describe the characteristics of an informal organization.**

   The informal organization is built on friendships and common desires. It, too, may have goals that may or may not coincide with the formal organization's goals. The informal organization has its own communications and behavior patterns, as well as a system of rewards and punishments to assure conformity. The informal organization has several important characteristics:

   Naturalness—The informal organization is natural and spontaneous; it does not ordinarily take on the characteristics of a social group as a result of an order or edict from higher authority. Instead, the informal group evolves and develops in response to conditions and needs of people in the organization.

Interactions (or group dynamics)—Group members interact with each other because they want to; they have a natural, spontaneous desire to do so.

Empathy—Members of a social group have a high degree of attraction and sympathy for each other. They like to be with each other. Their social inhibitions are at a minimum and they feel a lack of the type of restraint that results from expected disapproval of one's associates.

Social distance—Members of a social group do not feel too much social distance. That is, they do not feel that there are status or other types of barriers (ethnic, gender, and racial) between themselves and other members.

Democratic orientation—The social group has a strongly democratic orientation. The very essence of social group action is the attraction that members have for each other, supplemented by uninhibited communication and self-expression. Naturalness and freedom characterize effective social groups.

Leadership—Leaders tend to emerge naturally from the group.

Group pressures—One aspect of the social group is the pressure exerted to get the members to conform to group standards in thought and action. The phenomenon can be used either to thwart the goals of management or to facilitate their achievement.

Cohesiveness and unity—In order to endure, a social group must have a certain amount of cohesiveness. Members must have sufficient desire to belong, to keep the group together and in continued existence. In short, there must be enough attractiveness in group goals and associations to ensure their observance as a means of maintaining the group.

Chapter Review Questions

1. What is the *principle of hierarchy*?
2. What is the distinction between rank and title?
3. What six factors will affect the span of management?
4. Distinguish between vertical and horizontal differentiation.
5. What are some of the more common ways in which activities and personnel are grouped within police organizations?
6. Discuss the differences between tall organizational structures and flat organizational structures.
7. List and discuss four basic types of structural designs within police departments.
8. Why have the functions of detectives remained relatively unchanged over the history of policing?
9. What are the crime factors that impact investigation?
10. Identify and discuss the six models of investigative style commonly observed within the investigative function.
11. Identify major organizational differences between sheriff's offices and municipal police departments.
12. Identify the basic causes of tension between line and staff.
13. Describe the characteristics of the informal organization.

Critical Thinking Exercises

1. Learn from individual police officers. Contact your local police department and if possible, arrange for a ride-along. Interview the officer and inquire about his or her attitudes toward supervision, management, and leadership within the department. What statements can you make about the informal organization within the police department versus the formal structure of the department?

2. Compare and contrast the organizational structure of a major police department versus a major private corporation in the United States. What differences exist between the two types of structure? Can you find any similarities? What do you think are the advantages and/or disadvantages of each organizational structure?

3. Visit the web page of the New York Police Department at: http://www.nyc.gov/html/nypd/html/home/home.shtml.

4. How did the events of 9/11 impact the structure of the NYPD? Who is the head of the Intelligence and Counterterrorism Division of the NYPD? Do research on this person and describe his background and specific qualifications for this position. Do you think he is qualified to hold such a controversial position? Why or why not?

Key Terms

city-county consolidated governments	line and staff structure	sector policing
decentralization	line structure	span of management
functional structure	matrix (or grid) structure	specialization
horizontal differentiation	organizing	structure
informal organization	principle of hierarchy	vertical differentiation

Endnotes

[1] S. P. Robbins, *The Administration Process* (Englewood Cliffs, NJ: Prentice Hall, 1976), pp. 17–18.

[2] *The Republic of Plato,* trans. A. Bloom (New York: Basic Books, 1968), p. 47.

[3] For example, see Luther Gulick and L. Urwick, eds., *Papers on the Science of Administration* (New York: August M. Kelley, a 1969 reprint of the 1937 edition).

[4] O. W. Wilson and R. C. Mclaren, *Police Administration*, 3rd edition. (New York: McGraw-Hill, 1972), p. 79.

[5] Dale Willits and Jeffrey Nowacki, "The Use of Specialized Cybercrime Policing Units: An Organizational Analysis" *Criminal Justice Studies* 29, No. 2 (London: Taylor and Francis, 2016)

[6] Wilson and McLaren, *Police Administration*, p. 81.

[7] Ibid. p. 83.

[8] N. C. Kassoff, *Organizational Concepts* (Washington, DC: International Association of Chiefs of Police, 1967), p. 22.

[9] Wilson and McLaren, *Police Administration*, p. 56.

[10] Ibid.

[11] Gary W. Cordner, "Community Policing: Elements and Effects," in Roger G. Dunham and Geoffrey P. Alpert, *Critical Issues in Policing*, 6th edition (Long Grove, IL: Waveland Press, 2010), pp. 432–449.

[12] "City and County to Unify," *The Kansas City Star* (November 11, 2007), p. 1.

[13] Troy Lane, "Span of Control for Law Enforcement Agencies," *Police Chief Magazine* 73 (October 2006), p. 10. Retrieved from http://policechiefmagazine.org/magazine/index.cfm?fuseaction=print_display&article_id=1 (June 25, 2010).

[14] Ibid.

[15] D. A. Tansik and J. F. Elliot, *Managing Police Organizations* (Monterey, CA: Duxbury Press, 1981), p. 81.

[16] Ibid.

[17] U.S. Department of Justice, Community Relations Service, "Importance of Police-Community Relationships and Resources for Further Reading" in Toolkit for Policing (Washington, DC: Community Relations Service, 2016), p. 3.

[18] B. J. Hodge and W. P. Anthony, *Organizational Theory: An Environmental Approach* (Boston: Allyn & Bacon, 1979), p. 240.

[19] Richard Hall, *Organizations: Structure and Process* (Englewood Cliffs, NJ: Prentice Hall, 1972), p. 143.

[20] This Section Is a Synopsis of the "Nature and Process of -Differentiation" found in Hodge and Anthony, *Organizational Theory*, p. 249.

[21] Hans Toch, "Police Officers as Change Agents in Police Reform," *Policing and Society* 18, No. 1 (March 2008), pp. 60–71.

[22] Ronald Wells, "Intelligence-Led Policing: A New Paradigm in Law Enforcement" *PATC Bulletin* (Indianapolis, IA: PATC Law Enforcement Training Council, September 2009).

[23] Darlton E. Mcfarland, *Management: Foundations and Practices*, 5th edition. (New York: Macmillan, 1979), p. 316.

[24] Ibid., p. 309.

[25] B. J. Hodge and H. J. Johnson, *Management and Organizational Behavior* (New York: John Wiley & Sons, 1970), p. 163.

[26] Modified by Robert W. Taylor (July 2015). See Edward R. Maguire and Craig D. Uchida, "Measurement and Explanation in the Comparative Study of American Police," in *Measurement and Analysis of Crime and Justice*, Criminal Justice 2000, Vol. 4 (2000). See also Edward R. Maguire, *Organizational Structures in American*

Police Agencies: Context, Complexity and Control (Albany, NY: SUNY Press, 2003).

[27]W. Michael Phibbs, "Should Sector Policing Be in Your Organization's Future?" *FBI Law Enforcement Bulletin* (April 2010), pp. 1–2, 7.

[28]U.S. Department of Justice, Press Release, "Multi-Agency Investigation into East LA Gang Results in Federal RICO Indictment that Charges 38 Gangsters," (December 10, 2014).

[29]Richard Kitaeff, "The Great Debate: Centralized vs. Decentralized Marketing Research Function," *Marketing Research: A Magazine of Management and Applications* 6 (Winter 1993), p. 59.

[30]Anaheim Police Department (Anaheim, CA), "Community Policing Team Annual Report," 1994.

[31]Several critiques of experimental police methods have been noted in the literature. See Robert W. Taylor and Dennis J. Kenney, "The Problems with Problem Oriented Policing" (paper presented at the Academy of Criminal Justice Sciences Annual Meeting, Nashville, Tennessee, March 1991); Kenneth W. Findley and Robert W. Taylor, "Re-Thinking Neighborhood Policing," *Journal of Contemporary Criminal Justice* 6 (May 1990), pp. 70–78; Jerome Skolnick and D. Bayley, *Community Policing: Issues and Practices Around the World* (Washington, DC: National Institute of Justice, 1988); Jack Greene and Ralph Taylor, "Community Based Policing and Foot Patrol: Issues of Theory and Evaluation," in Jack Greene and Stephen Mastrofski (eds.), *Community Policing: Rhetoric or Reality?* (New York: Praeger, 1988), pp. 216–219; Stephen Mastrofski, "Police Agency Accreditation: The Prospects of Reform," *American Journal of Police* (May 15, 1986), pp. 45–81.

[32]Gary W. Cordner, "Written Rules and Regulations: Are They Necessary?" *FBI Law Enforcement Bulletin* 58 (July 1989), pp. 17–21.

[33]See Robert Michaels, *Political Parties* (New York: Dover, 1959).

[34]Jerry H. Ratcliffe, "Intelligence-Led Policing," in R. Worley, L. Mazerolle and S. Rombouts (eds.), *Environmental Criminology and Crime Analysis* (Portland, OR: Willan Publishing, 2008).

[35]Jerry H. Ratcliffe and Ray Guidetti, "State Police Investigative Structure and the Adoption of Intelligence-Led Policing," *Policing: An International Journal of Police Strategies and Management* 31 (2008), p. 1.

[36]The current fiscal crisis confronting many police departments, especially in California, over the past decade has prompted considerable effort in maximizing the efficiency of police agencies in general, and the investigative function more specifically. Many departments have conducted evaluations of staff and workload studies to meet this demand. Much of this section has been used in evaluation studies conducted by the author, Robert W. Taylor first originated with Dr. Jerry Dowling, Chief Marlin Price, and Dr. Larry Hoover, *An Evaluation of the Fort Worth, Texas Police Department—Staffing of the Investigative Function* (January 2002) *and Final Executive Report* (March 2002) (Huntsville, TX: JUSTEX Systems, Inc.).

[37]Steve Fainaru, "Oakland Police Force Restructuring Could Hinder Murder Investigations and More," *The New York Times* (May 15, 2011).

[38]John D. McCluskey, Jefferey M. Cancino, Marie Skubak Tillyer, and Rob Tillyer, "Does Organizational Structure Matter? Investigation Centralization, Case Clearances and Robberies," *Police Quarterly* 17, No. 3 (September 2014).

[39]Much of the early scholarly work on detective staffing, function and relationship within the organizational design of a police agency has been conducted during consulting projects. Foremost in this area of study is the work of our good friend, Dr. Jerry L. Dowling, Sam Houston State University. The only published work presented in this area by Jerry is as follows: "Analysis of Detective Staffing Patterns in Law Enforcement Agencies," paper presented to 41st Annual Meeting of the Academy of Criminal Justice Sciences, Las Vegas, Nevada, March 2004.

[40]President's Commission on Law Enforcement and Administration of Justice, *Challenge of Crime in a Free Society: Science and Technology Report* (USGPO: 1967). See https://www.ncjrs.gov/App/Publications/abstract.aspx?ID=42.

[41]Peter W. Greenwood, *The RAND Criminal Investigation Study: Its Findings and Impacts to Date* (Santa Monica, CA: RAND Corporation, 1979). See http://www.rand.org/pubs/papers/P6352.

[42]Frank Horvath, Robert T. Meesig, and Yung Hyeock Lee, *National Survey of Police Policies and Practices Regarding the Criminal Investigations Process: Twenty-Five Years After RAND* (East Lansing, MI: Michigan State University, 2001). See https://www.ncjrs.gov/pdffiles1/nij/grants/202902.pdf.

[43]See Peter Greenwood, Jan Chaiken, and Joan Petersilia, *The Criminal Investigation Process* (D.C. Heath & Co., Lexington, MA, 1977), p. 228.

[44]John Liederbach, Eric Fritsch, and Charissa Womack, "Detective Workload and Opportunities for Increased Productivity in Criminal Investigations," *Police Practice and Research: An International Journal* 1, No. 1 (December 2011), p. 60.

[45]See U.S. Department of Justice, *Data Collection: Law Enforcement Management and Administrative Statistics (LEMAS) Report: Local Police*, 2013. See http://www.bjs.gov/index.cfm?ty=tp&tid=71.

[46]Ibid.

[47]Ibid.

[48]James Q. Wilson, *Varieties of Police Behavior: The Management of Law and Order in Eight Communities* (Boston, MA: Harvard University Press, 1968).

[49]Martin Kaste, "Open Cases: Why One-Third of Murders in America Go Unresolved," *National Public Radio*, March 30, 2015. See: http://www.npr.org/2015/03/30/395799413/how-many-crimes-do-your-police-clear-now-you-can-find-out, and http://www.npr.org/2015/03/30/395069137/open-cases-why-one-third-of-murders-in-america-go-unresolved.

[50]Ibid.

[51]Kassoff, *Organizational Concepts*, pp. 31–38.

[52]National Sheriffs' Association. See http://www.sheriffs.org/content/faq.

[53]Ibid., pp. 22–26.

[54]John M. Pfiffner and Frank P. Sherwood, *Administrative Organization* (Englewood Cliffs, NJ: Prentice Hall, 1965), pp. 43–44.

CHAPTER SEVEN

LEADERSHIP

Learning Objectives

1. Identify and briefly describe any five key characteristics of effective senior police leaders.
2. Explain Drucker's distinction between leadership and management.
3. Define and describe Schafer's acts or omissions of ineffective police leaders.
4. Distinguish between a Police Chief's rational-legal authority and power.
5. Contrast socialized versus personalized power needs.
6. Identify and define the components which make up the leadership skill mix.
7. Describe each of Downs four leader styles.

INTRODUCTION

KNOWLEDGE OF LEADERSHIP IS *important because: (1) officers deserve serious and competent leadership; (2) leadership weakness can reduce unit effectiveness and be a precursor to conduct problems by officers due to a lack of corrective action; (3) leadership failures can result in civil liability problems (see Chapter 14, Legal Aspect of Police Administration); (4) personnel costs, including fringe benefits, may account for 80 or more percent of the police budget (see Chapter 12, Financial Management); (5) leadership style communicates what commanders think about the people they lead; (6) while some people might be "born leaders," everyone else has to learn about it and integrate that knowledge with their behavior in small steps; and (7) leadership mistakes can result in injuries and deaths to those who are led, as well as to members of the public.*

POLICE LEADERSHIP

Although effective leadership is desired within police departments and there is an abundance of training to help provide it, there is not substantial depth in the empirical research on effective police leadership processes.[1] Schafer argues that much of what is known is from small case studies, descriptive accounts, and anecdotal reports from "celebrity chiefs."[2] The police profession is a consumer of leadership theory. The theories relied upon are overwhelmingly developed by academics as general propositions and then researched almost entirely in non-police settings. When the theories are tested in police settings, the studies often involve small sample sizes that are largely not replicated. Moreover, leadership studies conducted by observation may consist of a cursory analysis lacking rigor and focusing only on the short-term impact.[3]

Often, leadership theories or portions of them work in law enforcement agencies. From this we can conclude that many aspects of leadership are universal, such as integrity and fostering meaningful participation. However, we are left to wonder if theories generated specifically from studies of law enforcement leadership would merely confirm what we know, or would they identify subtle but important differences between policing and other professions in terms of what constitutes "good" leadership?

Our preoccupation with crime, homeland security, and the need to be seen as "current" in terms of leadership theory has diverted attention from developing a passion about leadership excellence. Some of the barriers to such excellence include:

1. Insufficient effort and funding are devoted to leadership development at every level of our agencies, although our chief resource is people (see Chapter 12, Financial Management);

2. We need more strong leadership role models in law enforcement agencies. Perhaps the most potent way to change behavior in organizations is for leaders to openly model or "wear" the desired behavior consistently;

3. Law enforcement generally fails to identify potential leaders earlier in their careers. A modest start would be to give them small projects to showcase their abilities, staying out of their way as they grapple with their assignments, and giving them honest critiques; and

4. Ineffective police leaders are seldom demoted nor are they thoughtfully retrained. Instead, we manage around their shortcomings or transfer them to minor duties for which they are often over qualified, wasting valuable resources and allowing the continuation of a poor role model.[4] It is a practice that is simultaneously humane and costly.

Developing police leadership is not a one-time investment; like the maintenance on police vehicles, it should be conceived of as a continuing expenditure. To help keep our eyes on the ball, the cost of leadership should not be aggregated under training. It must be a separate line in the budget supported by an abundance of individual staff development plans. If leadership is really dispersed in our departments, then it must find its reality in the commitment of dollars.

Pearson-Goff and Herrington did a systematic review of the police leadership literature published in journals.[5] After applying filters such as only including empirical studies with a large sample size and using only reports written in English, they were left with 66 studies. Several of these were eliminated because of low relevance or other reasons, leaving 57 studies to be closely examined.[6] Those studies are based on the perceptions of officers of their senior police leaders.[7] Analysis of the data provided seven key characteristics of effective senior police leaders and five key activities in which they engaged (see Table 7.1).[8] Unifying these two factors is the view that senior police leaders are focused on providing a vision for the future and the mission.[9]

Implicitly, leadership is often thought of as being positive—a good thing, uplifting and guiding toward some important accomplishment. That is the major thrust of this chapter, although the dark side of leadership is also covered.

TABLE 7.1 PEARSON-GOFF AND HERRINGTON: KEY CHARACTERISTICS AND ACTIVITIES OF EFFECTIVE SENIOR POLICE LEADERS*

Seven Key Characteristics of Effective Senior Police Leadership	Five Key Activities
1. Ethical behavior, a genuine sense of integrity and honesty that encourages subordinates to do likewise with each other. 2. Trustworthy, being viewed within the law enforcement agency, in government, and across the community as a "straight arrow." 3. Legitimacy perceived as someone who still knows how to work the street as opposed to being desk bound and out of touch with the daily realities of policing. 4. Being a role model, serving as an example of the behavior expected from subordinates. 5. Communication, the capacity to share ideas, explain decisions, create support, and respond to criticism within the police department, across agencies, with stakeholders, and as a voice in government policy making. 6. Decision making, a competency in making decisions that move the agency forward, e.g., obtaining resources, removing performance barriers, and achieving goals. 7. Critical, creative/innovative, and strategic thinking ability, which entails looking to the future and determining what conditions need to be met or created to be successful.	1. Creating a shared vision that helps police department members know where they are going. 2. Engendering organizational commitment by strategies such as providing a system of rewards and power sharing, e.g., giving members a voice in some decisions or creating committees on which they can have input to policies and other matters. 3. Caring for subordinates involves a cluster of actions, illustrated by coaching, mentoring, training opportunities, engaging assignments, and participating on committees and projects that both challenge them and provide an opportunity to demonstrate their abilities. 4. Driving and managing change without which the status quo is perpetuated. Announcing change doesn't produce it. Change requires champions and senior police leaders are one important source of energy to help propel change from a plan to a reality. As an aside, lower ranking officers are more likely to cling to the status quo than quickly embrace change.[10] 5. Problem solving by senior leaders ordinarily does not involve easily resolved "garden variety problems." The less thorny problems have already been handled by mid-level or lower leaders. The more intractable problems end up on the desks of senior police leaders.[11]

*The present authors have added comments in both columns intended to be consistent with Pearson-Goff and Herrington's and to amplify their views. No reformulation of the original work is intended.

LEADER AND MANAGER

There are many definitions of leadership, each reflecting certain perspectives, but all incorporate the notion that the essence of leadership is interacting with others and influencing them. For example, **leadership** can be simply defined as the difference between pushing a string and pulling it or being a "difference maker." More completely, leadership has external and internal components; it is the process of:

1. Orientating police department to the larger environment, such as city council or county commission, the news media, civic organizations, and the general public; and

2. Influencing officers to use their energies willingly and appropriately to facilitate the achievement of the department's goals.

Leadership occurs in dyads (e.g., a chief and an assistant chief), small face-to-face groups, such as a command staff meeting; at the entire police department level; and externally as a representative/symbol of the department. Some argue that individual officers can provide leadership to themselves by *self-monitoring* their own behavior and learning from their mistakes, so they are not repeated. In this view self-leadership leads to enhanced performance. This line of thinking seems thin: Leaders need subordinates.

Quick Facts: The Dark Side of Self-Monitoring

Although not in a police setting, where competitive promotions are the usual case, a 2019 study found some evidence that effective self-monitoring can improve the likelihood of emerging as a leader. There is also a dark side to self-monitoring. People who are highly self-monitoring can be unduly influenced by the opinions of others. Stated differently, self-monitoring can result in making bad decisions because of a flawed perception by the self-monitoring person that others favor a particular decision.[12]

FIGURE 7.1 ▶ A Citizen Potawatomi Nation (CPN) community policing officer visits with senior citizens to learn of any needs or problems. The CPN is located on their reservation in Oklahoma with some 29,000 Native American members. The federal government has supported the development of community policing for local state, and tribal governments. (Courtesy of Citizen Potawatomi Nation)

However, Anderson's *Every Officer Is a Leader* effectively argues that officers must provide leadership to business owners, neighborhood associations, planning and zoning employees, and others outside of their agency to make community policing work[13] (see Figure 7.1).

There are diverse definitions of **leader** and **manager**. Those terms are also used imprecisely sometimes.[14] Occasionally, they are erroneously employed to mean the same thing and sometimes synonymously with *leadership* and *managing.*

Alimo-Metcalfe and Alimo-Metcalfe argue that many models of leadership are better regarded as management styles; *they maintain management is the content of a job and leadership is how it is carried out.*[15] Others argue that a person can be a leader, a manager, both, or neither and the mix of those skill sets and the responsibilities involved can vary over situations and time.[16] Another line of thought maintains effective administrators must be both leaders and managers. In that assessment leading and managing are co-dependent skill sets.

Quick Facts: Leadership and Management

Peter Drucker (1909–2005) was among the preeminent thinkers of his generation on these subjects, publishing 41 books. In *Essential Drucker: Management, the Individual, and Society* (2001), he viewed leadership as doing the right thing and management as doing things right.

Leader and manager can also be examined using three contrasting views: (1) placement in hierarchy, (2) organizational theory, and (3) role enactment:

1. In the first view, whether you are a leader, or a manager depends on where you are placed in the organization's hierarchy (see Table 7.2). Senior leaders are clustered at the top of an organization while managers are in non-line units "further down" the organizational chart and

"off to one side" with responsibility for staff functions, fewer people to supervise, less flexibility and usually less discretionary authority than line commanders. Illustrations of staff activities include strategic planning, quality control, crime analysis, professional standards, records, and public information/affairs.

2. In the second view, organizational theory, Weber notes that in the bureaucracy model each person and unit is under the direction/command of a higher office. It is from this arrangement that an organizational chart can be drawn. At the top of the pyramid is a lone figure, the police chief. By custom, people refer to the occupant of that office not only as "Chief" but also as "Our leader." Can there be other leaders in a police department? How

TABLE 7.2 DISTINCTIONS BETWEEN LEADERS AND MANAGERS USING PLACEMENT IN THE POLICE DEPARTMENTS HIERARCHY

Leaders	Managers
1. Are at or near the top	1. Occupy the middle ground between leaders and first-line supervisors
2. Have wide responsibilities.	2. Have narrower responsibilities.
3. Work on a broad stage, both outside and within the organization.	3. Are primarily directed toward those in their units.
4. Have both followers and subordinates.	4. Have subordinates.
5. Elevate how others do their jobs.	5. Make sure subordinates do their jobs.
6. Envision the future and are change oriented.	6. Are oriented toward shorter time frame, create agendas, maintain status quo.
7. Think strategically.	7. Think tactically.

would we know whether the commanders of various units on an organizational chart are leaders or managers? Arbitrarily, are those commanding line units "leaders," and staff commanders are "managers?" Should job descriptions be scrutinized to see which ones specify "leads" versus "manages"? Other than identifying "Our Leader," the bureaucratic model is not very illuminating on this issue.

3. Role enactment is the third view and may be the surest way of determining who is acting out of a leadership skill set and who does so out of a management skill set. However, this delineation of skills is not precise. Some skills, such as decision making, overlap. Role enactment is revealed by observing how a person with authority over the performance of others behaves. For example, those who are acting out of their leadership skill set tend to be visionaries who want to improve on the status quo whenever possible and will also unleash energy and creativity by trusting and empowering subordinates to come up with better ideas for doing things. Leaders know that they do not have a lock on good ideas and create the environment in which energy can be released and ideas generated. Those acting out of a management skill set may also do this, but in the main they have a bias toward maintaining the status quo, for example, refining or developing policies and the procedures supporting them and work within the established agency boundaries. One skill set is often restless with the status quo and the other tends to embrace it.

Of necessity, the challenge of leading and managing the activities of the department must be widely distributed.[17] Police departments, except for very small ones, cannot function without distributed authority. The extension of this reality is that law enforcement agencies need individuals who possess both leadership and managerial skill sets. Leadership and management skills are not mutually exclusive and are usually not coequal. It is perhaps inevitable that subconsciously or through introspection, officers recognize the mix of aptitudes they have and gravitate toward assignments that are a good match for their strongest skill set.

Police chiefs have multiple roles, such as preserving the trust and confidence of the public in the department, interacting with politicians, modeling and communicating values, envisioning the future, determining the operational philosophy, being a change agent and a budget gladiator, allocating resources, coordinating with other local departments, boards, and authorities, such as school and water, working with state officials with oversight authority on portions of departmental matters, for example, peace officer standards commissions, resolving conflicts, solving problems, recognizing and celebrating the achievements of officers, civilian staff, and the public (see Figure 7.2) and being a spokesperson. In state police, state patrol, larger county, and municipal departments, sheriffs and chiefs have the additional task of leading personnel at district stations/precincts "remotely."[18]

These tough roles and other factors lead to an average tenure for police chiefs of about 2.5 to 4.5 years.[19] The Law Enforcement Management Institute of Texas (LEMIT) provides research, continuing education, and training to Texas law enforcement executives. Its experience underscores the abbreviated tenure of police chiefs. LEMIT trained some 50 new chiefs annually in the early 1990s, a figure now grown to approximately 150.[20]

Some of this turnover is due to chiefs deciding that leading police departments simply takes too much out of them and their families. The exiting chiefs often dealt with multiple issues, many of which occurred both simultaneously and repetitively. The most prominent issues included fiscal restraints, service demands, political skirmishes, long hours, unions, and the usual assortment of criminal activities that vary across jurisdictions.

FIGURE 7.2 ▶ Peter Carey, then the Colorado Springs Police Chief, presents a Citizen's Award of Appreciation to an unnamed bank official who's courageously helped an officer overcome physical resistance from an alleged bank robber. Editor: Photo from https://www.afspc.af.mil/News/Features/Display/Article/731634/i-am-schriever-civilian-hero/ (Courtesy of U.S. Air Force)

FIGURE 7.3 ▶ A Missouri Grand Jury determined that Ferguson Missouri police officer Darren Wilson was justified in using deadly force against 18-year-old, African-American male Michael Brown, because he was defending his life. However, there were many who disagreed with this decision. This photo depicts a 2014 San Francisco demonstration march to the police station as part of their protest against both the shooting and the Grand Jury's decision. (Jay Shaw Baker/Nurphoto/Getty Images)

To this list former New Jersey State Police Superintendent Rick Fuentes adds that in the post-9/11 environment there has been a blurring of hometown and homeland security.[21] The multiple roles and tough problems also affect recruiting to fill vacant police leadership jobs; in some areas of the country, there are roughly 50 percent fewer candidates seeking those positions.[22]

Quick Facts: Police Chief Turnover: All Terminations Aren't Politically Motivated

A 2019 empirical study of police chief turnover examined two types of performance: (1) leadership performance and (2) departmental performance. Police chiefs rated as performing poorly were more likely to have left their positions involuntarily. In contrast, Chiefs rated as being effective were recognized as such and rewarded.

Other points made by the study include: (1) the ratings were made by currently employed Chiefs. This suggests there is some consensus between municipal officials responsible for police department oversight and "sitting chiefs" as to what constitutes a "good job." By extension, it also establishes that not every chief who is involuntarily separated can honestly assert their leaving was a "political hatchet job"; and (2) chiefs hired by a Mayor were less subject to involuntary turnover than those hired by a city council. This is attributed to the reality that a city council is made up of people with contradictory opinions, including whether the "right person" is leading the police department and what it should and shouldn't be doing. [27]

THE FALL OF POLICE LEADERS

Police leaders may be compelled to resign or are terminated for reasons beyond their control. Some of these dismissals are unfair because of a politically based, almost compulsive, need to have somebody to blame: Former Los Angeles Police Chief Bill Bratton believes that if you are going to mobilize support, you must innovate, and that involves taking risks. In Bratton's view, that means setting goals that can be measured, which is both a necessity[23] and some chiefs' undoing. Chiefs also act as change agents. "When you make changes, you make some people mad." A portion of them may become adversarial, meaning "enemies."[24] Sooner or later your enemies become 51 percent, leading to a shortened shelf life for chiefs.[25] A third of what are reported as voluntary resignations by police chiefs actually occur as an alternative to being fired.[26]

"Leadership is considered a set of positive traits; those lacking them are not true leaders"[28] and they fail because of their own inadequacies.[29] Schafer's survey of 304 leaders attending the FBI's National Academy identified ineffective "leaders" by their: (1) commission, doing things they shouldn't and (2) omission, the lack of needed skills and/or the inability to recognize or lack of willpower to do what is needed[30]

1. These five points are the *acts of commission* by police leaders:
   a. focusing on themselves over others, a "me first mindset";
   b. displays of ego/arrogance beyond the realm of healthy confidence and self-assurance;
   c. a closed mindedness demonstrated by the failure to listen to, and value, the ideas of others;
   d. micro-managing that reflects a lack of trust in subordinates. In this regard, a sergeant from a small municipal agency noted that micro-managers failed to delegate when appropriate; and
   e. being arbitrary and capricious, represented by inconsistent decision making and a lack of a systematic approach. Being able to anticipate the

likely decisions of their leaders allows subordinates to take actions and make decisions that support them. Capricious leaders also put personal relationships ahead of what is right, just, and consistent with past practices.[31]

2. Ineffective leaders can also be characterized by five points of omission:
   a. poor work ethic, revealed by laziness, doing the minimal necessary work, and essentially "retiring in place" (RIP). Police leaders with a poor work ethic are frequently late in their careers and have lost their enthusiasm and commitment. Concurrently, they display a negativity;
   b. failing to take action and make decisions in a variety of circumstances;
   c. ineffective communication, but not because they have weak written and verbal skills. Instead, they are unable or unwilling to have two-way conversations, don't explain their actions or decisions, and don't accept input;
   d. lack of appropriate interpersonal skills, considered as impoverished basic human relations skills. One survey respondent, an investigations supervisor from a small state agency, summarized this omission as "they fail to realize they are leading people"[34]; and
   e. integrity and forthrightness are among the bedrock values of policing; the lack of integrity erodes public respect and support. Inside of law enforcement agencies leaders who are seen by subordinates as being weak, lacking, or may have tarnished or lost their reputation for being trustworthy will not be able to lead for very long.[35]

Some police leaders, often unknowingly, set in motion events that will lead to their forced resignation or dismissal, or they may simply fail immediately. They may develop or have personality quirks or defects that result in them wounding or harming those they are supposed to be leading, creating

Box 7.2: A Tale of Two Police Chiefs: One Resigns and the Other is Fired

The Police Department (PD) consisted of 52 sworn officers and 11 civilians. Its Police Chief resigned after 26 years of service on the department amidst sexual misconduct charges. A report revealed nearly 800 pages of sworn statements from police officers and employees describing the former Chief as having sexually harassed female workers, repeatedly asking female employees out on dates, made unprofessional comments about their appearance and perfume, and sent them romantic poems. The most sensational allegations involve a female officer to whom the former chief sent something in the order of 100 photographs and 50 videos, some of which allegedly showed his sex organ. He also was described as having "vulgar temper tantrums" during meetings and degrading people in front of others. At least six people filed a suit against the city and its former chief for creating a hostile work environment. At some point, a report was be submitted to the Criminal Justice Standards and Training Commission to determine if the former chief's certification should be subject to a disciplinary procedure.[37]

The Chief of a four-officer Police Department was fired after surrendering on four felony charges involving a sexual relationship with a 14-year-old girl. Over video chat the man asked the victim to perform naked sexual acts and exposed himself to her multiple times. When they met in person, sometimes in the Chief's office, he would insert his hand inside of her underpants. According to the MPD's website, the Chief was a certified sexual assault investigator.[38]

These cases represent aberrant conduct that departs from the high-professional standards held by the men and women who serve law enforcement at the local, state, and federal levels. They are presented as a cautionary tale: People can have weak moments, without strong values and disciplined conduct, a fall will be on the horizon.

lingering problems, damaging morale, and reducing what they can get others to do willingly. The result is a smaller zone of effectiveness. Occasionally, the public posturing of Chiefs calls their leadership into question and when examined they are dismissed, or their contract is not renewed, or their position is abolished.

Misjudgments and character flaws by some police chiefs reveal themselves in a variety of activities. Among these are making personal use of items entered into the evidence room, for example, big-screen televisions and jewelry; sexually harassing or having sex or affairs with subordinates or members of the public (see Box 7.2); becoming aloof and remote, which results in reducing the communications sent to them, choking off their effectiveness; their drinking gets out of control; and they irritate subordinates by their maladaptive leadership styles, for example, "seagull chiefs" who don't give guidance on the front end, swoop in and poop on everyone when a problem arises, and fly away without providing any solutions.[36] All of these examples lead to the quick path out of the department.

Leaders also fail because they are toxic. They pit subordinates against each other, lie to them, undermine anyone who is seen as a threat, take credit for the ideas and accomplishments of others, create an image that they are defending the department from outside forces to distract subordinates, stifle constructive criticism, and make others scapegoats for their own failures.[39] They lack integrity, are incapable of introspection, are blind to their own shortcomings, shrink from hard decisions, and have a reckless disregard of how their actions affect others.[40] In the end, they are found out and lose their jobs, but they leave a legacy that the incoming chief must work hard to overcome, that is, gaining the trust of the rank-and-file.

Law enforcement leadership doesn't just mean occupying a position; reduced to its simplest, it means being a "difference maker." Leadership success depends on exhibiting positive leadership behaviors and avoiding a catastrophic error[41] (see Box 7.3). The absence or presence of competent leadership can often be gauged by simply watching and listening:

- Police officers, operating a dirty patrol vehicle, approached a motorist they had stopped for a traffic violation. The officers' interaction with the driver was superficially correct but had a definite underlying tone of arrogance.
- The chief of police of a medium-sized city chronically complained to anyone who would listen that his commanders "aren't worth anything" and that he was "carrying the whole department on his back."
- A visitor to a city approached an officer walking a beat and asked where the nearest car rental agency could be found; he replied, "What the hell do I look like, an information booth?" and walked away.
- A woman asked an officer standing on a street corner where the First National Bank Building was. The officer took the woman's arm, escorted her across the street, and said, "Lady, you see that big building on the corner where we were just standing? Well, if it had fallen, we'd have both been killed by the First National Bank."
- Based on limited new information, the commander of an investigation bureau reopened the case file on a convicted "no-good" who had already served 14 months for the offense in question. Subsequently, new evidence and a confession resulted in his release and the conviction of the actual perpetrator.

Box 7.3: "Chief Herbert's" Career Ending Mistake

A single statement produced a self-inflicted and fatal career wound. Herbert led a 38-officer department. A popular chief who came up through the ranks was asked to meet in closed session with the mayor and city council to discuss a raise for the police department.

Council members initiated the meeting because they wanted to do something extra for the officers. They proposed a 10 percent increase, to which Herbert, for reasons he couldn't later articulate, replied the officers would be well pleased with 6 percent, which is what they got. One council member felt Herbert had sold out the welfare of officers' families to curry favor with the council. The story was leaked to the newspaper and officers raged at "the betrayal." Officers began making secretive end runs around Herbert to some members of council, giving them inside information on the department. The council gradually sharpened its questioning of Herbert's decisions.

As the Fall election drew closer, two candidates for council made "things in the police department" a campaign issue. The rank-and-file waited until the tide was turning against Herbert before giving him a no-confidence vote. Faced with strong internal opposition and dwindling political support, Herbert retired.

LEADERSHIP, AUTHORITY, AND POWER

In this section, the important distinctions and examples between the authority and power that leaders have are covered.

Weber identified three sources of **authority**:

1. charismatic authority rests on the exceptional heroism, exemplary character, or sanctity of a person, such as Medal of Honor recipients, Mahatma Gandhi, the Pope, and the police chiefs mentioned in Chapter 1, *A History of Police Administration.*
2. traditional authority, illustrated by kings and queens; and
3. rational-legal authority, a grant of authority made by the formal organization, such as a city, to a *position.* Each successive incumbent of that position, for example, Chief of Police, uses that authority to fulfil his or her job responsibilities.[42]

French and Raven concluded that there were five types of power:

1. legitimate, the belief that someone has the right to make demands on how you do your job;
2. expert, derived from a person's expertise and skill;
3. reward, the ability to compensate others for their compliance;
4. coercive, the expectation that you will be disciplined for your failure to conform to legitimate expectations; and
5. referent, to become liked or respected to such a degree that subordinates willingly follow orders.[43] Whatever the source of a leader's authority, power is a separate concept.

The fact that a formal grant of authority has been made does not mean that the person receiving it is also automatically able to influence others to perform at all, let alone willingly (see Quick Facts: Authority, But Not Power).

Quick Facts: Authority But Not Power

Officer Murphy was among 50 officers to be promoted by the New York City Police Commissioner. Instead of accepting a handshake and his gold detective's shield, Officer Murphy placed it on the dais and walked out of the ceremony. Officer Murphy took this action to protest the department's investigation of allegations that his unit—the Brooklyn Narcotics Tactical Team—had mistreated prisoners and lied about evidence to shore up shaky arrests. Officer Murphy was not believed to be a target of this investigation. A ranking police official with 40 years of service said he had never seen anything like Murphy's actions before.[44]

This incident illustrates that, while the commissioner had the authority to promote Officer Murphy, he did not have the power to make him accept it. Some power to affect an officer's performance is inherent in positions with formal authority. But to a significant degree, **power**, as suggested by Barnard, is a grant made by the led to the leader.[45] A police leader whose subordinates refuse to follow orders is not without power; those officers may be given verbal or written reprimands, reassigned, suspended, or terminated.[46] The use of this type of power must be considered carefully; failure to invoke it may contribute to a breakdown in discipline and organizational performance; the clumsy use of it may contribute to morale problems or have other negative side effects, including calling into question the abilities of the leader (see Box 7.4). Moreover, disciplinary actions in police and other municipal departments are normally subject to appeal and review by a Civil Service Board or the provisions of the union contract.

Box 7.4: The Water Cooler Commando

A uniformed officer riding alone informed the dispatcher that he was stopping a motorist who may have been drinking. His sergeant, who had only been promoted and assigned to the squad two weeks previously, heard the transmission and came to the scene as a backup.

When the sergeant, a nine-year veteran, but who had not served in any "street" assignment for the past six years, arrived a Marine corporal had just gotten into a taxicab. The sergeant talked briefly with the corporal and walked back to the officer. Unseen, the cab eased away. When questioned, the officer told the sergeant that while the Marine had a few drinks, he was not impaired. The sergeant accused him of dereliction of duty for not charging a "fellow Marine" with DUI

The officer received a mild letter of reprimand. The "slap on the wrist" was widely viewed as the platoon commander reluctantly supporting a green sergeant. The squad saw the sergeant as a "water cooler commando" and didn't trust him. A more serious misstep several months later resulted in the sergeant being transferred to a minor staff position. Although the Sergeant oversaw several functions, he supervised nobody.

Leadership also arises, as demonstrated by the Hawthorne Studies, out of the informal side of an organization. In police departments, officers "give" power to more seasoned or decorated colleagues, listening carefully to their opinions and suggestions. In some cases, informal leaders take exception to new policies and procedures and have the potential to disrupt a unit's harmony. A related problem occurs when younger officers make sergeant, passing veteran officers. Dismissing them as "test takers," the more experienced officers may quietly "compete" with the new supervisor to influence the attitudes and actions of the unit. However, informal leaders can also provide support to newly minted leaders as they adjust to new responsibilities.

THE POWER MOTIVATION OF POLICE LEADERS

Power is an indispensable dimension of police departments; it requires that a person have a desire to play a key role in influencing the outcome of activities. Former Richmond, California, Police Chief Chris Magnus says about power, "I think being a chief is very seductive in terms of power and influence. It's hard not to get caught up in this racket. You sort of lose focus."[47]

As we have seen, power is both a grant from the formal organization to a position, as well as a grant from the led to the leader. Power, however, is not always used for the same purpose; the term "**power motivation**" refers to the reasons, intentions, and objectives that underlie the use of power.[48]

McClelland and his associates studied the motivations of leaders extensively and concluded there were three types of power:

1. a high achievement or a **socialized power** motivation—the need to have a positive impact on a police department's administration and operations;

2. a high power or **personalized power needs**—the need to be in control for selfish, self-aggrandizing reasons (see Table 7.3); and

3. **affiliation needs**—the desire to be liked and accepted.

Affiliation needs and aspirations are not true power needs because they reflect a greater preoccupation with being accepted and liked than with having an impact on events. Affiliation needs can mediate some degree of personalized power needs. The contexts for these motivations may also be important; there is limited evidence that in conflict situations, socialized power leaders may make better decisions than those with personalized power needs.[49]

The difference between personalized power and socialized power has practical implications. A police leader with personalized power needs will tend toward being authoritarian, making most decisions and tightly controlling work. An authoritarian chief believes that officers will not work without close supervision. This style of leadership ultimately leads to problems because as the lack of trust becomes apparent, officers chafe at the tight control, morale suffers, and departmental performance declines, often accompanied by a spike in turnover by officers seeking a better work environment. A study of the department may be called for and the report used as the basis for firing the chief.

In contrast, chiefs with socialized power tend to help people around them and have a stabilizing effect, are restrained in their use of power, share some of their power with subordinates, and are restrained and polite, helping people to achieve their potential. Leadership styles are discussed in greater detail later in this chapter.

THE LEADERSHIP SKILL MIX

Skill is how knowledge is translated into action. The leadership skills mix varies along the organizational chain from Chief to line-level managers..[50] There are three inter-related types of skills needed for effective leadership: a) human relations skills, b) conceptual skills, and c) technical skills.

TABLE 7.3 PERSONALIZED AND SOCIALIZED POWER NEEDS	
Police Leaders with Personalized Power Tend to Be	**Police Leaders with Socialized Power Tend to Be**
• Impulsive and erratic in their use of power	• Inhibited and self-controlled in their use of power
• Rude and overbearing	• Respectful of others' rights
• Exploitative of others	• Concerned with fairness
• Oriented toward strength	• Oriented toward justice
• Committed to the value of efficiency	• Committed to the value of working per se
• Proud	• Egalitarian
• Self-reliant; individualists	• Organization-minded; joiners
• Excited by the certitudes of power	• Ambivalent about power
• Competitive	• Collaborative
• Concerned with exceptionally high goals	• Concerned with realistic goals
• Defensive—protective of own sense of importance	• Non-defensive—willing to seek help
• Inspirational leaders	• Builders of systems and people
• Difficult to replace—leaves behind a group of officers who were dependent on the leader; does little to develop officers	• Replaceable by other managers—leave a system intact and self-sustaining
• Sources of direction, expertise, and control	• Sources of strength for others

Human Relations Skills

Human relations skills involve the capacity to interact positively with other people and are used at all levels of a police department and also externally. Examples include motivation, conflict resolution, and interpersonal communication skills. The single, most important human relations skill is communication; without it, nothing can be set in motion, and nothing underway can be guided.

As officers progress up the rank hierarchy of a police department, they typically become responsible for more people but have fewer people reporting directly to them. The human relations skills of a police department's top managers remain important, however, as they are used to win political support for the agency's programs and to obtain the resources necessary to operate them. In particular, the chief's human relations skills are critical, as this person is the department's key representative to the larger environment. The way in which he or she "comes across" is, to a certain degree, the way in which some significant others—such as the city manager and members of city council—will regard the police department. The question of the fairness of that fact aside, the practical implication is that the chief must be aware of and fulfill the symbolic leadership role.

Within the department, top management must communicate its goals and policies downward and be willing to receive feedback about them. As mid-level managers, lieutenants and captains play an important linking function, passing downward in implementable forms the communications they receive from top management and passing upward certain communications received from first-line supervisors. Because sergeants ordinarily supervise directly the greatest number of people, they use human relations with great frequency, often focusing on issues such as resolving interpersonal problems, communicating the department's vision, and providing guidance.

Conceptual Skills

Conceptual skills include the ability to understand and to interrelate various parcels of information that may seem unrelated, or those for which the meaning or importance is not immediately apparent. Although this skill is used at all levels of the police department, the standards for handling the information become less certain and the level of abstraction necessary to handle the parcels becomes greater as one moves upward. Illustrative is the difference between a sergeant helping a detective evaluate the legal significance of evidence and a chief envisioning a future for the department and how to create and maintain a culture that will support the innovations being considered.

Technical Skills

Technical skills vary by level within a police department. Uniformed sergeants assigned to field duties must be able to help develop and maintain the skills of officers in areas such as handling domestic violence calls. As one progresses upward toward middle and top management, the range of technical skills narrows, and conceptual skills come to predominate. In that upward progression, the character of the technical skills also changes from being operations oriented to management oriented and gradually includes new elements, such as budgeting, planning, and being responsible for decisions that must be made now, but their outcome/impact is not certain. To elaborate further, one may not be able to tell by the generic label whether a particular skill is, for example, technical or conceptual. To illustrate this point, an understanding of the many aspects of financial management (see Chapter 12, Financial Management) is a conceptual skill, but the actual preparation of the budget is a technical skill required of middle managers and those more senior.

THEORIES OF LEADERSHIP

Theories of leadership attempt to explain the factors associated with the emergence of leadership and the nature of leadership. This chapter examines leadership in terms of: 1) traditional leadership theory, 2) behavior and leadership styles theory, 3) contingency and situational theory, 4) transactional and transformational theories, 5) comparison of charismatic and transformational leadership, and 6) "new leadership": servant, spiritual, authentic, and ethical leadership.

Traditional Leadership Theory

There are two branches to traditional leadership theory: (1) great man and (2) the traits approach.

GREAT MAN THEORIES

"Great man" theories were advanced by Thomas Carlyle (1795–1881) and George Hegel (1770–1831).[52] Carlyle (see Figure 7.4) believed that leaders were unusually gifted individuals who made history. He may not have been entirely wrong—there is preliminary evidence that approximately 30 percent of the variation in leadership styles is accounted for by heredity, the balance being environmental influences, including leadership development opportunities and roles.[53] Reversing the direction of causality, Hegel argued that it was events that produced the "great man." As an illustration of this, Dwight Eisenhower (1890–1969) was an obscure Army Colonel in 1941, three years into World War II, he was a five-star General and later a two-term President. The "born leader" concept is associated with Francis Galton (1822–1911), who espoused that leaders were the product of genetics,[54] transmitted from one generation to the next one. If Galton is correct—that leaders are born—then arguably police departments may be wasting money on leadership development.

FIGURE 7.4 ▶ Thomas Carlyle: unusually gifted people make history. (Library of Congress Prints and Photographs Division [LC-USZ62-134797])

THE TRAITS APPROACH

The traits approach is a natural extension of great man theory. **Traits** are relatively stable predispositions to behave in certain ways; examples include being energetic, emotionally stable, and extroverted.[55] Field Marshal Montgomery, one of England's great World War II commanders,[56] believed that leaders were made, not born; however, they had certain traits, such as an infectious optimism, confidence, intellect, and the ability to be a good judge of character.

Beginning around 1910 and continuing through the 1950s, research on traits dominated the thinking about leadership. The research was so substantial that Allport and Odbert (1936),[57] Stogdill (1948),[58] and Goode (1951)[59] attempted to consolidate hundreds of studies and still ended up with lengthy lists of traits. The earlier traits research suffered from several deficiencies: (1) traits such as loyalty, diligence, and perseverance were difficult to define and hard to measure; (2) some traits aren't portable from one setting to another; (3) traits are variable in their importance; and (4) situational factors can diminish the importance of traits or cause others to be needed (e.g., creating a police department for a newly incorporated city).

TABLE 7.4 THE CORRESPONDENCE BETWEEN THE "BIG FIVE" AND SPECIFIC TRAITS

Big Five Personality Traits	Specific Traits
Surgency	Extroversion/Outgoing Energy/Activity level Need for power/Assertive
Conscientiousness	Dependability Personal integrity Need for achievement
Agreeableness	Cheerful/Optimistic Nurturing/Sympathetic/Helpful Need for affiliation
Adjustment	Emotional stability Self-esteem Self-control
Intelligence	Curious/Inquisitive Open-minded Learning oriented

Source: Courtesy of Gary Yukl, *Leadership in Organizations*, Upper Saddle River, NJ: Prentice Hall, 7th edition, 2010.

The traits approach was re-energized beginning in the 1970s as new methodological and statistical techniques were developed and older ones improved. Meta-analysis, first used in 1904 and since greatly enhanced, allows the results from many comparable studies to be analyzed; its use led to the "Big Five" model of traits. The **Big Five** is the result of efforts to find a small number of broad trait categories into which many specific traits can be fitted (Table 7.4).[60] In 2010, Erdle and colleagues confirmed the existence of a **Big Two** within the Big Five: (1) stability, consisting of emotional stability, agreeableness, and conscientiousness; and (2) plasticity, composed of extraversion and being open minded.[61]

Zaccaro concluded that there is mounting evidence that some traits are "precursors" of leadership effectiveness.[62] Emotional intelligence (EI) and social intelligence (SI) appear to be among them. EI and SI have been examined both as single traits and combined. Bar-On used a combined Emotional Social Intelligence (ESI) measure to help the Air Force identify potential recruiters who could be high performers. The use of ESI data resulted in nearly a 300 percent increase in selecting high-performance recruiters.[63]

EI is positively associated with the quality of peer relationships,[64] may account for a lack of progress among intelligent people in psychotherapy,[65] and helps manage stress. Units with higher levels of EI experience less task and relationship conflict, and when it occurs, it is less intense.[66] A study of EI in Nigerian police officers revealed that it was not related to gender, marital status, length of service, or age.[67,68] In an earlier study, Barbera et al. (2002) found evidence to the contrary, suggesting that the emotional and social intelligence may develop over time.[69] Bar-On called for more research into emotional intelligence, particularly with respect to a sense of well-being; happiness; raising and educating well-adjusted, productive, healthy children; and the search for a more meaningful life.[70] Ultimately, researchers may find that the amounts of EI and SI are less important than what combinations of them are related to effective leadership.

Riggio and Reichard concluded that another way to approach EI and SI was through the skills related to them. They developed a taxonomy—a classification system—for **emotional skills (ES)** and **social skills (SS)** (Table 7.5). ES as the ability to accurately perceive and appraise your own emotions and those of others, to regulate your own emotions, and to do so while adapting and responding to the needs of others.[71] Social skills are closely related to emotional skills and are defined as the ability to express one's self in social situations; the ability to "read" social situations, recognizing different social roles and expected behavior; and interpersonal problem solving.[72]

ES and SS are associated with being (1) more favorably viewed in social situations; (2) more confident; (3) a better public speaker; (4) more physically attractive; (5) more upwardly mobile in one's career; (6) seen as more effective by subordinates; and (7) savoir-faire, or seemingly able to know just what to do.[73]

Police officers have also weighed in on leadership traits. While they have some preference for leaders with greater field experience, the characteristics they most prefer in command, middle managers, and first-line supervisors are honesty, dependability, competency, and being broad minded.[74]

Organizational citizenship behavior (OCB) is composed of subtle things that employees do voluntarily and are not required or expected but contribute to overall organizational effectiveness.[75] Examples include police officers officially at the end of their tour of duty volunteering to back up a unit on a traffic stop or giving words of encouragement or suggestions to another detective who is working a tough, high-profile case. Several studies have found that overall the Big Five personality traits are positively associated with OCB. Although

TABLE 7.5 EMOTIONAL AND SOCIAL SKILLS

Skill	Example	Purpose
EI Skills		
Emotional Expressiveness	Chief communicates nonverbally, e.g., command presence, selection of seat at table, facial expression, posture, or gesture	Communicates place in hierarchy; approval and disapproval to subordinate commanders
Emotional Sensitivity	Chief receives and accurately interprets nonverbal (e.g., body language) expressions of members of command staff	Gains understanding of the needs and emotional states of others, enhances ability to establish rapport
Emotional Control	Chief controls the display of his/her emotions	Eliminates the immediate display of anger or other strong emotional responses, requires a high degree of self-monitoring. A self-indulgent display of anger may impair relationships and impede goal achievement. A premeditated display may be useful in reinforcing the Chief's priorities, policies, and programs.
SI Skills		
Social Expressiveness	Chief has command of language, evoking powerful images through well-crafted articulation	Increases Chief's effectiveness within the department, at external meetings, and before audiences, enhances performance as mentor and coach
Social Sensitivity	Chief accurately interprets verbal communications from others and monitors social situation	Chief tailors comments and interaction to the conversation or situation at hand, is "smooth"
Social Control	Chief manages how he/she presents him/herself to others; is tactful, but doing so doesn't reduce impact of message; conveys ability to "get things done"	Represents him/herself and department well, creates new opportunities, and responses to criticisms are seen as reasonable, thoughtful

Source: Adapted with restatement into a police framework and some reorganization from Ronald E. Riggio and Rebecca J. Reichard, "The Emotional and Social Intelligences of Effective Leadership," *Journal of Managerial Psychology* 23, No. 2 (2008), p. 172, Table 1.

OCB continues to be researched as a separate topic, by 2008, researchers were increasingly interested in a broader concept, **positive organizational behavior (POB)**. In at least some studies, POB included OCB as a component factor. Presently, POB lacks anything approaching a consensus definition, but it has the potential to do for current leadership interests what the Big Five did for traits research.

Counterproductive work behavior (CWB) also commands research interest. CWB is behavior that has a detrimental effect on relationships with other commanders and officers and/or on the efficiency of operations.[76] Examples include being verbally aggressive or rude to coworkers, emotional outbursts, engaging in anger-producing behavior, refusing to help a coworker, using demeaning language, and maintaining interpersonal conflicts with others.[77]

Behavior and Leadership Style Theories

Whereas trait theories attempt to explain leadership on the basis of what the leader is, behavioral theories try to do the same thing by concentrating on what the leader does.[79] These behaviors are often described in terms of leadership styles, meaning the continuing patterns of behavior as perceived and experienced by others that they use to characterize the leader. The behavior and leadership style theories were the main focus of researchers during the 1950s and 1960s.

LEWIN, LIPPITT, AND WHITE: AUTHORITARIAN, DEMOCRATIC, AND LAISSEZ-FAIRE

Although the three leadership styles these researchers studied had been previously identified, it was their 1939 study that systematized thinking about them.[80] The **authoritarian/autocratic leader** ("My way or the highway") makes all decisions, closely controls work, and is a micromanager; the **democratic leader** ("Let's talk about it") encourages individual or group participation in matters affecting the organization; and the **laissez-faire leader** (LFL) ("Whatever") takes a passive, "hands-off" posture. Only reluctantly do LFLs use the authority of their position; they do not make necessary decisions and delay taking any kind of action. This has the effect of providing subordinates with substantial autonomy.[81] LFLs provide only episodic leadership and that may be ineffectual. The larger the stakes, the more invisible LFLs become.

Quick Facts: The Perfect Chief Who Couldn't Get an Important Thing Done

Even if chiefs have all of the important traits, their efforts may amount to nothing. "Willow City," with 102 nonunionized officers, hired its first outside chief since the department was established in the early 1800s. Although "Chief Henry" had a strong task orientation, his relational skills were also excellent. He had impeccable education and training credentials and, on the basis of having led his former department to accreditation by the Commission on Accreditation of Law Enforcement Agencies (CALEA), Willow City hired him with the understanding he would do likewise with its department. However, it never happened.

His staff dragged their heels on assignments and otherwise thwarted "Chief Henry's" efforts. Rank-and-file officers were irrational in their opposition to him. For example, one officer told another something the chief had allegedly done.

The second officer replied that he knew the chief didn't do it "but would've if he thought he could get away with it." Even when "innocent," the chief was "guilty."

The negligible staff support, rank-and-file carping, and evaporating political support became powerful **leadership neutralizers**,[78] negating "Chief Henry's" efforts. Recognizing he had been rendered ineffectual, the chief resigned; his outstanding background produced nothing because he lacked the most essential trait of all: being an insider.

The assistant chief, a life-long local resident, was promoted to replace him and the department relaxed. However, "Willow City" has still not been accredited. Speculatively, the process may have become tainted by being deeply associated with an outsider.

Lewin, Lippitt, and White concluded that although the quantity of work was somewhat greater under the autocratic leader, autocracy could generate hostility and aggression. The democratically controlled groups were about as efficient as the autocratically controlled ones, but the continuation of work in the former did not depend on the presence of the leader. Under the laissez-faire leader, less work was produced, the work quality was poorer, and the work was less organized and less satisfying to members of the group.[82] A study of leader styles and officers attitudes in a mid-sized New England police agency confirmed the much earlier findings of Lewin, Lippitt, and White.[83]

LIKERT: MANAGEMENT SYSTEMS

In *New Patterns of Management* (1961) and *The Human Organization* (1967), Rensis Likert (1903–1981) echoed and extended Lewin, Lippitt, and White's work by specifying four different management systems (see Table 7.6). The names of

TABLE 7.6 LIKERT'S MANAGEMENT SYSTEMS

Organizational Variable	System 1	System 2	System 3	System 4
Leadership Processes Used Extent to which superiors have confidence and trust in subordinates	Have no confidence and trust in subordinates	Have condescending confidence and trust, such as master has to servant	Substantial but not complete confidence and trust; still wishes to keep control of decisions	Complete confidence and trust in all matters
Extent to which superiors behave so that subordinates feel free to discuss important things about their jobs with their immediate superior	Subordinates do not feel at all free to discuss things about the job with their superior	Subordinates do not feel very free to discuss things about the job with their superior	Subordinates feel rather free to discuss things about the job with their superior	Subordinates feel completely free to discuss things about the job with their superior
Extent to which immediate superior in solving job problems generally tries to get subordinates' ideas and opinions and make constructive use of them	Seldom gets ideas and opinions of subordinates in solving job problems	Sometimes gets ideas and opinions of subordinates in solving job problems	Usually gets ideas and opinions and usually tries to make constructive use of them	Always gets ideas and opinions and always tries to make constructive use of them

Source: The Human Organization by Rensis Likert. Copyright © 1967 McGraw-Hill Book Company. Used with permission of McGraw-Hill Book Company.

these systems are also used to describe leadership styles, and, for that reason, Likert's work is included in this section.

Authoritarian/autocratic police leaders, associated with Likert's Systems 1 and 2, have largely gone the way of the dinosaurs. The demise of the authoritarians is due to the world around them changing, becoming more liberal, as well as the perspectives and experiences associated with each new generation of workers entering law enforcement agencies. The characterization of these generations and their attributes vary somewhat in the research literature and are discussed in Chapter 9, Human Resource Management.

BLAKE AND MOUTON: THE MANAGERIAL GRID

Developed by Robert Blake and Jane Mouton,[84] the **Managerial Grid** has received a great deal of attention since its appearance in 1962 in the *Journal of the American Society of Training Directors*. The grid is part of the survey research feedback stem of organizational development and draws on earlier work done at Ohio State University and the University of Michigan.[85]

Depicted in Figure 7.5, the grid has two dimensions: concern for production and concern for people. Each axis, or dimension, is numbered from 1, meaning low concern, to 9, indicating high concern. The way in which a person combines these two

dimensions establishes a leadership style in terms of one of the five principal styles identified on the grid. The numbers associated with each of the styles reflect the level of concern for each of the two dimensions of the grid. For example, 9,1 indicates a maximum concern for production or the needs of the organization and a minimum orientation toward the needs of people in the organization. The first style number is always read off the production axis.

Some of the leadership styles identified previously can be related readily to the grid. Authoritarian leaders are represented by the 9,1 style; laissez-faire leaders by the 1,1; and democratic leaders by the 5,5. Additionally, the 9,1 and 9,9 styles are consistent, respectively, with the streams of thought summarized in Chapter 5 under the headings of "Traditional Organizational Theory" and "Open Systems Theory."

The leadership style of an individual can be identified by using a questionnaire based on the work of Blake and Mouton. According to the grid, one moves from the "best" to the "worst" styles going from 9,9 through 5,5; 9,1; 1,9; and 1,1. The most desirable combination of a primary and backup style is the 9,9 with a 5,5 backup.

A difficulty in using the grid questionnaire is that the data produced are no more accurate than the self-perceptions of

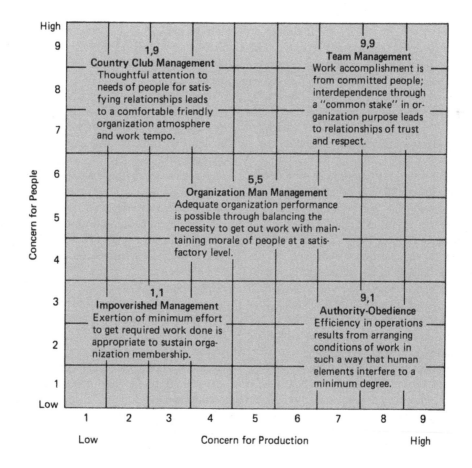

FIGURE 7.5 ▶ The Managerial Grid.

the person completing the instrument. When consulting with law enforcement agencies, one way to overcome this is to have each commander complete the instrument and then have each of his or her subordinates fill one out on how they experience the commander. Comparing these two sets of data provides useful information. Typically, more weight is given to the subordinate's combined data because they reflect how the leader is "coming across."

DOWNS: LEADERSHIP STYLES IN BUREAUCRATIC STRUCTURES

Downs[86] described four types of leader behavior in bureaucratic structures: (1) climbers, (2) conservers, (3) zealots, and (4) advocates.

Climbers are strongly motivated by power and prestige needs to invent new functions to be performed by their unit, particularly functions not performed elsewhere. If climbers can expand their functions only by moving into areas already controlled by others, they are likely to choose ones in which they expect low resistance. To protect their "turf," climbers tend to economize only when the resultant savings can be used to finance an expansion of their functions.[87] An example of a climber is a newly promoted major commanding the Patrol Division who argues that the Traffic Division should be "folded" into the Patrol Division.

The bias of **conservers** is toward maintaining things as they are. The longer a person is in the same job and the older one becomes, the lower one assesses any chances for advancement and the stronger one becomes attached to job security, all of which are associated with the tendency to become a conserver. Climbers can become conservers when they assess their probability for advancement and expansion to be low. Desiring to make their organizational lives comfortable, conservers dislike and resist change.[88] A Lieutenant with 19 years of service and no promotions in the last seven years would tend to be a conserver.

The peculiarities of the behavior of **zealots** stem from two sources: their narrow interest and their missionary-like energy, which they focus almost solely on their special interest. As a consequence, zealots do not attend to all of their duties and often antagonize other administrators by their lack of impartiality and their willingness to trample over all obstacles to further their special interest. Zealots rarely succeed to high-level positions because of their narrowness and are consequently poor administrators. An exception is when their interest comes into favor and they are catapulted into high office.[89] Some Commanders of Special Weapons and Tactics (SWAT) units may fall into the zealot category.

Unlike zealots, **advocates** promote everything under their jurisdiction. To those outside their units, they appear highly partisan, but within their units, they are impartial and fair, developing well-rounded programs. Loyal to their organizations, advocates favor innovation. They are also simultaneously more radical and more conservative than climbers. They are more radical in that they are willing to promote programs and views

that may antagonize politicians, superiors, and other powerful groups, such as the news media, if doing so helps their departments. They are more conservative because they are willing to oppose changes from which they might benefit but which would not be in the overall interest of their agencies.[90] Advocates may spring up anywhere in a police agency, confident and focused they are sometimes unaware of how others see them or simply don't care.

VAN MAANEN: STATION HOUSE SERGEANTS AND STREET SERGEANTS

In a study of a 1,000-officer police department, Van Maanen[91] identified two contrasting types of police sergeants: "station house" and "street." **Station house sergeants** had been out of the "bag" (uniform) before their promotions to sergeant and preferred to work in an office environment once they won their stripes; this preference was clearly indicated by the nickname of "Edwards, the Olympic Torch who never goes out" given to one such sergeant. Station house sergeants immersed themselves in the management culture of the police department, keeping busy with paperwork, planning, record keeping, press relations, and fine points of law. Their strong orientation to conformity also gave rise to nicknames as suggested by the use of "by-the-book Brubaker."

In contrast, **street sergeants** (see Figure 7.6) were serving in the field when they received their promotions. Consequently, they had a distaste for office procedures and had a strong action orientation, as suggested by such nicknames as "Shooter McGee" and "Walker the Stalker." Moreover, their concern was not with conformity but with "not letting the assholes take over the city."

In addition to the distinct differences already noted, station house sergeants and street sergeants were thought of differently by those whom they supervised: station house sergeants "stood behind their offices," whereas street sergeants "stood beside their officers." Each of these two different styles of working as a sergeant also has its drawbacks and strengths. Station house sergeants might not have been readily available to officers working in the field; however, they could always be located when a signature was needed and were able to secure more favors for officers than street sergeants were. Although immediately available in the field when needed, street sergeants occasionally interfered with the autonomy of their officers; unrequested, they responded to calls for service and handled them or, otherwise, at least in the eyes of their officers, "interfered."

A consideration of Van Maanen's work leads to some generalizations about the future careers of station house sergeants versus street sergeants. Station house sergeants are learning routines, policies, procedures, and polishing skills that will improve future promotional opportunities. Their promotional opportunities are further enhanced by contacts with senior police commanders who can give them important assignments and who may, if favorably impressed, influence future promotions. In contrast, street sergeants may gain some favorable publicity and awards for their exploits, but they are also more likely

FIGURE 7.6 ▶ A street sergeant on Staten Island, New York. Note his numerous decorations and five "hash marks" on his lower sleeve, each one denoting the completion of five years of service. (Robert Essel NYC/Getty Images)

to have citizen complaints filed against them, more likely to be investigated by internal affairs, and more likely to be sued. Consequently, very aggressive street sergeants are regarded by their superiors as "good cops" but difficult people to supervise. In short, the action-oriented street sergeant who does not "mellow out" may not go beyond a middle manager's position in a line unit, such as patrol or investigation.

Contingency and Situational Leadership Theories

Contingency leadership and situational leadership are similar; both postulate that there are no approaches that are always right. Contingency theory is somewhat broader, considering both leader capabilities and other factors in any given circumstance; **situational leadership** focuses more on what leaders should do.

TANNENBAUM AND SCHMIDT: FROM LEADER STYLES TO A CONTINGENCY MODEL

In 1958, **Tannenbaum and Schmidt** published "How to Choose a Leadership Pattern," which was the first situational leadership

theory, subsequently revising it in 1973 (see Table 7.7).[92] They asserted that the societal environment and organizational forces interplayed to form situations in which one leadership style would be more effective than other styles and leaders had to find that "good fit." Although we would now substitute other societal environment examples, Tannenbaum and Schmidt identified: (1) the younger generation's distrust of "establishment" organizations; (2) the civil rights movement with its call for more participation and influence for all people; and (3) a growing desire for workers to have a higher quality of life within the organizations that employ them. The organizational forces, stated here in a police context, are as follows:

1. Forces in the police leader, such as his or her value system, confidence in subordinate officers, leadership inclinations, and need for security in uncertain situations (e.g., "I can afford to be wrong on this one");

2. Forces in subordinate officers, including their knowledge, skills, and experience; more can reasonably be expected from a veteran squad than one that is light on experience; and

3. Forces in the department, formal and informal (e.g., a policy not to participate in federal immigration roundups or the practice of not arresting non-persistent panhandlers).

The most common criticism of Tannenbaum and Schmidt's theory is that while it discusses variables, including the leader, the subordinates, and the situation, the theory stops short of specifying how the variables are combined and translated into leadership behavior.[93]

FIEDLER: LEAST PREFERRED COWORKER (LPC)

Fiedler, a clinical psychologist, was originally interested in the relationship between psychotherapists and patients, later shifting his focus to leader-subordinate relationships.[94] His *A Theory of Leadership Effectiveness* (1967) attracted wide attention and has been subsequently modified several times. According to Fiedler, group effectiveness is a function of the interaction between the leader's esteem for his least preferred coworker (LPC) and three situational variables: (1) the task structure, (2) leader-subordinate relations, and (3) the power position of the leader.[95] Fiedler's use of "power" should be read to mean "authority" in the sense that Weber uses rational-legal authority; we have substituted "subordinate" where he used "member." Although Fiedler provides scales to determine the level of each of these three variables, only their short definitions are shown below:

1. **Task structure** refers to the degree a task is or is not clearly spelled out as to goals, methods of handling, and standards of performance. Arresting a motorist for drunk driving has high structure; by policy, there are a series of things that officers must do to properly perform the task. In contrast, the police reaction to a terrorist's detonation of a nuclear device in one of our major ports has low-task structure. There may

be no or only very general guidelines; there are many ways to approach the task; there may be more than one acceptable solution; or there may only be "Devil's Choices" meaning the only options are degrees of terrible. In the most extreme situations, the actual outcome of any solution may not be clearly foreseeable.

2. **Leader-Subordinate relations** are characterized by the extent to which commanders enjoy the confidence and goodwill of the officers they lead, and relations are cordial. Good relations make many things both possible and easier; poor relations render all things more difficult and if not corrected can become leadership neutralizers.

3. The **leader's position power** is the degree to which the commander has, or is perceived to possess by officers, the authority to reward or punish them for their performance.[96]

The LPC is a single individual with whom the leader presently works or another individual with whom he or she has worked in a different unit; someone who might be described in terms such as difficult, unpleasant, or uncooperative. Underlining LPC theory is the assumption that how leaders regard the person they least like is an indicator of their leadership preference. To determine whether leaders have a task or relationship orientation, they complete the LPC scale using pairs of descriptors (see Table 7.8).

TABLE 7.7 A CONTINUUM OF POLICE LEADERSHIP STYLES AND IMPACTS ON SUBORDINATES

Chiefs/ Supervisors Orientation	Characteristic Leadership Behavior	Impact on Subordinates
Overt Authoritarian/ Autocratic	**Authoritarian/Autocratic (AA) Leadership Level 1** AAs are not open minded and value their own thoughts/opinions over those of others. AAs tend to discourage dissenting views and often surround themselves with "Yes People." As a result, AAs forfeit growth opportunities and movement toward greater competency because Yes People don't give genuine feedback. AAs are decisive and make quick decisions, leading some officers to regard them as "often wrong, but never in doubt." If AAs make the right decisions in crisis and tactical situations, their decisive style is an asset. Although AAs crave total control of their departments, they, like other police leaders, can never achieve it because their control is diluted by: (1) federal and state investigative agencies and laws; (2) grand jury indictments and reports, court decisions, and consent decrees; (3) the actions of elected and appointed governmental officials and their legislative bodies; (4) local government charters and ordinances; and (5) any collective bargaining agreements. Communication between AAs and subordinates are usually one-way, telling them how to do their jobs. Real social interactions are limited and more often are superficial, e.g., "Who do you think is going to win the game?" The overt authoritarian approach may be rooted in a need to be in control for self-aggrandizing reasons. The Chief's motto is "My way or the highway."	**Authoritarian/Autocratic Leadership Level 1** Rank-and-file (RF) participation in the key processes of the department, e.g., planning, policy formulation, and decision making, is negligible to nonexistent. Officers are careful with whom they talk about job conditions out of fear of retribution, e.g., "Well, megalodon sharks were 60 feet long and disappeared thousands of years ago. Maybe the chief will be gone much sooner." Strict discipline contributes to a high turnover as evidenced by comments such as "You rarely get an 'attaboy' around here, but slip-up just a little and they stick it to you." Some officers who remain may not be of high caliber and/or have no or few other options for other careers. Others accept working for AAs because of the salary, fringe benefits, pension, and civil service job security. A third group of officers remain for only as long as it takes to achieve personal goals, such as finishing a degree or completing some family or other important personal obligation. In states where it is authorized, the collective bargaining process is a force that mediates AA leadership. Moreover, team policing, community policing, CompStat, intelligence-led and strategic policing require participation by officers, which tends to blunt, but not eliminate, AA behavior.

Chiefs/ Supervisors Orientation	Characteristic Leadership Behavior	Impact on Subordinates
Softer Authoritarian/ Autocratic	**Authoritarian/Autocratic Leadership Level 2** The core dynamics of Level 1 still prevail, but less overtly. Infrequently, to occasionally, AAs will "toss a bone" to the RF and informally or formally solicit its input by appointing a temporary committee and its chairperson to do so. The greater the importance of a topic to AAs, the less likely that RF input will be encouraged or solicited. AAs especially want their way on issues that are important to them. Input could jeopardize AAs preferred solutions.	**Authoritarian/Autocratic Leadership Level 2** Away from participation, but others are curious about it and become engaged with the department in a new way. AAs watch these reactions and the "quality" of their input closely.
Democratic Leadership Emerges	**Transitional Leadership Level 1** Agencies are in the initial stage of moving toward democratic leadership (DL), which is a precursor for the emergence of participatory leadership. A shift to DL may occur due to current or new chiefs concluding that input from department members, including the RF, could lead to improved decision making and generate higher levels of organizational commitment. The chief appoints more temporary committees and names the chairperson for each one. By memo, the authority of each committee is carefully limited to making a recommendation and the topic to be evaluated is carefully defined to prevent the committee from exceeding its role. Chiefs unsure what RF input might be and worry that it could create opposition to their own preferred course of action. They are also unsure of how and how far to proceed with the DL model. Sheriffs may be looking for something new to showcase in their re-election campaign and may be open to change they believe they can control.	**Transitional Leadership Level 1** Important decisions are still made at the highest level. Most department members have not yet served on any committee. Still, there are slowly increasing opportunities for wider RF input because leadership recognizes it is getting fresh information and some worthy recommendations. Some leaders in the department don't see any value to getting RF input, but are not overtly resistant to doing so. Still, among trusted friends, they express doubt about the process: "I've been on the job 12 years and some rookie knows more than me what the department needs to do?" The real issue: a handful of leaders are not sure they can or want to change and fear their job will become less important. The jobs of police leaders actually become more important because they make a shift from simply telling others what to do, to coaching them to achieve high performances.
Democratic Leadership Maturing	**Transitional Leadership Level 2** From lessons learned in Transitional Leadership 1, there is a broadening of the issues for which the input of subordinates is solicited. To some extent, the movement toward more involvement of officers is driven by new generations of officers who have an expectation they will be involved with the department's important processes. Leadership's acceptance of some recommendations in Transitional Leadership Level 1 from the temporary committees has made a positive impression on the RF. Committee work is no longer considered "busy work" or "show and tell."	**Transitional Leadership Level 2** A paradigm shift in leadership style is underway. Although not yet fully developed, RF participation in organizational processes and decisions is no longer considered novel. The RF is unsure of where participation will lead and how much of it they will be allotted, but the future seems to hold new and interesting possibilities. Existing unions may be suspicious, skeptical, or threatened by the budding changes. They may fear that growing participation could make the union less important.
Participative Leadership Emerges	**Participative Leadership Level 1** From lessons learned at Transitional Leadership Levels 1 and 2, the involvement of subordinates continues to be cautiously expanded. A few standing committees are appointed on "safe" subjects, such as training and equipment. The chief continues to select committee members, who can only make recommendations, but the committees elect their chairpersons.	**Participative Leadership Level 1** First-line supervisors feel they are in a bind. Their department is moving toward participative leadership, but their work in the field often requires quick action that doesn't allow for it. Supervisors are trained to use participatory leadership as a core model and situational leadership as needed.

(continued)

Chiefs/ Supervisors Orientation	Characteristic Leadership Behavior	Impact on Subordinates
	Involvement of community stakeholders begins or is expanded as the police department moves toward more departmental transparency. Departmental leaders have learned that some policy shifts, such as community engagement, must be treated as an organizational change intervention, and training to provide the new skills needed is provided. Some decisions normally made by mid-level and even senior leaders are being pushed to the lowest level in the department that they can be made effectively.	Situational leadership is an adaptive response where supervisors choose an appropriate leadership style for the demands of the situation and in consideration of the capabilities of subordinates and other resources, e.g., unilaterally directing subordinates to contain a just developed hostage situation while waiting for hostage negotiators to arrive. The new grants of authority and expanded role of first-line supervisors have a positive effect on them. Middle managers do not feel disenfranchised because they have their own new authority and roles.
Participative Leadership Maturing	**Participative Leadership Level 2** The chief seeks further opportunities to engage officers, e.g., establishes an electronic suggestion box on the department's intranet. More standing committees appear, such as awards and decorations, ethics, off-duty work, accident review, and homeland security. The departments issues or broadens its committee policy. While some ad hoc committees may still be appointed, the emphasis is on standing committees and their authority. Units elect their own representatives to committees and those members elect their respective chairpersons. The use of committees is now well institutionalized. Community engagement has evolved into a key focus and is accomplished by interactive websites, town hall meetings, and other mechanisms. Stakeholders participate in key organizational processes, such as serving on promotional boards and strategic planning groups. The use of civilian volunteers expands into increasingly important responsibilities. A volunteer coordinates the recruitment of people with special capabilities, e.g., conducting an annual survey of satisfaction with police services.	**Participative Leadership Level 2** Officers acting jointly develop outreach programs to serve special populations, such as teaching the elderly how to be less vulnerable to victimization and develop alcohol safety programs for bars and restaurants to reduce their liability for drunk drivers and to reduce the frequency of related arrests, accidents, and injuries. Some agencies employ 360-degree evaluations of officers and leaders, where each individual receives feedback from subordinates, peers, and their supervisors. Organizational citizenship is widespread with officers taking individual initiatives to help the department forward in small ways that may go unnoticed and larger ways such as volunteering to help with specific projects.
	Ad hoc committees/task forces are appointed in special circumstances. Assume there are a series of serious accidents that occurred during high speed police pursuits. A committee would be appointed and might include a cross section of the department, as well as stakeholders, e.g., government officials, community members, and the state patrol. Many of these developments are associated with the use of community policing, raising a chicken and egg question: Did community policing produce participative leadership or did that style of leadership foster it?	

Although Table 7.7 was referenced in the discussion of Tannenbaum and Schmidt's work, there it was prepared by Charles R. Swanson, Leonard Territo, and Robert Taylor to illustrate the concepts using police examples.

The LPC score determines whether a leader is task motivated (low LPC) versus being relationship oriented (high LPC).

A third group, the middle-LPC scorers, do not have a distinct preference for task or relationship approaches to leadership and have been somewhat ignored.[97] Low LPCs get their psychological subsistence from completing their assigned tasks and are less concerned about how their drive to complete assignments impacts their subordinates. Conversely, high LPCs derive their sense of well-being in the workplace by creating and maintaining satisfying interpersonal relationships. Further

TABLE 7.8 A PORTION OF FIEDLER LPC SCALE		
Descriptor	Scale	Descriptor
Unfriendly	1 2 3 4 5 6 7 8	Friendly
Considerate	8 7 6 5 4 3 2 1	Inconsiderate
Insincere	1 2 3 4 5 6 7 8	Sincere
Warm	8 7 6 5 4 3 2 1	Cold
Backbiter	1 2 3 4 5 6 7 8	Loyal

Source: Fred E. Fiedler and Joseph E. Garcia, *New Approaches to Effective Leadership* (New York: John Wiley & Sons, 1987), extracted from Figure 7.1, p. 71.

TABLE 7.9 DIFFERENCES BETWEEN FIEDLER'S TASK AND RELATIONSHIP MOTIVATED LEADERS	
Task Motivated (Low LPC)	**Relationship Motivated (High LPC)**
• Accomplishing tasks is paramount and the source of self-esteem	• The leader's self-esteem comes from having satisfying relationships with subordinates.
• Highly critical of subordinates who don't contribute to task completion; may call them "slugs," "worthless" or "despicable"; blinds them to leader's to subordinates good characteristics.	• A pleaser, the leader is reluctant to criticize, overlooks followers deficits and focuses on good attributes
• Leader is courteous and ingratiating when needs co-operation of subordinates.	• The leaders is consistently courteous and friendly
• Primary focus is completing tasks, but when accomplished the leader may turn to repairing relationships.	• The leader's primary focus is people, but may become more directive around assignments they feel competent about
• Subordinate expertise is important concern.	• To the leader, loyalty from subordinates is an important concern.

differences in these two types of leadership approaches are shown in Table 7.9. Fiedler considered leader behavior fairly stable and difficult to change. The interplay among task structure, leader-subordinate relations, and the power position of the leader produced situations that were more or less favorable to high- and low-LPC leadership preferences (see Table 7.10.)

LPC has been studied extensively; Vecchio's test of the model concluded that factors other than those specified in the model or different combinations of them were responsible for group performance.[98] Rice reviewed 25 years of research on it and found general support for the low-LPC and high-LPC leadership preferences.[99] Peters, Hartke, and Pohlmann reached the same conclusion.[100] Middle LPCers are less involved with both tasks and relationships and approach their jobs less emotionally than the other two LPC preferences.[101] Kennedy found that the middle-LPCers' leadership performance was higher than the other two leadership preferences within the parameters described by Fiedler's model.[102]

HOUSE: PATH-GOAL THEORY

Although there was an earlier version of **path-goal theory (PGT)** by Evans in 1970, it is more closely associated with

House, who built on Evan's work by formulating a more elaborate version that included situational variables (1971); it has been revised several times.[103] The central thought of PGT is that leaders should remove the obstacles that inhibit, make more difficult, or prevent individual subordinates from doing a good job.[104] Originally, PGT was not about leadership of groups or work units; it was a dyadic supervisor to an individual subordinate theory.[105]

In 1996, House's early work was reformulated as both an individual and work unit performance theory, stated here in law enforcement terms, that incorporates five notions: (1) the behavior of commanders is acceptable to subordinates to the extent to which it is seen as an immediate source of gratification or as a pathway to future satisfaction; (2) commanders can enhance subordinates' focus on goals to the extent that the commander's behavior increases motivation, builds task relevant skills, provides useful guidance, reduces obstacles to performance and organizational rewards, and provides the resources that subordinates need to do their job effectively; (3) commanders can increase subordinates' motivation by providing psychological support and linking their subordinates satisfaction of personal needs to job performance; (4) commanders

TABLE 7.10 MIX OF SITUATIONAL VARIABLES AND FAVORABLENESS TO HIGH- AND LOW-LPC PREFERENCES

Task Structure	Leader–Follower Relations	Leader's Position Power	Situation Favorable to Leader Preference
High	Good	Strong	Low LPC
High	Good	Low	Low LPC
Low	Good	Strong	Low LPC
Low	Good	Low	High LPC
High	Weak	Strong	High LPC
High	Weak	Low	High LPC
Low	Weak	Strong	High LPC
Low	Weak	Low	Low LPC

TABLE 7.11 HOUSE'S EIGHT LEADERSHIP BEHAVIORS

Leader Behavior	Descriptions
Path-Goal Clarifying	Clarifies subordinates' performance goals; the means to be used; the standards by which they will be evaluated; discusses the expectations about job performance which others may hold, e.g., merchants for an officer walking a beat, which should and shouldn't be honored; and judiciously uses rewards and discipline to shape performance.
Achievement Oriented	Achievement motivation is an individual's usually non-conscious desire to measure one's self against some standard of excellence or unique achievement. The ability of the leader to foster an achievement-oriented work unit will vary by the individuals assigned to it. Some officers are innately achievement oriented and motivated, "self-starters." Officers with lesser achievement motivation require more effort. In these officers, leaders must identify and arouse the subordinates' needs that will lead to a higher achievement motivation.
Work Facilitation	Consists of planning, scheduling, and organizing work; coordinating the work of subordinates; coaching, guiding, counseling, providing feedback, and mentoring them; reducing obstacles to their performance; eliminating bottlenecks to the resources they need; and authorizing them to take actions requiring the leader's prior approval.
Supportive	Supportive behavior provides psychological support to subordinates, especially when the task or incident is distressing, e.g., investigating child abuse and working the murder of another officer; supportive relationships reduce stress and make the leaders–subordinate relationship more satisfying; conversely, when work is satisfying and not dangerous or stressful, supportive behavior has little or no influence on subordinate's behavior.
Interaction Facilitation	Resolving disputes; facilitating communication; giving those in the minority the opportunity to voice their opinion; interaction facilitation may reduce voluntary absenteeism and attrition.
Group-Oriented Decision Process	Involves the way in which decisions that affect the group are made; group oriented decision making increases both the quality and acceptance of the decision; leader encourages full participation, inhibits domination by one subordinate or a faction, allows full search for alternatives, facilitates discussion of alternatives, and the group makes the decision.
Representation and Networking	Some work units have a high status and an easier time getting the resources they need from other units. Other units do not enjoy such a favorable situation. Leaders must be able to increase their unit's standing and perceived value to the larger organization and therefore their legitimacy to make claims on resources which will be honored.
Value Based	Value-based leaders receive extraordinary commitment from followers, tapping into their cherished beliefs, their identification with the leader, their support of organizational goals, and their self-worth and identities. Value-based leaders articulate the vision of a better future; display self-confidence and self-sacrifice in the interest of the vision; take risks to further the vision; communicate high-performance expectations for subordinates; and express confidence in their ability to meet those expectations.

must be role models. In a study of 2,130 officers, police leaders modeling ethical behavior was found to be significant in limiting unethical conduct when the modeling occurred in an interpersonal, as opposed to a more distant context;[106] and (5) work unit performance is enhanced by a commander encouraging collaborative support among subordinates, maintaining a good relationship between the work unit and the larger organization in which it is embedded and demonstrating to the larger department the importance of the work performed by the unit.

In his revised work unit model (1996), House specifies eight types of leadership behavior that is acceptable, satisfying, facilitative, and motivational to subordinates. The essence of PGT is that for leaders to be effective, they must engage in leader behaviors (see Table 7.11), which compensate for the deficiencies of subordinates, enhances their performance, and is instrumental to their individual and work unit performance and satisfaction.[107] It is unlikely that any single commander will have the ability to engage in the eight leadership behaviors all or even most of the time. Effective leaders are likely to select the behaviors with which they are most comfortable, based on their personality and abilities.[108]

DANSEREAU, GRAEN, AND HAGA: LEADER-MEMBER EXCHANGE (LMX)

Police officers know that their leaders treat subordinates differently, as do practitioners in other settings. Researchers, until LMX (1975),[109] made two wrong assumptions about leader behavior: (1) its effect on subordinates was homogenous or "averaged out," affecting their behavior "on average equally" or (2) leaders treated all subordinates in the same manner. The core of LMX is that leaders develop different types of relationships with their subordinates. Exchange relationships can be thought of as the unique quality of the interpersonal relationship between the leader and a subordinate, which also has practical consequences for both and the department. The "merit" of an officer is contingent on how well he or she fits with the values, attitudes, preferences, and outlook of the leader.

An LMX police leader divides officers into two different groups: in-group and out-group, with a small holding category,

"try-out" (see Figure 7.7). Through one-on-one encounters, the leader forms opinions about each officer, sometimes in as little as two weeks. Where the leader and an officer are "simpatico," like-minded, congenial, and develop trust and respect in each other, the officer goes to the in-group. Where the "fit" is not good, the officer goes to the out-group.

On rare occasions, a leader will move an officer from the out-group to the in-group, but this requires potent new evidence, such as clearing a string of burglaries or apprehending a serial killer. Newly hired officers always go to the try-out category. Experienced officers transferred into the unit usually have a reputation of some sort. Still, unless the leader has had prior personal experience with them, they go to "the try-out bin." The new hires and transfers do not know they are in the try-out bin; in time, they will come to notice the difference between being an in-group and out-group member. Ultimately, they will figure out which group they are in by the way the leader treats them.

In-group members receive more leader attention, have performance appraisals greater than merited, high-job satisfaction, faster career progression, a high level of organizational citizenship behavior (OCB), reduced turnover, and more diverse work assignments. Out-group members are given accurate performance appraisals and their characteristics are essentially the "flip side" of the in-groupers.[110]

In 1995, Graen and Uhl-Bien moved away from the in- and out-group model, reconceptualizing it as a continuum of leader and subordinate **relationships** (see Table 7.12).[111] In it, the purpose of the leaders is to form individual relationships with officers that will help them grow into the Mature Partnership stage to the betterment of leaders, subordinates, and the performance of the organization.

In Table 7.12, the progress from the Stranger stage to the Mature Partnership stage is not assured. Leadership methods may be ineffective. Moreover, some officers might simply want to do their job and go home, seeking nothing more than doing an honest day's work for a fair wage. Such officers may see policing not as a profession, just where they work to make a living. Their lack of a richer involvement might signal that their family is the first priority or that they want to put their energy into a family business, hobbies, or recreational pursuits. Thus, some officers are content to remain in the Stranger stage. Regression is possible also; officers in the Acquaintance stage and the Mature Partnership stage may return to an earlier stage if they become discouraged with their career or have personal events or losses, which adversely affect their job performance.

Beyond the three stages identified in Table 7.12, Graen and Uhl-Bien identify a fourth stage. This involves dropping an overlay of relevant Mature Partnership stage dyads over the task structure of the police department to maximize the use of talent. Developing a research framework to test this fourth stage has proven troublesome and therefore made it resistant to empirical study. Otherwise, the existing research for both the 1975 and 1995 iterations of LMX has generally been favorable. Much of the research on LMX has been on how it correlates with other characteristics, such as OCB, intelligence, gender, and cross-cultural implementations.

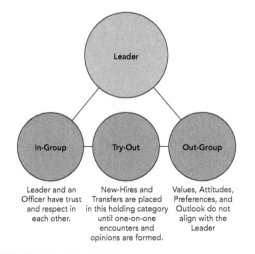

FIGURE 7.7 ▶ The LMX in-group and out-group model.

	Stages of Relationship		
Characteristic	**1** **Stranger Stage**	**2** **Acquaintance Stage**	**3** **Mature Partnership Stage**
Phase of Relationship Building	Although roles understood and shaped by rules, leader and follower feel each other out; e.g., "How are we going to relate to each other?" At some point, the leader or the follower must create opening to move the relationship forward on a career interest basis	Some sharing of personal and work information; relationship evolving; "putting meat on the bones of their relationship"	Relationship is at mature stage; mutual roles understood and well accepted
Type of Reciprocity	Formal and limited; leader expects follower to do job and follower does it, but no more	Some formalities of the relationship fade as leader and the follower explore reciprocity; e.g., leader offers new challenge in which follower has an interest	Full reciprocity; relationship has been tested and is dependable
Reciprocity Occurs	Immediately, but only within the job context	Some delay involved as the dynamics of reciprocity with the relationship are figured out; e.g., is immediacy of reciprocity most important or is an equivalent reciprocity received later acceptable?	On-going, comfortable; dynamics have been worked out
Leader–Follower Exchange	Leaders provide only resources needed to do job; followers meet basic job requirements	Followers may have access to additional benefits, e.g., being assigned to patrol a particular area, sent to special training classes	Highly developed; emotional component becomes more prominent: mutual respect, trust, loyalty, sense of mutual obligation
Mutual Influence	Mostly one-way, leader directing follower's job performance	Still mostly one-way, but some limited mutual influence	Bi-directional; genuine feedback can be provided without damage to relationship

TABLE 7.12 LIFE CYCLE LMX LEADERSHIP

KERR AND JERMIER: LEADERSHIP SUBSTITUTES AND NEUTRALIZERS

In 1978, Kerr and Jermier observed that in some situations, hierarchical leadership didn't seem to make much of a difference in what subordinates did, and under other circumstances, it even appeared to be irrelevant. Stopping well short of Miner's 1975 proclamation that the concept of leadership had outlived its usefulness,[112] they asked a startling question: "Are there variables in the work setting that can substitute for, or even neutralize, leader behavior?"[113] Earlier in this chapter, the Willow City case study established that leadership can be neutralized. Kerr and Jermier's work gives us a broader understanding of substitutes and neutralizers; it was conducted with reference to two styles of leadership: task oriented and relationship oriented. The model explores how the impact of leadership is contingent upon specific variables in the workplace.

Leadership substitutes are variables or factors that diminish the importance of leadership behavior or take its place entirely. Examples of substitutes are as follows: (1) Officers, who accurately perceive that they require little or no personal supervision by virtue of their training, job experience, knowledge, and job commitment—moreover, they may rankle under continuous supervision. (2) Officers with a professional orientation may be heavily influenced by an external organization, such as the National Tactical Officers Association (NTOA) and the opinions of qualified peers. (3) Sergeants are unlikely to find success trying to motivate officers who find police work intrinsically satisfying. (4) Close-knit peer groups may provide sufficient approval needs to diminish the efficacy of a sergeant using a relationship approach.

Neutralizers are variables that make task and relationship leadership approaches ineffective or impossible. An officer seriously considering leaving the department to work full-time on a graduate degree, attend law school, start a business, or with multiple external job opportunities is outwardly directed, away from the department. Guidance, support, or threats from a supervisor may have little saliency, no real importance, because the officer mentally has "one foot out the door." However, the department does hold one important card: the letter of recommendations leaders may be requested to write. Even going out the door, most officers do not want to "soil their nests." A few officers leaving an agency will tell one or more supervisors what "assholes" they are. Later, when these officers want a letter of recommendation or are seeking reinstatement to the department, they come to regret indulging themselves that way.

Officers who have a misperception of their own abilities and experience and think they don't need any supervision are neutralizers; they are a bad mix of arrogance and ignorance (faulty perception). The more consistently a leader and subordinates are separated by location, the greater the likelihood is that without special leader measures, his or her leadership will be seen as less important over time. Thus, chiefs with precincts need to do more than use technology to communicate with dispersed officers; they must also establish a personal presence by visiting those precincts. Other neutralizers include officers who are indifferent to the award system, a perception that leaders occupy a low status in the "food chain"; inflexible work guidelines that create unnecessary work; and leaders who one way or another inflict "wounds" on themselves, which lowers the regard in which their officers hold them.

Researchers have only found mixed support for this theory.[114] However, it still has practical significance in that it identifies factors leaders should consider when they ask themselves "How am I doing?" Perhaps the most important contribution of this theory is that it spawned interest in learning more about the role of trust in organizations. Lewicki, Wiethoff, and Tomlinson identified two types of trust in organizations: (1) calculus-based trust (CBT), in which the parties to a relationship must determine the costs of maintaining or severing it and (2) identification-based trust (IBT), based on a mutual understanding of each other's needs and wants.[115]

HERSEY AND BLANCHARD: SITUATIONAL LEADERSHIP THEORY

Although many situational variables are important to leadership—such as the demands of time, the leader, the led, superiors, the organization, and job demands—Hersey and Blanchard (1977) emphasize what they regard as the two key variables: (1) the behavior of the leader in the relationship to (2) the maturity of subordinates.[116] Maturity is defined in situational leadership as the capacity to set high but attainable goals, the willingness to take responsibility, and the education and/or experience of the individual or the group.[117] Age may be a factor, but it is not related directly to maturity as used in situational leadership theory.[118] An individual or group is not mature or immature in a total sense but only in relation to the specific task to be performed.[119] This task-relevant maturity involves two factors: job maturity, or the ability and technical knowledge to do the task, and psychological maturity, or feelings of self-confidence and self-respect about oneself as an individual.[120]

Table 7.13 summarizes the Hersey-Blanchard model, which includes references to task and relationship dimensions in the same manner as the Managerial Grid. Although it is easier said than done, the effective use of the Hersey-Blanchard model depends on police leaders developing or having a diagnostic ability and the flexibility to adapt their leadership styles to given situations.[121] Research on the model has been mixed; Cairns and colleagues (1998) found it intuitively appealing and empirically contradictory.[122] Perhaps, like several other theorists, Hersey-Blanchard model could be beneficially reformulated, employing emotional intelligence (EI) and social intelligence (SI) concepts.

TABLE 7.13 HERSEY AND BLANCHARD'S SITUATIONAL LEADERSHIP

Subordinates' (S) Capabilities	Hersey and Blanchard's Best Leadership Style	Corresponding Managerial Grid Style
Ss are insecure, may be rookies, and/or have lower levels of experience. Ss are not willing to perform the task and/or resist taking responsibility for it.	**Telling:** Relies on one-way communication with the unstated stance of "I have authority and you will obey." Gives them very specific directions and supervises Ss closely.	**9/1, Authority/Obedience** In authoritarian approach, task has high importance, but there is low concern for people. Work always comes first. Deviations usually result in discipline.
Ss are willing, but unable to accept responsibility for the task.	**Selling:** Need to engage Ss in a constructive conversation. Begin with emphasizing, "We are a team. What we do reflects on all of us." Provide step-by-step directions about how to execute the task and the importance of their role to the success of the department. Elicit and respond to questions. Engaging Ss in two-way communication is a key dynamic.	**9/9, Team Management** High concern for both work and people, tries to find ways to create "win" strategies for both tasks and people.
Ss know how the task should be performed but refuse to accept responsibility for doing it.	**Participating:** Superficially, leadership appears to be democratic with give and take in discussing the task and decision making about the task. However, it is always people first and task second. Makes appeals to their relationship to encourage accepting the task.	**1/9, Country Club Management** Wants relaxed atmosphere. Tries to protect Ss from censure by persons superior to supervisor for task not being performed.

VROOM, YETTON, AND JAGO: NORMATIVE DECISION-MAKING THEORY

Collaborative work between Vroom and Yetton (1973) and Vroom and Jago (1988) resulted in this theory, which is narrow in its focus—decision making—and not a general leadership model. It is "normative," stipulating under what conditions one leadership approach to decision making is more likely to be successful than another. Table 7.14 summarizes three leadership approaches to decision making: authoritarian, consultative, and group. Table 7.15 identifies eight contingency factors and the corresponding key questions/concerns leaders should consider. Research evidence for the initial model was adequate, but there were criticisms of it. The reformulation of the model in 1988 responded to those criticisms, and there was an impressive increase in research evidence supporting it. In one study, effective decisions were made 68 percent of the time using the normative model as compared to 32 percent using other methods.[123] Yukl concludes that it is "probably the best supported of the contingency theories of leadership."[124]

TABLE 7.14 VROOM-YETTON-JAGO NORMATIVE DECISION-MAKING MODEL

Leader Approach	Description	Decision Maker
Authoritarian	**A1**: Chief uses all information immediately available	Chief
	A2: Chief obtains any necessary information from staff members, may not disclose why the information is needed	Chief
Consultative	**C1**: Chief shares problem/situation/opportunity with relevant staff members individually; decision may or may not reflect input received	Chief
	C2: Chief convenes command staff or other group; gets their input, decision may or may not include any signs of influence from group	Chief
Group	**GI**: Chief and one subordinate work to solve a limited problem.	Group
	GII: Chief briefs group on situation without attempting to influence them as to the preferred solution. Chief may act as an equal to group members, careful not to use his/her status to influence the group or Chief may loosely "manage" the process with a light hand. The consensus decision of the group is accepted.	Group

TABLE 7.15 CONTINGENCY FACTORS IN THE NORMATIVE DECISION-MAKING MODEL

Contingency Factors	Key Questions/Concerns
Quality of Decision	How important is the quality of this decision, e.g., "just good enough" versus optimum
Leader Information	Does the chief have enough information to make a high-quality decision?
Follower Information	Do others have enough information to make a high-quality decision?
Structure of the Problem	Clear, action needed well known versus structure unclear, ill-defined, unfamiliar, alternatives need to be identified and evaluated
Goal Congruence	Are followers and organizational goals aligned, a "win-win" situation or in conflict, "win-lose"
Follower Conflict	Are followers divided on what the outcome should be? Failure to build consensus may lead to a lack of commitment/support
Commitment Probability	If an authoritarian decision made, will it matter to followers?
Commitment Required	How important is it to the Chief that follower commitment to the decision be substantial?

Transactional and Transformational Leaders

Burns (1978) contrasted transactional and transformational leaders, thinking of them as polar opposites.[125] Most leader-subordinate relationships are transaction based. **Transactional leaders** give something to get something. They motivate subordinates by appealing to their self-interest; contingent upon a subordinate doing a good job, the leader will provide favorable evaluations that produce raises and desired assignments. Each party to the transaction, or "bargain," is at least implicitly aware of the resources of the other, and the purposes of both are entwined.[126] To function, both parties to a bargain must have certain values, such as reliability, honesty, fairness, and reciprocity.[127] Commanders using a transactional leadership style clearly state their expectations for what subordinates need to do to fulfill their part of the bargain and they monitor their performances.

Essentially, **transformational leadership** emphasizes the upper levels of Maslow's needs hierarchy—esteem and self-actualization—to motivate subordinates[128] (see Chapter 5, Organizational Theory). These two levels of need include such factors as the need to test yourself against challenging work and standards, the quest for self-esteem and confidence, and autonomy in problem solving. Transformational leadership consists of several factors, referred to as the "Four I's" (see Table 7.16). The use of the "Four I's" was studied in a Royal Canadian Mounted Police (RCMP) detachment. It concluded that transformational leadership increased commitment, work satisfaction, and motivation.[129]

As conceived of by Burns (1978) and Bass (1985),[130] transformational leaders are inspirational; they motivate subordinates to "elevate their game," to go beyond their own self-interests for the good of the unit or department, making more and larger contributions than they had expected to make (see Table 7.15)[131]; in this process, police transformational leaders help subordinates grow personally and to develop their own capacity for leadership.[132] This help takes the form of individual attention to officers, empowering them, appealing to their ideals and values, and aligning their interests and the goals with the leader, the unit, and the department. This results in the subordinates' commitment to work "now," a well-articulated vision of the future, and strong organizational citizenship behavior.[133]

While accommodating the needs of officers, transformational leaders "send the same message" about their vision and the challenging goals ahead to everyone.[134] "Even when a chief has a vision, implementation is not always easy."[135] In some cases, the chief's vision may clash with those who do not support it. Resistance to the Chief's vision may take the form of a commander being slow to implement it, overemphasizing difficulties in applying it, or other obstruction.

Ideals and values are powerful forces; our Declaration of Independence (1776) rings with them: "All men are created equal ... with unalienable rights ... life, liberty, and the pursuit of happiness." Although not the sole contributor to gaining our independence from what was then the most powerful nation in the world, the words resonated and took deep root in the minds of our populace, evoking passion about them. Mohandas Gandhi (1869–1948), the Bapu, or Father of India, led his country to independence from England by advocating noncooperation and mass civil disobedience, tactics used by Dr. Martin Luther King, Jr., in the civil rights movement (see Chapter 1, The Evolution of Police Administration). Ironically, both men, who advocated peaceful resistance, were assassinated. However, their lives demonstrate how transformational leaders can use ideals and values to achieve enormous political and social change.

"Charismatic" and "transformational leadership" are used interchangeably by some theorists, largely because the first two of

---

TABLE 7.16 THE "FOUR I'S" OF TRANSFORMATIONAL LEADERSHIP

1. **Idealized Influence (IL):** Transformational leaders serve as role models, generating respect, trust, and admiration. They can be counted on to do the right thing and followers identify with them and emulate them. Chiefs who do not "walk the talk" cannot be transformational because followers quickly discount them.

2. **Inspirational Motivation (IM):** In a genuine manner, Chiefs behave in ways that motivate and inspire those around them. They manage the meaning of events, display optimism and enthusiasm, work hard, and actively demonstrate their own personal commitment to the vision of the future. The ability to communicate ideas nonverbally, verbally, symbolically, and in written form is an essential part of "winning hearts and minds."

3. **Intellectual Stimulation (IS):** Transformational Chiefs supportively probe their followers' progress toward creativity and innovation by questioning their assumptions, line of reasoning, and approach to solving persistent and new problems. This helps followers reframe problems and see new possibilities for their solution. Challenging assignments also stimulate growth. Ideas that are different from the Chief's are not just tolerated; they are encouraged.

4. **Individualized Consideration (IC):** The needs of individual followers for growth and accomplishment are attended to by coaching and mentoring, moving them to successively higher levels. Interactions with followers are personalized, e.g., the transformational Chief recalls past conversations about families and work, sees follower as whole person.

TABLE 7.17 BRITISH POLICE OFFICERS' (*N* = 1,066) PERCEPTIONS OF THEIR LEADERS

Element	Percent Disagree	Percent Agree	Total Percent
Behaves in a way that increases my motivation to achieve	23	77	100
Manages and leads in a way that I find very satisfying	30	70	100
Behaves in a way that has a positive effect on my job commitment	25	75	100
Behaves in a manner that has a positive effect on my self-confidence	23	77	100
Behaves in a manner that raises my sense of fulfillment for the job	22	78	100
Reduces my stress level by his/her approach to leadership	37	63	100
Leads and behaves in such a way that it increases my job satisfaction	32	68	100
Manages and behaves in a manner that increases my self-esteem	32	68	100
Has a leadership style that increases my organizational commitment	32	67	100
Acts in a manner that enables me to achieve beyond my expectations	35	65	100

Source: John Dobby, Jane Anscombe, and Rachel Tuffin, "Police Leadership: Expectations and Support" (Home Office: London, England, 2004), Table 4.2, p. 25. The six columns of data in Table 4.2's 6-point Likert Scale were collapsed by the present authors into "Disagree" and "Agree" categories and then converted to percentages.

the "Four Is" "idealized influence" and "inspirational motivation" were often combined together in early research as "charismatic leadership."[136] Indeed, some theorists maintain that there can be no transformational leadership without a charismatic leader. However, if the "Four Is" are studied individually, with no combining of the four factors, charismatic leadership becomes *one of the styles* that works with a transformational approach.[137] For example, a leader can be inspirational without being charismatic.[138] Subordinates can be drawn to the purposes, goals, and vision of an inspirational leader, without being drawn to the person per se as in charismatic leaders,[139] a pivotal and profound difference.

There is ample evidence supporting transactional and transformational leadership. Like transformational leadership, properly executed transactional leadership can result in trusting the leader, organizational citizenship behavior, and commitment; moreover, it may establish the foundation from which transformational leadership can develop.[140] Transformational leadership increases subordinates' job satisfaction[141]; its individual support of subordinates may help protect them from depression,[142] builds committed, cohesive work teams,[143] and produces organizational innovations, such as new approaches to doing the work.[144] Women are slightly more likely than men to use transformational leadership.[145]

A study of Texas police chiefs found there were slightly more transactional than transformational leaders.[146] A study of the "Four Is" in the Royal Canadian Mounted Police (RCMP) found support for them. Officers said that the first and foremost aspect of *idealized influence* (IF) was when commanders knew their "true north," leading their personal and professional lives consistent with the values of the RCMP.[147] The RCMP respondents said that *inspirational motivation* (IM) was not complete with respect to the use of community policing because while there was no active resistance to it, "buy-in" by officers wasn't 100 percent.

A RCMP commander reported that one of his approaches to *intellectual stimulation* (IS) was to assign unusual cases to a very experienced investigator and then team that person with someone who would learn and grow from being involved. As to *individualized consideration* (IC), another commander stated that the most effective tool was simply getting the right person in the right job.

The largest study of transformational leadership in a police setting was conducted in England by the Home Office (see Table 7.17). Overall, 70 percent of the 1,066 officers surveyed agreed with 10 statements reflecting a transformational approach. The roughly 30 percent who disagreed with those statements raise some interesting questions: (1) as time passes, will some of the 30 percent come to have a more favorable opinion of transformational leadership? (2) With more experience with transformational leadership will the 30 percent who are in disagreement with it increase? (3) Is 70 percent a saturation point or ceiling, above which any favorable increases will be negligible? And (4) could the 30 percent represent people who are uncomfortable with any major changes in their work environment that they view as unneeded or experimental?

Comparison of Charismatic and Transformational Leadership

Historically, **charisma** was thought to be a divine gift, bestowed on one who was favored by the "gods," an early characterization of the born leader. Leaders cannot declare that they are charismatic, nor can they be such if they are not successful (Figure 7.8). "Charisma" is a label that can only be authentically applied by subordinates. Charismatic leaders have certain traits:

1. their vision is a significant shift from the present status quo but still acceptable to subordinates;
2. they use new, unconventional strategies to implement the vision;

FIGURE 7.8 ▶ Three of the most successful allied leaders of World War II. England's Prime Minister Churchill (L) was energetic and inspirational. American General Eisenhower (C) was a strong administrator, building the allied coalition; although decisive he often relied on persuasion as opposed to simply giving orders. Field Marshal Montgomery (R) was an effective, but temperamental combat commander who made harsh criticisms of Eisenhower and other allied leaders after WW II. (Manchester Daily Express/SSPL/Getty Images)

3. they take risks and self-sacrifice to achieve the vision (e.g., possible loss of the chief's position);

4. they are less motivated by self-interest than by concern for subordinates;

5. they radiate a contagious confidence and enthusiasm;

6. they rely more on emotional appeals to subordinates than on the use of authority to get performance; and

7. they select a vision that is innovative, relevant to subordinates, and timely in its implementation.[148]

These traits are the "ideal version" of a charismatic leader; however, charisma also has a "dark side" (e.g., Hitler and Stalin). On a smaller scale, Charles Manson gathered a "family" of subordinates and in 1969 dispatched them to commit gruesome murders, including fatally stabbing actress Sharon Tate, who was nearly nine months pregnant.

It may not be possible to immediately differentiate whether charisma is positive or good; even charismatics who help their department and officers to substantial achievements may also do some damage to some officers along the way. Without dismissing the matter lightly, it is somewhat like breaking a few eggs to make an omelet, except the stakes are much higher: The impact on the lives of officers negatively affected can be catastrophic. Other aspects of charismatic leadership that are problematic include:

1. the desire of officers to be "in good standing" might inhibit useful criticisms from them;

2. widespread approval by officers can breed a dangerous sense of infallibility in chiefs;

3. excessive confidence by charismatic chiefs can lead them into dangerous mistakes; and

4. charismatic behavior inevitably breeds believers but also determined enemies who prefer to cling to more familiar ways and will opportunistically look for ways to discredit or remove the leader from office.[149]

Charismatic and transformational leadership has been used synonymously, described as overlapping, and sharply differentiated. Earlier charismatic leadership theories have been revised, causing some convergence with transformational leadership.[150] Not all charismatic leaders are transformational. While there are some similarities between charismatics and transformationals, there are also some important distinctions:

1. transformationals, by developing subordinates' abilities and eliminating unnecessary controls, make subordinates less dependent on them;

2. transformational leaders are more common, whereas charismatics are rare and their emergence depends upon circumstances being favorable for their leadership approach;

3. charismatics, as described earlier, elicit more diverse and extreme reactions; and

4. charismatics are much more attuned to managing their image.[151]

The "New Leadership" Theories: Servant, Spiritual, Authentic, and Ethical

Because these theories share some common characteristics, and for ease of reference, theorists have labeled them "neo-charismatic" or the "new leadership," independent from when they were actually initially formulated. In some fashion, they all attempt to explain how leaders:

1. take organizations on an upward trajectory to outstanding accomplishments;
2. engender extraordinary levels of subordinate motivation, trust, dedication, and loyalty;
3. use symbolic and emotionally appealing behaviors, such as envisioning, empowering, and supporting, to rally subordinates to their vision; and
4. employ leadership to increase subordinates' self-esteem, job satisfaction, and performance.[152]

They also fall short of being full leadership theories in that the linkage between leader behavior—the resulting subordinate behavior—and organizational outcomes are neither fully explained nor demonstrated.

SERVANT LEADERSHIP

Greenleaf (1904–1990) articulated the core notion of **servant leadership** (1977): The servant leader is servant first … making sure that other people's highest priority needs are met.[153] The idea is consistent with many of the teachings of the world's religions. Servant leadership (SL) includes the concepts of nurturing, defending, and empowering subordinates; helping them to be more complete persons, healthier, wiser, and more willing to accept their responsibilities; listening to their aspirations and frustrations; keeping actions consistent with their own values; and preparing people to lead when their opportunity comes.[154] Law enforcement agencies who have used SL include Boone, North Carolina; Casper, Wyoming; Hartford, Vermont; Coppell, Texas; and Peachtree City, Georgia.

A principal difference between transformational leadership and SL is that ultimately, the former focuses on organizational outcomes, whereas the latter's "wheelhouse" is subordinates.[155] Spears identifies 10 characteristics of SL:

1. *Listening*—SLers have a deep commitment to listen to others, apprehending both what is said and what is omitted. They are alert to emotional states and nonverbal cues;
2. *Empathy*—Empathy is the ability to vicariously understand and perhaps even experience (e.g., grief) what another person is feeling or a situation. Empathy approximates emotional intelligence and social intelligence, discussed earlier in this chapter;
3. *Healing*—Many relationships become strained or fractured. Uncomfortable, we avoid the other person involved and worry about what will happen. If we feel misunderstood, disappointed, injured, wounded, or betrayed, moving forward can be a difficult task.

The longer we remain in that state, the more we reduce the quality of what our personal and organizational lives can be. The healing brought about by a kind gesture, "closing the distance," a forthright, thoughtful, "air clearing" discussion, forgiveness, or similar action has enormous restorative powers for us and those with whom we are in some sort of a conflict. SLers heal themselves and subordinates. As a practical matter, many people make a habit of "never letting the sun go down on their anger"; they know lingering anger is destructive.

Disciplina was a minor Roman deity; from her identity, we derive *disciplina*, the Latin root word for discipline, *meaning to teach and to learn*. Properly conducted discipline can also be a healing act, correcting a situation and putting it into the past. The Biblical basis for this is the forgiveness of our sins: As far as the east is from the west so far has He removed our transgressions from us (Psalm 103:12). The "Bibles" of other world religions, such as the Torah and Koran, contain very parallel statements.

4. *Awareness*—This capacity strengthens SLers, helping them to stay in touch with themselves and their values and ethics;
5. *Persuasion*—SLers rely less on authority and more on persuasion and consensus, seeking others to join rather than simply telling them to do something;
6. *Conceptualization*—Whereas traditional leaders are often captured by the daily "tyranny of events" and focus on short-term operational needs, SLers look beyond day-to-day realities, further into the future, and see new opportunities, delicately balancing both time frames;
7. *Foresight*—Little has been written about the role of foresight in leadership; it is less like tactical and strategic planning and more akin both to awareness and intuitiveness. It allows SLers to draw upon past lessons, factors, and situations in the present, and the likely consequences of decisions about the future;
8. *Stewardship*—This characteristic means the responsible care of something entrusted to your care. In SL, the "prime directive" for stewardship is always the commitment to serve others;
9. *Commitment to the growth of people*—SLers are deeply committed to the personal, professional, and spiritual growth of each person in the organization; and
10. *Sense of community*—Our lives are dominated by large-scale organizations (e.g., employers, banks, health care, and school systems). In large part, the movement of families to villages and small towns is an attempt to live life differently, to create a sense of intimate belonging. City dwellers do the same thing without moving, creating their own, typically multiple, "communities" to which they can belong and from which they can derive meaning and psychological sustenance. SLers make organizations viable "communities."[156]

Box 7.5: The Warrior-Servant-Leader Code

- I am a Warrior-Servant-Leader.
- It is my duty in all that I do to Protect, Serve and Lead others with all my heart, mind and soul.
- I will Protect with courage.
- I will Serve with humility.
- I will Lead with compassion.
- In all my thoughts, words and actions I will ask myself:
  - Am I doing the right thing?
- At the right time?
- In the right way?
- For the right reasons?
- I will always strive to live up to my duty and not blame others when I fail.
- I will always strive to grow in my knowledge, understanding and skills of being a true Warrior-Servant-Leader.

Welsh conceptualized the role of police officers as "Warrior Servants." "Werreieor" was a 13th-century French word and also an old English word during the second half of that century denoting someone who is skilled in warfare or engaged in it. In modern English, the word is recognized as warrior. The police have been described as "fighting the war on crime" and "crime fighters."

In 2014, Welsh proposed the "hybrid" Warrior-Servant-Leader Code (see Box 7.5).[157] Had this existed in the 1960s, 1970s, 1980s and even into the 1990s, it may have been an easier "sell." Community policing took root as a national movement in the 1990s and subsequent ideas have also flourished. However, if the critics of police militarization and the proponents of the Guardian model make inroads in policing, the warrior-servant code may not flourish simply because of the warrior part of its name. The current demand for more and more community engagement by the police may not be quickly achievable in light of budget cuts and some communities wondering if they can really afford the policing they would like to have.

The deaths of unarmed African Americans by police during 2014–2015 appalled many Americans and there were many calls for reforms. The call for body cameras is reasonable, but some objectors claim they puts jurisdictions in the role of providing evidence for civil suits when there is police misconduct. This argument suffers from two flaws: (1) cameras exonerate many more than they convict. Moreover, evidence of wrongdoing saves police departments money by avoiding the expense of mounting a legal defense and (2) there is an important, but disturbing fact: some officers don't deserve the privilege of wearing a badge and need to be removed from the profession.

Much of the evidence about SL is from case studies and anecdotal accounts; although researchers are developing reliable scales to measure its concepts.[158] The sparse evidence on SL correlates with increased organizational citizen behavior, subordinate trust in the leader and the organization, job satisfaction, and some organizational effectiveness.[159] Some critics of SL believe that by definition the spiritual leader is so occupied with the needs of subordinates that legitimate, short-term, organizational needs become secondary in importance. Women, ethnic minorities, and others who have traditionally been held

to lesser roles may find the idea of SL unappealing.[160] More critically, Eicher-Catt believes it accentuates gender bias.[161] The theory also fails to take into account how SLers behave when the needs of the organization and the subordinates are in conflict (e.g., the downsizing seen in police departments during an economic downturn), as well as the possibility that the SLers' emphasis on humility, equality, and empowerment may be seen as weaknesses.[162]

SPIRITUAL LEADERSHIP

There are two major views about spiritual leadership:

(1) First, it is based on theology or religion based. This belief may produce an immediate visceral reaction so strong that the concept is quickly dismissed by some without taking the time to examine what it actually entails. Every time this happens, spiritual leadership loses another opportunity to flourish. Books authored by leadership gurus with titles like *Jesus, CEO* (1996), *What Would Buddha Do at Work?* (2002), and *Prophet Muhammad: The Hallmark of Leadership* (2015) seemingly imply that spiritual leadership is rooted in theological or religious beliefs. This may contribute to some headwind for wider use of spiritual leadership.

Thomas Jefferson (1743–1826) and other founding fathers were successful in creating Constitutional barriers that formed a wall between church and state. The Supreme Court has consistently upheld that position. For that reason, there can be no reasonable concern of a theological or religious based leadership existing in public sector organizations.

However, in the private sector, religious beliefs may legally affect business policies and practices. Illustratively, Truett Cathy (1921–2014), founder of Chick-Fil-A (1964), was deeply religious. Because of his beliefs, that business—whether company owned or operated as a franchise—is always closed on Sundays so people can go to church. Likewise, the Supreme Court exempted a private business, Hobby Lobby, from providing employees with certain types of birth control under "Obama Care" because of the company's religious beliefs. In what seems like a contradiction, Hobby Lobby does provide both Viagra and vasectomies. Parenthetically, the owner of Hobby Lobby is worth an estimated $6 billion dollars. At this writing on April 1, 2020,

TABLE 7.18 QUALITIES OF SPIRITUAL LEADERSHIP		
Vision	**Altruistic Love**	**Hope/Faith**
• Broad appeal to key stakeholders • Defines the destination and journey • Reflects high ideals • Encourages hope/faith • Establishes standard of excellence	• Trust/loyalty • Forgiveness/acceptance/gratitude • Integrity • Honesty • Courage • Humility • Kindness • Compassion • Patience/meekness/endurance • Excellence • Fun/work should be pleasurable/not endured	• Endurance • Perseverance • Do stretch goals • Excellence • Expectation of reward/victory • Do what it takes

Source: ©Louis W. Fry, "What Is Spiritual Leadership?" International Institute for Spiritual Relations, 2016.

Hobby Lobby continues to be open, but if employees contract COVID-19, they do not get sick pay. They have to use annual leave to get paid or take unpaid leave. On this issue, the company's assertion of religious beliefs don't seem to connect with corporate policy.

(2) Although spiritual leadership shares some values with theology and religion, those ideals are also found in many lands and times as well, including ancient Egypt, Greece, and Rome. In Western Europe, the Code of Chivalry for Knights and in Japan the Code of Bushido for samurai warriors espoused values such as honesty, hope, diligence, mercy, and politeness. It appears there was not a Code of Chivalry per se, but a set of shared and commonly understood values that are also acknowledged in literature. The Code of Bushido was much like that of chivalry's and evolved over hundreds of years beginning in the 8th century. In the remainder of this section workplace spiritual leadership is examined in its nontheological and nonreligious context.

Spirit is drawn from the Latin word for breath (spiritus) and in spiritual leadership refers to an abstract power that keeps people self-aware, invigorated, and connected to their vocational calling, workplace, and others.[163] Fry maintains that workplace spirituality meets an essential need of people, to have meaning in their lives and particularly in the workplace where they spend so much time.[164] More particularly, their calling to a vocation must provide a belief their lives are making a difference. As an illustration of the importance of work in our lives, when people ask us who we are, often our response is to tell people what we do, for example, "I'm a police officer." Spirituality connects us with higher values that otherwise may not be routinely accessible by us, giving meaning, purpose, and providing inner sustenance to our lives.[165]

Spiritual leadership emerges from the interaction of vision, altruistic love, and hope/faith; Table 7.18 summarizes the qualities of spiritual leadership identified by Fry.[166] "Vision" refers to a future state which appeals to a police department's members in a way that makes them want to achieve it.[167] The short version of "altruistic love" is that it is produced by a sense of harmony, wholeness, and well-being that springs from care, concern, and appreciation for ourselves and others.[168]

"Hope/Faith" is a belief rooted in values, attitudes, and behaviors that reveal officers are certain of reaching their goals.[169] It allows them to endure doubters, criticisms, setbacks, hardships, and even suffering to do so. Suffering may seem like an unusual word choice. However, officers who have stood in 30" or more of water directing traffic at an intersection flooded by a hurricane for many hours without relief know a degree of suffering. For spiritual leadership to flourish, leaders must model these qualities, most officers must respond to them, and ultimately those qualities could define an organization's culture.[170]

There is evidence that spiritual leadership can produce benefits important to officers and organizational performance, including increased senses of satisfaction, self-fulfillment, creativity, morale, and commitment, as well as mutual honesty and trust leading to greater cooperation between organizational members and work becoming an intrinsic motivator: the work itself motivates employees, instead of being something to just be endured.[171]

Police departments have long maintained associations with Chaplins from one or several faiths. The traditional role of Chaplins has been to tend to the needs of officers, for example, as a pastor or visiting them when hospitalized, accompany officers when they deliver death messages or other unpleasant news if a family's pastor cannot be identified or is unavailable, serve as a member of a crisis response team, be a link to a community's clerics, offer prayers at police functions, such as academy graduations and awards ceremonies, and related activities. Law enforcement agencies have also been more inclusive of religious leaders to help calm situations or otherwise involved them in departmental activities, such as community walks in support of, or against, various situations.

While there have been articles in the *FBI Law Enforcement Bulletin*, *The Police Chief*, and other journals on workplace spiritual leadership and the topic is also included in some

---

Quick Facts: Antidotes to Destructive Leadership

Servant, Spiritual, and other forms of altruistic leadership have the potential to prevent the development of destructive emotions or mediate their impact on organizational members. Such emotions can also hamper the performance of the organization itself. Destructive emotions may stem from a lack of positive core convictions about yourself, not getting what you want or think you deserve, and the loss of something valued, such as a relationship or job.

The four broad categories of destructive emotions are: (1) *fear*, including anxiety, worry, and apprehension; (2) *anger*, including, hostility, resentment, envy, jealousy, and hatred; (3) *sense of failure*, including such things as discouragement,

depressed moods, and various guilt feelings that lead to self-destruction; and (4) *pride*, which is dysfunctional, including prejudice, selfishness, and conceit.[172]

Altruistic leadership approaches can be an antidote to destructive emotions. It can ferment joy, peace, and serenity. Joy is a sense of gladness, delight, and lively pleasure about a past, present, or anticipated event. Peace is the condition of our minds when they are free of disturbance, agitation, or strife, sometimes described as "feeling balanced" or "in tune with the world." Serenity is that inner sense that all is well, giving rise to calmness, awareness, and clarity.

---

leadership courses, including those for police executives at the prestigious FBI National Academy (NA), accounts of law enforcement agencies adopting spiritual leadership are sparse. However, it seems more likely than not that at least pieces of spiritual leadership have made their way into policing.

AUTHENTIC LEADERSHIP

Partially in response to the mismanagement and "ethical meltdowns" of Fortune 500 companies[173] that wreaked so much havoc on the lives of employees and investors, substantial interest in **authentic leadership** (AL) began by the early 2000s. AL is more than being "real" or "genuine"—you can be a "real bastard" and "genuinely insensitive." AL is defined as:

(1) being deeply aware of how you think, behave, and are seen by others;

(2) being aware of your own and others' values/moral perspectives, knowledge, and strengths;

(3) understanding the context in which you and others operate; and

(4) being grounded by confidence, hopefulness, optimism, resiliency, and high-moral character.[174]

While aware of the opinions of others, ALers are not driven by their expectations, and moral character separates them from those who are merely "real" or "genuine." Chief Seabrooks is an advocate of authentic leadership, avowing that "I am about the truth and that does not change."

Avolio and Gardner (2005) argue that AL is the "root construct" that underlies transformational, charismatic, servant, spiritual, and ethical theories.[175] ALers can incorporate elements of all of these theories into their behavior. For example, an ALer may use a charismatic approach but may or may not be perceived as such by subordinates; likewise, when employing a transformational style, little or no emphasis may be placed on the proactive development of subordinates, although they may have a positive impact by modeling important behaviors.[176]

AL suffers from some of the same deficits that other leadership theories do: (1) there is an absence of a consensus definition; (2) the conceptual distinction between it and other "new"

leadership theories is not developed; (3) the claim of being a "root construct" is undemonstrated; (4) how long it will take before the effects of AL can be seen is unknown; (5) whether people can be trained to be authentic is questionable; (6) it fails to explain how authentic leaders should behave when dealing with authentically difficult subordinates; and (7) it is unknown how many "slips" authentic leaders can make before subordinates dismiss them as "unauthentic."[177] Until these difficulties are resolved, it is hard to imagine that large-scale studies can be usefully undertaken.[178]

ETHICAL LEADERSHIP

Ethical leadership is the consistent demonstration of moral values through personal actions, in interpersonal relationships, and the communication of those values to subordinates through two-way communication, reinforcement, and decision making.[179] Researchers have identified two components to ethical leadership: (1) the **moral person**, a fair and principled decision maker, who is altruistic, cares about people and the broader society and (2) the **moral manager** who proactively strives to reinforce subordinates' ethical behavior. Moral managers explicitly make ethics part of their leadership agenda by frequently communicating about it, modeling it, and using discipline to hold subordinates accountable for ethical lapses.[180] Discipline provides important learning to organizational members, who by the actions taken are able to reliably distinguish between what is acceptable behavior and what is not.[181]

At one level or another, transformational, servant, spiritual, authentic, and ethical leadership are concerned with being a good role model, integrity, and altruism or care for others. While ethical leaders keep their eye on modeling, communicating, and reinforcing moral values, the other "new" leadership styles have different preoccupations: (1) ultimately, transformational leaders are concerned about organizational outcomes or results; (2) servant leaders look to the needs of others; (3) spiritual leaders are interested in their own and their subordinates' spiritual survival; and (4) authentic leaders are keenly aware of how they think, behave, and are seen by others.

Ethical leadership matters because it influences what subordinates do. Ethical leaders are attractive role models who subordinates want to emulate—to be like. This increases ethical reasoning and action, even if the leader is not immediately present, stimulates organizational citizenship behavior, increases job satisfaction and trust in the leader, and reduces counterproductive subordinate behavior[182] (e.g., abuse of sick leave, being quarrelsome, and failing to complete assignments on a timely basis). Despite the interest in ethical leadership, Yukl notes that much of the research done has been superficial.[183]

Conclusion

Leadership is a slippery concept. It can be the traits exhibited by a leader, the manner or style in which the leader behaves, the way in which subordinates perceive the leader, how the leader affects the behavior and growth of subordinates, and the organizational performance leadership produces and sustains. In almost every situation, one or more leadership approaches will work. Many of the theories discussed produce similar affects; this fact is not surprising because researchers attempt to determine if the theories produce a fairly standard set of impacts on subordinates and organizational outcomes (e.g., increased trust and organizational commitment). This chapter describes "pure" or idealized models that rarely have a counterpart in the "real world." Ultimately, leadership is often a hybrid of things leaders do that are within their comfort zone.

Chapter Summary

Summary by Learning Objectives

1. **Identify and briefly describe any five key characteristics of effective senior police leaders.**

   Any five of these seven characteristics satisfies this objective: (a) *ethical behavior*, a genuine sense of integrity and honesty that encourages subordinates to do likewise with each other; (b) *trustworthy*, being viewed within the law enforcement agency, in government, and across the community as a "straight arrow"; (c) *legitimacy* perceived as someone who still knows how to work the street as opposed to being desk bound and out of touch with the daily realities of policing; (d) Being *a role model*, serving as an example of the behavior expected from subordinates; (e) *communication*, the capacity to share ideas, explain decisions, create support, and respond to criticism within the police department, across agencies, with stakeholders, and as a voice in government policy making; (f) *decision making*, a competency in making decisions that move the agency forward, for example, obtaining resources, removing performance barriers, and achieving goals; and (g) *critical, creative/innovative, and strategic thinking ability*, which entails looking to the future and determining what conditions need to be met or created to be successful then.

2. **Explain Drucker's distinction between leadership and management.**

   Leadership is doing the right thing. Management is doing thing right.

3. **Provide all five of Schafer's acts commission by ineffective police leaders.**

   These five points are: (a) *focusing on themselves over others*, a "me first mindset"; (b) *displays of ego/arrogance* beyond the realm of healthy confidence and self-assurance; (c) *a closed mindedness* demonstrated by the failure to listen to, and value, the ideas of others; (d) *micromanaging*, reflecting a lack of trust in subordinates. In this regard, a sergeant from a small municipal agency noted that micromanagers failed to delegate when appropriate; and (e) *being arbitrary and capricious*, represented by inconsistent decision making and a lack of a systematic approach. Being able to anticipate the likely decisions of their leaders allows subordinates to take actions and make decisions that support them. Capricious leaders also put personal relationships ahead of what is right, just, and consistent with past practices

4. **Distinguish between a Police Chief's rational-legal authority and power.**

   Rational-legal authority is a formal grant of authority made by an organization, for example, a city, to the *position* of Chief of Police. Each successive incumbent of that position uses that authority to fulfill his/her job responsibilities. Some power is inherent in a grant of authority to a police chief. To illustrate, A Chief may give a verbal or written reprimand, suspend an officer for up to a certain number of days, or "fire" an officer. Such actions by a Chief are normally subject to an appeal and review by a Civil Service Board or as provided for by union contract. However, to a large extent, power is a grant made by the led to the leader. Authority and power are related but separate concepts.

5. **Contrast socialized versus personalized power needs.**

Socialized power is defined as wanting/needing to have a positive impact on a police department's administration and operations. In contrast, personalized power needs include the need to be in control for selfish, self-aggrandizing reasons.

6. **Identify and define the components that make up the leadership skill mix.**

Human relations: the capacity to interrelate positively with other people who are at all levels of the police department. *Conceptual skills:* include the ability to understand and interrelate various parcels of information that seem unrelated or those for which the meaning or importance is not immediately apparent. *Technical skills:* these skills vary by level within the police department. A patrol sergeant must be able to help subordinates develop skills in handling domestic violence and other calls. As one progresses up toward middle and top management, the character of technical skills changes also, for example, budgeting skills.

7. **Describe each of Downs's four leader styles.**

Found in bureaucratic organizational structures, these four leader styles are: (1) climbers, who are strongly motivated by power and prestige needs to invent new functions for their unit, especially if they have not already performed elsewhere; (2) conservers, who have a bias of maintaining things as they are. The longer someone is in a job and the lower one assesses chances for advancement, the stronger one becomes attached to job security, all of which are associated with the tendency to become a conserver; (3) zealots' behavior stems from two sources, their narrow interest and the missionary-like energy they focus almost exclusively on their special interest; and (4) unlike zealots, advocates promote everything under their command. They appear highly partisan to outsiders, but within their units they are fair and impartial, developing well-rounded programs. They are loyal to their organization, favor innovation and are simultaneously more radical and more conservative than climbers. Advocates are more radical in that to promote their program and views they may antagonize politicians, superiors, other powerful groups, and the news media if it helps their department. They are more conservative because they are willing to oppose changes that might help their interests but is not in the best overall interest of their agency.

Chapter Review Questions

1. What are the seven key characteristics of "Effective Senior Police Leadership?"
2. What are the distinctions between Leaders and Managers?
3. Weber has identified three sources of authority. What are they?
4. McClelland and his associates studied the motivations of leaders extensively and concluded there were three types of power. What are they?
5. What are the major features of Conceptual and Technical Skills?
6. What is the major premise of the "Great Man Theory" as it relates to the understanding of leadership?
7. What is the major premise of the "Traits Approach" as it relates to the understanding of leadership?
8. What are the major characteristics of autocratic, democratic, and laissez-faire leaders?
9. What are the major characteristics of climbers, conservers, zealots, and advocates?
10. What are the basic optimal elements of Transactional Leaders?
11. What are the basic differences between Charismatic and Transformational Leaders?
12. What are the ten characteristics of Servant Leaders?

Critical Thinking Exercises

1. Reread the first case study in Box 7.2. For what reason(s) do you think the Police Chief was allowed to resign instead of firing him and charging him with any applicable crimes?

2. Assume that an area in a county with a population of about 78,000 was dissatisfied with services by the Sheriff's Office and incorporated as a totally new city of Flower Creek. You have been hired as its first Chief of Police. The Flower Creek Police Department does not yet exist. You have 12 months to organize and staff it. For now, your only support is an administrative secretary. You have authorization to hire four people for your command staff. When interviewing applicants for those positions what are the most important things to communicate to them about your leadership beliefs.

Key Terms

advocates
affiliation needs
authentic leadership
authoritarian/autocratic leader
authority
Big Five
Big Two
climbers
conceptual skills
conservers
counterproductive work behavior (CWB)
democratic leader
emotional skills (ES)
ethical leadership

"great man" theories
human relations skills
laissez-faire leader
leader
leadership
leadership neutralizers
leadership substitutes
manager
Managerial Grid
moral manager
moral person
organizational citizenship behavior (OCB)
path-goal theory (PGT)
personalized power needs

positive organizational behavior (POB)
power
power motivation
servant leadership
situational leadership
skill
social skills (SS)
station house sergeants
street sergeants
Tannenbaum and Schmidt
technical skills
transformational leadership
transactional leaders
zealots

Endnotes

[1] Joseph A. Schafer, "Developing Effective Leadership in Policing: Perils, Pitfalls, and Paths Forward," *Policing: An International Journal of Police Strategies and Management* 32, No. 2 (2009), p. 239.

[2] Ibid.

[3] Among the exceptions to this is Joseph A. Devine, An Analysis of the West Point Leadership and Command Program's Impact upon Law Enforcement Leadership, Dissertation in Partial Fulfillment of the Requirements for the Doctor of Education Degree, Seton Hall University, 2007.

[4] Developing Effective Leadership in Policing, pp. 247–250. The authors have extended some of Schafer's cogent points; any distortion or dilution is unintended.

[5] Mitchell Pearson-Goff and Victoria Herrington, "Police Leadership: A Systematic Review of the Literature," *Policing: A Journal of Policy and Practice* 8, No. 1 (2014), pp. 2–3.

[6] Ibid., pp. 3–4.

[7] Loc. Cit and p. 7.

[8] Ibid., pp. 4–5 and pp. 6–7.

[9] Ibid., p. 5.

[10] Loc. Cit.

[11] Ibid., pp. 6–7.

[12] Selin Kudret, Talya N. Bauer, and Berrin Erdogan, "Self-Monitoring Personality Trait at Work," *Journal of Organizational Behavior* 40, No. 2, (February 2019, Special Issue: *The Job Annual Review*), pp. 193–208.

[13] Terry D. Anderson et al., *Every Officer Is a Leader* (Boca Raton: St. Lucie Press, 2000), p. viii.

[14] J. Gregory Reynolds and Walter H. Warfield, "Discerning the Differences Between Managers and Leaders," *Educational Digest* 75, No. 7 (March 2010), pp. 26–29.

[15] Beverly Alimo Metcalfe and John Alimo-Metcalfe, "The Myths and Morality of Leadership in the NHS," *Clinician in Management* 12 (2004), p. 49.

[16] John P. Kotter, "What Leaders Really Do," *Harvard Business Review* (May/June 1990), pp. 103–111.

[17] See Brigitte Steinheider and Todd Wuestewald, "From the Bottom Up: Sharing Leadership in a Police Agency," *Police Practice and Research* 9, No. 2 (May 2008), pp. 145–163.

[18] On this point see Derrick J. Neufeld, Zeying Wan, and Yulin Fang, "Remote Leadership, Communication Effectiveness and Leader Performance," *Group Decision and Negotiation* 19, No. 3 (May 2010), pp. 227–246. For more extended information see Suzanne Weisband, *Leadership at a Distance* (New York: Lawrence Erlbaum Associates, 2008).

[19] On the low end, see Fred W. Rainguet and Mary Dodge, "The Problems of Police Chiefs: An Examination of the Issues in Tenure and Turnover," *Police Quarterly* 4, No. 3 (September 2001), p. 269 and on the high side, Steve Krull, *California Police Chief Demographic Study* (Sacramento: California Police Chiefs Association, 2004), p. 2.

[20] J. T. Murdaugh, Succession and the Police Chief: An Examination of the Nature of Turnover Among Florida

Police Chiefs, Doctoral dissertation, Florida State University, 2005, p. 103.

21 Jim Isenberg, *Police Leadership in a Democracy: Conversations with America's Police Chiefs* (Boca Raton: CRC Press, 2010), p. 28.

22 Phil Coleman, "New Ideas for Solving the Police Chief Recruitment Crisis" (Sacramento: League of California Cities, October 2007), p. 1.

23 Isenberg, *Police Leadership in a Democracy: Conversations with America's Police Chiefs*, p. 42.

24 Jill Leovy, "Little Job Security in Being a Police Chief," *Los Angeles Times*, May 5, 2002, p.1; http://articles.latimes.com/2002/may/05/local/me-dance5 (accessed July 27, 2015).

25 Loc. Cit.

26 Yudu Li and Ben Brown, "Police Chief Turnover in Texas: An Exploratory Analysis of Peer-Evaluation Survey Data Pertinent to Police Performance and Turnover," *Police Quarterly* 22, No. 4, December 2019, p. 6 on download printing.

27 Ibid., p. 9.

28 Joseph A. Schafer, "The Ineffective Police Leader: Acts of Commission and Omission," *Journal of Criminal Justice* 38, No. 4 (2010), p. 737.

29 Paul B. Thornton, "While Some Leaders Succeed and Others Fail," *Leader to Leader* 2011, No. 60, pp. 17–21, the police language was added by the authors; http://web.b.ebscohost.com/ehost/pdfviewer/pdfviewer?sid=f78f7e9f-d762-4092-8e57-90b636995817%40sessionmgr112&vid=8&hid=102 (accessed July 27, 2015).

30 Schafer, "The Ineffective Police Leader: Acts of Commission and Omission," p. 739.

31 Ibid., pp. 741–742 with restatement.

32 Restated from Scott Neumann, "Pennsylvania Police Chief Fired Months After Video Rants," NPR (National Public Radio), September 20, 2013, p.1; http://www.npr.org/sections/thetwo-way/2013/09/20/224462040/pennsylvania-police-chief-fired-months-after-video-rants (accessed July 26, 2015).

33 No author, "Mark Kessler Claims Video Rants Aimed to Snare Militia Members," LeighValleyLive.com, December 22, 2014, pp. 1–2; http://www.lehighvalleylive.com/breaking-news/index.ssf/2014/12/mark_kessler_claims_video_rant.html.

34 Ibid., p. 743.

35 Schafer, "The Ineffective Police Leader: Acts of Commission and Omission," pp. 742–743 with restatement.

36 Kenneth Blanchard, DreaZigarmi, and Patricia Zigarma, *Leadership and the One-Minute Manager: Increasing Effectiveness Through Situational Leadership* (New York: William Morrow, 1999), p. 38.

37 This account is drawn with restatement from Martin E. Comas, "Employees Tell Investigators That Ex-Casselberry Police Chief McNeil Bullied, Harassed Them for Years," *Orlando Sentinel*, July 26, 2015, 3 pp.; http://www.orlandosentinel.com/news/breaking-news/os-casselberry-police-harassment-documents-20150226-story.html (accessed July 26, 2015) and Steven Lemongello and Gal TzipermanLotan, "Casselberry Police Chief Bill McNeil Resigns Amid Sexual Misconduct Allegations," *Orlando Sentinel*, October 30, 2014, 2 pp.; http://

www.orlandosentinel.com/news/seminole/os-casselberry-police-chief-resigns-20141030-story.html (accessed July 26, 2015).

38 Drawn with restatement from Elise Schmelzer, "Maypearl Police Chief Fired After Surrendering on Four Felony Charges Alleging Sexual Relationship with Teen," *The Dallas Morning News*, July 22, 2015, 3 pp.; http://crimeblog.dallasnews.com/2015/07/maypearl-police-chief-surrenders-on-four-felony-charges-alleging-sexual-relation-with-teen.html (accessed July 26, 2015) and Jason Whitely and Monica Hernandez, "Former Maypearl Police Chief Surrenders on Child Sex Charges," WFAA8 ABC, July 23, 2015, 3 pp.; http://www.wfaa.com/story/news/crime/2015/07/22/maypearl-police-chief-surrenders-on-five-felony-charges/30519815 (accessed July 26, 2015).

39 Jean Lipman-Blumen, *The Allure of Toxic Leaders* (New York: Oxford University Press, 2005), pp. 19–20.

40 Ibid., pp. 21–22.

41 Melissa Horner, "Leadership Theory: Past, Present, and Future," *Team Performance Management* 3, No. 4 (1997), p. 276.

42 Max Weber, *The Theory of Social and Economic Organizations*, translated by A. M. Henderson and Talcott Parsons (New York: Free Press, 1947), p. 328.

43 J. R. French and B. Raven, "The Bases of Social Power," in D. Cartwright (ed.) *Studies in Social Power* (Ann Arbor: University of Michigan, Institute for Social Research, 1959), pp. 150–167.

44 Jacques Steinberg, "Police Officer Rejects Promotion," The *New York Times* (June 2, 1991). Although an older example, it is a perfect illustration of the point made in the text.

45 Chester Barnard also wrote on organizations as an open system. See *The Functions of the Executive* (Cambridge, MA: Harvard University Press, 15th edition, 1962). *Functions* was originally published in 1938. On many points, he must be read in the context of his own time. See Steven M. Dunphy and James Hoopes, "Chester Barnard: Member of the Elite?" *Management Decision* 40, No. 10 (2002), pp. 1024–1028.

46 The flip side of the coin is the question "Under what conditions do organizational members voluntarily elect to leave, stay and protest, or simply stay?" An important book addressing these issues is Albert O. Hirschman, *Exit, Voice, and Loyalty* (Cambridge, MA: Harvard University Press, 1970).

47 Isenberg, *Police Leadership in a Democracy: Conversations with America's Police Chiefs*, p. 119.

48 The description of power motivation styles is drawn, with restatement into a police context, from Jay Hall and James Hawker, "Interpreting Your Scores from the Power Management Inventory" (The Woodlands, Texas: Teleometrics International, 2000).

49 See Joe C. Magee and Carrie A. Langer, "How Personalized and Socialized Power Motivation Facilitate Antisocial and Prosocial Decision Making," *Journal of Research in Personality* 42, No. 6 (December 2008), pp. 1547–1559.

50 The basic model is drawn from Robert Katz, "Skills of an Effective Administrator," *Harvard Business Review* 33, No. 1 (1955), pp. 33–42. It continues to draw attention; see Robert L. Katz, "Skills of an Effective Administrator" (Cambridge, MA: Harvard Business Review, 2005).

[51] There is no shortage of skill models. For example, see Troy V. Mumford, Michael A. Campion, and Frederick P. Morgeson, "The Leadership Skills Strataplex: Leadership Skill Requirements Across Organizational Levels," *The Leadership Quarterly* 18 (2007), pp. 154–166. The model uses four skills: factors: cognitive, interpersonal, business, and strategic. See p. 156.

[52] Thomas Carlyle, *Heroes, Hero-Worship and the Heroic in History* (New York: A. L. Burt, 1902) and G. W. F. Hegel, *The Philosophy of History* (Indianapolis: Bobbs-Merrill, 1952).

[53] See R. D. Avery et al., "Developmental and Genetic Determinants of Leadership Role Occupancy Among Women," *Journal of Applied Psychology* 92, No. 3 (2007), pp. 693–706.

[54] Francis Galton, *Hereditary Genius: An Inquiry into Its Laws and Consequences* (New York: D. Appleton, revised with an American preface, 1887).

[55] Gary Yukl, *Leadership in Organizations* (Upper Saddle River, NJ: Prentice Hall, 2010), p. 190.

[56] Field Marshal Montgomery, *The Path to Leadership* (New York: Putnam, 1961), pp. 10–19. To some extent, Montgomery also holds with Carlyle in that the former asserted that the leader must be able to dominate and master the surrounding events.

[57] W. Allport and H. S. Odbert, "Trait-Names: A Psycholexical Study," *Psychological Monographs* 47, No. 211 (1936).

[58] Ralph M. Stogdill, *Handbook of Leadership: A Survey of Theory and Research* (New York: Free Press, 1974), p. 81 and "Personality Factors Associated with Leadership: A Survey of the Literature," *Journal of Psychology*, (January 1948), pp. 35–71.

[59] Cecil Goode, "Significant Research on Leadership," *Personnel* 25, No. 5 (1951), p. 349.

[60] For example, see Robert J. Allio, "Leadership—The Five Big Ideas," *Strategy and Leadership* 37, No. 2 (2009), p. 412.

[61] Stephen Erdle et al., "The General Factor of Personality and Its Relation to Self-Esteem," *Personality and Individual Differences* 48 (2010), p. 344.

[62] Stephen J. Zaccaro, "Trait-Based Perspectives of Leadership," *American Psychologist* 62, No. 1 (January 2007), p. 14, online access.

[63] Reuven Bar-On, "The Bar-On Model of Emotional-Social Intelligence," in P. Berrocal and N. Extremera, Guest Editors, Special Issue on Emotional Intelligence, *Psicothema* 17 (2005), p. 15.

[64] Lynda, Jiwen Song et al., "The Differential Effects of General Mental Ability and Emotional Intelligence on Academic Performance and Social Interactions," *Intelligence* 38, No. 1 (January 2010), pp. 137–143.

[65] Melanie B. Malterer, Samantha Glass, and Joseph Newman, "Psychotherapy and Trait Emotional Intelligence," *Personality and Individual Differences* 44, No. 3 (February 2008), pp. 733–743.

[66] Oluremi Ayoko, Victor Callan, and Charmine Hartel, "The Influence of Emotional Intelligence Climate on Conflict and Team Members' Reactions to Conflict," *Small Group Research* 39, No. 2 (April 2008), pp. 121–149.

[67] A. Oyesoji Aremu and T. Oluwayemisi, "Assessment of Emotional Intelligence Among Nigerian Police," *Journal of Social Science* 16, No. 3 (2008), p. 275.

[68] Oluremi Ayoko, Victor Callan, and Charmine Hartel, "The Influence of Emotional Intelligence Climate on Conflict and Team Members' Reactions to Conflict," *Small Group Research* 39, Issue 2 (April 2008), pp. 121–149.

[69] Kathryn L. Barbera et al., "Relating Emotional and Social Intelligence to Sex and Age," Nevada State Psychological Association Meeting, Las Vegas, May 17, 2003, p. 3.

[70] Reuven Bar-On, "Emotional Intelligence: An Integral Part of Positive Psychology," *South African Journal of Psychology* 40, No. 1 (April 2010), p. 46.

[71] Ronald E. Riggio and Rebecca J. Reichard, "The Emotional and Social Intelligences of Effective Leadership," *Journal of Managerial Psychology* 23, No. 2 (2008), p. 171.

[72] Ibid., pp. 172–173, 175–176.

[73] John D. Mayer and Peter Salovey, "What Is Emotional Intelligence?" In Peter Salovey and D. Sluyter (eds.), *Emotional Development and Emotional Intelligence* (New York: Basic Books, 1997), p. 10.

[74] Fatih Tepe, "Leadership Characteristics Among Command, Middle, and Line Level Police Department Personnel in the Era of Terrorism, Dissertation Abstracts International," *The Humanities and Social Sciences* 69, No. 7 (2002), p. 2564, 2009.

[75] Kuldeep et al. "Linking the Big Five Personality Domains to Organizational Citizenship Behavior," *International Journal of Psychological Studies* 1, No. 2 (December 2009), p. 73.

[76] Suzy Fox, Paul E. Spector, and Don Miles, "Counter Productive Work Behavior in Response to Job Stressors and Organizational Justice," *Journal of Vocational Behavior* 59 (2001), p. 292.

[77] Ibid., p. 297.

[78] Jennifer M. George and Garth R. Jones, *Organizational Behavior* (Addison-Wesley Publishing Company, 1999), p. 41.

[79] Gary Dessler, *Organization and Management: A Contingency Approach* (Englewood Cliffs, NJ: Prentice Hall, 1976), p. 158.

[80] See K. Lewin, R. Lippitt, and R. White, "Patterns of Aggressive Behavior in Experimentally Created Social Climates," *Journal of Social Psychology* 10 (May 1939), pp. 271–299; R. Lippitt and R. K. White, "The Social Climate of Children's Groups," in R. G. Baker, K. S. Kounin, and H. F. Wright (eds.), *Child Behavior and Development* (New York: McGraw-Hill, 1943), pp. 485–508; Ralph White and Ronald Lippitt, "Leader Behavior and Member Reaction in Three Social Climates," in Dorwin Cartwright and Alvin Zander (eds.), *Group Dynamics: Research and Theory*, 2nd edition (New York: Harper & Row, 1960), pp. 552–553; and Ronald Lippitt, "An Experimental Study of the Effect of Democratic and Authoritarian Group Atmospheres," *University of Iowa Studies in Child Welfare* 16 (January 1940), pp. 43–195.

[81] Bernard M. Bass and Ronald E. Riggio, *Transformational Leadership* (Mahwah, NJ: Lawrence Erlbaum Associates, 2nd edition, 2006), pp. 8–9.

[82] White and Lippitt, "Leader Behavior," pp. 539–545, 552–553.

[83]Stephen A. Morreale, "Perceived Leader Styles in Law Enforcement," Master's Thesis, Nova Southeastern University, 2002, p. 12, online access to abstract.

[84]Robert R. Blake and Jane Mouton, "The Development Revolution in Management Practices," *Journal of the American Society of Training Directors* 16, No. 7 (1962), pp. 29–52.

[85]The Ohio State studies date from the mid-1940s and identified the dimensions of consideration and structure; the University of Michigan studies date from the late 1940s and identified employee- and production-centered supervisors.

[86]Anthony Downs, *Inside Bureaucracy* (Boston: Little, Brown, 1967).

[87]Ibid., pp. 92–96.

[88]Ibid., pp. 96–101.

[89]Ibid., pp. 109–110.

[90]Ibid., pp. 107–109.

[91]John Van Maanen, "Making Rank: Becoming an American Police Sergeant," *Urban Life* 13, No. 2-3 (1984), pp. 155–176. The distinction between station and street sergeants is drawn from Van Maanen's work with some restatement and extension of views. The speculation about future career patterns is the work of the present authors.

[92]Robert Tannenbaum and Warren Schmidt, "How to Choose a Leadership Pattern," *Harvard Business Review* (May/June, 1973), pp. 162–180.

[93]Victor H. Vroom and Philip W. Yetton, *Leadership and Decision-Making* (Pittsburgh: University of Pittsburgh Press, 1973), p. 18.

[94]John B. Miner, *Organizational Behavior* (New York: Oxford University Press, 2002), pp. 320–321.

[95]Gary Yukl, "Toward a Behavioral Theory of Leadership," *Organizational Behavior and Human Performance* 6, No. 4 (July 1971), p. 434.

[96]Fred E. Fiedler and Joseph E. Garcia, *New Approaches to Effective Leadership* (New York: John Wiley & Sons, 1987), pp. 52–61.

[97]Afsaneh Nahavandi and Ali R. Malekzadeh, *Organizational Behavior* (Upper Saddle River, NJ: Prentice Hall, 1999), pp. 305–306.

[98]Robert P. Vecchio, "An Empirical Examination of the Validity of Fiedler's Model of Leadership Effectiveness," *Organizational Behavior and Human Performance* 19, No. 1 (June 1977), p. 203.

[99]R. W. Rice, "Construct Validity of the Least Preferred Coworker Scale," *Psychological Bulletin* 85, No. 6 (November 1978), pp. 1199–1237.

[100]Lawrence H. Peters, Darrell D. Hartke, and John T. Pohlmann, "Fiedler's Contingency Model," *Psychological Bulletin* 95, No. 2 (March 1985), pp. 274–285.

[101]*New Approaches to Effective Leadership*, pp. 76–77.

[102]John K. Kennedy, Jr., "Middle LPC Leaders and the Contingency Model of Leadership Effectiveness," *Organizational Behavior and Human Performance* 30, No. 1 (August 1982), pp. 1–14.

[103]Yukl, *Leadership in Organizations*, p. 228.

[104]R. J. House, "A Path Goal Theory of Leadership Effectiveness," *Administrative Science Quarterly* 16 (1971), pp. 321–329.

[105]Robert J. House, "Path-Goal Theory of Leadership: Lessons, Legacy, and a Reformulated Theory," *The Leadership Quarterly* 7, No. 3 (Autumn 1996), p. 325.

[106]L. Huberts, M. Kaptein, and K. Lasthuizen, "A Study of the Impact of Three Leadership Styles on Integrity Violations by Police Officers," *Policing* 30, No. 4 (November 2007), pp. 587–606. The findings are based on the responses of Netherlands police officers.

[107]"Path-Goal Theory of Leadership: Lessons, Legacy, and a Reformulated Theory," p. 348.

[108]Ibid., p. 347.

[109]Although not using the LMX designation, the first articulation of it was Fred Dansereau, George Graen, and William J. Haga, "A Vertical Dyad Linkage Approach to Leadership within Formal Organizations," *Organizational Behavior and Human Performance* 13 (1975), pp. 46–78.

[110]The descriptions of these two groups are drawn from Jun Liu and Xiaogu Liu, "A Critical Review of Leadership Research Development," *International Journal of Business and Management* 1, No. 4 (August 2006), pp. 7–8.

[111]George Graen and M. Uhl-Bien, "Relationship Based Approach to Leadership: Development of a Leader-Member Exchange (LMX) Theory of Leadership over 25 Years," *Leadership Quarterly* 6, pp. 219–247. The concepts were not clearly defined and understanding of them was partially derived by the context in which they were used. Our characterization of the authors' work is our best understanding of what they intended.

[112]J. Miner, "The Uncertain Future of the Leadership Concept," in James Hunt and Lars Larson (eds.), *Leadership Frontiers* (Kent, OH: Kent State University Press, 1975).

[113]Steven Kerr and John M. Jermier, "Substitutes of Leadership: Their Meaning and Measurement," *Organizational Behavior and Human Performance* 22, No. 3 (1978), pp. 377, 395.

[114]Margaret L. Williams and Philip Podsakoff, "A Preliminary Analysis of the Construct Validity of Kerr and Jermier's Substitutes of Leadership Scales," *Journal of Occupational Psychology* 61, No. 4 (1988), pp. 307–333.

[115]R. J. Lewicki, E. C. Wiethoff, and E. Tomlinson, "What Is the Role of Trust in Organizational Justice?" in Jerald Greenberg and Jason Colquitt (eds.), *Handbook of Organizational Justice* (Mahwah, NJ: Lawrence Erlbaum Associates, 2005), pp. 247–270.

[116]Hersey and Blanchard, *Management of Organizational Behavior*, pp. 160–161.

[117]Ibid.

[118]Ibid., p. 163.

[119]bid., p. 161.

[120]Ibid., p. 163.

[121]bid., p. 159.

[122]Thomas D. Cairns et al., "Technical Note: A Study of Hersey and Blanchard's Situational Theory," *Journal of*

Leadership and Organization Development 19, No. 2 (1998), pp. 113–116.

[123]Bernard M. Bass with Ruth Bass, *The Bass Handbook of Leadership* (New York: Free Press, 2008), p. 493.

[124]Yukl, *Leadership in Organizations*, p. 99.

[125]James McGregor Burns, *Leadership* (New York: Harper & Row, 1978).

[126]Ibid., pp. 4, 19–20.

[127]Yukl, *Leadership in Organizations*, p. 261.

[128]Bass and Bass, *The Bass Handbook of Leadership*, p. 619.

[129]Steven A. Murphy and Edward N. Drodge, "The Four Is of Police Leadership," *International Journal of Police Science and Management* 6, No. 1 (March 2004), pp. 1–15.

[130]See B. M. Bass, *Leadership and Performance* (New York: Free Press, 1985).

[131]V. R. Krishan, "Transformational Leadership and Outcomes," *International Journal of Value Based Management* 25, No. 5/6 (2005), pp. 19–33.

[132]Bass and Riggio, *Transformational Leadership*, p. 3.

[133]Ronald F. Piccolo and Jason A. Colquitt, "Transformational Leadership and Job Behaviors," *Academy of Management Journal* 49, No. 2 (2006), p. 327.

[134]Simon A. Moss and Somon Ngu, *Current Research in Social Psychology* 11, No. 6 (2006), p. 71.

[135]Isenberg, *Police Leadership in a Democracy: Conversations with America's Police Chiefs*, p. 115.

[136]Bass and Riggio, *Transformational Leadership*, p. 228.

[137]Ibid., pp. 228–229.

[138]Hersey and Blanchard, *Management of Organizational Behavior*, p. 163.

[139]Pat Welsh, "Are You a Warrior, Servant, and Leader?" *Law Enforcement Today*, January 3, 2014; http://www.lawenforcementtoday.com/2014/01/03/are-you-a-warrior-servant-and-leader (accessed August 1, 2015).

[140]Lee Whittington et al., "Transactional Leadership Revisited," *Journal of Applied Social Psychology* 39, No. 8 (August 2009), pp. 1860–1886.

[141]Yi-Feng Yang, "An Investigation of Group Interaction Functioning Stimulated by Transformational Leadership on Employee Intrinsic and Extrinsic Job Satisfaction," *Social Behavior and Personality* 37, No. 9 (2009), pp. 1259–1277.

[142]Fehmidah Munir, Karina Nielsen, and Isabella Gomes, "Transformational Leadership and Depressive Symptoms," *Journal of Affective Disorders* 120, No. 1–3 (January 2010), pp. 235–239.

[143]Rajinandini Pillai and Ethlyn Williams, "Transformational Leadership, Self-Efficacy, Group Cohesiveness, Commitment, and Performance," *Journal of Organizational Change Management* 17, No. 2 (2004), pp. 144–159.

[144]Rabia Khan, Abaid Ur Rehman, and Afsheen Fatima, "Transformational Leadership and Organizational Commitment," *African Journal of Business Management* 3, No. 11 (November 2009), p. 683.

[145]Roya Ayman and Karen Korabik, "Why Gender and Culture Matter," *American Psychologist* 65, No. 3 (April 2010), p. 164.

[146]Mary Sarver, Holly Miller, and Jennifer Schulenberg, "Leadership and Effectiveness: An Examination of the Leadership Styles of Texas Police Chiefs," Paper presented at the 2008 Annual Meeting of the American Society of Criminology, St. Louis, on-line access of abstract.

[147]Steven A. Murphy and Edward N. Drodge, "The Four Is of Police Leadership," *International Journal of Police Science and Management* 6, No. 1 (2004), p. 10. The description of all Four Is is drawn from this source.

[148]Yukl, *Leadership in Organizations*, p. 262.

[149]Ibid., pp. 272–274.

[150]Ibid., p. 285.

[151]Ibid., pp. 261 and 285–286.

[152]Robert J. House and Ram N. Aditya, "The Social Scientific Study of Leadership: Quo Vadis?" *Journal of Management* 23 (May/June 1997), pp. 409–473.

[153]Robert K. Greenleaf, *Servant Leadership* (Mahwah, NJ: The Paulist Press, 1977), p. 13.

[154]Yukl, *Leadership in Organizations*, p. 419.

[155]A. Gregory Stone, Robert Russell, and Kathleen Patterson, "Transformational Leadership: A Difference in Leader Focus," *Leadership and Organization Development* 25, No. 4 (2003), pp. 349–361.

[156]Larry Spears, "Practicing Servant-Leadership," *Lead to Leader Journal*, No. 34 (2004), approximately 3 pp., online access. The authors have restated portions of these 10 points and added commentary. No alteration of the author's position is intended.

[157]Pat Welsh, "Are You a Warrior, Servant, or Leader?" *Law Enforcement Today*, January 3, 2014; http://www.lawenforcementtoday.com/2014/01/03/are-you-a-warrior-servant-and-leader (accessed April 19, 2016).

[158]Yukl, *Leadership in Organizations*, p. 421.

[159]For example, see John E. Barbuto, Jr., "Scale Development and Construct Clarification of Servant Leadership," *Group and Organization Development* 31, No. 3 (2006), pp. 300–326.

[160]Mark McKergow, "Host Leadership," *International Journal of Leadership in Public Services* 5, No. 1 (March 2009), p. 20.

[161]Deborah Eicher-Catt, "The Myth of Servant-Leadership: A Feminist Perspective," *Women and Language* 28, No. 1 (Spring 2005), pp. 17–25.

[162]Yukl, *Leadership in Organizations*, p. 421.

[163]Bruce J. Avolio, Fred O. Walumbwa, and Todd J. Wheeler, "Leadership: Current Theories, Research, and Future Directions," *The Annual Review of Psychology* (2009), p. 438.

[164]Cathy Lynn Grossman, "Survey: 72% of Millennials 'More Spiritual than Religious,'" *USA Today* (April 27, 2010).

[165]Louis W. Fry, "Toward a Theory of Spiritual Leadership," *The Leadership Quarterly* 14 (2003), p. 702.

[166]Toward a Theory of Spiritual Leadership," pp. 703–705, 716.

[167]Ibid., pp. 702–705, 711.

[168]Yukl, *Leadership in Organizations*, p. 422.

[169]Laura Reave, "Spiritual Values and Practices Related to Leadership Effectiveness," *The Leadership Quarterly* 16, No. 5 (October 2005), pp. 655–687.

[170]Frank Markow and Karin Klenke, "The Effects of Personal Meaning and Calling on Organizational Commitment: An Empirical Investigation of Spiritual Leadership," *International Journal of Organizational Analysis* 13, No. 1 (2005), pp. 8–27.

[171]Maragret Benefiel, "The Second Half of the Journey," *The Leadership Quarterly* 16, No. 5 (October 2005), p. 727.

[172]Fry, "Toward a Theory of Spiritual Leadership," pp. 715–716.

[173]William L. Gardner et al., "Can You See the Real Me?" *The Leadership Quarterly* 16 (2005), p. 344.

[174]Cecily Cooper, Terri Scandura, and Chester Schriesheim, "Looking Forward But Learning from Our Past: Potential Challenges to Developing Authentic Leadership Theory and Authentic Leaders," *The Leadership Quarterly* 16, No. 3 (June 2005), p. 478.

[175]Bruce J. Avolio and William A. Gardner, "Authentic Leadership Development: Getting to the Root of Positive Forms of Leadership," *The Leadership Quarterly* 16, No. 3 (June 2005), p. 327.

[176]Ibid., p. 328.

[177]Cooper, Scandura, and Schriesheim, "Looking Forward But Learning from Our Past: Potential Challenges to Developing Authentic Leadership Theory and Authentic Leaders," pp. 481–483.

[178]Yukl, *Leadership in Organizations*, p. 427.

[179]M. E. Brown et al., "Ethical Leadership," *Organizational Behavior and Human Decision Processes* 97 (2005), p. 120.

[180]Michael E. Brown and Linda K. Trevino, "Ethical Leadership: A Review and Future Directions," *The Leadership Quarterly* 17, No. 6 (December 2006), p. 599.

[181]Ibid., p. 600.

[182]Ibid., pp. 610–611.

[183]Yukl, *Leadership in Organizations*, p. 416.

## CHAPTER EIGHT

PLANNING AND DECISION MAKING

Learning Objectives

1. Explain what planning is expected to accomplish.
2. Define what a plan is.
3. Discuss synoptic planning.
4. Identify the specific elements of administrative, procedural, operational, tactical, and strategic plans.
5. Discuss what planning can be expected to accomplish.
6. State Simon's concept of "bounded rationality."
7. Explain Lindblom's incremental decision making.
8. Describe Gore's decision-making process.
9. Explain the concept of the thin-slicing theory.
10. State the advantages of group decision making.
11. Discuss the liabilities of group decision making.
12. Explain the concept of brainstorming.

INTRODUCTION

PLANNING AND DECISION MAKING are both critical processes for effective police administration that are inevitably connected. These two processes are important steps toward establishing the direction and operation of a police department. Often, planning is precipitated by recognizing that a problem, either small or large, exists that needs to be addressed. That situation is sometimes referred to as problem-oriented planning.

Although natural and man-made disasters may not occur with regularity, there is still a need for effective planning and decision making that may save lives and reduce property losses. A well-prepared plan on the shelf is more valuable (even if it is never needed), than an extemporaneous plan created in haste. Planning is seldom a wasted effort although some events may briefly overcome any plan, such as a series of large organizational changes conducted too rapidly, which can confuse law enforcement officers about their roles and responsibilities and new missions thrust on agencies like homeland security. Even if a specific plan has not been developed to address an unanticipated crisis, having experience in dealing with the planning process can be very valuable. A classic example of this is when Apollo 13 was nearing the moon and was rocked by a series of events that made the survival of the crew very uncertain. It was only through continuous and improvised planning by the National Aeronautics and Space Administration (NASA) over 3 days that got the crew safely home.

In this chapter, we will examine elements of the planning and decision-making process. This will include the following: (1) planning; (2) planning as a process; (3) planning and time orientations; (4) synoptic planning; (5) other categories of plans; (6) the blending of the five types of planning; (7) decision making; (8) the use of computers in the decision-making process; (9) decision making during crisis events; (10) group decision making; (11) ethics and decision making; (12) common errors in decision making; and (13) improving decision making.

PLANNING

The planning landscape is crowded with many approaches and associated techniques. Together, they range from simple but effective schemes, to those based primarily on statistical analysis. While many organizations know the value of planning and do it well, others discover too late that their planning is woefully inadequate.

For example, the BP oil spill in the Gulf of Mexico in 2010 reflects a lack of in-depth planning. BP had template procedures to address emergencies, but when an oil rig explosion blew out an underwater well, the company took nearly 12 days to formulate its first plan of attack. The templates failed to consider, or adequately anticipate, an accident of such magnitude. The result was that a catastrophic amount of oil spilled into the Gulf, contaminating coastlines and wildlife around portions of the Gulf Coast. Consider what would happen if police organizations took a similar approach to planning, for example, stopping to formulate a response to a complex and fluid situation like the 2013 active shooter who murdered 12 people at the Navy Yard in Washington, DC (discussed in greater detail later in this chapter). In such cases, there is simply not enough time to stop operations while adjustments are made to a basic template.

Some police administrators may not have a full appreciation of the importance of planning because of their pattern of career development. If they have spent substantial portions of their careers in line divisions, such as patrol and investigative services, they may be field oriented to the degree that staff functions, such as planning, do not receive the executive attention or support that they deserve.

Planning is one of the most critical ingredients for the success of any organizational undertaking.[1] Police leaders must fully embrace the planning process in order to resolve problems and be prepared for the future. Sound planning and programs can reduce the opportunity for crimes to occur, as well as prevent some other unknown number of crises from occurring or at least to handle them more efficiently when they do occur, for example, hurricanes, earthquakes, and forest fires. Law enforcement agencies that are perpetually in crisis suffer from the absence of good leadership and have either no planning function or an unsupported and overwhelmed one. Such factors foster an environment where crisis is unfortunately predictable and further supported by an orientation that is too past or present oriented and only minimally oriented to the future, the proverbial "short time horizon." In contrast, effective planning can accomplish the following:

1. Improve/strengthen the analysis of problems.
2. Provide better information and data for decision-making.
3. Help to clarify goals, objectives, and priorities.
4. Foster a more effective allocation of resources.
5. Improve inter- and intradepartmental co-operation and coordination.
6. Enhance the performance of programs.
7. Clearly communicate the department's direction to all employees, other agencies, and the public.
8. Generate opportunities for community engagement.
9. Increase the commitment of personnel by involving them.

In short, competent planning is a sure sign of good police administration and enhances the ability of an administrator to make more effective and efficient decisions.[2]

PLANNING AS A PROCESS

The word **planning** achieved prominence in the vocabulary of criminal justice agencies when the federal grant-awarding Omnibus Crime Control and Safe Streets Act of 1968 became law. However, what was missing from that document was an explanation of what planning actually involved, or what it meant in the operation of criminal justice organizations. A plan essentially is a decision about a future course of action. The briefest definition of a plan is "How we get from here to there." Weiss[3] asserts that a primary purpose of planning is in evaluation, comparing "what is" with "what should be." Hudzik and Cordner[4] defined planning as "thinking about the future, thinking about what we want the future to be, and thinking about what we need to do now to achieve it." Stated more succinctly, planning involves linking present actions to future conditions. Mottley views planning as:

a management function concerned with visualizing future situations, making estimates concerning them, identifying the issues, needs and potential danger points, analyzing and evaluating the alternative ways and means for reaching desired goals according to a certain schedule, estimating the necessary funds and resources to do the work, and initiating action in time to prepare what may be needed to cope with changing conditions and contingent events.[5]

The SITAR Approaches to Planning

Planning can also be defined by the approaches used and they are sometimes referred to by the acronym SITAR:

1. **Synoptic**—This is a rational approach and still the dominant planning process in policing and elsewhere. Its roots are in England where rudimentary planning became an essential part of the Industrial Revolution (1760–1850). As society took advantage of manufacturing, people left their farms to find work in rapidly growing cities. Because the synoptic model is the dominant approach, it is also covered in greater detail in a subsequent section of this chapter.

2. **Incremental**—In 1959, Lindblom developed the concept of "muddling through" that challenged the notion of rationality in policymaking. In his view, policy decisions are made on the basis of "muddling through" or a series of limited comparisons of policy options, which reduces rationality. When muddling through is applied to planning in law enforcement agencies, the result is small, incremental changes made to existing plans. This perpetuates the status quo by making plans evolutionary but not revolutionary. It is disjointed because there are no larger, more comprehensive considerations and as a consequence incremental planning, which is more "now focused" than future oriented, is used.

3. **Transactive**—This relies on acquiring face-to-face knowledge of people's problems and not those of some anonymous group. It focuses largely on obtaining data by conversations with members of the target population. To some degree, community policing reflects transactive planning.

4. **Advocacy**—This model rests on the adversarial process of the legal profession and is usually applied to help the weak and disadvantaged against powerful interests, for example, government and business. In doing so, advocacy implicitly incorporates a more political view of planning. Paul Davidoff coined the term advocacy planning in 1965.

5. **Radical**—This rests on the notion that planning is most effective when done by lay people on neighborhood committees that best know their own problems. Ideally, those people feel empowered to collectively address their own problems. At its heart, radical planning incorporates Marxist thinking. Part of radical planning's bias is an almost urgent need to change the status quo.

PLANNING AND TIME ORIENTATIONS

One way or another, all plans have a time orientation and we instinctively think of them as being future oriented. A budget is a plan stated in financial terms; most law enforcement agencies have a one-year operational budget (see Chapter 11, Financial Management). Strategic plans are multiyear plans of usually three to five years. Tankha identified four types of planning approaches based on their time orientations. These approaches are "pure" in nature and in actual practice several of them may be used within a single agency.[6]

1. **Inactive Planning.** Law enforcement agencies that do little or no real planning where the process is markedly underemployed or altogether dormant implicitly rely on the **inactive planning** approach. Its underlying assumption is that things will continue to be as they are and it will be "business as usual." Its time orientation is substantially rooted in the present under the assumption that it's better than the past and not as dangerous as the uncertainties of the future. There is no systematic scanning of the environment to detect new opportunities. Such agencies are change resistant, even in the face of community calls for new responses to crime. In trying to sustain things as they are now, while the world around the agency changes, it is more likely than not that their services will degrade over time.

2. **Reactive Planning.** As its name suggests, it is in reaction to problems that have recently occurred and are being addressed or are presently happening and require an immediate response. It is both past and present oriented. Reactive departments are not leaders in innovation and are generally slow to change. Characteristically, reactive agencies make incremental changes cautiously, using the back edge of leading thoughts and technology. However, there are two exceptions to this:

   (1) They react as swiftly as possible to strong social/community pressures, such as issuing body-worn cameras to all of their uniformed officers, allowing more citizen participation in crime reduction efforts, or putting more video surveillance cameras in crime hot spots.

   (2) Also, assuming hypothetically that the federal Occupational Safety and Health Administration (OSHA) issued new guidelines on how certain classes of physical evidence such as body fluids should be collected and stored, the reactive agency would quickly mobilize resources to be in compliance.

3. **Preactive Planning.** This is centered on the future, attempting to predict changes in the larger environment. Once armed with this knowledge, preactive police agencies use it to acquire the skills and competencies they need in the future they envision.

4. **Proactive Planning.** This model has some similarities with the preactive approach. For example, proactive planning includes interactively engaging government agencies, examining "think tank" publications, assessing demographic analyses, and planning against the criminal use of technological developments or combinations of them. Where the preactive and proactive agencies part company is when the latter attempts to change anticipated future events that are likely to occur. For example, assume that a city's population of individuals who are between 18 and 24 years of age is expected to increase by 24 percent over the next three years because of the anticipated opening of a new technical college and the expected relocation of technology companies offering jobs to individuals within the same age bracket. With all the positive things these developments will bring, there are also some negatives. The population increase among younger adults falls into the 15–24 age range, a group of persons that is at high risk of both criminal activity and victimization. Just on this one issue the police department is searching for strategies and programs that will mediate those facts and "change" these future potential problems. There are other types of plans identified in the sections that follow.

Box 8.1: Reactive Planning and the Walk-Back from Body-Worn Cameras

The adoption of body-worn cameras is a relatively new trend in policing. In 2013, the National Institute of Justice (NIJ) and the Police Executive Research Forum (PERF) conducted a survey that indicated only 25 percent of police agencies nationwide used body-worn cameras. In 2016, NIJ conducted a subsequent survey on the same topic and found that nearly one-half (47 percent) of general purpose law enforcement agencies in the United States had acquired body-worn cameras. So, in the span of only three years, the rate of body-cam acquisition among U.S. police agencies had roughly doubled.

The lightning fast adoption of body-worn cameras was no doubt pushed at least in part by a series of notorious and highly publicized police citizen encounters during 2014 and 2015. We describe several of these encounters in Chapter 4 including police shootings that involved Michael Brown and Tamir Rice, as well as the in-custody death of Freddie Gray. Indeed, police agencies indicate that one of the primary reasons for their adoption of body-worn cameras was to reduce civilian complaints and agency liability.[7] Many police agencies responded to intense public pressure and scrutiny and reacted through the acquisition of body-worn cameras.

But the reactive trend toward body-cams has not been free of problems. There is evidence to show that at least some agencies are walking back from their hasty acquisition of the devices.[8] Some agencies, particularly those in smaller jurisdictions, dropped their body-worn camera programs citing cost as the major factor. Police administrators in those jurisdictions explain that buying the cameras and issuing them to officers is relatively cheap. But, laws in some state's requiring long term storage of the video makes the programs cost prohibitive. Costs associated with the storage of video footage can range anywhere from $10,000 to $30,000 annually for small departments, and up to $300,000 annually for larger agencies such as Arlington County (VA).

These agencies hastily implemented reactive plans to respond to intense political and community pressure for increased police transparency. They failed to think through and appropriately plan the implementation of the programs in terms of long-term costs. The trend toward acquisition of body-worn cameras underscores some of the problems and pitfalls of reactive organizational planning.

SYNOPTIC PLANNING

Synoptic planning, or the rational comprehensive approach, is the dominant tradition in planning. It is also the point of departure for most other planning approaches, which in general are either modifications of synoptic planning or reactions against it. The classic and most basic synoptic model had four steps: (1) goal setting, (2) identification of alternatives, (3) evaluation of the means against the end, and (4) implementation of the decision. Figure 8.1 represents a common version of the synoptic model. It is theoretically based on "pure" or "objective" rationality and attempts to ensure optimal achievement of desired goals from a given situation.[9] It can be more or less labor intensive depending how "deep" each component is considered.

This model is especially appropriate for police agencies, as it accommodates a problem-oriented approach to planning. It relies heavily on the problem identification and analysis phase of the planning process and can assist police administrators in formulating goals and priorities in terms that are focused on specific problems and solutions that often confront law enforcement.

Steps in Synoptic Planning

The steps in synoptic planning are designed to provide those involved in the planning process with a logical course of action as the model unfolds.[10] Using Figure 8.1 as a reference, a discussion of those steps follows:

Preparation for Planning. It is during this step that the police chief focuses the planning effort by issuing a memorandum that describes its organization, goals, responsibilities, methods, timeline, and desired results. Citizen participation in the planning process should be considered essential under most circumstances, and in many jurisdictions, this is considered a routine matter. Citizen participation is also fundamental to community policing. Community engagement gives citizens voices about what their police departments do and how they do it, which builds trust. The Chief's memorandum should include mention of any citizen involvement.

Box 8.2: Preparation for Planning and the Need for Citizen Involvement

Steps in the synoptic planning approach provide the police administrator a logical course of action that is proceeded by an important stage of preparation for planning. Citizen participation in this planning process is essential, particularly in the planning of all sorts of community policing strategies that demand citizen buy-in and participation. We outlined some of those strategies in Chapter 2 using the community policing models previously undertaken in Newport News (VA), Chicago (IL), and Minneapolis (MN).

Two of the authors were involved in a project to discern the level of agreement between citizens and police in one large southwestern police agency on some proposed changes to an existing community policing program.[11] The researchers used identical surveys of citizens and police to compare the views of the two groups on the relative importance of crime problems in the jurisdiction and the value of existing community policing strategies. We found that officers and citizens significantly differed in their assessment of the importance of specific crime problems and the value of community policing programs. Officers assigned greater importance to traditional violent and property crimes, while citizens assigned greater importance to problems more closely associated with community disorder such as drug use, unsupervised juveniles, and school-related problems. How can problem solving strategies work when citizens and police do not agree on which problems are most important to solve?

The study has implications for police administrators undertaking any sort of synoptic planning approach. Preparation for synoptic planning needs to include preparation and consideration of citizen inputs into the planning process. Community policing programming is one of the best but certainly not the only example of the point. Effective preparation for the planning of community policing strategies and/or any revisions to existing strategies should include an assessment of the degree of agreement between citizens and police on the prioritization of problems to solve in the community. This information needs to be collected in the preparation stage in order to increase the likelihood of successful synoptic planning and ultimately program implementation and success. This sort of planning process is otherwise likely to fail simply due to the lack of preparation and understanding of citizen priorities and how they may differ from those within the police organization.

Analyze the Present Situation, Problems, and Opportunities. There are multiple sources of information to describe the present situation, problems, and opportunities. These sources may include citizen satisfaction surveys, program evaluations, auditor reports, staff inspections results, the current history of lawsuits against the department, communications to and from unions, local newspaper coverage of the agency, and self-assessment for accreditation or reaccreditation. There are also tools that can be used to assess the broader environment that are useful in both short-term and strategic planning. One of these tools is the four-quadrant SWOT (strengths, weaknesses, opportunities, and threats) analysis, which was developed by Albert Humphrey at Stanford during the 1960s (see Figure 8.2). Its development is also credited to Edmund Learned, C. Christensen, Kenneth Andrews, and others.

Set Goals. Goals are future conditions or "states" that a police department wants to reach. The rule of thumb is to limit the number of goals to be accomplished within any given year to roughly five to seven, so that they may receive concentrated attention and become more likely to be attained. Of course, all goals are not equally important. Police organizations for example sometimes distinguish between "priority" goals and those that are "important" but less of a priority.

Goals communicate what we hope to become. They lift our vision from the "now" to the future, creating forward motion and driving performance as we strive to reach them. Goals establish a collective sense of responsibility and engender higher performance levels so that they may be achieved. We like being on winning teams whether it's selling Girl Scout cookies, scavenger hunts, the middle school quiz bowl, or sports. Departmental goals that are achieved provide law enforcement officers with professional satisfaction.

A goal should be stated in terms that allow for the measurement of progress. A goal statement should have three indispensable features: (1) time-phased, (2) quantitative, and (3) target specific. An example of these might be stated as follows: "During the year 2017, the Ocean View Police Department will reduce juvenile violent crimes by 6 percent." A goal may be difficult to achieve but must be realistically attainable. Goals often have subordinate or short-term objectives that represent milestones. For example, a subordinate objective may be stated as follows: In the first 31 days of 2017, the agency will complete the training of 100 percent of its officers

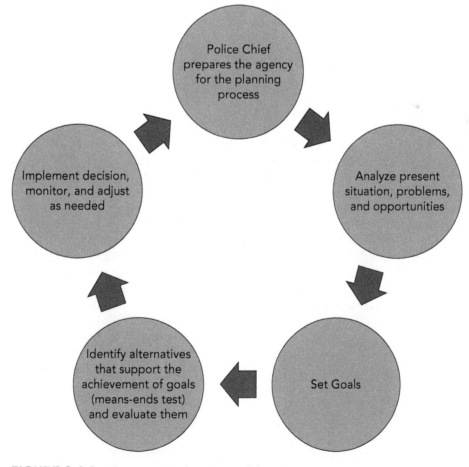

FIGURE 8.1 ▶ The synoptic planning model.

Determining *Strengths*	Identifying *Opportunities*
• How does our agency do on UCR Part 1 benchmarks?* • What does the most recent citizen survey tell us about their satisfaction with our services? • Are our previously defined mission-related skills better than average? • Are we properly trained for simultaneous large-scale/multiple shooter events? • What is our present reputation with the administration and political body? • How do our officers place in regional and national athletic, marksmanship, and SWAT competitions?	• What economic, social, technological, or other large-scale external shifts are favorable to us? • What innovations would reduce response time? • How can we meet the community's need for more engagement in crime fighting? • New grants available from the federal Department of Homeland Security that would bolster our capabilities in that area.
Determining Weakness*	**Identifying Threats**
• What programs or activities do not support our mission? • What deficiencies did the most recent financial and program auditors note? • How can we get annual voluntary separations below 9%?	• What economic, social, technological, or other large-scale external shifts are unfavorable to us? • Sworn and civilian salaries are not competitive.

* A benchmark is a comparison against a fixed standard, such as the national average for Uniform Crime Reports (UCR) Part 1 arrests for jurisdictions in our population range or relative to similar sized jurisdictions in our state or region.
** The answers to some questions in determining strengths may fall into this category.

FIGURE 8.2 ▶ SWOT analysis for a law enforcement agency.

who are assigned to field duties in the subject of conflict de-escalation.

Identify Alternatives. A simple truth is that alternative courses of action cannot be identified until a goal is selected. Often, there are several alternatives that are attractive. Alternatives proposed by members of the planning team should be worthy of genuine consideration. Brainstorming (discussed in detail later in this chapter) is sometimes done with suggestions recorded on a flip chart to get the "creative juices" flowing, including some suggestions that may seem frivolous. Some alternatives may be quickly discarded, but occasionally a seemingly frivolous alternative may spark useful conversations. A more thoughtful and deliberate discussion of alternatives may follow the brain-storming exercise. Discussions may be needed to flesh out alternatives that are closely related. When comparing alternatives, there are several easy-to-use tools that can be utilized. For example:

A. The Decision Matrix. This technique was developed by Stuart Pugh (1929–1993) and is both simple and elegant. Its steps are (1) identify and define the criteria against which all alternatives will be evaluated. Examples of such criteria include cost, sustainability, and compliance with CALEA standards; (2) develop the decision matrix; (3) have each member on the planning team score each alternative on all criteria with the points defined on an accompanying scale; (4) compute the total score for each alternative; and (5) discuss the higher scoring

alternatives and make a selection. The scores should be considered carefully but not without some flexibility. This also applies to the results obtained from the second tool discussed in this section. If judiciously used, there is a role for experienced judgment to supplement the results of the decision matrix.

Figure 8.3, the Pugh Decision Matrix worksheet, provides an example. For purpose of illustration, assume that Criterion A is "Increase Receiving Stolen Property Arrests by 15 percent." The criteria column may be lettered and may have a short definition for each criterion in it. Each criterion and its full definition should be readily viewable on flip charts, handouts, or a PowerPoint to make sure that team members consistently have the definitions before them. A Pugh Decision Matrix worksheet may have another column to the right of the criteria column where importance weights are assigned and which vary according to the perceived value of each criterion. When using weights, the score (see Figure 8.3) assigned to each criterion is multiplied by its associated importance weight. Each member of the planning team would complete the Figure 8.3 worksheet and subsequently all of the scores would be consolidated, displayed, and discussed to reach consensus. During these discussions, some excellent points are made, which may precipitate some rescoring by individuals. If the scores in Figure 8.3 were the averages for all raters, an agency may elect to only do a consensus discussion for Alternatives 3 and 4.

Date:_____   Rater:_____

Criteria	Scores for Alternative 1	Scores for Alternative 2	Scores for Alternative 3	Scores for Alternative 4
A	+2	+1	+3	+2
B	+2	+2	+3	+2
C	+1	+1	+3	+2
D	+1	+2	+3	+3
E	+2	+1	+1	+2
Total+	+8	+7	+13	+11
Total–	–0	–0	–0	–0
Final Score	+8	+7	+13	+11

The Scoring Scale:
+3 Far more than likely
+2 More than likely
+1 Likely, but no more than that
–1 Likely to fall short
–2 More than likely to fall short
–3 Far more than likely to fall short

FIGURE 8.3 ▶ Example of a Pugh Decision Matrix.

B. The Paired Comparison Method. The earliest writings about paired comparison were those of Witmer and Cohn (1894) and Kitchener (1901).[12] Their technique remains in wide use today with variants ranging from rudimentary to those dependent on statistical analysis.[13] As with the other tools discussed in this section, paired comparisons provide law enforcement decision makers with a systematic way of sorting out which alternatives "best" meets their agency's needs. For discussion purposes, there are five raters. A pool/set of criteria must be developed and defined. Hypothetically six of them are generated. The criteria essentially represent the "standards" against which all alternatives are individually evaluated on separate worksheets by decision makers. Figure 8.4 shows an individual worksheet for evaluating the first criterion, "How likely is this alternative to fully meet the goal?"

In Figure 8.4, Alternative A cannot be evaluated against itself, so the first rating involves the judgment of whether Alternative A is more likely than Alternative B to meet Criterion 1. Hypothetically, the number on the scale in Figure 8.4 that is consistent with the rater's judgment is entered into the worksheet; in this illustration it is a "7." Working from left to right across the

Alternatives	A	B	C	D	Sum of Rows	Rank of Alternative
A		7	9	9	25	2
B	5		7	3	15	3
C	9	9		9	27	1
D	5	5	3		13	4
Scale for Paired Comparison						

Scale	Definition	Explanation
1	Less than likely	The evidence does not suggest the possibility
3	Likely	The evidence suggests the possibility
5	More than likely	The evidence suggests a moderate possibility
7	Much more than likely	The evidence suggests a strong possibility
9	Absolutely likely	The evidence suggests a very strong possibility

FIGURE 8.4 ▶ Criterion 1: "How likely is this alternative to fully achieve the goal?"

worksheet, the other two numbers are, in turn, entered, 9 and 9. When the rater completing the worksheet is done entering ratings in the worksheet, the sum of the rows and the standing in the ranks are recorded. Although Alternative C is seemingly in good shape with 27 points, Alternative A has 25 points. There are two things to keep in mind: (1) this is the worksheet for just one of five raters and for this criterion and (2) there are five more criteria to be evaluated for each alternative.

Implement Decision, Monitor, and Adjust the Plan as Needed

The Chief of Police may assign a unit commander or designate a civilian project manager to implement the chosen alternative depending on the situation. The purpose of this assignment is to fix responsibility for its monitoring, progress, and success. The planning committee should have laid out an evaluation plan for the alternative selected and made sure the data for it is collected. If some needed evaluation data has not been collected, the evaluation plan must be adjusted on the authority of the person responsible for the implementation of the alternative or by the authorization of any steering committee to which he/she reports, and forms need to be devised to capture the data from the beginning.

Evaluation requires comparing what actually happened with what was planned for—and this may not be a simple undertaking.[14] Feedback must be obtained concerning the results of the implementation of the alternative, as well as the effectiveness and other impacts of it. Hudzik and Cordner[15] point out that evaluation completes one cycle of synoptic planning. The need to identify and resolve problems must be considered repetitively.

OTHER CATEGORIES OF PLANS

From an applications perspective, the planning process yields an end product—a plan. These can be categorized by use and are delineated into five groups:[16]

1. Administrative or Management Plans
2. Procedural Plans
3. Operational Plans
4. Tactical Plans
5. Strategic Plans

Administrative or Management Plans

This includes formulation of the department's mission statement, values, goals, and policies and procedures; the organizational structure, the functions, authority, and responsibilities of positions and units; the allocation of resources; sick leave, vacation time, court appearances, and other related topics.

Procedural Plans

This category of plans are ordinarily included as part of a police department's written directive system, a copy of which is assigned to every officer and is updated periodically. Procedural plans are the guidelines for the action to be taken under specific circumstances. For example, this could include the following: proper application of the use of force; responding to bank robberies; evidence handling; when and how to utilize canine teams; responding to domestic violence calls; informant management and dozens of other similar police matters.

Operational Plans

These are often called work plans and describe specific actions to be taken by line units (patrol officers, precinct groups, and/or division teams). Work plans are usually short and terse, giving both direction and time constraints in accomplishing a given task. In community policing ventures, the work plan usually focuses on a defined community need in a specific neighborhood.

Tactical Plans

These involve planning for emergencies of a specific nature at known locations. Some tactical plans are developed in anticipation of such emergencies as the taking of hostages at a prison or a jailbreak and are subject to modification or being discarded altogether in peculiar and unanticipated circumstances. Other tactical plans are developed for specific situations as they arise, such as how to relate to a demonstration in the park or a march on city hall as well as hosting political conventions. Although well-operated police agencies invest considerable effort in developing tactical plans, they may seldom or never be used. Nevertheless, their very existence stimulates confidence among field officers and lessens the likelihood of injury to officers, the public, and violators.

Sometimes even the best laid out tactical plans do not go exactly as planned because not every eventuality can be anticipated. A good example of this occurred in an **active shooter** situation on September 16, 2013, at the Washington, DC, Navy Yard that resulted in 12 individuals being killed and several others being injured.[17] The active shooter, Aaron Alexis, 34, was subsequently shot and killed at the scene by a Metropolitan Police Department officer who had first been fired upon by Alexis but was saved by his protective vest.[18] The following is a summary of the After Action Report resulting from this incident.

CASE 1

AFTER ACTION REPORT
OF THE WASHINGTON NAVY YARD ACTIVE SHOOTER EVENT

At the beginning of the incident, the streets were blocked off by the police (see Figure 8.5). One hundred seventeen law enforcement officers from various agencies entered the building to search for the gunman.[19] Many of the search teams consisted of officers or agents from a variety of different agencies. Despite the mixed composition of the teams, the team members quickly went to work searching for the shooter.

The harsh lessons of Columbine in Colorado,[20] in which the initial responding officers waited for the arrival of the Special Weapons and Tactics (**SWAT**) team, have forced law enforcement to adapt its response protocols and enter as quickly as possible in order to search for the shooter. Waiting for the specially trained SWAT teams or Emergency Response Team (ERT) officers to arrive and lead the tactical response is no longer considered an option during active shooter incidents.

The first officers on scene must form active shooter teams, make entry, and immediately begin searching for the shooter, moving as quickly, but prudently, as possible. They have also been trained to bypass downed victims, when

the gunman is still active, in order to find and neutralize the threat as quickly as possible. Those first officers may be all that stands between the gunman and even more victims.

The rapid entry of the first officers proved critical in stopping the gunman from taking the lives of even more people. Unlike the shooters in some previous tragedies, this active shooter did not take his own life when the first officers entered, but rather seemed determined to first evade and then engage law enforcement officers. The sheer size and maze-like layout of the building contributed to the active shooter's ability to evade and then ambush officers he encountered. However, upon entering the officers were able to neutralize the threat without further loss of life.

After prior training scenarios were reviewed, it was noted that law enforcement had conducted extensive active shooter training exercises and scenario-based drills in many different types of locations, but military bases were often excluded from the training even after a 2009 shooting at Fort Hood.[21] Also, civilian police department personnel may hold the mistaken belief that the personnel working

FIGURE 8.5 ▶ Upon responding to the active shooter call at the U.S. Navy Yard in Washington, DC, one of the first things the Metropolitan Police Department did was to block off all the intersections in the proximity of this facility. (Melina Mara/The Washington Post/Getty Images)

within gated military installations such as the Navy Yard are heavily armed and capable of defending against threats. The truth is that the majority of the individuals working on military bases are not armed. Out of the 14,000 workers at the Navy Yard, an extremely small number either possessed or had access to a firearm. In terms of an armed presence, the Navy Yard was really no different than other civilian agencies or private facilities that employ limited numbers of armed security personnel at entrances.

After Action Constructive Suggestions

There were two suggestions about how responding officers entered the buildings made during the review meetings with internal units and agency partners.

First, some reviewers indicated that the use of ballistic shields may have assisted in increasing the speed of officers' movement. Under the current training standard, officers were instructed to move as quickly and safely as possible to neutralize the threat. Officer perceptions as to the proper balance of speed and safety in those circumstances will likely differ; however, it was agreed that it was an important consideration for future tactical training. It was recommended that the police department should consider procuring ballistic shields as they provide officers with additional protection, which may increase their speed of movement. There are practical and financial considerations that make outfitting every officer in the department with certain equipment unfeasible. For example, many patrol officers are not in vehicles, but rather are on foot, bikes, motorcycles, or other modes that do not allow for carrying large pieces of equipment or large amounts of equipment.

A second issue that was raised in the after action assessment was that some personnel from other law enforcement agencies did not appear to be willing to take instructions or commands from the Washington, DC, Metropolitan Police Department's (MPD) forward operating commander, who was coordinating the entry of the active shooter teams. These law enforcement officers responded into the building on their own. It was reported that at least one law

enforcement officer indicated that he and his colleagues were federal officers and the Navy Yard was a federal facility, so they did not need "permission" to respond to the incident and enter the scene. Despite the truth of that statement, the officer was ignoring the much greater implications and increased risk created by an uncoordinated response. It was clear to all (or should have been) that Incident Command was operating and that MPD was the lead agency. This issue can ultimately be addressed through training and communication.

Recommendations

Neighboring law enforcement agencies, both federal and local, should conduct collaborative, interagency training exercises. By training together, officers from different agencies are able to develop trust and mutual understanding prior to responding together to an incident that may require a multiagency response. The tactical teams for the various regional agencies train together on a regular basis. MPD's Emergency Response Team (ERT) and the other area agencies' tactical operators are extremely familiar with one another's teams, tactics, and response plans. This familiarity should exist on additional levels throughout the agency—including patrol officers, field agents, and deputies—since these will often be the first personnel to arrive on the scene of an active shooter. Active shooter training should include different types of locations, including military bases. It is also important to note that even if a closed campus or gated facility has its own plans and protocols to respond to and manage a crisis, it is vital that the facility's personnel plan for the unexpected and this includes a larger-scale response.

The personnel from different agencies should receive standardized training, which results in a consistent understanding of tactics, communication, and approach. Collaborative training is also an opportunity to highlight the importance of a coordinated response by all involved. Ultimately, all personnel who arrive on scene should report to and be deployed by the incident commander.[22]

Quick Facts: Active Shooter Lessons

For more information on planning and training regarding responding to active shooter incidents, see Greg Ellifritz, "10 Lessons Learned from the New FBI Study on Active Shooters"; http://www.activeresponsetraining.net; Dan Marcou, "5 Phases of the Active Shooter Incident"; http://www.policeone.com/; and Office of Homeland Security, "Active Shooter Preparedness"; http://www.dhs.gov/active-shooter-preparedness.

Strategic Plans

A strategic plan can be used by administrators to set priorities, focus energy and resources, strengthen operations, ensure that employees and other stakeholders are working toward common goals, establish agreement around intended outcomes/results, and assess and adjust the organization's direction in response to a changing environment. It is a disciplined effort that produces fundamental decisions and actions that shape and guide what an organization is, who it serves, what it does, and why it does it. Strategic plans are longer than some other types of plans in duration, typically three to five years.

Quick Facts: Strategic Planning Example

For more information regarding strategic planning, see *Madison Police Department's Trust-Based Initiatives and Collaborative Efforts with Madison's Diverse Community*; https://www.cityofmadison.com/police/documents/trustbasedinitiatives.pdf.

BLENDING FIVE TYPES OF PLANS

In 2009, the City of Tampa, Florida, agreed to host the Republican National Convention in 2012. The entire planning process took three years and involved administrative, procedural, operational, tactical, and strategic planning. In the earliest planning stages, one of the major security concerns was that some individuals or groups might attempt to disrupt the convention. This did not occur to any significant degree because of this agency's careful planning. The steps that were taken in the planning process are summarized in "The Tampa Quick Look Analysis Report."

CASE 2

THE TAMPA QUICK LOOK ANALYSIS REPORT

The hosting of a national political convention posed unique planning and operational challenges. Due to their high-profile nature and the large number of attendees, national conventions have the potential to adversely impact public safety and security. Detailed documentation to guide local law enforcement on planning and operational best practices is sparse in these types of conventions.

In order to address this gap in knowledge and to respond to requests from law enforcement leaders, the U.S. Department of Justice's Bureau of Justice Assistance (BJA) worked in partnership with the Center for Naval Analyses (CNA) to provide technical assistance and support to local law enforcement security operations prior to and during the 2012 national conventions. The primary goal of the technical assistance was to develop an after action report (AAR) that documents key findings of the overall security planning and operations. CNA analysts were deployed to support public safety and security operations for the 2012 Republican National Convention (RNC) from August 26 through August 31, 2012.

In addition to this Tampa Quick Look Analysis Report, the lessons learned and best practices from this event will serve as a blueprint for future law enforcement agencies in charge of maintaining security. The BJA, with the support of CNA, documented key findings from the 2012 Democratic National Convention and the 2012 Republican National Convention in a comprehensive after action report.

The Tampa Police Department (TPD) understood the magnitude of the event and the potential for violent clashes between the police and demonstrators, and the high risk to officer safety. In reviewing the law enforcement response in previous similar large-scale events, it became clear to the Chief and Assistant Chiefs that a different philosophy had to be used to ensure the safety of attendees, demonstrators, and officers assisting in the response. This philosophy stressed an adherence to community policing strategies that are focused and based on protecting the constitutional rights of demonstrators while ensuring officers' safety.

In preparation for the event, the TPD developed and distributed a standard operating procedure, produced specifically for this event. This standard operating procedure outlined the department's missions and general policing philosophy. The TPD sought to:

- Protect the First Amendment rights of all persons;
- Conduct all operations in a safe and efficient manner; and
- Ensure that public safety services remain in full effect in the nonevent spaces for all affected jurisdictions.

To maintain uniformity and consistency of practices and protocols across the multiple agencies, TPD employed several strategies. It conducted training across the participating jurisdictions, provided officers with a pocket guide that referenced the department's use-of-force policy, held a training session for 1,900 crowd control officers, and provided all of the crowd control officers with identical uniforms. These actions ensured that the officers supporting the TPD operated as one unit, following the same procedures as one another and acting under one mission. Such a strategy is imperative in large-scale events where multiple agencies are involved.

During the event, CNA analysts observed discussions and noted key decisions, actions, and field operations as they related to critical functional areas, such as communications, intelligence, public information and media relations, and training. From these observations, CNA identified a number of best practices and lessons learned. Identified best practices were:

- **Pre-Event Planning:** Rigorous and robust planning prior to the event facilitated TPD's operations for several functional areas (e.g., training, tactical operations, logistics, communications, and traffic). Twenty-four subcommittees, an Executive Steering Committee, and a core planning team established effective operational plans, policies, and collaborative partnerships during the 28 months prior to the event that formed the basis for the successful execution of security operations. The TPD often cited the planning process and the operational plans that were developed as part of this multijurisdictional collaborative process as critical factors in ensuring the success of this event. Below are the key best practices that most influenced event-related security operations.

- **Pre-Event Training:** Training was disseminated in a number of different formats (e.g., scenario based, presentations, E-learning, and training videos) to ensure that officers clearly understood their roles and responsibilities. Training personnel was critical for ensuring that law enforcement officers accomplished their tasks while preserving the TPD's mission and policing philosophy. One example of the benefit that training provided was crowd control officers understanding their roles and expected behaviors in response to demonstrators exercising their freedom of speech.[23]

- **Personnel Recruitment:** The TPD recognized early in the planning process that event security would require a significant number of additional law enforcement personnel. To satisfy this requirement, the TPD recruited more than 5,500 state and local law enforcement officers from across the State of Florida. This enabled the effective provision of security to over 80 venues, 60 critical infrastructure sites, hundreds of delegates and VIPs, and thousands of event attendees. These additional law enforcement officers also provided a force reserve and the flexibility to meet potential/unanticipated challenges.

- **Communications and Situational Awareness:** The effective use of communications equipment and technology provided greater situational awareness for TPD

Commanders. Extensive criminal intelligence capabilities and video surveillance technologies (e.g., fixed cameras, mobile cameras on sources in the field) allowed TPD Commanders to make strategic response and resource-allocation decisions based on real-time information. Essentially, the enhanced video capabilities allowed TPD Commanders to have a virtual presence or "eyes on the ground" directly from the command center.

- **Legal Affairs:** Training was provided to improve the officers' understanding of the legal and civil rights issues involved in this type of event (e.g., First Amendment rights and privileges) and helped to ensure that officers understood that their mission included protecting the rights and civil liberties of the demonstrators as well as the ticket-holding attendees (e.g., delegates and invited guests). Though the number of demonstrators was far less than expected, the TPD still responded to a number of demonstrations throughout the event to ensure public order. Senior command staff and officials worked directly with the demonstrator groups, and this tactic appeared highly effective in quickly reducing tensions by allowing protestors "to be heard." In addition, the accessibility of senior officers in the field smoothed crowd control issues and allowed for rapid adjustments of strategy.

- **Command and Control:** TPD and the supporting law enforcement agencies effectively coordinated command and control of the event through a number of operations centers, daily meetings, and a common communication radio network (see Figure 8.6). The implementation of the Incident Command System (ICS) allowed for multiple jurisdictions to perform their duties in operational synchronicity, and ensured that communications and situational awareness were maintained from the field through the chain-of-command to the Chief of the Department. ICS and the interagency partnerships among TPD, neighboring local jurisdictions, federal agencies, local

FIGURE 8.6 ▶ During the Republican National Convention, the Tampa Police Department 911 Emergency Communications Bureau was set up with nine additional radio channels, four dedicated phone lines, and an RNC supervisor. The team monitored live video feeds, street cameras, and air service down links from the Tampa Police Department and the Hillsborough County Sheriff's Office. The information they gathered was then relayed to the numerous command centers and the 60 local, state, and federal agencies involved in the security operation. (Fitzcrittle/Shutterstock)

FIGURE 8.7 ▶ Police bike patrols were used extensively during the Republican National Convention in Tampa, Florida. They travel in formation throughout the Downtown Area, helping visitors find their way. Also, when demonstrators veered off the parade route bike officers rode ahead and blocked traffic on side streets to prevent accidents. The RNC bike patrol consisted of 200 officers who pedaled in for the event from 15 different Tampa Bay Area communities. (Terese Loeb Kreuzer/Alamy Stock Photo)

businesses, and community organizations played a significant role in the operational success of the event as evidenced by the minimal arrests and the perceptions of both the public and the department.

- **Crowd Management:** The use of bicycle patrols to quickly manage and cordon off crowds was particularly beneficial. Officers on bicycles were used to quickly respond to demonstrators and provided a soft barrier along the demonstration routes. Officers on bicycles often rode to the front of the demonstrator marches and blocked traffic providing safe routes for these demonstrators to exercise their constitutional rights. Using bicycles to manage the crowds proved more efficient than having officers mounted on horses, while still providing a strong police presence (see Figure 8.7).

- **Intelligence/Counterterrorism/Counter Surveillance:** The 2012 RNC was the first time the 700-megahertz long-term evolution (LTE), a National Public Safety Broadband Network, was used by local law enforcement. This network provided officers with interoperable voice, video, and data communications allowing sources in the field to use iPhones, operated under this LTE network, to send, via a secure network, live video of demonstrations and other intelligence information.

Identified lessons learned were:

- **Resource Allocation:** Obtaining and allocating personnel in an effective manner were issues that were apparent in both the planning and operational stages of the event. One issue that arose in planning for the event was that law enforcement planners and operators did not have a clear understanding of the role the Florida National Guard would play in security operations. Confusion existed about the number of guardsmen the Department of Defense would provide and the tasks these guardsmen could fulfill. In addition to this, during the event, it quickly became apparent that not all venue security personnel

were familiar with their assignments or their surroundings and as a result, there were inconsistencies in the security measures used at each checkpoint in the venue.

- **Personnel Tracking:** Although the Radio-Frequency Identification (RFID) equipment experienced technical difficulties in tracking and logging of personnel throughout the event, these difficulties were minimally disruptive to the overall operation. After the event, however, these technical difficulties and the lack of personnel tracking caused inefficiencies in processing payroll. As a result, in order to track the hours logged working, payroll personnel resorted to using sign-in sheets, which were often incomplete.

- **Financial/Grant Management:** Substantial time is needed to apply for federal funds, clear budgets, and obtain approval to begin to obligate and expend funds. This process should be considered carefully as part of the planning process. More details on grant management processes and procedures are outlined in *Managing Large-Scale Security Events: A Planning Primer for Local Law Enforcement Agencies*.

- **Credentialing:** The credentialing application process and instructions provided were unclear and undefined. In addition, rather than distributing credentials at one central location, each agency was individually provided credentials to issue. While this method was intended to be more efficient, it delayed the credentialing process due to the large volume of credentials needed. In retrospect, TPD recognized that the distribution of these credentials at a central location would have likely cut down on inconsistencies within the credential process and would likely have been a more efficient approach.

Overall, the TPD's operational response throughout the RNC was effective and aligned with its mission and planning objectives. Officers were prepared to deal with the incidents that arose and were able to maintain positive interactions with the demonstrators throughout the event.[24]

DECISION MAKING

This section provides an overview of selected milestones in the flow of thinking about decision-making. Planning is essentially a decision-making process and some of the terms used in this portion of this chapter will be familiar due to the earlier discussions in the "planning" portion of this chapter. The synoptic planning model parallels a number of steps involved in the rational comprehensive decision-making process, and both Pugh's decision-making matrix and paired comparisons are mainline decision tools.

Rational Comprehensive and Sequencing Models

The earliest writings on decision making are from the Frenchman, Nicolas de Caritat, Marquis de Condorcet (1743–1794).[25] In 1910, John Dewey (see Figure 8.8) developed a sequence of five steps for his "reflective thinking" model that morphed into the classical rational comprehensive model of decision making through the work of Simon, Brim et al., and others.[26] Knight eventually distinguished between risk and uncertainty, defining risk as knowing the probability of an adverse event happening and uncertainty as an unknowable risk.[27]

In 1960, Simon adapted reflective thinking into a three-step model to make it suitable for use in the context of organizational decisions. Two years later, Brim et al., elaborated on it as a six-step process:

1. Identification of the problem,
2. Obtaining necessary information,
3. Production of possible solutions,
4. Evaluation of solutions,
5. Selection of a strategy for performance, and
6. Implementation of the decision.[28]

From Dewey through Brim et al., the model remained sequential in the sense that each step occurred in the same order. The usual five or six steps in the rational comprehensive decision-making model are immediately recognizable as springing from the work of Dewey. During the mid-20th century, Barnard imported the term "decision making" from the language of public administration into business, where it was being discussed as "policy making" or "resource allocation."[29] The term quickly gained traction, perhaps because "policy making" could go on endlessly, but a decision implied the end of discussion and the beginning of the action phase.

Simon: Bounded Rationality

Beginning in 1947, Simon produced a series of challenges to the rational comprehensive notion that decision makers behaved with rationality[30] (see Figure 8.9). He argued that because decision makers did not acquire all of the relevant information about their decisions, the decisions were not fully rational. Instead, these decisions were sub-optimized by "bounded rationality." Simon described bounded rationality as:

> On one side, the individual is limited by those skills, habits, and reflexes which are no longer in the realm of the conscious... on a second side, the individual is limited by his values and those conceptions of purpose which influence him in making decisions... and on a third side, the individual is limited by the extent of his knowledge that is relevant to his job.[31]

According to Simon, the consequence of bounded reality was "satisficing." It produced decisions with which the decision makers were not fully *satis*fied, but neither did it

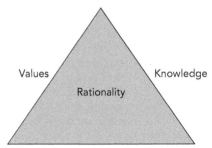

FIGURE 8.9 ▶ Simon's concept of bounded rationality.

produce much sacri*ficing*; instead, it resulted in decisions that were "good enough."

Lindblom: Muddling Through/Disjointed Incrementalism

Lindblom also challenged the rational model of decision making with his "**muddling through**" approach in 1959.[32] Rather than making sweeping changes, decisions, plans, and policies are changed by making small, successive incremental changes to them, tending to promote the status quo. Muddling through and a later term "disjointed incrementalism" are synonymous. Based on his study of government institutions in the United States, Lindblom concluded that the decision-making process is so fragmented and so complex, incorporating the interaction of various institutions, political entities, pressure groups, and individual biases, that rationality can have only a marginal effect. That is, the police administrator faces a set of limiting political factors, such as the mayor's wish to be re-elected, that prevent the decision-making process from being truly rational. For elected sheriffs, the political agendas can be so strong that rational decision-making is inhibited.

Lindblom's **incremental model** asserts that decision making is serial—that it is limited by time and resources as it gropes along successive paths where means and ends are not distinct, goals and objectives are ambiguous, and rationality cannot consistently thrive. Contending that police managers and administrators "play things safe" and opt to move very slowly in decision-making, Lindblom[33] proposes that managers "muddle through" problems rather than analytically choosing decisions. Lindblom's incrementalism provides both the police administrator and the public with a number of safeguards against error:

> In the first place, past experience has given police chief's knowledge about the probable consequence of any decision they are considering. Second, chiefs need not attempt big jumps forward because they don't expect their decision to be a final resolution of a problem. Their decision is just a first step . . . . Third, Chiefs are in effect able to "feel their way forward" as they move to each successive step. Lastly, Chiefs can often remedy an error fairly quickly.[34] While Lindblom's now older characterizations are not flattering, some police leaders still find them to be "a description of reality."[35]

Lindblom's incremental approach was recently found to be the most powerful predictor for explaining change over time in the share of the municipal budget going to police services. The study found that municipal budget decisions and the percentage of budgets allocated to police remained relatively stable over time and only changed incrementally.[36] The finding is consistent with the idea of "satisficing" where decision-makers make small incremental changes to municipal budgets and hope the outcome of the decision will be acceptable.

Although it was never an important challenge to the rational comprehensive model, in 1967 Etzioni produced a "third approach" to decision making that deserves mention beyond the rational comprehensive and muddling through approaches.

This third approach was "mixed scanning." Decision makers at various points could use aspects of the rational comprehensive approach and at others rely on disjointed incrementalism. Mixed scanning was vaguely worded and difficult to operationalize. As a consequence, it never took hold.[37]

Allison: Political and Organizational Models

Allison's[38] analysis of the 1962 Cuban missile crisis led him to the conclusion that the rational decision-making model, although most widely used, was seriously flawed. He provided two models that ran counter to the rational comprehensive model.

First, the organizational process model is based on the premise that few government decisions are exclusively the province or "property" of a single organization, particularly when making major policy decisions. Police agencies for example are subject to significant influences from entities in their immediate environment and in some instances even controlled by them. Just locally, there are mayors, city councils, district attorneys, courts, and business representatives, a small number of which cross the line from advocacy to improperly influencing or even controlling what the police do or not do.

Second, the government politics model holds that major government policies are rarely made by a single rational actor, such as the chief of police. Rather, policymaking and general decision-making are the outcome of a process of bargaining among individuals and groups to support various interests. Implicit in both of the models is that the decision maker requires direction from his or her internal staff as well as support from other government agencies in the making of important decisions. This is especially true during crisis situations.[39]

Gore: The Gut-Level Approach

In 1964, Gore[40] challenged the rational comprehensive model by identifying the crucial element of humanism in decision-making. He presents a **heuristic model**, appropriately referred to as "the gut-level approach," when considering action that may be taken. Many seasoned patrol officers assimilate their experiences as time passes, thus becoming "streetwise and develop the ability to anticipate events before they actually occur."

This streetwise dimension is captured in Gore's decision-making method for police administrators. In an antithesis to the rational model, Gore identifies a process by which a decision is the product of the maker's personality. Gore views the heuristic process as "a groping toward agreements seldom arrived at through logic ... the very essence of those factors validating a decision are internal to the personality of the individual instead of external to it."[41] Whereas the rational method is concrete, formalized by structure and calculations, the heuristic approach is nebulous, characterized by "gut feelings reaching backward into the memory and forward into the future."[42]

For Gore, decision-making is basically an emotional, nonrational, highly personalized, and subjective process. The facts validating a decision are internal to the personality of the individual instead of external to it. The key word in this statement is "validating"; it is intended to convey a sense of personal psychological approval or acceptance. The optimum situation is to select the decision alternative that creates the least anxiety about or disruption to the individual's basic needs and desires. Every "objective" decision should be modified to meet the emotional needs of the various members of the police department who will be affected by the decision.[43]

> Whereas the rational system of action evolves through the identification of causes and effects and the discovery of ways of implementing them, the heuristic process is a groping toward agreement seldom arrived at through logic. The very essence of the heuristic process is that factors validating a decision are internal to the personality of the individual instead of external to it. Whereas the rational system of action deals with the linkages between a collective and its objectives and between a collective and its environment, the heuristic process is orientated toward the relationship between that private core of values embedded in the center of the personality and its public counterpart, ideology. The dynamics of personality are not those of logic but rather those of emotion.[44]

In other words, although logic and reason may be the basic intellectual tools needed to analyze a given problem or to structure a series of solutions to a given situation, logic and reason may not prove to be completely effective in establishing intra-organizational agreement in connection with any given decision.[45]

Applauded for his contribution to the decision-making process, Gore has also been highly criticized as being too simplistic and nonscientific. Souryal[46] writes that "Gore's analysis is too unreliable.... It could complicate an existing situation, promote spontaneity, discredit the role of training and delay the advent of professionalism" in police organizations. This is an unfair assessment of the method. Gore views heuristic applications as adjuncts or alternatives to rational models. Further, some type of credibility must be assessed to that vague, unknown, and non-measurable entity we call experience, talent, streetwise, or a "sixth sense." It was these elements that Simon had so much trouble with in calculating his "bound and limited" argument regarding the rational model. In any event, Gore's contributions remain as an opposite of decision-making based solely on figures, formulas, and mathematical designs.

Recognition-Primed Decision Making (RPD)

This is a model based on a more naturalistic view of decision-making. While the previously discussed models focus on different courses of action and the selection of one course of action over others, RPD is distinguished by focusing more on the assessment of the situation, its dynamics, and the experience of the decision maker. Much like incrementalism and heuristic models, RPD asserts that formal models of decision-making are not possible in real-life situations, where decision makers are under time constraints and face poorly defined tasks, dynamic conditions, and ill-structured goals. RPD contains elements of the incremental and heuristic models and considers how a police official's experience affects his or her decisions. In RPD, police officials are primed to act in a situation and do not wait for a complete analysis of the facts before acting. Instead, elements of the situation are recognized as typical and action is taken based on previous experience. RPD relies heavily on the concept of satisficing, in which a solution is not so much optimal as it is sufficient, given the circumstances.[47] In other words, decision makers utilizing RPD identify an option that will suffice in a given situation based on past experiences with similar situations, then try to elaborate and improve on that option. Of course, the RPD model brings to mind questions about how decision makers react when they encounter situations that are absolutely not typical. In these cases, the RPD model states that the decision maker must identify anomalies in the situation and obtain as much information about the anomaly as possible in order to make a decision. The RPD model does not allow for much creativity or ingenuity in a situation, and it certainly allows for previous mistakes to be repeated. However, research indicates that RPD is the dominant form of decision-making used in command and control organizations.[48]

Thin-Slicing Theory

Gladwell, in his 2005 book *Blink*, described a model of decision-making called "thin-slicing." **Thin-slicing theory** states that, in situations where snap decisions are required (whether by a police administrator, a line officer, or anyone else in a decision-making capacity) instantaneous decisions can often be the best, particularly when paired with training and expertise.[49] Thin-slicing is clearly an offshoot of the heuristic model, as Gladwell maintains those decisions that are made in an instant can be equally good, or even better, than those made deliberately and with a lot of information. Thin-slicing incorporates more rationality than traditional heuristic models. Unconscious decision making, which Gladwell describes as "a kind of giant computer that quickly and quietly processes a lot of the data we need in order to keep functioning as human beings."[50] This allows decision makers to thin-slice, a rational response in which we find patterns based on very narrow slices of experience. According to Gladwell, our unconscious allows us to sift through situations that confront us, to the point that we throw out all irrelevant information and focus on the parts of the issue that are most relevant.

However, there is a dark side to rapid decision-making that is clearly not rational and Gladwell incorporates this into his theory. Often, unconscious attitudes and prejudices sneak into the decision-making process, leading thin-slicing astray. Under extreme pressure, researchers have found that decision makers tend to fall back on stereotypes and prejudices. The best way to counter this type of bias, according to Gladwell, is to train decision makers to slow down, even slightly, and find ways to mitigate the effects of stereotypes and biases by changing the environment where decisions might occur. This may at first glance seem paradoxical, and some might argue that Gladwell's concept of thin-slicing is at odds with itself because the theory asks that the decision maker go with his or her first reaction, but set rules ahead of time for the way that he or she might think. Gladwell acknowledges this but asserts that those with enough training and expertise are more able to extract the most meaningful amounts of information from the smallest, thinnest slice of an experience and are able to control the environment in which rapid cognition takes place.[51]

THE USE OF COMPUTERS IN DECISION MAKING

In the early 1960s, some federal government agencies began using "modern" mainframe computers. The less costly, but still powerful, minicomputer appeared in 1964 and 1965. Initially, computers were used to automate labor-intensive tasks, such as payroll calculations. Around that time, the phrase "garbage in, garbage out" gained currency, meaning that mistaken or poor quality input produced flawed results. In the mid-late 1960s, applications of computing to decision making largely centered on providing data to support decisions, which had the collateral effect of reinforcing the rational comprehensive approach to decision making, as did many other subsequent computer applications. However, in the 1960s and even into the 1970s, the veil had not yet been lifted on the seemingly miraculous other things computers could do in the realm of sophisticated problem analysis and decision-making.

Taking advantage of computer applications available now is particularly crucial to the future of intelligence-led/predictive policing and the research of the smart policing initiative.[52] Despite the advantages of powerful analyses, there is still much to learn about how computer analyses influence decision making. Many problems in how we make decisions have been attributed to limitations in how we memorize and process information, and computers are often used to overcome these restrictions. But because many computer systems have been developed without a full understanding of how people actually think, computers can lead people to make bad decisions. There are situations when it would have been better to follow gut reactions. Following your intuitions is much more difficult when you are sitting in front of a computer! The trick is to know when and when not to use gut reactions, something that most decision makers are not taught.[53] The field of computer science is currently focused on two broad, but related, fields of decision making:

1. Decision systems, which are decisions made by a computer. It does so using any of several forms of artificial intelligence (AI) and relies on its own particular knowledge base and inference or reasoning programming to reach decisions that would otherwise have to be made by a human. As an illustration, many police departments direct incoming nonemergency calls by automation; and

2. Decision sciences incorporating three subfields: normative, descriptive, and decision support; they all rest on the rational model. For present purposes, the most important of these is decision support, which also has three subfields: decision analysis (DA), operational research (OR), and decision support systems (DSS) (see Figure 8.10).[54]

Together, the three subfields of decision support gives the police powerful tools to quickly and efficiently examine staffing patterns and needs, distribution of the field force, conduct social network analysis (SNA) to discover the connection between criminals and their patterns, analyze the cost-effectiveness of using DNA to solve property crimes, crime mapping, hot-spot analysis, and other important problems.[55]

As has been seen in the riots following the Michael Brown shooting in Ferguson, Missouri, and the death of Freddie Gray in Baltimore, Maryland (both discussed in greater detail in Chapter 4, Politics and Police Administration), planning was inadequate. The police were either not allowed to be effective in controlling the situation because of political considerations, and/or decision makers did not know what action should be taken. Using

Decision Analysis (DA)	Operational/Operations Research (OR)	Decision Support Systems (DSS)
DA, popularly known as "applied decision theory" keeps breaking a decision problem into smaller sub problems that may be more manageable. In doing so, it considers factors like available information, alternatives, and uncertainties and presents the results as a decision model. Needed, but missing information produces a model that is "satisfactory" or "sufficiently good."	Similar to DA, OR uses analytical and mathematical models for decision support. However, OR differs in that it relies on higher-level mathematical modeling of questions or problems about the optimal way to manage scarce resources.	DSS is defined as interactive computer-based information systems intended to help users examine information databases, e.g., mine for data on wanted suspects with outstanding warrants, and utilize data and models to solve problems.

FIGURE 8.10 ▶ The three fields of decision support.[57] *Source:* These points are loosely derived with restatement from Marko Bohanec, "Decision Making: A Computer Science and Information Technology Viewpoint," *Interdisciplinary Description of Complex System* 7, No. 2 (2009), pp. 28, 32–33.

computer simulations, a 2008 study revealed what the optimal police responses should be when faced with a crowd control or riot situation, down to the placement of barricades. From decision support simulations, the on-scene commander can match crowd or riot behaviors with optimal response from pre-stored strategies to fit the tactical situation being faced.[56]

Decision Trees

When using a decision tree model, the probabilities for various outcomes are calculated for each branch of the tree. In the example used in Figure 8.11, the first branch of the trunk has three possible outcomes: (1) arrest at the scene by a patrol officer, (2) no arrest at the scene, and (3) arrest at the scene by a detective. Note in the figure that the probabilities for those three events total 1.0, which is the mathematical value for certainty; all possible outcomes for that branch of the example are accounted for. The next-higher branch of the decision tree deals with the various types of evidence obtained from investigation, and the final branches deal with the probability of arrest associated with the gathering of each type of evidence. Decision trees are very useful in analyzing situations and for reference when a series of decisions that flow from one event are involved. For example, decision trees would be useful to the commander of a detective bureau in formulating policy and guidelines on whether to continue an investigation based on the types of evidence and the

necessary allocation of organizational resources. In this regard, decision trees can be seen as a tool of operations research. If an administrator is facing a decision for which there are no actual data, a decision tree can still be useful in analyzing the situation and the "probabilities" can be the administrator's own subjective estimations based on experience. Decision tree models are commonly used in **e-learning software** programs that provide simulation-training scenarios to police officers and executives. The program changes and alternatives appear as the student makes various decisions that alter the precise path incorporated into the gaming simulation. These types of simulation software programs represent the latest technology in police training relating to officer and executive-level decision making (see Figure 8.11).

Alternative Decision-Making Models

Another attempt to outline various approaches to the decision-making process is Allison's[58] account of the 1962 Cuban missile crisis. He contends that the rational decision-making model, although most widely used, is seriously flawed. Allison presents two additional models (the organizational process model and the government politics model) to explain the decision-making during crisis events that police and other government agencies often face. The organizational process model is based on the premise that few government decisions are exclusively

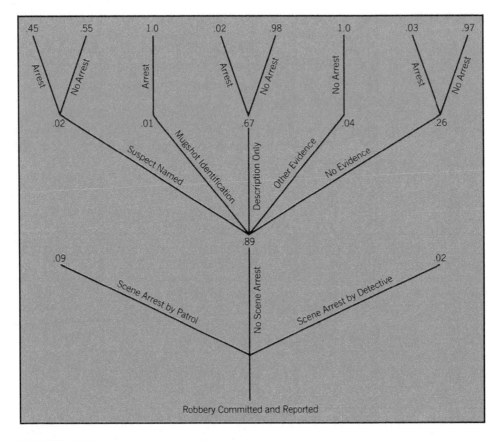

FIGURE 8.11 ▶ Decision tree of hypothetical probabilities of various outcomes in a robbery investigation.

the province of a single organization. In other words, police agencies are dependent on information and advice from other government units (such as the mayor's office, the FBI, and the district attorney's office) to make major decisions that affect public policy. The government politics model purports that major government policies are rarely made by a single rational actor, such as the chief of police. Rather, policymaking and general decision making are the outcome of a process of bargaining among individuals and groups to support those interests. Implicit in both of the models is that the decision maker requires direction from his or her internal staff as well as support from other government agencies in the making of important decisions. This is especially true during crisis situations.[59]

Operational Modeling

Other alternative models to decision making have evolved from the systems approach to management as described in Chapter 5, Organizational Theory. These techniques are vastly influenced by large, complex systems of variables. The application, collection, and analysis of data from decision making within the organization are called **operations research**.[60] In response to a need for a management science that addressed complex problems involving many variables, such as government planning, military spending, natural resource conservation, and national defense budgeting, operations research employs the use of mathematical inquiry, probability theory, and gaming theory to "calculate the probable consequences of alternative choices" in decision making.[61]

These approaches are highly sophisticated elaborations of the rational model using quantitative techniques. The weakness of the methods is in their practicality to real-world situations in which time and resources are not directly structured to gather intelligence about every problem and possible alternative. Further, these models assume that human biases will not enter the decision-making process. The most critical aspect of the approaches appears to be in their overriding insistence that decision-making is not a human activity but the product of some scientific, computerized, and unimpressionable robot that digests quantitative information. Wildavsky[62] has continually warned that the application of decision making to costs, benefits, resources, and budgets frequently results in the adoption of meaningless data, and places unwarranted stimuli into the process. For example, the RPD model is based on recognizing situations and knowing how to handle them.[63] Other types of alternative decision-making models come from notions popularized by best-selling books such as Gladwell's *Blink*.[64]

DECISION MAKING DURING CRISIS EVENTS

Police agencies, like all government organizations and private entities, are not immune to the necessity of effective decision making during crisis events. Thus far, we have examined decision making in law enforcement from the traditional aspects of planning, organizational needs, theoretical models, and administrative roles. However, two older major events remain as prime examples of protracted crisis events in which law enforcement control of a situation was at best, slipping away: (1) the raid of the Branch Davidian Compound in Waco, Texas, in 1993 and (2) the FBI siege of the Weaver family at Ruby Ridge, Idaho, in 1992. These types of events span hours, days, and even months to end and must *not* be confused with active shooter situations requiring immediate action. The purpose of this analysis is to bring applications of the various decision-making models to reality. It is not intended as a critical commentary, but rather as an effort to identify the commonalities of the incidents and the lessons derived. It should not be taken lightly that each incident began with a sense of duty, good faith, honor, and courage yet ended in tragic losses and damaged agency reputations.

The Branch Davidians, Waco, Texas (1993)

During the early 1990s, a young, charismatic religious leader began to develop a group of followers known as the Branch Davidians. The group settled slightly northeast of Waco, Texas, and began building a well-fortified compound in which to protect themselves from the outside world and the impending "Last Judgment Day." Their spiritual leader, David Koresh (commonly referred to by followers as "the Lamb of God"), was a high school dropout with a perceived mystical ability to teach from the apocalyptic Book of Revelation in the New Testament.

Police investigations of the Branch Davidians did not begin until late in 1992, when Alcohol, Tobacco, and Firearms (ATF) agents were contacted by a postal driver who reported seeing hand grenades in a partially opened package delivered to the Waco compound. As a result of the investigation, an arrest warrant for Koresh was issued, along with a search warrant to seek out additional illegal weapons and explosives at the Waco compound.

In the early morning hours of February 28, 1993, ATF tactical teams totaling approximately 75 people stormed the Waco compound. The agents were met with a fusillade of heavy gunfire. In the resulting exchange, four ATF agents and six Branch Davidians were killed. The incident prompted a 51-day standoff between federal agents and the Branch Davidians. Immediately following the initial confrontation between ATF and the compound occupants, the FBI assumed control of the operation. While negotiations during the ordeal were targeted initially at a peaceful resolution, the FBI began preparations to reenter the compound by force, using armored vehicles to break through heavily fortified walls and distribute a debilitating dose of CS tear gas. The gas was supposed to be nonlethal, would not permanently harm adults or children, and would not cause fire during the delivery stage. As time lingered and negotiations lulled, Attorney General Janet Reno gave orders to commence with the assault. At 6:00 a.m. on April 19, 1993, several M-60 military tanks, reconfigured with tear gas delivery booms, began breaking through the compound walls. Within hours of the operation, fire broke out. Fanned by 35-mile-per-hour winds, the fire raged, and the compound was rapidly incinerated. Seventy-two bodies were found among the remains, including several children.

The political flames of Waco linger. In 1999, the Texas Rangers and lawyers for the Waco survivors revealed a blatant cover-up by the FBI. For six years, the FBI insisted that the Branch Davidians burned their own compound and denied to Congress that its agents fired any flammable tear gas canisters in the attack on April 19, 1993. Renewed investigations revealed that not only did the FBI mislead Congress, but top decision makers may have overtly lied, finally admitting that the FBI did, indeed, fire at least two pyrotechnic M651 grenades at the Branch Davidian bunker. Even more troubling was the revelation that the U.S. military provided federal law enforcement agents with more than $1 million worth of support (supplying tanks, helicopters, aerial reconnaissance, munitions, and support personnel) during the standoff at Waco. At least 10 military advisers or observers attached to the U.S. Army's elite Delta Force were present at various times throughout the incident. The entire action came dangerously close to violating **the Posse Comitatus Act**, prohibiting the use of federal soldiers to act as police officers or in a law enforcement capacity within the borders of the United States. Further, Attorney General Reno admitted that her decision to allow the FBI to rush the Davidian compound was heavily based on tales of Koresh abusing children. Later, a Justice Department "clarification" said that there was no evidence of child abuse. According to Reno, the FBI convinced her that Koresh was a suicidal maniac bent on destroying himself and others within the compound; however, she was never shown a letter by Koresh, dated just days before the attack that promised that he would come out peacefully after completing his writing. The resulting publicity and trials caused serious questioning of the FBI's tactics, operations, and decision-making.

The Weaver Family, Ruby Ridge, Idaho (1992)

In March 1992, federal prosecutors indicted Randy Weaver, a known white separatist, on a charge of selling two sawed-off shotguns to an undercover federal informant. The job of arresting Weaver, who had fled to his secluded and fortified retreat at Ruby Ridge, Idaho, was assigned to the U.S. Marshal Service. On August 12, 1992, marshals began their surveillance of the Weaver's cabin and surrounding terrain under the code name "Operation Northern Exposure."

Nine days later, on August 21, Randy Weaver; his 14-year-old son, Sam Weaver; and a family friend, Kevin Harris, followed their dog into the woods adjacent to the cabin. Deputy U.S. marshals surveilling the cabin were discovered, and gunfire was exchanged between the two groups. Sam Weaver and one U.S. marshal were fatally wounded. Confusion and speculation about who fired first and whose bullets killed the two victims continued to plague the investigation. In any event, information soon reached Washington, DC, that federal agents were under attack at Ruby Ridge and that assistance was badly needed. The FBI deployed its Hostage Rescue Team (HRT) to the location, beginning an 11-day standoff between the FBI and the Weaver family.

Under normal circumstances, the HRT snipers followed specific rules of engagement that dictated the use of deadly force only under the threat of "grievous bodily harm." Although the reasoning behind changing this operational policy at Ruby Ridge and who was responsible for it are unclear, FBI snipers were told that they "could and should fire at any armed adult male" in the cabin. Hence, on August 22, one day after the initial confrontation and the deaths of Sam Weaver and a U.S. marshal, FBI snipers fired on cabin occupants to protect a surveillance helicopter. The resulting shots struck Kevin Harris and Vicki Weaver (Randy Weaver's wife), who was standing just inside the cabin, holding her infant child. Although Mrs. Weaver died of her wounds, FBI personnel did not learn of her death until Randy Weaver surrendered 9 days later.

The actions of the FBI were debated in Congress, and a special Senate judiciary subcommittee was formed to investigate the incident. Both Randy Weaver and Kevin Harris were acquitted of murdering the U.S. marshal in the initial confrontation.

Analysis of Decisions Made During Protracted Crisis Events

The on and off-site decision makers in these crises started out with a plan to follow a scripted step-by-step, rational model and adjust it if need be. However, the emotionality, stress, close attention by the national news media, the increasing situation complexity, and other factors may have resulted in impaired judgments about what to do. Arguably, any plans seemed successively overcome by rapidly occurring events and to some degree, control became an illusion. Like disjointed incrementalism on steroids, events spiraled beyond the planning horizon, beyond any real control, and they took on a life of their own. Faced with escalating casualties and collapsing planning time, toward the end it seems possible that decision makers relied on their "gut-level" feeling.

Janis and Mann have outlined a decision-making model, based on psychological conflict that emphasizes the decision-making process under stress.[65] Janis and Mann indicate that decision-making involves "hot" emotional influences, similar to Gore's theory and the need to make a decision inherently becomes more stressful. When a decision maker is faced with an emotionally consequential, no-win choice, how he or she copes with the problem depends on two major factors: hope and time. This process causes great stress, as the factors of hope and time are rarely within the control and purview of the decision maker. This can be uniquely observed in protracted, high-stress incidents involving the police, such as those observed in Waco and Ruby Ridge.

When the decision maker has control of time and has hope that conciliation is possible, that person's efforts are more likely to follow the desired pattern of the "vigilant decision maker."[66] The vigilant model closely resembles the rational comprehensive model. The vigilant decision maker (1) thoroughly canvasses a wide range of alternatives; (2) surveys a full range of objectives to be fulfilled and the values implicated by choice; (3) carefully weighs the costs and risks of negative consequences as well as the positive consequences that could come from each alternative; (4) intensively searches for new information relevant to further evaluation of the alternatives; (5) correctly assimilates and takes account of new information or expert judgment to which he or she is exposed, even when the information or judgment does not support the course of action initially preferred; (6) reexamines the positive and negative consequences of all known alternatives, including those originally regarded as unacceptable, before making a final choice; and (7) makes detailed provisions for implementing or executing the chosen course of action, with special attention to contingency plans that might be required if various known risks materialize.[67]

While Janis is better known among students of politics, policy, and management for his earlier work on "groupthink,"[68] his development with Mann of the concept of the vigilant decision maker has provided a practical model for measuring administrative responsibility. Most notable is Nagel's work in applying the decision-making theories of Janis and Mann to the 1985 MOVE incident in Philadelphia.[69] In his highly critical work, Nagel identifies several decision-making paradoxes that, unfortunately, are not uncommon in similar incidents (e.g., the Symbionese Liberation Army [SLA] shoot-out in Los Angeles in 1968, the American Indian Movement [AIM] siege of Wounded Knee in 1977, the FBI shootings at Ruby Ridge, and the ATF raid on Branch Davidians in Waco).

These paradoxes are identified and elaborated on by Taylor and Prichard.[70] All the incidents have commonality. They were all police precipitated—that is, each incident grew from the police advancing on the homes of well-armed, openly defiant, and hostile groups of individuals. Each incident grew from earlier encounters with the police, often highly charged, emotional encounters involving everything from civil and slander suits against the police for harassment to police-group shootings. In all of the incidents, the police intelligence concerning the actual location of the assault and/or the number of suspects and their armaments were in gross error. To complicate the issue, the primary decision maker was not at the scene. In both the Waco and Ruby Ridge incidents, critical decisions were made in Washington, DC, several thousand miles away. Then, too, the incidents were characterized by an overreliance on technology. Decision makers believed that tear gas would not ignite and burn but rather force hostages and suspects from their barricaded positions. The illusion of invulnerability also influenced each incident—who would believe that suspects would not surrender to a large, powerful, tactically trained, well-armed group of federal agents? This certainly was the case in the ATF raid on the Branch Davidians in Waco. The overreliance on intellectual rationality failed as police decision makers underestimated the power and control of a charismatic leader in a relatively small, religiously inspired group. Further, the belief that police SWAT agents could act as an effective, highly specialized military unit performing a "surgical strike" on a bunker belonged more in the movies than in reality. Police officers and agents are simply not experienced, trained, or equipped to handle such encounters. Contrary to popular belief, highly trained police tactical units must rely on meticulous timing, superlative intelligence,

surprise, and the ability to use deadly force effectively. None of these conditions existed in the protracted events of Waco and Ruby Ridge.

Finally, in each incident, the decision maker lost hope for a peaceful outcome. When such a condition occurs, the decision maker enters the downward spiral of "defensive avoidance."[71] The pattern is characterized by procrastination and delay, followed by shifting the blame and other ways of denying personal responsibility, followed by bolstering and gaining superficial support from others. The distorted view produced by bolstering results in a spreading of responsibility and an exaggerated value of the chosen course of action. More often than not, the chosen course is a "do something" reaction. As Janis and Mann state, the process of defensive avoidance "satisfies a powerful emotional need—to avoid anticipatory fear, shame, and guilt."[72] Delay followed by haste can result in wishful thinking, oversimplification of the problem, and the selection of the force option. Confusion, catastrophe, and denial soon follow.

Handling Crisis Events in the Future

Several new directions for handling such crisis events in the future can be developed from the lessons of the past. These recommendations have been adopted as policy for the FBI Critical Incident Response Group, created in 1994 as a response to the Waco and Ruby Ridge encounters. Recommendations for protracted conflict can be summarized as follows:

1. Nagel strongly argues that policies to deal with such events must be institutionalized.[73] That is, they must be concrete, written directives that reflect the overall philosophy of the department or agency. These policies must not be changed arbitrarily during a crisis event or for a specific operational strategy. Further, policies must identify key players and decision makers during such events. Who is the primary decision maker? Who is in charge of operational management? Who is in charge of coordination, communication, logistics, and so on? These are critical positions that must be identified in writing, well before an incident occurs.

2. Police agencies must adopt a philosophy that clearly articulates the importance of the safety and security of human life during such incidents. The force option through the use of SWAT team assault, selective sniper fire, and tear gas distribution must be last resorts. The primary philosophy must emphasize a patient, no-force negotiation strategy rather than a tactical solution for outcome. This is not a new concept. Bolz and others have pressed for this type of departmental philosophy for the past 25 years.[74]

3. Police agencies must consider withdrawal as a strategy. Certainly, in most of these cases, the police could have arrested the primary leaders of these groups outside the confinement of a barricaded compound. The use of more modern surveillance equipment using forward-looking infrared (FLIR) and wall-penetrating radar technology could do much to increase the accuracy

of intelligence and the development of an arrest plan before a barricaded standoff occurs.

4. Police executives must reconsider the role and use of SWAT teams. Their role must be limited to containment and deployment during search and arrest warrant executions. They should not automatically be deployed as a paramilitary group capable of executing high-risk operations requiring precision and exceptional teamwork unless their training skill level clearly establishes it. The routine comparison between police SWAT teams and military strike force teams (such as the Navy SEALS or Army Delta Force) must be broken. The rules of engagement for each unit are unique, as are their skills and outcomes when deployed.

5. Training for protracted conflicts must include the top-level decision makers as well as operational commanders and chiefs. Attorney generals, governors, city managers, mayors, councilpersons, and top police executives must be trained in coping with such conditions. Significant attention must be paid to the development of a policy that emphasizes the no-force negotiation option. Further, decision makers should be trained to recognize the characteristics of "defensive avoidance" and "groupthink" before courses of action are taken.[75] Mock scenarios and role playing should accompany the training.

6. During crisis events, outside and neutral referees or observers should assist in the situation. These individuals should be well versed in the no-force negotiation option and should act as "coaches" for the negotiation team. These individuals should have no ownership or responsibility in the situation and should be paid a fee for their time only. These are not high-level consultants but rather well trained, neutral observers with whom operational managers and top-level decision makers can review potential tactics and strategies. Outside observers must be protected from any type of potential ensuing liability through the agency involved. Their main purpose is to act as a "reality check and review" for actions to be taken by the police.

Decision-making during these types of protracted events, when the suspects appear to be anything but rational, is always a very difficult task. It is also a very human endeavor, and, as such, mistakes will inevitably occur. Remember that the purpose of studying these cases is not to criticize the agencies involved (hindsight is always 20-20) but rather to offer students and police executives alternatives to past experiences and tactics. No one decision-making model guarantees success. However, we owe it to the dedicated men and women who died in these past incidents to ensure that future decision makers always attempt to maximize the two most important factors in the negotiation strategy: hope and time. This can be accomplished by the judicious use of the force options of direct assault, selective sniper fire, and tear gas dispersal.

GROUP DECISION MAKING

Research on group decision making reveals that this approach has both advantages and disadvantages over individual decision-making. If the potential for group decision making can be exploited and its deficiencies avoided, it follows that group decision-making can attain a level of proficiency that is not ordinarily achieved. The requirement for achieving this level of group performance seems to hinge on developing a style of leadership that maximizes the group's assets and minimizes its liabilities. Because group members possess the essential ingredients for the solution, the deficiencies that appear in-group decisions reside in the processes by which group decisions are led and made. These processes can determine whether the group functions effectively or ineffectively. With training, a leader can supply these functions and serve as the group's central nervous system, thus permitting the group to emerge as a highly efficient entity.[76] The following section outlines advantages, disadvantages, and situations that may become an asset or liability depending largely on the decision-making skills of the administrator:

Advantages of Group Decision Making

GREATER TOTAL KNOWLEDGE AND INFORMATION

The sum of information in a group is always greater than any one of its members. Thus, problems that require the use of knowledge (both internal and external to the police agency) almost always give groups an advantage over an individual. If one member of the group, such as the police chief, has more knowledge on a subject, they may still be an asset by filling any gaps that exist, adding their own thoughts, or commenting on the points under discussion.

GREATER NUMBER OF APPROACHES TO MAKING A DECISION

Some of us get into ruts in our thinking, especially when problems arise that have similarities to ones we've encountered in the past. Almost instinctively, like being on cruise control, we have a quick and easy answer that might be correct. It may also get in the way of finding more creative solutions that work better if the stakes warrant the expenditure of more time. Sometimes, we do not need the optimal decision; we just need one that is "good enough." A group of police leaders may also have great "quick fixes," but their "fixes" may all be different. For example, one police administrator may insist that the best way to cope with the increasing number of robberies of local convenience stores in a community is to place the businesses under surveillance by specially trained police officers who can intervene effectively. Another police administrator might insist that the best way to reduce the number of robberies is through the implementation of crime prevention programs designed to use procedures that would make the businesses in question either less attractive or less vulnerable to robberies, for example, keep the amount of cash available to a minimum, put up cameras and height strips on the exit door, and remove large signs from the front of the store windows that block the view of passing patrol cars and other motorists. It is sometimes difficult to determine which approach or approaches would be most effective in achieving the desired goal. But undue persistence or allegiance to one method may imperil a decision group's willingness to be innovative.

PARTICIPATION IN PROBLEM SOLVING INCREASES ACCEPTANCE

Many effective solutions to problems require input, "shaping" or "tuning" by multiple members of the group. When last checked, no one has cornered the market on wisdom. Group participation in forging a decision increases its acceptance and implementation. Such a solution may be more effective than a hypothetically better solution that lacks acceptance. For example, a decision to establish a crime prevention program in a crime-riddled neighborhood must have support from the chief to individual beat officers. Although other measures to reduce crime, such as increasing the number of patrol officers or more attention to juvenile gang activity, might have a more substantial impact, it is important to remember that most of the program participants must support the effort.

BETTER COMPREHENSION OF THE DECISION

Of necessity, when a Chief gives an order to be executed by subordinate commanders the attending details, standards, timetable, desired outcome, and other matters cannot or

should not be ignored. If there is any ambiguity about the instructions being provided, a competent subordinate will quickly seek clarification. Thus, the chances for communication breakdowns are reduced greatly when the individuals who must work together in executing a decision have participated in making it. They not only understand the solution because they helped develop it but also are aware of the other alternatives that were considered and the reasons why they were discarded (see Figure 8.12).

Disadvantages of Group Decision Making

PEER PRESSURE

Peer pressure, whether it's articulated or unspoken, is a major force for increasing conformity. The desire to be a good group member and to be accepted may become more important than arguing for a position that is contrary to that held by most of the members of the group. This may especially be true when a newly promoted member joins an established decision-making group, for example, the command staff, and may be hesitant to quickly jump into the discussion. This is understandable, but deprives the new member of an important developmental experience and "short-changes" the group.

INDIVIDUAL DOMINATION

In some groups, a dominant individual may emerge and capture a disproportionate amount of the influence in determining

FIGURE 8.12 ▶ Open communication and increased communication increases effective group decision making.
© Joe Tabacca/Shutterstock.com

the final outcome. This does not necessarily equate to how much "air time" they get by talking frequently. Sometimes in groups, the most influential person is the one who patiently bides his/her time and waits to weigh in at exactly the most critical point of a discussion. In police circles, the influence of the chief's opinion is undeniable. Effective chiefs know they have two ears and one mouth and use them proportionately. They are excellent listeners, reining in a group with a few innocuous sentences to get things back on track only when the discussion has clearly gone far afield from its purpose. Even there, the discussion may be useful, revealing to chiefs some of the things that are on the minds of their command staffs.

CONFLICTING SECONDARY GOALS: WINNING THE ARGUMENT

When groups are confronted with a problem, the initial goal is to obtain a solution. However, in the absence of a quick consensus solution, the appearance of several alternatives causes individuals to have preferences, and, once these emerge, the desire to support a particular position is created. Converting those with neutral viewpoints and refuting those with opposing viewpoints now enter the problem-solving process. This is a normal group dynamic and a time for everyone to keep his or her "eye on the ball." It is not about winning; the goal is forging a good solution.

GROUPTHINK

The theory of **groupthink** was first introduced by Irving Janis in 1972.[77] Groupthink is a psychological phenomenon that most often occurs in cohesive groups that are isolated from other political and decision-making bodies. This condition often occurs within police leadership circles, especially during crisis events. The political pressure and stress to make a decision, coupled with the presence of a strong leader, escalate the condition. Groupthink is most often characterized by a serious lack of methodical procedure that forces a misperception of the problem and a hurried search for answers. During groupthink, there is considerable focus on a shared rationalization that bolsters the least objectionable alternative as a decision, a suppression of unfavorable outcomes, and an illusion of unanimity and invulnerability. Indeed, Janis and Mann warn that the decision-making process may be so intense that more effort is expended on striving for concurrence than on finding an appropriate decision.[78] During such conditions, the chief should strive to remain impartial, listening to ideas and alternatives. He or she must encourage members of the command staff who have been quiet to express their thoughts about suggested decisions. The chief should play the devil's advocate, questioning some views expressed, for example, what might go wrong and what the possible adverse consequences might be to the proposed actions. Chiefs also must accept criticism of their own judgments as well as those proposed by the group. Janis and Mann are quick to point out that groupthink occurs not only during crisis times but also during rather mundane policymaking meetings.[79] It is incumbent that the Chief,

as well as individual members of the group, be on guard for the signs and characteristics of groupthink.

One general defense to such a condition is continual, open debate and discussion. This requires a leadership style that has earned the chief the trust of the command staff, which by experience has learned there are no repercussions from such discussions. More recent research on the groupthink phenomenon suggests more specific remedies.[80] For example, the origins of groupthink occur as soon as one person states a potential solution to a problem in front of the group. This initial suggestion in front of the group influences the thinking of every person in the group in ways that contribute to like-minded groupthink. The solution is to allow members of the group to initially think about a problem and formulate solutions as individuals before the group meets. These individual suggestions for solutions should only be shared as a group after individuals have had a chance to formulate solutions to the problem on their own.

Potential Assets or Liabilities of Group Decision Making

DISAGREEMENT

Discussion sometimes leads to strong disagreement and fosters short-lived hard feelings among the command staff. However, this may also be the path to good decisions. The first of these outcomes of disagreement is a liability, especially with regard to the acceptance of solutions; the second is an asset, particularly where innovation is desired. A chief can treat disagreement as undesirable and thereby reduce both the probability of hard feelings and innovative thought. The skillful police administrator creates a climate for disagreement without risking hard feelings because properly managed disagreement can be a source of creativity and innovation. The chief's perception of disagreement is a critical factor in using disagreements. Other factors are the chief's permissiveness, willingness to delay reaching a solution, techniques for processing information and opinions, and techniques for separating idea elicitation from idea evaluation.

CONFLICTING VERSUS MUTUAL INTERESTS

Disagreement in discussions can take many forms. Occasionally, command staff members seemingly disagree with one another with regard to a solution, but when the disagreements are explored, it may be discovered that the solutions are in conflict because they are actually designed to solve slightly different aspects of the problem. Analysis of a problem may reveal that it is actually the proverbial "hairball," a cluster of entwined problems. If possible, the best approach is to separate the problems into parcels, each of which can be resolved by a single solution. Failing this because of their uniqueness, each problem has to be fitted with an appropriate solution. Here the saying, "I thought I knew what this conversation was about, but I'm mistaken" comes into play. Chiefs, or a command member who has spontaneously taken the role of a gatekeeper, must keep the discussions focused or conflict instead of cooperation will arise. A gatekeeper guides the exchange of information in a discussion. Parenthetically, in politics, the gatekeeper is the person who gets access to his/her principal or "boss."

RISK TAKING

Groups are more willing than individuals to reach decisions that involve risk. Taking risks is a factor in the acceptance of change, but change may represent either a gain or a loss. The best protection against the latter outcome seems to be primarily a matter of the quality of a decision. In a group situation, this depends on the leader's skill in using the factors that represent group assets and avoiding those that make for liabilities.

TIME REQUIREMENTS

In general, more time is required for a group to reach a decision than for an individual to reach one. Some problems require immediate decisions by individuals, such as a wounded officer down in the open with a barricaded subject still firing at the downed officer. The practice of moving a portion of a meeting or an entire meeting swiftly forward is likely to prevent a full discussion and have subsequent repercussions. A better tactic is to table the remaining portion of a meeting's agenda. Unskilled leaders tend to be either too concerned with reaching a solution and prematurely terminate a discussion or too anxious about getting input, allowing the discussion to digress and become repetitive.

WHO CHANGES

Unless it just immediately occurs, a consensus is reached because some members of a group change their views, not to just achieve consensus, but because they are persuaded by the points made by others. In group situations, who changes can be an asset or a liability. If persons with the most constructive views are induced to change, the end product suffers, whereas if persons with the least constructive points of view change, the end product is upgraded. Chiefs can potentially help upgrade the quality of a decision because their position allows them to elicit more information from a command staff member who has a strong idea but is in the minority. This "protection tactic" is a constructive factor because a minority viewpoint only has hope when the facts favor it.

Brainstorming is a type of group decision making developed initially in advertising to help trigger creativity. The idea behind brainstorming is to establish a group environment in which individuals can present any idea that seems to apply even remotely to the subject being considered with the understanding that criticism will be withheld unless it can somehow improve on the original idea.[81] Whiting identified specific procedures that improve the effectiveness of brainstorming sessions:

1. The sessions should last 40 minutes to an hour, although brief, 10- to 15-minute sessions may be effective if time is limited.

2. Generally, the problem to be discussed should not be revealed before the session.

3. The problem should be stated clearly, but not too broadly.

4. A conference table may be the best setting because a certain level of closeness invites contributions.[82]

One of the most important aspects of brainstorming is an existing environment in which it can occur. Brainstorming requires a level of trust between individuals who work together, for example, they would not be ridiculed, which does not exist in an unstable organization.[83]

COMMON ERRORS IN DECISION MAKING

Analysis of the decision-making process indicates that certain types of errors occur at a higher frequency than others. Nigro and Nigro[84] have indicated that these errors are: (1) cognitive nearsightedness, (2) the assumption that the future will repeat the past, (3) oversimplification, (4) overreliance on one's own experience, (5) preconceived notions/confirmation bias, (6) unwillingness to experiment, and (7) reluctance to decide/procrastination.[85]

Cognitive Nearsightedness

A human tendency is to make decisions that satisfy immediate needs and to brush aside, ignore, or fail to consider the long-range implications. Implicitly, the hope is that the decision will "have legs' and be durable, but this actually is counting on being lucky. The odds for such good fortune to occur consistently across all decisions are poor.

Assumption That the Future Will Repeat Itself

In making decisions, police officials must try to forecast future conditions and events. Social upheavals, economic collapses, terrorist attacks, technological breakthroughs, droughts, famine, petulance, and epidemics and a host of other variables make forecasting a tough business. In relatively stable periods of history, the assumption can be made with reasonable assurance that conditions will stay approximately the same and the government, politics, the community, crime and other factors will be within the range of past experience. The present period is, however, far from stable. However, very rarely do dramatic changes occur without some warning signals. Attention to small "flutters" may provide valuable indicators about future conditions. The police administrator must make the effort to be aware of these trends and develop strategies to cope with them.

Oversimplification

People may address the symptom of a problem because the cause may be too complex to understand. It is also easier to understand a simpler solution: It is more readily explained to others and therefore more likely to be adopted. The decision maker looking for an acceptable answer may take the first simple one even in preference to a somewhat more complicated alternative with a much better outcome.

Overreliance on One's Own Experience

In general, law enforcement practitioners place great weight on their own previous experience and personal judgment. Although an experienced police executive should be able to make better decisions than a completely inexperienced one, a person's own experience may still not be the best guide. Frequently, another police executive with just as much experience has a completely different solution and is just as certain that his or her solution to a problem is the most satisfactory one. In fact, past success in certain kinds of situations may be attributable to chance rather than to the particular action taken. Thus, there is frequently much to be gained by counseling with others whose own experience can add an important and uniquely different dimension to the decision-making process.

Preconceived Notions/Confirmation Bias

Decisions purportedly based on facts may actually reflect the bias of some police executives. They are particularly diligent about finding information that supports their bias, as well as any that can be used to counter other anticipated views. Decision makers may only appear as if they are proceeding in an orderly fashion from consideration of the facts to the conclusions derived logically from them. Some cases of administrative policymaking suffer from a similar defect: They are supported by a dangerously thin foundation of facts and untested assumptions.[86]

Unwillingness to Experiment

The best way in which to determine the workability of a proposal is to test it on a limited scale. However, pressure for immediate, large-scale action may convince a police chief that there is no time to proceed cautiously with pilot projects, no matter how sound the case for a slow approach, because grant opportunities are evaporating for some other reason. Police executives may be reluctant to request funding and other needed support for the small-scale test implementations of new programs out of a concern that such prudence may create doubts about the soundness of the programs. In all fairness to the cautious police administrator, sometimes this assessment has merit.

Reluctance to Decide/Procrastination

Even when in possession of adequate facts, some chiefs try to avoid making a decision. They may procrastinate until the need for a decision is eliminated by events that occur or have "analysis paralysis," constantly seeking more information to assure themselves they are doing the right thing. Barnard speaks of the natural reluctance of some people to decide:

> The making of a decision, as everyone knows from personal experience, is a burdensome task. Offsetting the exhilaration that may result from a correct and successful decision is the depression that comes from failure or error of decision and in the frustration that ensues from uncertainty.[87]

IMPROVING DECISION MAKING

Recognizing some of these common errors in decision-making can be a springboard for strengthening the ability to make good, ethical decisions in the future. Police executives fall into the trap of focusing on the outcome of a bad decision. Obviously, in the classic examples of Ruby Ridge and the Branch Davidians, the majority of us know *what* happened but are unable to fully articulate *why* it happened. We know about the number of people killed but do not necessarily focus on the process that led the decision makers to take the actions that they did. By looking at mistakes on a personal level, as well as looking at mistakes made by contemporaries, police executives have an opportunity to capitalize on what did not work so well in the past. Mauboussin discusses this process at length and encourages all decision makers to take three steps toward better decision-making: preparing, recognizing, and applying past mistakes to determine future courses of action.[88] Preparation is simply the process of gathering information about past mistakes and understanding why they happened. The goal, according to Mauboussin is "to recognize the kind of problem you face, how you risk making a mistake, and which tools you need to choose wisely."[89] Finally, Mauboussin suggests applying what you have learned about past mistakes in decision-making results in diminishing the opportunity for a repeat. Police executives should put together a mental toolbox of sorts to cope with situations as they come up. Filing away and flagging errors in decision making as they come up is an excellent way to avoid making the same mistake, no matter what the circumstances.

Box 8.3: The Law Enforcement Advancing Data and Science (LEADS) Program

A model for police improvement and public safety has taken hold over the course of the last two decades, a philosophy commonly referred to as "evidence-based policing." This topic was previously discussed within Chapter 2. Evidence-based policing involves the use of the best available research on the outcomes of police work to implement guidelines and evaluate agencies, units, and officers.[90] Put more simply, evidence-based policing is a movement to more effectively mesh research and police practice. Police administrators are increasingly expected to utilize findings from research to inform their organizational plans and decision making.

The idea seems like a no-brainer but is difficult to accomplish in the real world. One of the biggest problems in implementing evidence-based policing is a long-standing gap between scholars and police. Traditional police research is often conducted on topics that are not part of the common day-to-day concerns of many police administrators. Even in the case that researchers investigate topics of immediate concern, most published research articles are either inaccessible to police administrators due to online paywalls, or they lack the capacity to fully utilize the research because

they do not have the appropriate educational background or training.

One way to bridge the gap would be to empower law enforcement officers to better utilize and consume existing research or even help them to conduct their own research. The National Institute of Justice (NIJ) recently partnered with the International Association of Chiefs of Police (IACP) to create the Law Enforcement Advancing Data & Science (LEADS) Program.[91] The LEADS program seeks to identify and develop a degree of research expertise among mid-rank officers who will presumably become organizational leaders in the future. The program provides these officers support for research projects, literature reviews, and connections to subject matter experts in various areas important to police administrators. The goal is the production of "officer-driven research" on topics of direct concern to their agency that can be shared with like-minded research-oriented officers to determine what works in policing. The model should obviously bridge the gap between researchers and practitioners and allow them to better incorporate scholarship into the processes of organizational planning and decision making.

Chapter Summary

Summary by Learning Objectives

1. **Explain what planning is expected to accomplish.**

   It is expected to (1) improve the analysis of problems; (2) provide better information for decision making; (3) help to clarify goals, objectives, and priorities; (4) result in more effective allocation of resources; (5) improve inter- and intradepartmental cooperation and coordination; (6) improve the performance of programs; (7) give the police department a clear sense of direction; (8) provide the opportunity for greater public support; and (9) increase the commitment of personnel.

2. **Define what a plan is.**

   Stated succinctly, planning involves linking present actions with future conditions.

3. **Discuss synoptic planning.**

   Synoptic planning, or the rational comprehensive approach, is the dominant tradition in planning. It is also the point of departure for most other planning approaches, which in general are either modifications of synoptic planning or reactions against it. The

typical synoptic model is based on "pure" or "objective" rationality and attempts to ensure optimal achievement of desired goals from a given situation.

4. **Identify the specific elements of administrative, procedural, operational, tactical, and strategic plans.**

   (1) Administrative or management plans include formulation of the department's mission statement, goals, and policies; the structuring of functions, authority, and responsibilities; the allocation of resources; personnel management; and other concerns that are prevalent throughout the agency; (2) procedural plans are the guidelines for the action to be taken under specific circumstances and detail such matters as how evidence is to be sent or transported to the crime laboratory, the conditions under which male officers may search arrested females and the limits thereto, and how to stop and approach traffic violators; (3) operational plans describe specific actions to be taken by line units (patrol officers, precinct groups, and/or division teams); (4) tactical plans involve planning for emergencies of a specific nature at known locations; (5)

strategic planning is an organizational management activity that is used to set priorities, focus energy and resources, strengthen operations, ensure that employees and other stakeholders are working toward common goals, establish agreement around intended outcomes/results, and assess and adjust the organization's direction in response to a changing environment. This type of plan typically addresses events three to five years into the future.

5. **Discuss what planning can be expected to accomplish.**

   (1) Improve the analysis of problems; (2) provide better information for decision making; (3) help to clarify goals, objectives, and priorities; (4) result in more effective allocation of resources; (5) improve inter- and intradepartmental cooperation and coordination; (6) improve the performance of programs; (7) give the police department a clear sense of direction; (8) provide the opportunity for greater public support; and (9) increase the commitment of personnel.

6. **State Simon's concept of "bounded rationality."**

   Noting that human beings are "bounded" by a triangle of limitations, Simon said, "On one side, the individual is limited by those skills, habits, and reflexes which are no longer in the realm of the conscious… and on a second side, the individual is limited by his values and those conceptions of purpose which influence him in making decisions… and on a third side, the individual is limited by the extent of his knowledge that is relevant to his job."

7. **Explain Lindblom's incremental decision making.**

   Lindblom asserts that decision making is serial—that it is limited by time and resources as it gropes along a path where means and ends are not distinct, where goals and objectives are ambiguous, and where rationality serves no purpose. Contending that police managers and administrators "play things safe" and opt to move very slowly (incrementally) in decision making, Lindblom proposes that managers "muddle through" problems rather than analytically choosing decisions. In Lindblom's view, decision making that occurs through a series of incremental steps provides the police administrator (and hence the public) with a number of safeguards against error.

8. **Describe Gore's decision-making process.**

   For Gore, decision making is basically an emotional, nonrational, highly personalized, and subjective process. Therefore, the facts validating a decision are internal to the personality of the individual instead of external to it.

9. **Explain the concept of the thin-slicing theory.**

   It occurs in situations where snap decisions are required, whether by a police administrator, a line officer, or anyone else in a decision-making capacity; instantaneous decisions can often be the best, particularly when paired with training and expertise.

10. **State the advantages of group decision making.**

    (1) Greater total knowledge and information; (2) greater number of approaches to making a decision; (3) participation in problem solving increases acceptance; (4) better comprehension of the decision.

11. **Discuss the liabilities of group decision making.**

    (1) Social pressure; (2) individual domination; (3) conflicting secondary goals: winning the argument; (4) groupthink.

12. **Explain the concept of brainstorming.**

    Brainstorming is a type of group decision making developed initially in advertising to help trigger creativity. The idea behind brainstorming is to establish a group environment in which individuals can present any idea that seems to apply even remotely to the subject being considered with the understanding that criticism will be withheld unless it can somehow improve on the original idea. The practitioners of brainstorming have been able to determine some specific procedures that improve the effectiveness of brainstorming sessions.

Chapter Review Questions

1. Explain the advantage of planning within a police department.
2. Why is it that some police administrators may not fully appreciate the importance of planning?
3. What is it that effective planning can be expected to accomplish?
4. Tankha identified four types of planning approaches based on their time orientation. What are they?
5. What are the key lessons learned by law enforcement officers participating in the Republican National Convention?
6. What is the purpose of the decision tree used in robbery investigations?
7. What are some of the important recommendations, developed in this chapter, for handling future protracted crisis events?
8. List the steps decision makers should take when confronted with an ethical issue?
9. What are the most common errors in decision making?

Critical Thinking Exercises

1. **Operational Plan**. In recent years, there has been a dramatic increase in prostitution in your community, primarily involving women and young girls from Central and South American countries. You suspect that many of them have been illegally trafficked into the United States and are being forced into prostitution. However, your patrol officers and vice squad officers have very little experience in identifying and dealing with the issue of sex trafficking. You have therefore made a decision to begin to train those officers who are most likely to come in contact with these victims so they will be able to more effectively identify and assist them. However, in order to do so, you need to answer to the following questions:
   a. What are the venues where sex trafficking victims are most likely to be found?
   b. What are the specific indicators that a woman who is engaged in prostitution has been trafficked and is being forced to engage in this practice against her will?
   c. Who can you turn to assist in training your officers in better understanding the problem of sex trafficking in your community?
   d. Since you are aware that sex trafficking is a multijurisdictional problem how would you go about organizing a multiagency task force to deal with the issue?

2. **Decision Making**. In recent years, there has been a national trend for police departments to require individuals being promoted to supervisory or managerial positions to have earned a college degree. However, the agency you have recently taken over as police chief has educational requirements for promotion that are the same as those required at the entry level, namely, a high school diploma. You have made a decision that in the future individuals will not be considered for promotion unless they have earned a college degree. However, before you can accomplish this objective you will have to address the following questions:
   a. What timeline, if any, would you recommend before putting this change into effect?
   b. Would you have a modified educational requirement for those applying for the position of sergeant (AA or AS degree) than you would for those applying for higher ranks such as lieutenant, captain, and major (BA or BS)?
   c. Will you impose limits on the number of courses an officer can take at one time so their school work will not interfere with their work responsibilities?
   d. Will you be reimbursing officers for their college tuition? If so, will there be a contractual obligation for them to stay with the agency for a specified period of time in order to compensate the agency for the financial aid it provided?
   e. Are you prepared to make adjustments in the work schedules if officers choose to take classes on campus as opposed to taking their courses online?
   f. Will you require your officers to major in certain academic disciplines such as criminal justice or criminology or will they have the latitude to major in other disciplines (e.g., business administration, public administration, psychology, education, and so forth)?
   g. Who will you involve in the decision-making process, for example; a committee composed of officers within the agency, police union representatives, the mayor, city manager, and citizens?

Key Terms

active shooter
brainstorming
e-learning software
groupthink
heuristic model
inactive planning

incremental model
operational plan
operations research
planning
posse comitatus
proactive planning

reactive planning
SWAT
synoptic planning
thin-slicing theory

Endnotes

[1] Israel Stollman, "The Values of the City Planner," in *The Practice of Local Government Planning*, ed. Frank S. So et al. (Washington, DC: International City Management Association, 1979), p. 13.

[2] Ibid.

[3] Carol Weiss, *Evaluation Research: Methods of Assessing Program Effectiveness* (Englewood Cliffs, NJ: Prentice Hall, 1972), p. 7.

[4] John Hudzik and Gary Cordner, *Planning in Criminal Justice Organizations and Systems* (New York: Macmillan, 1983), p. 1.

[5] Charles M. Mottley, "Strategy in Planning," in *Planning, Programming, Budgeting: A System Approach to Management*, 2nd edition, ed. J. F. Lyden and E. S. Miller (Chicago: Markham, 1972), p. 127.

[6] See Sunil Tankha, Sustainable Corporations: Reconciling Wealth Creation with Global Sustainability, 15–16 (The Woodlands, TX: Houston Advanced Research Center, 1999. HARC is a non-profit organization founded in 1982). The authors have added the police context to the types of planning.

[7] There is a need for more research on the impact of body-worn cameras. Many of the earliest studies were limited in terms of methodology, and more recent studies suggest that the use of force rates of officers wearing body worn cameras may depend on officer discretion and that point at which police choose to activate the devices. See e.g., U.S. Department of Justice, Community Oriented Policing Services; Police Executive Research Forum, "Implementing a Body-Worn Camera Program: Recommendations and Lessons Learned," 2014; Hyland, SS (2018). "Body-Worn cameras in Law Enforcement Agencies, 2016," US Department of Justice, Office of Justice Programs, Bureau of Justice Statistics Bulletin.

[8] K. Kindy,"Some US Police Departments Dump Body camera Programs amid High Costs," *Washington Post* (January 21). Available at http://www.washingtonpost.com/national/some-us-police-departments-dump-body-camera-programs-amid-high-costs/2019/01/21/991f0e66-03ad-11e.

[9] The term "pure," or "objective rationality," is taken from the alternative planning models identified by Tony Eddison, *Local Government: Management and Corporate Planning* (New York: Harper & Row, 1973), pp. 19–23.

[10] The synoptic model is thoroughly discussed in Cushman, *Criminal Justice Planning*. Some of the following information relating to the model is paraphrased from that work.

[11] J. Liederbach, E. J. Fritsch, D. L. Carter, and A. Bannister, "Exploring the Limits of Collaboration in Community Policing: A Direct Comparison of Police and Citizen Views." *Policing: An International Journal of Police Strategies & Management* 31, No. 2, pp. 271–291.

[12] Patrick Slater, "Inconsistencies in a Schedule of Paired Comparisons," *Biometrika* 48, Nos. 3/4 (December 1961), p. 303.

[13] A good example of the statistical end is Kristi Tsukida and Maya R. Gupta, "How to Analyze Paired Comparison Data," UWEE Technical Report-2011-004, May 2011, Department of Electrical Engineering, University of Washington.

[14] Hudzik and Cordner, *Planning in Criminal Justice*, p. 196.

[15] Ibid.

[16] A number of sources identify plans according to their use; see O. W. Wilson, *Police Planning*, 2nd edition (Springfield, IL: Charles C. Thomas, 1962), pp. 4–7, and Vernon L. Hoy, "Research and Planning," in *Local Government Police Management*, ed. Bernard L. Garmire (Washington, DC: International City Management Association, 1977), pp. 374–375.

[17] This has been adapted from the After Action Report Washington Navy Yard September 16, 2013, Internal Review of the Metropolitan Police Department, Washington, DC, July 2014, pp. 28–30; http://www.policefoundation.org/wp-content/uploads/2015/05/Washington-Navy-Yard-After-Action-Report.pdf.

[18] The shooter in this incident, Aaron Alexis, 34 years old, was employed by Experts Inc., a subcontractor of Hewlett-Packard, as an independent contractor who provided information technology support services for the U.S. Navy at the installation. It was later learned that he may have been suffering from insomnia, pronounced bouts of anger, and possible psychological disturbances. It does not appear that he gave those who knew him or worked with him any prior warning or specific indication he planned on carrying out this shooting.

[19] The 117 officers that entered the building during the initial search for the shooter included officers and agents from DC Metropolitan Police Department

(MPD); U.S. Park Police (USPP); Naval District of Washington (NDW) Police; Naval Criminal Investigative Service (NCIS); Metropolitan Washington Airports Authority; U.S. Marshalls Service (USMS); Navy Contract Service Guards; and U.S. Navy, Department of Defense (DOD).

[20]The police response to "active shooter" scenarios changed following the terrible events of the Columbine, Colorado, massacre on April 20, 1999. In the Columbine School shooting, Eric Harris and Dillon Klebold murdered 13 people on the school campus before they committed suicide, bringing the total to 15 people dead. The first responding patrol officers told horrific stories of arriving at the scene and hearing shots fired and victims screaming for over 10 minutes, yet had no training or advanced weaponry to enter the school and stop the killing. This event, more than any other, changed police responses to similar events now classified as "active shooter" situations.

[21]On November 5, 2009, a mass murder took place at Fort Hood, near Killeen, Texas. Nidal Malik Hasan, a U.S. Army major and psychiatrist, fatally shot 13 people, which included 12 U.S. soldiers and a civilian police officer working at the base, and injured more than 30 others. See "Soldier Opens Fire at Ft. Hood; 13 Dead," CBS News/AP, November 5, 2009; http://www.cbsnews.com/news/soldier-opens-fire-at-ft-hood-13-dead/ (accessed August 29, 2015).

[22]There are similarities in the nearly 100 school shootings (in the United States and Canada since 1966) that make them significantly different than those of the protracted crisis discussed earlier. Most of the victims are school-age children, some as young as six years old, who were shot *randomly*; the shootings have little, if any, logical reason or purpose other than causing massive carnage and human death; the suspects are for the most part, also students, or at least student age (11–22 years), working alone; the vast majority of the suspects are white males with a history of school issues, including social conflict, disenfranchisement, and/or mental problems; the suspect's actions were planned and well-thought-out, and in some cases even rehearsed, with suspects bringing guns to the school before their planned event. The suspects even made threats that they wanted to hurt people but were not taken seriously; the suspects had easy access to firearms and were often well-armed with multiple weapons and ammunition; and in most cases, the suspect(s) commits suicide or is killed by the police. The need to act quickly in these types of scenarios often precludes the use of SWAT teams that must be called out with some delay. Further, the presence of an active shooter at the scene also requires that responding patrol officers take action to save lives and human destruction rather than cordon off the area and wait.

[23]Examples of the training materials used in both the RNC and DNC are available as part of the Appendix in *Managing Large-Scale Security Events: A Planning Primer for Local Law Enforcement Agencies.*

[24]Tampa Police Department, *Command, Control, and Coordination: A Quick-Look Analysis of the Tampa Police Department's Operations During the 2012 Republican National Convention,* available at: https://www.cna.org/sites/default/files/research/2012-RNC-Quick-Look.pdf.

[25]Sven Ove Hansson, "Decision Theory: A Brief Introduction" (Stockholm: Department of Philosophy and the History of Technology, Royal Institute of Technology, August 19, 1994), p. 9.

[26]John Dewey, *Democracy and Education* (New York: The Macmillan Company, 1916).

[27]Leigh Buchanan and Andrew O'Connell, "A Brief History of Decision Making," *Harvard Business Review* (January 2006), p. 5. The page numbers used are from a PDF file, https://hbr.org/2006/01/a-brief-history-of-decision-making (accessed July 12, 2015).

[28]Hansson, "Decision Theory: A Brief Introduction," pp. 8–9.

[29]Buchanan and O'Connell, "A Brief History of Decision Making," p. 1.

[30]Herbert A. Simon, *Administrative Behavior: A Study of Decision-Making Processes in Administrative Organization* (New York: First edition, Macmillan, 1947).

[31]Simon, *Administrative Behavior,* p. 40.

[32]Charles E. Lindblom, "The Science of Muddling Through," *Public Administration Review* 19, No. 2 (spring 1959), pp. 79–88.

[33]Charles F. Lindblom, The Policy-Making Process (Englewood Cliffs, NJ: Prentice Hall, 1968), p. 209.

[34]Lindblom, "The Science of Muddling Through," p. 86.

[35]Jack Kuykendall and Peter Unsinger, *Community Police Administration* (Chicago: Nelson-Hall, 1975), p. 132.

[36]J. Zhao, L. Ren, and N. P. Lovrich, "Budgetary Support for Police Services in US Municipalities: Comparing Political Culture, Socioeconomic Characteristics, and Incrementalism as Rival Explanations for Budget Share Allocation to Police," *Journal of Criminal Justice* 38, pp. 266–275.

[37]Buchanan and O'Connell, "A Brief History of Decision Making," p. 9.

[38]Graham T. Allison, *Essence of Decision: Exploring the Cuban Missile Crisis* (Boston: Little, Brown, 1971).

[39]Some of this discussion was excerpted from an excellent review of Allison's book by Robert B. Denhardt, *Theories of Public Organization* (Monterey, CA: Brooks/Cole, 1984), pp. 81–85.

[40]William J. Gore, *Administration Decision-Making: A Heuristic Model* (New York: John Wiley & Sons, 1964).

[41]Ibid., p. 12.

[42]Sam S. Souryal, *Police Administration and Management* (St. Paul, MN: West, 1977), p. 318.

[43]L. G. Gawthrop, *Bureaucratic Behavior in the Executive Branch* (New York: Free Press, 1969), pp. 98–99.

[44]Gore, *Administrative Decision-Making,* p. 12.

[45]Gawthrop, *Bureaucratic Behavior,* p. 99.

[46]Souryal, *Police Administration,* p. 319.

[47]C. Zsambock, and G. Klein, *Naturalistic Decision Making* (Mahweh, NJ: Erlbaum, 1997), p. 286.

[48]Ibid., p. 219.

[49]Malcom Gladwell, *Blink: The Power of Thinking Without Thinking* (New York: Little, Brown, 2005), pp. 10–14.

[50]Ibid., p. 11.

[51]Ibid., p. 253.

[52]Relatedly, see Suhaib Alzou'bi et al., "Artificial Intelligence in Law Enforcement, A Review," *International Journal of Advanced Information Technology* 4, No. 4 (August 2014), pdf file pp. 1–9; http://airccse.org/journal/IJAIT/papers/4414ijait01.pdf (accessed August 14, 2015).

[53]John Maule, "Why the Computer Isn't Always Right," Leeds University Business School, United Kingdom, March 8, 2010, p. 1; http://business.leeds.ac.uk/about-us/article/why-the-computer-isnt-always-right (accessed August 14, 2015).

[54]These points are loosely derived with restatement from Marko Bohanec, "Decision Making: A Computer Science and Information Technology Viewpoint," *Interdisciplinary Description of Complex System* 7, No. 2 (2009), pp. 23–24.

[55]Several of the topics in this paragraph are taken from Tombul Fatih and Cakar Bekir, "Police Use of Technology to Fight Against Crime," *European Scientific Journal* 11, No. 10 (April 2015), pp. 290–292.

[56]Conference paper: Johan Schubert et al., "A Decision Support System for Crowd Control," Proceedings of the 13th International Conference Command and Control Research Technical Symposium, Seattle, Washington, June 2008, p. 1.

[57]Ibid., pp. 28, 32–33.

[58]Graham T. Allison, *Essence of Decision: Exploring the Cuban Missile Crisis* (Boston: Little, Brown, 1971).

[59]Some of this discussion was excerpted from an excellent review of Allison's book by Robert B. Denhardt, *Theories of Public Organization* (Monterey, CA: Brooks/Cole, 1984), pp. 81–85.

[60]John Ott, "The Challenging Game of Operations Research," in *Emerging Concepts of Management*, eds. Max S. Wortmann and Fred Luthans (London: Macmillan, 1970), p. 287.

[61]Ibid.

[62]Aaron Wildavsky, *Speaking Truth to Power: The Art and Craft of Police Analysis* (Boston: Little, Brown, 1979), p. 84.

[63]Gary A. Klein, *Sources of Power: How People Make Decisions* (Cambridge, MA: MIT Press, 1998).

[64]In his book *Blink: The Power of Thinking Without Thinking* (New York: Little, Brown, 2005), Malcom Gladwell examines: Why are some people brilliant decision makers, while others are consistently inept? Why do some people follow their instincts and win and others end up stumbling into error? How our brains really work—in the office, in the classroom, in the kitchen, and in the bedroom? And why are the best decisions often those that are impossible to explain to others?

[65]Irving L. Janis and Leon Mann, *Decision Making: A Psychological Analysis of Conflict, Choice, and Commitment* (New York: Free Press, 1977).

[66]Ibid., chapter 1.

[67]Ibid., pp. 11–15.

[68]Irving L. Janis, *Victims of Groupthink* (Boston: Houghton Mifflin, 1972).

[69]John H. Nagel, "Psychological Obstacles to Administrative Responsibility: Lessons of the MOVE Disaster," *Journal of Policy Analysis and Management* 10, No. 1 (1991), p. 3.

[70]Robert W. Taylor and Leigh A. Prichard, "Decision-Making in Crisis: Police Responses to Protracted Critical Incidents" (paper delivered at the Academy of Criminal Justice Sciences Annual Meeting, Las Vegas, NV, March 13, 1996).

[71]The concept of "defensive avoidance" was first developed by Janis and Mann in *Decision Making*. However, Nagel uniquely applied the concept to reality in his article "Psychological Obstacles to Administrative Responsibility."

[72]Janis and Mann, *Decision Making*, p. 85.

[73]Nagel, "Psychological Obstacles," p. 21.

[74]The concept of a negotiated solution to crisis events has been developed over the past 25 years. See Frank A. Bolz and Edward Hershey, *Hostage Cop* (New York: Rawson, Wade, 1979); Ronald C. Crelinsten and Denis Szabo, *Hostage-Taking* (Lexington, MA: Lexington Books, 1979); Murray S. Miron and Arnold P. Goldstein, *Handbook for Hostage Negotiations: Tactical Procedures, Negotiating Techniques and Responses to Non-Negotiable Hostage Situations* (New York: Harper & Row, 1979); and Robert W. Taylor, "Hostage and Crisis Negotiation Procedures" in *Police Civil Liability*, ed. Leonard Territo (New York: Hanrow Press, 1984).

[75]See Nagel, "Psychological Obstacles"; Janis and Mann, *Decision Making*; and Taylor and Prichard, "Decision-Making in Crisis."

[76]N. R. F. Maier, "Assets and Liabilities in Group Problem Solving: The Need for Integrated Function," *Psychology Review* 74, No. 4 (1967), pp. 239–248. Much of the information in this chapter dealing with the discussion of group decision making was obtained from this source.

[77]See Irving L. Janis, *Victims of Groupthink* (Boston: Houghton Mifflin, 1972).

[78]Janis and Mann, *Decision Making*, pp. 398–400.

[79]Ibid.

[80]A. Markman, "The Problem-Solving Process That Prevents Groupthink," *Harvard Business Review* (fall), pp. 12–14.

[81]W. Gortner, *Administration in the Public Sector* (New York: John Wiley & Sons, 1977), p. 124.

[82]C. S. Whiting, "Operational Techniques of Creative Thinking," *Advanced Management Journal* 20 (1955), pp. 24–30.

[83]John Schafer, "Making Ethical Decisions: A Practical Mode," *FBI Law Enforcement Bulletin*, May 2002.

[84]Much of the information in this chapter dealing with the discussion of common errors in decision making was obtained from F. A. Nigro and L. G. Nigro, *Modern Public Administration* (New York: Harper & Row, 1977), pp. 226–232.

[85]D. Katz and R. L. Kahn, *The Social Psychology of Organizations* (New York: John Wiley & Sons, 1966), p. 285.

[86]Ibid.

[87]C. Barnard, *The Functions of the Executive* (Cambridge, MA: Harvard University Press, 1938), p. 189.

[88]Michael J. Mauboussin. *Think Twice: Harnessing the Power of Counterintuition* (Boston, MA: Harvard Business Press, 2009), pp. 137–143.

[89]Ibid., p. xvi.

[90]L. Sherman, "Evidence-Based Policing," *Ideas in American Policing* (July). Police Foundation.

[91]M. Q. Mcgough, "Research in the Ranks: Empowering Law Enforcement to Drive their own Scientific Inquiry," *National Institute of Justice Journal* 280 (January). Available at https://wwwnij.gov/journals/280/pages/research-in-the-ranks.aspx

## CHAPTER NINE

HUMAN RESOURCE MANAGEMENT

Learning Objectives

1. List 10 functions a police human resource unit might perform.
2. Identify the main objective of the Equal Pay Act.
3. Describe how the Age Discrimination in Employment Act is applied to law enforcement agencies.
4. Explain the four major theories of discrimination.
5. Name and explain two categories of sexual harassment.
6. Define *disability* and *reasonable accommodation*.
7. Briefly contrast exempt and nonexempt employees.
8. Define *validity* and *reliability*.
9. Explain the meaning of *discipline* and *progressive discipline*.
10. Explain how a discipline matrix works.
11. Describe the assessment center process.
12. Discuss the problem of identity loss that some officers experience in retirement.

INTRODUCTION

THERE ARE SOME COMPELLING *reasons to have a strong working knowledge of human resource management: (1) at least 80 percent of a law enforcement agency's annual operating budget is spent on personnel and personnel support costs; (2) an agency competes in the same labor market with businesses and other police organizations; it should strive to become the law enforcement employer of choice; (3) some number of personnel problems can be traced back to faulty human resource management practices; (4) serious mistakes by weak selection processes and inadequate training are inevitably revealed by the actions of officers; (5) high turnover costs not only result in repetitive selection and training costs, but drive down the experience level of patrol officers—a threat to the quality of service delivery; (6) achieving and maintaining a diverse work force is a strong element in working effectively with the different populations in our communities; (7) there is a maze of local, state, and federal laws and regulations pertaining to public sector employees; failure to understand and follow them will bring adverse attention to an agency and can result in litigation by employees; (8) a department embroiled in job discrimination litigation puts the community at a significant disadvantage when trying to recruit potential employers to relocate there; for some potential employers, it will be sufficient to scratch your city or county off their list; (9) valid and reliable promotional practices will identify leaders (see Chapter 7, Leadership) who can help maintain a high level of agency performance; and (10) a community needs and deserves the best possible law enforcement agency, whose effectiveness and image ultimately rests on the people that represent it.*

FUNCTIONS OF A POLICE HUMAN RESOURCES UNIT

In small jurisdictions, human resources (HR)/personnel services will largely be provided by the city's or county's central personnel office. As law enforcement agencies become progressively larger, they take on additional HR responsibilities. Larger departments may have a HR division, but in many agencies, HR management is a function within their Administrative or Personnel and Training Divisions.

Depending on the size of a law enforcement agency and the division of responsibilities with the central personnel office, a police HR unit may have oversight of the following functions:

1. Complying with Peace Officers Standards and Training Commission (POST) requirements and guidelines;
2. Maintaining currency with federal job discrimination laws;
3. Developing agency HR policies, subject to executive approval;
4. Recruiting and selecting sworn and civilian personnel;
5. Monitoring turnover, retention, and diversity;
6. Providing or contracting for psychological services (e.g., entry screening and critical incident counseling);
7. Delivering or contracting for academy, in-service, advanced, and managerial training;
8. Conducting special studies (e.g., staffing, benefits, and compensation surveys);
9. Administering benefits programs (e.g., health and life insurance and workers compensation);
10. Preparing payroll;
11. Directing labor relations;
12. Coordinating drug testing;
13. Administering promotional testing;
14. Managing intern programs;
15. Advising commanders on personnel matters;
16. Coordinating the employee evaluation process;
17. Organizing promotions and awards ceremonies;
18. Coordinating off-duty work;
19. Directing Professional Standards/Internal Affairs efforts;
20. Acting as personnel records custodian;
21. Preparing content for the agency's website;
22. Conducting job exit interviews to identify factors associated with turnover; and
23. Serving as liaison to the central personnel office.[1]

In preparing this list, a number of local law enforcement websites were visited. The City and County of San Francisco Police Department has an unusual and very useful function for a large agency, an American with Disabilities Act (ADA)

Coordinator who meets with personnel seeking an accommodation under that federal legislation, which is covered later in this chapter.

KEY FEDERAL LAWS PROHIBITING JOB DISCRIMINATION

In addition to the protections afforded by state laws, local ordinance, and civil service or merit commissions, there are several prominent federal laws prohibiting job discrimination. An overview of them is provided for general familiarity and not as a substitute for legal counsel. Some of these statutory laws are further referred to in a more specific context in subsequent sections of this chapter.

These laws discussed in this section are administered by the Department of Justice's **Equal Employment Opportunity Commission (EEOC)** and the **U.S. Department of Labor (USDOL)**. Despite the differences in the laws, the remedies available to plaintiffs are often similar or the same.

Job Discrimination Laws Administered by the Equal Employment Opportunity Commission

THE EQUAL PAY AND THE LILLY LEDBETTER FAIR PAY ACTS

The Fair Labor Standards Act (FLSA, 1938) was amended in 1963 by the **Equal Pay Act (EPA)**. Its main objective is to eliminate discrimination in wages based on gender. Still, it was not until 1970 that a federal court ruled in *Schultz v. Wheaton Glass Company* that for EPA purposes, the job of a woman did not need to be identical to a man's, only substantially similar. Although there has been progress, the EPA has never fully achieved its intended objective.

In 2009, the **Lilly Ledbetter Fair Pay Act (LLFPA)** was signed into law, overturning the Supreme Court's decision in *Ledbetter v. Goodyear Tire & Rubber Co.*, which held a discrimination charge under EPA had to be filed within 180 days of the date of the original compensation decision leading to the charge or within 300 days in jurisdictions that have a state or

local law prohibiting the same kind of compensation discrimination. The LLFPA carried a retroactive effective date of May 28, 2007, and vindicated EEOC's position that each discriminatory paycheck was a new violation.

LLFPA provided a brief victory to Mary Lou Mikula, who was hired as a grants coordinator for the Allegheny (PA) County Police Department.[3] After being hired, Ms. Mikula began inquiring about an adjustment in pay because she was doing work equal to a similarly situated male, but making $7,000 less annually. Ultimately, she litigated and the suit was dismissed by the District Court because it was not filed within the time limits existing at that time. That decision was upheld by the 3rd Circuit Court of Appeals just as the LLFPA act passed. On a rehearing and facts considered within the recently passed LLFPA, the 3rd Circuit reversed itself and Mikula's case was remanded for further proceedings, where the court ruled for the employer on other grounds. Box 9.1 summarizes a pay suit filed under a state equal pay act.

AGE DISCRIMINATION IN EMPLOYMENT ACT (ADEA)

The **Age Discrimination in Employment Act, ADEA** (1967), only forbids age discrimination against people who are age 40 or older and work in organizations with 20 or more employees.[4] ADEA forbids age discrimination in any aspect of employment, including hiring, job assignments, promotions, layoffs, training, fringe benefits, and any other term or condition of employment. Harassment of older workers, such as continuing offensive remarks about their age, may rise to the level of creating a hostile working environment and may also be actionable.

In *Smith v. City of Jackson* (2005), the U.S. Supreme Court reviewed a case filed by Jackson (Mississippi) police officers who were 40 years of age and older, who sued under a theory of disparate impact, alleging that their employer's new adopted pay plan was more favorable to younger officers and fell more harshly by comparison on older officers.[6] Factually, officers with less than five years tenure received higher raises than those with more service. The defendant, City of Jackson, argued that it had a legitimate, nondiscriminatory reason for the plan, desiring to raise starting salaries to the regional average. The Supreme Court affirmed the lower court's summary judgment in

---

Quick Facts: Gender and Other Pay Disparities

A 2020 study conducted by PayScale Consulting reveals that a woman working full time earns 81 cents for every dollar a man working full time earns on average. For Black and Hispanic women that figure is 75 cents for every dollar a man makes. However, the coronavirus pandemic of 2020 has made pay disparities even more acute as women are often the first to be laid off or furloughs. Women have a higher risk of suffering greater penalties in earnings as a result.

Women make up a much larger percentage of occupations in *Community and Social Services, Education, Library and Training, Office and Administrative Support,* and *Personal Care and Services,* which are areas that are more likely suffer suspensions, layoffs, or reduced hours of work. History has also shown that women often incur a pay penalty upon returning to work after an absence, on average about 7 percent less for the same position.[2]

Box 9.1: Officer Kristi Lougheed Wins Suit

Officer Lougheed was hired with 15 years of prior police experience by the Aberdeen, Washington, Police Department at Step 1, the lowest pay grade. She subsequently learned that some male counterparts, with less experience, were making more than she was. The Chief agreed at some point to move her to Step 2, which was only a modest increase, and Lougheed filed suit under the State of Washington's equal pay and antidiscrimination laws. A trial determined that Aberdeen had violated both laws and the city unsuccessfully appealed the decision. In mid-2015, Aberdeen agreed to pay Lougheed $375,000 for general damages, costs, litigation expenses, purge her personnel file of letters of reprimand, advance her to Step 4, and the Chief was to write a letter of apology.[5]

favor of the defendant, concluding that while there were other ways to achieve the city's goal, the method selected was not unreasonable.

Nassau County (New York) reached a voluntary settlement with the EEOC in 2008 on an age discrimination suit. Although protected by the ADEA, four Nassau County Police Department Marine Bureau officers with excellent records and no negative performance evaluations were transferred to precinct jobs that were less desirable and were replaced by younger officers. The plaintiff officers argued that the personnel actions were motivated by an attempt to get them to retire. The settlement included $450,000 in damages for the plaintiffs and other injunctive relief.[7]

ADEA has a public safety exemption provision to apply its provisions; local units of government can refuse to hire a person for a sworn position if the applicant is over their maximum age for hiring and the refusal to hire was part of a bona fide hiring or retirement plan and not a subterfuge to evade ADEA's purposes.[8] This position was reached in *Kannady v. City of Kiowa* (2010). It was undisputed that the City of Kiowa refused to hire the plaintiff because he was 45 years old and thus not eligible to participate in the state-operated Oklahoma Police Pension and Retirement System, which had a 45-year-old cutoff for membership since 1989. In response, Kannady filed an ADEA suit. The trial court dismissed the suit and upon appeal, the federal 10th Circuit Court of Appeals affirmed the District Court's decision.

Many states have also enacted age discrimination laws. In ten states there is no minimum number of employees required to sue for age discrimination, although the usual number specified by states often is in the 5–15 employee range. Some states also specify an age discrimination threshold younger than the federal threshold of 40.

TITLE VII (1972) OF THE CIVIL RIGHTS ACT OF 1964

Title VII prohibits discrimination in hiring, pay, promotion, firing, wages, job assignments, fringe benefits, and other terms and conditions of employment because of race, color, sex, national origin, or religion.[9] These five categories are referred to as **protected classes**. The law covers federal, state, and local governments, private employers with 15 or more employees, labor unions, and employment agencies. Although Title VII contains no references to lesbian, bisexual, gay, transgender, or queer people (LBGTQ+), EEOC asserts that they are included within the meaning of the "sex" class of Title VII.[10] In FY 2015, EEOC received 26,396 claims of sex discrimination, which represented 29.5 percent of all claims.[11] A key case on the way to EEOC's inclusion of LBGTQ+ people within the sex class of Title VII was *Barnes v. City of Cincinnati* (2005), the facts of which are summarized in Box 9.2.

Remedies for relief available to plaintiffs include (1) injunctive relief, a court order prohibiting future discrimination; (2) hiring, promotion, or reinstatement; (3) backpay with interest; (4) if discriminatorily denied a job or terminated and there is no current vacancy, frontpay will be ordered until a position is available. Frontpay may also be an appropriate remedy when employer-employee hostility would make a continuing employment relationship difficult; (5) compensatory damages, to make the victim financially whole for past losses and emotional distress; (6) attorney fees; (7) removal from personnel and all other files of discipline, adverse performance appraisals, and other actions related to the complaint ultimately filed, and (8) punitive damages, against nongovernmental entities, where the discrimination was undertaken with malice or reckless indifference.[12]

EEOC's enforcement of the law is based on four theories of discrimination. These theories apply both to Title VII violations and to the other job discrimination laws that EEOC administers:

1. ***Disparate treatment***—An applicant or officer may rightly believe that he or she has been dealt

Quick Facts: Limits on Compensatory and Punitive Damages Vary By Size of Employer

For employers with 15–100 employees, the limit is $50,000.

For employers with 101–200 employees, the limit is $100,000.

For employers with 201–500 employees, the limit is $200,000.

For employers with more than 500 employees, the limit is $300,000.[14]

Box 9.2: The Probationary Sergeant Who "Lacked Command Presence"

Phillip Barnes (PB) joined the Cincinnati Police Department as an officer. On the Sergeants' examination some 10 years later, he was placed 18th among 120 officers who took it. He was promoted to Sergeant and, like other recently promoted Sergeants, placed on probation. PB was living as a preoperative male-to-female transsexual, dressing as a man at work and a woman while off-duty, sometimes coming to work with arched eyebrows and lipstick on his face. This resulted in a reputation as a homosexual, cross dresser, or bisexual.

After reporting to District One on his first assignment as a Sergeant, a superior noted that PB had trouble completing documents, exercising judgment in the field, and completing assignments on time. Unlike other Sergeants on probation, PB was then evaluated by a different set of standards in a "new training program." A special six-page form was developed, used only for evaluating PB. He was not allowed to go to the field alone; was required to wear a microphone at all times; during the last weeks of his probationary period had to ride in a car with a camera in it, and was evaluated daily by seven Sergeants. One of the Sergeants who evaluated PB testified that the purpose of the program was to document every mistake he made so he could be failed on probation. The Sergeant also stated PB was targeted for failure although he was actually improving over the course of his probationary period.

This Sergeant warned PB that he was going to fail probation because he wasn't masculine enough. Prior to promotion a senior commander had counseled PB because he needed to stop wearing makeup and act more masculine, which was explained as an effort to correct grooming deficiencies.

Ultimately, a recommendation was made to fail PB during probation. This recommendation was rejected and instead PB was told to choose a mentor. At the beginning of that relationship PB got mediocre scores, which later collapsed to zeros in some categories as time passed. A second fail recommendation was made and accepted by the administration. PB was the only Sergeant to fail probation during an eight-year period.

Among the other characterizations of PB made during probation was that he lacked command presence, he failed to use proper radio procedures, his grooming and uniform appearance didn't meet standards, and he was dishonest on several occasions.

PB acknowledged that being a Sergeant was more difficult than he had expected, there was a difference in the duties of officer and Sergeant, and in some areas he did need to improve. At one point during probation, he sought help from the department's psychologist, stating problems during probation elevated his stress and that the problems would not have occurred but for his supervisors singling him out in the manner they did, which he found demeaning.

PB filed a sex discrimination suit under Title VII and prevailed at a jury trial The jury awarded him $150,000 in compensatory damages, $30,511 in back pay, and $140,000 in front pay. The District Court additionally awarded PB $527,888 in attorney fees and $25,837 in costs. The city appealed the case twice, both of which were denied. Phillip Barnes later became Philecia Barnes.

---

with unfairly by an employment decision. To rise to the level of a disparate treatment claim, the person must have been intentionally treated differently because of his or her membership in a protected class; the discrimination must be more than slight to be actionable.[13] Both compensatory and punitive damages can be awarded against a *nongovernmental employer*.

Black police officers in Houston filed a Title VII suit alleging racial discrimination. The officers complained they were excluded from serving in four divisions that prohibited officers from wearing beards. The department's position was that those divisions would be most likely to respond to chemical, biological, radiological, or nuclear attacks and the bearded black officers could not safely wear respirators. In *Stewart et al. v. City of Houston Police Department*, the District Court granted summary judgment to the defendant, the Houston Police Department, and the dismissal was affirmed by the Appellate Court (2010).[15]

In *Endres v. Indiana State Police* (2003), a Baptist officer refused assignment as a full-time gaming commission agent at a casino because gambling violated his religious belief that games

of chance were sinful.[16] The plaintiff requested other duties and was denied. The suit was dismissed with the court noting that juggling unpopular enforcement duties and the preferences of officers would be a daunting task to managers and create operational hardships.

Religious discrimination may also be litigated on Constitutional, as opposed to Title VII, grounds. An Orthodox Jewish Las Vegas detective, Steve Riback, sued his department (*Riback v. Las Vegas Metropolitan Police Department*) for religious discrimination because it would not allow him to grow a short beard or wear a yarmulke skullcap, even though he was on desk duty and not in contact with the public (see Figure 9.1). In 2009, this First Amendment case was settled with the plaintiff receiving $350,000, the right to grow a beard, and permission to wear a baseball cap in lieu of a yarmulke.[17] Newark Sunni Muslim police officers also successfully litigated a First Amendment claim, allowing them to grow beards in fulfillment of their religious practices (1999).[18] In its decision, the court noted that the department had already made an exception for African-American officers prone to develop infections from shaving (*Fraternal Order of Police Newark Lodge 12 v. City of Newark*).

FIGURE 9.1 ▶ Detective Steve Riback reviews his religious discrimination suit against the Las Vegas Metropolitan Police Department. (Photograph by Steve Riback)

2. **Adverse impact**—Prior to 1965, the Duke Power Company hired only African-Americans into the lowest-paying job classifications, while Whites were hired into better-paying positions. The two races worked in segregated departments and promotions were made within those racially divided departments. Based on the enactment of the Civil Rights Act of 1964, Duke Power was later required to change its employment practices.

In 1965, new applicants and employees seeking transfer to traditional White classifications were required to have a high school education and pass two aptitude tests. The tests excluded 94 percent of the minorities, but only 42 percent of the majority group. At that time in Duke Power's home state of North Carolina, only 12 percent of African-Americans had a high school education. Willie Griggs, an African-American employee of Duke Power, filed a class action suit under the Civil Rights Act of 1964.

In *Griggs v. Duke Power Company* (1971), the Supreme Court found for plaintiff, Griggs. The tests and the high school education requirement continued past discriminatory practice and both requirements were not job related. Griggs established the principle that the absence of discriminatory intent is unimportant and it is the consequences that matters. Although Duke Power's requirements were seemingly innocuous, their impact fell more harshly on African-Americans, excluding them from better-paying positions, creating an adverse impact. An adverse impact is an employment practice that, although lacking any discriminatory intent and on its face appearing to be neutral, an employer is prohibited from using because it has an unjustified impact on members of a protected class.

In 1978, the EEOC developed **Uniform Guidelines for Employee Selection Procedures**. The purpose of the Guidelines was to create a single set of principles designed to help covered employers comply with federal laws prohibiting employment practices that discriminated on the basis of race, color, sex, religion, and national origin. As defined by EEOC, "selection procedure" means any measure, or combination of measures or procedures, used as a basis for any employment decision. The term includes the full range of evaluation techniques from traditional paper and pencil tests, performance tests, training programs, probationary periods, and physical, educational, and work experience requirements through informal or casual interviews and unscored application forms.

Using the example of a written promotional test, a rough rule-of-thumb method of assessing adverse impact is the "**4/5ths rule**."[19] If the passing rate on the test for any race, sex, or ethnic group is less than 4/5ths, or 80 percent, of the passing rate for the group with the highest passing rate, an adverse impact exists (see Table 9.1).

In such a case, the employer must defend its practices or under EEOC guidelines adopt a selection process that is equally valid and reliable, reasonably meets the employer's legitimate business needs, and is less discriminatory, or go to trial. The replacement selection process might be a different written test or it could be an entirely different process, such as an oral board.

Law enforcement agencies are sensitive to the problems of adverse impact. However, as noted above, under EEOC guidelines, all adverse impact is not illegal, although defending such practices imposes a substantial burden. That is a fight, even if winnable, in which most employers don't want to engage. It is likely to be costly, time-consuming, reduce prospects for increasing diversity, tarnish the image of the employer, and make economic development a harder task because employers are reluctant to relocate their businesses to a city or county that can't effectively govern itself. The flip side is that abandoning the results of a test with adverse impact may result in a suit by officers who passed the test.

TABLE 9.1 EXAMPLE OF THE 4/5THS RULE APPLIED TO A POLICE PROMOTIONAL WRITTEN TEST[a]

Test Data	White Candidates	African-American Candidates	Totals
Took Test	400	100	500
Passed	120	10	130
Failed	280	90	370
Passing Rate	30%	10%	26%

[a]Adverse impact calculation: 10% (lowest passing rate)÷30% (highest passing rate) = 33.3 substantially less than 80 percent, indicating an adverse impact. To avoid adverse impact in this example, the African-American passing rate would have to be a minimum of 24 percent.

In *Ricci v. DeStefano* (2009), the Supreme Court ruled that New Haven, Connecticut, couldn't simply dismiss the results of promotional tests for Fire Lieutenant and Captain that produced adverse impacts because it feared Title VII liability. The data for an adverse impact was clear—under the 4/5ths rule, the minority passing rate was 34 percent, only 59 percent of the passing rates for majority officers. The Court concluded that before being used the tests had been subject to "painstaking analysis," New Haven had turned a "blind eye" toward its validity evidence, and another process that met the employer's needs was not available at that time.

A case with a fact situation striking similarity to *Ricci* is *Joe Oakley v. City of Memphis*. The 40 plaintiffs in Oakley included a racially and gender-mixed group of candidates that litigated over a promotional test to police major that Memphis discarded amid concerns about Title VII litigation despite strong possibilities for its defense. Both the trial and appeals court found for the defendant city of Memphis and plaintiffs appealed to the Supreme Court. In the wake of its decision in *Ricci*, the Supreme Court remanded Oakley for further consideration. Upon reconsideration, the plaintiffs prevailed. Note should be taken that both the original trial and appeals court decisions were based on the prevailing decisions prior to *Ricci*.

Quick Facts: Seattle's Rush to "Defund" and "Cut" the Police Department's Budget May Lead to "Adverse Impact"

In 2020, after months of confronting Black Lives Matter protests and the development of autonomous occupied zones (see Chapter 2, *Policing Today*, for a more detailed discussion), Seattle Police Chief Carmen Best, the first Black female chief to lead the Seattle Police Department (SPD), resigned. Chief Best's actions were in protest to Seattle City Council's newly proposed cuts in personnel in the department. Interestingly, Chief Best had initiated a new hiring program in Seattle in 2019 resulting in the addition of 110 officers (with over 40 percent of those new hires being persons of color). As a result of the city council's action attempting to "defund" the police, the SPD was forced to lay off nearly 100 officers. Ironically, since the department employees are governed by seniority (last hired, first to go), officers of color are disproportionately impacted

by these cuts, which may lead to claims based on adverse impact. (REUTERS / Alamy Stock Photo)

3. *Harassment*—Although technically harassment is a form of disparate treatment, EEOC recognizes it as a separate theory of discrimination.[20]

Harassment is a discriminatory, unwelcome action toward an individual on the basis of race, color, sex (including pregnancy), national origin, age, religion, disability, or genetic information. Unwelcome actions that may rise to the level of harassment include speech, touching, and other conduct that create an intimidating "hostile work environment" that employees reasonably should not have to endure. Mild teasing and occasional offhand comments will fall short of being recognized as creating a hostile environment; the conduct involved must be more severe or pervasive but need not be totally intolerable.[21] Gender harassment can occur without it being specifically sexual harassment[22] (e.g., "You're pigheaded like all other women").

A single significant act may constitute harassment. In *Chris Sanford v. Department of Veterans Affairs* (2009), the Associate Director grabbed the plaintiff's arm, turned him around, pushed him into a desk, and screamed at him.[23] The incident was sufficiently severe as to allow a claim of harassment to be made. However, the more usual situation is a pattern of continuing conduct. The more severe the harassing actions, the less need there is to show a pattern.

Sexual harassment is perhaps the most immediately recognizable form of harassment. The harasser may be an immediate supervisor, a supervisor in another unit, the agent of the employer, or an nonemployee, such as a package delivery person. The victim and harasser may be of the same gender; a victim may also be someone other than the person being harassed who finds the conduct offensive. There does not have to be an economic injury to the victim before a claim can be filed and the harasser's attention must be unwelcome. It is helpful if the victim informs the harasser that the conduct is not wanted and uses the employer's complaint system to document the circumstances of each such encounter.[24] Although victims of sexual harassment can be men, they are most often women; in rare occasions, they may be very young. A 14-year-old girl working in a Wichita, Kansas, fast-food restaurant was sexually harassed by the store manager almost immediately after being hired. One day after work he insisted on driving her home. Instead, he took the girl to his home and sexually assaulted her. The manager was later sentenced to eight years in prison. EEOC investigated and found that other girls were also sexually harassed, and sued the company, which settled the suit in 2002. The girl who was sexually assaulted received $150,000.[25]

Traditionally, **sexual harassment** has been categorized as (1) **quid pro quo**, from Latin, meaning an exchange or literally "something for something." It is constituted by unwelcome sexual advances, requests for sexual favors, and other verbal or physical conduct of a sexual nature when (A) submission to such conduct is either explicitly or implicitly a term or condition of an individual's employment or (B) submission or rejection of such conduct by an individual is used as the basis for employment decisions affecting that individual[26] and (2) **hostile environment** which is created when the prohibited and unwelcome behavior has the purpose or effect of unreasonably interfering with an individual's work performance or by creating an intimidating, hostile, or offensive working environment.[27]

Examples of conduct that contribute to a hostile work environment include crude language; displaying sexually suggestive cartoons, calendars, posters, photographs, sex toys, or pornographic material; unnecessary touching; off-color, lewd, and obscene jokes; sexually suggestive gestures and body language; references to sexual activity and questions about another's sexual life; social invitations to discuss a promotion, raise, performance appraisal, or other terms and conditions of employment; and demeaning or offensive language, such as "babe," or "work spouse."[28] In determining whether such unwelcome conduct may have established a hostile environment, a variety of factors are considered, such as frequency, severity, and whether the conduct is intimidating or humiliating.

Employers have a substantial responsibility in curbing all forms of prohibited harassment. Table 9.2 illustrates common elements in a sexual harassment policy. Such policies often include the names, telephone numbers, and physical and e-mail addresses of those outside of the department to whom sexual harassment can be reported. Not shown in Table 9.2 are the specific procedures related to the policy.

Box 9.3: Deputy Sues Sheriff, Alleges Sexual Harassment

Although the Sheriff avowed there would be no toleration of sexual harassment, he was self-described as a "touchy-feely person." Periodically, the sheriff had contact with a female deputy, making inappropriate or suggestive remarks and touching her in sexually aggressive ways. Subsequently, he insisted on hugging her when they encountered each other at work and would grab her buttocks. At one point, he required her to sit on his lap and forced a kiss on her lips, admonishing her that if she wanted a transfer or promotion, she had to choose him over her boyfriend. Some at work referred to the Sheriff as a "gropealope." These and other episodes made the plaintiff dread going to work. She resigned, filed suit, and prevailed at trial on appeal, the judgment of the trial court was affirmed.[29]

4. *Retaliation*—Unlawful retaliation can take one of two forms: (1) retaliation for participation and (2) retaliation for opposition.

Under retaliation for participation, employers are prohibited from retaliating against a job applicant or an employee because he or she made a charge, testified, assisted, or participated in any manner in an investigation, proceeding, or hearing involving a covered job discrimination claim; for the employee's expression or conduct to be protected from retaliation, it must make reference to a protected class or type of prohibited job discrimination.[30]

Under retaliation for opposition, employers cannot discriminate against an applicant or employee who opposed covered job discrimination practices or said so in response to the employer's questions. Protection is afforded so long as the opposition is based on a reasonable and good faith belief that the practice opposed is illegal. In the event, the practice opposed is not prohibited, the employee is still protected. However, if such opposition is unreasonable, in bad faith, deliberately false, or malicious there is no protection.[31]

THE PREGNANCY DISCRIMINATION ACT (PDA)

Pregnancy, childbirth, and related medical complications were not originally conceived of as discrimination issues. Still, some agencies developed policies to prevent such discrimination and the courts allowed litigation under the 1964 Civil Rights Act. To formalize what had previously been an ad hoc process and to promote uniformity of rights, the **Pregnancy Discrimination Act (PDA)** of 1978 was enacted. In some circumstances, the ADA, and the Family Medical Leave Act (FMLA) protections may also be invoked. The PDA is the primary law prohibiting discrimination against pregnant women and is applicable to businesses with 15 or more employees and all public employers.

Broadly, the act makes it illegal to discriminate in employment practices against a woman because of pregnancy, childbirth, or medical conditions arising from such.[34] Hiring a pregnant woman is not required, but such an applicant must be treated equal to all other candidates. Women applying for pregnancy leave cannot be required to give more than the 30 days notice mandated by the FMLA. Poor performance and attendance problems by pregnant women need not be tolerated

Quick Facts: Officer Sues for Retaliation, Actively Supported Wife's Disability Claim

A consent decree was entered into by the City of Colorado Springs and plaintiff Lance Lazoff in a retaliation case.[32] Both Mr. Lazoff and his wife were police officers. She filed an Americans with Disabilities Act (ADA) complaint, which he actively supported. Subsequently, he was denied promotion to Sergeant 16 times. The consent decree remedies included back pay and retroactive seniority.

TABLE 9.2 SEXUAL HARASSMENT POLICY STATEMENT

Policy
All Departmental employees have a right to work in an environment free from unsolicited and unwelcome conduct of a sexual nature. Sexual harassment is against the law and is prohibited conduct that will not be tolerated in the department. Violations will be swiftly investigated and appropriate action taken at the earliest possible point. It may be necessary to transfer the accused to another position pending resolution.
In addition to being legally wrong, sexual harassment is also misconduct that undermines the integrity of the employment relationship. All employees have a responsibility to prevent the development of a department climate that allows, supports, promotes, condones, tolerates, or ignores sexual harassment and are required to report violations orally or written at the earliest possible opportunity.
Reports of misconduct may be made with any of the following: (1) any departmental supervisor, including outside of the normal chain of command; (2) the Internal Affairs Unit; (3) the city's Human Resource Department or EEO Officer; (4) any Assistant City Manager or the City Manager; (5) the State Civil Rights Commission; and (6) the federal Equal Employment Opportunity Commission.
All supervisors are responsible for preventing sexual harassment by: (1) monitoring the workplace on a daily basis; (2) ensuring that employees understand their rights and requirements to comply with the law and this policy; (3) taking immediate corrective action when misconduct is observed even if the involved employee is outside the normal chain of command; and (4) reporting allegations and observed misconduct in writing to the Office of the Chief of Police within 24 hours of occurrence. Reports shall be hand carried by the initiating supervisor to the Office of the Chief of Police in a sealed envelope bearing no outer details to protect privacy.

Source: Drawn, with restatement for brevity, from the policies of the Denver, Colorado; Santa Cruz, California; and Peoria, Illinois, Police Departments.

Box 9.4: Pregnant Officer Fights Back After Lost Opportunity to Take Sergeant's Exam

New York Police Department Officer Akema Thompson learned that the first Sergeant's test in two years was going to be on the same day as her baby's due date. She also knew that the civil service gave a makeup test. After an exchange of correspondence, the most accommodation she received was civil service would allow her to sit on a cushion on the regular date for the test. In that same year, 1,376 women nationwide had pregnancy discrimination cases resolved in their favor.

Thompson solicited the support of her union, the Patrolmen's Benevolent Association, which sent three letters warning that the denial would alter the trajectory of Thompson's career and was unlawful. Her request for a makeup test, which the civil service had scheduled, was once again turned down. In 2014, the Legal Momentum, a women's advocacy group, took her case pro bono and filed suit against the city for pregnancy discrimination. The case was settled out of court and Thompson received $50,000 and was allowed to take the make-up test. The Legal Momentum got $15,000, and the city stipulated that pregnancy and child-related conditions would be grounds for a make-up examination in the future.[33]

Box 9.5: Six Officers Sue for Pregnancy Discrimination

Six Suffolk County (New York) Police Department (SCPD) female officers sued their employer on pregnancy discrimination grounds for denying women officers limited duty, desk-type jobs during their pregnancies. Until 2000, the SCPD provided access to such positions and then changed its policy to limit the use of such positions to officers injured on-duty. The SCPD also failed to provide bulletproof vests and gun belts that would fit pregnant women. The result was that women could not work for much of their pregnancies and were unpaid after exhausting their annual leave. The trial court found for the women in *Lochren et al. v. Suffolk County* and awarded damages and attorney fees. The plaintiffs appealed the amount of attorney fees and costs awarded to the Appeals Court, which discovered mathematical and other errors by the trial court, in awarding $578,704. The Appeals Court remanded those issues to the trial court. In 2010, the trial court awarded attorney fees and costs of $932,187.[35]

by an employer, but such employees cannot be held to a higher standard than any other employee. A woman cannot be forced from her job even if it exposes her to dangerous conditions although the employer should provide her with written notice of the hazards.

PREGNANT POLICE OFFICERS AND DEPARTMENTAL PRACTICES AND POLICIES

Findings from a major review of research studies lead to the question of whether existing law enforcement policies related to pregnant officers are sufficiently comprehensive and informative.

Some departments still lack policies regarding firearms training by pregnant officers. Although nonlead rounds are used by many law enforcement agencies, others still use leaded bullets. "Nonlead" rounds use no or very little lead and are sometimes called "green rounds" because they are also more ecofriendly. Lead toxicity is harmful to the fetus and exposure during pregnancy is associated with serious complications, including spontaneous abortion and hypertension. Well-ventilated indoor ranges can substantially mediate this problem. Noise toxicity is also related to acute disorders, including miscarriages. Lead and noise combined have a higher toxicity with significant consequences (e.g., heart lesions).[36]

Gun-cleaning solvents may not be safe and pregnant officers should not clean firearms. Heavy physical activity during the last trimester may injure the baby or the mother. Pregnant officers should not be tasered during training due to a risk of miscarriage. Chemicals at clandestine labs, haz-mat spills, and traffic accidents are also health risks, as are contact with potentially infectious subjects and violent assaults. Shift work and night duty are associated with preterm births.[37]

The International Association of Chiefs of Police (IACP) developed a policy, Pregnancy and Policing," in October 2010. Among its notable points: (1) women are important in policing as part of its diversity; (2) women should never have to choose between motherhood and livelihood; (3) there continue to be obstacles for women in law enforcement, including inadequate facilities and equipment; (4) male norms in place can create self-doubt; and (5) inadequate maternity policies and equipment for pregnant officers.[38] In 2011, The Women in Federal Law Enforcement (WIFLE) Foundation has also offered advisory pregnancy guidelines for federal law enforcement agencies.

The IACP properly notes that policies that automatically exclude women from regular duties from the onset of pregnancy are discriminatory, as are policies that afford no accommodation because it ultimately results in loss of seniority, health benefits, and pensions (see *United States of America v. Bill Sturch, Sheriff, Bryan County, Oklahoma*, 2009). No accommodation policies also deny departments the opportunity to retain valuable women officers. Automatically placing women on light duty status when they become pregnant also create some potential disadvantages: loss of off-duty employment, may be unable to maintain state certification as a peace officer, may be illegally excluded from competing for promotion, and adversely effecting opportunity for productivity and thus a potentially negative performance evaluation.[39]

According to the IACP, a sound policy keeps trained and experienced female officers working as long as reasonably possible and does not compel light duty until medically necessary, defers types of training that could interfere with the pregnancy, preserves seniority and all other employment rights, recognizes pregnancy as a transient or temporary condition, is based on medically sound information and not stereotypes, and prevents Title VII liability. The IACP policy also avoids the use of assignments that have a likelihood of encountering toxic chemicals, or pose other health risks, for example, raids on meth labs, chemical spills, intensive traffic enforcement, prolonged air travel, high-risk entries, SWAT Team duty, riot control, and prolonged stationary posts, all of which have a high possibility of producing trauma. The option to use maternity duty should be made available to the pregnant officer during the second trimester or when medically indicated and may include nonhazardous assignments, writing police reports, operating a radio, interviewing people, and clerical work.[40]

The IACP also recommends avoiding the following during maternity duty: alternating shifts, defensive tactics training, actual firearms training, patrol duties, extensive exposure to automobile exhaust fumes, standing for more than 30 minutes at a time, lifting more than 25 pounds, and exposure to high concentrations to toxins. During pregnancy, the department should seek a temporary weapon qualification exemption or arrange for an alternative firearms qualification.[41]

THE AMERICANS WITH DISABILITIES ACT (ADA) 1990

The **Americans with Disabilities Act (ADA)** was enacted in 1990 to guarantee equal opportunity to jobs for qualified individuals with disabilities and to provide covered individuals with other protections as well. The ADA Amendment Acts of 2008 provided broader protections to job seekers with disabilities and put in place less-restrictive interpretations of the law than those held by the courts. The law covers private employers, state and local governments, employment agencies, and labor organizations and is enforced by the U.S. Equal Employment Opportunity Commission.

Rochester, Michigan, is one of only a number of police departments that have been sued because they lacked the policies and equipment to properly handle deaf persons. With all of its resources and specialization, even the New York City Police Department entered into a settlement with the U.S. Department of Justice in 2009 to implement practices that would enhance effective communication when its officers are in contact with deaf

persons.[42] ADA further requires easy access and use by covered individuals to a wide range of facilities, including banks, theaters, recreational opportunities, transportation, hotel/lodging, child care centers, voting centers, restaurants, and assistance at self-serve gasoline stations.

ADA legislation has had a significant impact on the hiring and other human resource practices of law enforcement agencies. It makes it unlawful to discriminate in all employment practices with respect to covered individuals, including recruitment, hiring, pay, firing, promotion, job assignments, training, leave, lay-offs, and benefits. The law does not require that preferences be given to covered individuals.

In the employment context, a **qualified individual with a disability** is a job applicant or employee who meets legitimate skill, experience, education, or other requirements of an employment position that he or she seeks or holds.[43] The person must be able to perform the essential or core job functions versus the marginal requirements, with or without a **reasonable accommodation** for his or her disability by the employer; job requirements that screen out people with disabilities are legal only to the extent that they are job related and consistent with business necessity.[44] Examples of reasonable accommodations by employers include modifying equipment and facilities, redesigning jobs, modifying work schedules, and approving transfers to other vacant jobs that can be performed.[45] There are federal and some state tax credits for businesses to offset the cost of providing reasonable accommodations.

Accommodations cannot impose an "undue hardship" on employers, such as substantial expense. This is evaluated in terms of the employer's own circumstances. Accommodations will vary according to individual needs (e.g., an applicant may need a sign language interpreter during an interview, blind employees may need someone to read job instructions to them, and diabetics may need periodic breaks to eat properly and monitor their blood sugar and insulin levels).[46] Employers are not required to lower production or quality standards as an accommodation, nor must they provide one unless a request is made.[47]

With respect to an individual, a **disability** is (1) a physical or mental impairment that *substantially* limits one or more major life activities, (2) a record of such an impairment, or (3) a perception that a person has such an impairment.[48] Major life activities include but are not limited to by federal law, caring for one's self, performing manual tasks, seeing, hearing, eating, sleeping, walking, standing, lifting, bending, speaking, breathing, learning, reading, concentrating, thinking, communicating, and working.[49] Major bodily functions are also covered, including digestive, bowel, bladder, respiratory, circulatory, and reproductive functions.[50] Determining "substantial limitation" is a "common sense judgment"; the limitation need not totally prevent a major life activity nor rise to the level of a significant or severe restriction.[51] Although individuals may take "mitigating measures" to reduce or eliminate their impairment (e.g., insulin or use of a prosthetic limb), in ADA's view, the test of impairment is whether the person would have a substantial limitation of a major life activity without it.

GENETIC INFORMATION NONDISCRIMINATION ACT (GINA)

The **Genetic Information Nondiscrimination Act (GINA)** covers employers with 15 or more workers, labor unions, training programs, and employment agencies. It effectively extends the reach of Title VII of the Civil Rights Act of 1964. The law defines "genetic information" broadly; it includes information about an individual's genetic tests and the genetic tests and medical histories of "family members" (i.e., their diseases, disorders, and conditions). *Family members* means to the fourth degree (i.e., great-great-great grandparents). In addition to other provisions, GINA strictly limits the disclosure of genetic information and requires its storage in special medical files. The law provides for compensatory damages for violations, which make plaintiffs whole, restoring them, and punitive damages, which are intended to punish violators and deter future offenses.

Title I forbids the use of genetic information by health insurers. Excluded from the definition of genetic information are cholesterol and liver-function tests, the sex of a person, or his/her age. Blood tests are permitted to the extent that they are not designed to detect genotypes, mutations, or chromosomal changes.

Title II regulates the use of genetic information in the work setting. Employers cannot (1) use genetic information when making employment decisions about applicants and the terms and conditions of employment for employees (e.g., a law enforcement agency cannot refuse employment to applicants because they have a family history of cancer); (2) classify, segregate, or limit employees based on genetic information; (3) retaliate against someone who asserts opposition to actions or practices forbidden by GINA; or (4) request, require, purchase, or disclose genetic information about employees. For example, employers may not use a health risk questionnaire requesting family medical history unless an "exception" applies.

The law recognizes six narrow exceptions to acquiring genetic information: (1) the "water cooler" situation, when an employer overhears someone talking about a family member's illness; (2) accidental discovery acquisition through a newspaper obituary or other publicly available source (e.g., reading that an employee's mother died of heart failure); (3) voluntary participation in an employer's wellness program where the employee gives written consent; (4) when the information is required as part of a Family Medical Leave Act or similar state or local law provision to establish the medical necessity for which an employee is asking for leave (the Family Medical Leave Act is discussed in the next section of this chapter); (5) genetic testing that monitors the biological effects of toxic substances in the workplace, where program participation is voluntary or required by law; and (6) law enforcement agencies may request genetic information from employees to determine if they have contaminated forensic evidence and to identify human remains.

GINA took effect on November 21, 2009, and litigation involving it has been sparse during 2009–2015. There does not appear to be any GINA suits filed by police officers because of their department's disclosure of genetic information or against police departments by civilians for their disclosure of it.

Job Discrimination Laws Administered by the Department of Labor

The **Fair Labor Standards Act (FLSA)** was passed in 1938 and the U.S. Supreme Court upheld its constitutionality in 1941. It has been amended several times; most importantly for present purposes is that public employees became covered in 1986. It affects 130 million full-time and part-time private and public sectors employees.[52] In 1938, the federal minimum wage was 25 cents an hour; when adjusted for inflation, it now equates to $8.56 hourly.[53]

The goal of the original **Fair Labor Standards Act (FLSA)** (1938) was to create jobs in a struggling economy in the belief that business employers would rather pay normal or "straight time" to new employees than pay overtime to existing workers—1.5 times their normal hourly rate—when they worked more than 40 hours a week.[54] In 1974, Congress amended the FLSA to make it applicable to public sector employees; two years later in *National League of Cities v. Usery*,[55] the Supreme Court held the amendment to be unconstitutional. Subsequently, the Supreme Court reversed itself on this issue in *Garcia v. San Antonio Metropolitan Transit Authority* (1985),[56] ruling that Congress did have the authority to apply FLSA to state and local governments.

The purpose of the FLSA is to establish national minimum wage, work hours, overtime pay, child labor, and required record-keeping standards. Of concern here are the work hours and overtime provisions pertaining to law enforcement agencies:

1. FLSA does not require holiday, vacation, or sick leave days; shift differential pay, hazardous duty compensation, overtime pay for working holidays, specific work schedules, fringe benefits, meal breaks, a written notice of the reason a person is fired, or any type of severance pay or package.[57] It also does not speak to job-sharing arrangements. Such things may be provided by a police department as part of its HR program or by written agreement with the officers' union.

2. Nothing in the FLSA prevents employers from paying more than the national minimum wage of $7.25 an hour and has not increased since July 2009. Most states have enacted a higher minimum wage. For instance, New York and California were the first to commit to raising the minimum wage to $15 an hour by 2021. President Donald Trump signed Executive Order 13658 effective January 1, 2020, raising the minimum wage to workers performing work on a federal contract to $10.80 per hour.

3. Employees are grouped into two categories for purposes of overtime pay: (1) **nonexempt**—the group that is entitled to overtime pay and (2) **exempt**—the group that is not. Under the rule change effective January 1, 2020, to be classified as exempt, an employee must (1) be paid a predetermined and fixed annual salary, (2) be paid more than $684 weekly

or $35,568 annually, and (3) primarily perform bona fide executive, administrative, or professional ("white collar") duties as identified in the three-pronged "duties test:" (1) the *salary test*, which is covered above; (2) the *duty test*, which requires that the content of the job are directly related to the organization's management or general business operations and must be the principal, main, major, or most important duty of the employee; and (3) the *discretion and independent judgment test*, meaning the employee must exercise such judgment in matters of significance for the organization.[58] There are a number of exceptions to FLSA overtime provisions. Members of the "learned professions," such as medical doctors, lawyers, the clergy, registered nurses, pharmacists, teachers, and accountants are all examples. Coaches are exempt if they teach athletic concepts and skills, but athletic personnel who primarily recruit, have quality control responsibilities, or kindred positions are nonexempt.[59] If properly classified, exempt employees have no FLSA rights.

4. Employers with less than five law enforcement officers working during a seven-day week have a complete FLSA exemption from paying overtime for such weeks.[60] The law does not differentiate between full and part-time officers when counting the number of officers working.

5. Many private and public employers must pay overtime when the number of hours worked exceeds 40 hours during a week; for such employers, a "work week" may start on any day and consists of 7 consecutive 24-hour periods that total 168 hours. However, effective January 1, 2020, the general rules on compensable hours of work for fire and law enforcement officers was changed under Code of Federal Regulations, Title 29, Subpart C - Fire Protection and Law Enforcement Employees of Public Agencies. Specifically, Subsection 553.210-553.227 focuses on the exception of fire and police, redefining important elements of work duty, including "tour of duty" defined, compensable hours of work, sleep time, meal time, early and late relief and outside employment.

6. Overtime compensation must be paid at least as 1.5 times the employee's normal hourly rate. In lieu of overtime pay, law enforcement employers can award compensatory time on the same basis; "comp time" acts as a bank of additional vacation or days off time.

FLSA cases involving law enforcement officers as plaintiffs have not been substantial in recent years. Police officers were not entitled to compensation when putting on and taking off their uniforms and accompanying gear in *Bamonte, Cota, Perine et al. v. City of Mesa* (2010).[61] Although the officers were permitted, as a convenience, to change at the police station, there was no requirement to do so. The court contrasted the officers' situation with those working in a chemical plant who are mandated by the employer to change into and out of protective clothing on-site and who cannot safely perform their essential duties without doing so.

Adams et al. v. United States (2006) concluded that police officers commuting to and from work in an agency provided a "take-home car" are not entitled to be compensated under FLSA unless they perform some substantial police functions (e.g., working a wreck, intervening in a violent assault, or apprehending an offender).[62] In *Cleveland et al. v. City of Elmendorf, Texas* (2004), the court decided that small law enforcement agencies employing fewer than five officers need not count the unpaid service of reserve officers in determining whether they are FLSA exempt.[63] Compensation for K-9 officers caring for their dogs off-duty has been litigated under a variety of fact situations. As held in *Bull v. Customs and Border Protection Service* (2007), *Lewallen v. Scott County, Tennessee* (2010), and other K-9 cases, the courts have generally been favorable to FLSA claims by such officers. In cases not favorable to the plaintiffs, they asserted overtime, but failed to keep records, began litigation too late, or their suits were otherwise defective.

THE FAMILY MEDICAL LEAVE ACT

Enacted in 1993, the **Family Medical Leave Act's (FMLA)** intention is to help employees balance their career and family needs. States are allowed to enact more generous terms but cannot adopt more restrictive measures Although the federal government and a minority of the states had previously extended some benefits to same-sex partners, the Supreme Court's decision in *Obergefell v. Hodges* (2015) resulted in a substantial extension of those benefits. That decision rested on the equal protection clause of the 14th Amendment, which established a right to same-sex marriages. Among the new benefits for same-sex marriages are social security payments, FMLA leave to care for a sick spouse, and spousal benefits for someone married to a member of the armed forces.[64]

"Covered employers" must grant "eligible workers" a total of 12 workweeks of unpaid leave during any 12-month period for one or more of the following reasons:

- The birth of a child and to care for the newborn child within one year of birth; or

- The placement with the employee of a child for adoption or foster care and to care for the newly placed child within one year of placement; or

- To care for the employee's spouse, child, or parent who has a serious health condition; or

- A serious health condition that makes the employee unable to perform the essential functions of his or her job; or

- Any qualifying exigency arising out of the fact that the employee's spouse, son, daughter, or parent is a covered military member on "covered active duty; or

- Twenty-six workweeks of leave during a single 12-month period to care for a covered servicemember with a serious injury or illness if the eligible employee is the servicemember's spouse, son, daughter, parent, or next of kin (military caregiver leave)

Box 9.6: Can Officers Get FLSA Overtime Pay for Attending Mandatory Counseling?

In *Gibbs and Drew v. City of New York Police Commissioner Bratton and others* (2015), the court had to determine if mandatory counseling to save one's job required FLSA overtime pay for inpatient and after regular work hours outpatient counseling. Gibbs joined the NYPD in 2009 and was later assigned to the 63rd Precinct in January 2010 as a police administrative aide. In June, she was referred to the Counseling Service Unit (CSU) for coming to work on several occasions with alcohol on her breath (AOB). She met with a CSU counselor who documented that she drank after work nearly every day, for the last few months she drank in the morning, and drank the night before and on the morning of her first visit to CSU. Diagnosed as alcohol dependent, she initially resisted a 28-day inpatient treatment but finally relented. The release report states her prognosis was extremely poor and she needed to be more open and honest. Gibbs was paid her regular rate during inpatient treatment. She returned to work. On three different later occasions

Gibbs refused to participate in another 28 days impatient treatment. On her fourth refusal, her employment was terminated.

Because Drew, the second plaintiff, was nonsworn as a civilian employee at the Bronx Tow Pound lot, the particulars of her case do not warrant extensive comment here except to note that the court record, as far as it goes, reveals a successful recovery.

The court held that the extra hours spent in inpatient and outpatient counseling were not FLSA compensable. Those activities were not compensable because they were not part of the plaintiffs, indispensable primary duties. On another test, the court held that the counseling was not for the primary benefit of the employer. It did note that if Gibbs' rehabilitation had have been successful, the NYPD would receive some, but not a primary, benefit in that it would not have to go to the effort and expense of hiring and training a replacement.[65]

A "covered employer" is a business with at least 50 employees and all public sector organizations. An "eligible worker" is a person who has worked for the employer 12 continuous months and at least 1,250 hours immediately prior to the request for FMLA leave. Employers may require a medical certification of the condition of a covered family member or that of an employee. The employer may seek a second medical opinion about such certification. Employees seeking FMLA leave must give the employer 30 days notice except for "unforeseeable circumstances," in which case the employee must explain and provide answers to any questions about why the request was unforeseeable. The use of sick or vacation days may be permitted in conjunction with a request for FMLA leave; the use of those days does not count as part of the 12-week FMLA leave period.

THE POLICE PERSONNEL SELECTION PROCESS

Figure 9.2 summarizes police applicant processing, selection, and training. The flow of this chapter substantially parallels this figure.

Applicants and Recruiting

Minimum standards for the employment of law enforcement officers are established by each state's **Police/Peace Officer Standards and Training Commission (POST)** or similarly titled agency. Employers may establish further or higher standards. Recruiting is the process of attracting a pool of candidates from which well-qualified applicants can be selected. The

attractiveness of any pool of applicants can vary from one time to another. The economy has an impact on the number and quality of applicants for law enforcement positions; in a good economy the applicant pool is sometimes shallow, and in a down cycle, there are more quality applicants.[66] For instance, as the U.S. economy soured in 2007, the New York City Police Department received 54 percent more applications the next year and the FBI was sorting through 227,000 applications in 2009 for 3,000 openings.[67] The COVID-19 pandemic in 2020 has dramatically changed the way police do business. A 2020 IACP bulletin reports that 43 percent of all police agencies have stopped or significantly changed their response to calls for service, utilizing telephone, Internet, and teleconference systems to take reports remotely.[68] Many police agencies noted a 50 percent drop in calls for service, and 76 percent have provide officers with formal guidance in reducing the number of physical arrests, particularly during the federal and state shutdown. Certainly, the COVID-19 pandemic will have severe consequences for future police recruitment as 34 percent of police agencies in the United States and Canada have suspended academy training, without offering an alternative while 18 percent more agencies have suspended all in-person training and were using only online alternatives.[69] The long-term impact of the pandemic is still not known; however, it is safe to say that the traditional mechanisms of police recruitment and training will significantly change in the future. See Figure 9.3.

A study of 850 California academy recruits explored their views about the recruiting process and revealed:[70]

1. The top two reasons for joining a law enforcement agency were a desire to serve and a sense of adventure and excitement, although most recruits were also influenced by health and retirement benefits.

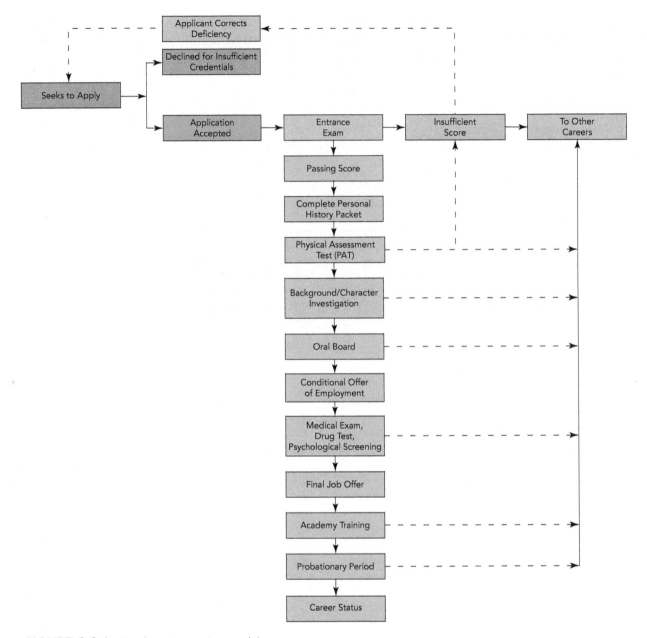

FIGURE 9.2 ▶ Applicant screening model.

2. The length of time it took to process their applications (54 percent) and the lack of personal contact and updates during the process (34 percent) were negative experiences.

3. The professional reputation of a potential employer (i.e., well respected) was a major attractor (86 percent).

4. The least productive recruiting strategies were traditional ones, such as advertising in newspapers.

5. The most productive recruitment strategies were websites with information and online application forms followed by contacts with officers who were friends or family members or other employee referrals.

6. Recruits had long-term interest in law enforcement; 20 percent were interested in a police career in elementary school and 50 percent by the time they graduated from high school.

A study surveyed 205 North Carolina state and local law enforcement agencies.[71] Respondents classified their recruiting techniques as passive (35 percent), neutral (34 percent), and aggressive (31 percent). Overall, the agencies' preferred methods of recruiting were word of mouth (95 percent), newspaper ads (83 percent), targeting community college students (72 percent), and the Internet (63 percent). With nearly 70 percent of the departments employing passive or neutral recruiting efforts, it is not surprising that 68 percent of them had no waiting or backlog list of qualified candidates. Their techniques were simply not very successful. For them, if police recruiting was survival of the fittest, they would be an endangered species.

FIGURE 9.3 ▶ Police recruitment and training, as well as the operational mechanisms of doing police work have significantly changed as a result of the COVID-19 pandemic. (STEFAN JEREMIAH/REUTERS/Alamy Stock Photo)

The California Peace Officers Standards and Training Commission recommends the following recruiting practices:[72]

1. Develop an overall plan that addresses a range of factors, including agency goals, the community's demographics, future number of officers needed, the skills that will be required, and diversity.

2. Profile the ideal candidate, review past successes, failures, and future opportunities, and identify best practices; one agency found that its most successful candidates were 27-year-olds, who had a stable employment history during the past two years, and at least two years of college.

3. Personalize the recruiting process; stay in contact with applicants, update them on their status with calls and letters, and let them know which staff members to call with questions.

4. Carefully select and train recruiters.

5. Build strong partnership with potential applicant pipelines (e.g., the military, educational institutions, and student associations).

6. Make officers recruiting ambassadors, provide them with excellent recruiting packets, and reward them for referrals and hires.

7. Streamline the recruiting process, cutting out bottlenecks; provide potential applicants with a self-administered form so they can decide if they have any disqualifiers.

8. Develop a plan to deliver recruiting messages using multiple means or channels.

9. Have an Internet presence that is easy to navigate with as few clicks as possible to accommodate the many people who use the Internet to sort through employment opportunities.

10. Use effective recruiting strategies, relying on proven techniques and being open to new possibilities. Thinking "outside the box," the Sacramento (California) Police Department began hosting a Law Enforcement Expo/Female Health and Fitness Challenge, with males allowed to participate. The orientation of the event significantly increased female hirings.

Recruiting strategies and the expenditure of any recruiting funds should be carefully considered in light of human resource objectives, and the results carefully scrutinized. A study of the recruiting practices of the Los Angeles Police Department (LAPD) found results that may vary elsewhere, but illustrate the point that successful recruiting requires careful thought. The site of a recruiting event yields differential results; as compared to recruiting on military bases, the LAPD produced three times the number of applicants at community colleges.[73] Recruiting at events that focused on employment (see Figure 9.4) produced more applicants than those at cultural celebrations and athletic events; events that charged an entry fee and advertised in advance were also productive.[74] Women are more likely than men to attend events.[75]

The cost of reaching applicants varies by the methods used and also may yield applicants with different characteristics. It costs the LAPD $29 to attract each applicant from its e-government recruiting site and $1,012 from radio advertising.[76] Asian and Pacific Islanders report significantly more exposure to the Internet than do other racial and ethnic groups; African-Americans report more exposure to events, for example, job fairs and direct mail than do other groups.[77] The LAPD advertises on only one television station, an Asian language

FIGURE 9.4 ▶ Police officer recruiting efforts are more productive when held on college campuses and at events that focus on employment. Knowing when and where to recruit new officers will become more important as calls for defunding the police escalate. (Craig Warga/Bloomberg/Getty Images)

channel, where it broadcasts ads in Korean, Chinese, and Tagalog; it is a cost-effective effort at $147 per applicant.[78] The cost of recruiting efforts must also be evaluated in the context of keeping a law enforcement agency's "brand" before the public in a positive light.

By 2007, the EEOC began focusing more attention on recruiting efforts to determine to what degree they were unbiased or discriminatory. Recruiting messages cannot express a preference for any race, sex, color, ethnic group, or religion. Although most police departments depend, to a degree, on word-of-mouth recruiting by its officers, in a nondiverse department it might constitute a barrier to equal employment opportunity and limit diversity. Likewise, homogenous recruiting occurs when law enforcement agencies fail to use minority newspapers or Internet job sites such as Asian Nation, which might also be a barrier to equal opportunity.

The professionalization of policing has long been linked to college education for police officers. Only 1 percent of agencies require a college degree, 9 percent a two-year degree, and another 8 percent, some college education; the high school degree is the basic educational credential for 81 percent of all agencies.[79] These requirements do not, however, reflect the actual numbers of police officers working in agencies who have some college to graduate or professional degrees.

The Entrance Examination

EEOC's Uniform Guidelines for Employee Selection requires that tests be valid and reliable. **Validity** means that a test actually measures what it is intended to measure and conclusions and decisions based on test scores are therefore appropriate and meaningful. The starting point to establish the validity of any test is a detailed job analysis.

A job description falls substantially short of being a job analysis because it is just a broad description of duties and responsibilities. Job analysis techniques can be used to identify (1) the important types of knowledge to test for on a written examination and the number of questions to be written for each knowledge area; (2) the skills to be measured in a single job simulation exercise, such as requiring an applicant to play the role of an officer who has been stopped by an elderly citizen who is hard of hearing, a little confused, and asking for directions. The importance of each skill needed for a job varies and each skill identified by the job analysis ordinarily has its own unique statistical weight. A series of job simulations may constitute an assessment center. Additionally, the job analysis can identify (3) the knowledge and skills to be tested by an oral board and (4) the physical tasks police officers must perform in carrying out their duties. Validity gives tests the quality of being job related.

Reliability means that if the same test was given again or in a parallel form to the same group of people, they would score substantially the same. Reliability speaks to getting consistent, rather than random, results.

Larger municipalities and counties can develop their own entry tests. However, because establishing test validity and reliability can be time-consuming and technically challenging, many police entry-level tests are purchased or rented from test providers. Such providers include POSTs, Police Chief and Sheriff Associations, the International Personnel Management Association (IPMA), and private companies. Typical entry-level areas tested include reading comprehension, basic mathematical calculations, grammar, spelling, reasoning, memory, vocabulary, and clarity of expression (see Table 9.3).

Passing scores on entry-level tests for all jobs in local government have traditionally been set at 70 by local civil service/merit boards. The courts have been disinclined to alter that standard when it has been challenged. Jurisdictions allow a failed candidate to retake the test after the passage of time (e.g., six months). To avoid potential liability, test administrators

TABLE 9.3 EXAMPLES OF VOCABULARY AND CLARITY OF
EXPRESSION QUESTIONS ON AN ENTRY-LEVEL EXAMINATION

Vocabulary: Select the word that has the closest meaning to the word in bold print.
1. The suspect's employer **corroborated** her alibi.
    a. doubted
    b. verified
    c. contradicted
    d. denied

Clarity: Compare the two statements. Pick the one that is most clearly stated.
    a. The hairs were gathered in a clear envelope by the evidence technician.
    b. The hairs were gathered by the evidence technician in a clear envelope.

make sure that all applicants take the test under the exact same conditions (e.g., everyone starts and stops at the same time, no one is allowed to use a cell phone, and lighting is adequate throughout the room). In large longitudinal studies published in 2009 and 2010, respectively, the passing rate on entry-level examinations for LAPD applicants was 84 percent versus 83 percent in Rochester, New York.[80]

Although entry-level tests are most often written or a job simulation exercise, assessment centers are also used. The key advantages to the written test are low cost, ease of administration, and rapid scoring. Entry-level tests cannot cover what applicants are expected to learn in the academy or on the job, only the things the knowledge and/or skills they are expected to bring to the job.

To a passing score on any federal entrance examination, the federal government will add five points for an honorably discharged veteran and 10 points for a disabled veteran or a recipient of a Purple Heart Medal for a combat wound. If a veteran is unable to use the preference points a mother, widow/widower, or spouse is entitled to them for federal employment purposes. Some law enforcement agencies have provisions to add points to qualifying veterans who make a passing score.

The Physical Assessment Test

The physical demands of police work are considerable at times. Illustratively, officers must have a level of strength and cardiovascular fitness to sustain themselves in a fight with a resisting subject or in pursuit of a subject fleeing on foot.[81] Physical fitness, condition, assessment, readiness, and agility tests are all intended to gauge the extent to which applicants can do so (see Figure 9.5). Physical assessment tests (PATs) are developed from a job analysis physical task inventory. The important tasks are translated into physical requirements by a qualified person, such as an exercise physiologist, and a battery of tests is developed to measure those attributes (e.g., bench pressing weights or doing push-ups to determine upper-body strength, as well as timed runs to gauge cardiovascular condition and endurance).

Many agencies rely on the standards and testing protocols of outside providers for PATs for the same reasons they use their entrance examinations. PATs are often assessed on a fail/pass basis, with applicants being excluded from further participation at any point in which they cannot pass a subtest of the PAT. Table 9.4 summarizes a PAT test battery.

FIGURE 9.5 ▶ Police applicants participating in a physical assessment test. (Courtesy of Fit Force, Inc.)

TABLE 9.4 PAT TEST BATTERY							
Vertical Jump	Bench Press	Bench Press*	Sit Ups	Agility Run	300 Meter Run	Push Ups	1.5 Mile Run
11.0–20.5"	90–205 lbs.	57–93%	25–42	17.8–22.0 seconds	56–92 seconds	12–34	14:05–19:48

*Percent of current body weight

Source: FitForce.

The EEOC prohibits requiring a medical examination before an applicant is offered a job contingent on passing it. Police departments have opted for two strategies to avoid liability if candidate injures himself or herself or dies in association with the PAT: (1) applicants are advised of all activities and potential dangers and must sign a waiver to participate or (2) the candidate must provide a "medical certification," stating that a physician has examined the candidate and that he or she can participate. EEOC allows the medical certification because it is not a full medical examination and no specific medical data are provided with the certification. A study of the Rochester, New York, Police Department found that 61 percent of those tested passed the physical agility test.[82]

Women have successfully challenged some PATs on the basis that they produce a discriminatory adverse impact. *United States v. City of Erie* (Pennsylvania, 2005) illustrates this problem. A police lieutenant was assigned to develop a new PAT, although he had none of the needed specialized education, training, or experience. Nonetheless, he developed a series of tests with cut-off scores. During its use, from 1996 to 2002, 71 percent of the men taking it passed versus only 13 percent of the female applicants. There was no job analysis or validity evidence and the court held the test to be neither job related nor consistent with the employer's business needs.[83]

A study by the University of Kentucky addressed the question "What percentage of currently employed full-time sworn officers in Kentucky police departments could pass the Police Officers Professional Standards physical agility test (PAT)?" A survey was sent to 286 police departments and 155 (54 percent) responded. Among responding agencies only 22 did recurring PAT of currently employed police officers. After statistically analyzing responses, the study estimated that between 58.5 percent and 72.7 percent of all currently employed full-time Kentucky police officers could pass the test.[86]

The Lie Detection/Truth Verification Examination and Background/Character Investigation

The **Employee Polygraph Protection Act (EPPA**, 1988) is administered by the federal Department of Labor (USDOL) and restricts the use of the *polygraph* and other mechanism of lie detection with respect to employees. An employer shall not:

1. require, request, suggest, or cause an employee or prospective employee to take or submit to any lie detector test;

2. use, accept, refer to, or inquire about the results of any lie detector test of an employee or prospective employee; or

3. discharge, discipline, discriminate against, deny employment or promotion, or threaten to take any such action against an employee or prospective employee for refusal to take a test, on the basis of the results of a test, for filing a complaint, for testifying in any proceeding or for exercising any rights afforded by the Act.[87]

Box 9.7: Corpus Christi Sued for Physical Test Gender Discrimination

The Corpus Christi, Texas, Police Department (CCPD) settled a suit by the U.S. Department of Justice involving gender discrimination in its PAT testing by agreeing to a consent decree. Eighty-two percent of male CCPD applicants passed the PAT, but only 33 percent of the women did so. Applying the previously explained EEOC 4/5ths "rule of thumb" to the CCPD case, the expected pass rate for women on the PAT should have been at least 65.6 percent (0.80 × 82) or about twice what actually occurred. The 4/5ths rule is not a prima facie case but does invite more scrutiny from many directions, including EEOC, those negatively effected, lawyers, law enforcement executives, city managers, and their human resources director.[84]

The CCPD consent decree required the city to pay $700,000 as back pay to female applicants who took and failed the challenged physical abilities test between 2005 and 2011 and who were determined to be eligible for relief. Also under the consent decree, some women who took and failed the challenged physical abilities test between 2005 and 2011 may receive offers of priority employment with retroactive seniority and benefits. Applicants interested in priority employment must pass the new, lawful selection procedure developed by Corpus Christi under the decree and meet other qualifications required of all applicants considered for entry-level police officer positions.[85]

Included within the meaning of lie detector are the **computerized voice stress analyzer (CVSA**, see Figure 9.6) and the similar Layered Voice Analyzer, which uses its own patented technology.

The EPPA provides certain exceptions, including screening security services employees (e.g., guards for banks and armored cars), national defense and security, certain portions of the pharmaceutical industry, some business-conducted investigations involving theft and fraud, and law enforcement agencies.[88] A national study found that even when combining the use of polygraphs and CVSAs, only 29 percent of the law enforcement agencies responding to the survey used them in the selection process.[89]

Studies of the accuracy of the polygraph and the CVSA vary considerably; to some degree this is due to the research design, whether the subjects were students playing a role versus "real-world" applications, and the training and experience of examiners. A National Academy of Sciences analysis labeled the evidence supporting the polygraph weak and lacking scientific rigor.[90] Still, other studies place its accuracy between 64 percent and 98 percent; the reports of CVSA accuracy are similar to those of the polygraph.[91]

In several federal court circuits, there has been somewhat of a relaxation of the practice of automatically barring lie detection results, although the clear majority view is that the scientific evidence is not sufficiently substantial.[92] Some state courts admit lie detection evidence if the parties to a proceeding stipulate to its admission prior to the test being administered; New Mexico allows its admission in state courts as scientific evidence.[93]

Consistent with the EPPA, when a lie detector is used with police applicants, it is primarily to verify the information on their detailed personal history questionnaire. In addition, applicants are asked an additional set of questions that are standard in each jurisdiction but vary somewhat across law enforcement agencies. Examples of these include whether they have ever used a different name or social security number, received an unfavorable work evaluation, been paid for work "under the table" or "off the books," used illegal drugs while working, falsified a time sheet, shoplifted or switched price tags, been involved in a fight, carried a weapon illegally, driven without a license or insurance, received a major discipline on a previous job, or been involved with a group that advocates violence, hate, racial prejudice, terror, or subversive activities. Thus, a lie detector examination mechanism is primarily used to (1) verify personal history information and (2) probe for particular things that may require special attention by the background/character investigator.

During lie detection examinations, applicants may be disqualified for deception, using countermeasures, or admitting actions that disqualify them (e.g., thefts and acts of family violence). Except for these reasons or closely allied ones, eliminating a candidate solely on the basis of a lie detection examination is not a good practice. Two large studies placed the passing rate for polygraph examinations at 63 percent and 70 percent.[94]

In *Mullen v. County of Suffolk* (2007), a polygraph examiner determined that a police officer applicant to the Ocean Beach (New York) Police Department was deceptive in responding to questions about his drug involvement.[95] The applicant was disqualified from further consideration and appealed that decision. The court ordered the polygraph evidence reviewed. The record was independently evaluated by the Vermont State Police, which concurred with the initial findings, and the plaintiff's suit was dismissed.

The background/character investigation is a specialized type of investigation and one best learned through training and the guidance of more experienced personnel. Like other types of

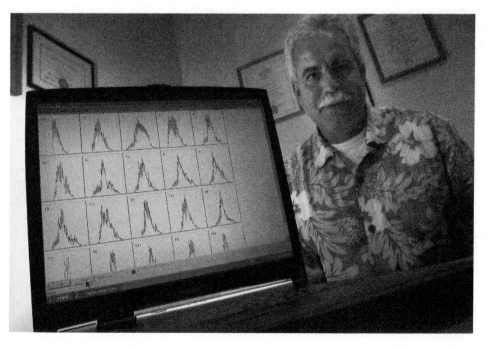

FIGURE 9.6 ▶ A San Diego Sheriff's Department Detective sits near a Computer Voice Stress Analyzer (CVSA) used to screen applicants seeking to be employed with that agency. The CVSA screening verifies statements made on the employment application and identifies areas that need further attention by the department's background investigators. (Dan Trevan/U-T San Diego/ZUMA Press/Newscom)

investigations, it requires strong attention to detail and executing all required steps. The first step is to review the applicant's personal history questionnaire and the findings of the lie detector examination. Combined, these documents will key the investigator to contradictions, inconsistency in details, admissions made that need to be discussed with the candidate, and other matters.

Prior to the initial meeting with the applicant, the investigator should prepare a series of questions to probe areas of concern and have information release forms ready for the applicant to sign (e.g., education, military, and credit). Any documents that the applicants are required to present should be copied and the originals returned to the applicant. The copies should be dated and countersigned by the applicant and the assigned investigator so it is clear where the documents came from and who received them. Documents that agencies commonly request from applicants include a current color photograph signed on the back, birth certificate/naturalization order, divorce decree, name change, social security card, restraining orders, selective service card (if subject to the draft), DD 214 record of military service, passport, driver's license, and POST training record if presently or previously serving as a peace officer in another state.

Even when presented with apparently genuine documents, verification of them is essential. An applicant submitted his documents, including an original DD 214. In the initial meeting with the applicant, the investigator asked about the three-month employment gap between his honorable discharge from the Coast Guard and his application to the law enforcement agency. The man related he and his wife had taken an extended vacation to "see the country." Nonetheless, the investigator had the man sign a military records release form. Once received, the record showed that the applicant had been separated from the Coast Guard twice. The first DD 214 was accurate in all respects. However, there had been no extended vacation. Several weeks after being discharged the applicant reenlisted and shortly thereafter weeks later was drunk, beat his wife badly, and assaulted the military authorities who came to his on-base quarters to handle a domestic disturbance complaint. The applicant told the investigator that he gambled his DD 214 would be accepted at face value or that the record of his second enlistment and dishonorable discharge would never be discovered.

Other aspects of the background investigation include checking references and interviewing family, friends, roommates, coworkers, landlords, neighbors, spouse and/or a former spouse, and such others as the investigator feels necessary. Prior to writing the final report on the candidate, it might be necessary to have a second interview to resolve any lingering questions. A study found that 8 percent of the applicants making it to the background stage are eliminated.[96]

The Oral Board

Oral board panelists cannot ask whatever suits them and then simply subjectively evaluate applicants; in the past, such shoddy practices were so rampant that Doerner characterized police oral interviews as a fallible practice that had outlasted their usefulness,[97] and Gaines and Lewis concluded that they were the largest source of errors in making decisions about people.[98] The use of oral boards has improved substantially over the past several decades, although there are still some jurisdictions whose use of entry and promotional oral boards lags behind best and legal practices.

An applicant oral board often has three members, one of whom may represent the central personnel officer or community and two who are supervisors in the law enforcement agency to which the candidate has applied. To satisfy legal requirements, the questions asked must be job related and not be impermissible. "Tell us about your writing skills; how good do you think they are?" or "Would you describe a time when you got really angry?" would be established as job related by any competent job analysis. In contrast, "When is your baby due?" or "What provisions will you make for child care?" may lead to a charge that the Pregnancy Protection Act and Title VII were violated if the person is not hired and otherwise qualified.[99]

The length of an oral board varies across agencies but often falls in the 20- to 45-minute range. The members must be adequately trained in using a well-developed scoring system and the questions must have been validated. Although shorter training times are common, eight hours of it, including the opportunity to evaluate multiple mock applicants, should provide the skills needed by panel members and a good level of defensibility if the adequacy of training is challenged. A good training method to calibrate the scoring by oral board members to the standards desired is to make digital motion pictures of the performance of six or so mock candidates and have experts make a written record of important behaviors noted and translate them into scores. When the actual board members are evaluating the same motion pictures, the written behavioral comments and scores of the experts and the board members are compared with the goal of having the behaviors noted and scores converge during the training.

As questions are asked at an oral board, each member makes his or her own notes. When the candidate leaves the room, each member reviews his or her own notes and translates them into a whole number score. As a protocol, every score of board members on each skill involved, such as oral communication, must be within one point. When there are discrepancies greater than that, the panel discusses the applicant's behavior until the discrepancy is resolved.

A portion of a scoring sheet for oral communication is shown in Table 9.5. A training manual provided to each panel member gives substantial guidance as to the exact types of behavior that place an applicant in each score level.

Conditional Job Offer

The **conditional job offer (CJO)** is a letter from the employing agency to the applicant offering a job contingent upon there being a funded position available and the applicant passing the medical, drug, and psychological screening. A CJO is usually

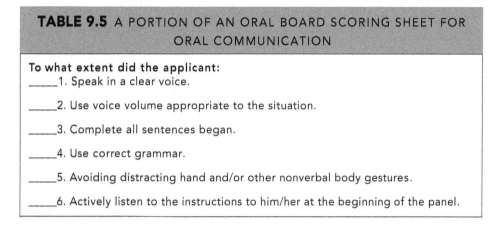

TABLE 9.5 A PORTION OF AN ORAL BOARD SCORING SHEET FOR ORAL COMMUNICATION

To what extent did the applicant:

_____1. Speak in a clear voice.

_____2. Use voice volume appropriate to the situation.

_____3. Complete all sentences began.

_____4. Use correct grammar.

_____5. Avoiding distracting hand and/or other nonverbal body gestures.

_____6. Actively listen to the instructions to him/her at the beginning of the panel.

extended only to the best qualified/most competitive candidates. An agency may not know exactly how many positions it has available because the new budget has not been finalized, and resignations, retirements, and terminations may be more or fewer than projected; thus, the need to condition the offer on a position being available.

The Medical Examination, Drug Test, and Psychological Screening

The purpose of this phase is to ensure that applicants can medically and psychologically perform the essential functions of a law enforcement officer. Some state POSTs have validated standards for medical, drug, and psychological screening. The exact sequence of these three tests varies and are often outsourced. In addition to the usual components of a health examination, an audio test is conducted to verify that candidates meet hearing standards. Vision is tested for acuity, narrowing, and color deficiency. Vision acuity must be correctable to a reasonable standard, such as 20/30. Drug screening is based on urine samples, although a handful of agencies use hair analysis, which can reveal drug use over a longer period of time.[100] The physical assessment test may be a surrogate for the medical examination; a study found that 95 percent of those who passed the PAT also passed the medical examination.[101]

Psychological tests used in police selection vary, although the Minnesota Multiphasic Personality Inventory (MMPI) is commonly used. The 2019 revision of it was designated MMPI-3 and builds on the history, research base, and strengths of the original MMPI first developed in 1942. It has 338 questions and can be administered in 30–50 minutes, about half the time for previous MMPI editions.[102]

The Inwald Personality Inventory (IPI) was developed for use with public safety officers and is not used with other high-risk occupations. It has gained supporters over the past two decades and is designed specifically for use in law enforcement agencies. A study found that combining the results from the MMPI-2 (an earlier edition of the MMPI-3), IPI, and Costa and McCrae's Neo Personal Inventory-Revised (Neo) contributed significantly to predicting recruit academy success.[103]

Psychological tests may be followed by up to a one-hour interview with a licensed clinical psychologist or a psychiatrist.

The Formal Offer of Employment

At this point in the selection process, there is a completed file for each applicant documenting the results of the selection process. The appointing authority ultimately decides on those to whom a formal offer of employment will be made, although civil service rules, union contracts, and politics may influence those decisions. In larger law enforcement agencies, the names on the formal offer list will have been compiled by a staff member for the chief's or sheriff's approval. As the size of the agency decreases, the probability increases that the chief executive of the agency has a more personal hand in picking many of those to whom a job offer will be extended.

The Recruit Academy

Based on a single major analysis, 12 percent of those taking the entrance exam make it to the academy; there is no significant difference between the success rates of men and women in it. Those with at least some college enter the academy at a marginally higher rate than those with a high school degree, as do applicants in their thirties compared to younger candidates. Among ethnic/racial groups, the ability to get into the academy ranged from 16 to 22 percent, with African-Americans lagging other groups.[104] Eighty-eight percent of males successfully completed academy training as compared to 81 percent of females.[105]

The length and content of the recruit academy/basic course is established by each state's Peace Officers Standards and Training Commission (POST). Individual law enforcement agencies can require training beyond the minimum established. The basic POST course in Texas is 618 hours, about 15.5 weeks, whereas the Austin Police Department operates a 32-week police academy with 1,280 hours on instruction. The national average for POST mandated entry training is 588 hours.[106]

Nationally, there are 626 academies providing entry-level training, employing 12,200 full-time instructors and about twice that number in part-time faculty.[107] Recruit academies must be certified by their state's POST. They may be operated by mid-sized to larger departments that allow smaller agencies to use a few seats at a nominal fee, by vocational/technical schools, community colleges, and by university police departments as a service to agencies in their region. If a state has a central police training facility, it may do some basic training, although the main effort of this type of facility is often focused on advanced/specialized courses. POSTs also require the completion of annual training to remain certified as a peace officer, with the national average being 24 hours.[108]

A study of 250 police academies concluded they failed to provide adequate training to investigate child sexual abuse.[109] The same criticism could also be made of preparation for other types of offenses (e.g., of white collar and organized crime, homeland security threats, human trafficking, and kidnapping). Almost any academy subject could benefit from additional training hours, but some useful topics simply cannot be squeezed into the overall time available. The academy's objective is to produce an adequate or better beginning generalist; within the resources available, often every additional hour added to one subject must be taken from some other subject area.

Police cadets socialize and drink more with their fellow recruits as compared with their previous circle of friends.[110] Scarfo found a significant relationship between education and police academy scores; however, military experience was not related to academy performance.[111] In a comparison between a traditional academy and one oriented toward community policing, more educated officers and women did better in the latter although overall recruits from both types of academies performed similarly.[112]

If a police academy is accredited with the Veterans Administration, veterans benefits can be used while attending it. A number of academies also have arrangements for trainees to earn college credits upon successful completion.

The New York City Police Department began a $1.5 billion project to develop a new police academy that will also be used for advanced training.[113] When fully developed, the new facility will look like a small city, including five-story buildings, a tactical village with movable walls so cadets cannot memorize the course, and a firearms range. Outdoors, trainees will be put through trench collapse and other scenarios. The facilities provide the setting to make a shift from predominately classroom-based instruction to more hands-on scenario training. The first phase of construction was completed at a cost of $750 million. In January 2015, the first academy class began at the new facility with 800 trainees.

Probationary to Career Status

The probationary period is the last step in the entry-level selection process and the opportunity to observe the recruit under actual work conditions. In many jurisdictions, probationary periods can be extended, although most often that flexibility is not needed. The length of police probationary periods and when they start varies (see Table 9.6), although one year following graduation from the police academy may be typical. Nationally, 4 percent of probationary officers are rejected.[114]

Following completion of the recruit academy, a probationary police officer is placed in a field training program to prepare officers to function on their own. The national average length for POST-mandated field training programs is 147 hours[115] although many jurisdictions have longer ones.

Officers in training (OITs) ride with a **field training officer (FTO)** whose primary responsibility is to demonstrate skills from a checklist and then develop the OIT's proficiency to perform them by certain points in the program (e.g., perform 25 traffic stops correctly by the end of week 4). FTOs are experienced officers; in many states, they must complete a POST-required certification course to ensure they are qualified for their duties.

The Mesa, Arizona Police Department (MPD), has a nationally recognized 19-week FTO program.[116] OITs are rotated through the department's patrol districts and must be supervised by at least three different FTOs. Daily Observation Reports (DORs) are completed by FTOs and become the basis for the Sergeant's Weekly Report (SWR) on each OIT under his or her supervision. OITs may acquire the needed proficiencies before the end of the 19-week program. If so, they are allowed to ride solo, although the supervising sergeant continues to fill out SWRs. In the MPD and elsewhere, those successfully completing the OIT program will be recommended for career status.

TABLE 9.6 ILLUSTRATIVE PROBATIONARY PERIOD LENGTHS	
Law Enforcement Agency	**Length**
Anchorage, Alaska	One year from the end of field training period, but not longer than 18 months from the date of hire.
Marion, Iowa	One year from date of hire
St. Paul, Minnesota	One year from Police Academy graduation
Wauchula, Florida	Six months, beginning with the first day assigned to a Field Training Officer
Montpelier, Vermont	Nine months, although the chief may extend it for three months. If the City fails to write a final probationary evaluation, the employee is deemed to have completed it satisfactorily

WORK GENERATIONS AND THE NEW RECRUITING

Recruits entering law enforcement have been shaped by forces such as their genetic predispositions and life experiences. After their academy training, the "locker room wisdom" is passed on to them, and they become socialized into the norms of the agency. In short, police work changes people. This section explores several generations of recruits who have entered law enforcement. While it is true that law enforcement agencies still change people and that, to a degree, each generation has changed policing, the more recent generations must be recruited with new messages attuned to their skills and values, as well as more generous benefits.

The Silent Generation

Born between 1925 and 1945, the **Silent Generation** is generally loyal, security conscious, and conforming.[117] They were born from the Great Depression until the end of World War II; as adults, many of the men served in the military and, like the women they married, they believe in the American way of life. The silent generation, with perhaps a rare exception, has passed through their law enforcement careers and retired. Recruiting members of this generation to jobs in police departments and supervising them did not present unusual challenges because of their experiences and values.

The Baby Boomers

Baby boomers have turned gray and are at or beyond normal retirement years, but are often reluctant to retire; 39 percent do not plan to retire until 66 or older and another 10 percent say they will never retire.[118] Born during 1946–1964, after millions of men and women returned home from the war, boomers grew up during a period of widespread social change. Early boomers personally experienced the unfolding of rock and roll, military service during the Vietnam War, civil rights demonstrations, the proliferation of drug use, assassinations, and all of the other manifestations of the turbulent 1960s (see Chapter 1, The Evolution of Police Administration). With some college or more, boomers are better educated and more liberal than their parents. As teenagers and young adults, they challenged conventional values, with the slogan "Never trust anyone over 30." Still, they were influenced by the strong work ethic of their parents. Ultimately goal and achievement oriented, the boomers are work focused and sacrificed, including some neglect of their families, to get ahead in their careers. Women had more career opportunities. Divorces were sometimes followed by second marriages to "start another family and get it right." Overall, 27 percent of baby boomers never married.[119]

Police departments did not hire boomers who admitted, or were discovered during the character/background investigation, to having used drugs. This eliminated some otherwise outstanding candidates, some of whom experimented with drugs while in the military. Eventually, departments softened their stance on drug use, although use of "hard" drugs was still an automatic disqualifier. Boomers were at the forefront as college education became more common in policing. Some supervisors routinely gave "college boys" lower performance appraisals than their less-educated counterparts. Sergeants were annoyed by the boomers' "disturbing tendency" to ask why things had to be done a certain way. To accommodate officers attending college, some received special work schedules, further irritating their routine-oriented supervisors. Authoritarian middle-managers were aggravated by the periodic written suggestions boomers submitted to improve operations, regarding them as a lack of respect for "proven methods." Eventually, the boomers proved their worth, even to skeptics, rising through the ranks to senior leadership positions with new styles of leadership. There are 30 million more boomers than the number of the next generation of workers, the "Xers."[120] When boomers finally retire it will create a loss of experience and institutional memory.

Generation X

Presently, **Generation X** makes up a large number of officers employed by police agencies. Many of them have retired and some are approaching or are in the tail end of their careers.[121] Birthed from 1965 to 1980, Xers are more ethnically diverse than boomers, grew up in families where both parents worked, and were the first generation of "latch-key" children.[122] More than one-half have divorced parents and one-third were physically or sexually abused, often by a stepparent.[123] Drive-by shootings, abortions, AIDS, school violence, and missing children were also part of their lives. Technologically, Xers tend to be computer fluent.

Early Xers grew to adulthood in a mixed economy; as toddlers their nation's economy was sound, but turned sour during the 1970s with stagflation. Stagflation, or a stagnant economy, is produced by a combination of a high unemployment and high inflation. It resulted in interest rates hitting 21.5 percent in 1980. As a result of stagflation, there was a noticeable migration of Xers back to their parents' homes to make ends meet.[124] The economic instability left Xers with concerns about their financial circumstances and retirement and with good reason: They are the first generation predicted to have a lower standard of living than that of their parents.[125] Xers marry later, delay having children, and expect their spouses to work; the women place a great emphasis on the family life many of them missed and are less inclined to sacrifice their families for career gain as the boomers did.[126] Rejecting the political platforms of the major parties, most Xers are independents (43 percent), followed by Democrats (30 percent) and Republicans (27 percent).[127] The three leading causes of death for Xers are automobile accidents, homicide, and suicide.[128]

Xers have been branded in various ways, including crybabies, grunge, and the lost generation. They have also been described in positive ways, including clear sighted, practical, intelligent, curious, good strategists and negotiators, seeing the whole person—not just the good or bad qualities, comfortable with diversity, and voracious learners.[129] There is some truth to these various characterizations because Xers are less homogeneous than boomers.

A Census Bureau study identified Xers' core values as equality, honesty, and respect in dealing with others, hard work, family values, and a sense of public service, which leads them to be high in volunteerism for social causes such as homelessness and social harmony.[130]

In the work setting, Xers have been restless; they welcome change and move from one employer to improve their financial circumstances and to be where they can make lasting contributions. At some point, Xers will run out of the number of times they can shift from one job to another and many settle down into something more like a conventional career as opposed to a succession of jobs with different employers. Managed properly they will go the extra mile and beyond to get things done well but will resist being micro-managed; given job autonomy, they are determined to succeed.[131]

Many police departments adapted their recruiting messages to attract Gen Xers, including (1) ensuring that the recruiting messages and their cultures are aligned to avoid turnover with repeated recruitment, screening, selection, and training costs; (2) communicating that policing is a noble, exciting public service career; (3) emphasizing that there are many career paths in law enforcement that will require life-long learning in order to be effective, giving them a sense of possibilities about their futures;[132] (4) highlighting that their sense of self-reliance is a substantial asset for them and their department; (5) illustrating how the Xers' skills at multitasking can be used; (6) underscoring that they will often be working without direct supervision, giving them desired flexibility and freedom in carrying out their job responsibilities;[133] and (7) giving them examples of how suggestions made by departmental members have improved operations.

As Xers entered law enforcement, some of their sergeants quickly noticed two characteristics that required attention: (1) their propensity to innovate occasionally made them somewhat resistant to supervision; sergeants lamented "I can tell them what to do until I'm blue in the face and they still do some part of the job their own damned way" and (2) their strong self-reliance and individuality led some patrol division Xers to emphasize a single or small number of duties, such as DUI enforcement, neglecting their broader responsibilities.

Generation Y: The Millenniums

Born during 1981–1994 and largely the children of baby boomers, **Generation Y** babies are entering our law enforcement agencies. The "Yers" have also been called the Millenniums, dot com babies, and "thumbers" because of the speed with which they can text message (see Figure 9.7). Less favorably, they have been tagged as Kids in Parents Pockets or "KIPPers," a slap at certain Yers prolonged dependence on their family of origin. Some of this dependency is created by overly supportive parents who get in the way of their children's journey to living as independent adults.

Raised in an era of gaming and rising modes of instant communication, social network sites (SNSs) have become a staple for Yers, including MySpace (2003), Facebook (2004), and Twitter (2006); they cruise Craigslist ads and subscribe to Internet dating services like Match.com (1995) and eHarmony (2005). Some SNSs target Yers, such as BrazenCareerist and MyYearBook, giving them forums to discuss their careers and workplace issues.

They are more optimistic than Xers, seek a better balance between work and the rest of their lives, have high expectations for their employers, enjoy diversity and challenges, prefer teamwork over individual efforts, feel a need to volunteer and fund-raise, desire honest feedback about their job performance,

FIGURE 9.7 ▶ A Generation Y student using the "thumber technique" to text. (Biddy O'Neill/Corbis/VCG/Getty Images)

Quick Facts: Use of Social Networking Sites (SNS)

Research by the Pew Research Center reveals SNS use in the United States is substantial: 76 percent of women and 74 of males use them. Eighty-five percent of those 18–49 are on SNS, but only 56 percent of those 65 or older are. In contrast, during an 18-month period between 2005 and 2006, the percentage of people 18–29 years old using SNS jumped from 9 percent to 49 percent.

SNS use is greater among those with a higher income, younger people, African-Americans, and Hispanics. Smartphones and tablets are key pieces of technology fueling the rise of SNS. A slight majority of SNS users, 52 percent, are on two or more sites.[135]

Worldwide, the four most popular SNS are (1) Facebook (1,100,000,000 users), (2) Twitter (310,000,000), (3) LinkedIn (255,000,000), and (4) Pinterest (250,000,000).[136]

Prensky coined the term "digital natives" to describe those raised in the immediate availability of information and images on the Internet. Later, the term came to be loosely defined as those born in 1980 and thereafter, a period that coincides with the beginning of Generation Y.

In 2015, the International Association of Chiefs of Police (IACP) released the results of a survey of 553 responding law enforcement agencies revealing 96 percent of them had an SNS presence. The most common use was for criminal investigations, for example soliciting leads for information or location of wanted persons (89 percent).[137]

Other uses made by law enforcement agencies using SNS include building a relationship and enhancing trust with the community being served, dissemination of information to protect the community, such as gas leaks in a neighborhood, school closings due to weather conditions, announcing where roadblocks will be set up in the future, recruiting, and missing persons information.

SNS can serve a key interest of governments generally and for police departments specifically in developing a reputation in the community for transparency.

and are unafraid to question authority. There is a trend toward traditional family values and Yers are spiritual about love, although not necessarily religious.[134]

Generations Z and Alpha

Generation Z, the "Zedders," fall in the birth range of 1995–2000 and now make up the bulk of young officers today. Some concerns have been expressed about their fascination with virtual realities that may lead to impoverished social and interpersonal skills. Beyond Zedders is the **Alpha Generation**, which will be the best educated of all of the generations and the most technologically sophisticated. Alphas are in their infancy with a birth cohort of 2011–2025.

The New Recruiting

The combination of Xers and Yers entering law enforcement has resulted in a better understanding that part of the process of recruiting officers might also be about recruiting their families, leading to the development of elaborate family information packages and videos about all aspects of a community, including job opportunities for spouses and departmental partnerships with children's day-care centers.

In addition to the usual benefits, such as life and disability insurance and deferred compensation plans, police recruiting tools have been elevated.[138] Although the practices of individual jurisdictions vary, officer incentives have become more varied[139] and may include relocation reimbursement; signing bonuses of $5,000 to $10,000; a stipend of $6,000 for graduation from the recruit academy and another $4,000 for completing the probationary period; allowing the use of GI Bill benefits while attending the academy; 45 or more college credits for academy completion; interest-free home loans up to $75,000 and forgiveness of home loans of up to $28,000 on the basis of 5 percent for each year of service;[140] increased vacation time and enhanced longevity pay and retirement systems. In some cities, officers retire with 20 years of service, based on 70 percent of the average of their three highest-paying years or 80 percent at 25 years. Some of these incentives "take a hit" in fiscally constrained environments; Los Angeles and Dallas are among large cities trimming such incentives.

Job flexibility and job sharing are used in law enforcement, but only to a small extent. Flexibility scheduling means that police departments present officers a choice of schedules within those established by the department; in contrast, job sharing means two or more officers share a single job.[141] Since 1999, the Orange County, California, Sheriff's Department has offered job sharing to its 4,000 members; the Huntington Beach, California, Police Department made it available to its 224 employees in 2001, and the Medina, Washington Police Department, allows 2 of its 12 members to job share. Job sharing reduces stress and absenteeism, increases job satisfaction, and allows valuable employees enough "wiggle room" to remain on the job.[142] For managing dwindling budgets and as a regular tool, job sharing may be attractive to personnel winding down their careers, as a prelude to their actual retirement. Used as a "decompression" period, job sharing would be beneficial in making the transition from work to retirement.

MILITARY CALL-UPS AND REINSTATEMENT

The substantial military commitments in Iraq and Afghanistan required the activation/call-up of National Guard and Reserve units as well as personnel in the Individual Ready Reserve (IRR), who do not participate in the two days a month "weekend drills" or the 14 days of annual training for unit members. While entire National Guard and Reserve units are called to active duty, members of the IRR are activated individually based on the need for their special skills, such as helicopter pilots.[143] Law enforcement officers from both categories have been activated.

How many law enforcement agencies have experienced personnel call-ups is somewhat of a question; two national studies came up with different answers: 21 percent and 44 percent.[144] In a 40-officer department, the loss of four officers represents a 10 percent drop in staffing, creating operational difficulties and generating overtime costs. Even in departments where call-ups have been minimal, the loss of a single key person can create an impact: In Youngstown, Ohio the SWAT Team's only qualified sniper was activated.[145] Some agencies have officers who have been deployed several times on tours of up to 16 months.

Administered by the USDOL, the purpose of the **Uniformed Services Employment and Reemployment Rights Act** (USERRA, 1994) is to encourage noncareer participation in the uniformed military service by eliminating barriers to such service, minimizing the disruption of the lives of those called to active duty, and prohibiting discrimination against them. The Palm Beach County (Florida) Police Benevolent Association filed a grievance when a deputy on military leave was allowed to take a promotional test elsewhere, asserting that the collective bargaining agreement made no allowance for such a test. The arbitrator found for the Sheriff's Office; the provisions of USERRA supersede collective bargaining agreements.[146]

Under USERRA, a police officer called to active duty must give advance notice of his pending absence to the department unless it is precluded by military necessity or otherwise impossible or unreasonable. The cumulative period of absence with that department cannot be longer than five years, and service separation cannot be under dishonorable or other punitive conditions. The officer must report back to duty on a timely basis or file a timely application for reemployment unless impossible or unreasonable.[147] Table 9.7 summarizes the reporting back to duty timelines.

> ### Quick Facts: The Five-Year Cumulative Absence
>
> An employer is legally obligated to support up to a five-year cumulative total of military service. However, not included in that total are: involuntary recall to active duty, drills for reserve and national guard (active "reserve") participation, training, annual training, and additional training requirements determined and certified in writing by the Service Secretary concerned to be necessary for professional development or for completion of skill training or retraining.

When called to active duty, officers can keep their individual and family health insurance for up to 24 months, although they may be required by their department to pay up to 102 percent of the full premium. USERRA also provides guidelines for seniority, pension, and other rights of returning officers who are returning from active duty call-up. The "escalator principle" requires reemployment at the position officers would have attained but for their military service. If the officer is not qualified for the escalator position, the employer must provide the nearest approximation to it or if that is not possible, to the premilitary service position.

Assuming the example of a state trooper called to active duty who misses a promotional examination, her employer is required to give her a make-up exam and promote her with back-dated seniority to the point she reasonably would have been expected to be advanced in rank.[148] A federal court approved a jury award of double-pay, $300,000 for emotional distress, and promotion without testing for a New York City Fire Department promotional candidate who was denied an opportunity for a make-up exam when the absence was due to his military service.[149]

TABLE 9.7 USERRA REPORTING OBLIGATIONS FOLLOWING MILITARY SERVICE	
Length of Service	**Reporting Requirement**
Service of 1 to 30 days	The beginning of the first regularly scheduled work day or 8 hours after the end of the military duty, plus reasonable commuting time from the military duty station to home
Service of 31 to 180 days	application for reinstatement must be submitted not later than 14 days after completion of military duty
Service of 181 or more days	application for reinstatement must be submitted not later than 90 days after completion of military duty

Source: Based on information from U.S. Department of Labor, No author, Your Rights Under Userra The Uniformed Services Employment and Reemployment Rights Act, undated, p. 1, http://www.dol.gov/vets/programs/userra/aboutuserra.htm#knowyourrights (accessed May 9, 2020).

The call-up of officers also raises some POST certification issues that should be included in an agency's policy on military activation. As an illustration, in Michigan, officers are not considered to have discontinued their law enforcement employment for license purposes, unless they voluntarily extended their active duty commitment. Upon return to their agencies, officers must provide a copy of their DD 214s (Certificate of Release or Discharge from Active Duty) or a DD 220 if the active duty lasts less than 90 days. If separated dishonorably, an investigation must be conducted to determine if the circumstances still allow POST licensing.

Activated officers may also be entitled to other rights under some state statutes and other federal laws (e.g., the federal **Servicemembers Civil Relief Act** [SCRA, 2003]). Some of SCRA's protections require that debts or leasing agreements entered into must predate the call to duty and the relief applying to them may be limited to the period during which the officer is on active duty or a short period thereafter. Key SCRA protections include (1) service members and their family members cannot be evicted from leased housing costing less than $2,932 monthly; (2) interest charged on debts cannot be greater than 6 percent; (3) if the officer receives permanent change of station orders, a housing lease can be terminated, if present at the new location for 90 days or more; (4) car leases can be terminated if the officer is called to duty for 180 days, or after entering the service, the officer executes a lease and is deployed outside of the continental United States for 180 days or more; (5) up to $250,000 of life insurance cannot be cancelled for nonpayment while on active duty; and (6) protections begin with the date of activation and may apply until as much as 180 days after return to civilian life.

Paul Sutton, a former police lieutenant, sued the City of Chesapeake, Virginia, claiming that contrary to USERRA he was denied reemployment after completing call-up service in the Coast Guard. Sutton had been employed with the police department from 1974 until he was activated in 2000. In 2007, he was denied reemployment and continued to serve on active duty until 2009, when he retired from the Coast Guard and litigated.

The federal court noted that Sutton had retired from the police department before going on active duty, cashing out his vacation and sick time, and that he began drawing a police pension. Sutton argued that his retirement should not be a barrier to reemployment. The court dismissed the suit, reasoning that to find for Sutton would be an expansion of rights beyond those contemplated by USERRA and his absence from the police department was greater than the law's five-year limitation.

Despite some difficulties created by a call-up of officers, law enforcement agencies are proud of their service. Such officers exhibit a strong commitment to our nation and often return with sharpened or new skills that are relevant to the police setting. However, inevitably someone will attempt to take advantage of a situation. A police officer claimed he was being called to active duty. However, the officer went to another city in the state and took a high-paying job in business. The employing agency continued to deposit money into the officer's bank account, reaching $8,700 before the scheme was discovered. Convicted of fraud, the officer lost his job and served a jail sentence of 90 days.[150]

EARLY INTERVENTION SYSTEMS

In reaction to public concerns about police abuse of force and the number of complaints being generated by some officers, early-warning systems (EWSs) began appearing in the late 1980s. The police departments of New York City, Oakland, Kansas City, Miami, and Miami Dade were early leaders in this movement.[151] Some law enforcement executives speculate that perhaps 10 percent of their officers cause 90 percent of the problems. Leaving aside speculation, it is true that a relatively small number of officers cause a lot of an agency's problems. Research somewhat supports this belief. An eight-year study of the San Francisco Police Department showed that of its 2,200 officers, just 100, roughly 5 percent of all sworn personnel, were associated with 25 percent of the use of force reports.[152]

EWS were subsequently modified and "rebadged" as **Early Identification and Intervention Systems (EIIS)**. In some agencies, EWS had developed a negative image with rank-and-file members because the term "problem officer" was closely associated with the program. In contrast, EIIS is framed as being a support system for officers and includes them in decision making.

Well-operated EIISs assumed even greater importance following the passage of the federal Violent Crime Control and Law Enforcement Act (1994). The Act authorizes the Attorney General to file lawsuits to reform police departments engaging in a pattern or practice of violating citizens' federal rights. Suits may also be brought by the Attorney General under the Omnibus Crime Control and Safe Streets Act (1968) and Title VII (1972) for discrimination by law enforcement agencies on the basis of race, color, sex, or national origin if they receive federal funds.[153]

Presently, many agencies have substituted the use of Early Intervention System (EI or EIS) for the EIIS designation. Whatever terminology is used, it is clear what began as the early warning system (EWS) has continued to evolve and mature.

About 40 percent of law enforcement agencies use EIs.[154] While manual EIs may work well in smaller departments, in larger agencies, the systems must be automated to be effective because of the volume of daily work that must be entered and analyzed. The Seattle Police Department's policy on their EI system/program characterizes it in the following ways.[155] It (1) is a risk management strategy that is neither punitive nor disciplinary in nature, which is separate from, but does not replace, the disciplinary system; (2) seeks to identify and change at-risk behaviors, although employees remain fully accountable for following policy and other performance standards; (3) supports officers by supervisors coaching, mentoring, performance feedback, identification of pathways to improve job performance, which may include appropriate training; (4) regards early identification information as confidential, except as may be required by law, policies, or union contract; (5) requires Sergeants, managers, and commanders to review early intervention thresholds at least weekly for their subordinates; (6) allows leaders to develop assessments before the preestablished threshold value has been not yet been reached if potentially problematic behavior is identified; (7) requires other leaders to review assessment reports and take appropriate action, such as developing a mentoring plan; and (8) provides that officers may review their files and report inaccuracies immediately to their supervisor.

The Phoenix, Arizona Police Department's (PPD) EI system is transparent. Officers can access their EIIS status online at any time and see where they stand in relation to the threshold standards that would trigger an EI identification, allowing them to be self-monitoring.[156]

Whenever a Phoenix officer is "tagged" by the EI, a case manager is automatically notified electronically. Case managers review each file to make sure that the identification is not a "false positive," an error. Once contacted, the actual supervisor of the officer involved has 21 days to complete the intervention review.[157] Officers are part of the intervention review process, helping to design the responses that are most helpful to them.

Ten years ago, only 27 percent of the agencies responding to a national survey reported using EIs, although that number is thought to be much higher now.[158] The number of variables tracked in an EI largely depends on whether it is a manual or automated system. Common variables include use of force reports, the ratio of use of force reports to arrests, the number of force incidents in which its use is questionable, citizen complaints, the numbers of resist arrests, the frequency of high-speed pursuits, assignment history, and disciplinary record. An EI system has "threshold values" that when reached result in an officer being "tagged" by the computer (e.g., two sustained citizen complaints in a three-month period or three in a year).[159]

The value of EIs is substantial: (1) it supports officers' desires to perform well, (2) it reduces the numbers of officers who might lose their jobs, (3) it protects the departments investments in its current workforce, and (4) it reduces or eliminates potential for officers' at-risk behaviors to advance to a legal liability or it damages the department's reputation in, and relationship with, the community. EIs have produced dramatic results in curbing citizen complaints and related performance indicators—the New Orleans Police Department reported a 62 percent drop in a single year.[160] Significant results from using EIs have also been reported in other countries; in Victoria, Australia, a 71 percent reduction over a 12-month period was achieved.[161]

DISCIPLINE

If law enforcement executives are to be held accountable for the performance of their agencies, they must have ways to control them. This system of controls is well-understood and includes staff inspections to make sure that policies are being followed; line inspection at roll call to verify officers are adhering to grooming, uniform, and other standards; financial audits; periodic evaluation of programs and units; and stringent selection procedures.

Discipline is part of the control system and, in some agencies, the wooden application of sanctions for violations of standards of conduct has made discipline synonymous with punishment—far from its actual meaning and intention. **Discipline** is related to three Latin words: (1) *disciplina,* or instruction to a disciple; (2) *discipulus,* or pupil; and (3) *discere,* or to learn, to acquire knowledge. Although discipline is often thought of as punishment, its core meaning is instruction. Police discipline serves important purposes: (1) modify/correct an officer's behavior, (2) deter future misconduct by the officer and other officers, (3) give departmental members notice that misconduct will not be condoned and communicate this stance to the public, (4) ensure the proper operation of the police department, (5) reinforcement of department values and standards, (6) reinforcement of training, (7) manage liability risks, and (8) establish respect for the disciplinary system by fair and impartial administration of it.[162] Not all investigations into alleged police conduct results in a disciplinary action. There are four possible outcomes to such investigations:

1. Unfounded: The investigation indicates that the subject officer's alleged actions relating to the Department policy, procedure, rule, regulation, or directive in question did not actually occur;

2. Exonerated: The investigation indicates that the alleged actions of the subject officer were within the policies, procedures, rules, regulations, and directives of the Department;

3. Not Sustained: There was insufficient evidence to either prove or disprove the allegation; and

4. Sustained: The subject officer's actions were found, by a preponderance of the evidence, to have been in violation of the Department policy, procedure, rule, regulation, or directive in question.[163]

By way of comparison, the "preponderance of evidence" standard to sustain an allegation against an officer is the lightest burden of proof in civil cases. In some states, the higher standard of "a clear and convincing" evidence in a civil case must be demonstrated. In a few states, the highest burden of proof in both civil and criminal cases is required, "beyond the exclusion of any reasonable doubt," the meaning of which is that no other logical explanation of the facts in the case is possible except as posited by the plaintiff or district attorney.

Standards of Conduct and Progressive Discipline

The standards of conduct for police officers are set forth in their oath of office; their agency's policies, rules, and regulations; local ordinances; state statutes; federal laws; and consent decrees (e.g., prohibition against racial profiling). In addition to departmental discipline, an officer's POST license may be in jeopardy in some fact situations (e.g., acts of **moral turpitude**, conduct that is contrary to honesty, justice, or good morals). Law enforcement agencies use a system of **progressive discipline**, incrementally increasing more serious penalties for transgressions. A progressive discipline system may include many of the following steps:

1. Verbal counseling;
2. Oral reprimand;
3. Written reprimand;
4. Monetary fine;
5. Transfer/reassignment;
6. Suspension without pay;
7. Loss of promotional opportunity;
8. Demotion; and
9. Termination.[164]

In some situations, progressive discipline is not possible and termination is the only reasonable course of action (e.g., an officer steals money from the informant fund or drugs from the evidence room). In some jurisdictions, monetary (e.g., New Jersey) fines may be used in lieu of a suspension when the absence of an officer is detrimental to public health, welfare, or safety; when the fine is restitution; or when the officer agrees to the fine.[165]

Administration of Discipline

Of necessity, the chief executive of a law enforcement agency must delegate the authority for discipline to individuals in the chain of command and to the professional standards/internal affairs (PS/IA) unit. Many agencies have clearly specified rules about what misconduct may be handled by the first-line supervisor, within a division, at the bureau level, or those that must be referred to PS/IA. In addition to unit commanders being required to refer more serious misconduct to PS/IA, such action may also be called for when officers from different divisions are involved. Criminal acts by officers employed by smaller law enforcement agencies are often investigated by an external agency, such as a nearby larger department or the state police. Larger agencies will usually refer such acts to their own investigative unit.

Entities outside of the department may also be involved in the disciplinary process. In some jurisdictions, civilian review boards (CRBs), and unions evaluate law enforcement agencies' completed internal affairs investigations and the chief's disciplinary decisions and may offer their own recommendation as to the appropriate sanctions. CRB members are usually appointed by the relevant local official, such as a mayor. CRBs can be relatively "toothless," with only the power to make recommendations. Alternatively, CRBs can receive complaints directly from the public, have an investigative staff and subpoena power, and are able to make disciplinary decisions on the cases that fall within the scope of their authority. Independent

monitors may be appointed by the mayor or other official or as part of a consent decree; they have no investigative power and their function is to scrutinize and report on the disciplinary process (e.g., why does it take so long to complete internal affairs investigations?). District attorneys do not want to prosecute police officers accused on a criminal act because they want to maintain a close working relationship with law enforcement agencies. In such cases, a special prosecutor may be temporarily hired for this purpose.

In addition to oral and written reprimands and suspensions, officers may lose privileges, such as (1) eligibility to work extra-duty assignments and grant provided overtime (e.g., driving while intoxicated checkpoints and patrol); (2) use of a take-home car; and (3) serving on specialty teams, such as scuba, search and rescue, canine, hostage negotiation, and SWAT.

All disciplinary actions are subject to review through the chain of command and may be appealed by the officer. Under collective bargaining agreements, disciplined officers may be able to grieve the action taken, potentially requiring a binding decision by a neutral arbitrator. A study analyzed 100 police cases selected at random from the Labor Arbitration Reports and compared them to another randomly selected 100 cases from nonlaw enforcement public agencies.[166] Law enforcement executives' disciplinary recommendations were sustained at a higher rate, suggesting better handling by them. An alternative explanation is that officers are held to a higher standard. A five-year study of arbitrator discipline decisions involving the Houston Police Department revealed that the sanctions being sought were reduced by a net amount of nearly 50 percent.[167]

Because much misconduct is relatively minor (e.g., violating grooming standards, being late to roll call, not keeping the department informed of current address, telephone number, and Internet address, writing on departmental walls, not providing a badge number and name to the person requesting it, maintaining desk in an unsatisfactory order, and ignoring a radio call), first-line supervisors play a primary role in the disciplinary process. This dictates that supervisors have substantial training in policies, forms, officers rights, and counseling techniques. On incidents referred to PS/IA, the first-line supervisor is no longer the key figure.

In cases of serious misconduct, the unit commander may immediately suspend officers pending the outcome of an investigation because (1) they are unfit for duty; (2) they would constitute a hazard to themselves or others if allowed to remain on the job; (3) the action is necessary to protect health, safety, order, or effective direction of services; or (4) they have been charged with a crime. Where immediate action is required in these situations, some law enforcement agencies often allow the first-line supervisor to place the officer on "temporary relief from duty," pending review by higher authority. Officers so relieved must ordinarily be advised of their duty status within 24 hours by the higher authority.

Officers may also be placed on administrative leave, with full pay and benefits, pending the completion of an investigation. In an unusual situation during 2010, an Arizona police chief was placed on administered leave as part of an ongoing inquiry into his leadership, including inconsistency in handling disciplinary actions.[168]

A barrier to PS/IA investigations continues to be the "blue wall," or code of silence. Although 83 percent of officers responding to a national survey rejected the notion that a code of silence is necessary for good policing, 25 percent reported whistle-blowing was not worth it and 67 percent indicated that those who report misconduct by their peers would get the "cold shoulder."[169] Fifty-two percent of the respondents said that it was not unusual to turn a blind eye toward improper conduct by other officers and 61 percent disagreed with the statement that police officers always report serious criminal violations involving abuse of authority by fellow officers.[170]

One study concluded that officers with at least some college were not better behaved than those with a high school degree.[171] A larger Florida analysis indicated that high school graduates made up about 50 percent of all law enforcement officers in the state but accounted for 75 percent of all disciplinary actions.[172] Among those who lost their POST certification, high school graduates were disproportionately represented also: 76 percent versus 12 percent for those with a bachelor's or higher degree.[173] An analysis of discipline in the New York City Police Department found no evidence of race, gender, or national origin bias.[174] In an unnamed large-city police agency, minorities were overrepresented in documented complaints, specifically those initiated by fellow officers and supervisors.[175]

In 2015, Hickman and Poore completed a study of complaints against police use of force. Part of that study was a review of the literature, which revealed:

1. A relatively small proportion of officers are responsible for a large proportion of complaints, but this has generally been linked to arrest activity and other measures of productivity;

2. On-view incidents and more "proactive" policing assignments may be more likely to lead to complaints than dispatched calls;

3. Minority citizens complain in numbers disproportionately greater than their representation in the population served, and this is particularly true for black citizens;

4. Minority officers are disproportionately the subject of citizen complaints, as well as internal (police-initiated) complaints;

5. There is wide variation in sustain rates across agencies, some of which is attributable to structural differences, but also to idiosyncrasies in the processing of complaints;

6. In general, sustain rates are lower for physical force complaints as compared to other types of complaints; and

7. Internal (police-initiated) complaints tend to have higher sustain rates than citizen complaints.[176]

The Discipline Matrix

The perceived or actual unfairness of discipline is a long-standing problem in law enforcement agencies. In traditional disciplinary systems, this condition has been exacerbated because (1) fact situations may appear the same or similar on the surface, but the variance in individual circumstances leads to lesser or greater sanctions, which have gone unexplained and (2) variance in the disciplinary measures taken by supervisors was seen as part of the essential discretion they needed to deal with misconduct. As a matter of informal practice in many traditional discipline departments, a probationary officer late to roll call is not likely to "catch a break" while a veteran officer with "credits" in the agency may "get by with a hard look or word or two" from some supervisors.

A **discipline matrix** is a formal schedule for disciplinary actions, specifying both the presumptive or presumed sanction to be imposed for misconduct and any reduction or increase in the presumptive sanction for mitigating or aggravating factors (see Table 9.8).[177] Its primary purpose is to develop consistency in discipline, eliminating disparities and ensuring those who commit similar acts of misconduct will be sanctioned *equally*, as adjusted for *fairness* based on their mitigating and aggravated circumstances.[178] Discipline matrixes incorporate the concept of progressive discipline.

A matrix system identifies categories of conduct or perhaps more accurately, misconduct; a typical figure *number of categories* seems to be six (see Table 9.9, with categories A–F). As partially illustrated in Table 9.10, under each category are lists of what policies, procedures, rules, or regulations fall within it. Sanctions to be imposed are also associated with each category (see Table 9.10) and may run from Level 1 (least serious, oral or written reprimand) to the highest level, termination, which Table 9.10 does not illustrate.

In actual use multiple tables are used in a matrix system; for purposes of illustration, Table 9.12 combines them, showing their interaction. If two or more charges against an officer arise from a single incident, a decision is made as to which one is the primary.

Matrix systems have been opposed by officers and unions when they have not been included in their development. In a few jurisdictions, there have been complaints by officers that supervisors have not been held to the same degree of accountability. Other critics wonder about the fairness of rank being an aggravation factor. When all is said and done, matrix systems are a leap forward and traditional discipline agencies should take a close look at them.

Legal Aspects of Discipline

Disciplining police officers also has a legal component to it; illustratively, to prevent disciplinary abuses, many states have enacted police officer bill of rights legislation; content related to discipline is also commonly included in collective bargaining agreements; and except for narrow restrictions in some areas, officers retain all of their Constitutional rights. These and related topics are covered in Chapter 14, Legal Aspects of Police Administration.

TABLE 9.8 ILLUSTRATIONS OF MITIGATING AND AGGRAVATING CIRCUMSTANCES

Mitigating circumstances may include, but are not limited to:

1. Willingness to accept responsibility and acknowledge wrongdoing;
2. The circumstances under which the rule was violated;
3. The culpable mental state of the officer in the commission of the violation;
4. Complimentary history, including awards, commendations and positive public recognition;
5. If minimal, the severity of the current offense and the lack of or minimal nature of any consequences caused by the current offense;
6. Prior work history, such as positive evaluations and/or work performance, or voluntary, advanced, job-related training; and/or
7. Minimal or lack of prior disciplinary history relative to the officer's years of service.

Aggravating circumstances may include, but are not limited to:

1. Injury or harm to a member of the public or an officer;
2. Endangerment to a member of the public or an officer;
3. The existence of an actual and demonstrable legal or financial risk to the department or the city (including, but not limited to, cases involving allegations of civil rights violations, unlawful search and seizure, excessive use of force or unlawful detention or arrest);
4. The supervisory or command rank of the officer who committed the violation. It is appropriate that the department have higher expectations for supervisors and commands officers and that they exercise greater judgement and restraint than subordinates;
5. The officer's prior disciplinary history;
6. Actual and demonstrable prejudice to the department;
7. Jeopardizing the department's mission and/or relationship with other agencies;
8. Loss or damage to city or private property;
9. A criminal conviction of the involved officer arising out of the underlying event;
10. Dishonesty on the part of the officer;
11. Prejudicial conduct regarding race, color, creed, national origin, ancestry, gender/sex (including pregnancy, childbirth, or caregiver status), sexual orientation, age, religion, political affiliation, physical or mental disability, military status, marital status, or other protected classifications;
12. Harassment or retaliatory conduct;
13. The culpable mental state of the officer in the commission of the violation; and/or
14. Unsatisfactory work history.

Source: These points are drawn with restatement and consolidation from the Denver Police Department, *Discipline Handbook*, revised September 6, 2012, pp. 23–24, https://www.denvergov.org/content/dam/denvergov/Portals/744/documents/handbooks/DPD_Handbook_Revised_9-6-2012.pdf (accessed May 13, 2016).

PERFORMANCE APPRAISAL

Performance appraisals are sworn by and at. Supporters claim that they are essential and detractors label them as "annual rituals," a "global scourge,"[179] and are based on the erroneous assumption that the supervisors completing them have sufficient relevant information to complete them accurately and do so without any bias or prejudice.

Assuming that the performance of individuals does not vary greatly, it is reasonably expected that their ratings would remain relatively stable. However, a study of 6,000 business employees reporting simultaneously to two different bosses revealed ratings ranging from "very weak" to "outstanding." Sixty-two percent of those receiving "outstanding" evaluations from the first boss got lower scores from their other boss.[180] This finding may reflect that one boss did not get as much effort as the other one; the duties were different and when working for one boss the

duties were not a good fit for the skill set for the employee; or flaws in the performance appraisal system itself.

A majority of 393 constables, sergeants, and staff sergeants surveyed across 15 Canadian cities reported that their performance appraisal system was "deficient."[181] Officers did not receive regular feedback during the rating period, had little or no input into the evaluation, the supervisors were not sufficiently trained in evaluation, and personality often triumphed over actual performance criteria.

The truth is that getting a performance appraisal system to have real meaning requires a substantial organizational commitment, a stream of informal feedback, good supervisory record keeping, employee participation, validated forms, and rater training. In broad terms, the purpose of ratings is to (1) reinforce organizational values, (2) have a basis for impartial personnel decisions, (3) reinforce performance expectations, (4) stimulate performance, (5) identify the officers' training needs,

TABLE 9.9 CATEGORIES OF CONDUCT IN A DISCIPLINE MATRIX

Category	Definition
A	Conduct that has a minimal negative impact on the operations or professional image of the department.
B	Conduct that has more than minimal negative impact on the operations or professional image of the department; or that negatively impacts relationships with other officers, agencies or the public.
C	Conduct that has a pronounced negative impact on the operations or professional image of the department; or on relationships with other officers, agencies, or the public.
D	Conduct that is substantially contrary to the values of the department or that substantially interferes with its mission, operations or professional image, or that involves a demonstrable serious risk to officer or public safety.
E	Conduct that involves the serious abuse or misuse of authority, unethical behavior, or an act that results in an actual serious and adverse impact on officer or public safety, or to the professionalism of the department.
F	Any violation of law, rule or policy which: foreseeably results in death or serious bodily injury to another person; or constitutes a willful and wanton disregard of department values; or involves any act which demonstrates a serious lack of the integrity, ethics or character related to an officer's fitness to hold the position of police officer; or involves egregious misconduct substantially contrary to the standards of conduct reasonably expected of one whose sworn duty is to uphold the law; or involves any conduct which constitutes the failure to adhere to any contractual condition of employment or requirement of certification mandated by law.

Source: Denver Police Department, *Discipline Handbook (2020)*, pp. 16–17.

TABLE 9.10 PARTIAL ILLUSTRATION OF RELATIONSHIP AMONG A CONDUCT CATEGORY À, POLICIES, LEVELS OF DISCIPLINE, AND SANCTIONS

Category A: Conduct that has a minimal negative impact on the operations or professional image of the department or that negatively impacts with other officers, agencies, or the public.

Policy Involved	1st Violation in Four Years	2nd Violation in Four Years	3rd Violation in Four Years
Giving testimonials, seeking publicity	Discipline level 1	Discipline level 2	Discipline level 3
Use of tobacco in police facilities	Discipline level 1	Discipline level 2	Discipline level 3
Personal appearance in court	Discipline level 1	Discipline level 2	Discipline level 3
Testifying in civil cases	Discipline level 1	Discipline level 2	Discipline level 3
Sanctions Table			
Mitigation	Not applicable	Oral reprimand	Written reprimand to 1 fined day
Presumptive	Oral reprimand	Written reprimand	2 fined days
Aggravated	Written reprimand	1–3 fined days	4–6 fined days

Source: Drawn from the Denver Police Department, *Discipline Handbook (2020)*, Appendix F, pp. 1–2.

and (6) extend recognition to those who perform their duties well. The results of performance appraisals are used to determine or influence:

1. pay raises;
2. eligibility for promotion;
3. shift bids/duty assignments;
4. career development decisions (e.g., attendance at the FBI National Academy);
5. eligibility for reinstatement;
6. layoffs/reduction in force decisions; and
7. terminations.

Officers satisfactorily completing their probationary periods are awarded career status and cannot be terminated except for serious misconduct. During financial emergencies, career-status officers can be furloughed indefinitely. Career-status officers are commonly rated once annually by their immediate supervisors. However, special circumstances may cause an evaluation to be written on an other than annual basis: (1) officer resignations and terminations and (2) transfers to another unit and promotions may trigger a probationary requirement for monthly or quarterly evaluations for a year.

In preparing a standard evaluation form, a supervisor considers notes he or she has made about the officer and the factors identified on the form such as adherence to safety procedures, relationships with coworkers and supervisors, report quality, commendations, complaints, attendance, and training.

Informally, some supervisors initially fill out the appraisal in pencil and at a preliminary meeting give the officer an opportunity to provide input that may alter the ratings. A similar practice is to give the officers to be rated a copy of the appraisal form and ask them to evaluate themselves. Before the actual rating conference, the supervisor's and officers' preliminary ratings are compared and discussed. By policy in many law enforcement agencies, officers headed toward an unsatisfactory rating must be advised of their deficiencies at least 90 days before the end of the rating period so they have an opportunity to improve.

Signing a performance appraisal is akin to signing a traffic ticket; the signature means that you have received a copy of it, not that you necessarily agree with it. Officers seldom formally appeal a performance appraisal; although they may ask that a statement prepared by them be attached to it for the record.

PROMOTIONS

Promotional tests can serve several objectives: (1) determining which candidates' names should be placed on the promotional roster; (2) reinforcing organizational change (e.g., when the Savannah, Georgia Police Department adopted community-oriented policing, all sworn personnel had to complete a 40-hour course in that philosophy. The next written promotional tests drew questions from the course material, communicating the message "you need to be on-board with COP if you plan to get promoted"); (3) refreshing familiarity with critically important policies, such as use of force and high-speed pursuits, by asking questions about them; (4) increasing the level of important knowledge in the organization through candidates studying the resource material for written tests; and (5) improving the candidates' understanding of their skill levels by their behaviors being tested in assessment centers, which roughly equate to a series of job simulations, and receiving feedback about their performance.

A dilemma for many law enforcement executives is the disparity between the limited number of promotional openings they have versus their large pool of well-qualified candidates. Even so, that pool might be more substantial were it not for the fact that some officers choose not to participate in promotional testing. Seventy percent of nonparticipating women and 51 percent of men do not want to be moved from their current assignment or shift.[182] They know that a transfer usually accompanies a promotion; by doctrine, a new supervisor should not lead those with whom they have worked as equals. Other reasons for nonparticipation include child-care/family responsibilities, not wanting supervisory responsibilities, and loss of overtime pay; overall, one in five potential candidates is simply not interested.[183]

Although infrequent, officers do cheat on promotional exams and supervisors sometimes help them to do so. An officer hired someone to take the Hudson County (New Jersey) Sheriff's Office's Sergeant's exam for him; both men were sentenced to prison terms on a variety of charges.[184] In Providence (Rhode Island), a chief directly or indirectly provided four favored candidates with an advance copy of the materials for a written exam, giving them more time to study, and also dictated who would score first, second, and third in the interview phase.[185]

With respect to the rules and testing processes used to identify those eligible for promotion, law enforcement officers want (1) clear and unambiguous guidelines, (2) the rules to be evenly applied to all candidates, (3) confidence in the integrity of the testing process, (4) a reasonable amount of material to study for a written test, and (5) prompt feedback on the results.[186]

The rules and practices that comprise the promotional system can be specified in departmental policy, civil service/merit rules, local ordinances, the city or county charter, or state statutes. Broadly, the promotional policy specifies who is eligible, what the steps in the promotional process are, how the final scores are calculated, and how officers passing the process will be selected from the eligibility roster. Policies must use carefully crafted language to avoid potential problems. A well-written promotional policy might specify that to be eligible for promotion to sergeant, "An officer shall have completed at least 36 months of continuous service with this agency on the date immediately preceding the administration of the written examination." In contrast, another policy might simply provide "Three years of police service must be completed to be eligible." Does that mean with the present agency? Could some of it be with another department? Do breaks in service affect eligibility? Assume an officer works for a department 32 months, then he resigns to work in at an insurance company. Eight months later, he is rehired by his former agency. After completing four months of service, is the officer eligible for promotion?

Promotional tests are subject to the same EEOC validity and reliability requirements as are entrance examinations and physical assessment tests. Despite these requirements, some agencies attempt to prepare their own written promotional tests. There are reasons they should be reluctant to do so: (1) most frequently they will not have conducted a validity study, (2) the perception or actuality of the test "getting out" is substantial, (3) the skills to write good test items may not exist in the department, (4) command officers teaching part-time in a criminal justice program are often selected to prepare the test. Some agency officers taking the promotional exam will have taken classes from them and have a perceived or real advantage, and (5) if the test results are challenged under Title VII, the prospects for successfully defending them are often dim. If other types of promotional tests are prepared internally (e.g., an oral board or an assessment center), they face the same hurdles as do written examinations.

Regardless of what form a promotional test takes, the reading level of the materials must be closely monitored. On average, high school graduates read at a tenth-grade level; only 35 percent of them achieve a "proficient" or higher level of performance.[187] Most law enforcement agencies require a high school diploma as an entry-level education requirement. In those departments, if the promotional materials are written at more than a tenth-grade level, a court may find the test is not job related. A related matter is a review of the job analysis study before each promotional cycle begins. Roughly, if an agency has no major shifts in operational philosophy, does not significantly reallocate tasks or have other major transitions, a job analysis study might remain in use for five years. However, a committee should carefully review the study annually, record comments about its currency, and certify in writing that in the group's judgment, it can be relied upon for the next promotional cycle. A more conservative approach is to conduct the annual reviews and do a new job analysis study every three years.

Written Promotional Tests

Written promotional tests from test providers come in three basic models:[190]

1. *Off-the-Shelf/Stock*—Test providers have validity data from a large number of departments from across the country that can be "transported" or used with virtually all other law enforcement agencies. The provider gives clients a list of the five to eight books from which the questions are drawn. The clients buy enough copies to establish a lending library for candidates. Some candidates buy their own books and small study teams pool their money to do the same thing. The test questions are generic and can be used with the "Anywhere U.S.A." police department. Off-the-shelf/ stock tests rent for about $15 per copy, with price breaks for larger orders. Additional sources of profit for providers include (a) a transportability study at a cost of roughly $1,500; (b) the sale or rental of candidate study guides, around $7.50 each; and (c) administration and/or scoring services.

2. *Custom-Developed*—The provider may have validity data from a large-scale study on which the test is based or can validate the test for use in a single agency. When the knowledge areas and the number of questions to come from each area are known, the test

---

Box 9.8: Suits Filed Alleging Opposing Discrimination Issues in 2019

Two important yet opposing federal lawsuits were filed in 2019 that challenges the very definition of "discrimination" for the future. Ironically, the opposing suits were filed in two areas geographically opposite in the country as well. The first suit was filed in June 2019 by a group of white San Francisco police officers claiming that lower-scoring black and female candidates were promoted over white and male contenders because of the department's race and gender quota system that favors minorities. According to the suit, the system creates a "pernicious atmosphere of confusion, obfuscation and blatant discrimination" against white officers. At the heart of the suit is whether an agency can develop quota lists that supersede "better" qualified applicants for the sake of diversity alone. The San Francisco Police Department is one of the most highly diverse departments in the country.[188] The second suit was filed just two months later in August 2019 by the U.S. Department of Justice against the Baltimore County Police Department alleging hiring discrimination during the initial written test for police officer recruits. Claiming that the test was unfairly biased because African American applicants failed the test at a higher and "statistically significant" rate than white counterparts. The Justice Department stated that the entrance exam tested reading, grammar, logic and other skills that were not relevant to the job of being a police officer or police cadet. The first part of the exam tested observations skills by having the applicant review a photograph and answer 15 questions about it. The second part had 85 questions on reading comprehension, "logical ordering," writing and grammar, and data interpretation. The suit alleges a "pattern and practice of discrimination" against African American applicants, stating that it is most important to have diversity among sworn police officers that reflect the community than pass tests which may well reflect a person's past educational and environmental conditions.[189] These two opposing suits may well define the issue of discrimination for future generations of police in our country, a topic that has historically caused much dissention in the ranks of American policing. Both suits were filed before the 2020 COVID-19 pandemic, a unique variable which may well impact the decisions in each case.

developer sits down with a liaison committee from the agency and they decide from which sources the test questions will come. This allows many questions to come from sources unique to the agency, such as the policy manual and training materials.

Custom test developers also write scenario questions that incorporate local information (see Table 9.11). Too many scenario questions on a test require more time to complete the test. An overly long test creates the danger that test fatigue will occur and applicants will not be able to perform at a level that reflects their actual knowledge. As a rule of thumb, 15–20 short scenario questions is probably a reasonable limit for a 100-item test.

Custom developers also charge a fee for a job analysis studies. If a sergeants test is going to be developed, all sergeants will be asked to complete the job analysis questionnaire. Job analysis fees vary widely depending on the number of job incumbents in the target position, but the fees range from several thousand dollars for a single rank in one department to over $100,000 for a statewide study. Custom test questions cost $35 to $60 each, with a minimum number, such as 75, plus a base fee of $250 to several hundred dollars more. Like off-the-shelf/stock providers, custom test providers provide other services, such as administration and scoring, for additional fees.

3. *Semicustom Tests*—These exams include stock questions plus some custom-written items. Providers may require that if a client selects this option, he or she must agree to use a minimum number of custom questions, such as 10 or 25, plus the base fee and charges for other services.

Study guides should be provided to all candidates taking a written test. It is also essential that law enforcement agencies conduct seminars on how to study and take multiple-choice exams. All sessions of seminars should be video recorded and placed on the department's intranet for four primary purposes: (1) candidates can review their own session to refresh their recollection, (2) those unable to attend can have access to the same information, (3) different questions will arise if there are multiple training sessions; everyone should have access to the same information, and (4) if controversies or litigation exist, the videos might be useful in defending the agency's practices. Although some argue that a video record may be used to bolster a plaintiff's case, they may also guide the agency to making a pretrial settlement, which avoids costly litigation and leads to mistake-free seminars.

The contents of a study guide often have the following elements: (1) information about the test; (2) study tips; (3) strategies for taking multiple choice tests; (4) creating a good study environment; (5) sample questions; and (6) the list of source materials from which the test is drawn.

Less frequently, two other elements are included in a study guide: (1) a copy of the test plan (see Table 9.12) and (2) copies of all source material. While many test providers simply supply a list of books, a test plan is narrower and more specific. If one purpose of written testing is to increase the level of knowledge in the agency, narrowing the amount of material to be studied encourages it by making preparation less formidable. Including all source material eliminates the need for the agency to establish a lending library and places everything candidates need to know in a single volume. In addition to permission costs to reprint all copyrighted material, which can range from $300 to as much as $800, printing each all-inclusive study guide of 350–425 pages ranges from $16 to $22. Besides its fairness to all candidates, the use of an all-inclusive study guide cuts down on complaints and grievances. Those who perform poorly on the written test often make the comment. "It's my own. Everything I needed was handed to me." Study guides do not inflate the results of the written test. Scores, typically range in the low 30s to the lower-mid-90s.

Promotional practices are not normally addressed in a collective bargaining agreement in detail. Union contracts often specify that a promotional vacancy must be filled within 60 or 90 days if the position is not abolished. Likewise, contacts may specify the study time allowed before the promotional test is administered. Most test providers recommend 60–90 days, and unions push for a 30- to 45-day period to get their members

---

TABLE 9.11 SCENARIO QUESTION USING LOCAL INFORMATION

Thirty-year-old Wilbur is 6'5" tall. He weighs 295 pounds. Wilbur is a mean drunk. He has a history of fighting in bars. Tonight, Wilbur is drunk in Charlie's Tavern on Hancock Avenue. Patrons there have seen Wilbur pick a fight. Wilbur is in the restroom. Milford comes in and sits at the bar. He is a timid man. Milford is 31 years old and 5'4". He weighs 140 pounds. Wilbur returns to the bar. He sees Milford. He reaches for the front of Milford's shirt. Then he pulls back his fist. He screams "I'm going to hit you hard! You'll be 6 months older when you quit rolling!" Milford passes out. He falls to the floor. Wilbur's actions violate which of the following offenses?

a. Menacing
b. Battery
c. Terrorist threats
d. Assault

TABLE 9.12 PORTION OF A TEST PLAN

2020 Columbus (Georgia) Police Department Sergeant Written Test Plan

KNOWLEDGE NUMBER	KNOWLEDGE AREA	APPROX. NUMBER OF QUESTIONS	SOURCE MATERIALS
K1	Basic legal standards (including state statutes; arrest, search and seizure laws; court procedures; warrants; rules of evidence; legal terms and definitions; legal rights of accused; civil liability)	10	• Bill of Rights • Columbus Consolidated Government Code. • Selected portions of Chapter 14. • Georgia State Statutes, Title 16. Selected Portions including: 5-20; 5-21; 5-23; 5-23.1; 5-24; 5-40; 5-41; 5-42; 5-72; 10-2; 10-20; 10-93; 10-94; 11-30; 11-31; 11-33. Title 17, 4-20. • Peace Officer Standards and Training Council. *Rules of Evidence.* Pages 2.3-1–2.3-15
K2	Correct and safe use of equipment	9	• CPD Policies and Procedures. 3-3: Firearms; 3-4: Discharging of Firearms; 3-11: Responsibility and Accountability of Police Equipment; 3-12: Permanently Assigned Vehicles; 3-14: Vehicle Operations; 3-15: Operations of Motor Vehicles While Responding to Requests for Police Services
K3	Investigative concepts, principles, methods, procedures, and practices (including crime scene search, physical evidence, and modus operandi of criminals)	21	• Swanson, CR, Territo, L., & Taylor, R.W. (2019). Criminal Investigation. New York: McGraw Hill. Pages 37–78. • CPD Policies and Procedures. 5-2: Criminal Process; 6-5: Property and Evidence Procedures; 7-1: Criminal Investigation; 7-2: Collection and Preservation of Evidence.
K4	Interview and interrogation concepts, principles, and practices	6	• CPD Policies and Procedures. 2-6: Inter-department Investigations; 5-2: Criminal Process; 7-1: Criminal Investigation • US Department of Transportation (2006). *DWI Detection and Standardized Field Sobriety Tests.* Pages VI-1 to VI-6.
K5	Columbus Police Department policies and procedures	10	• CPD Policies and Procedures. 1-7: Disciplinary Action; 3-1: Non-Deadly Force/Less Lethal Munitions; 3-2: Deadly Force; 3-7: Required Court Attendance; 3-10: Off-Duty Employment; 3-16: Motor Vehicle Pursuit; 3-17: Hot Pursuit, Extradition, and Fugitive Warrant; 3-25: Guidelines for the Release of Information; 4-4: Performance Evaluations; 4-8: Drug and Alcohol Testing Policy.
K6	Leadership and motivation concepts, practices, and principles	17	• Iannone, NF & Iannone, MP (2014). *Supervision of Police Personnel.* Upper Saddle River, NJ: Prentice-Hall. Pages 33–56, 147–155.
K7	Interpersonal and organizational communication concepts, principles, and practices	10	• Swanson, CR, Territo, L, & Taylor, RW (2017). *Police Administration.* Upper Saddle River, NJ: Prentice-Hall. Pages 346–375.
K8	Counseling and discipline concepts, principles, and practices (including administrative principles and practices)	17	• Whisenand, Paul M (2014). *Managing Police Organizations.* Upper Saddle River, NJ: Pearson Education. Pages 171–188, 262–276.

NOTES:

1. Questions may be drawn from any source cited regardless of the alignment of knowledge areas and sources shown above.

2. The number of questions drawn from each knowledge area is based on the 2010 job analysis conducted by the Carl Vinson Institute of Government. The number of questions on the actual written promotional test may vary somewhat from the exact number of questions shown in this test plan. Any such variation, if necessary, would be minor.

3. For the purposes of developing a test plan, the following K areas were merged due to similar source material: Investigative concepts (merged with Crime Scene Search, Physical Evidence, and Modus Operandi of Criminals); Leadership (merged with Motivation); Counseling and Discipline (merged with Administrative principles and practices).

4. Total number of questions is 100.

promoted quicker. Sixty days is actually ample study time if an all-inclusive study guide is provided, but 90 days provides a humane safety buffer for candidates who need operations, get married, go on vacation, have deaths in the family, emergencies, and become a primary caregiver under FMLA, or other related events.

Oral Boards and Assessment Centers

Promotional oral boards are conducted in the same manner as entry-level oral boards, although the questions are different, and therefore require no further elaboration. An *assessment center* is both a process and the place where the process is conducted. Such places might be a hotel, a technical school or community college, a civic center, or National Guard installation.[191] Police facilities are not a good choice for testing; to candidates, they reek of the possibility of command influence and lack a factually neutral feeling.

Assessment centers were first used to select German Army officers during World War I; during World War II, the British War Officer Selection Boards (WOSBs) employed them to find competent officers. The U.S. Office of Strategic Services (OSS), the forerunner of the Central Intelligence Agency, utilized them to screen for agents who could be infiltrated into enemy territory to gather intelligence. The first large-scale test of assessment centers in this country was carried out by AT&T.[192] By the mid-1980s, American law enforcement agencies began using assessment centers.

Assessment centers are an attractive alternative to written tests because they produce less or no adverse impact. As compared to both written tests and oral boards, assessment centers are more difficult to administer, use a great amount of officers' time, and are more costly. A sergeants assessment center for the Dallas Police Department processed 208 candidates at an average cost of $764.[193]

An **assessment center** consists of several exercises or job simulations designed to elicit behaviors from candidates that are established to be important to job success by a job analysis. At least one of the exercises must require candidates to interact with someone else. Usually panels of three trained assessors make notes about the behaviors and assign whole number scores to the behaviors tested. Behaviors are also referred to as dimensions or competencies.[194] Examples of dimensions are shown in Table 9.13. Several exercises are required so that candidates have multiple opportunities to have their behavior assessed by panels staffed by different teams of assessors.

Assessors must at least hold the rank for which a candidate is competing. Customarily, other law enforcement agencies allow their supervisors to serve as assessors for other departments with the tacit understanding that the favor will be returned. Assessor panels should reflect diversity. Departments should not use their supervisors in their own assessment centers because charges of favoritism, bias, and prejudice will discredit the process. Most often, assessors are paid no fee, although their travel, hotel, and meal costs are covered by the department hosting them.

Some law enforcement agencies do not host assessors well and have them evaluate too many candidates each day, which can lead to rating errors. Good hosting etiquette includes having per diem checks ready for the candidates on the first day of their training, arranging transportation to the agency's bank to cash them, the hotel room charge being directly billed to the department's account, bringing in varied and quality lunch meals, allowing assessors in departmental cars to fill up at the police motor pool, and arranging special tours of the city. Depending on the length of exercises, which influences the time needed to properly assess the candidates, assessors can reasonably see 8–12 candidates a day.

Table 9.14 provides examples of assessment center exercises; it assumes that the candidate is seeking promotion to the rank of sergeant. In each example, the candidate has just been promoted to sergeant and this is "day one" in that rank. The

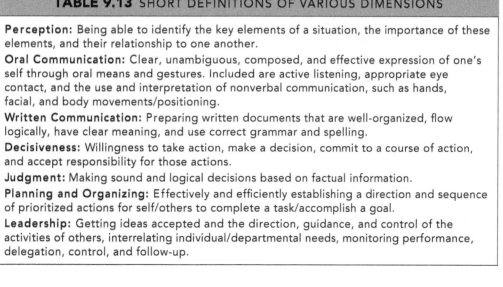

TABLE 9.13 SHORT DEFINITIONS OF VARIOUS DIMENSIONS

Perception: Being able to identify the key elements of a situation, the importance of these elements, and their relationship to one another.

Oral Communication: Clear, unambiguous, composed, and effective expression of one's self through oral means and gestures. Included are active listening, appropriate eye contact, and the use and interpretation of nonverbal communication, such as hands, facial, and body movements/positioning.

Written Communication: Preparing written documents that are well-organized, flow logically, have clear meaning, and use correct grammar and spelling.

Decisiveness: Willingness to take action, make a decision, commit to a course of action, and accept responsibility for those actions.

Judgment: Making sound and logical decisions based on factual information.

Planning and Organizing: Effectively and efficiently establishing a direction and sequence of prioritized actions for self/others to complete a task/accomplish a goal.

Leadership: Getting ideas accepted and the direction, guidance, and control of the activities of others, interrelating individual/departmental needs, monitoring performance, delegation, control, and follow-up.

TABLE 9.14 EXAMPLES OF ASSESSMENT CENTER EXERCISES

Type	Brief Description
Press Conference (PC)	The candidate must brief "members of news media" on an incident. Assessors may play the role of news media members or others may do it. Length: 5 min.
Role Play (RP): Citizen Meeting	The sergeant meets with agitated citizen who wants to complain about one of the sergeant's subordinates. A role play can be conducted with any subject matter. Variations include meeting with an officer who is a declining performer and selecting members of a robbery investigation task force from a pool of candidates. Length: 20 min.
In-Basket (IB)	The candidate replaces a sergeant who was killed in an accident while on vacation, had a heart attack and took a medical retirement, or is otherwise gone. His/her in-basket has been filled up pending the appointment of a replacement. The new sergeant must go through a stack of papers and make dispositions and write necessary memos. Length: 45 min to 3 hours.
The Written Problem Analysis (WPA)	The sergeant's boss has delegated a problem to be solved (e.g., abuse of sick leave). A packet of information about the problem is on the sergeant's desk. A memo must be written to the boss explaining the situation and making a recommendation. Length: 45 min to 2 hours.
Leaderless Group Discussion (LGD)	The candidate and four other sergeants have been assigned to discuss a problem (e.g., a large home subdivision has been hit with four to seven car burglaries in four of the last 10 days). A leader for the group has not been designated. Each candidate has the same packet of information. The group must come up with a consensus strategy to attack this problem. The LGD is hard to score and is unpopular with officers because it doesn't square with actual practice where someone is always in charge. Put differently, it lacks "face validity" to candidates. The use of LGDs appears to have been on the wane in industry and policing. Length: 45 to 60 min.
Video-Based	A DVD is made showing an officer making traffic stops and performing other duties. The sergeant is asked to identify the policy violations committed and write a memo to his/her Lieutenant. This format may also be used with other scenarios. Video length: 7 to 12 minutes followed by a 25 to 30 minute period to write the memo.

TABLE 9.15 EXAMPLE OF AN ASSESSMENT CENTER RATING SCALE

Rating	Definition of Behavior	Extent to Which Behavior Falls Short/ Exceeds Normally Expected Standards
1	*Unable to perform.* Completely unacceptable. Improvement required in every aspect of the dimension.	Completely unacceptable
2	*Needs much improvement.* Definite improvement needed in nearly all aspects of the dimension.	Clearly below acceptable
3	*Needs some improvement.* Approaches, but falls short, of acceptable on this dimension. Some aspects of standards met, but improvement needed.	Marginally unacceptable
4	*Satisfactory, Adequate.* Performs consistently at acceptable level on this dimension.	Acceptable
5	*Effective.* Consistently better than acceptable performance on this dimension, characteristically above acceptable standards.	Above acceptable
6	*Outstanding.* Demonstrates high degree of proficiency on this dimension. Far exceeds normally expected standards consistently.	Outstanding

types of exercises illustrated could be used for any rank. The length of time each exercise takes depends on its complexity; the times indicated are approximations.

A minimum of two, but usually three, trained raters observe each exercise, making their own notes during the exercise, and making their individual ratings after the candidate leaves the room (see Table 9.15). The individual ratings are then discussed by the assessor panel and the final whole number scores for that exercise formed in the same manner as described for entry-level oral boards. Each candidate's overall score is formed by combining the scores from each of the exercises (see Table 9.16).

TABLE 9.16 SERGEANTS ASSESSMENT CENTER SCORE SUMMARY SHEET

Candidate Name: <u>Joe Jones</u>

Candidate Identifier: <u>Badge 181</u>

Dimensions/ Exercises	Role Play 1	In-Basket	Press Conference	Role Play 2**	Average	Dimension Weight***	Total
Perception	6,5,6	5,5,5	4,5,5	6,5,5	5.16	8.23	42.46
Oral Communication	5,6,5	NM*	5,5,5	6,6,5	5.33	7.93	42.26
Written Communication	NM*	4,4,5	NM*	5,5,4	4.50	6.71	30.19
Decisiveness	5,6,5	5,5,5	3,4,4	4,5,5	4.66	7.33	34.15
Judgment	4,5,5	5,5,4	3,3,4	5,5,5	4.41	8.15	35.94
Planning & Organizing	5,5,5	5,6,5	3,4,4	6,6,5	4.91	6.82	33.48
Leadership	5,5,6	NM*	4,3,3	5,5,5	4.55	8.41	38.26
						Overall score:	256.7

*Not Measured.

** After Role Play 2 candidates returned to their office with the requirement to write a summary memo to their Lieutenant.

***Statistical importance of dimension to doing the job of a captain as derived from the job analysis study.

The number of exercises used in an assessment center is not a fixed requirement. Some assessment centers use six or so short exercises of perhaps 5–8 minutes each, while others might have three or four exercises that each last 15 or 20 minutes. Short exercises require little or no time for candidates to prepare. Often they are simply given a single sheet of paper with a few lines of information immediately before they begin the exercise.

The longer exercises require that candidates have more time to prepare. A typical cycle is 30 minutes of candidate preparation time followed by 15 or 20 minutes before the assessor panel. For purposes of illustration, a candidate may assume the role of a just-promoted sergeant. On his or her "first day" as a "sergeant," the candidate arrives at work and finds a stack of papers to review. At the end of 30 minutes, the "sergeant" is to go to the "lieutenant's office" to discuss what he/she has learned during the review period (i.e., an assessment center staff member will come get the "sergeant" from the preparation station and take him or her to the assessor panel). The staff member knocks on the "lieutenant's" door and announces, "Your new sergeant is here to see you." A role player previously trained for 8–16 hours for the "lieutenant's" part assumes the role of the lieutenant and greets the candidate directing him/her to sit at in front of the "lieutenant's desk. The lieutenant then asks a standard series of questions. The "meeting" ends when time expires or, when asked, the sergeant says he/she has nothing left to add. The length of time spent in the exercise room is not an assessed factor, only what the candidate accomplished. This information should also included in the instructions to the assessors and candidates.

The sergeant's preparation ("prep") station is set up like an office and includes staple removers, pads of papers, sticky notes, a dictionary, other accoutrements, and sometimes a telephone and/or computer. The telephone can be used to simulate the lieutenant calling him to add information or a requirement for their meeting. This call must be made at the same point in each candidate's preparation time. Many assessment centers allow candidates to bring their policy manual for reference and place a countdown timer on their desk so they know how much preparation time they have left. The candidate's policy manual must be checked before an exercise's preparation period begins to avoid allegations or the possibility someone had access to unauthorized material. Likewise, backpacks should not be allowed in the preparation room. The staff member administering the exercise also keeps time but is not in the room while the candidate prepares. In lieu of a telephone call, the staff member may knock on the door and announce "Here is a another piece of paper the lieutenant wants you to look over for the meeting." Like the telephone call, the paper must be delivered at the same time for each candidate (e.g., 6 minutes into the exercise).

Most commonly, the only feedback candidates get about their assessment center performance is a letter telling them how they scored on each dimension in the assessment center and where their overall score places them on the eligibility list. In the "Cadillac" of feedback, after candidates have received their feedback letter, they can sign up for a feedback session. Supervisors from other law enforcement agencies are trained in providing feedback, including ones that were assessors in that assessment center. Each feedback session lasts 30–60 minutes, during which time the candidate can review everything—literally every piece of paper—in his or her file. The videos from the interactive exercises are shown to the candidates; this vividly illustrates the scores given to the candidates and they can see the specific skills they need to improve upon. This approach uses feedback as a staff development opportunity and appears to reduce the number of disgruntled candidates.

Selection from the Promotional Roster

In selecting those to be promoted from a promotional roster, law enforcement executives are usually restricted in their choices by civil service/merit rules or other measures (e.g., the city charter or state law). All candidates on a **rank order** roster are listed from high to low based on their final passing scores. A rule of three can be used, meaning that for a single promotional vacancy, any one of the top three candidates can be selected. A variation is to use a rule of 5 or 10. When someone is promoted under the rule of three, the fourth-ranked candidate often becomes part of the next top three. This has the same effect on rules of 5 or 10.

Various jurisdictions provide that an otherwise eligible person cannot be passed over more than twice during the life of a promotional roster, although this rule does not appear to be common. Absent such a provision a person ranked first on a promotional list may "die on it" if others are chosen for nondiscriminatory reasons.[195] Depending on the applicable provisions of a promotional system, a candidate passed over for promotion may or may not be entitled to a reason, although the latter seems to be more usual.

An unknown number of agencies use an **all-qualified** promotional roster. It allows the executive to pick anyone on the list, which is alphabetized and the appointing authority does not know what the test scores were. From a risk management perspective, this provides an opportunity to virtually eliminate adverse impact in promotions because the chief or sheriff can ensure diversity when selecting from the promotional roster. However, the premise of a valid and reliable test is that higher scores are reasonably expected to be associated with higher performance of important job attributes. Stated somewhat differently, the primary purpose of testing is to make useful distinctions between people. All qualified lists simply separate the unqualified from the qualified and toss out the finer distinctions that undergird the notion of merit.

Banded promotional rosters are widely used. Their essence is placing candidates with similar scores into groups, called bands. The most common method of doing so is through any of several statistical processes. As a general rule, the highest-ranking band must be exhausted before selections are made from the next highest band.

There are two types of bands:

1. *Fixed bands*—All officers in the top band must be promoted before anyone in the next-highest-ranked band can be offered a promotion. There are two exceptions to this: (a) some systems provided that if no candidates in the top band accept a promotional offer, then someone from the next-highest band may be selected. For example, the last state police trooper in the top band might decline a promotion because it would mean moving her family to the far end of the state.

There may also be a provision that if two promotional opportunities are declined, the candidate's name is struck from further consideration from the life of the list, and (b) court orders to correct past discrimination may exist, functionally requiring either that lower-scoring minorities are "lifted into the top band" or are otherwise selected off of the promotional list.

2. *Sliding bands*—The width of the band is adjusted when all members holding the top score are exhausted. If the range of the scores in the top band is 88–93, then when all those with 93 are promoted, the bottom of the range is adjusted by including all of those who scored an 87. The promotion of those with the top score first is not required.

Banded systems have been criticized on the grounds that they invite bias, favoritism, and politics into promotional decisions. These fears loom larger when the chief executive and command staff do not enjoy the trust of the rank and file. Where collective bargaining is allowed, philosophical differences almost naturally exist about promotional decision making. The unions want their members treated equally and those responsible for making the decisions want some discretionary authority. A properly conceived banded system dispenses with at least the intensity of some of these fears by a written policy that clearly identifies the factors that will be used when making selections from within a band.

Using a strict rank order list to make promotions from is fraught with danger. In *Bridgeport Guardians v. City of Bridgeport*,[196] 68 percent of whites taking the test passed versus 30 percent of African-Americans, creating an adverse impact. Despite this impact, Bridgeport insisted on relying on a rank order list and litigation ensued. The court essentially saw this reliance as a pretext for discrimination and ordered the use of a banding system, which reduced, but did not totally eliminate, the adverse impact and reasonably met the employer's needs.

As was the case with new hires, the final step in the selection process for supervisors is the probationary period or **"working test."** Most of those promoted will successfully complete the probationary period for two reasons: (1) while promotional tests do not totally eliminate "false positives" (those who test well, but cannot do the job), they reduce the frequency with which that happens and (2) law enforcement agencies are reluctant to revert probationers to their previously held rank.

RETIREMENT COUNSELING

Retirement is not given much thought by newly hired officers. It is decades away and they are focused on beginning their careers and getting on the streets "doing police work." Unless a law enforcement agency provides retirement counseling, these eventually gray officers will arrive at retirement unprepared. Although many departments provide the counseling, the quality of it is not documented.

Officers may benefit in the long run from their agency offering retirement counseling with the content geared to the different stages of their career. In the earliest stage the content might emphasize the value of participating in a supplemental retirement account, the difference between a disability in the line of duty pension versus one that is not service connected, and in states where applicable, that a pension earned while married is divisible property. Later-stage counseling might include subjects such as changes in survivor benefits, tax exposure for withdrawals from supplemental retirement accounts, cost-of-living-adjustments (COLAs), and the effect of taking Social Security benefits at different ages.

Police unions and associations appear to have done a good job in keeping their members informed about matters affecting their retirement, particularly by providing up-to-date information on their websites. As the federal Pension Protection Act (PPA) of 2006 made its way through Congress, their websites carefully followed its progress. Parenthetically, for state and local police officers, the PPA eliminated the 10 percent penalty for early withdrawals from certain types of tax-sheltered savings plans and allows up to $3,000 in annual tax credits when health insurance costs are deducted directly from qualified plans.

Retirement creates challenges for police officers and can be stressful.[197] The Chief of the Lake Oswego, Oregon Police Department died unexpectedly from an apparent heart attack the night before his retirement ceremony.[198] Although the relationship between the chief's imminent retirement ceremony and heart attack is not certain, the proximity of the two events suggests that it may have been more than mere coincidence.

A common retirement problem is the loss of professional identity. Many people, when asked who they are, respond with both their names and what their job is. Retirement punches a hole in that identity, leaving officers unable to define themselves as anything other than what they were. Lacking plans to retire to something, some former officers become bored, drink more heavily, develop health problems, become despondent, and commit suicide.[199]

Important relationships may be disturbed as stressed retirees struggle with redefining themselves; they are more often at home, aimless, restless, and sometimes agitated.[200] A lack of long-term financial planning (e.g., the failure to create a supplemental pension or other streams of income such as rental property) may create financial pressures as retirees come to grips with the fact that their pension does not go as far as they thought it would.

The general consensus is that people fare better in retirement when, instead of just retiring from, they are retiring to something (e.g., a new job, devoting time to hobbies, travel, a family business, or learning a new skill like making jewelry or knives). In addition to other benefits, retirement counseling can implant the notion to simultaneously celebrate the end of one career while embracing the opportunity to reinvent oneself.

Chapter Summary

Summary by Learning Objectives

1. **List 10 functions a police human resource unit might perform.**

   Any 10 of these 23 functions will satisfy this objective. A police human resources (HR) unit may have oversight of the following functions:

   1. Complying with Peace Officers Standards and Training Commission (POST) requirements and guidelines;
   2. Maintaining currency with federal job discrimination laws;
   3. Developing agency HR policies, subject to executive approval;
   4. Recruiting and selecting sworn and civilian personnel;
   5. Monitoring turnover, retention, and diversity;
   6. Providing or contracting for psychological services (e.g., entry screening and critical incident counseling);
   7. Delivering or arranging for academy, in-service, advanced, and managerial training;
   8. Conducting special studies (e.g., staffing, benefits, and compensation surveys);
   9. Administering benefits programs (e.g., health and life insurance, and workers compensation);
   10. Preparing payroll;
   11. Directing labor relations;
   12. Coordinating random drug screening;
   13. Administering promotional testing;
   14. Managing intern programs;
   15. Advising commanders on personnel matters;
   16. Coordinating the employee evaluation process;
   17. Organizing promotions and awards ceremonies;
   18. Coordinating off-duty work;
   19. Directing Professional Standards/Internal Affairs efforts;
   20. Acting as personnel records custodian;
   21. Preparing content for the agency's website;
   22. Conducting job exit interviews to identify factors associated with turnover; and
   23. Serving as liaison to the central personnel office.

2. **Identify the main objective of the Equal Pay Act.**

   Its main objective is to eliminate discrimination in wages based on gender.

3. **Describe how the Age Discrimination in Employment Act is applied to law enforcement agencies.**

   ADEA has a law enforcement exemption provision; local units of government can refuse to hire a person for a sworn position if the applicant is over their maximum age for hiring and the refusal to hire was part of a bona fide hiring or retirement plan and not a subterfuge to evade ADEA's purposes.

4. **Explain the four major theories of discrimination.**

   1. *Disparate treatment*—An applicant or officer may rightly believe that he or she has been dealt with unfairly in an employment decision. To rise to the level of a disparate treatment claim, the person must have been intentionally treated differently because of his or her membership in a protected class; the discrimination must be more than slight to be actionable. Both compensatory and punitive damages can be awarded against a *nongovernmental employer*.

   2. *Adverse Impact*—An applicant or officer may rightly believe that he or she has been dealt with unfairly in an employment decision. To rise to the level of a disparate treatment claim, the person must have been intentionally treated differently because of his or her membership in a protected class; the discrimination must be more than slight to be actionable.

   3. *Harassment*—Although technically harassment is a form of disparate treatment, EEOC recognizes it as a separate theory of discrimination. Harassment is action toward an individual on the basis of race, color, sex (including pregnancy), national origin, age, religion, disability, or genetic information. Unwelcome actions that may rise to the level of harassment include speech, touching, and other conduct that create an intimidating "hostile work environment" that employees reasonably should not have to endure. Mild teasing and occasional offhand comments will fall short of being recognized as creating a hostile environment; the conduct involved must be more severe or pervasive, but need not be totally intolerable.

   4. *Retaliation*—Unlawful retaliation can take one of two forms: (1) retaliation for participation, meaning an employer retaliated against a job applicant or employee because he or she made a charge, testified, assisted, or participated in any manner in an investigation, proceeding, or hearing involving a covered job discrimination claim; for the employee's expression or conduct to be protected from retaliation, it must make reference to a protected class or type of prohibited job discrimination and (2) retaliation for opposition, which prohibits employers from discriminating against an applicant or employee who opposed covered job discrimination practices or said so in response to the employer's questions. Protection is afforded so long as the opposition is based on a reasonable and good faith belief that the practice opposed is illegal. In the event, the practice opposed is not prohibited, the employee is still protected. However, if such opposition is unreasonable, in bad faith, deliberately false, or malicious there is no protection.

5. **Name and explain two categories of sexual harassment.**

   Traditionally, sexual harassment has been categorized as (1) quid pro quo, from Latin, meaning an exchange or literally "something for something." It is constituted by unwelcome sexual advances, requests for sexual favors, and other verbal or physical conduct of a sexual nature when (a) submission to such conduct is either explicitly or implicitly a term or condition of an individual's employment or (b) submission or rejection of such conduct by an individual is used as the basis for employment decisions affecting that individual and (2) hostile environment, which is created when the prohibited and unwelcome behavior has the purpose or effect of unreasonably interfering with an individual's work performance or by creating an intimidating, hostile, or offensive working environment.

6. **Define *disability* and *reasonable accommodation*.**

   With respect to an individual, a disability is (1) a physical or mental impairment that *substantially* limits one or more major life activities, (2) a record of such an impairment, or (3) a perception that a person has such an impairment. In general, a reasonable accommodation is any change in the work environment or in the way things are customarily done that enables an individual with a disability to enjoy equal employment opportunities.

7. **Briefly contrast exempt and nonexempt employees.**

   Employees are grouped into two categories for purposes of overtime pay: (1) nonexempt—the group that is entitled to overtime pay and (2) exempt—the group that is not.

8. **Define *validity* and *reliability*.**

   Validity means that a test actually measures what it is intended to measure and conclusions and decisions based on test scores are therefore appropriate and meaningful. Reliability means that if the same test was given again or in a parallel form to the same group of people, they would score substantially the same. Reliability speaks to getting consistent, rather than random, results.

9. **Explain the meaning of *discipline and progressive discipline.***

Discipline is related to three Latin words: (1) *disciplina,* or instruction to a disciple; (2) *discipulus,* or pupil; and (3) *discere,* or to learn, to acquire knowledge. Although discipline is often thought of as punishment, its core meaning is instruction. Progressive discipline is incrementally increasing more serious penalties for transgressions.

10. **Explain how a discipline matrix works.**

A discipline matrix is a formal schedule for disciplinary actions, specifying both the presumptive or presumed sanction to be imposed for misconduct and any reduction or increase in the presumptive sanction for mitigating or aggravating factors.

11. **Describe the assessment center process.**

An assessment center consists of several exercises or job simulations designed to elicit behaviors from candidates that are established to be important to job success by a job analysis. At least one of the exercises must require candidates to interact with someone else. Usually, panels of three trained assessors make notes about the behaviors and assign whole number scores to each of the behaviors tested.

12. **Discuss the problem of identity loss that some officers experience in retirement.**

Loss of professional identity is a common retirement problem. Many people, when asked who they are, respond with both their names and what their job is. Retirement punches a hole in that identity, leaving officers unable to define themselves as anything other than what they were. Lacking plans to retire to something, some former officers become bored, drink more heavily, develop health problems, become despondent, and commit suicide.

Chapter Review Questions

1. What are five compelling reasons to have a working knowledge of human resource management?

2. What is the purpose of EEOC's Uniform Guidelines for Employee Selection?

3. Under FLSA, at what rate is overtime compensation paid?

4. Except for "unforeseeable circumstances" an employee seeking FMLA leave must give the employer how many days notice?

5. A California study revealed the top two reasons for joining a police department. What were they?

6. For police applicants, what are the top two negative experiences?

7. What is the primary responsibility of a Field Training Officer (FTO)?

8. Hickman and Poore's review of the literature of police use of force produced seven findings. What are four of them?

9. Why are police promotional assessment centers an attractive alternative to the use of written promotional tests?

Critical Thinking Exercises

1. Research the issue of the "gender pay gap" on the Internet. What factors do you think influences this gap: race, ethnicity, disability, access to education, age, personal lifestyle? Or a combination of all of these factor? Support your answer with real examples, and provide a plan to reduce this gap in policing.

2. Reread Box 9.8, "Suits Filed Alleging Opposing Discrimination Issues in 2019." Now, search the Internet for any resolution to either case. Do you think that white police officers should be able to sue for discrimination? How can white male officers claim discrimination when they belong to the majority power class in the United States?

Key Terms

adverse impact	assessment center	disability
Age Discrimination in Employment Act (ADEA)	baby boomers	discipline
	banded list	discipline matrix
all-qualified list	computerized voice stress analyzer (CVSA)	disparate treatment
Alpha generation		Early Identification and Intervention Systems (EIIS)
Americans with Disability Act (ADA)	conditional job offer (CJO)	

Employee Polygraph Protection
    Act (EPPA)
Equal Employment Opportunity
    Commission (EEOC)
exempt employee
Equal Pay Act (EPA)
Fair Labor Standards Act (FLSA)
Family Medical Leave Act (FMLA)
field training officer (FTO)
4/5ths rule
Generation X
Generation Y
Generation Z
Genetic Information Nondiscrimination
    Act (GINA)

harassment
hostile environment
Lilly Ledbetter Fair Pay Act
    (LLFPA)
moral turpitude
nonexempt employees
officer in training (OIT)
Peace Officers Standards and
    Training Commission
Pregnancy Discrimination Act
progressive discipline
protected class
qualified individual with a disability
quid pro quo
rank order

reasonable accommodation
reliability
retaliation
Servicemembers Civil Relief Act (SCRA)
sexual harassment
silent generation
Title VII
Uniform Guidelines for Employee
    Selection Procedures
Uniformed Services Employment and
    Reemployment Rights Act (USERRA)
U.S. Department of Labor (USDOL)
validity
working test

Endnotes

[1] These functions were originally taken on June 22, 2010, from 31 different police websites across the country that described their HR responsibilities. We did not keep a list of those agencies, but for the current edition we visited the websites of 16 local law enforcement agencies during August 31–September 1, 2015, to verify the list was still valid.

[2] PayScale Consulting, "The State of the Gender Pay Gap 2020," See https://www.payscale.com/data/gender-pay-gap (retrieved on May 6, 2020).

[3] Amy Onder, "Ledbetter Law Leads to Equal Pay Victory," *HR Magazine* 54, No. 12 (December 2009), p. 58, http://connection.ebscohost.com/c/articles/47554472/ledbetter-law-leads-equal-pay-victory (accessed September 1, 2015).

[4] The statements in this paragraph are drawn from U.S. Equal Employment Opportunity Commission, Age Discrimination, p. 1, http://www.eeoc.gov/laws/types/age.cfm (accessed August 31, 2015).

[5] Kyle Mitten, "City to Pay $375K as Part of Lougheed Settlement," *The Daily World* (Aberdeen, Washington), April 9, 2015, p. 1, http://thedailyworld.com/news/local/city-pay-375k-part-lougheed-settlement (accessed August 31, 2015).

[6] U.S. 288 (2005).

[7] Equal Employment Opportunity Commission, "Nassau County Police Department to Pay $450,000 for Age Bias," p. 1, October 23, 2008, http://www.eeoc.gov/eeoc/-newsroom/release/archive/10-23-08.html (accessed September 1, 2015).

[8] See 29 United States Code, Section 623 (j)(1)(A).

[9] No author, Laws Enforced by EEOC, Equal Employment Opportunity Commission, http://www.eeoc.gov/laws/-statutes, p. 1 (accessed September 1, 2015) and No author, Title VII of the Civil Rights Act of 1964, Equal Employment Opportunity Commission, http://www.eeoc.gov/laws/-statutes/titlevii.cfm (accessed August 31, 2015). This second source is the actual text of Title VII.

[10] No author, "Facts About Discrimination in Federal Government Employment Based on Marital Status, Political Affiliation, Status as a Parent, Sexual Orientation or Transgender (Gender Identity) Status, Equal Employment Opportunity Commission, p. 1, http://www.eeoc.gov/federal/otherprotections.cfm (accessed August 31, 2015). No author, "What You Should Know About EEOC and the Enforcement Protections for LGBT Workers," Equal Employment Opportunity Commission, p. 1, http://www.eeoc.gov/eeoc/newsroom/wysk/enforcement_protections_lgbt_workers.cfm (accessed August 31, 2015). No author, Remedies for Employment Discrimination, Equal Employment Opportunity Commission, http://www.eeoc.gov/employees/remedies.cfm (accessed August 31, 2015).

[11] No author, "EEOC Releases Fiscal Year 2015 Enforcement and Litigation Data (Equal Employment Opportunity Commission: Washington, DC, February 11, 2016), p, 1, http://www.eeoc.gov/eeoc/newsroom/release/2-11-16.cfm (accessed March 1, 2016).

[12] No author, *EEOC Training Institute Resources Guide: Employer Responsibilities* p. B-2 to B4, No author, Remedies for Employment Discrimination, Equal Employment Opportunity Commission, http://www.eeoc.gov/employees/remedies.cfm (accessed August 31, 2015), and Barbara L. Johnson, "Types of Damages Available in Employment Cases," American Bar Association, 2011 Conference, Toronto, Canada, August 4, 2011.

[13] Loc. cit.

[14] No author, Remedies for Employment Discrimination, Equal Employment Opportunity Commission, http://www.eeoc.gov/employees/remedies.cfm (accessed August 31, 2015).

[15] *Stewart et al. v. City of Houston Police Department*, No. 09-20680, U.S. Court of Appeals for the Fifth Circuit (2010).

[16] Benjamin P. Endres, Jr. and the *United States of America v. Indiana State Police*, No. 02-1247, United State Court of Appeals for the 7th Circuit 349 F.ed 922, U.S. App Lexis 23570 (2003).

[17] Carri Geer Thevenot, "Las Vegas Police Settle Officer's Lawsuit over Religious Clothing," *Las Vegas Review Journal*, January 23, 2009.

[18] *Fraternal Order of Police v. City of Newark*, 170 F.3d 359 (3d Cir, 1999).

[19] 41 Code of Federal Regulations (CFR) 60-3.4(D), 1978.

[20] Laurie Wardell and Michael K. Fridkin, *Title VII and Section 1981* (Chicago: Chicago Lawyers' Committee for Civil Rights Under the Law, October, 2009), p. 15.

[21] *Jackson v. County of Racine*, 474 F.3d 493 (7th Cir. 2007).

[22]*Hall v. Gus Construction Co.,* 842 F.2d 1010, 46FEP, Cases 57 (8th Circuit), 1988.

[23]*Chris Sanford v. Department of Veterans Affairs,* EEOC Appeal No. 0120082632 (2009).

[24]U.S. Equal Employment Opportunity Commission, Facts About Sexual Harassment, July 22, 2002, p. 1, http://www.eeoc.gov/facts/fs-sex.html (accessed September 2, 2015).

[25]U.S. Equal Employment Opportunity Commission, Fourteen-Year-Old Reports Sexual Harassment and Assault at Kansas Fast Food Restaurant, undated, p. 1, http://www.eeoc.gov/youth/case3.html (accessed September 2, 2015).

[26]U.S. Equal Employment Opportunity Commission, Policy Guidance on Current Issues of Sexual Harassment, March 19, 1999, p. 2, http://www.eeoc.gov/eeoc/-publications/upload/currentissues.pdf (accessed September 2, 2015) and Federal Code of Regulations, Title 29, Subtitle B, Chapter XIV, Part 1604, 1604.11, Sexual Harassment, August 31, 2015, https://www.google.com/webhp?sourceid=chrome-instant&ion=1&espv=2&ie=UTF-8#q=Federal+Code+of+Regulations%2C+Title+29%2C+Subtitle+B%2C+Chapter+XIV%2C+Part+1604%2C+1604.11%2C+Sexual+Harassment%2C+August+31%2C+2015 (accessed September 2, 2015).

[27]Policy Guidance on Current Issues of Sexual Harassment, p. 2.

[28]On some of these points, see *Robinson v. Jackson Shipyards,* 760 F. Supp 1486, Cases 971 (M.D. Fla), 1991.

[29]*King v. Macmillan,* U.S. Court of Appeals for the 4th Circuit, 594 F.3d 301 (2010).

[30]Wardell and Fridkin, Title VII and Section 1981, p. 24.

[31]Ibid.

[32]Civil Action No. 07-cv-02560-LTB-CBS, *The United States of America and Lance Lazoff v. City of Colorado Springs, Colorado,* in the United States District Court of Colorado (2008).

[33]Drawn with restatement from Rachel L. Swarns, "Pregnant Officer Denied Chance to Take Sergeant's Exam Fights Back," *The New York Times,* August 9, 2015.

[34]No author, Laws Enforced by the EEOC (Washington, DC: U.S. Equal Employment Opportunity Commission: Washington, DC, 2010), p. 1. http://www.eeoc.gov/laws/statutes (accessed September 4, 215).

[35]See *Lochren et al. v. County of Suffolk,* No. 08-2723-cv, United States Court of Appeals, 2nd Circuit (2009) and *Sandra L. Lochren, Sara A. Macdermott, Patricia O'brien, Kelly Mennella, Christine Blauvelt, and Miriam Riera, plaintiffs, v. County of Suffolk, defendants,* United States District Court, e.d. New York, March 23, 2010.

[36]The content in this paragraph is drawn from Fabrice Czarnecki, M.D., "The Pregnant Officer," *Clinics in Occupational and Environmental Medicine* 3, No. 4 (August 2003), pp. 641–648 and Karen J. Kruger, Fabrice Czarnecki, and Gary W. McLhinney, "Pregnancy and Policing: Are They Compatible?" Paper presented at the 2008 International Association of Chiefs of Police Annual Meeting, San Diego.

[37]Loc. cit.

[38]Drawn from Colonel Deborah J. Campbell, New York State Police, Karen J. Kruger, Funk and Bolton, and Randall H. Carroll, Chief of Police (Retired), speakers, Bellingham, Washington, "Pregnancy & Policy: A New Policy Makes Them More Compatible," International

Association of Chiefs of Police, October 2010, 28 pp., 1–28, http://www.aele.org/los2010kruger-pregnancy.pdf (accessed September 4, 2015) and no author, Pregnancy Guidelines for Federal Law Enforcement, May 1, 2011, Wifle Foundation, 8 pp., http://www.wifle.org/pdf/PregnancyGuidelines.pdf (accessed September 4, 2015).

[39]Loc. cit.

[40]Loc. cit.

[41]Loc. cit.

[42]Settlement Agreement Between the United States of America and the New York City Police Department, November 18, 2009.

[43]No author, Americans with Disabilities Act, Information for Law Enforcement, December 1, 2008, www.ada.gov/policeinfo.htm (accessed September 4, 2015).

[44]Loc. cit.

[45]U.S. Equal Employment Opportunity Commission, *Disability Discrimination,* undated, http://www.eeoc.gov/laws/types/disability.cfm (accessed September 6, 2015). Parenthetically, while the EEOC may or may not note the date a document is effective or placed on the Internet, it does note when documents are outdated.

[46]Loc. cit.

[47]Loc. cit.

[48]Americans with Disabilities Act (1990) as Amended (2008, effective January 1, 2009), Section 12103(1).

[49]Ibid., Section 12103(2).

[50]U.S. Equal Employment Opportunity Commission, *Questions and Answers on the Final Rule Implementing the ADA Amendments Act of 2008 the ADA Amendments Act* undated, p. 1, http://www.eeoc.gov/laws/statutes/adaaa.cfm (accessed September 6, 2015).

[51]Loc. cit.

[52]The points in this short paragraph, except for the last sentence, are taken from no author, Wage and Hour Division History, U.S. Department of Labor, 2009, p. 1, http://www.dol.gov/whd/about/history/whdhist.htm (accessed September 9, 2015).

[53]No author, Minimum Wage Since 1938, CNN Money, 2015, p. 1, http://money.cnn.com/interactive/economy/minimum-wage-since-1938 (accessed September 9, 2015).

[54]Michael E. Brooks, "The Fair Standards Labor Act and Police Compensation," *FBI Law Enforcement Bulletin* 73, No. 6 (June 2004), p. 1 and Ted H. Bartlestone, "Issues to Consider in Defending Overtime Claims Under the Fair Labor Standards Act," *Journal of the Missouri Bar* (November/December, 2009), p. 290.

[55]U.S. 833 (1976).

[56]U.S. 528 (1985).

[57]U.S. Department of Labor, "Handy Reference Guide to the Fair Labor Standards Act," November 2014, p. 2, http://www.dol.gov/whd/regs/compliance/hrg.htm (accessed September 9, 2015).

[58]See U.S. Department of Labor. Fact Sheet, May 2016, https://www.dol.gov/whd/overtime/final2016/overtime-factsheet.htm (accessed June 21, 2016).

[59]No author, Guidance for Higher Education Institutions on Paying Overtime Under the Fair Labor Standards Acr, Wage and Hour Division, United States Department of Labor, May 18, 2016, p. 7.

[60]Loc. cit.

61 *Fred Bamonte, Javier Cota, Ricardo Perine and other similarly situated employees v. City of Mesa (AZ)*, 598 F. 3rd 1217 (2010).

62 *Stephen S. Adams, et al. v. United States*, 471 F.3d 1321 (2006).

63 *David A. Cleveland, Mark S. Vojodich, Andres W. Aston, Brian Benavides v. City of Elmendorf, Texas*, 388 F.3d 522 (2004).

64 Brian Taylor, "Government Extending Federal Benefits to All Married Same-Sex Couples," NPR (National Public Radio), July 9, 2015, pp. 1–2, http://www.npr.org/sections/thetwo-way/2015/07/09/421489372/government-extending-federal-benefits-to-all-married-same-sex-couples (accessed September 11, 2015).

65 *Gibbs and Drew v. City of New York Police Commissioner Bratton and Others*, 2015 U.S. Dist. Lexis 7960 and 24 Wage and Hour Cas. 2d (BNA) 274

66 MaCherie Placide, "In Search of the Best," Paper presented at the Annual Meeting of the Midwest Political Science Association, Chicago, April 3–6, 2008 addresses the quality of recruits and recruiting difficulties. Also see Jeremy M. Wilson and Justin A. Heinonen, "Police Workforce Structures: Cohorts, the Economy, and Organizational Performance," *Police Quarterly* 15, No. 3 (September 2012), pp. 283–307.

67 Kevin Johnson, "Police Agencies Buried in Resumes," *USA Today*, March 12, 2009.

68 Cynthia Lum, Carl Maupin, and Megan Stoltz, "The Impact of COVID-19 on Law Enforcement Agencies," *IACP Bulletin* (Washington, DC: A Joint Report of the International Association of Chiefs of Police and the Center for Evidence-Based Crime Policy, George Mason University) April 13, 2020. See https://www.theiacp.org/sites/default/files/IACP-GMU%20Survey.pdf

69 Ibid., p. 2.

70 No author, *Recruitment and Retention Practices* (Peace Officers Standards and Training Commission: Sacramento, April 2006), drawn with restatement from pp. viii and 25–26. A national study of 49 state police agencies produced similar results; parenthetically, Hawaii has no state police force per se. See Thomas S. Whetstone, John C. Reed, Jr., and Phillip C. Turner, "Recruiting: A comparative Study of the Recruiting Practices of State Police Agencies," *International Journal of Police Science and Management* 8, No. 1 (Spring 2006), pp. 52–66.

71 Douglas L. Yearwood, *Recruitment and Retention Study Series* (North Carolina Criminal Justice Analysis Center: Raleigh, North Carolina, April 2003), p. i.

72 *Recruitment and Retention Practices*, pp. xi and 25–26. Also see no author, *POST Recruitment Strategic Planning Guide* (Peace Officers Standards and Training Commission: Sacramento, 2009).

73 Nelson Lim et al., *To Protect and Serve: Enhancing the Efficiency of LAPD Recruiting* (Santa Monica, CA: The RAND Corporation, 2009), p. xviii.

74 Ibid., p. xvii.

75 Ibid., p. 39.

76 Ibid., p. 40.

77 Ibid., p. 39.

78 Ibid., pp. 42 and 40.

79 Matthew Hickman and Brian Reaves, *Local Police Departments, 2003* (Washington, DC: Bureau of Justice Statistics, May 2006), p. 9.

80 Lim et al., *To Protect and Serve: Enhancing the Efficiency of LAPD Recruiting*, p. 60 and Michelle Comeau and John Klofas, *The Police Recruiting Process: Rochester: N.Y.*, p. 5.

81 See W. Payne and J. Harvey, "A Framework for the Design and Development of Physical Employment Tests and Standards," 53, No. 7 (July 2010), pp. 858–871.

82 Comeau and Klofas, *The Police Recruiting Process: Rochester: N.Y.*, p. 7.

83 *United States v. City of Erie*, 411 F.Supp.2d 524 (2005).

84 No author, "Justice Department Settles Sex Discrimination Lawsuit Against City of Corpus Christi, Texas, Police Department," U.S. Department of Justice Press Release, September 19, 2012, p. 1, https://www.justice.gov/opa/pr/justice-department-settles-sex-discrimination-lawsuit-against-city-corpus-christi-texas.

85 Loc. cit.

86 Charles Nathan Brown, Survey of Physical Agility Testing and Officer Fitness Levels in Kentucky Police Departments, Martin School, University of Kentucky, Spring 2005, p. 111.

87 No author, Fact Sheet #36: Employee Polygraph Protection Act of 1988, U.S. Department of Labor, July 2008, http://www.dol.gov/whd/regs/compliance/whdfs36.pdf (accessed September 16, 2015).

88 Code of Federal Regulations (CFR) 801.10, current to July 2, 2010.

89 Hickman and Reaves, *Local Police Departments*, p. 8.

90 No author, *Polygraph Testing May Be Flawed for Security Screening*, National Academy of Sciences, October 8, 2002, p. 1.

91 Charles Swanson, Neil Chamelin, Leonard Territo, and Robert Taylor, *Criminal Investigation* (New York: McGraw-Hill, 2006), pp. 218–219.

92 *United States, Petitioner v. Edward G. Scheffer* 523 U.S. 303 (1998). Also see Christopher Domin, "Mitigating Evidence? The Admissibility of Polygraph Results in the Penalty Phase," *University of California, Davis, Law Review* 43, No. 4 (April 2010), pp. 1461–1490 and Leonard Saxe and Gershon Ben-Shakhar, "Admissibility of Polygraph Tests: The Application of Scientific Standards Post-Daubert," *Psychology, Public Policy, and Law* 5, No. 1 (March 1999).

93 Ibid.

94 Lim et al., *To Protect and Serve: Enhancing the Efficiency of LAPD Recruiting*, p. 61.

95 *Thomas J. Mullen v. County of Suffolk, Supreme Court of the State of New York*, D16143 (2007).

96 Lim et al., *To Protect and Serve: Enhancing the Efficiency of LAPD Recruiting*, p. 60.

97 William G. Doerner, "The Utility of the Oral Board in Selecting Police Academy Admissions," *Policing: An International Journal of Police Strategies and Management* 20, No. 4 (1997), pp. 777–785.

98 Larry Gaines and Bruce Lewis, "Reliability and Validity of the Oral Board in Police Promotions," *Journal of Criminal Justice* 10, No. 5 (1982), pp. 403–420.

99 This section draws on the 38 years of experience of Charles Swanson in designing oral boards, job simulations, and

assessment, as well as training promotional panel members from over 26 states.

[100]T. Mieczkowski, "Drug Testing the Police: Some Results of Urinalysis and Hair Analysis in a Major U.S. Metropolitan Police Force," *Journal of Forensic Medicine* 3 (June 2004), pp. 115–122.

[101]Comeau and Klofas, *The Police Recruiting Process: Rochester: N.Y.,* p. 8.

[102]Martin Sellbom, Gary L. Fischler, and Yossef S. Ben-Porath, "Identifying the MMPI-2 Predictors of Police Integrity and Misconduct," *Criminal Justice and Behavior* 34, No. 8 (August 2007), pp. 985–1004. Also see Jane Framingham, Minnesota Multiphasic Personality Inventory (MMPI), PsychCentral, 2015, p. 1, http://psychcentral.com/lib/minnesota-multiphasic-personality-inventory-mmpi/?all=1 (accessed September 16, 2015). Updated information from the University of Minnesota Press, "MMPI-3 Development Update" December 2019. See https://www.upress.umn.edu/test-division/mmpi-3-announcement

[103]John T. Chinall and Paul Detrick, "The Neo PI-R, Inwald Personality Inventory and the MMPI-2 in the Prediction of Police Academy Performance: A Case for Incremental Validity," *American Journal of Criminal Justice* 27, No. 2 (March 2003), pp. 233–248.

[104]Lim et al., *To Protect and Serve: Enhancing the Efficiency of LAPD Recruiting,* pp. 61, 69–70.

[105]Matthew Hickman, *State and Local Law Enforcement Training Academies-2002* (Washington, DC: Bureau of Justice Statistics, 2005), p. iii.

[106]Hickman and Reaves, *Local Police Departments,* p. 9.

[107]Ibid.

[108]Ibid.

[109]Lawrence W. Daly, "Police Officers Do Not Receive Adequate Training to Prepare Them to Handle Child Sexual Abuse Investigations," *Issues in Child Abuse Accusations* 15, No. 1 (Winter 2005), p. 1.

[110]Patricia Obst and Jeremy Davey, "Does the Police Academy Change Your Life?" *International Journal of Police Science and Management* 5, No. 1 (2003), p. 31.

[111]Stephen J. Scarfo, "Validity Study Relationship Between Police Academy Performance and Cadet Level of Education and Cognitive Ability," *Applied H.R.M. Research* 7, No. 1 (2002), p. 39.

[112]Allison Chappell, "Police Academy Training: Comparing Across Curricula," *Policing: An International Journal of Police Strategies and Management* 31, No. 1 (2008), p. 52.

[113]Nadine Post, "Police Academy to Set Stage for Scenario-Based Training," *ENR: Engineering News-Record* 264, No. 6 (February 22, 2010).

[114]Hickman and Reaves, Local Police Departments, 2003, p. 8 and James Hannah, "Military Call-Ups Strain Police Forces in Ohio and Elsewhere," *The Enquirer* (Cincinnati, Ohio) February 20, 2003.

[115]Ibid., p. 9.

[116]For more details, including forms, see www.Mesaaz.gov/police/FTO.

[117]Francis L. McCafferty, "The Challenge of Selecting Tomorrow's Police Officers from Generations X and Y," *The Journal of the American Academy of Psychiatry and Law* 31, No. 1 (2003), p. 81. This note is only for the qualities of the silent generation. As a separate matter, McCafferty

uses a 1930–1948 birth range for this group. Our own reading of sources led us to use a 1925–1945 range.

[118]Population Division, U.S. Census Bureau, "Selected Characteristics of Baby Boomers," (Washington, DC, U.S. Census Bureau, 2009), from unnumbered PowerPoint presentation. Also see Jim Harter and Sangeeta Agrwal, "Many Baby Boomers Reluctant to Retire," Gallup Poll, January 20, 2014, p. 1, http://www.gallup.com/poll/166952/baby-boomers-reluctant-retire.aspx (accessed May 13, 2016).

[119]Ibid.

[120]Commission on Peace Officers Standards and Training (POST), Recruitment & Retention (Sacramento, CA: POST, 2006), p. viii.

[121]Eric P. Werth, "Adult Learning: Similarities in Training Methods and Recruits Learning Characteristics," *The Police Chief* LXXVI, No. 11 (November 2009), p. 1, online access.

[122]"The Challenge of Selecting Tomorrow's Police Officers from Generations X and Y," p. 80.

[123]Ibid.

[124]Melinda Crowley, Generation X Speaks Out on Civic Engagement and the Decennial Census: An Ethnographic Approach (Washington, DC: U.S. Census Bureau, June 17, 2003), p. 2.

[125]"The Challenge of Selecting Tomorrow's Police Officers from Generations X and Y," p. 80.

[126]Ibid., p. 80. Also see Marisa Dinatale and Stephanie Boraas, "The Labor Force Experience of Women from Generation X," *Monthly Labor Review* 125, No. 3 (March 2002), pp. 3–15.

[127]Elwood Carlson, 20th-Century Generations, *Population Bulletin* 64, No. 1 (2009), computed from Table 4, p. 11.

[128]"The Challenge of Selecting Tomorrow's Police Officers from Generations X and Y," p. 80.

[129]Ibid., p. 82.

[130]Generation X Speaks Out on Civic Engagement and the Decennial Census: An Ethnographic Approach, pp. 10–16.

[131]"The Challenge of Selecting Tomorrow's Police Officers from Generations X and Y," p. 82.

[132]Tamara Erickson, "Don't Treat Them Like Baby Boomers," *Business Week*, No. 4097 (August 25, 2008), p. 1, online access.

[133]Neil Simons, "Leveraging Generational Work Styles to Meet Business Objectives," *Information Management* 44, No. 1 (January/February 2010), p. 29.

[134]"The Challenge of Selecting Tomorrow's Police Officers from Generations X and Y," p. 81.

[135]No author, "Social Networking Fact Sheet," Pew Research Center, undated, but contents reveal it was written in late 2014 or 2015, http://www.pewinternet.org/fact-sheets/social-networking-fact-sheet (accessed March 2, 2016) and Maeve Duggan, Nicole B. Ellison, Cliff Lampe, Amanda Lenhart, and Mary Madden, "Social Media Update, 2014," Pew Research Center, January 9, 2015, p.1, http://www.pewinternet.org/2015/01/09/social-media-update-2014 (accessed March 2, 2016).

[136]No author: "Top 15 Most Popular Social Networking Sites," eBizMBA Rank, March 2016, p. 1, http://www.ebizmba.com/articles/social-networking-websites (accessed March 2, 2016).

[137]No author, "2015 Social Media Survey Results," International Association of Chiefs of Police, 2015, p. 1, http://www.iacp.org/portals/0/documents/pdfs/2015Social MediaSurveyResults.pdf (accessed March 2, 2016).

[138]See Christopher D. Licher, Devon Reister, and Christopher Mason, *Vermont Statewide Law Enforcement Study* (Chicago: I/O Solutions, Inc., 2006).

[139]See *Major Cities Chiefs and the Federal Bureau of Investigation, National Executive Institute, Retention: Understanding the Generations, Recruitment, and Selection*, Employee Leadership Development, 2007.

[140]Liz Martinez, Real Life Recruiting, Officer.com, online access, August 2006, pp. 2–3.

[141]Lisa Perrine, "Job Sharing: A Viable Option for Law Enforcement?" *The FBI Law Enforcement Bulletin* 78, No. 3 (March 2009), pp. 14–15.

[142]Lisa Perrine, "Is Job Sharing a Viable Option for Law Enforcement?" (Sacramento: California Commission on Police Standards and Training), 2007 Paper for Command College 41, p. 5.

[143]Donna Leinwand, "IRR Call-Up Puts Lives in Disarray," *USA Today*, August 5, 2004. Also see Leonard Territo, "Military Combat Veterans: What They Mean to Your Department," *Florida Police Chief*, August 2008, pp. 26–31. This comprehensive article also discusses the psychological issues facing returning Veterans and the necessity for re-entry psychological evaluation of returning police officers.

[144]Hickman and Reaves, *Local Police Departments*, 2003, p. 4.

[145]Hannah, "Military Call-Ups Strain Police Forces in Ohio and Elsewhere."

[146]Palm Beach County Sheriff's Office and PBC PBA, AAA Case No. 32-390-100713-04, 121 LA (BNA) 1624 (Smith, 2005; Reported 2006).

[147]United States Code, Sections 4301 to 4335, December 19, 2005.

[148]Code of Federal Regulations (CFR) 1002.193(6), current to July 1, 2010.

[149]*Fink v. City of New York*, 129 F.Supp.2d 511 (E.D. N.Y. 200 (1)).

[150]Missy Diaz, "Former Fla. Officer Gets 90 Days for Faking Military Call-Up," PoliceOne.Com, August 26, 2007. www.PoliceOne.com

[151]Samuel Walker, *Early Intervention Systems for Law Enforcement Agencies: A Planning and Management Guide* (Washington, DC: Office of Community Oriented Policing Services, 2003), p. 48.

[152]Susan Sward and Elizabeth Fernandez, "The Use of Force/Counting Without Consequence/Police System of Tracking Is Outdated, Often Ignored, SFGate.com, February 6, 2006. SFGate is the online version of the *San Francisco Chronicle*. The study covered 1996–2004.

[153]No Author, *Conduct of Law Enforcement Agencies, Civil Rights Division, U.S. Department of Justice*, current to July 7, 2010. www.Justice.Gov.

[154]Tami Abdollah, Los Angles Daily News, "Early Warning Systems Aim to Identify Problem Officers, September 7, 2014, p. 1, http://www.dailynews.com/government-and-politics/20140907/early-warning-systems-aim-to-id-troubled-police-officers (accessed March 2, 2016).

[155]Ibid., p. 2.

[156]Ibid.

[157]Ibid.

[158]Samuel Walker, *Early Warning Systems: Responding to the Problem Officer* (Washington, DC: Office of Justice Programs, July 2001), p. 2.

[159]*Early Intervention and Personal Assessment FAQs*, Phoenix (AZ) Police Department, p. 5.

[160]Walker, *Early Warning Systems: Responding to the Problem Officer*, p. 3.

[161]Stuart MacIntyre, Tim Prenzler, and Jackie Chapman, "Early Intervention to Reduce Complaints," *International Journal of Police Science and Management* 10, No. 2 (Summer 2008), pp. 238–250.

[162]Denver Police Department, *Discipline Handbook (2012)*, pp. 13–14.

[163]Ibid., p. 13.

[164]No Author, *Internal Affairs Policy and Procedures*, N.J. Office of the Attorney General, November 2000, pp. 11–20.

[165]Ibid.

[166]Helen LaVan, "Public Sector Employee Discipline: Comparing Police to Other Public Sector Employees," *Employee Responsibilities and Rights Journal* 19, No. 1 (March 2007), pp. 17–30.

[167]Mark Iris, "Police Discipline in Houston: The Arbitration Experience," *Police Quarterly* 15, No. 2 (June 2002), pp. 132–151.

[168]Lisa Halverstadt, *The Arizona Republic*, July 9, 2010.

[169]David Weisburd et al., *Police Attitudes Toward Abuse of Authority: Findings from a National Study* (Washington, DC: Bureau of Justice Statistics, 2000), 5.

[170]Ibid.

[171]Jennifer Manis, Carol A. Archbold, and Kimberly D. Hassell, "Exploring the Impact of Police Officer Education Level on Allegations of Police Misconduct," *International Journal of Police Science and Management* 10, No. 4 (Winter 2008), pp. 509–523.

[172]No Author, "For Florida Police, Higher Education Means Lower Risk of Disciplinary Action," *Law Enforcement News*, October 31, 2002, pp. 1 and 10.

[173]Ibid.

[174]James J. Fyfe et al., "Gender, Race, and Discipline in the New York City Police Department," paper presented at the Annual Meeting of the American Society of Criminology, Washington, DC, 1998.

[175]Jeff Rojek and Scott H. Decker, "Examining Racial Disparity in the Police Discipline Process," *Police Quarterly* 12, No. 4 (December 2009), pp. 388–407.

[176]Matthew J. Hickman and Jane E. Poole, "National Data on Citizen Complaints about Police Use of Force: Data Quality Concerns and the Potential (Mis)use of Statistical Evidence to Address Police Agency Conduct," Draft unpublished paper dated January 26, 2015, https://nacole.org/wp-content/uploads/Hickman.National-Data-on-Citizen-Complaints-about-Police-Use-of-Force_Data-Quality-Concern-and-the-Potential-Mis-Use-of-Statistical-Evidence-to-Address-Police-Agency-Conduct.DRAFT_.pdf

(accessed September 17, 2015). Hickman has previously published on police misconduct.

[177] With modification, from Samuel Walker, Conference Report, "The Disciplinary Matrix: An Effective Police Accountability Tool?" January 2003, University of Nebraska at Omaha.

[178] Ibid., with modification.

[179] Bernd Debusmann, "Performance Reviews—A Global Scourge," June 1, 2010. Online access http://blogs.Reuters.com/great-debate, p. 1.

[180] Ibid., p. 2.

[181] Larry M. Coutts and Frank W. Schneider, "Police Officer Performance Appraisal Systems: How Good Are They?" *Policing: An International Journal of Police Strategies and Management* 27, No. 1 (2004), pp. 67–81. Also see David Lilly and Sameer Hinduja, "Police Officer Performance Appraisal and Overall Satisfaction," *Journal of Criminal Justice* 35, No. 2 (March/April 2007), pp. 137–150.

[182] Thomas Whetstone and Deborah G. Wilson, "Dilemmas Confronting Female Police Officer Promotional Candidates," p. 69, in Jim Ruiz and Don Hummer, *Handbook of Police Administration* (Boca Raton, FL: CRC Press, 2008).

[183] Ibid.

[184] No Author, Former Police Officer Convicted in Hudson County Promotional Exam Cheating Case, N.J. Office of the Attorney General, March 6, 2006 press release.

[185] Gregory Smith, "Ex-Chief Who Helped Officers May Face Pension Cut," *The Providence (R.I.) Journal*, June 12, 2007.

[186] These points are repeatedly mentioned by agency personnel to Charles Swanson.

[187] Mark Schneider, "National Assessment of Educational Progress," February 22, 2007. http://NCES.ed.gov

[188] See Alaina Lancaster, "White San Francisco Police Officers Sue Claiming Discrimination," *The Recorder*, June 11, 2019.

[189] See Pamela Wood and Wilborn P., Nobles III, "U.S. Department of Justice Sues Baltimore County over Alleged Racial Discrimination I Police Department Hiring," *Baltimore Sun*, August 27, 2019

[190] Ibid.

[191] For the most current standards see, No Author, "Guidelines and Ethical Consideration for Assessment Center Operations, *International Journal of Selection and Assessment*," 17, No. 3 (September 2009), pp. 243–252.

[192] This history is recited in numerous publications; for example, see Kris Hogarty and Max Bromley, "Evaluating the Use of an Assessment Center Process for Entry Level Police Officer Selections in a Medium Sized Agency," *Journal of Police and Criminal Psychology* 11, No. 1 (March 1996), p. 27.

[193] George C. Thornton and Michael J. Potemra, "Utility of Assessment Center Promotion of Police Sergeants," *Public Personnel Management* 39, No. 1 (Summer 2010), p. 57.

[194] On the relationship of dimensions and exercises, see Filip Lievens, Stephen Dilchert, Deniz S. Ones, "The Importance of Exercise and Dimension Factors in Assessment Centers," *Human Performance* 22, No. 5 (November 2009), pp. 375–390.

[195] For example, see *Oliver v. Scottsdale*, 969 F. Supp. 564 (D.Ariz. 1996).

[196] F.2d 1140 (2nd Cir. 1991).

[197] On this point see Jim Ruiz and Erin Morrow, "Retiring the Old Centurion: Life After a Career in Policing: An Exploratory Study," *International Journal of Public Administration* 28, No. 13/14 (December 2005), pp. 1151–1186.

[198] Rick Bella, *The Oregonian*, OregonLive.com, Lake Oswego Police Chief Dan Duncan Dies, May 20, 2010.

[199] Michelle Perin, "Police Suicide," *Law Enforcement Technology* 34, No. 9 (September 2009), pp. 8, 10, 12, 14, and 16.

[200] Organizational culture and workload remain as key stressors; see P. A. Collins and A. Gibbs, "Stress in Police Officers: A Study of the Origins, Prevalence, and Severity of Stress-Related Symptoms with a County Police Force," *Occupational Medicine* 53, No. 4 (2003), p. 256. The findings are based on a sample of 1,206 officers.

PART 3 The Management of Police Organizations

This section addresses three core issues of managing law enforcement agencies that if mismanaged invariably lead to thorny problems: communication within the organization, the leaders' relationship with a unionized workforce, and obtaining financial resources and being a good steward of them.

In an earlier chapter it was asserted that communication was a crucial skill. This assertion was justifiable by a single sentence: Without communication, no new activities can be initiated and programs in progress cannot be steered. An agency that cannot be guided is akin to a ship without a rudder and renders leadership ineffective. Illustratively, the most common complaints that police officers have about their immediate supervisors is a lack of communication. Where this deficiency exists, officers lack clarity about what they are to do and it shakes confidence in their supervisors, sometimes leading to them having less influence with those they supervise. Chapter 10. "Organizational and Interpersonal Communication" examines these issues, including how to communicate effectively, the dangers when both senders and receivers miscommunicate, the importance of the grapevine, effective use of e-mail, using social networking sites for organizational purposes, proper use of such venues when officers are posting personal thoughts, cross-gender, multicultural, and trans generation communication, as well as the special attention that is required when relating to people with disabilities.

Chapter 11, "Labor Relations" traces the multiple forces that led to the creation of public sector collective bargaining. Among these forces were the maladaptive personnel practices used in some law enforcement agencies, such as uncompensated court appearances on off-duty days. There is no national public sector collective bargaining law. As a result, it was developed in a number of different states whose respective laws have both similar and different provisions for the bargaining process.

The traditional "big stick" in private sector collective bargaining has been the right of many categories of employees to strike, or withhold their services. This right is very limited or non-existent for public sector employees.

Although in the early days of police collective bargaining there were some strikes, they were notable exceptions and not widespread. This was followed by a period of unofficial job actions by officers, such as work slowdowns, for example, to put pressure on their unit of government by depriving it of revenue, officers only wrote traffic tickets for the most egregious violations. Deprived of the right to strike, states have provided various ways of resolving bargaining impasses short of the strike. However, unofficial job actions still occasionally occur. Chapter 11 also examines how the collective bargaining relationship is established, administered, its impact on police administration, involvement in the political process, and its setbacks in the last several years.

Frederick Mosher (1913–1990) was one of the preeminent scholars of public administration. One of Mosher's most concise and important observations about administration was the need for the administrator to operate as a gladiator and tactician in the budget process, underscores the importance of Chapter 12, "Financial Management." While Mosher's statement has always been true, it assumed even greater importance for law enforcement executives from December 2007 to 2009, a period that is called the Great Recession.

During this period the American economy went into a deep economic recession and its effect on many police agencies was profound. As an illustration, this chapter contains a case study of Stockton, California, where the police department was cut so severely that it could only respond to crimes-in-progress calls many hours of some days. The city went bankrupt and among the measures taken were substantial cuts to police pensions. Other common cost-cutting measures across the country included lay-offs, closing precincts and selling police patrol boats, motorcycles, mounted patrol horses, and helicopters, and slashing overtime spending. Some municipalities simply closed their police departments and contracted with the county for such services. The cuts went well beyond fat and muscle into hitting bone.

Although the Great Recession nominally ended in 2009, the recovery has been slow and may take a decade or more if there are no intervening economic problems. Some cuts to police budgets may never be restored because citizens are asking questions such as did we really need the police department we had. The COVID-19 pandemic and the resulting fall out from the death of George Floyd demanding changes to the police, including "defunding" the police, will be significant economic issues for the future. Financial management is much broader than someone adding and subtracting figures in different columns. Chapter 12 examines a full range of financial management information from what a budget is, budgeting as a political process, and budget formats and strategies. Most importantly, Chapter 12 discusses the massive impact of COVID-19 on the general economy and the future of police budgets.

## CHAPTER TEN

ORGANIZATIONAL AND INTERPERSONAL COMMUNICATION

Learning Objectives

1. Identify and describe the basic steps in the communication process.
2. Identify the major barriers to communication in terms of senders, receivers, and barriers involving both senders and receivers.
3. Understand the various communication strategies used by effective organizational leaders.
4. Identify and describe the various modes of organizational communication.
5. Understand specific issues associated with police communications across specific audiences.
6. Describe the most important electronic mediums of communication.

INTRODUCTION

COMMUNICATION IS A CRUCIAL FUNCTION

of police leadership. Without it, nothing can be started, monitored, guided, or stopped. On August 25, 2018, Hurricane Harvey made landfall on the coast of South-Central Texas. It impacted over 13 million people. That catastrophe provides a dramatic example of the importance of communication. Harvey destroyed 135,000 homes and generated $125 billion in property damages. It also caused 100 deaths.[1] However, the exemplary response of emergency personnel, including law enforcement from federal, state, and local agencies, was widely acclaimed for their constant use of communication.

Emergency communications were essential to the Houston Police Department's (HPDs) efforts. HPD Chief Art Acevedo was a thoughtful, decisive, and inspirational leader. Seemingly, he was everywhere, including storm preparation, and search and rescue efforts that saved many lives. His presence was magnified by numerous face-to-face conversations, as well as the use of an array of electronic communication platforms.

Acevedo personally led on-the-ground efforts to assess damages, communicate directly with citizens, and rescue victims. Members of the HPD ultimately rescued 3,500 people (see Figure 10.1). He also conducted on-the-scene press briefings to members of the media. Mobile devices, including cell phones, provided the only means of communication after the storm knocked out electrical services. The HPD maintained direct communications with citizens despite the ravages of the storm through mobile phones and social media platforms, particularly Twitter. During the first seven days of the crisis, Acevedo tweeted or retweeted on 180 different occasions, providing critical emergency bulletins and exhorting residents to remain calm in the face of the disaster. His leadership succeeded mainly through the skills of communication that defined him as a "commander, comforter, and cheerleader" in times of crisis.[2]

FIGURE 10.1 ▶ Houston Police Department Officer Daryl Hudeck, a member of the Special Weapons and Tactics Unit, carries a woman and her 13-month-old baby through the flooded waters caused by Hurricane Harvey to safety. In the first four days of this disaster, 4 trillion gallons of rain fell on Houston (David J. Phillip/ASSOCIATED PRESS).[3]

This chapter provides readers an in-depth understanding of the role of communication in determining the success of any police administrator. The chapter is divided into four primary sections. The first section provides an overview of the basics of communication, including: (a) steps in the communication process, (b) common barriers to communication, and (c) communication strategies employed by effective organizational leaders. These basics of communication provide a foundation for understanding how police administrators must communicate within the organizational structure of police agencies.

The second section overviews these organizational systems of communication in terms of: (a) multiagency communication, (b) downward communication, (c) upward communication, (d) horizontal communication, and (e) the more interconnected patterns of organizational communication commonly referred to as the grapevine.

The third section of the chapter provides direction in terms communicating with specific audiences across: (a) cultures, (b) genders, (c) generations, and (d) persons with various disabilities.

The fourth and final section of the chapter recognizes ongoing shifts in the ways in which police and their organizations communicate within the context of large-scale trends in technology and the most important electronic mediums of communication including: (a) e-mail, (b) mobile devices such as mobile phones and tablets, and (c) social media platforms including Facebook, Twitter, YouTube, and Nixle.

COMMUNICATION 101: THE BASICS

An explanation of communication begins with the basic problem that it cannot be examined as an isolated or discreet event. Communication is instead an interactive process rather than an event, so it must be understood as the sum of several independent and dynamic elements. An aggregate **communication** can be defined as the process by which senders and receivers interact in both professional and social contexts. In layman's terms, we can liken communication to the old adage, "It takes two to tango," where the communication needs (at least) two willing and able participants for the phenomenon to occur.

The first primary section of this chapter provides a foundation in the basics of communication that is a context for understanding the issues covered in subsequent sections of the chapter that are more specifically related to the work of police administrators. Three topics associated with the basics of communication are covered in this section: (a) steps in the communication process, (b) **communication barriers**, and (c) communication strategies for organizational leaders.

Steps in the Communication Process

Assume that a lieutenant on the midnight shift tells one of her sergeants there has been a dramatic increase in the number of burglaries in the sergeant's patrol sector during the past month. She "suggests" it might be caused by "a lack of focus and effort." The following steps occurred in that communication process:

Sender: The sender (the lieutenant) speaks face-to-face with the sergeant (the receiver). The authority and credibility of the sender are important determinants in how the sergeant reacts to the message, influencing how much attention it gets. It is probable the sergeant will take the message as a form of "encouragement" and take some action with his squad to reverse the situation.

Message: The heart of the communication event is the message, that is, the purpose or idea being transmitted. Many factors influence how a message is received. Among them are clarity, the alertness of the receiver, the complexity and length of the message, and how well the content is organized. Had the lieutenant composed her opening statement more succinctly and used specific language, it would have commanded greater attention and effort from the sergeant, for example, "You are responsible for reversing last month's surge in this sector's burglaries. You have three days to bring me a written plan on how you propose to do it. We'll go over it together."

Quick Facts: Words Matter

Mark Twain (1835–1910) understood the importance of communicating. He famously observed that the difference between the almost right word and the right word is the difference between lightening and a lightening bug.

Channel (medium): Several communication channels, or media, are usually available for sending messages in organizations. Often, messages are spoken (as in the example), written (increasingly electronic), or a combination. When a message is spoken, it is typically accompanied by nonverbal signs, such as a sigh, frown, smile, tight lips, hand gesture, a shake of the head, arched eyebrows, eyes narrowing or widening, or serious gaze.

Receiver: Communication is completed only when another party receives the message and understands it correctly. Perceptual distortions occur when the receiver has a flawed or atypical understanding of the message as compared to how it would commonly be understood. The receiver's cognitive bias is often at the heart of their misperception.

Cognitive bias occurs in communication when people receiving messages filter its meaning through their own experiences, understandings, and preferences, ignoring information to the contrary, and arriving at flawed understanding. Perceptual bias also occurs in other cognitive processes, such as recalling a memory, reasoning, and judgement.

Feedback: Messages sent back from the receiver to the sender are referred to as **feedback**. Without feedback, it is difficult to know whether a message has been received and understood. The feedback step may also include the receiver's reactions. If the receiver—in this case, the sergeant—takes appropriate action as intended by the lieutenant, then the message has been received and acted on satisfactorily. Effective interpersonal communication involves an exchange of messages between two people. The two communicators take turns being receivers and senders.

Environment: A full understanding of communication requires knowledge of the environment in which messages are transmitted and received. The organizational culture (attitudes and atmosphere) is a key environmental factor that influences communication. It is easier to transmit controversial messages when trust and respect are high as opposed to when they are low.

Noise: Distractions, such as noise, have a pervasive influence on the components of the communication process. However, within this context, **noise** can mean anything that disrupts communication, such as odors, fatigue, extreme heat/cold, sounds, static interference on radios, and movement around the communicators. Additionally, noise also encompasses the attitudes and emotions of the communicators, influenced by injuries, stress, fear, negative attitudes, and low motivation[4] (see Figure 10.2).

Communication Barriers

Barriers to communication, sometimes referred to as communication "breakdowns," can occur at any place in the system of basic steps described. Barriers can be the result of improper techniques on the part of either the sender or the receiver. Below we provide a review of the major barriers to communication including the (a) seven most common ways that senders hinder communication, (b) four most common ways that receivers hinder communication, and (c) three major barriers to communication that may involve both sender and receiver.

Sender Barriers:

1. *Ambiguous Purpose:* The sender is not clear about what the message is intended to accomplish.

2. *Failure to Adapt Message to Receiver:* The sender assumes incorrectly that the receiver has the knowledge necessary to understand the message and its intent and does not adapt the message to the intended receiver. The sender in some cases fails to account for differences between sender and receiver in terms of experiences and attitudes. For example,

---

Quick Facts: Failed and Absent Two-Way Communication Makes Situation Worse

A barricaded man in a small home waving a pistol was screaming deadly threats and screeching bizarre sounds. Two seasoned officers arrived and were trying to move people off of the street to safety and to assess the situation. A few minutes later, a Sergeant arrived at the scene. Until promoted recently, the Sergeant had served for three years in the Personnel Division. Very quickly, the Sergeant decided it was important to "Go in now" before someone in the neighborhood got shot.

The two officers reported they had followed policy and the tactical team would be there in approximately 25 minutes. Luckily, the team had been at the department's nearby firing range. Its commander was already in route. They recommended maintaining containment and getting direction by radio from the tactical team commander. Before they were finished with their briefing, the Sergeant reportedly said, "There could be hostages in there. They may not have even 25 seconds. Follow me" and started at a dash toward the carport, which was at the opposite side of the house where the man could be seen. Reluctantly, the two officers moved with him. Predictably, it ended badly. One officer was wounded in the leg and the subject was killed. The news media was highly critical of incident. The Mayor called for the State Police to investigate the encounter. The subject's wife filed a lawsuit over it, The Sergeant, who was on promotional probation, was reverted in rank and transferred to an inside position.

FIGURE 10.2 ▶ A basic model of the communication process. *Source:* A.J. Dubrin, *Human Relations: Interpersonal, Job-Oriented Skills,* 8th edition, © 2004. Reproduced by permission of Pearson Education, Inc., Upper Saddle River, NJ.

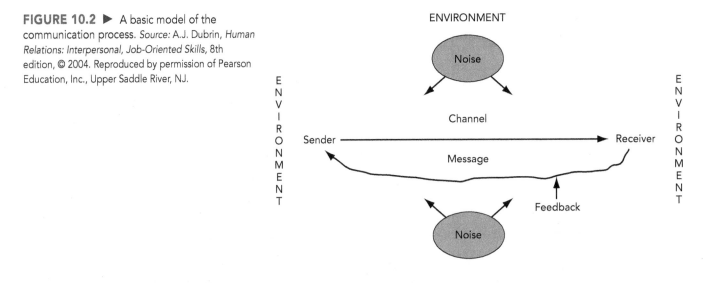

Quick Facts: What Happens When Senders and Receivers Both Miscommunicate?

Harvard Professor Henry Louis Gates, an African-American, was arrested at his home by Cambridge (Massachusetts) Police Sergeant James Crowley.

A neighbor saw two African-American men with backpacks on pushing against the door to the Gates home and called the police, thinking there was a burglary in progress. However, the neighbor had misread the situation. The two men at the door were Dr. Gates, the homeowner and his limo driver who were trying to open a jammed door. Before the police were on the scene, the limo driver had departed and Dr. Gates was inside his home.

Sgt. Crowley arrived with a man unknown to him in the house. The man refused to come outside and so

Sgt. Crowley entered the home. Dr. Gates, a Harvard Professor, showed Sgt. Crowley identification that established he lived there. At some point, an angry Dr. Gates followed Sgt. Crowley outside of the home and there was a confrontation between the two men. Gates was arrested for disorderly conduct, a charge that was later dismissed.

President Obama was critical of the arrest, calling it "stupid," but later invited both men to the White House. An independent report on the incident concluded that the arrest could have been avoided and was caused by a mutual "misunderstanding and failed communication."[5]

instructors in police academies adapt their presentation to the pre-service students, but when instructing seasoned officers, they calibrate their instruction to a different level, for example, they can rely on the fact the seasoned personnel have a much larger "police vocabulary," such as what acronyms mean.

3. *Inappropriate Medium:* The sender uses a communication medium not suited for the message. For example, some messages are better transmitted face-to-face, others in writing, while others are most effectively transmitted with the use of visual aids. Still others are best taught with direct, hands-on experience. Figure 10.3 displays a scale of sensory perceptions that can be useful as a guide in determining which medium of communication is most effective for a particular type of message.

4. *No Feedback Mechanism:* The sender does not develop a mechanism for receiving feedback to determine if the message was understood correctly.

5. *Failure to Respond to Feedback:* The sender does not interpret feedback correctly or fails to clarify the initial message when the receiver responds with misconceptions to the sender's initial statement.

6. *Failure of Language:* The sender uses language that causes the receiver to stop listening, reading, or receiving.

7. *Failure to Analyze Audience:* The sender analyzes the audience improperly, for example, assumes that every person in an emotional crowd on a street corner speaks English, ignoring the fact he or she is in a Somalian neighborhood.

Receiver Barriers:

1. *Misinterpretation of Meaning:* The receiver is a poor listener, observer, or reader and therefore misinterprets the meaning of the message.

2. *Improper Conclusions:* The receiver jumps to conclusions prior to the completion of the message.

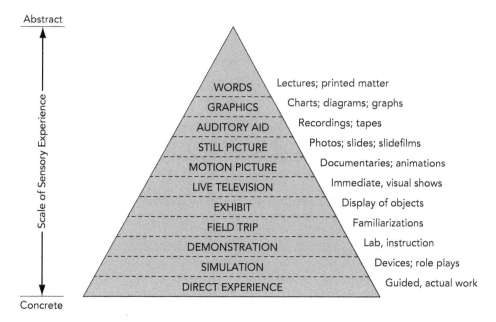

FIGURE 10.3 ▶ Scale of sensory perception.

3. *Selective Listening:* The receiver ignores the parts of a message that contradict his/her own assumptions, beliefs, and values.

4. *Lack of Focus:* The receiver has other concerns or emotional barriers, such as being mentally preoccupied or wondering if his or her family made it out of the city before a riot turned violent.

Barriers Involving Senders and Receivers:

1. *Distraction:* Noise, temperature, and other physical distractions

2. *Distance:* Distance or an inability to see or hear the message being sent

3. *Relational Differences:* Sender-receiver relationship, power structure, roles, and personality differences

The preceding sections are relevant to both leaders and the led. Those sections covered the steps in the communication process, as well the most common sources of communication breakdowns. The next section moves us from the basic concepts of communicating to issues of specific interest to law enforcement leaders.

Communication Strategies for Organizational Leaders

There is extensive information about how to communicate persuasively and effectively.[6] In this section, the focus is primarily on creating the high-impact communication that is associated with effective leadership. Both formal and informal leaders must be persuasive and dynamic communicators. Effective **interpersonal communication** skills often help informal leaders be selected for formal leadership positions. Suggestions for becoming an effective communicator include strategies on

speaking and writing, nonverbal communication, and some of the basic principles of persuasion.

Many people are already familiar with the basics of effective spoken and written communication, yet the basics, such as writing and speaking clearly, maintaining eye contact, and not mumbling, are only starting points. Most effective leaders have extra energy in their communication style. The same excitement is reflected in both their speaking and their writing styles. Kouzes and Posner underscore the importance of colorful language in communicating a vision (one of a Chief's most important functions) in these words:

> Language is among the most powerful methods for expressing a vision. Successful leaders use metaphors and figures of speech; they give examples, tell stories, and relate anecdotes; they draw word pictures; and they offer quotations and recite slogans.[7]

Senior police department members, mid-level managers, and government officials generally have exposure to the spoken words of Chiefs. However, the largest number of personnel are clustered at the bottom of the department. They will be less likely to have access to the Chief. Instead, what they get most often from the "higher-ups" are e-mail and written documents. However, if done well, those methods of communicating will exert considerable influence on officers. The following are some suggestions for dynamic and persuasive oral and written communication.

Be Credible

If speaking or writing is to be persuasive, most often it rests on the reputation of the person doing so (see Box 10.1). The foundation of persuasive communication is the essential quality of credibility. A simple definition of credibility is the standing to have people believe what you say. Being perceived as

Box 10.1: Can Rookie Officers Have Credibility?

Can newly minted police officers going to district court for the first time be credible witnesses? Certainly, if they have carefully prepared.

There are many things officers must do to be ready as a witness. A few examples illustrate what being prepared means. Unless rookies work drugs, undercover, or some similar special assignment, they should come in neatly dressed. Walk confidently and while doing so, visually take in the courtroom, including the jury. When taking the oath, speak evenly and loud enough to be heard. Don't slouch or fidget in the witness chair. Sit with your knees together. Don't cross your legs or you may distract the jury and influence them to wonder, "What in the world is that...stuff on the soles of his shoes?" Avoid moving your hands unnecessarily. Have command of your case and answer questions with a firm voice. Think about what the question asks and limit the response to the question. Officers may want the person they arrested to go to jail or prison, but they are there to tell the truth rather than to "win." Affirm points made by the defense counsel gracefully and not with a display of reluctance. Depart the court room with the dignity and confidence with which you entered it.

intelligent and knowledgeable are qualities associated with credibility. Synonyms for credibility include character, trustworthiness, reliability, and integrity. When people use these synonyms, they may unknowingly be imputing credibility to someone or some writing. In the police lexicon, if Chiefs are described as fair-minded, straight shooters, even-handed, tells it like it is, acts the same here as at City Hall, and in similar words, they have credibility.

Credibility has its consequences. With it, a Chief has an asset when dealing with tough decisions, such as abolishing units in budget cutback years and reassigning some members to other units. Credibility begets respect, which translates to fewer people "bucking" Chiefs. Conversely, with diminishing or little credibility, a Chief's shelf-life plummets and resignation or termination loom near.

An old axiom associated with credibility is the story of the "The Three Envelopes." A recently hired Chief from another state found a note on his desk from his fired predecessor: "I have prepared three numbered envelopes and left them in the center drawer. When you are in a tough situation, take out the first envelope out and act on it." About 11 months later, the City Manager was very unhappy about all the complaints from parents about the low number of school resource officers. She directed the Chief to immediately rectify the situation. The Chief took out the first envelope and read "Blame me." At a press conference, the Chief announced that "Without exception, all schools in the city would have two officers on duty every day until all students left. I inherited this situation from my predecessor. When Chief Dawson retired, he was negotiating with the school system director to provide some reimbursement for the additional police presence. About the same time, the school system director took a position in Kansas and the negotiations fell off everyone's radar. We have responded quickly and effectively to this situation and I am proud of the men and women in our department for making this work."

The controversy quickly subsided. Months later, some City Council members began asking if the Chief could find ways to make the department more efficient. The Chief hurried to his office and read from the second envelope, "Reorganize." The Chief did so and things soon returned to a normal state.

A year later, in a 10-day span, two officers totaled patrol cars and two liability suits were filed against the city. After an unpleasant 50-minute meeting with the City Manager, the Chief quickly opened the third envelope and read "Prepare three envelopes."

Gear the Message to the Listener

One generally accepted rule of persuasive communication is that a speaker must adapt the message to the listener's interests and motivation. A review of the evidence concludes that the average intelligence and experience level of the group is a key factor in designing a persuasive message. People with high intelligence tend to be more influenced by messages based on strong, logical arguments. Also, bright people are more likely to reject messages based on flawed logic.[8]

Persuade Group Members on the Benefits of Change

Sometimes, Chiefs are impeded by the slowness or unwillingness of department members to accept changes. To counter this "slowness of spirit," leaders should explain to department members how they will benefit from what is being proposed. Assume a Chief has decided to radically modify the department's high-speed pursuit policy (a topic discussed in greater detail in Chapter 14, Legal Aspects of Police Administration). In the past, the department's policy allowed officers considerable latitude to pursue fleeing motorists irrespective of the violation. However, the Chief is now seriously considering restricting the policy, so that officers will only be permitted to pursue violent felons.

"Selling" or persuading agency members is often done more effectively when the Chief takes the time to build consensus rather than to change the policy through administrative fiat. Instead of trying simply to order a change without any discussion, a slower but often more effective strategy is to win the support of key personnel within a reasonable time frame. Persuasion guru Jay Conger notes that successful persuasion often requires ongoing effort and suggests that the following sequence be followed:

- At the first meeting, appeal to them to consider the initiative carefully.
- At the second meeting, after they have had the opportunity to think about the modification, see if the key members have concluded that it is necessary to make adjustments in the policy.
- At the final meeting, it is imperative to have all the key members reach a consensus. If a consensus cannot be obtained and the final decision has been made to modify the policy, it is important that key personnel understand the importance of not undermining the policy with their constituents.[9]

Use Heavy-Impact and Emotion-Provoking Words

Certain words used in the proper context give power and force to a presentation. Used comfortably, naturally, and sincerely, these words project the image of a self-confident person. Closely related to heavy-impact language are emotion-provoking words. An expert tactic is to sprinkle one's speech with emotion-provoking—and therefore inspiring—words. Emotion-provoking words bring forth powerful images. For example, if a Chief wants to convince officers that a new, restrictive policy on high-speed pursuits will benefit them and others, he or she would call attention to certain facts that relate to injuries or deaths. For example, the new policy will reduce (a) the likelihood of their own injury or death, (b) the risk of injury or death to otherwise uninvolved motorists and their passengers, (c) the possibility of injury and death to fleeing motorist and their passengers in the fleeing vehicles, and (d) potential lawsuits against the officer and the agency. In rare cases, when a death has occurred, officers have been criminally charged, convicted, and sent to prison as a result of high-speed pursuits.

Support Presentation Points with Information and Data

Any message will be more persuasive if it is supported with information and data. Police administrators may support their message or more specific presentation points using a wide variety of sources depending on the nature of the communication. For example, statements made on the basis of findings from specific research studies should include citations and specific quotations from the research articles. The best sources to locate research articles to use in support of presentation points include the National Criminal Justice Reference Service (NCJRS), the National Federation of Scientists, and Google Scholar. The Federal government provides numerous useful sources to support talking points including the Bureau of Justice Statistics (BJS), the National Institute of Justice (NIJ), the U.S. Department of Justice (USDOJ), the Office of Justice Programs (OJP), the Office for Victims of Crimes (OVC), and the Office for Juvenile Justice and Delinquency Prevention (OJJDP).

State governments often provide data and other information resources through the Office of the Attorney General and state-level police training commissions (Figure 10.4). There are numerous private institutions and policy "think tanks" that sponsor and/or conduct policing research including the Police Executive Research Forum, Rand Corporation, the Brookings Institute, the Police Foundation, the Cato Institute, and the American Civil Liberties Union. Support for specific policy-related talking points as well as model policies and language may also be derived from police leadership organizations including the International Association of Chiefs of Police (IACP) and the National Sheriffs Association (NSA). Figure 10.4 provides a visual depiction of the use of visual aids in support of talking points on a new drone program.

Specific examples and statistics can be extracted from those various sources to support the previously discussed significant changes in the agency's high-speed pursuit policy. For example, the National Law Enforcement Officers Memorial Fund has reported that the second-leading cause of deaths of law enforcement officers is auto accidents (the leading cause was officers being shot in the line of duty). In 2018 for example, 50 officers died from traffic-related incidents, which is a statistic that would no doubt convince skeptical officers and support policy changes designed to increase officer safety.[11] These figures do not include the many thousands of police officers who have been seriously injured and disabled as a result of automobile accidents, many of which occurred during high-speed pursuits for what turned out to be, in many cases, minor traffic violations or misdemeanors.

Minimize Vocalized Pauses and Junk Words

Words and phrases can reduce or eliminate the impact of speech. Worse yet, a negative opinion of speakers and/or their agency may be created. Trite expressions, such as "you know," "you know what I mean," as well as distracting "mutterances" such as "umm" and "uhhhhhhh" should be eliminated. The use of parasitic words (also known as "junk words") conveys the impression of low self-confidence—especially in a professional setting—and detracts from a sharp communication image. The word "like" has emerged as one of the words used most frequently. For example, "I had a hard time trying to get handcuffs on this big guy I arrested. He was *like* screaming profanities and a crowd had gathered and was yelling *like* "Let him go. He didn't do anything" or "My sergeant was *like* so annoyed with me for being two minutes late for roll call." All of these can persuade your audience to "tune you out" because "junk words" reduce your credibility and by extension anything you are trying to communicate.

An effective way to decrease the use of these distracting vocalized pauses and extraneous words is to tape record or video record your presentation ahead of your conversation with someone and then play it back. Many of us are unaware we possess these shortcomings. It is always important to speak with precision and convey the impression of being articulate, well informed and confident.

FIGURE 10.4 ▶ The Office of the Attorney General building is shown here. State governments provide data and other information resources to the Office of the Attorney General. *Source:* Greater Irvine Chamber of Commerce, "Irvine Police Chief Mike Hamel Presents New Drone Program to Irvine Chamber of Commerce," December 18, 2018.[10] (Paul Brady Photography/Shutterstock)

Write Crisp, Clear Memos and Reports Using a Front-Loaded Message

According to Mercer, high achievers write more effective reports than do their less-highly achieving counterparts. Mercer examined the writing (memos, letters, and reports) of both high achievers and low achievers. He observed that the high achievers' writing was distinctive in that it had more active verbs than passive verbs, more subheadings and subtitles, and shorter paragraphs.[12]

It is more persuasive when key ideas are placed at the beginning of a conversation, an e-mail message, a paragraph, or a sentence. Front-loaded messages are particularly important for leaders because people expect them to be effective communicators.

Use a Power-Oriented Linguistic Style

A major part of being persuasive involves choosing the right linguistic style, which is a person's characteristic speaking pattern. According to Tannen, linguistic style is a combination of directness, pacing and pausing, word choice, and the use of such communication devices as jokes, figures of speech, anecdotes, questions, and apologies.[13] Linguistic style is complex because it includes the culturally learned signals by which people communicate what they mean, along with how they interpret what others say and how they evaluate others. The complexity of linguistic style makes it difficult to offer specific prescriptions

for using one that is power-oriented. However, there are several components of a linguistic style that will, in many situations, give power and authority to the communicator. Tannen and other language specialists list the following:

- To feel and project confidence you must know or learn enough about the topic you are presenting on to feel comfortable. For some of us, we have to over-prepare to feel "safe." It's better to have more knowledge than you need than to have under-prepared and be unable to answer a few questions.

- Nobody knows the future with absolute certainty. If asked a question about the impact of a new policy, you might say "I am confident this new use of force policy will reduce injuries deaths, and litigation." Alternatively, you might respond, "A great deal of thought and research went into developing this new policy. The policy wouldn't have reached the implementation stage if we weren't convinced it would be good for our officers, the public, and our community."

- Keep an open mind and accept verbal opposition to ideas, especially at staff meetings, rather than becoming upset and defensive.

- Emphasize direct rather than indirect talk, such as saying "I need your report by noon tomorrow" rather than "I'm wondering if your report will be available by noon tomorrow."

- Speak without expressing uncertainty, for example, "I will have my part of the strategic plan completed by no later than noon on the Wednesday before Thanksgiving. This will give the staff time to sift through the information."

- Know exactly what you want from a group before actually engaging with it. The chances of selling an idea increase to the extent that it is clarified in the mind of the presenter. The clearer and more committed the person is at the outset of the session, the stronger he or she will be as a persuader.

- Be sensitive to the possibility that your presentation is not taken as criticism directed at those who preceded you and who may still have powerful friends and supporters within the agency. For example, if an agency head says that "Our Research and Planning unit studied the problem of assaults on police officers. Their work produced very informative data. I believe our new policy of riding two officers in patrol cars in sectors where assaults on solo officers were higher will make it safer for our officers." By pointing to the new policy as data-driven, it's clear a predecessor is not being blamed for recent injuries to officers working dangerous sectors.[14]

Despite these suggestions for having a power-oriented linguistic style, Tannen cautions that there is no one best way to communicate. How one projects power and authority is often dependent on the people involved, the organizational culture, the relative rank of the speakers, and other situational factors. The power-oriented linguistic style is a general guideline.

Inspire Confidence Through Nonverbal Communication

Effective leaders are strong nonverbal and verbal communicators. Nonverbal communication is important because leadership involves emotion, which words alone cannot communicate convincingly.[15]

One research study concluded that when communicating about feelings 55 percent of the message is nonverbal, 38 percent is tone of voice, and 7 percent is the actual words spoken.[16] If true, the audience would miss 93 percent of a message about feelings by just focusing on the words spoken. Leaving aside the issue of whether the percentages are about right or whether they are applicable to presentations other than those about feelings, it remains true that effective leaders use nonverbal as well as verbal communications.

A self-confident leader not only speaks and writes with assurance but also projects confidence through body position, gestures, and manner of speech. Not everybody interprets these things in the same way. However, a mastery of the points that follow will project a self-confident leadership image that helps connect speakers and their audiences in positive ways:

- Use an erect posture when walking, standing, or sitting. Slouching and slumping are almost universally interpreted as an indicator of low self-confidence.

- Occasionally shift your eyes or physical move from one side of your audience to the other. At those locations make eye contact with people while speaking. It generates a feeling in the audience of having a connection with you and of being included.

- Speak clearly at a moderate pace, using a consistent voice-volume appropriate for the situation. Nervous people and those lacking in self-confidence tend to speak either too rapidly or very slowly. The volume of their voice also tends to lack consistently and will "break" at times.

- Smile frequently in a relaxed, natural-appearing manner.

- Gesture in a relaxed, non-mechanical way, including nodding your head or pointing toward others in a way that gives them positive recognition, such as indicating "You're right." [17]

A subtle mode of nonverbal communication is the use of time. Guarding time as a precious resource will help project an image of self-confidence and leadership. A statement such as "I have 15 minutes to go over this with you on Thursday at 4pm" connotes confidence and control. Other ways to communicate respect for your time and the time of others include starting and stopping meetings on time.

Your personal appearance also plays an important role in communicating non-verbal messages to others. People have more respect for, grant more privileges to, and listen more closely to those whose personal appearance is well-groomed, professional, and appropriate to the setting.

Attend to the Dynamics of Group-Level Communication

For our purposes, interpersonal communication is defined as the sharing of information between two persons. **Group communication** on the other hand involves interaction among three or more individuals in a face-to-face situation. The three or more people have a common need that is satisfied by the exchange of information.[18] There are important dynamics that can affect the group communication process including: (a) the size of the group and (b) the processes of group interaction.

One of the most important dynamics of group-level communication is the size of the group. The definition of group communication does not set limits on the ultimate size of the group. However, practical considerations inherent in the definition do define a maximum number of people who would be able to interact effectively. Individuals attending a professional sporting event may have common interests, but their opportunities for face-to-face interaction are likely limited to those seated in their immediate area or those standing in line at the refreshment stand. If we compare the Super Bowl, with an attendance of 100,000 people, to a group of five fans planning a tailgate party before the game, it is easy to see that the size of the group is a factor in determining the ability of individuals to communicate with each other.

The dynamics of group communications have been carefully analyzed.[19] Research established the natural size for purposes of defining group interactions between 3 and 20.[20] If the size of the group exceeds 20 people, the ability of individual members to influence each other is reduced. The nature of the gathering takes on more of the characteristics of a mass meeting or conference, in which one person may influence the group but the ability of individual members within the group to influence each other is limited. The size of the group has a direct bearing on the type of communication involved. Therefore, the discussion of communication is limited to groups that do not exceed 20 individuals.

Another one of the most important dynamics of group-level communication is the processes of group interaction. It is generally accepted that there are four phases in **group interaction**: (1) orientation, (2) conflict, (3) emergence, and (4) reinforcement.[21]

In the *orientation* phase, group members attempt to get to know each other and discover the problems that face the group. This may occur as strangers meet in a group for the first time, or it may happen with people who know each other and attend periodic meetings, such as staff meetings or roll call before the beginning of patrol shifts. If group members already know each other, then the orientation is aimed at common problems facing the group. These problems could range from determining what to do about a rash of accidents in departmental vehicles to deciding what to do about a new policy that limits off-duty jobs to 10 hours per week

The second phase, *conflict,* involves disagreement among the members of the group. This phase is characterized by an atmosphere of polarization and controversy. Using the previous two examples, the staff may be in conflict over using enhanced disciplinary action for more than two accidents in any 12-month rolling period versus termination. Patrol officers may be split about the new 12-hour cap on off-duty jobs and prefer the former 20-hour limit, while other officers may be relieved that they have a bona fide reason not to be working so many hours each week.

During the *emergence* phase of group interaction, there is more emphasis on positive statements and unity. This phase allows dissenting members to save face by moving toward the majority's position.

The final phase is *reinforcement*. In this phase, group members comment on the positive aspects of the group and its problem-solving ability.

The preceding discussion focused on the dynamics that normally occur in a problem-solving group; however, this interaction is usually present in most groups.[22] A police administrator may determine what phase a group is in by listening to the types of comments made by members of the group, and then use that information to express personal views in the most effective manner. Group interaction is an important aspect of any organization. Law enforcement administrators need to understand these group dynamics to carry out their duties and lead their organizations most effectively.

ORGANIZATIONAL SYSTEMS OF COMMUNICATION

The previous section focused on the basics of interpersonal and group-level communication. In this section the focus is **organizational communication**. The context for organizational communication in police agencies is job-related information. The organizational context creates both unique communication channels and challenges to effective communication. These organizational systems of communication are of obvious concern to police administrators. They work simultaneously with unique operational demands and more traditional bureaucratic requirements to accomplish the goals of police work.

Police departments, as well as all other organizations based on the bureaucratic model, must provide all employees with access to its formal communication systems. Predictably, for those systems to be effective, the hierarchical nature and associated chain of command features of such organizations must be accommodated.

Most police managers prefer formal communications systems over informal ones. That preference is based on circumstances including the fact that they can exert control over formal communications systems, and these systems are understandable, predictable, reliable, and automatically create records for future use. The use of the formal systems is variable. The wider responsibilities of leaders suggest that out of necessity, they make more frequent and varied use of the systems versus those at the bottom of the organization.

Multilevel and Multiagency Communication

Multilevel communication is essential to maintaining the functioning of units and individuals throughout a police department. Multiagency communication can be within a single jurisdiction and/or between departments in different jurisdictions, depending on the nature, magnitude, and severity of an incident. It may also be non-urgent, but important, such as sharing information on a matter of mutual concern.

Organizational communication occurs simultaneously at different levels or multiple levels of a police department and through various channels. Routine communications includes a radio request to have an accident reconstruction specialist come to a traffic accident scene, confirmation of attendance at the next staff meeting, transfers of personnel, and other related non-urgent matters. At the same time, a dispatcher may be broadcasting an alert for two people who just robbed a convenience store and severely beat the store clerk.

An illustration of the need for multi agency communication is when one agency cannot handle mass casualties and complex investigations caused by simultaneous suicide car bomb attacks at different locations such as an elementary school, an assisted living complex, the local airport, and a mall. Conversely, multi agency communication can also go badly, as shown in the next Quick Facts scenario.[23]

Quick Facts: The Boston Nuclear Attack Warning That Went Awry

Several years after the 9/11 attacks, an FBI Agent was called out of a meeting with approximately 100 local government officials, as well as some consultants. When the Agent returned, he reported on what was described as "heavy detail," an uncorroborated threat report that two Iraqis and four Chinese chemists might be conspiring to launch some sort of nuclear attack on Boston. The story quickly hit the newspapers and produced an uproar. After several days of investigation, the FBI concluded that the report was false. An unnamed FBI source blamed the uproar on officials in the meeting because information was leaked and some of them responded by saying the federal government was trying to make them scapegoats.[24]

Downward Communication

Law enforcement agencies substantially rest on the classical bureaucratic model discussed in Chapter 5, Organizational Theory. Bureaucracies have two key purposes: control and efficiency. Some of the ways in which control is achieved are: (1) reliance on the hierarchical organizational structure, (2) the chain of command, (3) formal selection processes for employment and advancement, (4) a division of labor with specialization, (5) written orders, rules, regulations, procedures, and administrative policies, (6) a system of records, (7) impartiality toward employees and the public, and (8) reliance on various methods of downward communication.

Downward communication is used by leaders to send orders, directives, goals, policies, procedures, memorandums, and so forth to employees at lower levels of the organization. Five types of downward communication within an organization can be identified:[25]

1. *Job instruction:* Provides information about officer duties and how to properly perform the associated tasks.

2. *Job rationale:* Explains why the job exists and why the tasks must be performed in a certain way, for example, to provide officer safety or comply with the requirements of new laws and court decisions.

3. *Procedures and practices:* During the police academy, attendees are provided with copies of police department written guidance, including policies, procedures, rules, and regulations. As these are updated or new ones issued, officers must acknowledge in writing their receipt and assert that they have read and understood them.

   In some cases, in-service training may also be provided to certain employees who need to understand a particular new policy, for example, on how to appropriately handle calls dealing with domestic violence involving police officers as aggressors or victims.

4. *Feedback:* Supervisors provide subordinate officers with information about their performance, both about what they are doing correctly, as well as areas that need improvement. This is done in informal conversations and formally during written performance appraisals. The goal for employees is to have a clear understanding of what they need to do going forward.

   Another type of performance feedback occurs when leaders call attention to performances ranging from unusually good to exceptional. With perhaps only a small number of exceptions, police departments have award systems. Examples include letters of commendation, years of service awards, Life Saving Medal, Officer of the Year, Distinguished Service, Purple Heart/Legion of Honor, and Medal of Valor/Honor. Most departments have a formal ceremony to present officers with their awards (see Figure 10.5). This may be a separate ceremony or a ceremony combined with promotions.

   Feedback on performance may also be provided at roll call, for example, "Officers Jackson and Ortego caught two burglars inside of Frank's Corner Mart." It may also be mentioned within a department's intranet.

5. *Indoctrination/Orientation/Assimilation:* While departments use different terms, new hires must have structured experiences to assist them in transitioning into an agency. In many departments, indoctrination begins during an applicant's background investigation. There is a joint applicant and significant other visit in the home that in addition to other purposes, gives a realistic job preview. Indoctrination continues in the Police Academy and goes on further while the new officer is working with a field training officer (FTO). During that experience, the new officer will work with several different FTOs to get a well-rounded experience. Even experienced officers need orientation experiences, for example, when a department changes from one sidearm to another or when the operational philosophy of an agency is changed, such as the shift from traditional policing to evidence-based policing.[26]

Studies of communications flow within complex organizations, including law enforcement agencies, repeatedly find that each level of management can act as a barrier to downward communication.[27] In a key study in downward communication, Dahle[28] established the efficacy of using oral and written media together. His findings revealed the following order of

FIGURE 10.5 ▶ At a special ceremony, these members of the Los Angeles Police Department received their department's highest and most prestigious award, the Medal of Valor. (Los Angeles Daily News/Zuma Press Inc./Alamy Stock Photo)

effectiveness for the various forms of downward communication. From most effective to least effective they are:

1. oral and written communication combined,
2. oral communication only,
3. written communication only,
4. the bulletin board, and
5. the organizational grapevine or system of horizontal informal communication Today, social media plays an important part of informal communication in any organization, including the police.

Dahle's work was published over 60 years ago before the advent of various forms of electronic communication covered in more detail later in this chapter. His work however remains important in terms of at least two key points: (1) the effectiveness of downward communication varies by which form is used and (2) multiple channels should be used. Police administrators need to consider which form of downward communication, or combinations of various forms of downward communication, provide the best way to overcome the most common barriers to downward communication.

Upward Communication

Upward communication is sent by a lower-level person to someone higher in their chain of command, sometimes reaching high ranking administrators, including the Chief. Police administrators understand the need for effective **upward communication** and many departments, such as Baltimore and Philadelphia, have recognition or money awards for suggestions that are: (1) innovative, cost or time saving, or improve safety, health, morale, or procedures or are of other noteworthy nature, and (2) adopted. A sound suggestion policy will have a section

listing ineligible suggestions, such as those already discarded or implemented, those that can be implemented by the submitter, matters that are already being worked on for implementation, contrary to union agreements or law, or are impractical.

From time to time, officers use suggestion boxes, memos, e-mail, or work through their associations or unions to present suggestions to leaders in a respectful way. What those leaders do with unsolicited input is variable in and across departments. However, it is a mistake if suggestions are simply glanced at, read, and filed without any further action. [29]

There should be a departmental culture that all suggestions deserve at least a courteous reply. Such action helps maintain morale. Input from below that is implemented should merit mention in the departments' newsletter and consideration for an award. Even with a system calibrated to be responsive to suggestions, there are barriers at work that can thwart the best of intentions, including (a) the structure of police agencies, (b) supervisors, and (c) subordinates. A discussion of these barriers follows.

The Hierarchical Structure as a Barrier

The hierarchical structure of police organizations can be a barrier to upward communication. Just as the physical distance between police headquarters and substations/precincts creates difficulties in communicating, for example, messages being carried to headquarters get misplaced/lost or the reception of them at headquarters is not cordial, "Most of those officers at the 5th Precinct are out of touch with what we are trying to do." Police departments may have seven or more layers of the chain of command. As communications pass through those layers messages become diluted, distorted, mischaracterized, or otherwise suffer changes that can alter the substance or meaning of them.

Supervisors as Barriers

This set of barriers to upward communication involves supervisors more directly. The attitudes of superiors and their listening behaviors play a vital role in encouraging or discouraging communication upward. If, in listening to a subordinate, a supervisor seems anxious to end the interview, impatient with the subordinate, or annoyed or distressed by the subject being discussed, a significant barrier to future communication may be created. Moreover, officers take an important lesson away from such situations: "The Sergeant writes my evaluation, which can affect my raise. There's only a down side to talking about things like this with him/her."

Likewise, when some supervisors realize subordinates have a complaint about a procedure or policy, they may consider the officer to be disloyal. The extension of this is those supervisors may not want to be associated with a "disloyal" officer and try to maneuver them to drop the matter with comments, such as "You've got a long way to go to retirement. Do you want to get tagged with a 'complainer' reputation?"

Conversely, discouraging subordinates from complaining in writing can also be considered an act of support. Examples include when officers are acting on a rumor, misunderstand the situation, and/or situations where the target of the complaint is someone "higher in the food chain" who is known to retaliate against perceived or actual criticism.

The Position of Subordinates as Barrier

The third set of barriers to upward communication involves the position of subordinates. Communication can flow more freely downward than upward because a superior may call in an officer to talk about a problem at will. Officers do not have the same freedom to intrude on the time of their superiors. If the immediate superiors of officers know the subjects of a requested meeting and avoid committing to them, the message is clear: I don't want any part of this.

Violating the chain of command by going over a superior's head overwhelmingly ends badly. A supervisor who wants to extract a "price" from a subordinate who violates the chain of command has numerous potential courses of action. The price may be taking disciplinary action just before a promotional test, which makes the officer ineligible to take the test. Other prices include transferring a transgressor to duties as far away from their homes as possible, assignment to unpopular duties, or placing them under a strict supervisor who frequently "writes up" miscreants.

Officers watch what happens in their department and learn from it. For some or even most subordinates, the old adage "Nothing ventured, nothing gained" does not make sense given their position within the organization. More conservative common adages are more easily followed by subordinates within agencies that do not value upward communication such as, "Nothing risked, nothing lost," "Better to be safe than sorry," or "I come in, do my job, and go home. Others can be crusaders, but not me."

Horizontal Communication

When an organization's formal communication channels are not open, the informal horizontal channels are almost sure to thrive as a substitute.[30] Horizontal communication refers to communication that is sent laterally across the organizational structure. If there is a disadvantage in **horizontal communication**, it is that it is much easier and more natural to achieve than vertical communication and, therefore, it often replaces vertical channels rather than supplementing them. The horizontal channels that replace weak or nonexistent vertical channels are usually informal in nature. Necessary formal horizontal channels are built into the system. Formal horizontal channels must be set up between various bureaus and divisions for the purposes of planning, task coordination, and general functions, such as problem solving, information sharing, and conflict resolution.

Horizontal communication is essential to effectively coordinating different parts of departments. Horizontal communication by peers promotes esprit de corps and teamwork. As an example, on shift change-over, an officer ending the evening watch tells several oncoming night shift detectives, "A guy who knows the street told me Jack Higgins may be pulling home burglaries again. He's not working and is flashing cash."

Psychologically, people may need informal horizontal communication. As a practical matter, it would continue to flourish even if discouraged by supervisors, and police managers would do well to provide for this need and thus allow peers to solve some of their own work problems together (see Figure 10.6).

Suppose, for example, that patrol sergeant A is having great difficulty communicating certain mutually beneficial information to detective sergeant B because the police department requires strict adherence to the chain of command in transmitting information. As indicated in Figure 10.6A, sergeant A would have to go up through the various hierarchical complexities of the patrol division and back down through the detective

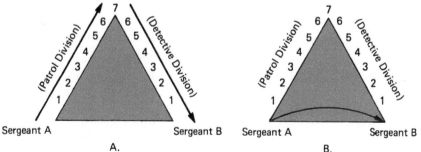

FIGURE 10.6 ▶ Horizontal lines of communication: (A) message path from sergeant A to sergeant B following the usual structured channels; (B) message path from sergeant A to sergeant B following Fayol's bridge.

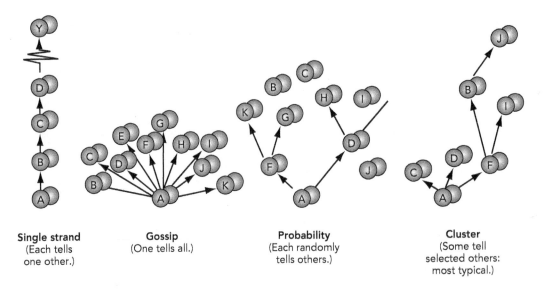

Single strand
(Each tells
one other.)

Gossip
(One tells all.)

Probability
(Each randomly
tells others.)

Cluster
(Some tell
selected others:
most typical.)

FIGURE 10.7 ▶ Grapevine patterns. *Source:* John W. Newstrom and Keith Davis, *Organizational Behavior: Human Behavior at Work,* 9th edition, p. 445. © 1993 McGraw Hill Companies. Reproduced with permission from The McGraw Hill Companies.

division to communicate with sergeant B. The time wasted and the level-to-level message distortion in the classically managed organization was recognized by Fayol[31] in 1916. Fayol proposed the creation of a horizontal bridge (see Figure 10.6B) that would allow more direct communications between individuals within an organization. The major limiting factor to the use of Fayol's bridge is a loss of network control and the subsequent weakening of central authority and the random transmission of messages throughout the system.[32]

Despite the need for formal horizontal communication, there may be a tendency among peers not to formally communicate task-related information horizontally. For instance, rivalry for recognition and promotion can cause competing subordinates to be reluctant to share information. Subordinates may also find it difficult to communicate with highly specialized people at the same level as themselves in other divisions.

In sum, formal horizontal communication channels are vital as a supplement to the vertical channels in an organization. Conversely, the informal horizontal channels, although socially necessary, can be detrimental to the vertical channels. They may also introduce false or distorted information into the agency.[33]

The Grapevine

The best-known system for transmitting informal communication is **the grapevine**, so-called because it meanders back and forth like a grapevine across organizational lines. The grapevine's most effective characteristics are that it is fast, it can be highly selective and discriminating, it operates mostly at the place of work, and it supplements and relates to formal communication. These characteristics can be divided into desirable or undesirable attributes.

The grapevine can be considered desirable because it gives management insight into employees' attitudes, provides a safety valve for employees' emotions, and helps spread useful information. Dysfunctional traits include its tendencies to spread rumors and untruths, its lack of responsibility to any group or person, and its uncontrollability. Attributes of the grapevine—its speed and influence—may work either to the good or to the detriment of the organization. The actual operation of the grapevine can be visualized in four ways (see Figure 10.7):[34]

1. **The single strand**—A tells B, who tells C, who tells D, and so on.

2. **The gossip chain**—A seeks and tells everyone, thus becoming the organizational Paul Revere.

3. **The probability chain**—A communicates randomly to D and F, then with the laws of probabilities, D and F tell others in the same manner.

4. **The cluster chain**—A tells three selected others; perhaps one of them tells two others and one of these tells one other person.

The grapevine is a permanent factor to be reckoned with in the daily activities of management, and no competent manager would try to abolish it. Rather, the astute manager should analyze it and consciously try to influence it.[35]

COMMUNICATION ISSUES AND SPECIFIC AUDIENCES

The first two primary sections of the chapter covered the basics of communication as well as organizational systems of communication more directly related to the job of the police administrator. This third primary section of the chapter covers communication issues that arise within the context of interactions between police and members of specific audiences, or particular citizen groups that share a certain attribute(s) of concern to officers and the police administrator. The specific communication issues covered within this section include those that involve: (a) cross-gender communication, (b) cross-cultural and multicultural communication, (c) cross-generational communication, and (d) strategies to more effectively communicate with persons with disabilities.

Cross-Gender Communication

Generally, an examination of the differences in the ways men and women communicate would be confined to scholarly books on linguistics or perhaps to books in the popular market that examine male-female relationships. However, it is essential that police supervisors who must evaluate the actions of their subordinates understand that men and women often communicate quite differently and may solve problems in dramatically different ways. A failure to understand these differences can result in erroneous evaluations of police officers' actions and even result in unfair criticism by fellow officers and superiors.

The following relevant scenario was witnessed by one of the authors.

A young woman pulled up to the gas station to fill up her car. While at the pump, her boyfriend pulled up behind her in his vehicle. They had a dispute the evening before and she walked out on him. He had been driving around looking for her when he observed her pulling into the filling station. Initially, she did not see him pull up. He exited his car, walked up to her from behind, forcefully turned her around and slapped her across the face. An off-duty police officer in plainclothes and in his personal car was filling up his car at an adjoining pump and witnessed the assault.

The officer immediately identified himself as a police officer and advised the man he was under arrest. The officer requested that the filling station attendant call for a patrol unit. Prior to the arrival of the patrol unit, the assailant was placed in the front seat of the off-duty police officer's car un-handcuffed. Two uniformed officers arrived in separate police cars. One was a male, and the other was a female.

The off-duty officer explained to the uniformed officers what he had witnessed and requested their assistance in filling out the necessary paperwork and transporting the assailant to the county jail. However, as the officers were conversing, the assailant, who was still agitated, was loudly expressing his anger at his female companion, who had apparently been out with another man the evening before. The female officer walked over to the assailant and in a very conciliatory way attempted to calm him down, which did not work. After a couple of minutes, the male officer became agitated with the prisoner still "running his mouth." He walked over to the assailant and, in very close physical proximity, said very angrily, "If you don't shut your damn mouth, your ass is really going to be in trouble." At that point, the man became quiet.

Now, let us assume that this scenario was being witnessed by a traditionally trained male supervisor. He might believe that the female officer should have been less conciliatory and more assertive and that her failure to be more assertive could have been interpreted as a sign of weakness by the arrested man, thereby encouraging him to become more belligerent. The supervisor might have assessed the male officer's approach as being more effective because he did, in fact, get the individual to quiet down and there were no further difficulties. However, let us assume, on the other hand, that the individual being arrested was sufficiently agitated that, when the agitated male officer spoke to him, he in turn responded angrily and decided he would rather fight than go peaceably to jail. If this had occurred, the outcome could have been quite different, and someone could have been injured or perhaps even killed.

The fact of the matter is that the female officer was behaving in a way that women in our society learn to behave when attempting to resolve a conflict—namely, in a non-confrontational, conciliatory, and nonphysical manner. In fact, this technique is recommended and employed in conflict resolution in facets of police work. There is some merit to the old proverb that "a soft word turneth away wrath."

Insights into the differences between the ways males and females communicate are important for police supervisors. Supervisors lacking such insight might unfairly judge the actions of the female officer. Worse yet, if a female officer is criticized, she may believe that, in order to be accepted by her peers and her supervisor, she has to be overly aggressive, more confrontational, and more physical. This is not to suggest that assertiveness is not a positive quality for police officers to possess. However, like anything else, too much can lead to unfortunate consequences.

Cross-Cultural and Multicultural Communication

The term culture can be applied to various population categories. However, it is normally associated with the attributes of race and ethnicity. The United States has long been considered a melting pot (or, as some have characterized it, a salad), for many races and cultures throughout its history. It is this diversity that both enriches and obstructs a law enforcement officer's involvement and interaction with other persons, groups, and cultures. With the increase of Southeast Asian refugees in some parts of the nation and more commonly the rapidly increasing Hispanic population within most regions of the United States, the problem of communicating with persons who do not speak English as a primary language has become a critical issue within the law enforcement community.[36]

Police organizations and administrators have begun to respond to the challenges posed by the need for increased cross-cultural and multicultural communication. For example, the development of a cross-cultural training course titled "Survival Spanish for Police Officers" began in 1986 at Sam Houston State University in Texas in a cooperative effort between the police academy and a faculty member of the university's Spanish department. The course grew from a minor part of the language component when it became apparent that cultural barriers were just as important as language barriers and had to be addressed in more detail.

Quick Facts: Hispanics as the Fastest Growing Minority

Persons described as Hispanic or of Latino ethnicity have been defined as those of Cuban, Mexican, Puerto Rican, South or Central American, or other Spanish culture or origin regardless of race. The Hispanic population is the largest minority group in the United States. In 2017, there were an estimated 58.9 million Hispanic people living in the United States, some 18.1 percent of our population.[37] The U.S. Census Bureau estimates that there will be 119 million Hispanic people in the United States by the year 2060. They will comprise 28.6 percent of the total population. An estimated 41 million U.S. residents or 13.4 percent of the U.S. population currently speak Spanish at home.[38]

Even with the awareness that minority populations continue to expand in the United States, the ability to communicate with these groups will continue to be a problem for many law enforcement agencies unless a concerted effort is made to address the problem such as that practiced by officers of the New York City Police Department. For many New York officers, their second language is simply part of their culture. Officer Michael Belogorodsky, a native of Ukraine, helped investigate a suspected con artist who had targeted non-English speakers by posing as a travel agent. After speaking in Russian with several alleged suspects, police arrested a 40-year-old man and charged him with stealing more than $26,000 from a dozen people. In Chicago, the nation's second-largest police force with roughly 13,000 officers, some 3,835 officers speak additional languages, most commonly Spanish, Polish, and German. The department recently required officers to take a 24-hour Spanish course during their academy training.

The Los Angeles Police Department has provided raises to over 3,000 officers who have become fluent in another language, or over one-third of the total number of officers in the department. And in Dallas, where 358 members speak Spanish and another 20 or so speak Asian languages, officers can earn an extra $150 a month after they become certified that they are fluent in another language. In Lexington, Kentucky, officers spend a year practicing Spanish and are then sent to Mexico to improve their language skills and learn about the culture. The department's Spanish speakers have increased from two to more than 100, according to the Vera Institute.

Recent census data shows more than 20 percent of Americans speak a language other than English and 12 percent are foreign-born. Many smaller cities are also attracting increasing numbers of immigrants. Managing that change is an ongoing challenge for police administrators.

Other Multicultural Issues

Officers should remember that most minorities have developed a sharp sense for detecting condescension, manipulation, and insincerity. There is no substitute for compassion as the foundation, and sincerity as its expression, in carrying out law enforcement services equally and fairly.

The first contact minorities have with law enforcement officers will either confirm or dispel suspicion as to how they will be treated. Proper pronunciation of a person's surname is an excellent place to begin contact with him or her. Surnames have histories and meanings that allow for conversation beyond the introduction. In working with immigrant, refugee, or native populations, it is helpful to learn a few words of greeting from those cultures. This willingness to go beyond what is comfortable and usual conveys the officer's intent to communicate.

Listening is fundamental to human relationships. The principles and manner of listening, however, differ among cultures. Asians and Pacific Islanders, for example, deflect direct eye contact in conversation as a sign of patient listening and deference. These groups therefore consider staring to be impolite and confrontational. Many Western cultures, on the other hand, value direct eye contact as a sign of sympathy or respect. Misunderstanding in the communication process will occur if some allowance is not made for these differences. Multicultural issues must be understood by all law enforcement officers. Understanding that "different" does not mean "criminal" will assist officers attempting to communicate in an environment that continues to be increasingly diverse.

Consider the following hypothetical scenario:

A cab driver from Nigeria runs a red light. An officer pulls him over in the next block, stopping the patrol car at least three car lengths behind the cab. Before the police officer can exit the patrol car, the cabbie gets out of his vehicle and approaches the officer. Talking rapidly in a high-pitched voice and making wild gestures, the cab driver appears to be out of control, or so the officer believes.[40]

As the officer steps from his car, he yells for the cab driver to stop, but the cabbie continues to walk toward the officer. When he is about 2 feet away, the officer orders the cabbie to step back and keep his hands to his sides. But the cab driver continues to babble and advance toward the officer. He does not make eye contact and appears to be talking to the ground.

Finally, the officer commands the cab driver to place his hands on the patrol vehicle and spread his feet. What began as a routine stop for a traffic violation culminates in charges of disorderly conduct and resisting arrest.

This scenario depicts problems that can potentially occur on the street absent appropriate and effective police training to address the multicultural issues commonly confronted by patrol officers. A simple traffic violation may escalate out of control and become more than a matter of miscommunication and common sense. The example represents different cultures colliding and producing unnecessary outcomes.

To understand the final outcome, we need to examine the breakdown in nonverbal communication. First, most Americans know to remain seated in their vehicles when stopped by the police. But the cab driver exited his cab because he wanted to show respect and humility by not troubling the officer to leave his patrol car. The suspect relied on his own cultural experience, which conveyed a completely different message to the officer, who viewed it as a challenge to his authority.

The cab driver then ignored the command to "step back." Most likely, this did not make any sense to him because, in his eyes, he was not even close to the officer. The social distance for conversation in Nigeria is much closer than in the United States. For Nigerians, it may be less than 15 inches, whereas 2 feet represents a comfortable conversation zone for most Americans.

Another nonverbal communication behavior is eye contact. Anglo Americans expect eye contact during conversation; the lack of it usually signifies deception, rudeness, defiance, or an attempt to end the conversation. In Nigeria, however, people often show respect and humility by averting their eyes. While the officer saw the cabbie defiantly "babbling to the ground," the Nigerian believed he was sending a message of respect and humility. Most likely, the cab driver was not even aware of his exaggerated gestures, high-pitched tone of voice, or rapid speech. But the officer believed him to be "out of control," "unstable," and probably "dangerous." Had the cab driver been an Anglo American, the officer's reading of the cabbie's nonverbal behavior would have been correct.

One of the primary results of a breakdown in communications is a sense of being out of control, yet in law enforcement, control and action are tantamount. Unfortunately, the need for control combined with the need to act often makes a situation worse. "Don't just stand there. Do something!" is a common admonition.

With the cab driver, the officer took control using his cultural common sense when it might have been more useful to look at what was actually taking place. Of course, in ambiguous and stressful situations, people seldom take time to truly examine the motivating behaviors in terms of culture. Rather, they view what is happening in terms of their own experiences, which is ethnocentric—and usually wrong.

Many law enforcement agencies have embraced cultural empathy. Others have made efforts to do so and are continuing their efforts. Those that have done little to nothing need to evaluate their stance, which requires experiencing as one's own the feelings and cultural orientations of another. These cultural orientations can usually explain why situations develop the way they do, and properly considered cultural awareness offers potential ways to address and mitigate misunderstandings between persons from different cultures.

Here's another scenario:

During face-to-face negotiations with police at a local youth center, the leader of a gang of Mexican American adolescents suddenly begins to make long, impassioned speeches, punctuated with gestures and threats. Other members of the group then join in by shouting words of encouragement and agreement.

A police negotiator tries to settle the group and get the negotiations back on track. This only leads to more shouting from the Chicano gang members. They then accuse the police of bad faith, deception, and an unwillingness to "really negotiate."

Believing that the negotiations are breaking down, the police negotiator begins to leave, but not before telling the leader, "We can't negotiate until you get your act together where we can deal with one spokesperson in a rational discussion about the issues and relevant facts."

At this point, a Spanish-speaking officer interrupts. He tells the police negotiator, "Negotiations aren't breaking down. They've just begun."

Among members of certain ethnic groups, inflammatory words or accelerated speech are often used for effect, not intent. Such words and gestures are a means of getting attention and communicating feelings.

Quick Facts: Multiculturalism and the New York City Police Department

One-third of NYPD employees can speak a second language. Of those, 785 are certified linguists, or expert translators, in 63 languages, including Bengali, Dari, Farsi, Arabic, and Urdu. Bilingual officers do everything from intelligence gathering to undercover work to community outreach. But New York police do not rely solely on their own officers.

Nearly all of the city's 76 precincts and most transit facilities are equipped with a dual-handset phone that can get a third-party translator instantly. There are software applications that allow the officer to speak English into the phone and then the words are spoken or displayed on the phone in Spanish.[39]

For example, during an argument, it would not be uncommon for a Mexican American to shout to his friend, "I'm going to kill you if you do that again." In the Anglo culture, this clearly demonstrates a threat to do harm. But in the context of the Hispanic culture, this simply conveys anger. Therefore, the Spanish word *matar* (to kill) is often used to show feelings, not intent.

In the gang scenario, the angry words merely indicated sincere emotional involvement by the gang members, not threats. But to the police negotiator, it appeared as if the gang was angry, irrational, and out of control. In reality, the emotional outburst showed that the gang members wanted to begin the negotiation process. To them, until an exchange of sincere emotional words occurred, no negotiations could take place.

Each culture presents arguments differently. For example, Anglo Americans tend to assume that there is a short distance between an emotional, verbal expression of disagreement and a full-blown conflict. African-Americans quite often believe differently.[41, 42] For African-Americans, stating a position with feeling shows sincerity. However, White Americans might interpret this as an indication of uncontrollable anger or instability and, even worse, an impending confrontation. For most African-Americans, threatening movements, not angry words, indicate the start of a fight. In fact, some would argue that fights do not begin when people are talking or arguing but rather when they stop talking.

Anglo Americans expect an argument to be stated in a factual-inductive manner. For them, facts presented initially in a fairly unemotional way lead to a conclusion. The greater number of relevant facts at the onset, the more persuasive the argument.[43] African-Americans, on the other hand, tend to be more affective-intuitive. They begin with the emotional position, followed by a variety of facts somewhat poetically connected to support their conclusions. African-Americans often view the mainstream presentation as insincere and impersonal, while White Americans see the Black presentation as irrational and too personal. Many times, arguments are lost because of differences in style, not substance. Deciding who's right and who is wrong depends on the cultural style of communication and thinking used.

Differences in argumentative styles add tension to any disagreement. As the Chicano gang leader presented his affective-intuitive argument, other gang members joined in with comments of encouragement, agreement, and support. To the police-negotiator, the gang members appeared to be united in a clique and on the verge of a confrontation.

Sometimes, Anglo Americans react by withdrawing into a super factual-inductive mode in an effort to calm things down. Unfortunately, the emphasis on facts, logical presentation, and lack of emotion often comes off as cold, condescending, and patronizing, which further shows a disinterest in the views of others.

Because of naive assumptions, the criminal justice community seldom views cross-cultural awareness and training as vital, yet as society and the law enforcement workforce become more diverse, the ability to manage cultural diversity becomes essential. Those agencies that do not proactively develop cultural knowledge and skills fail to serve the needs of their communities. More importantly, however, they lose the opportunity to increase the effectiveness of their officers.

Unfortunately, cross-cultural training in law enforcement often occurs after an incident involving cross-cultural conflict. If provided, this training can be characterized as a quick fix, or a once-in-a-lifetime happening, when in reality it should be an ongoing process of developing awareness, knowledge, and skills. At the very least, officers should know what terms are the least offensive when referring to ethnic or racial groups in their communities. For example, most Asians prefer not to be called Orientals. It is more appropriate to refer to their nationality of origin, such as Korean American, assuming the officer is positive about their nationality of origin. Likewise, very few Spanish speakers would refer to themselves as Hispanics. Instead, the term "Chicano" is usually used by Mexican Americans, while the term "Latino" is preferred by those from Central America. Some would rather be identified by their nationality of origin, such as Guatemalan or Salvadoran. Many American Indians resent the term "Native American" because it was invented by the U.S. government. They would prefer being called American Indian or being known by their tribal ancestry, such as Crow, Menominee, or Winnebago. The terms "Black American" and "African-American" can usually be used interchangeably. However, "African-American" is more commonly used among younger people.

Law enforcement executives need to weave cross-cultural awareness into all aspects of law enforcement training and realize it is not enough to bring in a "gender expert" after someone files sexual harassment charges or a "race expert" after a racial incident occurs. Three-hour workshops on a specific topic do not solve problems. Cross-cultural issues are interrelated; they cannot be disconnected.

Developing a Culturally Aware Workforce

What can the law enforcement community do to ensure a more culturally aware workforce? To begin, law enforcement professionals must know their own culture. All personnel need to appreciate the impact of their individual cultures on their values and behaviors. Sometimes, the best way to gain this knowledge is by intensively interacting with those who are culturally different. However, law enforcement professionals must always bear in mind that culture, by definition, is a generalization. Cultural rules or patterns never apply to everyone in every situation.

The next step is to learn about the different cultures found within the agency and in the community. However, no one should rely on culturally specific "guidebooks" or simplistic "dos and don'ts" lists. While such approaches to cultural awareness are tempting, they do not provide sufficient insight and are often counterproductive.

First, no guidebook can be absolutely accurate, and many cover important issues in abstract or generic terms. For example, several nations constitute Southeast Asia. Therefore, when promoting cultural awareness, law enforcement agencies should concentrate on the nationality that is predominant within their respective communities—that is, Vietnamese, Laotian, Cambodian, and so on. At the same time, these agencies should keep in mind that cultures are complex and changing. Managing cultural diversity also means being able to adjust to the transformations that might be occurring within the ethnic community thus necessitating the incorporation of this information into both police academy training as well as in-service training courses.

Second, relying on a guidebook approach can be disastrous if it does not provide the answers needed to questions arising during a crisis situation. It is much more useful to have a broad framework from which to operate when analyzing and interpreting any situation. Such a framework should focus on internal, not just external, culture. Knowing values, beliefs, behaviors, and thought patterns will assist law enforcement professionals to avoid catastrophic misunderstanding.

Law enforcement professionals should also understand the dynamics of cross-cultural communication, adjustment, and conflict. When communication breaks down, frustration sets in. When this happens, law enforcement reacts. This presents a potentially dangerous situation for officers because of the emphasis placed on always being in control. Understanding the process of cross-cultural interaction gives a sense of control and allows for the development of coping strategies.

Finally, law enforcement professionals should develop cross-cultural communicative, analytic, and interpretive skills. Merely having a casual familiarity about the history and religion of a particular culture or ethnic group will not in and of itself allow police officers to communicate effectively or understand someone from that group. Although the ability to communicate effectively is often best learned through experience, police officers can also gain valuable insights into the various facets of these groups by inviting respected leaders from these groups to participate in police academy or a specifically designed in-service training course. All related training should be designed to provide insights into important characteristics of these groups. These can also be accomplished by reading authoritative books about these groups or by listening to lectures from experts in the field. All of these combined will assist law enforcement officers in analyzing and understanding the ways in which people of different cultures or ethnic groups communicate and resolve conflict.

Cross-Generational Communication

The topic of generational differences in the workplace became increasingly popular within the news and business media over the last two decades.[44] The conventional wisdom

was that only a small portion of older people would adopt to what was then "new" technology such as mobile phones or social media platforms, while younger generations would make wholesale use of it. The conventional wisdom included for example the idea that members of generation x and the millennial generation needed to "stay connected" and preferred "multitasking" and "texting" more than those of older generations, or that millennials and members of generation x demanded immediacy and were more intolerant of delays in workflow than members of the baby boom generation.

The assumption that older people would not eventually adopt and utilize newer communication technologies and workplace norms was wrong. For example, you would be hard-pressed to find a significant number of Americans workers—no matter the generation—who currently do *not* need to "stay connected" for work, or have *not* become increasingly adept at "multitasking" in their job, or do *not* increasingly engage in "texting" or e-mail rather than personal conversations. These technology-based changes in how we work and communicate have caught up to us all over the course of the last 20 years and particularly since large-scale adoption of the smartphone (see Figure 10.8). Members of each generation change over time and adapt to broader societal trends, historical effects, and their approach to work and life as these are experienced.

Still, there are strategies that police administrators need to consider to promote communication and workplace efficiency between older and younger employees. For example,

FIGURE 10.8 ▶ A Hickory. North Carolina, Police Officer checks information on his cell phone. In the background, tents used by vendors at this craft show can be seen. (RidingMetaphor/Alamy Stock Photo)

the research on generational differences points to some trends occurring within the context of each successive generation in American society including: (a) increased focus on the individual, (b) increased self-esteem, (c) increased narcissism or emphasis on thinking about one's self, and (d) increased anxiety and depression.[45]

These trends seem to suggest that the digital revolution and newer communications technologies may be making each successive generation more self-aware and confident, but at the same time increasingly anxious and depressed. The trends also suggest that administrators within any formal organization need to increasingly attend to the personal well-being of those that they supervise. Effective mentoring of employees remains a core task within any organization. Younger (or simply newer) employees need to be informed of organizational expectations and provided timely and constructive feedback on their personal performance. Another thing is also certain: Some things are important to nearly all employees, regardless of age. Simple gestures like listening, acknowledging what others have said, and acting on their suggestions when appropriate are all signs of respect—no matter when you were born. People tend to appreciate being addressed with a "hello" or a "good-bye" or being greeted by name. Saying something like "yo, dawg" (meaning a friend and not a member of the canine variety) is probably not going to be appreciated by all generations.

The best solution to any observed problem in cross generational communication is to try to be considerate of the views of members of other generations. If someone from another generation says something problematic, or their manner or tone is causing a problem, efforts should be made to discuss it openly to resolve the situation.[46] The nature of formalized work relationships and particularly the hierarchical structure of police organizations and lateral hiring practices ensures that "older" workers will more often than not be responsible for supervising "younger" workers. Differences in modes of communication will naturally emerge across each successive generation. Effective police administrators recognize these generational gaps and adopt communication strategies to bridge them when necessary.

Communication with People with Disabilities

Thus far, our focus has been on organizational and interpersonal communication and the implicit orientation that people with no disabilities are involved. However, there are 41 million people in the United States with disabilities who are not institutionalized.[47] Depending on the area an officer patrols, relating to such people is an everyday occurrence, often with a number of different people. Those contacts are also ones that officers often feel uncomfortable with and/or have low confidence about handling them.

An underlying assumption is that we are dealing with individuals who do not have special needs that would affect their ability to engage in normal communication. However, there are millions of individuals living in the United States who have special needs,

FIGURE 10.9 ▶ A New York Police Officer leads a visually impaired man away from a crowded shooting crime scene. Note the man's red-tipped cane and their joined arms. The officer guided the man to an ATM and a drug store. Once sure the man could navigate his way home, the officer said good-bye. *Source:* David Handschuh and Ginger Adams Otis, *New York Daily News,* July 2, 2013.[48]

and law enforcement officers must be aware of the most effective means of communications in dealing with these individuals.

Within the special need groups are individuals who are blind (see Figure 10.9) or visually impaired, deaf or hard of hearing, mobility impaired, speech impaired, or have cognitive disabilities. The following suggestions are tools for law enforcement officers to use when assisting and communicating with special needs people.

Visual Impairment

- Speak to the individual as you approach him or her.
- State clearly who you are; speak in a normal tone of voice.
- When conversing in a group, remember to identify yourself to the person to whom you are speaking.
- Never touch or distract a service dog without first asking the owner's permission.
- Do not attempt to lead the individual without first asking. Also, allow the person to hold your arm, thus allowing him or her to control their own movements.
- Be descriptive when giving directions; verbally give the person information that is visually obvious to individuals

who can see. For example, if you are approaching steps, mention how many steps.

- If you are offering a seat, gently place the individual's hand on the back or arm of the chair so that the person can locate the seat.
- Tell the individual when you are leaving. [49]

Hearing Impairment

- Before speaking, get the person's attention with a wave of the hand or a gentle tap on the shoulder.
- Face the person and do not turn away while speaking.
- Try to converse in a well-lit area.
- Do not cover your mouth or chew gum.
- If a person is wearing a hearing aid, do not assume he or she can hear you clearly.
- Minimize background noise and other distractions whenever possible.
- When you are communicating orally, speak slowly and distinctly. Use facial expressions to reinforce what are you saying.
- Use visual aids whenever possible such as pointing to printed information on a citation or other document.
- Generally, for those who are deaf or hard of hearing, only one-third of spoken words can be understood by speech reading.
- When communicating in writing, keep in mind that some individuals who use sign language may lack good English reading and writing skills.
- If someone with a hearing disability cannot understand you, write a note to ask them what communication aids or service are needed.
- If a sign language interpreter is requested, be sure to ask via a note which language the person uses. American Sign Language (ASL) and Signed English are the most common.
- When interviewing a witness or a suspect or engaging in any complex conversation with a person whose primary language is sign language, a qualified interpreter is usually needed to ensure effective communication.
- When using an interpreter, look and speak directly to the deaf person and not to the interpreter.
- Talk at your normal rate or slightly slower if you normally speak fast.
- Only one person should speak at a time.
- Use short sentences and simple words. [50]
- If you telephone an individual who is hard of hearing, let the phone ring longer than usual. Speak clearly and be prepared to repeat the reason for the call and who you are.

- If you do not have a Text Telephone (TTY), dial 711 to reach the national telecommunications relay service, which facilitates the call between you and the individual who uses a TTY.

Mobility Impairment

- If possible, put yourself at the wheelchair user's eye level.
- Do not lean on a wheelchair or any other assistive device.
- Never patronize people who use wheelchairs by patting them on the head or shoulders.
- Do not assume the individual wants to be pushed—ask first.
- Offer assistance if the individual appears to be having difficulty opening a door.
- If you telephone the individual, allow the phone to ring longer than usual to allow extra time for the person to reach the telephone.

Speech Impairment

- If you do not understand something the individual says, do not pretend that you do. Ask the individual to repeat what he or she said and then repeat it back.
- Be patient. Take as much time as necessary.
- Try to ask questions that require only short answers or a nod of the head.
- Concentrate on what the individual is saying.
- If you are having difficulty understanding the individual, consider writing as an alternative means of communicating, but first ask the individual if this is acceptable. [51]

Cognitive Impairment

About 3 out of every 100 people have developmental disabilities, so it is likely that a law enforcement office will encounter an individual who experiences these or other associated cognitive impairments. A successful interaction with a person who has developmental disabilities or cognitive impairments can yield accurate and useful information while, at the same time, protecting his or her rights as an individual. [52]

- If you are in a public area with many distractions, consider moving to a quiet or private location.
- Be prepared to repeat what you say, orally or in writing.
- Offer assistance completing forms or understanding written instructions and provide extra time for decision making. Wait for the individual to accept the offer of assistance; do not "over-assist" or be patronizing.

- Be patient, flexible, and supportive. Take time to understand the individual and make sure that the individual understands you.[53]

ELECTRONIC MEDIUMS OF COMMUNICATION

The creation of the digital infrastructure, computer systems and networks, and various information technologies over the course of the previous decades has been nothing short of remarkable. The first electronic computer was manufactured in 1945. The military and banking systems began to utilize computer technologies during the 1960s. Consumers began purchasing and using "personal computers" in their homes during the 1980s. American workers across almost all sectors of the economy adapted to the desktop computer and e-mail during the 1990s. The Internet, or what was then popularly referred to as the World Wide Web, became familiar to most American during the latter half of that same decade. Mobile phones gained in popularity during the early 2000s, and the smartphone ultimately emerged and became an indispensable feature of modern life during the following decade. Information technologies are now fixtures of everyday life. Almost every form of interaction, business, and mode of communication relies on computers and network systems in some way.[54]

The revolution in information and communication technologies has obviously impacted law enforcement and the work of the police administrator, particularly with regard to communications. This fourth primary section of the chapter describes some of the ways that the revolution has altered organizational and interpersonal communications and the work of police executives. This section covers three of the most prevalent electronic mediums of communication including e-mail, mobile devices, and social media platforms.

E-mail

E-mail is a mainstay of the American workplace culture including the law enforcement industry. The first version of what would become known as E-mail was invented by computer engineers at the Massachusetts Institute of Technology (MIT) in 1965. CompuServe was the first online service to offer Internet-based e-mail service in 1989. Most Americans were introduced to e-mail in their workplace during the 1990s. The first version of Microsoft Outlook was released in 1993. Yahoo Mail followed in 1997. Google released the company's initial public version of Gmail in 2007.[55]

E-mail now dominates large blocks of time spent at work, particularly office-based workers. In 2017, there were 281.1 billion e-mails sent and received per day worldwide. The number of sent and received e-mails per day is expected to grow to 347.3 billion by 2023.[56] Surveys indicate that over one-half of all American adults check their e-mail multiple times per day and about 30 percent keep their e-mail accounts open throughout their workday.[57] Americans spend on average about three hours of every work day checking their work e-mail account.[58] The scholarly literature includes numerous references to an ongoing e-mail "epidemic" across the American workplace.

E-mail has inevitably become one of the most common mediums of communication for police administrators who, like the rest of us, spend many hours checking, sending, and receiving e-mails. The following suggested tips would do much to eliminate the unfortunate consequences that too often result from violations of commonsense etiquette in the use of e-mail.

- Maintain professionalism in e-mail correspondence. People who do not know you will form an impression based on what they read. As in any other business correspondence, business etiquette does not change when a message is digitized.
- Avoid flowery prose, which lengthens the message without adding value. Write in a sparse, tight manner. Limit the e-mail to a single topic and group the content in short paragraphs that are sequenced logically.
- Don't slow the system down with very large attachments, and avoid using the blind copy (BC) line; it suggests that there is something to hide.
- Respond to e-mail promptly, even if only to acknowledge initial receipt and that a more detailed response will follow.
- Check e-mail frequently but do not allow it to interrupt other scheduled tasks.
- Read and reread your e-mails for quality, tone, grammar, spelling, and punctuation before sending them. Do not rely solely on grammar or spell check to catch errors. Moreover, spell check may change the spelling of words, giving the message a different or ambiguous meaning.
- Remember that e-mail is not private correspondence and can easily become public without intent or consent. It is a permanent record of written communication.
- Do not use business e-mail for jokes or frivolous and offensive messages.
- If you write an e-mail while angry, even if provoked, don't send it until you can reread it in a calmer moment and are able to be more dispassionate. Venting in an e-mail reflects poorly on the sender.
- Deal with personal or sensitive issues in person, not through an impersonal electronic medium.
- Treat an e-mail inbox similar to a paper one: Review the document, act on it, and move on.
- The agency's e-mail is very effective in getting information to a number of people in an expeditious

fashion and to quickly, involve others, but do not send copies to persons who do not need to receive it.

- Use caution when responding to e-mails. How something is said in an e-mail language is just as important as what is said, no matter how emotional the issue or the contents of the e-mail received.[59]

Mobile Devices

Mobile devices such as smartphones and tablets have become the dominant mode of electronic communication for most Americans including police officers and police administrators. The forerunner to the smartphone, or the cellular telephone, initially became available to the public in 1983. The phone was "dumb"—you could only use it to make telephone calls—larger than the size of a brick, and cost $4,000.[60] Nokia introduced the first widely popular consumer handsets in the early 1990s. Sony Ericsson released the first popular cell phone that included a camera in 2002. Research in Motion (RIM) introduced the transformative Blackberry with 3G Internet connectivity in 2003. Apple pushed the trend toward "smart" devices (or mobile phones that perform many of the functions of a computer using a touchscreen and 4G Internet connectivity) with the introduction of the first iPhone in 2007.[61] Virtually every American adult currently owns a cellular phone of some type (95 percent), and 77 percent of adult Americans own a smartphone, with 55 percent of those also owning a tablet, another form factor that performs as a wireless computer with a touchscreen that is larger than a smartphone.[62] The revolution in wireless computing technology is complete and probably irreversible. The mobile device has become an indispensable part of modern life.

Smartphones and tablets are beginning to transform law enforcement and the manner in which police send and receive information in ways that were unimaginable just a couple of decades ago. The use of personal mobile phones by police on the street largely paralleled the emergence of the technology and the societal trends outline above. But the more recent trend toward department-issued smartphones has clearly quickened the pace of change in regard to police communications. The New York City Police Department (NYPD), for example, began issuing smartphones to all 36,000 officers in 2015. NYPD Cadets are now issued smartphones as part of their police academy training. On a single day in 2016, 5,500 NYPD officers logged onto their department issued cell phones and clicked on over 39,000 "notifications" or 911 calls for police service.[63] Likewise, the Police Foundation recently partnered with the Redlands (CA) Police Department to develop, implement, and evaluate the use of department-issued smartphones and tablets to over 100 officers.[64] These two programs can be used to show how the trend toward department-issued smartphones and tablets has begun to quicken change in police communications.

NYPD patrol officers use department-issued smartphones to more effectively communicate with citizens. The NYPD previously did not provide a way for citizens to contact officers directly in the field. Citizens who wanted to contact an individual patrol officer by phone called the precinct and were almost always forced to leave a message on a voice mail system shared by an entire squad of officers. Officers since the issuance of department smartphones now commonly provide their personal phone number to citizens including crime victims, witnesses, or other types of citizens. NYPD officers are now obviously more personally accessible to the citizens they serve.

Redlands (CA) police officers are issued smartphones as part of the partnership program with the Police Foundation. They utilize the devices through several customized software applications. The Field Interview (FI) phone app allows police to conduct field interviews directly through the software and immediately upload the information to the organization's records management system (RMS). Officers are provided access through the software to all of the searchable databases in real-time while they are in the field. The NearMe phone app allows officers to utilize crime mapping software directly from their phones. They can use crime mapping tools and select and search data fields including crime types, date and time ranges, geolocation data, and records of arrests, citations, and motor vehicle collisions—all from their mobile device in the field. The Police Flyers app allows officers to create and immediately distribute informational flyers including BOLOs directly from their mobile device.[65] These software applications seem like only the tip of the iceberg in terms of how mobile devices will become an increasingly important tool in terms of facilitating communications.

Social Media

Social media refers to a set of online tools that are designed for and focused on social interaction. These technologies, often referred to as communications "platforms," allow users to communicate and interact in order to exchange information of specific interest.[66] Social media platforms use Internet-based technologies that allow users to create content and enable interaction and communication across users through collaboration, information exchange, and networking.[67] This section provides information on these platforms, how police agencies have thus far utilized them, and descriptions of some of their limitations.[68]

Social media platforms originated as a means to connect individuals and promote the interpersonal communication of private citizens and groups, but these platforms have become more common with businesses and corporations as tool for marketing and sales. Social media platforms have more recently been recognized by public organizations including those within the realm of law enforcement as a way to accomplish many of the goals of policing including crime control, the improvement of public safety, and the promotion of collaborative ties with citizens.

American law enforcement can learn a great deal about social media from the corporate sector because businesses have already encountered some of the challenges of this type of communications medium. Businesses and corporations have more experiences than do public agencies in the identification of problems associated with the use of social media platforms and the use of strategies to mitigate them. Still, police departments are not corporations, businesses, nor even run-of-the-mill government agencies. They have unique powers and responsibilities along with a unique relationship with the public. Police need their own models, their own best practices, and their own discussions and philosophies about how to incorporate social media to achieve their unique purposes and goals.[69] There are four primary social media platforms most important to the objectives of police.

The Major Social Media Platforms

Facebook: Facebook is the most well-recognized and popular social media platform with 2.32 billion monthly active users worldwide and $55.8 billion in revenue in 2018. About 1.52 billion people log onto Facebook every day.[70] Users build communications networks through the identification of "friends" and adding them to a list of users authorized to view content. Users can also choose whether other users can "friend" them and gain access to privileged content.[71]

Law enforcement agencies often provide information and videos about news, arrests, promotions, academy class graduation, and other content. "Friends" of the police organization can opt to receive instant notification when the agency posts new information and content, and they can respond with their own comments. To illustrate, a law enforcement agency can post a Friday afternoon status update reminding "friends" of checkpoints targeting drunk driving. Every "friend" will get this information as they make plans for Friday night activities, and hopefully will remember to use a designated driver.[72]

Twitter: Twitter is the fifth most popular social media platform in the world, with 326 million active users worldwide including 67 million active users in the United States. Over 20 percent of American Internet users access Twitter. Twitter earned over $758 million in revenue in 2018.[73] Twitter is commonly referred to as a "microblogging" platform. Users exchange short content entries defined as "tweets" of up to 280 characters of text. Users may also upload and share videos of up to 2 minutes and 20 seconds in length. Twitter users build social networks by "following" other users and allowing other users to "follow" them. Twitter in terms of law enforcement is perhaps best viewed as a platform for the dissemination of crisis communications and emergency alerts. Police agencies can use Twitter to disseminate basic short communications instantly to followers rather than preparing, editing, and distributing full news releases.[74]

YouTube: YouTube is the world's second largest Internet search engine behind Google. The platform is dedicated to the creation and dissemination of video content. YouTube has 1.8 billion registered global users including 63 million daily users. The platform hosts over 5 billion videos. Users upload over 300 hours of video to the platform per minute.[75] YouTube users can create personal "channels" to create and upload video content and subscribe to other users specific channels to build a network. Many police departments utilize the platform to publish recruiting videos and news conferences at no cost to the agency, or even to promote new organizational strategies that may be more difficult or expensive to produce through traditional sources of media.[76]

Nixle: Nixle is a platform that is probably not as recognizable as the three previous platforms to the average citizen. Nixle is nonetheless important for law enforcement and police administration, since it was the first social networking platform to target government agencies as the primary audience. Nixle connects agencies of public safety, government, schools, and businesses using real-time two-way communications through text, e-mail, other social media platforms, and Nixle's proprietary mobile software application. Over 8,000 public agencies including police, fire, medical, and other public institutions subscribe to the platform.[77]

Similar to Twitter, Nixle is perhaps best utilized as a tool for the instant communication of emergency information to the public including severe weather events, evacuation orders, safety hazards, and security threats. Nixle's focus on government subscriptions has produced some partnerships of value to law enforcement. For example, Nixle was the first public networking site to partner with the National Law Enforcement Telecommunications System (NLETS). Because of this relationship, Nixle can house its servers in NLETS' secure facilities, resulting in an enhanced level of security and reliability for municipal agencies.[78] Nixle offers users the opportunity to have their own network that allows them to send secure instant emergency messages to all users in a designated geographic area.[79] This works well in communicating directly to those who need the information quickly. Users simply log in, enter their message, and then select the area on a map affected by the incident. The message goes only to users who choose to accept alerts in those areas. This ability to limit information distribution to those who need it offers a substantial advantage over other social media platforms.

Law Enforcement Utilization of Social Media

There is a range of information that can be used to find out how police agencies use social media platforms. For example, there have been two recent major surveys of American law enforcement agencies in regard to their use of social media. These surveys were conducted by the Police Executive Research Forum (2013) and the International Association of Chiefs of Police (IACP) in conjunction with the Urban Institute (2017). Taken together, these surveys provide a wealth of information important for police administrators.[80]

The IACP surveyed 539 American police agencies. The survey found that about 20 percent of the agencies started using social media by 2012, and an additional 35 percent of agencies had started using social media through 2015. The survey indicated that more than one-half of responding agencies claimed to use social media for a wide range of purposes including:

- public notification of safety concerns (91 percent),
- community engagement (89 percent),
- public relations (86 percent),
- traffic notifications (86 percent),
- solicitation of crime tips (76 percent),
- monitoring public sentiment (72 percent),
- investigative intelligence gathering (70 percent), and
- recruitment and vetting of job applicants (58 percent).

The PERF survey included more descriptive information regarding how agencies utilized social media platforms. For example, the Sacramento Police Department (SPD) reported that the agency is active on Facebook and Twitter and has used YouTube. The agency posts "dumb crook" stories, which are very popular. They also post all their press releases, including commendations to their employees as well as posting anniversaries of officers' deaths, which gets a considerable amount of attention as well. The SPD also puts video clips on their Facebook page, for example, crime prevention videos. In the last couple of years, there has been a significant increase in the amount of rapes committed (see Figure 10.10). The SPD analyzed the reports and found that at least 90 percent of the suspects and victims knew each other, and as a result they decided to find a way to educate the public about date rape and other types of rape in which the perpetrator is not a stranger. They have partnered with Women Escaping a Violent Environment (WEAVE) and started a campaign to post educational messages about the consequences of committing any kind of rape. The messages were designed for different groups of people. One targeted 16- to 25-year-olds, while another targeted those who were 25 years and older.

The Los Angeles County (CA) Sheriff's Department (LASD) reports that as technology changes, the public *expects* them to communicate in new ways. They now have the ability to instantly send out notifications when emergencies or other situations arise. The agency has also made major upgrades in their website and frequently sends department messages using the

FIGURE 10.10 ▶ The Facebook page for the Sacramento, California Police Department, available at: https://www.facebook.com/pages/Sacramento-Police-Department/137481202396.

various social media platforms popular with the public. The LASD realized that the general public usually does not have much of an opportunity to interact with the police unless they see them while on patrol or they do something wrong. But by using popular social media platforms, they are able to engage citizens who would like to have more interaction with the department. These new forms of communication allow the LASD to release news stories themselves instead of relying solely on traditional media outlets. One might expect this to lead to an antagonistic relationship with the local news media because police are no longer dependent on them anymore for communications. But in reality, they found it resulted in a closer relationship with the media. The media still likes to be the first ones to report police-related stories, so they are often given the story first. In addition, the agency still works closely with the media to provide accurate information. The overall effect is that most of the local media are reporting law enforcement stories in a more balanced and factual way.

The Boston Police Department also provided information on the use of social media. The Police Commissioner of the BPD noticed teens standing around the yellow tape at crime scenes and sending text messages. The commissioner thought that there might be a way for the agency to harness the information these individuals were gathering at the crime scene. The agency created an advertising campaign in which it set up the software that would be needed to develop a "text-to-tip" line. The program was so well received that people were texting in tips from across the country—not just from Boston—and they also saw a dramatic increase in the volume of calls to their 1-800 tip line. The BPD has also developed a blog to help them communicate with the public, and they have seen an incredible response to that. Their blog, bdnews.com, gets about 70,000 visitors a month. They have reached that number through the application of a variety of publicity techniques, including printing the websites on the side of all police vehicles. Having a visible website has helped the agency avoid any of the confusion that can occur when people put up fake websites that are created to appear as if they are official. The BPD has benefitted from having the blog as a forum to put out news about the department before the local papers. When people are getting their police news—both good and bad—straight from the law enforcement agency, it provides a higher level of assurance that the public is receiving accurate information and avoiding some of the sensationalizing that sometimes occurs when news agencies are racing to "break" the story.

Social Media and the Potential for Police-Community Collaboration

The information derived from the surveys conducted by PERF and the IACP are largely positive and imply that police agencies have already successfully adopted social media platforms as a way to make stronger connections between their agencies and the public. The surveys however rely on information provided entirely by police administrators themselves. Researchers may conduct what are referred to as content analyses instead of or in addition to surveys of law enforcement administrators in order to determine how police agencies have thus far utilized social media platforms. These content analyses simply involve an identification and measurement of the materials actually posted on the social media websites of police agencies rather than asking police administrators how they utilize social media.[81]

Studies based on content analyses of police social media websites provide at least three important findings. First, large municipal police agencies in the United States are typically very active on social media platforms, particularly Facebook. The most prolific agencies create close to 100 posts to their Facebook pages per month and have up to 14,000 Facebook followers. The rate of postings across the largest agencies however varied greatly, with some of the agencies much more active than others. Second, police agencies seem to most commonly use the platform for purposes other than public interaction. For example, agencies commonly use social media for the purposes of public relations or "push strategies," where agencies commonly post "good news" stories about the department for public dissemination. Other examples include "push and pull strategies," where police agencies use social media as a police blotter or the posting of crime and emergency bulletins.

The third major finding involves what police agencies are *not* typically accomplishing through their utilization of social media—true interactive dialogue with citizens. The first section of this chapter focused on the basics of communication and defined communication as a process where senders and receivers interact and send messages back and forth. Likewise, advocates of community policing demonstrate the need for collaboration between police *and* citizens to reduce crime and improve communities. Both basic communication and community policing are interactive and rely on the input of police and citizens in order to be successful. The research on police utilization of social media suggests that police have a ways to go in realizing the full potential of social media platforms in this regard. Most of what police agencies do on social media is in the form of one-way communication. Police post to the platforms again and again. They post public relations messages; they post crime bulletins; they post traffic updates. Citizens are in some cases allowed to respond and post, but there is currently very little dialogue or "back and forth" or multi-post threads involving police *and* citizen communications.

Perhaps the point can best be made using the traditional in-person community meeting between police and members of the public as an analogy for how many police agencies currently utilize social media platforms. Imagine that police called a community meeting (they set up a social media website). Members of the police department stand up and talk about agency performance measures and provide crime bulletins and traffic updates (police posts). Then, police speakers matter-of-factly announce that there will be no opportunity for public comments or questions, and then all police participants in the meeting get up and leave the premises without further comment. Citizens shout out questions and comments (citizen posts), but the police continue walking straight out of the door without responding to the comments or questions of citizens. Then police call another meeting (another police post) and the cycle repeats.

No police executive or officer would communicate in such ways at a face-to-face meeting with the public. Yet, that is the course of communications typical within the context of social media platforms such as Facebook. Communication takes at least "two to tango," and social media platforms have the potential to provide unending opportunities for police to communicate and collaborate with citizens, but only in the case that agencies utilize strategies designed to more effectively promote dialogue and interaction between citizens and police going forward.

Social Media and Police Indiscretions

The PERF survey suggests some more specific problems associated with the increased use of social media platforms by police agencies. More than one-half (57 percent) of responding agencies reported issues, disputes, or controversies resulting from employees' personal postings on social media sites. Moreover, additional evidence derived from research studies identifies a significant rise in citizen complaints and cases of disciplinary action relating to what has been recently defined as the most prevalent "indiscretions" of police officers using social media platforms.[82] Four different types of social media indiscretions have been identified in the literature:

- The posting of officer opinions that are perceived by the public to be extreme or prejudicial.
- The posting of information that threatens the personal safety of police officers themselves.
- The posting of information that divulges personal associations that may be defined as undesirable or that potentially undermine police integrity.
- The posting of information that undermines criminal proceedings and/or provides material that may be used to support the case of criminal defendants.[83]

Police officers in some egregious cases purposively release information through social media that is inappropriate and/or specifically not authorized to be released. But more commonly, officers commit social media indiscretions due to simple carelessness or ignorance of the dangers associated with the misuse or mismanagement of personal social media accounts. For example, many users are not aware that the default settings of popular social media platforms do not provide levels of privacy and security appropriate for users who are police officers. Facebook in particular includes certain "personalization" and "archival" features that potentially threaten police legitimacy. For example, followers of police users may indiscriminately identify them as law enforcement officers through the "tagging" feature. Police users who utilize archival features also allow others to investigate their personal "timeline" and identify facts about their personal histories or associations that can undermine both their personal integrity and that of the employing police agency.[84]

The PERF survey demonstrates on ongoing trend toward the development and enforcement of policies to guide officers in their use of both personal and organizational social media platforms. More than one-half of responding agencies (58 percent) indicated that their organization has implemented policies regarding what may or may not be appropriate for employees to post on social media sites. For example, the Northampton Police Department has developed the following instructions for their personnel to follow in order to avoid **police indiscretions** on social media.

- Photographs or other depictions of departmental uniforms, badges, patches, marked units, other departmental property, or on-duty personnel, including incident scenes, shall not be posted on Internet sites by department personnel without the approval of the Chief of Police.
- Employees are prohibited from posting, transmitting, and/or disseminating any pictures or videos of official departmental training, activities, or work-related assignments, without the expressed, written permissions of the Chief of Police.
- Employees shall treat as confidential, all the official business of the department.
- No employee shall release, either directly or indirectly, information concerning crimes, accidents, or violations of ordinances and/or statutes to persons outside the department, except as authorized by departmental policy under Public Information Function.
- No employee should gossip about the affairs of the department with persons outside the department.
- No sexual, violent, racial, ethically derogatory material, comments, pictures, artwork, video, or other references may be posted along with any department-approved reference.
- Employees shall not post any material on the Internet that brings discredit to or may adversely affect the efficiency or integrity of the Northampton Police Department. In disparage or harass, another department or city employee, as well as any other citizen.
- Employees shall not post any disparaging material about another police agency, employee, or citizen.
- Employees should consider the possible adverse consequences of Internet postings, such as future employment, cross-examination in criminal cases, and public, as well as private, embarrassment.
- Employees are reminded to exercise good judgment and demonstrate personal accountability when choosing to participate on social networking sites. Use of these types of sites while on duty shall be restricted to official departmental business only.

Police Management of Social Media Platforms

Police administrators need to consider at least three important factors in order to effectively manage organizational social media platforms.[85] The first important factor involves the selection of the best personnel to operate the platform. Social media management is really no different than many areas of police work: having the right people in the right places can make all of the difference. Having personnel in place who are already familiar and comfortable with the platforms will save time and training costs. A person familiar with the technology will be able to step into the technical side of the role very easily, and he or she will have more time available to devote to content development and other necessary tasks. However, if it were as simple as that, agencies could simply authorize access to the social media passwords to any 21-year-old officer fresh out of the academy. Police administrators should instead consider the appointment of personnel who command a grasp of the "big picture." It is important to find employees who have an understanding of the local politics and current events; who have an understanding of broad issues of department concern and the agency's official stance on them; and who have a level of foresight about the important issues that are likely to be forthcoming in the near future. This point cannot be overstated, as everything broadcast on social media, even down to a single tweet, amounts to a press release. And anything broadcast, if written in the wrong manner or with the wrong words, can instantly and irreparably bring negative attention to the agency.[86]

The second important factor in the management of social media platforms involves consideration of the proper **voice and tone** of communications. Consideration should be given to messaging voice and tone. As any public information officer will attest, the way that messages are delivered often has more impact than the actual content of the message. This is also true in the messages sent via social media. Consistency in voice is key. Each agency, particularly those using multiple posters, should strive for uniformity in how messages are conveyed. This can give the department an online identity that the public comes to recognize, appreciate, and depend on. Consider an agency that has two employees who share posting duties on the official department Twitter account. One employee may choose to tweet, "If you drink and drive tonight, we will arrest you, tow your car, and throw you in jail. Don't drink and drive." The other employee may take a softer approach, and choose to tweet, "If you are going out tonight, have fun, but please be safe and designate a nondrinking driver!" While there's nothing inherently wrong with either tweet, having both messages come from the same agency account on consecutive weekend nights will confuse followers and can even be off-putting. Having a consistent message delivered in a reliable and consistent voice makes the agency seem more professional and dependable (see Figure 10.11).

Many agencies choose to use a stoic and unemotional tone in their social medial platforms, a sort of 21st-century "just the facts, ma'am" approach. Consider, though, that several departments have had great social media success by relaxing the tone slightly when appropriate and by choosing to show some personality and even humor at times. Just like in-person interactions at a block party or at a local park, online social interactions give departments the chance to show the human side of their personnel. Agencies have long recognized that communities that get to know their officers usually like them. Social media platforms provide a means to accomplish the goals of community interaction and collaboration in the case that the appropriate organizational tone and messaging is employed.[87]

The third important factor in the management of social media platforms is consideration of the evolving role of the Public Information Officer (PIO) (previously introduced in Chapter 4 on the management of the media as a political consideration for police administrators). Not long ago, when a police agency wanted to communicate with a large number of citizens, the traditional mass media was pretty much the only game in town. The traditional news media not only controlled the mass distribution channels but also influenced how

FIGURE 10.11 ▶ Don't Drink and Drive messages from employees posting to an official department social media account need to be professional and dependable. (StacieStauffSmith Photos/Shutterstock)

the public viewed police.[88] Within this traditional context, large- and medium-size police agencies typically employed a Public Information Officer (PIO) whose primary focus was the dissemination and management of communications through traditional media sources such as radio, television, and newspapers.

The emergence of social media as a primary communications medium has fundamentally altered the role of the typical PIO.[89] The role of the traditional PIO has in some cases been augmented or even supplanted by personnel who act as full-time **social media managers** (SMM).[90] The effective management of organizational social media—whether accomplished under the auspices of a traditional PIO or the more recent SMM position—requires the performance of several important roles including the following.

- **Gatekeeper** of the flow of information through social media platforms from the organization to the public
- **Monitor** of public inputs on social media and the dissemination if necessary of public inputs to appropriate organizational channels
- **Expert** on social media trends and the operation of all major social media platforms.
- **Disseminator** of organizational communications to the most appropriate social media platform for public dissemination

Chapter Summary

Summary by Learning Objectives

1. **Identify and describe the basic steps in the communication process**

   The basic steps in the communication process involves senders, the message, a channel, receivers, feedback, environment, and noise.

2. **Identify the major barriers to communication in terms of senders, receivers, and barriers involving both senders and receivers**

   The major barriers to communication involving senders include ambiguous purpose, failures to adapt the message to the receiver, inappropriate mediums, no feedback mechanism, failure to respond to feedback, and failure to analyze the audience. The major barriers to communication in terms of receivers include misinterpretation of meaning, improper conclusions, selective listening, message rejection, and lack of focus. The major barriers to communication involving both senders and receivers include distraction, distance, and relational differences.

3. **Understand the various communication strategies used by effective organizational leaders.**

   The various communications strategies used by effective leaders are: credibility, gearing the message to the listener, persuading group members of the benefits of change, the use of heavy-impact and emotion-provoking words, consistently backing up conclusions with data, minimizing vocalized pauses and junk words, writing crisp, clear memos and reports using front-loaded messages, the use of power-oriented linguistic styles, inspiring confidence through nonverbal communication, and attending to the dynamics of group-level communications.

4. **Identify and describe the various modes of organizational communication**

   The various modes of organizational communication are multilevel and multiagency communication, downward communication, upward communication, horizontal communication, and the grapevine.

5. **Understand specific issues associated with police communications across specific audiences**

   There are specific issues involved in police communications across specific audiences including cross-gender communication, cross-cultural and multicultural communication, cross-generational communication, and communication problems associated with people with various forms of disability including visual impairment, hearing impairment, mobility impairment, speech impairment, and cognitive impairment.

6. **Describe the most important electronic mediums of communication.**

   The most important electronic mediums of communication are e-mail, mobile devices including mobile phones and tablets, and social media platforms including Facebook, Twitter, YouTube, and Nixle.

Chapter Review Questions

1. Discuss the steps in the communication process.
2. What are some of the barriers that result because of improper techniques used on the part of either the sender or receiver?
3. What are the seven most common sender communication barriers?
4. Why is it important to minimize vocalized pauses and junk words when communicating?
5. What are five types of downward communication within an organization?
6. The actual operation of the grapevine as a means of communication can be visualized in four ways. What are they?
7. Why is it so important for police officers to understand the need for effective cross-gender, cross-cultural and multi-cultural communication?
8. What types of special-need groups are police officers most likely to come in contact with and what are the most effective ways to deal with them?
9. What are the three most prevalent electronic mediums of communication?
10. What are the most common ways that law enforcement utilizes social media?
11. Four types of police officer social media indiscretions have been identified. What are they?

Critical Thinking Exercises

1. **Cross-Cultural Communication**. Your community has recently received a major influx of immigrants from a nonwhite, non-Judeo-Christian country.
   a. There have been some unfortunate clashes between your uniformed police officers and some young males from this community.
   b. You believe that many of these clashes have resulted because of a failure of your officers as well as members of this recently arrived immigrant community to understand important aspects of each other's culture.
   c. Who would you turn to provide the necessary training so your officers can become familiar with important aspects of the recently introduced culture in order to reduce some of the unfortunate misunderstandings and confrontations that have recently occurred?
   d. How would you go about identifying leaders within the newly arrived immigrant community who would be in a position to serve as a useful conduit with your agency in order to assist the recently arrived immigrants to better understand the expectations of your agency both in its personal and professional interactions?

2. **Management of Social Media Platforms**. You are the administrator of a small rural police organization that has a total of 10 sworn officers, including you, 2 sergeants, and 7 patrol officers. The organization does not currently have a presence in any of the major social media platforms, and there are no existing policies on officers' use of personal social media.
   a. Devise a policy that guides officer discretion in their personal and organizational use of social media.
   b. Determine which of the social media platforms would be most appropriate and effective in order to create a social media presence for your organization.
   c. Determine who will perform the duties of the social media manager in your organization and how that person will successfully perform those duties.

Key Terms

Channel
Communication barriers
Downward communication
Environment
Facebook
Feedback
Group communication
Group interaction

Horizontal communication
Interpersonal communication
Message
Nixle
Noise
Organizational communication
Police Indiscretions
Receiver

Sender
Social Media Manager
The grapevine
Twitter
Upward communication
Voice & Tone
YouTube

Endnotes

1. *World Vision,* "2017 Hurricane Harvey: Facts, FAQs, and How to Help." Available at http://www.worldvision.org/disaster-relief-news-stories/hurricane-harvey-fatcs.

2. G. Pennybacker, "Focus on the Social Media: Communication as a Function of Leadership." *FBI Law Enforcement Bulletin* (March 7). Available at http://leb.fbi.gov/articles/focus/focus-on-social-media-communication-as-a-function-of-leadership; J. Saul, "Meet the Houston Police Chief Who Helped Stop Hurricane Harvey from Becoming a Katrina Crisis," *Newsweek* (September 1). Available at http://www.newsweek.com/Houston-hurricane-flooding-police-chief-art-acevedo-austin-lessons-front-lines-658475

3. Available at https://abc30.com/weather/hurricane-harvey-heroes/2355221/ (accessed April 1, 2019).

4. A.J. DuBrin, *Human Relations: Interpersonal Job-Oriented Skills,* 8th edition (Upper Saddle River, NJ: Prentice Hall, 2004), pp. 42–46.

5. Krissah Thompson, "Arrest of Harvard's Henry Louis Gates Jr. Was Avoidable, Report Says," *Washington Post,* June 30, 2010; Katie Zezima, "Officer and Professor Faulted for Confrontation at Home," *New York Times* 159, No. 55088 (July 1, 2010), p. 21.

6. Andrew J. Dubrin, *Leadership* (New York: Houghton Mifflin, 2004), pp. 364–371, 373, 374.

7. James M. Kouzes and Barry Z. Posner, *The Leadership Challenge: How to Get Extraordinary Things Done in Organizations* (San Francisco: Jossey-Bass, 1987), p. 118.

8. Stephen P. Robbins and Phillip L. Hunsaker, *Training in Interpersonal Skills: Tips for Managing People at Work* (Upper Saddle River, NJ: Prentice Hall, 1996), p. 115.

9. Refer to Jay A. Conger, *Winning 'Em Over: The New Model for Management in the Age of Persuasion* (New York: Simon & Schuster, 2001).

10. Available at https://www.greaterirvinechamber.com/ambassador-of-the-month-archive/p/item/8494/irvine-police-chief-mike-hamel-presents-new-drone-program (accessed April 9, 2018).

11. Bill Chappell, "More Police Officers Died from Gunfire than Traffic Incidents in 2018, Report Says," National Public Radio, available at https://www.npr.org/2018/12/27/680410169/more-police-died-from-gunfire-than-traffic-incidents-in-2018-report-say (accessed April 15, 2019).

12. Michael W. Mercer, "How to Make a Fantastic Impression," *HR Magazine,* March 1993, p. 49.

13. Deborah Tannen, "The Power of Talk: Who Gets Heard and Why?" *Harvard Business Review* (September–October 1995), pp. 138–148.

14. Ibid. "How You Speak Shows Where You Rank," *Fortune,* February 2, 1998, p. 156; "Frame Your Persuasive Appeal," *Executive Strategies,* September 1998, p. 7; "Weed Out Wimpy Words: Speak Up Without Backpedaling, Qualifying," *Working Smart,* March 2000, p. 2.

15. Several of these suggestions are from *Body Language for Business Success* (New York: National Institute for Business Management, 1989), pp. 2–29, and "Attention All Monotonous Speakers," *Working Smart,* March 1998, p. 1.

16. Albert Mehrabian and M. Wiener, "Decoding Inconsistent Communications," *Journal of Personality and Social Psychology* 6 (1947), pp. 109–114.

17. Several of these suggestions are from *Body Language for Business Success* (New York: National Institute for Business Management, 1989), pp. 2–29, and "Attention All Monotonous Speakers," *Working Smart,* March 1998, p. 1.

18. Harvey Wallace, Cliff Roberson, and Craig Steckler, *Written and Interpersonal Communication Methods for Law Enforcement* (Upper Saddle River, NJ: Prentice Hall, 2001), pp. 39, 40. Reprinted by permission of Pearson Education, Inc., Upper Saddle River, NJ.

19. See Michael Burgoon, Judee K. Heston, and James McCroskey, *Small Group Communication: A Functional Approach* (New York: Holt, Rinehart & Winston, 1974), pp. 2–3, 12, 39.

20. See Robert Ardrey, *The Social Contract* (New York: Atheneum, 1970), p. 368, where the author theorizes that the range for a natural group is 11 or 12, and Marvin E. Shaw, *Group Dynamics* (New York: McGraw-Hill, 1971), which places the maximum number of persons at 20.

21. B. Aubrey Fisher, "Decision Emergence: Phase in Group Decision-Making," *Speech Monographs* 37 (1970), pp. 53–66.

22. Field, "The Abilene Paradox," p. 89.

23. Ibid., pp. 36–37.

24. Siobhan Gorman, "How Boston Terror Warning Went Awry," *National Journal* 37, No. 8 (February 19, 2005), p. 542.

25. Ibid., pp. 37–38.

26. D. Katz and R. L. Kahn, *The Social Psychology of Organizations* (New York: John Wiley & Sons, 1966), p. 239, as cited in Lewis, *Organizational Communication,* p. 38.

27. R.L. Smith, G.M. Richetto, and J.P. Zima, "Organizational Behavior: An Approach to Human Communication," in *Readings in Interpersonal and Organizational Communication,* 3rd edition, eds. R.C. Huseman, C.M. Logue, and D.L. Freshley (Boston: Holbrook Press, 1977), p.11.

28. T.L. Dahle, "An Objective and Comparative Study of Five Methods of Transmitting Information to Business and Industrial Employees" (PhD dissertation, Purdue University, 1954), as cited in Smith et al. "Organizational Behavior," p. 12.

29. E. Planty and W. Machaver, "Upward Communications: A Project in Executive Development," *Personnel* 28 (January 1952), pp. 304–319.

30. R.K. Allen, *Organizational Management through Communication* (New York: Harper & Row, 1977), pp. 77–79.

31. H. Fayol, *General and Industrial Administration* (New York: Pitman, 1949), p. 34.

32. Allen, *Organizational Management,* p. 78.

33. Ibid., pp. 78–79.

34. K. Davis, "Management Communication and the Grapevine," *Harvard Business Review* (September–October 1953), pp. 43–49, as cited by Lewis, *Organizational Communication,* p. 41.

[35]Lewis, *Organizational Communication*, pp. 41–42.

[36]Spanish is not the only language that officers will encounter. For a discussion of law enforcement agencies' experiences with Chinese, see C. Fredric Anderson and Henriettee Liu Levy, "A Guide to Chinese Names," *FBI Law Enforcement Bulletin*, March 1992, p. 10.

[37]United States Census Bureau, Newsroom, "Hispanic Heritage Month 2018, https://www.census.gov/newsroom/facts-for-features/2018/hispanic-heritage-month.html (accessed April 8, 2019).

[38]CNN Library, "Hispanics in the US Fast Facts," available at http://www.cnn.com/2013/09/20us/Hispanics-in-the-u-s-/index.html, (accessed March 8, 2019).

[39]Colleen Long, "Police Departments Offer Raises, Immersion Programs for Bilingual Cops," Associated Press, March 11, 2010. Writers Cristian Salazar in New York and Jeff Carlton in Dallas, and AP photographer Bebeto Matthews in New York contributed to this report.

[40]This section is adapted from Brian K. Ogawa, *Focus on the Future: A Prosecutor's Guide for Victim Assistance* (Washington, DC: National Victim Center, 1994).

[41]G. Weaver, "Law Enforcement in a Culturally Diverse Society," *FBI Law Enforcement Bulletin*, September 1992, pp. 3–7. (This discussion of cross-cultural diversity in communication was taken with modification from this source.)

[42]Thomas Kochman, *Black and White Styles in Conflict* (Chicago: University of Chicago Press, 1981).

[43]Edmund Glenn, D. Witmeyer, and K. Stevenson, "Cultural Styles of Persuasion," *International Journal of Intercultural Communication* 1 (1977), pp. 52–66.

[44]See e.g., Diana Oblinger, "Boomers & Gen-Xers, and Millennials: Understanding the New Students," *Educause Review* (July/August, 2003), p. 40; Diane Thielfoldt and Devon Cheef, "Generation X and the Millennials: What You Need to Know About Mentoring the New Generations," *Law Practice Today* (2010); Janna Anderson and Lee Rainie, "Millennials Will Benefit and Suffer Due to Their Hyperconnected Lives," Pew Research Center, February 29, 2012. http://www.pewinternet.org/2012/02/29/millennials-will-benefit-and-suffer-due-to-their-hyperconnected-lives/ (accessed June 15, 2015).

[45]Ibid.

[46]Linda A. Panszczyk, *HR How-To: Intergenerational Issues* (Chicago, IL: CCH KnowledgePoint, 2004), p. 168.

[47]No author, "Anniversary of Americans with Disabilities Act," U.S. Census Bureau, June 6, 2018, https://www.census.gov/newsroom/facts-for-features/2018/disabilities.html, (accessed April 11, 2019).

[48]https://www.nydailynews.com/new-york/springs-aid-visually-impaired-man-tense-shooting-scene-investigation-article-1.1388076, (accessed July 2, 2013).

[49]U.S. Department of Labor, Office of Disability Employment Policy; the Medial Project, Research and Training Center on Independent Living, University of Kansas, Lawrence, KS; and the National Center for Access Unlimited, Chicago, IL. About 9 percent of the American population is either deaf or hard of hearing. And as baby boomers reach their senior years, the percentage is going to increase. So the chance of an officer dealing with a deaf person or someone who is hard of hearing is a distinct possibility, which the officer should be prepared to deal with. Retrieved from http://www.dol.gov/odep/pubs/fact/comucate.htm, (accessed February 17, 2014).

[50]Amaury Muragado, "Dealing with the Deaf," *Police Beat*, September 20, 2013, http://www.policemag.com/channel/careers-training/articles/2013/09/dealing-with-the-deaf.aspx, (accessed February 17, 2014).

[51]U.S. Department of Labor, Office of Disability Employment Policy.

[52]Police Officer's Guide for Working with People with Developmental Disabilities and Achieving Positive Outcome, Community Mental Health for Central Michigan. http://www.thearcofmidland.org/wordpress/wp-content/uploads/2013/11/A-Police-Officers-Guide-for-Working-with-People-with-Developmental-Disabilities-and-Achieving-Positive-Outcome.pdf, (accessed February 17, 2014).

[53]U.S. Department of Labor, Office of Disability Employment Policy.

[54]R.W. Taylor, E.J. Fritsch, J. Liederbach, M.R. Saylor, and W.L. Tafoya, *Cyber Crime and Cyber Terrorism*, 4th edition (New York: Pearson, 2019).

[55]S. Gibbs, "How Did Email Grow from Messages Between Academics to a Global Epidemic," *The Guardian*, March 7, available at https://www.theguardian.com/technology/2016/mar/07/email-ray-tomlinson-history

[56]*Statista*, Number of Sent and Received Emails per Day Worldwide from 2017 to 2023. Available at https://www.statista.com/statistics/456500/daily-number-of-e-mails-worldwide

[57]R. Allen, "The American Inbox: The Modern State of Email in the Workplace." Available at https://www.smartinsights.com/email-marketing/American-inbox-modern-state-email-worrplace/

[58]C. Crandell, "Adobe Study Finds Email Is an Addiction," *Forbes*, August 26. Available at https://www.forbes.com/sites/chrstinecrandell/2015/08/26/adobe-study-finds-email-is-an-addiction/#b9164b2502ba

[59]James D. Sewell, "Handling the Stress of the Electronic World," *FBI Law Enforcement Bulletin*, August 2003, p. 14.

[60]Tigermobiles.com, "Evolution of the Mobile Phone." Available at http://www.tigermobiles.com/evolution/#start

[61]Ibid.

[62]*Pew Research Center*, Mobile Fact Sheet (February 5). Available at https://www.pewinternet.org/fact-shett/mobile/

[63]*CNET*, "This is NYPDs Official Crime-Fighting Phone" October 13. Available at http://www.cnet.com/news/nypd-new-york-police-offical-crime-fighting-windows-phone/

[64]*Police Foundation*, "Smartphones for Law Enforcement." Available at http://www.policefoundation.org/projects/smartphones-for-law-enforcement/

[65]Ibid.

[66]S.I. Bretschneider, and I. Mergel, "Technology and Public Management Information Systems: Where Have We Been and Where Are We Going," in *The State of Public Administration: Issues, Problems, and Challenges*, eds. D.C. Menzel and H.J. White (New York: M.E. Sharp, Inc.), pp. 187–203.

[67]L. Brainard, and M. Edins, "Top 10 US Municipal Police Departments and Their Social Media Usage." *American Review of Public Administration* 45, No. 6, pp. 728–745.

[68] J. Van Dijck, *The Culture of Connectivity: A Critical History of Social Media* (2013), New York: Oxford.

[69] Edward F. Davis III, Alejandro A. Alves, and David Alan Sklansky, *Social Media and Police Leadership: Lessons from Boston.* New Perspectives in Policing Bulletin (Washington, DC: U.S. Department of Justice, National Institute of Justice, 2014.) NCJ 244760, p. 2.

[70] Zephoria Digital Marketing, "The Top 20 Valuable Facebook Statistics Updated March 2019." Available at https://zephoria.com; Statista.Com, "Facebook's Annual Revenue from 2009 to 2018." Available at https://www.statista.com/statistics/268604/annual-revenue-of-facebook/

[71] L. Brainard, and M. Edins, " Top 10 US Municipal Police Departments and Their Social Media Usage." *American Review of Public Administration* 45, No. 6, pp. 728–745.

[72] Ibid.

[73] M. Iqbal, "Twitter Revenue and Usage Statistics 2018." Available at http://www.businessofapps.com/data/twitter-statistics/ (accessed March 8, 2019).

[74] "The Public Information Officer," pp. 4–5.

[75] A. Dogtiev, YouTube Revenue and Usage Statistics 2018. *Business of Apps*, January 7. Available at http://www.businessofapps.com/data/youtube-statistics/

[76] Ibid., p. 7.

[77] Nixle, About Nixle. Available at http://www.nixle.com/about-us/

[78] Ibid., p. 5.

[79] http://www.nixle.com (accessed June 16, 2015).

[80] Police Executive Research Forum, Social Media and Tactical Considerations for Law Enforcement. U.S. Department of Justice, Office of Community Oriented Policing Services: Washington, DC.
The Police Executive Research Forum (PERF) is a professional organization of progressive chief executives of city, county, and state law enforcement agencies. In addition, PERF has established formal relationships with international police executives and law enforcement organizations from around the globe. PERF's membership includes police chiefs, superintendents, sheriffs, state police directors, university police chiefs, public safety directors, and other law enforcement professionals. Established in 1976 as a nonprofit organization, PERF is unique in its commitment to the application of research in policing and the importance of higher education for police executives.
K. KiDeuk, "2016 Law Enforcement use of Social Media Survey: A Joint Publication by the International Association of Chiefs of Police and the Urban Institute." Justice Policy Center (February).

[81] See e.g., J.D. Lieberman, D. Koetzle, and M. Sakiyama, "Police Departments Use of Facebook: Patterns and Policy Issues," *Police Quarterly* 16, No. 44, pp. 438–462; A. Meijer, and M. Thaens, "Social Media Strategies: Understanding the Differences Between North American Police Department," *Government Information Quarterly* 30, pp. 343–350; L. Brainard, and M. Edins, "Top 10 US Municipal Police Departments and Their Social Media Usage," *American Review of Public Administration* 45, No. 6, pp. 728–745.

[82] A. Goldsmith, "Disgracebook Policing: Social Media and the Rise of Police Indiscretion," *Poling and Society* 25, No. 3, pp. 249–267.

[83] Ibid.

[84] Ibid.

[85] Dennis Burns and Zach Perron, "Considerations for Social Media Management and Strategy," *The Police Chief* (April 2014), pp. 30–32.

[86] Ibid., p. 31.

[87] Ibid.

[88] Ibid.

[89] A.M. Hughes, and L. Palen, "The Evolving Role of the Public Information Officer: An Examination of Social Media in Emergency Management," *Journal of Homeland Security and Emergency Management* (Online) 1547-7335. DOI: https://doi.org/10.1515/1547-7355.1976.

[90] See e.g., C. Hsiung, "Bringing Social Media Strategy into the 21st Century," *Police Chief* 83, No. 12 (December), pp. 24–27; R. Strain, "Social Media Manager in Law Enforcement," A Leadership White Paper Submitted in Partial Fulfillment Required for Graduation from the Leadership Command College, The Bill Blackwood Law Enforcement Management Institute of Texas (September).

## CHAPTER ELEVEN

LABOR RELATIONS

Learning Objectives

1. Identify and understand some of the factors that led to growth in the unionization of police.
2. Compare and contrast various models for collective bargaining for law enforcement officers.
3. State the two most widely used alternative dispute resolution methods and their common purpose.
4. Explain the ways in which the bargaining process is established including the process, opportunities for conflict, and negotiation.
5. Define collective bargaining grievances and the five steps to the grievance procedure.
6. Understand various job actions that may occur within the context of collective bargaining agreements including work stoppages, the vote of confidence, and work slowdowns and speed-ups.

INTRODUCTION

NO SINGLE FORCE IN *the past 60 years has had a greater impact on the administration of police agencies than collective bargaining by officers. Police unions represent a major force with which police managers must reckon. It is important for the police administrator to possess the following information in order to enhance their effectiveness in dealing with police unions: (1) the historical aspects of the creation of police unions in the United States, (2) the impact police unions have had on their communities and their respective agencies, (3) the general structure of laws governing collective bargaining for law enforcement officers, (4) how a bargaining relationship is formed, (5) the various job actions that police unions will sometimes take when they are dissatisfied with the negotiation process or other political issues arising in the community, (6) the most efficient ways for police administrators to handle job actions, and (7) collective bargaining trends.*

UNIONIZATION OF THE POLICE: A HISTORICAL PERSPECTIVE

From 1960 through the 1970s, a number of events combined to foster public-sector collective bargaining. These significant forces were: (1) the needs of unions to expand their membership, (2) the reduction of legal barriers, (3) police frustration with the perceived lack of support for their "war on crime," (4) personnel practices in police agencies, (5) salaries and benefits, (6) violence directed at the police, and (7) the success of other groups.[1]

The Needs of Labor Organizations to Expand Their Membership

In 1935, federal law gave private sector employees the right to bargain. As a consequence, until the 1960s, the attention of labor organizations was devoted almost entirely to organizing and enrolling members exclusively from the private sector. However, ultimately this exclusive focus effectively created a ceiling to union growth. Entrepreneurially, unions looked for another large group of employees to serve, which also benefited themselves.

In 1960, only 2 percent of the public workforce was unionized.[2] By 1965, there were 10.6 million employees in local, state, and federal governments, who were almost entirely non-unionized.[3] Therefore, unions coveted the possibility of organizing public employees in order to increase their membership rolls. Because there was and would be no national public sector collective bargaining law, unions worked in individual states to pass laws permitting it. Wisconsin became the first state to grant bargaining rights to municipal employees in 1959. One consequence of a lack of national legislation for public sector collective bargaining was that just a few states passed such laws. Across those states and the ones that later followed, there are similarities and differences, creating a patchwork of laws. When police collective bargaining occurs, it is substantially governed by the applicable state statute. In a few states where collective bargaining with public employees is not legally prohibited, it is provided for by ordinances enacted by county commissions and city councils. In this chapter, we will avoid repetitively distinguishing between state statutes and local ordinances.

Since 1983, there has been a continuing decline in private sector union memberships. In that year, unions represented one in every five workers. By 2020, unions represented only 1 in 10 workers.[4] The public sector membership rate in 2019 was 33.6 percent or five times that of the private sector's 6.3 percent. The most organized occupational group in 2019 was the protective services with 33.8 percent.[5] While membership in private sector unions has plunged downward, in the public sector it surged upward.

The decline in overall union membership was precipitated by[6] (1) new laws that rolled back the power of unions in states such as Indiana, Michigan, New Jersey, and Wisconsin with right to work laws. Such laws allow people to be employed without an obligation to join the applicable union, commonly called a union "closed shop," (2) manufacturers and other major employers preferred to expand into states with right to work laws. In 2020, there were 28 states with right to work laws;[7] (3) although there have been continuing increases in the number of retail and restaurant employees, unions historically have enjoyed only tepid success in organizing those sectors; and (4) The U.S. Supreme Court ruled in *Janus* (2018) that it is unconstitutional for unions to collect fees from non-consenting employees who were not union members.[8]

The Reduction of Legal Barriers

The first campaign to organize the police started shortly after World War I, when the American Federation of Labor (AFL) reversed a long-standing policy and issued charters to police unions in Boston, Washington, DC, and about 30 other cities. Berkeley, California Police Chief August Vollmer and many other police chiefs promptly condemned this move. Following the logic of the military analogy, they insisted that policemen could no more join a union than soldiers and sailors and therefore had no right to affiliate with the AFL.

FIGURE 11.1 ▶ Massachusetts State Guard marching people to jail who were suspected of committing crimes during the Boston police strike of 1919. Police Commissioner Curtis fired 1,117 striking police officers, replacing them with out-of-work World War I veterans. (Everett Collection Inc/Alamy Stock Photo)

Boston Police Commissioner E.U. Curtis refused to recognize the police union, forbade the rank and file to join it, and filed charges against several union officials. Commissioner Curtis called on the union to give up its charter and when it refused, it suspended more than a dozen policemen. As a result, three-quarters of the force went out on strike (see Figure 11.1). On orders from Governor Calvin Coolidge, the Commonwealth fired the strikers and destroyed the union. This action was applauded by President Woodrow Wilson, who called the strike "a crime against civilization."[9] The ill-fated Boston police strike provided an object lesson to officers and governments (see Figure 11.1). By 1920, that object lesson effectively ended all efforts to unionize the police in America for the next 40 years.[10]

States that enacted public sector bargaining laws removed the chief barrier to the unionization of public employees. After Wisconsin in 1959, other states that extended collective bargaining rights to at least some classes of public employees at an early date included California, Connecticut, Delaware, Massachusetts, Michigan, Oregon, Washington, and Wyoming. Many other states followed this lead, particularly from 1967 to 1974.[11] President John F. Kennedy granted limited collective bargaining rights to federal workers in 1962 by Executive Order 10988. The courts, too, were active in removing barriers; for example, in Atkins v. City of Charlotte (1969), the U.S. District Court struck down a portion of a North Carolina statute prohibiting public employees from being or becoming a union member as an infringement on the First Amendment right to free association.[12] While Atkins involved firefighters, the federal courts reached similar conclusions involving Atlanta police officers in Melton v. City of Atlanta (1971)[13] and a Colorado deputy sheriff in Lontine v. VanCleave (1973).[14]

Police Frustrations with a Perceived Lack of Support for Their War on Crime

During the 1960s and much of the 1970s, the police felt abandoned and isolated in their effort to control crime. This was caused by two factors: (1) perceived public hostility and (2) the impact of the due process revolution.

Perceived Public Hostility

A 1967 survey of a larger city police department revealed that over 70 percent of the officers felt an acute sense of citizen hostility or contempt.[15] In contrast, a survey conducted by the National Opinion Research Center that same year revealed that 77 percent of the respondents felt the police were doing a "very good" or "pretty good" job of protecting people in their neighborhoods.[16] These data notwithstanding, the police saw the public as hostile, and the most persuasive "evidence" of this emerged in the attempts to create civilian review boards, which carried several latent messages to police officers. First, it created anger with its implied allegation that the police could not, or would not, keep their own house in order. Second, it fostered the notion that politicians were ready to "throw the police to the wolves" and thus were part of "them."

The previously high public opinion of the police has declined dramatically in recent years. After a string of controversial police shootings, a 2015 Gallup poll found confidence in the police at its lowest in two decades, a mere 52 percent, matching the level in a 1991 poll taken after African-American motorist Rodney King was beaten by Los Angeles police officers.[17]

The Impact of the Due Process Revolution

Particularly among street-level officers, the reaction of the police to the due process revolution and associated Supreme Court decisions during the 1960s was one of dismay at being "handcuffed" in attempts to control crime. It tended to alienate the police from the Supreme Court and to contribute to a general feeling that social institutions that should support the police effort in combating crime were, instead, at odds with that effort.

Personnel Practices in Police Agencies

Past practices become precedent, precedent becomes tradition, and tradition in turn becomes the mighty anchor of many organizations, sometimes impeding change. By the late 1960s, the tendency to question the appropriateness of certain traditions was pervasive. Police rank-and-file members were no exception. This tendency was heightened by the increased educational achievement of police officers. Although management's general performance was often judged to be suspect, traditional and sometimes idiosyncratic personnel practices were the greatest concern, as these directly affected the individual officer.

Among the practices that were most distasteful to rank-and-file members were the requirement to attend, unpaid, a 30-minute roll call immediately before the 8-hour tour of duty; uncompensated court attendance during off-duty time; short-notice changes in shift assignments; favoritism in both work assignments and selection for attendance at prestigious police training schools; and arbitrary disciplinary procedures. Good performing veteran officers often didn't get written up for things a rookie did. If both the veteran and a rookie committed roughly the same infractions and got written up, more experienced officer got a mildly written letter of reprimand while the newer one got something more than that.

Gradually, the gap between officers and management widened. Officers began turning to employee organizations to rectify collectively the shortcomings of their circumstances. Subsequently, the solidarity of police officers was to prove a great benefit to employee organizations.

Salaries and Benefits

As did other government workers in the 1960s, police officers felt their salaries, fringe benefits, and working conditions were not adequate. In 1961, mining production workers were averaging $111 a week in earnings, lithographers $114, tire and inner-tube producers $127, and telephone line construction workers $133,[18] whereas the pay of police officers averaged far less. Even by 1965, the salary range for patrol officers in the larger cities—those with more than 100,000 in population—was only between $5,763 and $6,919 annually.[19]

The rank-and-file members believed increasingly that, if what was fairly theirs would not be given willingly, they would fight for it. In New York City, the Patrolmen's Benevolent Association (PBA) was believed to have been instrumental, from 1958 to 1969, in increasing entry-level salaries from $5,800 to $11,000 per year; obtaining longevity pay, shift differential pay, improving retirement benefits; and increasing the death benefit from $400 to $16,500.[20] In 1968, the Boston PBA, in negotiating its first contract, which required mediation, obtained increased benefits for its members, such as an annual increase of $1,010; time and a half for all overtime, including court appearances; and 12 paid holidays.[21]

However, in recent years, police unions have been called upon not only to fight for pay raises for their members but also to oppose and effectively deal with threatened pay cuts, reductions in pension benefits, paying a greater share of the cost of medical insurance, forced layoffs, and token raises (see Figure 11.2).

Violence Directed at the Police

In 1964, there were 9.9 assaults per 100 officers; in 1969, that figure rose to 16.9. Before 1968, the killing of police officers by preplanned ambushes was unheard of; in that year, there were seven such incidents.[22] The escalating violence had considerable psychological impact on the police, who saw themselves as symbolic targets of activists attacking institutional authority. Rank-and-file members began pressing for body armor, special training, the placement of special weapons in police cars, and sharply increased death benefits. The Islamic State has recently encouraged jihadists to kill American police officers, raising the specter that ambushes of the police may increase, even as many are calling for the demilitarization of the police.

Violence directed at police officers continues. Recent examples are as follows: (1) in 2020, a lone gunman shot and wounded one of two on-duty NYC officers sitting in their vehicle. He escaped the scene and later entered a police precinct, where he wounded another officer. When out of bullets, he tossed the gun away, and surrendered and (2) two Los Angeles Police officers were sitting in their police vehicle in 2019, when a man suddenly started shooting at them. A gunfight ensued and the man was fatally wounded.

The Success of Other Groups

During the 1960s, the police witnessed mass demonstrations on college campuses that used many of the tactics associated with the Civil Rights movement. The college campus protests were against the Vietnam War (see Figure 11.3). Among the campus demonstrations that were highly publicized were the University of Chicago (1965), Columbia University (1968), and San Francisco State College (1969). By 1970, campus demonstrations

FIGURE 11.2 ▶ Members of the New York City Patrolmen's Benevolent Association fight city hall plans to raise their annual salaries by only 1 percent. (Courtesy of Alamy, photograph by Luiz Rampelotto/Pacific Press/Alamy Live News)

FIGURE 11.3 ▶ A 1972 antiwar demonstration in San Francisco. America's involvement in the Vietnam War stretched from 1954 until 1973. During the 1950s, our troop level in Vietnam was roughly 800, reaching its height in 1968 at 549,500. As the war went on, opposition to it increased. The large-scale demonstrations effected America's policy, leading it to end the war. (J. G. Domke/Alamy Stock Photo)

reached the point that within 10 days of President Richard Nixon's announcement that he was expanding the Vietnam War and invading enemy sanctuaries in Cambodia, a total of 448 campuses were either shut down or otherwise affected by campus unrest.[23] One lesson the police learned from this is that collective action can produce results.

THE IMPACT OF POLICE UNIONS ON THE COMMUNITY

The existence of a police union impacts both the police department and the community itself. Unions do not just bargain and enforce agreements through litigation. They are much more active. Examples include financially supporting and campaigning for candidates running for local, state, and national offices, using the news media to shape public opinion on issues important to the unions, for example, why job protection clauses in agreements are essential, shaping the discussion on what the staffing of the police department should be, and demonstrating labor solidarity by joining public and private sector unions picketing employers. This section illustrates some of those impacts. Those selected for commentary are: (1) collective bargaining agreements (CBAs, also referred to as agreements and contracts) and discipline, accountability, and transparency; (2) police unions, local governments, and communities; (3) politics; and (4) financial impact.

Collective Bargaining Agreements and Discipline, Accountability, and Transparency

Police unions strive to protect the rights of their members.[24] They defend members whether the charges are minor or more significant, for example, drinking on duty or involvement in a controversial shooting incident. Although unions are not bound to support members in every disciplinary situation, they do provide consistent support. These actions are worthy ones for unions. However, in this process, it is certain that a small number of officers, whose misconduct is serious, escape being held accountable, that is, being disciplined or terminated.[25] Some observers also maintain this may result in other officers not being deterred from future misconduct.

Even while recognizing the unique responsibilities, dangers, and responsibilities of officers making split second life and death decisions, there are a growing number of voices arguing against CBAs and **Peace Officer Bill of Rights (POBR)** laws granting far more protection that ordinary government employees have. This and the results of police use of deadly force sometimes angers and mobilizes some groups, such as Black Lives Matter (see Figure 11.4). This is an issue that will not go away and will be very difficult to resolve.

The impact of police unions on discipline, accountability, and transparency is the issue that causes the greatest concern among community activists, public officials, and particularly police executives.[26] Most police collective bargaining occurs out of public sight (see Box 11.1), as does arbitration of grievances arising out of the agreement. Unions have negotiated agreements that provide strong rights for their members under investigation for misconduct (see Box 11.3).

Police unions have negotiated agreements that reduce the amount of control a department can exert over its disciplinary procedures.[27] Some of the most problematic provisions in this regard include those that prohibit the interrogation of officers for alleged misconduct until a specified period that typically ranges from 24 hours to two days.[28] Other provisions limit the consideration of prior disciplinary records by requiring that they be purged from an officer's personnel file and destroyed after an established time period. These and other similar types of provisions weigh heavily in the favor of officers suspected or accused of wrongdoing.

A study of 314 disciplinary cases in the Chicago Police Department between February 2010 and February 2017 revealed 85 percent of the cases supported by the union on behalf of the officers had their punishments reduced or overturned entirely. About half of the cases were decided by an independent arbitrator. In the remaining cases, union officials and Chicago's lawyers negotiated a settlement before arbitration, typically to receive a lesser discipline in exchange for officers withdrawing their grievances.[29] Speculatively, the charges against officers may have been too severe and correction was needed. However, how likely is it that overcharging officers occurred in 85 percent of the cases?

The **code of silence** or blue wall reinforces the difficulties created by contract articles in investigating, disciplining, and terminating officers who transgress. This code is totally independent

FIGURE 11.4 ▶ Throngs of protesters rally in New York City's Union Square, condemning the police shootings that resulted in the killing of two black men within a day of each other. One of the ironies of policing is officers must protect demonstrators' Constitutional rights to peacefully assemble and freedom of speech, even when the demonstrator's actions are critical of the police. (Courtesy of M. Stan Reaves/Alamy Live News)

Box 11.1: Police Unions Negotiating with Government Entities in Florida

Florida is among the states that do allow public attendance at agreement negotiations between a union and the employing government. The practice is made possible by "sunshine laws." At its simplest, Florida's sunshine law for public collective bargaining is divided into two parts: (1) when the public employer is meeting with its own side, for example, developing bargaining priorities and strategies, it is exempt from the sunshine law and (2) when the public employer is bargaining with the union, it is required to comply with the sunshine law. Essentially, sunshine laws are tools that support transparency by requiring governments and unions to operate openly "in the sunshine."[30]

---

of unions, which did not create it, have not endorsed it, and do not support it in any fashion. It is well-documented that many officers will not report acts of misconduct and/or crime by fellow officers. To do so means being shunned in the locker room, backups will be slow getting to the "rat's" location, and confrontations occur, as does vandalism to personal cars.

Police Unions, Local Governments, and Communities

Police unions have major advantages over their private sector counterparts. By taking advantage of the political process, they acquire a great deal more influence with the employers of their members, that is, unions can help elect the leaders with whom they deal. Presently, political contributions made by public sector unions are far more than those of their private sector counterparts. The ballot box advantage tilts to police unions in low turnout elections because they'll mobilize their supporters and friends.[31] Moreover, general public employee turnout for elections is higher than those employed in the private sector.

Historically, unions have focused on wages, benefits, and pensions for their members. Rarely did they push for hiring more people because it would dilute the money available for the benefit of current employees. Police unions now resist cutbacks and support adding additional officers. That translates to more dues and more people to move the union agenda forward. Further, unlike private sector employers, public employers often have a monopoly on services, such as electricity and water, which allows them to make incremental price increases to cover a budget shortfall from collective bargaining without creating meaningful opposition.[32]

Police unions in California and other states have fought efforts to make police use of force and disciplinary records transparent. The U.S. Department of Justice (USDOJ) found it challenging to investigate the Cleveland Police Department's (CPD) use of force because of the CPD's agreement with the union required the deletion of disciplinary records from departmental databases two years after the incident.[33] Nonetheless, the USDOJ was able to enter into a court enforceable agreement regarding the department's pattern or practice of excessive use of force. The degree to which court enforceable agreements produce the outcomes desired by USDOJ is unclear. A small study of 10 police departments under such agreements

produced interesting results. Half of the departments saw their use of force decline or remain the same during or after the agreements ended, but the other half saw use of force incidents increase.[34]

Two weeks before Freddie Gray died in Baltimore Police Department custody, police unions were successful in sidetracking major policing reforms under consideration by the Maryland legislature. The reforms could not have been enacted, signed into law, and operationalized in police departments, so they never could have saved Mr. Gray's life. Had those reforms become law, some lives would have been saved. This is an accounting of what might have been, played out in too many jurisdictions. All reformers can't be wrong and some or more of their recommendations must have merit.

There is also a record of police groups and unions occasionally supporting reforms. In the early 1900s, Chief August Vollmer instituted the Friday Crab Club. He met weekly with a group of police officers to review police actions, including use of force.[35] More recently, during his tenure as the new head of the Seattle Police Officers' Guild (SPOG) during 2014–2016, Ron Smith worked closely with the Chief of Police and other reformers implementing consent decree reforms from the U.S. Department of Justice to curb excessive use of force and racially biased policing. Smith told the Guild's member bias-free policing was important. If they didn't like it, they could go someplace that supported their view. While he was leading the SPOG no grievance or other actions were taken to block the reforms. A group of Seattle officers did file a suit against the new use of force policy, but Smith expressed disapproval and the SPOG did not join it.[36]

Police unions are occasional innovators of programs to protect their officers. In New York City, the Sergeants Benevolent Association announced a $500 cash award for civilians who assist NYPD officers to restrain persons who are resisting arrest. The Association cautioned people not to do so for the award because they could be injured. The Association advises as an alternative to assisting: Call 911 and get help for the officer instead. Ultimately, a police panel will determine eligibility for the award.[37] The Reverend Al Sharpton, a long time civil rights leader, saw the program as inciting vigilantes to violence against Black and Brown people, and incentivizing it monetarily, as unconscionable.[38]

Police unions sometimes provide support to community causes as shown by the examples from across the country:

1. The Combined Law Enforcement Association of Texas (CLEAT), the state's largest police union, championed the cause of two members of the El Paso Sheriff's Officers' Association struck by catastrophic illness. They were experiencing financial hardship and blocked by local policy from using sick leave days from a pool of 7,500 days contributed by other county employees. The CLEAT intervention resulted in rewriting of the eligibility rules for receiving days from the sick day pool and the issuance of specific instructions that the two men were to be made eligible.[39]

2. The Glendale, California, Police Officers Association (GPOA) started as a service organization to its member officers and firefighters. Its history begins in 1923, when it provided relief/assistance to police and fire fighters, for example, $3.00 a day for 12 weeks to members who were unable to work. In the 1950s, it sponsored a Police Boys Band, a basketball throwing contest, and a Little League baseball team. More recently, The GPOA still provides services to its members such as long-term disability and supplemental life insurance. It also gives back to the community through its "Cops for Kids" foundation, which raises money to help children in underprivileged families during the holidays, provides scholarships to local students, and financially supports other local events benefitting the youth of Glendale.[40]

3. The Fraternal Order of Police Lodge 108 in Seymour, Indiana, raises funds annually to provide Christmas gifts to children of low-income families. Teachers received a $5,000 donation from the Mattoon (Illinois) Police Union to purchase classroom supplies and buy essential clothing for needy children.

Communities don't just passively receive police services. Some actively demonstrate their appreciation for the sacrifices made to protect them. Two cities separated by 1,459 miles illustrate this point in different ways. Citizens of the Village of Ruidoso, New Mexico, are close to their officers. Residents handmade masks for officers to wear for safety during the COVID-19 pandemic (see Figure 11.5). In Dublin, Ohio, City Barbeque dropped off 40 pounds of cooked meats at Police Headquarters on New Year's Eve. It was their way of showing their love for officers protecting the city and unable to be with their families on a holiday. Such voluntary acts are appreciated by officers for their genuineness.

Politics and Police Unions

Historically, police unions have used their political muscle. Candidates for public office value and seek their endorsement. Multiple streams of change have hit public employee unions since the Great Recession of 2007-08. During 2011–2018, in a dozen or more states, such unions suffered losses in power.[41] They were attacked in some states by Republican Governors and legislatures, where efforts to weaken them have been successful. Illustratively, in Wisconsin the public sector collective bargaining law was amended to limit negotiated pay increases to no more than the annual increase in the consumer price index (CPI). Republican success in trimming the power of public employee unions is viewed in some circles as a move to weaken their usual support for Democrats. That could be the reason, but supporters of the changes argue that it's actually an austerity movement by Republicans. They point to the mountain of debt caused by generous pensions and health care costs. Those costs consume ever-increasing portions of state spending and are not sustainable.[42]

Unions are not oblivious to the turbulence in their environments. One way unions exercise political clout is through

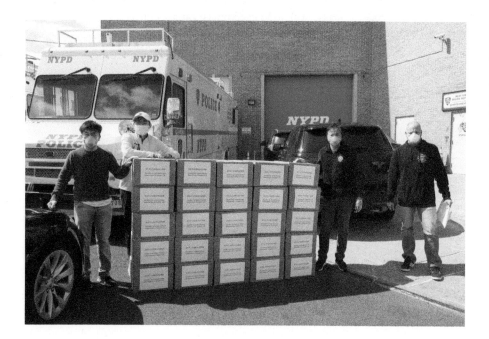

FIGURE 11.5 ▶ Volunteers of United Chinese Associations of Eastern U.S. donated 30,000 facemasks to the NYPD. Chinese American communities across the United States are donating medical supplies to hospitals, police stations, and local residents to help fight COVID-19. (Courtesy Xinhua via Getty)

political contributions. In 2019, public sector employee unions spent $160 million on such contributions.[43] These are meant to maintain union political support and proactively head off or reduce incursions to reduce union power; more recently, police unions are seemingly backing more Republican candidates. Symbolically, that may be interpreted as an olive branch to the Republican Party. The Fraternal Order of Police is the largest police union in the world with 355,000 members.[44] In 2016, it endorsed Republican candidate Donald Trump for President. The 100,000-member International Union of Police Associations (IUPA) also endorsed President Trump in his 2020 reelection bid.

Financial Impacts

Until most recently, police unions have been generally successful in negotiating good salary and fringe benefit packages for their members. The resulting contract provisions have no doubt impacted the finances of local jurisdictions. It is believed that the negotiations of police unions set the standard for negotiations by other municipal employees, although this proposition has not been the subject of empirical scholarship. It is not known to what extent negotiated police salaries and benefits force cities and counties to reduce expenditures for other services such as streets, parks, and libraries. On the positive side, it is generally accepted that the advent of police unionism in the late 1960s and early 1970s resulted in significant improvements in police salaries and fringe benefits. This has in turn helped to improve the relative attractiveness of law enforcement as a career over time.

Two recent trends threaten to upend these gains. First, the Great Recession of 2007–2009 dramatically threatened the financial well-being of both citizens and local governments.[45] U.S. household income dropped by 18 percent or more than $10 trillion. Thirty million people lost their jobs.[46] The impact of the Great Recession on law enforcement was substantial: (1) fiscal distress in state and local governments was widespread; (2) many communities could no longer afford their police departments so they closed them and contracted for police services from the Sheriff or a nearby city; (3) a portion of small cities simply ceased to exist, along with all of their departments; and (4) some police departments were cut so deeply they could only answer emergency calls and/or couldn't provide 24-hour service.[47] After the Camden, New Jersey, Police Department (CPD) laid off 163 officers, the department no longer responded to home burglaries and breaking and entering vehicles calls unless they were in progress. The CPD isn't an isolated case. Across the country, cities and counties made deep cuts in their workforces. Generally unable to make economic gains for members during the Great Recession, police unions focused on saving jobs and rights.

The second most recent trend influencing local government finances and by extension police salaries and benefits involves the COVID-19 global pandemic.[48] COVID-19 has caused an enormous loss of revenue for local jurisdictions. The ultimate financial impact of the pandemic on police salaries and benefits remains largely unknown, but there is a possibility that **concessionary bargaining** or police union "givebacks" will be widespread.

Givebacks are defined as a negotiated reduction in contract wages and benefits in exchange for which union members receive greater job security or other nonmonetary things of value. These may include government assurances regarding the availability of adequate quality personal protection equipment (PPE) for officers, the provision of paid administrative leave for officers required to stay home or quarantine, and/or waiving co-pays and out-of-pocket expenses associated with the testing and treatment of COVID-related illnesses among police officers (see Figure 11.6).[49]

A point to be kept in mind by both parties to concessionary and other negotiations is even if a police chief can make unilateral decisions regarding an existing agreement, the city may still have a duty to bargain with the police union over the *effects* of those decisions. Assume a police chief has the right to order officers to wear masks while on duty. Union members have a right to bargain over the quality of the masks, how long masks can be worn before they must be replaced, and how many replacement masks will be in each police car, as well as requiring the city to pay all associated costs.[50]

FIGURE 11.6 ▶ A Detroit Police Officer in the Narcotic unit wears a mask due to COVID-19 requirements. (Michael Matthews - Police Images / Alamy Stock Photo)

Quick Facts: Conflicts over COVID-19 Pay, Benefits, and Job Security

The Cleveland (Ohio) Patrolmen's Association requested monthly hazardous pay of $1,200 for 1,500 officers during the COVID-19 pandemic. Justification was stated as the extra responsibilities, risk of exposure, and stress on the officers and their families.[51] In California, Deputies in a Sheriff's Office did not support the request of civilian staff members for such pay. The City of Baltimore will have a $42 million deficit in its current fiscal year and a revenue shortfall of $100 million in the next one. The police and other departments will be forced by Baltimore to absorb large personnel cuts and pay cuts as well. The personnel cuts come at a time when violent crime is increasing. Baltimore wants to withdraw the officers' present $200 per paycheck COVID-19 supplement, a move that provoked angry opposition from the unions involved.[52]

MODELS GOVERNING COLLECTIVE BARGAINING FOR LAW ENFORCEMENT OFFICERS

Without question, the broadest grant of rights to law enforcement officers exists within collective bargaining agreements. Under collective bargaining agreements, the wages and benefits of law enforcement officers are guaranteed for the duration of the agreement. Most significantly, officers who dispute a decision of their employer concerning working conditions usually have the right to appeal that decision through a grievance procedure that culminates with a final and binding decision by a neutral third party. Laws regulating collective bargaining for state, county, and local police have developed on a state-by-state basis, and occasionally, on a local basis. Although public employee collective bargaining laws vary by state, the general thrust of the laws can be summarized in terms of three models of collective bargaining: 1) no bargaining and bargaining not required model, 2) meet and confer model, and 3) state and local government collective bargaining law model.

No Bargaining and Bargaining Not Required Models

Law Enforcement officers have no collective bargaining rights in North Carolina, South Carolina, Tennessee, and Georgia. In several of those states, it is statutorily prohibited and in others, there is no legal authorization for it. In Georgia, the Attorney General ruled in the absence of authorization, collective bargaining on behalf of law enforcement officers is illegal. There is a small number of states that have the **bargaining not required** model. In those states, collective bargaining is permitted but not required. Local enactments provide the legal basis to bargain.

Meet and Confer Model: Weak Bargaining Rights

A handful of states have **meet and confer** legislation and/or there are local enactments for it as well. This results in a variety of meet and confer authorizations. In general, they describe how officers select their representatives, the obligation of the parties to freely exchange information, meet for reasonable periods of time, bargain in good faith, and that agreements shall be in writing and approved by both a majority of the officers being represented and the governing body. Meet and confer does not provide for true collective bargaining because its provisions are symbolic. The public employer and the police union do not meet as equals. They meet to exchange opinions, information, and proposals on permissible topics. The government employer is charged with fully considering presentations made to it before taking any action. If there is a bargaining deadlock, there may or may not be a nonbinding impasse procedure. Whether or not there is an impasse procedure, the government employer is free to implementing its last best offer.[53] Union members refer to the meet and confer model as "collective begging."

State and Local Government Collective Bargaining Law Model

Most public employee bargaining is established by a state statute, which also creates a state agency to administer the bargaining law. The agency is often called a State Employees Relations Board (SERB). Other names are also used, such as Florida's Public Employees Relations Commission (PERC) and slight variations of it, for example, Public Employment Relations Board (PERB) in Washington, California New York, and Iowa, and the Michigan Employees Relations Commission (MERC). To avoid confusion, rather than continuously using different terms when referring to the state agency administering a collective bargaining law, "SERB" is used.

In addition to state laws, local ordinances, executive orders and case law also authorize and shape public sector collective bargaining. There are often separate guidelines for some classifications of employees, for example, teachers and law enforcement being common ones. There are exceptions to some of our representations, a portion of which is pointed out. To be sure of the legal status of public sector bargaining in your state, consult the documents establishing bargaining and a labor relations attorney, as needed.

The broadest grant of rights to law enforcement officers exists in collective bargaining agreements/contracts. They identify the wages, benefits, and other terms of employment, which can legally be bargained. The table of contents for a contract is often long and commonly found topics include union recognition, seniority, shift bidding, sick, vacation, military, personal, and funeral leave, disability procedures, severance pay, reinstatement of former officers, pensions, education benefits and pay, and drug testing.

The terms of contracts are guaranteed for the life of the contract, although unanticipated emergencies, such as the financial shortfalls caused by the Great Recession resulted in the "guarantees" being altered. COVID-19 has also quickly had that impact several months into the pandemic in the United States. The life of a contract may be limited by the applicable state statute. One state limits the duration to one year, but elsewhere the range appears to be no more than two years nor greater than seven years.

In 31 states most public employees can collectively bargain with employers on legally permissible subjects.[54] Only 12 states allow some members of public employee unions to strike. Police, fire, and other protective service providers are prohibited from doing so. When bargaining reaches a deadlock or impasse, states encourage a resumption of bargaining by requiring the use of one or more **alternative dispute resolution (ADR)** methods. The most common of these are mediation and/or fact-finding. If they fail to get police unions and employers back to the table, the use of binding arbitration method is mandatory, a subject covered later in this section.

To trigger a potential resolution, one party to the negotiations advises the other in writing: (1) negotiations are deadlocked, (2) an impasse exists and further bargaining would be unproductive, (3) mediation or fact-finding will be requested (whichever the state statute provides, (4) a description of the items on which there is a deadlock, and (5) the alternative dispute resolution intervention is being invoked. In some states, there is a statutory definition of when bargaining is deadlocked. In Texas, an impasse occurs when the parties can't resolve an issue or issues by way of a written agreement within 30 days after bargaining commenced. If mediation and/or fact-finding don't get the public employer and police union to resume negotiating, the final ADR, binding arbitration is usually mandated by law.

Good Faith Bargaining, Impasses, Mediation, and Fact-Finding

Public employers and unions are legally required to bargain in good faith until an impasse is reached. Declaring an impasse essentially means the parties are deadlocked and no further negotiating progress seems possible. At that point, an alternative dispute resolution **(ADR)** method is used to get negotiations re-started. The two most widely used ADRs are

mediation and **fact-finding**, which are non-judicial methods. Each of these forms of alternative dispute resolution may be used alone or in combination with the other. Neither a mediator nor a fact-finder has the authority to compel parties to accept their suggestions and recommendations. If both mediation and fact-finding are available, either or both parties may initiate a request for them in the order established by state law. Mediation and fact-finding are done privately, out of the public eye.

Mediation is the process of helping deadlocked bargaining parties return to the table and resolve their differences. Deadlock means the parties have concluded further negotiations will be unproductive.

Mediation may be used voluntarily or be mandated by law. It is attractive because it: (a) can be quickly scheduled. Mediators are often working on site rapidly; (b) can be completed reasonably quickly, (c) enhances the parties understanding of the others bargaining position, (d) replaces distrust/anger/hostility with objectivity, (e) helps the parties voluntarily reach an acceptable disposition of the issue(s) involved, (f) has a high success rate, (g) avoids, if successful, the parties having a decision imposed on them in binding arbitration, (h) allows a party to withdraw from the process at any point, and (i) is cost effective.[55]

Some SERBs evaluate and maintain a listing of qualified mediators. Upon request, a computer randomly generates the names of five mediators from the list. Selection is made by the parties alternating striking names until only one name remains.[56] Within some states, a random "custom" list of five mediators can be generated upon request by the parties, for example, mediators who have worked as a law enforcement officer. Some state laws put a deadline on completing mediation, such as 45 days.

The mediator, public employer, and the police union are required to sign confidentiality agreements before mediation can begin. Mediators can schedule, facilitate, and adjourn meetings, help draft proposals and recommendations, and otherwise be helpful to the goal of the resumption of bargaining, short of being an advocate for one of the parties. The neutral mediator meets privately with the parties individually and jointly to help them identify the real issues holding them apart, areas of potential agreement, and suggest ways to deal with the areas in which they are deadlocked. As catalysts to the bargaining process, mediators may provide unconsidered or unrecognized paths forward. Strong interpersonal communication skills are essential for mediators.

Mediators, the employee, and the police union held to their confidentially agreements about things learned during the mediation may not disclose them during negotiations or afterward. However, the mediator's written report, including its recommendations, is provided to the SERB and the parties involved. Among the components of the report are sections on deadlocked issues resolved and those that are unresolved. Within some states, the report may be made public if the employer and police union agree to such disclosure.

Quick Facts: Fact-Finding and Outcomes

Fact-finding outcomes tend to favor the public employer, resulting in lower wages for public employees, in the range of 2–5 percent less as compared to other dispute resolution procedures.[57]

Box 11.2: Example of Fact-Finder's Recommendation

Article 31. Section 1. Amount. Each police officer shall receive an annual uniform allowance in the amount of one thousand eighty-five collars ($1,085.00)

Employer Position
The Employer proposes to cut the annual uniform allowance by approximately 54%, reducing it to five hundred dollars ($500) annually, from one thousand eighty-five ($1,085.00). The Employer states that such a reduction is reasonable in view of its need to save wherever possible.

Union Position
The Union recounts that for at least four (4) negotiation cycles the Employer has offered nothing, and consistently asked for give-backs. This pattern has eroded the buying power of the bargaining unit, and contributed to the continuing downsizing of the police force. It believes the proposed uniform allowance reduction is not reasonable.

Finding and Recommendation
I find that the reduction in uniform allowance is not reasonable. There is no evidence in the record that the proposal is in any way related to the cost of uniforms.
I recommend existing language on this issue.

Source: This page is from a Fact Finder's Report to the City of Youngstown, Ohio, which was rejected by the city. See: https://media.wkbn.com/nxs-wkbntv-media-us-east-1/document_dev/2019/04/16/Fact%20Finder%20report_1555387202242_82651337_ver1.0.pdf, accessed May 1, 2020.

Fact-finding may be requested by either or both parties who have declared a bargaining impasse. The selection may be the same as for mediators, although in a several states, the SERB Executive Director may appoint a person or a three-person panel. As would also be done in mediation, a single party request for fact-finding would include a statement of the issues in dispute. This would trigger a requirement to send a copy of the request to the other bargaining party. The time and place of the first meeting of the fact-finder and the parties must be announced, which is 10 days in some states. That rule may be waived for cause by the fact-finder or in some states the SERB Executive Director. Once a hearing is announced, it may be jointly cancelled by the parties, but cancellation usually cannot be done unilaterally.

Before the first meeting, each of the deadlocked parties submits a brief to the fact-finder(s) containing pertinent information from their own perspective, for example, facts, precedents, statements, past practices. The non-requesting party may include unresolved issues it will raise during fact-finding. As a non-judicial method, fact-finding is conducted under relaxed rules of evidence. The fact-finders' powers include issuing subpoenas, administering oaths to witnesses, and compelling the production of records and other documents related to the issues at hand.

Direct or indirect communications with the fact-finders by an entity uninvolved with negotiations are forbidden. Fact-finders may also request statistical information and information from outside sources that may be helpful to their deliberations. Copies of the fact-finder report, including the recommendations for unresolved issues, are sent to the parties involved and to the SERB executive director. If the parties return to bargaining after the report is issued, it remains confidential. However, if there is any 10-day break in bargaining after the report's issuance, in many states, the SERB Executive Director may release the report. The result is public, and political pressures often cause the parties to return to the table to produce an agreement quickly.

Compulsory Interest Arbitration: Binding Arbitration

Compulsory interest arbitration is also called "binding arbitration." It resolves deadlocked issues arising out of negotiations for a new contract.[58] Mediation and/or fact-finding usually precede binding arbitration. **Binding arbitration** replaces the decision-making authority of the governmental employer and the police union with a single arbiter or a three-member panel of arbiters from outside of the community.[59] It is binding in that the deadlocked parties are required to sign a document before its commencement, committing the employer and the police union to accept the decisions of the arbiter(s) as final and forgoing legal appeals.

However, a small number of arbiters' decisions may still end up in court. Examples include the arbiters exceeded their authority, added an issue(s), the wording of an award is so ambiguous that what is required to implement it is lost, the arbiters failed to act in a neutral manner, and failed to comply with statutory guidelines for arbitration. Like mediation and fact-finding, binding arbitration operates less formally than a court trial. Nonetheless, binding arbitration is conducted more formally than both of them. There are two types of binding arbitration laws, reflecting differences in the latitude given arbitrators to render decisions. In **conventional arbitration,** the arbiter(s) has the authority to set the date, time, and place for hearings, providing reasonable notice to the parties, subpoena witnesses, administer oaths, conduct hearings, require the attendance of witnesses and the production of documents of all types the arbiter deems material, hear and rule on motions, and to make awards. In most states, there are statutory guidelines for making awards. The second type of binding arbitration is **final offer arbitration**. Final offer arbitration is also called "last best offer" (LBO) or baseball arbitration because of its similarity to settling salary disputes between major league players and their teams.[60] Final offer arbitration has two forms: (1) issue by issue and (2) total package. The processes and procedures are akin to conventional arbitration and require no elaboration. The most important distinction with conventional arbitration is the restricted scope of arbiters' decision making.

Unfair Labor Practices

States with collective bargaining laws list a number of labor practices deemed to be "unfair." The usual list of unfair labor practices includes the following.

- A refusal to bargain in good faith over subjects that are mandatory for bargaining[61]
- Interference, restraint, or coercion of employees because employees have exercised their collective bargaining rights
- The "domination" of a labor organization by an employer
- The failure to furnish information relevant to the collective bargaining process
- Inappropriate "interference" by an employer with the internal activities of a labor organization
- Discrimination against employees who have exercised their collective bargaining rights[62]

The usual form of challenging any of these practices is through the filing of an "unfair labor practice" or "prohibited practice" complaint with the state agency responsible for administering the collective bargaining laws. Most states have a relatively quick statute of limitations—some as short as six weeks—for the filing of such complaints.[63]

Categories of Collective Bargaining Topics

Where a law enforcement employer is obligated to bargain, the bargaining topics over which bargaining may be conducted are generally classified under one of three categories—mandatory, permissive, or illegal topics of bargaining.[64] Mandatory subjects of bargaining—usually those described as topics pertaining to wages, hours, and terms and conditions of employment—must be bargained if raised by either side.[65] Permissive subjects of bargaining—usually falling under the general heading of "management rights"—are those over which bargaining may occur but is not compelled.[66] Illegal subjects of bargaining are those over which the employer is forbidden by law from bargaining.[67] The distinction among the categories of bargaining subjects is particularly important when interest arbitration is the last step in the bargaining process because only mandatory subjects of bargaining may generally be referred to interest arbitration.[68]

Where the obligation to bargain exists, it has importance, not only when negotiations for an actual contract are being conducted but also during the term of the contract and after the contract expires. The obligation to bargain is continual, a characteristic that can significantly limit an employer's flexibility in making certain decisions. If a matter is a mandatory subject for bargaining, an employer cannot make changes in past practices affecting the matter without first negotiating with the labor organization representing its officers.[69] This restriction applies whenever a labor organization has been certified as the bargaining representative for employees. The continuing duty to bargain can even invalidate an employer's efforts to change its past practices even through enacting a charter amendment.[70]

Two cases from the state of Washington provide a good example of this so-called continuing duty to bargain. In one case, the collective bargaining contract covering a city police department had expired when the employer decided to change from a fixed-shift system, in which shifts were selected by seniority, to a system in which shifts rotated every few months. In the second case, the employer made changes in the method of allocating standby assignments. Even though a contract was in effect at the time of the changes, the contract did not address the method of standby assignment allocation. In both cases, the employers were held to have committed unfair labor practices by making the changes without first negotiating with their respective unions. The Washington State Public Employment Relations Commission held that, absent a clear waiver of the union's right to bargain, the continuing duty to bargain prohibited the implementation of any changes in such mandatorily negotiable hours of work issues.[71]

A labor organization can waive the right to bargain over changes in past practices in one of two ways: by "inaction" and by "contract." A waiver by inaction occurs when the labor organization has knowledge that the employer intends to make a change in past practice (or has actually made such a change) but fails to demand to bargain over the change in a timely manner.[72] Even a six-week delay in demanding the right to bargain has been held to waive bargaining rights.[73] In order to have a labor organization's demand to bargain held untimely, the employer generally must establish that it provided actual and timely notice of its intended action.[74]

A waiver by contract exists when the labor organization has contractually given the right to the employer to make changes in mandatory subjects of bargaining. To be effective, "contract waivers" must be specific and clearly articulated. For example, a management rights clause that generally gives the employer the right to establish hours of work would likely not be specific enough to allow the employer the unilateral right to change work shifts or to change from fixed to rotating shifts.

For bargaining rights to exist mid-contract, the labor organization must establish that the past practice the employer is intending to change has been consistent and long-standing.[75] The labor organization must also establish that there has been an actual change in past practices in order to demand bargaining during the term of the contract. In one case, the police association in New York City was attempting to bargain over a department directive that banned "hog-tying" of suspects. The court ruled the directive was not negotiable because the labor association failed to prove the existence of a past practice that allowed hog-tying, resting its decision on testimony that hog-tying was not taught during training and on the word of the supervisor of the patrol force that, in 41 years of service, he had never seen hog-tying used in the department.[76] In addition, an employer's right to make changes in mandatory subjects of bargaining can also be limited by a collective bargaining contract. Contractual clauses typically labeled "maintenance of benefits" or "existing conditions" forbid an employer from changing wages, hours, or working conditions. The contract covering Buffalo, New York police officers contains an example of such a clause:

> All conditions or provisions beneficial to employees now in effect which are not specifically provided for in this contract or which have not been replaced by provisions of this contract shall remain in effect for the duration of this contract, unless mutually agreed otherwise between the Employer and the Association.[77]

Maintenance of benefits clauses enhance a labor organization's ability to prevent changes in past practices. When under the general continuing duty to bargain, a labor organization has the ability to demand only that an employer bargain to impasse over changes in past practices that are mandatory negotiable; a maintenance of benefits clause allows a labor organization simply to refuse to agree to the change, even if the employer is willing to bargain over the issue. This distinction is particularly important in states where the bargaining process does not culminate with binding arbitration but, instead, allows an employer to unilaterally implement its last best offer on a bargaining issue.

When a topic is mandatory for bargaining, the employer must negotiate on the topic with the police union, not with individual union members. For example, because discipline is mandatorily negotiable, an employer would violate its bargaining obligation if it entered into a "last chance" contract with a troubled employee unless the employee's labor organization also was a party to the contract.[78] This ban on one-on-one contracts with individual union members is a strong one and has invalidated a wide variety of employer contracts with individual union members, including the payment of a signing bonus,[79] a contract with the newly hired officers that they will repay the costs of their training if they quit to go to work for another law enforcement employer,[80] and a contract with a probationary employee to extend the probationary period.[81]

ESTABLISHING THE BARGAINING RELATIONSHIP

The Process

Assuming the existence of a legal provision for collective negotiations, the process of establishing a bargaining relationship is straightforward, but also contains an opportunity for disputes. The mere fact that most members of a police department belong to a single organization does not mean that it automatically has the right to represent its members for the purpose of collective bargaining.[82] Those eligible to be represented may select an organization to which they already belong for this purpose, or they may select another one. This choice must be made in ways that conform to the applicable collective bargaining statute if the employee organization hopes to gain certification by SERB as the bargaining representative.

The union begins an organizing drive, working to get the 30 percent of the votes for each group of employees it seeks to represent to sign authorization cards, of which Figure 11.7 is typical. What constitutes an appropriate group is ordinarily defined by state law. The most common method of determining the appropriate group or unit determination, however, is for SERB or a similar administrative body to make decisions on a case-by-case basis, applying criteria stipulated in the legislation.[83] Among the criteria often identified are the desires of the employees, the "community of interests" shared by them, the need to avoid creating too many bargaining units, the effects on efficiency of operations, and the history of labor relations in the police department.

Once the 30 percent goal is reached, the union notifies the police department and an election is held. The union seeking to represent a class of employees must get 50 percent of the votes in the class, plus one more to win selection as the bargaining agent. If management believes that the union has obtained a majority legitimately and that it is appropriate for the class or classes of officers to be grouped together as proposed by the union, it will recognize the union as the bargaining agent of the officers that it has sought to represent. Once recognized by the employer, the union will petition the SERB for certification. In such cases, SERB does not check the authorization cards but only the appropriateness of the grouping of the officers. If the

INTEREST CARD
INTERNATIONAL UNION OF POLICE ASSOCIATIONS, AFL-CIO

DATE _____

I, the undersigned, hereby authorize the International Union of Police Associations, AFL-CIO,
to represent me for the purpose of collective bargaining with my employer.

_____
(Name of employer; and/or its successor)

and to seek an election for that purpose.
(PLEASE PRINT CLEARLY)   RANK _____

NAME _____   _____
                                                                                          Social Security Number

ADDRESS _____
                    Number and Street

_____
            City   State   Zip Code

HOME PHONE _____   WORK PHONE _____

SIGNATURE _____   WITNESS _____

FIGURE 11.7 ▶ A typical authorization card. *Source:* Reprinted with permission from the International Union of Police Associations.

grouping is deemed appropriate by SERB, the employee organization is certified as the bargaining representative.

If the employee organization is not recognized by management, it can petition SERB for an election; the petition must be accompanied by signed and dated representation cards from 30 percent of the group of employees the union seeks to represent. A secret vote is then held at the direction of the SERB, with the ballot including the union or unions that are contesting the right to represent the officers, along with the choice of no union. The union that receives a majority of the votes from among the officers who are eligible to be represented by the employee organization and who actually cast ballots is certified. Alternately, a majority of those casting ballots might vote for no union. In the event that no majority is achieved, a runoff election is necessary.

The Opportunity for Conflict

In establishing the bargaining relationship, there is ample opportunity for disputes to develop. Management may undertake a campaign to convince officers they are better off without the union at the same time the union is conducting its organizing drive. The employee organization may desire access to bulletin boards, meeting space, and mailing lists to publicize the advantages of unionizing to the officers, all of which management may not want to provide. The decision as to what is an appropriate grouping of officers for the purposes of collective bargaining, referred to as "unit determination," is significant and one about which management and the union may have sharp differences.

Questions such as the following may arise: Are lieutenants part of management and therefore not eligible for representation by the union for purposes of collective bargaining? Should detectives be in a bargaining unit by themselves? Such questions are important. Philosophically, both management and unions want to have large units, but for different reasons. Management wants to have the fewest number of units with which it must bargain because of the effort involved. Unions want to have as many units as the employee numbers can sustain because it creates more strength for them.[84] The union may know that it has the support of only one class of employees, detectives for example, and seek to represent them as a single bargaining unit. Management may feel that a particular union is too militant and, consequently, favors, as a part of a hidden agenda, the inclusion of detectives in a wider unit as a means of promoting the election of a more moderate union that is also seeking to represent employees.

What constitutes an appropriate unit may be defined by state law. The most common method of unit determination, however, is for SERB or a similar administrative body to make decisions on a case-by-case basis, applying certain criteria stipulated in the legislation.[85] Among the criteria often identified are the desires of the employees, the "community of interests" shared by the employees, the need to avoid creating too many bargaining units, the effects on efficiency of operations, and the history of labor relations in the police department.

NEGOTIATIONS

Selection of the Management and Union Teams

Figure 11.8 depicts one configuration of management and union bargaining teams. The union's chief negotiator will usually not be a member of the bargaining unit. He or she will be a specialist brought in to represent it. This ensures a certain level of expertise, an appropriate degree of objectivity, and an autonomy that comes from knowing, once the bargaining is over, he or she will not be working daily for the people sitting across the table. It is not automatic that the union president will be a member of the bargaining team, although customarily a union officer is, and often it is the president. Accompanying the union's chief negotiator and president will be two or three team members who have conducted in-depth research on matters relating to the bargaining issues and who will have various types of data, facts, and documents such as wage and benefit surveys, trends in the consumer price index, and copies of recent contracts for similarly sized jurisdictions. Although there will be only several union research team members at the table, they will have had assistance in gathering their information from others in the union.

The chief negotiator for management may be the director of labor relations or the human resources director of the unit of government involved or may be a professional labor relations specialist. Some jurisdictions prefer the latter because, if there are acrimonious occurrences, once the bargaining is over the director of labor relations can step back into the picture and assume a relationship with the union that is un-scarred by any incidents. The chief of police should not appear at the table personally, but a key member of the command staff who has his or her confidence should.

The way in which issues are presented, and the flexibility that both sides have, will impact strongly on how the bargaining sessions will go. Perhaps equally important are the decisions made as to who will represent each side at the table, and in what role. The proper training of all involved in the negotiation process is absolutely essential.

Personality Types to Be Avoided

There are certain personality types that should not be called upon to participate in the negotiation process. This includes individuals with "axes to grind," as well as those with sarcastic, acrid, or abrasive personalities. The purpose of bargaining is to produce a bilateral written contract to which both parties will bind themselves during its lifetime. This is not only a profoundly important task but also one that is sufficiently difficult without including people on either side who have an agenda other than negotiating in good faith or whose personalities create yet another obstacle. For these reasons, management must exercise careful consideration in deciding who will represent the police department at the table and, if necessary, influence the selection of the city's other representatives. The same logic applies to those selected by the union to be at the table (see Figure 11.8 for an example of management and union bargaining teams).

Preparing for Negotiations

Management can ill afford to simply wait until the employee organization prepares its demands and presents them. Effective action requires considerable effort on management's part before it receives the union's proposal. Management's negotiating team must be selected, agreement with the union obtained on the site where the negotiations will take place; the bargaining schedule established in conjunction with the union; and

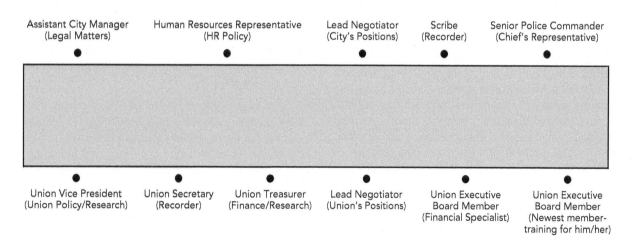

FIGURE 11.8 ▶ The management and union bargaining teams. Although the composition of management's and the union's bargaining teams varies somewhat from one jurisdiction to another and even within jurisdictions over time, the configuration shown here approximates the "typical" municipal situation. Occasionally, a member of the city council also sits in as an observer. *Source:* Courtesy of Chuck Foy, past president of the Arizona Conference of Police and Sheriffs Local 7077 and past president of the Peoria [Arizona] Police Officers Association.

various types of data and information gathered, tabulated, and analyzed. Although final preparations for negotiating will begin several months before the first bargaining sessions, the preparation process is a continuous one. Management should begin preparing for the next negotiations as soon as current negotiations are completed. The demands not obtained by the union in the past year may be brought up again in this year's bargaining sessions, and management should be prepared for this.

Various types of records should be kept and summaries made of such factors as the union membership; the types and outcomes of grievances; the costs of settling grievances; the numbers, kinds, and consequences of any contract violations by the employee organization; the subject matters brought before the union-management committee during the life of the expiring contract and the disposition of them; and the themes reflected in the union's newsletter. Additionally, just as the employee organization's bargaining team is doing, the management team must familiarize itself with changes in the consumer price index and the provisions of recent contracts in similarly situated jurisdictions and conduct its own wage and benefit survey or cooperate with the union on one.

From all of these sources, and others, it is essential that management do three things. First, it must anticipate what the union will be seeking and the relative importance of each demand to the union. Second, it must develop its position with respect to the anticipated preliminary demands it believes the union will present. Third, it must develop the objectives it seeks to achieve during the process of bilateral determination. If it is not already an institutionalized practice, arrangements should be made to have the union submit its demands in writing prior to the first scheduled round of negotiations. These demands may be submitted either in the form of a proposed contract or as a "shopping list," which simply lists the demands being made. The presentation of the demands in writing before the first bargaining session allows for a more productive use of the time allotted for the first negotiating session.

The Negotiating Sessions

The number of bargaining sessions can run from one to several dozen, lasting from 30 minutes to 10 or more hours, although half-day sessions are more common depending on how close or far apart the union and management are when they begin to meet face to face. Traditionally, any means of making verbatim transcripts, such as the use of a stenographer or tape recorder, have generally been excluded from the bargaining sessions because these would force "on the record" statements that tended to impede the progress of negotiations

At the first meeting, friendly conversation might be passed across the table, or there may be merely strained greetings before the formal session begins. Friendly conversation might suggest that rapid and amicable bargaining will follow but instead no mutually acceptable positions will be reached because the friendly conversation has veiled only thinly the hostility or aggressiveness of one or both sides, which quickly comes to the fore. On the other hand, strained greetings might

reflect the heavy responsibility of each party to the negotiations and quick progress may follow.

In the initial session, the chief negotiator for each party will make an opening statement. Management's representative will often go first, touching on general themes such as the need for patience and the obligation to bargain in good faith. The union's negotiator generally will follow this up by voicing support for such sentiments and will outline what the union seeks to achieve under the terms of the new contract. Ground rules for the bargaining may then be reviewed, modified as mutually agreed on, or developed. The attention then will shift to the terms of the contract that the union is proposing. Whatever terms a union is proposing will be carefully examined in a **"walk-through,"** during which time management will seek to learn what the union means by particular wording. This is a time-consuming process, but of great importance because both parties must have a common understanding of what they are attempting to commit each other to, or there will be frequent unresolved conflicts and many complex and expensive grievances filed during the lifetime of the contract.

For purposes of illustration, the union may have proposed that "vehicles will be properly equipped and maintained to protect the health and safety of officers." Discussion of this proposal may reveal that their expectations are much more specific:

1. This is to apply to all vehicles, including marked, semi-marked, and unmarked.
2. All vehicles will be replaced at 90,000 miles.
3. All vehicles will be equipped with radial tires.
4. Plexiglas protective shields will be installed between the front and rear seats in marked and semi-marked vehicles.
5. Shotguns or rifles in locking mounts accessible from the front seat will be provided in all marked and semi-marked cars.
6. First-aid kits of a particular type will be placed in all vehicles.
7. Two sets of Personal Protection Equipment (PPE) shall be in every car and inspected and maintained monthly by the city.

For bargaining purposes, the union may pre-categorized each clause in the proposed contract as being (1) "expendable," meaning that under certain circumstances it will be withdrawn as a symbol of good faith; (2) a "trade-off," indicating that it will be dropped as total or partial payment for obtaining some other benefit; (3) "negotiable," meaning that the benefit needs to be obtained in one form or another; and (4) "non-negotiable," meaning that the benefit is wanted exactly as proposed.[92] Management will study the information gained from the walk-through for several days and then both parties will return to the table. Management then will respond to the union's proposal by indicating which clauses it has (1) "accepted," (2) "accepted with minor modification," (3) "rejected," and (4) wished to make its own proposals and counterproposals. Management cannot simply reject a clause out of hand; to do so would not constitute bargaining in good faith. Instead, it must give a reason for the rejection that is reasonable, such as an actual inability to pay.

Having been told formally of management's position on the proposed contract, the bargaining begins, concentrating on the items upon which agreement can be reached immediately or fairly rapidly. Such an approach helps foster a spirit of mutualism that can be useful in dealing with the issues about which there are substantial differences. As bargaining enters the final stages, the issues that must be dealt with usually become fewer but also more difficult in terms of securing agreement.

At such points, "side trips" may threaten to make the sessions unproductive. These side trips might involve accusations and recriminations, or discussion of a disputed clause in philosophical or intellectual terms as a means of not dealing with the concrete realities that may be threatening and anxiety provoking for one or both parties. At these times, a caucus or even a slightly longer space of time than ordinary until the next session may give enough time for tempers to calm or for more perspective to be gained. At other times, the police union may feel the need to "up the stakes" by engaging in picketing as a form of political pressure.

Ultimately, unless a total impasse is reached, agreement will be obtained on the terms of a new contract. The union's membership will vote on the contract as a whole. If approved by the membership, the contract then goes before the necessary government officials and bodies, such as the legislative unit that appropriates the funds, for its approval.

GRIEVANCES

Why Grievances Are Inevitable

There is a notion that, once the bargaining is completed and a contract signed, the most difficult part of labor relations has been passed through and easy times are ahead. Such a notion is natural. Bargaining is high drama, with a great deal of attention focused on it by the news media and the community. The production of a contract acceptable to both the union and management is, in fact, a significant achievement. Beyond it, however, is the day-to-day administration of the contract during its lifetime where grievances occur. No matter how diligently the parties bargain, they cannot anticipate all possibilities, making grievances inevitable. Because the contract outlines the duties and rights of each party in its dealings with the other, it is ironically the basis not only for accord but also for conflict:

> It would be ideal for all concerned, including the public, if in the negotiation of the contract both parties were able to draft a comprehensive document capable of foreseeing and forestalling all potential disputes which might arise during its life. Unfortunately, perfection sets a high bar, particularly when the parties are pressured by tensions and an approaching deadline. It is not humanly possible in a collective bargaining relationship to draft a perfect document.[86]

Given the above, it is inevitable that questions will arise concerning the interpretation and application of the collective bargaining agreement. What is the meaning of a particular clause of the contract? How does it apply, if at all, to a set of facts that occurred after the contract was signed? Such questions are not uncommon during the life of the CBA.[87]

Defining Grievances

Whereas in common usage a grievance is a complaint or an expression of dissatisfaction by an employee with respect to some aspect of employment, what can be grieved formally is defined within the contract itself. Grievances may be limited to matters discussed specifically in the contract that are primarily contract-related, or that pertain to the job, as is seen in these clauses from three different contracts:

1. A grievance is defined as a complaint arising out of the interpretation, application, or compliance with the provisions of this contract.

2. For the purpose of this contract, the term "grievance" shall mean the difference or dispute between any police officer and the city, or a superior officer in the chain of command, with respect to the interpretation, application, claim or breach, or violation of any of the provisions of this contract, or with respect to any equipment furnished by the city.

3. A grievance, for our purposes, shall be defined as any controversy, complaint, misunderstanding, or dispute arising between an employee or employees and the City, or between the Brotherhood and the City.

The Grievance Procedure

The grievance procedure is a formal process that has been the subject of bilateral negotiations and is detailed in the contract. It involves seeking redress of the grievances through progressively higher levels of authority and may culminate in binding arbitration by a single or tripartite panel. Because the police union must equally share the cost of arbitration with management, the decision to take a grievance to the last step is customarily the prerogative of the union rather than the individual officer who is grieved. The shared arbitration costs do not include each parties' costs for preparing for arbitration, witnesses travel, and associated costs.

A typical sequence of grievance steps approximates the following:

Grievances shall be presented in the following manner and every effort shall be made by the parties to secure prompt disposition of grievances:

Step 1. The member shall first present his or her grievance to his or her immediate supervisor within five days of the occurrence which gave rise to the grievance. Such contact shall be on an informal and oral basis, and the supervisor shall respond orally to the grievance within five working days.

Step 2 Any grievance that cannot be satisfactorily settled in Step 1 shall be reduced to writing by the member and shall next be taken up by his/her division commander. Said grievance shall be presented to the division commander within five working days from receipt of the answer in Step 1. The division commander shall, within 5 working days, render his or her decision on the grievance in writing.

Step 3. Any grievance not satisfactorily settled in Step 2 shall be forwarded, in writing, within five working days, to the chief of police, who shall render his or her written decision on the grievance within five working days.

Step 4. If the grievant is not satisfied with the response of the chief of police, he or she will forward his written grievance within five working days to the city manager, who will have 10 working days to reply, in writing.

Step 5. If the grievance has not been settled to the satisfaction of the grievant in Step 4, the matter will be subject to arbitration. An arbiter will be selected, without undue delay, according to the rules of the American Arbitration Association. The arbiter will hold an arbitration hearing. When the hearing has ended, the arbiter will be asked to submit his/her award, in writing, within 15 days.

Enumerated in the agreement are not only the steps of the grievance procedure but also such matters as the manner of selecting the tripartite panel or the single neutral, along with their duties and powers. If the panel is used, management and the union each appoints one member, and those two appoint the third; where the two cannot agree on the neutral, the contract may provide for the referral of the choice of a chairperson to a designated agency,[88] such as the Federal Mediation and Conciliation Service, or a state agency. Where a single arbitrator is used, a variety of techniques are employed in selection, ranging from agreement on the person by the union and management on a case-by-case basis, to the appointment of a permanent arbitrator during the life of the contract, to having an outside agency submit a list of qualified arbitrators from which management and the union take turns eliminating names until only one remains or they agree to accept any of some number remaining, such as three.

The arbitration hearing is quasi-judicial, with more relaxed rules of evidence than are found in either criminal or civil proceedings. The burden of proof is on the grieving party, except in discipline cases, where it is always on the employer. The parties may be represented by legal counsel at the hearing, and the format will generally include obtaining agreement on what the issue is, an opening statement by each side (with the grieving party going first), examination and cross-examination of witnesses, and closing arguments in the reverse of the order in which the opening statements were made.

Arbitration Issues and Decision Making

Despite the many types of matters that can be and are grieved, the largest single category of cases, about 90 percent of the total, brought to an arbitration hearing are those involving discipline against an officer. Some arbitration decision making is not

difficult because one side, perhaps the union, chooses to take a losing case to arbitration because of its symbolic importance and the need to appear supportive of union members. This rationale can also be applied to management as well in order to show support for managers.

If an employee is found to have done what he or she has been accused of, the arbitrator may then consider certain factors that might mitigate the severity of the penalty, including the officer's years of service to the department; the provocation, if any, that led to the alleged offense; the officer's disciplinary history, including the number, types, and recency of other violations; the consistency with which the applicable rule is enforced; and the penalties applied for similar offenses by other officers.[96]

One study of arbitrated police grievances reveals that the officer involved in the grievance was assigned to uniformed patrol 84 percent of the time, another police officer was involved in the incident slightly more than half the time (56 percent of the cases), the grieving officer's supervisor supported him or her 14 percent of the time, and in exactly three-quarters of the cases, the involved officer had a clean disciplinary record.[97] Given that police unions must be selective in terms of the cases they take to arbitration, the results are not too surprising: The union won 77 percent of the grievances it took to arbitration.

A key advantage of arbitration is the speed with which issues are heard and a decision is made, as compared with seeking resolution of the dispute in court. The deadline for issuance of the award may be established by statute; the parties; a government authority, such as the SERB; the arbitrator, if he or she is acting as an independent; or the body appointing the arbitrator.[98] The AAA requires arbitrators to render their decisions in writing within 30 days of (1) the conclusion of the hearing; (2) the receipt of the hearing transcript, if one has been made; or (3) the receipt of posthearing briefs.[89] In general, except in such instances as fraud or bias by the arbitrator, the hearing officer's decision, where binding arbitration is provided for, will not be reviewed by the courts.

JOB ACTIONS

"Job action" describes several types of activities in which unionized police employees have historically engaged to express their dissatisfaction with a particular person, event, or condition or to attempt to influence the outcome of a matter pending before decision makers, such as a contract bargaining impasse. This section reviews job actions, including ones that are known to be prohibited in some or more places, to provide an understanding of how conflicted the relationship between public employers and police unions was in years past.

Work Stoppages

It is well understood that state and local legislation enabling police collective bargaining prohibits police strikes. That prohibition is commonly repeated in many CBAs. Largely unnoticed by outsiders is the success of management in many negotiations to eliminate other types of job actions. The City of Hasting, Nebraska's CBA with the Fraternal Order of Police, Lodge 9, illustrates this success:

> The Union shall neither cause nor counsel any person to hinder, delay, limit, or suspend the continuity or efficiency of any City function, operation, or service for any reason, nor shall it in any manner coerce, intimidate, instigate, induce, sanction, suggest, conspire with, promote, support, sponsor, engage in, condone, or encourage any person to participate in *any strike, slowdown, mass resignation, mass absenteeism, or any type of concerted work stoppage*. The Union shall not aid or assist any persons or parties engaging in the above prohibited conduct by giving direction or guidance to such activities and conduct or by providing funds, financial, and other assistance for the conduct or direction of such activities or for the payment of strike, unemployment, or other benefits to those persons or parties participating in such prohibited conduct and activities, provided, however, that the Union may provide legal representation.[90]

In jurisdictions with the above provision, job actions in which police officers can legally participate are seemingly limited to votes of no confidence and picketing. Although technically not job actions, police unions can engage in activities that can create controversies and problems for the public employer, such as media blitzes to support political candidates and promoting criticism of policies and decisions being considered or already announced.

The Vote of Confidence

The **vote of confidence**, which typically produces a finding of no confidence, has been used somewhat sparingly in law enforcement. Such a vote is how rank-and-file members signal their collective displeasure with the chief administrator of their agency. Although such votes have no legal standing, they sometimes generate a great deal of negative publicity that may lead to the police chief's resignation.

Work Slowdowns and Speedups

Work slowdowns occurred when officers wanted to flex their political muscle over bargaining impasses or demonstrate their opposition to leaders' inaction or taking what they see as flawed positions. Since at least 2015, accounts of police work slowdowns or speedups are virtually non-existent. Where several have demonstrably occurred, the union has denied their existence, pointing to other factors. Just before Christmas 2014, two NYPD officers were murdered as they sat in their police car. New York City officers feared for their safety and felt the opportunity for the deadly ambush was created by Mayor Bill de Blasio's lack of support for them. Without any known planning or encouragement from the police union, NYPD traffic citations and summons to appear in court for minor offenses, such as public drinking and public urination, plummeted by 94 percent,[93] causing a substantial reduction in city revenue. The union countered claims of a work slowdown by pointing to the Police Commissioner having officers work in pairs for safety, which created less area being covered. Ironically, the COVID-19 pandemic led to police departments essentially telling officers to start the equivalent of a work slowdown: for your safety and to halt the spread of the virus, limit arrests and use summons if action is necessary.

As a description, although officers continued to work during a **work slowdown**, they did so at a leisurely pace, causing productivity to fall. As productivity dropped, the government employer came under pressure to restore normal work production. This pressure may have been from within the unit of government itself. For example, a department urged officers to write more tickets, so more revenue was not lost. Or citizens complained to politicians and appointed leaders to "get this thing settled," so the police would answer calls more rapidly and complete the reports citizens need for insurance purposes.

Work speedups are another topic that has not appeared in searches of news accounts and other sources for many years. Although one may pop up in the future, it is all but a vanished species. Work speedups were a sharp acceleration of police enforcement activity resulting in the overproduction of one or more police services. Examples of speedups include "ticket blizzards" and sudden strict enforcements of usually ignored minor violations, such as jaywalking, littering, or smoking in prohibited areas. The union's intent is to so anger the public that citizens will direct their hostility toward public officials, using e-mails, text messages, phone calls, comments, and letters, who were in a position to solve or at least ameliorate the problem so the issue causing the union's dissatisfaction could be resolved politically in its favor.

Box 11.3: Two No Confidence Votes, Different Endings

In California, the Sebastopol Police Officers Association sent a confidential letter to the City Manager, the Assistant City Manager, Mayor and City Council members. The 2019 sharply worded letter revealed a vote of no confidence for Chief James Conner. City sources were shocked by the letter's harsh and condemning content.

Ten days later the Police Chief retired.[91]

During 2019, Effingham, Illinois, Mayor Bloemker took direct aim at the vote of no confidence for Chief Fuesting by members of the Fraternal Order of Police, which bargains for officers. The Mayor defended the Police Chief as a tireless fighter for best practices in management. With a negotiation for a new union contract on the horizon, the Mayor dismissed the vote as a "cheap parlor trick."[92]

Chapter Summary

Summary by Learning Objectives

1. Identify and understand some of the factors that led to growth in the unionization of police.

   There were several factors that led to the growth of police unions. These include: (1) the needs of unions to expand their membership, (2) the reduction of legal barriers, (3) police frustration with the perceived lack of support for their "war on crime," (4) personnel practices in police agencies, (5) salaries and benefits, (6) violence directed at the police, and (7) the success of other groups

2. Compare and contrast various models for collective bargaining for law enforcement officers.

   There are three primary models of collective bargaining for law enforcement covered in the chapter including: 1) No bargaining and bargaining not required, 2) meet and confer, and 3) state and local government collective bargaining law model. The first model is included in order to explain that in some states, there are laws that specifically forbid collective bargaining by police. The meet and confer model allows collective bargaining, however this model does not allow for true collective bargaining and severely limits the power of police unions to collectively bargain. The third model is the most complex. Collective bargaining is established by state statute and typically administered through a State Employee Relations Board (SERB). The broadest grant of rights to law enforcement officers to collectively bargain occurs within the context of this model.

3. State the two most widely used alternative dispute resolution methods and their common purpose.

   The two most widely used alternative dispute resolution methods are mediation and fact finding.

4. Explain the ways in which the bargaining process is established including the process, opportunities for conflict, and negotiation.

   The process involves union organizing efforts, methods for determining the appropriate bargaining unit, and union elections. Opportunities for conflict between the police union and the agency arise primarily within the context of decisions on who the union will represent. The negotiation phase includes the selection of the management and union teams, the process of preparation for negotiation, and the negotiation sessions themselves.

5. Define collective bargaining grievances and the five steps to the grievance procedure.

   A grievance within the context of collective bargaining involves disagreements as to the duties and rights of union members and management. The five steps involved in the grievance procedure include:

   Step 1. The member shall first present his or her grievance to his or her immediate supervisor within five days of the occurrence which gave rise to the grievance. Such contact shall be on an informal and oral basis, and the supervisor shall respond orally to the grievance within five working days.

   Step 2. Any grievance that cannot be satisfactorily settled in Step 1 shall be reduced to writing by the member and shall next be taken up by his/her division commander. Said grievance shall be presented to the division commander within five working days from receipt of the answer in Step 1. The division commander shall, within 5 working days, render his or her decision on the grievance in writing.

   Step 3. Any grievance not satisfactorily settled in Step 2 shall be forwarded, in writing, within five working days, to the chief of police, who shall render his or her written decision on the grievance within five working days.

   Step 4. If the grievant is not satisfied with the response of the chief of police, he or she will forward his written grievance within five working days to the city manager, who will have 10 working days to reply, in writing.

   Step 5. If the grievance has not been settled to the satisfaction of the grievant in Step 4, the matter will be subject to arbitration. An arbiter will be selected, without undue delay, according to the rules of the American Arbitration Association. The arbiter will hold an arbitration hearing. When the hearing has ended, the arbiter will be asked to submit his/her award, in writing, within 15 days.

6. Understand various job actions that may occur within the context of collective bargaining agreements including work stoppages, the vote of confidence, and work slowdowns and speed-ups.

   The various job actions that may occur are work stoppages, the vote of confidence, and work slowdowns and speed-ups. A work stoppage involves a strike or mass resignation, or mass absenteeism. The vote of confidence is a means for union members to express dissatisfaction with management. Work slow-downs and speed-ups involve collective actions by officers to alter normal workflows.

Chapter Review Questions

1. Votes of confidence were held in Sebastopol, California and Effingham, Illinois. What impact did each have and what explains the difference in outcomes?
2. What is concessionary bargaining?
3. What are two reasons binding arbitration decisions still may end up in Court?

4. What is the most common method of unit determination?
5. Why are the union's chief negotiators not usually a member of the union they represent?
6. When the union takes an officer's grievance to arbitration, what is the most common reason for the grievance?
7. What are two examples of work speedups?

Critical Thinking Exercises

First Exercise: Required Wearing of Body Armor

1. You are the new Chief of Police in the Broken Arrow, Oklahoma, Police Department. It is your first week on the job. By the CBA with the police union and reiterated in departmental policy, officers shall consider department-issued body armor as part of their daily-required on-duty attire. Yesterday, you saw Officer Miller was not wearing one. Although in a hurry to see the city manager, you asked about it. Her reply was "Chief, it's too hot, limits my upper body mobility, and is a danger to me." You explained the body armor policy, explaining wearing it was mandatory, not optional, and gave her a direct order to wear it at all times while on duty. This description of the brief conversation includes all of it.

2. Today, you stopped Officer Miller after roll call and asked where her body armor was. She said, "Chief, we had this conversation yesterday and my reasons haven't changed. It doesn't enhance my safety. Following that policy could get me killed."

3. There are several ways to approach this situation. As the new Chief, word of whatever you do will get around quickly and be an important first

impression of you. What alternatives do you consider and how do you handle this situation?

Second Exercise: The Peace Officers Bill of Rights (POBR) Assignment

1. You are Captain James of the Kuna (Idaho) Police Department (KPD), which is located in the wine country of the Western Snake River Valley. The KPD serves a resident population of 18,455 with a seasonal influx of approximately 40,000 tourists. Chief Kilpatrick has assigned you to prepare a recommendation for a topic sure to be raised by the police union in the upcoming negotiations, a Police Officers Bill of Rights (POBR) to be included in the new agreement.

2. Chief Kilpatrick directs you to compare the state POBR laws for California, Nevada, and New Mexico. Idaho does not have such a law.

3. You have to make a list of the elements in the POBRs state laws you feel would provide the best balance to protect managerial prerogatives, assure the community that officers are being held accountable, and provide protection for the individual rights of police officers.

4. Finally, identify what POBR elements you do not support and for what reason(s).

Key Terms

alternative dispute resolution	fact finding	vote of confidence
binding arbitration	final offer arbitration	walk-through
code of silence	job action	work slowdown
compulsory interest arbitration	mediation	work speed up
concessionary bargaining	meet and confer	
conventional arbitration	peace officer bill of rights	

Endnotes

[1]These themes are identified and treated in detail in Hervey A. Juris and Peter Feuille, Police Unionism (Lexington, MA: Lexington Books, 1973).

[2]Jeffrey Keefe, Laws Enabling Public-Sector Collective Bargaining Have Not Led to Excessive Public Sector Pay," Economic Policy Institute, October 16, 2015, p. 1, https://www.epi.org/publication/laws-enabling-public-sector-collective-bargaining-have-not-led-to-excessive-public-sector-pay, accessed March 28, 2020.

[3]Data 360; http://www.data360.org/dsg.aspx?Data_Set_Group_Id=228 (accessed June 21, 2015).

[4]Loc. cit.

[5]No author, "Economic News Release: Union Members Summary, U.S. Department of Labor, January 22, 2020, p. 1, https://www.bls.gov/news.release/union2.nr0.htm, accessed March 16, 2020.

[6]Loc. cit., with additions by the authors. National Right to Work Legal Defense Foundation; http://www.nrtw.org/b/rtw_faq.htm (accessed June 26, 2015).

[7]No Author, "Right to Work States: Everything You Need to Know. Upcounsel, 2021 (See https://www.upcounsel.com/right-to-work-states#:~:text='Right%2Dto%2DWork'%20Act%20of%201947%20affirms%20that,and%20fees%20to%20the%20union). Accessed February 24, 2021.

[8]Public Service Research Council, Public Sector Bargaining and Strikes (Vienna, VA: Public Service Research Council, 1976), pp. 6–9.

[9]Robert M. Folgeson, Big-City Police (Cambridge, MA: Harvard University Press, 1977), 193–195.

[10] Ibid, 193–195.

[11]See Janus v. American Federation of State, County, and Municipal Employees, Council 31, No. 16-1466, 585 U.S. ___ (2018).

[12]296 F. Supp. 1068, 1969.

[13]324 F. Supp. 315, N.D. Ga., 1971.

[14]483 F. 2d 966, 10th Circuit, 1973.

[15]President's Commission on Law Enforcement and Administration of Justice, Task Force Report: The Police (Washington, DC: U.S. Government Printing Office, 1967), p. 144.

[16]Ibid., p. 145.

[17]Suzannah Gonzales, "Opinion Poll: Confidence in Police Hits a 22-Year Low," The Columbus Dispatch, June 20, 2015; http://www.dispatch.com/content/stories/national_world/2015/06/20/confidence-in-police-hits-22-year-low.html (accessed June 26, 2015).

[18]From various tables, U.S. Department of Labor, Employment and Earnings 8, No. 4 (October 1961).

[19]Bureau of the Census, Statistical Abstract of the United States, 1975 (Washington, DC: U.S. Government Printing Office, 1975), p. 162.

[20]John H. Burpo, The Police Labor Movement (Springfield, IL: Charles C Thomas, 1971), p. 34.

[21]Albert, A Time for Reform, p. 29. Several studies have reported that market forces other than unions explain better the rise in public employees' salaries than does union activity.

[22]The data were extracted from the Federal Bureau of Investigation's Uniform Crime Reports (Washington, DC: U.S. Government Printing Office, 1965, 1970).

[23]William W. Scranton, Report of the President's Commission on Campus Unrest (Washington, DC: U.S. Government Printing Office, 1970), p. 18.

[24]Some 16 states also have Peace Officer Bills of Rights (POBR) statutes, which contain provisions similar to those in police union contracts.

[25]The purpose of discipline is to teach the correct behavior. To do so necessarily implies a continuing relationship. Appropriate discipline benefits officers by deflecting them from a potentially downward track of misconduct and departments benefit from this also. Termination differs from discipline in that there is no continuing relationship.

[26]Samuel Walker, "The Neglect of Police Unions: Exploring One of the Most Important Areas of American Policing," Police Practice and Research 9, No. 2 (May 2008), pp. 102–107.)

[27]See Stephen Rushin, "Police Disciplinary Appeals," University of Pennsylvania Law Review, Vol. 167, No. 3, February 2019, p.1220.

[28]Ibid.

[29]Jennifer Smith Richards and Jodi S. Cohen, "Chicago Police Win Big When Appealing Discipline," ProPublica Illinois, December 14, 2017, no page number, https://www.propublica.org/article/chicago-police-grievances, accessed March 28, 2020.

[30]Office of the Florida Attorney General, Government-in-the Sunshine Manual 2020, Vol. 42, p. 31, http://myfloridalegal.com/webfiles.nsf/WF/MNOS-B9QQ79/$file/SunshineManual.pdf, accessed April 2, 2020.

[31]The information in this paragraph is taken with restatement from Danial DiSalvo, "The Trouble with Public Sector Unions," National Affairs, No. 43, Spring 2020, No page numbers, https://lris.com/2020/03/24/kansas-city-police-officers-rent-trailers-to-skirt-residency-rule-union-leader-says, accessed April 2, 2020.

[32]Loc. cit.

[33]Stephen Rushin, "Police Union Contracts," Duke Law Journal, Vol. 66, No. 3, March 2017, pp. 1197–1198, https://lawcommons.luc.edu/cgi/viewcontent.cgi?article=1604&context=facpubs, accessed March 16, 2020.

[34]Adeshina Emmanuel, "How Union Contracts Shield Police Departments from DOJ Reforms," In These Times, June 21, 2016, http://inthesetimes.com/features/police-killings-union-contracts.html, accessed March 16, 2020.

[35]Adeshina Emmanuel, "How Union Contracts Shield Police Departments from DOJ Reforms," In These Times, June 21, 2016, http://inthesetimes.com/features/police-killings-union-contracts.html, accessed March 16, 2020.

[36]Ibid., pp, 764–766.

[37]Rob Nelson, "Police Union Offers $500 Award to Citizens Who Help NYPD Officers Restrain Suspects," ABC7NY, August 22, 2018, https://abc7ny.com/sergeants-benevolent-association-union-nypd-police-officers/4030054, accessed April 2, 2020.

[38]Safeed Shabazz, "Sharpton and Activists React to Police Union Call for Cirizenz to Help Cops," New Amsterdam News (New York City), August 30, 2018, p. 1, http://amsterdamnews.com/news/2018/aug/30/

sharpton-and-activists-react-police-union-call-cit, accessed March 30, 2020.

[39]CLEAT News, Victory for El Paso County, February 10, 2020, https://www.cleat.org/latest-news/victory-for-el-paso-county, accessed April 2, 2020.

[40]The information in this paragraph is taken with restatement from, No author, "About Glendale POA," Glendale POA, undated, https://glendalepoa.com/about, p. 1, accessed April 17, 2020.

[41]DiSalvo, "The Trouble with Public Sector Unions," p. 1.

[42]PEW Charitable Trust, "The State Pension Funding Gap, June 11, 2020. See: https://www.pewtrusts.org/en/research-and-analysis/issue-briefs/2020/06/the-state-pension-funding-gap-2018.

[43]BallotPedia News, " Public-Sector Unions Contributed Nearly $160 million to Political Candidates in 2019." October 4, 2019.

[44]See home page of Fraternal Order of Police at: www.fop.net.

[45]Erik Sherman, "Are We Headed for a Depression? Economists Weigh In," Fortune, April 4, 2020, https://fortune.com/2020/04/04/are-we-headed-for-a-depression-coronavirus-recession-markets-economy-predictions-2020, accessed April 17, 2020.

[46]Podcast, September 18, 2020, Representing the University of California Los Angele, Peter Cappelli and Iwan Barankay, and the University of Pennsylvania, Wharton School's David Lewin discuss the impact of the Great Recession on U.S. workers and the job market, https://knowledge.wharton.upenn.edu/article/great-recession-american-dream, April 6, 2020.

[47]Ibid.

[48]No author, "COVID-19 to Send Almost All G20 Countries into a Recession, The Economist, March 26, 2020, https://www.eiu.com/n/covid-19-to-send-almost-all-g20-countries-into-a-recession, accessed March 30, 2020.

[49]David J. Pryzbylski, "Do You Have a Duty to Bargain With Your Union Over Your Conoavirus Response Measures, The National Law Review, April 18, 2020, https://www.natlawreview.com/article/do-you-have-to-bargain-your-union-over-your-coronavirus-response-measures, accessed April 18, 2020.

[50]Ibid.

[51]Adam Ferrise, "Cleveland Police Union Wants Extra Money for Officers During Coronavirus Pandemic," April 15, 2020, Officer.com, https://www.officer.com/covid-19/news/21134141/cleveland-police-union-wants-extra-money-for-officers-during-coronavirus-pandemic, accessed April 16, 2020.

[52]Jessica Anderson, "Baltimore Police Union Told There Could be Pay Cuts, Layoffs, Because of COVID-19 Budget Shortfall," The Baltimore Sun, April 11, 2020, https://www.policeone.com/coronavirus-covid-19/articles/baltimore-police-union-told-there-could-be-pay-cuts-layoffs-because-of-covid-19-budget-shortfall-dJf0FMT0MtkZyKCP, accessed April 13, 2020.

[53]This paragraph summarizes California's meet and confer law. Portions of this paragraph are taken with restatement from Berry Wilkinson, "The Meet and Confer Obligations of Local Public Agencies," Berry & Wilkinson Law Group,

October 2008, http://berrywilkinson.com/documents/MeetandConferHandout.pdf, accessed April 15, 2020.

[54]Joseph E. Slater, "The Assault on Public Sector Collective Bargaining: Real Harms and Imaginary Benefits," American Constitution Society, June 2011, p. 2, https://www.acslaw.org/wp-content/uploads/2018/04/Slater_Collective_Bargaining.pdf, accessed March 17, 2020.

[55]The information in this paragraph is based on some restated thoughts from No author, Utah Mediation Best Practice Guide, Updated 2020, Utah Courts, https://www.utcourts.gov/mediation/docs/Mediation%20Best%20Practices%20Guide.pdf, accessed March 17, 2020; and Charles B. Craver, "The Use of Alternative Dispute Resolution Techniques to Resolve Public Sector Bargaining Disputes," Ohio State Journal. on Dispute Resolution, Vol.28, No. 1, 2013, https://papers.ssrn.com/sol3/papers.cfm?abstract_id=2197950, accessed March 17, 2020. The last source was very pertinent, but impervious to efforts to locate a normal cite. The available information is: No author identified, Dispute Resolution Techniques and Public Sector Collective Bargaining, Vol. 2.2, 1987, p. 288, https://kb.osu.edu/bitstream/handle/1811/76179/OSJDR_V2N2_287.pdf?sequence=1, accessed April 17, 2020.

[56]Loc.Cit.

[57]Jeffrey Keefe, "Laws Enabling Public-Sector Collective Bargaining Have Not Led to Excessive Public-Sector Pay," Economic Policy Institute, October 16, 2015, https://www.epi.org/publication/laws-enabling-public-sector-collective-bargaining-have-not-led-to-excessive-public-sector-pay, accessed April 16, 2020.

[58]Brian J. Malloy, "Binding Interest Arbitration in The Public Sector: A "New" Proposal for California and Beyond," Hastings Law Journal, Vol. 55, Issue 1, 2003, p. 245, https://repository.uchastings.edu/cgi/viewcontent.cgi?article=3541&context=hastings_law_journal, accessed April 7, 2020.

[59]No author, "What is Arbitration?" Mediate.com, reprinted by permission from HR.com, undated, https://www.mediate.com/articles/grant.cfm, accessed April 22, 2020. *Hillsdale PBA v. Borough of Hillsdale*, 644 A. 2d 564 (N.J. 1994).

[60]While there are a number of related rules, the barest explanation of baseball arbitration is when a player and his major league team agree to salary arbitration, both the team and the player submit their salary offers to a three-person panel of professional arbiters. Each side has one hour to present their case and a half-hour to rebut the other party's presentation. During deliberation, the arbiters consider other criteria, such as leadership contributions and the salaries of comparably situated players and pick one or the other offer without modification. The contract cannot be more than one-year and is not guaranteed if the player is released.

[61]*Hillsdale PBA v. Borough of Hillsdale*, 644 A. 2d 564 (N.J. 1994) and Village of Dixmoor, 16 PERI ¶2038 (Ill. SLRB Gen. Counsel 2000).

[62]See *California Correctional Peace Officers Association v. State California*, 25 PERC 32,015 (Cal. PERB ALJ 2000).

[63]*Borough v. Pennsylvania Labor Relations Board*, 794 A.2d 402 (Pa.Cmwlth. 2002).

400 CHAPTER 11 • LABOR RELATIONS

[64]A good early discussion of bargaining topics can be found in Clark, *The Scope of the Duty to Bargain in Public Employment, in Labor Relations Law in the Public Sector* 81 (A. Knapp ed. 1977).

[65]*Portland Firefighters Association v. City of Portland*, 751 P.2d 770 (Or. 1988).

[66]*Borough v. Pennsylvania Labor Relations Board*, 794 A.2d 402 (Pa.Cmwlth. 2002).

[67]A good early discussion of bargaining topics can be found in Clark, *The Scope of the Duty to Bargain in Public Employment, in Labor Relations Law in the Public Sector* 81 (A. Knapp ed. 1977).

[68]*City of Buffalo*, 13 NPER NY-13036 (N.Y. PERB 1990).

[69]*County of Perry*, 19 NPER IL-124 (Ill. LRB 2003).

[70]*Plains Township Police Bargaining Unit v. Plains Township*, 33 PPER ¶33,019 (Pa. LRB ALJ 2001).

[71]*City of Bremerton*, PEB ¶45,352 (Wash.) (CCH, 1987).

[72]*City of Iowa City*, 17 NPER IA-26005 (Iowa PERB ALJ 1995) delay of 90 days in filing unfair labor practice charge); *County of Nassau*, 35 NYPER ¶4583 (NY PERB ALJ 2002); *City of Reading*, 17 NPER PA-26132 (Pa. LRB ALJ 1995)); *City of Philadelphia*, 13 NPER PA-22042 (Pa. LRB Hearing Examiner 1991) (six-week delay between filing of unfair labor practice charge and violation of duty to bargain did not render the charge untimely).

[73]*Throop Borough*, 16 NPER PA-25012 (Pa. LRB ALJ 1993).

[74]*Law Enforcement Labor Services*, Inc. v. City of Luverne, 463 N.W.2d 546 (Minn.App.1990).

[75]*Peekskill Police Association*, 35 NYPER ¶3016 (N.Y. PERB 2002).

[76]*Caruso v. Board of Collective Bargaining of the City of New York*, 555 N.Y.S.2d 133 (A.D. 1990).

[77]Quoted in *Model Law Enforcement Contract, 1993 Edition* (Portland, OR: Labor Relations Information System, 1993).

[78]*Washington State Patrol*, 3 (8) Public Safety Labor News 7 (Wash. PERC 1995).

[79]*City of Grosse Pointe Park*, 14 MPER ¶32051 (Mich. ERC 2001).

[80]*City of Mt. Vernon*, 23 GERR 667 (New York) (BNA 1986).

[81]*Howard County*, 1 (9) Public Safety Labor News 5 (Fishgold, 1993).

[82]William J. Bopp, *Police Personnel Administration* (Boston: Holbrook HSS, 1974), p. 345.

[83]In this regard, see Stephen L. Hayford, William A. Durkee, and Charles W. Hickman, "Bargaining Unit Determination Procedures in the Public Sector: A Comparative Evaluation," *Employee Relations Law Journal*, 5, No. 1 (summer 1979), p. 86.

[84]See Richard S. Rubin et al., "Public Sector Unit Determination Administrative Procedures and Case Law," Midwest Center for Public Sector Labor Relations, Indiana University Department of Labor Contract J-9-P-6–0215, May 31, 1978.

[85]In this regard, see Stephen L. Hayford, William A. Durkee, and Charles W. Hickman, "Bargaining Unit Determination Procedures in the Public Sector: A Comparative Evaluation," *Employee Relations Law Journal*, 5, No. 1 (summer 1979), p. 86.

[86]Arnold Zack, *Understanding Grievance Arbitration in the Public Sector* (Washington, DC: U.S. Government Printing Office, 1974), p. 2.

[87]Loc.Cit.

[88]Zack, *Understanding Grievance Arbitration*, p. 4.

[89]Ibid.

[90]Collective Bargaining Agreement, City of Hastings, Nebraska and Fraternal Order of Police, Lodge 9,Fiscal Year 2014-2018, p. 19, https://www.cityofhastings.org/assets/site/coh/documents/doccentral/Police-Union-Contract1412352116.pdf, accessed April 17, 2020.

[91]Laura Hagar Rush, "Police Chief Resigns After No Confidence Vote, Sonoma West Times and News," October 9, 2019, http://www.sonomawest.com/sonoma_west_times_and_news/news/police-chief-to-retire-after-vote-of-no-confidence/article_341fa586-eab9-11e9-a801-6b180e5addfb.html, accessed April 14, 2020.

[92]Greg Sapp, ""Mayor Bloemker Takes Issue W/No Confidence Vote for Police Chief," Premier Broadcasting, Inc., April 29, 2019, http://www.thexradio.com/news/78-local-news/39108-mayor-bloemker-takes-issue-w-no-confidence-vote-for-police-chief, accessed April 14, 2020.

[93]Larry Celona, Shawn Cohen, and Bruce Golding, "Arrests Plummet 66% With NYPD in Virtual Work Stoppage," New York Post, December 29, 2019, https://nypost.com/2014/12/29/arrests-plummet-following-execution-of-two-cops, accessed April 18, 2020.

## CHAPTER TWELVE

FINANCIAL MANAGEMENT

Learning Objectives

1. State what COVID-19 likely means for state and local government budgeting.
2. Define a police operating budget and give five examples for which expenditures are made.
3. Give three definitions of the budget.
4. Explain why budgeting is inherently a political process.
5. Identify the sequential steps in the budget process and briefly describe them.
6. Contrast program budget and performance/performance-based budget formats.
7. Explain hybrid budgets and why they exist.

INTRODUCTION

THIS CHAPTER IS IMPORTANT *to the development of police leaders for the following reasons: (1) budgeting does not occur simply in a police context; it occurs within a larger framework of state laws and regulations, city or county charters, local ordinances, guidance from city/ county chief executives, finance officers, legislative bodies, regulations, the terms of collective bargaining agreements, citizen and special interest groups, the political climate, and the financial markets. Complete police administrators must understand the larger context and their own departmental budgeting practices to be effective, (2) essentially, three things fuel law enforcement agencies: funding, people, and information; continuous learning about all three is essential; (3) responsibilities in the budget process increase as the rank ladder is climbed; learning now prepares one for the future. Moreover, some agencies solicit budget input from all levels of the agency. In those instances, your knowledge of the budget will serve you well from the beginning of any career in law enforcement; (4) the budget process is closely watched by more senior appointed and elected officials, police associations and unions, auditors, and the news media; to a large degree the measure of police administrators is how well they prepare, present, and execute their department's budget; and (5) a reputation as a good financial manager is a major asset when facing cutbacks or seeking appropriations for new programs.*

THE ECONOMY AND POLICE BUDGETS: IMPACT OF THE GREAT RECESSION AND COVID-19

The Great Recession

The Great Recession received some attention in the last chapter, but there is more to be said about it. The main driver of the recession or economic slowdown was the number of mortgage loans extended to people who did not have an attractive credit history, referred to as subprime borrowers. Many borrowers had credit scores that were less than 700. Some did not use their credit wisely, occasionally missed payments, and some created more debt than they could service. All of these factors made them greater credit risks. Banks and other lenders charged them higher interest rates than credit-worthy borrowers.

Just fourteen months after the onset of the recession, CNN found that 84 percent of cities surveyed were in financial trouble.[1] The states also had their financial problems. Between 2009 and 2012, state budget shortfalls amounted to $376 billion. In 2010 alone, 39 states made mid-budget year cuts totaling $18.3 billion.[2] How did all of this indebtedness happen?

Indebtedness was caused by falling property values and increasing unemployment figures, which resulted in tax revenues to decline. Consumer spending slowed. People relocated to find greener economic pastures. Mortgage foreclosures, loan defaults, and personal bankruptcies spiked, and many businesses reduced the number of employees or were forced to close their doors. Other factors created more fiscal pressure. Illustratively, in Chicago during 2014–2015, lawsuits for police misconduct cost the city $106 million for settlements, judgments, legal fees, and other related expenses.[3] That amount was an additional staggering expenditure for Chicago, already saddled with billions of dollars in unfunded pension obligations. To trim the deficit, Chicago shutdown mental health clinics, reduced library hours, and raised fees for water, parking, and other services.[4] Elsewhere, some cities discovered their municipal charters prohibited reducing police salaries.

By 2015, some police departments had portions of their cuts restored, but other voices, for example, the Tea Party, continued to argue for smaller and more efficient government. With deep cuts in staffing, many law enforcement agencies were actually a thin blue line. Unpredictable events, such as hurricanes and pandemics stretched some agencies too far. Technology is a force multiplier for law enforcement agencies, but if staffing cuts are severe enough, technology cannot completely overcome the absence of officers.

The Great Recession effected many law enforcement agencies because it: (1) introduced fiscal distress, (2) reduced their resources, (3) forced leaders to make painful decisions, (4) left a lingering impact on many agencies, and (5) provided useful and sometimes painful lessons about financial management. The Great Recession required governmental employers to take a hard look at their unfunded liabilities, the largest of which were health care insurance, pensions, and annual cost of living adjustments (COLAs).

The purpose of COLAs is to reduce or offset the inflation rate. Assume a pension of $25,000, no COLAs, and an average of 2 percent inflation over 20 years in retirement. Absent any COLAs, the pension's real buying power becomes $16,697, meaning it has only retained 67 percent of its original value.[5]

Government employers bargained to have officers pay a larger amount for health care and put caps on some health expenditures. Changed pensions rules created savings in many jurisdictions. Examples include: (1) regardless of when people retired, they didn't receive any COLAs until age 60; (2) officers who retired before earning 20 years of service didn't receive COLAs until they were 65; (3) COLA's were capped at no more than 2.5 percent of retirees annual salary; (4) some states increased the age at which officers could begin drawing their retirement and used new calculations for how pensions were calculated. Instead of basing a pension on the highest three years of earnings times 2.5 percent- or 3 percent-times years of service, a portion of that calculation was changed to the highest earning five years of service, creating smaller pensions; and (5) some COLAs are automatic, set on a statutory calculation. By changing to be "ad hoc COLAs," retirees might not get a COLA in any given year.[6]

COVID-19 and Fiscal Health

The COVID-19 pandemic is a once in a generation event (see Figure 12.1). As a new disease, its reach is global. Efforts to reduce its impact have produced slow and modest results. Much of the history of COVID-19 is still to be written. Already we can identify major impacts on people, particularly frontline workers, from food delivery truck drivers to medical professionals who are exposed to multiple risks daily, homes become schools and offices, the burden of debt for medical treatment, the emotional strain from uncertainties, financial losses from the stock market, for example, its one-day drop of 3,000 points, and the sorrow of being unable to visit dying family members and attend their funerals. We also know the future economic impact on the United States will be greater than that of the Great Recession.

COVID-19 infected hundreds of thousands of us and caused a significant number deaths. Yet, we still cannot yet see the end.

The high end of projections for U.S. deaths is 240,000.[7] Harvard researchers assert social distancing, such as school closings and stay-at-home orders, may need to go on until 2022 unless more critical care capacity is available, or an effective vaccine quickly becomes developed.[8] Hopefully, new 2020 vaccines that have a 90-plus percent effectiveness rate will soon be available for first responders, like the police, as well as for general society. Economically, it is projected that 26 percent of all small businesses are *immediately* vulnerable to failing,[9] which represents 2 million business closings and 27.5 million lost jobs.[10] Beyond the 22 million who already filed for unemployment benefits, another 20.5 million people lost their jobs in late 2020.

The Economic Policy Institute (EPI) estimates total unemployment as a result of the COVID-19 pandemic in the United States to exceed 50 million people, or nearly 20% of our population by the end of 2021, the highest level since the Great Depression.[11] After EPI released its estimate, the White House opined unemployment may be even higher, 25 percent. In early 2020, unemployment was just 3.5 percent. America is in the grips of an economy, the likes of which we have never seen before. The pandemic produced enormous deficits due to the "twin terrors:" (1) The severe economic damage done by businesses closing, people out of work, substantially reduced industrial production, and miniscule consumer spending due to quarantines and social distancing, and (2) the actions taken in response, such as federal relief laws enacted by the Congress and signed into law.

The projected federal deficit just for 2020 was $3.7 trillion, increasing the federal deficit. The federal government has wide discretion with deficit budgeting. However, state governments,

FIGURE 12.1 ▶ New York, NY, April 14, 2020. The World Trade Center Transportation Center also provides shopping opportunities for the 250,000 passengers that pass through it daily. Normally crowded by commuters and tourists, it is eerily empty except for these police officers as people shelter during the COVID-19 pandemic. (Photograph Courtesy of K.C. Wilsey/FEMA)

Quick Facts: When Is a Balanced Budget Not a Balanced Budget?

A state or local government may adopt a balanced budget, which is based on analysts' projected revenue.

If there is a revenue shortfall, which happened during the Great Recession and COVID-19, the budget is no longer balanced. Jurisdictions handle this in several ways, including revising the budget. In some jurisdictions, it is an exception to not being able to operate with a deficit budget and the deficit is carried forward to the next budget cycle.[14]

except for Vermont, are required to produce a balanced budget, one that does not exceed total revenue. In fairness to Vermont, it usually brings in a balanced budget even though there is no legal compulsion to do so.[12] Generally, nearly 70 percent of state revenues come from two sources: incomes and general sales taxes. With so many people out of work and quarantining, state revenues have substantially been reduced. Examples for 2021 include Illinois ($7.4 billion), Massachusetts ($4.2–$7.2 billion), and Colorado ($2.4 billion). New York's 2022 revenue deficit is projected to be an astonishing $16 billion.[13] U.S. Senator Dirksen (1896–1969) famously said of budgeting, a billion here, a billion there, pretty soon you're talking real money. Unfortunately, COVID-19 has a lot of states talking real money deficits.

Local governments are also revenue starved for the same reasons. In 2020, the Mayor of Shreveport, Louisiana, proposed cuts of $19.3 million from the city budget due to the pandemic. The $61 million Police Department budget was targeted with a $4.5 million cut, a reduction of 7 percent. What all of this means is that austerity budgeting at the state and local levels is likely to be normal state of affairs for several years. There will be some easy choices for cuts, but those will be quickly used up. Cuts thereafter will be much harder.

Law Enforcement Agencies and Fiscal Stress

When under fiscal stress law enforcement agencies choose from strategies such as: (1) freezing new hires, not filling vacant positions or eliminating them, and freezing promotions; (2) cancelling recruit and many advanced training classes;[15] (3) requiring officers to take furlough/unpaid days off; (4) reducing salaries;[16] (5) closing precincts;[17] (6) delaying the purchase of replacement vehicles; (7) selling helicopters;[18] (8) closing police headquarters to the public;[19] (9) slashing police programs;[20] (10) eliminating mounted patrol, motorcycle, accident investigation, burglary, and marine patrol units;[21] (11) laying off officers and slashing overtime funding; (12) achieving reductions in force by not filling vacancies created by attrition; (13) replacing sworn officers with fewer and less-expensive civilians; and (14) increasing the numbers and breadth of assignments for volunteers.

The Great Recession and COVID-19 have severely tested the financial management skills of law enforcement executives. Even their best efforts have sometimes not been sufficient. Hundreds of small towns have abolished their police departments.[22] Typically, these small towns contract with the state police or a sheriff's office for minimal law enforcement services or consolidate with another law enforcement agency.

For many police departments, all nice to have, but not essential budget lines will be gone and further cuts will be into muscle and bone, affecting service delivery in ways that citizens can feel, such as such as increased response time, Slashed budgets are common when deficits are created because there are so many "budget busters" that cannot be foreseen—for example, natural disasters,[23] including hurricanes, tornadoes, earthquakes, floods, snow storms, mudslides, avalanches, and wildfires. For instance during the summers of 2018–2020, the states of Oregon, Washington, and California experienced massive forest fires that engulfed whole towns and caused massive property damage as well as loss of life. All three declared "state emergencies" that lasted for several months that tested the very limits of police and fire service personnel as well as producing massive budget shortfalls. To make matters worse, each state confronted significant protest and rioting stemming from the Black Lives Matter movement and the death of George Floyd. Already strained city budgets were tasked as police and fire personnel worked significant overtime. For instance, police and fire officers in Portland, Oregon experienced well over 100 consecutive nights of civil unrest necessitating hundreds of extra personnel to quell disturbances, protect property and be on duty for potential, large-scale burning, rioting and looting.

These types of events can add up to be huge budget busters, particularly when the myriad of normal, everyday circumstances continue to routinely occur, like searches for missing children, hunters, and seniors who walk away from their care situations, protracted industrial strikes, complex investigations involving serial offenders, unforeseeable surges in the price of gasoline, terrorist attacks, and the cost of using private labs to process key evidence in significant cases. Cutting staffing and reducing overtime funds in the police budget are not compatible strategies. If staff is slashed, overtime costs may exceed the budgeted amount. In very small departments, the budget may be "busted" by lesser events, such as having to replace a copier machine or buying a new patrol car because of an accident. Without question, the deep cuts resulted in some people becoming crime victims, some criminals escaped investigation and prosecution due to elimination of positions, and police work became more dangerous because of less or no backup on dangerous calls for service.

Ironically, the summer of 2020 also witnessed calls to "defund" the police or completely abolish the police. These were clearly controversial topics that resulted in a number of police chiefs resigning their positions in protest to budget cuts to their departments and external meddling by city councils. See Box 12.1.

Box 12.1: Camden, New Jersey: A Case Study in "Defunding" the Police

By: Jennifer Davis-Lamm, Caruth Police Institute and Robert W. Taylor, University of Texas at Dallas

In the wake of the death of George Floyd in May of 2020, calls for "defunding" the police began to echo through not just activist circles—but in mainstream media, politics, and in communities across the country. Use of the term "defund" has had varying connotations, however; for some, it means abolishing policing altogether, while others envision a re-prioritization of municipal funds toward services that would reduce police calls for service related to mental health, addiction, and family crises.

As defunding the police has become a hot topic, so too has the story of Camden, New Jersey. As pundits discuss what defunding might look like, many have pointed to the story of the town in New Jersey that, in 2012, dissolved its own police force and reimagined it as a county-wide public safety agency. At first glance, it seems like the perfect example of what defunding looks like—and indeed, the chief that oversaw the agency's transition has himself written op-eds seemingly in that context. But the metamorphosis of Camden Police Department into the Camden County Police Department was less of a reform measure and more an immediate reaction to a massive budget shortfall and a quickly growing violent crime rate.

In 2011, still reeling from a recession that resulted in reduced tax revenue and state funding, the city faced a $26.5 million budget *shortfall*. Nearly half of its police force was laid off, a total of 163, with only 260 officers left to battle a skyrocketing crime rate with response times that meant citizens were left waiting hours for critical assistance. In 2012, the city saw a record number of murders and assaults, and in a bid to address this issue, along with other budgetary issues and failing police/community relations, the city did something quite radical: It dissolved its police department.

All officers were laid off, though many were re-hired at a lower rate of pay, and the city shifted to a regional model of policing. The Camden County Police Department would serve not only the city, but the entire county jurisdiction with an emphasis on proactive, community-based policing strategies. Though other jurisdictions have been slow to sign on, residents did notice more community/police interaction. However, initially, to increase revenue to the city, there were also major increases in minor infractions, including offenses such as jaywalking, bicycle violations and tinted windows. Statistically, there were also increases in use of force complaints, and a specific use of force incident in 2014 that included the same type of controversial techniques used in the George Floyd case. An increase in police surveillance was also noted as the Camden County Police Department relied heavily on its Real Time Crime Center (fusion center) and other means of supervision, including CCTV, aerial surveillance, license plate readers, and more. This approach to policing is a far cry from more current "defund" rhetoric initiated in 2020, as increased police presence and surveillance is not generally part of the "defund" narrative.

Interestingly, since 2014, crime rates have fallen in the area, however, it is not clear that the re-organization of the police department had much impact on this issue. Local activists point to area gentrification as part of the reason for decreases in violent crime; further, those statistics mimicked falling crime rates throughout the state of New Jersey (and the rest of the country) during the same time period.

Regardless, while crime data may not lend much support to the reorganization of Camden's police force as a panacea, there are some legitimate takeaways: A partnership with New York University has yielded a use of force policy that emphasizes force as a last resort; the department has instituted a de-escalation training program; there are now policies that require intervention by officers if they see their counterparts using inappropriate force; the department has deployed significantly more officers on foot and on bikes in an effort to increase non-call contacts with the public; other agencies such as child welfare and mental health professionals respond to family disorder and suicide calls, and most importantly, there is a spirit of collaboration and responsiveness to the community relating to citizen complaints around increased surveillance, aggression and enforcement that has been lauded by community groups, including the local ACLU chapter. The greater Camden area now realizes that reduced police budgets must provide for better and more focused training of officers, while at the same time diverting money to be spent on local programming for the homeless, mental health assistance and domestic violence may fall beyond the police department's responsibility.

Quite interestingly, many calls for reform are originating from *within* police circles. The RAND Corporation recently noted that without exception, the only entity that has been made the "front line" in addressing almost every social problem in America is the police. Asking police officers to act as social workers, to respond to mental health crises, give aid to victims of violent crime, house the homelessness, feed the hungry, find treatment for substance abusers, and counsel couples engaged in domestic disputes may well be an unrealistic expectation for any individual and any one governmental agency. Defunding the police does not make sense if communities continue to ask their police departments to do the same job with fewer resources. In such an environment, we can all expect higher levels of disorder, violence, and crime. Since the George Floyd shooting, a number of police chiefs across the nation have either resigned or accelerated their retirements in protest to budget cuts arising from calls to defund the police. Top on that list was the resignation of Chief Carmen Best, the first Black female to lead the Seattle Police Department (SPD), who stepped down after the SPD budget was slashed by some 14 percent, resulting in a cut of over 100 officers. On the other hand, while Camden County Police Department is not necessarily a poster child for defunding and disbanding, it certainly points to

possibilities for reform and rebuilding community trust. At a time in our country, when there are highly polarized calls for police reform, it may be time to identify and build reforms that are likely to succeed, versus wholesale cuts to police budgets across our country.

Sources:

Adomaitis, G. (January 16, 2019). "6 Months Later, 6 Answers from Camden Police to Your Questions." *NJ.com.* https://www.nj.com/camden/2016/10/6_months_later_6_takeaways_from_camden_county_poli.html

American Civil Liberties Union. (May 18, 2015). "Policing in Camden has Improved, but Concerns Remain." *Aclu.org.* https://www.aclu.org/press-releases/policing-camden-has-improved-concerns-remain

Casiano, Louis. (September 9, 2020). "Police Chiefs Who Have Resigned or Retired Since George Floyd Death." *Fox News.com.* https://www.foxnews.com/us/police-chiefs-george-floyd.print

Fussell, Sidney. (July 1, 2020). "What Disbanding the Police Really Meant in Camden, New Jersey." *Wired.* https://www.wired.com/story/disbanding-police-really-meant-camden/

Holder, Sarah. (June 4, 2020). "The City that Remade Its Police Department." *Bloomberg Businessweek.* https://www.bloomberg.com/news/articles/2020-06-04/how-camden-new-jersey-reformed-its-police-department

Lockwood, B. and Brian R. Wyant. (2014). "Who Cares Who Protects Us? The Relationship Between Type of Police Coverage and Citizen Satisfaction with the Police." *Police Practice and Research,* 15(6), 461–475.

Maciag, Mike. (June 2014). Why Camden, N.J., is the Murder Capital of the Country, Disbanded Its Police Force. *Governing.com.* https://www.governing.com/topics/public-justice-safety/gov-camden-disbands-police-force-for-new-department.html

Policing Project. (2019). "Camden County Police Department Use of Force Policy." *Policing Project.* policingproject.org/camden

Thomson, J. (June 18, 2020) As Camden's Police Chief, I Scrapped the Force and Started Over. It Worked." *Washington Post.* https://www.washingtonpost.com/outlook/camden-police-chief-old-new-department/2020/06/18/37407536-b0b8-11ea-856d-5054296735e5_story.html

Wiig, A. (2017). "Secure the City, Revitalize the Zone: Smart Urbanization in Camden, New Jersey." Environment and Planning Commission: *Politics and Space,* 36(3), 403–422.

Vermeer, Michael J., Dulani Woods, and Brian A. Jackson. (August 2020), "Would Law Enforcement Leaders Support Defunding the Police? Probably—*If* Communities Ask Police to Solve Fewer Problems." *Perspective,* (Santa Monica, CA: RAND Corporation).

Quick Facts: The Distinction Between Budgeting and Accounting

Some police personnel are dismissive about budgeting, characterizing it as "accountant's work." The claim reveals a lack of understanding about how the two concepts are related. Budgeting is prospective, future oriented; accounting is retrospective, past oriented.[24]

FIGURE 12.2 ▶ Amid calls to "defund" the police, Glendale, Arizona police officers attended a tense city council meeting during which a $20 million reduction of the city's existing total budget was discussed. The cuts were not as deep as they feared. The police department lost 19 of 425 sworn and 14 of 152.5 civilian positions. (Ross D. Franklin/AP/Corbis)

POLITICS AND FINANCIAL MANAGEMENT

Anything done by government involves the expenditure of public funds.[25] Budgeting is inherently a political process because elected members of city councils, county commissions, state legislatures, and the Congress express their preferences when they vote on appropriations. Appropriators consider their own views, as well as those expressed by constituents, political donors, the news media, police unions, polls, special interest groups, lobbyists, and colleagues, as well as deals made to secure support for their own interests. Politics do not stop when a budget is adopted; in some circumstances, the politics can actually intensify during the time a budget is executed (see Figure 12.2). This is especially true when a law enforcement agency has scarce resources and must cut back or end different services. Some citizens and groups effected by such decisions will try to get their preferred services restored.

STATE AND LOCAL INFLUENCES ON FINANCIAL MANAGEMENT

Cities and counties are under the authority of their respective state governments, which have considerable authority over them, including financial management. Local governments cannot be created, nor can they levy taxes or deliver services without the prior approval of the state. Following the economic crash of 1929,

thousands of local governments went bankrupt because they could not meet their financial obligations. As a result, many states passed laws that regulate local finance in such areas as revenue sources, tax collection, level of permissible indebtedness, budgeting procedures, and audits. Typically, states prohibit cities and counties from borrowing to fund annual operating budgets; historically such borrowing signals bankruptcy was on the near horizon.[26] States also require detailed financial reports from local governments, which are carefully studied for signs of fiscal weakness.

In addition to whatever requirements the state establishes, local financial management is guided by a maze of other guidelines, including the city or county charter, ordinances, executive orders, regulations, and customary practices. The form of local government shapes who the dominant figures are in finance. In a strong mayor system, the mayor is the key player, whereas in the weak mayor form, the council is the predominant force. In a mayor-city manager system, the manager holds great power. These generalizations are affected by other factors, such as how much influence a long-serving finance director has accrued and the degree to which a city council is more or less activist in scrutinizing and revising the mayor's or city manager's budget.

KEY BUDGET TERMS

Every year, the most important statement governments make is their approved budgets because they reveal in financial terms what their priorities are. There are different ways to define a

budget. For example, it is a plan expressed in dollars. The use of financial resources to meet human needs and a contract between those who appropriate the money and those who execute the budget.[27]

A budget year is called a **fiscal year (FY)**, and it may coincide with the calendar year. Often, a FY runs from July 1 of one year until June 30 of the next year. A budget, which begins on July 1, 2021, and ends on June 30, 2022, is called the FY '22 budget. Some local units of government have changed their fiscal year to October 1 of one year until September 30 of the next year to coincide with the federal budget year and the funding of its grant programs. At various times, the Congress has considered adopting a biennial budget but never changed to one. In 1940, 44 states were using a **biennial budget**, which covers a two-year period, presently 19 states do so.[28] Budgets can also be defined as operating and capital:[29]

An **operating budget** usually covers a 12-month period and consists of annually recurring costs such as salaries, fringe benefits, uniforms, crime scene supplies, ammunition, training, telephone service, gasoline, and kindred expenses. Operating budgets are overwhelmingly funded by a city or county's annual stream of revenues into its general fund, with a few exceptions such as grants and donations. As its name suggests, the general fund contains a local government's revenues that are not obligated to other funds. Both operating and capital budgets must be approved by the appropriate legislative body which authorizes appropriations, such as a city council, county commission, state legislature, or the Congress.

Capital Improvement Plans (CIPs) of them slowly spread.[30] Capital budgets are made up of individual "high cost" capital improvement plans (CIPs). Across the United States, there is variation in how local governments define capital budget items. A "capital item" (high cost) varies by state, and across local governments. For example, in Minnesota, state guidance on capital budgets for small units of local government is different than for large ones.

Cars are defined in the capital budget in one jurisdiction, while in others it is part of the separate operating budget. Those definitions establish the *financial thresholds* that determine into which budget an item goes. As an example, in many jurisdictions purchasing an automobile is automatically in the capital budget regardless of its cost. In contrast, in New York City, unless the cost of purchasing a car is more than $35,000, its cost goes into the annual operating budget. The advantage of placing an item in the capital budget is that it can be paid

for over multiple years as opposed to one year in an annual operating budget.

Illustrations of CIPs include the purchase of land, major rehabilitation of buildings, construction of new facilities, sewer, gas, and water lines, bridges, dams, parks, and airports. Equipment and machines, such as increasingly sophisticated computers, vehicles, firearms, and forensic laboratory equipment, may also be in the capital budget. CIPs vary in terms of the number of years over which they are paid off and each of them are reviewed annually and adjusted. The subsequent maintenance of many newly acquired capital items, for example, cars, buildings, and a new police station, comes out of the operating budget. Some CIPs may be required as a matter of law, such as a court order to a county to build a new jail for the Sheriff's Office/Department because the existing one is antiquated and continuously overcrowded.

Unlike operating budgets, capital items, once paid for, are not annually recurring expenses because the item no longer appears in the budget. Commonly, capital items are paid for by multiple sources, including revenues, grants, and donations. Some jurisdictions have a preference to "pay as you go" as much as possible, but very large projects, such as purchasing a helicopter for surveillance and rescue, may force cities and counties to issue a bond, creating an indebtedness. Bond investors are repaid semiannually over a fixed number of years. The Government Finance Officers Association (GFOA) recommends that the operating and capital budgets should be distinctly separate and also considered separately by the legislative body appropriating the funds.[32]

THE BUDGET CYCLE

At its heart, the **budget cycle** is a stream of four sequential steps that are repeated at about the same time every year in a jurisdiction: (1) preparation and submission of the budget by all of a city or county's departments, which includes getting input from stakeholders, such as citizens and advisory boards (see Box 12.2); (2) review and approval by the legislative body, which usually involve public hearings and occasionally heated exchanges; (3) execution of the budget, meaning doing the actual things for which the funds were appropriated, including any budget adjustments after the budget is approved; and (4) the audit and evaluation.[33] An audit is an independent evaluation of something, for example, a law enforcement agency's

---

Quick Facts: Origination of the Term "Budget"

"Budget" comes from the French *bougette*, meaning a leather bag. Originally, it referred to the bag in which the Chancellor of the Exchequer carried budget documents to the English Parliament. Later, it came to mean the documents themselves.[31] The first Exchequer budget was taken to Parliament in 1284. The office of Chancellor of the Exchequer still exists in England.

Box 12.2: Citizen-Centric Reports (CCRs)

Citizens in the United States generally have multiple opportunities to learn about and provide input on budget priorities and appropriations. Such opportunities are enhanced by a technique loosely referred to as a "citizen guide," citizen-centric report, "performance report" or some similar title. The key objectives of citizen-centric reports are to increase the transparency of government and citizen participation in governance. The contents vary, but frequently incorporate color pie, bar graphs, and similar methods to summarize information about the budget, the accomplishments of the jurisdiction, and a survey of local citizens on their satisfaction with the city or county's services. Citizen guides are widely distributed in print and are often available on the city or country's website. The advantage of surveying citizens is that instead of a jurisdiction just *telling* people what the city or county has done, it is in a *listening* mode to the perceptions of citizens and may discover new opportunities or conditions that need correction.

Used precisely, a "Citizen-Centric Report" (CCR) refers to an initiative by The Association of Government Accountants (AGA) to give citizens numbers that they can understand. In plain language and limited to four pages, the AGA's CCR format answers four questions for citizens: (1) strategic objectives/what are we chartered (required) to do? This explains the mandated services to be provided; (2) how are we doing? This page is a performance report of key missions and services and AGA encourages that public input, such as a survey, be used to gather data. A usual survey question is, "How much confidence do you have in your police department?" This question is used with other departments as well; (3) what are the costs for servicing citizens and how is it paid for? On this third page, cost data is linked to the service delivery results, so citizens understand what each service costs; and (4) the last page covers challenges moving forward: What's next and future challenges, which summarizes emerging conditions and the economic outlook.

The more elaborate reports may also incorporate information from the International City/County Management Association's (ICMA's) National Citizen Survey (NCS), which asks questions in eight different community domains to determine citizen perceptions. Users jurisdictions can get data about their own community as well as comparative data for comparable jurisdictions. NCS may be used in lieu of the local survey or as a supplement. Law enforcement agencies may be able to hone their preparation skills for annual and other reports by studying the features of citizen-centric and other citizen guides on the Internet.

---

control of its petty cash fund, its annual expenditures, or its performance on key indicators, such as use of force incidents. Many of these four activities are going on simultaneously because different budget activities overlap.[34] For example, while a sheriff's, or police department is executing this year's budget, last year's budget is being audited and the next year's budget is being prepared.

Well before a police department starts preparing its budget, the F/FSD has been at work preparing the revenue forecast for the city, documenting the assumptions departments are required to make during budget preparation, such as percentage increases for gasoline or equipment service, and other data, including the budget preparation manual. These manuals focus on the technical aspects of putting the budget together and include laws, policies, definitions, forms, changes from last year's budget manual, and the **budget calendar** to be followed (see Figure 12.3).

The mayor or city/county manager then sends the budget manual to the department heads with specific guidelines on services to be emphasized and specific fiscal guidance as to the percentage the budget may increase or must decrease, the maximum, average percent raises for employees, limits on new positions and programs, and other fiscal data. Often, previous budget messages from the city/county manager, the budget preparation manual, and past budgets are available online, along with any software needed to prepare the budget.

Budget workshops are often held by the F/FSD to explain the process and establish uniformity in the budget process across departments.

As part of gathering information for the budget preparation manual, the mayor or city/county managers usually meet with their council or county commission to get their views on budget priorities. This helps avoid major conflict later in the budget process. Many jurisdictions conduct strategic planning and budget planning workshops at various points in the budget process to get citizen and city council/county commission input early in the process, especially with respect to goals, priorities, and target budget figures. These measures do not guarantee there won't be conflict later, but they do reduce potential for it. Occasionally, differences arise in budgeting over seemingly minor programs (see Quick Facts: Police Geese Restored in Budget).

Step One: Budget Preparation in the Police Department

In small police departments, those with roughly 10 or fewer officers, the chief's role in budget preparation is often limited.[36] Most frequently, strong mayors or city managers will have several conversations with such chiefs about their department and formulate the budget themselves or delegate its preparation. In larger departments with seven or eight layers of hierarchy, the

Date	Event
Mid-March	2021 budget request materials distributed to city departments
May 12	2021 budget requests due from city departments to Budget Office
Late July	Requested Budget Summary published in the Milwaukee Journal/Sentinel
Mid-August	Mayor's Public Hearing on the 2021 Budget
Late September	Mayor presents 2021 Proposed Executive Budget to the Common Council Common Council Chambers
Late September	Proposed Budget and Notice of Joint Public Hearing published in the Milwaukee Journal/Sentinel
October	Finance & Personnel Committee Hearings on the 2021 Proposed Budget
Early October 6:30 pm	Joint Public Hearing on the 2021 Proposed Budget Common Council Chambers 200 E. Wells St., 3rd Floor
October 30	Finance & Personnel Committee Budget Amendment Day
November 6 9:00 am	Budget Adoption Common Council Chambers

FIGURE 12.3 ▶ The Milwaukee 2020 budget calendar.

Quick Facts: Police Geese Restored in Budget

The Eatontown, New Jersey, city finance staff cut the budget $12,000 by eliminating the "Geese Police," a dog that chased the geese from Wampum Memorial Park. The city council's president expressed anger at the cut. One council member said the program was very effective, the cut would reduce park use, and the budget should be amended to fund the Geese Police.[35]

On the "left coast," there is an Oregon business, "Geese Guys," who use highly trained border collies to humanely eliminate high concentrations of Canada Geese from parks and other public areas. A single Canada Goose produces several pounds of "poop" daily. When there are larger populations of them, this creates a health hazard and eyesore, both of which reduce public use of such facilities. Where animal control departments are organizationally assigned to law enforcement agencies "geese herding" becomes a police responsibility.

---

budget process is more formal. In medium-sized and larger departments, the chief's budget is shaped by the guidance given by a city or county manager and, in that context, is a top-down process. In turn, police chiefs provide their guidance on priorities, programs, and staffing.

The budget is also built by reviewing, sometimes revising, and then combining the budget requests from smaller units to form much of the budgets of bureaus or divisions. The single most important element in a police budget is people and their support costs, such as salaries, medical insurance, life insurance, and pension benefits, as well as overtime and training. In many departments, personnel and personnel support costs may consume 80 or more percent of the budget, limiting what cuts can be made before staffing is affected.

In a tight budget year, some chiefs cut back on training dollars. This might make the budget work, but it is a poor strategy. Any chief who submitted a budget without dollars in it for preventive maintenance of the police fleet would be criticized. Yet, training is the preventive maintenance on people. It keeps

personnel fresh and at the cutting edge, prevents litigation or can be a defense to it, and is a means of importing new ideas and techniques into the police department. As to delaying the purchase of replacement vehicles, officers operating vehicles with 100,000 and more miles are using cars that may be dangerously worn out, no matter how well they have been maintained. These ideas are easily written, but when chiefs are ordered to cut their budget 20 percent, they have a very difficult task to perform. It's less about mathematically making the cuts and more about knowing the chaos and pain the cuts will bring to the men and women of the department and affect service to the community.

When the chief meets with bureau or division commanders to review their budget requests, it is an opportunity to reward the "faithful" and to informally discipline those who are seen as "not toeing the party line" and are therefore "disloyal." In lean budget years, however, it is harder to reward the faithful and easier to harm a wayward subordinate.

Chiefs are also concerned with budget strategy and making the best case for funding. If solid justifications cannot be made for programs, they should not be included in the request lest it set budget analysts in the F/FSD on a quest to also find other programs to cut. As a matter of strategy, chiefs may include some "fat" in the budget, so that they can withstand a certain degree of reductions. The fat is not wasteful spending. It represents new positions or programs the department would like to have and would make good use of but whose loss would not endanger the delivery of important services.

In fiscally strained years, when transmitting the budget to the finance director or mayor/city manager, the chief's cover letter may detail what cuts were necessarily made in his/her proposed budget for the next year and what their probable impact will be, and other difficulties created by them. Examples of difficulties included reduced response times, increased citizen dissatisfaction of their perception of the police and with police services, lower clearance rates, and future difficulties in recruiting. When a city or county's revenues are more robust, the Chief or Sheriff will cite accomplishments from the current budget, illustrated by success stories, and will call attention to the importance of new initiatives, and the lost opportunities and ills likely to arise if these initiatives are not funded. No matter what is happening in terms of the amount of crime, chiefs and sheriffs have an explanation that seemingly justifies a budget increase: If crime is up, more personnel and programs are needed to reduce it; if things are going well, new funding will help keep crime in check.

Step Two: Budget Review and Approval

At some point, the Mayor or city manager will meet with the police chief to review the department's request. Prior to that meeting, the F/FSD will have reviewed the budget and had discussions about it with the mayor or city manager. How the meeting goes with the city manager depends on many factors,

including the chief's reputation as a fiscal manager, his or her relationship with the city manager, the priorities and direction given by the city council, and the confidence the public has in the chief and the police department. Even recent events can affect the outcome. For example, assume that a chief has a street crimes unit whose tactics often include using decoys who are similar to the types of victims being targeted by predatory criminals (e.g., indigents, the elderly, and lone females). If in the past week, an offender was killed attempting to rob a decoy, the newspapers, and public sentiment may run toward disbanding this "killer" unit (see Box 12.3). No matter how effective the unit is, the question may become how much "bad press" can the city afford to have? Ultimately, the city manager and chief come to an understanding about the department's request. That understanding is reflected in the budget the city manager recommends to council.

When making their budget "pitch" to the city council, chiefs should be able to anticipate questions. For example, if the U.S. Department of Justice has just released a study on how the use of body cameras leads to a reduction in complaints against officers, the chief is likely to get this question: "Why aren't there body cameras in your budget?" Another question might be, "Last month, I read a news article which said it can now be determined when a fingerprint was left at a crime. Are we pursuing that?" In the final analysis, in some years, chiefs, no matter how skilled they are or how good a presentation they made, simply have to be political realists and gracefully take their "budgetary lumps." The budget approval process is depicted in Table 12.1.

Step Three: Budget Execution

This section deals with three key aspects of **budget execution**: (1) budget execution objectives, (2) budget execution adjustments, and (3) budget execution control.

Box 12.3: Elite New York Police Department's (NYPD) Street Crimes Unit (SCU) Disbanded

The NYPD's SCU was elite, comprised of between 100 and 150 officers. Officers voted who came into the unit because their lives depended on each other. The SCU was particularly effective in detecting those who surreptitiously carried guns despite the strict gun laws. The almost legendary successes of the SCU became a prime factor in its downfall.

Against the advice of the unit's commanding officer, it was expanded by roughly another 300 officers. It is believed the quality of unit personnel was reduced by this decision. In 1999, there was a wrongful fatal shooting while young and inexperienced SCU officers searched for a rapist suspect. The suspect, perhaps thinking the plainclothes officers were robbers, tried to move his wallet, which was mistaken for a move to draw a weapon.

Although the officers were indicted for murder, they were acquitted. In the backlash that followed SCU was disbanded in 2002 and as of 2015 had not been reactivated despite

some calls to do so in a city where gun crimes and violence are on the rise.[38] At some point, the functions of SCU were transferred to the Anti-Crime Unit.

At budget hearings before their city councils, chiefs must tread a narrow path. If they attempt to persuade council members to restore cuts made by city managers, the chiefs risk alienating their "bosses." Conversely, if the cuts have gone too deep, chiefs as a matter of public safety may feel obliged to appeal for some funds to be restored. Safer than initiating the appeal on their own, experienced chiefs may plant key questions with friendly members of council so that the discussion can be had without them openly spearheading the discussion. City managers know this game and can tolerate it, versus having their chiefs openly defy them. Generally, even council members who favor increasing the police budget may be reluctant to do so if it means voting for a tax increase.

TABLE 12.1 FY 2021: THE OPERATING BUDGET APPROVAL PROCESS

ORG	OBJ	Police Patrol	FY 2017 Actual	FY 2018 Actual	FY 2019 Actual	FY 2020 Budget	FY 2021 Mayor* Proposed	Council Approved	Percent Change
01474	6003	Payroll—Regular	4,283,889	4,428,791	4,612,450	4,497,410	4,510,787	4,510,787	0.30%
01474	6008	Special Officers/Events	67,297	90,414	149,508	60,480	122,823	112,823	86.55%
01474	6009	Payroll—Supplementary	202,006	226,554	188,437	240,000	140,000	140,000	–41.67%
01474	6020	Payroll—Overtime	137,398	204,775	127,687	84,000	125,000	125,000	48.81%
01474	6021	Court Time Travel	—	—	—	1,960	—	—	–100.00%
01474	6022	Shift Differential	113,690	125,089	117,547	124,460	124,460	124,460	0.00%
01474	6024	Callback	659,794	551,044	441,546	425,000	393,000	383,000	–9.88%
01474	6058	Uniform Maintenance	64,991	69,774	72,282	64,800	69,600	69,600	7.41%
01474	6156	Prisoner Meals	5,358	6,557	2,665	2,500	2,500	2,500	0.00%
01474	6302	Equipment Service	19,533	20,198	10,360	19,600	19,600	19,600	0.00%
		Totals:	5,553,956	5,723,198	5,722,482	5,520,210	5,507,770	5,487,770	–0.23%

*Or City/County Manager

BUDGET EXECUTION OBJECTIVES

Budget execution is the action phase of budgeting, the phase in which plans reflected in the police budget are put into operation.[39] During this phase, police chiefs:

1. must rigorously pursue achieving the goals of the agency;

2. document service gaps, the variance between the types and amounts of service delivery planned for versus actual demand;

3. provide timely information on expenditures, program accomplishments, and milestones for any CIP projects to senior appointed and elected officials, as well as the legislative body, such as city council, which appropriated the budget;

4. publicize police department successes; and

5. maintain budget execution control, a responsibility that is shared with the F/FSD and discussed in a subsequent section.

Budget Adjustments

It is said that people plan and fate laughs; like other types of plans, budgets must be monitored and adjusted as needed. Budget adjustments may increase or decrease a police department's budget (see Figure 12.4). Any financial changes proposed for an adopted budget must be approved by the legislative body that adopted it, for example, city council or county commission. In some states if the change reaches a certain dollar threshold, it requires the approval of the state.

There are six common methods of adjusting the budget: (1) accepting grants and donations; (2) transferring funds from one category to another, subject to any approval that is needed. A department head may have limited authority to do so and for larger transfers the approval of the legislative body, such

as city council, is required; (3) seeking a supplemental budget some months into the execution phase because of unforeseeable conditions or other grounds, for example, when it is clear that anticipated demands for police services are outstripping resources. An example of this is when a smaller community suddenly becomes a college spring break destination; (4) freezing expenditures when the city's or county's revenue collection may be slower than anticipated; (5) delaying expenditures due to signs of revenue shortfalls; and (6) the city council or county commission may reallocate funds from one department to another, reduce the budget in just one or a few departments or by an across the board cut such as 3.5 percent. Some of these methods and related topics are discussed in a later section of this chapter.

The Oregon Department of Revenue's *Local Budgeting Guide* recognizes the following reasons for changing an approved budget, some of which exist in its State Statutes:

1. An occurrence or condition that was not known at the time the budget was prepared requires a change in financial planning.

2. A pressing necessity creates a need for prompt action.

3. Unexpected funds are made available by another unit of federal, state, or local government (see Figure 12.4).

4. A request for services or facilities is received and the cost will be paid for by a private individual, corporation or company, or by another governmental unit, and the amount of the request could not have been known or known for certain at the time the budget was prepared.

5. Proceeds from the involuntary destruction, involuntary conversion, or sale of property have necessitated the immediate purchase, construction or acquisition of different facilities to carry on governmental operations.

City of
Evanston™

Memorandum

To: Hitesh Desai, Chief Financial Officer, Kate Lewis-Lakin, Budget Coordinator
From: Demitrous Cook, Chief of Police
Joseph Dugan, Deputy Chief of Police
Louis Gergits, Police Manager of Budget and Finance
Subject: Requested Budget Modification—Police Department Overtime
Date: August 13, 2019

Reason for Request:

The 2019 Police Department budget for total overtime (civilian overtime, police hire back, and special details) is $959,106. From 2014 to 2018, total overtime has ranged from a low of $1,464,628 in 2017 to a high of $1,697,453 in 2016, averaging $1,577,663. Increasingly, community organizations are requesting a police presence at public events and reimbursing the City for overtime incurred. Accordingly, police overtime expenditures and reimbursements will increase in 2020.

In 2018, the City was reimbursed revenue of $744,594 on the overtime ($344,594 over the budgeted revenue amount of $400,000). For 2019, the Department projects that the City will receive revenue of $826,000 to offset the anticipated overtime expense of $1,541,888. For the 2020 Budget to reflect the actual overtime expenses incurred and reimbursement received, budgeted overtime cost should be increased by $500,000 and budgeted reimbursement by $400,000.

FIGURE 12.4 ▶ The Evanston, Illinois, Police Department's request for a budget modification (adjustment). The original memorandum was edited and removed technical budgeting details that made it longer without adding educational value.

6. A sufficiently greater amount of ad valorem taxes than estimated are received during the fiscal year such that the difference will significantly increase the level of government operations that can be funded by those taxes in the current year.

7. A local option tax is approved by the voters and produces revenue that can be used in the current budget year.

8. Less income from taxes and other mechanisms is produced, requiring the governing body to reduce appropriations.[40]

BUDGET EXECUTION CONTROLS

Even if the budget is not changed during its execution, budget controls are crucial to public accountability for the use of resources entrusted to the unit of government involved. Means of control are specified by state law and regulations, city/county charters and ordinances, and the policies and procedures established by the F/FSD, and the police chief.

Budget controls serve several purposes: (1) ensuring that laws, regulations, and accepted accounting procedures are followed, (2) making sure the funds are expended for the purposes authorized by the appropriators, (3) protecting resources from mismanagement or fraud,[41] (4) eliminating waste to preserve public funds, (5) preventing deficit spending, (6) identifying problems so responsibility can be fixed and remedial action taken, and (7) identifying gaps in control procedures that must be rectified.

The single most important aspect of both external and internal controls is separating the responsibility for various functions, which promotes the benefits of specialization and limits the ability of a few people to misuse or corrupt the system. Thus, for example, the purchasing department obtains competitive bids for equipment, but a different office, accounts payable, actually writes the checks, the police department verifies the delivery of the equipment, and a separate inventory control office accounts for the placement and use of the equipment.[42]

External Controls.

External control is the control exercised on a police department's budget from outside of the police department. Each city or county's F/FSD is the primary external control agent for the police and other departments. The control methods here are illustrations; the full range of controls is much richer.

One universal method of external control is the allotment system. The F/FSD breaks each department's budget into portions, called **allotments**, which are amounts of money made available to the departments for specific periods of time, such as for a month or a three-month period, called a quarterly allotment. Allotments allow the F/FSD to time the availability of funding in the police department to the actual need for their expenditure. Therefore, allotments may vary in their amount from one month or quarter to another. This allows governments to invest funds not immediately needed. Freezing expenditures and cutting the budget are also external budget control measures.

In jurisdictions and particularly where there has been fraud or abuse in agencies, the F/FSD may conduct a "pre-audit" of transactions before purchases are made. The F/DSD periodically generates financial reports, such as Table 12.2, which they send to all departments. These budget status reports play a significant role in monitoring expenditures. The final element in external control is audit and evaluation, discussed later in this chapter, as it is also the fourth and last component of the budget cycle.

Internal Controls.

The objectives of a police department's financial control system include: (1) safeguarding access to, and use of, organizational assets, (2) verifying financial transactions (such as cash payments from the informant fund), (3) encouraging operational efficiency, and (4) fostering adherence to fiscal policies. Altogether, the fundamental purpose of internal controls is to prevent mistakes before they happen and to rectify them when they occur.

Examples of internal controls include breaking the overall budget for the police department into smaller, more easily managed amounts based on units or activities, often referred to as cost centers (see Table 12.3). Expenditures must be authorized in advance by appropriate documentation. Internal controls are crucial not only in the budget context but for the operation of the police agency as well. Illustrations of operational controls include policies on the use of tasers, impact weapons, pursuits, and use of deadly force.

Step Four: The Audit and Evaluation

Stated simply, an **audit** is a check on something; Governments audit themselves on an ongoing basis throughout the FY. Historically, annual audits were of a department's budget, expenditures, and financial management practices—a financial audit (**FA**). In most states, the annual FA is submitted to the Office of State Auditor, where it is reviewed, and any needed follow-up action taken. Financial auditors systematically collect and examine records and reports, conduct interviews, and otherwise rely on competent evidence to determine whether

1. required financial records and reports were made in a timely and complete form;
2. public funds were subject to any waste, fraud, or abuse;
3. unauthorized charges to the budget or reimbursements from the budget were made;
4. computations were accurate;
5. unauthorized transfers from one budget category to another were made;
6. procurement requirements were followed; and
7. expenditures were at or less than the approved budget.

Although there was some earlier movement, another type of annual audit began stirring in the late 1970s, determining how good of a job an agency was doing—a **performance audit (PA)**.

TABLE 12.2 A PORTION OF A POLICE DEPARTMENT'S FY 20 BUDGET STATUS REPORT, DATED DECEMBER 31, 2019

Approved	Expended to Date*	Encumbered*	Balance	% Expended
$1,710,788.00	$848,161.05	$0.00	$862,626.95	49.58%
$15,000.00	$5,374.47	$6,098.00	$9,625.53	35.83%
$6,000.00	$2,000.00	$0.00	$4,000.00	33.33%
$8,500.00	$3,500.57	$1,500.25	$4,999.43	41.18%
$3,100.00	$1,800.00	$0.00	$1,300.00	58.06%
$35,000.00	$17,213.81	$0.00	$17,786.19	49.18%
$22,000.00	$7,688.93	$634.39	$14,311.07	34.95%

The city's fiscal year is from July 1 of one year to June 30 of the following year. This budget status report is dated December 31, 2019 and represents the first six months of the fiscal year.

*Before a contract is signed or a purchase order issued, the F/FSD first determines if the funds are available in the budget. If they are, the amount involved is encumbered, meaning that it is held in reserve for payment upon delivery of the services or goods and encumbered funds are not part of the available balance in the budget.

TABLE 12.3 MAJOR COST CENTERS IN THE BRIGHTON, COLORADO, POLICE DEPARTMENT'S APPROVED FY '20 BUDGET

Cost Centers	FY 2020 Budget	Percent Change from FY '19
Patrol Operations	$10,033,520	7%
Police Support Operations	2,222,826	8%
Victim Services	576,868	–1%
Emergency Management	164,658	+8%
Police Grants and Contracts	77,000	+8%
Community Services	700,694	+13%
Total	$13,775,575	

Quick Facts: Audit Leads to Police Chief's Arrest

An audit was performed of the Greensburg (Indiana) Police Department's Evidence Room. Thirteen property receipts for cash were found, but no cash. According to subsequent court documents, the chief stole $73,000 from it and gambled it away. She lost another $57,000 of family money gambling that was intended to partially replace the missing cash. Her gambling problem also led her to charge $30,000 on a credit card. The chief was arrested for one count of felony theft and another of official misconduct and plead guilty.[45]

Today, in many jurisdictions, an "audit" often encompasses both financial and performance components. Because financial audits have a longer history, the standards for them are well established and they have a fixed focus to them.[43] The U.S. Government Accountability Office's (GAO) guidelines for both FAs and PAs are contained in its Government Auditing Standards (2018), commonly referred to as the "Yellow Book." It notes that the focus of a PA is variable, according to the purpose stated for its execution. PAs may focus on some aspect of a police department's performance (e.g., compliance with legal mandates, program effectiveness and results, or a prospective analysis, such as the future value of advanced training in conflict deescalation for police officers).[44]

The essence of all audits is that an independent party who has no stake in the outcome of the audit does the checking. To ensure the independence of auditors, some jurisdictions elect them, in others the legislative body, such as a city council or county commission, may appoint the auditor or a firm specializing in auditing governments will be retained.

Before an audit report is submitted in any unit of government, it is discussed with the chief of police and any errors of fact, representation, interpretation, or conclusion are corrected. If there is still content for which the auditor and the chief have differing opinions, the chief may write a **letter of exception**, setting forth the reasons why he or she believes that the audit report is wrong or manifestly unfair. After the city council reviews the audit report, the chief may be directed to appear before the council to answer questions, or the council may simply task the city manager or finance director to make sure that the police department takes any needed corrective action. No one enjoys criticisms because they identify weaknesses, yet a wise chief knows that correcting deficiencies is a pathway to enhanced performance and makes any needed changes without rancor.

BUDGET FORMATS

At the beginning of the 20th century, there was nothing resembling the budget cycle previously described in this chapter. The power center in budgeting was the legislative body and its respective committees. Budgeting was a chaotic process because there was no central point, such as a budget office, where budget requests from departments were reviewed or revised. Moreover, committees, rather than a legislative body as a whole, often had the authority to appropriate funds for departments. Lump sum budgets were requested by the departments without any supporting details and sent directly to the legislature. There was no uniform system of accounts because each department used its own method, and audits were either not done or decades went by between them.[46]

It is not surprising that legislative bodies had little interest in giving up their central role in budgeting. When President Taft submitted an executive budget for FY 1914, Congress received it coldly and practically ignored it.[47] However, strong reform forces were at work. In 1899, the Model Municipal Corporation Act, which proposed an executive budget under a mayor, received significant national attention. Executive budgets were also called for by New York Bureau of Municipal Research's *Making a Municipal Budget* (1907) and the National Municipal League's model 1916 city charter. Between roughly 1915 and 1925,[48] the executive budget and standard budget cycles and formats gained considerable use in local government. The passage of the Budget and Accounting Act (1921) by the federal government, created significant fiscal control advancements. Examples include the executive budget, independent audits, and what is now known as the Government Accountability Office (GAO), a nonpartisan component of the Congress, to conduct investigations for the Congress.

These events are important because they (1) explain why substantial emphasis was placed on the control orientation in the early stages of budget reform and (2) underscore that budget control remains at the heart of budget execution, regardless of the type of budget format used. The sections that follow address six major types of budget formats: (1) line item, (2) program and performance, (3) PPBS and zero-based, (4) priority based, and (5) hybrid. Additionally, service level, zero-line item, target, and community budgeting are briefly discussed.

The Line Item Budget

The **line item budget**, is the oldest and simplest budget format; it remains widely used today, although it is most closely associated with the period from 1915 to just after World War II. The line item is the basic system on which all other budget

TABLE 12.4 ONE SECTION OF THE NAPLES (FLORIDA) POLICE DEPARTMENT'S (NPDS) LINE ITEM FY 20 BUDGET NAPLES IS ON FLORIDA'S LOWER GULF COAST. THE NPD HAS 106 EMPLOYEES, 72 OF WHICH ARE SWORN POSITIONS

PERSONAL SERVICES	FY 18-19 ACTUAL	FY 18-19 ADOPTED BUDGET	FY 18-19 ESTIMSTED ACTUAL	FY 19-20 ADOPTED BUDGET	CHANGE FROM FY 18-19
510200 REGULAR SALARIES & WAGES	6,220,092	6,565,241	6,598,745	6,825,700	260,459
510300 SPECIALTY PAY AND LONGEVITY	161,306	171,249	181,665	298,625	127,376
510320 STATE INCENTIVE PAY	74,060	80,255	78,170	78,780	(1,475)
510330 EDUCATION REIMBURSEMENT	30,458	35,000	35,000	47,000	12,000
510400 OVERTIME	290,198	289,000	334,000	302,000	13,000
510410 SPECIAL DUTY PAY	142,094	175,000	185,000	185,000	10,000
510420 HOLIDAY PAY	167,729	170,535	164,167	176,432	5,897
525010 FICA	521,829	513,133	520,216	551,158	38,025
525030 RETIREMENT CONTRIBUTIONS	2,280,122	2,174,333	2,185,071	2,441,295	266,962
525040 LIFE/HEALTH INSURANCE	1,093,371	1,218,957	1,175,306	1,371,447	152,490
525070 EMPLOYEE ALLOWANCE	1,680	2,160	1,680	1,680	(480)
525220 STATE INSURANCE PREMIUM	718,404	610,00	700,000	700.000	90,000
TOTAL PERSONAL EXPENSES	$ 11,701,944	$ 12,004,863	$ 12,159,020	$ 12,979,117	$ 974,254

(Courtesy Naples, Florida Police Department[49])

formats ultimately rest because of its excellence as a control device. It gets its name from its nature: The amount that is requested, recommended, appropriated, and expended is associated with a particular item or class of items which appears as a separate numbered line in the budget (see Table 12.4).

Some limited workload indicators for past years and the forthcoming budget may also be included as part of a line item budget, although they are not used in a classical, or "pure" line item budget format. Such workload indicators may include one or a few of the following (1) arrests by various categories, (2) calls for service, (3) response times for emergency calls, (4) traffic citations issued, (5) accident investigations, (6) criminal investigations, (7) Uniform Crime Reports Part 1 Offenses per capita, and clearance rates.

In police departments large enough for functional specialization, there is an overall line item budget and that budget is broken down into smaller line item budgets for the various organizational entities (Cost centers), such as patrol, investigation, and crime prevention. These smaller budgets further facilitate control and serve as the basis of allocations within the police department. Cost centers can be used with any budget format. Table 12.5 summarizes the advantages and disadvantages of the line item budget format.

The Program Budget

The roots of the **program budget (PB)** spring from work by the (New York) Bureau of Municipal Research, which called for a new budget format in 1907. The term *program budget* was not established at that time, but its elements were clearly defined: "For each department, the budget shall be separated to show

the kinds of services to be provided."[50] The next year New York City adopted a PB. Both DuPont and General Motors used program budgeting during the 1920s and it was used by the federal government beginning in 1942. Program budgets were "center stage" from the 1940s until the 1960s, although they continue to be widely used by state and local governments.

A program is defined as a major group of several closely related activities or services. A PB consists of the following three essential elements: (1) a *program structure* composed of several closely related activities or services. These may be referred to as subprograms, or by some other term (see Figure 12.5); (2) goals, which may take one or more than one years to achieve. Some goals may also be pursued continuously, for example, Create a Safe Community; and (3) a line item budget.

Governments may include other features in their PBs, such as objectives. These are outcomes to be attained in one year or less, such as disrupt five open-air markets or increase police presence in the core business district. Crosswalks (see Figure 12.6) for linking programs, goals, objectives, and terms (time) may also be used. These are more likely to be used in larger jurisdictions and performance/performance-based budgets. There may also be a total staffing table for the program by rank and number of personnel and some performance metrics, which edges what is called a program budget toward a performance budget format. Table 12.6 summarizes the advantages and disadvantages of a program budget.[51]

This crosswalk is one entry from a longer document. "Scorecard" refers to the programs involved. Goals may take one or multiyears to achieve. "Objective(s)" represent specific activities which support the achievement of goals. In general, objectives are for one year

TABLE 12.5 ADVANTAGES AND DISADVANTAGES OF A LINE ITEM BUDGET

Advantages	Disadvantages
• Focus is on controlling expenditures • Simplest format • Expenditures organized around categories or object of expenditures (e.g., SWAT Training, Paper for Copy Machines, and Gasoline) Easy to prepare, present, and understand • Every item or class of items for which expenditures made is controlled • Control systems prevents overspending budget • "Behind" all other budget formats there is a line item budget for control	• Perpetuates the status quo: Once items become a line in the budget, they tend to stay there, creating inertia • No specific, measurable goals, without which police agencies have nothing to drive toward and measure their accomplishments/performance • No program structure (e.g., "DUI Enforcement" or "Abatement of Open-Air Drug Markets) • Budget changes tend to be incremental, small changes up or down in various categories • Inhibits reviews of what the valuable activities in the police department are versus the need to downsize, recombine, or eliminate some units that exist simply by the weight of tradition • Long-range planning is neglected • Limited information is provided to decision makers

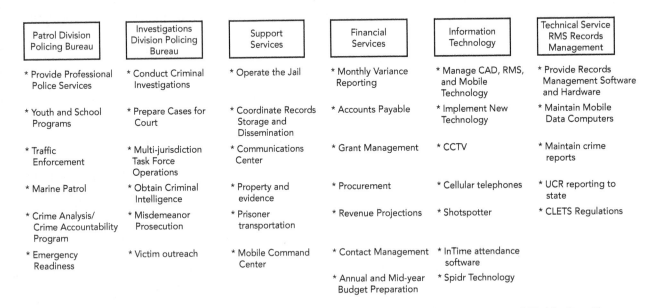

FIGURE 12.5 ▶ A portion of the program structure for the Richmond, California, Police Department's (RPDs) Budget. These six boxes are half of the programs used by the RPD. The units below them are subprograms. (Courtesy Richmond, California, Police Department)

of less. "Term" refers to length of the objectives in terms of short, intermediate, and long duration.

The Performance Budget/Performance-Based Budget (PB/PBB)

The (New York) Bureau of Municipal Research quickly improved on its program budget format by advocating that each program should now be accompanied by cost data, such as the cost for sweeping each mile of road. Such data is now included in what is called performance measures (PMs). The 1912 Taft Commission on Economy and Efficiency also called for a budget with cost data for the type of work being done. The weight of these two recommendations led to the adoption of what

is now called a **performance budget or a performance-based budget (PB/PBB)**.

The absence of computer systems made implementing the PB/PBB labor intensive and it soon developed a reputation for being costly to implement, and unwieldy. Many cities that were early adopters of PB/PBB, such as New York City, tried it briefly and quickly dropped it. In the 1930s, during the Depression, some cities (e.g., San Diego) made brief use of PB, although generally there was little experimentation with it until the 1950s.

Faced with a large debt from World War II, the federal government sought to achieve greater spending efficiency. In 1949, the Commission on the Organization of the Executive Branch (the "Hoover Commission") recommended a performance budget and Congress passed the Reorganization Act that same year

Scorecard	Goal	Objective(s)	Term
Business Processes and Customer Services	Reduce number of annual larcenies by 5% each year for 3 years	Increase number of assigned personnel to high theft from vehicle areas through blitz operations at targeted locations	Long
		Enhance coverage of Lock, Take or Hide message by concentrated social and multimedia campaigns	
		Work with the Office of Commonwealth Attorney to identify and prosecute repeat offenders	

FIGURE 12.6 ▶ A crosswalk, linking "scorecard," "goals," "objectives," and "terms." (Courtesy Leesburg, Virginia, Police Department[52])

TABLE 12.6 ADVANTAGES AND DISADVANTAGES OF A PROGRAM BUDGET

Advantages	Disadvantages
• Focus is on achieving broad police goals	• More labor intensive to develop than line item budgets
• Links programs, expenditures, and goals (e.g., 85% of citizens will feel safe)	• Some police goals are hard to measure.
• Budget justifications are concrete	• Ineffectual program may be difficult to reduce or cut due to political champions of it.
• Appropriators can easily shift resources from one program to another	• Lacks a full system of performance metrics, such as number of new gang graffiti eradicated within 24 hours of discovery
• An excellent management tool for police chiefs	• Doesn't reveal the relative priority of each program.
• Because of goal orientation, easier to explain to public and garner their support	
• Accountability	
• Data-driven decisions	

requiring its use. PB/PPB was used in the federal government in the1950s and part of the 1960s.

During the 1960s, the federal adoption of the Planning, Programing Budgeting System ended its use of PB/PBB and that format also lost momentum in state and local government. PPBS is discussed later in this chapter. PB/PBB regained some traction in state budgeting not later than the 1990s and also in local governments, but as the Great Recession played havoc with budgets, some jurisdictions retreated to a line item budget because there was simply less revenue over which to preside.[53] As the Great Depression receded, there was renewed interest in state and local government in PB/PBB and some of its techniques. To some degree, this interest was fed by the government transparency movement.

Presently, all 50 states and Puerto Rico use some form of performance measures in their budgets.[54] In local governments under 25,000, the PB/PBB is often not practical because of limited resources and perhaps insufficient expertise to implement it. However, the most significant contribution of PB/PBB may not be its form, but the substantial interest it has generated in PMs. Measuring what you are doing becomes the pathway to improved public service and being a better steward of resources allocated to the police department. Even in smaller jurisdictions there may be linkages between the budget and the outcomes produced, even if they are not robust. Even measurements of "Planned For" versus "Actual" for different activities, for example, number of burglaries investigated, is useful. Jurisdictions have to start where they are, with what they have, and seize the opportunity to improve going forward.

For present purposes, a PB/PBB is a planning tool linking the expenditures for each program to the achievement of goals. Its basic components are: (1) a program structure, (2) the attachment of goals to each program, (3) performance measures/metrics, and (4) a line item budget for control. PPB/PBB have increasingly added another optional feature: Objectives to Meet Goals. This feature identifies the activities that must be undertaken to achieve the goals. At the risk of oversimplification, a PB/PBB is essentially a program budget with performance measures/metrics (see Figure 12.7). Table 12.7 summarizes the advantages and disadvantages of a PB/PBB budget.[55]

As jurisdictions grow in size, their use of PMs increases. At some point they become more sophisticated, for example, Mayors are less likely to use PMs than city managers.[57] While descriptions of PB/PBB continue to vary, a common set of elements is: (1) a program/activity structure; (2) goals (multiyear effort to reach) and/or objectives (one year or less to achieve); (3) a description of the strategies to be used to achieve the goals/objectives; (4) the resources (allocations/expenditures) connected to the program/activity; (5) use of PMs; and (6) a line item budget undergirding it for control.

PMs are inherently comparative, such as the change in the number of burglaries of home burglaries in this budget year compared to the previous year or several years. Some PMs are based on **bench marking,** which is comparing your city versus other municipalities, preferably within the same state, of similar characteristics, for example, crime and demographics. Effectiveness, efficiency, and quality are also used as PMs. Illustrations of these are (1) effectiveness: improve average emergency call response

	___Actual 2017	___Actual 2018	___Target 2019	___Projected 2019	___Target 2020
Client Benefits/ Impacts					
Increase public safety and awareness					
# of media contacts	551	550	550	550	550
# of news releases distributed	83	85	100	85	100
# of social media followers	41, 187	50,863	48,000	51,000	53,000
Identify, assess and respond to					
Community needs					
% of favorable survey responses to					
Meeting community needs (1 year survey)	84%	84%	84	N/A*	85%
Strategic Outcomes					
Provide excellence in police services					
% from survey that are satisfied with	N/A	85%	85%	N/A*	85%
Department's overall performance					
Work Process Outputs					
Foster community relationships					
# of active neighborhood watch groups	140	75	140	80	100
Cultural responsiveness					
# of diversity initiatives/ meetings	40	24	35	25	25

FIGURE 12.7 ▶ Sample PB/PBB performance measures from the Appleton, Wisconsin, Police Department's 2020 Budget.[56]

TABLE 12.7 ADVANTAGES AND DISADVANTAGES OF A PB/PBB BUDGET

Advantages	Disadvantages
• Focus is on costs and performance measures. • As presently practiced, the limited and carefully selected cost measures substantially reduce expensive cost accounting techniques. • Provides sufficient data to decision to strengthen oversight by appropriators. • Performance measures assist police chiefs in allocating resources, a plus in strategic planning and management, as well as being able to demonstrate being responsive to the community, e.g., adding more school crossing guards at the request of the Parent Teacher Association (PTA). • Performance measures can be useful in program evaluation. • Chiefs can use on-going performance measurement data to guide and control current programs, identify deviations, and "keep things are on track." • Like Citizen Centric Reports, PBB makes government more transparent, enhancing government openness, which is associated with greater citizen satisfaction.	• May measure what is easy rather than what is important. • Expensive if extensive cost measures are used. • Can tell whether current programs are being done right, but not whether the right things are being done. • How do you determine if the results are "good enough"? Benchmarking? Ad hoc comments by appropriators, citizens, special interest groups? Citizen Centric Reports? • Additional resources dedicated to successful programs do not guarantee even better results. • May be time consuming to distinguish between poorly performing police programs that are under resourced and those that must be abandoned. • Some poorly stated performance measures may imply quotas and provoke public controversy, e.g., number of traffic citations to be issued.

time by 12 seconds in FY 2022 as compared to FY 2021; (2) efficiency: reduce average cost of original investigation of home burglaries by $1.00 in FY 20 as compared to FY 19; (3) quality: increase community trust in police services by three points in FY 2021 as compared to FY 2020. Quality data will be provided by an independent polling entity.

As currently practiced, the cost measures for PB/PBB are carefully selected because (1) meaningful measures are difficult to develop, (2) cost accounting requires a high level of expertise, and (3) it is expensive to collect and analyze the data for them. As a result, PMs are often based on available data, which may have limited value for budget and policy decisions.

The Planning, Programming Budgeting System (PPBS), and Zero-Based Budgeting (ZBB)

During the 1960s, federal government used the **Planning, Programming Budgeting System (PPBS)**. PPBS's dominant feature was planning and required extensive use of cost-effectiveness data. The process was cumbersome and unpopular with the federal agencies using it. PPBS made almost no headway in state and local government and by the very early 1970s it disappeared.

Another short-lived budget format in its pure form was **Zero-Based Budgeting (ZBB)**, developed at Texas Instruments in the early 1970s and introduced into the federal government in 1977 by President Carter. Pure ZBB requires that every governmental program or activity must justify its entire existence each new operating budget year. In ZBB, each program or activity requested in a budget is organized into a decision package (DP) and includes three alternative funding levels: eliminated or reduced, current, and enhanced. No program or activity is considered essential; its existence must be tightly justified. New service DPs could also be submitted. Police chiefs who used ZBB prioritized their DPs and appropriators determined what DPs would be funded at what level but tended to carefully consider their Chiefs' priorities. In later use, some activities did not need to be justified. Illustratively, a police department's Patrol Division did not require it many local governments. The massive paperwork required doomed ZBB as a budgeting process and it also faded, although here and there some use of DPs can be found as part of program or performance budgeting.

Today, ZBB is seldom encountered, although remnants are still found, for example, service-level budgeting and zero-line item budgeting. **Service-level budgeting (SLB)** assumes, unlike ZBB, that programs and activities have previously been justified. The key question is at what level should they be funded? Departments using SLB prepare a required number of packages for their programs and activities, each package describe a different level of service and cost for appropriators to consider. In "**zero-line item budgeting**" departments receive a blank budget request form with zeros filled in for each line item, instead of last year's budget or actual expenditures as the starting point. Departments must rebuild their budgets from the ground up and justify each line,[58] but do not use decision packages.

The Hybrid Budget and Participatory Budgeting

Hybrid budgets incorporate features of several different types of budget formats Budget formats can be described with a great deal more purity than actually exists in many real-world applications. The lone exception may be the line item, although occasionally a line budget with metrics is found. The reason for this lack of "pure" formats is that each jurisdiction, and by extension its police department, uses a system that meets their needs. History, unique city charter provisions, state laws and local ordinance, past practices, the preferences of key people in the budgeting process, and other variables contribute to the reality that many budgeting systems incorporate features from one or more formats. The test of a budget format is how it's constructed, not what it's labeled.

Getting public input on local governments' spending is not a novel idea. It is sought in various ways, for example, from community meetings and advisory boards. **Participatory budgeting (PB)** is a more structured way of doing the same thing. It is a process and not a budget format which influences a government's allocation of funds. Essentially, PB gives power over the public purse to people in the community, including youngsters and the homeless. Although it started in Brazil in 1989, it or some variant is getting increasing attention and use in recent years.

The PB process consists of the following steps: (1) a steering committee whose membership reflect the community creates the rules and how people will be able to participate; (2) the community can attend meetings or use online tools to brainstorm ideas; (3) the feasible ideas are turned into proposals by volunteer "budget delegate;" (4) residents can vote for the proposals they believe will best fit the needs of the community; and (5) local government funds and implements the winning proposals.[59] Local governments may have set aside a financial cap to fund winning proposals. Community donations, grants, and other sources are also used. In 2020, Seattle got community input on how to spend parks and street money with a "Your Voice, Your Choice" campaign. A sample of results includes improving basketball courts, adding benches in the parks, repairing a bridge over wetlands, and planting trees.

ASSET FORFEITURE, GRANTS, POLICE FOUNDATIONS, DONATION PROGRAMS, AND THE USE OF VOLUNTEERS

This section provides information about some of the common ways budget adjustments can be made, as well as several other topics, such as the use of volunteers.

Asset Forfeiture

In 11th-century England, horses, carts, and other property involved in a fatal accident were deemed *deodand* (literally, to be given to God) and forfeited to the king for "pious use." The practice was abandoned by an act of Parliament in 1846 due to the seizure of trains involved in fatal accidents.[60] Generally, property can be subject to forfeiture in the United States if it is (1) contraband, (2) the proceeds of criminal activity, (3) used to facilitate criminal activity, or (4) connected to criminal enterprise.[61]

Forfeiture laws were passed to deprive drug dealers of their profits and cripple them. Its application has gone substantially beyond that. In addition to their own state forfeiture laws, state and local law enforcement agencies have long been able to retain, unless otherwise directed by state laws, 80 percent of their seizures by asking the federal government under the Equitable Sharing program to "adopt" their seizures.[62] Between 2001 and 2018, the Departments of Justice and Treasury kept more than $42 billion through forfeitures.[63] Federal and state law enforcement agencies have guidelines of minimum values that a proposed seizure must meet or exceed, for example, $30,000 for aircraft, $15,000 for vessels, and $5,000 for cars for federal seizures.[64]

Civil asset forfeiture allows law enforcement to seize property they claim has been involved in a particular criminal activity. Such proceedings charge the property itself with involvement in a crime. Until relative recently, the owner of the property doesn't need to be charged with or found guilty of a criminal offense. A small number of states, for example, Michigan, have passed laws requiring a person's conviction of a crime before forfeiture can be pursued because of abuses (see Box 12.4). It is thought forfeiture laws incentivize law enforcement agencies seizing property, leading to some abuses (See Figure 12.8).

Grants

The largest amount of grant funds flowing to the police has always been through the federal government. Although a number of federal agencies, such as the Department of Homeland Security and the National Highway Traffic Safety Administration, provide grants for law enforcement agencies, the U.S. Department of Justice has provided a wider array of grant opportunities, such as those for community-oriented policing, reduction of gun and gang crimes, DUI abatement, enhancement of crime analysis, acquisition of new technologies, reduction of violence against women (including stalking and human trafficking), enforcement of protective orders, and date and domestic violence.

Some large corporation foundations have an interest in the police; the Met Life Foundation makes grants nationally to support innovative partnerships between community groups and the police to promote neighborhood safety and neighborhood revitalization.

One of the most spectacular awards to a law enforcement agency by a community foundation was made by the Caruth Foundation in 2008. The Dallas Police Department (DPD) received $9.5 million from it to train a new generation of leaders for the 21st century, leading to the creation of the Caruth Police Institute (CPI). An endowment for perpetual support was created with $6 million and the remaining $3.5 million was dedicated to startup costs. In 2010, CPI graduated the first class—23 DPD Lieutenants, who completed a six-week course taught by leading national experts. The graduates reported that the course taught them to think differently and to set higher goals. Even the smallest foundations, which may restrict applicant eligibility to one county, make police awards. Illustratively, the Harrison County (Indiana) Community Foundation funds small police projects, often for the acquisition of a single piece of equipment.

Police Foundations and Donations

Nonprofit police foundations have proliferated over the past 40 years, literally dotting the landscape from Los Angeles to New York City. Their prominence is such that the International Association of Chiefs of Police (IACP) has a Police Foundations Section. Police foundations are a conduit from the public and businesses that wish to promote excellence in their police departments through the donation of money, goods, and services.[68] The goal is to provide resources unavailable to departments through the budget process. Most police foundations serve multiple purposes, such as promoting wellness, recognizing valorous officers, and making purchases of equipment and newer technology, for example, license plate scanners.

COMPSTAT may have never been or its development delayed without a $15,000 check from the New York City Police Foundation, which was ready two days after the request was initiated.[69] The Philadelphia Police Foundation purchased drones for trained Philadelphia Police Department "pilots," renovated facilities, and established a Police Explorer Program. Summer camp attendance, mentoring for at-risk city youths, and technology to combat Internet crimes against children are provided by the Washington DC Police Foundation. The Salt Lake City Police

---

Box 12.4: The Perils of Forfeitures and the U.S. Supreme Court Cracks Down on Forfeitures

In Detroit, a party for some 130 people was held at a downtown Art Institute. Police flooded the party and seized 44 cars from attendees, one parked more than a mile away. Not known to attendees was the art institute had no liquor license and everyone there was therefore complicit in that crime. Inasmuch as the cars brought these desperados to the party, they were also guilty and therefore seized.[65] In the end, cars were returned at a fee of more than $1,000 each. Getting your car returned requires proof you were not engaged in a criminal activity and didn't know your car was being used in a crime or you did everything possible to prevent. Forfeited property has a low recovery rate for owners.

States laws regulating the distribution of forfeitures may be restricted or generous. Some allow none or 100 percent of the assets to be retained by the police. Missouri is one of eight states where asset forfeitures go to education and that distribution has not reduced police asset seizures.[66]

In *Timbs v. Indiana* (2019), a forfeiture case, the U.S. Supreme Court ruled for the first time that the 8th Amendment's prohibition against excessive fines was applicable to the States. By extension, it applies to local governments and may limit egregious seizures. It also offers up a Constitutional basis for challenging seizures.

FIGURE 12.8 ▶ City of Tenaha, Texas, which serves a community of 1,000. In a single year, Tenaha seized nearly $1.2 million in cash, mostly from out-of-town motorists. (San Antonio Express-News/ZUMA Press/Alamy Stock Photo)

Quick Facts: Black Asphalt

A private intelligence network has assisted law enforcement agencies across the country in seizing assets. The **Black Asphalt Electronic Networking & Notification System** has allowed agencies to share information about drivers, both criminal and innocent, including social security numbers, addresses, tattoos, and hunches about which drivers to stop. The driving force behind it also made a movie in 1989, Desert Snow, which trained law enforcement officers in recognizing potential stops.[67]

Foundation's Pay It Forward-Back to School take 50–60 underprivileged to purchase school supplies, get backpacks and gift certificates from Target for back to school clothing. Each child is matched with a police officer for their shopping. The day kicks off with breakfast, games, and other activities with police officers. Police foundations in smaller jurisdictions have a narrower focus and may be limited to a single purpose. Some police websites, like that for Oshkosh, Wisconsin prominently feature a donations section advising readers how to help the department by making donations.

Use of Volunteers

Police departments have long been aware of the advantages of involving volunteers. Often, this was limited to Reserve/Auxiliary police and a few other positions. In the midst of budget slashes, many agencies have, and seem likely to continue, a much more robust use of qualified volunteers. The volunteers often have diverse backgrounds in business, are well-qualified

retirees, or simply may be local citizens who want to help make a difference in their community. Among the uses made of volunteers are:

- bilingual services, including verbal and document translations.
- coordinate neighborhood watch programs.
- crime prevention activities.
- maintaining computer systems.
- counsel victims of domestic abuse.
- parking enforcement.
- crime scene protection.
- vacation checks.
- bike registration.
- traffic control.
- legal research.
- crime analysis.

Quick Facts: Volunteers in Police Service

VIPS has been an important catalyst to the movement toward broader use of volunteers. The International Association of Chiefs of Police (IACP) manages and implements the Volunteers in Police Service (VIPS) Program in partnership with the Bureau of Justice Assistance, U.S. Department of Justice. VIPS is administered by individual agencies and its origin was in President George W. Bush's 2002 State of the Union Address.

The VIPS Program provides support and resources for agencies interested in developing or enhancing a volunteer program and for citizens who wish to volunteer their time and skills with a community law enforcement agency. The program's ultimate goal is to enhance the capacity of state, local, campus, tribal, and territorial law enforcement to utilize volunteers. The VIPS staff shares information and resources with law enforcement agencies that want to expand their programs, increase the use of volunteers in existing programs, help citizens learn about and become involved in VIPS program.[70]

- purchasing.
- editing/writing departmental publications, for example, newsletters and brochures.
- administration of volunteer program.

- recruiting volunteers, especially those with specific skill sets.
- planning departmental events.
- communications and records assistance.

Chapter Summary

Summary by Chapter Objectives

1. **State what COVID-19 likely means for state and local government budgeting.**

   Austerity budgeting at the state and local levels is likely to be normal state of affairs for several years. Initially there will be some easy choices for cuts, but those will be quickly used up. Cuts thereafter will be much harder.

2. **Define a police operating budget and give five examples for which expenditures are made.**

   An **operating budget** usually covers a 12-month period and consists of annually recurring costs such as salaries, fringe benefits, uniforms, crime scene supplies, ammunition, training, telephone service, gasoline, and kindred expenses. Operating budgets are overwhelmingly funded by a city or county's annual stream of revenues into its general fund, with a few exceptions such as grants and donations.

3. **Give three definitions of the budget.**

   Those definitions are (1) a plan expressed in dollars, (2) the use of financial resources to meet human needs, and (3) a contract between those who appropriate the money and those who execute the budget.

4. **Explain why budgeting is inherently a political process.**

   Budgeting is inherently a political process because elected members of city councils, county commissions, state legislatures, and even Congress express their preferences when they vote on appropriations. The appropriators' personal views and those of their constituents, political donors, the news media, police unions, polls, special interest groups, lobbyists, colleagues, and other entities often shape these decisions, as well as deals to secure support for their own interests. Politics do not stop when a budget is adopted; in some circumstances, the politics can actually intensify during the time a budget is executed.

5. **Identify the sequential steps in the budget process and briefly describe them.**

   The **budget cycle** has four sequential steps that are repeated at about the same time every year in a jurisdiction: (1) preparation and submission of the budget by all of a city or county's departments, which includes getting input from stakeholders, such as citizens and advisory boards; (2) evaluation and appropriation by the legislative body, which may involve public hearings and occasionally heated exchanges; (3) execution of the budget and supplemental budgets, which means actually doing the things for which public funds have been appropriated; and (4) the audit, which is an independent evaluation of something, for example, a law enforcement agency's control of its petty cash fund, its annual expenditures, or its performance on key indicators, such as use of force.

6. **Contrast the program budget and performance/performance-based budget formats.**

   Program budgets appeared before performance-based budgets. A program budget structure is composed of several closely related activities or services. For instance, these may be referred to as subprograms, or by some other name. Program budgets have increasingly added "Objective to Meet Goals" that essentially identify the activities that must be undertaken to achieve the goals. In a program budget, stated goals that may take one, or more than one year to achieve are listed and some goals may be pursued continuously, like, "Create a Safe Community." Program budgets almost always have a line item budget within their structure for control. At the risk of oversimplification, a performance-based budget is essentially a program budget with performance measures/metrics added.

7. **Explain hybrid budgets and why they exist**

Hybrid budgets are not a "pure" budget format and incorporate features from two or more different formats. Many budgets are hybrids because of history, unique charter provision, state laws, local ordinances, past practices, the preferences of key people in the budget process, and for other reasons. It seems likely that the line item budget is used in a "pure" form far more than any other format. It dominates the budgets of the numerous small jurisdictions across the country and in larger cities and counties that use more advanced formats, the line item budget is often used for control.

Chapter Review Questions

1. Under fiscal stress, what are six strategies law enforcement agencies use to cut their budget?
2. What is the distinction between budgeting and accounting?
3. How are CIPs and a capital items related?
4. How are budgets prepared in small police departments?
5. What is the downside of large cutbacks of training funds?
6. What are the definitions of allotments and encumbrances?
7. How is bench marking used in budgeting?
8. How should participatory be implemented?
9. Why is it argued that law enforcement agencies should not receive any portion of the assets that are forfeited as the result of their investigative actions?

Critical Thinking Exercise

1. Read the section on performance audits. Assume you are a Sergeant in the Patrol Division. One of your officers hands you a report to approve that only states in the narrative section that the "Subject was injured while resisting arrest and transported to the hospital." Would you approve the report? Whether you would sign it or not, explain the rationale for your decision.

Key Terms

allotments
audit
biennial budget
budget
budget calendar
budget cycle

budget execution
capital improvement plan (CIP)
fiscal year (FY)
letter of exception
line item budget
operating budget

performance audit (PA)
performance budget (PB)
Planning, Programming Budget System (PPBS)
program budget
zero-based budget (ZBB)

Endnotes

[1]The federal government's definition of a small business varies: (1) The Affordable Care Act identifies a small business as having 50 employees or less and (2) the Small Business Administration has several definitions, the standard one being there are 500 or fewer employees.

[2]Tahmi Luhby, "84% of Cities in Money Trouble," CNN, February 4, 2009, p.1, http://money.cnn.com/2009/02/04/news/economy/city_troubles/?postversion=2009020418 (accessed May 27, 2016).

[3]Robert Jay Dilger, State Government Fiscal Stress and Federal Assistance (Washington, DC: Congressional Research Service, February 4, 2014), unnumbered summary page at the front of the document and National Governors Association and the National Association of State Budget Officers, "The Fiscal Survey of States," (Washington, DC: National Association of State Budget Officers, 2011), p. Xiii.

[4]Andrew Schroedter, "Chicago Police Misconduct-A Rising Financial Toll," Better Government News, January 31, 2016, p. 1. http://www.bettergov.org/news/chicago-police-misconduct-%E2%80%93-a-rising-financial-toll (accessed May 27, 2016).

[5]Charles Thomas, "City Council Passes Budget, Praises Mayor," ABC/WLS-TV Chicago, November 16, 2011, pp. 1–2, http://abc7.com/archive/8433801 (accessed May 28, 2016).

[6]No author, NASRA Issue Brief: Cost-of-Living Adjustments, November 2019, p. 1, https://www.nasra.org/files/

Issue%20Briefs/NASRACOLA%20Brief.pdf (accessed April 3, 2020).

[7] Ibid., multiple pages from a 32-page document.

[8] Sharon Begley, "It's Difficult to Grasp the Projected Deaths from COVID-19. Here's How They Compare to Other Causes of Death," STAT, April 9, 2020, https://www.statnews.com/2020/04/09/its-difficult-to-grasp-the-projected-deaths-from-covid-19-heres-how-they-compare-to-other-causes-of-death (accessed April 9, 2020).

[9] Stephen M. Kissler, et al., "Projecting the Transmission of SARS-CoV-2 Through the PostPandemic Period," *Science*, April 14, 2020, https://science.sciencemag.org/content/early/2020/04/14/science.abb5793 (accessed April 14, 2020).

[10] Joseph Parilla, Sifan Liu, and Brad Whitehead, "How Local Leaders Can Stave Off a Small Business Collapse from COVID-19," The Brookings Institution, April 3, 2020, https://www.brookings.edu/research/how-local-leaders-can-stave-off-a-small-business-collapse-from-covid-19 (accessed April 4, 2020).

[11] Samuel Stebbins, Unemployment: These Are Every State's Claims Since the Coronavirus Shut the Economy Down," *USA Today*, April 14, 2020, https://www.usatoday.com/story/money/2020/04/14/coronavirus-unemployment-claims-caused-covid-19-crisis-state/5130034002 (accessed April 16, 2020).

[12] Jared Walczak, "State Strategies for Closing FY 2020 with a Balanced Budget," Tax Foundation, April 2, 2020, https://taxfoundation.org/fy-2020-state-budgets-fy-2021-state-budgets (accessed April 9, 2020).

[13] No author, "States Grappling with Hit to Tax Collections," Center on Budget and Policy Priorities," updated May 4, 2020, https://www.cbpp.org/research/state-budget-and-tax/states-grappling-with-hit-to-tax-collections (accessed May 6, 2020).

[14] Loc. cit.

[15] WSLS10 (Television), Angela Hatcher, "Losing Troopers: Virginia State Police Hit Hard by Budget Cuts," online access, p. 3, WWW2.WSLS.com, November 11, 2008.

[16] Dustin Gardiner, "Phoenix Imposes Cuts on Police Pay in Late, Tense Session." The Republic, May 8, 2014, http://www.azcentral.com/story/news/local/phoenix/2014/05/08/phoenix-imposes-cuts-police-pay-late-tense-session/8838737 (accessed May 25, 2016). The police were not singled out for a pay cut. The council voted for a 1.6 percent pay cut for all employees to save $16.5 million in expenditures.

[17] Todd South, "Police Satellite Precincts Closing," *Chattanooga (TN) Times Free Press*, online access, February 4, 2010, TimesFreePress.com

[18] Jeff Brady, "Facing Budget Gap, Colorado City Shuts Off Lights," National Public Radio, February 14, 2010, online access, NPR.org

[19] Matt Bartosik, "Police Station: Sorry, We're Closed," NBCChicago.com, online access, July 29, 2009.

[20] Arlington (VA) Proposed Fiscal Year 2011 Budget Proposal.

[21] Maxine Bernstein, "Portland Police Propose Cutting Mounted Patrol and Leaving Some Positions Vacant to Balance Budget," PortlandLive.com, online access, January 14, 2010.

[22] In Minnesota alone in the past few decades, more than 100 small towns have disbanded their police department, merged with another one, or turned to their sheriff for services; See Tom Robertson, "Cass Lake Abolishes Police Force, Seeks Enforcement Deal with County," MPR News Q: Minnesota's On-Line News Source," online access, August 1, 2008.

[23] See Vicki Wilson, "Being Prepared for Disasters," *Government Finance Review* 23, No. 6 (December 2007), pp. 22–26 and Timothy McKeon, "Lessons from Recent Natural Disasters," *Municipal Finance Journal* 27, No. 4 (Winter 2007), pp. 27–53.

[24] Robert D. Lee, Ronald W. Johnson, and Philip G. Joyce. *Public Budgeting Systems*, 8th edition (Boston: Jones and Bartlett, 2008), p. 17.

[25] Roland N. McKean, *Public Spending* (New York: McGraw-Hill, 1968), p. 1.

[26] Robert J. Landry III and Cynthia S. McCarty, "Causal Factors Leading to Municipal Bankruptcies," *Municipal Finance Journal* 28, No. 1 (Spring 2007), p. 21.

[27] Aaron Wildavsky, *The Politics of the Budgetary Process*, 2nd edition (Boston: Little, Brown, 1974), pp. 1–4.

[28] James V. Saturno, "Biennial Budgets: Issues, Options, and Congressional Actions," Congressional Research Service, January 10, 2017, Summary Page, https://fas.org/sgp/crs/misc/R44732.pdf (accessed May 8, 2020).

[29] See David R. Shock, "Capital Budgets: The Building Blocks for Government Infrastructure," *Government Finance Review* 23, No. 3 (June 2007), pp. 16–22.

[30] Jill Wendorf, "Capital Budgeting from a Local Government Perspective," *SPNA Review* 1, No. 1 (May 2001), p. 76, accessed July 13, 2015.

[31] A. E. Buck, *The Budgets in Governments Today* (New York: Macmillan, 1945), p. 5.

[32] No author, "Presenting the Capital Budget in the Operating Budget Document," Government Finance Officers Association, October 2008, p. 1, http://www.gfoa.org/presenting-capital-budget-operating-budget-document (accessed July 13, 2015).

[33] Robert D. Lee, Ronald W. Johnson, and Philip G. Joyce, *Public Budgeting Systems*, 8th edition (Boston: Jones and Bartlett, 2008), p. 17.

[34] Ibid. p. 53.

[35] Sherrry Conohan. "Geese Police Fall Victim to Borough Budget Axe," *Atlanticville* (Manalapan, NJ, March 5, 2004, pp. 1–2, http://atl.gmnews.com/news/2004-03-05/Front_page/009.html (accessed July 16, 2015). This is an older incident, but is very illustrative of a how a minor budget line can become a major issue.

[36] Because sheriffs are elected and police chiefs appointed, there are some differences in city and county budgeting because as an elected official, a sheriff would be more independent. See LaFrance T. Casey and MaCherie, "Sheriffs' and Police Chiefs' Leadership and Management Decisions in the Local Law Enforcement Process," *International Journal of Police Science and Management* 12, No. 2 (Summer 2010), pp. 238–255.

[37] Sherrry Conohan. "Geese Police Fall Victim to Borough Budget Axe," *Atlanticville* (Manalapan, NJ, March 5, 2004, pp. 1–2, http://atl.gmnews.com/news/2004-03-05/Front_page/009.html (accessed July 16, 2015).

[38] Thomas A. Reppetto, "The Elite Unit the NYPD Must Revive to Fight Gun Crime," *New York Post*, January 11, 2015, p. 1, http://nypost.com/2015/06/11/the-nypd-needs-to-revive-its-elite-anti-gun-unit (accessed March 3, 2016).

[39]Robert D. Lee and Ronald Johnson, *Public Budgeting Systems* (Gaithersburg, MD: Aspen, 1998), p. 265. Also see the execution phase of the budget in No Author, North Carolina Budget Manual (Office of the State Budget and Management: Raleigh, NC), January 1, 2015.

[40]No author, Local Budgeting Manual (Oregon Department of Revenue: Eugene, Oregon, 2012), p. 65.

[41]See Jeffrey C. Steinhoff, "Forensic Auditing: A Window to Identifying and Combating Fraud, Waste, and Abuse," *Journal of Government Financial Management* 57, No. 2 (Summer 2008), pp. 10–18.

[42]The organizational placement of procurement, purchasing, payment of invoices, and property control varies. They may be clustered in a F/FSD or spread out over several departments. In very small units of government, one or two people working in the same office may perform these functions. For purposes of this text, we use a F/FSD that encompasses all of these functions, although in actual practice there are many variations.

[43]Mark Schelker, "Public Auditors: Empirical Evidence from U.S. States," *Center for Research in Economics, Management, and the Arts* (CREMA: Basel, Switzerland, 2008), p. 9.

[44]No Author, *Conducting Performance Audits in Accordance with the Yellow Book* (San Diego: Office of the City Auditor, 2009), pp. 4–6.

[45]Briefly summarized from Steve Jefferson, "Former Greensburg Police Chief Pleads Guilty to Charges," March 5, 2015, pp. 1–2, http://www.wthr.com/story/28128743/former-greensburg-police-chief-arrested-following-audit (accessed July 17, 2015). Although an older case, it has been kept because it illuminates the fact Chiefs, like other people, are occasionally brought down by their own weakness as opposed to a "plot against them."

[46]Allen Schick, *Budget Innovation in the States* (Washington, DC: Brookings Institution, 1971), pp. 14–15.

[47]A. E. Buck, *The Budget in Governments of Today* (New York: Macmillan, 1945), p. 5.

[48]In 1913, Ohio became the first state to adopt the executive budget.

[49]City of Naples (Florida), Adopted Budget Fiscal Year 2019–2020, https://www.naplesgov.com/sites/default/files/fileattachments/finance/page/8031/00_adopted_budget_19-20.pdf (accessed May 13, 2020).

[50]No Author, *Purpose and Methods of the Bureau of Municipal Research* (New York: Bureau of Municipal Research, 1907), p. 25.

[51]John Worrall, *Asset Forfeiture* (Washington, DC: Center for Problem-Oriented Policing, 2008), p. 5.

[52]Town of Leesburg (Virginia), Adopted Fiscal Year 2020–2021 Budget & Fiscal Years 2020–2025 Capital Improvements Program, p. 89, https://www.leesburgva.gov/home/showdocument?id=31568 (accessed May 12, 2020).

[53]Robert O'Harrow, Jr., Sari Horwitz, Steven Rich, "Holder Limits Seized-Asset Sharing Process That Splits Billions with Local, State Police," *The Washington Post*, January 16, 2015, p. 1, http://www.washingtonpost.com/investigations/holder-ends-seized-asset-sharing-process-that-split—bill-i-ons-with-local-state-police/2015/01/16/0e7ca058-99d4-11e4-bcfb-059ec7a93ddc_story.html (accessed July 20, 2015).

[54]See Richard D. Young, "Performance Based Budget Systems, Public Policy and Practice 2, No. 2, January 2003, about p. 4 of an unnumbered online copy, http://ipspr.sc.edu/ejournal/performancebudgets.asp and No author, "Budget Processes Spotlight: How States Use Performance Data" (The National Association of State Budget Officers: Washington, DC), August 4, 2015.

[55]Worrall, *Asset Forfeiture*, p. 5.

[56]City of Appleton (Wisconsin) 2020 Executive Budget and Service Plan, p. 408, https://www.appleton.org/home/showdocument?id=22992 (accessed May 12, 2020).

[57]David H. Folz, Reem Abdelrazek, and Teonsoo Chung, "The Adoption, Use, and Impacts of Performance Measures in Medium-Size Cities: Progress Toward Performance Management" University of Tennessee, undated paper, although the data for it was gathered in 2004, p. 5.

[58]No author, Zero-Based Budgeting: Modern Experiences and Current Perspectives (Government Finance Officers Association: Calgary, Canada, 2011), p. 7.

[59]No author, "How Does PB Work?" Participatory Budgeting Project, undated, https://www.participatorybudgeting.org/what-is-pb (accessed May 16, 2020).

[60]William Pietz, "Death of the Deodand," Res: Anthropology and Aesthetics 31, (Spring 1997), pp. 97–98.

[61]John Worrall, Asset Forfeiture (Washington, DC: Center for Problem-Oriented Policing, 2008), p. 5.

[62]Michael Sallah, et al., "Stop and Seize," *The Washington Post*, September 6, 2014, p. 3, http://www.washingtonpost.com/sf/investigative/2014/09/06/stop-and-seize/ (accessed July 20, 2015).

[63]Darpana Sheth, "The Police Can Take Your Stuff: The Civil Forfeiture Reforms We Still Need," The Heritage Foundation, August 22, 2019, https://www.heritage.org/insider/summer-2019-insider/the-police-can-take-your-stuff-the-civil-forfeiture-reforms-we-still (accessed May 11, 2020).

[64]Georgia Department of Public Safety Policy Manual, Policy 12.05, Asset Forfeiture, Revised April 9, 2019, p. 2.

[65]Jarrett Skorup, "Michigan Now Requires You to Be Guilty Before Losing Your Property," *Impact Magazine*, May 28, 2019, https://www.mackinac.org/26596 (accessed May 10, 2020), and Alyssa Hazelwood and Andrew Kloster, "The Motor City Wants Your Car Back: Civil Forfeiture in Detroit," *Impact Magazine*, Mackinac Center for Public Policy, https://www.mackinac.org/26596 (accessed May 10, 2020).

[66]No author, "Policing for Profit, Missouri Profile," The Institute for Justice, undated, but citations suggest no earlier than 2008, https://www.ij.org/asset-forfeiture-report-missouri (accessed July 20, 2015).

[67]"Stop and Seize," p. 1

[68]Pamela Delaney and Donald Carey, "Police Foundations Partnerships for the 21st Century," *The Police Chief* 74, No. 8 (2007), p. 1.

[69]Ibid. p. 2, http://www.policechiefmagazine.org/magazine/index.cfm?fuseaction=display_arch&article_id=1237&issue_id=82007 (accessed May 30, 2016).

[70]No author, VIPS-Volunteers in Police Service, International Association of Chiefs of Police, undated, p. 1, http://www.theiacp.org/VIPS (accessed July 7, 2015).

PART 4 The Management of Police Organizations

Some 50 years ago the police were described as a "terra incognita," an unknown land. Empirical research on this unknown land was sparse and there needed to be empirical research on every subject connected with it. Since that time we have learned much about policing, but there is still a great deal to learn. In the intervening years there has been a proliferation of studies on the subject of Chapter 13, "Stress and Police Personnel." Under stress, the body changes, for example, the heart rate accelerates, blood pressure increases, pupils dilate, and the mouth goes dry. Unsurprisingly, the greatest stressor for police officers is killing someone in the line of duty. Also addressed in this chapter are the negative physical and psychological impacts of alcohol and drug use on police performance; police suicide; police domestic violence; the impact of shift length on performance, the role of the police psychologist and the elements of a successful peer support program.

Chapter 14, "Legal Aspects of Police Administration," addresses the ever-changing landscape of laws, which are enacted by legislative bodies and interpreted by court decisions. Police enforcement of criminal laws is typically sound because it is an everyday activity. In contrast, while high speed pursuits, use of force, and kindred incidents are not uncommon across police agencies, officers understanding of the civil liability created by mistakes in these areas is less perfected.

Police leaders at every level must also be aware that their decisions or lack of appropriate action can also result in civil liability. For example, if an officer has been repeatedly disciplined for excessive use of force, but remains on the department assigned to field duties, and subsequently shoots someone several times, crippling them for life, when the use of deadly force is not authorized, the employing agency will be faced with a civil suit claiming that but for the agency wrongfully continuing to employ the officer, the plaintiff would not have suffered the life changing injury. In such a fact situation the department would have the difficult task of defending the officer's action and may settle out of court.

Depending on the particulars of a situation, officers and their leaders, in addition to civil liability, are further exposed to two other risks: (1) being charged with a criminal act and (2) loss of their certification from the state's Peace Officers Standards and Training Commission or similarly titled body, ending their law enforcement careers. Thus, the content of this chapter is central to the welfare of persons having contacts with officers and maintaining public confidence, as well as officers and their leaders, their families their agency, and their police profession.

Chapter 15, "Organizational Change," may well not have been an important topic when the policing philosophy in America was "aggressive preventive patrol in all areas at all times diminishes the opportunity for crimes to be committed." This philosophy held sway until roughly the advent of community policing. A whole series of refinements of community policing, as well as newer philosophies and programs, moved the importance of understanding organizational change into the important category. To no small extent other factors such as news events, political decisions, and technological innovations also propel changes in law enforcement agencies.

The Italian historian, government official, and thinker Machiavelli (1469–1527) observed in The Prince "There is nothing more difficult to take in hand, more perilous to conduct, or more uncertain of success than to lead in the introduction of a new order of things." President John Kennedy (1917–1963) concluded, "Trying to change the federal bureaucracy has the same effect as punching a curtain." Separated by four centuries two remarkable men reached the same conclusion: changing organizations is hard, uphill work that may not turn out well. Among the topics this chapter details is when changes should not be made, different change strategies, and how to heighten the possibilities when introducing change.

## CHAPTER THIRTEEN

STRESS AND POLICE PERSONNEL

Learning Objectives

1. Describe the perceptual, cognitive, and behavioral disturbances resulting from an officer's use of deadly force.
2. Explain why police officers are often reluctant to seek mental health services even when they need it.
3. Discuss some of the questions that police administrators must address in terms of drug use by police officers.
4. Examine the role the police psychologist plays in a psychological health wellness initiative.
5. Discuss the benefits and weaknesses in the use of peer support personnel.

INTRODUCTION

FOR THE PAST 50 YEARS, the topic of stress and its relationship to police work has been extensively studied by both the social science community and the police profession. As a result, there is now an abundance of police stress-related information available to the law enforcement executives to assist them in fully understanding and developing programs designed to reduce stress among their personnel.[1] Police administrators should be aware of the following stress-related information: (1) how stress is defined, (2) the relationship between diseases of adaptation and recent medical funding, (3) the ways in which personality type can impact positively or negatively upon job performance, (4) why the use of deadly force by police officers is consistently listed as the number one stress inducer, (5) why police officers are so reluctant to seek mental health services after a deadly force encounter even when needed and what can be done to overcome their reluctance, (6) understand what posttraumatic stress disorder and cumulative career traumatic stress are and recognize their major symptoms, (7) the negative physical and psychological impacts of alcohol and drug use on police performance, (8) the multiple aspects of police suicide and what can be done to prevent it, (9) police domestic violence and ways in which police departments can and should react to it, (10) the impact of shift length on performance, health, quality of life, sleep, fatigue, and extra duty employment, (11) stress reduction management techniques, (12) the police psychologist's role in a psychological health wellness initiative, (13) the elements of a successful peer support program, and (14) the functions and value of an employee assistance program.

WHAT IS STRESS?

Hans Selye, the researcher and theorist who pioneered the physiological investigation of stress, defines **stress** in the broadest possible terms as anything that places an adjustive demand on an organism (see Figure 13.1). Identified as "the body's nonspecific response to any demand placed on it," stress can be either positive (eustress) or negative (distress; see Table 13.1).[2] According to this distinction, many stressful events do not threaten people but provide them with pleasurable challenges. Illustrations of eustress include driving at top-end speeds, gambling, free climbing mountains, and sky diving. Arguably, volunteers for "high-speed" military units such as the U.S. Navy's SEAL Team 6, the U.S. Army's Delta Force, and SWAT Police Teams or undercover drug detectives may fall into this category. Fledgling entrepreneurs also face many stressful situations; some entrepreneurs crack under the distress and others experience eustress and succeed spectacularly. Illustratively, Bill Gates dropped out of college to pursue his computing interests and was the cofounder of Microsoft in 1975, and as of 2020 Forbes estimates that Gates' net worth is $118.4 billion.[3]

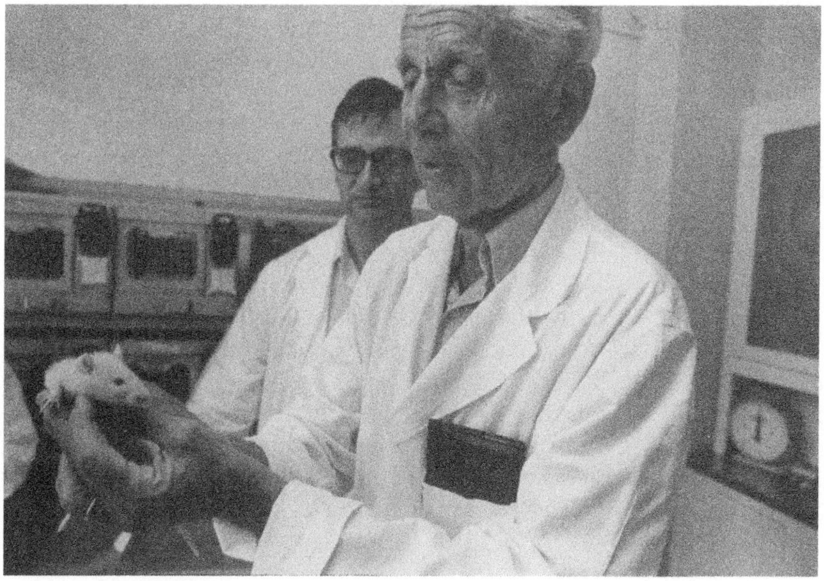

FIGURE 13.1 ▶ Dr. Hans Selye holds one of the many rats studied in meticulous detail to work out the actual nature of the mammalian stress response. *Source:* John Olson/The LIFE Images Collection/Getty Images.

TABLE 13.1 CHANGES TO THE BODY AT THE ALARM STAGE	
Heart rate increase	Blood flow increases to heart, lungs, and large muscles
Blood pressure increase	Perspiration, especially to palms
Large muscle groups tense	Digestive secretions slow
Adrenaline rush	Dry mouth due to saliva decrease
Increase blood sugar	Bowel activity decreases
Hypervigilance	Extremities become cool
Pupils dilate	Sphincters tighten
Increased hearing acuity	More white blood cells enter the bloodstream
Increased blood clotting	Cholesterol remains in the blood longer
Increased metabolism	Dilation of the lung passages and increased respiration

Source: Wayne Anderson, David Swenson, and Daniel Clay, *Stress Management for Law Enforcement Officers,* 1st edition, © 1995, p. 37. Adapted by permission of Pearson Education, Inc., Upper Saddle River, NJ.

Biological Stress and the General Adaptation Syndrome

Selye formulated the **general adaptation syndrome (GAS)** to describe how stress, on the biological level, can incapacitate an individual. The GAS encompasses three stages of physiological reaction to a wide variety of stressors: environmental agents or activities powerful enough in their impact to elicit a reaction from the body. These three stages are as follows:

- Alarm
- Resistance
- Exhaustion

The **alarm stage**, sometimes referred to as an emergency reaction, is exemplified on the animal level by the so-called fight-or-flight syndrome. When an animal encounters a threatening situation, its body signals a defense alert. The animal's cerebral cortex flashes an alarm to the hypothalamus, a small structure in the midbrain that connects the brain with body functions. The powerful hormone adrenocorticotropic (ACTH) is released into the bloodstream by the hypothalamus and is carried by the bloodstream to the adrenal gland, a part of the endocrine, or ductless gland, system. There, ACTH triggers the release of adrenaline, which produces a galvanizing, or energizing, effect on the body functions. The heart pounds, the pulse races, breathing quickens, the muscles tense, and digestion is inhibited. The adjustive function of this reaction pattern is readily apparent—namely, preparing the organism biologically to fight or to run away. When the threat is removed or diminished, the physiological functions involved in this alarm, or emergency reaction, subside, and the organism regains its internal equilibrium (see Table 13.1).

If the stress continues, however, the organism reaches the **resistance stage** of the GAS. During this stage, bodily resources are mobilized to deal with the specific stressors, and adaptation is optimal. Although the stressful stimulus may persist, the symptoms that characterized the alarm stage disappear. In short, the individual seems to have handled the stress successfully.

Under conditions of prolonged stress, the body reaches a point where it is no longer capable of maintaining resistance. This condition characterizes the **exhaustion stage**. Hormonal defenses break down, and emotional reactions that appeared during the alarm stage may reappear, often in intensified form. Further exposure to stress leads to exhaustion and eventually to death.[4]

DISEASES OF ADAPTATION AND RECENT MEDICAL FINDINGS

There is considerable agreement that some types of stress can worsen the symptoms of almost any condition, but recent medical research suggests there is little evidence that stress is the exclusive or the principal cause of any disease. For decades, it was accepted by the medical community that stress led to the overproduction of stomach acid, which caused duodenal ulcers. Stress does increase the amount of acid produced in the stomach, and there is no doubt that, once a person has a duodenal ulcer, acid makes the ulcer hurt. However, medical science has determined the ulcer is not caused by stress but rather by a bacterial infection, curable with antibiotics. Doctors also once believed that the inflammatory bowel diseases—Crohn's disease and ulcerative colitis—were caused by stress. They now know these diseases are caused by inherited tendencies toward abnormal inflammation in response to gut bacteria. Also, there is little evidence that stress causes asthma, although some patients have flare-ups more often at times of stress.[5]

The Role of Stress in Heart Disease

The role of stress in heart disease has received the most attention over the years, and with good reason. Like our ancestors, we all occasionally face the single, sudden, and extreme stressors that the stress response has evolved into in order to protect us from dangerous situations. However, unlike our primitive ancestors, the acute stressor is not caused by an approaching wild animal's intent on devouring us or the belief that we will soon be dead because we have been hexed by the local witch-doctor. Instead, it might result from a road rage situation when an angry motorist is attempting to run us off the road or perhaps someone is attempting to forcibly enter our home. Our response to such sudden and extreme stressors can protect us, but it can also trigger a powerful hormonal release that can have dire consequences if a person already has heart disease.

Perhaps even more important are the persistent, chronic, low-grade stressors experienced by almost everyone in a modern society, such as the recurring tension in dealing with an unpleasant supervisor, coworker, spouse, or child, or worrying about how to pay the bills this month. These chronic stressors, like sudden and acute stressors, can also affect the most common and lethal form of heart disease we face—atherosclerosis, sometimes called "hardening" of the coronary arteries.

Coronary atherosclerosis deforms artery walls and can ultimately block blood flow, starving the heart muscle of the oxygen it needs. Plaques of atherosclerosis cause symptoms in two ways. First, if the plaques grow large enough to significantly obstruct the flow of blood, the heart will not get the blood supply it needs when it is forced to work harder—for example, by exercise or by anger or fear. The heart is not actually damaged, but pain can occur whenever the heart is again forced to work hard. Second, plaque can rupture, either when the heart is working hard or even when a person is at rest and at peace. Plaque rupture causes a blood clot to form that suddenly and often completely stops the flow of blood through the artery.

Chronic stressors also contribute to heart disease indirectly if they lead us to overeating, underexercising, or smoking. Stress is a toxic emotional and physical response; anger, hostility, depression, and anxiety are examples of such toxic responses. Anxiety, for instance, involves apprehension combined with palpitations, fatigue, and shortness of breath. Some people respond to chronic stressors with remarkable equanimity. Others spend a substantial fraction of their day experiencing one or more of the toxic reactions. This is influenced in part by our genes but is also controllable with stress-management techniques (discussed later in this chapter). In addition, if these toxic reactions are not controlled, there is growing evidence that heart disease is more likely to occur and at an earlier age.[6]

Major Stressful Life Events

Sudden, major stressful life events can sometimes cause catastrophic results in people with underlying heart disease—including heart disease they did not know they had because it had never before caused symptoms. This could then result in the sudden outpouring of adrenalin resulting from a specific highly stressful event such as a police officer responding to an officer in need of assistance, or a felony in progress call. This can cause a plaque of atherosclerosis to rupture, which in turn can generate dangerous heart rhythms and sudden death.

In a paper published over 45 years ago in the *Annals of Internal Medicine*, internist and psychiatrist George Engel reconstructed the events in the hours before 170 people died suddenly. Particularly for women, Engel found that the most common trigger for sudden death was a major loss—of a spouse or self-esteem. For men, sudden danger (a constant companion for law enforcement officers) more often was a trigger. Even the excitement of pleasant experiences can have deadly effects.

STRESS AND PERSONALITY TYPE

The classification of personalities into major categories can be a very useful tool in assessing personality types. However, when discussing them it is important to remember that almost no one fits entirely into a single category but simply possesses a majority of the characteristics associated with that specific personality type.[8]

Type A Personality

- Under constant stress, much of which is self-generated
- Continuous pressure to accomplish
- Hostile and demanding
- Always in a hurry; sense of time urgency
- Continuing impatience
- Intense and ambitious
- Believes time should be used "constructively"

Quick Facts: Too Much Happiness Can Kill You

Sudden death can also follow a triumph or a happy ending to a long struggle. These include the reported sudden deaths of a number of individuals, including a just-released prisoner upon returning home, a man who had just scored his first hole in one, and an opera singer who was receiving a standing ovation. Even joy can disrupt silently diseased arteries.[7]

- Has difficulty relaxing and feels guilty when not working
- Compelled to challenge, and not understand, another type A personality

The qualities underlying type A characteristics include the following:

- Constant state of being "on guard"
- Hypermasculinity
- Constantly working against time
- Lack of insight into one's own psychological needs

The physiological implications are as follows:

- Seven times as likely to develop heart disease
- Higher cholesterol and triglyceride (blood fat) levels (sudden stress increases triglyceride; prolonged stress increases cholesterol)
- Clotting elements have greater tendency to form within coronary arteries
- Excess accumulation of insulin in blood

Type B Personality

- Less competitive and less rushed
- More easygoing
- Better able to separate work from play
- Relatively free of a sense of time urgency
- Ambitions are kept in perspective
- Generally philosophical about life

Type C Personality

- Appear to be quiet and introspective but are actually frustrated and suppress their anger
- They are at increased risk of developing cancer
- They are nonemotional, nonassertive and appease others to the point of self-effacement and self-sacrifice
- They suppress their own desires even if there is something they dislike
- Their lack of assertiveness results in tremendous stress and sometimes leads to depression
- They tend to be introverted, respectful, eager to please, and compliant
- They love details and can spend a lot of time trying to find out how things work and this makes them very suitable for technical jobs[9]

Type D Personality

- Have a negative outlook toward life and are pessimistic
- Might become socially withdrawn as a result of fear of rejection, even if they like to be around people

- They are famous for suppressing their emotions thus making them vulnerable to depression
- Like the type A personality, they are also more likely to develop cardiovascular problems[10]

Workaholic Personality

- This phrase was coined in 1968
- Similar to type A
- Has an addiction to work
- When absent from the job, may experience withdrawal symptoms similar to those of withdrawal from other addictions
- Is agitated and depressed when not working
- May account for up to 30 percent of the working world
- Other characteristics of workaholics include:
  - Readily buck the system; often bucked by the bureaucracy
  - Display well-organized hostility toward the system's imperfections
  - Obsessed with perfection in their work
  - Haunted by deep-seated fear of failure; will "play to win" at all games
  - Prefer labor to leisure
  - Constantly juggle two or more tasks (called multitasking)
- Many are overachievers and "get things done"
- Takes its toll and may result in:
  - Gastrointestinal problems
  - Cardiovascular disease
  - Divorce

The Pitfalls of Being a Workaholic—Police Work Addiction

The following is a cautionary tale based upon an actual case, using a fictitious name, which describes the potential health risks associated with being a workaholic.

Great leaders lead by example, and Police Chief William Smith was no exception. He was totally selfless and always available, arriving at work each morning before 8:00 and not leaving until everyone else had gone home. It was not uncommon to find him working on Saturday or Sunday. The deputy chief told those assembled at the church that he was actually reluctant to leave each night before the chief. Everyone felt sad that Chief Smith left a young family and even sadder that he should pass away in the prime of his life.[11]

Certainly, police officers are expected to put aside all other needs when duty calls, and, without question, duty does call. Commanders and officers alike must sustain an endless capacity to meet this demand. Communities hold fast to the expectation that the police will do all that can be humanly done and, at times, much more than should be expected of mere humans. Therein lies the great challenge for law enforcement officers and supervisors—maintaining a healthy balance in meeting *reasonable* responsibilities to the job, to themselves, and to their families.

Perhaps Chief Smith represents an extreme example of the dangers inherent in the work-addicted lifestyle. However, literature on work addiction asserts that work constitutes the drug of choice for some 30 percent of the population, for whom working is so vital to their emotional well-being that in fact they have become addicted to it.[12] While the actual mortality rate for work addiction may be low, the social lethality of this behavior proves overwhelming. These unfortunate individuals are predisposed to involve themselves—and their families—in a life not unlike that of Chief Smith's. Clearly, work addicts (or workaholics, the more common descriptor) cannot assess what is important in healthy lifestyle choices and, thus, experience a diminished quality of life. Regrettably, they do not suffer alone. They unwittingly share this pain with their families and colleagues alike.

Workaholics are married to their work. Their vows to love and honor their spouses above all "others" no longer hold meaning or possibility. No spouse and no family can compete with this all-consuming obsession.

Workaholics themselves are a key contributor to the unhealthy family patterns resulting from work addiction for a number of reasons. First, they may have grown up in a dysfunctional family system where role models taught unhealthy patterns of relating to others. Research indicates that the family origin contributes greatly to the development of the workaholic, and the roots of the workaholic's perfectionism often lie in childhood experiences.[13] In these dysfunctional homes, families reward children for good performance, not for who they are. They give praise and conditional love whenever children perform a certain way or meet certain high expectations. In adulthood, this same need for perfection is the basis for the obsession for work—everything must be done properly and always at a very high level of competence and perfection.

Second, the need for workaholics to feel dominant and "in control" may make them less able to relate to peers. They may interact more easily with older and younger people or those of lower status or socioeconomic level than themselves. This need for continually being in control of themselves and in charge creates tension in family relationships. The one constant

involved in this work mind-set devalues the quality of social interactions. Loved ones have a reasonable expectation that time spent together is time well spent and, therefore, they should not be made to feel that such time comes at the expense of personal productivity. Loved ones can sense when the workaholic is "just going through the motions." The same holds true for relationships with peer groups and clients. People have a strong sense for those who are too busy to make time to properly address issues. Conflict becomes inevitable, and everyone "gets drawn into the act by waltzing around the workaholic's schedule, moods, and actions."[14]

The self-imposed behavior of work addiction also causes physical symptoms. Excessive pumping of adrenaline resulting in abnormal blood pressure, heart trouble, stomach sensitivity, nervousness, and the inability to relax under any circumstances are commonplace. Workaholics report feeling pressure in their chests, dizziness, and lightheadedness.[15] Obviously, any long-term stress that manifests such symptoms as these can result in dangerous health consequences of many types. Chief Smith's protracted work addiction led to serious illness and his ultimate, untimely death.

Those people obsessed with work share the traits of others with such addictions as substance abuse, food dependencies, or sexual compulsions. A classic definition of a workaholic describes "a person whose need for work has become so excessive that it creates noticeable disturbance or interference with bodily health, personal happiness, and interpersonal relations, and with smooth social functioning."[16] The unique difference between work addiction and other addictions, however, is that supervisors often sanction work addiction. Supervisors and peers admire this so-called work ethic, and it can be both financially and professionally rewarding.

Workaholics become gradually more emotionally crippled as they become embroiled with the demands and expectations of the workplace. They are "addicted to control and power in a compulsive drive to gain approval and success."[17] The obsession with work grows out of the workaholic's perfectionism and competitive nature. As with other addictions, work is the "fix," the drug that frees the workaholic from experiencing the emotional pain of the anger, hurt, guilt, and fear in the other areas of the workaholic's life. Workaholics constantly focus on work, seeking to meet their personal emotional needs through their professions.

With this information in mind, law enforcement supervisors must understand the dangers that work addiction presents.

Quick Facts: The Deadly Effects of Stress on Police Officers

More law enforcement officers are likely to be killed by job-related stress than are killed by criminals. For every police officer slain by an assailant in the line of duty, countless others succumb to the insidious, long-range effects of job-induced pressures including alcoholism, drug abuse, domestic violence, posttraumatic stress disorder, and even suicide.[18]

These supervisors also must remember that they have an ethical responsibility to intervene when they observe the telltale signs of the work-addicted personality.

Perhaps the poet Robert Frost had Chief Smith in mind when he observed, "By working faithfully 8 hours a day, you may eventually get to be boss and work 12 hours a day." Certainly, expectations run high in the law enforcement profession. Establishing and maintaining relationships creates tremendous demands on time, resources, and energy; life balance easily becomes lost. The wise boss must understand and accept this reality.

STRESS IN LAW ENFORCEMENT

Police work is highly stressful; it is one of the few occupations in which an employee is asked continually to face physical dangers and to put his or her life on the line at any time. The police officer is exposed to violence, cruelty, and aggression and is often required to make extremely critical decisions in high-pressure situations.

The Highest Police Stressors

In order to assess which events generate the most stress for police officers Violanti and Aron distributed a 60-item Police Stress Survey (PSS) to a random sample of 110 officers in a large New York State police department.[19] Ninety-three percent of those sampled ($N = 103$) completed the PSS and returned it. The results of the survey reveal that the single-most-potent stressor was killing someone in the line of duty (79.38 percent) and close behind was the killing of a fellow officer (76.38 percent) (see Figure 13.2).

The empathy police officers have for victims is revealed by the fact that the fourth-most-potent stressor was handling child abuse cases (69.24 percent), which ranked ahead of other well-known stressors, such as engaging in high-speed chases (63.73 percent), using force (60.96 percent), responding to felony-in-progress calls (55.27 percent), and making death notices (52.59 percent).[20]

Perceptual, Cognitive, and Behavioral Disturbances Resulting from the Use of Deadly Force

Many police officers who have been involved in a deadly force shooting episode have described one or more alterations in perception, thinking, and behavior that occurred during the event,[23] and these are similar to those reported in military personnel following a firefight. Most of the following reactions can be interpreted as natural adaptive defensive reactions of an organism under extreme emergency stress:

- *Distortions in time perception* are most common, with the majority of officers recalling the shooting event as occurring in slow motion, although a smaller percentage reported experiencing the event as speeded up.

- *Sensory distortions* are also common and most often involve *tunnel vision*, in which the officer is sharply focused on one particular aspect of the visual field, typically the suspect's gun or weapon, while blocking out everything in the periphery. Thus, such distortions are also very common for officers who are engaged in high-speed pursuits. Similarly, "*tunnel hearing*" may occur, in which the officer's auditory attention is focused exclusively on a particular set of sounds, most commonly the opponent's voice, while background sounds are excluded. Sounds may also seem muffled or, in a smaller number of cases, louder than normal. Police officers have reported not hearing their own or other officers' gunshots. Thus, overall perceptual clarity may increase or diminish.

- *A sense of helplessness* may occur during the shooting exchange, but this may be underreported due to the potential stigma attached. A small proportion of service members report they "froze" at some point during the event:

Quick Facts: The Use of Deadly Force as a Major Source of Stress for Police Officers

When one considers the millions of encounters between police officers and citizens, fatal shootings by the police are rare occurrences. For example, following are the number of fatal police shootings for the four-year period from 2015 to 2018: 2015 – 995; 2016 – 963; 2017 – 987; and 2018 – 998.[21] Some of these killings are in self-defense, some are accidental, and others are to prevent harm to others. The sources of stress attached to an *officer-involved shooting* (OIS) are multiple, and include the officer's own psychological reaction to taking a life; the responses of his or her law enforcement peers and the officer's family; the rigorous examination by departmental investigators and administrators, and increasingly federal investigators who are trying to determine if there have been any civil rights violations; the possible disciplinary action resulting in suspension, demotion, or dismissal; the possibility of criminal prosecution and imprisonment; the possibility of civil litigation; and negative media attention.[22]

again, either this is an uncommon response or personnel are understandably reluctant to report it, especially in a culture like law enforcement, which places a premium on physical courage and disparages those who show any degree of timidity in the face of danger. In a series of interviews with police officers,[24] it was found that most of these instances of "freezing" really represented the normal *action-reaction gap* in which officers make the decision to shoot only after the suspect has engaged in clearly threatening behavior. In most cases, this brief evaluation interval is a positive precaution, to prevent the premature shooting of someone who does not pose a threat to the officer. But in situations where the ostensibly prudent action led to a tragic outcome, this cautious hesitation by an officer may well be viewed retrospectively by him or her as a fault: "If I hadn't hesitated to shoot, maybe my partner would still be alive."

- *Disturbances in memory* are commonly reported in shooting exchanges. About half of these involve impaired recall for at least some of the events during the shooting; the other half involve impaired recall for at least part of the officer's own actions; this, in turn, may be associated with going-on-automatic response. More rarely, some aspects of the event may be recalled with unusual clarity, sometimes characterized as a *flashbulb memory.* Over a third of the cases involve not a total loss of recall but a distortion of memory, to the extent that the shooter's

account of what happened differs markedly from the report of other observers at the scene; in such cases, they might be unfairly accused of lying.

FIVE BASIC PHASES OF THE POSTSHOOTING REACTION

1. The first phase occurs prior to the shooting itself and consists of *concern about being able to pull the trigger* when the time comes and not freezing up and letting one's fellow officers down.

2. The second phase is the *actual killing experience*, which is often done reflexively, with officers describing themselves as "going on automatic."

3. The third stage is that of *exhilaration* that comes from having been able to put one's training into action. This exhilaration, fueled by the release of huge amounts of adrenalin, can create a high or rush, which in some cases can give rise to what the military has characterized as "combat addiction." It has been described as the kind of "adrenalin overdosing" that can negatively impact a police officer's nervous system and lead to adverse reactions later on (i.e., hesitating to use deadly force when it is clearly justified or overreacting to situations that do not justify the use of deadly force).[26]

FIGURE 13.2 ▶ New York Police officers carrying casket of fallen officer Wenjian Liu who had been killed in an ambush shooting. *(Lev radin/Shutterstock)*

Quick Facts: The FBI Provides Four Categories of Situations That Present a Threat to Law Enforcement Officers

1. The suspect possesses a weapon or is attempting to gain access to a weapon.

2. The suspect is armed and running to gain the tactical advantage of cover.

3. A suspect with the capability of inflicting death or serious injury, with or without a weapon, is demonstrating an intention to do so.

4. The suspect is attempting to escape the vicinity of a violent confrontation in which he or she inflicted or attempted to inflict death or serious injury.[25]

---

4. The fourth phase[27] is what police psychologists[28,29] have called the *recoil, remorse, and nausea* phase. This follows the rush of exhilaration and is often associated with a close-range kill; this is the more common type of response experienced by police officers who tend to confront their adversaries in close quarters, rather than from a distance, which is often the case with military personnel.

For police officers, feelings of guilt or self-recrimination may be especially likely in cases where the decision to shoot was less than clear-cut or where the suspect's actions essentially forced the officer into using deadly force, such as botched robberies, violent domestic disputes, or **suicide by cop (SbC)**.[30] SbC occurs when an individual who intends to take his or her life uses the police to assist in accomplishing that objective by threatening to injure or kill the police officer, typically with a gun or some other similar deadly weapon (see Figure 13.3). The issue of SbC is discussed in greater detail in Chapter 14: Legal Aspects of Police Administration.

During the recoil/remorse phase, law enforcement service members may seem detached and preoccupied, going through the motions of their job duties, and operating on what could be characterized as "behavioral autopilot." In addition, they may be hypersensitive or even annoyed to well-meaning probing and congratulations by peers who make comments such as "Way to go, killer—the dirt bag deserved it."

Also, during this recoil phase, a variety of posttraumatic symptoms (discussed earlier) may be seen, most of which will resolve themselves in a few days or weeks.[31] Some of these will represent general posttraumatic reactions similar to those experienced by psychological trauma workers.[32]

5. The fifth phase,[33] *rationalization and acceptance*, can be a long process, and many law enforcement officers wrestle with this single event for a lifetime. As the officer begins to come to terms with the shooting episode, a similar resolution or acceptance phase may ensure, wherein the officer assimilates the fact that the use-of-deadly-force-action was necessary and justified in this particular instance.

FIGURE 13.3 ▶ A man, armed with what police would later learn were unloaded guns, confronted Chicago police officers. When the man refused to drop his guns and threatened to kill the officers, he was shot and killed. (AP Photos)

Even under the best of circumstances, resolution may be partial rather than total, and psychological remnants of the experience may continue to haunt the officer periodically, especially during future times of crisis. But in most cases, the officer is eventually able to return to work with a reasonable sense of confidence.[34]

However, in the worst cases, sufficient resolutions may never occur, and the officer enters into a prolonged posttraumatic phase, which may effectively end the officer's law enforcement career. In less severe cases, a period of temporary stress disability allows the officer to seek treatment, to eventually regain his or her emotional and professional bearings, and to ultimately return to the job. Still other officers return to work right away but continue to perform marginally or dysfunctionally until their actions are brought to the attention of superiors.[35]

POSTSHOOTING INTERVIEW

An important question about postshooting interviews is what the agency's policy should be as it relates to how, where, and when it should be conducted. It is very clear that the event itself can have very serious consequences on the officer's recollection of what happened and in some cases, a failure in this area may result in the officer being unfairly accused of lying. The International Association of Chiefs of Police (IACP) Police Psychological Services has provided guidelines suggesting that investigators should give officers time to recover after the incident before they conduct detailed interviews, with this recovery time ranging from a few hours to overnight.[36] Other experts have also supported this recommendation and suggested that officers would be better able to provide more accurate and thorough statements if they are allowed to wait at least 24 hours before questioning, thereby giving the officers time to rest and recuperate.[37]

Many agencies have embraced this suggestion and implemented policies requiring officers to wait before giving an interview or speaking to an investigator about an officer-involved shooting (OIS). In this respect, these departments have made a decision to treat their officers differently than civilian witnesses or suspects who are normally interviewed as soon as possible after the incident. The rationale for this differential treatment is the fact that sometimes victims who are seriously injured may die, witnesses may disappear, and suspects may flee.

Prior research has consistently determined that individuals' memories react strangely to stressful or traumatic events. This includes both officers and civilians alike who may experience serious perceptual and memory distortions.[38] The question is how to best minimize this phenomenon.

To this end, it might be best for agency protocol to allow for case-by-case flexibility when determining the timing and structure of interviews following an OIS. Investigators must remain sensitive to personnel who have likely just experienced one of the most traumatic events in their life while striving to obtain the most accurate information possible about the incident. For example, if investigators need precise intelligence, then it may be important for them to give the officers and civilian witnesses an initial walk-through of the incident without engaging in intensive probing detail that has been customary in the past. This walk-through may function as the "rehearsal" interview that helps trigger better memory recall later on. One expert has highlighted the value of this time delay in the interview process, stating that interviewers can consider "…providing enough brief information during an immediate on-scene 'walk-through' to get the investigation started."[39] Also, with the increasing use of body worn cameras as well as dashboard cameras some agencies are permitting their officers involved in confrontational situations with citizens to view the recordings before making either an oral or written statement.

PROVIDING MENTAL HEALTH SERVICES AFTER DEADLY FORCE ENCOUNTERS

Unfortunately, sometimes for good reason,[40] police officers have traditionally shunned mental health services, perhaps perceiving its practitioners as ferrets and shills who are out to dig up dirt that their departments can use against them.[41] More commonly, the idea of needing any kind of "mental help" implies weakness, cowardice, and lack of ability to do the job. In the environment of many departments, some officers realistically fear censure, stigmatization, ridicule, thwarted career advancement, and alienation from colleagues if they are perceived as the type who "folds under pressure." Still others in the department, who may have something to hide, may fear a colleague "spilling his guts" to the clinician and thereby blowing the malefactor's cover.[42,43,44,45,46]

But the goal of law enforcement psychological services following a critical incident should always be to make officers stronger, not weaker. At times a broken bone that has begun to heal crookedly has to be re-broken and reset properly for the individual to be able to walk normally again. While the rebreaking may hurt, the pain is temporary, and the effect is to restore and strengthen the limb. In the same way, an officer who is responding to critical incident stress with an ossified, malformed defensive mind-set that's impeding his or her job performance and personal life may need to have those defenses challenged in a supportive atmosphere, so he or she can benefit from a healthy resetting of his mental state to deal with life more adaptively and courageously. He or she needs to regain the psychological strength to learn to walk the path of life again.[47,48,49,50,51]

Therapeutic Strategies for Recovery and Resilience

In most cases, the effectiveness of any therapeutic strategy in fostering resilient recovery will be determined by the timeliness, tone, style, and intent of the intervention. Most effective psychological interventions with law enforcement officers and other service personnel share the following common elements.[52,53,54,55,56,57]

Brevity. Clinicians should utilize only as much therapeutic contact as necessary to address the present problem. The officer does not want to become a "professional patient."

Limited focus. Related to the above, the goal is not to solve all the officer's problems, but to assist in restabilization from the critical incident or cumulative stressors, and provide stress-inoculation for future incidents.

Directness. Therapeutic efforts are directed to resolve the current conflict or problem to reach a satisfactory short-term conclusion, while planning for the future if necessary.

Utilizing Cognitive Defenses for Resilience

In psychology, defense mechanisms are the mental tactics and strategies the mind uses to protect itself from unpleasant thoughts, feelings, impulses, and memories. While the normal use of such defenses enables the average person to avoid unnecessary conflict and ambiguity and to preserve the basic integrity of their personality and belief systems, most psychologists would agree that an overuse of defenses to wall off too much unpleasant thought and feeling leads to a rigid and dysfunctional coping style. Accordingly, much of the psychotherapeutic process involves carefully helping a patient to substitute pathological defenses with adaptive coping skills so that he or she can learn to deal with internal conflicts more constructively.

However, in the face of immediately traumatizing critical incidents, the last thing the affected person needs is to have his or her defenses stripped away. If a person sustains a broken leg on the battlefield, the medic binds and braces the limb as best as he can and helps the person to quickly hobble out of the danger zone, reserving more extensive medical treatment for a later, safer time and place. Similarly, for an acute psychological trauma, the proper utilization of psychological defenses can serve as an important psychological splint that enables the person to function in the immediate posttraumatic aftermath and eventually be able to productively resolve and integrate the traumatic experience when the luxury of therapeutic time and safety can be afforded.[58]

Indeed, whether in their regular daily work or following critical incidents, law enforcement and public safety personnel usually need little help in applying defense mechanisms on their own. Examples[59,60,61], here applied to coping with the aftereffects of a deadly force encounter, include the following:

Denial. "Put it out of my mind; focus on other things; avoid situations or people who remind me of it."

Rationalization. "I had no choice; things happens for a reason; it could have been worse; other people have it worse; most people would react the way I am."

Displacement/projection. "It was Command's fault for issuing such a stupid order; I didn't have the right backup; they're all trying to blame me for everything."

Refocus on positive attributes. "Hey, this was just a fluke – I'm usually a great marksman and first responder; I'm not gonna let this jam me up."

Refocus on positive behaviors. "Okay, I'm gonna get more training, increase my knowledge and skill so I'll never be caught in a no-win position like this again."

Janik[62] proposes that, in the short term, clinicians may actively support and bolster psychological defenses that temporarily enable the officer to continue functioning. Just as a physical crutch is an essential part of orthopedic rehabilitation when the leg-injured patient is learning to walk again, a psychological crutch is perfectly adaptive and productive if it enables the officer to get back on his emotional two feet as soon as possible after a traumatic critical incident. Only later, when he or she is making the bumpy transition back to normal life, are potentially maladaptive defenses revisited as possible impediments to progress.

Just as some orthopedic patients may always need one or another kind of assistive walking device, like a special shoe or a cane, some degree of psychological defensiveness may persist in officers so they can otherwise productively pursue their work and life tasks. Indeed, rare among us is the person who is completely defense-free. Only when defenses are used inappropriately and for too long—past the point where we should be walking on our own psychological legs—do they constitute a "crutch" in the pejorative sense.

POSTTRAUMATIC STRESS DISORDER (PTSD)

PTSD can be traced back to antiquity. It was called "soldier's heart" during the American Civil War, "shell shock" in the First World War, and "battle fatigue" in the World War II. In the Korea War, it was called "operational exhaustion." It was not until the Vietnam War that the term "posttraumatic stress disorder" was created when the American Psychiatric Association added the term to its list of recognized mental disorders.[63]

The Clinical Classification

In clinical classification, a *syndrome* is defined as a set of symptoms and signs that occur in a fairly regular pattern from patient to patient, under a given set of circumstances, and with a specific set of causes (even though individual variations may be seen).[64] By this definition, ***posttraumatic stress disorder***, or **PTSD**, is a syndrome of emotional and behavioral disturbance that follows exposure to a traumatic stressor or set of traumatically stressful experiences that is typically outside the range of normal, everyday experience for that person. As a result, there develops a characteristic set of symptoms.[65]

Symptoms of Posttraumatic Stress Disorder

Anxiety. The subject describes a continual state of free-floating anxiety or nervousness. There is a constant gnawing apprehension that something terrible is about to happen. He or she maintains an intensive hypervigilance, scanning the environment for the least hint of impending threat or danger. Panic attacks may be occasional or frequent.

Physiological Arousal. The subject's autonomic nervous system is always on red alert. He or she experiences increased bodily tension in the form of muscle tightness, tremors, restlessness, fatigue, heart palpitations, breathing difficulties, dizziness, headaches, and gastrointestinal or urinary disturbances. About one-half of PTSD subjects show a classic startle reaction: surprised by an unexpected door slam, telephone ring, sneeze, or even just hearing their name called, the subject may literally "jump" out of their seat and then spend the next few minutes trembling with fear and anxiety.

Irritability. There is a pervasive chip-on-the-shoulder, edginess, impatience, loss of humor, and quick anger over seemingly trivial matters. Friends get ticked off, coworkers shun the subject, and family members may be verbally abused and alienated. A particularly common complaint is the patient's increased sensitivity to children's noisiness or the family's bothering questions.

Avoidance and Denial. The subject tries to blot out the event from his or her mind, avoids thinking about the traumatic event and shuns news articles, radio programs, or TV shows that may be reminders of the incident. "I just don't want to talk about it," is the standard response, and the individual may claim to have forgotten important aspects of the event. Some of this is a deliberate, conscious effort to avoid reminders of the trauma; part of it also involves an involuntary psychic numbing that blunts most incoming threatening stimuli. The emotional coloring of this denial may range from blasé indifference to nail-biting anxiety.

Intrusion. Despite the subject's best efforts to keep the traumatic event out of his or her mind, the horrifying incident pushes its way into consciousness, often rudely and abruptly, in the form of intrusive images of the event by day and frightening dreams at night. In the most extreme cases, the individual may experience dissociative flashbacks or reliving experiences in which he or she seems to be mentally transported back to the traumatic scene in all its sensory and emotional vividness, sometimes losing touch with current reality. More commonly, the intrusive recollection is described as a persistent psychological demon that "won't let me forget" the terrifying events surrounding the trauma.

Repetitive Nightmares. Even sleep offers little respite. Sometimes, the subject's nightmares replay the actual traumatic event; more commonly, the dreams echo the general theme of the trauma but miss the mark in terms of specific content. For example, an individual traumatized in an auto accident may dream of falling off a cliff or having a wall fall on them. A sexual assault victim may dream of being attacked by vicious dogs or drowning in a muddy pool. The emotional intensity of the original traumatic experience is retained, but the dream partially disguises the event itself. This symbolic reconfiguration of dream material is, of course, one of the main pillars of Freudian psychoanalytic theory.[66]

Impaired Concentration and Memory. The subject complains of having gotten "spacey," "fuzzy," or "ditsy," has trouble remembering names, tends to misplace objects, loses the train of conversations, or can't keep their mind focused on work, reading material, family activities, or other matters. The subject may worry that he/she has brain damage or that "I'm losing my mind."

Sexual Inhibition. Over 90 percent of PTSD subjects report decreased sexual activity and interest; this may further strain an already stressed-out marital relationship. In some cases, complete impotence or frigidity may occur, especially in cases where the traumatic event involved sexual assault.

Withdrawal and Isolation. The subject shuns friends, neighbors, and family members, just wants to be left alone; and has no patience for the petty, trivial concerns of everyday life—bills, gossip, news events—and gets annoyed at being bothered with these piddles. The hurt feelings this engenders in those who are rebuffed may spur retaliatory avoidance, leading to a vicious cycle of rejection and recrimination.

Impulsivity and Instability. More rarely, the trauma survivor may take sudden trips, move from place to place, walk off the job, disappear from their family for prolonged periods, uncharacteristically engage in drunken binges, gambling sprees, or romantic trysts, make excessive purchases, or take dangerous physical or legal risks. It is as if the trauma has goaded the subject into a "what-the-hell—life-is-short" attitude that overcomes their usual good judgment and common sense. Obviously, not every instance of irresponsible behavior can be blamed on trauma, but a connection may be suspected when this kind of activity is definitely out of character for that person and follows an identifiable traumatic event. Far from taking such walks on the wild side, however, the majority of trauma survivors continue to suffer in numbed and shattered silence.

CUMULATIVE CAREER TRAUMATIC STRESS (CCTS)

In contrast to the condition posttraumatic stress disorder just discussed, officers may also experience trauma symptoms sporadically throughout a career as a result of being routinely exposed to many traumatic events over a period of time. This is classified as **Cumulative Career Traumatic Stress** (CCTS).[67]

The symptoms of CCTS are similar to PTSD, but rather than presenting suddenly as a result of a single traumatic event directly experienced by the officer, such as a shooting, the officer may experience one or a combination of symptoms sporadically throughout a career as he or she is exposed to a myriad of traumatic events over a period of years. The trauma symptoms that are experienced fail to fit the duration criteria of PTSD but are nonetheless frequently experienced and left unacknowledged. This in turn creates the potential to cause a slow and subtle deterioration of the officer's psychological and emotional stability. For example, an officer who has responded to a fatal motor vehicle collision may experience nightmares or flashbacks of the scene for a few days after the incident. This is especially true of those fatal traffic accidents that result in the death of a small child. Several months later, the officer may respond to another motor vehicle fatality or similar scene that brings back memories of the previously investigated serious collision.

Many times throughout a career, an officer may be involved in incidents that threaten his or her physical safety or which directly threatens the officer's life.[68] These events are typically quickly forgotten and are often viewed as a "part of the job." This cycle repeats itself throughout the officer's career. As past events are hopefully forgotten, new events trigger additional trauma symptoms and may exhume old memories.[69] CCTS involves the sporadic experience of trauma symptoms such as intrusive thoughts and memories of troubling incidents (via flashbacks or nightmares), emotional numbing, moodiness, anxiety, avoiding reminders of an incident/s, loss of hope, hypervigilance, memory and/or concentration problems, sleeping and/or eating problems, disconnection from family and friends, and hyperarousal (e.g., jumpiness, easily startled), among others. These symptoms typically will not last for more than a few days to a week but may be reexperienced at a later time either alone or in conjunction with other trauma symptoms.

There are a number of ways in which CCTS might adversely affect the officer. These include psychological problems, impaired job performance, marital/family problems, and diminished physical health to name a few. Implicit in the process of understanding why an officer may be experiencing the adverse reactions of CCTS is the understanding that these symptoms are normal reactions to the abnormal and unique demands of policing.

Vicarious Trauma Toolkit

Through an interdisciplinary and collaborative effort, law enforcement agencies now have an evidence-informed and discipline-specific resource to help them address the impact of the work on their members through key organizational responses.[70,71]

Since 2013, with funding from the U.S. Department of Justice's Office for Victims of Crime (OVC), Northeastern University's Institute on Urban Health Research and Practice in Boston, Massachusetts, has led the effort to create the Vicarious Trauma Toolkit (VTT).[72] The VTT, which was released in 2017, is a first-of-its-kind online toolkit developed by a multidisciplinary team of first responder organizations, including those representing law enforcement, victim service providers, emergency medical services, firefighters, and researchers. The International Association of Chiefs of Police (IACP) contributed a visiting fellow to the team. The toolkit moves beyond the usual focus on what the individual can do for "self-care" and attends to the duty and responsibility of professional organizations to sustain their staff using evidence-informed approaches. The interactive, online platform provides first responder organizations with a "Compendium of Resources" that contains nearly 500 items: policies, practices, and program descriptions; research literature; and links to websites, podcasts, videos, and testimonials from each discipline. Additionally, new tools created just for the VTT fill gaps in currently available resources, including an organizational assessment tool. Each item in the compendium has been vetted and sorted by discipline.[73]

ALCOHOL AND DRUG USE BY POLICE OFFICERS

Alcoholism and Police Officers

Alcohol abuse among police officers is a serious and widespread problem, with some studies estimating that it affects one-quarter of all police officers in the United States. Research

---

Quick Facts: The Cost of Problem Drinking

Problem drinking in the United States costs employers a staggering $10.7 to $20.7 billion per year in accumulated sick pay, lost productivity, accidents, and the consequences of bad workplace decisions. Some 60 percent of job absenteeism is attributable to alcoholic and other troubled employees, and these employees miss work 16 times more frequently than do their nontroubled colleagues. Moreover, nearly 90 percent of all industrial accidents are attributed to workers with either substance abuse or mental health issues.[75]

has revealed a strong connection between occupational stress and alcohol and drug abuse but also a strong subculture more among police officers that encourages drinking both for social and stress-reduction purposes. Alcohol consumption among police officers is also correlated with officer suicides and domestic violence, and many departments are beginning to recognize the liability in allowing this problem to go untreated.[74]

The Impact of the Police Culture and Character Traits on the Development of Alcoholism

Paradoxically, despite the significantly high risk for alcoholism and other related problems, law enforcement remains one of the most difficult groups to reach with intervention and prevention services, due largely to the insular and clannish nature of the police culture.[76]

Several researchers have also linked negative coping mechanisms with both alcoholism and drug abuse in law enforcement personnel[77] and suggest these negative coping skills may be embedded in character traits (specifically, tough-mindedness, and aggressiveness) typically associated with the "beat cop," which many departments may still look for in recruits despite a rapidly changing social environment. Another researcher suggests these character traits are "constant predictors of superior police performance" in a traditional, reactive law enforcement setting. However, the current trend in law enforcement is away from the reactive practices of patrol, rapid response, and investigation and toward a more proactive, community-oriented approach. The new skills required for this new approach include "problem solving, flexibility, good interpersonal and communication abilities, and a demeanor that is *authoritative* rather than authoritarian."[78]

Thus, officers who cling to the "old school" mind-set may suffer future shock in a rapidly evolving social climate. Even in the midst of social change, many police departments today continue to embrace many of the traditions of a bygone era, including the acceptance of drinking.[79] Factors such as the availability of alcohol both inside and outside of work, lack of departmental policies on drinking (or if they do exist, lax enforcement), lack of support mechanisms to help members deal with the stress, and—not by far the least—peer pressure, all contribute to the problem of drinking among police officers.[80] Bandura's Social Learning Theory[81] would view drinking as a *social cue* of the cultural group or subgroup with which one is involved. In the case of police work, drinking has been a time-honored way of "taking the edge off" the stresses of the job since the first New York City patrolman set out on their nightly rounds in the 1840s.

It has been suggested further that policing is especially conducive to alcoholism. Because police officers frequently work in an environment in which social drinking is commonplace, it is relatively easy for them to become social drinkers. The nature of police work and the environment in which it is performed provide the stress stimulus.

Traditionally, police departments adhered to the "character flaw" theory of alcoholism. This outdated philosophy called for the denunciation and dismissal of the officer with an alcohol problem. Today, police departments attempt to rehabilitate officers by employing a number of preventive and intervention programs.

Drug Use by Police Officers

Drug abuse by police officers has garnered a great deal of attention and as a result of this condition, police administrators have had to grapple with such issues as the following:

- What positions will the employee unions or other employee organizations take if drug testing is proposed?
- Who should be tested for drugs? Entry-level officers? Regular officers on a random basis? All officers before they are promoted? Personnel assigned to high-profile units, such as bomb disposal and special tactics and response?
- When does a supervisor have "reasonable suspicion" of a subordinate's drug use?
- Who should collect urine or other specimens and under what conditions?
- What criteria or standards should be used when selecting a laboratory to conduct the police department's drug testing program?
- What disciplinary action is appropriate when officers are found to have abused drugs?
- What duty does an employer have to rehabilitate employees who become disabled as a result of drug abuse?[82]

In recent years, issues concerning the testing of sworn officers for drugs have been debated and litigated. In the early days of such litigation, court rulings were sometimes wildly contradictory, with most courts striking down such requirements, typically on the basis that it was an unwarranted intrusion into officers' constitutional right to privacy.[83] Nevertheless, three major principles have emerged from the many random drug cases decided by the courts. The first is that drug testing—both on the basis of reasonable suspicion and when conducted on a random basis—does not violate the federal Constitution. The second is that, although drug testing may not violate federal Constitutional rights, it may not be permissible under the constitutions of some states. The third principle is that, in states that have granted collective bargaining rights to police officers (see Chapter 11, Labor Relations), drug testing cannot be unilaterally implemented by the employer. Instead, it must be submitted to the collective bargaining process.

The selection of officers for drug testing must be truly random and part of a clearly articulated drug testing policy. The courts will not support the police department's operation of a nonrandom drug testing program except when there is reasonable suspicion to test for the presence of certain drugs.[84] This generally involves a urine drug screen for the following drugs:

- Cannabinoids (Marijuana, Metabolite)
- Benoyldcgonine (Cocaine, Metabolite)

- Opiates (Codeine, Morphine, Hydrocodone, Hydromorphone, Oxycodone)
- Amphetamines (Amphetamine, Methamphetamine)
- Phencyclidine
- Barbiturates (Phenobarbital, Secobarbital, Pentobarbital, Butalbital, Amobarbital)
- Benzodiazepenes (Oxazepam, Nordiazepam, Alpha OH-Alprazolam, Temazepam)
- Propoxyphene
- Methadone
- Ecstasy
- Anabolic steroids[85]

POLICE SUICIDE

Suicide is a very real problem for law enforcement officers and their families. Most studies have shown that the number of officers lives lost to suicide exceeds those killed in the line of duty. A number of potential risk factors are unique to law enforcement. Law enforcement officers are regularly exposed to traumatic and stressful events. Additionally, they work long and irregular hours, which can lead to isolation from family members. Negative perceptions of law enforcement officers and discontent with the criminal justice system also play a role in engendering cynicism and a sense of despair among some officers. A culture that emphasizes strength and control can dissuade officers from acknowledging their need for help. Excessive use of alcohol may also be a factor, as it is for the population in general. Also, suspended police officers and those who are under investigation are 6.7 times more likely to kill themselves.[86]

Need for a Cultural Change in Law Enforcement

Unfortunately, in many law enforcement departments, the culture toward mental wellness or addressing emotional problems of any kind is one of disdain and avoidance. The presumption within this culture is often that the mere presence of an emotional problem indicates a weakness on the officer's part. That perception leads to the even more dangerous perception that being open about these issues can make the officer vulnerable, even to the point of losing their job. Significant progress in curbing officer suicide and enhancing officer mental wellness is only achievable if the culture does an about-turn toward openness and support for all aspects of officer health and wellness, particularly mental health.[87]

Also, to more effectively deal with this issue, it has been recommended that the chief executive should be proactive and speak directly to their officers about mental wellness and officer suicide. Hearing from the chief executive personally and candidly carries a tremendous amount of weight. In particular, a chief executive or others who have triumphed over their own

mental health issues should champion this subject and share their own success stories. In addition, one of the executives' most important tasks in this effort is to be held accountable for the review, improvement, and auditing of mental wellness and suicide prevention policies and practices. The chief executive should appoint and personally oversee a specific employee to begin such an agency review, including identification of resources needed and implementation deadlines. Such an assessment tool or "checklist" could include items such as those found in Table 13.2.

Stressors That May Contribute to Suicide or Mental Illness

While by no means an exhaustive list, the following identifies some of the stressors and indicators that officers encounter, which may cause officers to consider suicide or contribute to the development of mental illness.

- Accumulation of chronic stresses and daily hassles
- Exposure to horrific events or acute stresses
- Relationship events, including divorce or loss of major relationship; death of a spouse, child, or best friend, especially if by suicide; infidelity or domestic violence
- Shift work, as officers on midnight shifts may be higher suicide risks because of abnormal sleep patterns, which can impair their ability to make rational decisions
- High expectations of the profession, followed by perceived futility or social isolation
- Significant financial strain, such as inability to pay mortgages or car payments
- Diagnosis of serious or terminal illness
- Significant change in routine, such as a change of duty or pending or existing retirement[88]
- An internal affairs investigation resulting in disciplinary action, which could be career ending

Indicators of Police Officers Who May Be Contemplating Suicide

- Talking about wanting to die, seeking revenge, feelings of hopelessness, being trapped, being a burden to others, or in unbearable pain
- Increased risk-taking behavior or recklessness
- Looking for a way to kill oneself
- Emotionless, numb, angry, agitated, anxious, enraged, or showing extreme mood swings
- Giving away valued possessions
- Socially isolated or withdrawn
- Weight gain or loss
- Sleep deprivation or sleeping too much
- Cutting themselves
- Increased consumption of alcohol or drugs[89]

TABLE 13.2 SUGGESTED CHECKLIST FOR COMPREHENSIVE MENTAL WELLNESS AND SUICIDE PREVENTION PROGRAMS

Policy/Practice Review	To Do
Does you agency treat officer mental and physical safety and wellness equally?	A mental resiliency check is like a cholesterol check. Make sure that your officers are mentally fit.
Do you and your officers know the early warning signs of depression, other mental illness, and suicidal behavior?	Implement effective education and training initiatives, and aggressively (and routinely) publicize how officers can get the mental health assistance they need.
Do you have an effective Employee Assistance Program (EAP), peer support group, a consortium approach, or other mental health providers dedicated to law enforcement? Do you have a relationship with a local hospital with trusted doctors to treat officers?	Know what mental health assistance is available to your department, and find out how you can improve the quality of mental health services delivered to your officers.
What are your mental health intervention protocols for at-risk officers and after critical incidents?	Make sure that these protocols are effective and consistent.
Do your training programs from academy recruits to retirees include routine training on mental wellness and stress management? Do you incorporate these curricula at critical incident training?	Invest in this training throughout an officer's career. It is as important as firearms training or wearing bullet proof vests.
If you officers have a union, is the union on board with your mental wellness program?	The union might be the go-to contact for a line officer. Work with your unions to foster support for mental wellness programs.
Do you have clear guidance on confidentiality law and rules?	Confidentiality laws are complex and a failure to comply with them can have serious ramifications. Educate your agency.
Does employee self-reporting result in discipline or negative consequences, either intentional or unintentional? Do officers fear that self-reporting will result in discipline or even job loss? Do you have clear guidance on the laws and policies that govern when an officer's firearm must be removed due to mental health issues?	Fear of self-reporting may be one of the greatest barriers to achieving a healthy department. Change your culture so that officers are encouraged to self-report. When an officer sees another officer getting help without being degunned or debadged, it is very reassuring.
Are the policies in your department addressing suicide adequate?	Be sure you have an established notification and funeral policy in place for officers who die by suicide, to include outreach, education, support for family members and fellow officers, and media coordination.

Source: Breaking the Silence on Law Enforcement Suicides, Community Oriented Policing Services, U.S. Department of Justice, July 2013, p. 6.

Intervention Protocols

Identify, Evaluate, and Routinely Audit Mental Health Providers That Screen and Provide Services to Officers at Risk.

To identify early warning signs of mental health issues, mental illness, and suicidal behavior and implement successful intervention programs, departments must identify, evaluate, and routinely audit their mental health providers. These providers are the linchpin to the delivery of effective mental health care to officers in need. Symposium participants identified the types of providers typically used by law enforcement, and some of their respective benefits and drawbacks. Participants also made recommendations respective to each type of service to enhance the delivery of these services.

Whoever the providers are, be sure to not only identify and evaluate their services but also to routinely audit their quality and to track how often their services are used. This data is essential to obtaining necessary funding and to deploying effective resources where needed.

Peer Support Program

A **peer support program** along with carefully selected and trained peer support personnel have been recognized as being critical mental health resources for officers who are in crisis. (Discussed in much greater detail later in this chapter.)

Employee Assistance Programs (EAP)

EAPs (discussed in greater detail later in this chapter) provide no-cost, confidential assistance to an agency's employees (and sometimes their families) on health and wellness issues that impact work performance, such as stress management, substance abuse counseling, and mental health concerns.

Reinforce Family Connections

Families are a key resource to any successful early intervention program. Programs and information are important for family members in order for them to understand how they can support their significant other.

POLICE OFFICER DOMESTIC VIOLENCE

Given the stressful nature of police work, it is not surprising that officers sometimes have difficulty keeping what happened to them at work separate from their home lives. "Leave it at the office" is a common admonition to officers. While the intent of this message is clear, it is often hard to do so consistently and unfortunately, it sometimes manifests itself in domestic violence.[90]

The International Association of Chiefs of Police (IACP) Model Policy on Police Officer Domestic Violence defines it as follows:

It is any reported, founded, and/or prosecuted incident of domestic violence wherein a sworn police officer is the suspected offender. It is also an act of violence (threatened or actual) perpetrated by a police officer (on or off duty) or any police department employee upon his or her intimate partner. "Partner" refers to any individual (opposite or same sex) the officer has dated, cohabitated with, married, and/or has a child in common.[91] These definitions may be limited to the definitions in the law of each state. While not the focus of this policy, other forms of family violence (for example; child and elder abuse) should be addressed in a parallel manner.[92,93]

It is not known how many acts of **domestic violence** police officers commit in their own homes. The reasons for the nonreporting of such incidents include victims with low esteem who think they "got what they deserved," threats from their attackers of more severe physical harm if the victims do call the police, and the belief that fellow officers will not take action against "one of their own."

Personality Changes That Can Potentially Contribute to Marital Problems

Police officers occasionally develop new personality characteristics after joining the force, which may contribute to marital problems.[94,95,96] Law enforcement officers are distinct from other occupational groups because of their unique social role and status. This often contributes to the development of a distinct police subculture with its own norms and values.[97] The officer's "working personality"[98] can inadvertently extend into family life, leading to complaints about authoritative demands, overprotectiveness, or cynicism.[99,100]

The police culture emphasizes the traditional male gender role, which is characterized by aggression, competitiveness, and control.[101,102] The nature of police work requires that officers take charge of a situation, and they may use authoritative interrogation tactics to obtain information or aggression to assert superiority.[103] These behaviors do not translate into being an empathic, positive listener to either children or spouses.

Additionally, police officers are trained to remain in control of their emotions at all times.[104] Emotional control allows officers to respond instrumentally to a variety of potentially traumatic situations, but it may also lead to emotional detachment from other aspects of daily life that are unrelated to the job.[105,106] Spouses sometimes complain that officers are unable to "turn off" these mechanisms of authoritarianism and emotional control.[107] Therefore, the police culture creates an ambiguous situation in which officers are encouraged to maintain emotional control and a command presence at work, yet they are punished for doing so at home.[108] Mikkelsen and Burke[109] concluded that officers who perceive a greater need to hide their emotions also expressed greater work-family conflict.

The police culture may also tend to promote an "us-versus-them" mentality in which officers perceive their peers as the only reliable sources of support.[110] Officers may assume their spouses do not fully understand the conditions they face at work, or they may not want to subject their spouses to troubling accounts of violence and suffering.[111] Regardless of the rationale, emotional restriction is inconsistent with certain qualities that are usually deemed necessary for maintaining successful relationships, such as cooperation and a willingness to communicate emotions openly.[112]

Early Warning and Intervention

Of critical concern to departments is how to screen and select new officers to minimize the risk of hiring officers who may engage in domestic violence.[113] To understand the connection among the various forms of family violence, it is essential to investigate whether a candidate has a history or likelihood of engaging in child abuse, domestic violence, or elder abuse. The process of investigating candidates must be handled in two stages: (1) preemployment screening and investigation and (2) postconditional offer of employment.

PREEMPLOYMENT SCREENING AND INVESTIGATION

All candidates should be asked about any history of perpetrating child abuse, domestic violence, or elder abuse and past arrests or convictions for such crimes. They should be asked whether they have ever been the subject of a civil protective order. If the candidate answers positively to any of these questions or the department uncovers any information in the background check that indicates a history of violence, the candidate should be screened out of the hiring process.

During the background investigation, a check should be made for restraining orders issued in any jurisdiction where the candidate has lived.

POSTCONDITIONAL OFFER OF EMPLOYMENT

If the candidate's background investigation does not indicate a history of child abuse, domestic violence, or elder abuse, the department should proceed with a psychological examination, which should include indicators of violent or abusive tendencies. This portion of the screening process should be conducted by an experienced clinical psychologist or psychiatrist (see Chapter 9, Human Resource Management, for a more detailed discussion).

Zero Tolerance Policy

Departments must make it clear to all officers that the department has a zero tolerance policy on domestic violence, and the department should share this information with family members of the officer. Departments should look to develop a line of communication directly with the domestic partners of recruits and officers. For example, a department can hold a family orientation day prior to graduation from the police academy. Family members should be provided with instructions on whom to contact within the department if any problems arise. The dual purpose of establishing such contact is to underscore the department's zero tolerance policy, even with high-ranking members of the organization and to provide victims with an avenue for direct communication with a department employee who is trained in handling such calls.

Department Responsibilities

An individual or a family member of an officer may recognize early indicators of potential violence, such as issues of power and control. The power and control might take the forms of restricting contact with family and friends, requiring the partner to turn over his or her paycheck, and limiting activities outside the home. Victims may communicate their concerns "informally" at first, such as with calls to an officer's supervisor. These informal contacts must be treated with care, since this is a critical opportunity for a department to provide intervention using early intervention and prevention strategies. The model policy calls for a formal system of documenting, sharing, and responding to information from concerned partners and family members.

Departments need to provide officers and their families with nonpunitive avenues of support and assistance before an incident of domestic violence occurs. Departments must establish procedures for making confidential referrals to internal or external counseling services with expertise in domestic violence. These referrals can be made on the request of an officer or family members or in response to observed warning signs.

Officers will not be entitled to confidentiality anytime they or family members disclose to any member of the department that an officer has engaged in domestic violence. Confidentiality should be extended to partners or family members who report an officer as a matter of safety. A report of such criminal conduct must be treated as an admission or a report of a crime and investigated, both criminally and administratively.

Departments must understand that other officers may become involved in domestic violence situations by engaging in inappropriate activities that interfere with cases against fellow officers who are engaged in acts such as stalking, intimidation, harassment, or surveillance of victims, witnesses, and/or family members of victims or witnesses. If this occurs, these officers must be investigated and sanctioned and/or charged criminally where appropriate.

Supervisory Responsibilities

Typically, an abusive person engages in certain patterns of behavior. These may include repeated actions of increasing control directed at his or her partner preceding an incident of physical or criminal violence.

The early indicators of potential violence are not limited to home life; the department may detect warning signs in an officer's behavior prior to a domestic violence incident. Supervisors must receive specific training on warning signs and potential indicators of violent or controlling tendencies. Warning signs that may indicate a likelihood of violent behavior include increased use of force in arrest situations, drug/alcohol problems, frequent tardiness or absences, verbal disputes, physical altercations, and other aggressive behavior.

When supervisors become aware of a pattern of controlling or abusive behavior exhibited by officers, the supervisors have a responsibility to document the information and notify their immediate ranking supervisor, who will then inform the chief in accordance with the department's chain of command. After making proper notification, supervisors should inform officers that the behaviors have been documented. A recommendation can be made to officers that they participate voluntarily in a counseling or support program to address the identified issue or behavior.

In cases in which behavior violates departmental policy, a department can seize the opportunity to mandate participation in a batterer intervention program in addition to any appropriate sanctions.

Early prevention and intervention strategies employed by a department at this phase of the continuum have tremendous potential not only to reduce future violence but also to save victims' lives and officers' careers. The services that can be made available include the following:

- Employee assistance program referral (discussed later in this chapter)
- Internal professional counseling (police psychologist)
- External professional counseling (contract/referral)
- Advocacy support from local agencies
- Peer support program (with clear reporting and confidentiality guidelines)

The department will need to ensure that the quality and expertise of these resources are sound. Collaboration with local domestic violence victim advocacy organizations is recommended.

Police Officer Responsibilities

As part of a department's zero tolerance policy, all officers need to understand their responsibility to report definitive knowledge they have concerning domestic violence on the part of an officer. Departments must be prepared to investigate and possibly sanction and/or charge criminally any officer who fails to report such knowledge or to cooperate with an investigation.

In addition, all officers need to know they will be investigated and sanctioned and/or charged criminally if they engage in activities such as stalking, surveillance, intimidation, or harassment of victims or witnesses in an attempt to interfere with investigations of other officers accused of domestic violence.

In the event that an officer is the subject of a criminal investigation and/or a protective or restraining order, the officer is responsible for informing his or her supervisor and providing copies of the order and timely notice of court dates regardless of the jurisdiction.

Incident Response Protocols

A department's response to 911 calls involving police officer domestic violence immediately sets the tone for how a situation will be handled throughout the remainder of the continuum. Further, the unique dynamics between the offending and responding officers (e.g., collegiality and rank differential) often make on-scene decisions extremely difficult.

A department must take the following actions, all of which are critical steps in responding to allegations of domestic abuse by police officers:

Communications officer/dispatcher documentation—When a call or report of domestic violence involves a police officer, the dispatcher should have a standing directive to document the call and immediately notify both the on-duty patrol supervisor and the chief of police. This directive ensures that key command personnel receive the information and prevents the call from being handled informally.

Patrol response—Any officer arriving at the scene of a domestic violence call or incident involving a police officer must immediately request the presence of a supervisor at the scene, regardless of the involved officer's jurisdiction.

On-scene supervisor response—The on-scene supervisor has responsibilities for the following:

- Securing the scene and collecting evidence
- Ensuring an arrest is made where probable cause exists
- Removing weapons in the event of an arrest
- Considering victim safety
- Notifying the police chief or sheriff if the incident occurs outside the officer's jurisdiction

The on-duty supervisor must respond to the call and assume all on-scene decision making. Leaving the decision making to officers of lesser or equal rank to the suspect officer puts the responding officer in a difficult situation. The presence of a ranking officer on the scene resolves this problem. The policy recommends that, in police officer domestic violence cases, no fewer than two officers, with at least one of senior rank to the accused officer, be present. This is also the case when serving arrest warrants and civil protective orders.

Crime scene documentation—Recanting or reluctant witnesses and victims are not uncommon when domestic violence occurs. Police on the scene of a 911 call must take specific actions to document all evidence, including color photographs/videotape of injuries, overturned/damaged furniture, interviews of neighbors and family members, and threats from the officer. Documentation of this evidence will be essential to the successful prosecution of the case with or without the victim's presence in court.

Arrest decisions—Policies on arrest for domestic violence incidents vary among state, county, and local jurisdictions. In all cases, responding officers should base arrest decisions on probable cause. When a crime has been committed, an arrest will be made, as in all other cases. The on-scene supervisor is responsible for ensuring an arrest is made if probable cause exists or for submitting written documentation to explain why an arrest was not made. All officers need sufficient training to enable them to determine which party is the primary (i.e., dominant) aggressor in domestic violence situations. Every effort should be made to identify the primary aggressor to avoid the unwarranted arrest of victims.

Weapon removal—If an arrest is made, the on-scene supervisor will relieve the accused officer of his or her service weapon. Some police officers may have several weapons at their home. Where multiple weapons are present, removing only the service weapon of the officer leaves the victim entirely vulnerable to further violence. While federal, state, and local laws vary on how and when such weapons can be removed, police have broad powers to remove weapons in certain circumstances, particularly if an arrest is being made. Where application of the law is questionable, the on-scene supervisor should suggest that the officer in question voluntarily relinquish all firearms. The supervisor can also simply ask victims if they want to remove any weapons from the home for safekeeping by the department. When no arrest has been made, the on-scene supervisor should consider removing the accused officer's weapon as a safety consideration.

After weapons are removed, decisions need to be made about how long they will or can be held. Where court orders of protection are in place, these orders may also affect decisions on gun removal or seizure.

When the accused officer is the chief, director, or superintendent of the department, a specific protocol must be in place to document and report the incident to the individual who has direct oversight for the chief, director, or superintendent.

When police respond to a domestic violence incident involving an officer from another jurisdiction, all responding officers, investigators, and supervisors will follow the same procedures to be followed if responding to a domestic violence complaint involving an officer from their own department. The on-scene supervisor will notify the chief of police from the accused officer's department verbally as soon as possible and in writing within 24 hours of the call.

Departments may be faced with domestic violence situations where the victim is a police officer. If this occurs, standard domestic violence response and investigation procedures should be followed. The department should take steps to protect the privacy of the officer and make referrals to confidential counseling services. The department should not allow the reported incident to impact negatively on the assignments and evaluation of the victimized officer.

If both the victim and the offender in a domestic violence situation are police officers, the protocols established by the department should remain substantially the same. Safety of the victim should be the paramount concern. In the event that an order of protection has been issued, a department will need to make careful decisions concerning work assignments for accused officers pending administrative and criminal investigations. Gun removal in this situation becomes extremely complex. In the development of the policy, individual departments should seek legal guidance to ensure that the rights of all concerned are protected.

> *Department follow-up*—The department or supervisor should require a debriefing of all officers involved in a response to the scene of a police officer domestic violence case and may include communications officers. At the debriefing, the department's confidentiality guidelines should be reviewed. In addition, a command-level **critical incident** management review of every domestic violence case involving an officer should be conducted.

The department must take responsibility for conducting an assessment to determine the potential for further violence on the part of the accused officer. A specifically trained member of the command staff should review a domestic violence lethality checklist (discussed later in this chapter) of risk factors with the accused officer. In addition, the evaluation should be supplemented by interviews with the victim, witnesses, and family members. Information gained from the assessment should be used to determine appropriate sanctions, safeguards, and referrals. The command officer assigned as the victim's principal contact should discuss the risk factors with the victim as part of safety planning.

DOMESTIC VIOLENCE LETHALITY ASSESSMENT FOR FIRST RESPONDERS

Law enforcement agencies are increasingly providing their first responders with a **domestic violence lethality assessment form** and accompanying them with instruction to assist them in more systematically evaluating the extent to which someone may be in grave danger of being seriously injured or killed (see Figure 13.4).

Purpose of the Lethality Assessment: This evidence-based Lethality Assessment form is a user-friendly, straightforward instrument that predicts danger and lethality in domestic incidents between intimate or former intimate partners to a high degree. Research shows that **only 4 percent of intimate partner murder victims ever used domestic violence (DV) services.** This Assessment encourages victims in high danger to seek domestic violence program services to prevent serious injury or death.

Step 1—Fill out the Assessment Form with the victim.

Step 2—If any of the first three answers are yes, ask the victim to call the agency's local advocacy agency and ensure that they make contact. You may need to dial the number for them if they are upset.

Step 3—If they talk to someone, check the box that they spoke to a hotline counselor.

Step 4—If they answer yes to one of the first three questions but do not want to speak to a hotline counselor right away, note the victim's safe phone number to call and fax the Lethality Assessment to the appropriate DV organization at the bottom of the form.

Step 5—If the victim answers yes to the first three questions, or a significant number of follow-up questions are yes, but they refuse to speak to a hotline counselor advise the victim that in your opinion, he/she is in high danger for lethality and you highly encourage them to seek DV program services.

Step 6—Provide them with a DV resource card and case number.

Step 7—Fax all Lethality Assessment forms to the appropriate DV organization listed on the bottom of the form regardless of the answers or whether or not the victim answered any of the questions.[114]

POLICE OFFICER HOMICIDES AND SUICIDES

Police officers work in an occupational culture premised on violence. They also have firearms available, a lethal method for both suicide and homicide.[115] Police officers may be more prone to violence at home due to their exposure at work. Studies have shown the estimated incidence of domestic violence among police officers (25–40 percent) is significantly higher than in the general population (16 percent).[116] Because of job-related factors, police officers appear to be disproportionately at risk for homicide-suicide. They have access to guns, which some use as instruments of violence against others or themselves, usually with lethal results. Domestic violence appears to be heavily implicated in police homicide-suicide. The police

SANTA CLARA COUNTY DOMESTIC VIOLENCE
LETHALITY ASSESSMENT FOR FIRST RESPONDERS

Date:	Case #:
Officer:	Agency:
Victim:	Offender:
Victim's Safe Numbers to Call: Home: Cell: Work:	Would you like to provide names/phone numbers of 2 people that can reach you? 1. 2.

Is the victim monolingual/limited English proficient? If yes, what language do they speak?

☐ Check here if the victim did not answer any of the questions.

If the victim answers YES to any of questions 1–3, please call the appropriate domestic violence crisis hotline and have the counselor speak with the victim.

1. Has your current or previous partner ever used a weapon against you or threatened you with a weapon?	☐ Yes ☐ No ☐ No Answer
2. Have they threatened to kill you or someone else?	☐ Yes ☐ No ☐ No Answer
3. Do you think your current or previous partner might try to kill you?	☐ Yes ☐ No ☐ No Answer

If the answers to the above questions are NO but at least 4 of the questions below are YES please contact the hotline.

4. Do they have a gun or can they easily get one?	☐ Yes ☐ No ☐ No Answer
5. Have they ever tried to choke/strangle you?	☐ Yes ☐ No ☐ No Answer
6. Are they violently or constantly jealous or try to control most of your daily activities?	☐ Yes ☐ No ☐ No Answer
7. Have you left or separated from your partner after living together or being married?	☐ Yes ☐ No ☐ No Answer
8. Are they unemployed?	☐ Yes ☐ No ☐ No Answer
9. Have they tried to commit suicide?	☐ Yes ☐ No ☐ No Answer
10. Do you have a child that he knows is not his?	☐ Yes ☐ No ☐ No Answer
11. Do they follow or spy on you or leave threatening messages?	☐ Yes ☐ No ☐ No Answer

12. Is there anything else that worries you about your safety? If yes, what concerns do you have?

Officers are encouraged to call the hotline whenever they believe the victim is in a potentially lethal situation regardless of the victim's responses to the questions above.

Check one:	☐ Victim screened in based on responses ☐ Victim screened in based on the belief of officer	☐ Victim did not screen in	
Did the victim speak with the hotline counselor?		☐ Yes	☐ No

NORTH COUNTY HOTLINE: YWCA Support Network 1-800-572-2782 FAX: 408-295-0608			**CENTRAL COUNTY HOTLINE:** Next Door Solutions 408-279-2962 FAX: 408-441-7562
	SOUTH COUNTY HOTLINE: Community Solutions 1-877-363-7238 FAX 408-782-9469 54		

PLEASE FAX THIS DOCUMENT TO THE APPROPRIATE DOMESTIC VIOLENCE AGENCY

FIGURE 13.4 ▶ Santa Clara County domestic violence lethality assessment for first responders. *Source:* Domestic Violence Protocol for Law Enforcement, Police Chiefs Association of Santa Clara County, California, March 2014, p. 54.

culture encourages control, aggression, authoritarianism, domination, a strong sense of entitlement, and other conduct that correlates with aggressive behavior at home.[117]

Exposure of police officers to violence and aggression may increase the risk of homicide-suicide. Several studies have suggested associations of suicide and aggression.[118] Farberow and colleagues[119] compared suicide completers with accident victims, and concluded that suicide completers were more likely to have histories of angry outbursts. Other associations noted in relation to suicide are hostility and irritability. Officers considering suicide may be more likely to have a history of violence and act violently in a greater variety of relationships, especially spousal.[120]

The following summarized news stories show the potential for such a tragic event.[121]

Case 1

The Tacoma, Washington Police Chief, killed his wife and then himself during a violent domestic dispute. Two weeks prior to the incident, the chief had arrived at his estranged wife's house and attempted to gain entry. She called the Sheriff's Department and told the Sheriff's operator her estranged husband was attempting to forcibly enter the house. She also advised them that he was the Chief of the Tacoma, Washington Police Department, and that he was armed. The Sheriff's Department did not respond to take a report even though it was their agency's standard procedure to do so. Two weeks after this initial encounter when the news broke about the Chief's divorce battle and allegations of his forcible attempt to gain entry into the house occupied by his wife city officials still insisted that the Chief was doing a good job. City Attorney Robin Jenkinson rejected an internal proposal by other city officials that the Chief be disarmed feeling this was a civil matter. The following day the Chief shot his wife and himself.

Case 2

A 33-year-old Police Deputy Inspector shot his 38-year-old wife several times, killing her. It happened during an argument the couple had in their car. The officer had earlier approached his wife in a cafeteria and ordered her into the car. He later committed suicide. During the month prior to the homicide, the wife told friends she felt threatened and afraid. However, she never filed any claims or notified the police. He was well known as a campaigner against domestic violence, and only weeks earlier had received praise for his efforts in the protection of women.

Case 3

A county Sheriff's Office jailer shot his four-year-old son, his wife, and then himself. The jailer called 911 and informed the dispatcher of the situation prior to turning the weapon on himself. Shortly after the killings, the Sheriff said that the jailer had been in good spirits and had not exhibited signs of depression or agitation at any time prior to the homicides. Last week, the Sheriff investigated allegations made by the jailer's wife, accusing the sheriff's office of not acting on information regarding

abuse at the hands of her husband. The wife's father said Friday that he contacted County officials multiple times to report domestic abuse, but officials did not act. He alleges that his daughter was the victim of physical abuse and said that he had witnessed his daughter with black eyes.

THE IMPACT OF SHIFT LENGTH ON PERFORMANCE, HEALTH, QUALITY OF LIFE, SLEEP, FATIGUE, AND EXTRA-DUTY EMPLOYMENT

In the past, most law enforcement agencies had traditionally deployed their patrol officers based on a 40-hour work week in which personnel work five consecutive, 8-hour shifts, followed by 2 days off.[122] However, in recent years, an increasing number of agencies have moved to some variant of a compressed workweek (CWW) schedule in which officers work four 10-hour shifts per week or three 12-hour shifts (plus a time adjustment to make up the remaining 4 hours of the standard 40-hour workweek). While this trend toward CWWs has been increasing, there have been few, if any, rigorous scientific studies examining the advantages and disadvantages associated with these work schedules for officers and their agencies.

Recently, a study was funded by the U.S. Department of Justice to examine any potential issues associated with compressed workweek. This was done by implementing a randomized block experiment in Detroit (MI) and Arlington (TX), in which the blocks include site (i.e., Detroit, Arlington) as well as shift (day, evening, and midnight) in order to examine the effects of the three shift lengths on various outcomes. Work performance was measured using both laboratory simulations and departmental data. Health, quality of life, sleep, sleepiness, off-duty employment, and overtime hours were measured via self-report measures including surveys, sleep diaries, and alertness logs. Fatigue was measured using both objective, laboratory-based instruments, and subjective reports of sleepiness.

The results revealed no significant differences between the three shift lengths on work performance, health, or work-family conflict. There were, however, important differences where the other outcomes were concerned. Officers working 10-hour shifts, for example, averaged significantly more sleep and reported experiencing a better quality of work life than did their peers working 8-hour shifts. And officers working 12-hour shifts experienced greater levels of sleepiness (subjective measure of fatigue) and lower levels of alertness at work than those assigned to 8-hour shifts. The results suggest that CWWs are not likely to pose significant health risks or result in worsened performance and that 10-hour shifts may offer certain benefits not associated with 8-hour shifts, whereas 12-hour shifts may have some disadvantages over 8-hour shifts. Importantly, those on 8-hour shifts averaged significantly less sleep per 24-hour period and worked significantly more overtime hours than those on 10- or 12-hour shifts. As such, a 10-hour shift may

---

Quick Facts: Shift Work and Potential Health Problems

Recent studies on shift work and police health confirm, to some degree, there are certain risks for health problems for officers working night shift. For example:

- Officers who regularly had fewer than 5 hours of sleep had significantly poorer artery health than those who typically had more than 6 hours of sleep.
- Over a period of seven years, male officers who worked night shifts had significantly poorer cardiovascular health than those who worked day shifts.

- Officers who worked nights and had less than six hours of sleep had four times as many metabolic syndrome components than officers working the day shift. The metabolic syndrome is a collection of five components that predict heart disease, including waist size, blood pressure, weight, glucose, cholesterol, and triglyceride levels.[123]

---

be a viable alternative to the traditional 8-hour shift in larger agencies; however, caution is advised when considering 12-hour shifts due to increased levels of self-reported fatigue/sleepiness and lower levels of alertness. Indeed, researchers have noted that individuals tend to underestimate their levels of fatigue, so officers may be more fatigued than they reported while working 12-hour shifts. Additionally, past research has shown increased risks for accidents with increasing numbers of hours worked. It is for these reasons that caution should be exercised when agency leaders consider adopting 12-hour long shifts. Finally, the reduced levels of overtime usage for those working 10- and 12-hour shifts suggests the possibility for cost savings for agencies employing compressed schedules. These findings are consistent with many past findings; however, the lack of randomized controlled trials has limited the utility of past studies.

SLEEP DEPRIVATION AS A STRESS INDUCER

Although sleep deprivation is often not thought of as a stress factor, it can be a significant factor in the creation of stress. For example, sleep deprivation can cause the following to occur in police officers:

- Increased mood swings
- Impaired judgment
- Decrease in adaptability to certain situations
- Heightened sense of threat
- Increased anxiety or depression
- Increased chances of mental illness (e.g., officers may develop posttraumatic stress disorder or bipolar disorder)
- Reduced eye-hand coordination
- Weight gain
- Pain (e.g., backaches and headaches)
- Inability to relax (e.g., cause restless sleep and provoke heightened alert response)
- Gastrointestinal problems (e.g., loss of appetite or abdominal distress)
- Damage to the cardiovascular system (e.g., causing heart disease, arteriosclerosis, or congestive heart failure)
- Use of more sick leave
- Inappropriate uses of force more frequently
- More vehicle accidents
- More accidental injuries
- Greater difficulty dealing with the community members and other law enforcement agencies
- Higher likelihood of dying in the line of duty[124,125]

Quick Fact: Effects of Shift Work on Officer Safety and Wellness

An interesting study was conducted that compared the effects of sleep deprivation and blood alcohol levels on reaction times. The results concluded that sleep loss was more potent than alcohol in its effect on reaction time.

The following comparisons were observed within a 24-hour period:

- No sleep—equivalent to 0.19 blood alcohol level as measured by breath ethanol concentration

- Two hours of sleep—equivalent to 0.102 blood alcohol level
- Four hours of sleep—equivalent to 0.095 blood alcohol level
- Six hours of sleep—equivalent to 0.045 blood alcohol level [126]

Quick Facts: Microsleep: Falling Asleep Without Knowing It

Microsleep is a brief sleep episode, maybe a few second, during which people fall asleep without realizing they are asleep. In essence, the brain falls asleep ahead of the body. The brain needs adequate sleep to prevent accidents and injury during the night shift. When sleep is insufficient, the brain has a slower response and lapses into a lack of attention and slowed reactions. As sleepiness increases, lapses get more frequent and longer in duration—and there is an increasing loss in muscle tone (e.g., eyelids, hands) that contributes to an even greater risk.[129]

Sleep Deprivation Can Cause Work-Related Accidents

One study found that four out of eight officers involved in on-the-job accidents and injuries were impaired because of fatigue.[127] Such accidents include automobile crashes that were due to officers' impaired eye-hand coordination and propensity to nod off behind the wheel. Other work-related injuries come from accidents that occur when officers have impaired balance and coordination.

Despite the impact of fatigue, many officers continue to work double shifts, triple shifts, and second jobs. Some work well over 1,000 hours of overtime a year. Excessive work with inadequate rest over a long period of time can make officers sleep-deprived—53 percent of officers report an average of 6.5 hours of sleep or less.[128]

STRESS REDUCTION MANAGEMENT TECHNIQUES

Some police officers think that stress is just "a fairy tale—something that those who can't hack it can blame for their problems." Thus, the first step is for officers to recognize that unchecked stress can cause them to be sick more frequently, to engage in self-destructive behaviors (such as substance abuse or suicide), to live life less fully, to lose their families, and simply to be more uncomfortable every day than they need to be. The second step for officers is to monitor their own bodies and actions for stress, even though this capacity for self-awareness and introspection is difficult for some people to develop. Simply put, officers need to be in touch with what they are feeling, to think about what they have said and done, and to ask, "Why?" The final step is to eliminate or reduce stress by engaging in the following so-called **stress inoculation activities**.

- Exercise rigorously for 20–30 minutes at least three times per week.
- Maintain a proper diet, including minimizing the intake of foods high in salt and cholesterol.
- Develop leisure interests and hobbies, such as hiking, tying fishing flies, rock climbing, gardening, collecting stamps, writing poetry and fiction, learning a foreign language, and photography; in other words, learning new things that excite and refresh the mind.

- Meditate and pray.
- Avoid maladaptive responses to stress, such as smoking and drinking.
- Establish support groups.
- Develop a network of friends, including people outside the department.
- Monitor yourself. Refer yourself for help before you have to be referred; you will avoid some problems, reduce others before they become entrenched, and get more out of the helping process.
- Use relaxation techniques, such as biofeedback, yoga, progressive muscle relaxation, tai chi, imagery, and breathing exercises.
- Make sure that your career and other expectations are consistent with your actual situation.[130]

THE POLICE PSYCHOLOGIST'S ROLE IN A PSYCHOLOGICAL HEALTH WELLNESS INITIATIVE

The role of a police psychologist in psychological health wellness initiatives can vary on a number of dimensions, mostly determined by the individual needs of the department or agency hiring the psychologist or contracting for the psychologist's services. However, there are specific ways in which a psychologist can function more effectively if the goal of the relationship with the department involves fostering a comprehensive psychological health and resiliency initiative.[131]

In order for a psychologist to be an effective part of a psychological health initiative, there must be clarity on the part of the department, the officers, and the psychologist on the functions being served. For example, delineating the role of the psychologist as evaluator for fitness for duty from that of the psychologist providing officer support, resources, and consultations is important in building relationships. The police psychologist will ideally have the ability to work with training units on developing wellness trainings at the primary prevention level on a variety of topics that can help officers to buffer stress. In addition to standard stress management and suicide awareness trainings, officers can often make use of primary prevention training to develop skills in the areas that can lead to a cumulative buildup of stress for an officer. At the secondary level, the police psychologist who successfully collaborates with other department officer resources, such as peer support teams, chaplaincy programs, and veteran assistance and reintegration programs, will enhance the connections between these efforts and the psychologist's services.[132]

More specifically, police psychologists must exhibit their willingness to work as a team by first of all demonstrating great respect for the natural healing resource of the police brotherhood. Peer supporters are the specially trained colleagues of other officers (discussed later in this chapter). They play an important role in the first-line response to officers who are experiencing stress, distress, or impairment. If the police psychologist can earn the respect, trust, and collegiality of the peer support providers, then peer support will act as a natural bridge to the psychologist when the peer encounters an officer in need of the special services available only from the mental health provider. Psychologists will need to play an important role in facilitating such collaborations. A consultation and client-centered approach is the hallmark of effective psychological assistance and central to the training of psychologists. Such skills can be extremely valuable in the effort to foster teamwork and establish a psychological health initiative.[133]

A police psychologist can and should perform the traditional roles of providing an assessment of a potentially suicidal individual if the officer has reached the stage of obvious impairment, as well as implementing or arranging the appropriate type of tertiary prevention. However, the police psychologist who adopts a focus on "problem solving for people in crisis" in carrying out these professional activities can do much to reduce the stigma associated with using both secondary and tertiary suicide prevention programs and, in that way, help to prevent an officer from becoming impaired and suicidal. A police psychologist is a specialist in stress management and helps to reverse the downward cascade of poorly managed stress before it becomes distress, impairment, and ultimately problem behaviors (e.g., suicidal thoughts or acts, substance abuse, or dysfunctional relationship dynamics on the job or at home). Police officers are natural problem solvers who do not like to ask for help, but they are smart enough to seek out the experts and the specialists for DNA analysis, complex data analysis and management, or whatever else it takes to get the job done. Consulting with a police psychologist regarding the maintenance of the officer's most important "piece of equipment"—his or her health and wellness—is just smart police work. The police psychologist who can serve as a consultant to the officer in this way can serve a valuable role.[134]

PEER SUPPORT PROGRAM

Elements of a Successful Program

The idea of peer support dates back to the early 1970s with efforts within police agencies such as Boston, New York, and Chicago to deal with alcoholism in their police ranks.[135] Citing the successes of groups such as Alcoholics Anonymous, Police Officer Ed Donovan, who had been attending AA meetings to deal with his own abuse issues, formed the Boston Police Stress Program. Donovan and his colleagues were able to convince the Boston Police Commissioner to implement what we would now call a peer support program for police officers and their families, perhaps the first of its kind in the nation. The peer support concept holds that police employees are more likely to discuss psychological and emotional issues with someone who understands their job and the types of stress they may undergo, rather than with a psychological professional who may have expertise but lacks a comprehensive or adequate insight into the officer's problem, which may be directly related to specific aspects of police work or the police culture. This approach at ensuring the emotional health of law enforcement personnel assumes that a basic level of training is necessary, and empathy is particularly critical, in allowing the paraprofessional, in this sense, to provide necessary support and to be able to listen. Finn and Tomz[136] have identified benefits and weaknesses of peer supporters. Among those positives, they suggest that such peer support personnel:

- provide instant credibility and ability to empathize,
- assist fellow employees who are reluctant to talk with mental health professionals,
- recommend the program to other employees by attesting credibly to its confidentiality and concern,
- provide immediate assistance due to accessibility,
- detect incipient problems because of their daily contact with coworkers, and
- are less expensive than professionals.

Among the weaknesses are:

- They cannot provide the professional care that licensed mental health practitioners can;
- They may try to offer full-scale counseling they are not equipped to provide;
- They may be rejected by employees who want to talk only with a professional counselor;
- They may be avoided by employees because of the fear that problems will not be kept confidential;
- They require time, effort, and patience to screen, train, and supervise; and
- They may expose themselves and the department to legal liability.

Identifying the Elements of a Successful Peer Support Program

In establishing a peer support program within a criminal justice agency, it is important that those responsible for planning and implementation take a comprehensive approach to their task. Robinson and Murdoch,[137] for example, recommend that the following steps be considered when beginning a peer support program:

- determine that there is support for the program.
- develop a master plan.
- seek input from all relevant sections of the organization.
- develop policy.
- educate the organization regarding the program.
- integrate regional and central functions.
- integrate peer and mental health support.
- building in a review process.

Selection of the Team

Selection of a competent and respected peer support team is of vital importance. Robinson and Murdoch[138] describe characteristics that the manager of a peer support program would most likely want to look for in potential candidates, that is, personnel whom:

- have a good rapport with their colleagues and respect for members of management and the organization's union;
- possess good listening skills and are sensitive to the problems that others experience;
- understand ethical behavior defined by the agency's peer support program, especially in terms of confidentiality;
- display a willingness to learn how to provide good peer support and crisis response;
- have enough time in their personal and professional lives to dedicate themselves to the cause.

Other necessary qualities of effective peer support team members include the following:

- Acceptance of other people who differ in race, ethnic origins, gender, and lifestyles
- Emotional stability
- Trustworthiness
- Ability to connect with others
- Ability to demonstrate empathy
- Self control
- Self awareness

As is the case with the employment of good law enforcement officers, the selection process for peer support team members is critical to the ultimate success of the program. Candidates for positions on a peer support team may be "nominated" by themselves or recommended by other personnel within the agency; nominations by other members of the team are particularly valuable. Those responsible for selection then must ensure the past performance of the individual indicates future success in this new role; that performance evaluations of previous supervisors, both formal and documented and informal through one-on-one conversations, reflect the qualities necessary for this position; and that other personnel in the agency recognize the individual as trustworthy, worthy of respect, and capable of meeting the needs of individuals in time of crisis. Past training and education serve as further indicators of the preparation, interest, and motivation of the individual in providing peer support services.

Training of Agency Members

In the discussion of any aspect of law enforcement, there is no substitute for effective training. Basic training for peer support members must provide the minimum skills required for successful performance on the job including:

- agency expectations, policies, and procedures;
- sources and manifestations of law enforcement stress;
- basic debriefing and deescalation skills;
- interpersonal communications skills, particularly active listening;
- crisis intervention skills;
- problem-solving skills;
- recognition of symptoms of acute or chronic stress;
- recognition of suicidal warning signs;
- availability of and appropriate referral to local mental health and support resources;
- legal and professional responsibilities as a peer support team member; and
- confidentiality concerns.

Advanced training should enhance those skills and knowledge given at the basic level and could include more intensive classroom or online training.

In addition, ongoing or continuing training of team members should focus on lessons learned from cases handled by the specific peer support team, on changes and improvements in contacts available in support of the peer support team and its members, and on new developments in the emotional support of law enforcement personnel.

Training of agency personnel, especially supervisors, is also a necessity for a successful peer support program. Such training serves a three-fold purpose: (1) to ensure that personnel can recognize early warning signs of other personnel in distress; (2) to ensure that all personnel know methods and protocols by which peer support personnel can be involved in providing assistance; and (3) to emphasize the importance of peer support to all personnel within the agency.

An important part of the training process is the effective "selling" of the program to agency personnel. An active program of education and training must foster awareness of the program's existence. It becomes imperative that agency personnel ultimately understand the relevance of the program to meeting their needs and see seeking services of the program as a viable option to dealing with their personal problems.

EMPLOYEE ASSISTANCE PROGRAMS

Although their evolution has been slow in development, a variety of employee assistance services are currently available within police departments.[139] The growth of **employee assistance programs (EAPs)** in the law enforcement field can be traced back to the early 1950s.[140] Many programs, such as those initiated in Boston, New York, and Chicago, were created to deal primarily with alcohol abuse.

In the 1970s, agencies such as the Los Angeles Sheriff's Office, the Chicago Police Department and the San Francisco Police Department expanded their programs to include problems not related to alcohol. In 1980, mental health professionals began providing personal and job-related counseling services to FBI personnel. Mental health professionals were also used to assist FBI managers with a variety of employee-related matters.

By 1986, many of the largest police departments in the United States had formed "stress units" or other sections to provide help for officers having personal or occupational difficulties. In the early 1990s, the U.S. Customs Service provided stress-management training for both its supervisory and its nonsupervisory personnel throughout the country.[141] The majority of law enforcement agencies with 100 or more officers now have written policies regarding providing counseling assistance services for their officers.[142]

Chapter Summary

Summary by Learning Objective

1. **Describe the perceptual, cognitive, and behavioral disturbances resulting from an officer's use of deadly force.**

   Distortions of time perception are most common, with the majority of officers recalling the shooting event as occurring in slow motion, although a smaller percentage reported experiencing he even as speeded up; (1) *sensory distortions* are also common and most often involve *tunnel vision*, in which the officer is sharply focused on one particular aspect of the visual field, typically the suspect's gun or weapon, which blocking out everything in the periphery; (2) *a sense of helplessness* may occur during the shooting exchange, but this may be underreported due to the potential stigma attached; (3) *disturbances in memory* are commonly reported in shooting exchanges. About half of these involve impaired recall for at least some of the events during the shooting; the other half involve impaired recall for at least part of the officer's own actions; this, in turn, may be associated with going-on-automatic response.

2. **Explain why police officers are often reluctant to seek mental health services even when they need it.**

   Unfortunately, sometimes for good reasons, police officers have traditionally shunned mental health services, perhaps perceiving its practitioners as ferrets and shills who are out to dig up dirt that their departments can use against them. More commonly, the idea of needing any kind of "mental help" implies weakness, cowardice, and lack of ability to do the job. In the environment of many departments, some officers realistically fear censure, stigmatization, ridicule, thwarted career advancement, and alienation from colleagues if they are perceived as the type who "folds under pressure." Still others in the department, who may have something to hide, may fear a colleague "spilling their guts" to the clinician and thereby blowing the malefactor's cover.

3. **Discuss some of the questions that police administrators must address in terms of drug use by police officers.**

   What positions will the employee unions and other employee organizations take if drug testing is proposed? (1) Who should be tested for drugs? Entry-level officers? Regular officers on a random basis? All officers before they are promoted? Personnel assigned to high-profile units, such as bomb disposal and special tactics and response? (2) When does a supervisor have "reasonable suspicion" of a subordinate's drug use?: (a) Who should collect the urine or other specimens and under what conditions? (b) What criteria or standards should be used when selecting a laboratory to conduct the police department's drug testing program? (c) What disciplinary action is appropriate when officers are found to have abused drugs? (d) What duty does an employer have to rehabilitate employees who become disabled as a result of drug abuse?

4. **Examine the role the police psychologist plays in a psychological health wellness initiative.**

   The police psychologist will ideally have the ability to work with training units on developing wellness trainings at the primary prevention level on a variety of topics that can help officers to buffer stress. In addition to standard stress management and suicide awareness trainings, officers can often make use of primary prevention training to develop skills in the areas that can lead to a cumulative buildup of stress for an officer. At the secondary level, the police psychologist who successfully collaborates with other department officer resources, such as peer support teams, chaplaincy programs, and veteran assistance and reintegration programs, will enhance the connections between these efforts and the psychologist's services.

5. **Discuss the benefits and weaknesses in the use of peer support personnel.**

Benefits:

Provide instant credibility and ability to empathize; assist fellow employees who are reluctant to talk with mental health professionals; recommend the program to other employees by attesting credibility to its confidentiality and concern; provide immediate assistance due to accessibility; detect incipient problems because of their daily contact with co-workers; are less expensive than professionals.

Weaknesses:

Cannot provide the professional care that licensed mental health practitioners can; may try to offer full-scale counseling they are not equipped to provide; may be rejected by employees who want to talk only with a professional counselor; may be avoided by employees because of a fear that problems will not be kept confidential; require time, effort, and patience to screen, train and supervise; may expose themselves and the department to legal liability.

Chapter Review Questions

1. Describe the three stages of the general adaptation syndrome, as described by Hans Selye.

2. According to recent medical findings, what is the relationship between diseases of adaption and stress?

3. What are the major characteristics of the type A personality, type B personality, type C personality, type D personality, and the workaholic?

4. The FBI provides four categories of situations that present a threat to law enforcement officers. What are they?

5. What recommendations were made regarding the postshooting interview of police officers?

6. Why have police officers traditionally shunned mental health services, even when it's obvious they need help?

7. What is posttraumatic stress disorder (PTSD)?

8. How does cumulative career traumatic stress (CCTS) differ from posttraumatic stress disorder?

9. What is the Vicarious Trauma Toolkit?

10. Alcohol-related problems manifest themselves in police officers in a number of ways. What are they?

11. What are some early warning interventions police departments can employ to minimize the risk of hiring officers who might engage in domestic violence?

12. What are the indicators that an officer may be contemplating suicide?

13. What are some of the services police departments can make available to reduce the incidents of domestic violence among their officers?

14. If a police supervisor notices a pattern of controlling or abusive behavior in an officer, what steps should be taken?

15. What role can the police psychologist play in the health and wellness of individual law enforcement officers in an agency?

16. What characteristics should managers be looking for in those members of their agency who are interested in participating on a peer support team?

Critical Thinking Exercises

1. **Cumulative Career Traumatic Stress (CCTS).** During the past 50 years, there has been a surge of public and professional attention focused on the psychological and physical effects of continuous exposure to traumatic stressors. Typically, individuals exposed to chronic traumatic stress or the victims of abuse for a period of time in their lives are those who are exposed to traumatic experiences or events as part of their profession. This includes individuals who serve as emergency personnel and are often continually exposed to high levels of traumatic stress and intense emotional experience resulting from exposure to traumatic and critical events. You should answer the following questions:

a. How does CCTS differ from posttraumatic stress disorders?

b. What are the behavioral manifestations of CCTS?

c. In what ways may CCTS adversely affect a police officer in his or her job performance?

d. What intervention counseling strategies would you suggest be employed in dealing with someone suffering from CCTS?

2. **Homicide-Suicide in Police Families.** Police officers work in an occupational culture premised

on violence. Evidence indicates that they are more prone to violence at home and that the rate of domestic violence is significantly higher for police officers than it is for the general population. You should answer the following questions:

a. What are the factors that are most likely to make police officers disproportionately at risk for homicide-suicide?

b. What is the best course of action a police department can take to anticipate and then prevent homicide-suicide among its police officers?

c. Of what value is a domestic violence lethality assessment scale for first responders having calls involving police officers who are involved in domestic violence situations?

Key Terms

alarm stage
cumulative career stress
domestic violence lethality assessment form
employee assistance programs (EAPs)
exhaustion stage
general adaptation syndrome (GAS)

peer support program
posttraumatic stress disorder (PTSD)
resistance stage
stress
stress inoculation activities
suicide by cop (SbC)

type A personality
type B personality
type C personality
type D personality
Vicarious Trauma Toolkit
workaholic personality

Endnotes

[1] For a complete review of the most current programs and techniques being used by police departments see: Leonard Territo and James D. Sewell, *Stress Management in Law Enforcement*, 4th edition (Durham, NC: Carolina Academic Press, 2019).

[2] H. Selye, *Stress Without Distress* (Philadelphia: Lippincott, 1974), p. 60.

[3] Carter Coudriet, "Bill Gates Again World's Second-Richest Person After One Day Behind Arnault," Real Time Net Worth, Forbes Magazine.https://www.forbes.com/profile/bill-gates/?sh=35a4d9a9689f/(accessed December 4, 2020)

[4] Selye, *Stress Without Distress*, pp. 35–39.

[5] Anthony L. Komaroff, "The Usual Suspect," *Newsweek* 25 (February 2009), pp. 52–53.

[6] Ibid.

[7] Ibid.

[8] M. Farouk Radwan, "A B C D Personality Types," Segen's Medical Dictionary, 2012.

[9] Ibid.

[10] Ibid.

[11] Gerard J. Sloan and Jean M. Casey, "Police Work Addiction: A Cautionary Tale," *FBI Law Enforcement Bulletin* (June 2003), pp. 13–17. (This discussion of workaholics was adapted from this article.)

[12] B. E. Robinson, *Chained to the Desk* (New York, NY: New York University Press, 1998), p. 3.

[13] B. Killinger, *Workaholics: The Respectable Addicts* (Buffalo, NY: Firefly Books, 1991).

[14] Supra note 1, 75.

[15] Supra note 2.

[16] W. E. Oates, *Confessions of a Workaholic* (New York, NY: Abingdon Press, 1971), p. 4.

[17] Supra note 2, 6.

[18] For a complete review of the ways in which these various factors have deadly effects upon police officers see: Territo and Sewell, *Stress Management in Law Enforcement.*

[19] John M. Violanti and Fred Aron, "Police Stressors: Variations in Perceptions Among Police Personnel," *Journal of Criminal Justice* 23, No. 3 (1995), pp. 287–294.

[20] Ibid., p. 347.

[21] FBI "Crime in the United States, 2019," Expanded Homicide Data, Uniform Crime Report, Department of Justice, FBI, Washington, DC, 2019.

[22] C. Baruth, "Pre-Critical Incident Involvement by Psychologists," in J. T. Reese and H. A. Goldstein, eds., *Psychological Services for Law Enforcement* (Washington, DC: USGPO, 1986), pp. 413–417.

[23] Alexis Artwohl, "Perceptual and Memory Distortion During Officer-Involved Shootings," *FBI Law Enforcement Bulletin* (October, 2002), pp. 18–24. (This discussion was adapted from this article.)

[24] Ibid., pp. 18–24.

[25] Laurence Miller, "Police Deadly Force Encounters: Psychological Reactions and Recovery Patterns," in Leonard Territo and James D. Sewell, eds., *Stress Management in Law Enforcement*, 4th edition (Durham, NC: Carolina Academic Press, 2019), pp. 116–117.

[26] Bruce A. Rodgers, *Psychological Aspects of Police Work: An Officer's Guide to Street Psychology* (Springfield, IL: Charles C Thomas, 2006).

[27] D. A. Grossman, *On Killing: The Psychological Cost of Learning to Kill in War and Society* (New York: Little, Brown, 1996).

[28] E. Nielsen, E. "Traumatic Incident Corps: Lessons Learned," in J. Reese, J. Horn, and C. Dunning, eds., *Critical Incidents in Policing* (Washington DC: US Government Printing Office, 1991), pp. 221–226.

[29]M. B. Williams. "Impact of Duty-Related Death on Officers' Children: Concepts of Death, Trauma Reactions, and Treatment," in J. M. Violanti and D. Paton, eds., *Police Trauma: Psychological Aftermath of Civilian Combat* (Springfield: Charles C Thomas, 1999), pp. 159–174.

[30]Suicide by Cop (SbC) refers to an individual who wishes to die and uses the police to affect the goal. For more details, see D. B. Kennedy, R. J. Homant, and R. T. Hupp, "Suicide by Cop," *FBI Law Enforcement Bulletin* (August, 1998), pp. 21–27.

[31]W. Anderson, D. Swenson, and D. Clay, *Stress Management for Law Enforcement Officers* (Englewood Cliffs: Prentice Hall, 1995).

[32]M. A. Borders and C. H. Kennedy, "Psychological Interventions After Disaster in Trauma," in C. H. Kennedy and E. A. Zillmer, eds., *Military Psychology: Clinical and Operational Applications* (New York: Guilford, 2006).

[33]Grossman, *On Killing.*

[34]L. Miller, *Practical Police Psychology: Stress Management and Crisis Intervention for Law Enforcement* (Springfield, IL: Charles C Thomas, 2006).

[35]L. G. Bender and others, *Critical Issues in Police Discipline: Case Studies* (Springfield, IL: Charles C Thomas, 2005).

[36]Geoffrey P. Alpert, John Rivera, and Leon Lott, "Working Toward the Truth in Officer-Involved Shootings: Memory, Stress, and Time," *FBI Law Enforcement Bulletin*, May 2012, pp. 5 and 6.

[37]D. Grossman and B. K. Siddle, *Critical Incident Amnesia: The Physiological Basis and the Implications of Memory Loss During Extreme Survival Situations* (Millstadt, IL: PPCT Management Systems, 1998).

[38]Alpert, op cit., pp. 5–6.

[39]Alexis A. Artwohl, "Perceptual and Memory Distortions in Officer-Involved Shootings," *FBI Law Enforcement Bulletin*, October 2002, p. 22.

[40]Laurence Miller, "Police Deadly Force Encounters: Psychological Reactions and Recovery Patterns," in Leonard Territo and James D. Sewell, eds., *Stress Management in Law Enforcement* (Durham, NC: Carolina Academic Press, 2019), pp. 127–129.

[41]D. J. Max, "The Cop and the Therapist." *New York Times*, December 3, 2000, pp. 94–98.

[42]L. Miller, "Tough Guys: Psychotherapeutic Strategies with Law Enforcement and Emergency Services Personnel. *Psychotherapy* 32 (1995), pp. 592–600.

[43]L. Miller, "Law Enforcement Traumatic Stress: Clinical Syndromes and Intervention Strategies," *Trauma Response* 6, No. 1 (2000), pp. 15–20.

[44]L. Miller, *Practical Police Psychology: Stress Management and Crisis Intervention for Law Enforcement* (Springfield, IL: Charles C Thomas, 2006e).

[45]L. Miller, "Police Officer Stress: Syndromes and Strategies for Intervention," in S. M. F. Clevenger, L. Miller, B. A. Moore, and A. Freeman, eds., *Behind the Badge: A Psychological Treatment Handbook for Law Enforcement Officers* (New York: Routledge, 2015), pp. 202–221.

[46]L. Miller, *The Psychology of Police Deadly Force Encounters: Science, Practice, and Policy* (Springfield, IL: Charles C Thomas, 2017 in press).

[47]L. Miller, *Practical Police Psychology: Stress Management and Crisis Intervention for Law Enforcement* (Springfield, IL: Charles C Thomas, 2006e).

[48]L. Miller, *METTLE: Mental Toughness Training for Law Enforcement* (Flushing, NY: Looseleaf Law Publications, 2008b).

[49]D. Rudofossi, *Working with Traumatized Police Officer-patients: A Clinician's Guide to Complex PTSD Syndromes in Public Safety Personnel* (Amityville, NY: Baywood, 2007).

[50]D. Rudofossi, *Death, Value and Meaning Series. A Cop Doc's Guide to Public Safety Complex Trauma Syndrome: Using Five Police Personality Styles* (Amityville, NY, US: Baywood Publishing Co., 2009).

[51]H. Toch, *Stress in Policing* (American Psychological Association, Washington, DC, 2002)

[52]T. H. Blau, *Psychological Services for Law Enforcement* (New York: Wiley, 1994).

[53]S. M. Conn, *Increasing Resilience in Police and Emergency Personnel* (New York: Routledge, 2018).

[54]L. Miller, *Practical Police Psychology: Stress Management and Crisis Intervention for Law Enforcement* (Springfield, IL: Charles C Thomas 2006e).

[55]L. Miller, *METTLE: Mental Toughness Training for Law Enforcement* (Flushing, NY: Looseleaf Law Publications, 2008b).

[56]C. S. Fullerton, J. E. McCarroll, R. J. Ursano, and K. M. Wright, "Psychological Responses of Rescue Workers: Firefighters and Trauma," *American Journal of Orthopsychiatry* 62 (1992), pp. 371–378.

[57]S. R. Wester and J. Lyubelsky, "Supporting the Thin Blue Line: Gender-Sensitive Therapy with Male Police Officers," *Professional Psychology: Research and Practice* 36 (2005), pp. 51–58.

[58]J. Janik, "What Value Are Cognitive Defenses in Critical Incident Stress," in J. Reese, J. Horn, and C. Dunning, eds., *Critical Incidents in Policing* (Washington DC: US Government Printing Office, 1991), pp. 149–158.

[59]Durham et al., 1985 [does not appear anywhere else in the article].

[60]V. E. Henry, *Death Work: Police, Trauma, and the Psychology of Survival* (New York: Oxford University Press, 2004).

[61]S. E. Taylor, J. V. Wood, and R. R. Lechtman, "It Could Be Worse: Selective Evaluation as a Response to Victimization," *Journal of Social Issues* 39 (1983), pp. 19–40.

[62]Janik, in *Critical Incidents in Policing*, pp. 149–158.

[63]Mark Thompson, "Unlocking the Secrets of PTSD," *Time*, March 26, 2015, p. 42.

[64]Laurence Miller, "Stress, Traumatic Stress, and Posttraumatic Stress Syndromes," in Leonard Territo and James D. Sewell, eds., *Stress Management in Law Enforcement*, 3rd edition (Durham, NC: Carolina Academic Press, 2013), pp. 13–16.

[65]American Psychiatric Association, *Diagnostic and Statistical Manual of Mental Disorders*, 4th edition, text revision (Washington DC: American Psychiatric Association, 2000); C. L. Meek, "Evaluation and assessment of post-traumatic and other stress-related disorders," in C. L. Meek, ed., *Post-traumatic Stress Disorder: Assessment, Differential Diagnosis, and Forensic Evaluation* (Sarasota, FL: Professional Resource Exchange, 1990), pp. 9–61; H. Merskey, "Psychiatric Aspects of the Neurology of Trauma," *Neurologic Clinics* 10 (1992), pp. 895–905; L. Miller, "Civilian Posttraumatic Stress Disorder: Clinical Syndromes and Psychotherapeutic Strategies," *Psychotherapy* 31 (1994), pp. 655–664; L. Miller, *Shocks*

to the System: Psychotherapy of Traumatic Disability Syndromes (New York: Norton, 1998); L. Miller, "Ego Autonomy and the Healthy Personality: Psychodynamics, Cognitive Style, and Clinical Applications," Psychoanalytic Review 85 (1998), pp. 423–448; L. Miller, Counseling Crime Victims: Practical Strategies for Mental Health Professionals (New York: Springer, 2008); L. Miller, Criminal Psychology: Nature, Nurture, Culture (Springfield, IL: Charles C Thomas, 2012); H. C. Modlin, "Traumatic Neurosis and Other Injuries," Psychiatric Clinics of North America 6 (1983), pp. 661–682; R. S. Parker, Traumatic Brain Injury and Neuropsychological Impairment: Sensorimotor, Cognitive, Emotional, and Adaptive Problems in Children and Adults (New York: Springer-Verlag, 1990); H. Weiner, Perturbing the Organism: The Biology of Stressful Experience (Chicago: University of Chicago Press, 1992).

[66]L. Miller, Freud's Brain: Neuropsychodynamic Foundations of Psychoanalysis (New York: Guilford, 1991); L. Miller, Criminal Psychology: Nature, Nurture, Culture (Springfield, IL: Charles C Thomas, 2012).

[67]Ellen K. Marshal, "Cumulative Career Traumatic Stress (CCTS): A Pilot Study of Traumatic Stress in Law Enforcement," in Leonard Territo and James D. Sewell, eds., Stress Management in Law Enforcement, 3rd edition (Durham, NC: Carolina Academic Press, 2013), pp. 372–373.

[68]C. Alexander, "Police Psychological Burnout and Trauma," in J. M. Violanti and D. Paton, eds., Police Trauma: Psychological Aftermath of Civilian Combat (Springfield, IL: Charles C Thomas, 1999), pp. 54–64; P. Bonifacio, The Psychological Effect of Police Work (New York: Plenum Press. 1991); J. T. Fennel, "Psychological Stress and the Peace Officer, or Stress—A Cop Killer," in G. Henderson, ed., Police Human Relations (Springfield, IL: Charles C Thomas, 1981), pp. 170–179.

[69]T. H. Blau, Psychological Services for Law Enforcement (New York: John Wiley & Sons, 1974); C. M. Davidson, I. Fleming, and A. Baum, "Post-traumatic Stress as a Function of Chronic Stress and Toxic Exposure," in C. E. Figley, ed., Trauma and Its Wake: Traumatic Stress, Theory, Research, and Intervention (New York: Brunner/Mazel, 1986), pp. 57–77; C. M. Dunning, "Postintervention Strategies to Reduce Police Trauma: A Paradigm Shift," in J. M. Violanti and D. Paton, eds., Police Trauma: Psychological Aftermath of Civilian Combat (Springfield, IL: Charles C Thomas, 1999), pp. 269–289.

[70]Michael Rizzo and C. J. Scallon, "Burnout, Stress and Fatigue: How the Vicarious Trauma Toolkit Provides Public Safety Agencies National Resources and Promising Practices," in Leonard Territo and James D. Sewell, eds., Stress Management in Law Enforcement, 4th edition (Durham, NC: Carolina Academic Press, 2019), pp. 514 and 515.

[71]Ibid.

[72]For a more detailed discussion of the Vicarious Trauma Toolkit (VTT) see: https://vtt.ovc.ojp.gov/

[73]Rizzo and Scallon, "Burnout, Stress and Fatigue," p. 515.

[74]James Genovese, "Alcoholism Among Law Enforcement Personnel: Its Unique Challenges," The Milestone Group, n.d., http://www.milestonegroupnj.com/?page_id=348 (accessed May 31, 2015).

[75]Ibid.

[76]Ed. Donovan, "Programs Need Caring Touch to Reach Law Enforcement Enforcers," Alcoholism & Drug Abuse Weekly 6, No. 35 (1994), pp. 3–4.

[77]P. Shanahan, A Study of Attitudes and Behaviours: Working in the Police Force Today and the Role of Alcohol (Sydney, Australia: Elliott and Shanahan Research, 1992); Elliot and Shanahan Research, Alcohol and Other Drugs in the Workplace: A Benchmark Survey Comparing two Victorian Organisations (Sydney: Elliot and Shanahan Research, 1994); J. M. Violanti, "Coping in a High Stress Police Environment," Journal of Social Psychology (1993), pp. 717–730; J. D. Davey, P. L. Obst, and M. C. Sheehan, "It Goes with the Job: Officers' Insights into the Impact of Stress and Culture on Alcohol Consumption Within the Policing Occupation," Drugs, Education, Prevention, and Policy 8, No. 2 (2001), pp. 141–149.

[78]R.C. Lumb and R. Breazeale, "Police Officer Attitudes and Community Policing Implementation: Developing Strategies for Durable Organizational Change," Policing and Society 13, No. 1 (2002), pp. 91–106.

[79]Davey et al., "It Goes with the Job."

[80]Ibid.

[81]A. Bandura, Social Foundations of Thought and Action: A Social Cognitive Theory (Englewood Cliffs, NJ: Prentice-Hall, Inc., 1986).

[82]Newlun v. State Department of Retirement Systems, 770 P. 2d 1071 (Wash. App. 1989). Relatedly, McElrath v. Kemp, 27 Govt. Emp. Rel. Rep. (BNA) 605 (D.D.C. 1989), deals with an alcoholic employee who had relapses after being treated and was terminated but was reinstated later.

[83]Will Aitchison, The Rights of Police Officers, 3rd edition (Portland, OR: Labor Relations Information System, 1996), pp. 228–233, is the source of the information in this paragraph, with restatement by the authors.

[84]Delaraba v. Nassau County Police, 632 N. E. 2d 1251 (N.Y. 1994).

[85]Cincinnati, Ohio Police Department, Administrative Regulation #52 (06/07), Manual of Rules and Regulations: 15.110 Alcohol and Drug Testing of Department Personnel, revised 02/26/15, p. 6, http://www.cincinnati-oh.gov/police/assets/File/Procedures/15110.pdf (accessed June 11, 2015).

[86]Melanie Hamilton, "Special Report on Police Suicide: Cop Killer," Police 27, No. 5 (2003), pp. 18.

[87]Breaking the Silence on Law Enforcement Suicides, Community Oriented Policing Services, U.S. Department of Justice, July 2013, pp. 4–17. The remainder of the discussion of police suicide was obtained from this document with modifications.

[88]Ibid.

[89]Office of the Surgeon General and National Action Alliance for Suicide Prevention, 2012 National Strategy for Suicide Prevention: Goals and Objectives for Action (Washington, DC: U.S. Department of Health and Human Services, September 2012, p. 19), http://www.armyg1.army.mil/hr/suicide/docs/10%20Sep%202012_NSSP_Final.pdf (accessed June 11, 2015).

[90]L. D. Lott, "Deadly Secrets: Violence in the Police Family," FBI Law Enforcement Bulletin, November 1995, pp. 12–15. This discussion was adapted from this article.

[91]Police Officer Domestic Violence, Concepts and Issues Paper, Developed by the International Association of Chiefs of Police, April 1999.

[92]These definitions may be limited to the definitions in the laws of each state. While not the focus of this policy, other forms of family violence (e.g.,child and elder abuse) should be addressed in a parallel manner.

[93]In order to access the Model Policy on Police Officer Domestic Violence, as well as the accompanying Concepts and Issues Paper log onto www.theiacp.org and click on Publications (under Information Resources) then scroll down to "Police Officer Domestic Violence Information," this will lead you to links to each of the two documents.

[94]Kerry Karaffa, Linda Openshaw, Julie Koch, Hugh Clark, Cynthia Harr, and Chris Stewart, "Perceived Impact of Police Work on Marital Relationships," in Leonard Territo and James D. Sewell, eds., *Stress Management in Law Enforcement* (Durham, NC: Carolina Academic Press, 2019), pp. 255 and 256.

[95]R. Borum and C. Philpot, "Therapy with Law Enforcement Couples: Clinical Management of the 'High-Risk Lifestyle,'" *Journal of Family Therapy* 21 (1993), pp. 122–135.

[96]L. A. Gould, "A Longitudinal Approach to the Study of Police Personality: Race/Gender Differences," *Journal of Police and Criminal Psychology* 15 (2000), pp. 41–51.

[97]V. E. Kappeler, R. D. Sluder, and G. P. Alpert, *Forces of Deviance: Understanding the Dark Side of Policing* (Long Grove, IL: Waveland Press, Inc. 1998).

[98]V. E. Henry, *Death Work: Police, Trauma, and the Psychology of Survival* (New York, NY: Oxford University Press. 2004), p. 13.

[99]Borum and Philpot, "Therapy with Law Enforcement Couples."

[100]E. Kirschman, M. Kamena, and J. Fay, *Counseling Cops: What Clinicians Need to Know* (New York, NY: The Guilford Press, 2013).

[101]A. M. Moller-Leimkuhler, "Barriers to Help-Seeking by Men: A Review of Sociocultural and Clinical Literature with Particular Reference to Depression," *Journal of Affective Disorders* 71 (2002), pp. 1–9.

[102]S. R. Wester and J. Lyubelsky, "Supporting the Thin Blue Line: Gender-sensitive Therapy with Male Officers," *Professional Psychology: Research and Practice* 36 (2005), pp. 51–58.

[103]L. D. Lott, "Deadly Secrets: Violence in the Police Family," *FBI Law Enforcement Bulletin* 64 (1995), pp. 12–16.

[104]L. N. Blum, *Force under pressure: How cops live and why they die* (New York, NY: Lantern Books, 2000).

[105]P. Finn, V. Talucci, and J. Wood, "On-the-Job-Stress in Policing: Reducing It and Preventing It," *National Institute of Justice Journal* (2000), pp. 18–24.

[106]Kirschman et al., *Counseling Cops.*

[107]L. Miller, "Police Families: Stresses, Syndromes, and Solutions," *The American Journal of Family Therapy* 35 (2007), pp. 21–40.

[108]E. Kirschman, *I Love a Cop: What Police Families Need to Know*, 2nd edition (New York, NY: The Guilford Press, 2007).

[109]A. Mikkelsen and R. Burke, "Work-Family Concerns of Norwegian Police Officers: Antecedents and Consequences," *International Journal of Stress Management* 11 (2004), pp. 429–444.

[110]R. H. Woody, "Family Interventions with Law Enforcement Officers," *The American Journal of Family Therapy* 34 (2006), p. 99.

[111]H. Toch, "Stress in Policing," (Washington, DC: American Psychological Association, 2002).

[112]L. Miller, "Police Families: Stresses, Syndromes, and Solutions." *The American Journal of Family Therapy* 35 (2007), pp. 21–40.

[113]André Ivanoff, "Police Suicide Study Recommends Additional Training, Counseling," *Columbia University Record* 20, No. 2 (September 16, 1994), http://www.columbia.edu/cu/record/record2002.14.html (accessed June 11, 2015).

[114]Domestic Violence Protocol for Law Enforcement, Police Chiefs Association of Santa Clara County, California, March 2014, p. 55.

[115]John M. Violanti, "Homicide-Suicide in Police Families: Aggression Full Circle," in Leonard Territo and James D. Sewell, eds., *Stress Management in Law Enforcement*, 4th edition (Durham, NC: Carolina Academic Press, 2019), pp. 288 and 289.

[116]E. Pam, "Police Homicide-Suicide in Relation to Domestic Violence," in D. C. Sheehan and J. I. Warren, eds., *Suicide and Law Enforcement* (Washington, DC: US Government Printing Office, 2001).

[117]Ibid.

[118]K. Romanov, M. Hatakka, E. Kesinen, H. Laaksonen, J. Kaprio, R. J. Rose, and M. Koskenvuo, "Self-Reported Hostility and Suicidal Acts, Accidents, and Accidental Deaths: A Prospective Study of 21,443 Adults Aged 25–59," *Psychosomatic Medicine* 56 (1994), pp. 328–336.

[119]N. L. Farberow, H. K. Kang, and T. A. Bullman, "Combat Experience and Postservice Psychosocial Status as Predictors of Suicide in Vietnam Veterans," *Journal of Nervous and Mental Disease* 178 (1990), pp. 32–37.

[120]J. D'Angelo, "Addicted to Violence: The Cycle of Domestic Abuse Committed by Police Officers," in D.C. Sheehan, ed., *Domestic Violence by Police Officers* (Washington, DC: US Government Printing Office, 2000), pp. 149–161.

[121]John M. Violanti, "Homicide-Suicide in Police Families: Aggression Full Circle," *International Journal of Emergency Mental Health* 9, No. 2(2007), pp. 101–102.

[122]Karen L. Amendola, David Weisburd, and Edwin E. Hamilton, *The Impact of Shift Length in Policing on Performance, Health, Quality of Life, Sleep, Fatigue, and Extra-Duty Employment*, Final Report Submitted to the National Institute of Justice, December 12, 2011. (This discussion was adapted from the abstract of this document appearing on page 4.)

[123]John M. Violanti, "Effects of Shift Work on Officer Safety and Wellness," in Leonard Territo and James D. Sewell, eds., *Stress Management in Law Enforcement*, 4th edition (Durham, NC: Carolina Academic Press, 2019), pp. 174 and 175.

[124]B. J. Vila and D. J. Kenney, "Tired Cops: The Prevalence and Potential Consequences of Police Fatigue," (pdf, 6 pages) *National Institute of Justice Journal* 248 (2002), pp. 16–21.

[125]U.S. Department of Justice, Office of Justice Programs, "How Fatigue Affects Health" (Washington, DC: National Institute of Justice, The Research, Development, and Evaluation

Agency of the U.S. Department of Justice, January 6, 2009), http://www.ojp.usdoj.gov/nij/topics/law-enforcement/stress-fatigue/health.htm (accessed May 5, 2010).

126 John M. Violanti, "Effects of Shift Work on Officer Safety and Wellness," in Leonard Territo and James D. Sewell, eds., *Stress Management in Law Enforcement*, 4th edition (Durham, NC: Carolina Academic Press, 2019), p. 173.

127 B. J. Vila, *Tired Cops: The Importance of Managing Police Fatigue* (Washington, DC: Police Executive Research Forum, 2000).

128 D. J. Dijk, D. F. Neri, J. K. Wyatt, J. M. Ronda, E. Riel, A. Ritz-De Cecco, R. J. Hughes, A. R. Elliott, G. K. Prisk, J. B. West, and C. A. Czeisler, "Sleep, Performance, Circadian Rhythms, and Light-Dark Cycles During Two Space Shuttle Flights," *American Journal of Physiology* 281 (2001), pp. R1647–R1663.

129 Christof Koch, "Sleeping While Awake," *Scientific American* (November 1, 2016), http://www.scientificamerican.com/article/sleeping-while-awake.

130 Many of these factors are identified in Robert W. Shearer, "Police Officer Stress: New Approaches for Effective Coping," *Journal of California Law Enforcement* 25, No. 4 (1991), pp. 97–104.

131 Scott Allen, Christine Jones, Frances Douglas, and Daniel Clark, "A Comprehensive Approach to Destigmatizing Mental Health Issues in Law Enforcement," *The Police Chief* 81 (March 2014), pp. 34–38.

132 Ibid., p. 36.

133 Ibid.

134 Ibid., p. 37.

135 James D. Sewell, "Elements of a Successful Peer Support Program," in Leonard Territo and James D. Sewell, eds., *Stress Management in Law Enforcement*, 4th edition (Durham, NC: Carolina Academic Press, 2019), pp. 473–479. (This information was originally prepared for Grant 2012-CK-WX-K019 awarded by the U.S. Department of Justice, Office of Community Policing Services, to St. Petersburg College Regional Community Policing Institute. However, it has been modified for this book.)

136 Peter Finn and Julie Esselman Tomz, "Using Peer Supporters to Help Address Law Enforcement Stress," *FBI Law Enforcement Bulletin* 67, No. 5 (1998), pp. 10–18.

137 Robyn Robinson and Patricia Murdoch, *Establishing and Maintaining Peer Support Programs in the Workplace*, 3rd edition (Elliot City, MD: Chevron Publishing, 2003).

138 Ibid.

139 Max Bromley and William Blount, "Criminal Justice Practitioners," in William R. Hutchison, Jr., and William G. Emener, eds., *Employee Assistance Programs* (Springfield, IL: Charles C Thomas, 1997), p. 400.

140 J. T. Reese, *The History of Police Psychological Service* (Washington, DC: U.S. Department of Justice, 1987).

141 C. Milofsky, E. Astrov, and M. Martin, "Stress Management Strategy for U.S. Customs Workers," *EAP Digest* 14, No. 6 (1994), pp. 46–48.

142 Bromley and Blount, "Criminal Justice Practitioners," p. 401.

## CHAPTER FOURTEEN

LEGAL ASPECTS OF POLICE ADMINISTRATION

Learning Objectives

1. Explain the three general categories of torts. How do they differ?
2. Define "acting under the *color of state law*." How does this statement relate to Section 1983 actions?
3. Explain and describe a *Bivens* action.
4. List and describe the negligence theories applicable to police supervision and management.
5. Describe procedural and substantive due process.
6. Explain a *Brady* violation?
7. Explain when rules infringing on the free speech of officers might be upheld.
8. Describe the circumstances in which an officer may use deadly force?
9. List the four elements that must be proven in order to sue the police for negligence in a high-speed pursuit.
10. Describe how a department can reduce liability in high-speed pursuits.
11. Relate the focus of most training programs regarding emotionally disturbed persons.
12. Describe the balancing test related to alcohol and drug testing in the police workplace.

INTRODUCTION

ONE OF THE PRIMARY characteristics of our nation's law is its dynamic nature. Rules of law are developed by legislation, regulation, and by court decision. In this chapter, we talk about the fluid nature of our lawmaking system as it applies to police and police executives. It is important to understand the legal aspects of police administration because (1) police officers understand criminal law because they deal with it on a daily basis; however, they have a relatively poor understanding of civil law; (2) civil law addresses private injuries that lead to liability and subsequent monetary damages due to negligence; (3) the major areas of litigation against the police fall under Title 42, U.S. Code, Section 1983, and usually involve negligent hiring, negligent assignment and retention, negligent supervision, and/or negligent training; (4) police officers have constitutional rights that are enjoyed by all citizens within the United States including the rights and liberties that address privacy, free speech, search and seizure, and self-incrimination; and (5) most civil actions against the police arise from the misuse of firearms and deadly force, use of for[ce]...

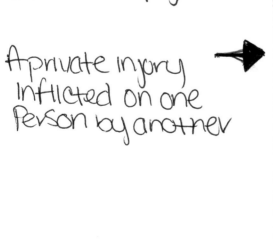

A tort is Pg. 465

A private injury inflicted on one person by another →

...as an authoritative basis for action. Police administrators should always seek qualified legal counsel whenever they face a problem or a situation that appears to have legal ramifications. A primary objective of this chapter is to make police administrators more capable of quickly determining when they face such a problem or situation.

LIABILITY FOR POLICE CONDUCT

One of the most troubling legal problems facing police officers and police departments in recent years has been the expanded impact of civil and criminal **liability** for alleged police misconduct. It is commonplace to hear police spokespersons complain that law enforcement officers are widely hampered by the specter of being undeservedly sued for alleged improper performance of duty. Although one can argue that the magnitude of police misconduct **litigation** may be overstated, the amount of litigation appears to be increasing and is apparently accompanied by a movement toward larger monetary damage awards.

Basic Types of Police Tort Actions[1]

Law can be divided into two parts: criminal law and civil law. Police officers and other criminal justice practitioners are generally more familiar with criminal law because they deal with it on a daily basis. Each "piece" of the law addresses a specific type of action. For instance, criminal law focuses on crimes, whereas civil law applies to torts.

Barrineau defines a crime as a public injury, an offense against the state, punishable by fine and/or imprisonment. It is the violation of a duty one owes the entire community; the remedy for a breach of such duty is punishment (fine or imprisonment) imposed by the state. Crimes are exemplified in the FBI Crime Index (generally speaking, they are murder, aggravated assault, robbery, rape (sexual battery), burglary, larceny over $200.00, auto theft, and arson), wherein each crime is composed of specific elements and has an affixed penalty.

On the other hand, a **tort** is a private injury inflicted on one person by another person for which the injured party may sue in a civil action. Such action may bring about liability that leads to an award of money damages. Tort actions encompass most personal injury litigation. The injured party initiates the lawsuit and is called the **plaintiff**. The sued person is called the **defendant** and is often referred to as the *tort feasor*.[2]

One example of a tort action brought against police officers is an allegation of criminal behavior, such as assault and battery (police brutality). More commonly, they are civil actions brought about by claims of false arrest, false imprisonment, invasion of privacy (through illegal search and seizure), negligence, defamation, or malicious prosecution.[3] Most of the suits against police officers fall into three general categories: negligence torts, intentional torts, and constitutional torts.[4]

NEGLIGENCE TORTS

Our society imposes a duty on individuals to conduct their affairs in a manner that does not subject others to an unreasonable risk of harm. This responsibility also applies to criminal justice practitioners. If a police officer's conduct creates a situation recognizable as dangerous by a reasonable person in like circumstances, the officer will be held accountable to those injured as a result of his or her conduct.

In **negligence** suits, defendants are not liable unless they foresaw or should have anticipated that their acts or omissions would result in injury to another. The key in negligence suits is the standard of the reasonably prudent person, also referred to as **reasonableness**. Was the care provided at the same standard that a reasonably prudent person would observe under a given set of circumstances?[5] Examples of negligence involving police officers often arise from pursuit driving incidents in which the officers violate common traffic laws, such as speeding, running a stop sign, or failing to control their vehicles, resulting in the injury or death of another person.

INTENTIONAL TORTS

An intentional tort is the voluntary commission of an act that to a substantial certainty will injure another person. It does not have to be negligently done to be actionable. Intentional torts are therefore *voluntary* and *deliberate* acts, such as assault, false arrest, false imprisonment, and malicious prosecution.

CONSTITUTIONAL TORTS

The duty to recognize and uphold the constitutional rights, privileges, and immunities of others is imposed on police officers and other criminal justice practitioners by statute, and violation of these guarantees may result in a specific type of civil suit. Most of these suits are brought under Title 42, U.S. Code, Section 1983, in federal court.

In our system of government, there are court systems at both federal and state levels. However, federal courts are intended to be courts of somewhat limited jurisdiction and generally do not hear cases involving private, as opposed to public, controversies unless a question of federal law is involved or the individuals involved in the lawsuit are residents of different states. Even

then, the suit can be decided in a state court if both parties to the controversy agree to have the dispute settled there. As a result, most tort suits have been brought in state courts.

Title 42, U.S. Code, Section 1983

A major trend in the area of police misconduct litigation is the increase in the number and proportion of these suits that are being brought in federal court. The most common legal vehicle by which federal courts can acquire jurisdiction of these suits is commonly referred to as a **1983 action**. This name derives from the fact that these suits are brought under the provisions of Section 1983 of Title 42 of the U.S. Code. This law, passed by Congress in the aftermath of the Civil War and commonly referred to as the Civil Rights Act of 1871, was designed to secure the civil rights of the recently emancipated slaves. It prohibits depriving any person of life, liberty, or property without due process of law. Specifically, Section 1983 states:

> Every person who, under color of any statute, ordinance, regulation, custom, or usage of any State or Territory, subjects, or causes to be subjected, any citizen of the United States or any other person within the jurisdiction thereof to the deprivation of any rights, privileges, or immunities secured by the Constitution and laws, shall be liable to the party injured in an action at law, suit in equity, or other proper proceeding for redress.[6]

After 90 years of relative inactivity, Section 1983 was resuscitated by the U.S. Supreme Court in the landmark case *Monroe v. Pape* (1961).[7] In this case, the Court concluded that, when a police officer is alleged to have acted improperly (e.g., in conducting an illegal search), that officer can be sued in federal court by alleging that he or she deprived the searched person of his or her constitutional right under the Fourth Amendment to be free from unreasonable searches and seizures. A critical element of Section 1983 is that the violation must have occurred while the officer was acting "under color of State law"—that is, while the officer was on duty and acting within the scope of employment as a sworn police officer. Unless there is direct personal participation by police supervisory personnel, they are not generally liable for Section 1983 damages, even if there are

---

Quick Facts: Americans for Effective Law Enforcement (AELE)

The Americans for Effective Law Enforcement (AELE) is a nonprofit agency founded in 1967, and today it is one of the most highly respected sources of legal advice and training for police officers. The AELE holds workshops on legal issues that affect police officers and administrators, such as the use of force, sudden and in-custody death, and discipline and internal investigations. Officers and administrators who attend special training courses are eligible to earn Certified Litigation Specialist credentials, which honor those who pursue litigation-related studies and increase

their understanding of public agency litigation. The AELE is also a resource for officers and administrators facing legal action. The agency can offer legal advice or refer officers to local attorneys or expert witnesses. The AELE also offers monthly newsletters, including the *Law Enforcement Liability Reporter* and the *AELE Monthly Law Journal*, both available on its website at www.aele.org. The website also offers an extensive law library, organized by topics of interest to law enforcement officers.

broad allegations of failure to properly train and supervise police officers who are liable in the Section 1983 lawsuit.[8]

Bivens Action

Section 1983 is the primary civil rights statute involved in litigation against municipal and state police officers. However, the statute rarely applies to federal agents (such as officials of the FBI, Secret Service, and Drug Enforcement Administration) because its terms require that the plaintiff be acting under "color of State law." Federal officials can be sued under one of two complaints. The first is a **Bivens action** for a violation of constitutional rights. The *Bivens* action applies only to the individual, not to the government. The second is a tort action against the United States under the Federal Tort Claim Act (FTCA).[9] Both actions can be combined into one lawsuit.

Essentially, a *Bivens* action is a judicially created counterpart to a Section 1983 tort action. The Supreme Court has permitted suits against federal officials (not, however, against the United States) for violations of constitutional rights that would otherwise be the subject of a Section 1983 action against a state or local officer. Its name is derived from the landmark case *Bivens v. Six Unknown Federal Narcotics Agents* (1971), wherein the Supreme Court held that a cause of action for violation of the Fourth Amendment (search and seizure clause) can be inferred from the Constitution itself.[10] Hence, federal courts have jurisdiction to hear federal question cases involving suits against federal employees in their individual capacities.[11]

In summary, there are three basic types of tort actions that can be brought against police for misconduct: traditional state law torts, Section 1983 torts, and *Bivens* torts. It is important to understand these classifications because the type of tort action brought will determine who can be sued, what kind of behavior will result in liability, and which immunities might be available to the defendants.

WHO CAN BE SUED?

At common law, police officers were held personally liable for damage caused by their own actions that exceeded the boundaries of permissible behavior. This rule applied even if the officer was ignorant of the boundary established by the law. As unjust as many of such results may seem, the rule establishes one of the traditional risks of policing.

A more difficult question concerns whether the supervisors of the officer and/or the government unit by which he or she is employed can be sued for that individual's misbehavior. Generally, an effort to impose liability on supervisors for the tortious conduct of their employees is based on the common-law doctrine of *respondent superior*. That doctrine, also called **vicarious liability**, developed along with the growth of industrial society and reflected a conscious effort to allocate risk to those who could afford to pay for the complaint of damages.[12]

As could be expected, the growing area of negligence as a Section 1983 cause of action has caused concern within police supervisory ranks. The courts have supported several negligence theories applicable to police supervision and management. The following is a discussion of important negligence cases and subsequent legal development in this area.[13]

Negligent Hiring

The law enforcement administrator and the local government entity have a duty to "weed out" those obviously unfit for police duty. Further, the courts have held that an employer must exercise a reasonable standard of care in selecting persons who, because of the nature of their employment (such as policing), could present a threat of injury to members of the public.[14] Further, in 1997, the Supreme Court held that law enforcement and government entities could be held liable under Section 1983 if the plaintiff's injury was an obvious and direct consequence of a bad hiring decision on the part of an agency. In this case, an officer was hired by a local police department *after* it was discovered that the officer had lied on his original application and had been convicted of a felony, barring him from police service under state regulatory agencies.[15]

Negligent Assignment, Retention, and Entrustment

Police administrators who know or should have known of individual acts or patterns of physical abuse, malicious or threatening conduct, or similar threats against the public by officers under their supervision must take immediate action. If an internal investigation sustains an allegation of such serious conduct by an officer, appropriate action by a police chief could be suspension—followed by assignment to a position with little or no public contact—or termination. A police chief failing to take decisive action when required could be held liable for future injuries caused by the officer. In addition, entrustment of the "emblems of office" (e.g., a badge, a gun, or a nightstick) subjects a municipality and appropriate administrators of a municipal agency to liability whenever injury results from the known misuse of such emblems. In other words, administrators and supervisors have a duty to supervise errant officers properly.[16]

Negligent Direction and Supervision

The administrator and/or supervisor have the duty to develop and implement appropriate policies and procedures. Therefore, a written manual of policies and procedures is an absolute must. This manual must provide clear instruction and direction regarding the position of police officer, be widely disseminated, and be accompanied with training so that all officers understand the significance of the manual.[17] Further, the courts have held that supervisors must "take corrective steps" where evidence indicates that official policy is being abridged and/or the public is being placed at an "unreasonable risk" because of the actions of a police officer. Inaction on the part of the police supervisors and/or administrators is enough to establish negligence if there is a pattern or custom of police abuse and accession to that custom by police supervisors and/or administrators.[18] For example, the failure of a police sergeant to order

FIGURE 14.1 ▶ Police chases often end an accident. Here, a U.S. Capitol police officer gave chase to a female driver who rammed the barrier gate in an attempt to gain illegal entry to the White House. Shots were fired and the suspect was killed; the officer was also injured but did recover. © B Christopher/Alamy Stock Photo

the termination of a high-speed pursuit of a minor traffic violator through a congested downtown business area that results in serious personal injuries or deaths to members of the public is sure to bring litigation based on an allegation of failure to supervise (see Figure 14.1).

Negligent Training

The local unit of government and the administrator or supervisor of a police department have an affirmative duty to train their employees correctly and adequately. In a recent landmark case (*City of Canton v. Harris*), the Supreme Court limited the use of inadequate police training as a basis for Section 1983 actions. The Court held that inadequate police training may form the basis for a civil rights claim "where the failure to train amounts to **deliberate indifference** to the rights of persons with whom the police come in contact" and that such official indifference amounts to "policy or custom." Therefore, it is incumbent on the plaintiff to prove that the training program is inadequate as to the expected duties of an officer and that the deficiency of training is closely related to the ultimate injury.[19]

The two areas of negligence that have been the greatest sources of litigation under Section 1983 in recent years have been negligent supervision and negligent training. Incidents arising out of the use of deadly force and use of force, and pursuit driving have certainly raised significant questions regarding training and are covered later in this chapter.

A second difficult question with respect to who may be sued for damages caused by police misconduct concerns the liability of the police department and the government unit of which the department is a part.[20] Individuals pursuing damage claims under Section 1983 against local government officials and state officials who are sued in their individual rather than official capacities will have to overcome the defense available to such

parties of "qualified, good-faith immunity." Such official immunities are not creatures of Section 1983; they arose from traditional, common-law protections that were historically accorded to government officials. Basically, the good-faith immunity doctrine recognizes that public officials who exercise discretion in the performance of their duties should not be punished for actions undertaken in good faith. Imposing liability on public officials in such situations would inevitably deter their willingness to "execute ... [their] office with the decisiveness and the judgment required by the public good."[21]

Over the years, the courts have struggled to develop a test for good faith. In 1975, the Supreme Court articulated such a test that considered both the official's state of mind when he or she committed the act in question (the subjective element) and whether the act violated clearly established legal rights (the objective element).[22]

However, seven years later, the Supreme Court decided that the subjective element of the text should be dropped, leaving only the standard of **objective reasonableness**.[23] Now a court must determine only whether the law at issue was "clearly established" at the time the challenged action occurred. Furthermore, if the plaintiff's allegations do not show a violation of clearly established law, a public official asserting good-faith immunity will be entitled to dismissal of the lawsuit before it proceeds further.[24]

The immunities available to state and local officials are generally designed to protect individuals from liability arising out of the performance of official acts. With the Eleventh Amendment providing similar protection to the states, the question of the immunity of a local government was raised. Initially, the Supreme Court concluded that Congress had not intended to apply 42 U.S.C. 1983 to municipalities, thereby giving municipalities what is called "absolute," or unqualified, immunity from suit.[25] On reexamination of this issue in the 1978 case *Monell v. Department of Social Services*,[26] the Court decided that Congress had intended for Section 1983 to apply to municipalities and other local government units. The Court further concluded that, although certain other immunities were not available to an individual who was responsible for Section 1983 violations. The Court made it clear that local government entities will be liable under Section 1983 only when that government's policies or official procedures can be shown to be responsible for the violation of federally protected rights.

Unfortunately, the *Monell* decision did not fully articulate the limits of municipal liability under Section 1983. The result has been considerable litigation to establish when a deprivation of federally protected rights actually results from enforcement of a municipal policy or procedure and at what point an official's actions can be fairly treated as establishing the offending policy.[27]

More recently, the Supreme Court has held that "single acts of police misconduct" do not, by themselves, show that a city policy was involved in the alleged tortious act.[28] Generally, a plaintiff must show a pattern of negligence or deliberate indifference by the agency.[29]

SCOPE OF LIABILITY

In general, state tort actions against police officers provide a greater scope of liability than do the Section 1983 and *Biven* suits. That is, in tort actions under state law, a greater range of behavior is actionable.

The types of torts under state law that commonly are brought against police officers can be categorized as intentional or negligence torts. An intentional tort is one in which the defendant knowingly commits a voluntary act designed to bring about certain physical consequences. For example, the tort of assault is the purposeful infliction on another person of a fear of a harmful or offensive contact. If X points an unloaded pistol at Y, who does not know the pistol is unloaded, X has created in Y an apprehension that Y is about to experience a harmful contact from a bullet. X voluntarily lifts the pistol and points it at Y, fully expecting that it will cause Y to be apprehensive about being hit by a bullet. Thus, X is liable to Y for the intentional tort of assault.

The tort of negligence involves conduct that presents an unreasonable risk of harm to others that, in turn, is the proximate cause of an actual injury. Whereas in an intentional tort, the consequences following an act must be substantially certain to follow, in the tort of negligence the consequences need only be foreseeable. When X drives through a stop sign, even if unintentionally, and hits the side of Y's car, X's behavior presents an unreasonable risk of harm to others and is the proximate cause of the damage to Y's car. Although X would have been negligent for "running the stop sign" even without hitting the other car, he or she would not have committed the tort of negligence in that no injury was caused.

The Supreme Court has limited the scope of liability in reference to negligence as an element of deprivation of constitutional rights in Section 1983 and *Bivens* actions. In *Daniels v. Williams* (1986), the petitioner sought to recover damages as a result of injuries sustained in a fall caused by a pillow negligently left on the stairs of the city jail in Richmond, Virginia. The Court held that the petitioner's constitutional rights were "simply not implicated by a negligent act of an official causing *unintentional* loss or injury to life, liberty, or property."[30] This case has had a profound impact on limiting Section 1983 and *Bivens* actions to intentional torts; hence, the sheer volume of such cases has significantly decreased in past years. It is important to note, however, that the Supreme Court "has not changed the rule that an intentional abuse of power, which shocks the conscience or which infringes a specific constitutional guarantee such as those embodied in the Bill of Rights," still implicates serious liability.[31]

As noted earlier in this chapter, many lawsuits against police officers are based on the intentional torts of assault, battery, false imprisonment, and malicious prosecution.[32] Suits against police officers for intentional torts can be brought as state tort actions, Section 1983 suits, or *Bivens* suits. Although suits against police officers for negligence torts can be brought as state tort actions, the issue is not so clear-cut with regard to Section 1983 and *Bivens* suits.

Generally, damages assessed in civil litigation for negligence are ordinary (compensatory) damages that are paid by the employing government entity (or its liability insurance carrier) on behalf of the defendant officer. Therefore, as a general rule, the individual employee is not required to pay ordinary damages that result from a civil negligence suit. This is so because, normally when government employees are performing their duties within the scope of employment, they are deemed to be the agents or representatives of the employing agency and therefore not personally liable for their acts. However, where punitive damages are assessed for conduct that is grossly negligent, wanton, or reckless, individuals who have been responsible for such acts are personally liable and, generally speaking, these assessments are not absorbed by the employing government entity or by liability insurance. Thus, law enforcement employees who act in reckless, wanton, or grossly negligent manners will be subject to and personally liable for punitive damage awards.

In this constantly changing area of the law, the Supreme Court has established a rule that police are entitled to "qualified" immunity for acts made in good faith that can be characterized as "objectively reasonable." In *United States v. Leon*,[33] the Court focused on the objectively ascertainable question of whether a reasonably well-trained officer would have known that the act committed was illegal. Subsequently, following that logic the Court held that, if police personnel are not "objectively reasonable" in seeking an arrest warrant, they can be sued personally for many damages, despite the fact that a judge has approved the warrant. In fact, the Court stated that a judge's issuance of a warrant will not shield the officer from liability if a "well-trained officer in [his] position would have known that his affidavit failed to establish probable cause and that he should not have applied for the warrant."[34] However, the Court modified its position in a later case when an FBI agent conducted a warrantless search of a resident's home for a fugitive by holding that an alleged unlawful warrantless search of an innocent third party's home does not create an exception per se to the general rule of qualified immunity. The Court held that the relevant question is whether a reasonable officer would have believed the search lawful once the clearly established law and the information possessed by the agent were taken into consideration and, if the answer is yes, whether the agent is protected by qualified immunity from civil liability.[35] This standard was upheld in 2001 and 2009.[36]

As with many areas of the law, lower courts have somewhat modified this landmark decision. In 1987, a U.S. district court found that qualified immunity protects all but the plainly incompetent or those who knowingly violate the law.[37] And in 1992, a federal court ruled that law enforcement officers are protected by immunity from "bad guesses in gray areas" but are liable for "transgressing obviously bright lines of law,"[38] essentially leading the way for protective immunity for officers honestly attempting to do their job. This was affirmed again in *Pearson et al. v. Callahan* in 2009.[39] Still, whereas public officials exercising discretion (e.g., judges and prosecutors) have absolute immunity for their unreasonable acts, the only person in the system left to sue for damages for a wrongdoing will be the police officer, unless his or her acts can be attributed to the policy or procedural custom established by the employing government agency.

TRENDS IN TORT LIABILITY FOR POLICE SUPERVISORS AND ADMINISTRATORS

Although there has been a reluctance to hold police supervisors and administrators liable for the misbehavior of their subordinate officers, some courts have been increasingly willing to extend liability to these officials where the plaintiff has alleged negligent employment, improper training, or improper supervision.[40]

Under negligent employment, a police official can be held liable for his or her failure to conduct a thorough investigation of a prospective employee's suitability for police work if he or she hires an applicant with a demonstrated propensity "toward violence, untruthfulness, discrimination, or other adverse characteristics."[41] Of course, under this theory, the injuries suffered by the plaintiff would have been the result of the negative trait that had been demonstrated by the individual before employment as an officer. If the negative trait is not demonstrated until after employment, a party injured by the officer may be able to sue a police official successfully for negligently retaining the officer or otherwise failing to take appropriate remedial action. In some

circumstances, the official may not be able to dismiss an officer who has demonstrated unfitness, but the official still might be found liable if he or she negligently assigns the unfit officer to duties where the public is not protected adequately from the officer's particular unfitness. Finally, the official is potentially liable for negligently entrusting a revolver to an officer who has a history of alcohol or other drug abuse or the misuse of a weapon.

Suits alleging that police officials have improperly trained a police officer have been particularly successful where firearms were involved in inflicting the injury. Courts have stressed that the "law imposes a duty of extraordinary care in the handling and use of firearms"[42] and that "public policy requires that police officers be trained in the use of firearms on moving and silhouette targets and instructed when and how to use them."[43] Suits alleging lack of necessary training are also becoming increasingly successful in cases involving the use of physical force to overcome resistance, the administration of first aid, pursuit driving, and false arrest.[44]

Another emerging theory of recovery against police officials is an allegation of failure to properly supervise or direct subordinate officers. This type of suit is typically brought where officials have failed to take action to rectify a recurring problem exhibited in the conduct of police operations by subordinates.[45] An interesting development in this area concerns the situation

FIGURE 14.2 ▶ Police officers responding to hostage and/or barricaded suspect situations often require specialized training in crisis negotiations and the use of firearms. In this case, a man was taken hostage at a local television station while the suspect shouted demands from the control room. After hours of skilled negotiations by local detectives, the hostage was released without harm, avoiding potential liability stemming from the incident. (Roberto Pfeil/AP Images)

in which the police department issues a written directive that establishes a policy more stringent than the law requires. In several cases involving such a situation, the courts have held that the written directive establishes a standard of conduct to which police officers must conform or face the possibility of civil liability for their actions.[46]

The last area to which courts have given increased attention concerns cases in which it is alleged that the police officer failed to provide needed medical care to people with whom the officer came in contact.[47] Although the incidents giving rise to such allegations can occur in a variety of situations, they seem to occur with greatest frequency when the plaintiffs have been in custody or have been mistakenly thought to be intoxicated when they actually were suffering from a serious illness. These cases are based on four categories of recovery: (1) failure to recognize and provide treatment for injury, (2) failure to provide treatment on request, (3) failure to provide treatment on recognition of an injury, and (4) negligent medical treatment. Suits in the first three categories may allege either negligent conduct or intentional behavior. Court rulings suggest that police officers who ignore classic signs of illness, such as a heart attack, are depriving arrestees of their Fourteenth Amendment right to receive medical care as a pretrial detainee. To prove that an officer is subject to liability because he or she failed to provide medical treatment requires a showing that the officer acted with deliberate indifference to the serious medical needs of an arrestee.[48] Recent cases have affirmed that holding.[49] Some courts have held that police officers do not have a duty to care for injured persons with whom they come in contact,[50] although such a holding is not likely to occur when the injured person is in their custody.

MISUSE OF FIREARMS AND DEADLY FORCE

There is no topic that weighs heavier on the mind of police administrators today than that of the misuse of firearms and deadly force by police officers. Because of the 2014–2020 incidents in Ferguson, Missouri; Charleston, South Carolina; Cincinnati, Ohio; Baltimore, Maryland; Minneapolis, Minnesota; Louisville, Kentucky, and more, departments are keenly aware that not only is there tragedy in the lives lost due to potential misuse of force, but there is also massive liability. It's not small thing that departments (and by proxy, their communities) have to pay out millions in damages due to such events, but even worse, such questionable shootings erode trust, put officers on edge, and can affect police/community relations for years.

To be clear, in the spate of high-profile officer shootings that made the news between 2014 and 2020, not all of them involved explicit wrongdoing by the officers at the time of the shootings. In a few cases, the officers perhaps failed to deescalate a situation properly, leading to a confrontation where deadly use of force was necessary. In other cases, the facts

backed the officers' actions. It's also worth noting that use of force is applied in about 1.9 percent of the nearly 40 million police/citizen contacts over the period of one year.[51] However, even one "bad" police shooting is too many—and, hence, there are far too many.

Unfortunately, in the past, police officer training has too often focused on the issue of how to shoot and not when to shoot. Many times when a problem does arise relating to the use of deadly force, it is not that the officer failed to qualify at the police pistol range or that the weapon malfunctioned but that the officer made an error in judgment.

The police chief and his or her legal counsel must question whether this error in judgment was merely a human error resulting from the pressure of the moment or whether the police department failed to provide proper guidelines to the officer. If proper guidelines were made available to the officer, did the police department incorporate these guidelines into its formal training program?

Let us examine what areas a use-of-deadly-force policy should cover and the formalized mechanisms by which officers can be trained to understand this policy.

Tennessee v. Garner (1985)

Until 1985, the courts nationwide had not established a standard of law regarding the use of deadly force. Likewise, law enforcement agencies had not developed a standard, written directive that would establish national guidelines. While most large police agencies had established use-of-deadly-force policies, those policies certainly were not consistent in form or content.[52]

On March 27, 1985, all this started to change when the Supreme Court ruled unconstitutional a Tennessee law that permitted police officers to use deadly force to effect an arrest.[53] The Tennessee statute on the police use of deadly force provided that if, after a police officer has given notice of an intent to arrest a criminal suspect, the suspect flees or forcibly resists, "the officer may use all the necessary means to effect the arrest."[54] Acting under the authority of this statute, a Memphis police officer shot a juvenile, Garner, as he fled over a fence at night in the backyard of a house he was suspected of burglarizing. The officer ordered him to halt, but he failed to stop. The officer then fired a single shot and killed him. The officer used deadly force despite being "reasonably sure" that the suspect was unarmed and believing him to be 17 or 18 years old and of slight build. The suspect's father subsequently brought an action in federal district court, seeking damages under 42 U.S.C.S. 1983 for asserted violations of his son's constitutional rights. The district court held that the statute and the officer's actions were unconstitutional. The court of appeals reversed and the Supreme Court affirmed the Court of Appeals' decision.

The Supreme Court held that the Tennessee statute was unconstitutional insofar as it authorized the use of deadly force against, as in this case, an apparently unarmed, nondangerous, fleeing suspect. Such force may not be used unless necessary to prevent the escape and the officer has probable cause to believe that the suspect poses a significant threat of death or serious physical injury to the officer or others. The Court's reasoning was as follows:

1. Apprehension by the use of deadly force is a seizure and subject to the Fourth Amendment's reasonableness requirement. To determine whether such a seizure is reasonable, the extent of the intrusion on the suspect's rights under that amendment must be balanced against the government interests in effective law enforcement. This balancing process demonstrates that, notwithstanding probable cause to seize a suspect, an officer may not always do so by killing him or her. The use of deadly force to prevent the escape of all felony suspects, whatever the circumstances, is constitutionally unreasonable.

2. The Fourth Amendment, for purposes of this case, should not be construed in light of the Common-Law rule allowing the use of whatever force is necessary to effect the arrest of a fleeing felon. Changes in the legal and technological context mean that the rule is distorted almost beyond recognition when literally applied to criminal situations today.

Whereas felonies were formerly capital crimes, few felonies are now. Many crimes classified as misdemeanors or nonexistent at Common Law are now felonies. Also, the Common-Law rule developed at a time when weapons were rudimentary. The varied rules adopted in the states indicate a long-term movement away from the Common-Law rule, particularly in the police departments themselves; thus, that rule is a dubious indication of the constitutionality of the Tennessee statute. There is no indication that holding a police practice, such as that authorized by the Tennessee statute, will severely hamper effective law enforcement.

3. While burglary is a serious crime, the officer in this case could not reasonably have believed that the suspect—young, slight, and unarmed—posed any threat. Nor does the fact that an unarmed suspect has broken into a dwelling at night automatically mean he or she is dangerous.

Box 14.1: Defining Key Terms in U.S. Code 42, Section 1983 Litigation Cases

Two key terms are used in Section 1983 litigation cases against police agencies. It is important to understand that these terms have been defined through the landmark Supreme Court cases, *Graham v. Connor* (1989) and *City of Canton v. Harris* (1989)

Objective Reasonableness: What is "objective reasonableness" from a legal perspective? Quite simply, it is the Constitutional standard to which an officer's actions will be evaluated. In *Graham v. Connor*, the Supreme Court set forth several guidelines to be taken into consideration when evaluating an officer's use of force. These evaluation guidelines include one overarching direction to anybody who chooses to opine about an officer's force response:

The calculus of reasonableness must embody allowance for the fact that police officers are often forced to make split-second judgments—in circumstances that are tense, uncertain, and rapidly evolving—about the amount of force that is necessary in a particular situation.

After a person understands this one overarching premise, the following questions may be used to help determine if an officer's actions were "objectively reasonable?":

- Would another officer, with the same or similar training and experience, facing the same or similar circumstances, act in a same or similar manner?
- In Graham, the SCOTUS provided several other factors to examine when evaluating an individual officer's use of force. What was the severity of the crime at issue? What was the physical threat to the officer? What was the level of resistance offered by the suspect? Did the suspect comply with lawful orders presented by the officer? What did the officer believe at the action time force was use? And, what were the actions or inactions of the suspect at the time deadly force was used, understanding that the suspect's actions dictate the level of force to be used?
- Without the benefit of 20/20 hindsight or "Monday morning quarterbacking" and based solely on the totality of the facts known to the officer at the time the force was applied, were his or her actions proper under established law at the time and were his or her actions reasonable in light of the facts and circumstances confronting him or her.

Deliberate Indifference: In order to hold a city or other governmental body liable for the acts of its police officers, it is not enough to simply show that an individual officer violated another person's constitutional rights while acting in the course and scope of their employment. For instance, an officer uses unreasonable force such as striking a noncombative suspect in the head with a heavy flashlight while the person is handcuffed. Indeed, the Court, primarily in *City of Canton v. Harris* (1989), has incorporated a theory of liability that holds that municipalities, and other government entities are liable only if they have the following:

1. an official policy, practice or custom, or lack sufficient policy to guide and direct officers while performing their work;
2. of which the policymaker, in most cases, the Chief of Police or Sheriff knew or should have known would violate the Constitution or a person's Constitutional right(s); following our example, the Chief of Police developed a policy indicating that officers were authorized to use heavy flashlights like batons, and there was no policy or training that prohibit striking a person in the head with said weapons. Surprisingly, there was no policy that prohibited striking noncombative suspects while in handcuffs;
3. the custom, practice, or policy was "deliberately indifferent" to the probability that the policy violates the Constitution. Continuing with the above example, is it reasonable to believe that officers should be trained in using a baton versus a heavy flashlight? That officers should be prohibited by policy from striking noncombative suspects in handcuffs? And most importantly, that the failure to have such training and policy violates a suspect's Constitutional rights;

4. the policy, practice, or custom, of failure to have an enforced policy was the "moving force" leading to the Constitutional violation; that is, the plaintiff must show that the action was taken with a requisite degree of culpability and must demonstrate a direct causal link between the action and the deprivation of a person's federal right. Having a policy that authorizes police officers to strike a person in the head with a flashlight, having no proper training in the use of a baton versus a heavy flashlight, and failing to prohibit officers from striking a handcuffed suspect directly led to the suspect suffering brain injury while in the custody of the police.

Sources: Board of County Commissioners of Bryan County, Oklahoma v. Brown, 520 U.S. 397 (1997) City of Canton v. Harris, 389 U.S. 378 (1989) Edward Flosi, "Use of Force: Defining 'Objectively Reasonable' Force, PoliceOne, February 8, 2017. Flanagan v. City of Dallas, Tex., 48 F.Supp.3d 941 (2014) Graham v. Connor, 490 U.S. 386 (1989) Kisela v. Hughes, 584 U.S. ____ (2018) Karen Blum, "Making Out the Monell Claim Under Section 1983," Touro Law Review, Vol. 24: No. 3, Article 2 (2012) Merritt v. County of Los Angeles, 875 F. 2d 765 (1989) Victor Kappeler, "How Ojvteive is the 'Objective Reasonableness' Standard in Police Brutality Cases?" EKU Police Studies Online December 10, 2013.

Graham v. Connor (1989)

Another landmark case related to the use of force started innocuously enough: Dethorne Graham, a maintenance worker in Charlotte, North Carolina, asked a friend to drive him to a convenience store when he felt a diabetic episode creeping up on him. He went into the store in search of orange juice to offset an insulin reaction. However, once inside the store, he left without purchasing anything after seeing that many people were waiting in line. A patrol officer (Officer M.S. Connor) sitting outside the convenience store saw him dart from the store and into the car and suspected that Graham had just committed a robbery. The car was stopped, and despite the pleas of the driver and Graham, the officer asked the suspects to stay inside the car as he investigated. Disobeying a lawful order of a police officer, Graham got out of the car and ran around it twice, he the lost consciousness as he sat on a nearby curb. Believing him to be drunk, officers subsequently handcuffed Graham. During the incident, Graham gained consciousness and begged officers to check his wallet for an ID card that detailed his medical condition.

Their reaction was to slam his head (face first) into the hood of the car. Graham suffered injuries that included a broken foot, cuts, bruising, an injured forehead, and a long-term ringing in his ear. He sued under Section 1983, and the Supreme Court ruled lower courts had errored in applying the Due Process Clause, instead of the Fourth Amendment, in analyzing an excessive force claim: "Because the Fourth Amendment provides an explicit textual source of constitutional protection against this sort of physically intrusive government conduct, that Amendment, not the more generalized notion of substantive due process, must be the guide for analyzing these claims."[55] Hence, the Court explained that, "As in other Fourth Amendment contexts…the 'reasonableness' inquiry in an excessive force case is an objective one: the question is whether the officers' actions are 'objectively reasonable' in light of the facts and circumstances confronting them, without regard to their underlying intent of motivation."[56] The Court went on to establish a major three-prong test of reasonableness for use-of-force cases in the future:

- First, what was the severity of the crime that the officer believed the suspect to have committed or was committing at the time of the encounter?
- Second, did the suspect present an immediate threat to the safety of officers or the public?
- Third, was the suspect actively resisting arrest or attempting to escape?

Graham also offered one of the most important narratives about police use of force, from Chief Justice William Rehnquist:

The reasonableness of a particular use of force must be judged from the perspective of a reasonable officer on the scene, rather than with the 20/20 vision of hindsight. The calculus of reasonableness must embody allowance for the fact that police officers are often forced to make split-second judgments—in circumstances that are tense, uncertain and rapidly evolving—about the amount of force that is necessary in a particular situation. The test of reasonableness is not capable of precise definition or mechanical application.[57]

It is interesting, using the perspective on reasonableness to consider some of the more prominent use-of-force cases from the past several years. Though the emotion from these cases may run high—the *Graham* decision makes clear that the standard of reasonableness emanates from *the officer's perception at the time of the crisis that results in the shooting.* See Box 14.2.

In August 2019, the State of California passed a new police use-of-force law that restricts when a police officer can used deadly force. Most importantly, the law attempts to eliminate the concept of "reasonableness" as determined from the officer's perception at the time of the crisis. Rather, the new California law restricts lethal force by an officer to when it is necessary in "defense of human life" as perceived by a "reasonable officer" and based on the "totality of circumstances" at the time of the use of deadly force. It also emphasizes "deescalation" as effective alternative to lethal force. Essentially, the California law attempts to usurp the Supreme Court of the United States by making officers prove that there was an "imminent threat of death or serious bodily injury," before using deadly force.[58]

Police will then be evaluated on the facts they knew leading up their actions. The new California law is often referred to as the "Stephon Clark Law" stemming from an egregious shooting of a 22-year-old black man (Stephon Clark) who was shot and killed in his grandmother's backyard (in March 2018) after Sacramento police officers said they mistook the cell phone in his hand for a gun. California Assembly Bill 393, or *The California Act to Save Lives*, has been called a compromise law between law enforcement lobbying groups and civil rights organizations.[59]

The new law that took effect on January 1, 2020, has far reaching ramifications for officer prosecutions stemming from a use-of-force incidents and the civil liability that may ensue from such actions. There are also significant issues that relate to internal police policy and training that must be immediately implemented for adherence to the new law.[60] The California law is currently untested at the U.S. Supreme Court level. It is possible that the *Graham v. Connor* decision will be revised, especially in the wake of the rash of high-profile, use-of-force incidents that have plagued our country—but as of this writing (early 2020), it remains the dominant test for use-of-force considerations.

Box 14.2: The Tragic Consequences of "Swatting"

"Swatting" is defined as making a hoax call to Emergency 9-1-1 designed to draw an immediate and large response from law enforcement, usually a "**S**pecial **W**eapons **A**nd **T**actics—SWAT" team. The calls are usually described by the caller as serious in nature, often involving a threat of imminent danger to the occupants at a specific location, and/or threats to responding officers. In many cases, the identity of the caller is hidden from authorities through the use of common "spoofing" technology that not only hides the name of the original perpetrator, but also makes the call look like it is actually originating from the victim's phone or address.

The consequences of "swatting" calls are obvious. Officers, as well as victims, are placed in harm's way as police rush to immediate calls for help. Officers have died in traffic accidents as they responded to would-be emergency situations; and innocent elderly victims have tragically suffered heart attacks as SWAT teams suddenly descended on their residence.[61]

In the past, most targets of "swatting" calls were aimed at well-known actors and musicians, as well as various politicians. FBI officials indicate that "swatting" calls have dramatically increased in the last 10 years, from 400 in 2011 to more than 1,000 today.[62] More importantly, the targets are no longer just celebrities but have now become common individuals involved in all sorts of disputes and arguments. The problem has even crept into the sporting world, as a group of hoaxers called in a bomb threat to a large sporting event, causing a long delay of the televised game as well as the evacuation of an entire hotel.[63] This kind of dangerous online harassment has drawn the ire of Massachusetts Congresswoman Katherine Clark (herself a victim of a swatting attack in 2016). She has introduced legislation to make "swatting" a federal crime.[64]

The Andrew Finch Case

On December 28, 2017 at approximately 5:00 in the afternoon, 28-year-old Andrew Finch was relaxing and enjoying the post-holidays with his family, when a SWAT team from the Wichita (Kansas) Police Department descended on his home…ten seconds later, he was fatally shot in the head! The events of this horrific incident were set in motion by "Call of Duty-WWII" gamers squabbling over a minor bet of $1.50. One of those gamers, Tyler Barriss, called the Wichita 9-1-1 Center from Los Angeles, and reported that a man was suicidal, had killed his father, and was holding others hostage at gunpoint… at the supposed address in Wichita of a second gamer. However, the address was wrong… the gamer did not live at that address … Andrew Finch and his family did.

A 10-person Wichita SWAT team, and 3 members of the Sedgwick County Sheriff's Office responded to the emergency call. Andrew Finch exited the house in alarm with his hands in the air, however during the first ensuing seconds, he became "startled," dropped his hands and reached into his waistbelt, a police sniper (believing that Finch was going for a weapon) fired from 50 yards away, striking Andrew Finch in the head and killing him. Immediately after the shooting, members of the family "surrendered" to police with their hands up, were cuffed, and forced to wait in below-freezing temperatures for over an hour, as bewildered police officers attempted to sort out their mistake.[65] The original prank caller, 25 year-old Tyler Barriss was soon arrested in LA. Investigation revealed that he had conducted other 'swatting calls' numerous times in the past. Barriss was charged with multiple felonies including involuntary manslaughter and cyberstalking. He plead guilty to these charges and was sentenced to 20 years in prison.

The family of Andrew Finch filed a federal (42 U.S.C., Section 1983) excessive force claim against the Wichita police officer and the City of Wichita Police Department alleging that Andrew Finch was "unjustifiably shot and killed" less than 10 seconds after encountering the police.[66] Further, court documents revealed that officers did indeed, arrive at the scene in response to a hoax ('swatting') call and that the Wichita Police Department failed to recognize the call as a hoax, failed to de-escalate the situation, and failed to properly train and supervise WPD officers during a critical incident.[67] Hence, the family seeks monetary damages through the lawsuit, in an amount exceeding $25 million for the loss, pain and suffering of an innocent father and son.

While the tragic events of December 28, 2017 cannot be undone and the life of Andrew Finch cannot be saved, police agencies today are now taking steps to prevent these types of incidents from happening in the future; such actions include increasing awareness of the crime of "swatting" to the general public and making sure that their officers and specifically their tactical team(s) are aware of the phenomenon. Another step aimed at reducing liability and increasing officer/citizen safety includes the development of an alert database that flags potential addresses as well as past addresses where victims of "swatting" have occurred. The database is then shared with agencies in a wide jurisdiction of these potential targets so that emergency responders can be aware that the call may well be a "swatting" hoax before they arrive at the scene.[68] (David Ryder/Getty Images)

Evaluation of Written Directives

As suggested earlier, when an alleged wrongful death case is being evaluated, the adequacy of the police department's policy must be considered. Generally speaking, an adequate policy addresses the following topics: defense of life and fleeing felons, juveniles, shooting at or from vehicles, warning shots, shooting to destroy animals, secondary guns, off-duty weapons, and registration of weapons (see Figure 14.3).

DEFENSE OF LIFE AND FLEEING FELONS

State laws and departmental policies still remain fairly diverse even after *Garner*, although with narrower bounds. No longer can these provisions leave officers virtually untethered, as in the extreme case of one small American town whose only gun guidance to its officers was the homily "Never take me out in anger; never put me away in disgrace."[69]

The range of firearms policies hereafter is likely to be from the "defense-of-life" regulations, which permit shooting only to defeat an imminent threat to an officer's or another person's life. At the other extreme, a minimal compliance with the *Garner* rule permits shooting at currently nonviolent, fleeing suspects who the officer reasonably believes committed a felony involving the threat but not the use of violence. Both approaches are currently employed by many large police departments.

The defense-of-life approach significantly reduces the possibility of wrongful death allegations. Policy cannot be developed for every instance in which an officer encounters. As an example, officers often respond to highly dangerous calls such as robbery in progress, domestic violence with a weapon, or man with a gun. In some of these incidents, the subject involved is not actually trying to commit a crime, but is more intent on taking their own life. Originally discussed in Chapter 13, suicide by cop (SbC) incidents pose a unique challenge to the *Graham* decision. See Box 14.3.

JUVENILES

For the most part, police departments do not instruct their officers to make a distinction between adults and juveniles in using deadly force, unless it is readily apparent that the individual is a juvenile. This is not based on a callous disregard for youthful offenders; rather, it is based on the pragmatic view that an armed juvenile can kill with the same finality as an armed adult. Further, it is often difficult, if not impossible, to tell if an offender is a juvenile or an adult.

SHOOTING AT OR FROM VEHICLES

The trend in recent years has been to impose severe limitations on police officers shooting at or from vehicles except as the ultimate measure in self-defense or the defense of another when the suspect is using deadly force by means other than the vehicle.

Some of the reasons presented against shooting at or from vehicles are difficulty in hitting the target, ricochets striking innocent bystanders, population densities, difficulty in penetrating the automobile body and steel-belted tires, inability to put a stop to the vehicle's momentum even when the target suspect is hit, damage that might result from causing the vehicle to go out of control, difficulty in hitting a moving target, and striking of an innocent passenger in the fleeing vehicle.[70]

There is little question that, if a motorist is trying to run a police officer down and the officer has no reasonable means of escape, then the officer has every right to defend his or her life. What often happens, however, is that the officer starts shooting at a vehicle when he or she is no longer in danger. For example, if a vehicle attempts to run a police officer down and the officer is able to take evasive action and get out of harm's way, under the provisions of many police departments' policies, the officer is no longer permitted to shoot at the vehicle because the officer is no longer in danger. Naturally, if the driver turns the vehicle around and goes back toward the officer, the officer once again has the right to protect his or her life.

WARNING SHOTS

There seems to be a general consensus among administrators that department policies should prohibit warning shots, as they may strike an innocent person. Privately, however, officials might fear something else: Officers shooting at and missing a suspect may claim that they were merely firing a warning shot and attempt to avoid answering for their actions. In addition, police officials point out that warning shots rarely accomplish their purpose, especially if suspects know that officers will not or cannot shoot them.[71]

SHOOTING TO DESTROY ANIMALS

Police departments generally allow their officers to kill an animal in self-defense, to prevent substantial harm to the officer or others, or when an animal is so badly injured that humanity requires its relief from further suffering. A seriously wounded or injured animal may be destroyed only after all attempts have been made to request assistance from the agencies (i.e., humane society, animal control, or game warden) responsible for disposal of animals. The destruction of vicious animals should be guided by the same rules set forth for self-defense or the defense and safety of others.[72]

SECONDARY GUNS

Police officers in the United States are all conspicuously armed with a revolver or semiautomatic handgun. This fact is recognized and for the most part approved by our citizenry. A second fact not commonly known is that many police officers also carry a concealed secondary weapon. There are stated reasons for the practice: Officers are concerned about being disarmed (with sound justification) during a confrontation, officers are less likely to be caught off guard when confrontation is not anticipated, and officers can less conspicuously be prepared to protect themselves during routine citizen stops. Regardless of the rationale, the practice is considered acceptable by knowledgeable police officials but treated by many police administrators as something understood but not formally admitted.

FIGURE 14.3 ▶ Two Special Weapons and Tactics (SWAT) officers watch a third SWAT officer use a one-man door ram, which appears to be a Broco's Enforcer model. Manual rams are used to achieve rapid forced entry into a premise, for example, officers have search and arrest warrants for drug offenses and they reasonably believe that those inside are flushing drugs down the toilet. (Photo courtesy of the National Tactical Officers Association. www.ntoa.org)

A major criticism of backup weapons is that they may be intended as "throwaways" in the event an officer shoots an unarmed suspect. In order to protect the officer from such allegations, it is generally recommended that there be a strict policy of registering all backup guns with the department.[73]

OFF-DUTY WEAPONS

The rationale for officers to be armed while off duty is based on the assumption that police officers within their own jurisdictions are on duty 24 hours a day and are therefore expected to act in their official capacity if the need to do so occurs. This, for the most part, was the policy of many police departments. Until recently, an officer who failed to comply with this regulation was subject to disciplinary action if a situation occurred that needed police action, such as responding to a robbery in progress, and the officer could not respond because he or she was unarmed.

Many police departments now make being armed while off duty optional but still compel their officers to register with the department any weapons they choose to wear off duty and to qualify regularly with the weapons. Most police departments also designate the type of ammunition the officers may carry in all weapons they use, regardless of whether they are used on duty or off duty.[74]

REGISTRATION OF WEAPONS

Most police departments require their officers to use only department-approved weapons on and off duty and further require that the weapons be inspected, fired, and certified safe by the departments' armorers. Further, the firearms must be registered with the departments by make, model, serial number, and ballistics sample.[75]

Box 14.3: Suicide by Cop (SbC): An Officer's "Worst Nightmare!"

Individual police use of deadly force must be clearly consistent with the standards created by the U.S. Supreme Court in *Graham v. Conner* (1989), whereby the court articulated the "objective reasonableness test" in cases arising from claims of excessive use of force by police. The court ruled that the extent to which the use of force is reasonable must be judged using the perspective of a reasonable officer on the scene. The decision recognizes the need to evaluate police actions in light of the circumstances that confront police, which are at times stressful and uncertain.[76] This discussion focuses on incidents where the subject is attempting to commit suicide by forcing the police to shoot them. The phenomenon is well-documented in the literature as *Suicide by Cop (SbC)*.

Police responding to a call regarding an armed suicidal subject are often confronted with this type of highly volatile and dangerous encounter. There are numerous and well-documented cases wherein officers were either wounded, killed, or forced to kill a suicidal assailant during these types of incidents. In many of these cases, the assailant openly voiced their intent to force police officers to shoot them because of a perceived (e.g., suspect had a toy gun or a package that they said was a bomb), or a real threat (indeed, the suspect was armed with a gun or knife). Again, these types of situations are commonly recognized both among police and scholars as cases of *Suicide by Cop (SbC)* incidents, whereby suicidal subjects "seek to bring about their own death by provoking armed police officers to shoot them."[77]

Incidents of Suicide by Cop (SbC) have been empirically verified by researchers in studies designed to distinguish cases as self-inflicted suicide or suicide attempts from cases objectively classified as SbC cases. A series of five empirical studies conducted during the late 1990s supported the conclusion that roughly 10 percent of police deadly force incidents involved SbC situations.[78] However, more recent studies noted in the Police Executive Research Forum, *Suicide by Cop: Protocol and Training Guide*[79] reveal that

the actual number may be much higher. In each year from 2015 to 2018, there were approximately 900 to 1,000 officer-involved homicides in the United States.[80] Various estimates, as high as 29 percent or more, may well be classified as "Suicide by Cop" incidents.[81] Hence, officer safety issues and reactions to these types of incidents are valid, legitimate, and reasonable based on their professional experience and on available, widely recognized, and scholarly research.

Interestingly, the research reveals several primary indicators identified by scholars to distinguish and characterize SbC situations. The first, and most important statistically significant indicator of SbC is "communicated intent" where the individual is known to have explicitly communicated a suicidal intention during or before the incident. Often, the individual expresses verbalizations of hopelessness and their actual intent to be "killed by the cops." This indicator often includes past verbal and nonverbal communications to commit suicide as well as actual previous attempts to commit suicide.[82] The second statistically significant indicator of SbC is "showed intent" where the individual indicates nonverbal suicide intent through life-threatening or criminal behavior with a lethal weapon or what appears to be a lethal weapon. This includes past histories of criminal behavior, drug and alcohol problems, documented psychiatric issues, and incidents of domestic violence. The final indicator is "planned intent," "showed intent," or "demonstrative behavior" often associated with the initial call for police to the location of the subject. For instance, armed robbery was the most frequent reason for initial officer interventions; however, general disturbance, domestic violence, and "person with a weapon" calls were close behind. In other words, the subject acted in a manner in which they knew the police would respond to, immediately and aggressively as a weapon or harm to others were commonly associated with the type of call or encounter presented. Upon arrival to the scene, the subject then points a weapon or reaches for a weapon threatening either an innocent bystander or the officer, immediately escalating the situation.[83] Lord and Sloop have identified this concept as an "outrageous act" characterized as the action taken by the subject that first brings them to the attention of the police.[84]

One of the most recent treatises on SbC, articulates 15 indicators recognized and associated with such encounters. These include:

- The subject is barricaded and refuses to negotiate.
- The subject has just killed someone, particularly a close relative, his mother, wife, or child.
- The subject says that he has a life-threatening illness.
- The subject's demands of police do not include negotiations for escape or freedom.
- The subject has undergone one or more traumatic life changes (death of a loved one, divorce, financial devastation, etc.).
- Before the encounter, the subject has given away all of his money or possessions.
- The subject has a record of assaults.
- The subject says he will only surrender to the person in charge.

- Subject indicates that he has thought about planning his death.
- The subject has expressed an interest in wanting to die in a "macho" way.
- The subject has expressed interest in "going out in a big way."
- Subject expresses feelings of hopelessness or helplessness.
- The subject dictates his will to negotiators.
- The subject demands to be killed.
- The subject sets a deadline to be killed.[85]

Certainly, every indicator is <u>not</u> present in every incident. However, the above factors can provide a "tip" for responding officers to understand that a suicidal person may be preparing to die. Without compromising officer or public safety, deescalation techniques aimed at a peaceful resolution should be employed. These techniques might include effectively communicating to the subject that his or her situation can be resolved peacefully, talking softly and with understanding toward the suspect, and using other crisis intervention techniques[86] may prevent these types of high-risk encounters from being an officer's "worst nightmare."

Familiarization with the Department's Policy

It does a police department little good to have an adequate use-of-deadly-force policy if its officers are not familiar with all aspects of that policy. Following are some examples of formalized administrative means by which officers can become familiar with their agencies' policies:

- *Recruit training*—Instructions dealing with the deadly force policy should be incorporated into the unit of instruction dealing with firearms training. As suggested earlier, the judgmental aspects of using deadly force are as important as the hands-on skill development of police officers in firearms training. Such a unit of instruction should involve a discussion of the numerous situations that officers will typically encounter and what course of action would keep these officers in strict compliance with their departments' policies and minimize wrongful deaths.

- *Field training officer*—The field training officer to whom a rookie officer is assigned immediately upon graduation from the police academy is responsible for continuing the training process started by the police academy and for evaluating the suitability of the rookie for police work. Such programs frequently incorporate training features designed to reinforce topics covered in the formal classroom setting of the academy. This component of the training program should be examined to be certain it deals with the topic of police use of deadly force.

- *Roll-call training*—A part of this training, which typically occurs just prior to the officers going on patrol, can be spent in reviewing newly developed departmental policies, procedures, and regulations, including those dealing with the use of deadly force.

- *In-service training*—In-service training classes typically range from one to five days (see Figure 14.4). It is quite clear that the *Garner*[87] decision has resulted in many police departments rethinking and rewriting their use-of-deadly-force policies. The importance of the *Garner* decision will not be fully appreciated if a police department merely rewrites its policy and hands it out to its officers with no explanation. It is imperative that some explanation be provided, preferably by legal counsel, so that there is no misunderstanding about what this policy means. This familiarization and orientation can occur in conjunction with the firearms requalification training that officers have to go through regularly, or it can be treated within the context of an in-service training course.[88]

Quick Facts: Body-Worn Cameras and Use of Force

Research and Brett Chapman, National Institute of Justice, "Body-Worn Cameras: What the Evidence Tells Us," NIJ Journal. Issue 280 January 2019. See: https://www.ncjrs.gov/pdffiles1/nij/252035.pdf on body-worn cameras indicates that the use of the technology may reduce use-of-force incidents by up to 50 percent.

Source: Tony Farrar, "Self-awareness to being watched and socially desirable behavior: A field experiment on the effect of body-worn cameras on police use-of-force," *Police Foundation.* See: http://www.policefoundation.org/content/body-worn-camera

FIGURE 14.4 ▶ Police use of deadly force requires extensive training in firearms techniques that can be validated and documented by qualified personnel. Virtual and simulation training programs provide real-world police encounters that hopefully decrease the number of officer-involved shootings as well as the subsequent number of police litigations. (Sgt Parker Gyokeres/U.S. Air Force photo)

POLICE USE OF FORCE AND LESS-LETHAL WEAPONS

Law enforcement agencies must walk a careful line in American society. While police officers are responsible for maintaining peace and order, this is complicated by a multitude of factors unique to each and every situation. When an officer responds to a call for service or reacts to observed criminal behavior in the field, that officer must either quell the disturbance or apprehend a suspect, sometimes through the use of force. Police use of force is most often justifiable and legal, particularly when overcoming resistance during arrests or in course of protecting themselves or others from harm.[89]

There is a general, usually unrealistic, societal expectation of increasingly more technical and sophisticated weapons available to police agencies. This is propagated in the entertainment industry. Television and big-screen productions tend to display deadly force in black and white; the evil doer misses or inflicts minor wounds while heroes are incredibly accurate and kill painlessly and from great distances. Less-lethal weapons in the entertainment arena can be viewed through a similar lens. The public, raised on science fiction like Star Trek©, expects phaser-like weapons that can incapacitate without causing permanent harm or death. Viewers watch as the fictitious recipient is usually rendered unconscious from a single application of a less-lethal weapon and recovers almost immediately. This creates a massive discrepancy between reality and the portrayal of **less-lethal weapons** in popular media. While less-lethal weapons are used without the intent to cause permanent injury or death, they still have the potential to cause death or serious injury. However, these weapons are ordinarily less harmful

and hence, less lethal than the projectiles fired from firearms.[90] Common less-lethal weapons used in policing include chemical weapons such as oleoresin capsicum (OC) or pepper spray, bean-bag guns, net guns that shoot a web around suspects, and controlled energy devices (CEDs).

TASERS®

A CED is a device designed to deploy electricity throughout the body of the target to temporarily cause loss of muscle control. Throughout the history of law enforcement in America, there have been many devices that loosely fit this description, including "cattle prods" or "stun guns." Such devices allow electricity to be deployed on contact with the skin or within close distances. Over the past several years, the technology for these devices has become more advanced, allowing the user to apply the device more accurately and from greater distances. Although greatly accepted as a less-lethal weapon option by many local, county, state, and federal police agencies, they have also been met by community concerns about safety, misuse, and overuse. TASER® International[91] is the company best known for producing CEDs. Their product has become so well-known that the name "TASER®" has become synonymous with "CED," much like the name "Band-Aid" is to a plastic bandage.[92]

According to the Government Accounting Office, TASERS® are now used by more than 10,000 law enforcement agencies across the United States.[93] TASERS® shock a person with 50,000 volts and create intense pain and discomfort by involuntary constrictions of skeletal muscles in order to gain compliance on the part of the suspect. A person being shocked or "tased" is conscious and the event is designed to last for five seconds or less; however, the newest version of the weapon is designed to produce up to three cycles of five seconds (15 seconds). While application of the electrical current is possible by contacting the end of the device to the skin, the uniqueness of the TASER® weapons lies in its ability to be applied from greater distances. Powered by high-pressure air probes that are similar to darts, the probes are fired while tethered to the handheld device on wire that can reach from 15 to 31 feet. However, in order for the device to be effective in gaining compliance, both probes must strike the target, preferably with a spread of about 1 foot between the probes.

Liability and Less-Lethal Weapons

While empirical research on police use of force has increased over the last 50 years, only limited attention has been paid to use-of-force encounters wherein the police used "less-lethal weapons" generally, and the TASER® specifically. Alpert and Dunham have focused on use-of-force encounters and police injuries and have demonstrated that the greatest likelihood of officer injury occurs when they attempt to control a suspect by punching, kicking, take-down, wrestling, and joint locks.[94] These types of incidents account for almost 70 percent of injuries. Research findings also reveal a higher likelihood of injury to the suspect when officers use canines, bodily force, and impact weapons (e.g., batons and riot sticks) as well. Generally, research reveals that few problems occur when healthy subjects are shocked or "tased" for less than 15 seconds.[95] Even though the bulk of research shows that the use of less-lethal weapons reduces injury, there have been several highlighted incidents across the nation that have peaked interest in the use of such weapons and influenced public opinion (see Figure 14.5).[96]

Most departments using TASERS® place the weapon within their continuum of force policy and provide extensive training on the use of the weapon. Most importantly, recent research[97] using data from 12 local police departments representing more than 24,000 incidents found that the use of physical force (e.g., striking, wrestling, and come-along holds) by police increased the odds of injury to both suspects and officers. Conversely, the use of less-lethal weapons (such as OC spray or TASERS®) decreased the odds of injury to suspects and officers. When used appropriately as trained, and controlled through use-of-force policy, the employment of less-lethal weapons (such as OC spray and TASERS®) against healthy suspects reduces injury overall; by reasonable extension, the use of less-than-lethal weapons also reduces the number and severity of potentially successful liability claims brought against the police.[98] To further reduce liability, officers should follow many of the suggestions designed to reduce liability during use-of-deadly-force encounters as proscribed above, be well-trained on each type of less-lethal weapons, be familiar with policies relating to their use, and receive periodic in-service training to update their skills and the usage of such devices.

FIGURE 14.5 ▶ The use of pepper spray against Occupy protestors at UC Davis in California in 2011 raised public debate about police use of less-lethal weapons. (JASNA HODZIC/epa european pressphoto agency b.v./Alamy Stock Photo)

SITUATIONAL USE OF FORCE OPTIONS

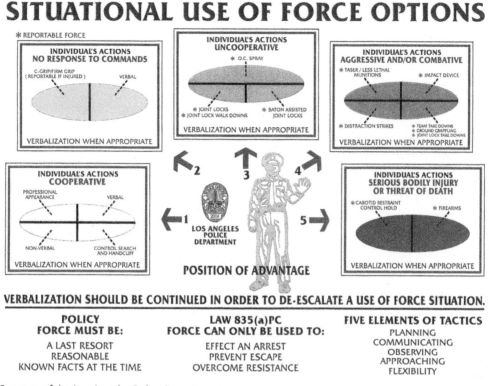

Courtesy of the Los Angeles Police Department.

POLICE LIABILITY AND HIGH-SPEED PURSUIT

The legal theory underlying most pursuit-related lawsuits is that the police were negligent in conducting a pursuit.[99] A negligence action is based on proof of the following four elements: (1) the officer owed the injured party a duty not to engage in certain conduct, (2) the officer's actions violated that duty, (3) the officer's negligent conduct was the proximate cause of the accident, and (4) the suing party suffered actual and provable damages.[100] Negligence litigation focuses on the alleged failure of an officer to exercise reasonable care under the circumstances.

Duty Owed

Courts first determine the duty owed in a pursuit situation by examining the officer's conduct in light of relevant laws and department regulations. With the exception of some police departments that prohibit all pursuits, police officers have no duty to refrain from chasing a criminal suspect, even when the risk of harm to the public arising from the chase is foreseeable and the suspect is being chased for a misdemeanor.[101] In *Smith v. City of West Point*,[102] the court stated that police "are under no duty to allow motorized suspects a leisurely escape."[103] However, police do have a duty of care with respect to the manner in which they conduct a pursuit. This duty is derived from state statutes, court decisions defining reasonable care, and departmental pursuit policies.

Statutes in most jurisdictions confer a special status on police and other authorized emergency vehicles, exempting them from certain traffic regulations, such as speed limits, traffic signals, and a right of way.[104] Statutes exempting emergency vehicles from ordinary traffic regulations generally make the privilege conditional on (1) the existence of an actual emergency, (2) the use of adequate warning devices, and (3) the continued exercise of due care for the safety of others. Whether a government unit or its officers can be held liable depends in large part on the construction of such statutes. As a general rule, police drivers are not liable for negligence as a matter of law solely because they disregard a traffic regulation during an authorized emergency run. However, these statutes provide no protection against liability for an officer's reckless driving. Drivers of emergency police vehicles have a statutory duty to drive with due regard for the safety of others.

Court decisions defining the reasonable care standard constitute a second source from which to derive a duty owed by police pursuit drivers. Most courts have translated the reasonable care standard into a duty to drive with the care that a reasonable, prudent officer would exercise in the discharge of official duties of a similar nature.[105] "Reasonable care" is a relative term depending on the exigencies of the situation and the degree of care and vigilance reasonably dictated by the circumstances of the chase.

A third source from which to derive a duty owed by police pursuit drivers is department policy. A law enforcement organization's policies, procedures, and training material concerning high-speed pursuits are generally admissible as evidence in

---

Quick Facts: The Statistics of Police Pursuits and Chases

A recent National Highway Traffic and Safety Administration (NHTSA) analysis revealed that over 11,500 people, including 6,300 fleeing suspects, were killed in police pursuits from 1979 to 2013; that is an average of 329 a year—nearly one person a day. The number also includes more than 5,000 innocent bystanders and passengers killed, and countless more injured as a result of high-speed and dangerous pursuits often initiated by the police for minor traffic infractions. In addition, State of California records of 63,500 police chases from 2002 through 2014 revealed:

- Most chases ended quickly—76 percent were over within five minutes.

- The vast majority (a whopping 89 percent) were initiated for vehicle-code violations or traffic infractions, including speeding, vehicle theft, reckless driving, and missing license plate or expire registration (nearly 5,000 cases).

- Only 5 percent of the cases were developed in an effort to arrest a suspected for a violent crime (e.g., robbery, kidnapping, assault, or murder). Only 168 cases out of over 63,500 cases in 13 years (less than 0.03 percent) sought a known suspect for murder.

- Nearly a 1,000 cases were initiated for safety violations like not wearing a seat belt or not wearing a helmet for motorcycle rider.

- In 90 cases, police chased suspect for "driving too slowly."

Source: Thomas Frank, "High Speed Police Chases Have Killed Thousands of Innocent Bystanders," *USA Today* (July 30, 2015). See http://www.usatoday.com/story/news/2015/07/30/police-pursuits-fatal-injuries/30187827/

---

lawsuits against the department or its officers for the negligent operation of a pursuit vehicle.[106] For example, in order to ascertain the standard of care applicable to a particular pursuit situation, a court could admit into evidence a police department regulation defining the proper speeds at which police cars responding to emergency calls were supposed to enter intersections when proceeding against red traffic signals. Depending on the jurisdiction involved, departmental pursuit policies may be merely a guideline to assist juries in determining the reasonableness of pursuit conduct, or they may actually constitute a duty owed, the violation of which would be considered negligent.

Proximate Cause

Liability must be based on proof that police conduct in breaching a duty owed was the **proximate cause** of a pursuit-related accident. Proximate cause is difficult to establish in cases involving the intervening negligence of other drivers, such as a case in which a fleeing motorist collides with an innocent person. In such cases, some courts impose liability on the officer and the department if the accident was a foreseeable consequence of police negligence.[107] For example, if police pursue without activating their emergency/flashing lights and siren and an innocent citizen enters an intersection without being warned of the pursuit and collides with the pursued vehicle, the police may be liable because the accident was the proximate and foreseeable result of their failure to adequately warn other drivers of the pursuit. In *Nelson v. City of Chester, Ill.,*[108] the court held that the city's breach of its duty to properly train its police officers in high-speed pursuit might be found to be the proximate cause of the pursued driver's death, notwithstanding the contributing negligence of the pursued driver.

Legal barriers to civil actions, such as immunity, have been removed in many jurisdictions by a combination of legislation and judicial decisions, even though the extent of immunity continues to vary.[109] Statutes in most states have limited sovereign immunity to discretionary as opposed to ministerial decisions. Accordingly, the decision to pursue is viewed as discretionary, rendering the public entity immune, but the manner of pursuit is a ministerial decision for which there is no general grant of immunity. *Rhodes v. Lamar*[110] used this bifurcated approach to hold that the decision to institute a pursuit is a discretionary decision for which a sheriff enjoyed sovereign immunity, but liability was not precluded if the pursuit was conducted in a manner that violated a reasonable duty of care. In *Fagan v. City of Vineland*, the Court of Appeals allowed the municipality to be sued directly under Section 1983 when the pursuit causing a constitutional tort was pursuant to municipal policy or custom. Furthermore, the court allowed the municipality to be held liable for lack of training its officers in high-speed pursuit even if none of the officers involved in the pursuit at issue violated the Constitution.[111]

Federal Civil Rights Act

Pursuit-related liability under the federal Civil Rights Act, 42 U.S.C. 1983, requires proof that an officer's conduct violated a constitutionally protected right.[112] In *Cannon v. Taylor*,[113] the Court of Appeals for the Eleventh Circuit concluded that "a person injured in an automobile accident caused by the negligent, or even grossly negligent, operation of a motor vehicle by a police officer acting in the line of duty has no Section 1983 cause of action for violation of a federal right."[114] The Supreme Court in *County of Sacramento v. Lewis* decided that a police officer does not violate the Fourteenth Amendment's guarantee of substantive due process "by causing death through deliberate or reckless indifference to life in a high-speed automobile chase aimed at apprehending a suspected offender."[115] The only violation of substantive due process occurs when there is a purpose to cause harm unrelated to the arrest. Automobile negligence actions are grist for the state law mill, but they do not rise to the level of a constitutional deprivation.[116] The common thread running through the cases is that negligent conduct during a pursuit does not suffice to trigger jurisdiction under Section 1983. However, a municipality can be held liable under Section 1983 if there was no or inadequate high-speed pursuit training for its officers, even when the officers involved with a pursuit were not individually negligent.[117]

Certain techniques employed by police during a pursuit may raise constitutional issues cognizable under 1983. For example, in *Jamieson By and Through Jamieson v. Shaw*[118] the court held that the constitutionally permissible use-of-force standard set forth by the Supreme Court in *Tennessee v. Garner*[119] was violated when a passenger in a fleeing vehicle was hurt when the vehicle hit a so-called deadman roadblock after officers allegedly shined a bright light into the driver's eyes as the vehicle approached the roadblock. In *Bower v. County of Inyo*,[120] a high-speed pursuit of over 20 miles ended when the fleeing suspect was killed when his vehicle hit a tractor-trailer that police had placed across the road as a roadblock. The Court of Appeals held that police use of a roadblock could constitute a constitutional violation of substantive due process if it was designed as an intentional deathtrap where the approaching driver does not have a clear option to stop because the roadblock is concealed around a curve or inadequately illuminated. The Supreme Court went further in stating that the deceased driver was unreasonably "seized" when the roadblock was placed completely across the highway in a manner likely to kill the driver and that the police officers were liable under the Fourth Amendment and Section 1983 for the use of excessive force.[121]

Factors Determining Liability

Pursuit-related litigation usually involves an inquiry into whether the manner in which the pursuit was conducted was reasonable under the circumstances of that case. Each pursuit situation is different and requires a particularized assessment. Following is a brief discussion of certain factors that most frequently determine the extent of pursuit-related liability.

PURPOSE OF PURSUIT

This factor relates to the need or reason for a pursuit. Does the purpose of the pursuit warrant the risks involved? What is the nature and seriousness of the suspected offense? Is the fleeing motorist suspected of committing a serious crime or only a misdemeanor? Was the motorist already operating the vehicle in a reckless and life-threatening manner before the pursuit started or had the motorist committed a minor, nonhazardous traffic violation prior to the pursuit but then started driving in a reckless and life-threatening manner after the pursuit was initiated? Is there a need for immediate apprehension or has the suspect been identified so that apprehension at a later time is possible?

DRIVING CONDITIONS

This factor involves a general assessment of equipment, the weather, roadway and traffic conditions, and the experience and personal ability of the drivers involved in the chase.

USE OF WARNING DEVICES

The use of adequate visual and audible warning devices, such as flashing lights and a siren, not only is a statutory mandate for most pursuit situations but also ensures to the greatest extent possible that other vehicles and pedestrians are alerted to approaching emergency vehicles and to the need to yield the right of way.

EXCESSIVE SPEED

Whether a particular speed is excessive depends on the purpose of the pursuit, the driving conditions, and the personal ability of a police driver to control and effectively maneuver the vehicle. Speed when crossing an intersection against a light or sign is an especially critical consideration, since statistics suggest that most pursuit-related collisions occur at intersections.[122] Liability may be based on the failure to sufficiently decrease speed when approaching an intersection so that a complete stop can be made to avoid a collision.

DISOBEYING TRAFFIC LAWS

Pursuit vehicles are statutorily obligated to use due care for the safety of others when disobeying traffic laws, such as operating a vehicle on the wrong side of the road, passing on the right, going the wrong way on a one-way street, passing in a "no passing" zone, or proceeding against a traffic signal. These dangerous and high-risk driving situations should be avoided because police are generally held liable for any resulting accidents.[123]

ROADBLOCKS

Special care is required when using roadblocks to ensure that innocent persons are not placed in a position of danger and that the fleeing motorist is afforded a reasonable opportunity to stop safely.[124] To reduce the risk of liability, it is recommended that roadblocks be used only when authorized by a supervisor and only as a last resort to apprehend a fleeing motorist who is wanted for a violent felony and who constitutes an immediate and serious threat. Although the Supreme Court stated that a roadblock could be a Fourth Amendment unreasonable seizure granting Section 1983 liability,[125] the Court of Appeals for the First Circuit qualified the definition of "seizure" to apply to roadblock accidents constituting a "misuse of power" as opposed to the "accidental effects of otherwise lawful governmental conduct."[126]

TERMINATION OF PURSUIT

Every police department's pursuit policy has a provision dealing with termination of pursuit. When officers are expected to terminate varies considerably, depending on the agency's philosophy. Some agencies allow their officers very broad latitude, while others greatly restrict officers' actions. Policies generally fall into one of three models:[127]

1. *Judgmental*—Allowing officers to make all major decisions relating to initiation, tactics, and termination.

2. *Restrictive*—Placing certain restrictions on officers' judgments and decisions.

3. *Discouragement*—Severely cautioning or discouraging any pursuit, except in the most extreme situations.

However, despite these variations in department policies, a noticeable trend has been emerging. Increasingly, police departments are permitting their officers to pursue only individuals who are known to have committed dangerous felonies—that is, murder, felonious assault, rape, robbery, kidnapping, and so on. This trend is occurring because it is becoming increasingly difficult to justify pursuits that result in injuries and the death of innocent third parties, as well as the injuries and death of police officers. Another reason for the dramatic shift in these policies has been because of the enormously high-monetary judgments imposed by juries for injuries to innocent third parties.

Alpert[128] and Beckman[129] show that the vast majority of pursuits are for traffic violations and/or misdemeanors and not felonies. The issue of when the violator would eventually stop was addressed by Alpert.[130] He interviewed 146 inmates who had fled from the police and who were confined to jails in three cities: Omaha, Nebraska; Miami, Florida; and Columbia, South Carolina. Over 70 percent of the suspects said that they would have slowed down "when I felt safe" whether the pursuit was on a freeway, on a highway, or in a town. The phrase "when I felt safe" was interpreted by the respondents as outdistancing the police by 2.2 blocks on surface streets, 2.3 miles on highways, and 2.5 miles on freeways. Fifty-three percent of the suspects responded that they were willing to run at all costs from the police in a pursuit, and 64 percent believed that they would not be caught; however, 71 percent said that they were concerned with their own safety, and 62 percent stated that they were concerned with the safety of others while engaged in a chase.[131]

Thus, law enforcement agencies that allow their officers broad discretion in pursuit can expect a greater number of arrests of violators who flee. However, they can also expect to have more uninvolved third parties injured or killed, as well as more police officers injured and a greater number of lawsuits. Conversely, those departments that have more restrictive policies can expect more conservative results. The final decision is ultimately left to the chief administrator of the agency.

Departmental Responsibility for Liability Reduction

To reduce the risks and liability associated with vehicular pursuits, law enforcement organizations must carefully evaluate their pursuit policies, training, supervision, and postincident evaluations. Liability reduction is accomplished through sound management controls and a reduction in the number of pursuit-related accidents.

POLICY DEVELOPMENT

The function of a well-written pursuit policy is to state the department's objectives, establish some ground rules for the exercise of discretion, and educate officers as to specific factors they should consider when conducting a vehicular pursuit. Where feasible, a comprehensive policy statement should give content to terms such as "reasonable" and "reckless" and provide officers with more particularized guidance. A policy should be tailored to a department's operational needs, geographical peculiarities, and training capabilities. A written policy also provides a basis for holding officers accountable for their pursuit-related conduct.

TRAINING

Lack of adequate training may contribute to many pursuit-related accidents. The natural tendency for many police drivers is to become emotionally involved and therefore lose some perspective during a pursuit. They are also required to drive different police vehicles with unique handling characteristics under

---

Box 14.4: Dallas, Texas Police Department Institutes a Restrictive Vehicle Pursuit Policy

The Dallas Police Department has one of the most restrictive vehicle pursuit policies in the United States, and the policy appears to be saving officers' and citizens' lives. Since the policy was enacted at the beginning of 2007, individual officers and the police unions have been critical, indicating that the policy is "soft on criminals" and encourages traffic violators not to stop for the police. Several officers indicated that the policy actually undermined their ability to "catch criminals." However, the policy has dramatically decreased the numbers of officers and citizens killed and injured in the city of Dallas as the result of a police vehicle pursuit, and

crime rates remain among the lowest in Dallas for decades. The policy is still at odds with many officer's desires to chase down the bad guys, but for newer officers, the policy is just the way things have always been.

Note that the policy places the entire decision on the officer. The highlighted area indicates that the officer must be able to immediately articulate why he or she is engaging in a chase and that the immediate need to apprehend the offender (via a police pursuit) outweighs the safety of other members of the community who might be endangered by the chase. (Courtesy Dallas Police Department)

Dallas Police Department General Order
301.00 Emergency Vehicle Operation

Revised 09/18/20

301.07   Vehicle Pursuits

A. Purpose - The purpose of this policy is to establish guidelines for making decisions with regard to vehicular pursuits.

B. Philosophy - General Order 906.01 B., states "protection of human life is a primary goal of the police department; therefore, police officers have a responsibility to use only the degree of force necessary to protect and preserve life." Initiating or participating in a vehicular pursuit presents a danger to the officers involved, the suspect, and the general public. Accordingly, the decision to initiate a pursuit must be based on the pursuing officer's conclusion that the immediate danger to the officer, public and suspect created by the pursuit is less than the immediate or potential danger to the public should the suspect remain at large.

C. Definition - A Pursuit is defined as an active attempt by an officer in an authorized emergency vehicle to apprehend a fleeing suspect in a motor vehicle who is attempting to elude the officer. A suspect is considered to be fleeing upon making any overt action intended to avoid arrest. For the purpose of this order, violators who follow all traffic regulations after an officer initiates a traffic stop and are merely failing to yield to the authorized emergency vehicle are not considered to be fleeing. The term "Chase" will be considered synonymous with "Pursuit".

D. Decision to Initiate Pursuit
1. The decision to pursue must be based upon facts and circumstances known to the officer.
2. In deciding whether to pursue, an officer must take the following pursuit risk factors under consideration:
   a. road, weather and environmental conditions.
   b. population density, vehicle and pedestrian traffic.
   c. relative performance capabilities of both the authorized emergency vehicle and the suspect's vehicle.
   d. seriousness of the offense.
   e. presence of other persons in the police vehicle.
   f. age of offender.
   g. whether or not the offender's identity is known, and
   h. any circumstance under which the pursuing officer will be unable to maintain control of the emergency vehicle.
3. An officer may initiate a pursuit under the following circumstances:
   a. When the officer has probable cause to believe that a felony involving the use or threat of physical force or violence has been, or is about to be, committed, and the officer reasonably believes that the immediate need to apprehend the offender outweighs the risk to any person of collision, injury or death, or
   b. to assist another law enforcement agency that has initiated a pursuit under the same circumstances.
   c. All other pursuits are prohibited.
4. Officers will not pursue a motorist whose only offense is driving while intoxicated if the actions of the driver escalate beyond merely failing to yield to the emergency vehicle.

E. Manner of Operation While in Pursuit
1. The emergency warning lights, siren, and emergency vehicle headlights will be used at all times while operating Code 3.
2. Only police vehicles equipped with operable emergency warning lights and sirens will participate in the pursuit of a fleeing vehicle.
3. Unmarked vehicles without roof mounted emergency warning light systems will not become involved in a pursuit. Supervisors in unmarked vehicles will follow the chase using a Code 1 response.
4. If a pursuit is initiated by a motorcycle, the motorcycle will abandon the pursuit when a four-wheel unit with roof mounted emergency warning light systems joins the pursuit.
5. Vehicles with passengers (prisoners, witnesses, suspects, complainants or other non-police personnel who have not signed a waiver of liability) will not become engaged in pursuits.
6. Paddy Wagons will not become engaged in pursuits.

---

various road and weather conditions. It is easy to lose control of a vehicle that is driven beyond its or the driver's capabilities, and law enforcement organizations can be held liable for failing to provide adequate driver training to prepare officers to handle vehicles safely in pursuit situations.[132] The extent and type of training required depend on a department's operational needs and objectives. A minimal level of cost-effective training can be accomplished by emphasizing defensive driving techniques and

carefully instructing officers about departmental pursuit policies and relevant state regulations concerning the operation of emergency vehicles.

SUPERVISION

Police departments are responsible for providing adequate supervision of officers involved in a pursuit. Experts who have studied the emotionalism and psychology associated with pursuits recommend that, as soon as possible after a pursuit has been initiated, a supervisor who is not in any of the pursuit vehicles be tasked with the responsibility of supervising the pursuit.[133] The supervisor who is not immediately involved is in a better position to oversee objectively the pursuit and decide whether it should continue and under what circumstances. The supervisor should track the location of the pursuit, designate the primary and secondary pursuit vehicles, and maintain tight controls on the desire of other officers to get involved or parallel the action. Effective communication between the pursuing vehicles and the supervisor is essential. The failure to transmit information concerning the location of a pursuit, the offense for which the pursuit was initiated, and other information required by departmental policy, such as the speed of vehicles, traffic conditions, and whether the pursued vehicle is ignoring traffic lights and signs may contribute to a subsequent accident because the supervisor lacks sufficient knowledge to order a pursuit terminated.

EVALUATION AND DOCUMENTATION

Law enforcement organizations should provide for an ongoing process of evaluation and documentation of pursuit-related incidents. All pursuits, including those successfully terminated without an accident, should be routinely critiqued to determine whether departmental policy was followed and the extent to which any policy modification, training enhancement, or other remedial action is warranted.

VEHICLE PURSUITS AND THE USE OF DEADLY FORCE

In an interesting mix of case law, the Supreme Court decided (2014) that police officers have an affirmative duty to end "grave risks" to the community. In *Plumhoff v. Rickard*, the Court straddled both vehicle pursuit and use-of-deadly-force case law. The case involves several West Memphis (AR) police officers who ended a high-speed vehicle pursuit by firing their weapons 12 times at a man fleeing from them in a vehicle. The court, in this decision, held that the officers' actions were reasonable in that the police chase caused a "grave public safety risk" to the wider community. As a result, the use of deadly force to end dangerous vehicle pursuits is justified in cases where the "totality of the circumstances" would make such action reasonable under *Graham v. Connor.*[134]

LIABILITY AND EMOTIONALLY DISTURBED PERSONS

Forty percent of persons suffering from serious mental illness will be arrested at least once during their lifetime. For this reason, it is imperative that progressive law enforcement agencies assume responsibility for evaluating potentially dangerous situations and recognizing those individuals suffering from various forms of mental illness. These individuals are commonly referred to as **emotionally disturbed persons (EDPs)**.[135]

Police responses to EDPs are determined to some degree by the manner in which the contact is initiated. The largest percentage of police officer contacts with EDPs are a result of on-the-street observations of bizarre, disruptive, or abnormal behavior. These encounters often end in an arrest of the subject for a relatively minor charge (e.g., disturbing the peace, disorderly conduct, vagrancy, or loitering), especially if alcohol use can be easily detected (see Figure 14.6). In other cases, the police receive complaints on an EDP as a result of a family disturbance or neighborhood problem. In either event, officers are often confronted by an individual with whom they have had prior contact (perhaps multiple prior contacts) and

FIGURE 14.6 ▶ Police officers often encounter vagrants near public buildings, business entrances, and parks. Removing emotionally disturbed people, homeless vagrants, and panhandlers is often a very delicate issue. (Mark Boster/Los Angeles Times/Getty Images)

one who might suddenly and without provocation burst into a violent confrontation, endangering everyone at the scene. As a result, many police departments are beginning to address this issue through basic and advanced training. For example, the Washington State Criminal Justice Commission has developed a unique curriculum focused on five key areas:

1. Recognizing abnormal behavior and mental illness (neuroses, psychoses, and psychopathic/sociopathic behavior);

2. Dealing with suicidal subjects (true versus parasuicidal behavior);

3. Developing crisis intervention skills (legal considerations in subject committal, tactical responses to handling the EDP, and responses to mental disturbance calls);

4. Developing awareness and knowledge of community services (interim facilities, hospital and emergency services, and community care homes); and

5. Recognizing and caring for Alzheimer's patients (physical cues and behavior).[136]

Other departments have also developed specialized in-service courses designed to provide more information to officers. The Monterey County Police Chief's Association has developed a Crisis Intervention Team (CIT) Academy in San Jose, California. The academy has distinguished itself through community collaboration and is well respected as a training model by the legislature and law enforcement community in California. The CIT Academy provides a 40-hour intensive training course that includes role playing, interactive participation of people with mental illness (consumers), identification of various symptoms and signs of medication use by consumers, crisis negotiation skills and tactics, panel discussions and feedback, visits to interim-type housing facilities, suicide and crisis training, and a constant review of all countywide protocols and incident procedures.[137] The training focuses on developing the most useful tool available to officers on the street: the ability to communicate in a nonthreatening manner.

The effective training of police officers in dealing with EDPs should result in two significant changes. First, there should be fewer incidents in which the use of force is necessary, thereby increasing officer safety. Second, effective training will provide a strong defense to litigation, should the department become entangled in litigation arising from the handling of an EDP.

Case law on the subject is still evolving. In 2015, the Supreme Court declined to expose two San Francisco police officers to liability under the Fourth Amendment after they shot a mentally ill woman who was brandishing a knife and making death threats. The incident occurred in August 2008, when a San Francisco city social worker called police after he was threatened by Teresa Sheehan when he went to check on her at the group home where she lived. When Sheehan refused to open the door to the officers, they let themselves in with the key provided by the social worker, and the officers were confronted with Sheehan, who was holding the knife. The officers called for back-up but decided that Sheehan presented an imminent threat and entered her room before back-up arrived, with their guns drawn. After Sheehan could not be subdued with the use of less-lethal weapons (pepper spray), the officers opened fire, wounding Sheehan. She later sued for claimed violations of the Fourth Amendment and the Americans with Disabilities Act (ADA), a 1990 law that requires government programs to take steps to accommodate the disabled.

In *City and County of San Francisco v. Sheehan*, the Court ruled that the officers did not violate the Constitution on their first entry into Sheehan's room and that the use of force on entering the second time was "reasonable," but it did not address whether the two officers were liable on Sheehan's constitutional claim that the Fourth Amendment required them to accommodate her mental condition. Hence, no landmark case exist that could have documented and established officer's duties under similar circumstance involving EDPs and the ADA—officers were immune to that specific claim.[138] However, the Department of Justice generally holds that Title II of the ADA includes all operations and activities of a police department, including the provision of reasonable accommodations during an arrest. So despite the lack of clarity from the Supreme Court and the inconsistency among lower courts related to whether the ADA requirement of reasonable accommodation applies to arrest, "a law enforcement agency may be subject to an enforcement action by the DOJ if reasonable accommodations are not provided during an arrest when dealing with a subject who is mentally ill."[139]

Box 14.5: Portland Police and Oregon Try to Impact Police Handling of Emotionally Disturbed Persons

Amid a rash of highly controversial shootings throughout the State of Oregon, the legislature passed Senate Bill 111 (SB 111) in late 2007, to be in force by the end of 2008. The law requires each county in the state to develop a plan regarding the use of deadly physical force by law enforcement officers. The purpose of the committee composed of various law enforcement executives within each of Oregon's

36 counties was to develop a deadly physical force plan to meet specific criteria:

- Develop proper training on the use of deadly force for police officers on a local and state-wide basis.

- Provide mechanisms for support for officers, civilians, and families of a community involved in a deadly force incident.

- Develop a specific process or protocol for investigating a deadly force incident.
- Determine whether the use of deadly force complied with applicable federal, state, and local law as well as the individual police department police.
- Stimulate research and interest on the issue of police use of deadly force.

Unfortunately, Oregon continues to suffer under the specter of questionable police use of deadly force. On January 29, 2010, an unarmed Aaron M. Campbell was shot in the back by members of the Portland Police Bureau SWAT team as he exited his apartment complex. Campbell, a person with a violent past including weapons charges and resisting arrest, had reportedly been suicidal after the death of his sister. During a bungled communication, officers mistakenly believed that Campbell made threatening gestures and the ensuing 50 rounds fired by the police was caught on video and widely dispersed on YouTube (see http://www.youtube.com/watch?v=_iwyd4ZHBUc).

The questionable shooting sparked an outrage in the city, with numerous public demonstrations and the firing of Chief of Police Rosie Sizer on May 12, 2010, in part for $1.6 million settlement for yet another questionable police-involved death. James A. Chasse, a skid-row bum with a history of mental illness was chased by police after allegedly urinating on the street. Witnesses indicated that police officers tackled, tased, and kicked Chasse as he laid defenseless on the ground. He died in the backseat of a police cruiser from injuries that included 26 breaks to 16 ribs and a punctured lung.

It is precisely these types of questionable incidents that cause significant strain between the police and public, and demand that police act appropriately in handling emotionally disturbed persons. The Portland Police Bureau remains under a Federal Consent Decree since 2012.

Sources: See http://www.leg.state.or.us/07reg/measpdf/sb0100.dir/sb0111.c.pdf (Retrieved July 20, 2010); "Why James Chasses' Story Matters to Portland," *The Oregonian*, May 11, 2010; "Man Shot and Killed by Police, KPTV.com (February 1, 2010), see http://www.kptv.com/news/22383908/detail.html; Carol Cratty, "Portland Police, Justice Department Agree on Excessive Force Reform," *CNN* (December 17, 2012), see: http://www.cnn.com/2012/12/17/justice/portland-police-justice-department/.

FEDERAL CONSENT DECREES

The violent beating of Rodney King by several police officers in Los Angeles in 1991 shook the consciousness of the United States and set in motion one of the most sweeping mechanisms for controlling the police outside of civil litigation. After a high-speed pursuit stemming from a speeding violation, no less than 20 officers from the California Highway Patrol (the agency initiating the pursuit), the Los Angeles School District, the Los Angeles County Sheriff's Office, and the Los Angeles Police Department responded to incident. Four LAPD officers were charged with the assault of King with a deadly weapon and the use of excessive force, as they were videotaped hitting, kicking, and tasing King. The ensuing trial ended with deadlocked jury and the acquittal of the officers. The incident triggered the 1992 Los Angeles riots in which 53 people were killed, 2,000 more were injured and millions of dollars of property damage occurred. The then Governor Pete Wilson activated the California National Guard in an effort to restore order.

As a result, the largest crime bill in the history of the United States, the 1994 Violent Crime Control and Law Enforcement Act was passed by Congress and signed into law by President Bill Clinton. The law provided for 100,000 new police officers, over $9.5 billion in funding for prison and another $6.1 billion in funding for community prevention programs. The law also funded the development of the Community Oriented Policing Services office within the U.S. Department of Justice (COPS Office) for another $14 billion aimed at not only hiring but also significantly training police officers in community policing programs aimed at bringing the police and minorities closer together. The law also gave, for the first time in American history, the federal government under the guidance of the U.S. Department of Justice, the power to sue local and state jurisdictions over a "pattern and practice" of policing that violated

Quick Facts: Officer Sues the Suspect

In an interesting turn of events, a white Chicago police officer counter-sued the estate of Quintonio LeGrier, an African-American teenager shot dead by the officer the day after Christmas, 2015. The officer, Robert Rialmos alleged that the 19-year-old LeGrier assaulted him with a baseball bat and caused him to suffer extensive trauma and posttraumatic stress. He argues that he had no other choice but to use deadly force against the teenager to save his life. He is seeking more than $10 million in damages. In the first-of-its-kind lawsuit, the officer's emotional as well as operational actions are considered in this controversial case involving police use of deadly force—one of many that have riddled the Chicago Police Department.

Source: Catherine E. Shoichet, Jeffrey Acevedo, and Tony Marco, "Chicago Cop Who Killed Quintonio LeGrier Sues Teen's Estate for $10 million" (Chicago, IL: CNN, February 9, 2016). See: http://www.cnn.com/2016/02/07/us/chicago-police-officer-sues-quintonio-legrier-estate/

federal law or the U.S. Constitution. The impact of such suits has been dramatic in policing over the past two decades. The suits essentially compel the defendant jurisdiction to change their practice through what is commonly known as a **federal consent decree**. Specific agencies agree to demanded changes over specified timeframes that are formalized in a "memoranda of understanding" and enforced by external and neutral federal monitors that oversee the changes and subsequent compliance by the agency.

The first case of federal suit or consent decree was brought against the Pittsburgh (PA) Police Department in 1997 for a "pattern and practice" of police abuse, particularly against the black community.[140] Since that time, nearly 30 cities have entered into consent decrees with the Department of Justice, including a large variety of agencies such as Los Angeles Police Department (CA), Cincinnati and Cleveland Police Departments (OH), New Orleans Police Department (LA), Portland Police Bureau (OR), Detroit Police Department (MI), the New Jersey State Police, the Virgin Islands Police Department, Seattle Police Department (WA), Albuquerque Police Department (NM), and Missoula Police Department (MT). The importance of these consent decrees cannot be overstated in reforming rogue police agencies and department.[141] Transformational change within police cultures is difficult at best and in many instances, changing patterns of abuse and excessive force as well as abhorrent behavior requires significant time and focused external effort. Police agencies, as well as individual officers, must be accountable for their actions; federal consent decrees have made such an impact.[142]

Box 14.6: Police Sexual Violence (PSV): An Emerging Law Enforcement Issue

by John Liederbach and Robert W. Taylor

Police sexual violence (PSV) has emerged as a critical issue for law enforcement agencies. PSV is the most egregious form of police sexual misconduct and involves sexual harassment and violence—including rape and violent sexual assaults—perpetrated by police officers against victims who are most often women. The PSV issue has surfaced within the context of recent high-profile cases that clearly demonstrate the problem. The city of San Diego (CA), for example, recently (2015) paid $5.9 million to settle a civil lawsuit involving a former San Diego Police Department officer who groped a woman in a public restroom while on-duty. The officer was found guilty of 12 different sex-related charges perpetrated against five different women during a previous criminal trial.[143] Other cases in Los Angeles (CA), Eugene (OR), Nassau County (NY), Houston (TX), Milwaukee (WN), Oklahoma City (OK), and Chicago (IL) have also raised the specter of PSV. The International Association of Police Chiefs (IACP) has recognized PSV as an important problem for police agencies and has held official roundtable discussions and published policy recommendations that describe sex-related misconduct as an issue that "warrants the full attention of law enforcement leadership."[144]

Police work affords ample opportunities to rogue police officers to perpetrate acts of sexual deviance and violence. Opportunities for sex-related misconduct derive from the context of the job. Police commonly patrol alone and largely free from any direct supervision. Police commonly encounter citizens who are vulnerable, usually because they are victims or criminal suspects. Police–citizen interactions often occur in the late-night hours that provide low-public visibility and ample opportunities to those officers who are able and willing to take advantage of them to commit acts of sexual deviance and to perpetrate sex crimes.[145]

Cases of sex-related police misconduct and crime have been described as "hidden" offenses that are likely to go unreported; and hence, difficult to document and study. However, there is a limited but growing line of empirical research designed to identify and describe the problem of PSV. One of the earliest studies on the phenomenon is authored by Kraska and Kappeler.[146] They use published opinions of the federal district courts in Section 1983 actions to identify and describe cases that mostly involved the use of strip or body cavity searches by police; but also, less commonly involved sexual assaults or rape. Other studies use published court opinions to focus on PSV liability under state tort law, and the Section 1983 liability of individual officers engaged in PSV.[147] Walker and Irlbeck identify what they refer to as the national problem of "driving while female."[148] Police in these cases use the pretext of alleged traffic violations to sexually harass or abuse female drivers. A follow-up report also includes victims of sexual misconduct who were prostitutes or teenagers involved in police "explorer" programs. Rabe-Hemp and Braithwaite explore recidivism among police who perpetrate sex crimes. Their findings suggest that PSV is a "pattern prone" offense that often involves recidivist officers who victimize multiple persons; and, that many police accused of sex crimes manage to escape penalties and maintain police certification by moving from one jurisdiction to another.[149]

A 2019 national-scale study of police officer crime includes a database of more than 16,370 arrest case of police crime (2005–2019) involving over 13,686 individual, nonfederal sworn law enforcement officers. The arrested officers were employed by more than 4,772 state, local and special law enforcement agencies throughout the United States.[150] The study identifies and describes cases in which police officers were arrested for criminal offenses associated with sex-related misconduct through a content analysis of published newspaper articles. The study identified 669 arrests of police officers across the United States for sex-related crimes from 2005 to 2012. Males were the perpetrator in all but six of these cases; and were patrol officers (on duty) in the vast majority of the cases (81.4 percent). The most serious offense charged in over 20 percent of these cases was forcible rape (*n* = 118) in just one three year period (2005–2007). There were also 107 cases of forcible fondling, 59 cases involving statutory rape, 54 cases involving forcible sodomy, and 39 cases involving child pornography. The study found that victims of sex-related police crime are typically female and younger than 18 years of age. The study overall demonstrates that the most egregious forms of PSV are not isolated events, a situation that presents considerable challenges to law enforcement executives.[151]

Indeed, the underlying theme of this research suggests that police sexual violence is not a new phenomenon, but one that has existed for many decades and continues to flourish within the police subculture. Historically, police administrators have portrayed cases of police sexual violence as encounters between consenting participants that involved females who were attracted to the uniform and the badge. The scenario provided plausible deniability to officers who were sexual predators and administrators who lacked the empathy to acknowledge these crimes and, more importantly, the courage to punish them. Many of the victims of police sexual violence are legally exposed; meaning, that in many cases, the females are easy to discredit because they are often women who are vulnerable, alone, drunk, or otherwise compromised when they are pulled over. This is the exact strategy that police agencies have used in their defense for failing to address such problems during civil litigation brought by victims who are survivors of police sexual violence.[152]

Police Sexual Violence (PSV) often occurs while the officer is working alone at night, with little or no direct supervision, and often hidden from public view. Victims of PSV are usually those who are most vulnerable to police power and abuse, oftentimes suspects of drug or alcohol-involved crimes such as DUI, or prostitutes or adult entertainment dancers who work late at night. (Jeremy Woodhouse/DigitalVision/Getty Images)

ADMINISTRATIVE DISCIPLINE: DUE PROCESS FOR POLICE OFFICERS

The Fifth and Fourteenth Amendments to the Constitution state that "no person shall be ... deprived of life, liberty, or property, without **due process** of law."

Liberty and Property Rights of Police Officers

There are two general types of situations in the disciplinary process in which an employee of a law enforcement agency can claim the right to be protected by the guarantees of due process.[153] The first type involves those situations in which the disciplinary action taken by the government employer threatens **liberty rights** of the officer. The second type involves a threat to **property rights**.

Liberty rights have been defined loosely as rights involving the protection and defense of one's good name, reputation, and position in the community. It has, at times, been extended further to include the right to preserve one's future career opportunities as well. Thus, when an officer's reputation, honor, or integrity is at stake because of government-imposed discipline, due process must be extended to the officer.[154]

It should be noted that the use of the "liberty rights" approach as a basis for requiring procedural due process has proven extremely difficult. The Supreme Court further restricted the use of this legal theory by holding that it can be utilized only when the employer is shown to have created and publicly disseminated a false and defamatory impression about the employee.[155]

The more substantial and meaningful type of due process guarantee is that pertaining to the protection of one's property. Although the general concept of property extends only to real estate and tangible possessions, the courts have developed the concept that a person's property also includes the many valuable intangible belongings acquired in the normal course of life, such as the expectation of continued employment. However, not all employees are entitled to its protection.

The courts have consistently held that an employee acquires a protected interest in a job (property interest or right) only when it can be established that there exists a justifiable expectation that employment will continue without interruption except for dismissal or other discipline based on just or proper cause. This expectation of continued employment is sometimes called "tenure" or "permanent status."[156]

Federal courts have been inclined to read employment laws liberally so as to grant property rights whenever possible. For example, the Fifth Circuit Court of Appeals found that a city employment regulation that allowed termination "only for cause" created a constitutionally protected property interest.[157] A federal district court held that a Florida statute (Section 112.532), known as the "Law Enforcement Officers' and Correctional Officers' Bill of Rights," created a property interest in employment because of its disciplinary notice provisions.[158] That approach is consistent with those of other jurisdictions in which state statutes have been interpreted to give property interests in a job to local government employees.[159]

Once a liberty or property right has been established, certain due process guarantees attach to protect the employee. The question becomes, what process is due?

The question of due process for police officers falls into two categories: **procedural due process** and **substantive due process**. The former, as its name implies, refers to the legality of the procedures used to deprive police officers of status or wages, such as dismissal or suspension from their job. Substantive due process is a more difficult and elusive concept. Simply, substantive due process is the requirement that the basis for government disciplinary action be reasonable, relevant, and justifiable.

Procedural Due Process

One of the 20th century's preeminent administrative law scholars, Kenneth Culp Davis, identified 12 main elements of a due process hearing:

> (1) timely and adequate notice, (2) a chance to make an oral statement or argument, (3) a chance to present witnesses and evidence, (4) confrontation of adverse witnesses, (5) cross-examination of adverse witnesses, (6) disclosure of all evidence relied upon, (7) a decision based on the record of evidence, (8) a right to retain an attorney, (9) a publicly compensated attorney for an indigent, (10) a statement of findings of fact, (11) a statement of reasons or a reasoned opinion, and (12) an impartial deciding officer.[160]

The courts have not examined all the trial elements in the context of the police disciplinary process. However, some cases have held that police officers must be informed of the charges

on which the action is based,[161] be given the right to call witnesses,[162] be confronted by the witnesses against them,[163] be permitted to cross-examine the witnesses against them,[164] be permitted to have counsel represent them,[165] have a decision rendered on the basis of the record developed at the hearing,[166] and have the decision made by an impartial hearing officer.[167]

A question that has proven particularly troublesome for the courts is whether due process requires that an evidentiary hearing be held before the disciplinary action being taken. In *Arnett v. Kennedy*, a badly divided Supreme Court held that a "hearing afforded by administrative appeal after the actual dismissal is a sufficient compliance with the requirements of the Due Process Clause."[168] In a concurring opinion, Justice Powell observed that the question of whether a hearing must be accorded before an employee's removal "depends on a balancing process in which the government's interest in expeditious removal of an unsatisfactory employee is weighed against the interest of the affected employee in continued public employment."[169] In *Mathews v. Eldridge*, the Supreme Court set forth the competing interests that must be weighed to determine what process is due to (1) the private interest that will be affected by the official action; (2) the risk of an erroneous deprivation of such interest through the procedures used and the probable value, if any, of additional or substitute procedural safeguards; and (3) the government's interest, including the function involved and the fiscal and administrative burdens that the additional or substitute procedural requirement would entail.[170]

In 1985, the Court further clarified the issue of pretermination due process in *Cleveland Board of Education v. Loudermill*.[171] The Court found that public employees possessing property interests in their employment have a right to "notice and an opportunity to respond" before termination. The Court cautioned that its decision was based on the employees also having an opportunity for a full posttermination hearing. Therefore, assuming that a public employee will be able to challenge the termination in a full-blown evidentiary hearing after the fact, pretermination due process should include an initial check against mistaken decisions—essentially, a determination of whether there are reasonable grounds to believe that the charges against the employee are true and support the proposed action. The Court went on to describe an acceptable pretermination procedure as one that provides the employee with oral or written notice of the charges against him or her, an explanation of the employer's evidence, and an opportunity to present his or her side of the story. The Court reasoned that the government interest in the immediate termination of an unsatisfactory employee is outweighed by an employee's interest in retaining employment and the interest in avoiding the risk of an erroneous termination.[172] In 1997, the Court ruled that public employees do not have the right to a hearing before suspension without pay as long as the suspension is short, the effect on pay is insubstantial, and the employee is guaranteed a postsuspension hearing.[173]

Thus, it is clear that public employees who can legitimately claim liberty or property right protections of due process for their jobs are guaranteed an evidentiary hearing. Such a hearing should be conducted before disciplinary action is taken unless the prediscipline protections just mentioned are provided, in which case the full-blown hearing could be postponed until afterward.

For administrators with a collective bargaining relationship with their employees, where minimal procedural safeguards are provided in contractual grievance provisions, that avenue of relief may provide an acceptable substitute for constitutionally mandated procedural rights.[174]

Substantive Due Process

As mentioned earlier, due process requirements embrace substantive as well as procedural aspects. In the context of disciplinary action, substantive due process requires that the rules and regulations on which disciplinary action is predicated be clear, specific, and reasonably related to a valid public need.[175] In the police environment, these requirements present the greatest challenge to the commonly found departmental regulations against conduct unbecoming an officer or conduct that brings discredit on the department.

The requirement that a rule or regulation be reasonably related to a valid public need means that a police department may not intrude into the private matters of its officers in which it has no legitimate interest. Therefore, there must be a connection "between the prohibited conduct and the officer's fitness to perform the duties required by his position."[176] In addition, the conduct must be of such a nature as to adversely affect the morale and efficiency of the department or have a tendency to destroy public respect for and confidence in the department.[177] Thus, it has been held that a rule prohibiting unbecoming conduct or discrediting behavior cannot be applied to a police officer's remarks that were highly critical of several prominent local figures but were made to a private citizen in a private conversation in a patrol car and were broadcast accidentally over the officer's patrol car radio.[178]

The requirements for clarity and specificity are necessary to ensure that (1) the innocent are not trapped without fair warning, (2) those who enforce the regulations have their discretion limited by explicit standards, and (3) where basic First Amendment rights are affected by a regulation, the regulation does not operate unreasonably to inhibit the exercise of those rights.[179]

The courts' applications of these requirements to unbecoming conduct and discrediting behavior rules have taken two courses. The first course, exemplified by *Bence v. Breier*, has been to declare such regulations unconstitutional because of their vagueness. In its consideration of a Milwaukee Police Department rule that prohibited "conduct unbecoming a member and detrimental to the service," the court found that the rule lacked inherent, objective content from which ascertainable standards defining the proscribed conduct could be fashioned. Like beauty, their content exists only in the eye of the beholder. The subjectivity implicit in the language of the rule permits police officials to enforce the rule with unfettered discretion, and it is precisely this potential for arbitrary enforcement which is abhorrent to the Due Process Clause.[180]

The second course taken by the courts has been to uphold the constitutionality of the regulation because, as applied to the officer in the case at hand, it should have been clear to him that his behavior was meant to be proscribed by the regulation. Under this approach, the court is saying that there may or may not be some circumstances in which the rule is too vague or overbroad, but the rule is constitutional in the present case. Thus, it should be clear to any police officer that fleeing from the scene of an accident[181] or making improper advances toward a young woman during the course of an official investigation[182] constitutes conduct unbecoming an officer or conduct that discredits the police department.

Many police departments also have a regulation prohibiting neglect or dereliction of duty. Although on its face such a rule seems to possess some of the same potential vagueness and over breadth shortcomings characteristic of the unbecoming conduct rules, it has fared better in the courts because the usual disciplinary action taken under neglect-of-duty rules nearly always seems to be for conduct for which police officers could reasonably expect disciplinary action. The courts have upheld administrative sanctions against officers under neglect-of-duty rules for sleeping on the job,[183] failing to prepare for planned demonstrations,[184] falsification of police records,[185] failure to make scheduled court appearances,[186] failure to investigate a reported auto accident,[187] and directing a subordinate to discontinue enforcement of a city ordinance.[188] The courts have refused to uphold disciplinary action against a police chief who did not keep 8-to-4 office hours,[189] and against an officer who missed a training session on riot control because of marital problems.[190]

Damages and Remedies

In determining an employee's entitlement to damages and relief, the issue of whether the employer's disciplinary action was justified is important. For example, when an employee's termination was justified but procedural due process violations occurred, the employee can recover only nominal damages in the absence of proof of actual compensable injuries deriving from the due process violation. On proof of actual injury, an employee can recover compensatory damages, which would include damages for mental and emotional distress and damage to career or reputation.[191] However, injury caused by the lack of due process when the termination was justified is not compensable in the form of back pay.[192]

CONSTITUTIONAL RIGHTS OF POLICE OFFICERS

Police officers have the same individual rights that all citizens within the United States are afforded under the U.S. Constitution. Even though they have been given significant training, held to a higher standard of conduct, and are subject to public and legal scrutiny, they still enjoy the same protections afforded to everyone else in our society.

Free Speech

The First Amendment of the U.S. Constitution prohibits Congress from passing any law "abridging the freedom of speech." It has been held that the due process clause of the Fourteenth Amendment makes this prohibition applicable to the states, counties, and cities as well.[193]

Although freedom of speech is one of the most fundamental of all constitutional rights, the Supreme Court has indicated that "the State has interests as an employer in regulating the speech of its employees that differ significantly from those it possesses in connection with regulation of the speech of the citizenry in general."[194] Therefore, the state may place restrictions on the speech of its employees that it could not impose on the general citizenry. However, these restrictions must be reasonable.[195] Generally, disputes involving the infringement of public employee speech will be resolved by balancing the interests of the state as an employer against the employee's constitutional rights.[196]

There are two basic situations in which a police regulation or other action can be found to be an unreasonable infringement on the free speech interests of an officer. The first is when the action is overly broad. A Chicago Police Department rule prohibiting "any activity, conversation, deliberation, or discussion which is derogatory to the Department" was ruled overly broad because it prohibited all criticism of the department by police officers, even if the criticism occurred in private conversation.[197] The same fate befell a New Orleans Police Department regulation that prohibited statements by a police officer that "unjustly criticize or ridicule, or express hatred or contempt toward, or ... which may be detrimental to, or cast suspicion on the reputation of, or otherwise defame, any person."[198]

The second situation in which a free speech limitation can be found unreasonable is in the way in which the government action is applied. The most common shortcoming of police departmental action in this area is a failure to demonstrate that the statements by the officer being disciplined adversely affected the operation of the department.[199] Thus, a Baltimore police regulation prohibiting public criticism of departmental action was held to have been applied unconstitutionally to a police officer who was president of the police union and who had stated in a television interview that the police commissioner was not leading the department effectively and that "the bottom is going to fall out of this city."[200] In this case, no significant disruption of the department was noted. However, when two officers of the Kinloch, Missouri Police Department publicly complained of corruption within city government, the court held that the "officers conducted a campaign ... with complete disregard of chain of command motivated by personal desires that created disharmony among the 12-member police force."[201] Because the allegations were totally unfounded and were not asserted correctly through channels instituted by state "whistle-blower" procedures, the dismissals were upheld.

A more recent basis for enforcing employees' First Amendment freedom of speech is that of public policy. The Court of Appeals for the Eighth Circuit held that discharging an employee who violated the police department's chain of command by reporting misconduct to an official outside of the city violated the employee's First Amendment rights. The court reasoned that the city's interest in maintaining discipline through the chain-of-command policy was outweighed by the public's vital interest in the integrity of its law enforcers and by the employee's right to speak out on such matters.[202] Generally, speech about corruption or criminal activity within the officer's law enforcement agency is very likely to be given protection under the First Amendment, especially when such speech is protected by a state "whistle-blower statute."[203] Central to a successful claim under a whistle-blower statute is that the employee show that discipline resulted from the employee's reporting of a violation of the law. Essentially, there must be an element of retaliation against the employee for publicly reporting illegal conduct.[204] The employee need only have a reasonable belief that illegal conduct has occurred and need not have absolute proof of the illegality.[205]

It appears that one's right to speak openly about the policies of a police department may well depend on four important factors: (1) the impact of the statements on the routine operations of the department, (2) the truth of the statements, (3) the manner in which the statements are made regarding existing policy orders involving chain-of-command and state whistle-blower regulations, and (4) the position occupied by the officer. For instance, statements made by dispatchers, clerks, and first-line officers in a large department that have relatively little impact might be given much more tolerance than supervisory or command personnel complaining of departmental policy because the degree of influence, validity, and credibility significantly increases with rank.

Other First Amendment Rights

A basic right of Americans in our democratic system of government is the right to engage in political activity. As with free speech, the government may impose reasonable restrictions on the political behavior of its employees that it could not impose on the citizenry at large. It is argued that, if the state could not impose some such restrictions, there would be a substantial danger that employees could be pressured by their superiors to support political candidates or causes that were contrary to their own beliefs under threat of loss of employment or other adverse action against them for failure to do so.[206]

At the federal level, various types of partisan political activity by federal employees are controlled by the Hatch Act. The constitutionality of that act has been upheld by the Supreme Court.[207] Many states have similar statutes, which are usually referred to as "little Hatch" acts, controlling political activity by state employees. The Oklahoma version of the Hatch Act, which was upheld by the Supreme Court,[208] prohibited state employees from soliciting political contributions, joining a partisan political club, serving on the committee of a political party, being a candidate for any paid political office, or taking part in the management of a political party or campaign. However, some states, such as Florida, specifically prohibit local governments from limiting the off-duty political activity of their employees.

Nonpolitical associations are also protected by the First Amendment. However, it is common for police departments to prohibit officers from associating with known felons or other persons of bad reputation on the basis that "such associations may expose an officer to irresistible temptations to yield in his obligation to impartially enforce the law, and ... may give the appearance that the community's police officers are not themselves honest and impartial enforcers of the law."[209] Sometimes, the prohibition is imposed by means of a specific ordinance or regulation, whereas in other instances, the prohibition is enforced by considering it conduct unbecoming an officer. Of course, if the latter approach is used, the ordinance or regulation will have to overcome the legal obstacles discussed earlier, relating to unbecoming conduct or discrediting behavior rules.

As with rules touching on the other First Amendment rights, rules prohibiting associations with criminals and other undesirables must not be overly broad in their reach. Thus, a Detroit Police Department regulation that prohibited knowing and intentional associations with convicted criminals or persons charged with crimes except in the course of an officer's official duties was declared unconstitutional because it proscribed some associations that could have no bearing on an officer's integrity or the public's confidence in an officer. The court cited as examples an association with a fellow church member who had been arrested on one occasion years ago and the befriending of a recently convicted person who wanted to become a productive citizen.[210]

The other common difficulty with this kind of rule is that it is sometimes applied to situations in which the association has not been demonstrated to have had a detrimental effect on the performance of the officer's duties or on the discipline and efficiency of the department. Thus, one court has held that a police officer who was a nudist but was fully qualified in all other respects to be a police officer could not be fired simply because he was a practicing nudist.[211] On the other hand, another court upheld the firing of a police officer who had sexual intercourse at a party with a woman he knew to be a nude model at a local "adult theater of known disrepute."[212] The court viewed this behavior as being of such a disreputable nature that it had a detrimental effect on the discipline and efficiency of the department.

In 2005, the Supreme Court determined that the police department could terminate an officer for selling a sexually explicit videotape of himself, in which he identified himself as a police officer. The Court ruled that, even though the activities of the officer took place outside the workplace, the department "demonstrated legitimate and substantial interests of its own that were compromised by the officer's speech" and the activities did not fall under free speech protections.[213]

The First Amendment's protection of free speech has been viewed as protecting means of expression other than verbal utterances.[214] That issue as it relates to an on-duty police officer's personal appearance was addressed by the Supreme Court decision in *Kelley v. Johnson*,[215] which upheld the constitutionality of a regulation of the Suffolk County, New York Police Department that established several grooming standards for its male officers. The Court in *Kelley* held that either a desire to make police officers readily recognizable to the public or a desire to maintain an esprit de corps was a sufficiently rational justification for the regulation. The issue of personal grooming and style continues to be a subject of hot debate in departments across the nation, particularly as officers move closer to their constituencies through community policing endeavors.

Searches and Seizures and the Right to Privacy

The Fourth Amendment to the U.S. Constitution protects "the right of the people to be secure in their persons, houses, papers, and effects, against unreasonable searches and seizures." This guarantee protects against actions by states and the federal government.[216] Generally, the cases interpreting the Fourth Amendment require that, before a search or seizure can be effectuated, the police must have **probable cause** to believe that a crime has been committed and that evidence relevant to the crime will be found at the place to be searched. Because of the language in the Fourth Amendment about "persons, houses, papers, and effects," for years the case law analyzed what property was subject to the amendment's protection. However, in *Katz v. United States* (1967)[217] the Supreme Court established

---

Quick Facts: Police Membership in Hate Groups

Recently, a police officer was forced to resign in San Francisco because of racist text messages, and a police officer and a lieutenant in the Anniston, Alabama police department were terminated following the discovery of a YouTube video that showed their participation in a neo-Confederate, white supremist group called the *League of the South (LOS)*. In both of these cases, the officers had extensive Facebook pages that depicted their racist perspectives on all minorities, and members of the gay, lesbian, and transgender population. The Anniston case, the group was identified by the Southern Poverty Law Center as a "hate group" which strongly supported the city's action. However, at the heart of the matter is whether an officer can be terminated for his or her own personal perspectives of race or their membership in a "civic club" even if that club, although legal and lawfully formed, expresses extreme bigotry, racism and hate (e.g., Proud Boys, the KKK, neo-Nazi groups, and Skinheads). The answer is clear when a policy exists within the department that prohibits actions of racism or hate that would violate the spirit of the U.S. Constitution and/or embarrass the department. In these cases, as well as in many others, racial bigotry cannot and will not be tolerated in police organizations.

a two-pronged test that accounted for both property and the *privacy expectations* of a person.[218] The two prongs are: (1) the person has an expectation of privacy, which is a subjective test and (2) the expectation of privacy is reasonable in the fact situation. This test has been used in decisions that affect not only police officers, but employees in other sectors of our economy as well. In this section we examine how these decisions have specifically impacted officers' right to privacy with respect to departmental supplied lockers, communication devices (such as cell phones and radios), and equipment generally.

In a case involving a police officer suspected of gambling, the Supreme Court held that the use of a pen register did not require the same constitutional safeguards as those surrounding a wiretap. The pen register uses a "trap-and-trace" device that records phone numbers and the duration of each call but does not capture any type of communication between parties. The Court reasoned that no warrant or probable cause was needed, as the Fourth Amendment was applicable to captured communication only and that there was no reasonable expectation to privacy regarding the actual phone number.[219]

The Fourth Amendment usually applies to police officers when at home or off duty as it would to any other citizen. In general, police officers cannot sustain a reasonable privacy expectation claim when using government issued/departmental lockers,[220] communications devices, and other equipment, for example, cars, desks, and filing cabinets. Many police agencies reinforce the applicable court decisions by formal policy, noting that all departmentally owned items such as lockers, desks, and cell phones may be opened and inspected at any time by an appropriate representative for both routine inspection as well as in the course of an investigation. Some agencies even go into such detail as to require the use of a department-issued lock on lockers, and prohibit the use of secondary/private locks. Further, in a landmark case in 2010, the Court ruled unanimously that a search of a police officer's personal, and sometimes sexually explicit, text messages on a city-owned pager was constitutional, even though it was conducted without a warrant.[221] By extension of previous case logic, cell phone communications and e-mail on a city-owned cell phone or computer would also not be protected material and the officer does not have a constitutional right to privacy regarding these devices. Again, there appears not to be an expectation of privacy for officers when using government-owned devices or equipment.

Another situation involves the ordering of officers to appear at a lineup. Requiring someone to appear in a lineup is a seizure of his or her person and, therefore, would ordinarily require probable cause. However, a federal Appeals Court upheld a police commissioner's order to 62 officers to appear in a lineup for the purpose of identifying officers who had allegedly beaten several civilians. The court held that, in this situation, "the governmental interest in the particular intrusion (should be weighed) against the offense to personal dignity and integrity." Because of the nature of the police officer's employment relationship, "he does not have the full privacy and liberty from police officials that he would otherwise enjoy."[222]

To enforce the protections guaranteed by the Fourth Amendment's search-and-seizure requirements, the courts have fashioned the so-called *exclusionary rule*, which prohibits the use of evidence obtained in violation of the Fourth Amendment in criminal proceedings. However, in a series of cases, the Supreme Court has redefined the concept of "reasonableness" as it applies to the Fourth Amendment and the exclusionary rule. In *United States v. Leon* and the companion case of *Massachusetts v. Sheppard*, the Court held that the Fourth Amendment "requires officers to have reasonable knowledge of what the law prohibits" in a search.[223] In essence, *Leon* and *Sheppard* began to develop the concept of "totality of circumstances" confirmed in *Illinois v. Gates*—that is, that evidence cannot be suppressed when an officer is acting "under good faith" whether or not a warrant issued is good on the surface.[224] These cases have far-reaching implications in civil actions against police officers, in that officers enjoy the benefits of qualified immunity when they are acting in good faith and under the belief that probable cause does exist.[225] Indeed, the Court has held that only a clear absence of probable cause will defeat a claim of qualified immunity.[226]

Finally, the exclusionary rule and the previously mentioned cases have an important bearing on disciplinary hearings involving the police. In *Sheetz v. Mayor and City Council of Baltimore*, the court held that illegally seized drugs in the possession of an officer could be used in an administrative discharge proceeding against that officer.[227] The Court reasoned that only a bad-faith seizure would render the evidence inadmissible because the police are not motivated to seize illegally for the purpose of use in an administrative discharge proceeding; hence, the exclusionary rule was not applicable, and the officer's firing was upheld.

Right Against Self-Incrimination

On two occasions, the Supreme Court has addressed questions concerning the Fifth Amendment rights of police officers who are the subjects of investigations. In *Garrity v. New Jersey*,[228] a police officer had been ordered by the attorney general to answer certain questions or be discharged. The officer testified, and the information gained as a result of his answers was later used to convict him of criminal charges.

The Fifth Amendment protects an individual from being compelled "in any criminal case to be a witness against himself."[229] The Supreme Court held that the information obtained from the police officer could not be used at his or her criminal trial because the Fifth Amendment forbids the use of coercion of this sort to extract an incriminating statement from a suspect.

In *Gardner v. Broderick*,[230] a police officer had declined to answer questions put to him by a grand jury investigating police misconduct on the grounds that his answers might tend to incriminate him. As a result, the officer was dismissed from his job. The Supreme Court ruled that the officer could not be fired for his refusal to waive his constitutional right to remain silent. However, the Court made it clear that it would have been proper for the grand jury to require the officer to answer or face discharge for his refusal, as long as the officer had been informed that his answers could not be used against him in a criminal case and the questions were related specifically, directly, and narrowly to the performance of his official duties. The Court felt that this approach was necessary to protect the important state interest in ensuring that the police officers were performing their duties faithfully.

In its ruling, the Supreme Court set forth a basic standard for disciplinary investigations of police officers. Referring to *Garrity*, the Court ruled that although a police agency can conduct an administrative investigation of an officer, it cannot in the course of that investigation compel the officer to waive his or her privilege against self-incrimination. As it has been interpreted, *Garrity* requires that before a police agency can question an officer regarding an issue that may involve disciplinary action against the officer for refusal to answer questions, the agency must do the following:

1. Order the officer to answer the questions.
2. Ask questions that are specifically, directly, and narrowly related to the officer's duties.
3. Advise the officer that the answers to the questions will not be used against the officer in criminal proceedings.[231]

If the officer refuses to answer appropriate questions after being given these warnings and advisement, then he or she may be disciplined for insubordination.

As a result of these cases, it is proper to discharge police officers who refuse to answer questions that are related specifically and directly to the performance of their duties and who have been informed that any answers they do give cannot be used against them in a criminal proceeding.[232]

Historically, it was not uncommon for police departments to make use of polygraph examinations in the course of internal investigations. The legal question that has arisen most frequently is whether an officer can be required to submit to such a procedure under threat of discharge for refusal to do so. There is some diversity of legal authority on this question, but the majority of courts that have considered it have held that an officer can be required to take the examination.[233]

An Arizona court overturned a county merit system commission's finding that a polygraph examination could be ordered only as a last resort after all other investigative efforts had been exhausted and held that

> a polygraph is always proper to verify statements made by law enforcement officers during the course of a departmental investigation as long as the officers are advised that the answers cannot be used against them in any criminal prosecution, that the questions will relate solely to the performance of official duties, and that refusal will result in dismissal.[234]

The use of polygraph examinations as a viable tool for internal affairs investigations was further strengthened by a state court in 2008.[235] The Massachusetts appeals court found that the Plymouth police department did not violate the state's statute by requiring a police officer who was accused of sexually molesting two minors to take a polygraph test for suspicion of criminal misconduct. After refusing to take the examination, the officer was terminated for "just cause."

On the other hand, a more recent decision of the Florida Supreme Court held that the dismissal of a police officer for refusing to submit to a polygraph test constituted "an unjust and unlawful job deprivation." Further, the court recognized that granting to public employers a carte blanche authority to force employees to submit to unlimited questioning during a polygraph test would conflict with the employees' constitutional right of privacy and would abrogate their protection against self-incrimination.[236]

Further, the use of a polygraph test to screen job applicants for police jobs has fallen under severe criticism. In 1987, a federal judge declared the test to be both unconstitutional and unreliable and ordered the city of Philadelphia to reconsider the applications of individuals denied positions because of their failure to pass a polygraph test. Conversely, the court of appeals reversed the district court holding and stated that the use of polygraph tests for preemployment screening did not violate either equal protection or substantive due process.[237]

As a result of these cases and the resulting ambiguity concerning polygraph testing and the Fifth Amendment, most jurisdictions have limited the use of the polygraph by statute and/or administrative regulation. Also, most agencies have developed extensive internal policies to limit the use of the polygraph and to expressly detail circumstances in which the test may be used to corroborate officer statements.

OTHER GROUNDS FOR DISCIPLINARY ACTION

Although police officers enjoy the same constitutional rights as other citizens within the United States, they are clearly held to a different standard of conduct both on and off the job. In many cases, their actions do not rise to the level of a criminal complaint yet still become the grounds for disciplinary actions that may result in termination and loss of career.

Conduct Unbecoming an Officer

By far, the largest number of police disciplinary cases arise under rules prohibiting conduct unbecoming an officer. These rules have traditionally been vague and overly broad in order to control officers both on and off duty.[238] Most "conduct unbecoming" regulations have been challenged for being unconstitutionally vague.[239] The basis of this claim rests in the concept of reasonableness as applied to the misconduct.[240] In a leading case, the California Supreme Court held that the permissible application of a "conduct unbecoming" regulation turns on whether the officer could reasonably anticipate that his or her conduct would be the subject of discipline:

> We construe "conduct unbecoming" a city police officer to refer only to conduct which indicates a lack of fitness to perform the functions of a police officer. Thus construed, [the rule] provides a sufficiently specific standard against which the conduct of a police officer in a particular case can be judged. Police officers ... will normally be able to determine what kind of conduct indicates unfitness to perform the functions of police officer.[241]

A wide variety of conduct has been held to fall appropriately within the scope of a "conduct unbecoming" regulation. It is important to note that the regulation must reasonably warn the officer of what type of conduct would be considered unbecoming and that said conduct would tend to affect the officer's performance of his or her duties adversely or cause the department to fall into public disrepute.[242] Some of the activities that commonly fall within the scope of a "conduct unbecoming" regulation and that have been upheld by the courts include associating with crime figures or persons with a criminal record,[243] verbal abuse and swearing,[244] off-duty drinking and intoxication,[245] criminal conduct,[246] dishonesty,[247] fighting with coworkers,[248] insubordination,[249] and a number of improprieties involving sexual activity, including promiscuity and fraternizing with known prostitutes.

One of the more interesting and recent cases involving "conduct unbecoming an officer" involved the Federal Bureau of Investigation in 2009. In *Doe v. U.S. Department of Justice*,[250] Doe argued that the FBI failed to show that his off-duty misconduct affected the "efficiency of the service" of his employment. The FBI's Office of Responsibility developed an investigation revealing that Doe had videotaped his personal sexual activities with women, including two women in his division, and that he might have done so without their consent. Doe was terminated for "unprofessional conduct"—conduct unbecoming an agent of the Federal Bureau of Investigation. Although an external review by the Merit Systems Protection Board (MSPB) supported the FBI's decision to fire Doe, the Federal Circuit Court of Appeals ruled that the FBI failed to address how Doe's off-duty and personal conduct negatively impacted the agency's "ability to perform" its mission. Further, the court ruled that the FBI failed to point out a violation of a specific internal policy that fit the circumstances of the conduct. Consequently, the MSPB's decision was reversed and remanded, and John Doe continues to be a Special Agent with the FBI. The case appears to reaffirm the concept that cases resting on "conduct unbecoming an officer" must not be overly vague, must indeed violate specific policies, and the behavior must be shown to negatively impact the agency in some manner.

Brady Violations

In a landmark 1963 case (*Brady v. Maryland*),[251] the U.S. Supreme Court ruled that the suppression of any evidence by the prosecution favorable to the accused violates the due process clauses of the Fourth and Fourteenth Amendments of the Constitution. As a result, prosecutors were compelled to disclose to the defense any and all evidence that might be exculpatory for the accused—meaning any evidence that could possibly clear the suspect must be presented to the defense. Such evidence could include physical evidence, fingerprints, DNA, photographs, and the alike, which conflicts with the prosecutor's evidence, and any evidence that could impeach the credibility of a prosecution witness.

More importantly for police administrators, in a follow-up case, *Giglio v. United States* and other *Brady* progeny cases,[252] the Court extended that obligation to share exculpatory information with the defendant to include information concerning the credibility of the prosecution's witnesses, including individual police officers. As a result, police agencies must disclose to the prosecution, who must disclose to the defense, any exculpatory or impeachment evidence that demonstrates that a witness is lying about specific facts in a case or is generally unworthy of belief. Evidence of this nature is often referred to as "*Brady* material." Failing to disclose such evidence is a "*Brady*" violation that can lead to dismissal of the criminal case and civil (U.S. Code 42, Section 1983) cases brought against the individual prosecutor, the police department, and the officer for violation of the suspect's constitutional rights.

LYING

Brady cases have had a dramatic effect on the credibility of individual police officers as witnesses. Because the prosecution is bound to reveal any possible impeachment evidence regarding its own witnesses, an officer's internal affairs records and

---

Box 14.7: Female Police Officers Still Have to Fight for the Right to Breastfeed on Duty, Despite Federal Law that Permits It

A police officer in Washington, DC, has raised concern about the lack of private lactation rooms for female officers.

In a case that challenges gender stereotypes and perceptions of police officers, female officers in many police departments have had to fight to have a secure, clean place to pump milk for their babies.

In 2011, the Affordable Care Act amended the Fair Labor Standards Act to hold that employers must provide a place, *other than a restroom*, that is shielded from view and free from intrusion in order for employees to express breast milk. However, police agencies have been slow to adapt to this change. The Metropolitan Police Department in Washington, DC, led by Cathy Lanier, was still directing employees as late as 2014 to bathroom stalls for the purposes of pumping—an unsanitary and unsavory practice that also had the effect of humiliating lactating police officers.

Officers have also reported that supervisors required them to log in and out when they pumped, taking note of the amount of time that they spent and requiring them to take leave when they pumped outside of their lunch hour. This is not illegal but does create difficulties for female police officers with young children.

The federal law is clear on the availability of private and appropriate lactation rooms, however—but many female officers feel that they will be retaliated against or mocked if they press the issue. For now, many police moms are forced to seek space in restrooms, utility closets and even patrol cars in order to provide milk for their infants.

Source: Emily Miller, "DC police department violates federal breastfeeding law," November 12, 2014. Retrieved on August 7, 2015 from: http://www.myfoxdc.com/story/27370521/dc-police-department-violates-federal-breastfeeding-law

any documented report where the officer lied or was untruthful must be presented as *Brady* material. Such officers simply cannot testify in court without being impeached; hence, their ability to work as a police officer is seriously compromised. For this reason, many police departments now have policies that terminate an employee for lying.

Social Network Sites

Although past incidents of lying and untruthfulness form the basis for impeaching the individual officer under *Brady*, there are indeed other issues that warrant discussion. Postings on social network sites have recently been entered into evidence in successful attempts to discredit police officers. Take, for example, officers who have posted racy and/or nude photos of themselves on their Facebook page, or pictures of officers taking drugs or drinking excessively on YouTube, or statements by officers that are offensive, racist, and show extreme bias on Twitter or a local blog. These examples show not only poor judgment on the part of the officer, but in the worst case, provide potential evidence for impeachment during a trial. While the behavior does not comport to *Brady* technically, this type of material can still be used to impeach the officer's credibility. As a general rule, the following "tips" are offered for police using social networking sites:

- *No nudity or sexually explicit pictures*—This includes pictures of you or you with a friend who is disrobed. Understand that your Facebook pictures and YouTube videos can easily be presented in court.

- *No drug taking or excessive alcohol postings*—Keep private "partying" photos to a minimum.

- *No gun glorification*—Keep your weapon and other police equipment off your social networking sites, and keep pictures of you in uniform off your social network sites.

- *Avoid bashing the department and keep rumors quiet*— Not only does this alleviate issues previously discussed that may indeed "interfere with the official business of the department" but also protects you from potential civil actions if the statements are found to be untrue.

- *Restrict personal information and manage your privacy settings*—Remember that suspects use the computer as well and that personal information relating to your address and family may place you in harm's way.[253]

Sexual Conduct and Sexual Orientation

The cases in this area tend to fall into two general categories: cases involving adultery and cases involving homosexuality. Most cases are in general agreement that adultery, even though committed while the police officer is off duty and in private, created a proper basis for disciplinary action.[254] The courts held that such behavior brings adverse criticism on the agency and tends to undermine public confidence in the department. However, one case involving an Internal Revenue Service agent suggests that to uphold disciplinary action for adultery, the government would have to prove that the employing agency was actually discredited; the court further stated that the discreditation would not be presumed from the proof of adulterous conduct.[255]

More recently, the Supreme Court justices appeared to be divided on the issue of extramarital sexual activity in public employment. In 1984, the Court of Appeals for the Sixth Circuit held that a Michigan police officer could not be fired solely because he was living with a woman to whom he was not married (a felony under state law). In 1985, the Supreme Court denied review of that decision over the strong objection of three justices who felt the case "presented an important issue of constitutional law regarding the contours of the right of privacy afforded individuals for sexual matters."[256]

In cases involving sexual improprieties that clearly affect an officer's on-the-job performance, the courts have had far less controversy. In a series of cases, the courts have consistently supported the disciplinary action attached to the department's "conduct unbecoming" regulation, including cases in which officers were cohabiting or in which the sexual activities were themselves illegal (e.g., public lewdness, child molestation, sexual activity with prostitutes, and homosexuality).[257] In fact, the courts have upheld internal regulations barring the employment of spouses, in part because of the concern for an officer's work performance.

The issue of homosexual activity as a basis for discharge was presented to the Supreme Court. Oklahoma had a law permitting discharge of schoolteachers for engaging in "public homosexual activity." The lower court held the law to be facially overly broad and therefore unconstitutionally restrictive. The Supreme Court affirmed the decision.[258] Another federal court held that the discharge of a bisexual guidance counselor did not deprive the plaintiff of her First or Fourteenth Amendment rights. The counselor's discussion of her sexual preferences with teachers and other personnel was not protected by the First Amendment. Her equal protection claim failed because she did not show that the heterosexual employees would have been treated differently for communicating their sexual preferences.[259]

In an equally important federal case involving 13 lesbian deputies terminated from the Broward County, Florida Sheriff's Department, the Supreme Court held that homosexuals are not a suspect class accorded strict scrutiny under the equal protection clause and, therefore, the dismissal did not deprive the plaintiffs of any constitutional or equal protection right.[260] However, in 2003, the Supreme Court ruled that state sodomy laws are unconstitutional,[261] nullifying many police departments' argument that homosexuality is a criminal violation that is a viable basis for discharging a police officer.

Although there has yet to be a clear reversal of previous court rulings on gay and lesbian protections in the workplace, there have been a number of decisions made at the circuit court level that support discrimination (including discrimination against trans-gender individuals) as sex discrimination. In addition, the Supreme Court ruling in *Obergefell v. Hodges* on June 26, 2015, legalizing same-sex marriage tends to support the equality of gay and lesbians in the workplace. As a result of this shifting tide of legal opinion, the Equal Employment Opportunity Commission developed a statement following the ruling: discrimination against an individual because of that person's sexual orientation is a violation of Title VII. The Commission accepts and investigates charges alleging sexual-orientation discrimination in employment.[262]

Residency Requirements

A number of local governments have established requirements that all or certain classes of their employees live within the geographical limits of the jurisdiction. These residency requirements have been justified by the governments imposing them as desirable because they increase employees' rapport with and understanding of the community. When police officers were concerned, it has been asserted that the presence of off-duty police has a deterrent effect on crime and results in chance encounters that might lead to additional sources of information.

Before 1976, challenges to the legality of residency requirements for public employees dotted the legal landscape. In 1976, the Supreme Court, in *McCarthy v. Philadelphia Civil Service Commission*, ruled that Philadelphia's residency requirement for firefighters did not violate the Constitution.[263]

Since the *McCarthy* decision, the legal attacks on the residency requirements have subsided. The cases now seem to be concerned with determining what constitutes residency. The most obvious means of attempting to avoid the residency requirement (by establishing a second residence within the city) appears doomed to failure unless the police officer can demonstrate that he or she spends at least a substantial part of his or her time at the in-city residence.[264] A strong argument has been made that in areas where housing is unavailable or prohibitively expensive, a residency requirement is unreasonable.[265] In upholding the application of such requirements, courts have focused on the issues of equal enforcement and the specificity of the local residency standard.[266]

Moonlighting

Traditionally, the courts have supported the authority of police departments to place limits on the outside employment of their employees.[267] Police department restrictions on moonlighting range from a complete ban on outside employment to permission to engage in certain endeavors, such as investments, rental of property, teaching of law enforcement subjects, and employment designed to improve the police image. The rationale in support of moonlighting prohibitions is that "outside employment seriously interferes with keeping the [police and fire] departments fit and ready for action at all times."[268]

However, in a Louisiana case, firefighters offered unreputed evidence that moonlighting had been a common practice before the city banned it; during the previous 16 years, no firefighters had ever needed sick leave as a result of injuries suffered while moonlighting, there had never been a problem locating off-duty firefighters to respond to an emergency, and moonlighting had never been shown to be a source of fatigue that was serious enough to impair a firefighter's alertness on the job. Under these circumstances, the court ruled that there was not a sufficient basis for the prohibition on moonlighting and invalidated the ordinance.[269]

It is important to note that, in several cases involving off-duty, moonlighting officers (as private security guards or store detectives), the same legal standards imposed on sworn officers acting in the capacity of their jobs apply. The Court has held that off-duty officers act "under color of State law" and are subject to Section 1983 liability while working in a private security or "special patrolman" capacity.[270] Therefore, it follows that police agencies and departments may be liable under the same ramifications, opening up a new wave of future litigation involving police officer off-duty employment.

Alcohol and Drug Testing

It is common for police departments to require that their officers not be under the influence of any intoxicating agent while on duty. Even in the absence of such specific regulation, disciplinary action has been upheld when it was taken against an officer who was suspected of being intoxicated while on duty by charging him or her with neglect of duty or violation of a state law.[271]

Regulations that prohibit being under the influence of an intoxicating or mind-altering substance have been upheld uniformly as reasonable because of the hazardous nature of a police officer's work and the serious impact his or her behavior or misbehavior is sure to have on the property and safety of others. The necessity to require a clear head and rational action, not confused by alcohol or drugs, is clear.[272] A Louisiana court upheld a regulation that prohibited an officer from consuming alcoholic beverages on or off duty to the extent that it caused the officer's behavior to become obnoxious, disruptive, or disorderly.[273]

Effective enforcement of regulations against an officer being under the influence of drugs or alcohol will occasion situations when a police supervisor or administrator will order an officer to submit to one or more tests to determine the presence of the prohibited substance in the subject's body. It has been held that a firefighter could be ordered to submit to blood sampling when reasonable grounds existed for believing that he or she was intoxicated and that it was permissible to discharge the firefighter for his or her refusal to comply with the order.[274] More recently, the courts have also been asked to review police department policies that require officers to submit to urinalysis for the purpose of determining the presence of drugs or alcohol. In *United States v. Jacobsen*, the Supreme Court defined the concept of search and seizure:

> A "search" occurs when an expectation of privacy that society is prepared to consider reasonable is infringed. A "seizure" of property occurs when there is some meaningful interference with an individual's possessory interests in that property.[275]

According to the Supreme Court, removing urine from an individual's body is a search within the meaning of the Fourth Amendment. Consequently, when a government agency tests an employee's urine, due process must be applied, which involves providing probable evidence of illegal activity. In the case of public employer drug testing, the search is justified from the beginning, when "reasonable grounds exist for suspecting that the search will turn up evidence of work-related drug use."[276]

A reasonable search depends on a "balancing test" set forth by Justice Sandra Day O'Connor:

> A determination of the standard of reasonableness applicable to a particular class of searches requires balancing the nature and quality of the intrusion on the individual's Fourth Amendment interests against the importance of the governmental interest alleged to justify the intrusion. In the case of

searches conducted by a public employer, we must balance the invasion of the employee's legitimate expectations of privacy against the government's need for supervision, control, and the efficient operation of the work place.[277]

The Supreme Court has ruled on two cases that have become landmarks for drug testing in the public sector. In *Skinner v. Railway Labor Executives' Association*, the Court upheld a mandatory drug testing program in cases in which the government had no reasonable suspicion about any particular public employee but had a substantial interest in maintaining public safety.[278] In a case even more important to police agencies, the Court considered in *National Treasury Employees Union v. Von Raub* whether the U.S. Customs drug testing program was constitutional. The customs service drug-tested employees who sought a promotion to positions that required seizing or safekeeping illegal drugs, carrying firearms, or handling classified documents. The Court held that such employees have a "diminished expectation of privacy" and that drug testing is a minimal intrusion that is far outweighed by the government's interests to keep the public and citizenry safe.[279]

The prevailing view appears to be that totally random, unscheduled drug testing is unacceptable but that particular officers can be required to submit to urinalysis if there exists a "reasonable suspicion" that the officer has been using a prohibited substance or is involved in an incident involving citizen safety.[280] For instance, in 2007, the New York Police Department instituted a new drug and alcohol policy regarding critical incidents involving the police. If an officer fires his or her weapon either on or off duty or is involved in a traffic accident that causes injury or death, a portable breathalyzer test is automatically given as a condition of employment. If the breathalyzer test concludes a blood alcohol level of 0.08 or greater, the officer is immediately placed on administrative leave and an Internal Affairs investigation is opened.[281] More importantly, advanced alcohol and drug testing is then conducted through blood tests or urinalysis. The results of such compulsory tests are appropriate evidence for introduction in administrative discharge proceedings.[282]

Decisions involving other government employees and similar kinds of personal intrusions (e.g., strip searches of prison guards) seem to support the view that random testing is unreasonable under the Fourth Amendment.[283] However, without a definitive decision from the Supreme Court on random drug testing, lower federal court decisions concerning public agency personnel appear to allow random drug testing without reasonable suspicion of individual drug abuse if (1) an employer knows that drugs are used in the workplace, (2) the testing will not totally disrupt the employee's privacy expectation, and (3) the jobs are "safety-sensitive" in nature.[284]

In an attempt to skirt the issue of mandatory or random testing, some departments have incorporated drug testing as a "usual and customary" part of a required medical examination. For instance, the Philadelphia Police Department requires a medical examination for all individuals attempting to secure employment under the following conditions: (1) when an officer is first hired, (2) when an officer is transferred to a "sensitive" position (i.e., vice and narcotics division, SWAT, and hostage negotiation teams), (3) when an officer is promoted to a higher rank, and (4) when an officer returns to duty after an extended period of time (e.g., long illness, disability, or suspension). Drug abuse is viewed as a medical malady and is subject to disclosure, similar to the findings of other tests that show spinal problems, poor vision, hearing loss, and the like. Hence, drug testing can be viewed as a routine part of the medical examination for preemployment to a new position.

Chapter Summary

Summary by Learning Objectives

1. **Explain the three general categories of torts. How do they differ?**

   Negligence, intentional, and constitutional torts are the three general categories of torts. Negligence torts focus on whether an individual conducted his or her affairs in a manner that does not subject others to an unreasonable risk of harm. Intentional torts are the voluntary commissions of an act that has a substantial certainty to injure another person—it does not have to be negligent. Constitutional torts deal with the duty to recognize and uphold the constitutional rights, privileges, and immunities of others.

2. **Define "acting under the color of state law." How does this statement relate to Section 1983 actions?**

   "Acting under color of state law" means that when the action under question occurred, the individual officer was on-duty and acting within the scope of his or her employment. It extends the Title 42, U.S. Code, Section 1983 civil rights statute to apply to plaintiffs in municipal and state police officers only; it does not relate to federal officers (such as agents with the FBI or DEA), as they act under federal jurisdiction.

3. **Explain and describe a *Bivens* action.**

   A *Bivens* action applies to federal officials, and it is a judicially created counterpart of Title 42, U.S. Code, Section 1983 that allows federal courts to hear federal litigation cases involving suits against federal employees in their individual capacities. In this manner, agents of the federal government (e.g., FBI, DEA, U.S. Marshall Service, and ICE) can be sued by individuals

4. **List and describe the negligence theories applicable to police supervision and management.**

   Negligent hiring means that employers must exercise a reasonable standard of care in not selecting persons who, because of the nature of their job, could present a threat of injury to members of the public. Negligent assignment, retention, and entrustment means that police administrators who know of or should have known of individual acts or patterns of behavior by police officers that could threaten the public must take immediate action to remedy said situation or be subject to liability. Negligent direction and supervision means supervisors have the duty to develop and implement appropriate policies and procedures. Negligent training deals with the fact that the local or state unit of government, acting through their administrator of a police department, have an affirmative duty to train their employees (officers) correctly and adequately.

5. **Describe procedural and substantive due process.**

   Procedural due process refers to the legality of the procedures used to deprive police officers of status or wages, such as dismissal or suspension from their job. Substantive due process is the requirement that the basis for government disciplinary action be reasonable, relevant, and justifiable.

6. **Explain a *Brady* violation.**

   Police agencies must disclose to the prosecution, who must disclose to the defense, any exculpatory or impeachment evidence that demonstrates that a witness is lying about specific facts in a case, or is generally unworthy of belief. Evidence of this nature is often referred to as "*Brady* material." Failing to disclose such evidence is a "*Brady*" violation that can lead to dismissal of the criminal case and civil (U.S. Code 42, Section 1983) cases brought against the individual prosecutor, the police department, and the officer for violation of the suspect's constitutional rights.

7. **Explain when rules infringing on the free speech of officers might be upheld.**

   When there are reasonable motives for a department to infringe upon those rights; when those motives are not overly broad; and when statements by employees adversely affect the operation of a department.

8. **Describe the circumstances in which an officer may use deadly force?**

   An officer may use deadly force only in defense of life and against fleeing felons who the officer reasonably believes committed a felony involving the threat of violence.

9. **List the four elements that must be proven in order to sue the police for negligence in a high-speed pursuit.**

   The officer owed the injured party a duty not to engage in certain conduct; the officer's actions violated that duty; the officer's negligent conduct was the proximate cause of the accident; and the suing party suffered actual and provable damages.

10. **Describe how a department can reduce liability in high-speed pursuits.**

    To reduce risks and liabilities associated with vehicular pursuits, law enforcement organizations must carefully evaluate their pursuit policies, training, supervision, and postincident evaluations.

11. **Relate the focus of most training programs regarding emotionally disturbed persons.**

    The primary focus of most training programs regarding emotionally disturbed persons (EDPs) is recognizing behavior that indicates that officers are dealing with EDPs and communicating with those persons in a nonthreatening manner.

12. **Describe the balancing test related to alcohol and drug testing in the police workplace.**

    The balancing test relating to alcohol and drug testing involves balancing the nature and quality of the intrusion of the individual's Fourth Amendment protections against the importance of the governmental interest that justifies the intrusion.

Chapter Review Questions

1. What are the three general categories of torts?
2. Explain the meaning of "acting under the color of state law" as it relates to U.S. Code 42, Section 1983 actions.
3. What is a *Bivens* action?
4. What are the primary negligence theories applicable to police supervision and management?
5. Describe procedural and substantive due process.
6. What is the major three-prong test of reasonableness for all use-of-force cases in the future established in *Graham v. Connor*?
7. What are federal consent decrees and how important are they in reforming the police?
8. What is PSV?
9. Discuss the importance of the 2015 landmark case, *Obergefel v. Hodges*.
10. Identify when department rules and policies might infringe on the free speech of officers.
11. What is a *Brady* violation?
12. Describe the circumstances when an officer can use deadly force.
13. Identify the four elements that must be proven in order to sue the police for negligence in a high-speed pursuit.
14. Describe a police department's responsibility in reducing liability in high-speed pursuits.

15. Identify the desired outcomes of effective training of police officers in dealing with emotionally disturbed persons.

16. List the *Garrity* warnings; why was this case so instrumental in investigating police officers of wrongdoing?

17. Why is "conduct unbecoming an officer" such a controversial issue?

18. Describe the "balancing test" as referred to in alcohol and drug testing in the workplace.

Critical Thinking Exercises

1. Do you think body-worn cameras will have the effect of increasing or decreasing *Brady* violations? Why or why not?

2. Should a police officer have the right to use personal social media platforms, like Facebook and Twitter, to give his or her opinion of the police department even though those opinions might be critical of their department? Do you think that an officer's right to be critical of a department or an incident, specifically one that might involve racist or bigoted officers be protected under their First Amendment rights? Why or why not?

3. Visit the AELE Law Enforcement Legal Center website at http://www.aele.org/. Navigate to their "Special Issues in Law Enforcement" section at http://www.aele.org/hotissues.html. Do you think that these legal updates are something that the average patrol officer is aware of? Do you think that it's necessary for patrol officers to know these legal updates? Why or why not? If you were an administrator or executive of a law enforcement agency, how would you make sure that patrol officers kept abreast of such information?

Key Terms

1983 action
Bivens action
defendant
deliberate indifference
due process
emotionally disturbed persons (EDPs)
federal consent decree
less-lethal weapon

liability
liberty rights
litigation
negligence
objective reasonableness
plaintiff
police sexual violence (PSV)
probable cause

procedural due process
property rights
proximate cause
reasonableness
substantive due process
tort
vicarious liability

Endnotes

[1]Much of this section is adapted, with additions, from H. E. Barrineau III, *Civil Liability in Criminal Justice* (Cincinnati: Anderson, 1987), pp. 3–5.

[2]Ibid., p. 3.

[3]False arrest is the arrest of a person without probable cause. Generally, this means making an arrest when an ordinarily prudent person would not have concluded that a crime had been committed or that the person arrested had committed the crime. False imprisonment is the intentional illegal detention of a person. The detention that can give rise to a false imprisonment claim is any confinement to a specified area and not simply incarceration in a jail. Most false arrests result in false imprisonment as well, but there can be a false imprisonment after a valid arrest also, as when the police fail to release an arrested person after a proper bond has been posted, the police unreasonably delay the arraignment of an arrested person, or authorities fail to release a prisoner after they no longer have authority to hold him or her. "Brutality" is not a legal tort action as such. Rather, it must be alleged as a civil (as opposed to a criminal) assault and/or battery. Assault is some sort of menacing conduct that puts another person in reasonable fear that he or she is about to have a battery committed on him or her. Battery is the infliction of harmful or offensive contact on another person. Harmful or offensive contact is contact that would be considered harmful or offensive by a reasonable person of ordinary sensibilities. See Clarence E. Hagglund, "Liability of Police Officers and Their Employers," *Federation of Insurance Counsel Quarterly* 26 (summer 1976), p. 257, for a good discussion of assault and battery, false arrest, false imprisonment, and malicious prosecution as applied to police officers.

[4]Although a fourth category (strict liability tort action) does exist in the wider body of law, such a general category is rare in police officer litigation. Therefore, for the purposes of this book, strict liability actions are not discussed. Under strict liability, one is held liable for one's act, regardless of intent or negligence. The mere occurrence of certain events will necessarily create legal liability. A good example of such cases is often found in airplane disasters in which the air transportation company is strictly liable for the passengers' health and well-being, regardless of other factors.

[5]*Black's Law Dictionary*, 4th edition (St. Paul, MN: West, 2004), p. 470.

[6]Title 42, U.S. Code, Section 1983.

[7]See *Monroe v. Pape*, 365 U.S. 167, 81 S. Ct. 473 (1961). The plaintiff and his family sued 13 Chicago police officers and the city of Chicago, alleging that police officers broke into their home without a search warrant, forced them out of bed at gunpoint, made them stand naked while the officers ransacked the house, and subjected the family to verbal and physical abuse. The court held that the definition of "under color of State law" for Section 1983 purposes was the same as that already established in the criminal context and concluded that, because Section 1983 provides for a civil action, the plaintiffs need not prove that the defendants acted with a "specific intent to deprive a person of a federal right" (365 U.S. at 187). The court also held that municipalities (such as the city of Chicago, in this case) were immune from liability under the statute, although the Supreme Court later overruled this part of *Monroe v. Pape*, holding that municipalities and other local governments are included among "persons" open to a Section 1983 lawsuit. See *Monell v. Dept. of Social Services of the City of New York*, 436 U.S. 658, 98 S. Ct. 2018 (1978). (Citations to case opinions give the volume number in which the opinion is located followed by the name of the reporter system, the page number, the court if other than the Supreme Court, and the year in which the opinion was rendered.)

[8]The resuscitation of Section 1983 hinges on the misuse and abuse of power imbued to individuals acting as police officers. All municipal and county law enforcement officers take an oath to uphold and enforce the laws of a specific state in which their municipality resides. Therefore, municipal police officers are squarely within the confines of Section 1983. "Misuse of power," possessed by virtue of state law and made possible only because the wrongdoer is clothed with the authority of state law, is action taken "under the color of law." *United States v. Classic*, 313 U.S. 299, at p. 326, 61 S. Ct., 1031, at p. 1043 (1941) as quoted in *Monroe v. Pape*. Thus, private citizens cannot be sued under Section 1983 unless they conspire with state officers. (See *Slavin v. Curry*, 574 F. 2d 1256 [5th Cir. 1978], as modified by 583 F. 2d 779 [5th Cir. 1978].) Furthermore, if a state officer has immunity to a Section 1983 lawsuit, private citizens who conspired with him or her do not have "derivative immunity" to the lawsuit. (See *Sparks v. Duval County Ranch Co., Inc.*, 604 F. 2d 976 [5th Cir. 1979], at p. 978.) In addition, see *Sanberg v. Daley*, 306 F. Supp. 227 (1969), at p. 279.

[9]Most tort actions against the U.S. government must be brought under the FTCA. The FTCA is a partial waiver of sovereign immunity, with its own rule of liability and a substantial body of case law. Federal employees can be sued for violation of constitutional rights and for certain Common-Law torts. For more information, see Isidore Silver, *Police Civil Liability* (New York: Mathew Bender, 1987), Section 1.04, from which this material is taken.

[10]See *Bivens v. Six Unknown Federal Narcotics Agents*, 403 U.S. 388, 91 S. Ct. 1999 (1971). See also Silver, *Police Civil Liability*, Section 8.02.

[11]Silver, *Police Civil Liability*, Section 8.02.

[12]See William L. Prosser, *Handbook of the Law of Torts*, 4th edition (St. Paul, MN: West, 1971), p. 69, for a good discussion of the philosophical basis for and development of the doctrine of vicarious liability.

[13]Although this list does not include all types of negligence theories regarding 1983 action against police supervisors and managers, it does provide a starting point in understanding this issue. This part has been adapted from Barrineau, *Civil Liability*, pp. 59–60.

[14]See *Peter v. Bellinger*, 159 N.E. 2d 528 (1959); *Thomas v. Johnson*, 295 F. Supp. 1025 (1968); *McKenna v. City of Memphis*, 544 F. Supp. 415 (1982), affirmed in 785 F. 2d 560 (1986); *McGuire v. Arizona Protection Agency*, 609 P. 2d 1080 (1908); *Di Cosal v. Kay*, 19 N.J. 159, 450 A. 2d 508 (1982); *Pontiac v. KMS Investments*, 331 N.W. 2d 907 (1983); and *Welsh Manufacturing Division of Textron, Inc. v. Pinkertons, Inc.*, 474 A. 2d 426 (1984).

[15]See *Board of the County Commissioner of Bryan County v. Brown*, 117 S. Ct. 1383 (1997).

[16]See *Moon v. Winfield*, 383 F. Supp. 31 (1974); *Murray v. Murphy*, 441 F. Supp. 120 (1977); *Allen v. City of Los Angeles* (No. C-9837), LA Sup.Ct. (1975); *Stengel v. Belcher*, 522 F. 2d 438 (6th Cir. 1975); *Dominguez v. Superior Court*, 101 Cal. App. 3d 6 (1980); *Stuessel v. City of Glendale*, 141 Cal. App. 3d 1047 (1983); and *Blake v. Moore*, 162 Cal. App. 3d 700 (1984).

[17]See *Ford v. Breiser*, 383 F. Supp. 505 (1974); *Dewel v. Lawson*, 489 F. 2d 877 (10th Cir. 1974); *Bonsignore v. City of New York*, 521 F. Supp. 394 (1981), affirmed in 683 F. 2d 635 (1st Cir. 1982); *Webster v. City of Houston*, 689 F. 2d 1220 (5th Cir. 1982), reversed and remanded on the issue of damages in 739 F. 2d 993 (5th Cir. 1984); and *District of Columbia v. Parker*, 850 F. 2d 708 (D.C. Cir. 1988), cert. denied in 489 U.S. 1065, 109 S. Ct. 1339 (1989).

[18]See *Marusa v. District of Columbia*, 484 F. 428 (1973); *Webzster v. City of Houston*, supra note 22; and *Grandstagg v. City of Borger*, 767 F. 2d (5th Cir. 1985), cert. denied in 480 U.S. 917, 107 S. Ct. 1369 (1987).

[19]*City of Canton v. Harris*, 389 U.S. 378, 103 L. Ed. 412, 109 S. Ct. 1197 (1989), at pp. 1204–1205; *Merritt v. County of Los Angeles*, 875 F. 2d 765 (9th Cir. 1989); *Owens v. Haas*, 601 F. 2d 1242 (2nd Cir. 1979), cert. denied in 444 U.S. 980 (1980).

[20]Prosser, *Handbook of the Law of Torts*, pp. 977–978.

[21]*Scheuer v. Rhodes*, at p. 240.

[22]*Wood v. Strickland*, 420 U.S. 308, 95 S. Ct. 992 (1975).

[23]*Harlow v. Fitzgerald*, 457 U.S. 800, 102 S. Ct. 2727 (1982).

[24]*Mitchell v. Forsyth*, 472 U.S. 511, 105 S. Ct. 2806 (1985).

[25]*Monroe v. Pape*, supra note 7.

[26]436 U.S. 658, 98 S. Ct. 2018 (1978).

[27]See, for example, *Rookard v. Health and Hospitals Corp.*, 710 F. 2d 41 (2d Cir. 1983).

[28]*Oklahoma City v. Tuttle*, 471 U.S. 808, 105 S. Ct. 2427 (1985); but see *Pembauer v. Cincinnati*, 475 U.S. 469, 106 S. Ct. 1292 (1986).

[29]M. S. Vaughn et al., "Assessing Legal Liabilities in Law Enforcement: Police Chief's Views," *Crime and Delinquency* 47, No. 1 (January 2001), p. 22.

[30]*Daniels v. Williams*, 474 U.S. 327, 106 S. Ct. 662 (1986).

[31]*New v. City of Minneapolis*, 792 F. 2d 724, at pp. 725–26 (8th Cir. 1986). See also *McClary v. O'Hare*, 786 F. 2d 83 (2nd Cir. 1986).

[32]Hagglund, "Liability of Police Officers," p. 257.

[33]*United States v. Leon*, 468 U.S. 897, 104 S. Ct. 3430 (1984).

[34]*Malley v. Briggs*, 475 U.S. 335, 106 S. Ct. 1092 (1986).

[35]*Anderson v. Creighton*, 483 U.S. 635, 107 S. Ct. 3034 (1987).

[36] *Saucier v. Katz*, 533 U.S. 194, 121 S. Ct. 2151 (2001). See also *Pearson et al. v. Callahan*, 07–751 (494 F3d 891) (January 21, 2009).

[37] *Malley v. Briggs*, 475 U.S. 335, 341 (1986).

[38] *Maciarello v. Summer*, 973 F. 2d 295, 298 (1992).

[39] *Pearson et al. v. Callahan*, 07–751 (494 F3d 891) (January 21, 2009).

[40] Schmidt, "Recent Developments."

[41] Ibid., p. 198.

[42] *Wimberly v. Patterson*, 183 A. 2d 691 (1962), at p. 699.

[43] *Piatkowski v. State*, 251 N.Y.S. 2d 354 (1964), at p. 359.

[44] Schmidt, "Recent Developments," p. 199.

[45] *Fords v. Breier*, 383 F. Supp. 505 (E.D. Wis. 1974).

[46] *Lucas v. Riley*, Superior Court, Los Angeles County, CA (1975); *Delong v. City of Denver*, 530 F. 2d 1308 (Colo. 1974); *Grudt v. City of Los Angeles*, 468 P. 2d 825 (Cal. 1970); *Dillenbeck v. City of Los Angeles*, 446 P. 2d 129 (Cal. 1968).

[47] *AELE Law Enforcement Legal Defense Manual*, "Failure to Provide Medical Treatment," Issue 77–6 (1977).

[48] *Watkins v. City of Battle Creek*, 273 F. 3d 682, 685–686 (6th Cir. 2001).

[49] *Carter v. City of Detroit*, 480 F. 3d 305, 310, 311 (6th Cir. 2005).

[50] *AELE Law Enforcement Legal Defense Manual*, "Failure to Provide Medical Treatment."

[51] International Association of Chiefs of Police." Emerging Use of Force Issues: Balancing Public and Officer Safety," March 2012. Retrieved on August 2, 2015 from http://www.theiacp.org/portals/0/pdfs/emerginguseofforceissues041612.pdf.

[52] Kenneth James Matulia, "The Use of Deadly Force: A Need for Directives in Training," *The Police Chief* (May 1983), p. 30.

[53] Kenneth James Matulia, "A Balance of Forces: Model Deadly Force and Policy Procedure," *International Association of Chiefs of Police* (1985), pp. 23, 24. See also *Tennessee v. Garner*, 471 U.S. 1, 105 S. Ct. 1694 (1985). While this citation is relatively old, many of the basic positions held here are reiterated in the Commission on Accreditation for Law Enforcement Agencies (CALEA), Model Policy for Use of Force and Use of Deadly Force (2010).

[54] *Tennessee v. Garner*, supra note 17.

[55] *Graham v. Connor*, 109 s Ct. 1865, 1872 (1989).

[56] Ibid.

[57] Ibid.

[58] See Assembly Bill No. 392, Chapter 170, State of California, *Legislative Counsel's Digest*, Filed with the Secretary of State, August 19, 2019.

[59] See Anita Chabria, "California Police Use-of-Force Bill Advances after Black Live Matter, Families Drop Support," *Los Angeles Times*, May 29, 2019.

[60] Jill Cowan, "What to Know About California's New Police Use-of-Force Law," *New York Times*, August 20, 2019,

[61] FBI Stories, "The Crime of 'Swatting:' Fake 9–1–1- Calls Have Real Consequences," September 3, 2013. See: https://www.fbi.gov/news/stories/the-crime-of-swatting-fake-9-1-1-calls-have-real-consequences1

[62] No Author, "Swatting Could Become a Federal Crime," *The Economist*, January 12, 2019. See: https://www.economist.com/united-states/2019/01/12/swatting-could-become-a-federal-crime

[63] FBI Stories, "Don't Make the Call: The New Phenomenon of 'Swatting," February 4, 2008. See: https://archives.fbi.gov/archives/news/stories/2008/february/swatting020408

[64] Dan Tynan, "The Terror of Swatting: How the Law Is Tracking Down High-Tech Prank Callers," *The Guardian*, April 15, 2016. See also No Author, "Swatting Could Become a Federal Crime," *The Economist*, January 12, 2019. See: https://www.economist.com/united-states/2019/01/12/swatting-could-become-a-federal-crime

[65] Much of the above description of this incident was taken from court documents, See *Lisa G. Finch et al. vs. City of Wichita, Kansas, et al.*, In the U.S. District Court for the District of Kansas, Case No. 18-cv-1018-JWB-ADM; and Aviva Shen, "The Hidden Police Violence Behind a 'Swatting' Death," The Appeal, May 16, 2018. See: https://theappeal.org/the-hidden-police-violence-epidemic-behind-a-swatting-death-2bb00f43cb5a/

[66] See *Lisa G. Finch et al. vs. City of Wichita, Kansas, et al.*, In the U.S. District Court for the District of Kansas, Case No. 18-cv-1018-JWB-ADM. See: https://www.ksn.com/wp-content/uploads/sites/13/2019/11/Finch-Lawsuit-Pretrial-Order-07915478965.pdf

[67] Ibid.

[68] Owen S. Good, "Wichita Cops Start Flagging Potential Swatting Addresses," *Polygon*, August 25, 2019.

[69] *Tennessee v. Garner*, supra note 179.

[70] Matulia, "A Balance of Forces," p. 72.

[71] Catherin H. Milton, Jeanne Wahl Halleck, James Lardnew, and Gray L. Albrecht, *Police Use of Deadly Force* (Washington, DC: Police Foundation, 1977), p. 52.

[72] Matulia, "A Balance of Forces," p. 52.

[73] Ibid., p. 77.

[74] Ibid.

[75] Ibid., p. 78.

[76] Robert W. Taylor and John Liederbach, "Police Use of Deadly Force," in Controversies in Policing, 2nd edition, Q. C. Thurman and A. L. Giacomazzi, eds. (Cincinnati, OH: Anderson Publishing, Fall 2004).

[77] D. Best, A. Quigley, and A. Bailey, "Police Shootings as a Way of Self-Harming: A Review of the Evidence for 'Suicide by Cop' in England and Wales Between 1998 and 2001," *International Journal of the Sociology of Law* (2004), pp. 349–361.

[78] See H. Range. Hutson, D. Anglin, J. Yarborough, K. Hardaway, M. Russell, J. Strote, M. Cantor, and B. Blum, "Suicide by Cop," *Annals of Emergency Medicine* (1998), pp. 665–669; D. Kennedy, R. J. Homant, and R. T. Hupp, "Suicide by Cop," *FBI Law Enforcement Bulletin* (August 1998), pp. 21–27; Vivian Lord, "One Form of Victim Precipitated Homicide: The Use of Law Enforcement Officers to Commit Suicide." Paper presented at the annual meeting of the Academy of Criminal Justice Sciences, 1998; Richard Parent and S. Verdun-Jones, "Aspects of Use of Deadly Force in British Columbia," *Policing: An International Journal of Police Strategies and Management* (1998). pp 432–448; and E. F. Wilson, J. H. Davis, J. D. Bloom, P. J. Batten, and S. G. Kamara, "Homicide or Suicide? The Killing of Suicidal Persons by Law Enforcement Officers," *Journal of Forensic Sciences* 43, pp. 46–52.

[79] See *Suicide by Cop: Protocol and Training Guide*, https://www.policeforum.org/suicidebycop (retrieved June 2020).

[80] "Fatal Force," *The Washington Post*. See: https://www.washingtonpost.com/graphics/2019/national/police-shooting-2019/

81Christina L. Patton and William J. Fremouw, "Examining 'Suicide by Cop': A Critical Review of the Literature," *Aggression and Violent Behavior* (2016), pp. 107–120.

82Vivian B. Lord and M. W. Sloop, "Suicide by Cop: Police Shooting as a Method of Self-Harming," *Journal of Criminal Justice* (2010), pp. 889–895

83See: Vivian B. Lord and M. W. Sloop, "Suicide by Cop: Police Shooting as a Method of Self-Harming," *Journal of Criminal Justice* (2010), pp. 889–895; Vivian Lord, "Factors Influencing Subjects Observed Level of Suicide by Cop Intent," *Criminal Justice and Behavior* (2012), pp. 1633–1646; Kris Mohandie and J. Reid Meloy, "Clinical and Forensic Indicators of "Suicide by Cop," *Journal of Forensic Science* (2000), pp. 384–389; Kris Mohandie, J. R. Meloy, and P. I. Collins, "Suicide by Copy Among Officer Involves Shooting Cases," *Journal of Forensic Science* (2009), pp. 456–462; and Ralph H. DeSimillein and Adamma Okorafor, "Suicide by Cop: What Motivates Those Who Choose This Method?" *Current Psychiatry* (2017), pp. 47–52.

84Vivian B. Lord and M. W. Sloop, "Suicide by Cop: Police Shooting as a Method of Self-Harming," *Journal of Criminal Justice* (2010), pp. 889–895.

85Barry Perrou, *Suicide by Cop: 15 Warning Signs that You Might Be Involved*, Calibre Press (Northbrook, IL: 2019).

86See "Suicide by Cop Protocol for Responding Officers" by Dr. John Nicoletti, as presented in *Suicide by Cop: Protocol and Training Guide*, https://www.policeforum.org/suicidebycop (retrieved June 2020).

87471 U.S. 1, 105 S. Ct. 1694 (1985).

88Matulia, "A Balance of Forces," p. 78.

89C. Mesloh, M. Henych, and R. Wolf, Conducted Electrical Weapons and Resolution of Use of Force Encounters. In M. W. Kroll, and J. D. Ho (eds.), *TASER® Conducted Electrical Weapons: Physiology, Pathology and Law* (New York: Springer Science and Business Media, 2009). Much of this section on TASERS and the Police Use of Less-Lethal Weapons has been adapted from Ross Wolf, "TASERS and Electronic Control Devises," LETN Video: *Electronic Control Devices* Courseware 111–0510 (Carrollton, TX: Critical Information Network, 2010).

90C. Mesloh, R. Wolf, M. Henych, and F. Thompson, "Less Lethal Weapons for Law Enforcement: A Performance-Based Analysis," *Law Enforcement Executive Forum* 8, No. 8 (2008), pp. 133–149.

91See TASER International at: www.taser.com

92Ross Wolf, "TASERS and Electronic Control Devises," LETN Video: *Electronic Control Devices* Courseware 111–0510 (Carrollton, TX: Critical Information Network, 2010).

93U.S. General Accounting Office, TASER Weapons: Use of TASERS by Selected Law Enforcement Agencies (Washington, DC: USPO, 2005).

94Geoffrey P. Alpert and Roger G. Dunham, *Understanding Police Use of Force: Officers, Suspects, and Reciprocity* (Cambridge, NY: Cambridge University Press, 2004). See also Geoffrey P. Alpert, "Police Use-of-Force, Less Lethal Weapons, and Injuries: Findings from a National Study," *Police Quarterly*, (forthcoming, 2010).

95Ibid.

96Incidents involving TASERS that have caused death and serious injury continue to dot the newspapers across the United States and Canada. For a discussion of concerns involving less-lethal weapons and a description of specific highlighted events, see a series of reports by Amnesty International (London: Amnesty International) at — www.amnestyusa.org: 1) "USA Amnesty International's Continuing Concerns about TASER Use (2006); Excessive and Lethal Force? Amnesty International's Concerns about Deaths and Ill-Treatment Involving Police Use of TASERS (2004); USA: Police Use of Pepper Spray—Tantamount to Torture (1997) and the American Civil Liberties Union (ACLU) at—www.aclu.org: (1) Pepper Spray Update: More Fatalities, More Questions (1995) and (2) Stun Gun Fallacy: How the Lack of TASER Regulation Endangers Lives (2005).

97See John M. MacDonald, Robert J. Kaminski, and Michael R. Smith, "The Effect of Less-Lethal on Injuries in Police Use-of-Force Events," *American Journal of Public Health*, 99, No. 12 (December 2009), pp. 2260–2274; and M. R. Smith, R. J. Kaminski, J. Rojek, G. P. Alpert, and J. Mathis, "The Impact of Conducted Energy Devices and Other Types of Force and Resistance on Police and Suspect Injuries," *Policing: An International Journal of Police Strategies and Management* 30 (2007), pp. 443–426.

98Geoffrey P. Alpert, "Police Use-of-Force, Less Lethal Weapons, and Injuries: Findings from a National Study," *Police Quarterly*, 2010.

99Daniel L. Schofield, "Legal Issues of Pursuit Driving," *FBI Law Enforcement Bulletin*, May 1988, pp. 23–30. This discussion was adapted from this source.

100Richard G. Zivitz, "Police Civil Liability and the Law of High-Speed Pursuit," *Marquette Law Review* 70, No. 237 (1987), pp. 237–279.

101*Jackson v. Olson*, 712 P. 2d 128 (Or. App. 1985).

102457 Do. 2d 816 (Miss. 1985).

103Ibid., at p. 818.

104See generally Annotation, "Emergency Vehicle Accidents," *American Jurisprudence, Proof of Facts* (St. Paul, MN: West, 1985), p. 599.

105See *Breck v. Cortez*, 490 N.E. 2d 88 (Ill. App. 1986).

106See generally Annotation, "Municipal Corporation's Safety Rules or Regulations as Admissible in Evidence in Action by Private Party Against Municipal Corporation or Its Officers or Employees for Negligent Operation of Vehicle," *American Law Review*.

107See *Fiser v. City of Ann Arbor*, 339 N.W. 2d 413 (Michigan 1983).

108733 S.W. 2d 28 (Mo. App. 1987).

109For a general discussion of immunity, see David Charlin, "High-Speed Pursuits: Police Officer and Municipal Liability for Accidents Involving the Pursued and an Innocent Third Party," *Seton Hall Law Review* 16, No. 101 (1986). While this citation is relatively old, many of the basic positions held here are reiterated in the Commission on Accreditation for Law Enforcement Agencies (CALEA), Model Policy for Police Pursuits (2010).

110490 So. 2d 1061 (Fla. App. 1986).

111*Fagan v. City of Vineland*, 22 F. 3d 1283 (3rd Cir. 1994).

11242 U.S.C. 1983 provides in relevant part: "Every person who, under color of any statute, ordinance, regulation, custom, or usage, of any State of Territory, subjects or causes to be subjected, any citizen of the United States or other person within the jurisdiction thereof to the deprivation of any rights, privileges, or immunities secured by the

Constitution and laws, shall be liable to the party injured in an action at law, suit in equity, or other proper proceedings for redress."

[113]782 F. 2d 947 (11th Cir. 1986).

[114]Ibid., at p. 950.

[115]See *County of Sacramento v. Lewis*, 98 F. 3d 434 (1998).

[116]Ibid.

[117]See *Allen v. Cook*, 668 F. Supp. 1460 (W.D. Okla. 1987). See also *Fagan v. City of Vineland*, supra note 202.

[118]772 F. 2d 1205 (5th Cir. 1985).

[119]471 U.S. 1, 105 S. Ct. 1694 (1985). The Supreme Court held that the use of deadly force to apprehend an unarmed fleeing felon was an unreasonable seizure that violated the Fourth Amendment.

[120]817 F. 2d 540 (9th Cir. 1987). In *City of Miami v. Harris*, 490 So. 2d 69 (Fla. App. 1985), the court held that a city can be liable under 1983 for a pursuit policy that is adopted with a reckless disregard of whether such policy would cause loss of life without due process.

[121]*Brower v. County of Inyo*, 489 U.S. 593, 109 S. Ct. 1378 (1989).

[122]A discussion of empirical studies regarding pursuits is set forth in Geoffrey P. Alpert, "Questioning Police Pursuits in Urban Areas," in R. G. Dunham and G. P. Alpert (eds.), *Critical Issues in Policing: Contemporary Readings* (Prospect Heights, IL: Waveland Press, 1989), pp. 216–229.

[123]*Jackson v. Olson*, supra note 192.

[124]See Annotation, "Municipal or State Liability for Injuries Resulting from Police Roadblocks or Commandeering of Private Vehicles," 19 *American Law Review* 4th 937.

[125]*Brower v. County of Inyo*, supra note 212.

[126]*Horta v. Sullivan*, 4 F. 3d 2 (1st Cir. 1993), at p. 10.

[127]Edmund Fennessy, Thomas Hamilton, Kent Joscelyn, and John Merritt, *A Study of the Problem of Hot Pursuit by the Police* (Washington, DC: U.S. Department of Transportation, 1970).

[128]Geoffrey P. Alpert, "Questioning Police Pursuit in Urban Areas," *Journal of Police Science and Administration* 15 (1987), pp. 298–306.

[129]Eric Beckman, "Identifying Issues in Police Pursuits: The First Research Findings," *The Police Chief* (July 1987), pp. 57–63.

[130]Geoffrey P. Alpert, *Police Pursuit Policies and Training* (Washington, DC: U.S. Department of Justice, Office of Justice Programs, National Institute of Justice, May 1997), pp. 1–8.

[131]Ibid.

[132]See, for example, *Nelson v. City of Chester, Ill.*, 733 S.W. 2d 28 (Mo. App. 1987); *Biscoe v. Arlington County*, 738 F. 2d 1352 (D.C. Cir. 1984).

[133]Alpert, "Questioning Police Pursuits in Urban Areas," pp. 227–228.

[134]*Plumhoff v. Rickard*, 188 L. Ed. 2d 1056 (U.S. May 27, 2014).

[135]International Association of Chiefs of Police, *Dealing with the Mentally Ill: Concepts and Issues* (Alexandra, VA: IACP Law Enforcement Policy Center, December 1, 1997).

[136]Washington Criminal Justice Training Commission (WCJTC), *Crisis Intervention Skills: Abnormal Behaviors, Mental Illness, and Suicide* (Seattle: WCJTC. 2000).

[137]Michael Klein, "Law Enforcement's Response to People with Mental Illness," *Law Enforcement Bulletin* (February 2002), pp. 12–16.

[138]*City & Cnty of San Francisco v. Sheehan*, 575 U.S. ____ (2015).

[139]Michael J. Oh. "Encountering Mentally Ill People and Potential Liability Under the Americans with Disabilities Act," *Police Chief Magazine* (July 2014).

[140]Robert C. Davis, Christopher W. Ortiz, Nicole J. Henderson, Joel Miller, and Michelle K. Massie, *Turning Necessity into Virtue: Pittsburgh's Experience with a Federal Consent Decree* (Washington, DC: Vera Institute of Justice, September 2002).

[141]Joe Domanick, "Police Reform's Best Tool: A Federal Consent Decree," *The Crime Report* (July 15, 2014).

[142]Police Executive Research Forum (PERF), *Civil Rights Investigations of Local Police: Lessons Learned* (Washington, DC: PERF, July 2013). Available online at: http://www.policeforum.org/assets/docs/Critical_Issues_Series/civil%20rights%20investigations%20of%20local%20police%20%20lessons%20learned%202013.pdf

[143]D. Littlefield, "Arevalos Victim Settles for $5.9 Million," *San Diego Union-Tribune* (September 25, 2014).

[144]International Association of Chiefs of Police *Addressing Sexual Offenses and Misconduct by Law Enforcement: Executive Guide* (Washington DC: Alexandria, VA: International Association of Chiefs of Police, 2011), p. 1.

[145]Phillip Matthew Stinson, Sr., John C. Liederbach, Steven L. Brewer, and Brooke E Mathna, "Police Sexual Misconduct: A National-Scale Study of Arrested Officers," *Criminal Justice Policy Review*, April 2014. Published Online: DOI 10.1177/0887403414526231

[146]Peter B. Kraska and Victor E. Kappeler, "To Serve and Pursue: Exploring Police Sexual Violence Against Women," *Justice Quarterly* 12, No. 1 (1995), pp. 85–111. Published online: DOI:10.1080/07418829500092581

[147]See Michael S. Vaughn, "Police Sexual Violence: Civil Liability Under State Tort Law," *Crime and Delinquency* 45, No. 3 (1999); and Sarah Eschholz and Michael S. Vaughn, "Police Sexual Violence and Rape Myths: Civil Liability Under Section 1983," *Journal of Criminal Justice* 29, No. 5 (2001). Published online: DOI:10.1016/S0047–2352(01)00104–0

[148]Samuel Walker and Dawn Irlbeck, *Police Sexual Abuse of Teenage Girls: A 2003 Update on Driving While Female* (Omaha, NE: University of Nebraska at Omaha, Department of Criminal Justice, Police Professionalism Initiative, 2003).

[149]C. E. Rabe-Hemp and J. Braithwaite, "An Exploration of Recidivism and the Officer Shuffle in Police Sexual Violence," *Police Quarterly* 16, No. 2 (2013). DOI: 10.1177/1098611112464964

[150]Phillip Matthew Stinson, "The Henry A. Wallace Police Crime Database," (Bowling Green, OH: Bowling Green University. See: https://policecrime.bgsu.edu/

[151]Phillip Matthew Stinson, Sr., John C. Liederbach, Steven L. Brewer, and Brooke E. Mathna. Ibid.

[152]Phillip Matthew Stinson, John Liederbach, and Robert W. Taylor, "Police Sexual Violence: Exploring the Context of Victimization," *Sexual Assault Report* (Princeton, NJ: Civic Research Institute April 2020.

[153]See, generally, Joan Bertin Lowy, "Constitutional Limitations on the Dismissal of Public Employees," *Brooklyn Law Review* 43 (summer 1976), p. 1; Victor G. Rosenblum, "Schoolchildren: Yes, Policemen: No—Some Thoughts About the Supreme Court's Priorities Concerning

the Right to a Hearing in Suspension and Removal Cases," *Northwestern University Law Review* 72 (1977), p. 146.

[154]*Wisconsin v. Constantineau*, 400 U.S. 433, 91 S. Ct. 507 (1970); *Doe v. U.S. Department of Justice*, 753 F. 2d 1092 (D.C. Cir. 1985).

[155]*Codd v. Velger*, 429 U.S. 624, 97 S. Ct. 882 (1977). See also *Paul v. Davis*, 424 U.S. 693, 96 S. Ct. 1155 (1976), which held that injury to reputation alone does not constitute a deprivation of liberty. See also *Swilley v. Alexander*, 629 F. 2d 1018 (5th Cir. 1980), where the court held that a letter of reprimand containing untrue charges that was placed in an employee's personnel file infringed on his liberty interest.

[156]See *Board of Regents v. Roth*, 408 U.S. 564, 92 S. Ct. 2701 (1972); *Perry v. Sinderman*, 408 U.S. 593, 92 S. Ct. 2694 (1972); *Arnett v. Kennedy*, 416 U.S. 134, 94 S. Ct. 1633 (1974); *Bishop v. Wood*, 426 U.S. 341, 96 S. Ct. 2074 (1976). Also see Robert L. Rabin, "Job Security and Due Process: Monitoring Administrative Discretion through a Reasons Requirement," *University of Chicago Law Review* 44 (1976), pp. 60–67, for a good discussion of these cases; see also *Bailey v. Kirk*, No. 82–1417 (10th Cir. 1985) and Carl Goodman, "Public Employment and the Supreme Court's 1975–76 Term," *Public Personnel Management* 5 (September–October 1976), pp. 287–289.

[157]*Thurston v. Dekle*, 531 F. 2d 1264 (5th Cir. 1976), vacated on other grounds, 438 U.S. 901, 98 S. Ct. 3118 (1978).

[158]*Allison v. City of Live Oak*, 450 F. Supp. 200 (M.D. Fla. 1978).

[159]See, for example, *Confederation of Police Chicago v. Chicago*, 547 F. 2d 375 (7th Cir. 1977).

[160]Davis, *Administrative Law*, p. 242.

[161]*Memphis Light Gas & Water Division v. Craft*, 436 U.S. 1, 98 S. Ct. 1554 (1978).

[162]*In re Dewar*, 548 P. 2nd 149 (Mont. 1976).

[163]*Bush v. Beckman*, 131 N.Y.S. 2d 297 (1954); *Gibbs v. City of Manchester*, 61 A. 128 (N.H. 1905).

[164]*Morrissey v. Brewer*, 408 U.S. 471, 92 S. Ct. 2593 (1972).

[165]*Goldman v. Kelly*, 397 U.S. 254, 90 S. Ct. 1011 (1970). See also *Buck v. N.Y. City Bd. of Ed.*, 553 F. 2d 315 (2d Cir. 1977), cert. denied in 438 U.S., 98 S. Ct. 3122 (1978).

[166]*Morrissey v. Brewer*, supra note 70.

[167]*Marshall v. Jerrico, Inc.*, 446 U.S. 238, 100 S. Ct. 1610 (1980); *Hortonville J.S.D. No. 1 v. Hortonville Ed. Assn.*, 426 U.S. 482, 96 S. Ct. 2308 (1976); *Holley v. Seminole County School Dist.*, 755 F. 2d 1492 (11th Cir. 1985).

[168]94 S. Ct. 1633, 416 U.S. 134 (1974), at p. 157.

[169]Ibid., at pp. 167–168.

[170]96 S. Ct. 893, 424 U.S. 319 (1975), at p. 335.

[171]105 S. Ct. 1487, 470 U.S. 532 (1985).

[172]Ibid., at p. 1494.

[173]See *Gilbert v. Homar*, 520 U.S. 924 (1997).

[174]*Gorham v. City of Kansas City*, 590 P. 2d 1051 (Kan. S. Ct. 1979); *Winston v. U.S. Postal Service*, 585 F. 2d 198 (7th Cir. 1978).

[175]*Bence v. Breier*, 501 F. 2d 1185 (7th Cir. 1974), cert. denied in 419 U.S. 1121, 95 S. Ct. 804 (1975).

[176]*Perea v. Fales*, 114 Cal. Rptr. 808 (1974), at p. 810.

[177]*Kramer v. City of Bethlehem*, 289 A. 2d 767 (1972).

[178]*Rogenski v. Board of Fire and Police Commissioners of Moline*, 285 N.E. 2d 230 (1972). See also *Major v.*

Hampton, 413 F. Supp. 66 (1976), in which the court held that an IRS rule against activities tending to discredit the agency was overbroad as applied to a married employee who had maintained an apartment for illicit sexual liaisons during off-duty hours.

[179]*Grayned v. City of Rockford*, 92 S. Ct. 2294, 408 U.S. 104 (1972), at pp. 108–109.

[180]*Bence v. Breier*, supra note 81, at p. 1190.

[181]*Rinaldi v. Civil Service Commission*, 244 N.W. 2d 609 (Mich. 1976).

[182]*Allen v. City of Greensboro, North Carolina*, 452 F. 2d 489 (4th Cir. 1971).

[183]*Petraitis v. Board of Fire and Police Commissioners City of Palos Hills*, 335 N.E. 2d 126 (Ill. 1975); *Haywood v. Municipal Court*, 271 N.E. 2d 591 (Mass. 1971); *Lewis v. Board of Trustee*, 212 N.Y.S. 2d 677 (1961). Compare *Stanton v. Board of Fire and Police Commissioners of Village of Bridgeview*, 345 N.E. 2d 822 (Ill. 1976).

[184]*DeSalvatore v. City of Oneonta*, 369 N.Y.S. 2d 820 (1975).

[185]*Marino v. Los Angeles*, 110 Cal. Rptr. 45 (1973).

[186]*Guido v. City of Marion*, 280 N.E. 2d 81 (Ind. 1972).

[187]*Carroll v. Goldstein*, 217 A. 2d 676 (R.I. 1976).

[188]*Firemen's and Policemen's Civil Service Commission v. Shaw*, 306 S.W. 2d 160 (Tex. 1957).

[189]*Martin v. City of St. Martinville*, 321 So. 2d 532 (La. 1975).

[190]*Arnold v. City of Aurora*, 498 P. 2d 970 (Colo. 1973).

[191]*Carey v. Piphus*, 435 U.S. 247, 98 S. Ct. 1042 (1978).

[192]*County of Monroe v. Dept. of Labor*, 690 F. 2d 1359 (11th Cir. 1982).

[193]*Gitlow v. New York*, 268 U.S. 652, 45 S. Ct. 625 (1925).

[194]*Pickering v. Board of Education*, 88 S. Ct. 1731, 391 U.S. 563 (1968), at p. 568.

[195]*Keyishian v. Board of Regents*, 385 U.S. 589, 87 S. Ct. 675 (1967).

[196]*Pickering v. Board of Education*, supra note 100.

[197]*Muller v. Conlisk*, 429 F. 2d 901 (7th Cir. 1970).

[198]*Flynn v. Giarusso*, 321 F. Supp. 1295 (E.D. La. 1971), at p. 1299. The regulation was revised and later ruled constitutional in *Magri v. Giarusso*, 379 F. Supp. 353 (E.D. La. 1974). See also *Gasparinetti v. Kerr*, 568 F. 2d 311 (3rd Cir. 1977), cert. denied in 436 U.S. 903, 98 S. Ct. 2232 (1978).

[199]*In re Gioglio*, 248 A. 2d 570 (N.J. 1968); *Brukiewa v. Police Commissioner of Baltimore*, 263 A. 2d 210 (Md. 1970); *Kannisto v. City and County of San Francisco*, 541 F. 2d 841 (9th Cir. 1976), cert. denied in 430 U.S. 931 S. Ct. 1552 (1977). Compare *Magri v. Giarusso*, supra note 104; *Hosford v. California State Personnel Board*, 141 Cal. Rptr. 354 (1977); and *Simpson v. Weeks*, 570 F. 2d 240 (8th Cir. 1978).

[200]*Brukiewa v. Police Commissioner of Baltimore*, supra note 105.

[201]*Perry v. City of Kinloch*, 680 F. Supp. 1339 (1988).

[202]*Brockell v. Norton*, 732 F. 2d 664 (8th Cir. 1984).

[203]See *Perez v. Agostini*, 37 F. Supp. 2d 103 (D.P.R. 1999); *Dill v. City of Edmond, Oklahoma*, 155 F. 3d 1193 (10th Cir. 1998); *Cahill v. O'Donnell*, 7 F. Supp. 2d 341 (S.D.N.Y. 1998); *Hadad v. Croucher*, 970 F. Supp. 1227 (N.D. Ohio 1997); *Saunders v. Hunter*, 980 F. Supp. 1236 (M.D. Fla. 1997); *Forsyth v. City of Dallas, Texas*, 91 F. 3d 769 (5th Cir. 1996); and *Glass v. Dachel*, 2 F. 3d 733 (7th Cir. 1993).

[204]Adapted from Will Aitchison, *The Rights of Law Enforcement Officers*, 4th edition (Portland, OR: Labor Relations Information System, 2000), p. 298.

[205]See *Lytle v. City of Haysville*, 138 F. 3d 857 (10th Cir. 1998), and *Frederick v. Department of Justice*, 73 F. 3d 349 (4th Cir. 1996).

[206]*Broaderick v. Oklahoma*, 413 U.S. 601, 93 S. Ct. 2908 (1973), and *Reeder v. Kansas City Bd. of Police Comm.*, 733 F. 2d 543 (8th Cir. 1984).

[207]*United Public Workers v. Mitchell*, 330 U.S. 75, 67 S. Ct. (1947): *U.S. Civil Service Commission v. National Association of Letter Carriers*, 413 U.S. 548, 93 S. Ct. 2880 (1973).

[208]*Broaderick v. Oklahoma*, supra note 112.

[209]*Sponick v. Detroit Police Dept.*, #15396, 49 Mich. App. 162, 211 N.W.2d 674 (Mich. App. 1973).

[210]*Sponick v. City of Detroit Police Department*, 211 N.W. 2d 674 (Mich. 1973), at p. 681. But see *Wilson v. Taylor*, 733 F. 2d 1539 (11th Cir. 1984).

[211]*Bruns v. Pomerleau*, 319 F. Supp. 58 (D. Md. 1970). See also *McMullen v. Carson*, 754 F. 2d 936 (11th Cir. 1985), where it was held that a Ku Klux Klansman could not be fired from his position as a records clerk in the sheriff's department simply because he was a Klansman. The court did uphold the dismissal because his active KKK participation threatened to cripple the agency's ability to perform its public duties effectively.

[212]*Civil Service Commission of Tucson v. Livingston*, 525 P. 2d 949 (Ariz. 1974).

[213]*City of San Diego v. John Roe*, 543 U.S. 77, 125 S. Ct. 521 (2005).

[214]See, for example, *Tinker v. Des Moines School District*, 393 U.S. 503, 89 S. Ct. 733 (1969).

[215]425 U.S. 238, 96 S. Ct. 1440 (1976).

[216]*Mapp v. Ohio*, 367 U.S. 643, 81 S. Ct. 1684 (1961).

[217]*Katz v. United States*, 389 U.S. 347, 88 S. Ct. 507 (1967).

[218]Ibid.

[219]*Smith v. Maryland*, 442 U.S. 735, 99 S. Ct. 2577 (1979), and *Chan v. State*, 78 Md. App. 287, 552 (1989). The "expectation to privacy" clause was developed in *Katz v. United States*, supra note 12, a case that involved warrantless electronic surveillance of a public telephone booth. The Court said that "the Fourth Amendment protects people, not places. What a person knowingly exposes to the public, even in his own home or office, is not subject to Fourth Amendment protection. But what he seeks to preserve as private, even in an area accessible to the public, may be constitutionally protected... . There is a two-fold requirement, first that a person have exhibited an actual expectation of privacy, and second that the expectation by one's society is prepared to recognize it as reasonable/legitimate."

[220]See *People v. Tidwell*, 266 N.E. 2d 787 (Ill. 1971).

[221]See *Ontario v. Quon* 529 F.3rd 892 (2010).

[222]*Biehunik v. Felicetta*, 441 F. 2d 228 (2nd Cir. 1971), cert. denied in 403 U.S. 932, 91S.Ct. 2256 (1971).

[223]*United States v. Leon*, 468 U.S. 897, 104S.Ct. 3430 (1984), and *Massachusetts v. Sheppard*, 468 U.S. 981, 104 S. Ct. 3424 (1984).

[224]*Illinois v. Gates*, 462 U.S. 213, 103 S. Ct. 2317 (1984).

[225]The concept of the "good faith-reasonable belief" defense as either a qualified or an absolute immunity has significant case history. See Isadore Silver, *Police Civil Liability* (New York: Matthew Bender and Company, 1987), Chapters 4 and 7.

[226]See *Floyd v. Farrell*, 765 F. 2d 1 (1st Cir. 1985); *Malley v. Briggs*, 475 U.S. 335, 106 S. Ct. 1092 (1986); *Santiago v. Fenton*, 891 F. 2d 373 (1st Cir. 1989); and *Hoffman v. Reali*, 973 F. 2d 980 (1st Cir. 1992).

[227]*Sheetz v. Mayor and City Council of Baltimore, Maryland*, 315 Md. 208 (1989).

[228]385 U.S. 493, 87 S. Ct. 6126 (1967).

[229]The states are bound by this requirement as well. *Malloy v. Hogan*, 378 U.S. 1, 84 S. Ct. 489 (1964).

[230]*Gardner v. Broderick*, 392 U.S. 273, 88 S. Ct. 1913 (1968).

[231]These procedural rights in police disciplinary actions have often been referred to as the "Garrity Rights." They were developed through a series of cases; see *Lefkowitz v. Turley*, 414 U.S. 70, 94 S. Ct. 316 (1973), and *Confederation of Police v. Conlisk*, 489 F. 2d 891 (1973), cert. denied in 416 U.S. 956, 94 S. Ct. 1971 (1974). Further, as the rights appear here, see Aitchison, *The Rights of Law Enforcement Officers*, p. 118.

[232]See *Gabrilowitz v. Newman*, 582 F. 2d 100 (1st Cir. 1978). Cases upholding the department's authority to order an officer to take a polygraph examination include *Eshelman v. Blubaum*, 560 P. 2d 1283 (Ariz. 1977); *Dolan v. Kelly*, N.Y.S. 2d 478 (1973); *Richardson v. City of Pasadena*, 500 S.W. 2d 175 (Tex. 1973); *Seattle Police Officer's Guild v. City of Seattle*, 494 P. 2d 485 (Wash. 1972); *Roux v. New Orleans Police Department*, 223 So.2d 905 (La. 1969); *Coursey v. Board of Fire and Police Commissioners*, 234 N.E. 2d 339 (Ill. 1967); *Frazee v. Civil Service Board of City of Oakland*, 338 P. 2d 943 (Cal. 1959); and *Hester v. Milledgeville*, 777 F. 2d 1492 (11th Cir. 1985). Cases denying the department's authority include *Molino v. Board of Public Safety of City of Torrington*, 225 A. 2d 805 (Conn. 1966); *Stape v. Civil Service Commission of City of Philadelphia*, 172 A. 2d 161 (Pa. 1961); and *Farmer v. Fort Lauderdale*, 427 So. 2d 187 (Fla. 1983), cert. denied in 464 U.S. 816, 104 S. Ct. 74 (1983).

[233]*Eshelman v. Blubaum*, supra note 141, p. 1286.

[234]*Farmer v. City of Fort Lauderdale*, supra note 141.

[235]*Furtado v. Town of Plymouth*, 451 Mass. 529, 888 N.E.2d 357 (Mass. 2008).

[236]*Faust v. Police Civil Service Commission*, 347 A. 2d 765 (Pa. 1975); *Steward v. Leary*, 293 N.Y.S. 2d 573 (1968); *Brewer v. City of Ashland*, 86 S.W. 2d 669 (Ky. 1935); *Fabio v. Civil Service Commission of Philadelphia*, 373 A. 2d 751 (Pa. 1977).

[237]*Anderson v. City of Philadelphia, Pennsylvania*, 668 F. Supp. 441 (1987), reversed by 845F. 2d 1216 (3rd Cir. 1988).

[238]See Aitchison, *The Rights of Law Enforcement Officers*, pp. 58–62.

[239]See *Bigby v. City of Chicago*, 766 F. 2d 1053 (7th Cir. 1985), cert. denied in 474 U.S. 1056, 106 S. Ct. 793 (1986); *McCoy v. Board of Fire and Police Commissioners* (Chicago), 398 N.E. 2d 1020 (1979); *Davis v. Williams*, 588 F. 2d 69 (4th Cir. 1979); *Parker v. Levy*, 417 U.S. 733, 94 S. Ct. 2547 (1974); *Bence v. Brier*, 501 F. 2d 1184 (7th Cir. 1974), cert. denied in 419 U.S. 1121, 95 S. Ct. 1552 (1977); and *Gee v. California State Personnel Board*, 85 Cal. Rptr. 762 (1970).

[240]Whether or not reasonable people would agree that the conduct was punishable so that an individual is free to steer a course between lawful and unlawful behaviors is the key to "reasonableness." See *Cranston v. City of Richmond*, 710 P. 2d 845 (1986); and *Said v. Lackey*, 731 S.W. 2d 7 (1987).

[241] *Cranston v. City of Richmond*, supra note 148.

[242] See *City of St. Petersburg v. Police Benevolent Association*, 414 So. 2d 293 1982; and *Brown v. Sexner*, 405 N.E. 2d 1082 (1980).

[243] *Richter v. Civil Service Commission of Philadelphia*, 387 A. 2d 131 (1978).

[244] *Miller v. City of York*, 415 A. 2d 1280 (1980), and *Kannisto v. City and County of San Francisco*, 541 F. 2d 841 (1976), cert. denied in 430 U.S. 931, 97 S. Ct. 1552 (1977).

[245] *McIntosh v. Monroe Police Civil Board*, 389 So. 2d 410 (1980); *Barnett v. New Orleans Police Department*, 413 So.2d 520 (1982); *Allman v. Police Board of Chicago*, 489 N.E. 2d 929 (1986).

[246] *Philadelphia Civil Service Commission v. Wotjuski*, 525 A. 2d 1255 (1987); *Gandolfo v. Department of Police*, 357 So.568 (1978); *McDonald v. Miller*, 596 F. 2d 686 (1979).

[247] *Monroe v. Board of Public Safety*, 423 N.Y.S. 2d 963 (1980).

[248] *Redo v. West Goshen Township*, 401 A. 2d 394 (1979).

[249] *Brase v. Board of Police Commissioners*, 487 N.E. 2d 91 (1985).

[250] See *John Doe v. U.S. Department of Justice*, 565, F.3d 1375 (Fed Cir. 2009).

[251] See *Brady v. Maryland*, 373 U.S. 83 (1963).

[252] See *Giglio v. United States*, 405 U.S. 150 (1972) and expansion of the *Brady* duty in *United States v. Agurs*, 427 U.S. 97 (1976), *United States v. Bagley*, 473 U.S. 667 (1985), *Kyles v. Whitley*, 514 U.S. 419 (1995), and *Youngblood v. West Virginia*, 547 U.S. (2006).

[253] Adapted from Richard Weinblatt, "Top 10 Social Networking Tips for Police," Policeone.com (August 25, 2009). Retrieved on July 24, 2010.

[254] *Major v. Hampton*, 413 F. Supp. 66 (1976).

[255] *City of North Muskegon v. Briggs*, 473 U.S. 909 (1985).

[256] *National Gay Task Force v. Bd. of Ed. of Oklahoma City*, 729 F. 2d 1270 (10th Cir. 1984).

[257] See *Whisenhund v. Spradlin*, 464 U.S. 964 (1983), and *Kukla v. Village of Antioch*, 647 F. Supp. 799 (1986), co-habitation of officers; *Coryle v. City of Oil City*, 405 A. 2d 1104 (1979), public lewdness; *Childers v. Dallas Police Department*, 513 F. Supp. 134 (1981); and *Fout v. California State Personnel Board*, child molesting; *Fugate v. Phoenix Civil Service Board*, 791 F. 2d 736 (9th Cir. 1986), sex with prostitutes; and *Doe v. Commonwealth Attorney*, 425 U.S. 901, 96S. Ct. 1489 (1976), *Smith v. Price*, 616 F. 2d 1371 (5th Cir. 1980), and *Bowers v. Hardwick*, 478 U.S. 186, 106 S. Ct. 2841 (1986), sodomy as a state law prohibiting homosexuality.

[258] *Bd. of Ed. v. National Gay Task Force*, 729 F. 2d 1270 (10th Cir. 1984), affirmed in 470 U.S. 903, 105 S. Ct. 1858 (1985).

[259] *Rowland v. Mad River Sch. Dist.*, 730 F. 2d (6th Cir. 1984), cert. denied in 470 U.S. 1009, 105 S. Ct. 1373 (1985).

[260] *Todd v. Navarro*, 698 F. Supp. 871 (1988).

[261] *Lawrence v. Texas*, 539U.S. 558, 123 S. Ct. 2472 (2003).

[262] "What you should know about the EEOC and the enforcement protections for LGBT Workers." Retrieved August 6 from: http://www.eeoc.gov/eeoc/newsroom/wysk/enforcement_protections_lgbt_workers.cfm

[263] *McCarthy v. Philadelphia Civil Service Comm.*, 424 U.S. 645, 96 S. Ct. 1154 (1976).

[264] *Miller v. Police of City of Chicago*, 349 N.E. 2d 544 (Ill. 1976); *Williamson v. Village of Baskin*, 339 So.2d 474 (La. 1976); *Nigro v. Board of Trustees of Alden*, 395 N.Y.S. 2d 544 (1977).

[265] *State, County, and Municipal Employees Local 339 v. City of Highland Park*, 108 N.W. 2d 544 (1977).

[266] *Hameetman v. City of Chicago*, 776 F. 2d 636 (7th Cir. 1985).

[267] *Cox v. McNamara*, 493 P. 2d 54 (Ore. 1972); *Brenkle v. Township of Shaler*, 281 A. 2d 920 (Pa. 1972); *Hopwood v. City of Paducah*, 424 S.W. 2d 134 (Ky. 1968); *Flood v. Kennedy*, 239 N.Y.S. 2d 665 (1963). See also *Trelfa v. Village of Centre Island*, 389 N.Y.S. 2d 22 (1976). Rules prohibiting law enforcement officers from holding interest in businesses that manufacture, sell, or distribute alcoholic beverages have also been upheld. *Bock v. Long*, 279 N.E. 2d 464 (Ill. 1972); *Johnson v. Trader*, 52 So.2d 333 (Fla. 1951).

[268] Richard N. Williams, *Legal Aspects of Discipline by Police Administrators*, Traffic Institute Publication No. 2705 (Evanston, IL: Northwestern University, 1975), p. 4.

[269] *City of Crowley Firemen v. City of Crowley*, 264 So. 2d 368 (La. 1972).

[270] See *Rojas v. Alexander's Department Store, Inc.*, 654 F. Supp. 856 (1986), and *Reagan v. Hampton*, 700 F. Supp. 850 (1988).

[271] *Reich v. Board of Fire and Police Commissioners*, 301 N.E. 2d 501 (Ill. 1973).

[272] *Krolick v. Lowery*, 302 N.Y.S. 2d 109 (1969), at p. 115, and *Hester Milledgeville*, 598 F. Supp. 1456, at p. 457, n. 2 (M.D. Ga. 1984), modified in 777 F. 2d 1492 (11th Cir. 1985).

[273] *McCracken v. Department of Police*, 337 So. 2d 595 (La. 1976).

[274] *Krolick v. Lowery*, supra note 229.

[275] 466 U.S. 109, 104 S. Ct. 1652 (1984), at p. 1656.

[276] *National Federation of Federal Employees v. Weinberger*, 818 F. 2d 935 (1987). See also related cases: *National Treasury Employees Union v. Von Raab*, 816 F. 2d 170 (1987), and *Lovvorn v. City of Chattanooga, Tennessee*, 846 F. 2d 1539 (1988).

[277] *O'Connor v. Ortega*, 480 U.S. 709, 107 S. Ct. 1492 (1987).

[278] 489 U.S. 602, 109 S. Ct. 1402 (1989).

[279] Supra note 195.

[280] *City of Palm Bay v. Bauman*, 475 So.2d 1322 (Fla. 5th DCA 1985). Officers can be required to submit to urinalysis if there is a "reasonable suspicion" that the officer has been using a prohibited substance (including alcohol), see *Jackman v. Schembri*, 635 NYS.2d 30 (A.D. 1995)[1996 FP72].

[281] The New York Policy was challenged and upheld in *Lynch v. City of New York*, 589 F.3rd 94 (2d Cir. 2009).

[282] *Walters v. Secretary of Defense*, 725 F. 2d 107 (D.C. Cir. 1983).

[283] *Security of Law Enforcement Employees, District Counsel 82 v. Carly*, 737 F. 2d 187 (2d Cir. 1984); *Division 241 Amalgamated Transit Union v. Suscy*, 538 F. 2d 1264 (7th Cir. 1976) cert. denied in 429 U.S. 1029, 97 S. Ct. 653 (1976); *McDonnell v. Hunter*, 612 F. Supp. 1122 (S.D. Iowa 1984), affirmed in 746 F. 2d 785 (8th Cir. 1984).

[284] For a comprehensive review of the cases in this area, see Gregory P. Orvis, "Drug Testing in the Criminal Justice Workplace," *American Journal of Criminal Justice* 18, No. 2 (spring 1994), pp. 290–305.

## CHAPTER FIFTEEN

ORGANIZATIONAL CHANGE

Learning Objectives

1. Explain why change occurs in law enforcement agencies.
2. Discuss five situations when change should not be initiated.
3. Analyze three models of change in organizations.
4. Discuss the role of the rank and file in organizational change.
5. Explain why organizational change sometimes fails.
6. Describe how to make organizational change succeed.
7. Describe the role of technology in police organizational change.
8. Discuss a few ways in which policing may change in the coming years.

INTRODUCTION

IT HAS LONG BEEN *said in policing circles that cops hate two things: change; and the way things are! That old adage is humorous but also adeptly sums up the organizational frustrations for many police officers and executives. Law enforcement is notoriously slow to change, but when things do happen, it often results in longstanding cultural norms, creating uncertainty and tension.*

Organizational change is stressful, even in the best of circumstances. But in law enforcement, change often requires both structural and cultural adjustments that impact an organization's legitimacy, officer morale, union or association relationships, and community relations. And organizational change in policing is a phenomenon that is occurring at warp speed. For instance, outrage over the deaths of several unarmed black men in 2014 and 2020 has led to calls to adopt principles of fair and impartial policing, examine use of force and hiring policies, demilitarize crowd control measures, improve community relations, and expand the role of technology. Furthermore, generational issues within the workforce are driving massive changes in police culture as well.

Police administrators in the current climate and the near future must understand and adapt to these factors in order to lead their organization successfully. This chapter discusses elements of organizational change, including (1) what drives change in law enforcement; (2) what limits change in law enforcement; (3) models of organizational change; (4) the role that politics plays in organizational change; (5) the role of officer culture in organizational change; (6) the role of technology in organizational change; (7) why change sometimes fails; (8) how to increase the chances of organizational success; and (9) the future of policing.

WHY CHANGE OCCURS

In any organization, there can be any number of catalysts for change. Law enforcement agencies, however, are in a unique position when it comes to change: they sit at a complex intersection of social issues, politics, and community service. Each of those facets both influence and are influenced by changes in policing organizations. This is why police administrators face particularly stressful and difficult challenges when making decisions related to organizational change. The following provides some concrete examples as to "why" police agencies change.

Reaction to Crisis

After September 11, 2001, the mission of police organizations in America—particularly those in major metropolitan areas—fundamentally changed. Never before had police departments been charged with securing the nation by preventing the next terrorist attack on the homeland. Historically, that was the role of the federal government and did not include state and local police agencies. As discussed in Chapter 3, the Posse Comitatus Act actually made it illegal for federal troops to be used in law enforcement purposes primarily because their role was relegated to national security interests; blurring the role between police and the military was prohibited. However post-9/11, police agencies began to take a much more active role in antiterrorism by gathering intelligence, monitoring communities for terror activity, militarizing their SWAT operations, and equipping fusion centers with the technology to allow the analysis of massive amounts of data and information.[1]

Further, we are currently witnessing a major crisis that may again, fundamentally change policing. The 2014–2020 shootings of unarmed black men by local police, such as Michael Brown, Samuel DuBose, Walter Scott, and George Floyd as well as the in-custody deaths of Sandra Bland, Freddie Gray, and Eric Garner have caused a major public outcry and prompted calls for police agencies to re-examine the way they do business. External constraints as well as internal self-reviews have prompted significant changes in policing, from training to internal investigations to public outreach. In the wake of these incidents, departments are struggling to address inherent bias within officer culture, deescalation techniques, and community relations—all of which could have major implications related to organizational structure and procedure (see Box 15.1).

As discussed in the previous chapter, the Civil Rights Division of the U.S. Department of Justice has the right to sue police agencies anywhere within the jurisdiction of the United States under the 1994 Violent Crime Control and Law Enforcement Act. While forced change is rarely seen as a positive influence in policing, the impact of a federal consent decree on police reform has not gone unnoticed.[2] For those agencies currently under such "memorandums of understanding," the ability of an external entity to monitor rogue police cultures and agencies and develop a set of "best practices" has been the pathway to change. Effective policing should not be violent and should not be biased but rather

Box 15.1: Actions in Wake of Police-Community Unrest

(MICHAEL REYNOLDS/epa european pressphoto agency b.v/Alamy Stock Photo)

Police confront protesters in Baltimore, Maryland, following the funeral of Freddie Gray in April, 2015. Similar unrest was witnessed throughout 2020 beginning with the death of George Floyd in Minneapolis, Minnesota in May, 2020

An Associated Press analysis identified at least 40 measures passed by 24 states that addressed issues highlighted by the events in Ferguson, MO, in the summer of 2014:

Body Cameras: Sixteen states passed measures that directly addressed officer worn cameras that can record interactions with an individual during a specific incident as well as general interactions with the public. Some states (Arizona, Maryland, and Louisiana) merely created committees to further study the issue or recommend policies on how the cameras should be used by local and state agencies, while other states (Illinois and Oregon) passed rigorous laws setting standards for when police must use the cameras and how long the videos must be stored. Other states (Colorado, Connecticut, South Carolina, and Texas) approved various grant programs to help local agencies purchase cameras and associated equipment and still other states (Florida, North Dakota, and Oklahoma) passed laws limiting the access of camera videos to the public. Finally, some states (North Carolina, Alaska, and Washington) simply did not address the issue or had previous legislation that governed the use of body-worn cameras by police.

Citizen Cameras: Several states (California and Oregon) affirmed the right of citizens to video or take photos of police officers conducting business or acting while on duty. Other states (Colorado and Connecticut) passed laws that held police agencies liable for interfering with citizens filming, taking videos, or photographing police officers in the scope of their duty.

Use of Deadly Force—Chokeholds: As a reaction stemming from the death of Eric Garner by an NYPD officer in Staten Island, New York, in July 2014, some states (Nevada, Tennessee, Illinois, and the District of Columbia) have laws that severely limit the police use of the carotid artery chokehold, or any other type of choke hold unless the officer is in a "life-or-death" situation. These laws classify chokeholds as "the use of deadly force."

Military Equipment: Concerned that some tactical weaponry such as riot gear, grenade launders, assault rifles, and armored vehicles, for example—are transferred from the U.S. Department of Defense with little oversight or justification creating a culture of aggression within police agencies and forces, several states (Montana, New Jersey, and New York) passed laws prohibiting local police to acquire former military equipment without specific authorization and oversight. These laws severely restrict the acquisition of military equipment by police and stem from President Barack Obama's special report entitled, *Review of Federal Support for Local Law Enforcement Equipment Acquisition*, December 2014.

Training for Police Officers: Forty-nine states have commissions that develop, implement, and administer training curriculum for police. These entities now require inclusion of issue-specific courses in basic as well as in-service police training focused on deescalation. The two most cited areas of training include (1) *crisis intervention training* that prepares officers to better respond to situations involving people with mental health problems and alternatives to lethal force when interacting with potentially dangerous people in the community and (2) *racial bias training* providing police officers with tools to help them reduce the effect of bias on their decision-making particularly during arrest. One state (Montana) enacted legislation that provided counseling for officers found to have engaged in race-based traffic stops and dictated that state training courses must "stress understanding and respect for racial and cultural differences and the development of effective, noncombat methods of carrying out law enforcement duty in a racially and culturally diverse environment"

(Montana State Law, Section 44-2-117). Further, several states (Colorado, Connecticut, Maryland, Rhode Island, and Illinois) passed legislation that either addressed and curtailed racial bias or profiling by police or required racial demographic data on subjects to be collected regularly and reported to state agencies for oversight.

Sources: Associated Press, "State Actions in Wake of Ferguson's Upheaval," August 2, 2015; and National Conference of State Legislatures (NCSL), *Law Enforcement Overview* (May 29, 2015). See: http://www.ncsl.org/research/civil-and-criminal-justice/law-enforcement.aspx.

imbue from the *Bill of Rights* those guarantees and liberties to which every police officer in this country swears their first and most important oath ... to uphold U.S. Constitution.

Fluctuating Crime Rates

As crime rates fluctuate, police organizations often adapt to address these primary indicators of safety and concern. Increasing the number of patrol officers to combat rising crime rates may involve significant organizational change—perhaps a tactical unit or special program was shifted in order to free-up personnel for such a change. Agencies may adapt new strategies—like hotspots policing—to attack a specific problem, requiring dedicated units, new task forces and partnerships, new technology, additional training, additional community outreach, and a new outlook on crime reduction altogether. Conversely, if crime rates decrease dramatically, specialized units may be disbanded altogether or reorganized to tackle another problem.

Technological Advances

Rapid change is often associated with the introduction of new technology. Witness the complex and rapid change that has occurred in global society over the past two decades with the introduction of the Internet or the impact on lives due to new innovations in medicine in just the last five years. Consider the discussions in Chapter 2 relating to COMPSTAT, intelligence-led policing, evidence-based policing, and GIS—and how they fundamentally changed the way police organizations go about doing their job.[3] Currently, and as discussed in Chapter 4, body-worn cameras are being touted as the next instrument of change within policing—and the technology will certainly require major resource commitments from agencies, infrastructure adjustments, policy and procedural changes, and new organizational considerations.

Funding and Economic Decline

Budgetary concerns obviously affect any organization—and in policing, money can be tied to every level of organizational effort. In a survey by the Police Executive Research Forum (PERF) in 2010, 78 percent of police agencies surveyed reported that they had experienced budget cuts as a result of the recession that began in 2008; by 2012, 51 percent reported that they were *still* experiencing cutbacks due to lingering effects of the downturn.[4] One significant result of the 2008 recession has been the

steady and rapid decline of employee benefits to police officers across the nation. Despite market rebounds, by 2015, many pension plans were still struggling as a result of the massive losses sustained in the economic collapse that devastated stock and real estate holdings on which many pension funds were dependent upon. Coupled with an ever-aging workforce, police agencies witnessed an unprecedented number of retirements that further stressed the situation. For instance, in San Diego and other California communities, police officers facing a slashing of work and retirement benefits simply quit—or retired before change legislation was enacted causing further negative impact on already stressed funds. Department across the country, and especially in hard-hit California, massive reductions in pension plans approved as a result of economic crisis continues to hamper recruitment efforts.[5] Certainly, the impact of COVID-19 on local economies s will continue to hamper any increase in police budgets in the future. This is particularly true with new calls for "defunding" the police in the aftermath of the George Floyd death in 2020. Chapters 2 (Policing Today) and Chapter12 (Financial Management) highlight these issues in our communities.

Unfortunately, economic decline for most cities interprets into fewer officers for the police department. Dwindling numbers of police have several negative effects on a community: (1) more proactive programs that focus on crime-specific areas are reduced, as well as more community-based strategies give way to the primary, reactive police mission of answering calls for service at the patrol level; (2) reactive policing usually results in higher crime rates as little if any proactive work is focused on crime-specific issues; (3) the reduction of community-based programs often hinder larger efforts to improve relationships between the police and different sectors of the community, particularly minority areas; (4) this leads to a vicious downward cycle of maintaining the reactive functions of patrol over more progressive strategies that attempt to improve police transparency, legitimacy, and organizational change; and (5) the resulting end is often highlighted by community distrust and anger toward the police.

More obvious effects can be seen in program cuts and organizational shifts as a result of budget adjustments. PERF's research revealed that 32 percent of agencies reported freezing recruitment of new officers, and 23 percent had implemented officer layoffs. Fifty-eight percent of agencies in 2010 reported a reduction of services to the community; in a 2012 follow-up, that number had dropped to 44 percent. Furthermore, 45 percent of police agencies had discontinued or significantly reduced specialty units as a result of a poor local economy, and 51 percent of agencies reported that they were eliminating or cutting back on plans to acquire new technology (see Box 15.2).[6] Considering that technology (like maintaining a database of problem officers in policing, or providing more advanced use-of-force training to recruits) plays a crucial role in the advancement of policing and that most cutting-edge policing strategies require sophisticated information systems and/or fusion centers (See Chapter 3 on Terrorism, Intelligence and Homeland Security) to be monitored and hence, evaluated—and that technology is the inherent cornerstone of a much-demanded implementation of body-worn cameras across the country—it becomes obvious that organization change within policing often requires significant economic funding.

Politics

Chapters 1, The Foundation of Police Administration and Chapter 4, Politics and Police Administration documented the historical linkages and issues of politics in policing in the United States and clearly the professional era of policing argued successfully to eliminate politics out of law enforcement. However, this has rarely been the case. The reality is that law enforcement agencies are legitimate governmental entities given the authority to enforce the laws of the government—making them inherently political. Police organizations are impacted greatly by what goes on in voting booths, city halls, district attorneys' offices, state legislatures, and the White House.

The most obvious organizational effects from political meddling often occur in agencies where leadership is elected— namely sheriff's offices. In those cases, when a new sheriff is elected, an organization can experience tremendous turnover and major structural change to accommodate a new leader's agenda or mandate. However, elections can greatly change law enforcement agencies that *are not* led by elected officials. For instance, the election of new mayors and the subsequent appointment of new city managers can result in incumbent police chiefs being replaced in order to better fit with an incoming administration's agenda—or, simply because of personality

---

Box 15.2: The Effect of Economic Downturn on Police Agencies

A Police Executive Research Forum survey revealed the organizational consequences of the crisis.

Change in Department Structure	% of Police Agencies that Are Implementing the Change
Discontinuing or significantly reducing **specialty units**	45%
Consolidating units	25%
Consolidating services with other departments	22%
Reducing public access hours at district stations	18%
Closing/consolidating **district stations**	8%
Contracting out for services	7%
Demoting staff in certain ranks	4%
Privatizing some police services	3%

Redeployment Strategy	% of Departments that Are Implementing the Change
Altering **shift times**	44%
Changing **patrol levels in** defined areas	34%
Handling **crime scene processing with** patrol officers	32%
No longer sending **investigators** immediately for certain crimes	30%
Alternative **call handling** strategies (phone or Internet)	25%
Changing **investigative priorities**	24%
Changing **response policies** for calls for service	19%

Source: Police Executive Research Forum, "Policing and the Economic Downturn: Striving for Efficiency Is the New Normal." See: http://www.policeforum.org/assets/docs/Critical_Issues_Series/policing%20and%20the%20economic%20downturn%20-%20striving%20for%20efficiency%20is%20the%20new%20normal%202013.pdf.

clashes. Police chief positions are largely political appointments, with the chief serving at the pleasure of city officials. If a mayor or city manager is, for example, unhappy with the performance of the police department, they may dismiss the chief and seek change through the administration of a new leader. There can be real expenses to this type of political change. It can be unsavory and kill officer morale when unqualified or marginally competent people with unbridled ambition successfully use politics to their personal advantage at the considerable expense of others or when the use of politics interferes with the timely and effective implementation of a new or exciting strategy.

Political meddling from outside of the city organizational structure can also have significant impact. For example, a newly elected District (County) or State's Attorney may signal change in prosecutorial decisions that greatly impact policing in that community. Illustratively in Dallas (Texas), a newly elected district attorney suddenly closed a digital forensics lab inside the Dallas Police Department. The closure was not due to financial issues, but rather the political whims of the newly elected DA, whose office in the past had funded the lab.

The lab had been processing digital evidence for police agencies in the entire Metroplex area of over 7 million people, relating to homicide, sexual abuse, child pornography, and various financial crimes.[7] The closure meant that police agencies were left scrambling to find other resources for the processing of digital evidence, forcing organizational changes from small movements like increasing overtime limits for detectives with backlogged cases, to more substantial impacts like adding significant personnel to new units within the department or assembling task forces to process digital evidence for growing numbers of cases.

A Changing Workforce

Conventional wisdom would dictate that the aging sector of the workforce—namely the *Baby Boomers*, who are those born between 1946 and 1964—are leaving policing in large numbers, as they reach retirement age. However, recent economic downturns have actually slowed their retirement in some communities—as pension funds scramble to catch up, and as the cost of living rises, many older police officers are hesitant to leave.[8] Policing, as with other public sector positions, has witnessed this trend more acutely than the private sector. Previous generations of police officers have managed to adapt to the traditional organizational structure without too many issues. The leadership of most police organizations is still very much indoctrinated in a paramilitary model of leadership. However, some policing scholars believe that dramatic change in the workforce of American policing is about to occur.

Contemporary employees, who include *Millenials* (1981 through 1994), and *Generation Zers* (1995 through 2010) are fundamentally different than their predecessors—not content to plow through monotonous paperwork, conform to a stagnant set of rules and regulations, and/or endure the hardship of working for an incompetent manager simply for the sake of getting a paycheck. These employees have been described in the literature as very conscientious, self-assured, and value-centered. Studies have shown Millenials and Generation Zers to be more likely to thrive in collaborative environments than Baby Boomers (1945 through 1964) or Gen Xers (1965 through 1980), better at recognizing the value of technology and embracing it as a vital part of their work; more accepting of diversity as a strength in the workplace; and better at multitasking in their jobs.[9]

However, they also lack many of the attributes that current police agencies value highly: namely, the ability to focus on a key issue or see a project through to its end. To deal with such issues, and to fully capitalize on the more positive qualities these generations bring, police agencies may need to change their organizational training model to focus on mentoring and coaching over a longer term than a traditional training academy. Generation Zers and Millenials also have a tendency to want to see career progression much more quickly than their predecessors. For current officers and managers, 20 years was not an abnormal amount of time to ascend to a leadership rank in police agencies. However, the contemporary generation of police wants much faster-growing careers and expects to move up through the ranks much more quickly. Faced with a slow-moving organization structure and bureaucracy, traditionally without many employee incentives, retention of officers will be problematic—an issue that has never confronted most police agencies. The contemporary generation will be much more likely to leave in pursuit of career fulfillment outside of law enforcement.[10] In response, police organizations today may have to institute career pathway programs that emphasize opportunities and delineate ways to achieve them and work with police unions and associations to adapt the promotional process to this new, shifting paradigm of employees. Further, contemporary police officers are also much more interested in accommodations in the workplace that improve their quality of life and their family's quality of life than their predecessors. Contemporary officers often seek more of a work/life balance and identify things like maternity/paternity leave and flexible scheduling as important to them as paid

Quick Facts: The Race Gap in America's Police Departments

According to an article in the *New York Times*, the percentage of white police officers is more than 30 points higher than in the communities they serve. Minorities make up only a quarter of police forces across the county. Therefore, more than three quarters of the cities on which the Census Bureau has collected data have a police department that is disproportionately white relative to the local community population.

Source: Jeremy Ashkenas and Haeyoun Park, "The Race Gap in America's Police Departments," *The New York Times* (April 8, 2015).

overtime and vacation. In the future, police agencies that have traditionally been wedded to the 24/7 law enforcement practice over 365 days, with newer officers bearing the burden of the midnight shift and adapting to the complexities of "seniority," may find the significant challenges in keeping the most qualified candidates to the profession. One chief recently lamented as a top recruit left his department after graduating first in the academy, "He didn't want to work nights ... how can you expect to be a police officer and not work nights?"

Another significant difference from past generations that will undoubtedly be a challenge to police agencies in the future is the bureaucratic structure of command control. As explained in Chapter 5, "Organizational Theory" and Chapter 6, "Organizational Design," chain of command and management requires written documents that pass through ranks of progressive responsibility of an organization, with direction following, again in writing down through the organization. By design, these steps take time and reflection with a focus on preserving organizational order and control. Today's contemporary employees demand immediate feedback—a result of technological capabilities like instant text messaging, the ubiquity of e-mail, and social media—mainstays in everyday life of contemporary employees. Today's officers expect much more timely responses with coherent and rationale for decisions than their predecessors and will most certainly impact officer morale, employee retention and productivity, and police organizational dynamics in the future.[11]

As the demographics of the country change, police organizations will also change to become more diverse (see Figure 15.1).[12] Population shifts in and of themselves don't necessarily drive this change. For example, a recent examination by the Associated Press of Census Data found that 49 out of 1,400 police departments served majority Hispanic populations; in many cases, these departments served communities that were vastly majority (over 80 percent) Hispanic. However, the demographic make-up of those departments was still well over 50 percent white.[13] Police agencies have long struggled with recruiting minority applicants. The events of 2014 and 2015 have highlighted, once again, the imbalance of power between races within our country. As citizens and government alike begin to focus on this issue in the future, recruitment and retention strategies that focus on minorities, ethnicities, and lifestyles will force organizational change. Nothing heralds this change more than the Supreme Court actions ruling to legalize and recognize same-sex marriages in the landmark case, **Obergefell v. Hodges**. Organizationally, this ruling required that accommodations be made to allow employees to add their same-sex spouses to employer insurance policies, broadened the application of existing leave policies, and opened the availability of retirement and pension benefits to same-sex spouses. While it is too soon to assess the impact that this ruling may have on overall police demographics and organizational change, it does seem likely that police organizations—long considered to be socially conservative—may be headed for massive organizational and cultural change. The Supreme Court ruling directly points to public agencies that will be more inclusive of gay employees, particularly since sweeping legal rulings related

FIGURE 15.1 ▶ New York Police Department (NYPD) Chaplin Iman Khalid Latif offers the opening prayer at the NYPD's Muslim Officers Society scholarship dinner. Founded in 2009 to promote patriotism and advance the interests of its members, the Society is recognized by the NYPD as an employee organization for sworn and civilian personnel. Such organizations reflect the continuing movement of law enforcement agencies toward a diverse workforce. (Courtesy of New York Police Department)

to discrimination against lesbian, gay, bisexual, and transgender (LGBT) employee hiring and promotional practices are on the immediate horizon in the wake of the Equal Employment Opportunity Commission's 2015 statement that such discrimination is illegal under federal law.[14]

A New Paradigm Shift

As discussed in Chapter 2, "Policing Today," paradigms are ways or models of conducting business and they often have an accompanying set of rules and procedures. Max Weber's bureaucratic model can be thought of as a paradigm; when new paradigms are developed, they have the potential for causing significant organizational change. Police scholars have identified several major and important paradigm shifts in policing over the past three decades. These certainly include (1) the advent of new technology to include vast information and communication systems that have broaden the police role from crime fighter to a much more intelligence-driven, national security-oriented police officer backed by fusion centers and array of federal task forces; (2) individual identification by DNA, which has created demands for new skills, training, and procedures in criminal investigation, especially in the areas of evidence identification, collection, preservation, and processing, as well as quantum leaps in clearing decades-old cold cases and exonerating those who were erroneously convicted in the past; and (3) the shift from the traditional, reactive model of policing characterized by random-moving police cars responding to calls for service to the widespread adoption of community-based, predictive police models that are evaluated through rigorous evidence-based techniques. It is too soon to say that the uprising of community outrage over police-involved shootings and in-custody deaths of African-Americans in Minneapolis, Minnesota, Louisville, Kentucky, Ferguson,

Quick Facts: Heraclitus (circa 500 BCE)

Heraclitus was a Greek philosopher of the late 6th-century BCE. He believed that most people sleep-walk through life, not really understanding what is truly going on about them. His work was criticized by his predecessors like Homer, Pythagoras, and Hesiod; however, he was the first to recognize that human values should be a central part of philosophy and to suggest a spiritual (metaphysical) foundation for scientific inquiry. He may have been highly cynical about his fellow man and criticized by his contemporaries as well as the great ancient philosophers Plato and Aristotle; however, his observations on man and the organizations of this world may be spot on: *"The Only Constant in Life Is Change!"*

Source: Internet Encyclopedia of Philosophy, "Heraclitus (fl.c. 500 B.C.E.)." See: https://www.iep.utm.edu/heraclit/

Missouri; Baltimore, Maryland; and Cleveland, Ohio, has contributed to yet another tangible paradigm shift—though it may be on the horizon as body-worn cameras and an emphasis on deescalation training and fair and impartial policing practices become the emphasis of the day. Then too, the impact of COVID-19 and more radical calls to "defund" and even abolish the police may well gain strength in cities where police reform fails to meet community expectations. See Box 15.5.

Regardless, however important these new policing perspectives and strategies may be to improving police legitimacy and to crime reduction, they have exacerbated already existing staffing shortages in state and local law enforcement agencies, strained technology and training budgets, and forced agencies to "do more with less."

WHEN CHANGE SHOULD NOT BE MADE

Because change is a perilous process, some thought should be given to whether it should be undertaken in the first place. Among the conditions that indicate contemplated change should be delayed are as follows:

1. The knowledge, skill, or other resources needed to carry out the change effectively do not exist inside the department.
2. An appropriately experienced external **change agent** is not presently available.
3. The effort of making the change is greater than any benefits to be derived. Former Georgia Governor Zell Miller expressed this as "the juice isn't worth the squeezing." This principle can also be stated as "all motion isn't progress; some of it is just thrashing around."
4. Collateral damage, such as abandonment by key supporters or significant union opposition, may lead chiefs to use their limited stack of "political chips" on another issue of greater concern to them and the community.
5. Too much change is already underway in the department and the nature of the change is not sufficiently important to make now, versus its potential for personnel to feel confused about priorities or conclude that the organization is becoming unstable.

ORGANIZATIONAL CHANGE MODELS

There is an old story about a boy who wanted his dog to have a short tail. But rather than hurt the dog by cutting the tail off all at once, the boy sliced an inch off at a time. This story illustrates what is described as "pain level" associated with gradual and radical change strategies in public organizations. One camp maintains that it is better to implement change swiftly (radical change) and get the upheavals that follow done and over with; the other camp wants to implement changes incrementally over time (gradual change) so that personnel have an opportunity to adjust to new realities and requirements. Proponents of radical change argue that when change is gradual, unanticipated events can derail the effort before it can be completed and that it gives opponents time to organize themselves to thwart further implementation. Kurt Lewin's three-step model on organizational change is a general model of the likely impact on police members when authoritarian and participative strategies using wide input and involvement are used as the basis for gradual radical organizational change; as noted in Chapter 7, leadership is not a spectator sport. Regardless of whether change is gradual or radical, the chief cannot sit passively on the sidelines to see how it turns out—he or she must actively help lead the change.

While some changes can be accomplished through the pronouncement by chiefs, especially in very small departments, larger departments are more complex and therefore require greater planning, the use of more sophisticated techniques, and wide involvement to garner crucial input and support before moving forward to the implementation phase. This often involves the use of organizational development (OD). In Chapter 5, "Organizational Theory," the OD process was defined and described. To briefly review, OD is an applied behavioral science method of changing organizations through long-term efforts designed to improve the work culture and work processes.

In this section, two models of **directed change** are presented. The first one, **Lewin's three-step model**, was selected because it is one of the oldest, simplest, and yet, the most durable. The second model, the **traditional action research model**, represents a fairly typical change process. If the second one seems somewhat familiar, it may be due to the fact that planning was covered in an earlier chapter (see

Chapter 8, "Planning and Decision Making"). The traditional action research model is simply a special type of planning. Both Lewin's three-step model and the Traditional Action Research Model rely on the use of organizational development (OD). In addition, the **Burke-Litwin model** of change, a more practical than theoretical exercise, will be presented.

Kurt Lewin's Three-Step Model on Organizational Change

This model involves three sequential steps (see Figure 15.2):

1. *Unfreezing*—Officers, like all other people, get into their "comfort zones." Before change can occur, they have to be "unfrozen" from the perceptions and behaviors that are presently part of who they are and how they approach their jobs. Often, this is accomplished by creating a sense of urgency that the present way of doing things is deficient in some way and that a shift to some new procedures will produce better results more efficiently. This tactic is known as "disconfirmation" because, to some degree, it invalidates what is presently being done. The heart of unfreezing is making people be receptive to change.

2. *Moving*—This is a transitional phase in which officers actually experience the changes that were planned; there will be less resistance if officers are, to the maximum extent possible, included in the planning process and feel that they have some impact in shaping events. While chiefs do make top-down decisions that constitute major change, such as to begin using COMPSTAT, there is ample room to involve sworn and civilian personnel from across the agency on the details of implementation, such as the design of forms to capture data and what types of data are most useful for planning various types of operations. The use of officers on task forces or committees cannot be

symbolic or gratuitous; such motives will be "sniffed out" immediately and provoke an unpleasant set of dynamics for the chief to preside over.

3. *Refreezing*—The purpose of this phase is for officers to make permanent the changes they experienced in the previous phase, part of the normal way in which they see things, think about them, and behave. Some of the refreezing can be accomplished by appealing to the professionalism of officers—"When we get this thing fully up and running, everybody in the state will be looking at us, wondering how we got so far ahead of them." However, drawing upon the lessons learned from the shift from traditional policing to community policing, resistance tapered off and refreezing occurred faster when departmental awards were realigned with community policing goals, such as recognition for enrolling 25 businesses in a crime prevention program. Thus, as part of any large-scale change process, the use of awards to reinforce the desired behaviors should be carefully considered.

Traditional Action Research Model

There are many organizational development (OD) change models; however, most of them approximate the traditional action research model with the following five steps (see Figure 15.3):

1. *Recognizing the Need for Change*—Without this awareness, it is simply "business as usual" for police agencies. The change awareness may come from the need to implement the provisions of a Supreme Court decision or a consent decree entered into in partial settlement of a civil liability suit. The department's planning and research unit may have identified lapses in performance that need to be addressed or unusual opportunities on which to capitalize, such as the availability of federal grants to implement

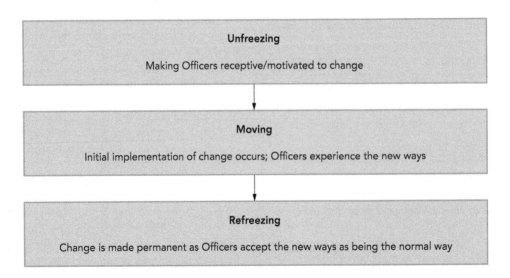

FIGURE 15.2 ▶ Kurt Lewin's three-step model on organizational change.

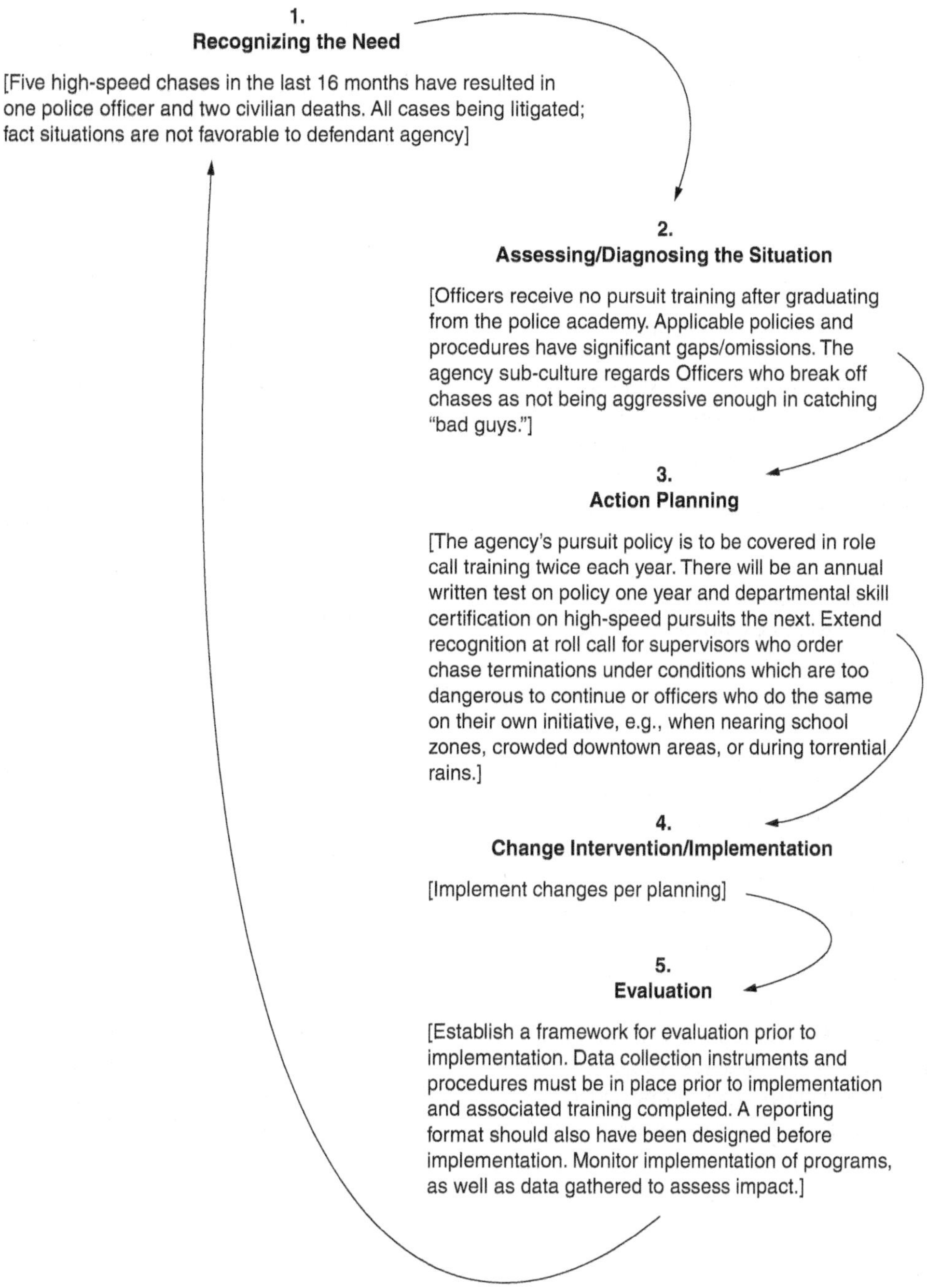

1.
Recognizing the Need

[Five high-speed chases in the last 16 months have resulted in one police officer and two civilian deaths. All cases being litigated; fact situations are not favorable to defendant agency]

2.
Assessing/Diagnosing the Situation

[Officers receive no pursuit training after graduating from the police academy. Applicable policies and procedures have significant gaps/omissions. The agency sub-culture regards Officers who break off chases as not being aggressive enough in catching "bad guys."]

3.
Action Planning

[The agency's pursuit policy is to be covered in role call training twice each year. There will be an annual written test on policy one year and departmental skill certification on high-speed pursuits the next. Extend recognition at roll call for supervisors who order chase terminations under conditions which are too dangerous to continue or officers who do the same on their own initiative, e.g., when nearing school zones, crowded downtown areas, or during torrential rains.]

4.
Change Intervention/Implementation

[Implement changes per planning]

5.
Evaluation

[Establish a framework for evaluation prior to implementation. Data collection instruments and procedures must be in place prior to implementation and associated training completed. A reporting format should also have been designed before implementation. Monitor implementation of programs, as well as data gathered to assess impact.]

FIGURE 15.3 ▶ Traditional action research model.

community policing programs or to upgrade crime scene investigation capabilities. Individual officers, supervisors, command staff members, or the union may make written recommendations in the form of memos or completed staff work that leads to change. Additionally, any of the situations discussed in the earlier section "Why Change Occurs" can take place, such as a new chief being hired with a mandate to make specific changes in the department's operating philosophy, organizational structure, programs and policies, and procedures.

2. *Assessing/Diagnosing the Situation*—Two fundamental tasks in assessing the situation must be executed flawlessly: (a) determining the opportunity or the problem—care must be taken to make sure that attention is given to the real problem and not a symptom of it and (b) determining the gap or difference between what is now happening and what the department would like to have happen. In order to accomplish these twin objectives, data must be gathered. Sources of such data include 911, training, and other records, surveys of personnel and clients, and reviews of disciplinary records and litigation trends.

3. *Action Planning*—The gap or difference between what is happening and what is desirable is the zone of impact, where meaningful change can occur if something significant is selected to work on. The chief must decide who will be in charge of the change process. Internal candidates for this responsibility know the organization, its capabilities, and its personnel but may lack the necessary skills to lead an effective intervention or may not have the time to devote to the change effort. External consultants don't have any "baggage" because people in the department typically don't know them, but they lack the depth of knowledge about the department an insider would have. Although outsiders come with a certain amount of instant credibility, any missteps they make are often judged harshly with biting comments such as "If he's the expert and making big bucks, how come we've got such a mess on our hands?"

As mentioned earlier, it is crucial to involve people from throughout the department and to have a continuous stream of information flowing to all personnel through posting on the department's intranet, announcements at roll call, information posted on bulletin boards, and the dissemination of memos and newsletters. When officers don't know what is going on, the rumor mill works overtime, seldom to the benefit of the process or the changes being implemented.

In many instances, officers serve on one or more task forces or committees involved in the change. For example, officers may be appointed to a steering task force, which has overall responsibility for the change, or the information coordination committee, which is charged with providing the continuing and timely flow of information to everyone in the department. Many lower-ranking officers are field-oriented and may chafe at being in meetings, particularly if they become restless at the slow progress being made initially, cannot immediately see any benefit from the work of the committee, or have doubts about whether it can really make a difference.[15] Ultimately, a written plan identifying the process to be used and the results desired will be produced during the action planning phase, with responsibilities assigned for all activities.

4. *Change Intervention/Implementation*. This is when the action plans are implemented. It is not the end of the process but rather the end of the beginning. As the various activities are set in motion, their progress must be carefully monitored against the time lines and standards established during the previous phase.

5. *Evaluation*. This is best accomplished by a series of informative, scheduled reports, and periodic personnel checking through observation and conversations with personnel involved at various levels of the department. The two most common needs during this time are (a) the need to further articulate or increase the level of detail in plans and (b) the need to initiate corrective action because the time lines initially set were too ambitious and cannot be met or the activities have somehow otherwise gotten off track (e.g., an equipment supplier cannot make delivery as previously agreed upon). As the decision makers receive evaluative information, the process loops back to step 1, recognizing the need for change, and the process repeats itself.

The Burke-Litwin Model

The ability to adapt and undertake organizational transformation when it's necessary is essential to adopting new policing models, preventing crime, and maintaining a good relationship with the community. While the previous models recognize this and incorporate organizational development theory, the Burke-Litwin model of change explores the various drivers of change and ranks them in order of importance[16].

1. **External Environment:** In policing, this would encompass crime rates, politics, the economy, and the community perception of police. Police leaders must be very cognizant of such changes and, indeed, should be able to prepare their organization when such shifts begin to occur within the environment.

2. **Mission and Strategy:** Previously discussed in Chapter 2, these changes are a strategy as a reaction to external forces. Police executives should recognize the necessity for changes in strategy and be able to articulate those to staff.

3. **Leadership:** The ways in which changes are perceived and implemented by line officers and law enforcement staff largely depends on the actions and attitudes of police leaders.

4. **Organizational Culture:** This is extraordinarily important for law enforcement. Culture is a huge part of policing, with traditions and procedures an integral part of organizational and even personal identity. Understanding that culture comes with a certain set of expectations from the organization and that prevailing organizational values must be respected will help with transition. Changes that can feel like an attack on organizational culture (e.g., the curtailment of vehicle chases in many jurisdictions) may require dialogue through multiple channels and ongoing employee input to strike the right balance between culture and organizational need.

5. **Structure:** Police leaders will need to assess the impact on relationships, responsibilities, and division of labor that a change will have.

6. **Systems:** These are the policies and procedures related to both people and operations of the organization.

7. **Management Practices:** How do managers/police executives work within the mission and strategy of the organization? Does the way that they treat and direct

officers and other personnel reflect the agency's overall values, mission, and strategies?

8. **Work Unit Climate:** Often, a change will impact the immediate working environment of officers or other employees; this can include work hours (such as a shift change), personnel (redeployments), or locations. In these cases, police executives will need to manage such change sensitively, as it may evoke a range of responses from personnel.

9. **Task Requirements and Individual Skills/Abilities:** Are there personnel with appropriate skill sets within the organization to carry out the necessary change? If not, will training be sufficient, or should outside consultants or new team members be brought in?

10. **Individual Values and Needs:** Organizational dynamics are greatly affected by individual personnel. When implementing change, it is critical to recognize the ways that individual styles, skills, abilities, and attitudes may come together in order to both capitalize on their potential and mitigate their risks.

11. **Motivation Level:** Are employees motivated to make a change? Or is the change an unpopular or misunderstood one? Recognizing and maintaining (or augmenting, if necessary) that the level of motivation throughout a change is critical to success.

12. **Individual and Overall Performance:** It is crucial to understand the level of performance in key areas such as productivity, budgetary adherence, crime reduction and be able to establish baselines to measure the effects of change.

Various Levels of Change

Not all change is momentous. However, the wider the scope of the change and the greater the number of people significantly impacted are, the more difficult it is to implement, sustain, and institutionalize it. For example, assume that historically in a department the ranking patrol supervisor at the scene of a serious crime was in charge of the scene. A new policy is issued; stating whenever detectives are dispatched to the scene of a serious crime, they are in command of all aspects of conducting the on-site investigation. Usually, this would affect the job of patrol sergeants and, although they would grouse at the loss of authority, the change would be implemented without any significant turbulence or opposition. In fact, some sergeants would simply say, "It's fine by me; it's one less thing I have to worry about." But when there is large-scale directed change, "more people are going to be ticked off and eating Rolaids." While some policy changes can be made without controversy, others will provoke opposition; an excellent example of this is when an agency goes to a very restrictive high-speed chase policy and rank-and-file officers feel that their "hands are being tied when it comes to catching bad guys."

When automobiles started becoming more commonplace, police chiefs assigned their best officers to traffic duty because they would be coming into contact with wealthy and professional citizens who could afford the cars. In a sense, police professionalism had its first modest start in traffic units; officers assigned there considered themselves elite. Once in a while, that leftover manifestation of this fact still appears.

Recently, a consultant finished a major organizational study of a police department with 200 sworn officers. One of his recommendations was that the traffic division (TD) be eliminated and all personnel from the TD be transferred to the patrol division. However, in order to maintain a high level of ability to investigate serious personal injury and fatality accidents, each patrol division shift would be assigned several of the best qualified TD accident investigators, who would continue to specialize in the same jobs they formerly held. The rest of the TD officers would be assigned to patrol duties. The reason for the recommendation was that the TD, whose members considered themselves the elite of uniformed officers, had become increasingly dysfunctional over a period of years. Among the indicators of this was that no traffic unit worked past 10:00 p.m., meaning that TD officers were not working during some of the prime hours for driving while intoxicated (DWI) enforcement. Moreover, compared with similarly sized cities, the TD officers generated fewer cases, despite having more personnel, used more sick leave than other officers in the department, and were often antagonistic to personnel in other divisions. They were often characterized as prima donnas by other officers in the department because of their reluctance to handle any other types of police incidents other than traffic accidents and traffic law enforcement. The change was implemented but not without great upheaval. Some TD officers and supervisors attempted to have the change killed before it was implemented by politicians who began to voice various concerns, pro and con, about the change. Some experienced TD officers left to take jobs in police departments in several nearby, smaller municipalities. The chief, who had risen through the ranks internally and had only recently been appointed, felt that the "change was long overdue, but messy." The mayor, who had appointed the chief, dismissed the controversy by noting that "You can't make an omelette without breaking a few eggs; we can't have a few malcontents trying to make policy." Slowly, things changed. DWI arrests went up because there were more officers working during the prime enforcement hours for them, response times to calls for service improved slightly because there were more patrol officers on duty to answer calls, and the number of traffic accidents declined marginally each month.

As the positive aspects of the change were "kicking in," a radical shift occurred that no one had foreseen. After some discussion and study, the city's voters approved merging their police department under the sheriff's office, which had a traffic unit. The benefits of the city police department having gone through a hard, large-scale organizational change were lost when the two agencies actually combined operations 18 months later. Under the sheriff, the former TD officers remembered who had supported the elimination of their division and made life difficult for them whenever they could, although slowly that behavior seemed to lessen over time. Thus, in large organizational change, there can be some lingering unanticipated difficulty for years beyond when the change actually happens.

Box 15.3: Police Recruiting: A Case for Organizational and Cultural Change

An image from NYPD's recruiting page online shows community interaction, as opposed to tactical imagery relied upon in the past. (Terese Loeb Kreuzer/Alamy Stock Photo)

Fundamental organizational change in police agencies doesn't generally happen slowly: we've seen many organizations pivot quickly in the aftermath of Ferguson to focus on community/police relations. But one area that is evolving at a slower pace is that of police recruitment and hiring—and the effects of that slow evolution are starting to become obvious. Nearly 66 percent of police agencies report declining numbers of applicants; major cities such as Nashville, Dallas and New York all report officer shortages due to a lack of new recruits.[17]

Some experts point to an otherwise healthy job market as the culprit—people are attracted to jobs with higher wages—but others see something more fundamental at play. First, policing has a PR problem due to multiple high-profile use-of-force incidents against black men; second, rigid organizational constraints limit the applicant pool in our changing society; and finally, organizational culture in law enforcement has funneled certain types of people into policing at the exclusion of others.

We've already examined the ways police organizations are changing as a result of negative attention on law enforcement by many American citizens and due to police legitimacy concerns. Less confrontational approaches to public order may help some potential applicants feel better about their role in a police agency, and agencies largely seem to be aware of that. Recruiting materials have changed from highlighting tactical pursuits and militaristic images to showing more community engagement and emphasizing collaborative approaches to policing.

Other changes include allowing those traditionally excluded from the applicant pool to apply. Tattoos, once forbidden, are now allowable in some agencies (with restrictions); prior drug use that was once an immediate disqualification is acceptable in a growing number of agencies. Minor drug use in adolescence, for example, may not be a hindrance. Agencies have also adopted breastfeeding friendly policies to attract more women and have increased outreach to LGBTQ communities to bring in more diverse applicants.

But organizational culture can also hinder women, LGBTQ applicants, and others from applying for police work: long-standing biases against pregnant officers (coupled with legitimate safety concerns) can be discouraging, and policing has long had a history of unease with the LGBTQ community. Organizational changes, such as adopting policies that promote the recognition and mitigation of implicit biases, are being undertaken in agencies across the country. Additionally, police recruiters are looking for applicants outside of criminal justice programs or the military: social sciences, such as psychology, social work, and liberal studies may produce qualified applicants who possess attributes that fit community policing paradigms that require creativity, interpersonal skills, and relationship building. Agencies have also begun implementing "grow-your-own" programs that rely on partnerships with local educational institutions to provide a pipeline to policing for qualified students.

THE ROLE OF THE POLICE CULTURE IN ORGANIZATIONAL CHANGE

The dominant mind-set of police departments, police reformers, appellate judges, and criminal justice scholars—in short, of nearly everyone who thinks about policing and its problems—is, and always has been, that policing needs strong, top-down management. However, in many ways, police officers necessarily collaborate in the shaping of their work environment.[18] Partners assigned to the same patrol car discuss how they should spend their time and the best ways of responding to known problems in familiar places. Teams of officers plan undercover stings. At a more indirect level, police officers have a say in organizational planning and policy making through strongly supported police unions as well as identity-based caucuses of police officers' groups such as minority officers, women officers, or gay or lesbian officers. And even without pressure from below, wise sergeants, lieutenants, and captains—like wise supervisors in any occupation—find ways to enlist the rank and file in the process of cooperative problem solving. Arguments for systematically involving front-line employees in workplace decision making have gained extraordinarily broad currency over the past several decades, in the public sector and the private sector alike—but not in policing. This is so despite the increasing frequency with which police executives speak in terms of team management, shared organizational outcomes, and aligning police managerial systems with the private sector employment relations practices.[19,20]

Three overlapping arguments are commonly made for involving rank-and-file officers in the decision-making process:

- It heightens morale and commitment.
- It develops democratic skills and habits.
- It makes for better decisions.

Scholars addressing this issue emphasize how police decision making could be improved by securing what is called *diffused and seminal intelligence* of the police culture, *craft knowledge, street knowledge*, or *context-specific knowledge*.[21] It includes not only the kind of micro-level sociological understanding all good officers acquire about their beats but also a hands-on feel for best practices, innovative ideas for improving those practices, and a thorough, nuanced understanding of their fellow offices—who can be trusted, who shirks responsibility, who cuts corners, and who is prone to violence. Thus, line officers can collectively offer not only richer and more nuanced *answers* to central problems of policing but also distinctive and important *questions*—questions different than, and complementary to, the ones typically posed by police executives and typically pursued by scholars.

In addition, if the policy is strongly opposed by the rank-and-file members of the agency, they could decide to flex their political muscle in opposition to it as reflected in the following Box 15.4.

WHY ORGANIZATIONAL CHANGE EFFORTS SOMETIMES FAIL

While organizational change is ubiquitous and necessary, it is also tenuous. As any organization prepares itself to manage the challenge of a planned change, it must be aware of the various threats that might be present that could inhibit the success of the change effort. Despite proper strategy selection, elaborate planning and resourcing, and strong administrative commitment, evaluation research shows that many attempts at major organizational change fail.[22]

Threats to the success of a planned organizational change can take many forms, both internal and external to the organization. External threats to change initiatives can present themselves as budgetary setbacks, a lack of support or misunderstandings from citizens, or opposition by a newly elected politically powerful official. Internal threats to change initiative also come in many forms. These include, but are not limited to, a lack of leadership commitment, a conflicting organizational culture, or as earlier suggested in this chapter, a lack of support, or understanding from the employees involved in the change.[23]

Models Regarding Change

There are three models regarding officer receptivity to planned organizational change:

1. A life experiences/life chances model
2. An officer/organizational subculture model
3. An organizational/structural model

The first model, the life experiences/life chances model, examines the influence of officers' ascribed and achieved status attributes, as measured by their sociodemographic and work experience characteristics. Although sparse, the extant literature suggests that some officer sociodemographic and work experience characteristics (race, gender, education, and years of service) are associated with their receptivity to change[24] and that female, minority, college-educated, and less-experienced officers are more open to organizational changes. Because policing

---

Box 15.4: Change Successfully Blocked by Rank-and-File Officers Labeling It a "Quota System"

The Ogden (Utah) City Council decided to drop a controversial police performance evaluation plan that included 18 factors, including a score for the number of traffic tickets given. This followed a period during which the wife of an officer who drove a van used to display signs critical of the traffic quota and Mayor Godfrey. Within hours, the officer was placed on administrative duty, although the police chief maintains this was due to other alleged actions by the officer. A two-day "blue-flu" was also used, with officers calling in "sick" during it. City officials agreed to meet with the officers to discuss the ticket quota system and after the meeting decided to rescind the ticket quota system.

Source: "Ogden Rescinds Ticket Quota for Police," The Associated Press and Local Wire, August 16, 2006.

has traditionally been a field dominated by white males and not requiring a college degree, the presence of women, minorities, and college-educated officers among the more recent recruits to the profession constitutes a form of organizational change aimed at diversifying and professionalizing the ranks. Such officers tend to be less wedded to more traditional models of policing and, likewise, are less integrated into the police subculture.[25]

The second rival model, the subculture of policing model, addresses the effects of officers' work orientation on their receptivity to planned organizational change. In particular, the influence of officer cynicism, traditionalism, as well as their crime-control and service work orientations. Those officers who most adhere to elements of the subculture of policing (i.e., have high scores on measures of cynicism, traditionalism, and a strong crime control orientation) are least receptive to organizational change, especially those that involve service activities and partnerships with community members to solve noncrime-related social problems. Conversely, those who hold a strong social orientation are most receptive of such change.

The final model, the organizational/structural model, asserts that officers' receptivity to change is a function of their perceptions of the extent to which their agency is prepared for such a change. This model also examines the association between officer receptivity to change and their perceptions of agency readiness with regard to the adequacy of officer training, administrative commitment, resource distribution, and reorganization.

Additionally, new research has found that a person's reaction to organizational change can be "so excessive and immediate, that some researchers have suggested it may be easier to start a completely new organization than to try and change an existing one."[26] In a police agency, this obviously isn't possible, but it does illustrate the difficulty in getting officers to accept change. The field of neuroscience offers some insight into this, finding that there are three main approaches to change that can actually trigger negative chemical and neurological changes in people:

1. Under preparation for change, which means that it comes as a surprise to personnel.
2. Motivation for change via either expressed or implied threat.
3. Leading change from the top of an organization without involving or communicating with lower ranks.

All of these approaches can induce limbic responses in people, affecting basic emotions and drives. Any or all of these can trigger fear, anxiety, and anger about their social status, their autonomy, their relationships with others, and about fairness and certainty within their jobs. Scientific studies have shown that these feelings activate the same circuitry in the brain that physical threats—such as pain—do.[27] Change, in these circumstances, can be literally painful and organizationally counterproductive.

WAYS TO MAKE ORGANIZATIONAL CHANGE SUCCESSFUL

To accomplish organizational change, the police manager needs a combination of will and skill to seize the opportunity to make the needed changes. The basic recommendations that follow can help managers seize opportunities for change in their departments.

Use Coaching as a Tool to Facilitate Organizational Change

Coaching, when provided by a carefully selected peer or supervisor, can be an invaluable tool for assisting officers in accepting change. If done properly, it can provide officers with increased awareness and information about the benefits of the change (i.e., requiring a two-year college degree for promotion to sergeant and a four-year bachelor's degree for a promotion to the rank of lieutenant and above). It can also give officers an opportunity to express any negative emotions they might be feeling about the change and provide them with the opportunity to express precisely why they are opposed to the new policy.[28] If properly handled, coaching can give the officers inclined to resist the change an opportunity for self-evaluation and a chance to consider how the organizational change could affect them in a very positive way.

Once an administrator has made a decision to implement a change and has moved into an action stage, carefully selected coaches who support the change process should work with potentially resistant individuals as they move through the change process. The coach can provide social and emotional

---

Quick Facts: The Brutal Fact: About 70 Percent of All Change Initiatives Fail

Just how hard is organizational change? Research suggests that between 50 and 80 percent of the time, the major results that were anticipated are *not* produced. Most initiatives—installing new technology, downsizing, restructuring, or trying to change organizational culture—have very low success rates.

Source: Nitin Nohria and Michael Beer, "Cracking the Code of Change," *Harvard Business Review*, May–June 2015.

support for the change process and can help the individual being coached accept the change in such a way as to make it easier to be implemented.

Individual and group coaching is just one tool for facilitating the change process in organizations; however, it should be given serious consideration. The organization as a whole must find ways of informing its employees about the benefits of the new program, ways of raising an awareness of the pros and cons of changing or not changing, and ways of reinforcing and supporting employees as they go through the change process.[29]

Coaching can be a critical part of this change process because it focuses on the individual's own agenda. It can also provide an effective process to assist officers in dealing with all the other changes they or their police organizations feel necessary to implement.[30]

Set Flexible Priorities

Police managers should plan their reform agendas very carefully but be prepared to change plans quickly. Effective managers always juggle their plans, putting some on hold while pursuing others. Priorities may vary with the manager's personal interests, the recent political history of the department, or new pressures being put on the department. They may also vary with issues largely unrelated to the police, such as a municipal election that has resulted in a shift in political power. There are reform agendas that will improve police performance, agendas that will heal community conflicts, and agendas that will advance personal careers. These are not always the same.

In any given situation, there may be issues that police managers feel are very important but they have found that their ideal goals are strategically impossible to accomplish. Thus, police managers should set potentially achievable goals. This is not to advocate timidity in setting such goals but merely to counsel against overreaching folly.[31]

Assemble Resources

In order to effect successful organizational change, police managers should accumulate political and other resources to strengthen their credibility and persuasiveness. It is important to have as many allies as possible. How these resources are accumulated, and which ones are chosen, depend very much on the personal style of the players in question. Police chiefs, for example, are often faced with the choice of whether to build support in the community, in the department, with local elected officials, or some combination. Because community coalitions shift, however, it is important to seek a broad base of support from citizen leaders, media, prosecutors, state legislators, and others.[32]

Seize Opportunities

With priorities set and resources in line, a police manager should be ready for a wide range of opportunities for change. These opportunities can be defined as events that can throw the spotlight on police policy and provide a "case in point" justification for an organizational change proposal.

Ironically, opportunities often come disguised in crises, and managers must resist the initial impulse to think first of damage control. In some cases, it may be advantageous for managers interested in change to embrace a crisis and make the most of it. Several generic kinds of events provide opportunities to capitalize on crises to achieve reform.

For example, dramatic tragedies can sometimes provide an opportunity for making needed improvements in department procedures. In one department, the death of an officer who employed an improper tactic in a traffic stop led to the development of a training course on traffic stop safety, as well as expanding the training on other officer survival skills. Other crime-related crises can also be used to bolster requests for additional police officers and financial resources. The dramatic death of an officer or uninvolved innocent third party during a high-speed pursuit for a minor traffic violation may provide an opportunity for a chief law enforcement officer who supports a more conservative pursuit policy to impose restrictions that had been heretofore resisted by rank-and-file officers.

Local or nationwide studies of a police department or policing in general on similar related issues can provide support for the chief's reform agenda. Even if a report is critical, the chief may be able to use its conclusions for the benefit of the department.

Budget crises and fiscal restraint—even layoffs—provide opportunities for questioning traditional practices and making hard choices. As a matter of fiscal necessity, for example, many departments have reordered their priorities, adopted various forms of call screening, and started to refer some kinds of calls to nonpolice organizations. For a chief who has long argued that the police cannot do everything, dramatic news about city tax shortfalls that have become endemic in recent years can provide the political opportunity to make needed changes.[33]

Create Opportunities

No matter how skillfully a police manager seizes opportunities, major items on the reform agenda may still have to be left unaddressed because of political or other reasons. The times may be so sensitive or so complex that no naturally occurring event opens a window for them. However, in some rare cases, police reformers have created their own opportunities by initiating publicity concerning police problems. However, such actions should be undertaken only after consultation with the city manager or mayor to avoid having important individuals being publically "blindsided" or "embarrassed."

In highly publicized situations, police at various ranks have tried to create public debate through leaks or whistle blowing, with attendant press coverage. More quietly, some top executives have sought to freshen their agencies by airing out some of their own dirty laundry in order to provoke the press into demanding reforms sought by the executives themselves. Another way to call attention to departmental problems is to launch an internal investigation or commission a study. Clear proof of misconduct provides a firm excuse for radical changes, and investigations are often the best way to produce that proof. Studies can be used to make people remember an old problem or to demonstrate the existence of a new one.[34]

Follow Through

In all these seized and nurtured opportunities, reform depends on more than just a single press conference. Announcing a planned change or signing an executive order is not usually enough to make change happen. Without a concerted follow-up effort, many or most reforms may die.[35]

Another important model that helps us understand the organizational transformation process is proffered by Dr. John Kotter. Kotter's process is logical and detailed, making it an ideal way to categorize change in police agencies. The **Kotter Model of Successful Change** is composed of eight steps as diagrammed in Figure 15.4:

1. **Establish a sense of urgency:** Most change in law enforcement is inherently urgent, particularly when it involves a reaction to a crisis—like rising crime rates—or a paradigm shift to quell community distrust of police. Nonetheless, police leaders should examine the environment that has led to the need for change, identify and discuss potential problems and opportunities, and create a catalyst for the change.

2. **Form a powerful coalition:** Police leaders should bring community organizers, police union or association leaders, and diverse group of informal leaders from throughout the agency together to develop strategies to achieve change.

3. **Create a vision:** What will the transformation look like? The coalition should identify a means to direct the change effort.

4. **Communicate the vision:** Use formal and informal channels of communication to ensure that everyone understands the new vision and strategies. The coalition responsible for guiding the change should use their formal and informal leadership to teach new behavior and lead by example.

5. **Empower others to act on the vision:** Remove obstacles to change by removing or revising structures, policies, and procedures that may undermine the new vision.

6. **Plan for and create short term wins:** Planning for tangible improvements in performance will allow officers and other staff to see results; for example, in implementing a new community policing program, a department can hold a community event where a good turnout will be noticeable to employees. In that case, the department can credit employees with their role in the positive turnout, further creating buy-in to the change.

7. **Consolidating improvements and creating still more change:** Continuing to refine and reinvigorate the processes behind the change by taking opportunities to use increased buy-in from personnel to make additional tweaks to systems, policies, and procedures.

8. **Institutionalizing new approaches:** Emphasize the links between the organizational change and any benefits/successes as a result of that change. Prioritize leadership development and succession planning to continue to vision and strategies put in place; anchor changes in organizational culture.[36]

INFORMATION TECHNOLOGY AND CHANGE

We have previously discussed the ways in which technology can drive change; recall in Chapter 2, "Policing Today," that GIS, COMPSTAT, and fusion centers have revolutionized policing. Technology, as a driver of change, is extraordinarily powerful—so much so that there is an entire field of change management theory that deals with information technology (IT). Morton's theory of change management, for example, looks at how change should occur with IT as an impetus. Morton asserts that it is critical that such change be made after several issues have been accomplished: First, people issues must be resolved through training and education, so that individuals have time to grapple with, and take on expanded roles utilizing the new technology. Second, management processes that

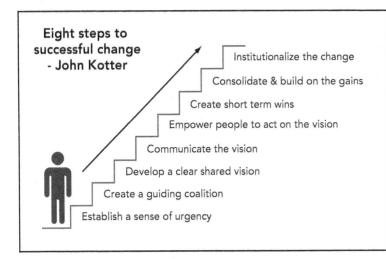

FIGURE 15.4 ▶ Kotter's eight step model of successful change. See http://tie575changemodel.wikispaces.com/Kotter%27s+8-step+model.

redistribute power and control must be presented and accepted within the organization. Third, the organizational structure must change in order to provide effective administration and management for the new technologies. Fourth, new strategies must be developed and accepted within the organization that develops a long-term plan for future technology in relation to the overall goals and objectives. And finally, after the previous steps have been accomplished, the new technology is implemented.[37] Essentially, Morton advocates for groundwork being laid, organizationally speaking, before a change is undertaken. Technological changes, particularly, evoke that limbic response in people; they fear it will complicate their jobs, or that they won't know how to operate or adapt to the technology. Worse yet, they may fear that their job is in jeopardy to the implementation of new technology. Police officers often feel similarly, however, that they manifest their dissatisfaction with statements associated about hindering their interaction with the community, or that this change will make it more difficult to "catch criminals," or that the change is simply another "duty" on top of an already full day of answering calls for service, citizen interactions, meetings, and report writing.

Some of these technological transformations are not specific to policing; social changes that have been facilitated by technology have had an impact on organizational change. Changes in the way that we, as a society, communicate have had a major hand in police organizational change. For instance, recalling our discussion on generational issues earlier in this chapter that instant messaging and web connectivity have created a generation of people who are used to tech-based communication, instant feedback, and immediate gratification. These expectations often carried into the workplace. Some agencies have embraced this phenomenon—for example, using virtual roll calls where officers can be briefed before their shifts via e-mail and check in using mobile devices. Other departments have implemented secure applications for personnel to give constant and continuous feedback and suggestions to supervisory and command staff.[38] And, the impact of social media cannot be overstated; social media has revolutionized the way police interact with each other as well as the community. Patrol, crime control strategies, community relations, personnel management, and the functions of the public information officer (PIO) are all vastly impacted by today's social media technology. For instance, PIO officers once responded to media requests, coordinated press conferences, and directed media mobilizations to crisis events; now, social media has allowed police departments to control their message, to get in front of potentially negative stories by offering their version of events before the media can break the story, and to inform the media of staging areas and other events with a simple Tweet or Facebook post. Social media has singlehandedly allowed PIO officers to transform from reactive entities to proactive public relations-style units.

Social media has also transformed the way police organizations communicate with the public. In years past, engaging the community meant deploying personnel into neighborhoods as time and budgets allowed—perhaps holding crime watch meetings, hosting community events, or even conducting "knock

and talk" programs where officers went door to door to assess problems and solicit tips and solutions. While those programs are all still enormously valuable, social media has allowed police agencies to fill-in the gaps and give communities the opportunity to have a dialogue with police agencies. Sometimes that dialogue is negative—but that in and of itself can be valuable feedback in identifying areas where police need to increase outreach and improve their interaction with citizens. Frequently, though, social media yields tips on crimes, gives the public insight into day-to-day law enforcement processes, and creates goodwill. These functions have all led to changes within police organizations—from the way internal affairs handles citizen complaints to the way that community affairs offices get the word out about specific events or informing the public of dangerous situations, wanted and suspicious persons, or even critical incidents like terrorist attacks and natural disasters.

Social media has also transformed the job of police recruiting offices. A decade ago, police recruiters traveled extensively to find new applicants and relied on background checks to ensure that they were a good fit for their agencies. Today, recruiters can make connections with potential recruits through social media advertising and direct messaging; background checks now include a thorough vetting of an applicant's social media sites. Applicants who post inflammatory content, express viewpoints that run counter to law enforcement values, and who have had the lack of foresight to remove photos of themselves in intoxicated states or compromising positions are now weeded-out before these characteristics become apparent in their work—and before they can embarrass the departments that hire them.

As discussed in Chapter 2, "Policing Today" and Chapter 10 "Organizational and Interpersonal Communication," social media has also caused some systemic changes within departments; policies and procedures have had be carefully updated to balance free speech of employees with the best interests of the organization. Never before have police organizations had to be so concerned with what their officers were saying in their off time—now with a screenshot and a share button, racist/sexist/classist ramblings or shared memes from an off-duty officers can become a major story in local, state, and even national news, causing major heartburn and damaging legitimacy for law enforcement institutions. Ten years ago, social media policies could probably not be found in more than a couple of police agencies' standard operating procedures in the United States. Today, just under 72 percent of all police departments in the United States have some sort of social media policy to guide and direct operations.[39]

Technology has also driven transformational change in the arena of crime control. The very nature of many crimes has changed as a result of new technology. For instance, people don't carry as much cash as they used to, forcing criminals to resort to identity theft and cybercrime to line their pockets. Many departments have found themselves scrambling to identify tech-savvy personnel to work on these complex issues and crimes, and having to restructure financial crimes units to keep up with the caseloads. Tools like GPS trackers have changed the way auto theft and other burglary investigators do business; surveillance cameras can now give clear pictures of criminal activity, enhancing the potential for suspects to be caught. Complex banking and security software can make organized crime and money laundering perpetrators much more easily identifiable to investigators—though the downside to this is that it may push the commission of such crimes to organizations such as Russia and China. For small departments without any type of experience in international locations, that reality will certainly engender some organizational adaptation.

The final area to consider when discussing technology as an impetus for change in a police organization is that of infrastructure. Unfortunately, many planners do not see the whole scope of technology change or implementation. Any major IT change requires connectivity, and connectivity requires infrastructure like bandwidth, cellular/microwave towers, generators, servers, hardware, and software. The demand for broadband access in a major city police department is staggering, considering that the massive needs required by police IT entities (e.g., dispatch, patrol officer's cell phones, wireless computers in patrol cars, downloads of dash-cam footage, downloads of body camera footage, fusion center computing, GIS, closed circuit cameras, crime mapping, websites, and crime watch apps). Increasing speed and broadband access will most likely be critical for a police agency to implement a necessary change or expansion of IT. The accompanying budgetary increase for such change may be staggering, adding to the stress of implementation. For example, a patrol station that is in an area of town surrounded by hills or tall buildings may not accommodate a microwave tower (or tower array) necessary for the massive amount of data that comes with police IT needs. Rural departments may not have the proper fiber optic infrastructure to accommodate fast Internet connectivity. However, despite the challenges that infrastructure can present, technology has the potential to truly revolutionize the way police organizations function in our rapidly changing society.

POLICING IN THE FUTURE: EVERYTHING CHANGES

For students of criminal justice—or even just consumers of current events—the term "post-George Floyd" is probably one that has become ingrained in the consideration of policing and police administration. As has been discussed throughout this text, that particular event in Minneapolis, Minnesota followed by additional instances of use of force or in-custody deaths against African-Americans by police—has become a flashpoint for the discussion about the future of policing. And indeed, it's difficult to forecast the future of the police organization without acknowledging the effects of the death of George Floyd. In a nutshell, police organizations will have to become more responsive to the communities that they serve. They will have to strive to become a reflection of those communities, and they will have to work hard to eliminate bias in their ranks and gain

the trust of the community through cooperation, communication, and—in some instances—some measure of reconciliation. This will absolutely run counter to the command and control style of policing that some agencies are used to, and it will require major ideological transformations in law enforcement. Training, recruitment, and crime control practices will all be touched by these shifts—making this both an exciting and challenging time to be in the field of law enforcement.

But beyond that, the infusion of contemporary employees into the workplace, the effects of complex economic and social drivers, and advances in technology will all combine to change the landscape of law enforcement. In very short order, policing will evolve and change, with experts predicting the most change in the following areas:

1. **Predictive policing:** Advances in IT and infrastructure improvements will take intelligence-led policing to the next level. Real-time analytics will allow intelligence to be drawn from data about crime and crime trends—allowing police to see patterns that may be actionable for purposes of crime prevention and response.[40]

2. **Changes in traditional police response:** Economic realities combined with technological opportunities may mean that police no longer respond to certain nonviolent property crimes. Victims may be able to report minor burglaries and thefts via online portals, and burglar alarm calls may require secondary verification before police are dispatched.

3. **Next Generation 9/11:** New capabilities in smartphones and Internet protocol (IP)-enabled dispatch systems mean emergency services infrastructure may be enhanced in the near future. This can improve response time, enhance dispatch efficiency through better geo-location, allow for text and photo-based reporting, and give better service to disabled citizens.[41]

4. **Body-worn cameras:** These cameras (as well as police vehicle dash-cameras) are seen as a panacea for use-of-force incidents and will likely become ubiquitous in police agencies in the coming years, though it remains to be seen what effect they will really have on police-citizen encounters.

Police leadership will also see major changes in the coming years. The Police Executive Research Forum survey, 61 percent of police chiefs who participated said that their agencies would be experimenting with some kind of organizational structure change in the coming two to five years. In many cases, this involves a new emphasis on developing future leaders, through career pathway opportunities and specialized leadership training that highlights developing and building relationships with communities over tactical considerations.

Organizations may also begin to experiment with flatter bureaucratic structures that impose fewer communication barriers, allow quicker response and adaptation, and establish clear lines of responsibility. Middle management positions tasked mainly with information sharing may be able to be streamlined, particularly since e-mail and cell phones make communication between front-line officers and administration quick and virtually painless.[42]

Ultimately, this is a challenging time for police officers and administrators alike as they navigate issues in police legitimacy, procedural justice, technology, and community relations, as well as other important medical, social and economic events (see Box 15.5). It's hard to say what the outcome of all these transitions will be, but it's worth noting that the public absolutely demands that police undertake them. Therefore, it's not a question of whether all of the disparate 18,000 law enforcement agencies across this country undergo some level of change; it's a question of how well the leaders and the officers will embrace their future, as they transform to earn and maintain community trust and keep crime at bay.

Box 15.5: Adapting to Massive Change in The Future; The Impact of COVID-19, Police Use-of-Force, Racial and Social Unrest, and the Potential "Defunding" of the Police

One thing is for sure, the year 2020 will soon not be forgotten. It not only marked the beginning of a new decade but also initiated an era that will forever be characterized by massive change in policing. Indeed, the world will be forever changed from the impact of the COVID-19 pandemic. Huge national and international loss of life, as well as debilitating economic conditions may well mark the next decade, all starting in 2020.

Police officers are "essential workers" and as such have faced much higher rates of exposure and transmission to the COVID-19 virus than their counterparts in business and government. On August 14, 2020, President Donald Trump signed into law the "Safeguarding America's First Responder Act," ensuring that officers that died or became ill from the COVID-19 virus would be covered by death and disability benefits. The law provides a "general presumption" that any first responder (including all federal, state, and local police/law enforcement officers) that contract the COVID-19 virus did so "while acting in the line of duty." According to the Police Officer's National Memorial and the Officer Memorial Page, deaths of police officers since the beginning of 2020 have far outpaced police officer deaths from more traditional causes like gunfire, vehicle accidents, or heart attacks. In fact, the number of deaths of police officers due to COVID-19 in 2020 exceeded the number of officers killed as a result of the terrorist strike on the World Trade Center in New York on 9/11/2001!

Causes of Death for Police Officers in 2020

COVID-19	210 officers
Gunfire	45 officers
Automobile Accidents	20 officers
Vehicle Assaults	13 officers
Heart Attacks	6 officers
Inadvertent Gunfire	5 officers
Other, including 9/11-related illnesses, drowning, stabbing, duty illnesses, fire, motorcycle accidents, etc.	29 officers
TOTAL:	**328 officers**

Clearly, COVID-19 has changed the workplace. At some point in the future, we will move on from the pandemic, leaving our facemasks behind and daring to encroach within 6 feet of each other. What will the "new" normal look like for police when the pandemic is gone. According to some reports, over 65 percent of employers provided mechanisms for employees to work from home. With the help of online meeting software like Zoom and Teams, employees may well choose the comfort and safety of their own surroundings versus returning to the workplace. For police officers, there will *never* be a choice; they will continue to report to work each day after the pandemic in the same manner as they did before, ready to serve their communities face-to-face on patrol. For police department staff and administrative employees, the COVID-19 pandemic has clearly shown that the police function may continue absent the workplace environment. The virtual workplace will mean a change in operations within policing circles, simply because staff and support positions will undoubtably continue to work remotely. Further, technology will become the life blood of the organization, as the abilities to timely communicate will continue to transform the workplace. In policing, that may mean, more discriminate selection of what types of calls for services are actually necessary for a live contact from an officer. Many departments are experimenting with more precise call-taking centers that use filters to initiate officer contact, more commonly referred to as differential police response. Some agencies have been doing business in this manner for years, particularly in addressing alarms. However, such a response will have to be learned and most importantly, accepted by the community. This is particularly true as police departments look at significantly reduced budgets from the lingering COVID-19 pandemic, economic turndown, and calls to "defund" the police stemming from the deaths of unarmed Black citizens at the hands of the police. Several cities have already significantly reduced police department budgets without understanding the consequence of such cuts on violent crime rates and the general safety of individuals in their community. For instance, after defunding their police department budget, the city of Minneapolis, MN (the city where George Floyd died) witnessed a significant spike in violent crime; the numbers of robberies, aggravated assaults, rapes, and murders rose quickly.

Then too, officers may need to develop new skills to address more serious problems, while other agencies address more commonplace issues like shoplifting, minor theft and vandalism, and homelessness. Some cities have called for new agencies to address social problems commonly referred in the past to the police, such as panhandling, homelessness, vandalism, and the like. Even more serious calls involving mental health crises, domestic violence, and suicide may well be the responsibility of a different responding agency than the police.

Time deadlines have already been replaced with more fluid schedules even in the most stringent of areas, like court proceedings and probation/parole visits which are experimenting with online meetings and other technological innovations that replace person-to-person contact. The traditional face-to-face meeting may well be a thing of the past in the workplace including the criminal justice setting. Pundits have predicted that each area of business and government will settle on a balance between in-person versus virtual meetings. However, no where in policing will there be the need for more competence in addressing change than in police leadership and administration. Amazingly, over 25 police chiefs, including those from major cities like Rochester (NY), Seattle (WN), Portland (OR), Nashville (TN), Milwaukee (WI), Dallas (TX), Richmond (VA), Atlanta (GA), Louisville (KY), and Los Angeles (CA), either resigned or accelerated their retirement since the killing of George Floyd on May 25, 2020. Chiefs, managers, supervisors, and leaders will have to be much more skilled in dealing with complexity and ambiguity. Much of their emphasis will shift from managing day-to-day operations to more strategic thinking, planning and decision making. The police culture must change as well, with a much greater emphasis on adapting to various transformations in the workplace. This includes acceptance of diversity, as well as self-monitoring and self-governing, elements currently under scrutiny in policing by communities of color.

Quoting an old English expression from a Chinese curse seems to accurately describe the future of policing, "we certainly live in interesting times!"

Sources: John Bacon, "Cop Killer: COVID-19 Could Eclipse 9/11 in Causing Police Officer Deaths," *USA Today*, September 4, 2020. See https://www.usatoday.com/story/news/health/2020/09/04/coronoavirus-police-officer-deaths-could-surpass-9-11/5689683002 Louis Casiano, "Police Chiefs Who Have Resigned or Retired Since George Floyd Death," *Fox News*, September 9, 2020. See https://www.foxnews.com/us/police-chiefs-george-floyd Megan Henny, "Minneapolis City Council Alarmed by Surge in Crime Months After Voting to Defund the Police," *New York Post*, September 16, 2020. See https://nypost.com/2020/09/16/minneapolis-city-council-alarmed-by-crime-surge-after-defunding-police/ Michael J. D. Vermeer, Dulani Woods, and Brian A. Jackson, "Would Law Enforcement Leaders Support Defunding the Police—If Communities Ask Police to Solve Fewer Problems," *Perspective*, RAND Corporation, August 2020. Sarah Kirby, "5 Ways COVID-19 Has Changed Workforce Management," *World Economic Forum*, June 2, 2020. See https://www.weforum.org/agenda/2020/06/covid-homeworking-symptom-of-changing-face-of-workforce-management/

Chapter Summary

Summary by Learning Objective

1. **Explain why change occurs in law enforcement agencies.**

   Change occurs in reaction to a crisis; due to fluctuating crime rates; because of technological advances; due to funding changes and economics; because of politics; because of changing workforces; and because of changing paradigms or models of policing.

2. **Discuss five situations when change should not be initiated.**

   (1) The knowledge, skill, or other resources needed to carry out the change effectively do not exist inside the department.

   (2) An appropriately experienced external change agent is not presently available.

   (3) The effort of making the change is greater than any benefits to be derived.

   (4) Collateral damage, such as abandonment by key supporters or significant union opposition, may lead chiefs to use their limited stack of "political chips" on another issue of greater concern to them and the community.

   (5) Too much change is already underway in the department and the nature of the change is not sufficiently important to make now, versus its potential for personnel to feel confused about priorities or conclude that the organization is becoming unstable.

3. **Analyze three models of change in organizations.**

   Kurt Lewin's three-step model on organizational change involves three sequential steps: (1) *unfreezing*, or making people be receptive to change; (2) *moving*, or the transitional phase in which officers actually experience the changes that were planned; and (3) *refreezing*, where officers make permanent the changes they experienced in the previous phase.

   The TRAC model recognizes the need for change; assesses and diagnoses the situation; involves action planning; implements and intervenes; and includes ongoing evaluation.

   Finally, the Burke-Litwin model ranks various drivers of change from most to least important: the external environment; mission and strategy;

leadership; organizational culture; structures; systems; management practices; work unit requirements; tasks and skills; individual values and needs; motivation level; and individual and overall performance.

4. Discuss the role of the rank and file in organizational change.

Line officers can collectively offer not only richer and more nuanced *answers* to central problems of policing but also distinctive and important *questions*—questions different than, and complementary to, the ones typically posed by police executives and typically pursued by scholars. In addition, if the policy is strongly opposed by the rank-and-file members of the agency, they could decide to flex their political muscle in opposition to it.

5. Explain why organizational change sometimes fails.

Threats to the success of a planned organizational change can take many forms, both internal and external to the organization. External threats to change initiatives can present themselves as budgetary setbacks, a lack of support or misunderstandings from citizens, or opposition by a newly elected politically powerful official. Internal threats to change initiative also come in many forms. These include, but are not limited to, a lack of leadership commitment, a conflicting organizational culture, or as earlier suggested in this chapter, a lack of support or understanding from the employees involved in the change. There is some research that also points to neurological resistance to change, as it evokes feelings such as fear, alienation, and other negative emotions.

6. Describe how to make organizational change succeed.

Coaching, when provided by a carefully selected peer or supervisor, can be an invaluable tool for as-

sisting officers in accepting change. Additionally, police managers should plan their reform agendas very carefully but be prepared to change plans quickly. In order to effect successful organizational change, police managers should accumulate political and other resources to strengthen their credibility and persuasiveness. Police managers should also seize opportunities, create opportunities and always follow through. Additionally, John Kotter described eight additional steps to success in organizational change: establish a sense of urgency; form a powerful coalition; create a vision: communicate the vision; empower others to act on the vision; plan for and create short-term wins; consolidate improvements and create still more change; and institutionalize new approaches.

7. Describe the role of technology in police organizational change.

Technology is a major impetus for change in police organizations. It has changed the way crime is analyzed (e.g., fusion centers, GIS); the way agencies communicate with the public (social media); the ways police agencies establish legitimacy (body-worn cameras); and more. It also affects internal budgets, internal administration, and internal policies and procedures.

8. Discuss a few ways in which policing may change in the coming years.

Law enforcement organizations will have to respond to citizen calls for transparency and fair and impartial policing through training, technology, and administrative policies and procedures. Predictive policing, enabled by technology, will allow quicker responsiveness. New modes for police responsiveness—including innovative dispatch systems—will also come online. Police organizations will also evolve to include specialized leadership training for its commanders and may become flatter structures as communication capabilities decrease the need for multiple levels of administration.

Chapter Review Questions

1. Identify seven recurring reasons why change occurs in law enforcement agencies.
2. Identify actions that many states have taken to address issues in wake of recent police-community unrest.
3. Explain the importance of the 2015 landmark case, *Obergefell v. Hodges*.
4. State five reasons when change should not be made.
5. What are the three steps in Kurt Lewin's model on organizational change?
6. What are the five steps in the traditional action research model?
7. What are the 11 drivers of change identified in the Burke-Litwin model?
8. What are the most common overlapping arguments commonly made for involving rank-and-file employees in workplace decision making?
9. Why do organizational change efforts sometimes fail?

10. What are ways to make organizational change succeed?

11. Identify the eight steps in Kotter's model for successful change.

12. Discuss and identify Mortons theory of change management involving information technology.

13. According to Orlando Patterson, what are the real problems confronting America's inner cities?

14. Identify the four areas where experts predict that the most change will occur in policing in the future.

Critical Thinking Exercises

1. Envision a change that you would make in your local law enforcement agency. Using the Burke-Litwin Model of Change, describe how you would implement your ideas.

2. Visit the website for the Police Executive Research Forum—PERF (policeforum.org) to browse publications and documents about police organizations that have adopted major changes in their organization. Do you think that similar changes could be made within any law enforcement agency or are certain agencies more adaptive to change than others? Why or why not?

3. Search the Internet to find articles and literature on organizational change in the private sector. Why is creating organizational change so difficult? Do you think that change is easier in the private sector versus the public sector? Why or why not?

Key Terms

Burke-Litwin Model
change agent
directed change

Kotter Model of Successful Change
Lewin's three-step model

Obergefell v. Hodges
traditional action research model

Endnotes

[1] Robert W. Taylor and Charles R. Swanson, *Terrorism, Intelligence and Homeland Security* (Upper Saddle River, NJ: Pearson, 2015). See specifically Part III: Responding to the Challenges of Terrorism.

[2] Joe Domanick, "Police Reform's Best Tool: A Federal Consent Decree," The Crime Report (July 15, 2014).

[3] Brian A. Jackson, Victoria A. Greenfield, Andrew R. Morral, and John S. Hollywood, *Police Department Investments in Information System Technology* (Santa Monica, CA: RAND Corporation, 2014).

[4] Police Executive Research Forum, "Policing and the Economic Downturn: Striving for Efficiency Is the New Normal," February 2013. Retrieved on July 17, 2015 from http://www.policeforum.org/assets/docs/Critical_Issues_Series/policing%20and%20the%20economic%20downturn%20%20striving%20for%20efficiency%20is%20the%20new%20normal%202013.pdf,

[5] http://www.bloomberg.com/news/articles/2015-01-26/pensions-hobble-police-hiring-as-san-diego-seeks-boots-on-street.

[6] Police Executive Research Forum (PERF), ibid.

[7] Tanya Eiserer, "Dallas DA disbands digital forensics lab after 8 months," WFAA, July 31, 2015. Retrieved on July 31, 2015 from: http://www.wfaa.com/story/news/local/dallas-county/2015/07/dallas-das-digital-forensics-lab-shuttered-after-8-months/31/30968707/.

[8] James P. Henchy, "Ready or Not, There They Come: The Millenial Generation Enters the Workforce."

[9] Anthony Batts, Sean Michael Smoot, and Ellen Scrivner, "Police Leadership in a Changing World," National Institutes of Justice: New Perspectives in Policing. July 2012. Retrieved on July 5 from: https://www.ncjrs.gov/pdffiles1/nij/238338.pdf.

[10] Bob Moritz, "The US Chairman of PwC on Keeping Millenials Engaged," *Harvard Business Review*, November 2014.

[11] Anthony Batts, Sean Michael Smoot, and Ellen Scrivner, "Police Leadership in a Changing World," National Institutes of Justice: New Perspectives in Policing. July 2012. Retrieved on July 5 from: https://www.ncjrs.gov/pdffiles1/nij/238338.pdf.

[12] "Diversity in Law Enforcement: A Literature Review," U.S. Department of Justice Civil Rights Division Office of Justice Programs and US Equal Employment Opportunity Commission. January 2015. Retrieved July 27, 2015 from: http://www.cops.usdoj.gov/pdf/taskforce/Diversity_in_Law_Enforcement_Literature_Review.pdf.

[13] Eileen Sullivana and Jack Gillam, "Analysis: Hispanic Police Officers Scant in Police Forces Despite Growing Populations," *Fort Worth Star-Telegram*, September 8, 2014. Retrieved on July 19, 2015 from: http://www.star-telegram.com/news/local/community/fort-worth/article3872396.html.

[14] "What You Should Know About EEOC and the Enforcement Protections for LGBT Workers," Equal Employment Opportunity Commission. Retrieved July 25, 2015 from: http://www.eeoc.gov/eeoc/newsroom/wysk/enforcement_protections_lgbt_workers.cfm.

[15]Hans Toch and J. Douglas Grant, *Police as Problem Solvers* (Washington, DC: American Psychological Association, 2005), p. 342.

[16]W. Warner Burke and George H. Litwin, "A Causal Model of Organization Performance and Change," *Journal of Management* 18, No. 3 (1992), pp. 523–545.

[17]Tom Jackman, "Who wants to be a police officer? Job applications plummet at most U.S. departments," *Washington Post*, December 8, 2016. Retrieved at https://www.washingtonpost.com/crime-law/2018/12/04/who-wants-be-police-officer-job-applications-plummet-most-us-departments/?utm_term=.739dd5ebef0f.

[18]David Alan Sklansky and Monique Marks, "The Role of the Rank and File in Police Reform," *Policing and Society* 18, No. 1 (March 2008), pp. 1–6. (This discussion was adapted with permission from this source.)

[19]E. McLaughlin and K. Murji, "Resistance Through Representation: 'Storylines,' Advertising and Police Federation Campaigns," *Policing and Society* 8, No. 4 (1998), pp. 367–399.

[20]M. Silvestri, "'Doing' Police Leadership: Enter the 'New Smart Macho,'" *Policing and Society* 17, No. 1 (2007), pp. 38–58.

[21]H. Toch and J. D. Grant, *Police as Problem Solvers: How Frontline Workers Can Promote Organizational and Community Change*, 2nd edition (Washington, DC: American Psychological Association, 2005).

[22]John K. Cochran, Max L. Bromley, and Matthew J. Swando, "Sheriff's Deputies' Receptivity to Organizational Change," *Policing: An International Journal of Police Strategies & Management* 25, No. 3 (2002), pp. 507–529. (This discussion was adapted from this source.)

[23]R. Aragon, "Community-Oriented Policing: Success Insurance Strategies," *The FBI Law Enforcement Bulletin* 66 (1997), pp. 8–18.

[24]A. J. Lurigio and W. G. Skogan, "Winning the Hearts and Minds of Police Officers: An Assessment of Staff Perceptions of Community Policing in Chicago," *Crime and Delinquency* 40, No. 3, (1994), pp. 315–330.

[25]John K. Cochran, Max L. Bromley, and Matthew J. Swando, "Sheriff's Deputies' Receptivity to Organizational Change," *Policing: An International Journal of Police Strategies & Management* 25, No. 3 (2002), pp. 507–529.

[26]Walter McFarland, "This Is Your Brain on Organizational Change," *Harvard Business Review*, October 16, 2012.

[27]Ibid.

[28]Richard C. Lumb and Ronald Breazeale, "Police Officer Attitudes and Community Policing Implementation: Developing Strategies for Durable Organizational Change," *Policing and Society* 13, No. 1 (2002), p. 99.

[29]Ibid.

[30]Richard C. Lumb and Ronald Breazeale have developed a training program to prepare supervisors to address and resolve problems before they affect either employees or the organizations. The results of this study can be found in ibid., pp. 100 and 101.

[31]Lawrence W. Sherman, Albert M. Greenfield Professor of Human Relations in the Department of Sociology and director of the Fels Center of Government, University of Pennsylvania, and Anthony V. Bouza, former chief of police, Minneapolis, Minnesota, in *Local Government Police Management*, 4th edition (Washington DC: International City/County Management Association, 2003), p. 440.

[32]Ibid., p. 440.

[33]Ibid., pp. 440, 441.

[34]Ibid., p. 441.

[35]Ibid.

[36]This section was adapted from John P. Kotter. "Leading Change: Why Transformation Efforts Fail," *Harvard Business Review*, January 2007.

[37]Michael Morton, "The Corporation of the 1990s: Information Technology and Organizational Transformation," Oxford University Press, 1991.

[38]Anthony Batts, Sean Michael Smoot, and Ellen Scrivner, "Police Leadership in a Changing World," National Institutes of Justice: New Perspectives in Policing. July 2012. Retrieved on July 5 from: https://www.ncjrs.gov/pdffiles1/nij/238338.pdf.

[39]International Association of Chief of Police, "IACP Center for Social Media: 2014 Survey Results," Retrieved on July 26, 2015 from: http://www.iacpsocialmedia.org/Resources/Publications/2014SurveyResults.aspx.

[40]Police Executive Research Forum, "Future Trends in Policing," 2014. Washington, DC: Office of Community Oriented Policing Services.

[41]Christopher Moraff, "8 Ways American Policing Could Change This Year," NextCity Politics. Retrieved on July 18, 2015 from: https://nextcity.org/daily/entry/police-technology-changes-2015.

[42]Police Executive Research Forum, "Future Trends in Policing," 2014. Washington, DC: Office of Community Oriented Policing Services.

GLOSSARY

1983 action: a tort action by which federal courts obtain jurisdiction of suits that involve the deprivation of any rights, privileges, or immunities secured by the Constitution by an individual acting under color of any statute, ordinance, regulation, custom, or usage of any state.

4/5ths rule: a rule of thumb used to determine whether adverse impact has occurred, not a legal standard.

active shooter: describes an individual who is still at the scene of an event and actively engaged in continuing to attempt to injure or kill people at the scene.

administrative theory: also called management theory and the principles approach, sought to find "universal" principles of management that could be used in any setting; also see traditional organizational theory.

administrative/management plans: this includes formulation of the department's mission statement of values, goals, and policies and procedures; the organizational structure, the functions, authority, and responsibilities of the positions; the allocation of resources; sick leave, vacation time, court appearance; and other related topics.

adverse impact: an employment practice, which although lacking any discriminatory intent and on its face appearing to be neutral, an employer is prohibited from using because it has an unjustified impact on members of a protected class.

advocates: leadership style described by Downs; such leaders promote everything under their control.

affiliation needs: the desire to be accepted and liked.

Age Discrimination in Employment Act (ADEA): (1967), forbids age discrimination in any aspect of employment for those 40 or older.

air raid wardens: persons in WW II who patrolled to make sure that during "black outs" no lights were showing that could assist enemy submarines in identifying targets if they shelled our coast. Also used to prevent enemy submarines or aircraft from using lights to assist in their navigation. Police and civic groups shared this duty across the country.

alarm stage: the component of general adaptation syndrome that puts the body on a "fight-or-flight" alert by releasing hormones that produce an energizing effect on the body.

all-hazard: able to support operations during an emergency that is either human-made or natural.

allotments: small amounts into which a budget is broken and given to the police department monthly or quarterly, instead of giving all of it at once to the police department.

all-qualified list: promotional roster method in which anyone on the list can be selected in any order.

Alpha generation: born 2011–2025, projected to be besteducated and most technologically sophisticated.

al-Qaeda: a radical Islamic, Middle Eastern terrorist organization formally led by the late Osama bin Laden and Ayman al-Zawahiri; it was responsible for the attacks against the United States on September 11, 2001.

Americans with Disability Act (ADA): (1990), provides equal opportunity to jobs for qualified persons with a disability as well as other protections. Job requirements that screen out people with disabilities are legal only to the extent they are job related and consistent with business necessity.

anabolic steroids: a group of synthetic hormones usually derived from testosterone, that promote storage of protein and the growth of muscle tissue.

Argyris, Chris: developed maturity-immaturity model postulating that traditional organization forms get in the way of workers' development.

assessment center: consists of several exercises or job simulations designed to elicit from candidates the behaviors found to be important to job success by the job analysis.

audit: an independent verification by someone who has no stake in the outcome; audits can be financial or programmatic.

authentic leadership: (1) being deeply aware of how you think, behave, and are seen by others; (2) awareness of your own and others' values/moral perspectives, knowledge, and strengths; (3) understanding the context in which you operate; and (4) being grounded by confidence, hopefulness, optimism, resiliency, and high moral character.

authoritarian/autocratic: a leadership style; makes all decisions, closely controls work, a micromanager, "my way or the highway."

authority: Weber identified three sources: charismatic, traditional, and rational legal. In police departments, it is a formal grant to a position; the incumbent uses it to accomplish organizational goals. Also see power.

baby boomers: born 1946–1964, many still employed by law enforcement agencies, reaching the end of their careers; grew up in era of widespread social change.

banded list: promotional roster method in which candidates with similar scores are grouped together.

bargaining not required model: the model for police-sector collective bargaining law in which collective bargaining is not statutorily required by the state.

behavioral systems theory: sees organizations as made up of the behavior of individuals and groups, wanted to make organizations more democratic and participative. Founded by Lewin.

benchmarking: the practice of comparing one's organizational performance to those that are recognized leaders in the field or otherwise relevant competitors.

biennial budget: a two-year police budget.

bifurcation: the "flash-point" when chaos overcomes normal conditions in an agency and forces it in a new direction in terms of priorities and tactics. See cosmology.

Big Five: the traits approach produced long lists of traits; using meta-analysis, five broad trait categories were identified into which the longer lists of traits could be fitted: surgency, conscientiousness, agreeableness, adjustment, and intellectance. See Big Two.

Big Two: a refinement of the Big Five: stability and plasticity.

binding arbitration: a judgment made by a neutral third party to settle a dispute between labor and management, in which both parties agree in advance to abide by the result.

***Bivens* action:** a judicially created counterpart to a 1983 action that gives the federal courts jurisdiction over torts involving federal officials.

Black Asphalt: the short name for a particular company that teaches police agencies how to identify enforcement opportunities that provide opportunities for subsequent asset forfeitures.

Black Codes: laws quickly adopted in southern states following the Civil War to repress African-Americans.

Black September Organization (BSO): terrorist group.

blue flu: a job action in which officers organize mass absences on the pretext of sickness for the purpose of protest against their employer.

bootlegger: someone who smuggled illegal alcohol during prohibition; also referred to people who hid a flask in their boot or held one to their leg with a garter.

brainstorming: this is a type of group decision making developed initially in advertising to help trigger creativity. The idea behind brainstorming is to establish a group environment in which individuals can present any idea that seems to apply even remotely to the subject being considered with the understanding that criticism will be withheld unless it can somehow improve on the original idea.

budget: a government's priorities expressed in financial terms, a plan stated in financial terms, the use of resources to meet human needs, a contract between the appropriators and those who execute the budget.

budget adjustment: during the course of executing a police department's budget it may be adjusted upward or downward only by the action of the local legislative body, such as a city council or county commission. There are six common methods of making budget adjustments.

budget calendar: a schedule of events for the preparation and approval of a budget.

budget cycle: a four-step, sequential process repeated annually in government.

budget execution: the action phase of budgeting, budget implementation.

buffering: stores inputs (e.g., gasoline) to avoid disruption of services if supply is interrupted; also see negative entropy.

bum blockades: police-staffed blockades established by some cities during the Depression to turn immigrants away at the city limits who would be a drain on local government resources if allowed to enter.

bureaucratic model: organizational form often called classical, mechanistic, and a closed system; comprised eight characteristics.

Burke-Litwin Model: a change model that recognizes and incorporates organizational theory by exploring and ranking the various drivers of change.

business concerns: owners are the primary beneficiaries.

butterfly effect: small, helpful, self-initiated acts have a ripple effect, causing others to become energized and helpful.

caliphate: an Islamic state in which the political and religious leader are the same.

capital budget: groups together multiple large-scale, nonrecurring projects such as the construction of a new police station and has a multiyear time horizon, often five years.

capital improvement plan (CIP): a single capital improvement project, a component of a capital budget.

CAPS: **C**hicago **A**lternative **P**olicing **S**trategy; one of the largest and most comprehensive community policing initiatives in the United States, conducted by the Chicago Police Department during the 1990s.

carpetbaggers: Northerners who came to the South following the Civil War, so called because their suitcases were cheaply made of second-hand carpet.

Challenge of Crime in a Free Society: 1967 government report calling for improvements across the criminal justice system.

change agent: an individual or a group from within or outside the police department that stimulates, guides, facilitates, and stabilizes the change process.

chaos theory: an organizational state of nonequilibrium produced by a crisis event that exceeds anything we can imagine. See cosmology and bifurcation.

charismatic leadership: Charisma was originally thought to be a gift of abilities from above; failures cannot be charismatic, nor can leaders proclaim themselves to be such. Charismatic leaders have seven traits, including having an innovative vision, inspiring and developing followers, and leading their departments to superior performances.

Chavez, Cesar: farm worker and later civil rights activist, fought for better working conditions and pay for migrant pickers.

citizen oversight: This is a process by which people who are not sworn officers are involved in some way in the review of citizen complaints against police officers.

city council: Acts as the chief legislative and policy-making body of a city.

city manager movement: style of city government that began in Stanton, Virginia, in 1908.

city manager: a professional administrator who is recruited for certain skills and training and is appointed by the city council.

city-county consolidated governments: a city and county that have merged into one unified jurisdiction, having the powers and responsibilities of both a municipal corporation (city) and the administrative division of a state (county).

Civil Rights Act of 1964: federal law that invalidated Jim Crow laws; Title 7 forbade discrimination by businesses, unions, and federal agencies on the basis of sex, race, color, religion, or national origin in hiring, promoting, and firing. Title 7 did not apply to state and local governments until 1972. See Equal Employment Opportunity Act of 1972.

climbers: leadership style described by Downs; such leaders invent new functions for their units.

code of silence: refusal of officers to testify against other officers who are accused of misconduct.

CODEFOR: **C**omputer **O**ptimized **DE**ployment—**F**ocus **O**n **R**esults; one of the first experiments in the COMPSTAT process, used in Minneapolis, Minnesota, designed specifically to reduce crime and improve the efficiency and effectiveness of the police department.

coding: to prevent overload, an organization codes or prioritizes messages so that important messages get to the right place quickly; citizens with minor problems wanting to talk to the Chief find themselves redirected and talking to some other official.

cognitive maps: accumulated sense making produces "mental understandings" that help us navigate our world. See sense making.

collective bargaining: negotiation between an employer and a labor union, usually regarding issues such as wages, benefits, hours, and working conditions.

colors: outlaw motorcycle gang patches and insignias that represent the club's name and chapter; usually wore on a denim jacket or vest.

Commission on Accreditation of Law Enforcement Agencies (CALEA): created in 1979 with the support of police associations; this private body accredits law enforcement agencies that meet its list of standards.

commonweal organizations: the public at large is the beneficiary (e.g., law enforcement agency).

communication: the process by which senders and receivers interact in both professional and social contexts.

Community-Oriented Policing Services (COPS): a federal grant program.

community-oriented policing (COP): early 1980s policing philosophy that essentially provided custom-tailored police services to neighborhoods and business districts. Used interchangeably with problem-oriented policing (POP).

community policing: a policing philosophy that focuses on general neighborhood problems as a source of crime; community policing is preventive, proactive, and information-based.

COMPSTAT: a police methodology using the most accurate and timely information to identify crime and social problems within a given geographic area and then to develop strategies designed to stop or prevent them from occurring in the future; COMPSTAT holds police administrators accountable for their decisions, tactics, and strategies aimed at reducing crime.

computerized voice stress analyzer (CVSA): a lie detection mechanism.

conceptual skills: the ability to understand and interrelate various parcels of information that seem unrelated or whose meaning or importance is not immediately apparent.

conditional job offer (CJO): an employment offer made contingent on passing a medical screening.

conservers: leadership style described by Downs; such leaders exhibit bias toward maintaining things under their control.

cosmology: chaos event that overwhelms us; beyond the worse conditions we could imagine; problems of magnitude, complexity, and durability on a scope not seen by us before.

counterproductive work behavior (CWB): behavior that has a detrimental effect on relationships with coworkers and/or the efficiency of operations.

crime analysis: the organization of massive quantities of raw data and information relating to reported crime in an effort to identify trends and patterns and then to forecast specific events from the statistical manipulation of these data.

critical infrastructure and key resources (CI/KRs): the important facilities, buildings, and installations that provide basic services within a community, such as transportation and telecommunications systems, water and power lines, electronic data systems, key bridges and waterways, emergency facilities, and private sector industries and businesses that are essential for the defense and security of the United States.

culture: the beliefs and behaviors characteristic to a particular ethnic, racial, or other population.

cumulative career stress: this is distress that often results from officers being exposed routinely to traumatic events over an extended period of time, sometimes years.

decentralization: the process of distributing the administrative functions or powers of an organization among all levels of the structure.

deep web: a secret part of the World Wide Web, not accessible through regular Internet browsing or search engines; accessible from dynamic websites that require the use of an application program called "Tor" that allows encrypted conversations.

defendant: the person or organization being sued; also called a tort feasor.

deliberate indifference: a legal standard that involves more than negligence; the conscious or reckless disregard of the consequences of one's acts or omissions.

democratic: a leadership style; encourages individual and group participation, "let's talk about it."

detainer: a written request issued by ICE to a local jurisdiction requesting 48 hours advanced notice before a person in their custody is released so ICE may take him or her into its custody. Compliance with a detainer is a voluntary "immigration hold" because it is not a legal document such as a court order or a warrant.

Dillinger, John: bank robber killed in Chicago by FBI agents in 1934, marking the end of the lawless era.

directed and saturation patrols: more of a police tactic than a style, directed patrol usually involves the directing of patrol officers to specific locations during their patrol shift; saturation patrol concentrates *additional* officers on specific locations at specific times in an attempt to efficiently deploy officers as well as deter and prevent crime.

directed change: a carefully planned, formal action designed to bring about a new condition.

disability: under ADA: (1) physical or mental impairment that substantially limits one or more major life activities; (2) a record of such impairment; and (3) a perception of such impairment.

discipline: the core meaning is to teach or instruct.

discipline matrix: a formal schedule for disciplinary actions, specifying both the presumptive or presumed sanction to be imposed for misconduct and any reduction or increase in the presumptive sanction for mitigating or aggravating factors.

disparate treatment: an EEOC theory of discrimination; a member of a protected class is intentionally discriminated against in an employment decision.

domestic violence lethality assessment form: used to assist law enforcement officers in objectively assessing the potential dangers to a victim of domestic violence.

double-loop learning: causes organizations to reconsider whether they are pursuing the right.

downward communication: communication used by management to send orders, directives, goals, policies, and so on, to employees at lower levels of the organization.

due process: a guarantee of fairness in legal matters that requires that all legal procedures set by statute and court practice must be followed for every individual, so that there is no prejudicial or unequal treatment.

dustbowl: term for dried-out prairie states, where good topsoil blew away; many immigrated from those states to seek a better life. See okies.

Early Identification and Intervention Systems (EIIS): a nonpunitive way for a police department to identify and change officers' at-risk behaviors that could result in legal liability or damage its relationship with the community. It is therefore a tool to support officers and a tool to manage the department.

Earth Liberation Front (ELF), Animal Liberation Front (ALF): the two most infamous, single-issue, ecoterrorist groups active in the United States; they are responsible for significant destruction of property caused by arson and vandalism and sometimes resort to more violent means to express their message.

e-government: provides citizens with online access to many governmental services.

e-learning software: computer-based training software designed to incorporate case studies and simulation in the learning experience.

emotional skills (ES): the ability to accurately perceive and appraise your own emotions and those of others, to regulate your own emotions, and to do so while adapting and responding to the needs of others.

emotionally disturbed persons (EDPs): individuals suffering from various forms of mental illness that may complicate interactions with police officers.

employee assistance programs (EAPs): programs made available by employers to help employees having personal or occupational difficulties.

Employee Polygraph Protection Act (EPPA): limits the use of lie detectors by employers, provides a law enforcement exception.

entropic process: open systems concept; all organizations face the prospect of moving toward decline, disorganization, and death.

equifinality: there are multiple ways to achieve goals.

Equal Employment Opportunity Act of 1972: law that amended Title 7 of the Civil Rights Act of 1964 to include state and local units of government.

Equal Employment Opportunity Commission (EEOC): a unit within the U.S. Department of Justice (USDOJ) that administers several key job discrimination laws. EEOC recognizes four theories of discrimination.

Equal Pay Act (EPA): (1963), prohibits wage discrimination based on gender.

ethical leadership: consistent demonstration of moral values though personal actions, in interpersonal communications, and the communication of values to followers. Two components: (1) moral person and (2) moral manager.

ethics: rules and standards governing conduct.

evidence-based policing (EBP): a style of policing using the best available research to guide, manage, and evaluate police operations within a community.

exception principle: routine matters should be handled at the lowest possible organizational level that they can be properly addressed, and unusual events, above or below standards, should be brought to the attention of higher-level managers.

exempt employee: not entitled to overtime pay under FLSA.

exhaustion stage: the point in general adaptation syndrome when resistance can no longer be maintained and the body's defenses against stress begin to break down.

Fair Labor Standards Act (FLSA): (1938, private sector; 1985, public sector), establishes national minimum wage, work hours, overtime pay, child labor, and record-keeping requirements.

Family Medical Leave Act (FMLA): (1993), provisions to help employees balance their career and family needs. Mandates unpaid leave by covered employees for eligible workers for up to 12 weeks during any 12-month period for four specific reasons.

federal consent decree: a federal lawsuit against a city or state jurisdiction that has an established "pattern and practice" of violating the Constitutional rights of people within their jurisdiction.

feedback: messages sent from the receiver to the sender in a communication.

field training officer (FTO): guides the field training of a recent basic/academy graduate; see officer in training.

fiscal year (FY): the 12-month period usually covered by a budget; also see biennial and capital budgets as exceptions.

force-field analysis: a decision-making tool developed by Lewin. Also see behavioral systems theory.

Forces Act: federal legislation (1870) to combat Ku Klux Klan.

Fosdick, Raymond: author who played a major role in the Cleveland Foundation Study.

Freedmen's Bureau: federal agency that provided assistance to African-Americans after the Civil War.

frontier closing: 1890—the official date set by the federal government for the "closing of the frontier," a key point in the transition from a rural to an urban society.

functional structure: a modified line and staff structure that brings together trained specialists and specialized resources under a single manager to accomplish a core responsibility.

functional supervision: one person supervises a function, even if it cuts across several organizational units.

fusion centers: data centers within police agencies that serve as intelligence hubs and clearinghouses for all potential relevant homeland security and crime information that can be used to assess local terror threats and aid in more traditional anticrime operations.

Garfield, President: U.S. president assassinated by frustrated patronage seeker; event gave momentum to passage of Pendleton Act.

general adaptation syndrome (GAS): the biological and physiological reactions, caused by stress, that may eventually incapacitate an individual.

Generation X: born 1965–1980, the largest generation working in law enforcement presently; grew up in mixed economy; first-generation latch key children; tend to be computer fluent. Many departments adapted their recruiting practices to attract Gen Xers.

generation x: those born between 1965 and 1980.

Generation Y: born 1981–1994, largely the children of baby boomers, recently entering law enforcement agencies. Tend toward traditional family values; spiritual, but not necessarily religious.

generation y: those born between 1981 and 1994.

Generation Z: born 1995–2010, the "Zedders," little known about them; fascination with virtual realities may lead to impoverished social and interpersonal skills.

Genetic Information Nondiscrimination Act (GINA): (2008), limits the use of genetic information, provides a law enforcement exemption.

geographic information systems (GIS): the integration of automated database operations and high-level mapping to analyze, manipulate, and manage spatial data, particularly relevant to crime analysis and forecasting.

grapevine: a system of informal information that meanders across organizational lines.

"great man" theories: two contrasting views: (1) events that must be responded to produce the great man and (2) great men are "born leaders," exceptionally endowed; one of two branches of traditional leadership theory, the other being the traits approach.

Great Recession: a major downturn in the American economy that began in December 2007 and was officially declared over in 2009, although the recovery has been slow.

grievance: an official expression of dissatisfaction brought by an employee or an employee organization as the initial step toward resolution through a formal procedure.

group communication: interaction among three or more individuals in a face-to-face situation where all parties have a common need that is satisfied by the exchange of information.

group interaction: a process that has four phases: orientation, conflict, emergence, and reinforced.

groupthink: decision making by a group, characterized by a lack of both creativity and individual responsibility.

Gulick, Luther: coined the most famous acronym of administration: POSDCORB.

harassment: a discriminatory, unwelcome action toward an individual on the basis of race, color, sex (including pregnancy), national origin, age, religion, disability, or genetic information. Sexual harassment is perhaps the most well-known type of harassment.

Harrison, President: U.S. president accused of "prostitution of the public service."

hate crimes: harms (usually violent crimes) committed against an individual because of his or her perceived race, religion, ethnicity, gender, and/or sexual orientation.

Hawthorne effect: people being studied behave differently because they like the attention they get; part of a study by the human relations school at the Hawthorne Electrical Plant.

Herzberg, Frederick: developed motivation-hygiene theory.

heuristic model: a simplified, gut-level method of decision making that emphasizes internal personality attributes of the decision maker.

Hispanic American Police Command Officers Association (HAPCOA): established 1973, HAPCOA provides training and other opportunities for its members.

homegrown terrorism: instances where U.S. citizens and residents convert to radical Islamic extremism and conduct terrorist acts.

homeostasis: when an organization is "in balance."

horizontal communication: communication among peers.

horizontal differentiation: an organizational design that is structured based on activity rather than rank.

hostile environment: created when the prohibited and unwelcome behavior has the purpose or effect of unreasonably interfering with the individual's work performance or by creating an intimidating, hostile, or offensive working environment.

hot-spot policing (HSP): a geographically based approach to crime-fighting focused on in-depth analysis of "places" and times, and deploying police officers to those locations that account for the majority of calls for service and crime in a community.

human relations school: saw traditional organizational theory as ignoring the human element and sought changes; helped set the stage for the emergence of organizational humanism; see Hawthorne effect.

human relations skills: the capacity to interrelate positively with other people.

hybrid budget: budget formats that incorporate features from one or more other budget formats versus being purely one type of format.

immaturity versus maturity: see Argyris.

improvised explosive devices (IEDs): homemade explosive devices and bombs, these "booby-trap" explosives are designed to cause extensive bodily injury or death and are usually located along roads or streets in conflict areas. IEDs are responsible for the majority of the casualties of U.S. troops in Iraq and Afghanistan.

inactive planning: this type of planning is based on the assumption that things will continue to be as they are and will be "business as usual." Its time orientation is rooted in the present under the assumption that it is better than the past and not as dangerous as the uncertainty of the future. There is no systematic scanning of the environment to detect new opportunities.

incremental model: this model contends that police managers and administrators "play things safe" and opt to move very slowly (incrementally) in decision making.

informal organization: an unofficial structure within an organization, often based on personal relationships, that has its own goals, communications, and behavior patterns.

intelligence: data and information that have been evaluated, analyzed, and produced with careful conclusions and recommendations for future decision makers and policymakers.

intelligence-led policing (ILP): arising from the 9/11 terrorist attacks, ILP is a relatively new policing style focused on offenders, not crime incidents, using intelligence analysis to prevent crime.

internal subsystems: in open systems theory, the internal unifying forces of an agency that prevent fragmentation of the organization and transform inputs into outputs.

International Association of Chiefs of Police (IACP): a professional organization of chiefs of international, federal, state, and local police agencies of all sizes.

International Association of Police Women (IAPW): organization founded in 1969, roots in organization date back to 1926.

interpersonal communication: the process of message transmitting between two people to create a sustained shared meaning.

Islamic State (ISIS): a radical Islamic terrorist group that quickly rose in the Middle East in 2014; previously known as the Islamic State in Iraq and the Levant (ISIL). (The Levant is a geographical region on the edge of the Eastern Mediterranean Sea composed of Syria, Jordon, Lebanon, and Israel and more recently referred to as ISIS or the Islamic State in Iraq and Syria.)

isomorphism: resource-dependent agencies tend to mirror the complexities and demands of their environments; when agencies receive signals from important others, they develop responsive policies and programs.

jihad: a "holy war," a concept perverted by radical Islamists to justify a physical war against the West; a perversion of the concept proscribed in the Holy Qur'an and *not* representative of mainstream Islam.

Jim Crow laws: southern laws that repressed African-Americans, enacted 1880–1960, followed the Black Codes.

job action: a label used to describe several types of activities in which employees may engage to express their dissatisfaction with a particular person, event, or condition or to attempt to influence the outcome of a matter pending before decision makers, such as a contract bargaining impasse.

judiciary: This is a system of courts of law that administer justice.

Kansas City Preventive Patrol Study: part of the trilogy of research and experiments that rocked policing in the early 1970s.

King, Martin Luther Jr., Reverend: distinguished leader in the Civil Rights movement.

KKK: Ku Klux Klan, organization founded as a social club in 1866, quickly turned to terrorizing African-Americans.

Knapp Commission: studied corruption in the NYCPD, identifying meat- and grass-eaters.

Kotter Model of Successful Change: an eight-step process model that identifies a logical and ideal way to implement successful change in police agencies.

laissez-faire: a leadership style; takes passive, "handsoff" approach, reluctantly use the authority of one's position, "whatever."

leader member exchange (LMX): theory by Dansereau, Graen, and Haga; those who are like the leader go to the in-group, those unlike the leader go to the outgroup, and those about whom the leader is unsure, go to the try-out bin (1975). See life cycle LMX theory (1995).

leader: can be contrasted with manager: (1) management is the content of a job, being a leader is how you get it done; (2) one person may be a leader, manager, both, or neither; and (3) a leader is identified by the position he or she occupies in the department's hierarchy. Leaders and managers can be differentiated by the variables identified in Table 7.1. See leadership.

leadership: (1) relating the police department to the larger/external environment and (2) influencing officers to use their energies willingly and appropriately to achieve the department's goals.

leadership neutralizers: as described by Kerr and Jermier, those who make leadership ineffective or impossible.

leadership substitutes: as described by Kerr and Jermier, those who diminish or take the place of formal leadership.

least preferred coworker (LPC): Fiedler's theory that underlining LPC is the assumption that how leaders treat their LPC is an indicator of their leadership preference. The relationship of that preference has three situational variables: (1) task structure, (2) leader-follower relations, and (3) the power position of the leader determines group effectiveness.

less-lethal weapon: As their name reflects, less-lethal weapons are used without the intent to cause permanent injury or death. Common less-lethal weapons include chemical weapons such as oleoresin capsicum (OC) or pepper spray, bean-bag guns, net guns that shoot a web around suspects, and controlled energy devices (CEDs) like Tasers.

letter of exception: a letter written by a chief of police to whatever office authorized the audit contesting one or more findings by the auditor.

Lewin, Kurt: founder of behavioral systems theory. Also see force-field analysis.

Lewin's three-step model: a change model that has three sequential steps: (1) unfreezing, (2) moving, and (3) refreezing.

Lexow Committee: committee that in 1894–1895 examined corruption in the New York Police Department.

liability: legal responsibility for a person's or an organization's acts or omissions.

liberty rights: rights involving the protection and defense of one's good name, reputation, and position in the community.

Lilly Ledbetter Fair Pay Act (LLFPA): (2009), law that states that each discriminatory paycheck is a new violation.

line and staff structure: an organizational structure that retains basic elements from line structure but adds auxiliary and administrative support units.

line item budget: budget whose focus is on controlling expenditures; each object of expenditure has a separate line in the budget.

line structure: the oldest, simplest, and clearest form of organizational design; authority flows from the top to the bottom of the organization in a clear and unbroken line.

litigation: a lawsuit or another question to the court that resolves a legal matter or question.

lone wolf (wolves): a violent attack by a single perpetrator (or small group), acting alone, without any direction, or assistance from an organization or outside group.

lynching: initially a severe beating, later synonymous with illegally hanging someone; initially meant rough justice.

machine politics: see political machine.

management systems: as described by Likert, a continuum of four leader styles.

manager: See leader.

Managerial Grid: Blake and Mouton's theory that balances two considerations: (1) concern for people and (2) concern for task to produce five distinct leadership styles.

Maslow, Abraham: developed the five-level hierarchy of human needs.

matrix (or grid) structure: an organizational design that assigns members of functional areas to specific projects, such as a task force.

McGregor, Douglas: developed Theory X and Theory Y, two contrasting sets of assumptions about workers.

McVeigh, Timothy: individual convicted of the Oklahoma City bombing and murders, executed in 2001; he stated that he wanted to get revenge for Ruby Ridge and Waco.

Mechanistic organizational structure: Mechanistic organizational structures are set up to run like a machine, tightly controlled, error free and producing a sustained, unflawed output. They incorporate many of the features of the bureaucratic structure, for example, a hierarchy, chain of command, and specialization, and much of the communication is vertical or top-down. Mechanistic organizations are also called "closed systems" because their boundaries are conceived of as being fairly impermeable to outside influences. Many theorists use mechanistic, closed system, and bureaucracies synonymously.

meet and confer model: referred to by some as "collective begging" because the laws or agreements establishing it confer little or no rights on employees. In the meet and confer model least friendly to employees, neither the employer nor the employees are required to meet. Such meetings are an opportunity, not a requirement.

military model: police theory that there is a war against crime and the police are front-line soldiers.

moral manager: ethical leadership concept, a fair and principled decision maker, who is altruistic, cares about people and the larger society.

moral person: ethical leadership concept, proactively strives to reinforce followers' ethical behavior.

moral turpitude: conduct contrary to honesty, justice, or good morals.

motivation-hygiene theory: two sets of factors, motivators and hygiene; hygiene factors, if met, don't motivate someone, but unmet they are a source of dissatisfaction. See Herzberg.

muckrakers: journalists and writers who exposed corruption and other abuses.

mutual benefit association: an association whose primary beneficiary is its members (e.g., a police union).

narco-terrorism: acts of insurgency by narcotics and drug traffickers aimed at influencing the policies of a specific government or society through violence and intimidation; the violent disruption of legitimate governmental services and security in a specific area.

National Advisory Commission on Civil Disorders: government report on riots in 1968; also known as the Kerner Commission after the group's Chair.

National Association of Asian American Law Enforcement Commanders (NAAALEC): founded in 2002, an organization fostering leadership, fraternal enrichment, and advancement.

National Association of Women Law Enforcement Executives (NAWLEE): established to address the unique needs of women holding senior positions in law enforcement.

National Commission on Law Observance and Law Enforcement: first comprehensive national study of police, 1929.

National Criminal Justice Reference Service (NCJRS): online reference source for criminal justice students, scholars, practitioners, and the public.

National Organization of Black Law Enforcement Executives (NOBLE): founded in 1976, NOBLE works toward the elimination of racism and bias with the law enforcement field.

National Prohibition Act: see Volstead Act, prohibition.

National Sheriffs Association (NSA): chartered in 1940, the NSA, like other professional organizations, provides education, training, and information resources to its members.

natural soldiering: the natural inclination of workers not to push themselves.

needs hierarchy: five levels of needs that explain human motivation; see Maslow.

negative entropy: the capacity to resist decline or death; see buffering.

negligence: the failure to exercise the care toward another person that a reasonable person would do in the same circumstances; also includes taking action that a reasonable person would not take; negligence is accidental.

neighborhood-oriented policing: a style of community policing fostered by Lee P. Brown in Houston, Texas, that focused on crime and social problems in select neighborhoods or districts.

networked organizations: organizations that are heavily dependent on informational technology, often comprised geographically dispersed units, horizontal communication accounts for most message traffic, their existence is panned and bound together by contract, may be single purpose or continuous in operation. Units are not part of same organization; they are autonomous, but collaborative. See virtual organizations.

new public management (NPM): began in 1980s, called for greater use of business practices to achieve greater efficiency.

noise: anything that disrupts communication, including the attitudes, the emotions of the receiver, such as stress, fear, negative attitudes, and low motivation.

nonexempt employees: entitled to overtime pay under FLSA.

normative decision-making theory: leadership model by Vroom, Yetton, Jago; not a general model of leadership; narrowly focuses on three leadership approaches to decision making and provides the greatest probability for a good decision, contingent upon follower characteristics.

normed: a norm is a statistical average of performance by a well-defined population. In the case involving the Colorado Springs Police Department suit by women who did not run a distance in an absolute time, a normed score for the plaintiffs would be the average time on the run for women in various age groups, that is, adjusted for both gender and age.

Obergefell v. Hodges: The 2015 supreme court landmark case recognizing and legalizing same-sex marriages across the United States.

objective reasonableness: A court-developed standard imposed under the Fourth Amendment "reasonableness" inquiring as to whether an officer's actions are "objectively reasonable" in light of the facts and circumstance of a specific incident. Would a reasonable officer confronted with the same or similar circumstances make the same decisions and conduct the same actions under review? The "objective reasonableness" test acknowledges that police officers are often forced to make splitsecond decisions under highly stressful conditions relating to the amount of force necessary in a particular incident.

officer in training (OIT): a recent academy graduate under the supervision of a field training officer.

Okies: term for immigrants from dust bowl states, many of them from Oklahoma.

open systems theory: a grouping of separate, but interdependent components that work together to achieve common goals.

operating budget: a recurrent budget for salaries, fringe benefits, uniforms, training, telephone service, and kindred expenses.

operational plans: often called "work plans" and describe specific actions to be taken by line units, such as patrol officers, precinct group, and/or other division teams.

operations research: the application, collection, and analysis of data from decision making within an organization.

organic organizations: organic organizations recognize that they have permeable boundaries and are therefore codependent with the larger environment in which they are embedded. Knowing they face an unstable environment, organic organizations are adaptable and nimble on their feet. Organic and open systems are used synonymously. Mechanistic and organic organizations can be thought of as opposite ends of a continuum.

organizational citizenship behavior (OCB): the extra things followers do that are not required but contribute to organizational effectiveness. See POB.

organizational development (OD): a change management process.

organizational humanism: 1950–1960s movement by theorists that called for the softening or elimination of many of the features of the bureaucratic model; see human relations school.

organizing: the process of determining the formal structure of task and authority relationships best suited to accomplish a mission.

path-goal theory (PGT): theory by House, 1996; revised his 1971 theory. The essence of PGT is that for leaders to be effective, they must engage in leader behaviors that compensate for the deficiencies of their subordinates, enhance their performance, and are instrumental to their individual and work unit performance and satisfaction.

patronage: in the worst sense, rewarding voters for their loyalty rather than their ability; useful in appointing qualified supporters who can help politicians implement their policies.

Peace Officers Standards and Training Commission (POST): a state-level organization that sets standards for police employment, basic and annual training, special certifications (e.g., use of radar, license revocations and other matters).

Peel, Sir Robert: driving force behind the London Metropolitan Police (1829).

Pendleton Act: federal legislation (1883) establishing the U.S. Civil Service Commission.

performance audit (PA): ordinarily a study to see how well a subunit or the whole organization is achieving its performance objectives. With some questionable shootings in 2014 and 2015, some audits are examining whether officers are following their use of force policies and writing all of the reports they should with the detail needed in them to constitute a professional report. One such study concluded that the officers were not writing all of the reports they should to keep use of force statists low and often simply wrote short passages, like arrested person was injured while resisting arrest and transported to the hospital.

performance budget (PB): also referred to as a performance-based budget (PBB), which focuses on results-based budgeting (RBB). In theory, a PB has four characteristics.

personalized power needs: the desire to be in control for selfish, self-aggrandizing reasons.

Pinkerton National Detective Agency: a private detective agency that excelled at tracking down outlaws.

plaintiff: the injured party that initiates a legal action.

Planning, Programming Budget System (PPBS): a budgeting innovation used in the federal government from the mid-1960s to the early 1970s; little use of it in state and local government.

planning: a process that links present actions to future conditions.

Police Administration: book authored by O. W. Wilson, known for many decades as the "Bible" of police administration, reasserted professional model of policing.

Police Executive Research Forum (PERF): group formed to do research and public policy work of interest to the larger jurisdictions founding it.

police sexual violence (PSV): an egregious form of sexual misconduct that involves sexual harassment and violence, including rape and other sexual assault, perpetrated by police officers against women.

political machine: a tightly controlled political party headed by a boss or small autocratic group whose purpose was to repeatedly win elections for personal gain, often through graft and corruption.

politics: In the negative sense, this refers to attempts to impose external, partisan political influence on the operation of a police department. In the positive sense, means the governance of the city.

Politics: the process of acquiring and maintaining control over a government, including its policies, administration, and operations.

Popular Front for the Liberation of Palestine (PFLP): terrorist organization.

POSDCORB: planning, organizing, staffing, directing, coordinating, reporting, and budgeting; also see Gulick.

positive organizational behavior (POB): a broader cluster of organizational behaviors that contribute to its overall success; OCB is included within POB by some researchers. See OCB.

posse comitatus: prohibits the use of federal soldiers to act as police officers in a law enforcement capacity within the borders of the United States.

posttraumatic stress disorder (PTSD): a psychological reaction that occurs after experiencing a highly stressful event outside the range of normal human experience.

power: when a formal grant of authority is made, some power inherently accompanies it to maintain standards, correct deficiencies, and discipline as needed. However, even with authority and power, leaders may not be able to compel others to perform. To a significant degree, power is a grant made by the led to the leader. Also see authority.

power motivation: see affiliation, personalized power, and socialized power needs.

predictive policing: a proactive policing style that uses information and analytical tools to prevent crime while using the fewest police resources possible.

Pregnancy Discrimination Act: PDA (1978), the Act makes it unlawful to discriminate against women in employment practices because of pregnancy, childbirth, or medical conditions rising from such.

principle of hierarchy: a requirement that each lower level of the organization be supervised by a higher level.

proactive planning: this is the attempt to change or anticipate events in the future that are likely to occur.

probable cause: Arising from the Fourth Amendment, probable cause is the standard by which a police officer has the authority to make an arrest, conduct a personal or property search, or to obtain a warrant for arrest; a set of facts and circumstances that would lead a reasonable person to believe that a crime has occurred and that a specific person is responsible for that crime.

problem-oriented policing: originally branded by Herman Goldstein, this style of policing addresses reoccurring social problems within a community through an innovative, four-step model called SARA.

procedural due process: the legality of the procedures used; in this case, to deprive police officers of status or wages.

procedural plans: the guidelines for the action to be taken under specific circumstances and address such matters as the use of force, high-speed pursuits, evidence handling, K-9 teams, sexual predators, domestic violence, hate crimes, cold case investigation, and form of management and dozens of other matters that permeate the agency.

program budget: focuses organized around programs/activities, has line item budget for control.

progressive discipline: slowly increasing the severity of sanctions unless a higher level is immediately required (e.g., termination).

prohibition: national prohibition officially lasted from 1919 to 1933.

property rights: rights involving the protection of one's property; in some cases, an individual's right to his or her job is considered a property right.

prosecutor: This is the public officer within a jurisdiction who represents the citizenry of a state or county who charges and prosecutes individuals who are alleged to have committed a crime.

protected class: a Title VII (1972) designation, race, color, sex, national origin, or religion.

proximate cause: an event that directly results in another event, particularly injury due to negligence or an intentional, wrongful act.

Public Employment Relations Commission: an administrative body, often on a state level, responsible for administering legislation related to union bargaining.

public interest organizations: these are organizations such as the American Civil Liberties Union (ACLU) and the National Association for the Advancement of Colored People (NAACP), which play an important role in police accountability, especially as it relates to allegations of police misconduct.

qualified individual with a disability: job applicant or employee who meets the employer's legitimate requirements for the position sought or held and is able to perform the essential/core functions with or without a reasonable accommodation by the employer.

quid pro quo: "something for something," a category of sexual harassment.

racial profiling: this is the consideration of race as a key factor in police decisions to stop and interrogate citizens.

RAND Criminal Investigation Study: part of the trilogy of research and experiments that rocked policing in the early 1970s.

rank order list: promotional roster method in which candidates are listed in their rank order. Selections are usually made from the list using a rule of 3, 5, or 10.

ration books: to divert as much food as possible to support service members fighting in WW II, national food rationing was instituted in the United States in 1942. Each person was issued a book of stamps that established the amounts of various types of foods he/she could have. Also see victory gardens.

rational-legal authority: authority is granted by the organization to the occupant of a position who uses it to accomplish organizational goals, a Weber-supplied concept.

reactive planning: this is the reaction to problems that have presently occurred and are being addressed or are presently happening and require a response. It is both past and present oriented.

reasonable accommodation: employers may tell applicants what the selection process consists of and whether they will need a reasonable accommodation by the employer. Examples of selection accommodations include large-print examinations and scheduling a wheelchaired applicants' interview on the first floor rather than the second floor where there is no elevator. After a conditional job offer is extended, employers may ask whether a reasonable accommodation is needed for any aspect of the job (e.g., modifying the equipment the person will use).

reasonableness: a standard applied to many legal questions in which it must be determined if conduct or action was reasonable in the eyes of the court.

recognition-primed decision making (RPD): method of decision making that focuses on the assessment of the situation, its dynamics, and the experience of the decision maker.

Reformation Period: reformers sought to free policing from political abuses and corruption; had two needs: arouse apathetic public and a conceptual model to drive it.

reformatted bureaucracy: a shift from close adherence to traditional organizational theory/closed system views to a neoclassical or neo-Weberian view that includes open systems precepts.

reliability: if the same test or a parallel form is given to the same group, substantially the same results will occur; results are not random.

residency requirements: rules from the Depression era, stating that before hiring, person had to live in a community six months or a year; intent was to protect jobs for local tax-paying residents.

resistance stage: the second step in general adaptation syndrome, exemplified by specific responses to continued stress by the body in order to optimize adaptation.

results-based budget (RBB): see performance budget.

retaliation: one of four EEOC theories of discrimination; two types: (1) retaliation for participation and (2) retaliation for opposition.

roid rage: an outburst of violent or aggressive behavior caused by taking large doses of anabolic steroids.

Ruby Ridge: 1992 Idaho standoff involving Weaver family and a friend and federal agents; fatalities on both sides; Weavers were seen by far-right groups as martyrs to federal government.

sanctuary movement: some people fleeing violence in Central America during the 1980s entered this country illegally. To prevent them from being returned to their home country some sympathetic churches gave them sanctuary, hiding and caring for them. This practice spread to city and counties and soon officials in those jurisdictions placed limits on the amount of assistance their public safety agencies could provide to the federal government with respect to illegal immigrants.

SARA: a cyclical, four-step problem-solving methodology designed to enhance community policing: **S**canning, **A**nalysis, **R**esponse, and **A**ssessment.

scientific management: finding the "one best way" to accomplish a task; see F. W. Taylor and traditional organizational theory.

sector policing: an innovative and proactive approach to structuring law enforcement crime-fighting strategies, personnel deployment, allocation of resources, and accountability to a geographical zone or area.

sense making: how people and organizations process their experiences and what they do with them. See cognitive maps.

servant leadership: as described by Greenleaf, primary orientation is the theory that leaders should first be servants, meeting the legitimate needs of their followers.

service organizations: an organization whose specific clientele is the primary beneficiary (e.g., clients of a community health center).

Servicemembers Civil Relief Act (SCRA): (2003), provides protections to service members, including those called to active duty; key provisions apply to leasing arrangements, the amount of interest that debtors can charge, and life insurance.

sexual harassment: a specific type of harassment, two categories: (1) quid pro quo and (2) hostile environment; violates Title VII.

sheriffs: Usually elected, with a custodial role in the detention of prisoners and serving as bailiffs in the court.

silent generation: born 1925–1945, loyal, security conscious, and conforming are key attributes. Almost entirely retired from law enforcement.

single-loop learning: allows organizations to make corrections and continue operations; see double-loop learning.

situational leadership: leadership model by Hersey and Blanchard; relates the behavior of the leaders to the maturity of followers; identifies the most probable successful leader behaviors for each level of maturity.

skill: how knowledge gets translated into action.

slave patrols: groups that hunted down fugitive slaves, administered impromptu punishments as they saw fit, and dispersed slave meetings; continued through the end of the Civil War.

snatch racket: 1920s and 1930s gangster term for kidnappings.

social media: a type of Internet-based resource integrating user-generated content with user participation.

social skills (SS): the ability to express oneself in social situations; the ability to "read" social situations; recognizing different social roles and expected behavior; and interpersonal problem solving; closely related to ES.

socialized power needs: the desire to have a positive impact on the department's operations and administration.

span of management: the number of personnel a supervisor can personally manage effectively.

speakeasies: illegal bars during federal prohibition.

specialization: a division of labor wherein specific jobs and tasks are allocated to meet different responsibilities with those specially qualified or trained to perform them.

spiritual leadership: leadership divided into two camps: those who are more overtly religious and those who define spirituality in another way. People can be spiritual without being religious, seeking meaning in their lives. Spiritual in this sense means having a closer connection with one's higher values and morality. Spiritual leadership taps into followers' higher-order needs (e.g., challenging work that is socially meaningful). See spiritual survival.

spiritual survival: (1) transcendence, a sense of being called to a profession and (2) membership, a sense of belonging.

spoils system: see patronage.

standard of reasonableness: in *Graham v. Connor,* the Supreme Court held that the standard of reasonableness emanates from the officer's perception at the time of the crisis that resulted in the use of deadly force.

station house sergeants: as described by Van Maanen, such sergeants work inside, have a strong conformity orientation, are immersed in the police department's management culture, and make contacts that can help career.

strategic plans: typically longer in duration than other kinds of planning, usually planning for events three to five years into the future.

street sergeants: as described by Van Maanen, such sergeants have a distaste for office procedures, are action oriented, are more likely to be investigated and sued, and may not advance beyond middle management.

street-level bureaucrats: government workers in direct contact with clients who use discretion on how to implement public policy (e.g., police officers and field social workers).

stress: anything that places an adjustive demand on the organism.

stress inoculation activities: activities that help eliminate or reduce stress.

strong mayor: In this form of government, the mayor is elected to office and serves as the chief executive of the city.

structure: an organizational design that assigns members of functional areas to specific projects, such as a task force.

substantive due process: the requirement that the basis for government disciplinary action be reasonable, relevant, and justifiable.

suicide by cop (SbC): a situation involving an individual who wishes to die and uses the police to affect that goal.

SWAT: special weapons and tactics police teams often used by the police during critical incidents such as barricaded felons, hostage situations, and felony search warrants.

synoptic planning: also known as the rational comprehensive approach and is the dominant tradition in policing.

systematic soldiering: keep production rates low so quotas don't increase.

tactical plans: these involve planning for emergency of a specific nature at known locations.

Tannenbaum and Schmidt: authors who identified a theory of leader styles (1958), revising it to a full situational leadership theory (1973).

Taylor, F. W: father of scientific management.

team policing: an attempt to reshape how police resources were used by reducing specialization and enlarging the role of uniformed patrol officers. Part of the trilogy of research and experiments that rocked policing in the 1970s.

technical skills: skills that are essential to doing a job; vary by level within a police organization (e.g., identifying physical evidence vs. preparing a budget).

temperance movement: late 19th-century antialcohol movement; church based.

tenure: This is a period, or term, during which a position is held.

terrorism: the threat of and/or use of violence to achieve a specific set of political objectives or goals.

Theory X-Theory Y: see McGregor.

thin-slicing theory: the concept that instantaneous or quick decisions made by well-trained and experienced administrators may often be better than those made more deliberately and with significantly more information and time.

Title VII: (1972), law that amends the Civil Rights Act of 1964; prohibits job discrimination in employment based on race, color, sex, national origin, or religion.

Tor network: Synonymous for the "deep web"; see deep web.

tort: a private injury inflicted on one person by another person, for which the injured party may sue in a civil action.

traditional action research model: a five-step change model consisting of the following: (1) recognizing the need for change, (2) assessing/diagnosing the situation, (3) action planning, (4) the intervention, and (5) evaluation.

traditional organizational theory: has three stems, bureaucracy, scientific management, and administrative theory; the centerpiece of organizational theory during 1900–1950.

traditional policing: a style of policing based on response to calls for service after the activity has occurred; traditional policing is reactive and incident driven, often utilizing random moving patrol cars.

traits approach: relatively stable predispositions to behave in a certain way; since roughly 1910, there has been interest in identifying the traits leaders have. Also see great man theory.

transactional leadership: leadership style that gives something (rewards) to get something (performance by followers). TLers appeal to the self-interest of followers. A basic system of reciprocity. Followers are motivated by lower levels of Maslow's needs hierarchy.

transformational leadership: leadership style that inspires followers to "elevate their game," go beyond self-interests, and make more and larger contributions than they had originally intended. In the process, transformational leaders help them to grow personally and professionally, to develop their own capabilities for leadership. Transformational leaders appeal to followers' ideals and values, aligning them with the organization's.

Two Medal of Honors: "Teddy" Roosevelt (1858–1919) and Mary Edwards Walker.

type A personality: the personality type characterized by an intense and ambitious mind-set, which puts the person under constant stress and physiological strain.

type B personality: the personality type characterized by a more easygoing state of mind than the type A personality.

type C personality: the personality type characterized as nonemotional, nonassertive, quiet, and introspective but actually frustrated and suppresses anger.

type D personality: the personality type characterized as pessimistic and socially withdrawn and as a result fears rejection.

U.S. Department of Labor (USDOL): administers some job discrimination laws in addition to other responsibilities.

undocumented immigrant: an individual who does not qualify for admission into the United States has entered the country illegally by crossing the border without full inspection or has violated the terms of legal admission.

unequal badge: term that describes African-American officers in some southern communities who, until the early 1960s, only walked beats in African-American business and entertainment districts; by custom, African-American officers were often not allowed to arrest Caucasians because an "ugly incident" leading to rioting might occur.

Uniform Guidelines for Employee Selection Procedures: "Uniform Guidelines," 1978, developed by EEOC to create a single set of selection principles designed to help covered employers comply with federal laws prohibiting employment decisions that discriminated against members of protected classes.

Uniformed Services Employment and Reemployment Rights Act (USERRA): (1994), encourages noncareer participation in the uniformed military service by eliminating barriers to such service, minimizing the disruption of the lives of those called to service and prohibiting discrimination against them.

untouchables: Treasury agents under Elliot Ness assigned to Chicago who couldn't be corrupted.

upward communication: communication used by lower-level employees.

validity: quality of a test that means it actually measures what it is intended to measure.

vertical differentiation: an organizational design based on levels of authority within an organization.

vicarious liability: a legal doctrine also known as "respondent superior" imposing liability on supervisors and managers for the tortious conduct of their employees.

virtual organizations: organizations that arise spontaneously to an urgent need; there is no planning or contract; participation is voluntary and members can withdraw at any time; there is not a command and control structure; they usually disappear when the single purpose that brought them together is accomplished.

Vollmer, August (Gus): father of modern law enforcement.

Volstead Act: National Prohibition Act; see prohibition.

vote of confidence: reflects how rank and file members signal their collective displeasure with the chief administrator of their agency.

Waco: Texas city where, in 1993, there was a 51-day federal siege of the Branch Davidian Compound led by David Koresh; ended with federal fatalities and perhaps 75 or more Branch Davidian deaths; federal authorities were sharply criticized, but no wrongdoing was found.

Watergate Scandal: petty burglary that ultimately led to President Nixon's resignation.

Weber, Max: founder of modern sociology whose name is synonymous with bureaucracy.

Wickersham Commission: see National Commission on Law Observance and Law Enforcement (1929).

Wilson, O. W.: chief of several jurisdictions; studied under Vollmer; his *Police Administration* has been regarded as the "Bible" of police administration for decades.

work slowdowns: officers continue to work but do so at a leisurely pace causing productivity to fall.

work speedups: an acceleration of an activity resulting in over production of one or more types of police services.

workaholic personality: this personality type is similar to a type A, and can result in serious physical and psychological consequences.

working test: the probationary period for a position.

zealots: leadership style described by Downs; such leaders have narrow interests, focus almost entirely on them.

zero-based budget (ZBB): in pure form, every program in a budget starts from "zero" and must be justified each year. Three alternative service levels are prepared for each program. As practiced in less stressful economic times, departments "have" 75 or 80 percent of their prior year's budget and use from there.

zero-tolerance policing (ZTP): a focused police strategy built on the philosophy that visible signs of social decay often lead to more serious crimes in a specific neighborhood; emphasis then, should be on strict enforcement of the law for even minor crimes of disorder.

INDEX